Lecture Notes in Computer Science

Lecture Notes in Computer Science

Edited by G. Goos and J. Hartmanis

194

Automata, Languages and Programming

12th Colloquium
Nafplion, Greece, July 15–19, 1985

Edited by Wilfried Brauer

Springer-Verlag
Berlin Heidelberg New York Tokyo

Editor

Wilfried Brauer
Fachbereich Informatik der Universität
Rothenbaumchaussee 67/69, 2000 Hamburg 13, FRG

CR Subject Classifications (1985): 4.1, 4.2, 5.2, 5.3

ISBN 3-540-15650-X Springer-Verlag Berlin Heidelberg New York Tokyo
ISBN 0-387-15650-X Springer-Verlag New York Heidelberg Berlin Tokyo

Printed in Germany

Printing and binding: Beltz Offsetdruck, Hemsbach/Bergstr.
2145/3140-543210

ICALP is the annual European summer conference on theoretical computer science sponsored by the European Association for Theoretical Computer Science (EATCS).

ICALP stands for International Colloquium on Automata, Languages and Programming, but this conference series intends to cover all important areas of theoretical informatics such as automata theory, formal language theory, analysis of algorithms, computational complexity, computability theory, mathematical aspects of programming language definition, logic and semantics of programming languages, program specification, theory of data structures, theory of data bases, cryptology, VLSI structures.

Previous colloquia were held in Antwerp (1984), Barcelona (1983), Aarhus (1982), Haifa (1981), Amsterdam (1980), Graz (1979), Udine (1978) Turku (1977), Edinburgh (1976), Saarbrücken (1974) and Paris (1972).

ICALP'86 will again be held in France: from July 15 to July 19, 1986, in Rennes.

ICALP'85 is being organized by the National Technical University of Athens in cooperation with the University of Hamburg. The conference is held at a very attractive location: Nafplion, the first capital of Greece, situated on the Eastern coast of the Peloponnese.

All the work related to the setting up of the scientific program was done in Hamburg. The final selection meeting of the program committee took place in Hamburg on January 28, 1985. The program committee (selection meeting participants underlined) consisted of:

K.R. Apt, Paris
J. Berstel, Paris
C. Böhm, Rome
W. Brauer, Hamburg
J. de Bakker, Amsterdam
J. Diaz, Barcelona
J. Gruska, Bratislava
B. Monien, Paderborn
C. Papadimitriou, Athens
J. Paredaens, Antwerp
M. Paterson, Warwick
A. Paz, Haifa
A.L. Rosenberg, Durham
A. Salomaa, Turku
D.S. Scott, Pittsburgh
I.H. Sudborough, Evanston
E. Welzl, Graz
D. Wood, Waterloo
Y. Yannakakis, Murry Hill

A great number of referees (see page IX) assisted the program committee members in their hard and difficult task. I would like to express my gratitude to all those persons who participated in the arduous selection process (every paper was sent to 4 program committee members who again often asked competent referees for assistance). In particular I thank those who did the final selection in a very laborious, intense and concentrated meeting. My thanks go also to the members of the Hamburg local arrangements committee: M. Kudlek (chairman), H. Bramhoff, H. Carstensen, V. Diekert, K.-J. Lange, M. Jantzen. In particular I am indebted to the program committee secretary, Mrs. H. Durry, for her special engagement and excellent work.

The organisation of the conference itself is carried out by the Greek organizing committee:

F. Afrati
L. Kirousis
F. Makedon
D. Maritsas
C.H. Papadimitriou (co-chairman)
G. Papageorgiou
E.N. Protonotarios (co-chairman)
D. Tsichritzis

In particular I would like to mention and thank Miss F. Afrati and C. Papadimitriou for their very close and helpful cooperation in dealing with matters concerning the conference.

I would also like to express my thanks to Mr. Th. Ottmann and his crew of the Karlsruhe University for the nice printing and quick distribution of the Call for Papers.

ICALP'85 received the largest number of paper submissions in ICALP history: 205 papers from the following countries:

Australia, Austria, Belgium, Brazil, Bulgaria, Canada, China, Czechoslovakia, Denmark, Federal Republic of Germany, Finland, France, German Democratic Republic, Great Britain, Hungary, Israel, Italy, Japan, Netherlands, Poland, Romania, South Africa, Spain, Sweden, Switzerland, U.S.A.

The time schedule of the conference allowed for the acceptance of only 49 papers.Therefore the selection was very difficult and we had to reject many good papers. The selection criteria were originality, technical quality and relevance; for the final evaluation the referee grading scale published in EATCS Bulletin 20 (June 1983), p. 31, was used. All accepted papers are included in these proceedings - many thanks to their authors for being in time.

I would like to thank very much all those who submitted papers for presentation at ICALP.

As usual, the ICALP'85 program offers two invited lectures: by A. Pnueli and L. Lovász, whose papers are also published in these proceedings; in addition, there is a special invited lecture on "Theory and Practice" given by D. Knuth in the ancient Greek theatre of Epidaurus. The program committee thanks all three invited lecturers for having accepted our invitation.

We are all very grateful for the special support given by the National Technical University of Athens, Ministry of Culture and Science, Ministry of Research and Technology, National Tourist Organization of Greece, OLYMPIC Airways, I.B.M., City of Nafplion and University of Hamburg.

Last but not least I would like to mention the excellent cooperation with Springer-Verlag and in particular with Mrs. I. Mayer.

Hamburg, April 1985

Wilfried Brauer
Program Committee Chairman

12th International Colloquium on

Automata , Languages and Programming

ICALP'85

July 15-19, 1985

Nafplion, Greece

TABLE OF CONTENTS

L. Lovász
Vertex Packing Algorithms 1

A. Pnueli
Linear and Branching Structures in the Semantics and Logics of Reactive Systems 15

D. Beauquier, M. Nivat
About Rational Sets of Factors of a Bi-Infinite Word 33

M. Ben-Or, O. Goldreich, S. Micali, R.L. Rivest
A Fair Protocol for Signing Contracts 43

G. Bilardi, F.P. Preparata
The Influence of Key Length on the Area-Time Complexity of Sorting . 53

L. Bougé
Repeated Synchronous Snapshots and their Implementation in CSP 63

W. Bucher, A. Ehrenfeucht, D. Haussler
On Total Regulators Generated by Derivation Relations 71

B. Chazelle, H. Edelsbrunner
Optimal Solutions for a Class of Point Retrieval Problems 80

B. Chazelle, L.J. Guibas
Fractional Cascading: A Data Structuring Technique with Geometric Applications 90

M. Chrobak
Hierarchies of One-Way Multihead Automata Languages 101

R. Cole
Partitioning Point Sets in 4 Dimensions 111

M. Coppo
A Completeness Theorem for Recursively Defined Types 120

P.-L. Curien
Categorical Combinatory Logic 130

J.W. de Bakker, J.N. Kok
Towards a Uniform Topological Treatment of Streams and Functions on Streams 140

J.W. de Bakker, J.-J. Ch. Meyer, E.-R. Olderog
Infinite Streams and Finite Observations in the Semantics of Uniform Concurrency 149

P. De Bra
Imposed-Functional Dependencies Inducing Horizontal Decompositions . 158

J. Engelfriet, H. Vogler
Characterization of High Level Tree Transducers. 171

Ph. Flajolet
Ambiguity and Transcendence 179

S.J. Fortune
A Fast Algorithm for Polygon Containment by Translation 189

M. Fürer
Deterministic and Las Vegas Primality Testing Algorithms 199

H.N. Gabow, M. Stallmann
Efficient Algorithms for Graphic Matroid Intersection and Parity . 210

J.A. Goguen, J.-P. Jouannaud, J. Meseguer
Operational Semantics for Order-Sorted Algebra 221

C.A. Gunter
A Universal Domain Technique for Profinite Posets 232

G. Hansel
A Simple Proof of the Skolem-Mahler-Lech Theorem 244

J. Hartmanis, N. Immerman
On Complete Problems for NP∩CoNP 250

M. Hennessy
An Algebraic Theory of Fair Asynchronous Communicating Processes . 260

T. Hortalá-González, M. Rodríguez-Artalejo
Hoare's Logic for Nondeterministic Regular Programs:
A Nonstandard Completeness Theorem 270

K. Hrbacek
Powerdomains as Algebraic Lattices 281

M. Jerrum
Random Generation of Combinatorial Structures from a Uniform
Distribution 290

J.H. Johnson
Do Rational Equivalence Relations have Regular Cross-Sections? . . 300

H. Jung
On Probabilistic Time and Space 310

R.G. Karlsson, J.I. Munro, E.L. Robertson
The Nearest Neighbor Problem on Bounded Domains 318

M. Kaufmann, K. Mehlhorn
Routing through a Generalized Switchbox 328

V. Keränen
On k-Repetition Free Words Generated by Length Uniform Morphisms
over a Binary Alphabet 338

J. Kortelainen
Every Commutative Quasirational Language is Regular 348

Th.G. Kurtz, U. Manber
A Probabilistic Distributed Algorithm for Set Intersection
and its Analysis 356

G.M. Landau, M.M. Yung, Z. Galil
Distributed Algorithms in Synchronous Broadcasting Networks 363

K.G. Larsen
A Context Dependent Equivalence Between Processes 373

M. Li
Lower Bounds by Kolmogorov-Complexity 383

M. Luby, P. Ragde
A Bidirectional Shortest-Path Algorithm with Good Average-Case
Behavior 394

M.G. Main, W. Bucher, D. Haussler
Applications of an Infinite Squarefree CO-CFL 404

Z. Manna, R. Waldinger
Special Relations in Automated Deduction 413

K. Mehlhorn, A. Tsakalidis
Dynamic Interpolation Search 424

P. Orponen, D.A. Russo, U. Schöning
Polynomial Levelability and Maximal Complexity Cores 435

J.E. Pin
Finite Group Topology and p-adic Topology for Free Monoids 445

S. Sippu, E. Soisalon-Soininen
On the Use of Relational Expressions in the Design of Efficient Algorithms 456

A.P. Sistla, M.Y. Vardi, P. Wolper
The Complementation Problem for Büchi Automata with Applications to Temporal Logic 465

C. Stirling
A Complete Compositional Modal Proof System for a Subset of CCS . 475

P.J. Varman, I.V. Ramakrishnan
On Matrix Multiplication Using Array Processors 487

U. Vishkin
Optimal Parallel Pattern Matching in Strings 497

J. Zwiers, W.P. de Roever, P. van Emde Boas
Compositionality and Concurrent Networks: Soundness and Completeness of a Proofsystem 509

Author Index 520

LIST OF REFEREES

I.J.J. Aalbersberg
K.R. Apt
E. Astesiano
F. Aurenhammer
G. Ausiello
J.L. Balcázar
R. Barbuti
J. Barcelo
J. Beauquier
J.A. Bergstra
J. Berstel
A. Bertoni
R.S. Bird
F. Blanchard
L. Boasson
C. Böhm
D.P. Bovet
H.A. Bramhoff
S.D. Brookes
W. Bucher
H. Carstensen
R. Cases
A. Chandra
C. Choffrut
M. Coppo
G. Costa
N. Cot
B. Courcelle
M. Crochemore
K. Culik II
D. de Baer
J.W. de Bakker
P. de Bra
W.P. de Roever Jr.
M. Dezani
J. Diaz
V. Diekert
U. Dieter
H. Edelsbrunner
J. Engelfriet
H. Erkiö
E. Fachini
M. Fontet
S. Fortune
N. Francez
J. Gabarro
J.H. Gallier
R. Gerth
O. Goldreich
O. Grumberg
J. Gruska
I. Guessarian
Y. Gurevich
M. Gyssens
D. Harel
T. Harju
M. Hofri
F. Honsell
H.J. Hoogeboom
D. Janssens
M. Jantzen
J.H. Johnson
J. Karhumäki
R. Karlsson
H.C.M. Kleijn
J.W. Klop
J.N. Kok
E. Korah
D. Kozen
M. Kudlek
M. Kunde
K.-J. Lange
P.A. Larson
M. Latteux
D. Lehmann
S. Levialdi
A. Lin
A. Llamosi
G. Longo
B. Lorho
W.F. McColl
A. Maggilo-Schettini
J.A. Makowsky
H. Mannila,
I. Margaria
A. Martelli
G. Mauri
L.G.L.T. Meertens
J.-J.Ch. Meyer
P.A. Miglioli
E. Moggi
B. Monien
U. Montanari
C. Montangero
S. Moran
U. Moscato
A. Nijholt
H. Oberquelle
F.J. Oles
F. Orejas
M. Ornaghi
P. Orponen
Th. Ottmann
M. Overmars
J. Pachl
C. Papadimitriou
D.M.R. Park
M. Paterson
A. Paz
M. Penttonen
D. Perrin
S. Porat
M. Protasi
Y. Raz
W. Reisig
C. Reutenauer
J.M. Robson
S. Ronchi della Rocca
A.L. Rosenberg
G. Rote
W. Rounds
G. Rozenberg
K. Ruohonen
J. Sakarovitch
A. Salomaa
D. Scott
G. Seroussi
M. Sharir
I. Shinar
O. Shmeli
G.M. Silberman
E. Speckenmeyer
I.H. Sudborough
F.B. Schneider
R. Schulz
M. Steinby
J. Stern
J.M. Steyaert
M. Tarzi
H.R. Tirri
B. Trakhtenbrot
E. Ukkonen
G. Vagkini
R. Valk
P. van Emde Boas
J. van Leeuwen
M. van den Bergh
J. Veijalainen
B. Venneri
M. Venturini Zilli
R. Verraedt
H. Vogler
O. Vornberger
E.G. Wagner
E. Welzl
D. Wood
M. Yannakakis
J.A. Yebra
M. Yoeli
M. Zacchi
S. Zaks
J. Zwiers

VERTEX PACKING ALGORITHMS

L. Lovász
Department of Computer Science
Eötvös Loránd University
H-1088 Budapest, Hungary

Introduction

Vertex packing is one of the most well-known NP-hard combinatorial optimization problems. To all probability this means that we will never find a polynomial-time algorithm which would solve this problem for all graphs. Nor can we expect to find a good characterization of the optimum value.

But there are several interesting special classes of graphs for which the vertex packing problem can be solved in polynomial time, and most of the algorithms which solve it for these special cases are far from being trivial. The vertex packing problem, simple and general as it is, may be viewed as a good testing ground for various algorithmic ideas: linear programming, decomposition methods, augmentation, branch and bound, enumeration. New classes of graphs for which the vertex packing problem is polynomial time solvable are being discovered frequently. Yet, it seems to be worth while to give a little survey of some of the most important algorithmic ideas and their applications.

1. Linear programming

This is a very general approach to NP-hard combinatorial optimization problems, which yields many nicely solved special classes and sometimes surprisingly good practical results . In this survey we shall formulate our arguments for vertex packing, even though the basic idea carries over to virtually any combinatorial optimization problem.

Let G be a graph with vertex set $V(G) = V$ and edge set $E(G) = E$. We denote by $\alpha(G)$ the maximum number of independent (i.e. mutually non-adjacent) points in G. The (unweighted) vertex packing problem is to determine this number.

Often this problem occurs in a weighted form: we are also given a weighting $w: V \to \mathbb{Q}_+$ of the vertices of the graph, and we want to find an independent set with maximum total weight. We shall denote this maximum by $\alpha(G,w)$.

For each subset A of V, let $\chi^A \in \mathbb{R}^V$ denote the incidence vector of the set A. Let us form the convex hull of all vectors χ^A, where A ranges through all independent subsets of V. We call this polytope the *vertex packing polytope* of G and denote it by VP(G).

Now an easy argument shows that

$$\alpha(G,w) = \max \{w.\chi^A\colon A \text{ independent}\} = \max \{w.x;\ x \in VP(G)\}.$$

So we may view the weighted vertex packing problem as the problem of maximizing a linear objective function over a convex polytope. This is almost a linear program, except that the convex polytope is not given in a form suitable for linear programming algorithms: it is not defined as the solution set of a system of linear inequalities. It is known that every polytope has a description by linear inequalities; the question is, how to find this description.

Some inequalities suggest themselves. For each vector χ^A in the definition of the vertex packing polytope, and hence also for each vector in VP(G), we have

(1) $$x \geq 0$$

and also

(2) $$x_i + x_j \leq 1$$

for any two adjacent points i and j of G. The inequalities (1) and (2) define a polytope, and it is easy to see that the integral points in this polytope are precisely the incidence vectors of independent sets of points. However, the solution set of (1) and (2) may be strictly larger than VP(G). In fact, (1) and (2) describe VP(G) if and only if the graph G is bipartite. For this case, we could use this method, and an appropriate linear programming algorithm (simplex, eelipsoid or Karmarkar) to solve the vertex packing problem. In this case, however, much more efficient direct methods are available, based on flow theory.

As a next step, consider the minimal non-bipartite graphs, i.e. the add circuits. Clearly, every odd circuit of length $2k+1$ contains only k independent points. This can be translated into the language of linear inequalities as follows:

$$(3) \quad \sum_{i \in C} x_i \leq \frac{1}{2}(|C|-1)$$

for each odd circuit C in the graph. The inequalities (3) do not follow from (1) and (2). Unfortunately, even these inequalities are not sufficient to describe VP(G) in general; e.g. if G is the complete 4-graph K_4, then the point (1/3, 1/3, 1/3, 1/3) satisfies all of the inequalities (1), (2) amd (3), but it does not belong to VP(K_4). However, there are quite interesting classes of graphs for which these inequalities do suffice. Let us call a graph with this property *t-perfect*. Obviously, every bipartite graph is t-perfect, and Fonlupt and Uhry (1982) showed that it remains t-perfect if one new point is added to it and connected to arbitrary points of the bipartite graphs. Boulala and Uhry (1979) showed, answering a question of Chvátal, that every series-parallel graph is t-perfect. Another interesting family of t-perfect graphs consists of those planar graphs in which exactly two faces have an odd number of vertices. A general sufficient condition for t--perfectness was given by Gerards and Schrijver (1985): if a graph does not contain, as a subgraph, a subdivision of K_4 such that all four circuits corresponding to the triangles of the original K_4 are odd, then the graph is t-perfect. It turns out, however, that such graphs can all be glued together (in a somewhat complicated but well-described sense) from the more special examples mentioned above. In spite of this rather substantial amount of work, no complete characterization of t-perfect graphs is known. In particular, we do not know if this property is in P. It is not even trivial that this property is in co-NP; this, however, can be derived from the algorithmic considerations that follow. It is not known if t-perfectness is in NP.

Suppose now that we consider a t-perfect graphs, i.e. (1), (2) and (3) suffice to describe VP(G). There is still a substantial difficulty with the application of linear programming methods to this system: namely, (3) consists in general of exponentially many inequalities, and so the input size of the system is exponentially large in terms of the natural input size of the problem. Fortunately, an important property of the ellipsoid method overcomes this difficulty, at least in a theoretical sense (it is not clear whether practically more efficient linear programming algorithms, like the simplex method or Karmarkar's algorithm, can be succesfully extended in this way). It follows from the general results on the ellipsoid method (see Grötschel, Lovász and Schrijver 1981, 1984) that to be able to optimize any linear objective function over VP(G) in polynomial time, it suffices to have a polynomial time subroutine to check whether or not a given vector x belongs to VP(G).

So let us see how this can be achieved. Let $x \in \mathbb{Q}^V$ be given. Then we can check if x satisfies (1) and (2) by straightforward substitution. Assume that these are indeed satisfied. In order to check the inequalities (3), we first consider the substitution

$$y_{ij} = 1 - x_i - x_j$$

for each edge $ij \in E$. Then (1) and (2) imply that

(4) $$0 \leq y_{ij} \leq 1,$$

while (3) is transformed into the following class of inequalities:

(5) $$\sum_{ij \in E(C)} y_{ij} \geq 1$$

for each odd circuit C. If we view y_{ij} as the "length" of the edge ij (which is non-negative by (4)), then (5) says that every odd circuit in the graph has length at least 1.

Now the shortest odd circuit in any graph can be determined by $|V|$ shortest path computations. This is done as follows. We double each vertex v of the graph, to get two new vertices v' and v''. We connect u' to v'' by an edge iff u and v are adjacent in G, and assign to each new edge the same length as that of the corresponding edge of G. Then we find a shortest $v'v''$-path in this new graph for each v. It is easy to see that the shortest one among these paths corresponds in G to a shortest odd circuit. So the validity of (5), and thus the validity of (3), can be checked in polynomial time. Hence the vertex packing problem can be solved for t-perfect graphs in polynomial time.

The algorithm sketched above is due to Grötschel, Lovász and Schrijver (1985). In this same paper some further classes of valid inequalities for VP(G) are studied, and shown that their validity for a given vector x can be checked in polynomial time. This leads to various analogues of t-perfectness; unfortunately, no really interesting classes of graphs are known to be"perfect"in this sense, although research in this direction is active.

There is, however, one very natural class of ineqalities valid for VP(G), which leads to a most important class of graphs and also to one of the most involved polynomial time vertex packing algorithms for this class. It is clear that the incidence vector of any independent set, and hence also every vector in VP(G), satisfies the inequality

(6) $$\sum_{i \in K} x_i \leq 1$$

for each complete subgraph K of G. The inequalities (6) are usually called the *clique constraints*. Note that the "line constraints" (2) are special cases of (6). A graph for which (1) and (6) suffice to describe VP(G) is called *perfect*. Of course, (1)and (6) do not in general suffice to describe VP(G), i.e. not every graph is perfect; the simplest examples of non-perfect graphs are odd cycles of length at least 5 and their complements. (It is conjectured by Berge that these are the only non-perfect graphs minimal with respect to inclusion as an induced subgraph.)

We cannot go into the theory of perfect graphs here; let us just refer to the monograph of Golumbic (1980) and to the collection of papers edited by Berge and Chvátal (1984). Many interesting classes of graphs are perfect; most notable are perhaps *chordal graphs* (graphs in which every circuit longer than 3 has a chord), *comparability graphs* (obtained from a poset by connecting two elements by an edge iff they are comparable), line-graphs of bipartite graphs, and the complements of these.

Turning to the algorithmic aspects of perfect graphs, let us remark that it is an outstanding open problem to characterize these graphs. More exactly, it is not too difficult to show that perfectness is in co-NP, but it is not known whether or not it is in NP or in P. One may hope that eventually sufficiently many "building blocks" and "glueing rules" will be found so that all perfect graphs can be built up from these blocks by the given glueing rules; such a program, however, has only been succesfully finished for some special classes of perfect graphs. This, however, is more closely related to the topic of our next section, decomposition methods, and we shall discuss an example there.

It is a natural idea to try to use the polyhedral description (1) and (6) of the vertex packing polytope of perfect graphs to obtain a polynomial time vertex packing algorithm in a similar way as we did for t-perfect graphs. (6), of course, contains exponentially many inequalities in general, but we have seen that this is not crucial. But here a new difficulty arises: if we want to check whether or not a vector $x \in \mathbb{Q}^V$ satisfies tha inequalities (6), then - viewing the entries of x as weights - we obtain the problem of checking whether or not each clique in the graph has weight at most 1. This problem is, in turn, equivalent to the problem of finding a maximum weight clique, which is just the same as the (weighted) vertex packing problem for the complement graph. So all this affort (including an application of the ellipsoid method) just took as back to the original problem!

The way out is to find a much larger (infinite) class of inequalities valid for VP(G), and then find a way to check whether these are satisfied. The method is based on the paper (Lovász, 1979), and is elaborated in (Grötschel, Lovász and Schrijver 1980, 1984, 1985). Let $(u_i: i \; V)$ be vectors in $\mathbb{R}^n$ for some large n (e.g. $n = |V|$ will do). This system of vectors is called an *orthonormal representation* of G if

(7) $\|u_i\| = 1$ (for all $i \in V$)

and

(8) $u_i . u_j = 0$ (for every non-adjacent pair (i,j) of vertices).

Let, furthermore, $c \in \mathbb{R}^n$ be any other vector of unit length. Consider the inequality

(9) $\sum_{i \in V} (c.u_i)^2 x_i \leq 1.$

Then it is not too difficult to show that the incidence vector of any independent set (and hence also every vector in VP(G)) satisfies (9). It is also easy to see that every clique constraint occurs among the constraints (9). Hence for perfect graphs (and in fact only for perfect graphs) the solution set of (1) and (9) is just the vertex packing polytope. For non-perfect graphs, the solution set of (1) and (9) is not even polyhedral. But, in spite of the complicated definition and the structural complexity, the solution set of (1) and (9) behaves nicely: one can optimize any linear objective function over it in polynomial time. This algorithm is based on the ellipsoid method and on some more involved linear algebra, and we cannot go into the details of it here. Unfortunately, the method seems to be impractical, although work is being done to make it applicable to graphs with at least 40-50 vertices.

It seems to be worthwhile, however, to formulate one special consequence of the method. Let G be any graph, and let $\overline{\chi}(G)$ denote the minimum number of complete subgraphs of G which cover all the vertices. (Note that this is just the chromatic number of the complement of G.) The following inequality is trivial:

$$\overline{\chi}(G) \geq \alpha(G). \tag{10}$$

For perfect graphs, one has equality here; in fact, perfect graphs are characterized (and often defined) by the condition that (10) holds with equality for each induced subgraph of them. Then the algorithm mentioned above implies the following:

There exists a function $f(G)$, *computable in polynomial time, such that*

$$\overline{\chi}(G) \geq f(G) \geq \alpha(G).$$

It may be interesting to point out that α is an NP-function in the sense that the property of the pair (G,k) that $\alpha(G) \geq k$ is in NP. The function $\overline{\chi}$ is a co-NP-function in an analogous sense, and by the result above, they can be separated by a P-function. It would be interesting to collect more examples of such "sandwich" results.

We conclude this section with emphasizing that the polynomial time vertex packing algorithm for perfect graphs mentioned above is non-combinatorial and impractical. For special classes of perfect graphs, several practically very efficient combinatorial algorithms are known to solve this problem. To find such an algorithm for perfect graphs is a major unsolved problem in this area.

2. Decomposition methods

This section contains some more loosely connected algorithms for vertex packing in various special classes of graphs.

Let us start with *chordal graphs*, which have been mentioned before as special perfect graphs. They are precisely those graphs in which every circuit longer than 3 has a chord. The key property of these graphs is that they contain at least one (in fact, at least two) *simplicial vertices*, i.e. vertices whose neighbours form a complete subgraph. So every chordal graph can be obtained by starting with a single point, and repeatedly adding a new vertex and connect it to the vertices of a complete subgraph of the previously defined graph. Conversely, every graph obtained this way is chordal.

This recursive construction of chordal graphs makes it easy to solve various algorithmic problems for them. If we want to find a maximum independent set (unweighted), then we may consider any simplicial vertex v. Then there will be a maximum size independent set containing v. For, let T be any maximum independent set, and assume that $v \notin T$. Then T must contain a neighbor u of v, or else v could be added to T. Now $T - u + v$ is another maximum independent set containing T. But if there exists such a maximum independent set, then deleting v and all of its neighbors from G, the independence number $\alpha(G)$ drops by exactly one. Hence we can proceed trivially.

This idea was extended to the weighted case by Frank (1976). Let $w: V \to \mathbb{Q}_+$ be any weighting of the vertices of the graph G, and suppose that we want to find an independent set with maximum weight. Consider again a simplicial point. By the same argument as above we see that every (inclusionwise)maximal independent set, so in particular every maximum weight independent set, contains exactly one point of the complete subgraph Q_v formed by v and its neighbors. So if we subtract any constant from the weights of the points of Q_v, then we obtain an equivalent problem. It also follows that if any vertex in Q_v has smaller weight than v, then it will not occur in any maximum weight independent set and so it can be deleted from the graph. So we may assume that $w(v)$ is a smallest weight in Q_v and also that $w(v) = 0$. But then deleting v from the graph we obtain an equivalent problem on a smaller chordal graph.

A third algorithmic problem for chordal graphs which is very easily solved is that of finding a maximum weight complete subgraph; equivalently, to solve the weighted vertex packing problem for the complement of a chordal graph..The point is that a chordal graph with n vertices contains at most n maximal complete subgraphs, which follows trivially by induction, using the existence of a simplicial vertex. In fact, all maximal complete subgraphs can be easily listed.

Another example for a class of graphs for which the number of cliques (maximal complete subgraphs) is polynomially bounded is the class of line-graphs. These are obtained from an arbitrary graph H by considering the edges of H as vertices of its line-graph L(H), and by connecting two of them if and only if they have an endpoint in common. Cliques in L(H) correspond to triangles and stars in H, and so their number is at most $\binom{|V(H)|}{3} + |V(H)|$. Thus the problem of finding a maximum weight clique in a line-graph is again easily solved e.g. by inspecting all cliques.

Balas (1984) found a different kind of decomposition trick which makes use of the kind of property discussed above. Let G be a graph whose vertices can be partitioned into two classes V_1 and V_2 such that the subgraph G_i induced by V_i has only polynomially many inclusionwise maximal independent sets, and these sets can be explicitly found (e.g. G_i may be the complement of a chordal graph, or the complement of a line-graph). Then a maximum weight independent set can be found in G in polynomial time as follows. Let $A_1,\dots,A_r$ be the maximal independent sets in G_1 and $B_1,\dots,B_s$ be the maximal independent sets in G_2. Let H_{ij} denote the subgraph of G induced by A_i B_j. Then every independent set in G is an independent set in at least one of the graphs H_{ij}, and so to find a maximum weight independent set in G, it suffices to find a maximum weight independent set in each H_{ij}, and take the best of these. But each H_{ij} is a bipartite graph, and so this is easily accomplished.

We now come to a more involved decomposition algorithm. Let us return to the line-graphs. It is clear that the vertex packing problem for L(H) is equivalent to the matching problem (the problem of finding a maximum cardinality/weight set of mutually disjoint edges). So this problem is well-solved by the results of Edmonds (1965). The question naturally arises whether this algorithm can be extended to any class more general than line-graphs.

Line-graphs can be characterized by a list of 9 excluded induced subgraphs (Beineke 1970). The simplest and as we shall see most important of these is the *claw*, or *3-star*, consisting of 3 independent vertices and a fourth vertex joined to each of them. If we try to translate some of the fundamental manipulations with matchings to line-graphs (e.g. alternating paths), then it is mostly the non-existence of a claw which plays a role. So it is natural to try to solve the vertex packing problem for claw-free graphs (i.e. for graphs not containing a claw as an induced subgraph). This turned out quite a bit more difficult then the matching problem, but eventually Sbihi (1980) and Minty (1980) found polynomial-time algorithms for this. Sbihi's algorithm is faster; Minty's, on the other hand, extends to the weighted case. Here we shall describe a third algorithm, which only concerns the unweighted case.

The reduction priciple applied below can be stated as follows. Let G be any graph. For a subset $X \subseteq V$, we denote by $N(X)$ the set of neighbors of X (excluding the points of X). Let $\alpha(X)$ denote the independence number of the graph induced by X.

(11) Lemma. Let $X \subseteq V$ be any set of vertices such that $\alpha(X) = k$, $\alpha(Y) > k$ for each $X \subset Y \subseteq V$, and $\alpha(N(X)) \leq 2$. Construct a new graph G' by deleting the vertices in X, and by connecting two as yet non-adjacent points in $N(X)$ by a new edge iff they can be extended by k points of X to an independent $(k+2)$-subset of G. Then

$$\alpha(G') = \alpha(G) - k.$$

The proof of this lemma is straightforward. We shall apply this lemma in two situations.

First, consider any point v. We say that v is *regular*, if its neighborhood can be partitioned into two complete subgraphs, and *irregular* otherwise. Suppose that G contains an irregular point v. Note that by claw-freeness, $\alpha(v \cup N(v)) \leq 2$. Let X be a maximal superset of $v \cup N(v)$ which still has $\alpha(X) \leq 2$. Then it follows by a lengthy but not too difficult argument that

$$\alpha(N(X)) \leq 2,$$

and so the reduction method of Lemma (11) applies. It is also important to see that the smaller graph G' constructed in Lemma (11) is again claw-free. So if G contains an irregular point then we can reduce the problem to a smaller graph.

Suppose now that all vertices of G are regular. Then for each vertex v we can find two cliques Q_{v1} and Q_{v2} which contain v and cover every neighbor of v. Next we check whether any of these cliques satisfies $\alpha(N(Q_{vi})) \leq 2$. If so, the construction of Lemma (11) can again be applied with $X = Q_{vi}$. Again, the graph G' constructed in the Lemma turns out to preserve claw-freeness. So again we have reduced our problem to a smaller graph.

Finally, the case remains when each Q_{vi} has three independent neighbors. Then one can show that the graph G is already a line-graph (this is not quite straightforward; for details see e.g. Lovász-Plummer 1985). So we may use any polynomial-time matching algorithm to solve the vertex packing problem for G.

When implemented carefully, this algorithm has running time $O(n^4)$, where n is the number of vertices in G. It is interesting to remark that one of the bottlenecks is that one has to check $O(n)$ times if a graph $N(Q_{vi})$ has three independent points. This is trivial in $O(n^3)$ time. Several collegues (J. Nesetril, F.Chung, R.Karp, M.Karpinski) have pointed out to me that using fast matrix multiplication procedures, this can be improved to $O(n^{2.5})$. Using this observation, the running time of our algorithm can be improved to about $O(n^{3.5})$.

This raises the more general question: given a graph G and an integer $k \geq 3$, how fast can we check if $\alpha(G) \leq k$? This is trivial in $O(n^k)$ time, and fast matrix multiplication procedures enable us to improve this to about $O(n^{5k/6})$. It would be interesting to decide if the factor 5/6 in the exponent could be replaced by an arbitrarily small factor for k large enough.

It is not clear just how far the above decomposition idea can be pushed. Can we go on and solve the vertex packing problem for line graphs, i.e. the matching problem, by similar reduction tricks? I feel not, but I could not find any way to formalize this negative feeling. The crucial point seems to be that we find cutsets X of vertices with $\alpha(X) \leq 2$. Claw-freeness itself says that the trivial cutsets, namely the neighborhoods of points have this property; in the above arguments we have used less trivial cutset. Which are those graphs which can be decomposed along such cutsets entirely, and is the vertex packing problem polynomially solvable for such graphs? If we replace $\alpha(X) \leq 2$ by $\alpha(X) \leq 1$, then we obtain just the class of chordal graphs, and we have seen that the vertex packing problem for such graphs can be solved easily by decomposition methods.

A further open problem is whether the above idea can be extended to the weighted case. Related to this is the problem of finding the facets of the vertex packing polytope of claw-free graphs.

A decomposition procedure of similar nature, but different from the above, was introduced by Hammer, Mahadev and de Werra (1985). Let G be a graph which does not contain a claw or a "net" (a graph consisting of a triangle and an independent triple, poined by three independent edges). We shall call such a graph *CN-free*. Let u be any vertex and $v_1,\ldots,v_k$ its neighbors (so far in an arbitrary order). Construct a new, smaller graph G' as follows:

(a) delete u as well as all v_i such that v_i is adjacent to each v_j with $j > i$;

(b) connect each pair of (previously non-adjacent) vertices in $N(u)$ by a new line, and connect a vertex $r \in V - N(u) - u$ to a vertex v_i by a new line if r is connected to every v_j such that $j > i$ and v_i and v_j are non-adjacent.

Then

$$\alpha(G') = \alpha(G) - 1.$$

This suggests a recursive procedure to determine the independence number of CN-free graphs. Unfortunately, when applying the above procedure, we may loose the CN-freeness of the graph. But Hammer, Mahadev and de Werra showed how to choose the original ordering of the neighbors (upon which the procedure is essentially dependent) so that CN-freeness is preserved.

So the Hammer-Mahadev-deWerra procedure works only for a subclass of claw-free graphs; but for these graphs it gives a total decomposition, while our algorithm sketched before only reduces the problem to line-

-graphs, for which the problem can be solved by different, and quite involved, methods, namely by matching theory. It would be interesting to find other classes of graphs for which some straightforward decomposition procedure determines the independence number in polynomial time.

REFERENCES.

E.Balas (1984): Lecture in Osnabrück, August.

L.W.Beineke (1970): Characterizations of derived graphs, *J.Combin. Theory* 6, 129-135.

C.Berge and V.Chvátal, eds., (1984): *Topics on Perfect Graphs*, Annals of Discrete Math. 21; North-Holland.

M. Boulala and J.P.Uhry (1979): Polytope des independentes d'un graph series-parallele, *Discrete Math.* 27, 225-243.

J.Edmonds (1965): Maximum matching and a polyhedron with 0,1-vertices, *J.Res.Natl.Bureau of Standards* B 69, 125-130.

J.Fonlupt and J.P.Uhry (1982): Transformations which preserve perfectness and h-perfectness of graphs, *Annals of Discrete Math.*16, 83-95.

A.Frank (1976): Some polynomial algorithms for certain graphs and hypergraphs, *Combinatorics*, Proc. 5th British Combin.Conf., Aberdeen 1975; Utilitas Mathematica, 211-226.

A.M.Gerards and A.Schrijver (1985): Matrices with the Edmonds-Johnson property, working paper, Inst. of Operations Research, Univ.Bonn.

M.Golumbic (1980): *Algorithmic Graph Theory and Perfect Graphs*, Academic Press.

M.Grötschel, L.Lovász and A.Schrijver (1981): The ellipsoid method and its consequences in combinatorial optimization, *Combinatorica* 1, 169-197.

M.Grötschel, L.Lovász and A.Schrijver (1984): Geometric methods in combinatorial optimization, *Progress in Combinatorial Optimization*, Proc. Silver Jubilee Conf. Waterloo 1982; Academic Press, 167-183.

M.Grötschel, L.Lovász and A.Schrijver (1985): Relaxations of vertex packing, *J. Combin. Theory* B (submitted)

P.L.Hammer, N.V.R.Mahadev and D.de Werra (1985): The struction of a graph: Application to CN-free graphs, *Combinatorica* 5 (to appear)

L.Lovász (1979): On the Shannon capacity of a graph, *IEEE Trans. Inform. Theory* 25, 1-7.

L.Lovász and M.D.Plummer (1985): *Matching Theory*, Akadémiai Kiadó - North-Holland.

G.Minty (1980): On maximal independent sets of vertices in claw-free graphs, *J.Comb.Theory* B 28, 284-304.

N.Sbihi (1980): Algorithme de recherche d'un stable de cardinalité maximum dans un graph sans étoile, *Discrete Math.* 29, 53-76.

Linear and Branching Structures in the Semantics and Logics of Reactive Systems

Amir Pnueli
Department of Applied Mathematics
The Weizmann Institute of Science
Rehovot, 76100 Israel

Introduction

When a formal model is suggested as the appropriate formalization of an intuitive (or natural) structure or phenomenon, there are two basic questions that are related to its validity.

The first question is whether the level of abstraction, i.e. the choice between the features of the structure that are modelled and those which are ignored, is the right one. The second question is the consistency between the intuitive notion and its formal model, namely, can one display a behavior expressible by the features that are included in the model, which is not shared by the other.

Both these questions are very difficult to settle, since, relating a formal to an informal notions, they can never be settled by formal means. Usually they are easier to refute by exhibiting a counter example. In the positive direction, the best we can hope for is the gradual accumulation of successful applications of the model as well as failures of alternatives.

A very helpful evidence is provided by reductions from independently developed alternative formalisms. When sufficient evidence has been accumulated, the associated formal model or theory is eventually promoted to the status of *thesis*. This has been the case for example with Church's thesis that formalizes the intuitive notion of effective computability by the formal notion of Turing Machine computability.

A more recent thesis is Scott's which claims that computability is equivalent to domain continuity, and in a broader framework identifies domain theory and denotational semantics as the appropriate formal models for studying sequential programs.

An important part of institutionalizing a formal model is a clarification of its limitations and range of applicability. For example, none would suggest using denotational semantic as the tool for analyzing the time complexity of a program, since this was one of the details that the designers of the formal model have intentionally decided to ignore or abstract away.

In some cases, a rivalry between two competing formalisms is not settled over a reasonable period, while convincing evidence is accumulated on both sides. In these cases the eventual result may be the establishment of accepted *dichotomy* or dual theory. Such was the case, for example, with Euclidean vs. non Euclidean geometry and the particle-wave dual view of light in classical physics. An important part in the acceptance of a dichotomy is again the clarification and delineation of the domains of applicability of each of the views.

Coming back to our more modest area, that of formalization of programming concepts, we find at least one such accepted dichotomy or dualism. It involves the alternative power domains constructions suggested for treating non-deterministic but sequential programs. The powerdomain associated with the Egli-Milner ordering [Pl1] is certainly different from the Smyth powerdomain [Sm]. However, it is clear that one approach should be preferred to the other depending on the way we wish to treat the existence of divergent computations. If the possibility of divergence is considered so catastrophic that in this case we do not care what the convergent computations may produce, we should use the Smyth ordering. Otherwise we should take the Egli-Milner ordering.

In this presentation I would like to suggest the institution of yet another dichotomy, namely the dichotomy between the branching and linear views of reactive systems. Instituting such a dichotomy implies agreeing that both are acceptable views of such systems, and investigating their respective domains of applicability, hoping to clarify the manner in which they complement each other.

The modest evidence that I offer here in support of this suggestion is to show that the distinction between the branching and linear views is a division that cuts across at least three different approaches to the formalization of reactive systems. These are formalization by process equivalences, by exterior semantics and by programming logics. By demonstrating a mapping between the controversies existing in each of these approaches, we hope to convince the reader that these are but three different aspects of the same controversy, which therefore has an existence independent of any particular framework.

Relational vs. Reactive or Sequential vs. Concurrent?

The question of linear vs. branching semantics arises naturally when we study *reactive* systems. Reactive systems are those systems whose behavior and specification cannot be adequately expressed by *relational* semantics, i.e. they cannot be satisfactorily described as computing a relation between an input and a corresponding output state. Typically, reactive systems are best described as maintaining an interaction with their environment. Some of the interaction may also include a final result, but other reactive systems such as operating systems, airline reservation systems and process control systems are never expected to terminate, so the notion of a final state which is essential to relational semantics is meaningless in such systems. A different case is that of a system that in its entirety does compute a relation, but it employs several modules that operate concurrently and maintain an interaction in order to achieve this common goal. In such cases the global specification of the entire system might very well be relational, but the specification of each module must be reactive. This supports our general feeling (see [Pn2], [HPn]) that the important distinction is not between sequential and concurrent systems but between the *relational* and *reactive* views of such systems.

A Simple Language for Processes

In order to illustrate our arguments we will use a very minimal language for *processes* (synonym for reactive systems). It combines the simplest concepts of CCS ([M1]) and the communication construct of TCSP ([BHR]).

We consider a *finite* set of *observable* actions Σ.

- Λ is the terminal process that can do no action. It is equivalent to NIL and STOP in CCS, TCSP respectively.
- If p is a process then so is ap, the process that may execute a and then behave like p (become p). We would often abbreviate $a\Lambda$ to a.

- If p and q are processes then so is $p+q$, the process that may behave both as p and as q.
- If p and q are processes and $A \subseteq \Sigma$ is a subset of actions then $p \parallel_A q$ is the process resulting from the concurrent activation of p and q requiring synchronization of p and q on any actions included in A.

It is straightforward to give operational semantics to terms in this language. For processes p and q and action $a \in \Sigma$, we denote by $p \xrightarrow{a} q$ the possibility of p executing the action a and becoming q (See [HM]). The rules defining this relation are:

1. $ap \xrightarrow{a} p$
2. $p \xrightarrow{a} r \Rightarrow (p+q) \xrightarrow{a} r$ and $(q+p) \xrightarrow{a} r$
3. $a \in A,\ p \xrightarrow{a} p',\ q \xrightarrow{a} q' \Rightarrow p \parallel_A q \xrightarrow{a} p' \parallel_A q'$
4. $a \notin A$ and $p \xrightarrow{a} r \Rightarrow p \parallel_A q \xrightarrow{a} r \parallel_A q$ and $q \parallel_A p \xrightarrow{a} q \parallel_A r$

In particular, there are no a and q such that $\Lambda \xrightarrow{a} q$, i.e. Λ can perform no action.

Note that this is the fragment of finite terms of CCS/TCSP which does not consider the unobservable action τ of CCS or its equivalent internal selection operator $\sqcap$ of TCSP.

Actually we will be even more minimal and assign semantics only to the sublanguage consisting of Σ,a, Λ and $+$, i.e. not including the $\parallel$ operator.

A Roadmap

Before we delve into the different formalization approaches and illustrate the branching vs. linear dichotomy in each, we present the following table which summarizes the entries belonging to each approach and division:

Approach: / View	Semantics by Equivalences	Exterior Semantics (Modeling)	Semantics by Logics
Branching	Observational Equivalence [M2]	Trees [FHLR]	STL [GS3], [GS2] HML [HM] RTL [BR]
Linear	Testing [dNH] Trace Congruence	Linear [FLP] Failures [BHR] Readiness [OH]	Linear TL [BKP]

Semantics by Equivalence

A bold step has been taken by Milner in his definition of the semantics of CCS ([M2]) in stating that the semantics of a programming language is fully specified when we provide the appropriate equivalence relation between programs. For those who insist that a semantics should be associated with some mapping or assignment of meanings, the provided mapping is that the meaning of a program P is the equivalence class of all programs that are equivalent to P. If one must have a more explanatory semantics using mapping into other domains (as we discuss in the next section) then at least this mapping should be ***fully abstract*** with respect to the specified equivalence. That is, two programs that map to different objects in the semantic domain must not be equivalent.

The notion of equivalence introduced for assigning semantics to CCS is ***observational equivalence***. For the definition of observational equivalence we only need the transition relation $p \xrightarrow{a} q$ defined by the operational semantics.

Observational equivalence is the ***largest*** symmetric relation $\approx$ between processes that satisfies:

$p \approx q$ and $p \xrightarrow{a} p' \Rightarrow$ There exists a q' such that $q \xrightarrow{a} q'$ and $p' \approx q'$.

For example, let us consider the two processes $a(b+c)$ and $ab+ac$. We usually picture such processes by synchronization trees in which an action corresponds to an edge and $+$ to branch splitting:

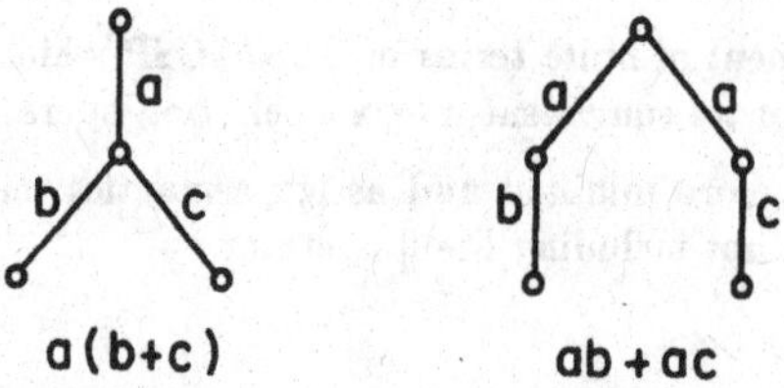

We claim that $a(b+c) \not\approx ab+ac$. We start by showing that $b \not\approx b+c$. This is because $b+c \xrightarrow{c} \Lambda$ while the process b (i.e. $b.\Lambda$) has no c successor. Now, observe that $ab+ac \xrightarrow{a} b$ while the only a successor of $a(b+c)$ is $b+c \not\approx b$.

On the other hand we can show that $a(b+c) \approx a(c+b)$. As a matter of fact Hennesy and Milner show in [HM] that the following four axioms completely characterize the relation $\approx$.

A1.	$x+(y+z)=(x+y)+z$	Associativity
A2.	$x+y=y+x$	Commutativity
A3.	$x+x=x$	Idempotence
A4.	$x+\Lambda=x$	Nullity

A question that naturally arises when we wish to apply this proof system is whether we can substitute *equals for equals* in any context. Thus, let $C(t)$ be a process in which t appears as a subterm. Suppose that we know that $t \approx t'$ by observational equivalence, can we infer that $C(t) \approx C(t')$. A relation that satisfies this requirement (i.e. $t \approx t' \Rightarrow C(t) \approx C(t')$ for every context C) is called a ***congruence***. Fortunately, for the simple language that we consider, observational equivalence is also a congruence. This holds even when we allow contexts that use the parallel composition construct $\|_A$.

In some sense observational equivalence can be described as taking the maximalistic approach: what is the maximal distinction between processes that we can externally observe? A dual approach would be to look for the minimal distinction, i.e. what processes must we distinguish.

First we observe that we must distinguish between processes that differ in their ***maximal traces***.

If the following is a sequence of transitions:

$$p = p_1 \xrightarrow{a_1} p_2 \xrightarrow{a_2} \cdots \xrightarrow{a_k} p_{k+1}$$

then we say that the sequence $a_1, a_2, \ldots, a_k$ is a ***trace*** of p. It is called a ***maximal*** trace if p_{k+1} is ***terminal***, i.e. has no possible successors. With each process p we can associate the set of its maximal traces $Tr(p)$. Thus, $Tr(a(b+c)) = Tr(ab+ac) = \{ab, ac\}$. We could try to define an equivalence $\sim_{Tr}$ by letting $p \sim_{Tr} q$ iff $Tr(p) = Tr(q)$. However, it is easily shown not to be a ***congruence***. We already observed that $a(b+c) \sim_{Tr} (ab+ac)$. However if we substitute these two processes in the context $ab \parallel_\Sigma (\ )$ we find that they behave differently.

In fact $Tr(ab \parallel_\Sigma a(b+c)) = \{ab\}$ while $Tr(ab \parallel_\Sigma ab+ac) = \{a, ab\}$

To see how we obtain a as a maximal trace consider the transition

$$ab \parallel_\Sigma (ab+ac) \xrightarrow{a} b \parallel_\Sigma c$$

and the term $b \parallel_\Sigma c$ is terminal (actually represents a deadlock).

Consequently we define the stronger relation of ***trace congruence*** $\sim$ which is defined to be the largest congruence which is contained in the trace equivalence $\sim_{Tr}$.

According to this definition $a(b+c) \not\sim ab+ac$.

It is easy to show that trace congruence contains observational equivalence, which means that it does not distinguish processes that are observationally equivalent. This containment is in fact strict as can be shown by the following two processes

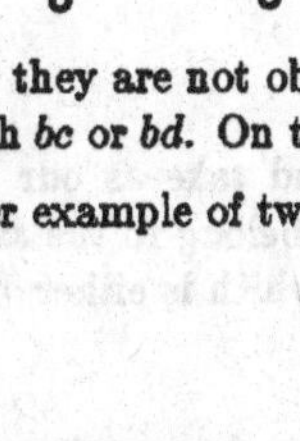

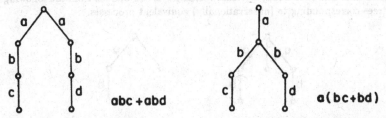

abc + abd

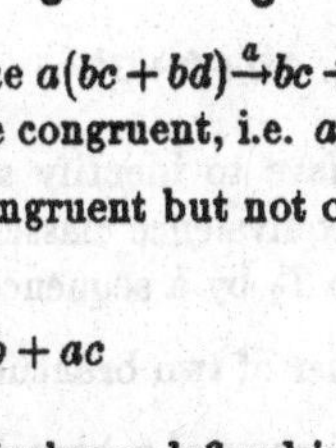

a(bc+bd)

Clearly they are not observationally equivalent since $a(bc+bd) \xrightarrow{a} bc+bd$ which is inequivalent to both bc or bd. On the other hand they are trace congruent, i.e. $abc+abd \sim a(bc+bd)$.

Another example of two processes that are trace congruent but not observationally equivalent is

$$ab + ac + a(b+c) \sim ab + ac$$

Trace congruence is very similar to the testing equivalence defined in [dNH]. Actually, for the simple language we consider here the two relations are identical.

An argument that we may advance in order to claim that trace congruence is the right equivalence relation is that when we observe a complete system from outside, the only observable behavior is given by the maximal traces. Specifying an internal module, we only need as much detail that will guarantee replaceability. That is, two alternate modules that agree on this level of detail should be completely interchangeable in the sense that exchanging one by the other will not change the external behavior. Hence trace congruence seems to be precisely the relation we are looking for.

We shall not at this point explain why observational equivalence is associated with the branching view while trace congruence corresponds to the linear view. This will be clarified when we consider the next approach. At this stage it is sufficient to observe that we have identified two distinct equivalence relations, the observational one strictly smaller (hence stronger) than the other. We also explained the motivation leading to each of them which may be summarizes as:

For OE: Distinguish as much as you can, based on external observations.

For TC: Distinguish only these processes that may cause in some context different external behaviors of the full system.

Exterior Semantics

The more traditional approach to semantics is by mapping programs to some well understood domain, such as the domain of functions or relations for the relational case. It is quite clear that in the reactive case the semantic object must reflect the ongoing performance of the process it models and not just the final result. There are two natural candidates for such mappings.

Under the ***branching*** view we associate with each process the ***computation tree*** (also called synchronization tree) that represents all the possible behaviors of the process. This association is so simple for our language that we will not give a formal definition. We have been using such trees already in the previous sections in order to illustrate processes. Unfortunately this association does not yield a fully abstract semantics as can be seen from the following example of the trees corresponding to (observationally) equivalent processes.

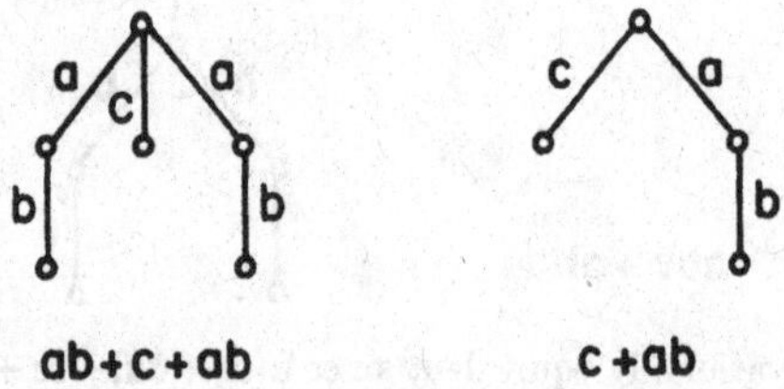

Consequently we have to identify several computation trees and take as our semantic domain the domain of equivalence classes. Two trees T_1 and T_2 will belong to the same class if we can get from T_1 to T_2 by a sequence of transformation each of which is either

a) Exchanging the order of two branches,

b) Creating additional copy of a branch and its associated subtree and appending it to the same node.

c) Deleting one of two identical subtrees hanging from the same node.

Operation a) is unnecessary if we define the domain as consisting of unordered trees. It is quite clear that these three operations reflect the obvious axioms $x + y = y + x$ and $x + x = x$ respectively. Consequently the tree equivalence we defined is almost identical to the observational equivalence we started with, and it is not very surprising that now it yields a fully abstract semantics.

Let us move directly to the linear semantics. The view taken here is that we should associate with a process the set of all of its computations. As we already observed, since this corresponds to the trace equivalence it is not strong enough. Let us return to the example of the two processes $a(b+c)$ and $ab+ac$ which were trace equivalent but not trace congruent. Inspecting the context that uncovered their differences we observe that it discovered the potential of deadlock in one that did not exist in the other. It is clear that the potential of deadlock is related to the branching structure of the process. Thus, $a(b+c)$ differs from $ab+ac$ in that the first can deadlock after performing a only if neither b nor c were available for synchronization. The other process may perform a and deadlock for lack of b alone or similarly for lack of c.

Once we realize that the missing element is the characterization of the deadlock potential associated with a process, it is very easy to come up with following suggestion:

<u>Broom Semantics:</u>

For each node n in the synchronization tree form the trace leading to this node (the stick) followed by the brush part that represents all the actions that are immediately possible from n.

Thus for $a(b+c)$ we obtain the following brooms:

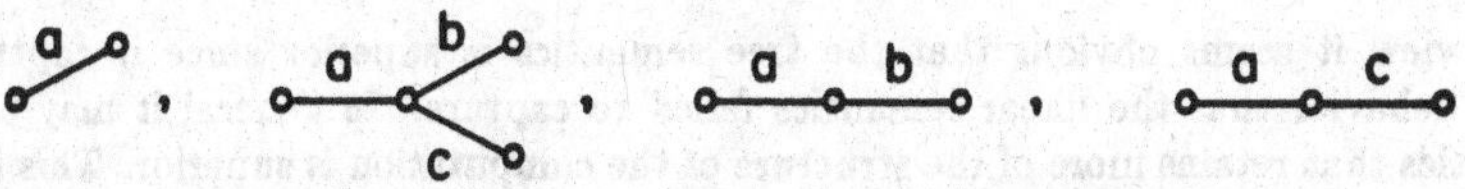

while for $ab+ac$, we obtain the following broom collection:

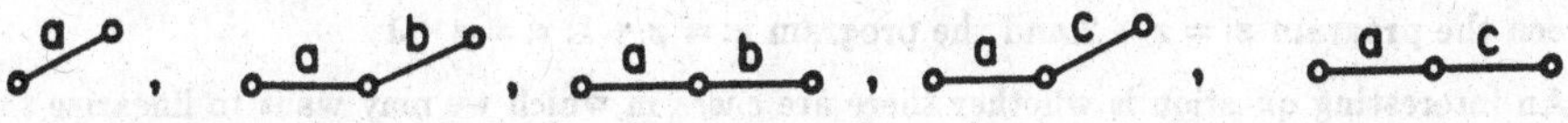

It is not difficult to realize that the broom semantics is nothing else than the ***acceptance*** semantics of [FLP], the ***readiness*** semantics of [OH] and when complementing the brush with respect to Σ is the ***failure*** semantics of [BHR]. For the process $a(b+c)$ this is usually represented as the set:

$$\{<\epsilon,\{a\}>,\ <a,\{b,c\}>,\ <ab,\{\ \}>,\ <ac,\{\ \}>\}$$

However, this semantics is not yet satisfactory. Observe that the two processes $ab+ac+a(b+c)$ and $ab+ac$ that we claimed to be trace congruent, produce the following broom sets respectively:

$$\{<\epsilon,\{a\}>,\ <a,\{b\}>,\ <ab,\{\ \}>,\ <a,\{c\}>,\ <ac,\{\ \}>,\ <a,\{b,c\}>\}$$

and

$$\{<\epsilon,\{a\}>,\ <a,\{b\}>,\ <ab,\{\ \}>,\ <a,\{c\}>,\ <ac,\{\ \}>\}$$

which are not equal.

If we examine more closely the guilty party, i.e. $<a, \{b, c\}>$ we find that it does not convey new information that is not already provided by the other brooms in the collection. What it tells us that is possible for the process to perform a and get to a state such that if ***neither*** b ***nor*** c are available it will deadlock. But this is already represented by another broom in the collection, e.g. $<a, \{b\}>$ which ensures deadlock in the situation that neither b nor c are available. We may therefore define a broom $<\sigma, S>$ with $\sigma \in \Sigma^*$, $S \subseteq \Sigma$ to be ***redundant*** in a collection C, if the collection contains another broom $<\sigma, S'>$ with $S' \subseteq S$. We may eliminate a redundant broom from a collection. Therefore from now on we will only consider collections with no redundant brooms.

It is not difficult to prove that the broom semantics is fully abstract with respect to trace congruence. Furthermore, in addition to inducing an equivalence relation among processes it also induces an ***ordering*** compatible with the equivalence. The ordering is defined by

$$P \sqsubseteq Q \quad \text{iff} \quad Br(P) \subseteq Br(Q)$$

This ordering is a very useful addition to the axiomatic system characterizing trace congruence. It has been proposed both in [dNH] and [BHR], but with inverted sense (i.e. they write $Q \sqsubseteq P$ whenever we write $P \sqsubseteq Q$).

It is obvious that the broom semantics captures more of the branching structure of the synchronization trees than just the traces. But the branching element that it captures is very limited.

At first view it seems obvious that the tree semantics is superior since it captures a difference in behavior that the linear semantics failed to capture. In general it may appear that a semantics that retains more of the structure of the computation is superior. This is not, however, the case since by the ideal criterion of ***full abstractness*** a semantics should be only as detailed as is necessary in order to distinguish between programs that must be distinguishable. Thus, conventional denotational semantics of relational programs is considered to be superior to operational semantics because it does not contain sufficient detail to be able to distinguish between the program $x := x + 2$ and the program $x := x + 1; x := x + 1$.

An interesting question is whether there are cases in which we may want to linearize the synchronization tree in a different manner.

Let us consider an alternative parallel composition construct, that we denote by $\bowtie$. The main difference between this construct and $\|$ is in the synchronization convention. The $\bowtie$ construct is modelled after the ***broadcast*** primitive suggested by Harel in [Ha]. According to this convention a process may perform any action at will, but once such an action a is performed, all the processes that can do a now must perform it together.

This can be expressed in the operational semantics by replacing clauses (3) and (4) by:

(3′) $p \xrightarrow{a} p', \quad q \xrightarrow{a} q' \Rightarrow p \bowtie q \xrightarrow{a} p' \bowtie q'$

(4′) $p \xrightarrow{a} r$ and $q \stackrel{a}{\not\rightarrow} \Rightarrow p \bowtie q \xrightarrow{a} r \bowtie q$
and $q \bowtie p \xrightarrow{a} q \bowtie r$

Here $q \stackrel{a}{\not\rightarrow}$ means that q cannot perform an a transition.

Naturally this modification cannot affect the observational equivalence of processes that do not contain parallel composition. It does however modify the strength of trace congruence. To see this consider the following two processes:

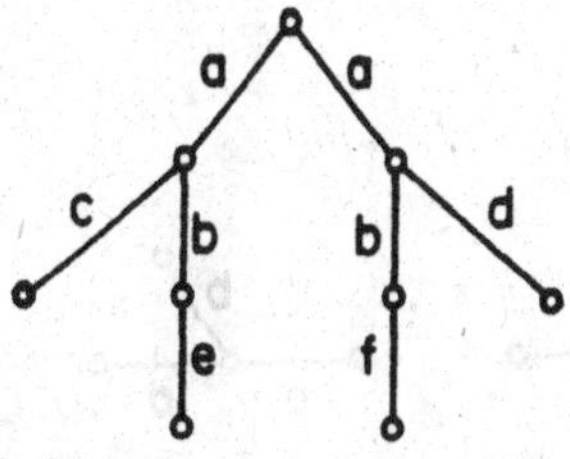

a(c+be) + a(d+bf)

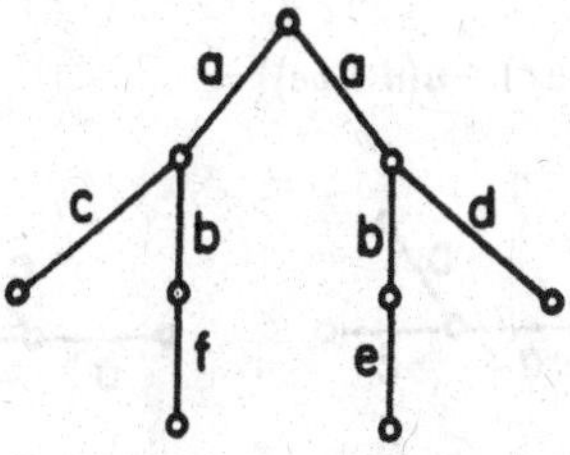

a(c+bf) + a(d+be)

They are obviously not observationally equivalent. They are trace congruent relative to || since the broom semantics of both yields:

$\{\langle\epsilon, \{a\}\rangle, \langle a, \{b, c\}\rangle, \langle ac, \{\ \}\rangle, \langle ab, \{e\}\rangle, \langle abe, \{\ \}\rangle, \langle a, \{b, d\}\rangle, \langle ad, \{\}\rangle, \langle ab, \{f\}\rangle, \langle abf, \{\}\rangle\}$.

However they are not trace congruent relative to $\bowtie$. To see this run them in parallel with $a(c+be)$.

We obtain:

$Tr(a(c+be) \bowtie a(c+be)+a(d+bf)) =$
$\{ac, abe, acd, adc, acbf, abef, abfe, adbe\}$

$Tr(a(c+be) \bowtie a(c+bf)+a(d+be)) =$
$\{ac, abef, abfe, acd, acbe, abe, adc, adbe\}$

In this case the additional consideration is not that of deadlock, since under this communication regime no process may deadlock. There is however the consideration that in performing *abe* the first process must be ensured that no *c* event will happen between the *a* and *b* events. The second process must require the same but for the *d* event that may divert it from following the *abe* route.

A closer examination shows that the appropriate linearization of the synchronization tree that corresponds to broadcast communication is the:

Barbed Semantics

Draw maximal traces of the tree, however at each node mark the immediately available actions which the trace decided to ignore.

This will give the following barbed traces:

$Barb(a(c+be)+a(d+bf)) =$

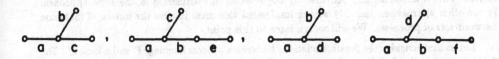

while

$$\text{Barb}(a(c+bf)+a(d+be)) =$$

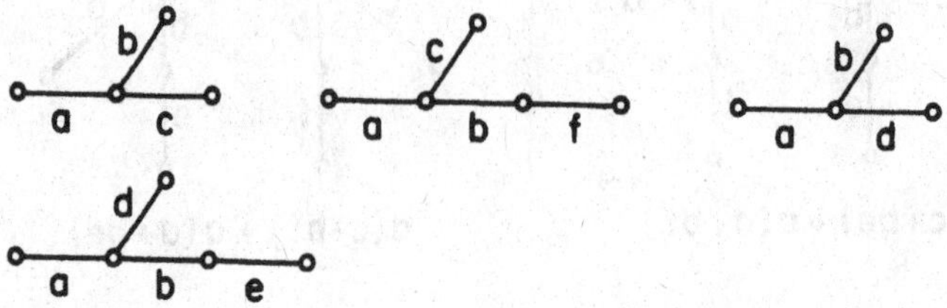

which obviously differ.

We may use the fact that changes in the communication construct affect the semantics and induced equivalence even of the nondeterministic fragment (that does not use communication), as a criticism against trace congruence and a praise for the stability of observational equivalence. But the same argument may be turned around and marked as an advantage of the trace congruence.

After all, we managed quite well to deal with nondeterminism in the relational framework as long as no concurrency or communication were introduced. Consequently, the need to apply behavioral analysis even to the non communicating fragment arose only because of the presence of communication in the context. Therefore any behavioral approach that is not sensitive to changes in the communication mechanism must be too detailed.

Semantics by Logics

The observation that logic can serve as a tool for defining the semantics of programs dates back to the pioneering work of Floyd ([Fl]) and Hoare ([H]). By this approach the semantics of a program P is defined as the set of all formulas in the logic that P satisfies. Basic to this approach is the definition of the relation of satisfaction between a program and a formula. More recently, the logic approach to the semantics of programs has been extended to cover also concurrent and reactive systems. (See [OG], [Pn1], [AFR] and many others).

Of course, the utility of logics in programming goes much beyond merely defining a semantics. Particularly in the realm of reactive systems, programming logics have proved to be of utmost importance for the specification, verification and systematic development of such systems. Naturally, the same may be claimed for the two other approaches to formalization. There is however an inherent advantage to the logic approach, which is the ability to deal with *partial specifications*. Thus, it is often the case that we wish to establish that a given process satisfies a particular property (e.g. safety, liveness, etc.) without considering its full specification. This is automatically provided by the relation of satisfaction in the logic approach. In the other approaches, the only way to implement this must involve the notion of inclusion between *sets* of processes. We will return later to this point.

Let us first consider the possible relations between a process language $\mathbf{P}$ and a logic $\mathcal{L}$. The first requisite is the definition of the satisfiability relation between a program and a formula. There are two ways to do this:

a) **Indirectly, via intermediate semantics. In this method we map the programs first into a semantic domain that may be either operational or denotational, and then define satisfiability of formulas by the semantic object. In some sense this was the approach used in [Fl] for relational programs and in [HM] for reactive processes.**

b) **Directly in a syntax directed manner. This was the approach used in [H] for relational programs and in [BKP1] for concurrent programs.**

Once the satisfaction relation is defined, we may associate with each process p the *set* of formulas that is satisfies $\Phi(p)$. This association induces an equivalence relation between processes, $\equiv_\Phi$, by which

$$p \equiv_\Phi q \Leftrightarrow \Phi(p) = \Phi(q).$$

Actually it also induces an ordering between processes which is compatible with the above equivalence:

$$p \sqsubseteq_\Phi q \Leftrightarrow \Phi(p) \subseteq \Phi(q).$$

Hennesy and Milner formulated in [HM] the notion of *adequacy* of a logic with respect to a given equivalence relation on a language of processes. By their definition a logic is adequate for a given process language equipped with a native equivalence relation $\approx$ if the equivalence induced by the logic $\equiv_\Phi$ coincides with the native equivalence $\approx$. by their formulation: $p \not\approx q$ iff there exists a formula $\varphi \in \mathcal{L}$ which is satisfied by one of the processes but not by the other.

However, this requirement of adequacy is the weakest requirement of compatibility between a process language and a logic. A symptom of its weakness is that the same simple logic, HML, suggested in [HM] is adequate for both the language of *finite* CCS terms as well as for the language that allows recursion.

A stronger compatibility requirement is *expressivity*. A logic $\mathcal{L}$ is said to be *expressive* for the process language $\mathbf{P}$, if for every process $p \in \mathbf{P}$, there exists a *characteristic formula* $L(p) \in \mathcal{L}$ such that

a) **For every processes p and q,**

$$p \models \mathcal{L}(q) \Leftrightarrow p \approx q$$

b) **For every process p and a formula φ,**

$$p \models \varphi \Leftrightarrow L(p) \rightarrow \varphi.$$

It is not difficult to see that these two requirements also imply:

c) $p \approx q \Leftrightarrow L(p) \equiv L(q).$

and adequacy.

Note that having an expressive logic for a language enables the reduction of the verification problem by a) and the equivalence problem by b) into the validity problem within $\mathcal{L}$ with obvious advantages.

The program of developing logics which are expressive for observational equivalence over CCS, has been persistently pursued by Graf and Sifakis in a series of papers [GS1], [GS2], [GS3].

An even stronger association between processes and logic is established when we have an inverse translation that associates with each formula $\varphi \in \mathcal{L}$ a *set* of processes, $P(\varphi)$ that contains all the processes satisfying φ. Abstractly, we can always consider $P(\varphi)$, however we call a process language *expressive* for a logic, if the translation $P(\varphi)$ is *syntactic*. Of course, to obtain such expressivity we must enrich the process language by operators that construct process sets.

Obvious candidates are the set constructors, $\cup$, $\cap$ and complementation, but we obviously need some more. Again we cite [GS3] where such operators have been suggested even though they are not presented as process operators but rather as logic operators. In fact, once we have a pair consisting of a process language $\mathbb{P}$ and a logic $\mathcal{L}$ which are mutually expressive, there is no longer a reason to distinguish between the two. For example problems in the logic such as the validity of $\varphi \rightarrow \psi$ can be reduced to inclusions of process sets in the process language, i.e. $P(\varphi) \subseteq P(\psi)$.

This brings us to the observation that a process language deserves to be called a specification language, rather than a programming language, only if it contains operators that construct sets of processes.

Coming back to particular logics that are appropriate for our simple language, we have again the choice between branching and linear logics. This is not the place to give a full account of the controversy between branching and linear temporal logics. The interesting reader may review its development through [BMP], [CE], [QS], [La], [EH].

The relevant facts are that on one hand we have the linear time temporal logic as defined for example in [GPSS]. On the other hand there are the intermediate level branching time logics which include UB of [BMP], CTL of [CE] the branching logic used in [QS] and also the μ-calculus presented in [Ko].

In a comparison between the linear version and these versions, Lamport concluded in [La] that they are incomparable. For example the linear logic statement of fairness $\Box\Diamond p \rightarrow \Box\Diamond q$ which states that every computation, in which p happens infinitely many times also achieves q infinitely many times, cannot be expressed in any of these logics.

In the other direction there are properties expressible in branching logics that cannot be expressed in the linear version. The simplest one is the existence of a computation that sometime realizes p.

A more sophisticated fairness property discussed in [QS] states that no computation ever looses the potential for realizing p.

Lamport also claimed that the properties expressible in branching time and not expressible in linear time are often not very useful in actual specifications. For example the fact that a program *may* sometimes produce p is not something that can be depended on, and therefore should not be included in a specification.

In response to this criticism, Emerson and Halpern produced in [EH] a maximalistic branching time logic, CTL*, which can obviously express everything that is expressible in the linear logic plus the additional things that can only be expressed in branching logics. For example it may state the property that every computation that never looses the potential of realizing p would eventually realize it.

In line with the other comparisons that we do in this paper it seems that the interesting comparison is between CTL* and the linear logic. And the conclusion we would like to draw is that, indeed, CTL* has a higher expressive power (just as observational equivalence is stronger than trace congruence)but do we really need this extra power in all cases?

Branching Logic

In this section we show that the HML logic suggested in [HM] is not only adequate for observational equivalence over the simple language of finite terms as has already been shown in [HM] but is also expressive for this language.

The logic consists of the constants T and F, the positive boolean connectives $\wedge$ and $\vee$, and the modalities $[a]\varphi$ and $<a>\varphi$ for every $a \in \Sigma$. We have chosen not to include negation, but its addition would not change much.

We follow [HM] in defining the satisfaction relation between processes and formulas, using the operational semantics:

- $p \models T$, $p \not\models F$ for every process p.
- $p \models \varphi \vee \psi$ iff either $p \models \varphi$ or $p \models \psi$.
- $p \models \varphi \wedge \psi$ iff both $p \models \varphi$ and $p \models \psi$.
- $p \models <a>\varphi$ iff there exists a p' such that $p \xrightarrow{a} p'$ and $p' \models \varphi$.
- $p \models [a]\varphi$ iff for every p' such that $p \xrightarrow{a} p'$ it follows that $p' \models \varphi$.

We proceed to show that HML is expressive for observational equivalence over our language. We define the translation $L: \mathbf{P} \rightarrow \mathcal{L}$ that produces for each process $p \in \mathbf{P}$ its characteristic formula $L(p)$.

$$L(\Lambda) = \bigwedge_{a \in \Sigma} [a]F \qquad \text{(also denoted by tt)}$$

$$L(ap) = <a>L(p) \wedge [a]L(p) \wedge \bigcirc a$$

$\bigcirc a$ is an abbreviation for *only* a, and stands for $\bigcirc a = \bigwedge_{b \in \Sigma - \{a\}} [b]F$.

In order to define $L(p_1 + p_2)$ we prove by induction that for each $p \in \mathbf{P}$ the characteristic formula $L(p)$ has the following normal form:

$$L(p) = \left(\bigwedge_{i \in I} <a_i>\varphi_i \wedge \bigwedge_{b \in \Sigma} [b]\psi_b \right)$$

Superscripting I and ψ_b by 1 or 2 corresponding to the two processes p_1 and p_2, we define:

$$L(p_1 + p_2) = \bigwedge_{i \in I^1 \cup I^2} <a_i>\varphi_i \wedge \bigwedge_{b \in \Sigma} [b](\psi_b^1 \vee \psi_b^2)$$

Consider for example the characteristic formula for the processes $a(b+c)$ and $ab+ac$. We abbreviate in this presentation $<a>p \wedge [a]p$ by $\langle\!\lbrack a \rbrack\!\rangle\, p$

$$L(a(b+c)) = \langle\!\lbrack a \rbrack\!\rangle\, (<b>tt \wedge <c>tt \wedge [a]F \wedge [b]tt \wedge [c]tt)$$
$$\wedge [b]F \wedge [c]F$$

$$\begin{aligned} L(ab+ac) = & <a>[<b>tt \wedge [a]F \wedge [b]tt \wedge [c]F\,] \wedge \\ & <a>[<c>tt \wedge [a]F \wedge [b]F \wedge [c]tt\,] \wedge \\ & [a]\Big[\Big([<b>tt \wedge [b]tt \wedge [c]F\,] \vee [<c>tt \wedge [b]F \wedge [c]tt\,]\Big) \wedge [a]F\Big] \\ & \wedge [b]F \wedge [c]F \end{aligned}$$

It is not difficult to verify that these two formulas are not equivalent.

It is possible to prove that the characteristic translation satisfies the requirements for expressivity. We refer the reader to [GS3] for another translation and also for a possible back translation from the logic into the process language. [GS2] also contains a treatment of the case of infinite processes.

Linear Logic

While the branching axiomatization of processes can be described as ***structural***, in the linear axiomatization we adopt a more ***operational*** view.

This is an obvious consequence of the linear interpretation by which a process is viewed as a generator (or acceptor) of possible behavior sequences. The logic then states a sequence property, and a formula is considered to be a valid specification for a process if all the sequences generated by the process satisfy the process.

Consider the process $a(b+c)$. Our linear characterization for it would be:

$$L(a(b+c)) = d(a) \vee <a>(d(b,c) \vee <b>d \vee <c>d)$$

Where the following abbreviations are used:

$d(a)$ – deadlocked, waiting for a-synchronization.

$<a>p$ – eventually will do a, and after it follow with p.

Thus the above description states that every execution of the process will either deadlock initially because of a missing a-synchronization from the environment, or will eventually perform a and then will either deadlock waiting for either b or c, or eventually perform b or c and deadlock waiting for nothing, i.e. terminate.

Since disjunctions distribute over the $<a>$ modality, the above is equivalent to:

$$d(a) \vee <a>d(b,c) \vee <a><b>d \vee <a><c>d$$

which precisely captures our broom semantics.

We will give now a more precise explanation of the operators involved. For simplicity we assume a distinction between actions performed by the process and those performed by the environment.

A particular state predicate $\imath$ means that currently no action is taken by the process.

The modality $<a>p$ is an abbreviation for

$$<a>p = \imath \mathcal{U}(a \wedge \bigcirc p).$$

That is, after a finite period in which the process is not active it will perform a and then proceed with p.

The deadlock statement is actually structured as follows:

$$d(a_1,\ldots,a_k) = \Box \imath \wedge \Box na(a_1) \wedge \cdots \wedge \Box na(a_k)$$

where $na(a_i)$ implies that no a_i is ever available from the environment.

This structuring explains why

$$d(a_1) \vee d(a_1, a_2) = [\,\Box \imath \wedge \Box na(a_1)] \vee [\,\Box \imath \wedge \Box na(a_1) \wedge \Box na(a_2)] \equiv d(a_1)$$

or more generally, for each $S_1 \subseteq S_2$

$$d(S_1) \vee d(S_2) \equiv d(S_1)$$

which is required by the broom semantics.

The cannonical translation from processes to logic formula is easily defined by:

$$L(\Lambda) = d$$
$$L(a_1p_1 + \cdots + a_kp_k) = d(a_1,\ldots,a_k) \vee \bigvee_{i=1}^{k} <a_i>L(p_i)$$

We can show that it is expressive for trace congruence. One advantage of the linear approach is that we can easily extend the semantic mapping L to cover parallel composition. To do this properly we slightly modify the communication regime in order to identify the partner responsible for any action. Then we will split Σ into Δ and $\overline{\Delta}$ and allow synchronization only between matching actions, i.e. a and $\bar{a}$. Again we stipulate that no process may perform both a and $\bar{a}$. Then we may redefine $na(a)$ as $\neg\bar{a}$ and $\imath$ for the process p as $\bigwedge_{a\in\Sigma(p)} \neg a$, that is, no action for which p is responsible is currently performed. With these modifications we may define:

$$L(p \parallel_A q) = L(p) \wedge L(q) \wedge \bigwedge_{a\in A} \Box(a \equiv \bar{a})$$

That is, a computation of $p \parallel_A q$ must satisfy both $L(p)$ and $L(q)$ and also obey the restriction that for any $a \in A$, performance of a must be accompanied by a performance of $\bar{a}$.

More details about the linear formalization of communicating proceses are available in [BKP2] .

We conclude this section by showing how to modify the temporal semantics when considering broadcast communications.

The required clauses are:

$$L(a_1p_1 + \cdots + a_kp_k) = \bigvee_{i=1}^{k} \Big((\imath \wedge \bigwedge_{j=1}^{k} \neg\bar{a}_j)\mathcal{U}(a_i \wedge \bigcirc L(p_i)) \Big)$$
$$L(p \,|\!|\!| \, q) = L(p) \wedge L(q)$$

In this description we insist that while waiting in front of $\Sigma_{i=1}^{k} a_i p_i$ no matching $\overline{a}_i$ occurs.

It is possible to check that this temporal semantics is compatible with both the barbed semantics and its associated trace congruence.

Conclusions

In this presentation we reviewed the dichotomy between branching and linear views of reactive systems as they are reflected in three different approaches to the formalization of reactive systems. Hopefully we succeeded in convincing the reader that these views are distinct and represent different attitudes to the desired level of abstractness in the semantics of reactive systems. The branching view is always more detailed than the linear view, and the important question that should be left open for the user of the approach, is whether this additional detail is necessary for his application.

In this presentation we only considered the branching vs. linear dichotomy in the treatment of nondeterminism. A very similar dichotomy exists in the treatment of concurrency itself, namely between the partial order (hence acyclic graph) representation of causality and concurrency and its linearization by all the total orders consistent with this partial order. We suggest a similar study for the identification of the elements captured in the partial order which are lost in the linearization.

References

[AFR] Apt, K.R., Francez, N., DeRoever, W.P. A Proof System for Communicating Sequential Processes, *TOPLAS 2*, 3 (1980) 359–385.

[BBKM] de Bakker, J.W., Bergstra, J.A., Klop, J.W., Meyer, J.J.C. Linear Time and Branching Time Semantics for Recursion with Merge, 10th ICALP, *LNCS* 154 (1983) 39–51.

[BHR] Brookes, S.D., Hoare, C.A.R., Roscoe, A.W. A Theory of Communicating Sequential Processes, *JACM* 31 (1984) 560–569.

[BKP1] Barringer, H., Kuiper, R., Pnueli, A. Now You May Compose Temporal Logic Specifications, *16th ACM Symposium on Theory of Computing* (1984) 51–63.

[BKP2] Barringer, H., Kuiper, R., Pnueli, A. A Compositional Temporal Approach to a CSP-like Language, *Proc. of IFIP Conference, the Role of Abstract Models in Information Processing*, Vienna (1985).

[BMP] Ben Ari, M., Manna, Z., Pnueli, A. The Temporal Logic of Branching Time, *Acta Informatica* 20 (1983) 207–226.

[Br1] Brookes, S.D. A Semantics and Proof System for Communicating Processes, 2nd Conference on Logics of Programs, Springer Verlag *LNCS* 164 (1983)68–85.

[Br2] Brookes, S.D. On the Relationship of CCS and CSP, 10th ICALP, Springer Verlag *LNCS* 154 (1983) 83–96.

[BR] Brookes, S.D., Rounds, W.C. Behavioral Equivalence Relations Induced by Programming Logics, 10th ICALP, Springer Verlag *LNCS* 154 (1983) 97–108.

[CE] Clarke, E.M., Emerson, E.A. Design and Synthesis of Synchronization Skeletons using Branching Time Temporal Logic, Proc. of an IBM Workshop on Logics of Programs, *LNCS* **131** (1981) 52–71.

[dN] De Nicola A Complete Set of Axioms for a Theory of Communicating Sequential Processes, Foundations of Computation Theory, Springer Verlag *LNCS* **158** (1983) 115–126.

[EH] Emerson, E.A., Halpern, J.Y. 'Sometimes' and 'Not Never' Revisited: On Branching Versus Linear Time, 10th ACM Symposium on Principles of Programming Languages (1983).

[FHLR] Francez, N., Hoare, C.A.R., Lehmann, D., DeRoever, W.P. Semantics of Non-Determinism, Concurrency and Communication, *JCSS 19* **3** (1979).

[Fl] Floyd, R.W. Assigning Meanings to Programs, Proc. Symposium on Applied Mathematics, *AMS*, 19 (1967).

[FLP] Francez, N., Lehmann, D., Pnueli, A. A Linear History Semantics for Languages for Distributed Programming, *Theoretical Computer Science* **32** (1984) 25–46.

[GPSS] Gabbay, D., Pnueli, A., Stavi, J., Shelah, S. On the Temporal Analysis of Fairness, 7th ACM Symposium on Principles of Programming Languages (1980) 163–173.

[GS1] Graf, S., Sifakis, J. A Modal Characterization of Observational Congruence on Finite Terms of CCS, 11th ICALP, *LNCS* **172** (1984).

[GS2] Graf, S., Sifakis, J. A Logic for the Specification and Proof of Controllable Processes of CCS, Proceedings Advanced Institute on Logics and Models for Verification and Specification of Concurrent Systems, La Colle Surs Loupe (1984).

[GS3] Graf, S., Sifakis, J. A Logic for the Description of Non-Deterministic Programs and Their Properties, *IMAG*, Grenoble (1985).

[H] Hoare, C.A.R. An Axiomatic Approach to Computer Programming, *CACM 12*, 10 (1969).

[Ha] Harel, D. Statecharts: A Visual Approach to Complex Systems, Technical Report CS84-05, Weizmann Institute of Science.

[HM] Hennesy, M., Milner R. Algebraic Laws for Nondeterminism and Concurrency, *JACM 32* 1 (1985) 137–161.

[HPn] Harel, D., Pnueli, A. On the Development of Reactive Systems, Proceeding Advanced Institute on Logics and Models for Verification and Specification of Concurrent Systems. La Colle Sur Loupe (Oct. 84).

[HP] Hennesy, M., Plotkin, G. A Term Model for CCS, 9th Conference on Mathematical Foundations of Computer Science, *LNCS* **88** (1980) 261–274.

[Ko] Kozen, D. Results on the Propositional μ-calculus, 9th ICALP, *LNCS* **140** (1982) 340–359.

[La] Lamport, L. "Sometimes" is Sometimes "Not Never", 7th ACM Symposium on Principles of Programming Languages (1980) 174–185.

[M1] Milner, R. Fully Abstract Models of Typed λ-calculi, *Theoretical Computer Science* (1977).

[M2] Milner, R. A Calculus of Communicating Systems, *LNCS* **92** (1980).

[M3] Milner, R. A Calculi for Synchrony and Asynchrony, *Theoretical Computer Science* *25*, **3** (1983) 267–310.

[NH] de Nicola, R., Hennesy, M.C.B. Testing Equivalences for Processes, 10th ICALP, *LNCS* **154** (1983).

[OG] Owicki, S., Gries, D. An Axiomatic Proof Technique for Parallel Programs, *Acta Informatica* **6** (1976).

[OH] Olderog, E.R., Hoare, C.A.R. Specification Oriented Semantics for Communicating Processes, 10th ICALP, *LNCS* **154** (1983) 561–572.

[Pl] Plotkin, G.D. A Powerdomain Construction, *SIAM Journal on Computing 5*, **3** (1976) 452–487.

[Pn1] Pnueli, A. The Temporal Semantics of Concurrent Programs, *Theoretical Computer Science*, **13** (1981) 45–60.

[Pn2] Pnueli, A. In Transition from Global to Modular Temporal Reasoning about Programs, Proc. Advanced Institute on Logics and Models for Verification and Specification of Concurrent Systems, La Colle Sur Loupe Springer Verlag (Oct. 84).

[QS] Queille, J.P., Sifakis, J. Fairness and Related Properties in Transition Systems—A Temporal Logic to deal with Fairness, *Acta Informatica* **19** (1983) 195–220.

[RB] Rounds, W.C., Brookes, S.D. Possible Futures, Acceptances, Refusals and Communicating Processes, 22nd IEEE Symposium Foundations of Computer Science (1981) 140–149.

[Sm] Smyth, M. Powerdomains, *JCSS 16*, **1** (1978).

[St] Stirling, C. A Complete Modal Proof for a Subset of SCCS, Mathematical Foundations of Software Development, Springer Verlag, *LNCS* **185** (1985) 251–266.

ABOUT RATIONAL SETS OF FACTORS OF A BI-INFINITE WORD

D. Beauquier - M. Nivat
L.I.T.P. - Université Paris VII

Abstract

In this paper, we consider the sets $F(u)$ of finite factors of bi-infinite words u, upon a finite alphabet A. A natural question about this notion is : are there several bi-infinite words which have the same set of finite factors. We prove that, if $F(u)$ is rational, then, there exists a unique bi-infinite word which has $F(u)$ as set of finite factors iff $F(u)$ has a non-exponential complexity (the complexity of $F(u)$ is the function $n \to \mathrm{Card}(F(u) \cap A^n)$) ; and if this condition is realized, in fact, $F(u)$ has a sub-linear complexity (there exists a constant C such that $\mathrm{card}(F(u) \cap A^n) \leq n+C$ for large enough integers n).

Furthermore, the proof gives a characterization of bi-infinite rational words : u is rational iff $F(u)$ is a rational set of non-exponential complexity.

Introduction

The theory of infinitary rational sets built by Buchi, McNaughton and Muller [2, 4, 6, 9] is well known today. Whereas the one of bi-infinitary rational sets is just arising [1, 7] except the first results of Thue [9].

Nevertheless, it is quite natural to consider, if $\mathcal{A} = (Q,F)$, $F \subset Q\times A\times Q$, is a finite automaton, the set of bi-infinite paths $\ldots, q_{-n}, a_{-n}, q_{-n+1}, \ldots q_{-1}, a_{-1}, q_o, a_o, q_1, a_1, \ldots, q_n, a_n, q_{n+1}, \ldots$ of $\mathcal{A}$ such that for every $z \in Z$, $(q_z, a_z, q_{z+1}) \in F$, and the set of connected bi-infinite words : $\ldots a_{-n} \ldots a_{-1} a_o a_1 \ldots a_n \ldots$ Extending the acceptance condition for infinite words, $\mathcal{A}$ is provided with distinguished sets T_g and T_d of repeated states, respectively on the left and on the right.

If $\mathcal{A} = (Q, F, T_g, T_d)$, the set ${}^{\omega}\mathcal{A}^{\omega}$ of bi-infinite words accepted by $\mathcal{A}$ is the set of the $\ldots a_{-n} \ldots a_{-1} a_o a_1 \ldots a_n \ldots$ such that there exists a path $\ldots q_{-n}, a_{-n}, q_{-n+1}, q_{-1}, a_{-1}, q_o, a_o, q_1, \ldots q_n, a_n, q_{n+1} \ldots$ in $\mathcal{A}$ verifying the condition :

$$\mathrm{card}\,\{n \in N \mid q_{-n} \in T_g\} = \mathrm{card}\,\{n \in N \mid q_n \in T_d\} = \omega$$

A set of bi-infinite words, L, is said rational iff there exists a finite automaton $\mathcal{A}$ such that $L = {}^{\omega}\mathcal{A}^{\omega}$. It is proved [7] that L is rational iff L is a finite union of sets ${}^{\omega}(Gi)\, Mi (Di)^{\omega}$ where Gi, Mi, Di are rational sets of finite words ; and, obviously the bi-infinite word u belongs to ${}^{\omega}(Gi)\, Mi(Di)^{\omega}$ iff u is equal to $\ldots g_{-n} g_{-n+1} \ldots g_1 m d_1 \ldots d_n d_{n+1} \ldots$ with $g_{-n} \in Gi$, $m \in Mi$, $g_n \in Di$.

The bi-infinite word u is said rational iff the set $\{u\}$ is rational ; it is then clear that u is rational iff $u = {}^{\omega}g\, m\, d^{\omega}$ for some $g, m, d \in A^+$.

Let u be a bi-infinite word, and $F(u)$ the set of its finite factors. Under an hypothesis of rationality for $F(u)$, we give in this paper a characterization of the sets $F(u)$ such that $F(u) = F(v) \Rightarrow u = v$, by the increase of the number of their elements of length n.

We prove that if $F(u) = F(v) \Rightarrow u = v$, then $\mathrm{card}(F(u) \cap A^n)$ grows up at most like $n+C$. We set up a converse : if $\mathrm{card}(F(u) \cap A_n)$ grows up less $F(u) = F(v) \Rightarrow u = v$. Furthermore, in this case, u is a rational bi-infinite word (the converse is obviously true).

So, we also obtain a characterization of rational bi-infinite words.

I. Preliminaries

A is a finite alphabet. A^* is the set of finite words written on the alphabet A.

The empty word is denoted by ϵ. $A^+ = A^* \setminus \{\epsilon\}$. We denote by A^ω (respectively ${}^\omega A$) the set of infinite words on the right (respectively on the left).

For every word of $A^* \cup A^\omega$, u^R is the *reverse image* of u : $u^R \in A^* \cup {}^\omega A$.

For $X \subset A^*$, we denote by X^ω the set of infinite words on the right of the form $x_1x_2 \ldots x_n \ldots$ $(x_n \in \setminus \{\epsilon\})$. And ${}^\omega X = ((X^R)^\omega)^R$.

A *dotted bi-infinite word* is an element of A

A *bi-infinite word* is an equivalence class for shift in the set A^Z : two dotted bi-infinite words u and v are equivalent iff there exists an integer p such that for every $n \in Z$, $u(n+p) = v(n)$.

Every $(u,v) \in A^\omega \times A^\omega$ defines a unique bi-infinite word denoted by u^Rv, which is the equivalence class of the dotted bi-infinite word w such that :

$$w(n) = v(n) \quad \text{for} \quad n > 0 \quad \text{and} \quad \omega(n) = u(1-n) \quad \text{for} \quad n \leq 0.$$

The relation $\underline{[}$ *"is factor"* is defined in the set of finite, infinite or bi-infinite words by :

$$f \,\underline{[}\, g \quad \text{iff} \quad \exists\, g_1, g_2 \;\; g = g_1 f g_2$$

If f and g are finite words, $|g|_f$ is the number of occurrences of f in g : $|g|_f = \mathrm{card}\{(g_1,g_2) \in A^* \times A^* / g = g_1fg_2\}$.

Let u be a word, we denote by $F(u)$ the set of finite factors of u. If $X \subset A^*$ $F(X) = \bigcup_{u \in X} F(u)$

If $u \in A^*$ $FD(u)$ (respectively $FG(u)$) is the set of right factors (respectively left factors) of u.

If $u \in A^*$ FD(u) (respectively FG(u)) is the set of right factors (respectively left factors) of u.

A sequence (α_n) of finite words is completely increasing for the relation $\sqsubseteq$ iff for every n :

$\exists \beta_n, \gamma_n \in A^* \quad \alpha_{n+1} = \beta_n \alpha_n \gamma_n$

Every completely increasing sequence (α_n) has a upperbound which is the bi-infinite word $u = \ldots \beta_1 \beta_0 \alpha_0 \gamma_0 \gamma_1 \ldots$ (be careful, this bound is not unique, as proved by this example

Let $\alpha_0 = b$ and for every $n \geq 0 \quad \alpha_{n+1} = a\alpha_n\alpha_n a$.

This sequence (α_n) is completely increasing in two manners :

First, $\alpha_{n+1} = \beta_n \alpha_n \gamma_n$ with $\beta_n = a$ and $\gamma_n = \alpha_n a$
whence $u = {}^{\omega}a\ \alpha_0\alpha_0 a\alpha_1 a \ldots \alpha_n a \ldots \in \overleftrightarrow{\{\alpha_n / n \in N\}}$

Secondly $\alpha_{n+1} = \beta'_n \alpha'_n$ with $\beta'_n = a\ \alpha_n$ and $\gamma'_n = a$
whence $u' = \ldots a\alpha_n \ldots a\alpha_1 a\alpha_0\alpha_0 a^{\omega} \in \overleftrightarrow{\{\alpha_n / n \in N\}}$

And clearly $u \neq u'$.)

Let $X \subset A^*$. *The bi-limit of X* denoted by $\overleftrightarrow{X}$ is the set of bi-infinite words which are upper-bound of a completely increasing sequence of elements of X.

A finite automaton $\mathcal{A}$ on the alphabet A is a 4-uplets (Q,F,I,T) :

- Q is the set of states
- $F \subset Q \times A \times Q$ is the set of transitions
- I and T are two subsets of Q.

$\mathcal{A}$ is said to be *reduced* if for every $q \in Q$, there exists $q_0 \in I$, $q_t \in T$ and a path $q_0 \xrightarrow{u} q \xrightarrow{v} q_f$.

$\mathcal{A}$ is said *deterministic* if for every $q \in Q$, $a \in A$, card$(F \cap \{q\} \times \{a\} \times Q) \leq 1$. A finite word u is *recognized* by $\mathcal{A}$ iff there exists $q_0 \in I$, $q_t \in T$ and a path $q_0 \xrightarrow{u} q_t$.

$\mathcal{A}^*$ is the set of finite words recognized by $\mathcal{A}$.

A subset $X \subset A^*$ is *rational* iff there exists a finite automaton $\mathcal{A}$ such that $X = \mathcal{A}^*$.

A bi-infinite word u is recognized by A iff there exists some pairs $(q_n,x_n) \in Q \times A$, $(n \in Z)$ such that $(q_n,x_n,q_{n+1}) \in F$ and $card\{n < 0 / q_n \in I\} = card\{n > 0 / q_n \in T\} = \omega$, and $\ldots x_{-n}\ldots x_{-1}x_0x_1\ldots x_n\ldots$ is an element of the class u.

We denote by ${}^{\omega}A^{\omega}$ the set of bi-infinite words recognized by A. A part $L \subset {}^{\omega}A^{\omega}$ is *rational* iff there exists a finite automaton A such that $L = {}^{\omega}A^{\omega}$.

It is known that L is rational iff L is a finite union of parts of ${}^{\omega}A^{\omega}$ of the form ${}^{\omega}XYZ^{\omega}$, where X,Y,Z are rational parts of A^*. Then, it is easy to characterize rational parts of ${}^{\omega}A^{\omega}$ with only one element :

Lemma I.1 Let $u \in {}^{\omega}A^{\omega}$. $\{u\}$ is rational iff there exists $f,g,h \in A^+$ such that $u = {}^{\omega}fgh^{\omega}$.

Our purpose is to study the properties of the set of factors of a bi-infinite word.

II. Set of finite factors of a bi-infinite word :

Definition A set $X \subset A^*$ is a covering if it satisfies :

1) $F(X) = X$ (X is factorial)
2) $\forall u \in X \ \exists a,b \in A \ aub \in X$
3) $\forall f_1,f_2 \in X, \exists f_3 \in X \ f_1,f_2 \in F(f_3)$.

One can verify immediately that for every bi-infinite word u, F(u) is a covering. The converse will be proved l&ater. Let $u \in {}^{\omega}A^{\omega}$, and C be a covering. By definition :

if $F(u) \subset C$ then C *covers* u
if $F(u) = C$ then C *covers exactly* u.

A covering C *is thin* if it covers exactly a unique bi-infinite word : $\exists !\, u \in {}^{\omega}A^{\omega}\ C = F(u)$.

Example $C = a^*b^*$ C is a thin covering.

It covers exactly only the bi-infinite word ${}^{\omega}ab^{\omega}$.

Let C be a covering, a word $f \in C$ is a *sparse factor* of C iff $\exists N \in \mathbb{N}\ \forall g \in C\ |g|_f \leq N$.

A word $f \in C$ is a *singular factor* of C iff :

$$\forall g \in C\ |g|_f \leq 1.$$

The three following lkemmas are properties about coverings.

Lemma II.1 Let C be a covering. One of the two following properties holds :
- C has not sparse factor
- C has a singular factor.

Sketch of the proof :

We prove that, if f is a sparse factor then, if g is of minimal length among the words such that $|g|_f$ is maximal, then g is a singular factor.

Lemma II.2 Let C be a covering which has a singular factor f, then C is thin and, moreover :

a) $\forall (m,n) \in N^2 \; \exists ! \; g_m, f_n \in A^* \times A^* \quad g_m f f_n \in C$ and $|g_m| = m \; |f_n| = n$

b) $\exists ! \; (u,v) \in A^\omega \times A^\omega \; C = F({}^R v \; f \; u)$

c) $v^R f u = \overleftrightarrow{(A^* f A^* \cap C)}$

Sketch of the proof:

a) The existence of g_m and f_n proceeds from the point 2) of the definition of a covering, the unicity from the point 3).

b) and c) are clear consequences of a).

Lemma II.3 Let C be a covering without singular factor. Then :

a) for every $f_1, f_2 \in C$, there exists $f_3 \in C$ such that f_1 and f_2 are factors of f_3 and an occurrence of f_1 in f_3 precedes an occurrence of f_2 in f_3, i.e. :

$\exists f_4, f_5, f_6, f_7 \in A^* \quad f_3 = f_4 f_1 f_5 = f_6 f_2 f_7$ and $|f_4| \leq |f_6|$

b) there exists a bi-infinite word u such that $C = F(u)$

Sketch of the proof

- If a) is not true, then there exists sparse factors in C
- We build a bi-infinite word u exactly covered by C in the following manner :

We order the elements of C : $C = \{f_o, f_1, f_2, \ldots\}$

And we define two sequences of words (l_n) and (l'_n) : $l_o = f_o$

l'_o is the first word belonging to C which can be written $a_o l_o b_o$ $(a_o, b_o \in A)$.

For every n, l_{n+1} is the shortest word of C which contains an occurrence of l'_n preceding an occurrence of f_{n+1} and l'_{n+1} is the first word of C which can be written $a_{n+1} l_{n+1} b_{n+1}$ $(a_{n+1}, b_{n+1} \in A)$. Then, the sequence (l'_n) is completely increasing and there exists words α_n, β_n, such that $l'_{n+1} = \alpha_n l'_n \beta_n$. Then the word $u = \ldots\alpha_n \ldots \alpha_o l'_o \beta_o \ldots \beta_n \ldots$ is a upperbound of (l'_n). One can verify that $C = F(\{l'_n \mid n \in N\}) = F(u)$.

There is a corollary of the two last lemmas, namely the following proposition.

Proposition II.4 For every covering C, there exists a bi-infinite word u exactly covered by C, i.e. such that C = F(u).

Our purpose is now to characterize thin rational coverings.

III. Thin rational coverings

Lemma III.1 Every rational covering is recognized by a finite deterministic automaton $\mathcal{A} = (Q,F,I,T)$ such that :

- $Q = I = T$
- $\forall q \in Q\ \exists q',q'' \in Q\ \exists a,b \in A\ (q',a,q) \in F$ et $(q,b,q'') \in F$

Such an automaton will be said trimmed.

The proof is left to the reader.

Lemma III.2 If C is a covering recognized by a finite trimmed deterministic automaton $\mathcal{A}$, thyen, the set of non sparse factors of C is the set of the factors of the loops iof $\mathcal{A}$.

The proof is easy to be done (a loop of $\mathcal{A}$ is a word $g \in A^+$ such that then exists $q \in Q : q \xrightarrow[\mathcal{A}]{g} q$.)

Lemma III.3 If C is a rational covering which has a singular factor, then :

a) C is of the form $F(g^* f h^*)$ where $g,h \in A^+$ and f is a singular factor.

b) C covers exactly a unique bi-infinite word that is the word ${}^{\omega}g\ f\ h^{\omega}$

c) $\exists K \in N\ \forall n \in N\ n \leq Card(C \cap A^n) \leq n+K$.

Sketch of the proof

It suffices to use the lemma I.1 and the lemma II.2 to obtain a) and b). c) is a simple computation of the number of factors of length n in ${}^{\omega}g\ f\ h^{\omega}$.

Lemma III.4f C is a rational thin covering without singular factor, then :

a) C is of the form $F(g^*)$

b) C covers exactly the unique bi-infinite word ${}^{\omega}g^{\omega}$

c) $\exists K \in \mathbb{N}\ \exists N \in \mathbb{N}\ \forall n \geq \mathbb{N}\ card(C \cap A^n) = K$.

Sketch of the proof :

a) Using a trimmed automaton which recognizes C, we build a bi-infinite word $u = {}^{\omega}g_1 g_2 v$ which is covered by C exactly and such that $F(v) = C$.
Symmetrically there exists a bi-infinite word $u' = w g_2 g'_1{}^{\omega}$ covered exactly by C. So $F(v) = F(g'_1{}^*) = C$, since C is thin.

b) is an easy consequence of a)
and c) is a simple computation.

These lemmas allow us to state the following theorem :

Theorem III.5 If C is a rational thin coverirng, there exists a constant K such that for every n, $card(C \cap A^n) \leq n+K$.

Remark The proposition is no longer true if C is not a rational set. Indeed let $u = {}^{\omega}bacac^2ac^3a\ldots ac^nac^{n+1}a\ldots$ and $C = F(u)$. It is clear that C is thin and one can easily prove that $card(C \cap A^n)$ increases like a polynomial function of degree two.

We have now to state a converse result.

IV. Complexity of a rational covering

We use here a wellknown tool which is the complexity of a set of words [3].

Definition Let C be a covering on an alphabet A.

For every integer n, we define $c(n) = card(C \cap A_n)$ c *is the complexity* of C. It is said to be :

(1) *exponential* iff there exists two reals $a,b > 1$ such that for n large enougn $a^n < c(n) < b^n$

(2) *sub-linear* iff there exists two integers A and B such that for n large enough $n + A < c(n) < n + B$

(3) *constant* iff there exists an integer K such that for n large enough $c(n) = K$.

The main result is the following.

Theorem IV.1 Let C be a rational covering. Then, C has a complexity exponentail, sub-linear or constant.

At once, we can see that the result does not hold if C is not rational as it is proved by this example :

$u = {}^{\omega}bacac^2a\ldots ac^n\ a\ c^{n+1}a\ldots$

$C = F(u)$ has not an exponential, sub-linear, nor constant complexity.

The proof is based upon a result which first requires some definitions :

a set $C \subset A^*$ is <u>transitive</u> if :

for every $u,v \in C$ there exists $\omega \in A^*$ such that $uwv \in C$. A deterministic finite automaton (Q,F,Q,Q) is <u>irreducible</u> if every state is accessible from every other.

At last, an elementary cycle of an automaton A is a path $q_o \xrightarrow{u_1} \ldots \xrightarrow{u_n} q_n$ such that for every $i,j < 0 \leq i < j < n \Rightarrow q_i \neq q_j$ and $q_o = q_n$.

The result we use is proved in [4], though stated in a very different way.

<u>Proposition IV.2</u> [4] A rational factorial and transitive set is recognized by an irreducible automaton.

<u>Sketch of the proof of theorem IV.1</u> :

If C has a singular factor, then C is a thin covering and C has a sub-linear complexity (lemma III.3).

Else C is a rational transitive set (it is an easy consequence of lemma II.2). So there exists an irreducible automaton A which recognizes C (Prop. IV.2).

Now, the result is clearly obtained from the two following lemmas :

<u>lemma 1</u> : If A has two distinct elementary cycles with the same beginning then C has an exponential complexity

<u>lemma 2</u> : If A has not two distinct elementary cycles with the same beginning then the graph of A is reduced to an elementary cycle and C has a constant complexity (C has the form $F(g^*)$).

We can state the following more precise results :

<u>Proposition IV.3</u> If C is a rational covering whose complexity is not exponential, there exists words $f,g,h \in A^+$ such that $C = F(g^*)$ or $C = F(f^*gh^*)$.

We have now to state a converse of the theorem III.5.

<u>Theorem IV.4</u> If C is rational covering whose complexity is not exponential, then C is thin and the unique bi-infinite word exactly covered by C is rational.

Sketch of the proof

It is based upon theorem IV.1, its proof and the following statement : if C is a covering such that there exists a word $u \in A^+$ verifying $C = F(u^*)$ then C is thin and covers exactly only the word ${}^{\omega}u^{\omega}$.

Theorem IV.4 provides us with a simple characterization of rational bi-infinite words :

Proposition IV.5 The bi-infinite word u is rational iff the set of its finite factors $F(u)$ is rational and has a non exponential complexity.

As a complement of theorem IV.4, let us mention two points :

- first, a result proved by J.J. Pansiot [7] which was the starting point of the present work

Proposition IV.6 Let C be a covering such that for n large enough, $card(C \cap A^n) \leq n$, then C is thin and the bi-infinite word exactly covered by C is of the form : ${}^{\omega}g^{\omega}$ $(g \in A^+)$.

Actually, in that case, for $n \geq |g|$, $card(C \cap A^n)$ is not only bounded by n but is even constant. A very direct proof of Prop. IV.6 is given in [7].

secondly a remark made by L. Pierre permits to conclude this work on the following statement which shows that a thin covering without singular factor is rational.

Proposition IV.7 A covering C without singular factors is thin iff there exists $g \in A^+$ such that $C = F(g^*)$.

Sketch of the proof :

Let C be a covering. A property (P) is defined as follows :

(P) : $\forall f \in C \; \exists f_1, f_2 \in A^+ \; |f_1| = |f_2|$ and $f_1 \neq f_2$ s.t. $ff_1, ff_2 \in C$. It is proved that :

a) if C verifies (P) then the set of bi-infinite words u such that $F(u) = C$ has the cardinality of $\mathbb{R}$.

(An injective map is built (using (P)) from $\{1,2\}^{\mathbb{N}}$ into $\{u \in A^{\mathbb{Z}} \; / \; F(u) = C\}$

b) if C doesn't verify (P), then C is thin and rational. So $C = F(g^*)$ (lemma III.4).□

References

[1] BEAUQUIER D., 1984, Bilimites de langages reconnaissables, à paraitre dans *Theoret. Comput. Sci.*

[2] BUCHI, J.R., 1962, On a decision method in restricted second order arithmetic, in Logic, Methodology and Philosophy of Science, (Proc. 1960 Internat. Cong.), *Stanford University Press*, Stanford.

[3] EHRENFEUCHT A., LEE R.P., ROZENBERG G., 1975, Subwords complexities of various classes of deterministic developmental languages without interactions, Theoretical Computer Science 1 p. 59-76.

[4] EILENBERG, S., 1974, Automata, Languages and Machines, Vol. A, *Academic Press*, New York, Vol. B, 1976.

[5] FISCHER R., 1975, Sofic systems and graphs Monats. Math. 80 179-186.

[6] McNAUGHTON, R., 1966, Testing and generating infinite sequences by a finite automaton, *Information and Control*, 9, 521-530.

[7] NIVAT M., PERRIN D., 1982, Ensembles reconnaissables de mots bi-infinis, Proc. 14th A.C.M. Symp. on Theory of Computing, 47-59.

[8] PANSIOT J.J, 1984, Lecture Notes in Computer Science No 166 STACS 84, Bornes inférieures sur la complexité des facteurs des mots infinis engendrés par morphismes itérés, p. 230-240.

[9] THOMAS W., 1981, A combinatorial approach to the theory of ω-automata, *Inform. Control*, 48, 261-283.

[10] THUE A., 1906, Uber unendliche Zeichenreihen, Norske Vid. Selsk. Skr. I. Mat. Nat. Kl. Christiania No 7, 1-22.

A Fair Protocol for Signing Contracts

(Extended Abstract)

Michael Ben-Or [1] Oded Goldreich [2] Silvio Micali [3] Ronald L. Rivest [4]

ABSTRACT

Assume that two parties, A and B, want to sign a contract over a communication network, i.e. they want to exchange their "commitments" to the contract. We consider a contract signing protocol to be *fair* if, at any stage in its execution, the following hold: the **conditional probability** that party A obtains B's signature to the contract *given* that B has obtained A's signature to the contract, is close to 1. (Symmetrically, when switching the roles of A and B).

Contract signing protocols cannot be fair without relying on a trusted third party. We present a fair, cryptographic protocol for signing contracts that makes use of the *weakest possible form of a trusted third party (judge).* If both A and B are honest, the judge will never be called upon. Otherwise, the judge rules by performing a simple computation, without referring to previous verdicts. Thus, no bookkeeping is required from the judge. Our protocol is fair even if A and B have very different computing powers. Its fairness is proved under the very general cryptographic assumption that functions that are one-way in a weak sense exist. Our protocol is also optimal with respect to the number of messages exchanged.

---

[1] Institute of Mathematics and Computer Science, Hebrew University, Jerusalem, Israel.
Work done when visiting MIT's Lab. for Comp. Sc. Supported by a Weizmann Postdoctoral Fellowship.

[2] Computer Science Dept., Technion, Haifa, Israel.
Currently in the Lab. for Comp. Sc., MIT. Supported by a Weizmann Postdoctoral Fellowship.

[3] Laboratory for Computer Science, MIT, Cambridge, MA 02139, USA.
Supported by NSF Grant DCR-8413577 and an IBM Faculty Development Award.

[4] Laboratory for Computer Science, MIT, Cambridge, MA 02139, USA.
Supported by NSF Grant MCS80-06938.

1. Introduction

Let A, B,... be users who can exchange messages over a communication network. For example, they may be the users of the ordinary mail system, or of a telephone network, or a modern computer network.

We will assume that a *Signature Scheme* S is adopted in the network. Two key properties are required from a signature scheme. First, *unforgeability*: only user U can create U's signature on message m. Second, *universal verification*: any other user should be able to verify that U's signature on message m is indeed a valid one. An instance of a signature scheme may be provided by ordinary "hand-written" signatures. Hand-written signatures are believed to be hard to forge and can be universally verified as trusted notary publics keep samples of each user's signature. Another instance of a signature scheme, more suitable for computer networks, is a "digital signature scheme". This notion was introduced by Diffie and Hellman [DH] and first implemented by [RSA]. The strongest notion of security for a digital signature scheme was suggested and concretely implemented (based on a weak and general complexity assumption) by Goldwasser, Micali and Rivest [GMR]. An historical account on the problem of digital signature can be found in [GMR].

We now describe the problem of "fair" contract signing. Two users, A and B, have negotiated over the network a contract *CONT* and now want to obtain each other's signature on it. In essence, the problem of signing a contract consists of exchanging signatures of an ordinary message, but with the additional constraint that the exchange must be "simultaneous". Therefore,

. *"a signature to a contract" does not necessarily consist of of applying the signature scheme to the text of the contract.*

In general, a signature of A to *CONT* is a set of messages that only A can generate on input *CONT*, e.g. *some* of these messages may be generated by applying the signature scheme S. A good contract signing protocol should satisfy the following (informal) conditions.

1) *Viability*: If both parties follow the protocol properly, then at its termination, each will have his counterpart's signature to *CONT*.
2) *Fairness*: If one party, say A, follows the protocol properly then at any stage during its execution, B has A's signature on *CONT* if and only if also A has B's signature on *CONT*.

The fairness condition is hard to satisfy, essentially because "simultaneity" is hard to meet in our discrete world [EY]. Thus, in order to successfully implement a contract signing protocol, it is necessary to relax and, at the same time, to formalize the fairness condition. The meaningfulness of a solution to the contract signing problem will depend on the acceptability of the definition used to approximate the intuitive notion of fairness. Two main approaches to approximating fairness have been considered. The first one, interprets simultaneity as deriving from equal computational effort. This approach, meaningful only if both parties are assumed to have equal computing power, suffers from some inherent additional disadvantages. The second approach, interprets the simultaneity of two events as very high probability that one event happens if and only if the second event happens.

1.1 Computational Approaches to Fairness

Even [E], Blum [B] and Even, Goldreich and Lempel [EGL], proposed a computational interpretation of approximate fairness. This approach requires that at any stage during the execution of the protocol, the computational effort required from the parties in order to get each other's signature to *CONT* be approximately equal. Informally, a protocol is said to satisfy this definition of fairness if, during its execution, for both parties the computational difficulty of computing the counterpart's signature to CONT decreases by equal amounts at each step, till it vanishes.

This approach suffers from the following major weaknesses.

1) This definition of fairness is meaningful only if both parties are assumed to have "equal computing power". Otherwise, at some step of the protocol, one party may find the remaing computational effort, necessary to obtain his counterpart's signature, to be feasible; while the same effort may be beyond the power of his counterpart. Such "equal computing power" was assumed by all the above mentioned researchers.

   We feel that assuming "equal computing power" is both unrealistic in practice and undesirable from a theoretical point of view. In real life, parties may often have different computing power (e.g. consider a large commercial firm and an individual). Also, it is difficult for a party to estimate accurately the computing ability of the other party (one can always pretend to be less powerful).

   [Jumping ahead, let us point out that the probabilistic approach, as well as our protocol, is valid even if the parties have very different computing power.]

2) As observed by Rackoff, this approach to fairness is *prone to the devastating effect of "early stopping"*. Assume party B stops the execution of the protocol prematurely, at a point when each party will need 10 years of computing time to obtain his counterpart's signature on *CONT*. Should A keep computing for the next 10 years or should she give up and hope that B is doing the same and thus will never have her signature? The situation effectively binds A to the contract without offering any priviledges. In fact, if she acts as if the contract is not binding, B has the option, by investing 10 years of computation time, to enforce the contract and to put her in serious legal trouble. Though this approach was developed for two parties only, it should be noticed that *the dilemma created by early stopping cannot be settled in court by a judge that rules deterministically.*

   [If the judge is allowed to rule probabilistically, then our protocol is optimal. In particular, if one party stops prematurely, the other will invoke the (probabilistic) judge with the following guarantee. If the judge rules that *CONT* is binding when B appeals then, with high probability, he also rules so in case A appeals.]

3) A third difficulty arises with this approach that may not be inherent, but is certainly a formidable one: the difficulty of proving the fairness of a protocol in this sense. Proving that certain problems cannot be efficiently solvable seems to be hard. Proving that the computational difficulty of certain problems decreases by a fixed amount, when releasing some "partial information", seems even harder. The correctness of Blum's protocol [B] follows from the assumption that a particular computational problem, related (but not known to be computationally equivalent) to integer factorization, is infeasible. Unfortunately, this problem has been shown to be efficiently solvable by Hastad and Shamir [HS]. The correctness of Even Goldreich and Lempel's protocol [EGL] follows from the assumption that "ideal" trapdoor one-way permutations exist and the assumption that "uniformly-hard" one-way functions f exist. By this they mean that given $f(x)$ and k bits of (information about) x, where x is n-bit long, the best algorithm for computing x essentially consists of trying all the 2^{n-k} possibilities for the remaining bits. This is a very strong assumption. Even's protocol [E] (as well as its simplified version [G]) requires, in addition to the existence of a uniformly-hard one-way function, an extra non-mathematical assumption: that the contract's subject has a fixed and known value.

   [In comparison, the correctness of our protocol follows from a much weaker and more general complexity assumption: the existence of one-way functions f. Such f's need not be "ideal" or uniformly-hard.

In particular, it may be that half of the bits of x are easy to compute on input $f(x)$. We only require that (all of) x is not efficiently computable on input $f(x)$. In case the communication network is a computer network or a telephone network, we also need particularly strong digital signature schemes. Such schemes have been proved to exist under simple complexity assumption by [GMR].]

1.2 A Probabilistic Approach to Fairness

Rabin [R] proposed to sign contracts with the help of a trusted third party that, at regular intervals (say each day), publicly broadcasts a randomly chosen integer between 1 and 100. Parties A and B can then sign contracts by agreeing on a future date D and exchanging signed messages of the form: "I am committed to *CONT* if integer i is chosen at date D". A goes first. B will send his i-th message *only if* he gets A's i-th message Similarly A sends her $i+1$-st message *only if* she receives B's i-th message. It should be stressed that all messages should be exchanged prior to date D. B may try to cheat by not sending his i-th message after receiving A's i-th message. The advantage he gains by doing so is not too large: the probability that he will have a signed contract, on date D, but A will not, equals 1/100. In this sense, the protocol is "fair".

How can this be made formal? We have two possible alternatives:

1) Requiring that the probability that "B has A's signature on *CONT* but A does not have B's" is small.

2) Requiring that the difference between 1 and the conditional probability that "A has B's signature on *CONT*", given that "B has A's signature to *CONT*", is small.

Notice that the second condition implies the first. We believe that the conditional probability is a better measure for fairness, since it better models the intuitive notion of fairness as simultaneity ("if B has the signature then A has it too" and vice versa).

In formalizing the definition of fairness we will use a "security" parameter k which will constitute, together with *CONT*, the input to the protocol. We also use a function μ from integers to the 0-1 inteval. μ will serve as our measure of "negligible" probability; namely, we will not care about events occuring with probability less than $\mu(k)$. For example, one may choose $\mu(k)=2^{-k}$ or $\mu(k)=k^{-c}$ for some positive integer c. The parties are allowed to make random choices during the execution of the protocol. So is the third party, if he is called into play.

Definition: A contract signing protocol is *μ-fair for A* if, on input k and *CONT*, in case A follows the protocol properly, the following holds. At any stage, during the execution of the protocol, in which the probability that B has A's signature to *CONT* is greater than $\mu(k)$, the conditional probability that "A has B's signature to *CONT*", given that "B has A's signature to *CONT*", is at least $1 - 1/k$.
Here the probabilities are taken over all the random choices of A, B and the third party (in case he is called into play).
A protocool is μ-fair if it is μ-fair both for A and B.

For example, if the trusted third party of Rabin's protocol is parametrized, so that on input k it randomly selects an integer between 1 and $l(k)$, then the protocol would be μ-fair if and only if $l(k) \geq \mu(k)^{-1} \cdot k$. In fact, after A has sent i messages, but before B has replied, the conditional probability that "A has B's signature to the contract" given that "B has A's signature to the contract" equals $1-1/i$.

1.3 Intervention by a Third Party

We believe that the definition of μ-fairness is the correct one. However, it cannot be enforced without the intervention of a third party.

Theorem 1: Let $\mu(k)$ be smaller than 1, for every k. Then no viable, μ-fair two-party protocol for signing contracts exists, without the intervention of trusted third parties.

A proof of Theorem 1 will appear in the final version of this paper. The proof is not hard once the right formalization is reached.

Relying on the existence of a trusted third party is indeed a drawback, but preferable to assuming equal computing power. It is certainly preferable to accepting the disruptive effect of "early stopping" inherent in the computational approach to fairness.

Since a μ-fair protocol must rely on a trusted third party, its quality will depend on the role that such a party plays in it: The more "inconspicuous" and efficient the third party is, the better the solution is. The third party we use is a probabilistic judge (algorithm). The judge is inactive until he is invoked. The judge can rule on whether a contract is binding, in the presence of only one party. Furthermore, the judge is invoked only in case of dispute and does not need to store past verdicts. The mildness of the (third party's) intervention in our solution can be demonstrated by comparing it with other forms of trusted third parties proposed in previous solutions to the contract signing problem.

A simple, folklore solution to signing contracts is a cancellation center which stores all invalidated contracts (see [EGL]). A contract is signed by exchanging messages of the form: "I'm committed to *CONT* unless I've deposited a cancellation notice in the center by date D", where D is some future date. This naive solution suffers from serious practical drawbacks. The paperwork involved in maintaining the cancellation center is tremendous. Even more disturbing is the fact that if A wants to convince C that she (A) has B's signature to *CONT*, A must get a certificate from the cancellation center that *CONT* was not cancelled. This is the case even if both A and B are honest and wish to execute the protocol properly.

As discussed in section 1.2, Rabin [R] proposed the use of a trusted third partywhich broadcasts randomly chosen integers at fixed times. We point out that this third party must always be active, regardless of the honesty of all parties and of whether its output is being referred to.

2. Optimal Fair Protocols for Parties with Different Computing Power

In this section we develop a viable and fair protocol, without relying on the equal resources assumption. During the execution of the protocol, the probability that a party obtains his counterpart's signature to *CONT* grows from zero to one. This growth must be moderate to satisfy the fairness requirement.

In subsection 2.1, we give a tight lower bound on the number of messages exchanged in a viable, μ-fair protocol. In subsection 2.2, we exhibit a protocol which achieves this lower bound. The heart of our solution is the efficiency of the implementaion of the judging procedure, suggested in subsection 2.3.

2.1 On the Number of Messages Exchanged in a μ-Fair Protocol

A protocol for contract signing is a sequence of message exchanges hereafter called *steps.* In each step one of the parties sends a message to the other. Without loss of generality, no party sends messages in two consecutive steps; i.e. each party alternately sends and receives messages. Let us denote the party which sends [receives] a message in step i by S_i [R_i]. Let E_i denote the event "after step i, party R_i has S_i's commitment to *CONT*", i.e. enough information so that the judge will rule that the contract is binding for S_i.

Following is an analysis of the implication of the μ-fairness requirement on the number of steps in a viable protocol. This number may be a function of the security parameter k. For simplicity, we assume here that the number of steps is independent of the contract *CONT*. Let us denote by $\#(k)$ the number of steps in a viable μ-fair protocol, on input the security parameter k and the contract *CONT*. By the viability requirement, we have

$$Prob(E_{\#(k)}) = 1$$

(since upon termination of the protocol the probability that each party has his counterpart's signature to *CONT* is 1.) By the μ-fairness, if $Prob(E_i) \geq \mu(k)$ $(1 \leq i \leq \#(k))$ then

$$Prob(E_{i-1}|E_i) \geq 1 - \frac{1}{k}.$$

This implies

$$Prob(E_{i-1}) \geq (1-\frac{1}{k}) \cdot Prob(E_i)$$

(since $\dfrac{Prob(A)}{Prob(B)} \geq Prob(A|B)$ for any two events A and B).
In order to minimize $\#(k)$ we set $Prob(E_i) = (1-1/k)^{\#(k)-i}$, $1 \leq i \leq \#(k)$. Finally, $Prob(E_1)$ is set to $\mu(k)$, so that the fairness requirement is not violated by the first step. Thus, $\#(k)$ and the $Pr(E_i)$'s are easily bounded by expressions depending on k and $\mu(k)$. Namely,

Theorem 2: Every viable, μ-fair protocol for signing contracts has length at least $\#(k) = k \cdot \log \mu^{-1}(k)$. Furthermore, the probability that after step i one party has his counterpart's signature to *CONT* does not exceed $(1-1/k)^{\#(k)-i}$. (The logarithm is taken to the natural base.)

A reasonable choice of $\mu(k) = poly(log\ k)^{-1}$ yields $\#(k)=\Omega(k \cdot \log k)$.

2.2 The Proposed Protocol

Our protocol makes use of the signature scheme of the network. For the purpose of this extended abstract, it will be convenient to decouple the analysis of a contract signing protocol from the security of the underlying signature scheme used in its implementation. In fact, if the network is, say, the ordinary mail system, the signature scheme in use (like pen-written signatures, fingerprints, etc.) may not be easy to analyze mathematically. This decoupling can be done by assuming that the signatures used in the implementation are totally unforgeable. Namely, for each message m and user A, the probability that another user (B) can produce A's signature on m is zero. (Independent of B's computing power.) It should be stressed that *digital* signature schemes cannot possibly be unforgeable in this sense, and problems might arise when implementing our protocol with a "concrete" digital signature scheme. In fact, the "security" of a contract signing protocol cannot exceed the "security" of the underlying signature scheme, but it may be *much* less. This is so because the protocol, in its concrete implementation, may interact badly (in an unpredictable manner) with the signature scheme. However, this is not the case with respect to the protocol presented in this extended abstract:

Our protocol remains fair when implemented with high quality signature schemes as the ones in [GMR].

The formal version of the above statement and its proof will appear in the final write-up. We now present our protocol for signing contracts. As before, the parties to the protocol will be denoted by A and B and the contract they wish to sign will be denoted by *CONT*. We assume that *CONT* also specifies the security parameter k and the function μ, the name of the party that goes first in the protocol (A in the description below) and the name of the party which goes second (B). Recall that $\#(k)=k \cdot \log \mu^{-1}(k)$.

The Protocol for A and B

0A) A chooses $l=\lceil \#(k)/2 \rceil$ arbitrary messages $a_1, a_2, \ldots, a_l$, with the only restriction that they were not used before by A.
(A's signatures to these messages will be hereafter referred to as A's secrets.)
A sends to B the following declaration (signed): "$CONT, a_1, a_2, \ldots, a_l$".

0B) B chooses l arbitrary messages $b_1, b_2, \ldots, b_l$, with the only restriction that they were not used before by A.
(B's signatures to these messages will be hereafter referred to as B's secrets.)
B sends to A the following declaration (signed): "$CONT, b_1, b_2, \ldots, b_l$".

(for $1 \leq i \leq l$)

iA) A sends her signature on a_i to B.

iB) B sends his signature on b_i to A.

Handling early stopping : If the entire protocol is not completed within T time units, party X invokes the judge with inputs the initial declarations (steps 0A and 0B), $CONT$, X, and the secrets of Y (X's counterpart) in X's possession.

The Judge's Procedure

On inputs the signed initial declarations, $CONT$, X and m secrets of Y, the judge checks whether the secrets are valid signatures, of X's counterpart, according to the protocol. If so, he then chooses an integer e (hereafter referred to as *the edge*) between 1 and $2l$ *as specified in section 2.3.* The same edge e is chosen every time $CONT$ is brought before the judge. The probability distribution of the edge is, essentially, the following.

$e = 1$ with probability $p_1 = (1-\frac{1}{k})^{2l-1}$.

$e = i$, $1 < i \leq 2l$, with probability $p_i = (1-\frac{1}{k})^{2l-i} - (1-\frac{1}{k})^{2l-(i-1)}$.

If $X=A$ and $m \geq \lfloor e/2 \rfloor$ or if $X=B$ and $m \geq \lceil e/2 \rceil$ then the judge rules that $CONT$ is binding. In this case, the judge waits for T time units to pass and then sends his signed verdict to both parties.

Notice that if both parties are honest and complete the protocol within T time units, the judge will never be invoked. In fact both will have all the counterpart's secrets, a number greater than or equal to any possible choice of the edge. This fact can be easily verified by any other party. Problems may arise only if one of the parties prematurely terminates the protocol, say after ι ($< \#(k)=2l$) steps. In such a case determining the "sufficient number of counterpart's secrets" is of importance and is done by the judge as described above. Notice that the parties cannot know the value of the edge during the execution of the protocol. This is achieved by delying the answer of the judge. Note that the above probability distribution by which the edge is chosen makes the protocol μ-fair and corresponds to the probability distribution of Theorem 2. Thus our protocol is of shortest length among all the μ-fair protocols. Namely,

Theorem 3: For function μ, there exists a viable, μ-fair protocol, for signing contracts, of length $\#(k) = k \cdot \log \mu^{-1}(k)$. (Here the logarithm is taken to the natural base.)

2.3 On the Determination of the Edge

Selecting the edge so that $Prob(e=i)=p_i$ is easy of one flips unbiased coins. (Let $q_0=0$, $q_i=\sum_{j=1}^{i} p_j$. Randomly select 0 and 1 with equal probability to construct the binary expansion a real number α between 0 and 1. Stop the construction of α as soon as $q_{i-1} \leq \alpha < q_i$, for some i. In this case the edge is chosen to be i.)

Recall that the judge was required to always use the same edge for the same contract. (The reader may note that failing to do so may creates conflicting verdicts; and furthermore, give advantage to parties who keep appealing to court many times with the same contract.) Using the same edge for the same contract can be accomplished if the judge operates as follows. Once he chooses an edge e with respect to a contract *CONT*, he stores the pair (e, *CONT*), and uses e again any time that the *CONT* is brought before him. This solution can hardly be considered efficient, as the judge must keeps record of all previous verdicts. It is our goal to free the judge from any bookkeeping. We do this by using the "poly-random functions" of Goldreich Goldwasser and Micali [GGM].

In [GGM] it is shown how to use any one-way (in a very weak sense [L]) function to efficiently construct a set of functions that are "very few" in number, deterministic and fast computable, but *possess all the statistical properties of truly random functions with respect to an observer with polynomially bounded resources.* Their deterministic construction, given as input a constant c and a randomly chosen n-bit long string r, outputs a determinstic, polynomial-time algorithm f_r. This algorithm, on input a n-bit long string x, outputs a n^c-bit long string $f_r(x)$. These functions (deterministic algorithms) f_r's cannot be distinguished from random functions by any probabilistic polynomial time algorithm that asks and receives the value of a function at arguments of its choice. (Here by a random function, we mean a function randomly selected with uniform probability from the set of all functions from n-bit strings to n^c-bit strings.)

Let us now show how to use this result in order to free the judge from bookkeeping. The judge randomly selects a n-bit string r once and for all. No other random choices are ever done by the judge. When invoked with *CONT* and all other inputs, the judge computes $f_r(CONT)$ and uses it (instead of flipping coins) to determine ths choice of the edge. This way of operating essentially maintains μ-fairness. It can be shown that the conditional probability that "A has B's signature on *CONT*" given that "B has A's signature on *CONT*" is greater than $1 - 1/k - 1/n^c$, for all constants c and sufficiently large n. (This follows from the properties of the poly-random functions, else all functions easy to evaluate can also be easily inverted.) We stress that the μ-faireness of protocol holds even if the parties are given the edges relative to other contracts of their choice.

In the above we assume n to be large enough so that all contracts have length smaller than n. There is no need to assume so: it is sufficient that each contract starts with an n-bit string C uniquely associated to it. Half of the bits of C are chosen by A and the remaining half by B. As long as one party never uses the same bits for another contract, then no matter how "trickly" the second party will choose the second half of C, the same security is maintained. This greatly improves the efficiency of the scheme.

Why poly-random functions?

Poly-random functions improve previous results of Blum and Micali [BM] and Yao [Y] on pseudo-random number generators. They present deterministic algorithms that transform a truly random (but short) secret seed to a long pseudo-random bit-sequence passing polynomial time statistical tests. Such high quality pseudo-random number generators may not be straightforwardly applied in our context. For example

1) Using *CONT* or part of it as input to the generator does not work. The parties may also do so and determine the edge as well.

2) Using the bit by bit "exclusive or" of *CONT* and some fixed key *r* (randomly and secretly selected by the judge) as input to the generator, may not work. In fact, these generators are proved to produce "random" outputs only on randomly and independently selected inputs. In our setting, knowledge of the edges relative to previous contracts, may help in predicting the edge relative to a new contract.

Remark: Above, we have suggested that the edge be determined by the judge. An alternative method for determining the edge (i.e. determining a fraction in the interval [0,1]) is described below. Each party has a one-way function associated with him. At step 1 of the protocol, each party chooses randomly a fraction in the interval [0,1], applies his one-way function to the binary extension of this fraction and appends the result to his declaration (which is only then signed). The fraction (which determines the edge) is agreed to be the sum reduced modulo 1 of these fractions. This way, the edge will be determined during the first step of the protocol, by both parties. However, none of them knows at that point what the edge is.
Although this solution appeals to be more elegant, it suffers from a serious drawback. In order to rule, the judge must find out the fractions chosen by both parties. This requires either that both parties appear in court or that the judge knows to invert the one-way functions of all users. Both requirements are highly undesirable from a practical point of view. Note that when the edge is chosen by the judge, the judge is able to rule even if only one party appears in court.

2.4 Summary and Further Discussion

Let us first sum up the properties of our solution (which consists of a two-party protocol and a judge-procedure):

1) It satisfies both the viability and the fairness requirements, *without using* the "Equal Computing Power" assumption. It is not prone to "early stopping". Furthermore, unlike other solutions, our solution requires the intervention of a trusted third party and a "time out" mechanism in a very mild sense.

2) A third party (a judge) intervenes only in case of dispute. In this case the judge can rule even if only one party appears in court. Furthermore, no bookkeeping is required from the judge!

3) The protocol is *optimal* in the sense that it can be implemented and proven fair under the minimum possible intractability assumption: the existence of one-way functions and secure signature schemes. (The judge-procedure which involves the use of random functions requires a slightly stronger assumption [GGM].)

4) The protocol is *optimal* in the sense that it uses the minimum number of message exchanges needed to satisfy the μ-fairness requirement.

5) The protocol is very easy to execute. Also the judging-procedure is conceptually simple and only requires the examination of *two* messages (the signed initial declaration and the last received secret).

Acknowledgments

We wish to thank Shimon Even and Adi Shamir for very illuminating discussions.

References

[B] Blum, M., "How to Exchange (Secret) Keys", *ACM Trans. on Comp. Sys.*, Vol. 1, No. 2, 1983, pp. 175-193. Also in the *Proc. of the 15th ACM Symp. on Theory of Computation*, 1983, pp. 440-447.

[BM] M. Blum and S. Micali, "How to Generate Cryptographically Strong Sequences of Pseudo-Random Bits", *SIAM Jour. on Computing*, Vol. 13, Nov. 1984, pp 850-864 (Preliminary version: Proc. 23rd IEEE Symp. on Foundations of Computer Science, 1982, pp 112-117.)

[BR] Blum, M., and Rabin, M.O., "Mail Certification by Randomization", in preparation.

[DH] Diffie, W., and Hellman, M.E., "New Directions in Cryptography", *IEEE Trans. on Inform. Theory*, Vol. IT-22, No. 6, November 1976, pp. 644-654.

[E] Even, S., "A Protocol for Signing Contracts", TR No. 231, Computer Science Dept., Technion, Haifa, Israel, 1982. Presented in *Crypto81*.

[EGL] Even, S., Goldreich, O., and Lempel, A., "A Randomized Protocol for Signing Contracts", *Advances in Cryptology: Proceedings of Crypto82*, (Chaum D. et. al. eds.), Plenum Press, 1983, pp. 205-210. A better version will apear in the *Comm. of the ACM*.

[EY] Even, S., and Yacobi, Y., "Relations Among Public Key Signature Systems", TR No. 175, Computer Science Dept., Technion, Haifa, Israel, 1980.

[G] Goldreich, O., "A Simple Protocol for Signing Contracts", in *Advances in Cryptology: Proceedings of Crypto83*, (Chaum D., ed.), Plenum Press, pp. 133-136, 1984.

[GGM] Goldreich, O., Goldwasser, S., and Micali, S., "How to Construct Random Functions", *Proc. of the 25th IEEE Symp. on Foundation of Computer Science*, 1984, pp. 464-479. To appear, *Journal of ACM*

[GMR] Goldwasser, S., Micali, S., and Rivest, R.L., "A *Paradoxical* Solution to the Signature Problem", *Proc. of the 25th IEEE Symp. on Foundation of Computer Science*, 1984, pp. 441-448.

[HS] Hastad, J., and Shamir, A., "The Cryptographic Security of Truncated Linearly Related Variables", to appear in the proceedings of the *17th STOC*, 1985.

[L] Levin, L.A., "One-way Functions and Pseudorandom Generators", to appear in the proceedings of the *17th STOC*, 1985.

[R] Rabin, M.O., "Transaction Protection by Beacons", TR-29-81, Aiken Computation Laboratory, Harvard University, 1981.

[RSA] Rivest, R.L., Shamir, A., and Adleman, L., "A Method for Obtaining Digital Signatures and Public-Key Cryptosystems", *Comm. of the ACM*, Feb. 1978, pp. 120-126.

[Y] Yao, A.C., "Theory and Application of Trapdoor Functions", *Proc. of the 23rd IEEE Symp. on Foundation of Computer Science*, 1982, pp. 80-91.

THE INFLUENCE OF KEY LENGTH ON THE AREA-TIME COMPLEXITY OF SORTING

G. Bilardi* and F. P. Preparata**

(EXTENDED ABSTRACT)

Summary. Recently discovered lower bounds for the area-time complexity of VLSI sorting of n k-bit keys exhibit a dependence upon the key length. On this basis, keys can be classified into short ($k \leq \log n$), long ($k \geq \log n$) and intermediate-length. Intermediate-length keys have been heretofore the object of investigation; this paper investigates the other two cases and confirms the inherent validity of the bounds for short and long keys by exhibiting optimal or near-optimal VLSI networks.

1. Introduction

In spite of the enormous research activity on sorting algorithms over the past two decades, this problem does not cease to offer extremely intriguings questions, particularly when novel computational models reveal heretofore unsuspected facets. Such situation occurs in the VLSI computation environment, where the nature of sorting exhibits an interesting dependence upon the length of the keys being sorted. This phenomenon, previously noticed on an intuitive basis by a number of authors [1,6,7,8], has been recently characterized in a quantitative manner by several area-time lower bounds. These results lead to a classification of the key lengths into intervals in each of which the sorting operation is characterized by different aspects. Moreover, in each interval of key lengths, the lower bounds indicate the presence of different computational and regimes, depending on the speed of operation.

In this paper, we explore the tightness of the lower bounds by constructing sorting networks for different key lengths and different speeds. Indeed, the proposed constructions are optimal or near-optimal, thus substantiating the validity of the lower bounds analysis. The interest of these results goes beyond the understanding of sorting per se; indeed they show that the novel techniques by which the lower bounds have been derived enable one to explore and characterize aspects of VLSI computation not captured by previous instruments.

Formally, the (n,k)-sorting problem is defined as follows:

(1) The input is a sequence of n k-bit keys, each a member of a finite set of integers.

(2) The output is a rearrangement of the input keys, so that they form a nondecreasing sequence.

We now state the lower-bound results with some pertinent remarks.

Theorem 1. (Short Keys). Any VLSI (n,k)-sorter, with $1 \leq k \leq \log n$ satisfies ($r = 2^k$):

This work was supported in part by an IBM predoctoral fellowship and by NSF grant ECS-84-10902.
(*) Department of Computer Science, Cornell University, Ithaca, NY 14853
(**) Coordinated Science Laboratory, University of Illinois, Urbana, IL 61801

$$AT^2 = \Omega(nr) \text{ for } T \in [\Omega(\log n), O(\sqrt{r})] \quad (1)$$

$$AT = \Omega(n\sqrt{r}) \text{ for } T \in [\Omega(\sqrt{r}), O(n/\sqrt{r})] \quad (2)$$

Theorem 2. (Intermediate-Length Keys). Any VLSI (n,k)-sorter, with $\log n < k < 2\log n$, satisfies:

$$AT^2 = \Omega(n^2(k - \log n)^2) \text{ for } T \in [\Omega(\log n), O(\sqrt{n(k-\log n)})] \quad (3)$$

Theorem 3. (Long Keys). Any VLSI (n,k)-sorter, with $2\log n = k \leqslant k^*$, where $k^* = \theta(2^{\beta\sqrt{n\log n}}\sqrt{\log n/n})$, satisfies

$$AT^2 = \Omega(kn^2\log n) \text{ for } T \in [\Omega(\log n), O(\sqrt{n\log n})] \quad (4)$$

$$AT^2 = \Omega(kn\sqrt{n\log n}) \text{ for } T \in [\Omega(\sqrt{n\log n}), O(k\sqrt{n/\log n})] \quad (5)$$

Theorem 4. (Very Long Keys). Any VLSI (n,k)-sorter, with $k > k^*$, satisfies

$$AT/\log A = \Omega(kn) \text{ for } T \in [\Omega(\log kn), O(\sqrt{n\log n}\, k/k^*)] \quad (6)$$

$$AT = \Omega(kn\sqrt{n\log n}) \text{ for } T \in [\Omega(\sqrt{n\log n}\, k/k^*), O(k\sqrt{n/\log n})] \quad (7)$$

Sorting of keys of intermediate length has been the focus of considerable attention [9]. With the further restriction $k\text{-}\log n = \theta(\log n)$ Theorem 2 has been proved in [7], and optimal networks have been proposed in [10, 7, 11, 12]. More recently the lower bound (3) has been extended to cover the case $k\text{-}\log n = o(\log n)$ [5] for which optimal circuits are described in [5], where an alternative proof of (3) is also given.

The above mentioned work has shown that bisection flow [1] determines the area-time complexity of sorting of intermediate-length keys. For the other ranges of key lengths instead, the derivation of the lower bounds [4,5] has required the development of a novel technique, called "square tessellation", whose focus is the study of the information flow across the boundary of a set of square cells that tessellate the layout region. When the mechanism forcing the flow is functional dependence (of output variables upon input variables whose respective I/O parts are on opposite sides of the cell boundary), the tessellation technique yields bounds on the AT^2-measure, like (1) and (4), and subsumes the bisection technique as a special case. When the mechanism forcing the flow is the storage saturation of the tessellation cells, the tessellation technique leads to bounds on the AT-measure, like (2), (5) and (7). Bound (6) is derived by a yet different technique, crucially based on the assumption that gates have bounded fan-in; this technique generalizes ideas previously applied to binary addition in [13] and [14].

An interesting feature of Theorems 1, 3, and 4 is the emergence of two distinct regimes: the "slow" regime governed by the AT-measure, and the "fast" regime, governed by the AT^2-measure for short and long keys, and by the AT/log A-measure for very long keys. As we shall see, these regimes will characterize the upper bounds as well.

When considering VLSI algorithms one must specify whether the I/O ports lie exclusively on the chip boundary or not. In the first case we are dealing with *boundary chips*. Theorems 1, 2, 3, and 4 apply to general chips (non-boundary chips). Somewhat stronger results can usually be obtained for boundary-chip designs.

2. Networks for Sorting a Multiset of Short Keys ($k \leqslant \log n$).

2.1. *The Algorithm*

Given a multiset of keys $S \subseteq U = \{0, 1, \ldots, 2^{k-1}\}$, with $r = 2^k$, let $\mu(j)$ be the *multiplicity* of $j \in U$ in S, and let the r-component vector $(M_S(i) = \sum_{j \leqslant i} \mu(j) : i = 0, \ldots, 2^{k-1})$ be the *distribution* of S. The distribution is an efficient encoding for multisets of short keys, and is additive with respect to the union, i.e., $M_{S \cup R}(i) = M_S(i) + M_R(i)$ for any two multisets S and R.

We now propose the following new sorting algorithm, specifically tailored to short keys, which makes crucial use of distribution encoding.

1. (ENCODE) Subdivide the input multiset $\{X_0, \ldots, X_{n-1}\}$ into $d = n/r$ submultisets of r keys each, and compute the distribution of each submultiset.
2. (TALLY) Sum the d distributions (as r-component vectors) obtained in Step 1, to produce the distribution of the entire input multiset.
3. (BROADCAST) Replicate this distribution d times.
4. (DECODE) From the i-th replica of the distribution obtain the r consecutive output keys $Y_{ir}, Y_{ir+1}, \ldots, Y_{ir+r-1} (i = 0, 1, \ldots, d-1)$, with a suitable decoding procedure.

The rationale for Step 4 is the wish to deploy decoders comparable to the corresponding encoders; this in turn creates the need for Step 3.

2.2. *Transcoding Operations*

We consider the transcoding operations (Steps 1 and 4), i.e., list-to-distribution transformation and its inverse (for example, for $U = \{0, \ldots, 7\}$, list $\{0,1,1,2,4,4,4,6,7,7\}$ corresponds to distribution $(1,2,1,0,3,0,1,2)$).

(1) *List-to-distribution* (encoding). Given a multiset $S = \{X_0, \ldots, X_{n-1}\}$ drawn from U the sorted list $Z = (Z_0, \ldots, Z_{n+r-1}) = \mathrm{SORT}(S \cup U)$, has, the form $(0, \ldots, 0, 1, \ldots, 1, \ldots, r-1, \ldots, r-1)$, i.e. it is the concatenation of r runs the $(i+1)$-st of which contains $\mu(i) + 1$ symbols i. If the rightmost element of run $i, \ldots, i$ is in position b, then $b = M(i) + i$. Since the rightmost element of each run is readily detected, one locally transforms sequence

Z to sequence $W prime$ as follows

$$W'_b = \begin{cases} b - Z_b & \text{if } Z_{b+1} \neq Z_b, \text{ that is } W'_b = M_{S \cup U}(Z_b)) \\ n & \text{if } Z_{b+1} = Z_b \end{cases}$$

Then, the smallest r terms of $W = \mathrm{SORT}(W')$ form the distribution vector $(M_S(i) : i = 0, \ldots, r-1)$. Therefore encoding is done by a sorter of $(n+r)$ k-bit keys.

(2) *Distribution-to-list* (decoding). Given the distribution $M = (M(0), \ldots, M(r\text{-}1))$ of a multiset S we want to obtain S as a sorted list $(Y_0, \ldots, Y_{n-1})$. Letting $H = (0, 1, \ldots, n-1)$ we define the sorted list $W = (W_0, W_1, \ldots, W_{n+r-1}) = \mathit{MERGE}(M, H)$, where the elements originally in H have been

tagged (one bit) for easy identification. If $h \in H$ is such that $M(i\text{-}1) \leqslant h < M(i)$, then $Y_h = i$. Thus, in W, an element $h \in H$ follows exactly $M(0), \ldots, M(Y_{h-1})$ and $0, \ldots, h-1$, and occupies the position of index $(Y_h + h)$. Therefore, if we replace each term W_b of W coming from M with $b - W_b = Y_b$, and unmerge W on the basis of the tag bit, we obtain Y. Thus the decoding can be done by a suitable merging network, or, if we wish, by a sorter of $(n+r)$ $\log n$-bit numbers.

The same technique can be used to extract the subsequence $(Y_{ir}, Y_{ir+1}, \ldots, Y_{ir+r-1})$ of Y by simply replacing H with $H' = (ir, \ldots, ir+r\text{-}1)$. In the latter case a minor modification enables us to work with numbers of $(k+1)$ bits rather than $\log n$. Indeed, we can transform M by replacing $M(j)$ by ir whenever $M(j) < ir$, and by $(i+1)r$ whenever $M(j) > (i+1)r$, without affecting the order of the elements of sequences H' and M. The relevant portion of the sequence, denoted $(\overline{M}_i(ir), \ldots, \overline{M}_i(ir+r-1))$ consists of r terms, where $M_i(h)$ is given by the $(k+1)$ least significant bits of $M(h)$.

2.3. *The Network*

We discuss first a nonpipelined version of a network implementing the above algorithm, and then we obtain the area-time trade-off by means of a pipelined version.

We recall that n, $r = 2^k$, and $d = n/r$ are all powers of 2, and we introduce the sequences of the input and of the output sequences of the sorter $S_i \triangleq (X_{ir}, X_{ir+1}, \ldots, X_{ir+r-1})$, and $R_i \triangleq (Y_{ir}, Y_{ir+1}, \ldots, Y_{ir+r-1})$. We also consider the distribution $M_i = (M_i(0), \ldots, M_i(r-1))$ of S_i, whose components have $k+1$ bits.

The nonpipelined version of the sorting network is the cascade of four parts, illustrated in Figure 1, each performing one of the four steps of the algorithm.

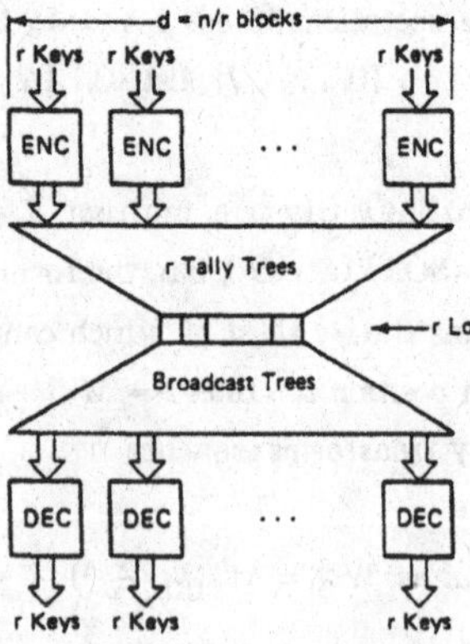

Figure 1. Structure of the network for sorting a set of short keys.

(a) ENCODERS $E_0, \ldots, E_{d-1}$, each capable of computing the distribution of a given (r,k)-multiset. Encoder E_j inputs S_j and computes M_j. Each encoder has r input lines and r output lines. I/O operations on words are bit-serial.

(b) TALLY TREES $TL_0, \ldots, TL_{r-1}$, each a full binary tree on d leaves, where a node at distance l from the leaves is equipped with an $O(l)$-bit storage and a l-bit operand carry-save adder, and is connected to its father by $O(l)$ wires. The j-th leaf of TL_h is connected to the h-th output line of encoder E_j, from which it will read- in bit serial fashion, least-significant-digit (LSD) first- the distribution value $M_j(h)$. By summing $M_0(h), \ldots, M_{d-1}(h)$, TL_h computes $M(h)$. Thus each tree tallies d k-bit numbers to produce a $(k+logd) = logn$-bit results. The operation of a tally tree is illustrated in Figure 2.

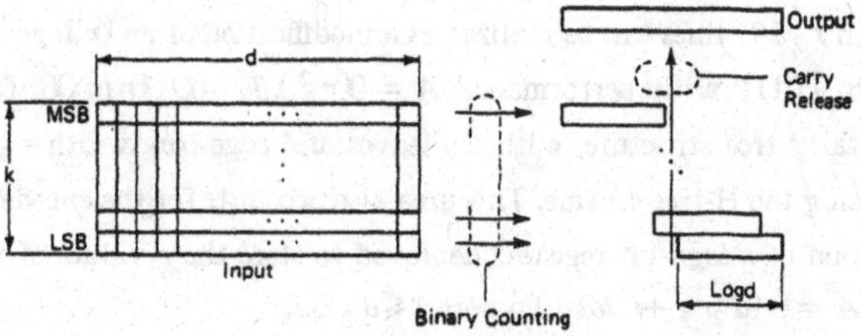

Figure 2. Tally-tree function.

First, for each bit position we obtain a $logd$- bit count of its 1's (this is done by suitable adders at the nodes of the tree); next the bit-counts are added with the correct alignment (carry-release) at the root of the tree. Each of these additions is performed in $O(1)$ time on a redundant carry-save representation. The conversion from carry-save to standard is done at the end of the step in time $O(k)$. Note that at any time only one *level* of the tree is occupied by data generated by a given bit position.

(c) BROADCAST TREES $BC_0, \ldots, BC_{r-1}$, are similar in structure to the tally trees, differing only in the functional capabilities of their nodes. The h-th leaf of BC_j is connected to the h-th input line of decoder D_j, to which the value $\overline{M}_j(h) \bmod r$ must be transmitted. Let j_0 be such that $j_0 r \leqslant M(h) \leqslant (j_0+1)r$. Then leaves $0,1,\ldots, j_0-1$ of BC_h must receive the value r, leaf j_0 receives $M(h) \bmod r$, and leaves $j_0+1, \ldots, d-1$ must receive the value 0; this is done by a scheme that activates the path to leaf j_0 on the basis of the $logd$ most-significant bits of $M(h)$, on which the k least-significant bits are subsequently sent.

(d) DECODERS. $D_0, \ldots, D_{d-1}$, each capable of computing the portion r_i of the output sequence from the appropriate modified distribution of the entire input multiset. The I/O operations are performed with protocol similar to the one used by the encoders.

An important remark is that the above network has period k. Therefore it can be used in a pipe-line fashion with this period. This leads to the final sorting network. Letting $d = d_1 d_2$ and $r = r_1 r_2$ (since d and r are powers of 2, so are their factors), the network has d_2 encoders and d_2 decoders, each with r_2 input and output lines. Corresponding, there are r_1 tally and broadcast trees, each with d_2 leaves. In this network, a given encoder will process d_1 different multisets (E_j will process $S_j, S_{j+d_2}, \ldots, S_{j+d-d_2}$), and a given decoder will compute d_1 different subsequences of the output (D_j computes $r_j, r_{j+d_2}, \ldots, r_{j+d-2}$). Each of the $r_1 d_1$ "wavefronts" (r_i wavefronts for each of the d_i subproblems) has a depth of k bits, so that the period of the network matches the depth of each pipelined wavefront.

2.4. *Area-Time Performance*

We shall focus on encoders and tally trees, since decoders and broadcast trees are respectively analogous.

An encoder with r_2 I/O lines can be realized as a modification of an $(r, logr + \theta(logr))$-sorter of the type proposed in [7,11], with performance $A = O(r_2^2), T = O(kr/r_2)$), for r_2 in the range $\sqrt{kr} \leqslant r_2 \leqslant r$. The tally tree structure, with d_2 leaves and edge-bandwidth r_2, can be laid out in $O(d_2 r_2^2)$ area, by using the H-tree scheme. This area also accounts for the encoder modules. Finally, adding the contribution of r $logn$-bit registers deployed to store the r values of the distribution, we obtain a global area $A = O(d_2 r_2^2 + r\ logn)$ where $1 \leqslant d_2 \leqslant d$.

Since, an encoder spends $O(kr_1 d_1)$ time to process the $r_1 d_1$ data wavefronts and a similar performance is achieved by the tally trees when used in pipeline, (with the addition of $logd_2$, the depth of the pipe), T is the form (for suitable constants C_1 and C_2)$T = C_1(C_2 kr\ d_1 + logd_2)$. By choosing appropriate values for r_2 and d_2 in their respective permissible ranges, we obtain the following result.

Theorem 5. An (n,k)-sorter can be constructed, for $1 \leqslant k \leqslant logn$, with the following performance ($r = 2^k, d = n/r, C_2$ a suitable constant). If $(1+C_2 r)k > logn$, then

$$AT^2 = O(nrk^2) \text{ for } T \in [\Omega(logn), O(\sqrt{kr})]$$

and

$$AT = O(n\sqrt{r}k^{3/2}) \text{ for } T \in [\Omega(\sqrt{kr}), O(k^{3/2}n/\sqrt{r}\ logn)].$$

If $(1+C_2 r)k \leqslant logn$, then

$$AT = O(n\sqrt{r}k^{3/2}) \text{ for } T \in [\Omega(logn), O(k^{3/2}n/\sqrt{r}\ logn)].$$

Remark. Comparing the results of Theorem 5 with lower bounds (1) and (2), we note gaps of $O(k^2)$ for AT^2 and of $O(k^{3/2})$ for AT. This minor suboptimality can be attributed to inefficiencies in the representation of multisets ($O(kr)$ bits rather that the information-theoretic $O(r)$).

3. Networks for Sorting a Multiset of Long and Very Long keys (k ⩾ 2logn)

3.1. *The Algorithm.* It is useful to define the quantity $d \triangleq k/logn$ and to express bounds (4) and (5) in terms of d, as $AT^2 = \Omega(d(nlogn)^2)$ and $AT = \Omega(d(nlogn)^{3/2})$. These forms, which are linear in d, suggest the decomposition of the problem in d subproblems, whose solutions can be combined at small cost. Therefore, we shall decompose each key into d blocks of consecutive bits, and simultaneously process homologous blocks of different keys. We assume $n = 2^\nu$.

Let the arrays $(X_i^j : 0 \leqslant i < n, 0 \leqslant j < k)$ and $(Y_i^j : 0 \leqslant i < n, 0 \leqslant j < k)$, denote the input and output data (each row is a key, each column a bit position- see Figure 3). We also let $X_i(h) = (X_i^{(h+1)\nu-1}, \ldots, X_i^{h\nu})$ denote the h-th block of X_i and $X(h)$ denote the $n \times \nu$ array whose rows are $X_0(h), \ldots, X_{n-1}(h)$.

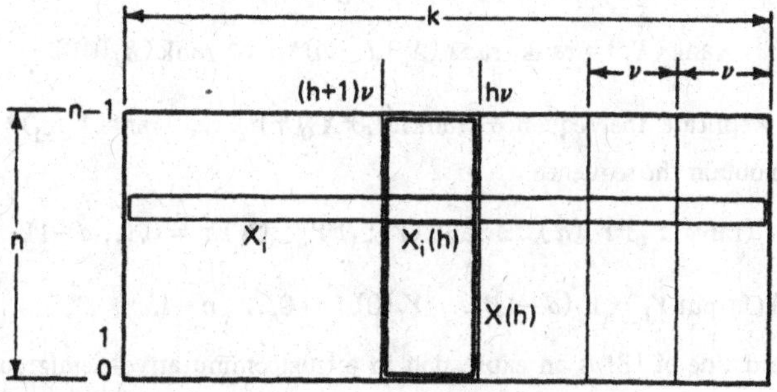

Figure 3. Nomenclature for input data.

It is obvious that, for given h, $(Y_0(h), \ldots, Y_{n-1}(h))$ is a permutation of $(X_0(h), \ldots, X_{n-1}(h))$. This permutation is functionally dependent on the values of the bits in blocks $h, h+1, \ldots, d-1$. For each key X_i in multiset $\{X_0, \ldots, X_{n-1}\}$ we define $\mathrm{rank}(X_i) = |\{j : X_j < X_i\}|$. It is crucial, for our application, that equal keys have the same rank. We now have the following technical lemma:

Lemma. Let X (an integer represented in binary) be a member of a multiset S. If X is viewed as the concatenation $L*R$ of two strings L and R, then

$$\mathrm{rank}(X) = \mathrm{rank}(L * \mathrm{rank}(R)).$$

By repeated application of this lemma we obtain

$$\mathrm{rank}(X_i) = \mathrm{rank}(\mathrm{rank}(X_i(d\text{-}1)) * \ldots * \mathrm{rank}(X_i(h)) * \ldots * \mathrm{rank}(X_i(0))),$$

i.e. the rank of the concatenation is the rank of the concatenation of the ranks. This property allows us to reduce the computation of the rank of long keys to the computation of the rank of small substrings of keys. The computation of the rank of the substrings is solved by the following procedure, based on sorting.

A. (EXTEND) Given a multiset $\{C_0, C_1, \ldots, C_{n-1}\}$, extend C_i to a new string $\overline{C}_i = C_i * i$, $i = 0, \ldots, n-1$, where i is represented with logn bits.

B. (SORT) Sort $\overline{C}_0, \ldots, \overline{C}_{n-1}$ to obtain a sorted sequence $\overline{Y}_0, \ldots, \overline{Y}_{n-1}$. Then $\overline{Y}_i = C_{\pi(i)} \pi(i)$, $i = 0, \ldots, p-1$, where $\pi(0), \ldots, \pi(n-1)$ is a permutation of $0, \ldots, n-1$.

C. (RANK) Compute $\mathrm{rank}(C_{\pi(i)})$ as one plus the maximum index j such that $C_{\pi(j)} < C_{\pi(i)}$. If no such index exists, then let $\mathrm{rank}(C_{\pi(i)}) = 0$.

D. (EXTRACT) Form a new set of keys $Z_i = \pi(i) * \mathrm{rank}(C_{\pi(i)}) * C_{\pi(i)}$, and sort.

Using the above procedure as as subroutine, we have the following divide-and-conquer sorting algorithm:

1. (DIVIDE) Decompose the input keys $X_0, \ldots, X_{n-1}$ into d blocks $\nu = logn$ consecutive bits each, so that $X_i = X_i(d-1)* \ldots * X_i(h)* \ldots * X_i(0)$.

2. (SUBPROBLEMS) For each $h = 0, \ldots, d-1$, compute rank $(X_0(h)), \ldots,$ rank$(X_{n-1}(h))$ with respect to multiset $\{X_0(h), \ldots, X_{n-1}(h)\}$.

3. (MARRY) Compute the ranks of the X_i's using the formula

$$\text{rank}(X_i) = \text{rank}(\text{rank}(X_i(d-1)) * \ldots * \text{rank}(X_i(0))). \qquad (8)$$

4. (ROUTE) Replicate the sequence (rank$(X_0)*X_0(h)$,..., rank$(X_{n-1})* X_{n-1}(h) : h = 0, \ldots, d-1$), to obtain the sequence

$$(\text{rank}(Y_0)*Y_0(h), \ldots, \text{rank}(Y_{n-1})*Y_{n-1}(h) : h = 0, \ldots, d-1).$$

5. (OUTPUT) Output $Y_i = Y_i(d-1)* \ldots *Y_i(0), i = 0, \ldots, n-1$.

The right-hand side of (8) is an expression in a (noncommutative) semigroup whose elements are sequences of n numbers, and whose operation computes the sequence of the ranks of the concatenation of two sequences. In general, the computation of (10) is viewed abstractly as a computation tree; the implementation of the above algorithm as a VLSI network rests crucially on the structure of this computation tree.

3.2 *The Network*

Several implementations are possible for the above algorithm. Here we outline one which is appropriate to non-boundary layouts. Another implementation more appropriate for boundary layouts is described in [5].

The network has the structure of a fully balanced binary tree on d leaves; each node of the tree corresponds to a module. A leaf receives the keys in a block and computes their ranks (i.e., it is $(n, 2\ logn)$- sorter); an internal node computes the ranks of the concatenation of the sequences produced by its two offspring nodes. All modules on the same level of the tree (levels are numbered 0, 1,..., $logd$-1, starting from the leaves) are identical. We denote by l_j and t_j, respectively, the side length and the computation time of the modules on level j; correspondingly, L_j and T_j respectively denote analogous quantities for the subtree, whose root is at level j.

We begin by describing the structure of the network for designs governed by the AT^2-measure, i.e. for $T \in [\Omega(logn), O(\sqrt{nlogn})]$ see Theorem 3). Depending upon the value of the key length k, it is convenient to group the levels of the tree into stages. The objective is to realize an H-layout whose area is of the same order as the area of its leaves.

1. *Basic Stage* (Level 0). The module of the basic stage is a standard area-time optimal $(n, 2logn)$-sorter with time T_0 and $l_0 = \theta(nlogn/T_0)$.

2. *Accelerating Stage* (Levels $1, \ldots, J_1 = 2log(T_0/logn)$). As the level j increases the modules are $(n, 2logn)$-sorters with decreasing computation time (and increasing area). Specifically, for any $1 < \epsilon < \sqrt{2}$, we have $l_j = l_0\epsilon^j$ and $t_j = T_0/\epsilon^j$. Thus we have $l_j = L_{j-2} + l_0\epsilon^j = l_0 2^{j/2}/(2/\epsilon^2 - 1)$ and

$$L_{J_1} = l_0 2^{\log(T_0/\log n)}/(2/\epsilon^2-1) = O(n),\ T_{J_1} = \sum_{j=1}^{J_2} t_j < T_0\epsilon/(\epsilon-1),$$

that is, the order of computation time has been maintained and the overall area has grown to $O(n^2)$. For given computation time $T_0(1+\epsilon/(\epsilon-1))$ this portion of the network provides an AT^2-optimal implementation for $k \leqslant K_1 = \log n . 2^{J_2} = T_0^2/\log n$.

3. *Fast stage* (Levels $J_1+1, \ldots, J_2 = J_1 + cT_0/\log n$, for any constant $c > 0$). All modules of any level j in this stage are "fast" $(n, 2\log n)$-sorters with $l_j = O(n)$ and $t_j = O(\log n)$. We easily obtain

$$L_{J_2} = L_{J_1} 2^{(J_2-J_1)/2} = O(n\, 2^{cT_0/2\log n}),\ \ T_{J_2} = T_0(1+\frac{\epsilon}{\epsilon-1}+c).$$

Note that this portion of the network provides an AT^2-optimal implementation for $k \leqslant K_2 = K_1 2^{cT_0/\log n}$.

4. *Superfast Stage* (Levels $J_2+1, \ldots, J_3 = J_2 + c'T_0$ for any constant $c' > 0$). This stage can be deployed only if $T_0 \geqslant (2/c)(\log n)^2$. Indeed, in such case, $L_{J_2} = O(n^2)$ is of the same order as the sidelength of a module that performs the concatenation of the ranks in time $O(1)$ by using a redundant representation. This type of module is appropriately called a "ranker". More specifically, for a multiset $\{X_0, \ldots, X_{n-1}\}$, we construct the $n \times n$ matrix of *ternary* entries whose component (i,j) represents the result of comparing X_i and X_j. Rank(X_i) is then readily extractible from i-th row of the comparison matrix. It is also clear that the matrix of the concatenation of two rankings is obtained by a simple local operation on corresponding entries of their matrices. Thus for each level j in this stage, we have $l_j = O(n^2)$ and $t_j = O(1)$, whence

$$L_{J_3} = L_{J_2} 2^{(J_3-J_2)/2} = O(n\, 2^{cT_0/2\log n + cT_0/2}),\ \ T_{J_3} = T_0(1+\frac{\epsilon}{\epsilon-1}+c+c').$$

Here again, the resulting network provides an AT^2-optimal implementation for $k \leqslant K_3 = K_2 2^{c'T_0/2}$.

Note that for $i = 1,2,3$ $K_i = \log n . 2^{J_i}$ and $L_{J_i} = l_0 2^{J_i/2}$. Since $J_3 = 2\log(T_0/\log n) + cT_0/\log n + c'T_0$, we see that for $T_0 = \theta(\sqrt{n\log n})$ K_3 is of the same order as k^*, defined in Theorem 3.

For designs governed by the AT-measure (i.e. for $T \in [\Omega(\sqrt{n\log n}.\max(1, k/k^*)), O(k\sqrt{n/\log n}\,])$, for given k and T we select an AT^2-optimal network corresponding to $k' = kT/\sqrt{n\log n}$ and $T' = \sqrt{n\log n}$ and use it sequentially k/k' times. This achieves AT-optimality.

Thus we obtain:

Theorem 6. A VLSI (n,k)-sorter whose performance attains the lower bound of Theorem 3 can be constructed for all $k \geqslant 2\log n$ if $T = \Omega(\log^2 n)$, and for all $k \in [2\log n, (T/\log n)^2 2^{cT/\log n}]$ (for every $c > 0$), if $T = o(\log^2 n)$.

Suppose now that for $T_{J_3} = \theta(\sqrt{n\log n})$ we extend the "superfast stage" for J additional levels. This realizes an $(n, \log n . 2^{J_3+J})$-sorter with area $l_0^2 . 2^{J_3+J}$ and computation time $T_{J_3}+J$. Since both T_{J_3} and J_3 are $\theta(T_0)$, we have $T_{J_3} = (J_3)$ and $T_{J_3}+J = O(J_3+J) = O(\log A)$. If we consider the product AT/logA for this network we obtain:

$$AT/logA = O(nlogn\,2^{J_3+J}) = O(nk)$$

i.e., this network is (AT/logA)-optimal. For values of k and T in the (AT/logA)-region, we select an (AT/logA)-optimal network corresponding to $T' = log(k'n)$ and $k' = (T'/T)k$ and use it sequentially k/k' times. This achieves AT/logA-optimality and we have:

Theorem 7. A VLSI (n,k)-sorter whose performance attains the lower bound of Theorem 4 can be constructed for all $k > k^*$.

The only range where a gap between lower and upper bounds remains is for $T = o(log^2 n)$ and $(T^2/logn)2^{cT/logn} < k < 2^T/n$, a range where the lower bound is of the AT^2 form, as given in (4).

Note. After the submission of the paper, we have learnt that bounds (1) (see [15]), and (3) have been independently obtained by A. Siegel, and that other optimal constructions for several ranges of k and T have been proposed by R. Cole and A. Siegel [16].

REFERENCES

1. C. D. Thompson, "A Complexity Theory for VLSI," Ph.D. Thesis, Dept. of Comp. Science, Carnegie-Mellon Univ.; August 1980.
2. R. P. Brent and H. T. Kung, "The chip complexity of binary arithmetic," Journal of the ACM, vol. 28, n. 3, pp. 521-534; July 1981.
3. J. Vuillemin, "A combinatorial limit to the computing power of VLSI circuits," *IEEE Trans. on Comp.* vol. C-32, n. 3., pp. 294-300, March 1983.
4. G. Bilardi and F. P. Preparata, "Square tessellation techniques for area-time lower bounds," submitted for publication.
5. G. Bilardi, "The Area-Time Complexity of Sorting," Ph.D. Thesis, Univ. of Illinois, 1984.
6. J. D. Ullman, *Computational Aspects of VLSI*, Computer Science Press; 1983.
7. F. T. Leighton, "Tight bounds on the complexity of parallel sorting," Proc. 16th Annual ACM Symposium on Theory of Computing, Washington, D. C., pp. 71-80; April 1984. (Also *IEEE Trans. on Comp.* April 1985).
8. A. Siegel, "Optimal area VLSI circuits for sorting," submitted for sub. publication.
9. C. D. Thompson, The VLSI complexity of sorting, *IEEE Trans. Comp.*, vol. C-32, n. 12, pp. 1171-1184; Dec. 1983.
10. G. Bilardi and F. P. Preparata, "An architecture for bitonic sorting with optimal VLSI performance," *IEEE Trans. Comp.*, vol. C-33, n. 7, pp. 640-651; July 1984.
11. G. Bilardi and F. P. Preparata, "A minimum area VLSI network for *O(logN)* time sorting", Proc. 16th Annual ACM Symposium on Theory of Computing, Washington, D. C., pp. 64-70; April 1984. (Also see *IEEE Trans. on Comp.* April 1985.)
12. G. Bilardi and F. P. Preparata, "The VLSI optimality of the AKS sorting network," *Information Processing Letters*, to appear.
13. R. B. Johnson, "The complexity of a VLSI adder," *Information Processing Letters*, vol. 11. n. 2, pp. 92-93; October 1980.
14. G. M. Baudet, "On the area required by VLSI circuits," manuscript.
15. A. Siegel, "Minimal Storage Sorting Circuits," *IEEE Trans. Comp.*, vol. C-34, n. 4; April 1985.
16. R. Cole and A. Siegel, "Optimal VLSI network that sort a numbers in an arbitrary, fixed range", manuscript.

REPEATED SYNCHRONOUS SNAPSHOTS AND THEIR IMPLEMENTATION IN CSP.
(extended abstract)

by
Luc Bougé
LITP, Université Paris 7,
2 Place Jussieu, 75251 Paris, France.(*)

Abstract

A new version of the Snapshot algorithm of Chandy and Lamport is presented. It considers synchronous communications and partially ordered semantics. It allows for repeated snapshots. Its implementation in the language CSP is described: it is symmetric, generic and bounded in storage. It yields a symmetric and generic solution to the classical Distributed Termination Detection problem of Francez.

Introduction

Several recent works have drawn attention to the notions of **local and common knowledge** in distributed computing ([FHV 84], [HM 84], [Le 84]). Consider for example a network of communicating sequential machines. Each machine manages a private store. Its **internal state** is thus in general a local knowledge. Moreover, as remarked by Lamport ([La 78]),**time** must also be regarded as a local knowledge. A given machine may only acquire some relative knowledge ("after", "before") about time in other machines by means of message synchronization. In such a framework, the notion of global state is meaningless: as in quantum mechanics, there is an irremovable trade-off between time and space ([LeL 77]).

On the other hand, the notion of the global state of a system plays a central role in many problems in distributed computing. A classical one is for example deadlock detection. This problem is well-known in the area of Distributed Data Bases (see e.g. [HC 83]). It was also identified by Francez ([Fr 80]) in distributed computing, in the framework of Hoare's language CSP ([Hoa 78]). It was called there the Distributed Termination Detection problem.

However, most of work on those subjects led to a bushy forest of ad-hoc solutions, without tackling directly the central notion of global state. Only recently Chandy and Lamport ([Ch 83], [CL 84], [La 84]) and Dijkstra ([Dij 83]) took a decisive step forwards by introducing the notions of a **snapshot** and of a **stable property**.

Informally, a snapshot of a given computation is a global state which could have been observed by some external observer equipped with a suitable global clock (any space-time referential which satisfies Lamport's Clock Axioms of [La 78]). A snapshot can thus be viewed as a **possible past** of the system.

Consider now predicates such as "The system is deadlocked", "Some process has terminated" or "All processes have completed their required work". All those predicates enjoy the following property: once they hold then they continue to hold. Such predicates are

---

* The author is also affiliated with
Laboratoire d'informatique, UER Sciences, Université d'Orléans,
rue de Chartres, 45046 Orléans, FRANCE.

called stable. To test a stable predicate on a given computation, it suffices to "imagine" a snapshot of this computation: if the predicate is true for the snapshot then it is true for the current state of the system. This is basically the principle of the Snapshot algorithm of Chandy and Lamport. It yields in particular straightforward and elegant solutions to detect deadlock or distributed termination in a distributed environment.

In this paper, we focus on the use of the Snapshot algorithm in the framework of the language CSP. In a first section, we rework the presentation of the (Single) Snapshot algorithm of Chandy and Lamport in the case of **synchronous communications** and **partially ordered semantics**. The improved version of this algorithm which handles **repeated snapshots** is described in section 2. Its properties are studied. Section 3 describes the implementation in CSP of this algorithm. This implementation is used to propose a **symmetric, generic** and **bounded in storage overhead** solution to the Distributed Termination Detection problem.

Related work

Much work has been done on the Distributed Termination Detection problem in CSP. Early solutions were not satisfactory because of the "freezing" ([Fr 82]): the original computation and the distributed termination detection waves were mutually exclusive. Next solutions were not symmetric because one prescribed process had to initiate the detection waves ([DS 80], [FRS 81], [FR 82], [MC 82], [DFG 83]). Then symmetric solutions were described. Rana ([Ra 83]) proposed a symmetric solution using global time-stamps. This solution is not bounded in storage. Moreover, it is incorrect on several points as indicated in [AR 84]. Apt and Richier ([AR 84], [Ri 84]) improved the solution of Rana by using virtual (logical) clocks instead of real ones. Again, their solutions are not bounded in storage. Also, they use a predefined Hamiltonian circuit of the graph and are thus not generic. Our solution via snapshots is not freezing, symmetric, generic and bounded in storage overhead.

The Snapshot algorithm is briefly (and somewhat cryptically) described in [Ch 83]. Chandy considers asynchronous (buffered) messages and partially ordered semantics.

A precise description can be found in [Dij 83] in the framework of abstract asynchronous machines. Two versions of the algorithm are studied. The first one uses white and red machines. The second one uses additional markers. Dijkstra considers an interleaving semantics.

The work by Lamport [La 84] considers asynchronous machines and partially ordered semantics. It contains an extensive discussion of the notion of global state (see also [La 78]) and reworks the description of [Dij 83]. But his algorithm does not allow for repeated snapshots. Also no indication is provided for a practical implementation of the algorithm, nor complexity evaluation.

A very elegant approach to the Snapshot algorithm is described by Morgan ([Mo 85]). It shows that above versions of the algorithm can in fact be factorized into two separate algorithms.

- A modified version of the Snapshot algorithm where *global time* is available to all processors. Its correctness is then straightforward.
- A *clock synchronization algorithm* which simulates some weak kind of global clock from local clocks (for instance Lamport's one in [La 78]).

The reader is advised that the two previous works and ours were carried out independently.

1. The Single Snapshot algorithm

This section describes briefly the framework of synchronized distributed systems. It uses a partially ordered semantics (also called non-interleaving semantics or causal semantics). We then sketch the (Single) Snapshot algorithm of Chandy and Lamport ([Ch 83], [CL 84], [La 84], [Mo 85]). Details and proofs omitted here can be found in the above references and in the extended version of this paper ([Bou 84a]). We rather focus on the intuitive explanation of the underlying framework and of the purpose of the algorithm.

1.1. Synchronized distributed systems

A **sequential process** can produce atomic events sequentially. Events are assumed to be uniquely identified. There exists three kinds of events: internal events which may occur without any reference to the outside world, receiving a message of a given type on a given incoming channel and sending a message of a given type along a given outgoing channel. Each process manages an internal (local) state which can only be modified by the occurrence of its own events. Initial states are fixed. A given state determines the set of events which may occur next. A given state together with the occurrence of an allowed event determines the next state.

A **distributed system** is a finite directed graph whose vertices are sequential processes and edges are one-way communication channels. A system is **synchronized** if no message of a given type can be sent along a channel before the receiver is ready to receive a message of this type on this channel. For an external observer, the transmission looks then *instantaneous* and *atomic*. Sending and receiving a message are in fact the *same* event.

A **computation** of a system is defined as follows ([La 84]). Consider for each process P a (totally ordered) sequence of events from the initial state. Identify the events of sending and receiving a given message (the system is synchronized). This set of events is then a computation if no cycle has been thereby introduced among the total orders. The resulting global partial order is called the **causality order**. Computations are partially ordered by inclusion. A computation is finite if its set of events is finite. It is maximal if it is maximal for inclusion among all computations. Otherwise, it is partial. Partial computation are exactly left-closed subsets of maximal computations (a partially ordered set C is left-closed if $f \in C$ and $e \leq f$ imply $e \in C$).

The usual notion of a global state is meaningless in this framework. Instead we define the notion of a **slice** ([La 84], also called a cut). Let C be a partial computation of a system. For each process P consider the internal state of P after the last event produced by P in C (it is undefined if P produced infinitely many events in C). The slice associated to C is then the collection of those internal states. A slice can be viewed as a *possible* global state of the system which *could* have been observed by some external observer equipped with a suitable clock. Conversely, all such possible (observable) global states are slices.

If slices associated with different partial computations are distinguished in some way (see [Ch 83] for example) then we have the following property. Let P_0 and P_1 be two partial computation with slices S_0 and S_1. Then $P_0 \subseteq P_1$ iff S_0 is observed before S_1 by any observer which can observe both.

Let B be a predicate on the slices S of a system. B is **stable** if B is monotonic: if $P_0 \subseteq P_1$ and B holds for S_0 then B holds for S_1. Examples of such predicates have been given in the introduction. We say that the system is stable if B holds. Then whenever a system is stable it remains stable for ever afterwards. As stated by Dijkstra ([Dij 83])

> the purpose of the Snapshot algorithm is to collect such (local) state information that, on the account of it, (global) stability can be detected.

1.2. White processes, red processes and markers waves

The main idea it to equip processes with some control facility which allows them to exchange messages of a special type called markers. For the time being, we assume the existence of an **external analyser** ([Mo 85]) which can exchange information with processes (probably with some delay; it is not a global observer). At some point of their computation, processes sample their internal state (take a snapshot of it) and report it to the analyser. Markers rules shall guarantee that those various sampling occur at consistent times so that the resulting collection of local states is actually a slice (a global snapshot) of the computation. The analyser can then test whether B holds for this slice and notify this information to all processes. Because B is stable, if a process is notified by the analyser that B holds then it knows that B holds for ever from that time on (this is even eventual common knowledge in the sense of [HM 84])

The word "basic" refers here to the original system whereas "marked" refers to the system equipped with markers. Following Dijkstra, a process is **white** if it has not yet sampled its local state. Otherwise, it is **red**.

Markers rules

1) Initially all processes are white. A white process turns red by suspending its basic computation and sampling its *basic* internal state. Then it resumes its basic computation but does not send any basic message along a channel before having sent a marker along it.
2) A white process can turn red spontaneously at any time.
3) A white process is always ready to receive markers. On receiving a marker it turns immediately red.

4) A red process is always ready to receive markers. On receiving a marker it ignores it. A red process sends only a finite number of markers. A red process eventually reports its sampled internal state to the analyser. A red process cannot turn back white.

5) A white process eventually turns red.

We now state without proof the main properties of systems equipped with markers. The **projection** of a marked computation is the partially ordered set of events obtained by forgetting all about markers and colors. It can be seen that it is actually a basic computation.

Property 1.1

Each process samples exactly once its local state and eventually reports it to the analyser.

Property 1.2

Let C be the projection of a marked computation. The local states reported to the analyser constitute a slice SSS of C associated with a finite partial computation SSC.

The analyser waits for all local states to be reported before testing whether B holds. From that time on, all partial computations of the system contain SSC (SnapShot partial Computation). Thus if B holds for SSS (SnapShot global State) then it holds when processes are notified by the analyser that it actually holds. We say then that B is **detected**.

Property 1.3

1) The projection of a maximal marked computation is a maximal basic computation.

2) Let C be a maximal basic computation and S_0 be a slice of C associated with a finite partial computation C_0. Then there exists a maximal marked computation which has C as projection, S_0 as SSS and C_0 as SSC.

The above property shows that introducing markers does not disturb basic computations. No basic computation is lost. Any finite slice may be snapshot by the analyser.

2. The Repeated Snapshot algorithm

Unfortunately, the above algorithm is rather unsatisfactory. If B happens to become true only after some process has turned red then detection is no more guaranteed. We need therefore to allow the system to initiate repeated snapshots if the first one is not successful. It suffices to introduce a rule to whiten processes. Yet, one must be careful enough to avoid that different markers waves interfer. An easy solution is to label markers with the number of their wave, but the number of needed waves is obviously not bounded in general. We therefore prefer to strengthen slightly the markers rules. A red process can turn back white only after having sent and received *all* markers it could ever exchange within the current wave. We modify thus rule 4 as follows.

Markers rules (cont'd)

4') A red process accepts at most one marker on each incoming channel and sends at most one marker along each outgoing channel.

4") A red process which has exchanged exactly one marker on each adjacent channel since it turned red for the last time and which has reported its latest sampled local state to the analyser eventually turns back white.

Here again, we must be careful enough to avoid that the analyser gets confused with the successive waves of reports. Again, an easy solution is to number reports. We prefer to restrict the behaviour of the analyser so that it does not accept a new wave of reports until it has completed the current one.

Analyser rule

The analyser collects exactly one local state from each process at each round. It does not accept any more report until it has tested whether B holds on the current snapshot slice and notified the result to all processes.

Observe that results may be notified to processes after they have turned back white and then red again. The analyser works thus highly asynchronously with respect to processes. We now state some properties of those modified rules.

Property 2.1

A process samples its basic local state and reports it to the analyser exactly once while it is red. For any n, all processes eventually turn red for the nth time.

Let SSS_n be the collection of local states reported to the analyser within the nth round. Let SSC_n be the set of basic events produced by processes before they turn red for the $(n+1)^{th}$ time.

Property 2.2

Let C be the projection of a marked computation. SSS_n is a slice of C associated with the finite partial computation SSC_n for all n.

This guarantees that results notified by the analyser are consistent. As in part 1, if the analyser reports that B holds then B actually holds for ever from that time on, and this is eventual common knowledge. We now state the converse property.

Property 2.2 (cont'd)

Let C be the projection of a marked computation and let C_0 be a finite partial computation of C. Then there exists an integer n such that $C_0 \subseteq SSC_n$.

Thus if B happens to be true for some finite partial computation then it will eventually be detected. Those modified rules meet thus our requirement. Unfortunately we have to pay for that. Nothing prevents the system to get overflooded by markers waves. Processes may perfectly spend all their time turning from white to red and then from red to white. More precisely, we have the following projection property.

Property 2.3

1) The projection of a maximal marked computation is a (possibly partial) basic computation.
2) Let C be a maximal basic computation and let S_0 be a slice of C associated with a finite partial computation C_0. Then there exists a marked computation which has C as projection, S_0 as SSS_0 and C_0 as SSC_0.

We thus need a way to prevent white processes from turning red spontaneously "too often". This can be viewed as some kind of fairness requirement about the interleaving between the processing of markers and the basic computation. A possible solution is to strengthen rule 2.

Markers rules (cont'd)

2') A white process can turn red spontaneously only if it has produced at least one basic event since the last time it turned red spontaneously.

This guarantees that maximal infinite marked computations have infinite (but not necessarily maximal) basic computations as projection. But this new rule may cause deadlock in markers processing. Consider for example a distributed system whose all computations are finite. Then eventually by property 2.2 the analyser will collect the final global state of the system. No more basic event can be produced afterwards, and a process may then only turn red spontaneously at most one time. Eventually, all processes will be waiting for a marker and none will be allowed to initiate the wave.

This kind of situation can be easily avoided by improving slightly the analyser. Assume that the analyser, besides testing whether B holds in the current snapshot slice, tests also whether this slice corresponds to a final state of the basic computation. If it can detect that no more basic event can ever be produced (this is also a stable predicate) then it notifies it to processes together with the truth value of B. When a process is notified that the basic computation is maximal then it can take the appropriate action (halting for example). Halting can moreover be synchronized by strengthening rule 4". If processes may not turn back white before the analyser has notified results to them then all processes will halt at the end of the same markers wave.

3. Application to CSP

Because communications in CSP are synchronous, the Repeated Snapshot algorithm above can be easily implemented in this language. This section sketches briefly this implementation and its applications. It assumes from the reader good familiarity with CSP. The original description of the language is in [Hoa 78]. An interleaving operational semantics is given in [Plo 82], and some insights into a partially ordered one are given in [Rei 84]. Omitted details can be found in [Bou 84a].

3.1. Implementation

A **CSP distributed system** is a CSP program of the form

$$P :: [P_a || P_b || ...]$$

where each process P_u is **sequential** (no nested parallelism). We disregard here the Distributed Termination Convention of CSP and assume that no failure occur. We assume that the communication graph is **strongly connected** and that all processes P_u are in Distributed Normal Form ([AC 85])

P_u :: [Init
*[$Guard_1 \rightarrow Comm_1$
▪ $Guard_2 \rightarrow Comm_2$
▪ ...]]

where all input/output commands are in the guards of the while-loop.

The **internal state** of a process P_u is defined by the value of its program counter together with the values of all its variables. The Repeated Snapshot algorithm is implemented by adding extra initialization commands, extra guarded commands to the main loop and prefixing original guarded commands by extra boolean guards or assignments. Moreover we require that all variables and message types which are used in those extra constructs are new. This guarantees that the projection of a marked computation is actually a partial computation of the original system. In this framework, we consider the execution of a guarded command of the main while-loop as a *single* event.

Rule 2' is implemented by adding a new variable *moved* which is reset to true each time a basic guard is chosen, and to false each time the process turns spontaneously red. A new variable *red* is set to true each time the process turns red, and reset to false each time its turns back white. We transform thus each original guarded command of the process to

▪ $Guard_p \rightarrow Comm_p$; moved := true

and we add the following new guarded command

▪ ¬red; moved → red := true; moved := false; SAMPLE

The function SAMPLE samples the current internal *basic* state of the process.

We define two new arrays *received*[*1..k*] and *sent*[*1..l*] which records receipt and sending of markers. We assume that in-neighbours of P_u are $P_{in(1)}, ..., P_{in(k)}$ and its out-neighbours $P_{out(1)}, ..., P_{out(l)}$. The following new guards implement rules 4' and 4''. Indices i and j range over [1..k] and [1..l].

▪$_i$ ¬ received[i]; $P_{in(i)}$?marker()
→ received[i] := true;
[red → skip ▪ ¬ red → red := true; SAMPLE]

▪$_j$ red; ¬ sent[j]; $P_{out(j)}$!marker() → sent[j] := true

Rule 1 is implemented by transforming further each guarded command containing an output command to some out-neighbour $P_{out(j)}$ as follows.

▪ (¬ red OR sent[j]); $Guard_p \rightarrow Comm_p$; moved := true

We now have to implement the analyser. In fact, each process plays here the role of the analyser. Information is diffused over all processes using a classical Wave strategy ([Schn 84], [Bou 84a]). Each process manages a new variable *info*, initially empty. Each time a process learns some information which it does not already know (by receiving it or by sampling its own internal state) then it forwards it to all its out-neighbours by sending messages of a new type *forward*. Eventually, all processes know exactly all available information because the communication graph is strongly connected.

The Analyser rule is implemented by arrays similar to those used above for markers. As soon as a process detects that an in-neighbour of its stores a complete slice then it refuses any more message from it. All processes store eventually the **same** slice, and each of them can then perform the appropriate tests. When it is done, it sets a new variable *done* to true. In particular, if this slice corresponds to a blocked state (deadlocked or terminated) then each process can set a new variable *halt* appearing in all guards to false. This forces thus the proper termination of the system.

Finally, rewhitening of processes is implemented by a boolean guarded command. RESET resets all new variables but *moved* to their initial value.

$$\bullet \text{ red; done; } \Lambda_i \text{ received[i]; } \Lambda_j \text{ sent[j]} \\ \rightarrow \text{red := false; RESET}$$

3.2. The Distributed Termination Detection problem

The Distributed Termination Detection problem was set by Francez ([Fr 80]). Consider a CSP distributed system P as above. Assume that P never fails, that its communication graph is strongly connected and that all computations of P are finite. The problem is to transform P into an equivalent system whose all computations properly terminate.

Because P is in Distributed Normal Form, P may get blocked only if all its processes are at their external while-loop. The predicate B "P is deadlocked or P has terminated" is thus actually a predicate on the *slices* of P's computations as defined above. It is moreover stable. We can thus apply the CSP version of the Repeated Snapshot algorithm to this problem. As stated at the end of section 3.1, it suffices to force proper termination as soon as B holds. It can be shown that the implementation described in section 3.1 can be made ***symmetric, generic*** and ***bounded in storage overhead*** ([Bou 84], [Bou 85]). If all processes of the original system play equivalent roles then so do all processes of the transformed system; in particular, no (hidden) monitor or starter is needed. The transformation can be made locally at each process without reference to its external environment. If all variables of the original system are bounded, so are those of the transformed system; this would not hold if markers were stamped with their wave number.

4. Conclusion

We have described here an improved version of the Snapshot algorithm of Chandy and Lamport. It considers synchronous communications between sequential machines and allows for repeated snapshots.

We have presented an implementation of it in the language CSP. It enjoys nice properties such as symmetry, genericity and bounded storage overhead. The components of the original distributed program are transformed independently. The transformation depends only on the local topology of the communication graph. In particular, no predefined Hamiltonian circuit is needed.

In this implementation, processes cooperate to diffuse information over the network. Our implementation allows as much nondeterminism and parallelism as possible according to the general philosophy of the language CSP.

The storage overhead induced by the algorithm for each process is $O(n^2)$ where n is the number of processes (the size of internal states is taken as a constant). At most $O(n^2)$ control messages are exchanged on each channel within each stability detection wave. There are at most as many such waves as the number of steps taken by the original program. However, because of the high degree of nondeterminism and parallelism, worst-case evaluations do not reflect the average behaviour of the algorithm. In the case of a ring with n vertices, a detection wave may for example consist of $O(n)$ messages.

As a side-effect, it provides a solution to the Distributed Termination Detection problem of Francez. To our current knowledge, it is the first one which enjoys the properties of symmetry, bounded storage overhead and genericity.

Acknowledgment

This work could not have been done without the encouragement and the help of Krzysztof R. Apt. Thanks also to P. Gastin for helpful remarks.

Literature

[AC 84] K.R. Apt and Ph. Clermont, Two normal form theorems for CSP programs, in preparation (1984).

[AR 84] K.R. Apt and J.L. Richier, Real time clocks versus virtual clocks, Rept. No. 84-34, LITP, Univ. Paris 7, Paris (1984).

[Bou 84] L. Bougé, Symmetric election in CSP, Rept. No. 84-31, LITP, Univ. Paris 7, Paris (1984), submitted for publication.

[Bou 84a] L. Bougé, More about the snapshot algorithm: repeated synchronous snapshots and their implementation in CSP, Rept. No. 84-56, LITP, Univ. Paris 7, Paris (1984).

[Bou 85] L. Bougé, Symmetry and Genericity for CSP distributed system, Rept. No. 85- , LITP, Univ. Paris 7, Paris (1985) in preparation.

[Ch 83] K.M. Chandy, Paradigms for distributed computing, in: Proc. 3rd Conf. on Found. of Soft. Technology and Theory of Computer Science, Bengalore, India (1983) 192-201.

[CL 84] K.M. Chandy and L. Lamport, Distributed snapshots: determining the global state of distributed systems, Rept. No. TR-LCS-8401, Univ. Texas, Austin, Texas (jan. 1984), submitted for publication (1984).

[Dij 83] E.W. Dijkstra, The distributed snapshot algorithm of K.M. Chandy and L. Lamport, Letter No. EWD864a (1983).

[DFG 83] E.W. Dijkstra, W.H.J. Feijen and A.J.M. van Gasteren, Derivation of a termination detection algorithm for distributed computations, Inf. Proc. Letters 16 (1983) 217-219.

[DS 80] E.W. Dijkstra and C.S. Scholten, Termination detection for diffusing computations, Inf. Proc. Letters 11 (1980) 1-4.

[FHV 84] R. Fagin, J.Y. Halpern and M.Y. Vardi, A model-theoritic analysis of knowledge: extended abstract, IBM Research Laboratory, San Jose, Calif. (1984).

[Fr 80] N. Francez, Distributed termination, ACM Trans. Prog. Lang. Syst. 2 (1980) 42-55.

[FR 82] N. Francez and M. Rodeh, Achieving distributed termination without freezing, IEEE Trans. Soft. Eng. SE-8 (1982) 287-292.

[FRS 81] N. Francez, M. Rodeh and M. Sintzoff, Distributed termination with interval assertion, in: J. Diaz and I. Ramos, eds., Proc. Int. Coll. on Formalization of Programming Concepts, Peniscola, Spain, Lecture Notes in Computer Science 107 (Springer, Berlin, 1981).

[Hoa 78] C.A.R. Hoare, Communicating sequential processes, Comm. ACM 21 (1978) 666-677.

[HC 83] T. Herman and K.M. Chandy, A distributed algorithm to detect and/or deadlock, Rept. No. TR LCS-8301, Dept. of Computer Science, Univ. of Texas, Austin, Texas (1983).

[HM 84] J. Halpern and Y. Moses, Common knowledge in a distributed environment, Computer Science Dpt., Stanford Univ., Calif. (1984).

[La 78] L. Lamport, Time, clocks and the ordering of events in a distributed system, Comm. ACM 21 (1978) 558-565.

[La 84] L. Lamport, Lecture Notes prepared for the Advanced Course on Distributed Systems - Methods and Tools for Specification, Computer Science Inst., TUM, Munchen, Germany (1984).

[Le 84] D. Lehmann, Knowledge, common knowledge and related puzzles (extended summary), Inst. of Math. and Computer Science, Hebrew Univ., Jerusalem, Israel (1984).

[LeL 77] G. Le Lann, Distributed systems - towards a formal approach, in: B. Gilchrist, ed., Information Processing 77 (North-Holland, Amsterdam, 1977) 155-160.

[Mo 85] C. Morgan, Global and logical time in distributed systems, Inf. Proc. Letters (1985), to appear.

[MC 82] J. Misra and K.M. Chandy, Termination detection of diffusing computations in communicating sequential processes, ACM Trans. Prog. Lang. Syst. 4 (1982) 37-42.

[Plo 82] G. Plotkin, An operational semantics for CSP, in: D. Bjorner, ed., Formal Description of Programming Concepts, IFIP TC-2 Working Conference, Garmish-Partenkirchen, Germany (1982) 185-208.

[Ra 83] S.P. Rana, A distributed solution to the distributed termination problem, Inf. Proc. Letters 17 (1983) 43-46.

[Rei 84] W. Reisig, Partial order semantics for CSP-like languages and its impact on fairness, in: J. Paradaens, ed., Automata, Languages and Programming, Lecture Notes in Computer Science 172 (Springer, Berlin, 1984) 403-413.

[Ri 84] J.L. Richier, Distributed termination in CSP - symmetric solution with minimal storage, Rept. No. 84-49, LITP, Univ. Paris 7, Paris (1984).

[Schn 84] F.B. Schneider, Lecture Notes prepared for the Advanced Course on Distributed Systems - Methods and Tools for Specification, Inst. for Computer Science, TUM, Munchen, Germany (1984).

On Total Regulators Generated by Derivation Relations [1]

Extended Abstract

W. Bucher, A. Ehrenfeucht* and D. Haussler**

Institutes for Information Processing, Technical University of Graz, A-8010 Graz, Austria.

*Department of Computer Science, University of Colorado, Boulder, Colorado 80302, USA.

**Department of Mathematics and Computer Science, University of Denver, Denver, Colorado 80208, USA.

All correspondence to Bucher or Haussler.

Abstract. A derivation relation is a total regulator on Σ^* if for every language $L \subseteq \Sigma^*$, the set of all words derivable from L is a regular language. We show that for a wide class of derivation relations $\overset{*}{\underset{P}{\Rightarrow}}$, $\overset{*}{\underset{P}{\Rightarrow}}$ is a total regulator on Σ^* if and only if it is a well-quasi-order (wqo) on Σ^*. Using wqo theory, we give a characterization of all non-erasing pure context-free (OS) derivation relations which are total regulators.

Introduction.

While most results on finite automata and regular languages are constructive in the sense that the machines and expressions involved can be effectively given, occasionally one comes across a completely non-constructive result. An example is the following result of

[1] The authors gratefully acknowledge the support of NSF grants IST-8317918 and MCS-8110430, and the Austrian Bundesministerium fuer Wissenschaft und Forschung. Part of this work was conducted while the third author visited the Institutes for Information Processing at the Technical University of Graz and the other part while the first author visited the University of Denver. We would like to thank our respective host institutions for these generous invitations.

Haines ([*HAI*]). We say that a word y is a supersequence of a word x if the sequence of letters of y contains the sequence of letters of x as a subsequence. For any language L, consider the language of all words (over a fixed alphabet) which are supersequences of words in L. This language is always regular. Thus, using J. H. Conway's terminology ([*CON*]), the operation of closing a language by adding all words which are supersequences of words in the language is a *total regulator*, since it converts *any* language L into a regular language. For an arbitrary recursive language L this construction cannot be effective, since this would allow us to solve the emptiness problem for recursive languages ([*LEE*]).

In this paper we look further into Conway's notion by investigating total regulators generated by closure under the more common types of derivation relations in Formal Language Theory. For any particular derivation relation $\overset{*}{\underset{P}{\Longrightarrow}}$ defined on words over an alphabet Σ, we will say that $\overset{*}{\underset{P}{\Longrightarrow}}$ is a total regulator on Σ^* if for any $L \subseteq \Sigma^*$, the language of words derived from words in L by $\overset{*}{\underset{P}{\Longrightarrow}}$ is a regular language. Haines' result can be easily cast in this form. For example, if $\Sigma = \{a, b\}$, $P = \{a \to aa \mid ab \mid ba, b \to bb \mid ba \mid ab\}$ is a pure context-free production system (OS scheme) then for any $x, y \in \Sigma^+$, y is a supersequence of x if and only if $x \overset{*}{\underset{P}{\Longrightarrow}} y$.

Haines' result can be derived from earlier results in the theory of well-quasi-orders, given in Higman's seminal paper ([*HIG*]). In [*EHR*], a more general connection between regularity and well-quasi-orders is exhibited, and a generalized version of the Haines/Higman result is given in terms of derivation by repeated insertion of words chosen from a fixed, unavoidable set. Here we carry these results further be showing that for a wide class of derivation relations, including those generated by propagating (non-erasing) OS schemes, $\overset{*}{\underset{P}{\Longrightarrow}}$ is a total regulator on Σ^* if and only if $\overset{*}{\underset{P}{\Longrightarrow}}$ is a well-quasi-order on Σ^* (Theorem 1.1). We then characterize the OS schemes which generate well-quasi-orders on Σ^* using the notion of unavoidability as defined in [*EHR*] (Theorem 2.1). The generalized Haines/Higman result from [*EHR*] is easily obtained as a corollary of this characterization. Another combinatorial result that follows from Theorem 2.1 is given at the end of Section 2. In Section 3 we give some preliminary results toward a more algebraic characterization of OS total regulators.

Several applications of the theory of well-quasi-orders have recently appeared in the literature ([*RUO*], [*LAT*], [*DER*]). It is hoped that the basic results on well-quasi-orders given here will lead to further applications of the theory in these and other areas. In this context, we note that [*LAT*] uses the Haines/Higman result, which is a special case of our characterization theorem, and the main regularity result from [*RUO*] can be derived from the fact that for the OS scheme with $\Sigma = \{a, b\}$ and $P = \{a \to aa \mid aba, b \to bb \mid bab\}$, $\overset{*}{\underset{P}{\Longrightarrow}}$ is a total regulator, which also follows directly from this theorem.

Several immediate directions for further research remain. These are discussed in detail in Section 4. The primary open problem is whether or not the characterization of propagating OS total regulators given by Theorems 1.1 and 2.1 is effective (i.e. is the criterion given in Theorem 2.1 a decidable property of propagating OS schemes). In addition, even if we can establish that $\overset{*}{\underset{P}{\Longrightarrow}}$ is a total regulator by showing that P satisfies the criterion of Theorem 2.1, the regular languages generated by applying this total regulator can not always be effectively given, as mentioned above. J. van Leeuwen ([*LEE*]) has explored the extent to which the Haines/Higman total regulator is effective, and demonstrated that the closure of any context-free language under this total regulator is an effectively given regular language. We have no similar results for an arbitrary propagating OS total regulator $\overset{*}{\underset{P}{\Longrightarrow}}$. In fact, even when R is the regular language language derived from a single letter $a \in \Sigma$ under $\overset{*}{\underset{P}{\Longrightarrow}}$, we cannot give any recursive bounds on the size of the smallest automaton for R in terms of the size of P. It remains to be seen if the non-constructiveness in our results is merely an artifact of our choice of methods or whether it indicates some deeper intractability of the problem.

Notation

For basic definitions in Formal Language Theory we refer the reader to [*HAR*]. Our conventions are as follows. For a finite alphabet Σ, Σ^* denotes the set of words over Σ, λ denotes the empty word and $\Sigma^+ = \Sigma^* - \{\lambda\}$. For $w \in \Sigma^*$, $|w|$ denotes the length of w and $\#_a(w)$ the number of a's in w for any $a \in \Sigma$. A *production system* is a pair (Σ, P) where P is a finite set of productions $P = \{u_1 \to v_1, \ldots, u_k \to v_k\}$ where $u_i \in \Sigma^+$, $v_i \in \Sigma^*$ for $1 \le i \le k$. If for all i, $1 \le i \le k$, $|u_i| \le |v_i|$, (Σ, P) is *propagating (length–increasing)*; if $|u_i| < |v_i|$ then (Σ, P) is *strictly propagating*; if $|u_i| = 1$ then (Σ, P) is an *OS scheme*. $u \to v_1 \mid v_2 \mid \cdots \mid v_k$ is shorthand for $u \to v_1, u \to v_2, \ldots, u \to v_k$. $RHS_P(u) = \{v : u \to v \in P\}$. $RHS_P = \{v : u \to v \in P$ for some $u\}$. If $x = x_1 u x_2$ and $y = x_1 v x_2$, where $x_1, x_2 \in \Sigma^*$ and $u \to v \in P$, then $x \underset{P}{=>} y$. $\overset{*}{\underset{P}{=>}}$ denotes the reflexive and transitive closure of $\underset{P}{=>}$.

Section 1. Well-quasi-orders and total regulators

We begin by defining the notion of a total regulator, and characterizing this class of relations using the theory of well-quasi-orders (see below). We will restrict ourselves to relations of the following type, which includes many of the common types of derivation relations in Formal Language Theory.

Definition 1.1. A *quasi–order* is a reflexive and transitive relation. A quasi-order $\le$ on Σ^* is *multiplicative* if for all $x_1, x_2, y_1, y_2 \in \Sigma^*$, $x_1 \le x_2$ and $y_1 \le y_2$ implies that $x_1 y_1 \le x_2 y_2$. The quasi-order $\le$ is *length–increasing* if $x \le y$ implies that $|x| \le |y|$.

Example 1.1. Let (Σ, P), with $P = \{u_1 \to v_1, \ldots, u_k \to v_k\}$, be a finite production system. Then $\overset{*}{\underset{P}{=>}}$ is a multiplicative quasi-order on Σ^*. If P is length-increasing then $\overset{*}{\underset{P}{=>}}$ is length-increasing.

Definition 1.2. For a quasi-order $\le$ on Σ^*, $w \in \Sigma^*$ and $L \subseteq \Sigma^*$, let $cl_\le(w) = \{x \in \Sigma^* : w \le x\}$, $cl_\le(L) = \bigcup_{y \in L} cl_\le(y)$. If $\le$ is the derivation relation $\overset{*}{\underset{P}{=>}}$ defined by some OS scheme (Σ, P), we write $cl_P(w)$ for $cl_\le(w)$, similarly $cl_P(L)$ for $cl_\le(L)$. The quasi-order $\le$ is a *regulator* (on Σ^*) if $cl_\le(L)$ is regular for all regular $L \subset \Sigma^*$, $\le$ is a *total regulator* (on Σ^*) if $cl_\le(L)$ is regular for any $L \in \Sigma^*$. A (total) regulator of the form $\overset{*}{\underset{P}{=>}}$, where (Σ, P) is an OS scheme, is also called an *OS* (total) regulator. It is a *propagating* OS (total) regulator if the OS scheme is propagating.

By the results of Haines ([*HAI*]), the supersequence relation given in the Introduction is one example of a propagating OS total regulator, but much simpler examples can be given.

Example 1.2. Let $\Sigma = \{a, b\}$ and let $P = \{a \to b, b \to a \mid bb\}$. Then for any $x, y \in \Sigma^+$, $x \overset{*}{\underset{P}{=>}} y$ if and only if $|x| \le |y|$. Thus for nonempty $L \subseteq \Sigma^+$, $cl_P(L) = T = \{x \in \Sigma^* : |x| \ge k\}$ where k is the length of the shortest word of L. For $L' = L \cup \{\lambda\}$, $cl_P(L') = T \cup \{\lambda\}$. Hence $\overset{*}{\underset{P}{=>}}$ is a propagating OS total regulator.

An OS total regulator which is not propagating was also given by Haines.

Example 1.3. Let $\Sigma = \{a, b\}$ and let $P = \{a \to \lambda, b \to \lambda\}$. Then for any $x, y \in \Sigma^+$, $x \overset{*}{\underset{P}{=>}} y$ if and only if x is a supersequence of y. This quasi-order is the inverse of the supersequence total regulator discussed in the Introduction, and is also a total regulator by the results of Haines ([*HAI*]). In fact, Haines' argument generalizes to show that the inverse of any total regulator is also a total regulator.

Haines' results can easily be derived from the more general theory of well-quasi-orders, introduced by Higman ([*HIG*]). We give only the basic definitions and results from this theory which will be needed in what follows. For a more complete treatment, the reader is refered to [*KRU*].

Definition 1.3. A quasi-order $\leq$ on a set S is a ***well-quasi-order*** (wqo) on S if and only if for each infinite sequence $\{x_i\}_{i\geq 1}$ of elements in S, there exist $i<j$ such that $x_i \leq x_j$.

Proposition 1.1. ([*HIG*]) Let $\leq$ be a wqo on a set S and let $\leq^E$ be the quasi-order on the set $F(S)$ of finite sequences of elements from S, defined by $<s_1,...,s_k> \leq^E <t_1,...,t_l>$ if and only if there exists a subsequence $<t_{i_1},...,t_{i_k}>$ of $<t_1,...,t_l>$ such that $s_j \leq t_{i_j}$ for $1 \leq j \leq k$. Then $\leq^E$ is a wqo on $F(S)$. ▪

Proposition 1.2. ([*EHR*]) Let $\leq$ be a quasi-order on Σ^* which is wqo on L_1, $L_2 \subseteq \Sigma^*$. Then $\leq$ is a wqo on $L_1 \cup L_2$ and if $\leq$ is multiplicative, then $\leq$ is a wqo on L_1L_2. ▪

Proposition 1.3. Let $\leq_1$ be a wqo on a set S. If $\leq_2$ is a quasi-order on S such that $x \leq_1 y$ implies that $x \leq_2 y$, then $\leq_2$ is a wqo on S.

Proof. This follows directly from the definition. ▪

Proposition 1.4. Let $\leq$ be a multiplicative quasi-order on Σ^*, and $x_1,...,x_k,y_1,...,y_k$ be words in Σ^+ such that $x_i \leq y_i$ holds for $1 \leq i \leq k$. If $\overset{*}{\underset{P}{=>}}$ is a wqo on Σ^* for the production system (Σ,P), where $P = \{x_1 \rightarrow y_1, \cdots, x_k \rightarrow y_k\}$, then $\leq$ is a wqo on Σ^*.

Proof. This follows easily from Proposition 1.3. ▪

In [*EHR*], a generalized Myhill/Nerode theorem for regular languages is given wherein the usual notion of a finite congruence on Σ^* is replaced by that of a multiplicative wqo on Σ^* (here our terminology varies slightly from that of [*EHR*]). A consequence of this result is the following.

Proposition 1.5. For any multiplicative wqo $\leq$ on Σ^*, $\leq$ is a total regulator on Σ^*. ▪

For a wide class of derivation relations, this result can be strengthened to provide a characterization of the total regulators. Surprisingly, the same characterizaton applies to weaker forms of the concept of total regulator, in which it is only required that the closure of any language be recursive.

Theorem 1.1. If $\leq$ is a length-increasing, multiplicative, decidable quasi-order on Σ^*, then the following three properties are equivalent.
(i) $\leq$ is a wqo on Σ^*.
(ii) $\leq$ is a total regulator on Σ^*.
(iii) $cl_{\leq}(L)$ is recursive for every subset L of Σ^*. ▪

Section 2. The Main Theorem

We now restrict our attention to derivation relations generated by OS schemes. Since, for propagating OS schemes, these relations fall into the general category of relations covered by Theorem 1.1, we know that a derivation relation of this type is a total regulator if and only if it is a wqo on Σ^*. Therefore we investigate the circumstances under which an OS scheme generates a wqo on Σ^*. In the case of propagating schemes, this leads to a characterization of the total regulators. We need the following concepts.

Definition 2.1. A subset L of Σ^+ is ***unavoidable***, if there exists a number $k_0 \in \mathbf{N}$ such that for all $w \in \Sigma^*$, $|w| > k_0$, w has a subword in L, i.e. $w = w_1xw_2$ for some $w_1, w_2 \in \Sigma^*$, $x \in L$. The smallest such number k_0 is called the ***avoidance bound*** for L.

It is clear from the definition that if L is unavoidable with avoidance bound k_0, then $\{x \in L : |x| \leq k_0\}$ is also unavoidable with avoidance bound k_0. Hence any infinite unavoidable language contains a finite unavoidable subset.

Definition 2.2. Let (Σ,P) be an OS scheme. Then, for $a \in \Sigma$,
$LEFT_P(a) = \{ax : x \in \Sigma^+, \text{ and } a \overset{*}{\underset{P}{=>}} ax\}$,
$RIGHT_P(a) = \{xa : x \in \Sigma^+, \text{ and } a \overset{*}{\underset{P}{=>}} xa\}$,
$DUAL_P(a) = LEFT_P(a) \cap RIGHT_P(a) = \{axa : x \in \Sigma^*, a \overset{*}{\underset{P}{=>}} axa\}$,

$MIXED_P(a) = LEFT_P(a) \cup RIGHT_P(a)$.
$LEFT_P = \bigcup_{a \in \Sigma} LEFT_P(a)$ and $RIGHT_P$, $DUAL_P$, and $MIXED_P$ are defined similarly.

The main result of this paper can now be stated as follows.

Theorem 2.1. Let (Σ,P) be an OS scheme. Then the following properties are equivalent.
(i) $\overset{*}{\underset{P}{\Rightarrow}}$ is a wqo on Σ^*.
(ii) $DUAL_P$ is unavoidable on Σ^*.
(iii) $MIXED_P$ is unavoidable on Σ^*.

The proof of Theorem 2.1 is somewhat involved, and is accomplished with a sequence of lemmas. The first lemma formalizes the following observation. If (Σ,P) is a strictly propagating OS scheme such that RHS_P is unavoidable with avoidance bound k_0, then any word in Σ^* can be parsed by repeatedly replacing the leftmost occurrence of a subword in RHS_P with a letter that derives it in such a way that all replacements occur within the first k_0+1 letters of the word and the final result is a word of at most k_0 letters. This "leftmost shift-reduce" parse of an arbitrary word yields a k_0-depth bounded "derivation" for any word in terms of the regular substitution S_P described below.

Definition 2.3. Let (Σ,P) be a propagating OS scheme and for each letter $a \in \Sigma$, let Z_a be a variable. Let $Z = \{Z_a : a \in \Sigma\}$ and let P' be the set of left linear productions defined by $P' = \{Z_a \to Z_b w,\ Z_a \to bw : a \to bw \in P\}$. Then $S_P(a)$ denotes the regular substitution on Σ^* defined by $S_P(a) = L(G_a) \cup \{a\}$, where $G_a = (Z \cup \Sigma, \Sigma, P', Z_a)$.

$S_P(a)$ is the set of all strings obtained from a by repeatedly replacing leftmost symbols by right hand sides of corresponding rules in P. The subscript P will be omitted when the production system P is clear from the context.

Lemma 2.1. Let (Σ,P) be a strictly propagating OS scheme such that RHS_P is unavoidable with avoidance bound k_0. Let $F = \{w \in \Sigma^* : |w| \leq k_0\}$. Then $\Sigma^* = S^{k_0}(F)$. ∎

We make the following definitions in analogy with those in Definition 2.2.

Definition 2.4. A production $a \to x$ is ***left bordered (right bordered)*** if $x \in a\Sigma^+$ ($x \in \Sigma^+ a$). An OS scheme (Σ,P) is ***left (right)*** bordered if each production in P is left (right) bordered. (Σ,P) is ***dual bordered*** if each production in P is both left and right bordered. (Σ,P) is ***mixed bordered*** if each production in P is either left or right bordered.

The essence of the argument that whenever $DUAL_P$ is unavoidable, $\overset{*}{\underset{P}{\Rightarrow}}$ is a wqo (i.e. (ii) implies (i) in Theorem 2.1) is contained in the following result.

Lemma 2.2. If (Σ,P) is a dual bordered OS scheme, then $\overset{*}{\underset{P}{\Rightarrow}}$ is a wqo on $S^k(F)$ for every $k \geq 0$ and finite set $F \subseteq \Sigma^*$. ∎

To complete the proof of Theorem 2.1 we must look now at the relationship between the unavoidability of $MIXED_P$ and that of $DUAL_P$. It is obvious that whenever $DUAL_P$ is unavoidable then $MIXED_P$ is unavoidable, since $DUAL_P \subseteq MIXED_P$. The essential part of the converse can be given in two steps.

Lemma 2.3. Let (Σ,P) be a mixed bordered OS scheme such that RHS_P is unavoidable with avoidance bound k_0. Then $LEFT_P$ is unavoidable with avoidance bound less than or equal $k_1 = k_0((k_0-1)|\Sigma|+1)^{k_0}-1$. ∎

Lemma 2.4. Let (Σ,P) be a left bordered OS scheme such that RHS_P is unavoidable with avoidance bound k_0. Then $DUAL_P$ is unavoidable with avoidance bound at most $k_1 = k_0((k_0-1)|\Sigma|+1)^{k_0}-1$. ∎

The above lemmas can be easily combined to give a proof of Theorem 2.1. For mixed bordered OS schemes, Theorem 2.1 gives a very simple (and easily decidable) characterization of those schemes which generate wqo's.

Corollary 2.1. If (Σ,P) is a mixed bordered OS scheme, then $\overset{*}{\underset{P}{\Rightarrow}}$ is a wqo on Σ^* if and only if RHS_P is unavoidable. ▪

For any mixed bordered OS scheme (Σ,P), if $x \overset{*}{\underset{P}{\Rightarrow}} y$ then y is a supersequence of x. Hence all of the wqos generated by mixed bordered schemes under the conditions of Corollary 2.1 are refinements of the supersequence wqo discussed in the Introduction. One might conjecture that a characterization as in Corollary 2.1 could be given for a larger class of OS schemes which enjoy this property, e.g. for the class of embedding schemes, where an OS scheme (Σ,P) is called *embedding*, if for each production $a \to x \in P$, x can be written in the form $x = x_1 a x_2$, with $x_1, x_2 \in \Sigma^*$. However, such a generalization of Corollary 2.1 is impossible, as shown by the following example.

Example 2.1. Let $\Sigma = \{a, b, c\}$ and let P be given by the productions $a \to aa \mid aba \mid acba$, $b \to bb \mid bab$, $c \to cc \mid aca \mid bcb \mid bca$. It is readily verified that RHS_P is unavoidable on Σ^*. However, $\overset{*}{\underset{P}{\Rightarrow}}$ is not a wqo since it can be shown that for no numbers $m, n, m > n$, the relation $(abc)^n \overset{*}{\underset{P}{\Rightarrow}} (abc)^m$ holds.

On the other hand, Corollary 2.1 does generalize previous results on wqo refinements of the supersequence relation generated by repeated insertion of words from a fixed unavoidable set ([*EHR*]).

Definition 2.4. An OS scheme (Σ,P) is an ***insertion system*** if there exists a finite set $X \subseteq \Sigma^+$ such that $P = \{a \to ax \mid xa : a \in \Sigma, x \in X\}$. In this case (Σ,P) is the ***insertion system generated by*** X.

Insertion systems were originally introduced in [*EHR*] in a slightly different way, but it is easy to see how their definition relates to ours.

Corollary 2.2. ([*EHR*]) For a finite set $X \subseteq \Sigma^+$, if (Σ,P) is the insertion system generated by X, then $\overset{*}{\underset{P}{\Rightarrow}}$ is a wqo on Σ^* if and only if X is unavoidable.

Proof. Clearly, RHS_P is unavoidable if and only if X is unavoidable. Consequently, Corollary 2.2 follows from Corollary 2.1. ▪

As a final example of the use of the wqos given by Corollary 1.1, consider the following proof that "history always repeats itself in ever more elaborate ways".

Definition 2.5. Let Σ be a finite alphabet of "events" and let $\lesssim$ be a total order which ranks the events in Σ. A sequence y of events is an ***elaboration*** of a sequence x, if $x = a_1 \cdots a_k$ for some $a_1, \ldots, a_k \in \Sigma$, and $y = y_1 \cdots y_k$ for some $y_1, \ldots, y_k \in \Sigma^+$, where for each i either $y_i = a_i$ or $y_i = a_i b_1 \cdots b_n a_i$ for some $n \geq 0$, $b_j \in \Sigma$ and $a_i \lesssim b_j$, $1 \leq j \leq n$.

Thus we obtain an elaboration of x by replacing each event a of x by a series of events which begins and ends with a, such that no intermediate event has a smaller rank than a.

Corollary 2.3. If Σ is an alphabet and $\lesssim$ is a total order on Σ, then every infinite sequence $\{x_i\}_{i \geq 1}$ of strings in Σ^+ contains strings x_i, x_j, with $i < j$, such that x_j is an elaboration of x_i. ▪

3. Monoid-representations

While in Section 2 total regulators generated by propagating OS schemes where characterized by an unavoidability criterion, in this section an attempt is made to describe such total regulators in a more algebraic way, corresponding to the well known characterization of regular languages in terms of congruences of finite index (finite monoids, resp.). The first result in this section can be seen as the natural extension of this characterization to regulators defined by OS schemes (see Def. 1.2).

Theorem 3.1. For an OS scheme (Σ,P), $\overset{*}{\underset{P}{\Rightarrow}}$ is a regulator on Σ^* if and only if there is a finite monoid M, a morphism $h : \Sigma^* \to M$, and a multiplicative quasi-order $\leq$ on M such that for all $a \in \Sigma$ and $x \in \Sigma^*$, $a \overset{*}{\underset{P}{\Rightarrow}} x$ iff $h(a) \leq h(x)$. ▪

The above theorem suggests the following definition.

Definition 3.1. Let (Σ,P) be an OS scheme, let M be a monoid, $h : \Sigma^* \to M$ a morphism, and $\leq$ a multiplicative quasi-order on M. The triple $(M, h, \leq)$ is called a *(monoid-) representation* of (Σ,P) if for all $a \in \Sigma$ and $x \in \Sigma^*$, $a \overset{*}{\underset{P}{=\!=\!>}} x$ holds iff $h(a) \leq h(x)$. $(M, h, \leq)$ is a *finite (monoid-)representation* of (Σ,P) if M is finite.

Theorem 3.1 can now be restated as follows: For an OS scheme (Σ,P), $\overset{*}{\underset{P}{=\!=\!>}}$ is a regulator if and only if (Σ,P) has a finite monoid-representation.

It seems natural to try to characterize wqo's (total regulators) defined by OS schemes in terms of monoid-representations. So far we only have partial answers to this problem, and we restrict ourselves to presenting the following sufficient condition on M to guarantee that $\overset{*}{\underset{P}{=\!=\!>}}$ is a total regulator.

Theorem 3.2. Let (Σ,P) be an OS scheme and let $(G, h, \leq)$ be a monoid-representation of (Σ,P) where G is a finite group. Then $\overset{*}{\underset{P}{=\!=\!>}}$ is a total regulator on Σ^*. ▪

There are wqo's (and hence total regulators) defined by OS schemes which cannot be represented in a finite group in the sense of Definition 3.1. For example, the OS scheme (Σ,P) with $\Sigma = \{a,b\}$, $P = \{a \to aa \mid aba,\ b \to bb\}$ defines a wqo $\overset{*}{\underset{P}{=\!=\!>}}$ by Corollary 2.1. On the other hand, if $(G, h, \leq)$ is a representation of (Σ,P) with G a finite group containing n elements, then $h(a) = h(ab^n)$, and consequently $a \overset{*}{\underset{P}{=\!=\!>}} ab^n$, which is a contradiction. This shows that (Σ,P) cannot be represented in a finite group.

In the rest of this section we briefly discuss the question which triples $(M, h, \leq)$ - where M is a finite monoid, $h : \Sigma^* \to M$ is a morphism, and $\leq$ is a multiplicative quasi-order on M - are monoid-representations of some OS scheme. To this end, let for such a triple and for $a \in \Sigma$

$$L_a' = \{x \in \Sigma^* : h(a) \leq h(x),\ a \neq x\},$$

and let $\bar{\Sigma} = \{\bar{a} : a \in \Sigma\}$ be a barred copy of Σ, $\Sigma \cap \bar{\Sigma} = \phi$. Define a substitution σ on Σ^* by $\sigma(a) = \{a,\bar{a}\}$, $a \in \Sigma$, and a substitution ρ on $(\Sigma \cup \bar{\Sigma})^*$ by $\rho(a) = \{a\}$, $\rho(\bar{a}) = L_a'$. For $a \in \Sigma$, let

$$L_a = L_a' - \rho(\sigma(L_a') \cap \Sigma^*\bar{\Sigma}\Sigma^*).$$

L_a is the set of words in L_a' which cannot be obtained from other words in L_a' by substituting words from some sets L_b', $b \in \Sigma$. By construction, L_a is effectively regular for each $a \in \Sigma$.

Lemma 3.1. Let M be a finite monoid, let $h : \Sigma^* \to M$ be a morphism and let $\leq$ be a multiplicative quasi-order on M.

(i) Let (Σ,P) be an OS scheme not containing any rule of the form $a \to a$. If $(M, h, \leq)$ is a representation of (Σ,P) then $\bigcup_{a \in \Sigma} L_a$ is finite and (*) $\bigcup_{a \in \Sigma}\{a \to x : x \in L_a\} \subseteq P \subseteq \bigcup_{a \in \Sigma}\{a \to x : x \in L_a'\}$.

(ii) Conversely, if $\bigcup_{a \in \Sigma} L_a$ is finite, then for any finite set P of productions satisfying (*), the triple $(M, h, \leq)$ is a representation of (Σ,P). ▪

As a consequence of Lemma 3.1, it is decidable whether a triple $(M, h, \leq)$ is monoid-representation of some OS scheme (Σ,P) : it suffices to test whether the regular sets L_a are finite. Moreover, there is essentially a unique OS scheme represented by $(M, h, \leq)$, namely $(\Sigma, \bigcup_{a \in \Sigma}\{a \to x : x \in L_a\})$. This decision problem is not trivial, since there are triples $(M, h, \leq)$ for finite M and multiplicative $\leq$ which are not representations of any OS scheme.

Example 3.1. Let $\Sigma = \{a,b\}$. Let M be the syntactic monoid of $L = (ab^2b^*)^*a$, let $h : \Sigma^* \to M$ be the canonical morphism mapping $x \in \Sigma^*$ to its class modulo L and let the quasi-order $\leq$ on M be the equality relation. A simple computation shows that $L_b' = \phi$,

$L_a' = L - \{a\}$, and $L_a = ab^2b^*a$. Consequently, $(M, h, \leq)$ is not monoid-representation of any OS scheme.

However, if M is a finite group, then $(M, h, \leq)$ is a representation of some OS scheme (Σ, P). It should be noted that because of Theorem 3.2, $\overset{*}{\underset{P}{=>}}$ is then a total regulator.

Theorem 3.3. If G is a finite group, $h : \Sigma^* \to G$ a morphism and $\leq$ a multiplicative quasi-order on M, then there is an OS scheme (Σ, P) with representation $(G, h, \leq)$. ▪

Example 3.2. Let C_3 be the (additively written) cyclic group with elements 0, 1, 2, let $\Sigma = \{a, b\}$, let $h : \Sigma^* \to C_3$ be defined by $h(a) = 1$, $h(b) = 2$, and $\leq$ by $i \leq j$ iff $i = j$. A straight forward computation shows that $L_a = \{bb, aba\}$, $L_b = \{aa, bab\}$, i.e. $(C_3, h, \leq)$ is a representation of the OS scheme (Σ, P) with $P = \{a \to bb \mid aba, b \to aa \mid bab\}$. This result could also be established directly by observing that $a \overset{*}{\underset{P}{=>}} x$ (resp. $b \overset{*}{\underset{P}{=>}} x$) holds if and only if $\#_a(x) - \#_b(x) \equiv 1 \; mod \; 3$ (resp. $\#_a(x) - \#_b(x) \equiv 2 \; mod \; 3$).

It remains an open problem to characterize those OS total regulators which have a representation in a group.

Section 4. Open Problems

The primary open problem remaining is to show that it is decidable whether or not a propagating OS scheme generates a total regulator. While Theorem 2.1 gives a characterization of such systems, we have been unable to show that this characterization is effective. One approach to this problem would be to investigate the pumping properties of OS total regulators, hoping to find one which is both necessary and sufficient, and effective.

Let (Σ, P) be a propagating OS scheme, and consider the following "pumping" properties:

a) For all $w \in \Sigma^+$ there exist k, l with $k < l$ such that $w^k \overset{*}{\underset{P}{=>}} w^l$

b) For all $w \in \Sigma^+$ there exists $k > 1$ such that $w \overset{*}{\underset{P}{=>}} w^k$

c) For all $w \in \Sigma^+$ there exist $a \in \Sigma$, $w_1, w_2 \in \Sigma^*$ and $k \geq 1$ such that $w = w_1 a w_2$ and $a \overset{*}{\underset{P}{=>}} (a w_2 w_1)^k a$.

While it appears that each of these pumping properties is stronger than the previous one, it can be shown that in fact they are all equivalent for propagating OS schemes. Thus since (a) is obviously implied whenever $\overset{*}{\underset{P}{=>}}$ is a wqo on Σ^*, they are all necessary pumping properties of propagating OS total regulators. Are they sufficient? We have no counterexample.

While these pumping properties are not effective as given, if it can be shown that, for example, (b) implies that $\overset{*}{\underset{P}{=>}}$ is a wqo on Σ^* then this, combined with Theorem 2.1, would provide an effective characterization of propagating OS total regulators. The effectiveness follows by considering two semi-algorithms: one which tests if $w^2 w^* \cap cl_P(w) = \phi$ for larger and larger w, and the other which checks if F is unavoidable in Σ^* for larger and larger finite subsets F of $DUAL_P$ (or $MIXED_P$).

One appealing aspect of this approach is that property (c) already comes close to implying that $DUAL_P$ is unavoidable in Σ^*. In fact, (c) implies for any word $w \in \Sigma^+$, that w^* contains a word with a subword in $DUAL_P$. Hence we might say that if property (c) holds, then $DUAL_P$ is "periodically unavoidable". Choffrut and Culik II ([*CC*]) have shown that for any regular language $R \subseteq \Sigma^+$, R is unavoidable if and only if it is periodically unavoidable in the above sense. We know that this property does not hold for all languages; $L = \{ww : w \in \Sigma^+\}$, where Σ has at least three letters, is an example of a language which is periodically unavoidable but not unavoidable. However, if it holds for all context-free languages, then (c) would imply that $\overset{*}{\underset{P}{=>}}$ is a wqo on Σ^*, since $DUAL_P$ is context-free. Hence we would like to know the status of the following:

Conjecture A For any context-free language $L \subseteq \Sigma^+$, L is unavoidable in Σ^* if and only if it is periodically unavoidable, i.e. if and only if for all $w \in \Sigma^+$, w^* contains a word with a subword in L.

It should be noted that Conjecture A would follow from the stronger conjecture that whenever the syntactic congruence of a context-free language is periodic, then the language is regular (see [*AUT*]); however a counterexample to this conjecture has recently been given by M. Main ([*MAI*]).

Another open problem is to generalize the characterization theorem (Theorem 2.1) to arbitrary length-increasing production systems (i.e. word replacement systems). In addition, it would be nice to know what role such systems play within the class of all length increasing wqo's. By Proposition 1.4, whenever a length-increasing multiplicative quasi-order contains a wqo generated by a finite production system, then it is a wqo. At present we have no counterexample to the following "converse" of this statement:

Conjecture B. For any length-increasing multiplicative wqo $\leq$ on Σ^* there exists a finite production system (Σ, P), with $P = \{u_1 \to v_1, \ldots, u_k \to v_k\}$, $u_i, v_i \in \Sigma^+$ and $u_i \leq v_i$ for all i, $1 \leq i \leq k$, such that $\overset{*}{\underset{P}{\Rightarrow}}$ is a wqo on Σ^*.

References

[AUT] J.M. Autebert, J. Beauquier, L. Boasson, M. Nivat, Quelques problems ouverts en theorie des languages algebriques, *RAIRO Inf. Theor.* **13** (4) (1979) 363-378.

[CC] C. Choffrut, K. Culik II, On extendibility of unavoidable sets, *Dis. Appl. Math.*, **9** (1984) 125-137.

[CON] J. H. Conway, *Regular Algebra and Finite Machines* (Chapman & Hall, London, 1971) pp. 63-64.

[DER] N. Dershowitz, Orderings for term-rewriting systems, *Theor. Comp. Sci.* **17** (1982) 279-301.

[EHR] A. Ehrenfeucht, D. Haussler, G. Rozenberg, On regularity of context-free languages, *Theor. Comp. Sci.* **27** (1983) 311-332.

[HAI] L. H. Haines, On free monoids partially ordered by embedding, *J. Combin. Th.* **6** (1969) 94-98.

[HAR] M. A. Harrison, *Introduction to Formal Language Theory* (Addison-Wesley, Reading, MA. 1978).

[HIG] G. Higman, Ordering by divisibility in abstract algebras, *Proc. London Math. Soc.* **3** (2) (1952) 326-336.

[KRU] J.B. Kruskal, The theory of well-quasi ordering: A frequently discovered concept, *J. Combin. Theory (Ser. A)* **13** (1972) 297-305.

[LAT] M. Latteux, G. Rozenberg, Commutative one-counter languages are regular, *J. Comp. Sys. Sci.* **29** (1984) 54-57.

[LEE] J. van Leeuwen, Effective constructions in well-partially-ordered monoids, *Discrete Math.*, 21 (1978) 237-252.

[MAI] M. Main, An infinite squarefree co-CFL, *Inf Proc. Let.*, to appear.

[RUO] K. Ruohonen, A note on off-line machines with 'Brownian' input heads, *Disc. App. Math.* **9** (1984) 69-75.

OPTIMAL SOLUTIONS FOR A CLASS OF POINT RETRIEVAL PROBLEMS

Bernard Chazelle and Herbert Edelsbrunner

Brown Univ. and Techn. Univ. Graz

Abstract

Let P be a set of n points in the Euclidean plane and let C be a convex figure. We study the problem of preprocessing P so that for any query point q, the points of P in $C + q$ can be retrieved efficiently. If constant time suffices for deciding the inclusion of a point in C, we then demonstrate the existence of an optimal solution: the algorithm requires $O(n)$ space and $O(k + \log n)$ time for a query with output size k. If C is a disk, the problem becomes the well-known *fixed radius neighbor* problem, to which we thus provide the first known optimal solution.

1. Introduction

Let P be a set of n points in the Euclidean plane E^2, and let C be a convex figure. We study the complexity of the following problem: preprocess P so that for any query translate $C_q = C + q$ of C the points in $P \cap C_q$ can be retrieved efficiently. Intuitively, a query corresponds to an arbitrary displacement of C without rotation. We demonstrate the existence of a solution that is optimal in space and time, provided that C satisfies certain weak computational conditions. Specifically, we describe a data structure that requires $O(n)$ space and $O(k+\log n)$ time to answer a query with output size k. The only assumption necessary to the validity of the algorithm is that constant time suffices for deciding whether a point is contained in C. A few other primitive operations must be assumed for the sake of preprocessing. If such operations can be executed in constant time, the data structure can be constructed in $O(n^2)$ time.

The generality of the setting allows a uniform solution of several problems which have been treated separately in the past. If C is a disk, the problem becomes the well-known *fixed-radius neighbor problem* [BM,C1,CCPY]. The best solution to this problem achieves optimal retrieval time at the cost of $O(n(\log n \log\log n)^2)$ space [CCPY], but also handles queries with non-fixed radius. If C is a triangle or a rectangle then we have restricted versions of the *triangular* and *orthogonal range search* problems

---

Authors' current address: B. Chazelle: Dept. of Computer Science, Box 1910, Brown Univ., Providence, RI 02912, USA. H. Edelsbrunner: Inst. Inf. Proc., Techn. Univ. Graz, Schiesstattg. 4a, A-8010, Graz, Austria. The first author was supported in part by NSF grant MCS 83-03925.

[EKM,CY,EW and K,W,C2]. Again, optimal retrieval time is achieved only with superlinear space. Other shapes which C may assume include ellipses or hybrid convex figures bounded by a constant number of analytic curves. We look at the special case where C is a convex m-gon and m is considered a variable of the problem. For this case, we describe a solution requiring $O(n+m)$ space and $O(k+\log n \log m)$ time to compute a k-point answer.

2. The Geometric and Computational Backdrop

In this section we introduce relevant geometric notions and address the computational assumptions we have to make.

Let E^2 denote the Euclidean plane and endow it with a system of Cartesian coordinates x and y. The directions determined by the x and y axes are referred to as *horizontal* and *vertical*, respectively. Let A be a subset of E^2. We assume that the reader is familiar with the concepts of interior $\underline{\text{int}}A$, closure $\underline{\text{cl}}A$ and boundary $\underline{\text{bd}}A$. For two points $a = (a_x, a_y)$ and $b = (b_x, b_y)$, we have $a + b = (a_x + b_x, a_y + b_y)$, and for a real λ, $\lambda a = (\lambda a_x, \lambda a_y)$. These operations are naturally extended to subsets A, B of E^2, i.e. $A + B = \{a + b \mid a \in A, b \in B\}$ and $\lambda A = \{\lambda a \mid a \in A\}$. For any point q, $A + q = A + \{q\}$ is called a *translate* of A and is denoted A_q. A is *convex* if for any points a_1 and a_2 in A, the point $\lambda a_1 + (1-\lambda)a_2$ lies in A for each λ such that $0 \le \lambda \le 1$. The smallest convex set that contains A is called the *convex hull* of A, denoted $\underline{\text{conv}}A$. The convex hull of $\{a, b\}$ is called a *segment*.

The model of computation is the standard RAM with infinite real arithmetic —a traditional assumption in computational geometry. Let C be a convex closed figure with non-empty interior. We leave C essentially unspecified and therefore must make a minimum number of assumptions on the primitive operations allowed with respect to C. First, we consider the intersection of the boundaries of two translates of C. We define $S(v, w) = \underline{\text{bd}}(-C)_v \cap \underline{\text{bd}}(-C)_w$, for two points v and w in E^2. By convexity of C, $S(v, w)$ is either empty or consists of at most two possibly degenerate segments, and thus can be represented in a constant amount of space. This concept is naturally extended to the case where v and w are infinitesimally close: this gives $S(v, w) = S(v, l) = \underline{\text{bd}}(-C)_v \cap \underline{\text{bd}}(-C + l)$, for l the line that contains v and w (see Fig.1 for an illustration of the two cases).

We call C *computable* if (i) constant time suffices to test for any point p in E^2 whether or not p is contained in C, and (ii) constant time suffices to compute $S(v, w)$ for any two, potentially infinitesimally close, points v and w in E^2. In the remainder of this section, we elaborate on the primitive operations needed and introduce the notion of *silo*. Let L (resp. R) in $\underline{\text{bd}}C$ be the point with minimal (resp. maximal) x-coordinate, and maximal y-coordinate if not unique.

Lemma 1. If C is computable, L and R can be determined in constant time.

Proof: Let l be the vertical line through the origin $O = (0, 0)$. Since C is computable, $S(O, l)$ and the lower endpoints a and b of the two vertical segments that constitute $S(O, l)$ can be determined in constant time. Let $a_x < b_x$; we then have $L = -b$ and $R = -a$. ∎

We immediately derive

Lemma 2. Let C be computable, let p be a point in E^2 and l be the vertical line through p. Constant time suffices to decide whether

1. C is to the right of l,
2. $C \cap l \neq \emptyset$ and (2.1) p is above C, (2.2) p is contained in C, (2.3) p is below C,
3. C is to the left of l.

Proof: Since C is computable, case 2.2 can be distinguished from the other cases in constant time. If case 2.2 does not apply, then compute L and R (Lemma 1) and observe that C contains $\underline{\text{conv}}\{L, R\}$. If $p_x < L_x$ (resp. $p_x > R_x$) then case 1 (resp. case 3) applies. Otherwise, case 2.1 (resp. case 2.3) applies if p_y is greater (resp. smaller) than the y-coordinate of $l \cap \underline{\text{conv}}\{L, R\}$. ∎

The algorithmic part of this paper uses the so-called *silos* as substitutes for $-C$. Let v be a point and $r(v)$ be the vertical *ray* with v as lower endpoint. The figure $-C + r(v)$ is termed the *silo* $T(v)$ of v (Fig.2). Obviously, $T(v)$ is the set of points q such that C_q intersects $r(v)$. $\underline{\text{bd}}T(v)$ consists of two vertical rays $-L + r(v)$ and $-R + r(v)$, and the lower part of $\underline{\text{bd}}(-C)_v$. The silos of two points v, w are translates of each other. Therefore, $\underline{\text{bd}}T(v) \cap \underline{\text{bd}}T(w)$ is empty or consists of a single point, segment, or ray, provided that $v_x \neq w_x$. Let $\text{maxx}(v, w)$ be the maximal x-coordinate of a point in $\underline{\text{bd}}T(v) \cap \underline{\text{bd}}T(w)$. The following technical result will be of interest in Section 4.

Lemma 3. For any pair of points v, w in E^2 with $v_x \neq w_x$ and $\underline{\text{bd}}T(v) \cap \underline{\text{bd}}T(w) \neq \emptyset$, $\text{maxx}(v, w)$ can be computed in constant time.

Proof: Assume wlog that $v_x < w_x$. Three cases must be distinguished:

1. $-R + w$ is below $(-C)_v$ (this is equivalent to "v is above C_{-R+w}" or "$v + R - w$ is above C" and, by Lemma 2, is decidable in constant time). Then $-R + w$ is below $T(v)$ and $\text{maxx}(v, w) = -R_x + w_x$ (Fig.2(a)).
2. $-L + v$ is below $(-C)_w$. Then $\text{maxx}(v, w) = -L_x + v_x$ by the same reasoning as in case 1.
3. Otherwise, $\text{maxx}(v, w)$ is the x-coordinate of the rightmost point of $S(v, w)$ which lies below $\underline{\text{conv}}\{-L + u, -R + u\}$, for $u = v, w$ (Fig.2(b)). ∎

3. Clearing the Way for the Main Algorithm

Let P be a set of points in E^2 and C a computable figure: C is closed, convex, and has non-empty interior. To retrieve $P \cap C_q$, for query point q, we store subsets of points in separate structures. These subsets are defined by a regular decomposition of E^2 into parallelograms. This section describes the particular decomposition and shows the relevance of silos.

Let L and R be the extreme points of C as introduced in the previous section. The segment $s = \underline{\text{conv}}\{L, R\}$ partitions C into two figures: C_a contains the points above and on s and C_b the points below s. Since C is computable, so are C_a and C_b. The algorithm considers each figure in turn. Because of symmetry, we may assume that C is now C_a, hence $s \subseteq \underline{\text{bd}}C$.

Let M be a point in $C \setminus s$ that allows a line through M to be both parallel to s and tangent to C (Fig.3). L, R, and M induce the decomposition of E^2 in the following way: Let $X = \frac{1}{2}(R - L)$ and $Y = \frac{1}{2}(M - N)$, with N the vertical projection of M onto s. We change the coordinate system so that point $(i,j) = iX + jY$, and call $c_{ij} = \{p = (p_x, p_y) \mid i \leq p_x < i+1, j \leq p_y < j+1 \text{ and } i, j \text{ integers}\}$ a *cell*. $\mathcal{G} = \{c_{ij}\}$ for all integers i, j is a decomposition of E^2 (Fig.3). Note that M can be determined in constant time, and that the new coordinates of a given point can be computed in constant time. The limited interaction between the cells of $\mathcal{G}$ and translates of C justifies the introduction of $\mathcal{G}$. We have

Lemma 4. For any q in E^2, C_q intersects at most nine cells of $\mathcal{G}$.

Proof: By construction of $\mathcal{G}$, C_q intersects cells of three consecutive rows and columns of $\mathcal{G}$. Nine cells lie in the intersection of three rows and three columns. ∎

If C_q intersects a cell c, the intersection always is of a particular kind. Let N, E, S, W denote the four edges of $\underline{\text{bd}}c$ with the natural association of north–above, east–right, south–below, and west–left. We say that C_q is D-grounded if $C_q \cap D$ equals the orthogonal projection of $C_q \cap \underline{\text{cl}}c$ onto D, for $D = N, E, S, W$. C_q is said to be *grounded* if it is D-grounded for at least one assignment of D to N, E, S or W. We have

Lemma 5. Let q be a point in E^2 and c a cell of $\mathcal{G}$ such that $C_q \cap c \neq \emptyset$. C_q is grounded with respect to c.

Proof: Let T be the triangle with vertices $L+q$, $R+q$ and $M+q$. Evidently, $T \subseteq C_q$ and C_q is D-grounded if T is. Define $s_1 = \underline{\text{conv}}\{L+q, R+q\}$, $s_2 = \underline{\text{conv}}\{R+q, M+q\}$, and $s_3 = \underline{\text{conv}}\{M+q, L+q\}$. Observe that

if T is not S-grounded then $\underline{\text{int}}c \cap s_1 \neq \emptyset$,

if T is not E-grounded then $\underline{\text{int}}c \cap s_2 \neq \emptyset$,

if T is not W-grounded then $\underline{\text{int}}c \cap s_3 \neq \emptyset$.

So T is not grounded only if $\underline{\text{int}}c$ intersects each edge of T. We prove that this is not possible: to obtain $\underline{\text{int}}c \cap s_1 \neq \emptyset$, s_1 must be above S. The line supporting N then intersects T in a segment longer than one. As a consequence, N cannot intersect s_2, say, and so neither can E. ∎

Note that we proved more than is asserted in Lemma 5: C_q is guaranteed to be D-grounded for at least one assignment of D to E, S, or W.

Lemmas 4 and 5 form the basis of the algorithm. The idea is to identify the at most nine cells that intersect C_q, and for each cell retrieve the points of P in C_q. Lemma 5 guarantees that for each cell the interaction with C_q is grounded. Each non-empty cell c (that is, $c \cap P \neq \emptyset$) is equipped with a data structure $\Delta_D(c \cap P)$, for each direction D from $\{N, E, S, W\}$. A high-level description of the algorithm for answering a query C_q follows:

Step 1: Determine the non-empty cells in $\mathcal{G}$ that intersect C_q.

Step 2: For each such cell c do:

Step 2.1: Find an assignment of D to N, E, S, W such that C_q is D-grounded with respect to c.

Step 2.2: Use $\Delta_D(c \cap P)$ to retrieve the points in $c \cap P \cap C_q$.

Next we sketch possible implementations of Steps 1 and 2.1 and relegate Step 2.2. to Section 4.

Computing Intersecting Cells

After some preliminary sorting, the non-empty cells c_{ij} in $\mathcal{G}$ can be computed in $O(n \log n)$ time, with $n = |P|$. These cells can be stored in a linear array, lexicographically sorted with respect to (i, j). Using binary search (Lemma 2), $O(\log n)$ time suffices to determine the rows that contain cells which intersect C_q, and then to identify all cells that intersect C_q.

Computing Ground Orientation

Let C_q be a query translate of C and let c_{ij} be a cell in $\mathcal{G}$ which intersects C_q. The following procedure can be used to determine an assignment of D to E, S or W such that C_q is D-grounded.

Case 1: C contains $(i, j) - q$ or $(i+1, j) - q$; then set $D := S$.

Case 2: C contains $(i, j+1) - q$; then set $D := W$.

Case 3: C contains $(i+1, j+1) - q$; then set $D := E$.

4. The Main Retrieval Algorithm

The four (or three) data structures to be assigned to a non-empty cell c are built according to the same procedure; so we limit our presentation to S-grounded queries. Recall the subproblem to be solved: given a non-empty cell c and a query point q such that C_q is S-grounded with respect to c, retrieve all points in $P \cap c \cap C_q$. The basic approach is to specify the locus of queries q yielding the same answer. Exhaustive characterization of the regions is prohibitively expensive, however, but the philosophy of *filtering search* can be applied to keep down the storage requirement [C2]. In a nutshell, this notion involves amortizing the search over the output size.

Although straightforward, the following facts are fundamental for our approach.

Observation 6. Point p lies in C_q if and only if q lies in $(-C)_p$.

Define $P_c = P \cap c$. We have

Lemma 7. Let c be a cell such that C_q is S-grounded, and let p be a point of P_c. Then p is in C_q if and only if q is in $T(p)$.

Proof: If $p \in C_q$ then $q \in (-C)_p \subseteq T(p)$. Conversely, if $q \in T(p)$ then $p \in -T(-q) = C_q + r$, with $r = \{(0, r_y) \mid r_y \leq 0\}$. By S-groundedness of C_q, $c \cap C_q + r = c \cap C_q$ and $p \in C_q$. ∎

Lemma 7 suggests replacing each point p of P_c by silo $T(p)$ and reporting all silos that contain q (Fig.4). We develop this idea next: let $P_c = \{p_1, \ldots, p_m\}$, with the ordering such that p_i precedes p_j in lexicographical order if $i < j$. Since the difference in x-coordinates of any two points in P_c is less than one, $U = \bigcup_{1 \leq i \leq m} T(p_i)$ is connected. We call $L(P_c) = \underline{\text{bd}}U$ the *layer* of P_c. By definition of $T(p)$, $L(P_c)$ is an unbounded connected curve, monotone in x, i.e. any vertical line intersects $L(P_c)$ in at most one (possibly degenerate) segment (Fig.4). $L(P_c)$ can be considered to consist of a sequence of "edges": for p_i in P_c, we call $L(P_c) \cap \underline{\text{bd}}T(p_i) - (\bigcup_{1 \leq j < i} \underline{\text{bd}}T(p_j))$ the *edge* e_i of P_c. Obviously, two distinct edges cannot properly intersect and $L(P_c) = \bigcup_{1 \leq i \leq m} e_i$. Intuitively, e_i is the contribution of $T(p_i)$ to $L(P_c)$. If some part of $L(P_c)$ is contained in $\underline{\text{bd}}T(p_j)$, for several j, then the smallest j is chosen. If e_i is empty, then p_i is called *redundant* and we define $\underline{\text{ext}}P_c = \{p \in P_c \mid p \text{ non-redundant}\}$. We describe salient properties of $L(P_c)$ and detail its construction.

Observation 8. Let $e_{k_1}, \ldots, e_{k_t}$ ($t = |\underline{\text{ext}}P_c|$) be the sequence of edges on $L(P_c)$ from left to right.

(i) $\text{maxx}(p_{k_i}, p_{k_{i+1}})$ is the x-coordinate of the right endpoint of e_{k_i} and the left endpoint of $e_{k_{i+1}}$, for $1 \leq i \leq t-1$ (see also Lemma 3).

(ii) $k_i < k_{i+1}$, for $1 \leq i \leq t-1$.

For the construction of $L(P_c)$, we choose to represent its edge-list in a linear array A, so that the indices of the edges in sorted order appear from left to right. The construction takes the points in the order of their indices (so we assume that an initial sorting phase has been previously performed). When p_i is processed, $L(\{p_1, \ldots, p_{i-1}\})$ is treated as a stack: a possibly empty sequence of points at the end of A is deleted and p_i is possibly added. A formal description of the algorithm follows:

$A[1] := 1$; $top := 1$;
for $i := 2$ **to** m **do**
  unless p_i **and** $p_{A[top]}$ share the x-coordinate **then**
    while $top > 1$ **and** $maxx(p_{A[top-1]}, p_{A[top]}) \geq maxx(p_{A[top]}, p_i)$ **do**
      $top := top - 1$
    endwhile
    $top := top + 1$; $A[top] := i$
  endunless
endfor

It is obvious that $L(P_c)$ can be constructed in $O(m)$ time. The following result is crucial for the ensuing developments.

Lemma 9. Let $L(P_c) = (e_{k_1}, \ldots, e_{k_t})$, C_q a translate of C that is S-grounded with respect to c, and $r = \{(q_x, r_y) \mid r_y \leq q_y\}$.

(i) r intersects $L(P_c)$ if and only if $C_q \cap P_c$ is non-empty.

(ii) Let $e_{k_l} \cap r \neq \emptyset$; then p_{k_l} lies in C_q.

(iii) There are indices i and j, with $i \leq l \leq j$, such that $C_q \cap \underline{\text{ext}}P_c = \{p_{k_i}, \ldots, p_{k_j}\}$.

Proof: Assertions (i) and (ii) follow directly from Lemma 7. To prove (iii), assume that C_q contains p_{k_i} and p_{k_j} but not p_{k_l} for some $i < l < j$. By Lemma 7, q lies in $T = T(p_{k_i}) \cap T(p_{k_j})$. Since p_{k_l} is not redundant, $T \subseteq T(p_{k_l})$ which implies that C_q contains p_{k_l} — a contradiction. ∎

If $L(P_c) = (e_{k_1}, \ldots, e_{k_t})$ and C_q are given, the points in $C_q \cap \underline{\text{ext}}P_c$ can be retrieved in $O(\log k_t)$ time as follows:

Step 1: Using binary search, determine l such that e_{k_l} intersects with r, the vertical ray falling down from q (if $1 < l < k_t$ then $\text{maxx}(p_{k_{l-1}}, p_{k_l}) < q_x \leq \text{maxx}(p_{k_l}, p_{k_{l+1}})$).

Step 2: If l exists then set $i:=j:= l$. While $p_{k_{i-1}}$ (resp. $p_{k_{j+1}}$) is in C_q, report it and set $i:= i-1$ (resp. $j:= j+1$).

We are now ready to describe the underlying data structure $\Delta_S(P_c)$. Essentially, $\Delta_S(P_c)$ is the (nested) family $\mathcal{L}(P_c) = (L_1, \ldots, L_k)$ of *layers* of P_c defined as follows: Let $P_{c,1} = P_c$ and $P_{c,k} = P_{c,k-1} - \underline{\text{ext}}P_{c,k-1}$, for $k > 1$. Let K be the largest index such that $P_{c,K} \neq \emptyset$, and $L_k = L(P_{c,k})$ for $1 \leq k \leq K$. $\mathcal{L}(P_c)$ necessitates $O(m)$ space and can be easily constructed in $O(m^2)$ time. Furthermore,

Observation 10. Let $\mathcal{L}(P_c) = (L_1, \ldots, L_K)$ be the family of layers of P_c and let C_q be S-grounded with respect to c. Let r be the vertical ray falling down from q. Then $r \cap L_i \neq \emptyset$ only if $r \cap L_j \neq \emptyset$, for $j < i$.

This remark leads to a procedure for retrieving the points in $C_q \cap P_c$.

```
i := 1; stop := false;
repeat determine edge e of L_i that intersects r.
    if e exists then
        report the points in C_q ∩ extP_c,i and set i := i + 1
            else set stop := true
    endif
until stop
```

The complexity of the procedure is $O(k \log m)$, where k is the number of points reported. $O(k + \log m)$ can be achieved by applying the *hive-graph* of [C2] to $\mathcal{L}(P_c)$. This graph connects L_i with L_{i-1}, for $2 \leq i \leq K$, in such a way that

(i) the knowledge of the edge in L_{i-1} that intersects r allows us to find the intersecting edge in L_i in constant time,

(ii) $O(m)$ space suffices to store $\mathcal{L}(P_c)$.

To describe the application of the hive-graph, it is convenient to change the representation of a layer L_i: in addition to $(k_1, \ldots, k_t)$ we store the sequence B_i of x-coordinates $(\text{maxx}(p_{k_1}, p_{k_2}), \ldots, \text{maxx}(p_{k_{t-1}}, p_{k_t}))$, $k_t = |\underline{\text{ext}}P_{c,i}|$. B_i subdivides the x-axis into t non-overlapping intervals, each belonging in the obvious manner to an index in $\{k_1, \ldots, k_t\}$. The hive-graph is obtained by the following procedure:

set $B_k^* := B_k$ **for** $k = 1, \dots, K$;

for $i := K-1$ **to** 1 **do**

pick every other x-value in B_{i+1}^* and merge the chosen values with B_i. Let B_i^* be the resulting list. For each value a in B_i^*, set up a pointer to the largest b in B_{i+1}^* with $b \le a$.

endfor

Figure 5 illustrates the connections between schematic layers that are introduced by the hive-graph. It is a straightforward exercise to verify that the hive-graph satisfies properties (i) and (ii) above. Details can also be found in [C2]. All this leads to the main result of this paper.

Theorem 11. Let P be a set of n points in E^2 and C a convex computable figure. There exists a data structure that stores P in $O(n)$ space such that $O(k + \log n)$ time suffices to retrieve all points of P lying inside a query translate C_q. The data structure can be constructed in $O(n^2)$ time.

We list a number of immediate consequences.

Corollary 12. For n points in E^2, $O(n)$ space and $O(k + \log n)$ time suffice to retrieve the k points within a fixed radius of an arbitrary query point.

It seems worthwhile to note that for the fixed radius problem C is a disk, thus making the partition into an upper and lower part unnecessary since both parts lead to the same decomposition of E^2. Another interesting special case arises when C is a convex polygon with m edges and m is considered a parameter of the problem. In this case, C violates the requirement of being computable. This can be fixed by allowing the primitive operations to take $O(\log m)$ time (this is motivated by the existence of a trivial algorithm for detecting whether a point lies inside a convex m-gon in $O(\log m)$ time). Our method yields

Corollary 13. Let C be a convex polygon with m edges in E^2. A set P of n points can be stored in $O(n+m)$ space such that $O(k + \log m \log n)$ time suffices to retrieve the k points of P lying inside a query translate of C.

5. Discussion

The problems examined in this paper fall into a general class involving a fixed set of objects and d-dimensional queries. A query is d-dimensional if it can be specified by d parameters; in this paper $d = 2$. By contrast, more difficult problems like orthogonal or triangular range search are respectively four- and six-dimensional. Studying the complexity of retrieval problems along this taxonomy appears to be of great methodological value. In general, can the complexity of query problems be asserted within a theory based on the dimensionality of queries?

Let us briefly recall the main tools used in this paper:

1. transforming the problem,
2. using a decomposition of E^2 into cells and introducing silos,

3. exploiting layers of silos to speed up searching,

4. connecting layers into a hive-graph.

All of these ideas have appeared —in most cases separately— in the computational geometry literature layers and transformations were exploited to give an optimal solution to the case where halfplanes are quer ranges [CGL]. There, too, the structure shared the connection of layers into a hive-graph. The notion of silo is closely related to the somehow dual concept of α-hull developed in [EKS]. Finally, using decomposition into cells seems almost as old as the field itself [K].

REFERENCES

[BM] Bentley, J.L., Maurer, H.A. *A note on Euclidean near neighbor searching in the plane*, Inform. Process Lett. 8 (1979), 133–136.

[C1] Chazelle, B. *An improved algorithm for the fixed-radius neighbor problem*, Inform. Process. Lett. 1 (1983), 193–198.

[C2] Chazelle, B. *Filtering search: A new approach to query-answering*, Proc. 24th Ann. Symp. Found Comp. Sci. (1983), 122–132.

[CCPY] Chazelle, B., Cole, R., Preparata, F.P., Yap, C.K. *New upper bounds for neighbor searching*, Tech Rept. CS–84–11 (1984), Brown Univ.

[CGL] Chazelle, B., Guibas, L.J., Lee, D.T. *The power of geometric duality*, Proc. 24th Ann. Symp. Found Comp. Sci. (1983), 217–225.

[CY] Cole, R., Yap, C.K. *Geometric retrieval problems*, Proc. 24th Ann. Symp. Found. Comp. Sci. (1983) 112–121.

[EKM] Edelsbrunner, H., Kirkpatrick, D.G. Maurer, H.A. *Polygonal intersection search*, Inform. Process Lett. 14 (1982), 74–79.

[EKS] Edelsbrunner, H., Kirkpatrick, D.G., Seidel, R. *On the shape of a set of points in the plane*, IEE Trans. Inform. Theory, IT–29 (1983), 551–559.

[EW] Edelsbrunner, H., Welzl, E. *Halfplanar range search in linear space and $O(n^{0.695})$ query time*, Rep F111, Inst. Inform. Proc., Tech. Univ. Graz, Austria, 1983.

[K] Knuth, D.E. *Sorting and Searching - The art of computer programming*, III, Chapter 6.5, Addison Wesley, Reading, 1973.

[W] Willard, D.E. *New data structures for orthogonal queries*, SIAM J. Comput., Vol. 14, No. 1 (1985) 232–253.

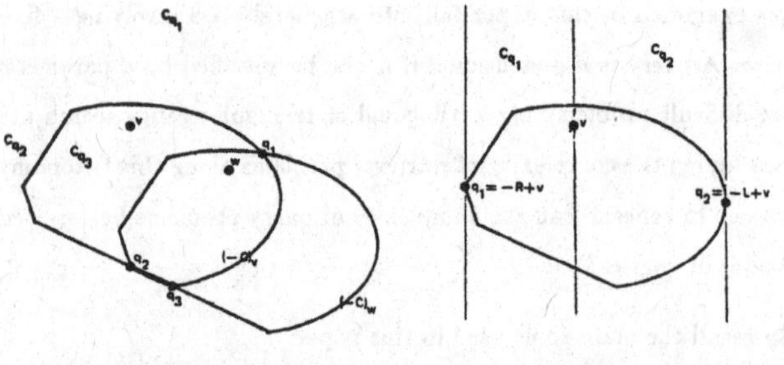

(a) $S(v,w)=\{q_1\}\cup\underline{conv}\{q_2,q_3\}$. (b) $S(v,l)=\{q_1,q_2\}$.

Figure 1. Support-sets.

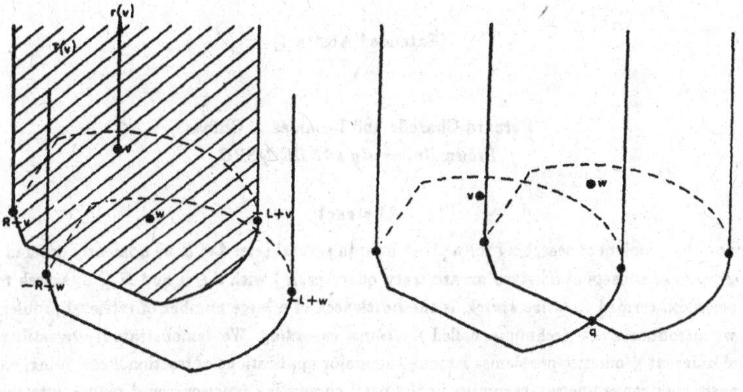

(a) $\max x(v,w)=-R_x+w_x$. (b) $\max x(v,w)=q_x$.

Figure 2. Intersection of two silos.

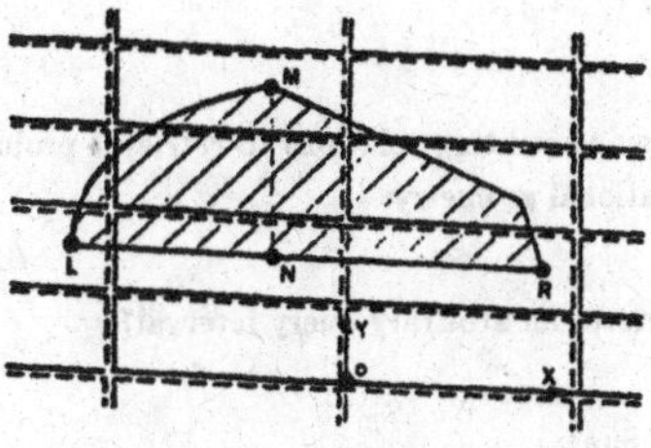

Figure 3. Decomposing C and E^2.

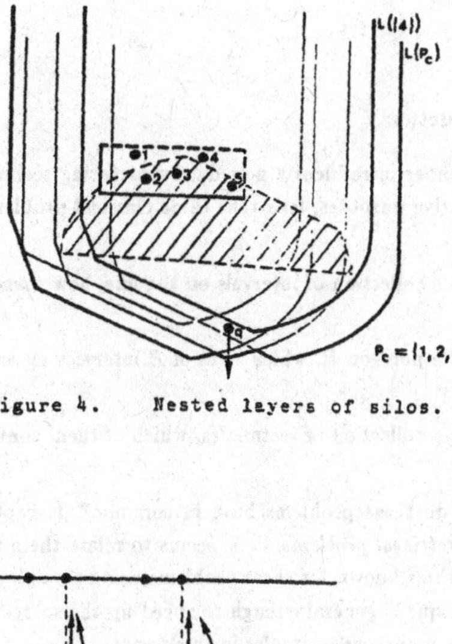

Figure 4. Nested layers of silos.

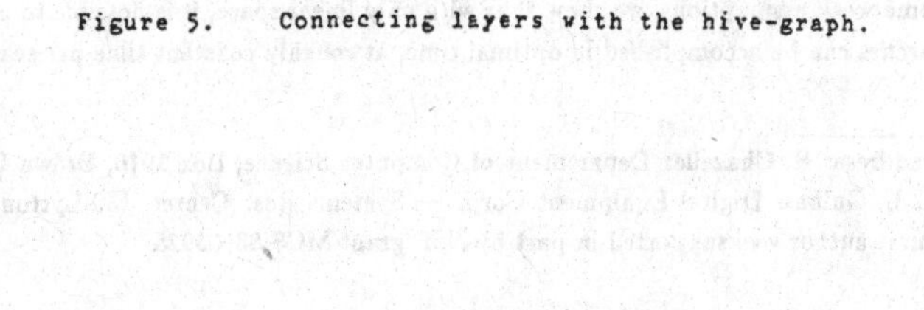

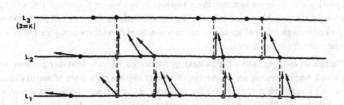

Figure 5. Connecting layers with the hive-graph.

FRACTIONAL CASCADING: A DATA STRUCTURING TECHNIQUE WITH GEOMETRIC APPLICATIONS

(Extended Abstract)

Bernard Chazelle and Leonidas J. Guibas
Brown University and DEC/SRC

Abstract

We examine the problem of searching for a given item in several sets. Let $\mathcal{U}$ be a linearly ordered universe and C be a finite collection of subsets of $\mathcal{U}$; given an arbitrary query (x, H) with $x \in \mathcal{U}$ and $H \subseteq C$, search for x in each set of H. This operation, termed *iterative search*, is the bottleneck of a large number of retrieval problems. To perform it efficiently, we introduce a new technique, called *fractional cascading*. We demonstrate its versatility by applying it to a number of different geometric problems. Among the major applications of fractional cascading, we find improved methods for answering range queries, searching in the past, computing functions on d-ranges, intersection searching, solving general extensions of classical retrieval problems, answering visibility questions in the context of ray-tracing, etc.

1. Introduction

This paper introduces a new data structuring technique for improving existing solutions to retrieval problems. For illustrative purposes, let's take three classical problems in computational geometry:

1. Given a collection of intervals on the line, how many of them intersect an arbitrary query interval?

2. Given a polygon P, which sides of P intersect an arbitrary query line?

3. Given a collection of rectangles, which of them contain an arbitrary query point?

What do these problems have in common? Except for the fact that they each fall into the broader class of *geometric retrieval problems*, little seems to relate them together in one way or the other. Yet, we can speed up the best algorithms known for these problems using a single common technique, which we call *fractional cascading*. This novel technique is general enough to speed up the solutions not only of these three problems but of a host of others; we will give numerous examples in this paper.

In a nusthell, fractional cascading is an efficient strategy for dealing with the following problem, termed *iterative search*: let G be a graph whose vertices are in one-to-one correspondence with a set of sorted lists; given a query consisting of a key x and a subgraph π of G, search for x in each of the lists associated with the vertices of π. This problem has a trivial solution involving repeated binary searches. Fractional cascading shows that it is possible to do much better. Under some weak assumptions, we show that with only linear space, it is possible to organize the set of lists so that all the searches can be accomplished in optimal time, at roughly constant time per search.

Authors' current address: B. Chazelle: Department of Computer Science, Box 1910, Brown University, Providence, RI 02912, USA. L. Guibas: Digital Equipment Corp. — Systems Res. Center, 130 Lytton Ave., Palo Alto, CA 94301, USA. The first author was supported in part by NSF grant MCS 83-03925.

As will appear clearly later on, iterative search is a fundamental component of most query-answering algorithms. Let's take Problem 3, for instance: *given a collection of rectangles, which of them contain an arbitrary query point?* Briefly, the data structure for this problem with the most efficient asymptotic performance is a complete binary tree whose nodes point to auxiliary lists. Answering a query involves tracing a path in the tree, searching for a given value (in effect, one of the coordinates of the query point) in *each* auxiliary list associated with the nodes visited. Here, as well as in many other algorithms for retrieval problems, iterative search is the main computational bottleneck. For this reason, it is imperative to treat the problem in an abstract setting, so the results obtained be directly applicable to as many problems as possible.

Following this approach, we present an optimal solution to iterative search, which we then apply to a number of retrieval problems. By doing so, we are able to improve upon a host of previous complexity results. It is worth noting, as will become apparent when we go into applications of fractional cascading later on, that this technique can be usefully thought of as a post-processing step that can be applied to speed up already existing solutions of various problems.

This paper has four main parts: in §2, we give an overview of the fractional cascading technique; in §3 and §4 we illustrate the power of the technique on two specific examples, and in §5 we list a number of other applications.

2. Fractional Cascading

2.1. Preliminaries

We consider a graph $G = (V, E)$ of $|V| = n$ vertices and $|E| = m$ edges. G is undirected and connected, and it may contain loops or multiple edges. In addition to this classical graph structure, we have associated with each vertex v of G a *catalog* C_v, and associated with each edge e a *range* R_e. A catalog is an ordered collection of values, which without loss of generality we will take to be a sorted list of real numbers. A range is an interval of $\Re$. We will refer to our graph G, together with the associated catalogs and ranges, as a *catalog graph*. For convenience, we assume that if K is an endpoint of a range $R_{(u,v)}$, then K appears as a distinct element in the catalogs C_u and C_v associated with the endpoints of the edge (u, v). With this assumption, the storage required to store a catalog graph is $O(s)$, with $s = \sum_{v \in V} |C_v|$.

Definition 1. A catalog graph is said to have *locally bounded degree d* if for each vertex v and each value $x \in \Re$ the number of edges incident on v whose range includes x is bounded by d.

Definition 2. A *generalized path* π in G is a sequence of vertices $v_1, v_2, \ldots, v_p$ and corresponding edges $e_2, \ldots, e_p$ such that for each vertex v_i, $i > 1$, the edge e_i connects v_i to a vertex v_j of the path, with $j < i$.

Definition 3. A *multiple look-up query* is a pair (x, π), where x is a key value in $\Re$ and π is a generalized path of G. The value x *must* fall within the range of every edge of π. If it does not, the query is invalid. The path π may be specified *on-line*, i.e., one edge at a time.

Note that if G has bounded degree it also has locally bounded degree, but the converse is not true in general. With these definition, we can now state the *iterative search problem*.

> Given a multiple look-up query (x, π), look up x successively in the catalogs of the vertices specified by π, and for each catalog C, determine $\sigma(x, C)$, the *successor* of x in C; that is, the smallest value present in the catalog that is greater than or equal to x (or $+\infty$ in none exists). If π is given on-line, then the reporting is to be done on-line as well.

Without any preprocessing whatsoever, the catalog graph takes up $O(s)$ space, and the query can be answered in time $O\left(\sum_{i=1}^{p} \log(|C_{v_i}|)\right)$. Another method is to merge all the catalogs into a master catalog M, and then for each catalog C keep a correspondence dictionary between positions in C and positions in M. If we do this, then we can look up x in M once and for all when a query is specified, and subsequently for each vertex of π simply follow the appropriate correspondence dictionary to locate x in the catalog of that node in constant time. Unfortunately the correspondence dictionaries altogether take up space $\Omega(n \sum_{v \in V} |C_v|)$, which is not $O(s)$. *Fractional cascading* is a technique for reducing the query time required for a multiple lookup, while increasing storage costs by at most a constant factor. The strategy followed by fractional cascading is to do only one binary search at the beginning, and then, as each vertex v of π is specified, locate x in C_v with only constant additional effort. Our main result is

Theorem 1: Let G be a catalog graph of size s and locally bounded degree d. In $O(s)$ space and time, it is possible to construct a data structure for solving the iterative search problem. The structure allows multiple look-ups along a generalized path of length p to be executed in time $O(p \log d + \log s)$. If d is a constant, this is optimal.

2.2. The Fractional Cascading Technique

We give a brief overview of the technique, omitting details and special cases. In general terms, fractional cascading involves adding to the catalog graph a number of additional structures whose aim is to facilitate look-ups between neighboring catalogs. Each catalog C_v is enlarged with additional keys to produce an *augmented* catalog A_v. For each edge e of G connecting nodes u and v we define a list of *bridges*, D_{uv}, as an ordered collection of elements common to both A_u and A_v, whose values lie in the interval R_e; From this definition, it follows that each bridge in D_{uv} has a *companion* bridge in D_{vu}, and vice versa. We require that a bridge should be associated with a *unique* edge of G. A pair of consecutive bridges associated with the same edge defines a *gap*. Let a_u and b_u be two consecutive bridges in D_{uv} and let a_v (resp. b_v) be the companion bridge of a_u (resp. b_u). The gap of b_u consists of each element of A_u positioned strictly between a_u and b_u and each element of A_v positioned strictly between a_v and b_v. The element b_u (resp. b_v) is called the *upper bridge* of the gap. A key property of the structure built by fractional cascading is the so-called

Gap-Invariant: No gap can exceed $6d - 1$ in size (Fig.1).

Catalogs and augmented catalogs are represented by linked-list structures. Each record in C_v consists of two one-word fields (*key-field, pointer to next key*). The *next key* refers to the element in C_v immediately following the current key in increasing order. The last key's pointer field is used as a sentinel. The structure for A_v is more complex. It is essentially a doubly-linked list with additional information on bridges. A record consists of nine fields, each of one word unless specified otherwise. From left to right we have,

1. *key-field*: stores the value K of the element.
2. *successor-pointer*: holds a pointer to the successor of K in C_v.
3. *up-pointer*: points to the next element in A_v (sentinel if last).
4. *down-pointer*: points to the previous element in A_v (sentinel if first).
5. *back-pointer*: if element is a bridge in D_{vw}, then points to the previous bridge in D_{vw}. Special value to indicate if element is lower endpoint of a range. Set to *null* if element is not a bridge.
6. *bridge-pointer*: if element is a bridge, then points to companion bridge. Set to *null* otherwise.
7. *edge-field*: if element is a bridge in D_{vw}, then stores label of edge vw. Set to *null* otherwise.
8. *count-field*: if element is a bridge, stores size of gap of which it is the upper bridge. Set to *null* otherwise.
9. *scrap-field*: two words of memory to serve as temporary pointers during updates.

The above collection of structures has the following two fundamental properties:

A. If we know the location of a value x in the augmented catalog A_v, for some $v \in V$, then we can compute the location (i.e. successor) of x in C_v in exactly one step.

B. If we know the location of a value x in the augmented catalog A_v, and $e = (v, w)$ is an edge of G such that x is in the range R_e, then we can compute the location of x in A_w in $O(d)$ time.

A. is immediate. From the position of $K = \sigma(x, A_v)$ in A_v follow up-pointers until a bridge is found that connects to A_w. To do so, check the edge-field of every element visited. At that point, follow the bridge-pointer and traverse A_w following down-pointers until x has been located. Because of the gap-invariant, these two traversals can be accomplished in $O(d)$ comparisons. A. and B. show that a multiple look-up query (x, π) can be answered very efficiently, provided that the position of x in A_{v_1} is known, where v_1 is the first vertex in π.

Let's now turn to the construction of these structures. The overall algorithm consists of two nested loops. For each vertex v of G, in turn, we consider the elements of C_v in increasing order and insert them into A_v one at a time.

Before inserting an element we make sure that *all* the gap-invariants have been restored since the previous insertion. Note that before any element of C_v has been inserted into A_v, this augmented catalog is likely to contain elements originating from other catalogs. Therefore we must implement the insertion by merging C_v into A_v. Each insertion of a given element of C_v may cause serious changes in A_v caused by the restoration of gap-invariants. After each insertion of a new key into A_v, we update the count-fields, and only then split excessive gaps into smaller ones. Splits will have the effect of additional insertions, so count-fields must be checked again, and so forth. This two-pronged process ceases as soon as all gap-invariants have been restored. Here is an overview of these operations.

Stage 1: *Insert new key* — Follow up-pointers from position of previous insertion in A_v. The scrap-field is turned *on* to indicate that the element has just been inserted, and a pointer to the new record is added to a set *count-queue.*

Stage 2: *Update count-fields* — For each pointer in the count-queue, retrieve the element to which it points and update the count-field of every gap containing the element. To do so, connect the elements inserted at the previous step into various linked lists, using scrap-fields; a scheme which allows us to "jump" over older elements without having to look at them. Every gap exceeding $6d - 1$ is inserted into a *wide-gap* queue.

Stage 3: *Restore gap-invariants* — If the wide-gap queue is not empty, remove its top element and split the gap of the upper bridge to which it points. To do so, merge all the elements of the gap into a temporary linked list, and split it into j groups of $3d$ elements (except for the last one which has between $3d$ and $6d - 1$ elements). This leads to the introduction of j gaps, all of which have size $3d$ (except possibly for the last one). Iterating on this process for each member of the wide-gap queue will restore all gap-invariants locally. Of course, the introduction of new bridges necessitates going back to stage 2. For this reason we must turn *on* the scrap-fields of these new bridges and insert them into the count-queue.

We recap the basic flow of operations. Stage 1 is called to insert a new key. At this point, stage 2 updates all count-fields. Stage 3 is then called to restore the gap-invariants. At termination, all gaps will have acceptable size, *if we discount the new elements that stage 3 has created.* To remedy this discrepancy, we call stage 2 again to obtain the list of flawed gaps. Stage 3 is then called again, and the process iterates in this way until stage 2 fails to reveal any flawed gaps. It is important to ensure that stage 2 and stage 3 operate completely separately. All count-fields must be correct before restoring any gap-invariant and all gaps must be valid (up to the discrepancies caused by newcomers) before stage 2 is called again into action. Thus, we can prove by induction that this process will terminate and produce the desired structure.

2.3. The Complexity of Fractional Cascading

We examine the storage requirement first. Each gap has a *piggy-bank* holding tokens and credits. A token will buy 10 words of memory, that is, one record in A_v. A token is worth d credits.

At all times, each gap of size g has at least $2\max(0, g - 3d)$ credits in its piggy-bank.

To handle an initial insertion (stage 1), we grant each new key three tokens. One of them is ample to cover the key itself. The other tokens are exchanged for $2d$ credits: two of them are deposited in the space piggy-bank of each containing gap; the remaining credits are thrown away. Note that this transaction preserves the piggy-bank invariant. To handle stage 3, we distribute the tokens of the piggy-bank into packets. The highest new gap is of size between $3d$ and $6d - 1$; it receives a packet equal to twice the excess of its size over $3d$. This packet goes into its own (new) piggy-bank. Each of the other gaps thus receives a packet of $6d$ tokens. Since, however, each has size $3d$, their piggy-banks do not need any tokens at all. Each gap will then give $3d$ tokens to each of its upper bridges. Two of them are deposited into the piggy-bank associated with each of the gaps containing their endpoints. This leaves at least $d + 2$ credits, which is more than one token, so the bridge can then pay for its own record. Extra credits are ignored. As a net result, only $3s$ tokens must be used to account for all the space used, so this space is $O(s)$. More precisely, only 30 words of memory are necessary per catalog element (on the average).

By a similar reasoning, it is possible to show that the construction time is $O(ds)$. To summarize, in $O(s)$ space and $O(ds)$ time, it is possible to construct a data structure for solving the iterative search problem. The structure allows multiple look-ups along a generalized path of length p to be executed in time $O(dp + \log s)$. A canonical transformation of the graph G (which we will omit) allows us to improve this result and achieve the bounds of Theorem 1.

Getting started — One of the points we have deliberately left aside is the initial location of a query value in the fractional cascading structure. Rather than using, say, arrays in which binary searches can be performed, we resort to a scheme that is in full harmony with the previous discussion. To each vertex v of G, attach an extra edge connecting v to a new vertex $g(v)$, called the *gateway* of v. $g(v)$ will have an augmented catalog attached to it but no catalog per se. The edge $(v, g(v))$ is called a transit edge; its range is $(-\infty, +\infty)$. The augmented catalog of $g(v)$ is required to have exactly three elements. When the preprocessing takes place, if $A_{g(v)}$ should end up with fewer than three elements, it is not created. On the other hand, if it ends up with more than three elements, another gateway is attached to it. This process might go on for a while, creating a chain of new vertices emanating from each vertex of G. Only the last vertex in the chain is called a gateway; all the others are called transit vertices. It is clear that every time a new gateway is created, there are enough tokens around to pay for this creation. To answer a query we perform the initial search in A_v by starting at the gateway of v, which will take $O(\log s)$ time. Close examination of the gateway chain structure reveals a strong affinity with B-trees. As it turns out, a B-tree can be looked at as a gateway chain: to do so, think of each level in the tree as one augmented catalog.

Dynamic Fractional Cascading — It is possible to generalize our construction algorithm so as to handle arbitrary insertions (or deletions, but not both) in $O(\log s)$ amortized update time. Actually, if the time for the initial location is not counted and we have a RAM (and not just a pointer machine), constant time suffices, using the *find-split-add* algorithm of [IA] (derived from [GT]). Mixed insertions and deletions seem more difficult. A lazy deletion scheme allows optimal updates in the augmented catalogs, but an efficient *find-link-split-add-delete* algorithm is needed in order to keep the correspondence between A_v and C_v. As suggested to us by J. Ian Munro [Mu], this can be done with a straightforward extension of van Emde Boas' stratified tree [V,VKZ]. This gives efficient updates but, unfortunately, costs a factor of $\log\log s$ in query time. The lower bound of $\Omega(\log\log s)$ provided in [KMR] for a related problem might be an indication that dynamization is inherently difficult in this context.

Recently, Fries, Mehlhorn, and Näher [FMN] have shown that by imposing a lower bound on the gap size, it is possible to handle deletions in a way similar to insertions. Their method has the same performance as our lazy deletion mechanism, but is more in harmony with the general technique; also it strenghtens the aforementioned analogy with B-trees.

3. Intersecting a Polygonal Path and a Line

In this section we investigate the following problem: we are given a polygonal path P and wish to preprocess it into a data structure so that, given any query line l, we can quickly report all the intersections of P with l. The obvious method for solving this problem simply checks each side of P for intersection with l. This method requires storage $S = O(n)$, where n is the length of P, and has query time $Q = O(n)$. Using fractional cascading we are able to develop a technique that gives $S = O(n \log n)$ and $Q = O(\log n + k \log \frac{n}{k})$ (k = size of the output). Until now, only the general method given in [Ch] for segment intersection search would give a fast query time, but at a cost of quadratic storage. The approach we propose is based on the recursive application of the following observation:

Lemma 1. A straight-line l intersects a polygonal line path P if and only if l intersects the convex hull $CH(P)$ of P.

Let $F(P)$ and $S(P)$ denote respectively the first and second halves of the path P, i.e., the subpaths of P consisting of the first $\lfloor n/2 \rfloor$ and second $\lceil n/2 \rceil$ edges. Then our algorithm involves computing the intersections directly if $|P| = 1$, else recursively calling itself on $F(P)$ and $S(P)$, provided that $l \bigcap CH(P) \neq \emptyset$. Since we are allowed to preprocess P, it is to our advantage to precompute and store all the convex hulls we may need. We can do this by a recursion similar to the above, where after having $CH(F(P))$ and $CH(S(P))$, we obtain $CH(P)$ by applying any linear-time algorithm for computing the convex hull of two convex polygons. The overall data structure that we thus build is best thought of as a binary tree T whose n leaves are the edges of our path P (which coincide with their own convex hulls and from left to right occur in the same order as in P). Interior nodes of the tree correspond in an obvious way to sub-paths of P and store the convex hull of their respective sub-path (Fig.2).

The tree T of convex hulls clearly takes $O(n \log n)$ space to store. The total time for computing it is also $O(n \log n)$ since, by the above discussion, it can be expressed by the recurrence $T(n) = 2T(\lfloor \frac{n}{2} \rfloor) + O(n)$. We must now look more closely at the implementation of our intersection algorithm. We decide whether to descend into a subtree by testing for intersections between the convex hull stored in its root and the line l. Even if we were to report only one intersection, the total cost of all these tests would be

$$\Omega\Big(\sum_i \log \frac{n}{2^i}\Big) = \Omega(\log^2 n),$$

since it costs $O(\log m)$ to test for intersection between a convex polygon of m sides and a line, and in T we must trace at least one path down to the intersected edge. This is already too expensive, so some additional weaponry must be brought into the battle. This is where fractional cascading comes in.

The underlying tree T is a perfectly good graph of bounded degree. However, how are we to view the "two-dimensional" (convex polygon, line) intersection problem as one of a look-up in a one-dimensional catalog? The answer is again given by a simple observation. Let $c_1, \ldots, c_m$ be the vertices of a convex polygon given in clockwise order, and let $c_i x$ be the horizontal ray emanating from c_i towards $x = +\infty$. We define the slope of an edge $c_i c_{i+1}$ as the angle $\angle(c_i x, c_i c_{i+1}) \in [0, 2\pi)$. It is well-known that since C is convex there exists a circular permutation of the edges of C such that the sequence of slopes is non-decreasing. This sequence is unique (barring collinear edges), and is called the ***slope-sequence*** of C.

Lemma 2. Let s and s' be the two slopes of l obtained by giving the line its two possible orientations; if we know the positions of s and s' within the slope-sequence of a convex polygon C, we can determine whether C and l intersect in constant time.

Proof: In effect the positions in the slope-sequence tell us the vertices of C where the tangents parallel to l occur. The line l will intersect C if and only if it lies between these two tangents. ∎

Thus we view each node x of T as containing a catalog consisting of the slope-sequence of the convex polygon associated with x. To these catalogs over T we apply fractional cascading. The result is a more elaborate structure, but one still only requiring space $O(n \log n)$. The data structure allows us to implement *all* the (convex polygon, line) intersection tests required by our algorithm, except for the one at the root, in constant time per test. By the previous lemma, any time we need to decide whether to descend into a subtree, we just look up the slopes of l in that subtree's root catalog and find the answer in constant time! There is, of course, an $O(\log n)$ cost at the root of T to get the whole process started. As a net result, the cost of our intersection algorithm is now reduced to $O(\log n+$ size of subtree of T actually visited), since once we pass the root, we spend only constant effort per node visited. Our claimed query time bound of $O(\log n + k \log \frac{n}{k})$ now follows from a technical fact: Let T be a perfectly balanced tree on n leaves and consider any subtree S of T with k leaves chosen among the leaves of T. Then, $|S| \leq k\lceil \log n \rceil - k \lfloor \log k \rfloor + 2k - 1$. We have finally shown

Theorem 2. Given a polygonal path P of length n, it is possible in time $O(n \log n)$ to build a data structure of size $O(n \log n)$, so that given any line l, all k intersections between l and P can be reported in time $O(\log n + k \log \frac{n}{k})$.

4. Slanted Range Search

Let E^2 be the Euclidean plane endowed with a Cartesian system of axes (Ox, Oy). The term ***aligned rectangle*** refers to the Cartesian product $[a, b] \times [0, c]$, for some positive reals a, b, c. The ***aligned range search*** problem involves preprocessing a set V of n points so that for any aligned rectangle R, the set $V \cap R$ can be computed efficiently. McCreight [Mc] has described a data structure, called a ***priority search tree***, which allows us to solve this problem in optimal space and time (other optimal solutions can be found in [Ch]). The data structure requires $O(n)$ space and offers $O(k + \log n)$ response-time, where $k = |V \cap R|$ is the size of the output. Can the priority search tree be extended to solve a more general class of range search problems? For example, consider adding one degree of freedom to the previous problem. Let's define an ***aligned trapezoid*** as a trapezoid with corners $(a, 0), (b, 0)$ and $(a, c), (b, d)$, where $c > 0$ and $b > a$. In the ***slanted range search*** problem, the set to be computed is of the form $V \cap R$, where R is an aligned trapezoid (Fig.3). Since slanted range search is strictly more general than aligned range search, previous solutions are inadequate. Instead, we turn to a slightly more complicated data structure, which we develop in two stages. First, we outline a linear space data structure whose response-time is $O(\log^2 n + k \log n)$ ($k =$ output size). This solution is then improved by application of fractional cascading.

A special case of slanted search has been solved by Chazelle, Guibas and Lee [CGL]: given a query line L, report all points of V on one side of L. The algorithm, which is optimal in both space and time, is intimately based on the notion of ***convex layers***, a structure obtained by repeatedly computing and removing the convex hull of V. This preprocessing partitions the point-set into a hierarchy of subsets, each of which lends itself to efficient searching. For the purpose of slanted range search, we introduce a dichotomy in the recursive construction of layers. To begin with, observe that without loss of generality we can assume that all points in V have distinct x-coordinates. Next, we introduce the notion of ***lower hull*** of the point-set V, denoted $L(V)$. If $a_1, \ldots, a_i, a_{i+1}, \ldots, a_j$ are the vertices of the convex hull of V, given in counterclockwise order with a_1 (resp. a_i) the point with minimum (resp. maximum) x-coordinate, $L(V)$ is defined as the sequence of points $a_1, \ldots, a_i$. If V consists of a single point, $L(V) = V$.

We are now ready to describe the data structure. It is constructed recursively by associating the list $D(v) = L(V)$ with the root v of a complete binary tree G of size n. Let W be the points of V not in $L(V)$, and let $l(v)$ (resp. $r(v)$) denote the left (resp. right) child of vertex v. The data structure $D(l(v))$, associated with $l(v)$, is defined as the sequence of points $L(W')$, where W' is the leftmost half of W. $D(r(v))$ is defined similarly with respect to the rightmost half of W (Fig.4). The contruction procedure is executed by calling $BUILD$(V,root).

$BUILD(C, v)$

begin
If $C = \emptyset$ **then stop**
$D(v) \leftarrow L(C)$
$W \leftarrow C \setminus L(C)$
Let α be the $\lceil \frac{|W|}{2} \rceil$th largest x-coordinate in W.
$BUILD(W \bigcap \{x \le \alpha\}, l(v))$
$BUILD(W \bigcap \{x > \alpha\}, r(v))$
end

Any vertex of G that has not been assigned a data structure can be deleted. Each data structure $D(v)$ is now refined as follows: let $D(v) = \{(x_1, y_1), \ldots, (x_m, y_m)\}$ be the lower hull at node v, with $x_1 < x_2 < \ldots < x_m$. The two pieces of information of interest at node v are:

1. $\mathrm{Abs}(v) = \{x_1, \ldots, x_m\}$, the sorted list of x-coordinates in $D(v)$;
2. $\mathrm{Slope}(v) = \{\frac{y_2 - y_1}{x_2 - x_1}, \ldots, \frac{y_m - y_{m-1}}{x_m - x_{m-1}}\}$, the sorted list of edge-slopes in $D(v)$.

For explanatory purposes, we describe the query-answering process in two stages. A preliminary phase marks selected vertices of G using two colors, *blue* and *red*. The red vertices are then used as starting points for the second stage of the algorithm, where the remaining candidate vertices are examined. We successively describe the algorithm, prove its correctness, and examine its complexity. As a convenient piece of terminology, we introduce the notion of an *L-peak*. Let L be the line passing through the two points (a, c) and (b, d), and let L^- be the half-plane below L. We define the L-peak of $D(v)$ as the point of $L^- \bigcap D(v)$ whose orthogonal distance to L is maximum (break ties arbitrarily). The L-peak of $D(v)$ is 0 if $L^- \bigcap D(v) = \emptyset$.

Stage 1: The algorithm is recursive and starts at the root v of G. In the following, $D(v)$ is regarded as the polygonal line with vertices $(x_1, y_1), \ldots, (x_m, y_m)$. The query trapezoid $R = \{(a, 0), (b, 0), (a, c), (b, d)\}$ falls in one of three positions with respect to $D(v)$:

1. $D(v)$ intersects the vertical segment $r_a = \{(a, y) \mid 0 \le y \le c\}$ at some edge $[(x_{i-1}, y_{i-1}), (x_i, y_i)]$: as long as the point (x_i, y_i) is defined and lies in R, report it and increment i by one. If $D(v)$ does not intersect r_a but intersects the segment $r_b = \{(b, y) \mid 0 \le y \le d\}$ at some edge $[(x_j, y_j), (x_{j+1}, y_{j+1})]$, then perform a similar sequence of operations. As long as the point (x_j, y_j) is defined and lies in R, report it and decrement j by one. As a final step, mark v blue. If v is a leaf of G then return, else recurse on both $l(v)$ and $r(v)$.
2. $D(v)$ is completely to the left or to the right of R, i.e., $x_m < a$ or $x_1 > b$: return.
3. None of the above: mark v red and return.

Stage 2: As long as there are some unhandled red vertices left in G, pick any one of them, say v, mark it "handled" and perform the following sequence of operations: compute (x_i, y_i), the L-peak of $D(v)$, and report it if it happens to lie in R. Initialize j to $i + 1$. As long as the point (x_j, y_j) is defined and lies in R, report it and increment j by one. Next, re-initialize j to $i - 1$; as long as the point (x_j, y_j) is defined and lies in R, report it and decrement j by one. Mark red $l(v)$ and $r(v)$. If the L-peak is not in R, just return.

The description of the algorithm will be complete after a few words on the implementation of its basic primitives. The case-analysis of *Stage 1* is performed by binary search in $\mathrm{Abs}(v)$ with respect to a and b. In *Stage 2*, the L-peak of $D(v)$ is computed by performing a binary search in $\mathrm{Slope}(v)$ with respect to the slope of L. Of course, the marking of vertices is for explanatory purposes only and is not necessary.

2. The Partition is Separating

We make the notion of a partition precise.

Definition: [Y1] Let S be a set of n points in d-dimensional space. A *partition* Π for S is a pair $(\mathbf{R},\mathbf{P})$, where $\mathbf{R}$ is a set of disjoint open regions and $\mathbf{P}$ is a set of $(d-1)$-dimensional surfaces, such that every point of S either lies in a region $R \in \mathbf{R}$, or on a surface $P \in \mathbf{P}$. A region $R \in \mathbf{R}$ is said to be a δn*-region* with respect to Π if at least δn points of S are contained in $R \bigcup_{P \in \mathbf{P}} P$ (i.e. the remaining open regions of $\mathbf{R}$ contain at most $(1-\delta)n$ points). We say $\Pi = (\mathbf{R},\mathbf{P})$ is a δn*-partition* if every $R \in \mathbf{R}$ is a δn-region.

We describe our partition next. As an aid to our intuition, we start by giving a partition Π of 3 dimensional space. We have 4 partitioning planes: P, Q, R_1, R_2 (see figure 1). R_1 and R_2 are parallel; further, we only use parts of the planes R_1 and R_2, as illustrated in figure 1. It is clear these surfaces define 8 disjoint, open regions.

Lemma 1: Any plane, M, intersects at most seven of the regions defined by Π.

Proof: The approach used in this proof, and in the proof of lemma 2, was suggested by Edelsbrunner [E]. Let us consider the intersection of P, Q, R_1, and R_2 with M; we refer to these intersections as P, Q, R_1 and R_2, where there will be no ambiguity. We will show that at most seven faces are defined on M; we can then deduce that M intersects at most seven of the regions defined by Π. Consider the four open sets in M defined by P and Q; we refer to these sets as quadrants. Let R be parallel to R_1 and R_2 and pass through $P \cap Q$. Then R does not intersect at least one pair of opposite quadrants. Only one of R_1 and R_2 can intersect either of the quadrants in this pair; without loss of generality suppose that R_1 is the only plane that intersects either of the quadrants in this pair. But R_1 can intersect at most one of the quadrants in this pair, since R_1 is parallel to R. We deduce that P, Q, R_1, and R_2 define at most seven faces on M. □

The partition Π in 4 dimensions uses 8 planes: $P, Q, R_1, R_2, S_1, S_2, S_3, S_4$. R_1 and R_2 are parallel, as are S_1, S_2, S_3, and S_4. P, Q, R_1, and R_2 have the same form as in the 3 dimensional case; let us label the 8 resulting regions, as before, as shown in figure 1 (we also label the four regions defined by P and Q as shown in figure 1). We keep just those parts of S_i that intersect the regions U_i and U_{4+i}, $1 \le i \le 4$; henceforth, when we refer to S_i (or R_j) we intend the surface consisting of the parts we have kept. Let W_{2j} and W_{2j-1} be the two regions obtained from partitioning U_j by S_i $(j=i,4+i)$, $1 \le i \le 4$.

Lemma 2: Any 3 dimensional hyperplane M intersects at most 15 of the 16 regions defined by Π.

Proof: Again, let P, Q, R_i, S_j refer to the intersection of these surfaces with M. We show that the planes P, Q, R_i, S_j define at most 15 regions on M, and deduce that M can intersect at most 15 of the regions defined by Π. Consider the eight open sets defined by the planes P, Q, R_1 and R_2; we refer to these sets as octants. Let R be parallel to R_1 and R_2. Fix R. P, Q, and R define a set of octants, that we associate in the natural way with the octants already defined. Consider the plane S, parallel to the planes S_j, passing through $P \cap Q \cap R$. S does not intersect at least one pair of opposite octants. Consider the corresponding pair of

5.3. Intersection Problems

6. **Counting Interval Intersections** – It is possible to store n intervals in $O(n)$ space so that for any query interval q the number of intervals intersecting q can be computed in $O(\log n)$ time. The preprocessing requires $O(n \log n)$ time. Improvement of $O(\log n)$ space [BW] or $O(\log n)$ time [E].

7. **Simple Polygonal Path $\bigcap$ Query Line** – Given a simple polygonal path P of length n, it is possible in time $O(n \log n)$ to build a data structure of size $O(n)$, so that given any line l, if l intersects P in k edges, then these edges can be reported in time $O(\log n + k \log \frac{n}{k})$ — see §3. Previous algorithm using $O(n^2)$ space and $O(k + \log n)$ time [Ch].

8. **Visibility Problems** – Ray-tracing is an important operation in computer graphics: it involves computing the trajectory of a ray of light as it is reflected and refracted by various obstacles. We can show that *tracing* the first k hits of a query ray of light inside a simple polygon with n vertices can be done in $O(\log n + k \log \frac{n}{k})$ time, using $O(n)$ space [CG].

5.4. Combinatorial Searching

9. **Explicit Iterative Search** – Consider a set of p catalogs of combined size n. There exists an $O(n)$ space data structure such that given a query value x and any sub-collection of m catalogs, x can be searched in the specified catalogs in $O(m \log \frac{p}{m} + \log n)$ time. Improvement of a logarithmic factor in time over naive method.

10. **A Space-Compression Scheme** – Data structures such as segment-trees [BW] and range-trees [BS] are suboptimal, space-wise. It is possible to eliminate some of their redundancy and thus save storage, but this entails considerable degradation in response-time. Fractional cascading can be used, however, to slow down the rate of degradation. For example, segment-trees and range-trees can be redefined to take up $O(n \frac{\log n}{\log \log n})$ space as opposed to $O(n \log n)$, while the search time increases by a factor of $\log^{\epsilon} n$, for any $\epsilon > 0$.

11. **Iterative Search Extensions of Retrieval Problems** – Consider a typical occurrence of orthogonal range search. A query involves retrieving the names of all employees in a company, whose attributes fall in a certain range. What is often desired, however, is not so much the names of the employees but additional information about them. To satisfy this request will involve looking up some files (i.e. catalogs) associated with each employee. Unfortunately, this extra work cannot be integrated within, say, a more general range search problem. The only recourse is then to search separately the files of each employee selected by the range search. In the best case, this may multiply the running time of the algorithm by a logarithmic factor. We can show that with fractional cascading *no extra work* need be done in order to retrieve the complementary information desired. This fairly striking result does not apply only to range search but to most retrieval problems studied in the literature.

6. Concluding Remarks

The contribution of this paper has been to introduce a new data structuring technique, *fractional cascading*, which is general enough to be applied to a large class of retrieval problems. An attractive aspect of fractional cascading is that it can often be used as a post-processing step to speed up existing solutions to various problems.

This work started as an attempt to unify three data structuring techniques: the *layered* structure of [W], the *hive-graph* of [Ch], and a combination of these two structures [Co,EGS]. Interestingly, all these techniques can now be regarded as special cases of fractional cascading.

Among the remaining open questions, first and foremost is the problem of understanding how stringent the bounded degree requirement really is. Also, deciding whether fractional cascading can be dynamized without loss in query time is an interesting open question. Finally, can fractional cascading be applied to more complex search structures, such as planar subdivisions? A positive answer to this question would have interesting consequences on a large number of proximity problems.

Acknowledgments: We wish to thank R.E. Tarjan for many valuable comments, and J.I. Munro for a helpful discussion on set-splitting algorithms.

REFERENCES

[BS] Bentley, J.L., Shamos, M.I. *A problem in multivariate statistics: Algorithms, data structures and applications*, Proc. 15th Allerton Conf. Comm., Contr., and Comp. (1977), 193–201.

[BW] Bentley, J.L., Wood, D. *An optimal worst-case algorithm for reporting intersections of rectangles*, IEEE Trans. Comput., Vol. C–29 (1980), 571–577.

[Ch] Chazelle, B. *Filtering search: A new approach to query-answering*, Proc. 24th Ann. Symp. Found. Comp. Sci. (1983), 122–132.

[CG] Chazelle, B., Guibas, L.J. *Visibility and intersection problems in plane geometry*, Proc. ACM SIGGRAPH Symp. Comp. Geom., June 1985.

[CGL] Chazelle, B., Guibas, L.J., Lee, D.T. *The power of geometric duality*, Proc. 24th Ann. Symp. Found. Comp. Sci. (1983), 217–225.

[Co] Cole, R. *Searching and storing similar lists*, Tech. Report No. 88, Courant Inst., New York Univ. (Oct. 1983).

[DM] Dobkin, D.P., Munro, J.I. *Efficient uses of the past*, Proc. 21st Ann. Symp. Found. Comp. Sci. (1980), 200–206.

[E] Edelsbrunner, H. *Intersection problems in computational geometry*, Ph.D. Thesis, Tech. Report, Rep. 93, IIG, Univ. Graz, Austria (1982).

[EGS] Edelsbrunner, H., Guibas, L.J., Stolfi, J. *Optimal point location in a monotone subdivision*, to appear.

[FMN] Fries, O., Mehlhorn, K., Näher, St. *Dynamization of geometric data structures*, manuscript, March 1985.

[GT] Gabow, H.N., Tarjan, R.E. *A linear-time algorithm for a special case of disjoint set union*, Proc. 15th Ann. SIGACT Symp. (1983), 246–251.

[IA] Imai, H., Asano, T. *Dynamic segment intersection with applications*, Proc. 25th Ann. Symp. Found. Comp. Sci. (1984), 393–402.

[KMR] Karlsson, R.G., Munro, J.I., Robertson, E.L. *The nearest neighbor problem on bounded domains*, these proceedings.

[Mc] McCreight, E.M. *Priority search trees*, Tech. Rep., Xerox PARC, CSL–81–5 (1981).

[Mu] Munro, J.I. *Personal communication*, February 1985.

[O] Overmars, M.H. *The design of dynamic data structures*, PhD Thesis, University of Utrecht, The Netherlands, 1983.

[V] van Emde Boas, P. *Preserving order in a forest in less than logarithmic time and linear space*, Info. Proc. Lett. 6, 3 (1977), 80–82.

[VKZ] van Emde Boas, P., Kaas, R., Ziljstra, E. *Design and analysis of an efficient priority queue*, Math. Systems Theory 10 (1977), 99–127.

[W] Willard, D.E. *New data structures for orthogonal queries*, SIAM J. Comput., Vol. 14, No. 1 (1985), 232–253.

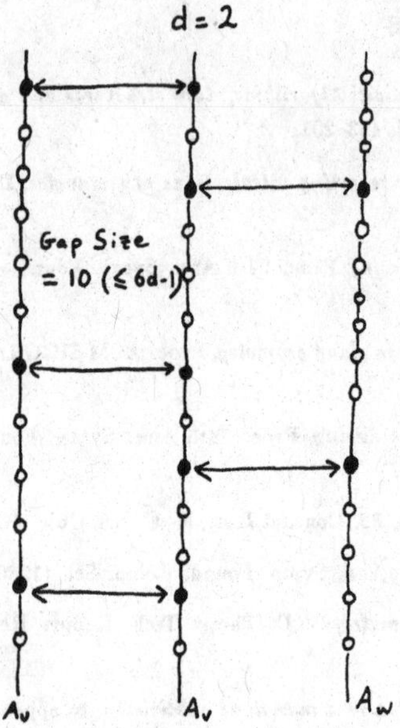

Figure 1

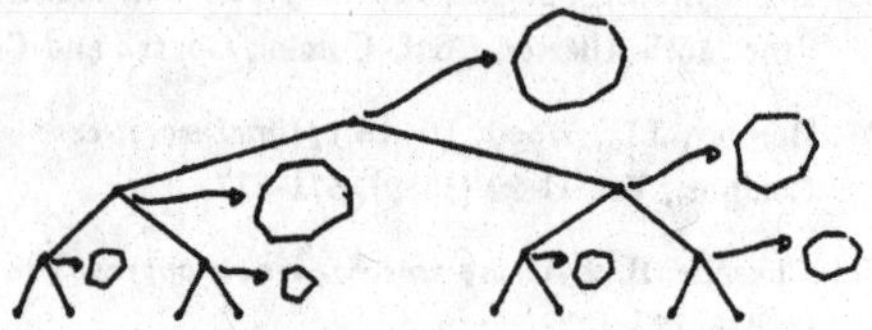

Figure 2

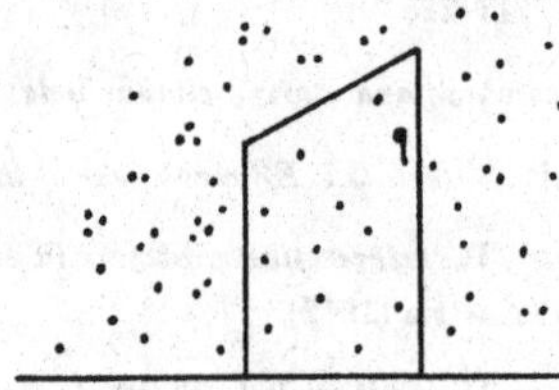

Figure 3

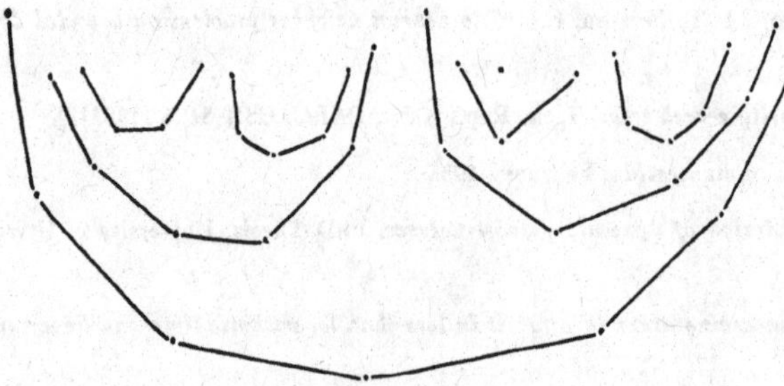

Figure 4

Hierarchies of one-way multihead automata languages

Marek Chrobak
Institute of Informatics
Warsaw University
PKIN VIII p., 00-901 Warsaw, Poland.

Abstract. Let DPDA(k) (resp. NPDA(k)) be the class of languages recognized by one-way k-head deterministic (resp. nondeterministic) pushdown automata. The main result of this paper is that for each $k > 0$ $DPDA(k) \subsetneq DPDA(k+1)$ and $DPDA(k) \subsetneq NPDA(k)$.

Notation. We will consider the following automata:
dfa(k) - a one-way k-head deterministic finite automaton,
nfa(k) - a one-way k-head nondeterministic finite automaton,
dca(k) - a one-way k-head deterministic counter automaton,
nca(k) - a one-way k-head nondeterministic counter automaton,
dpda(k) - a one-way k-head deterministic pushdown automaton,
npda(k) - a one-way k-head nondeterministic pushdown automaton.

If x(k) is a type of automata then X(k) is the class of languages recognized by x(k) automata. For example, NFA(3) is the class of languages recognized by nondeterministic finite automata with 3 heads. When k is not specified then k = 1 is assumed. By REG we denote the class of regular sets: REG = DFA = NFA.

A language L is said to be strictly n-bounded if there are n distinct symbols $a_1, \dots, a_n$ such that $L \subseteq a_1^* a_2^* \dots a_n^*$. L is strictly bounded if it is strictly n-bounded for some n. Since we will consider only stricly bounded languages we will say simply "bounded" instead of "strictly bounded".

Introduction. Given a class of multihead automata, the following problems are usually considered:

(1) are k+1 heads better than k?

(2) are nondeterministic automata better than deterministic ones?

(3) closure properties.

These problems were already considered for many types of automata. The first definition of multihead automata appeared in early 60's in Piatkowski [16]. He defined there a dfa(k) and soon after Rosenberg [17,18] investigated problems (1) - (3) for dfa(k)'s. Unfortunately, the proofs in [18] were incorrect (see [2]). The first progress was made in 1975 when Ibarra and Kim [12] proved that DFA(2) $\subsetneq$ DFA(3). These classes were separated by the language consisting of the words $a^i b^j c^k$, in which at least two of i,j,k are equal. A different proof of this inequality was given by Sudborough [19].

The full solution to (1) for one-way automata was presented in 1978 by Yao and Rivest [20], who proved that the language

$$L_b = \{ w_1 \# \ldots \# w_{2b} \mid w_i \in \{0,1\}^* \text{ and } w_i = w_{2b+1-i} \text{ for } i = 1,\ldots,2b \}$$

is in DFA(k) for $b \leq \binom{k}{2}$ but is not in NFA(k) for $b > \binom{k}{2}$. This gives us two hierarchies for one-way finite automata: DFA(k) $\subsetneq$ DFA(k+1) and NFA(k) $\subsetneq$ NFA(k+1) for every $k > 0$. They showed also a language in NFA(2) which is not in any DFA(k), what implies immediately the positive answer to the problem (2). The proof was by a clever counting argument, using some observations of Rosenberg about the behaviour of a dfa(k) on words in L_b. Their technique (called often "cutting and pasting" or "fooling") was applied by Miyano [14] to prove similar results for counter automata: DCA(k) $\subsetneq$ DCA(k+1), NCA(k) $\subsetneq$ NCA(k+1), DCA(k) $\subsetneq$ NCA(k) for every $k > 0$. Hromkovic [9] used suitably modified cutting and pasting to prove some non-closure properties of DFA(k). Problems (1) - (3) were also considered for so-called simple multihead finite automata, that is such automata that only one head sees input symbols, the other k-1 heads can detect only the endmarker [1,13].

We have not yet mentioned one-way multihead pushdown machines. The reason is that all problems (1) - (3) for these automata are still open, except the simple case k = 1. They seem to be too powerfull to fool them using counting arguments. Note that a nfa(k) has at most $O(n^k)$ configurations. The proof of Miyano [14] was possible because a nca(k) has $O(n^{k+1})$ configurations, that is still polynomially many. But a npda(k) may have then $O(2^n)$ because the number of possible contents of the pushdown store is expotential. This makes the application of counting arguments to fool a npda(k) rather unlikely. Also the semilinear property of npda(k) languages [10,11] is of no use to us, it can be applied only to separate the whole class of multihead pushdown automaton languages from other classes of languages, not possesing this property.

These problems were overcome partially by Miyano [15], but his definition of multihead automata differs from the one in [7]: the input tape has no endmarkers and the automata accept by entering an accepting state. He proved that for these machines k+1 heads are better than k. The proof is by reduction to the analogous problem for two-way automata, so in essence it is a proof by diagonalization.

In this paper we introduce a new technique for proving separation results which can be looked upon as a refinement of the so-called cycle technique. The cycle technique is based on the following observation:

Suppose that a dfa A has a^n on input, where n is greater than the number of the states of A. During the computation A must eventually enter a cycle and let s be the number of A's moves in this cycle. Then A accepts a^n iff A accepts a^{n+s}. If A is a dfa(k), for $k > 1$, then the situation is more complicated. In fact, so far this technique was used only for k = 2. We investigate the behaviour of A on n-bounded inputs, where n is fixed. Usually the witness language is chosen to be at most 4-bounded. For such inputs we can consider only "boundary configurations", that is such configurations in which one of the heads enters a new block of symbols on the input. It is important here to note that for fixed A and n the number of boundary configurations in each computation is bounded by a constant. The positions of the heads in consecutive boundary configurations are related by some linear equations and the coefficients in these equations depend only on the description of A. An investigations of these relations, usually by considering numerous cases, allows us to fool A by pumping the input and forcing it to accept a word which should not be accepted.

The cycle technique was used by Ibarra and Kim [12] to separate DFA(2) and DFA(3). Note that their witness language is 3-bounded. Hromkovic [17] also used similar ideas to investigate closure properties of DFA(2). We will refine this technique to prove the following theorem:

<u>Theorem 1</u>. Let x be one of the following types of automata: fa,ca,pda. Then for each $k > 0$

(a) $DX(k) \cap B_2 \subsetneq DX(k+1) \cap B_2$,

and for each $k > 1$

(b) $DX(k) \cap B_2 \subsetneq NX(k) \cap B_2$.

For k = 1 and x = fa we have NFA(1) = DFA(1) = REG. For x = ca,pda, it is not difficult to prove that $DX(1) \cap B_2 \subsetneq NX(1) \cap B_2$.

So, in particular, we obtain that DPDA(k) $\subsetneq$ DPDA(k+1) and DPDA(k) $\subsetneq$ NPDA(k) for $k > 0$, what solves some long open problems about multihead pushdown automata. Theorem 1 strengthens also the known hierarchy results from [14,20] because it states that they hold even for 2-bounded languages. Can we use here 1-bounded languages? No. For suppose that L is a 1-bounded language in NPDA(k). Then, by the semilinear property, the subset of N consisting of all possible lengths of the words in L is a finite union of arithmetic sequences. Therefore L is regular. In consequence we obtain that for 1-bounded languages all considered hierarchies collapse to regular sets. Thus we can say that, in a sense, Theorem 1 is "optimal".

We prove also that:

Theorem 2. Let x = dfa,dca,dpda. Then for $k > 1$ X(k) is not closed under union, intersection and concatenation.

Theorem 2 also holds for k = 1 and x = dca,dpda. For x = dpda Theorem 2 solves some open problems stated by Harrison and Ibarra [7]. For x = dfa the above results were already proved by Hromkovic [9].

The proofs. We introduce first a new device. By a one-way k-head 1-bounded pushdown automaton (dpda(k,1) in short) we mean a dpda(k) with pushdown alphabet $a_0, a_1, \ldots, a_l$ such that in every configuration the contents of the pushdown store is in $a_0 a_1^* \ldots a_l^*$ (a_0 denotes the bottom of the stack). In other words, a dpda(k,1) cannot push a_i onto the stack when the top symbol is a_j, for $i < j$. A dpda(k,1) is a generalization of bounded pushdown automaton introduced by Greibach [6]. As usual, DPDA(k,1) is the class of dpda(k,1) languages.

Let $L_n = \{1^x 2^{ix} \mid x \in N,\ 1 \leq i \leq n\}$. The symbol 3 denotes the endmarker of the input tape. We will use languages L_n as witness languages in our proof.

The most difficult step of the proof is the following lemma.

Lemma 1 (Fundamental Lemma). For every $k > 0$ and $l \geq 0$ there exists n such that $L_n \notin$ DPDA(k,1).

Proof (sketch). We will consider sets $D_i = \{(x, ix) \mid x \in N\}$ and some other subsets of N^2 called seminets and semisectors. A seminet is a set of points in N^2 distributed regularly in the plane. A semisector is an intersection of a seminet and an angle (the set of points between two lines), possibly minus some finite set. The formal definitions are not necessary here. A 0-seminet is a seminet containing (0,0).

Let $X \subseteq N^2$ and suppose that there exist $I \subseteq N$, a 0-seminet P and finite sets $R, S \subseteq N^2$ such that

$$X = \left[\left(\bigcup_{i \in I} D_i\right) \cap P - R\right] \cup S.$$

Informally, X is almost equal to the intersection of a finite sum of some D_i's with a 0-seminet. From the properties of 0-seminets it follows also that X has infinitely many points from every D_i, for $i \in I$. If the above equality holds then we define: rank(X) $= |I|$. If such I,P,R,S do not exist then rank(X) is undefined. The reader may imagine X as a broom-shaped subset of N^2 and rank(X) as the minimal number of lines containing X. Using some properties of seminets it can be proved that this definition is correct, that is there is at most one set I for X with the required property.

Let k,l and a dpda(k,l) A be fixed and take $n = (4k+4)^{4k+1}$. The reader may find it surprising that n does not depend on l. Lemma 3 below may serve here as an explanation because it implies that dpda(k,2k+1)'s over 2-bounded languages are as powerfull as all dpda(k,l)'s. In other words, a dpda(k,l) cannot make an essential use of more that 2k+1 blocks of the stack.

From the assumption that $L(A) = L_m$ for some $m > n$ we will derive a contradiction.

Boundary configurations are defined similarly as for a dfa(k) except that we must also consider changes of the top symbol on the stack. For a configuration K define the mode of K to be the vector $(q,e_1,e_2,\dots,e_k,i)$, where q is the state of A in K, e_j is the symbol scanned by the j-th head and i tells that a_i is on the top of the stack in K. Then K is boundary if either it is an initial configuration or else the preceding configuration had a different mode. In contrast to a dfa(k), A may have arbitrarily many boundary configurations on a fixed input. For example, when the pushdown stores only a_0 A may make alternatively push(a_1) and pop. So we prove first that if a dpda(k,l) accepts a 2-bounded language then there is a dpda(k,l) accepting the same language which has at most 4k+1 boundary configurations in every computation.

So suppose that A has at most 4k+1 boundary configurations in every computation and consider the tree ET whose nodes are labelled by modes. The labels, in order from the root to the leaves, correspond to the boundary configuration of A. The root E_0 is labelled by $(q_0,1,\dots,1,0)$. An edge $E \rightarrow F$ corresponds to the pass of A from the boundary configuration corresponding to E to the one corresponding to F. Therefore the depth of ET is 4k. For example, take k = 2, l = 1 and consider the following sequence of boundary configurations: A pushes a_1 onto the stack, the first head reaches a symbol 2, the second head reaches a symbol 2, the second head reaches the endmarker, the stack becomes empty, the first head reaches the endmarker. The corresponding path in ET is: $(q_0,1,1,0) \rightarrow (q_1,1,1,1) \rightarrow (q_2,2,1,1) \rightarrow (q_3,2,2,1) \rightarrow (q_4,2,3,1) \rightarrow (q_5,2,3,0) \rightarrow (q_6,3,3,0)$, where q_0 is the initial state of A and $q_1,\dots,q_6$ are the states occuring in the above boundary configurations.

Suppose now that E,F are nodes of ET and F is a son of E. Then either the pass from E to F is long (A enters a cycle) or short (A does not enter a cycle). If G is another son of E then F,G are twins if their labels differ only on the first position (state) and either both passes $E \to F$ and $E \to G$ are long or both are short. We can always assume that if the top of the stack is a_i and A pushes a symbol different from a_i then this symbol is a_{i+1}. Thus all sons of E are grouped into at most 2(k+1) clusters, where each cluster contains only twins and no twins are in different clusters.

Now we consider the flow of pairs $(x,y) \in N^2$ (corresponding to inputs 1^x2^y) through ET, from E_0 to the leaves. 1^x2^y is accepted by A iff (x,y) reaches a leaf with an accepting state in its label. Let N(E) be the set of all $(x,y) \in N^2$ such that $1^x2^y \in L(A)$, which flow through a node E. Suppose that $L(A) = L_m$ for some $m > n$. Then

$$N(E_0) = \left\{(x,y) \in N^2 \,\middle|\, 1^x2^y \in L(A)\right\} = \bigcup_{i=1}^{m} D_i, \text{ so } \mathrm{rank}(N(E_0)) = m.$$

Let E be a node of ET with rank(N(E)) = r. N(E) is divided into 2k+2 subsets corresponding to the clusters of the sons of E. It can be proved that this subsets fit into the definition of rank. From this we derive that there is a cluster $F_1,\ldots,F_s$ such that $\mathrm{rank}(Y) \geq r/(2k+2)$ for $Y = N(F_1) \cup \ldots \cup N(F_s)$. Now we have come to the key point of our proof. The number of F_i's may be large, as large as the number of the states of A. So it seems that Y may be divided into many sets $N(F_i)$ of small rank. However, using some number-theoretic and ...geometric arguments we show that this is not true. Namely, there is some i such that $\mathrm{rank}(N(F_i)) = \mathrm{rank}(Y) \geq r/(2k+2)$. Informally speaking: if there are r sets D_i whose infinite subsets flow through E then, no matter how many sons E may have, there must exist a son F of E with the property that r/(2k+2) sets D_i have infinite subsets flowing through F.

Let E_i, for each i, be obtained by the above procedure by taking it to be E, where E is E_{i-1}. It is easy now to observe that $\mathrm{rank}(N(E_{4k}))$ depends only on k and m. By some simple calculations we obtain that if $m > n$ then $\mathrm{rank}(N(E_{4k})) \geq 2$.

Now, if q is the state in the label of E_{4k} then q must be accepting, because $N(E_{4k})$ contains elements of some D_i, $1 \leq i \leq m$. In fact we have something more: $N(E_{4k})$ must contain infinite subsets of two different sets D_i. From some properties of the sets N(E) we derive then that $N(E_{4k})$ must also contain a point (x,y), where x does not divide y. Therefore we have a contradiction: $1^x2^y \in L(A)$ (because (x,y) reaches E_{4m} with an accepting state) but $1^x2^y \notin L_m$ (because y/x is not an integer). This completes the proof. ■

Lemma 2. For each $k > 0$, $l \geq 0$ $DPDA(k,l) \cap B_2 \subsetneq DPDA(k+1,l) \cap B_2$.

Proof. From Lemma 1 there exists m such that $L_m \in DPDA(k,l)$ but $L_{m+1} \notin DPDA(k,l)$. Let $L_m = L(A_1)$ for a dpda(k,l) A_1. We will show a dpda(k+1,l) A_2 recognizing L_{m+1}. First, A_2 places its (k+1)-th head on the first symbol 2. Next, it simulates the moves of A_1, except that when A_1 moves its first head then A_2 moves also its (k+1)-th head m+1 cells forward. If A_1 accepts then A_2 accepts too. Moreover, A_2 accepts when its first head reaches the first symbol 2 and its (k+1)-th head reaches the endmarker simultaneously. ■

Proof of Theorem 1 for x=fa,ca. (a) follows immediately from Lemma 2 because $DFA(k) = DPDA(k,0)$ and $DCA(k) = DPDA(k,1)$. (b) follows from the following claim: For every $k > 0$, $l \geq 0$ $DPDA(k,l) \cap B_2 \subsetneq NFA(2) \cap B_2$. To prove this we recall that if $L \in DPDA(k,l)$ then L has the semilinear property [10,11]. But every such a 2-bounded language can be recognized by a nfa(2). We left the proof to the reader. This gives the inclusion. The inequality follows from Lemma 2. ■

Remark. Similarly as in Lemma 2, one can prove that for $k > 0$ $DFA(k) \cap B_2 \subsetneq DCA(k) \cap B_2$. ■

In order to finish the proof of Theorem 1 we prove first the following lemma.

Lemma 3. For each $k > 0$ $DPDA(k) \cap B_2 = DPDA(k,2k+1) \cap B_2$.

Proof (sketch). The inclusion ($\supseteq$) is obvious. To prove the other one observe that a dpda(k) A on a 2-bounded input must enter a cycle when increases the stack while the symbols scanned by the heads do not change. So the contents of the pushdown are always of the form

(a) $x_1 y_1^{r_1} z_1 x_2 y_2^{r_2} z_2 \ldots x_l y_l^{r_l} z_l$,

where $l = 2k+1$ (because there may be at most 2k changes of the symbols scanned by the heads) and the words x_i, y_i, z_i are from some finite set of words. A dpda(k,l) simulating A stores (a) as

$a_1^{r_1} a_2^{r_2} \ldots a_l^{r_l}$, and the x_i, y_i, z_i are stored in the memory. ■

The proof of Theorem 1 for x = pda. From Lemma 2 and Lemma 3 we obtain:

$$DPDA(k) \cap B_2 = DPDA(k,2k+1) \cap B_2 \subsetneq DPDA(k+1,2k+1) \cap B_2$$
$$\subseteq DPDA(k+1,2k+3) \cap B_2 = DPDA(k+1) \cap B_2.$$

This gives us Theorem 1 (a). The proof of (b) is analogous to the one for x = fa,ca. ■

The proof of Theorem 2. It is enough to prove that for every $k > 1$, $l \geq 0$ DPDA(k,l) is not closed under union, intersection and concatenation. From Lemma 1 there is m such that $L_m \in$ DPDA(k,l) but $L_{m+1} \notin$ DPDA(k,l). Obviously $L_{m+1} - L_m \in$ DPDA(k,l). But $L_{m+1} = L_m \cup (L_{m+1} - L_m)$, so DPDA(k,l) is not closed under union. Since DPDA(k,l) is closed under complement, it cannot be closed under intersection. Observing that for $L, L' \subseteq 1^*2^*$ $L \cup L' = (L \cup \{\varepsilon\})(L' \cup \{\varepsilon\}) \cap 1^*2^*$, we obtain that DPDA(k,l) is not closed under concatenation. ■

Final remarks. We have applied our technique to multihead deterministic finite, counter and pushdown automata. We believe that it is more general, that it can be applied to prove other hierarchies of languages providing that these languages are defined by deterministic automata and that they have the semilinear property. For example, only slight changes in our proof are necessary to prove results analogous to Theorem 1 and Theorem 2 for simple multihead automata [1,13] (not necessarily finite).

Our method cannot be applied to nondeterministic automata. This follows from the following, easily proved fact:

Fact. For every $n, k > 0$ $\mathrm{NPDA}(k) \cap B_n \subseteq \mathrm{NFA}(n) \cap B_n$.

Thus the classes $\mathrm{NPDA}(k) \cap B_n$ do not form an infinite hierarchy with respect to the number of heads. The same concerns finite and counter automata. We believe, however, that such a hierarchy exists when we let n depend on k.

Another drawback of our technique is that it is not effective, that is, we do not determine which L_m separates k-head and (k+1)-head automata languages, we only prove that it exists. The problem is to find the maximal n such that $L_n \in$ DPDA(k,l). We only know that this n is much greater than one would expect. For example: $L_2 \in$ DFA(2) and $L_{11} \in$ DFA(3).

In case of two-way automata the analogues of Theorem 1 (a) are already known [22,23,24], even for 1-bounded languages [25,26]. As for the problems (2) and (3), the only separation results known are these for 1-head counter machines in [21].

Acknowledgements. This paper is a part of my Ph.D. dissertation. I am grateful to prof. A. Salwicki and dr. W. Rytter for their help and comments. Because of the insufficiency of space I could not satisfy the requests of the referees to give more details of the proofs. I promise to do this in the full version of this paper which will appear elsewhere.

References

1. P.Ďuriš, J.Hromkovič, One-way simple multihead finite automata are not closed under concatenation, Theoret. Comput. Sci. 27 (1983) 121-125.
2. R.W.Floyd, Review 14,353 of 18 , Comput. Rev. 9 (1968) 280.
3. S.Ginsburg, The Mathematical Theory of Context-Free Languages, McGraw-Hill, New York, 1966.
4. S.Ginsburg, E.H.Spanier, Bounded Algol-like languages, Trans. Amer. Math. Soc. 113 (1963) 333-368.
5. S.Ginsburg, E.H.Spanier, Bounded regular sets, Proc. Amer. Math. Soc. 17 (1966) 1043-1049.
6. S.A.Greibach, An infinite hierarchy of context-free languages, J.Assoc. Comput. Mach. 16 (1969) 91-106.
7. M.A.Harrison, O.H.Ibarra, Multi-tape and multi-head pushdown automata, Inform. Control 13 (1968) 433-470.
8. J. Hromkovič, Closure properties of the family of languages recognized by one-way two-head deterministic finite state automata, Proc. 10th MFCS, Lecture Notes in Comput. Sci. 118, 1981, 304-313.
9. J.Hromkovič, One-way multihead deterministic finite automata, Acta Inform. 19 (1983) 377-384.
10. O.H.Ibarra, A note on semilinear sets and bounded reversal multihead pushdown automata, Inform. Proc. Letters 3 (1974) 25-28.
11. O.H.Ibarra, C.E.Kim, A useful device for showing the solvability of some decision problems, J. Comput. System Sci. 13 (1976) 153-160.
12. O.H.Ibarra, C.E.Kim, On 3-head versus 2-head finite automata, Acta Inform. 4 (1975) 193-200.
13. K.Inoue, I.Takanami, A.Nakamura, T.Ae, One-way simple multihead finite automata, Theoret. Comput. Sci. 9 (1979) 311-328.
14. S.Miyano, A hierarchy theorem for multihead stack-counter automata, Acta Inform. 17 (1982) 63-67.
15. S.Miyano, Remarks on multihead pushdown automata and multihead stack automata, J. Comput. System Sci. 27 (1983) 116-124.
16. T.F.Piatkowski, N-head finite-state machines, Ph.D. Dissertation, University of Michigan, 1963.
17. A.L.Rosenberg, Nonwriting extensions of finite automata, Ph.D. Dissertation, Harvard University, 1965.
18. A.L.Rosenberg, On multihead finite automata, IBM J. Res. Develop. 10 (1966) 388-394.
19. I.H.Sudborough, One-way multihead writing automata, Inform. Control 25 (1976) 1-20.

20. A.C.Yao, R.L.Rivest, k+1 heads are better than k, J. Assoc. Comput. Mach. 25 (1978) 337-340.
21. M.Chrobak, Variations on the technique of Duris and Galil, to appear in J. Comput. System Sci. 30 (1985).
22. O.H.Ibarra, Characterizations of some tape and time complexity classes of Turing machines in terms of multihead and auxiliary stack automata, J. Comput. System. Sci. 5 (1971) 88-117.
23. O.H.Ibarra, On two-way multihead automata, J. Comput. System Sci. 7 (1973) 28-37.
24. B.Monien, Transformational methods and their application to complexity problems, Acta Inform. 6 (1976) 67-80, Corrigenda: Acta Inform. 8 (1977) 95.
25. B.Monien, Two-way multihead automata over a one-letter alphabet, RAIRO Inform. Theoret. 14 (1980) 67-82.
26. J.I.Seiferas, Techniques for separating space complexity classes, J. Comput. System Sci. 14 (1977) 73-99.

Partitioning Point Sets in 4 Dimensions

Richard Cole†
Courant Institute of Mathematical Sciences
New York University
New York, NY 10012

Abstract: We introduce a new type of partition called a parallel planes partition. We prove there exists a parallel planes partition of any set of n points in 4 dimensions. This partition yields a data structure for the half-space retrieval problem in 4 dimensions; it has linear size and achieves a sublinear query time.

1. Introduction

The half-space retrieval problem is the following. Given a set of n points in d-dimensional Euclidean space, preprocess them so as to be able to answer queries of the following form: how many points lie in a given half space. (A variant of the problem, the *listing problem*, is to ask for a list of the points in the half space.) It is assumed that many such queries will be made. Thus it is reasonable to preprocess the set of points and to amortize the cost of this preprocessing over the (many) queries. What we are concerned with is the query time and the space used by the data structure for holding the preprocessed information. We note that a naive searching algorithm takes linear time. Thus we aim for a sublinear search time and a data structure using linear space.

Recently, an elegant approach to this problem was discovered by Willard [W]. There are two basic lemmas underlying his construction. First, a set of n points can be partitioned by two straight lines into 4 sets, so that each (open) set holds at most $n/4$ points. This leads to a recursive storage of the points in a 4-way balanced tree. Second, any line only intersects 3 of the 4 sets defined by the two partitioning lines. This implies that in carrying out a half-space query at most three of the four subtrees of the root need be explored further. Recursive application of this observation yields a sublinear search time. (it is convenient to speak of a line, or plane, *missing* a set S when the line, or plane, does not intersect S.)

By tuning his data structure (dividing the set into 6 equal parts with 3 lines, rather than 4 parts with 2 lines) Willard obtained a linear-sized data structure which allowed a query time of $O(n^{0.77})$. (Henceforth we will not refer to the size of the data structure, for it is always linear in this paper.) Subsequent work by Edelsbrunner and Welzl [EW] improved the search time to $O(n^{0.695})$.

Using the same approach Yao [Y1,Y2] obtained a similar result in 3 dimensions. She proved that any set of n points can be divided by 3 planes into 8 equal sized sets. This yields an algorithm for the half-space retrieval problem with a sublinear query time. Dobkin and Edelsbrunner [DE1,E] then further improved the algorithm that is derived from this partition, obtaining a search time of $O(n^{0.89})$.

---

†This work was supported in part by NSF grant DCR-84-01633 and by an IBM faculty development award.

In d-dimensions, we seek to partition the set of n points into 2^d subsets, using d hyperplanes, so that each subset contains at least αn points, for some constant $0 \le \alpha \le 2^d$. Such a partition would yield an algorithm for half space retrieval, with sublinear search time, similar to Willard's. Avis [A] showed that for $d \ge 5$ there exist sets of n points for which there is no such partition. While not proving that there is no algorithm with a sublinear search time, this result does have a somewhat negative flavor.

We show a partitioning result for sets of n points in 4 dimensions. We show that there is a partition (which we call a parallel planes partition) such that each of the 16 sets defined by the partition contains at least $n/32$ points (loosely speaking; we are more precise in the next section). This partition immediately yields an algorithm for the half-space retrieval problem in 4 dimensions with a query time of $O(n^{0.9767})$. Further applications of the partition result include the circle retrieval problem [Y] and other query problems [DE2]. Our work extends these results to one higher dimension; for example, our partition implies that there is an algorithm for the sphere retrieval problem with a sublinear query time.

An interesting aspect of our work is that the partition is not by 4 planes (in fact it uses parts of 8 planes). So the result proved by Avis is not applicable to our construction. This opens up the prospect of finding similar partitions for point sets in 5 or more dimensions. Also, it suggests one might look for other partitions enjoying the following properties:

(a) Every set in the partition should contain some constant fraction of the points.

(b) Any plane misses at least one of the sets defined by the partition.

We call such a partition a *separating partition*. A separating partition immediately yields an algorithm for half space retrieval, of the form given by Willard, having a sublinear search time. A caveat should be made here. In Willard's data structure it is necessary to be able to perform half space queries on the separating lines, if they contain any of the points. Similarly, to obtain an efficient algorithm from a class of separating partitions, we need to be able to perform half space queries on the separating surfaces, and these queries must be performed as fast as the general queries. (Our partition uses 3 dimensional planes for the separating surfaces, and for these surfaces the requirement is met.)

Recently and independently, A Yao and F. Yao showed that there exists a separating partition in d dimensions, for any d. Their partition divides the set of points into 2^d equal sized sets [Y3]. This result is stronger than the one presented in this paper.

There has been considerable related work in this area. The data structures we have been describing are static; Fredman has proved lower bounds on the complexity of dynamic data structures for this problem [F]. When considering the listing problem we often use a different measure for the query time, $Q(n)$. $Q(n)$ is chosen so that the time taken to report the s points in a half space is $O(s+Q(n))$. The goal has been to achieve a fast query time $Q(n)$, while dropping the requirement for the data structure to have linear size [CY,CGL]. We will not consider these problems further, however.

In the next section we describe the form of our partition, prove that it is separating, and deduce the search time for the resulting algorithm. In section 3 we prove the partition exists.

2. The Partition is Separating

We make the notion of a partition precise.

Definition: [Y1] Let S be a set of n points in d-dimensional space. A *partition* Π for S is a pair $(\mathbf{R},\mathbf{P})$, where $\mathbf{R}$ is a set of disjoint open regions and $\mathbf{P}$ is a set of $(d-1)$-dimensional surfaces, such that every point of S either lies in a region $R \in \mathbf{R}$, or on a surface $P \in \mathbf{P}$. A region $R \in \mathbf{R}$ is said to be a $\delta n-$*region* with respect to Π if at least δn points of S are contained in $R \bigcup_{P \in \mathbf{P}} P$ (i.e. the remaining open regions of $\mathbf{R}$ contain at most $(1-\delta)n$ points). We say $\Pi = (\mathbf{R},\mathbf{P})$ is a $\delta n-$*partition* if every $R \in \mathbf{R}$ is a δn-region.

We describe our partition next. As an aid to our intuition, we start by giving a partition Π of 3 dimensional space. We have 4 partitioning planes: P, Q, R_1, R_2 (see figure 1). R_1 and R_2 are parallel; further, we only use parts of the planes R_1 and R_2, as illustrated in figure 1. It is clear these surfaces define 8 disjoint, open regions.

Lemma 1: Any plane, M, intersects at most seven of the regions defined by Π.

Proof: The approach used in this proof, and in the proof of lemma 2, was suggested by Edelsbrunner [E]. Let us consider the intersection of P, Q, R_1, and R_2 with M; we refer to these intersections as P, Q, R_1 and R_2, where there will be no ambiguity. We will show that at most seven faces are defined on M; we can then deduce that M intersects at most seven of the regions defined by Π. Consider the four open sets in M defined by P and Q; we refer to these sets as quadrants. Let R be parallel to R_1 and R_2 and pass through $P \cap Q$. Then R does not intersect at least one pair of opposite quadrants. Only one of R_1 and R_2 can intersect either of the quadrants in this pair; without loss of generality suppose that R_1 is the only plane that intersects either of the quadrants in this pair. But R_1 can intersect at most one of the quadrants in this pair, since R_1 is parallel to R. We deduce that P, Q, R_1, and R_2 define at most seven faces on M. □

The partition Π in 4 dimensions uses 8 planes: P, Q, R_1, R_2, S_1, S_2, S_3, S_4. R_1 and R_2 are parallel, as are S_1, S_2, S_3, and S_4. P, Q, R_1, and R_2 have the same form as in the 3 dimensional case; let us label the 8 resulting regions, as before, as shown in figure 1 (we also label the four regions defined by P and Q as shown in figure 1). We keep just those parts of S_i that intersect the regions U_i and U_{4+i}, $1 \le i \le 4$; henceforth, when we refer to S_i (or R_j) we intend the surface consisting of the parts we have kept. Let W_{2j} and W_{2j-1} be the two regions obtained from partitioning U_j by S_i $(j=i,4+i)$, $1 \le i \le 4$.

Lemma 2: Any 3 dimensional hyperplane M intersects at most 15 of the 16 regions defined by Π.

Proof: Again, let P, Q, R_i, S_j refer to the intersection of these surfaces with M. We show that the planes P, Q, R_i, S_j define at most 15 regions on M, and deduce that M can intersect at most 15 of the regions defined by Π. Consider the eight open sets defined by the planes P, Q, R_1 and R_2; we refer to these sets as octants. Let R be parallel to R_1 and R_2. Fix R. P, Q, and R define a set of octants, that we associate in the natural way with the octants already defined. Consider the plane S, parallel to the planes S_j, passing through $P \cap Q \cap R$. S does not intersect at least one pair of opposite octants. Consider the corresponding pair of octants defined by P, Q, R_1, and R_2. Only one of the planes S_j can intersect either of the octants in this pair; without loss of generality suppose S_1 is this plane. But S_1 intersects at most one of these octants, since S_1 is parallel to S. Hence P, Q, R_1, and R_2 define at most 15 regions in M. □

In the next section we show there exists such an $n/32$-partition; we call it a *parallel planes partition.* We deduce

Lemma 3: There exists a linear size data structure for half space retrieval in 4 dimensions which allows a query time of $O(n^{0.9767})$.

Proof: The search structure is built as described in Willard's paper, and as outlined in the introduction. A bound $T(n)$, for the search time is given by the following recurrence.

$$T(n) = \max\,[c + \sum_{i=1}^{15} T(n_i) + \sum_{i=1}^{8} S(m_i)], \quad n \geq 2,$$

$$T(1) = c$$

where $\sum_{i=1}^{15} n_i \leq 31n/32$, $\sum_{i=1}^{15} n_i + \sum_{i=1}^{8} m_i \leq n$, $n/32 \leq n_i \leq 3n/32$, $S(m_i)$ is the time to carry out a half space query on a data structure for a 3 dimensional space containing m_i points, and c is a constant.

The right hand side is largest when $n_i = 31n/15\cdot 32$ and $m_i = n/8\cdot 32$, giving the solution

$$T(n) = 15T(31n/15\cdot 32) + O(n^{0.89}), \text{ or}$$

$$T(n) = O(n^\alpha), \text{ where } \alpha = \frac{\log 15}{\log 32\cdot 15/31}$$

that is, $T(n) = O(n^{0.9767})$.

3. Existence of the Partition

We show there is an $n/32$ parallel planes partition of any set S of n points in 4 dimensions. This section provides a proof of existence and not an algorithm. There are two major concerns in our construction. The first is to select each plane in such a way that it is unique. The second concern arises because our construction involves certain parameters which may vary. The concern is to ensure that the planes vary continuously with these parameters.

It is simpler to carry out our construction on a connected body for then we can use theorems from analysis. So we extend the definition of a δn-partition in the natural way to a set consisting of one, or several continuous bodies of total mass n. (The formal details are left to the reader.) As described in [DE1] we replace each point by a sphere of radius ϵ centered at that point; the sphere is of uniform density and has mass 1. ϵ is chosen sufficiently small so that if a plane intersects k of the spheres then there is a plane intersecting the corresponding k points. Call the new set the *sphere set.*

Lemma 4: [DE1] If there is a δn-partition Π' of the sphere set then there is a δn-partition Π of the point set S.

We transform the set further. Let B be a (large) rectangular box containing the spheres. The space in B, not occupied by spheres, is filled with matter of uniform density and total mass m ($<<1$). m is chosen so that $\lceil \delta n - m \rceil = \lceil \delta n \rceil$. (in our construction $\delta = 1/32$, so that $m = 1/100$ suffices.) Call this the *continuous set.*

Lemma 5: If there is a $\delta(n+m)$-partition Π' of the continuous set then there is a δn-partition of the point set S.

Proof: Clearly a $\delta(n+m)$-partition of the continuous set implies a $[\delta n-(1-\delta)m]$-partition of the sphere set, and hence of the point set S. On a point set this is a $(\lceil \delta n-(1-\delta)m \rceil)$-partition, which by assumption is a δn-partition. □

Thus to obtain our result it suffices to show that a body S, of mass n, has an $n/32$-partition. We use the following two lemmas in our construction.

Lemma 6: [W] Given a connected body S of mass n, in two dimensional Euclidean space, and given a line L forming an $n/2$-partition of S, there is a unique line K such that L and K form an $n/4$ partition. Furthermore, K varies continuously with L.

Willard did not prove exactly this theorem, but the proof would be identical to Willard's. The fact that S is connected guarantees uniqueness.

Lemma 7: (Borsuk-Ulum theorem [L]). Let f be a continuous function, f: $\mathbf{S}^d \to \mathbf{R}^d$. Then there is an $\underline{x}$ such that $f(\underline{x}) = f(-\underline{x})$.

Definition: f is an *even* function if for all $\underline{x}$, $f(\underline{x}) = -f(-\underline{x})$.

Corollary: If f is an even, continuous function, f: $\mathbf{S}^d \to \mathbf{R}^d$, then there is an $\underline{x}$ such that $f(\underline{x}) = f(-\underline{x}) = \underline{0}$.

We build the planes described in the previous section. At times we will project onto 2 or 3 dimensional spaces; where no ambiguity will result we will name by P the projection of P, etc. We construct P, Q, R_i, S_j, in turn.

We choose P to be the bisector of S normal to $\underline{w}$, a direction vector. We note P is unique, varies continuously with $\underline{w}$, and is reversed when $\underline{w}$ is reversed. We define the other planes, in part, in terms of $\underline{w}$ and a set of coordinate axes on P. Since we are going to vary $\underline{w}$, and we wish the coordinate axes to vary continuously, we need to show how to define the axes in terms of some original set of axes.

Let $\underline{w}$, $\underline{x}$, $\underline{y}$, $\underline{z}$ be the 4 mutually perpendicular axes. And let $\underline{w_0}$, $\underline{x_0}$, $\underline{y_0}$, and $\underline{z_0}$ be some initial set of mutually perpendicular axes. Suppose $\underline{w} = (a,b,c,d)$ (i.e. $\underline{w} = a\underline{w_0}+b\underline{x_0}+c\underline{y_0}+d\underline{z_0}$). Then we define $\underline{x}$, $\underline{y}$,

$\underline{z}$ to be, respectively, $(-b,a,-d,c)$, $(-c,d,a,-b)$, $(-d,-c,b,a)$. It is easy to check the 4 axes are perpendicular and that they vary continuously with $\underline{w}$. (We were guided by the definition of quaternions and we are indebted to Colm O'Dunlaing for suggesting this approach.)

It is convenient to use spherical coordinates to refer to the orientation of $\underline{w}$ with respect to the axis system $\underline{w_0}$, $\underline{x_0}$, $\underline{y_0}$, $\underline{z_0}$; let (θ,ϕ,ψ) be this orientation. It is clear P is unique and varies continuously with (θ,ϕ,ψ), since S is a connected body.

We choose Q to intersect P parallel to the $\underline{x}$ and $\underline{y}$ axes. In addition, we would like P and Q to form an $n/4$-partition. By projecting parallel to $\underline{x}$ and $\underline{y}$, this becomes the 2 dimensional problem described in lemma 6. We deduce such a Q exists and is unique. Further Q varies continuously with (θ,ϕ,ψ), and is reversed when this orientation is reversed.

We choose R_1 and R_2 so that P, Q, R_1 and R_2 form an $n/16$-partition. Before describing our choice of R_1 and R_2 it is convenient to give another definition and to prove a lemma. We generalize the notion of a k-hull/center introduced in [CSY,Y1].

Definition: The δm-hull of a body of mass m consists of the set of points p, such that any plane through p has mass $\geq \delta m$ to either side.

Lemma 8: A closed, compact body B of mass m in $\mathbf{R}^{d-1}$ has a non-empty m/d-hull.

Proof: We first show that the body has a non-empty $(m/d-\epsilon)$-hull, H_ϵ, for all $\epsilon>0$. We also show H_ϵ is compact. Since $H_\epsilon \supset H_\delta$, for $\epsilon>\delta$, we deduce $\bigcap_{\epsilon>0} H_\epsilon \neq \emptyset$. But $\bigcap_{\epsilon>0} H_\epsilon$ is the m/d-hull.

We show H_ϵ is non-empty. Consider the set Π consisting of the half spaces S, where S is defined by a $(d-1)$-dimensional plane, such that the mass of that part of the body in S is exactly $m/d+\epsilon$. Then the intersection of d of these spaces contains mass $\geq 5\epsilon$, and thus is non-empty. By Helly's theorem [YB], we deduce the intersection of all the half spaces is non-empty. But this intersection is contained in H_ϵ; hence H_ϵ is non-empty.

We now show H_ϵ is compact. We observe H_ϵ is closed (from the definition of ϵm-hulls). In addition, H_ϵ is contained in B, a compact set. So H_ϵ is compact. □

We are able to reduce the choice of R_1 and R_2 to a 3 dimensional problem. We do this by choosing R_1 and R_2 to intersect P parallel to the $\underline{x}$ axis. We then project parallel to the $\underline{x}$ axis. Recall R_1 and R_2 are parallel. Let K_l be the $n/4$-hull of T_l. Let c_l be the center of gravity of K_l, considered as a body of uniform density. Let $\underline{l_1}$ and $\underline{l_2}$ be the vectors parallel to the lines from c_1 to c_3 and from c_2 to c_4, respectively. We choose both R_1 and R_3 to be parallel to both $\underline{l_1}$ and $\underline{l_2}$; also we choose R_1 to pass through c_1 and c_3, while we choose R_2 to pass through c_2 and c_4. We note $\underline{l_1}$ and $\underline{l_2}$ are not parallel (for if they were, by projecting parallel to the $\underline{y}$-axis, which is not parallel to either $\underline{l_1}$ nor $\underline{l_2}$, we obtain the situation shown in figure 2, with $\underline{l_1}$ and $\underline{l_2}$ ostensibly parallel, a contradiction). Thus R_1 and R_2 are well defined planes. Clearly they are unique. Since the sets K_l (and thus the points c_l) vary continuously with (θ,ϕ,ψ), we deduce that R_1 and R_2 vary continuously with these angles also. Also R_1 and R_2 are reversed when (θ,ϕ,ψ) is reversed. Because R_1 and R_2

pass through c_1 and c_3, c_2 and c_4, respectively, we know that each set U_i, $1 \le i \le 8$, has mass $\ge m/16$, and $\le 3m/16$.

It remains to define the planes S_i. Recall that these planes are required to be parallel. So let $\underline{s}$ be the normal to the planes S_i. Let ρ be the angle between $\underline{s}$ and $\underline{r}$, the normal to the planes R_1 and R_2. By choosing the angles (ρ,θ,ϕ,ψ) appropriately, we aim to obtain planes S_i, such that S_i bisects both the sets U_i and U_{4+i}, $1 \le i \le 4$. It is convenient, in defining the planes S_i to normalize so that the sets U_j each have mass 1. We then define S_i, to be the unique plane bisecting $U_i \cup U_{4+i}$, $1 \le i \le 4$.

We have yet to explain how $\underline{s}$ is chosen. We want to choose $\underline{s}$ uniquely, given $\underline{r}$ and ρ; we achieve this by choosing $\underline{s}$ to lie in a plane determined by $\underline{r}$. Let $\underline{w}' = \underline{r}$, and suppose $\underline{x}'$, $\underline{y}'$, $\underline{z}'$ are defined in terms of $\underline{w}_0$, $\underline{x}_0$, $\underline{y}_0$, $\underline{z}_0$, in the same way as $\underline{x}$, $\underline{y}$, and $\underline{z}$ were, given $\underline{w}$. Then we restrict $\underline{s}$ to lie in the $\underline{w}'$-$\underline{z}'$-plane. So $\underline{s}$ is uniquely defined by $\underline{r}$ and ρ. Also, $\underline{s}$ varies continuously with (ρ,θ,ϕ,ψ), and hence so do the planes S_i, $1 \le i \le 4$. When (θ,ϕ,ψ) is reversed, since both $\underline{r}$ and the coordinate axes are reversed, $\underline{s}$ is also reversed. When ρ is also reversed, $\underline{s}$ is reversed again, and thus returns to its original orientation. Thus, when (ρ,θ,ϕ,ψ) is reversed, the planes P, Q, R_1, and R_2 are all reversed, while the planes S_i are unchanged.

We show how to choose the angles (ρ,θ,ϕ,ψ) so that each of the S_i are bisectors of the two sets U_i and U_{4+i}, $1 \le i \le 4$. We define a function $f(\rho,\theta,\phi,\psi)$, $f\colon \mathbf{S}^4 \to \mathbf{R}^4$, with f continuous and even. Thus we can apply the corollary to the Borsuk-Ulum theorem. f is chosen in such a way that when $f(\underline{x}) = \underline{0}$, the planes S_i bisect the sets U_j as required.

f is defined to be the vector (f_1,f_2,f_3,f_4); the f_i are defined below. Let S_i divide U_j ($= U_i$ or U_{4+i}) into W_{2j-1} and W_{2j}, with W_{2j} on the positive side of the dividing plane. Let t denote the (normalized) mass of the set T; by a normalized mass we intend the mass of the set T, where the mass of each set U_j is normalized to be equal to 1. We define $f_1(\underline{x}) = w_1(\underline{x}) - w_9(\underline{x})$, $f_2(\underline{x}) = w_3(\underline{x}) - w_{11}(\underline{x})$, $f_3(\underline{x}) = w_5(\underline{x}) - w_{13}(\underline{x})$, and $f_4(\underline{x}) = w_7(\underline{x}) - w_{15}(\underline{x})$.

Lemma 9: f is an even, continuous function.

Proof: It is clear f is continuous. We show $f_1(\underline{x}) = -f_1(-\underline{x})$. We note $w_1 + w_9 = w_2 + w_{10}$ (since S_1 bisects $U_1 \cup U_5$), and $w_1 + w_2 = w_9 + w_{10}$ (since $t_1 = t_3$). So $w_1 = w_{10}$ and $w_2 = w_9$. As observed above, when the orientation $\underline{x} = (\rho,\theta,\phi,\psi)$ is reversed the planes P, Q, R_1, and R_2 are all reversed, while the planes S_i have the same orientation. Hence $U_i(-\underline{x}) = U_{i+4}(\underline{x})$ and $U_{i+4}(-\underline{x}) = U_i(\underline{x})$, $1 \le i \le 4$, while $W_i(-\underline{x}) = W_{i+8}(\underline{x})$ and $W_{i+8}(-\underline{x}) = W_i(\underline{x})$, $1 \le i \le 8$. It follows that $f_1(-\underline{x}) = w_1(-\underline{x}) - w_9(-\underline{x}) = w_9(\underline{x}) - w_1(\underline{x}) = -f_1(\underline{x})$; similarly for f_2, f_3, and f_4. We deduce f is even. □

When $\rho = 0$ or π, $\underline{r}$ and $\underline{s}$ are parallel, so f remains constant despite any variation of (θ,ϕ,ψ). Hence $f\colon \mathbf{S}^4 \to \mathbf{R}^4$. Applying the corollary to the Borsuk-Ulum theorem we deduce there is a value $\underline{x}$ such that $f(\underline{x}) = \underline{0}$. But then $f_1(\underline{x}) = 0$ so $w_1 = w_9$, which implies $w_1 = w_2$. Similarly, all the other sets U_j are bisected. Since the mass of U_j lies between $m/16$ and $3m/16$, it follows that the mass of each W_i lies between $n/32$ and $3n/32$. We deduce

Theorem: The planes P, Q, R_i, S_j, $1 \le i \le 2$, $1 \le j \le 4$, form an $n/32$-partition.

We briefly discuss an algorithm for finding a parallel planes partition. It is clear that any parallel planes partition can be transformed while maintaining the following two properties:

(a) The points in the closure of each region defined by the partition are unchanged.

(b) Each of the following planes passes through at least 4 points: P, Q, at least one of the R_i, and at least one of the S_j.

This implies that there are only $O(n^{16})$ possibilities to check, thereby giving a polynomial time algorithm. It seems likely that there should be a more efficient algorithm. One possibility is to try to apply Megiddo's technique [M], as illustrated in [CSY].

References

[A] D. Avis, Non-Partitionable Point Sets, manuscript, McGill University.

[CSY] R. Cole, M. Sharir, C. Yap, On *k*-hulls and Related Problems, STOC, 1984, pp.154-166.

[CGL] B. Chazelle, L. Guibas, D. Lee, The Power of Geometric Duality, FOCS, 1983, pp.217-225.

[DE1] D. Dobkin and H. Edelsbrunner, Organizing Points in Two and Three Dimensions, manuscript.

[DE2] D. Dobkin and H. Edelsbrunner, Space Searching for Intersecting Objects, FOCS, 1984, pp.387-392.

[E] H. Edelsbrunner, private communication.

[EW] H. Edelsbrunner and E. Welzl, Halfplane Range Search in Linear Space and $O(n^{0.695})$ query time, Tech. Rep. F111, Graz University, 1982.

[F] M. Fredman, The Inherent Complexity of Dynamic Data Structures which Accommodate Range Queries, FOCS, 1980, pp.191-199.

[L] S. Lefschetz, Introduction to Topology, Princeton University Press.

[M] N. Megiddo, Applying Parallel Computation Algorithms in the Design of Serial Algorithms, 4(1983), pp.852-865.

[W] D. Willard, Polygon Retrieval, *SIAM J. Comput.*, 11(1982), pp.149-165.

[Y1] F. Yao, A 3-Space Partition and its Applications, Proc. 15th STOC, 1983, pp. 258-263.

[Y2] F. Yao, private communication.

[Y3] F. Yao, private communication, to appear, with A. Yao, in STOC 85.

[YB] I. M. Yaglom and V.G. Boltyanskii, Convex Figures, Holt, Rinehart and Winston, Translation (1961).

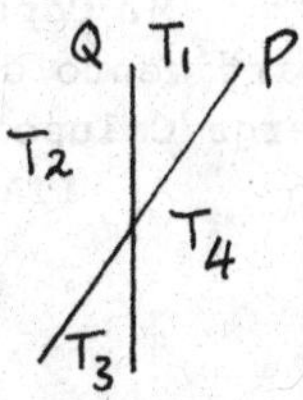

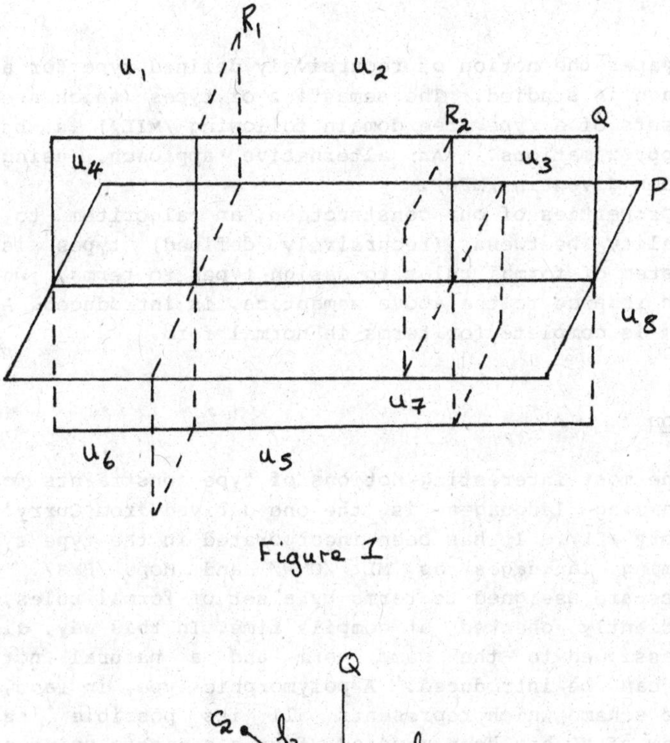

Figure 1

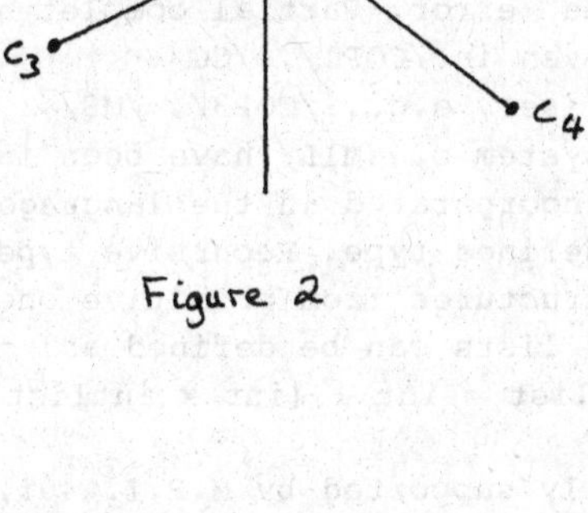

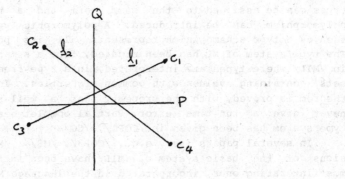

Figure 2

A COMPLETENESS THEOREM FOR RECURSIVELY DEFINED TYPES

M. Coppo (*)
Dipartimento di Informatica
V. Valperga Caluso 37 - 10125 Torino
ITALY

Abstract

In this paper the notion of recursively defined type for a functional language is studied. The semantics of types (which are interpreted as subsets of a type-free domain following /MIL/) is built by successive approximations. An alternative approach, using metic spaces, has been given in /MPS/.

Using the properties of our construction, an algorithm to decide semantic equality beetween (recursively defined) types is given. Moreover a system of formal rules to assign types to terms, which is complete with respect to the above semantics, is introduced. A recursive subsystem is complete for terms in normal form.

1. Introduction

One of the most interesting notions of type constraints for functional programming languages is the one derived from Curry's Functionality Theory /CF/. It has been incorporated in the type system of some programming languages as ML /GMW/ and Hope /BMS/. In this approach types are assigned to terms by a set of formal rules, which can be efficiently checked at compile time. In this way, different types can be assigned to the same term and a natural notion of polymorphism can be introduced. A polymorphic type, in fact, can be seen as a type scheme which represents all its possible instances. The type system of ML has been studied, from a semantic point of view, in /MIL/ where types are interpreted, in a type-free domain, as subsets containing values with common properties. In /MIL/ a soundness theorem is proved, with the property that a well-typed program can never give a run-time error. Partial completeness results for this type system has been given in /COP1/, /CG/.

In several papers (see, e.g., /COP3/, /MS/, /MPS/) some extensions of the basic system of /MIL/ have been introduced. One of the most intersting ones, incorporated in the language ML itself, is the notion of recursively defined type. Recursive types allows the definition of complex data structures from primitive ones. For example ,in ML, the type of integer lists can be defined as:

intlist = int + (int x intlist)

(*) Research partially supported by M.P.I. 40%, Gruppo Nazionale su Architetture e Linguaggi per la Programmazione Logica e Funzionale.

where int is the basic type of integers and +, x denote the operators of disjoint sum and cartesian product. Recursive types can be also used to overcome some limitations of the basic system. For example (we borrow this example from /MOR/, /MPS/), in the basic system no type can be assigned to the fixpoint combinator

$$Y = \lambda f.(\lambda x.f(xx))(\lambda x.f(xx))$$

However, if we introduce a new type $\emptyset$ satisfying

$$\emptyset = \emptyset\text{->}\mu$$

(where μ represents an arbitrary type and $\emptyset\text{->}\mu$ is the type of all functions which map elements of type $\emptyset$ into elements of type μ) we can assign type $(\mu\text{->}\mu)\text{->}\mu$ to Y in the following way. Let $e{:}\mu$ denote the assignment of type μ to term e. Assuming $x{:}\emptyset$ $(=\emptyset\text{->}\mu)$ (where x is a variable) we have $(xx){:}\mu$. Then, assuming $f{:}\mu\text{->}\mu$, we have $f(xx){:}\mu$ and $\lambda x.f(xx){:}\emptyset\text{->}\mu$ $(=\emptyset)$ (see section 4 for a formal definition of type assignment rules). This last statement implies $(\lambda x.f(xx))(\lambda x.f(xx)){:}\mu$ and, then, $Y = \lambda f.(\lambda x.f(xx))(\lambda x.f(xx)){:}(\mu\text{->}\mu)\text{->}\mu$.

The problem of giving an interpretation to recursive types is not a trivial one. It has been first solved by McQueen, Plotkin and Sethi /MPS/ by introducing a metric on the space of ideals over the semantic domain and by defining the interpretation of a recursive type as the fixpoint of a continuous and contracting function on this space. The motivations for the introduction of a metric topology is the fact that the function type constructor -> is not monotonic in its first argument with respect to the ordering of ideals given by set inclusion and, then, -> is not continuous in the Scott topology over the domain of ideals. A more general approach is that of Cartwright /CAR/, who introduces a richer domain of intervals where ideals corresponds to maximal (and incomparable) elements. In this domain the type constructor -> is continuous and a fixpoint construction can be used to solve recursive type equations.

In this paper we will introduce a different (and, in the author's opinion, more intuitive) method to give an interpretation to recursive types by defining it by successive approximations following, in some sense, the construction of the semantic domain. Also in our approach, however, types will turn out to be ideals and we will easily prove that each type equation has a unique solution. By this result our interpretation of types and the ones of /MPS/, /CAR/ coincide.

Using the properties of our construction we will also show that the problem of deciding the (semantic) equality of two (recursively defined) types can be reduced to the problem of deciding the equality of two (possibly infinite) regular trees, which is well-known to be recursive. Moreover, in section 4, we will introduce a formal system to assign types to terms which is complete with respect to the above semantics. This system, in its full formulation, is not recursive. Hovever, we can extract a recursive subsystem (defined by the usual type assignment rules /MIL/ plus a rule to handle type equality) which is complete for terms in normal form.

In order to avoid unnecessary technical complications we will prove these results for a language in which the only type constructor is ->. They can easily be extended to other type constructors, like x (cartesian product) and + (disjoint sum). Only disjoint sum causes some technical difficulties in the proof of the completeness theorem, which can be overcome using the technique of /CG/.

Lastly, our definition of type semantics should be generalizable without much difficulty to a type language containig universal and existential quantifiers over types (as in /MPS/). This richer language includes also the notion of polymorphism as intended in ML /MIL/. On the other hand, we do not know if (the natural extension of) our type assignment system is complete also for this language.

The complete proofs of the results are given in /COP4/.

2. The language and its semantics.

In this section we will introduce a simple functional language with its semantics. We will also recall some properties of the domain construction which are useful in the following.

Syntax

The set of expressions of our language is defined by

$$e ::= V \mid C \mid (e_1 e_2) \mid \lambda x.e \mid \text{fix } x.e$$

where V is a set of variables and C a set of constants. We assume that C contains integer and boolean constants as well as the usual primitive first-order functions on them.

Semantics

Let N^+ and T^+ be the complete lattices obtained respectively from the sets of integers and boolean values by adding to each a bottom (⊥) and top (⊤) element, and $W = \{ ? \}$ be a one-point lattice. The semantic domain D satisfies the equation

$$D = N^+ + T^+ + W + [D\text{->}D]$$

where + represents disjoint sum and [D->D] is the space of all continuous functions (in Scott topology) form D to D. The use of lattices instead of the more usual c.p.o.s (/MIL/, /MPS/) is needed only to overcome some thecnical difficulties in the proof of the completeness theorem stated in section 4. All other results hold in general for c.p.o.s. The domain D is built using the classical Scott's inverse limit construction (/SCO/, see also /PLO/ for a more general category-theoretic setting). We assume the reader to be acquainted with Scott's construction. We will shortly survey it to fix notations.

Starting from $D_0 = \{\bot\}$ a chain of approximations of D is built by defining $D_{n+1} = N^+ + T^+ + W + [D_n\text{->}D_n]$ and embedding each D_n in D_{n+1} by a suitable projection pair (i_n, j_n) where $i_n:[D_n\text{->}D_{n+1}]$ and $j_n:[D_{n+1}\text{->}D_n]$. The inverse limit of this chain can be defined as the domain $D = \{\langle x_n \rangle_{n\varepsilon\omega} \mid x_n = j_n(x_{n+1})\}$. Each D_n can be embedded in D. If $x\varepsilon D$ we identify x_n with its projection in D. So we have $x = \bigcup\{x_n \mid n\varepsilon\omega\}$ and, if $n < k$, $D_n \subseteq D_k \subseteq D$. Lastly, to simplify notations, we will identify the elements of N^+, T^+, W, $[D\text{->}D]$ with their projections in D.

The semantics of our language is given in the standard denotational style (see /STO/). Let H:C->D be an interpretation of constants and *:DxD->D be defined as

$$x_1 * x_2 = x_1 \in [D\text{->}D] \text{ -> } x_1(x_2), ?$$

The semantic equations are the following (where r:V->D is an environment)

1. $[c]_r = H(c)$ for $c\in C$
2. $[x]_r = r(x)$ for $x\in V$
3. $[e_1 e_2]_r = [e_1]_r * [e_2]_r$
4. $[\lambda x.e]_r = \lambda v.[e]_{r[v/x]}$
5. $[\text{fix } x.e]_r = Y[\lambda x.e]_r$

where $Y = \bigcup\{\lambda f.f^n(\bot) \mid n\in\omega\}$ is the least fixed point operator on D. Equation 3 specify a call-by-name semantics. However this choice is essential only in the proof of the completeness theorem (in its full formulation), to assure invariance of interpretations of terms under reduction. All other results hold also for call-by-value semantics (as defined, for example, in /MIL/).

3. Types

Syntax

Let $R = \{\phi_1,\dots,\phi_n\}$ be a finite set of type variables and K be a finite set of type constants (in this paper we assume K ={ int, bool}). The set $T_{K,R}$ of types over K, R (ranged over by μ,ν,ρ) is defined by

$$\mu ::= R \mid K \mid \mu_1\text{->}\mu_2$$

A <u>system of type equations</u> (over R) is a set E of equations of the shape $\phi_i = \mu_i[\phi_1,\dots,\phi_n]$ $(1\le i\le n)$ where $\mu_i[\phi_1,\dots\phi_n] \in T_{K,R}$ denotes a type with (possible) occurrences of $\phi_1,\dots,\phi_n$.

For example, $E_1 = \{\ \phi_1=\text{int}\text{->}\phi_2\ ,\ \phi_2=\phi_1\text{->}\phi_2\ \}$ is a system of type equations over $\{\phi_1\ ,\ \phi_2\}$.

We will use $\equiv$ to denote syntactic identity. Let E be a system of type equations (over R), the relation $\simeq_E \subseteq T_{K,R}\times T_{K,R}$ is defined by

$\mu\simeq_E\nu$ iff either $\mu\notin R$ and $\mu\equiv\nu$
or $\mu\equiv\phi$ for some $\phi\in R$ and $\phi=\nu \in E$

In the following we will assume E to be understood and we will write simply $\simeq$ instead of $\simeq_E$.

Semantics

Following /MIL/, /COP1/, /MPS/ types will be interpreted as subsets of the domain D. Let $[\mu]$ denote the interpretation of type μ. Basic types are interpreted in the following way

$[\text{int}] = \{d \mid d=\bot \text{ or } d\in N^+ \text{ and } d\neq T_N\}$
$[\text{bool}] = \{d \mid d=\bot \text{ or } d\in T^+ \text{ and } d\neq T_T\}$

where T_N, T_T are, respectively, the top elements of N^+, T^+. Our interpretation of types will be consistent with the usual interpretation of -> (/MIL/, /MPS/), in the sense that $[\mu\text{->}\nu] = [\mu]\text{->}[\nu]$ where if $A, B \subseteq D$, the subset $A\text{->}B \subseteq D$ is defined by

$$A\text{->}B = \{d \mid d=\bot \text{ or } d\varepsilon[D\text{->}D] \text{ and } \forall e\varepsilon A\ d(e)\varepsilon B\}$$

Type interpretations are built by successive approximations. Let $A_n, B_n \subseteq D_n$. Define $A_n\text{->}^{n+1}B_n \subseteq D_{n+1}$ in the following way

$$A_n\text{->}^{n+1}B_n = \{d\varepsilon D_{n+1} \mid d=\bot \text{ or } d\varepsilon[D_n\text{->}D_n] \text{ and } \forall e\varepsilon A_n\ d(e)\varepsilon B_n\}$$

For all integers n and tpyes $\mu\varepsilon T_{K,R}$, now, we define $[\mu]^n$ (the approximation of $[\mu]$ in D_n) in the following way

1. $[\mu]^0=\{\bot\}$ for all $\mu\varepsilon T_{K,R}$
2. $[int]^{n+1}= [int]$
   $[bool]^{n+1}= [bool]$
3. if $\mu\tilde{=}\nu\text{->}\rho$ then $[\mu]^{n+1}= [\nu]^n\text{->}^{n+1}[\rho]^n$.

For example, if $\emptyset=\emptyset\text{->}\emptyset\ \varepsilon\ E$, we define

$$[\emptyset]^0= \{\bot\} \quad , \quad [\emptyset]^1= [\emptyset]^0\text{->}^1[\emptyset]^0= \{\ \bot,\ \lambda x.\bot\ \}\ \ldots$$

The interpretation of type μ is then defined by

$$[\mu] = \{\ x \mid \forall n\varepsilon\,\omega\ \ x_n\varepsilon[\mu]^n\}\ .$$

The fitness of this definition is assured by the following results.

3.1 Lemma. (i) $[\mu]^n$ is an ideal (i.e. a downward closed, directed complete subset) in D_n.
(ii) $[\mu]_n \subseteq [\mu]_{n+1}$.

3.2 Theorem. (i) $[\mu]$ is an ideal in D.
(ii) If $\mu \tilde{=} \nu\text{->}\rho$ then $[\mu] = [\nu]\text{->}[\rho]$.

Theorem 3.2(ii) proves that the interpretation of types satisfies the equations in E. Indeed, given a set E of equations, there is a unique way of interpretig types with ideals , consistent with the interpretations of basic types and of -> , which satisfies E.

3.3 Theorem. Let $[\ ]^*$ be any interpretation of types satisfying E and such that, for all types μ, $[\mu]^*$ is an ideal. Then $[\mu]^* = [\mu]$.

By this theorem our interpretation of types and the one of /MPS/ coincide. Lastly, as in /MIL/ , /MPS/ we can easily show that neither ? nor (in our case) belong to any type.

Properties of type equality

In the last part of this section we show that semantic equality between types is easily decidable. Given a system of type equations E over R and $\mu, \nu\ \varepsilon\ T_{K,R}$ define

$$\mu\tilde{=}\nu \text{ iff } [\mu]=[\nu]$$

The relation $\tilde{=}$ is obviously closed under substitution of type variables with the r.h.s. of the corresponding equations in E, but this is not enough to characterize it. Take, for instance, $E_2 = \{ \emptyset_1 = \emptyset_2 \to \emptyset_1 , \emptyset_2 = \emptyset_1 \to \emptyset_2 \}$. We can easily show $\emptyset_1 \cong \emptyset_2$ but this cannot be proved by substitution.

A type system E over R can be interpreted as a set of regular equations between trees /COU/ or, equivalently, as a system of fix-point equations /CKV/. Let $K' = K \cup \{\bot\}$, where $\bot$ is a new constant with obvious meaning, and define, for each type $\mu \varepsilon T_{K,R}$ and integer n, the term μ_n over $K' \cup \{\to\}$ in the following way

1. $\mu_0 = \bot$ for all $\mu \varepsilon T_{K,R}$
2. $int_{n+1} = int$, $bool_{n+1} = bool$
3. If $\mu \cong \nu \to \rho$ then $\mu_{n+1} = \nu_n \to \rho_n$

μ_n can be seen as a labelled tree (with labels over $K' \cup \{\to\}$) of maximum depth n. As it is well known /CKV/, in the continuous term algebra over $K' \cup \{\to\}$ each type μ can be interpreted as the (possibly infinite) tree $t(\mu)$ defined by $t(\mu) = \bigsqcup \{ \mu_n | n \varepsilon \omega \}$. In the system of type equations E_2 , for example, we have $(\emptyset_1)_2 = (\bot \to \bot) \to \bot \to \bot$ and it is easy to see that $t(\emptyset_1) = \{ \bot, \bot \to \bot , (\bot \to \bot) \to \bot \to \bot ,\ldots\} = t(\emptyset_2)$.

The interpretation of types can be easily extended to terms of $T_{K'}$ by assuming $[\![\bot]\!] = \{\bot\}$. So we have $[\![\mu]\!]^n = [\![\mu_n]\!]^n$, where $\mu \varepsilon T_{K,R}$. It is then obious that $t(\mu) = t(\nu)$ impliy $\mu \cong \nu$. It is not hard to prove that also the converse is true

3.4 Theorem. Let $\mu, \nu \ \varepsilon \ T_{K,R}$ .Then $\mu \cong \nu$ iff $t(\mu) = t(\nu)$.

$t(\mu) = t(\nu)$ is known to be a recursive predicate /CKV/, hence $\cong$ is recursive. Actually the algorithm to decide $t(\mu) = t(\nu)$ is quite simple and efficient, and suitable for practical purposes.

4. Type assignment.

In this section we will introduce a complete set of formal rules to assign types to terms. To get completeness (with respect to the above semantics) we must introduce an infinitary rule (APP) and, hence, our system will not be decidable. By eliminating rule (APP), we obtain a subsystem which is complete only for a subset of terms. The present formulation of the type assignment system follows /COP2/, to which we refer for more motivations and insight.

To define rule (APP) we need the notion of set of approximants of a term. let --> indicate the notion of β-reduction of the lambda-calculus /BAR/, extended by assumig fix x.e --> e[fix x.e/x]. We will always consider terms modulo α-conversions of bound variables. A term is in normal form iff it is irreducible.

Let Ω be a new constant. The set of approximate normal forms (ranged over by a) is defined as the minimal set N containing $V \cup C \cup \{\Omega\}$ and such that $\lambda x.a \ \varepsilon \ N$, $ca_1 \ldots a_n$, $xa_1 \ldots a_n \ \varepsilon \ N$ (n>0) whenever $a, a_1, \ldots, a_n \ \varepsilon \ N$. The approximant $\omega(e) \varepsilon N$ of a term e is defined by

1. $\omega(\Theta e_1 \ldots e_n) = \Theta\, \omega(e_1) \ldots \omega(e_n)$ $(n \geq 0 , \Theta \ \varepsilon \ V \cup C)$
2. $\omega(\lambda x.e) = \lambda x.\omega(e)$

3. $\omega((\lambda x.e)e_1 \ldots e_n) = \Omega \quad (n>0)$
4. $\omega((\text{fix } x.e)e_1 \ldots e_n) = \Omega \quad (n \geq 0)$.

Observe that we do not assume $\lambda x.\Omega = \Omega$, as in other notions of approximation /HYL/. In fact, in D, $\lambda v.\perp$ do not coincide with $\perp$. The set of approximants A(e) of a term e is defined by

$$A(e) = \{ a \mid e \dashrightarrow e' \text{ and } a = \omega(e') \}$$

In call-by-name semantics the value $[e]_r$ of a term e (in an environment r) is preserved by reduction. Moreover, for each term e, the set $\{ [a]_r \mid a \in A(e) \}$ is directed and its l.u.b. is $[e]_r$.

4.1 Theorem. $[e]_r = \bigcup \{ [a]_r \mid a \in A(e) \}$.

A similar result has been proved, for a syntactic model, in /LEV/. A proof for interpretations in D can be given following the method of Wadsworth and Hyland /HYL/ for models of the pure lambda-calculus.

We can now give the formal rules to assign types to terms and to approximate normal forms. Let $e:\mu$ denote the assignment of type μ to term e. A basis B is a set of assignments $x:\mu$, where $x \in V$, which represent the assumptions of a deduction. We assume that to each constant $c \in C$ it is assigned a type $\tau(c)$. An assertion $B \vdash e:\mu$ means that type μ is deducible for e from the assumptions in B. The formal rules for type assignment, written in the style of /DM/, are the following.

(ASS) $\quad \dfrac{}{B \vdash x:\mu} \quad$ if $x:\mu \in B$

(CON) $\quad \dfrac{}{B \vdash c:\tau(c)} \quad$ where $c \in C$

(UND) $\quad \dfrac{}{B \vdash \Omega:\mu} \quad$ for all types $\mu \in T_{K,R}$

(->I) $\quad \dfrac{B \cup \{x:\mu\} \vdash e:\nu}{B \vdash \lambda x.e:\mu \to \nu}$

(->E) $\quad \dfrac{B \vdash e_1:\mu \to \nu \qquad B \vdash e_2:\mu}{B \vdash (e_1 e_2):\nu}$

(EQT) $\quad \dfrac{B \vdash e:\mu \qquad \mu \cong \nu}{B \vdash e:\nu}$

(APP) $\quad \dfrac{B \vdash a:\mu \quad \text{for all } a \in A(e)}{B \vdash e:\mu}$

Rule (EQT) is meaningful since we have proved that $\cong$ is a decidable relation. Rule (UND) is motivated by the fact that $\perp \in [\mu]$ for all types μ (recall that ideals are downward closed), while rule (APP) is motivated by the approximation theorem and the fact that type interpretatins are directed complete.

Obviously B $|-$ e:μ is not a recursive predicate. Indeed it is Π_1^0 complete (see /COP2/). We can define a more effective subsystem by deleting rules (UND) (and (APP)). This subsystem contains the usual type assignment rules (/MIL/, /DM/) plus rule (EQT) to handle type equality. Let $|-_0$ denote formal derivability in it. In this system we have no way to assign types to terms of the shape fix x.e , so we must drop this kind of expressions from our language. Using the decidability of ≅ , we can easily prove that $|-_0$ is recursive for terms in normal form. We conjecture that it is recursive also for arbitrary terms without occurrences of the fix operator.

In ML /MIL/, types can be assigned to terms of the shape fix x.e by a rule

$$\text{(FIX)}\quad \frac{B \cup \{x:\mu\} \;|\!-\; e:\mu}{B \;|\!-\; \text{fix } x.e:\mu}$$

We have not introduced this rule since, here, we are mainly interested in completeness properties and rule (FIX) is not complete (see /COP1/ for examples).

In the introduction we have given an informal proof of $|-_0$ Y:(μ->μ)->μ assuming ∅=∅->μ . Note that, using rule (APP), we can prove $|-$ Y:(μ->μ)->μ without assuming any type equation. In fact we have A(Y) = { $\lambda f.f^n(\Omega)$ | $n \varepsilon \omega$} and we can easily prove $|-\lambda f.f^n(\Omega)$:(μ->μ)->μ for all n (using rule (UND) to assign type μ to Ω).

We say that an environment r <u>respects</u> a basis B iff r(x)ε[μ] whenever x:μ ε B . The semantic counterpart |= of |- is then defined by

$$B \;|\!=\; e:\mu \quad \text{iff} \quad \text{for all } r \text{ respecting } B\ [\![e]\!]_r \varepsilon [\mu].$$

The soundness of the formal system can be proved by induction using 3.2 and 4.1.

<u>4.2</u> <u>Theorem</u>. B |- e:μ => B |= e:μ .

By soundness a typed term cannot denote ? or ⊤ .

To prove the completeness of the system we must put some (rather weak) restrictions on the interpretations of constants in C. Let μ be a basic or first order type (μ is a first order type iff μ = k->ν where k is a basic type and ν is either a basic or a first order type). A value vε[μ] <u>strongly</u> <u>belongs</u> to type μ (notation: $v\varepsilon_s[\mu]$) iff

1. v ≠ ⊥
2. if μ = k->ν then $\forall v' \notin [k]\ v(v')=?$ and $\forall v' \varepsilon_s [k]\ v(v') \varepsilon_s [\nu]$.

An interpretation of constants is <u>well</u> <u>behaved</u> iff, for all cεC, τ(c) is either a basic or a first-order type and $H(c)\varepsilon_s[\tau(c)]$. In the statements of Theorem 4.3 and Corollary 4.4 we assume that the interpretation of constants is well-behaved.

4.3 Theorem. $B \models e:\mu \Rightarrow B \vdash e:\mu$.

As a simple consequence of the proof of theorem 4.3 we have the following partial completeness result for the system $\vdash_0$.

4.4 Corollary. If e is in normal form then $B \models e:\mu \Rightarrow B \vdash_0 e:\mu$.

This result holds also for call-by-value semantics.

The proof of the completeness theorem uses a technique introduced in /COP1/, /COP2/. The main idea is to associate to each type μ an element $t_\mu \varepsilon [\mu]$ such that $t_\mu \varepsilon [\nu]$ implies $\mu \cong \nu$. Then, given a basis B, we define r_B as the environment such that $r_B(x)=t_\mu$ iff $x:\mu \ \varepsilon$ B and $r_B=\top$ otherwise. We can then prove that $[e]_{r_B} \varepsilon [\mu]$ iff $B \vdash e:\mu$. The completeness theorem follows immediately.

Note that our formulation of rule (EQT) is essential to get a complete system. For example, in the system E_2 introduced in section 3, we have $\{x:\phi_2\} \models x:\phi_1$ and we need rule (EQT) to prove $\{x:\phi_2\} \vdash x:\phi_1$. If we eliminate rule (EQT), we get a type assignment system which is complete for the basic type system (i.e. without type equations).

References

/BAR/ H. Barendregt - The lambda-calculus: its syntax and semantics. North-Holland 1981.

/BMS/ R. Burstall, D. Mc Queen, D. Sannella - Hope: an experimental applicative language. Proc. of the Lisp Conference, Stanford (1980), 136-143.

/CAR/ R. Cartwright - Types as intervals. Proc. of 12-th ACM Symposium on Principles of Programming Languages, New Orleans (1985).

/CKV/ B. Courcelle, G. Kanh, J. Vuillemin - Algoritmes d'equivalence et de reduction a des expressions minimales, dans une class d'equations recorsives simples. Proc. of ICALP '74, Lecture Notes in Computer Science 14, Springer-Verlag, 200-213.

/COP1/ M. Coppo - On the semantics of polymorphism. Acta Informatica 20 (1983), 159-170.

/COP2/ M. Coppo - Completeness of type assignment in continuous lambda models. Theoret. Comput. Sci. 29 (1984), 309-324.

/COP3/ M. Coppo - An extended polymorphic type system for applicative languages. Proc of MFCS '80, Lecture Notes in Computer Science 88, Springer-Verlag, 194-204.

/COP4/ M. Coppo - A completeness theorem for recursively defined types. Internal report, University of Turin (1984).

/CG/ M. Coppo, E. Giovannetti - Completeness results for a polymorphic type system. proc. of CAAP '83, Lecture Notes in Computer Science 159, Springer-Verlag, 179-190.

/COU/ B. Courcelle - Fundamental propeties of infinite trees. Theoret. Comput. Sci 25 (1983), 95-169.

/CF/ H. Curry, R. Feys - Combinatory Logic I. North-Holland 1958.

/DM/ L. Damas, R. Milner - Principal type schemes for functional programs. Proc. of 9-th ACM Symposium on Principles of Programming Languages, Albuquerque (1982).

/GMW/ M. Gordon, R. Milner, C. Wadsworth - Edinburgh LCF. Lecture Notes in Computer Science 78, Springer-Verlag 1979.

/HYL/ J. Hyland - A syntactic characterization of the equality in some models of the lambda-calculus. J. London Math. Soc. 12 (2) (1976), 361-370.

/LEV/ J. Levy - An algebraic interpretation of the λ- β-K-calculus and an application to a labelled λ-calculus. Theoret. Comput. Sci. 2 (1976), 97-114.

/MIL/ R. Milner - A thery of type polymorphism in programming. J. Comput. System Sci. 17 (1978), 348-375.

/MOR/ J. Morris - Lambda-calculus models of programming languages. Ph. D. Thesis, Sloan Scool of Management, MIT(1968).

/MPS/ D. Mc Queen, G. Plotkin, R. Sethi - An ideal model for recursive polymorphic types. Proc. of the 11-th ACM Symposium on Principles of Programming Languages, 165-174.

/MS/ D. Mc Queen, R. Sethi - A higher order polymorphic type system for applicative languages. Proc. of 1982 Symposium on Lisp and Functional Programming, 243-252.

/PLO/ G. Plotkin - The category of complete partial orders: a tool for making meanings. Summer Scool on Foundations of Artificial Intelligence and Computer Science, Pisa 1978.

/SCO/ D. Scott - Continuous lattices - in F. Lawvere ed., Toposes Algebraic Geometry and Logic, Lecture Notes in Mathematics 274, Springer-Verlag 1972, 97-136.

/STO/ J. Stoy - Denotational Semantics. MIT Press 1977.

CATEGORICAL COMBINATORY LOGIC

P-L. Curien

CNRS-Université Paris VII, LITP, Tour 55-56 1er étage,
3 Place Jussieu, 75221 PARIS CEDEX 05

ABSTRACT

The paper presents the connection between λ-calculus and cartesian closed categories both in an untyped and purely syntactic setting. More specifically we establish a syntactic equivalence theorem between what we call categorical combinatory logic and λ-calculus with explicit products and projections, with β and η-rules as well as with surjective pairing. "Combinatory logic" is of course inspired by Curry's combinatory logic, based on the well known S,K,I. Compiling λ-calculus happens to be natural and provokes only $n \log n$ code expansion (which is achieved only with infinitely many S,K-like combinators). Moreover categorical combinatory logic is entirely faithful to β-reduction where combinatory logic needs additional rather complex and unnatural axioms to be. The paper is intended as a mathematical foundation for developing implementations of functional programming languages based on a "categorical abstract machine", as developed in forthcoming papers.

1. Introduction

The motivation for studying calculi of combinators is that implementing the β-rule of the λ-calculus, and more generally parameter passing mechanisms of programming languages involves some difficulties with the scope of variables, so that getting rid of variables at compile time may yield both efficient and safe interprets. Among the numerous approaches to eliminate variables, two of them are of particular interest:

- the use of Curry's combinators S,K,I, as suggested by D. Turner [Tu]: a precise comparison with the categorical approach developed here is outside the scope of the paper; we shall only justify the claims in the abstract;
- the so called De Bruijn's notation [Bru] (which is implicit in many closure based implementations of functional languages) for λ-expressions, replacing the names of the bound variables by their binding height, i.e. the number of λ's between the variable and its binding λ in the expression; actually, as we shall see, compiling λ-expressions into categorical code factorizes through getting its translation in De Bruijn's notation, and more specifically what remains to be done is just textual transformation.

Introducing categorical combinators starting from the λ-calculus is best done by using an intuition on types, and trying to describe the meaning of typed λ-expressions then quite naturally leads to categorical combinators. We refer to our companion paper on typed categorical combinatory logic [CuTCCL] for such an approach. Since we do not want to introduce types here, even for the sake of intuition, we shall use a much steeper way, more akin to a machine description. Anyway we take here the risk of trying to convince the reader rather by the magic of "pushing symbols" than by a thorough semantic motivation. We suppose some acquaintance with λ-calculus (we refer to [Bare]). In the syle of P. Landin's SECD machine [Lan], imagine the computation of λ-expressions as some compound action of a code *applied* to an environment. Imagine moreover that the environment has a binary tree representation. Then the following can be said on the three constructors of the pure λ-calculus:

- variable: x represents the access to the x-part of the environment: hence the action may be viewed as the *composition* of some actions of going or *projecting* from a node to its *first* or *second* son.
- application: the action of MN may be conceptually decomposed as follows: first combine, or put aside, or *pair* the actions of M and N, then perform the *application*

-abstraction: $\lambda x.M$ cannot act directly on the environment in this kind of evaluation: the involved mechanism was called closure by P. Landin. Entering into it is out of the scope of the present paper, but is central to our categorical abstract machine [CouCuMau]. What we want to suggest may be phrased as follows: $\lambda x.M$ will only give rise to an action if a context $(\lambda x.M)N$ is reached. Then M will act on a modified environment, a combination, or *couple* of the current environment and the result of the computation of N. So M has two arguments, whereas $\lambda x.M$ has only one: the environment; the point is that the second argument has been abstracted, i.e. that some *currying* is involved.

We have introduced all the categorical combinators but one, the *identity* which we shall see does not arise when compiling λ-expressions into categorical combinatory logic, but when simulating a β-reduction on the categorical code.

Now our categorical kit is complete and the play can begin. Summarizing we have composing, identity, pairing, first and second projections, currying and application. So far for the code itself representing λ-expressions as compound actions. The interface with the environment needs to enlarge our kit to applying and coupling (yes, applying is different from application, coupling from pairing). However, in the untyped setting, applying and coupling are not primitive and may be defined.

We suppose a basic familiarity with equational theories (as in [HuOp] for example).

2. Categorical combinatory logic

2.1. Definition

The **pure categorical combinatory logic CCL** is the algebra of terms built from a set *Var* of variables over the following signature:

-*Id* , *Fst* ,*Snd* , *App*, called respectively **identity, first projection, second projection** and **application,** of arity 0

-Λ, called **currying,** of arity 1

-∘ , < >, called respectively **composition** and **pairing,** of arity 2 •

We use the following notation:

$-<M_1,..,M_n> = <..<M_1,M_2>,..,M_n>$

Now we state the equations which will allow to establish the correspondence between **CCL** and **λc**, the λ-calculus extended with products and projections, to be defined below.

2.2. Definition

$CCL\beta\eta SP$ is the following set of equations:

$(Ass)\ (x \circ y) \circ z = x \circ (y \circ z)$ $(IdL)\ Id \circ x = x$ $(IdR)\ x \circ Id = x$
$(Fst)\ Fst \circ \langle x,y \rangle = x$ $(Snd)\ Snd \circ \langle x,y \rangle = y$ $(DPair)\ \langle x,y \rangle \circ z = \langle x \circ z, y \circ z \rangle$
$(Beta)\ App \circ \langle \Lambda(x), y \rangle = x \circ \langle Id, y \rangle$ $(D\Lambda)\ \Lambda(x) \circ y = \Lambda(x \circ \langle y \circ Fst, Snd \rangle)$
$(AI)\ \Lambda(App) = Id$ $(FSI)\ \langle Fst, Snd \rangle = Id$

We write $CCL\beta = CCL\beta\eta SP - AI - FSI$ •

The reader may check that one gets a more compact, equivalent version of $CCL\beta\eta SP$ by replacing $DPair + FSI$ by $SPair$, and $Beta + D\Lambda + AI$ by $App + S\Lambda$, where

$(SPair)\ \langle Fst \circ x, Snd \circ x \rangle = x$
$(App)\ App \circ \langle \Lambda(x) \circ Fst, Snd \rangle = x$
$(S\Lambda)\ \Lambda(App \circ \langle x \circ Fst, Snd \rangle) = x$

The reader acquainted with categories will recognize the set of equations defining the cartesian closed categories (Ass, IdL, IdR for categories, $Fst, Snd, SPair$ for products, $App, S\Lambda$ for function spaces), except that there are no types and no equation for the terminal object.

The following consequence of $CCL\beta\eta SP$ will be useful.

$(Beta')\ App \circ \langle \Lambda(x) \circ y, z \rangle = x \circ \langle y, z \rangle$

We first show that we can define application and couple operators satisfying the equations which are naturally expected, typically

$(\Lambda(x).y).z = x.(y,z)$

where we have denoted application by "." for the sake of clarity. However we shall rather omit the "." in the sequel, and denote application by mere juxtaposition.

2.3. Definition

We define the operations "$>$", "$<$" of arity 1, "." (**application**, denoted by simple juxtaposition) and ( ) (**couple**) of arity 2 as follows (for any A,B):

$A^{>} = \Lambda(A \circ Snd)$ $A^{<} = App \circ \langle A, Id \rangle$ $AB = (A \circ B^{>})^{<}$ $(A,B) = \langle A^{>}, B^{>} \rangle^{<}$

We use the following notation: $A_1A_2..A_n = (..(A_1A_2)..)A_n$

moreover we agree that application has stronger precedence than composition.

Finally let **RA** = $\{B \in$ **CCL**$\mid B =_{CCL\beta\eta SP} B \circ \Lambda(Snd)\}$ •

For the categorists again, the intuition behind this definition traces back to the bijective correspondence between $1 \rightarrow A \Rightarrow B$ and $A \rightarrow B$, for all objects A,B in a cartesian closed category with terminal object 1.

2.4. Lemma

For all terms $A \in$ **CCL**, $B \in$ **RA** the following holds

(1) $(A^{>})^{<} =_{CCL\beta\eta SP} A$
(2) $B =_{CCL\beta\eta SP} B \circ A$
(3) $(B^{<})^{>} =_{CCL\beta\eta SP} B$

Moreover $CCL\beta\eta SP \vdash CCL + Quote$ where CCL is the following set of equations:

$(id)\ Id\,x = x \quad (ass)\ (x \circ y)z = x(yz)$

$(fst)\ Fst(x,y) = x \quad (snd)\ Snd(x,y) = y \quad (dpair)\ \langle x,y\rangle z = (xz,yz)$

$(app)\ App(x,y) = xy \quad (d\Lambda)\ \Lambda(x)yz = x(y,z)$

and *Quote* is the following set of equations:

$(Quote\,1)\ \Lambda(Fst)x \circ y = \Lambda(Fst)x$

$(Quote\,2)\ App \circ \langle x \circ \Lambda(Fst)y, z\rangle = xy \circ z$

$(Quote\,3)\ \Lambda(x)y = x \circ \langle \Lambda(Fst)y, Id\rangle$

Proof:

$(A^{>})^{<} = App \circ \langle \Lambda(A \circ Snd), Id\rangle =_{Beta} (A \circ Snd) \circ \langle Id, Id\rangle =_{Ass,Snd,IdR} A$

$B \circ A =_{def} (B \circ \Lambda(Snd)) \circ A =_{Ass,D\Lambda,Snd} B \circ \Lambda(Snd) =_{def} B$

$(B^{<})^{>} = \Lambda((App \circ \langle B, Id\rangle) \circ Snd) =_{Ass,DPair,IdL} \Lambda(App \circ \langle B \circ Snd, Snd\rangle)$
$=_{2,2} \Lambda(App \circ \langle B \circ Fst, Snd\rangle) =_{S\Lambda} B$

For the other equations we first show

$CCL\beta\eta SP,\ Quote\,2 \vdash Quote\,3$

$CCL\beta\eta SP,\ Quote\,3,\ ass,\ fst,\ snd,\ dpair,\ app \vdash id,\ d\Lambda$

Here is for *Quote* 3.

$\Lambda(x)y =_{IdR} \Lambda(x)y \circ Id =_{Quote\,2} App \circ \langle \Lambda(x) \circ \Lambda(Fst)y, Id\rangle$
$=_{Beta'} x \circ \langle \Lambda(Fst)y, Id\rangle$

For *id*, we first get by *Quote* 3

$(4)\ \Lambda(Snd)x =_{Quote\,3} Snd \circ \langle ..,Id\rangle =_{Snd} Id$

$Id\,x =_{4,snd} (\Lambda(Snd)(y,x))(Snd(y,x)) =_{app,dpair,ass} (App \circ \langle \Lambda(Snd), Snd\rangle)(y,x)$
$=_{Beta,Snd,snd} x$

For $d\Lambda$ we first show

$(5)\ \Lambda(Fst)y = \Lambda(Snd \circ Fst)(z,y)$

$\Lambda(Fst)y =_{snd,ass} (\Lambda(Fst) \circ Snd)(z,y) =_{D\Lambda} \Lambda(Fst \circ \langle Snd \circ Fst, Snd\rangle)(z,y)$
$=_{Fst} \Lambda(Snd \circ Fst)(z,y)$

By (5) we obtain the following instance of $d\Lambda$.

$(6)\ \Lambda(Fst)yz =_{5,fst} (\Lambda(Snd \circ Fst)(z,y))(Fst(z,y))$
$=_{app,dpair,ass} (App \circ \langle \Lambda(Snd \circ Fst), Fst\rangle)(z,y) =_{Beta,Ass,Fst,IdR,snd} y$

Finally we may prove $d\Lambda$ using *Quote* 3.

$\Lambda(x)yz =_{Quote\,3} (x \circ \langle \Lambda(Fst)y, Id\rangle)z =_{ass,dpair,6,id} x(y,z)$

We are left with the other equations, say *ass* and *Quote* 1.

$x(yz) =_{def} (x \circ ((y \circ z^{>})^{<})^{>})^{<} =_3 (x \circ (y \circ z^{>}))^{<} =_{Ass,def} (x \circ y)z$

(3) may be applied since we verify $y \circ z^{>} \in$ **RA** (same argument as to prove (2)).

For *Quote* 1 we first establish

$(7)\ \Lambda(Fst)x =_{def} App \circ \langle \Lambda(Fst) \circ x^{>}, Id\rangle =_{Beta',Fst} x^{>}$

$\Lambda(Fst)x \circ y =_7 x^{>} \circ y =_2 x^{>} =_7 \Lambda(Fst)x$ since $x^{>} \in$ **RA** ∎

3. The λc-calculus

The **pure λc-calculus λc** is built from a set *Var* of **variables**, which are the basic λ-expressions. The other λ-expressions (or terms) are built by

-**application:** if M,N are terms, then MN is a term
-**abstraction:** if x is a variable and M is a term, then $\lambda x.M$ is a term
-**couple:** if M,N are terms, then (M,N) is a term
-**first projection:** if M is a term, then $fst(M)$ is a term
-**second projection:** if M is a term, then $snd(M)$ is a term

We use the following notation:
-$(M_1,..,M_n) = (..(M_1,M_2),..,M_n)$
-$M_1M_2..M_n = (..(M_1M_2)..M_{n-1})M_n$
-$\lambda x_1x_2..x_n.M = \lambda x_1.(\lambda x_2.(..(\lambda x_n.M)..))$ •

The sets of free and bound variables are denoted by $FV(M), BV(M)$. M/u is the subterm at occurrence u (for instance $(\lambda x.xy)/02 = y$). $M[u \leftarrow N]$ is the term obtained by replacing the occurrence u by N in M.

The theory $\beta\eta SP$ of the λc-calculus is defined by

(β): $(\lambda x.M)N = M[x \leftarrow N]$	(η): $\lambda x.Mx = M$ if $x \not\in FV(M)$	
(fst) $fst((M,N)) = M$	(snd) $snd((M,N)) = N$	(SP) $(fst(M),snd(M)) = M$

The λc-calculus may be coded inside the λ-calculus, but only the conversions fst and snd may be simulated, and not SP, as was shown by H. Barendregt [BaPair]. This indeed justifies introducing the extension λc of the λ-calculus.

4. Translating between the two syntaxes

As suggested in the introduction, most of the work to get a categorical translation of a λ-expression has been done by De Bruijn. Here is an elementary description of De Bruijn's numbering. Let M be a λ-expression (i.e. a term of λc), say $M = \lambda y.(x,y)(\lambda x.y)$

We replace bound variables by the number of λ's between the variable ant its binding λ (not including it). This yields $\lambda.(x,0)(\lambda.1)$

We still have x, which is free, and it is rather unsatisfactory: it would be nicer to have just numbers. The trick is to put M in a closed context, say $P = \lambda xtz.M$

Then we shall say that the De Bruijn's translation of M is $\lambda.(2,0)(\lambda.1)$ relative to the sequence x,t,z, because, in P, 2 is just the number we get for the concerned occurrence of x. Now a categorical term is obtained by merely interpreting the λ-calculus abstraction, coupling and projections by currying, pairing, composing with Fst or Snd on the left, while application is interpreted by the defined operator S

$S(A,B) = App \circ \langle A,B \rangle$

(it deserves its name since $S(x,y)z = (xz)(yz)$ follows from ass, $dpair$ and app)

Finally numbers are interpreted by the composition of a second projection and the same number of first projections, i.e. an access in the environment.

This is consistent with the suggestions in the introduction. Our example becomes

$\Lambda(App \circ \langle\langle Snd \circ (Fst \circ Fst), Snd \rangle, \Lambda(Snd \circ Fst)\rangle)$

This example introduces the following formal definition.

4.1. Lemma

Let $M, x_0,..,x_n$ be as in the definition above. $M_{DB(x_0,..,x_n)}$ is defined by:

$$x_{DB(x_0,\dots,x_n)} = Snd \circ Fst^i \text{ if } i \text{ is minimum s.t. } x=x_i$$
$$(\lambda x.M)_{DB(x_0,\dots,x_n)} = \Lambda(M_{DB(x,x_0,\dots,x_n)})$$
$$(MN)_{DB(x_0,\dots,x_n)} = App \circ <M_{DB(x_0,\dots,x_n)}, N_{DB(x_0,\dots,x_n)}>$$
$$(M,N)_{DB(x_0,\dots,x_n)} = <M_{DB(x_0,\dots,x_n)}, N_{DB(x_0,\dots,x_n)}>$$
$$fst\,(M)_{DB(x_0,\dots,x_n)} = Fst \circ M_{DB(x_0,\dots,x_n)}$$
$$snd\,(M)_{DB(x_0,\dots,x_n)} = Snd \circ M_{DB(x_0,\dots,x_n)}$$

Moreover the following properties hold:

$M_{DB(x_0,\dots,x_n)} = N_{DB(x_0,\dots,x_{i-1},y,x_{i+1},\dots,x_n)}$ where $N = M[x_i \leftarrow y]'$

$M_{DB(x,x_0,\dots,x_n)} = M_{DB(x_0,\dots,x_n)} \circ Fst$ if $x \not\in FV(M)$

$M[x_0 \leftarrow N^0,\dots,x_n \leftarrow N^n]_{DB(y_0,\dots,y_m)} = M_{DB(x_0,\dots,x_n)} \circ <z \circ Fst^{m+1}, N^n_{DB(y_0,\dots,y_m)},\dots,N^0_{DB(y_0,\dots,y_m)}>$

where we suppose $FV(N^0) \cup .. \cup FV(N^n) \subset \{y_0,..,y_m\}$ and where z is any variable ▪

The last property is very significant: ***it means that the categorical composition mirrors the λ-calculus substitution***. More technically the presence of z in the equation corresponds to the intuition that the environment is made of its useful part, and "the rest", i.e. z.

Now we detach a branch of the principal result of the paper: the following proposition shows that one may simulate the β and η-conversions on the terms obtained by the translation of De Bruijn. The following property is the key of the simulation.

4.2. Lemma

Let $A \in$ **CCL**. We write $P(A) = <A \circ Fst, Snd>$. The following holds:

$Fst^m \circ P^n(A) =_{CCL\beta\eta SP} P^{n-m}(A) \circ Fst^m$ if $1 \le m \le n$ ▪

4.3. Proposition

Let $M, N \in \lambda c$ and $x_0,..,x_n$ be s.t. $FV(M) \cup FV(N) \subset \{x_0,..,x_n\}$. The following holds:

$M =_{\beta\eta SP} N \Rightarrow M_{DB(x_0,\dots,x_n)} =_{CCL\beta\eta SP} N_{DB(x_0,\dots,x_n)}$

Proof: We only have to prove the properties for a single conversion step. Let w be the occurrence concerned by the conversion of M, i.e. s.t. M/w is the redex. We first examine β-conversion. One checks easily that if $M/w = (\lambda x.M_1)M_2$, and if we write $M_{DB(x_0,\dots,x_n)}/w = S(\Lambda(A_1),A_2)$, then

$N_{DB(x_0,\dots,x_n)} = M_{DB(x_0,\dots,x_n)}[w \leftarrow B]$

where B is obtained from A_1, A_2 as follows: let u be s.t. $A_1/u = n!$, and $h_\lambda(u,A_1)$ the number of λ's above u in A_1; replace the subterms at such u's by

- $n-1!$ if $n > h_\lambda(u,A_1)$
- A_2^{+n} if $n = h_\lambda(u,A_1)$, where A_2^{+n} is obtained from A_2 by replacing the occurrences v s.t. $A_2/v = j!$ and $j \ge h_\lambda(v,A_2)$ (this situation corresponds to a free variable occurrence) by $j+n$.

Now we show that this machinery of numbers is performed by $CCL\beta\eta SP$. We get

$S(\Lambda(A_1),A_2) =_{def} App \circ <\Lambda(A_1),A_2> =_{Beta} A_1 \circ <Id,A_2> =_{Ass,DPair,D\Lambda} A$

where A is the term obtained from A_1 by replacing the occurrences u of $n!$ by $A(u) = n! \circ P^m(<Id,A_2>)$, where $m = h_\lambda(u,A_1)$. We proceed by cases.

-$n>m$:

$A(u) =_{def,Ass} (Snd \circ Fst^{n-m}) \circ (Fst^m \circ P^m(<Id,A_2>)$
$= (Snd \circ Fst^{n-m}) \circ (<Id,A_2> \circ Fst^m) =_{Ass,Fst} Snd \circ (Fst^{n-m-1} \circ Fst^m) =_{def} n-1!$

-$n=m$:

$A(u) = Snd \circ (<Id,A_2> \circ Fst^m) =_{Ass,Snd} A_2 \circ Fst^m$

So we have to examine the effect of composing a term with Fst^m. As above we have

$A_2 \circ Fst^m =_{SimBeta} A'$

where A' is obtained from A_2 by replacing the occurrences v s.t. $A_2/v=j!$ by $A'(v) = j! \circ P^i(Fst^m)$, where $i=h_\lambda(v,A_2)$. We proceed again by cases:

- $j \geq i$: then
  $A'(v) =_{Ass} (Snd \circ Fst^{j-i}) \circ (Fst^i \circ P^i(Fst^m))$
  $= (Snd \circ Fst^{j-i}) \circ Fst^{m+i} =_{def} m+j!$
- $j<i$:
  $A'(v) = Snd \circ (P^{i-j}(Fst^m) \circ Fst^j)$
  $=_{def} Snd \circ (<P^{i-j-1}(Fst^m) \circ Fst, Snd> \circ Fst^j) =_{Ass,Snd} j!$

-$n<m$: as in the last subcase

$A(u) =_{CCL\beta\eta SP} n!$

We have reached B.

Now we prove the simulation of the η-reduction. We suppose that $N/w = \lambda x.M_1 x$ where $x \notin FV(M_1)$. Let $M_{DB(x_0,\dots,x_n)}/w = A$. Then

$N_{DB(x_0,\dots,x_n)} = M_{DB(x_0,\dots,x_n)}[w \leftarrow B]$ where $B = \Lambda(S(A^{+1},0!))$

We are left to prove $A =_{CCL\beta\eta SP} \Lambda(S(A^{+1},0!))$,

which results of the above reasoning since $A =_{IdR,AI,D\Lambda} \Lambda(App \circ <A \circ Fst, Snd>)$

Finally for the conversions fst, snd and SP, we remark that the translation transforms them into conversions Fst, Snd and $SPair$ ∎

A more cautious treatment of the proof above (using $DPair$ in particular) allows to make the proposition more precise. Let us consider $CCL\beta$ as a rewriting system by orienting the equations from left to right: a β-reduction is simulated by a derivation (i.e. a sequence of elementary reduction steps) of $CCL\beta$.

For η the system obtained by adding the rule $x \longrightarrow \Lambda(App \circ <x \circ Fst, Snd>)$ (obtained by reversing $S\Lambda$) to $CCL\beta$ simulates the reversed η-reductions, i.e. $M \longrightarrow \lambda x.Mx$.

The De Bruijn's translation of a term is variable free; we need to recover the free variables somehow. This is done by applying the De Bruijn's translation to a symbolic environment. The following definition contains this trick as well as the inverse translation, which is rather obvious.

4.4. Definition

With every term M of λc s.t. $FV(M) \subset \{x_0,\dots,x_n\}$ we associate a term M_{CCL} of **CCL** defined by

$$M_{CCL} = M_{DB(x_0,\dots,x_n)}(x,x_n,\dots,x_0) \quad (x \text{ is distinct from } x_0,\dots,x_n)$$

With every term A of **CCL** we associate a term $A_{\lambda c}$ of λ**c** defined as follows:

$x_{\lambda c} = x$

$Id_{\lambda c} = \lambda x.x \quad Fst_{\lambda c} = \lambda x.fst(x) \quad Snd_{\lambda c} = \lambda x.snd(x) \quad App_{\lambda c} = \lambda x.fst(x)snd(x)$

$(A \circ B)_{\lambda c} = \lambda x.A_{\lambda c}(B_{\lambda c}x) \quad <A,B>_{\lambda c} = \lambda x.(A_{\lambda c}x, B_{\lambda c}x) \quad \Lambda(A)_{\lambda c} = \lambda xy.A_{\lambda c}(x,y)$

(with variables x,y not belonging to $V(A) = FV(A_{\lambda c})$, $V(B) = FV(B_{\lambda c})$).

We write
$M_{CCL,\lambda c} = (M_{CCL})_{\lambda c}$, and likewise for other compositions of translations ▪

One checks that M_{CCL} does not depend on the choice of the sequence $x_0,..,x_n$ modulo $CCL\beta$

We remark that $M_{CCL,\lambda c} = M_{DB,\lambda c}(x, x_n, .., x_0)$
(we replace $DB(x_0,..,x_n)$ by DB when no confusion may arise).

The following lemma shows that the translation $_{\lambda c}$ has the expected behaviour w.r.t. the application and couple operators.

4.5. Lemma

For all terms A, B of **CCL** the following holds (with $u \notin FV(A_{\lambda c})$):

$$(A^{>})_{\lambda c} = \lambda u. A_{\lambda c} \quad (A^{<})_{\lambda c} = \lambda u. (A_{\lambda c} u) u \quad (AB)_{\lambda c} = A_{\lambda c} B_{\lambda c} \quad (A, B)_{\lambda c} = (A_{\lambda c}, B_{\lambda c})$$ ▪

Now we come to our main result (see discussion for some explanation about its attribute "First").

4.6. First equivalence theorem

For all terms $M, N \in \lambda c$, $A, B \in$ **CCL** the following holds:

(1) $M =_{\beta\eta SP} N \Rightarrow M_{CCL} =_{CCL\beta\eta SP} N_{CCL}$

(2) $A =_{CCL\beta\eta SP} B \Rightarrow A_{\lambda c} =_{\beta\eta SP} B_{\lambda c}$

(3) $M_{CCL,\lambda c} =_{\beta\eta P} M$

(4) $A_{\lambda c, CCL} =_{CCL\beta\eta P} A$

Proof: (for a full proof we refer to [CuTh]) (1) has been proved above. (2) and (3) are routine. We only check (4) for composition; we use the fact that if $x \notin FV(M)$, then $M_{DB(x, x_0,..,x_n)} =_{CCL\beta} M_{DB(x_0,..,x_n)} \circ Fst$

$(A \circ B)_{\lambda c, CCL} =_{def} \Lambda(App \circ \langle A_{\lambda c, DB} \circ Fst, App \circ \langle B_{\lambda c, DB} \circ Fst, Snd \rangle\rangle) u$

$=_{Quote 3} (App \circ \langle A_{\lambda c, DB} \circ Fst, App \circ \langle B_{\lambda c, DB} \circ Fst, Snd \rangle\rangle) \circ \langle \Lambda(Fst) u, Id \rangle$

$=_{Ass, DPair, Fst, Snd, Quote 2, ind, IdR} A \circ B$ ▪

Now we show as a corollary of this theorem that $CCL\beta\eta SP$ is equivalent to $CCL + FSI$ plus an extensionality axiom.

4.7. Corollary

For all terms A, B of **CCL** the following holds:

$A =_{CCL\beta\eta SP} B$ iff $CCL, FSI, ext \vdash A = B$

where ext is the following (first-order, but not equational) axiom:

$(ext) \quad Ax = Bx \Rightarrow A = B$ (x occurs neither in A nor in B)

Proof: The equations of $CCL\beta\eta SP$ (except FSI) are easily checked using CCL and ext.

Reciprocally we prove $Ax =_{CCL\beta\eta SP} Bx \Rightarrow A =_{CCL\beta\eta SP} B$

Indeed we have $(Ax)_{\lambda c} =_{def} A_{\lambda c} x$

Since $Ax =_{CCL\beta\eta SP} Bx$ we get

$A_{\lambda c} x =_{\beta\eta SP} B_{\lambda c} x$ and $A_{\lambda c} =_{\eta} \lambda x. A_{\lambda c} x =_{\beta\eta} \lambda x. B_{\lambda c} x =_{\eta} B_{\lambda c}$

whence we conclude

$A =_{CCL\beta\eta SP} A_{\lambda c, CCL} =_{CCL\beta\eta SP} B_{\lambda c, CCL} =_{CCL\beta\eta SP} B$ ▪

Another corollary is a result of functional completeness.

4.8. Corollary (Functional completeness)

For every term $A \in$ **CCL** s.t. $V(A) \subset \{x_0,...,x_n\}$ there exists a unique closed term A^* modulo $CCL\beta\eta SP$ s.t.

$$A =_{CCL\beta\eta SP} A^*(x_n,...,x_0)$$

Proof: Roughly take $A^* = A_{\lambda c,DB}$ ■

The same result, expressed in a semantic setting, was shown using a different method by J. Lambek [LamSco].

Notice finally that due to the presence of surjective pairing (*SP* or *SPair*) there is probably no chance of getting confluence of the set of rules underlying $CCL\beta\eta SP$ or even $CCL\beta$ (it is easily checked that *FSI* is needed to get local confluence), as was proved formally for λc by J. Klop [Klo].

5. Discussion

We have achieved a first order purely equational description of a calculus fully equivalent to the λ-calculus with products and projections. Curry's combinatory logic may also be endowed with a set of equations, the so-called Curry axioms [Cur], rendering it equivalent to the λ-calculus (without products). But the Curry axioms are rather ad hoc whereas the equations of $CCL\beta\eta SP$ are just the untyped and equational version of the well known diagrams of category theory (or set theory for whom is afraid of categories). As for the other claim of the abstract, the only code expansion in De Bruijn's translation is when a variable becomes a number n which needs place $\log n$ to be stored, so that we get a worst case $n \log n$ expansion. The same result is achieved in the framework of classical combinators S,K by an elegant rephrasing of D. Turner's most efficient abstraction algorithm, recently proposed by R. Kennaway and R. Sleep [KenSl], but this rephrasing involves infinitely many combinators.

This paper has two companion papers [CuTCCL] and [CuEq]. The first one investigates the typed categorical combinatory logic; our First equivalence theorem extends easily to a typed version: the Second equivalence theorem. However in the typed case the application and couple operators cannot be defined, they have to be primitive. In the same paper the typed categorical combinatory logic is formally related to cartesian closed categories (where roughly the terminal object replaces the application and couple) through a Third equivalence theorem.

On the other hand the relation of pure λ-calculus with categories was first suggested (among others in [BeSy],[Sco]) using a universal object in a typed framework rather than by extracting an untyped calculus from cartesian closed categories. The second companion paper follows this approach and gives rise to a Fourth equivalence theorem; it also discusses a general setting of equivalences of equational presentations of the kind manipulated in our equivalence theorems and shows how they induce semantic equivalences between their models.

Models of $CCL\beta\eta SP$ appeared independently of our work in [LamSco], where they are called *C*-monoids. But there the setting is semantic rather than syntactic, and the underlying translations are not so "operational" in character: what we believe original in our approach is the connection with De Bruijn's ideas, and the simulation of β-reductions by rewrite rules rather than just equationnally.

Finally the lasr outcome is a "categorical abstract machine" where each categorical combinator (more precisely, each of the signs involved in their concrete syntax) corresponds to a very simple machine instruction. As an example the three signs "<" , "," , ">" involved in $<A,B>$ correspond to instructions "push","swap" and "mkpair" with meanings, roughly, push register onto stack, exchange register and top of stack, make a "cons" from top of stack and register and let the register point on the tree obtained in this way (hence the register contains a pointer on a tree). All this will be explained in a forthcoming paper with G. Cousineau, who significantly improved a first proposal of the author , and a postgraduate student, M. Mauny [CouCuMau]. We strongly believe that simple, easy to prove and very efficient implementations of functional programming languages can be developed using the categorical combinators.

A synthetic reference for these topics is [CuTh].

6. References

[Bare] H. Barendregt, The Lambda Calculus: its Syntax and Semantics, North Holland (1981).

[BaPair] H. Barendregt, Pairing without Conventional Constraints, Z. Math. Logik Grundlag. Math. 20, 289-306 (1974).

[BeSy] G. Berry, Some Syntactic and Categorical Constructions of Lambda-calculus models, Rapport INRIA 80 (1981).

[Bru] N.G. De Bruijn, Lambda-calculus Notation without Nameless Dummies, a Tool for Automatic Formula Manipulation, Indag Math. 34, 381-392 (1972).

[CouCuMau] G. Cousineau, P-L. Curien, M. Mauny, The Categorical Abstract Machine, Rapport LITP 85-8, Université Paris VII, January 1985.

[CuTh] P-L. Curien, Combinateurs Catégoriques, Algorithmes Séquentiels et Programmation Applicative, Thèse d'Etat, Université Paris VII (Décembre 83), to be published in english as a monograph.

[CuTCCL] P-L. Curien, Typed Categorical Combinatory Logic, CAAP 85 (Berlin).

[CuEq] Syntactic Equivalences Inducing Semantic Equivalences, EUROCAL 1985 (Linz).

[Cur] H.B. Curry, R. Feys, Combinatory Logic, Vol.1, North Holland (1958).

[HuOp] G. Huet, D. Oppen, Equations and Rewrite Rules: a Survey, in Formal Language Theory: Perspectives and Open Problems, R. Book Ed., Academic Press, 349-405 (1980).

[KenSl] J.R. Kennaway, M.R. Sleep, Combinator Strings, internal report of the University of East Anglia (1982).

[Klo] J.W. Klop, Combinatory Reduction Systems, PhD Thesis, Utrecht (1980).

[LamSco] J. Lambek and P. Scott, Introduction to Higher Order Categorical Logic, to be published by Cambridge University Press (1984).

[Lan] P.J. Landin, The Mechanical Evaluation of Expressions, Computer Journal 6, 308-320 (1964).

[Sco] D. Scott, Relating Theories of the Lambda-calculus, in To H.B. Curry: Essays on Combinatory Logic, Lambda-calculus and Formalism, ed. J.P. Seldin and J.R. Hindley, Academic Press (1980).

[Tu] D.A. Turner, A New Implementation Technique for Applicative Languages, Software Practice and Experience, Vol.9, 31-49 (1979).

Towards a uniform topological treatment of streams and functions on streams

*J.W. de Bakker**
*J.N. Kok***

Centre for Mathematics and Computer Science
P.O. Box 4079, 1009 AB AMSTERDAM, The Netherlands

ABSTRACT

We study the semantics of functional languages on streams such as Turner's SASL or KRC. The basis of these languages is recursive equations for (functions on) finite or infinite sequences. The paper presents a start towards a mathematical (denotational) description of such languages using tools from metric topology. The description is based on the Banach fixed point theorem and a restricted version of a typed lambda calculus. To a system of recursive stream (function) declarations a system of functions is associated in an appropriate topological domain. These functions have to be contracting in certain arguments and non distance increasing in others; a syntax is designed which ensures the right interplay between these conditions. Nondeterminism is handled by considering compact sets of streams, and preservation of compactness is another important technical issue. Not all concepts in a language such as KRC are covered, and some indications on possible extensions of the framework are provided.

1. Introduction

We present a semantic study of languages with streams and functions on streams as exemplified by Turner's languages SASL and KRC. The tools we use are from metric topology; ultimately, our model relies on Banach's fixed point theorem for contracting functions on a complete metric space.

A *stream* is a finite or infinite sequence of values from a set V. (The examples below always take for V the set of integers.) A *program* is a set of recursive declarations of streams and stream functions, together with an expression to be evaluated with respect to the declarations.

Example: $< v \leftarrow 1 \cdot v_1(v),\ \ v_1 \leftarrow \text{var}\ z\ :(head(z)+1) \cdot v_1(tail(z))\ \ |\ v >$, we see two declarations, viz. that of the stream v and of the stream function v_1. The expression to be evaluated is v itself. In v_1, the formal z is used which can have a stream (or, in general, a set of streams) as actual. "$\cdot$" denotes concatenation, and "|" separates the declarations from the main program expression. The functions *head* and *tail* are as usual. The intended meaning of v is the infinite sequence $1 \cdot 2 \cdot 3 \cdots$.

Our main task is the development of a semantic framework to assign meaning to declarations of streams and stream functions. First, we define various *metrics.* The distance d between two streams is smaller if the elements where they exhibit their first difference occurs further to the right in the streams. For example, $d(23,24)= \frac{1}{2}$, $d(123,124)= \frac{1}{4}$. By standard topological methods, we extend this metric to sets of streams and to stream functions. Section 2, on topological preliminaries, collects these definitions. Also, the important notions of contracting, non distance increasing, and continuous functions are introduced, and various properties of compactness needed below are described. In fact, compactness, as a limit case of finiteness, is the topological counterpart of the familiar notion of bounded nondeterminism present in various order theoretic approaches.

Section 3 presents the definitions of the syntax and the semantics of our language. The syntax is designed in such a way that the associated semantic functions have the right contracting c.q. non distance increasing properties, as developed in section 4. Two main themes arise here: in a declaration such as $(v \leftarrow \cdots v \cdots)$, recursive occurrences of v have to be *guarded* by some expression (e.g. $v \leftarrow \cdots s \cdot v \cdots$) in order to ensure contractivity. Moreover, in order to guarantee that such contractivity is preserved throughout, stream functions of the type $(v_1 \leftarrow \text{var}\ z\ : \cdots z \cdots)$ have to be non distance increasing in z. Appropriate syntactic categories are introduced in order to enforce the right combination of these properties. The format of the syntax follows the usual pattern of a typed lambda calculus, restricted, however, to ground types and first order functional types. We envisage no problems in generalizing this aspect of the syntax.

* Supported in part by ESPRIT project 415: Parallel Architectures and Languages
** Supported by the Netherlands Organisation for the Advancement of Pure Research (Z.W.O.), grant 125-20-04.

The main theorem of the paper is in section 4 where the basic contractivity result, for functions associated with a set of declarations, is established. The intended meaning of the declared streams or stream functions as unique fixed points by Banach's theorem is then immediate. A minor issue to be faced is the possibility that a "guarding" term s in $s.v$ has the empty word in the set $[\![s]\!]\gamma$ denoting its meaning.

Section 5 treats a program as a pair consisting of a set of declarations and an expression. In the latter, we can be more liberal as to the allowed functions occurring in it, since it has only calls (and no declarations) of recursive objects.

Section 6 discusses some limitations and possible extensions. First we discuss functions which, instead of being contracting or non distance increasing, allow a *bounded* increase in distance. The problems which arise in this case are related to those studied by Wadge [22]. Secondly, with a more refined syntax we can also cater for the use of external (i.e. not programmer declared) functions which are not required to be contracting or non distance increasing. However, we then must restrict the way in which such functions occur in our expressions. Thirdly, we mention an important case of a function declaration which is allowed in KRC but does not fit into the present framework (a "permutation" function). We expect that the use of Painlevé limits (rather than of Cauchy sequences of compact sets with respect to the Hausdorff distance) will be useful here, but we have not worked out this idea.

Functional programming in general, and programming on streams in particular, have received wide attention in recent years. For the general background we refer, e.g., to [9] and references contained therein. It will be clear from the above that the languages SASL and KRC [20,21] have been a source of inspiration to us. Further references concerned with programming on streams are [8,10,12,15,23].

Our use of topological techniques goes back to the work of Nivat and his coworkers (e.g. [1,16]). Many of the technical results we use below are also described or applied in [4,5].

An order-theoretic approach to stream semantics is also possible; a basic reference is Broy [6], see also [7] for a more introductory presentation. Advantages of the metric approach are that certain distinctions can be made, in particular between contracting, non distance increasing and (only) continuous functions, which have no direct order-theoretic counterpart. Also, contractivity leads to the attractive situation that uniqueness of fixed points is ensured. However, further work is needed to cope with the problem of unguarded recursion in a topological setting. For connections between metric, order-theoretic, algebraic approaches in general see [17], [18], [19].

2. Topological preliminaries

Let M, M_1, M_2 be metric spaces with (bounded) distances d, d_1, d_2. A function $\phi : M_1 \rightarrow M_2$ is called *continuous* whenever for each sequence $\{x_i\}_i$ in M_1 and $x \in M_1$ such that $x = \lim_{i\to\infty} x_i$, we have $\phi(x) = \lim_{i\to\infty}\phi(x_i)$, ϕ is called *contractive* whenever, for each $x,y \in M_1$, $d(\phi(x),\phi(y)) \leqslant c \,.\, d(x,y)$ for some constant c with $0 \leqslant c < 1$, and ϕ is called *non distance increasing* whenever for each $x,y \in M_1$, $d(\phi(x),\phi(y)) \leqslant d(x,y)$.

Given a metric space (M,d), d is said to be an ultrametric on M if it satisfies the 'strong triangle inequality': for all $x,y,z \in M$ $d(x,z) \leqslant \max\{\, d(x,y), d(y,z)\,\}$.

Let (M,d) be a complete metric space. For $X,Y \subseteq M$ we define the so called Hausdorff distance

$$\hat{d}(X,Y) = \max(\sup_{x\in X} d'(x,Y)\,,\, \sup_{y\in Y} d'(y,X)) \text{ with } d'(x,Y) = \inf_{y\in Y} d(x,y).$$

By convention $\inf \varnothing = 1$ and $\sup \varnothing = 0$. We now define some spaces obtained from other spaces.

Let $P_{comp}(M)$ denote the non empty compact subsets of M, let $[M_1 \rightarrow M_2]$ denote the non distance increasing functions from $M_1 \rightarrow M_2$, and let $M_1 \times \cdots \times M_n$ be the Cartesian product of $M_1, \cdots, M_n$. We give these spaces the following metrics:

- $(P_{comp}(M),\hat{d})$: Hausdorff metric induced by the metric on M,
- $([M_1 \rightarrow M_2], e)$: $e(\phi_1,\phi_2) = \sup_{x\in M_1} d_2(\phi_1(x),\phi_2(x))$,
- $(M_1 \times \cdots \times M_n, d)$: $d(<x_1,\cdots,x_n>, <\bar{x}_1,\cdots,\bar{x}_n>) = \max_{i\in\{1,\cdots,n\}} d_i(x_i,\bar{x}_i)$.

2.1. Theorem. *If M, $M_1, \cdots, M_n$ are complete metric spaces then the following spaces with the above defined metrics are also complete: $P_{comp}(M)$, $[M_1 \rightarrow M_2]$, $M_1 \times \cdots \times M_n$.*

(i) If $\{X_i\}_i$ is a Cauchy sequence of compact sets in $(P_{comp}(M),\hat{d})$ then there exists a limit and this limit is compact. For details see [4].
(ii) Let $\{\phi_i\}_i$ be a Cauchy sequence in $[M_1 \rightarrow M_2]$. Define $\phi' : M_1 \rightarrow M_2$ by $\phi'(X) = \lim_i \phi_i(X)$. Then we have $\lim_i \phi_i = \phi'$ and $\phi' \in [M_1 \rightarrow M_2]$.
(iii) omitted □.

2.2. Lemma. *If $d, d_1, \cdots, d_n$ are ultrametrics then the above defined metrics are also ultrametrics.*

A well known classical result is Banach's fixed point theorem:

2.3. Theorem. *Let M be d-complete and let $T : M \to M$ be d-contractive. Then T is continuous and has exactly one fixed point X, satisfying $X = \lim_i T^i(X_0)$ for any $X_0 \in M$.*

The following theorem is due to Michael (see [14]). It says that if we 'flatten' compact sets in a certain way we have again a compact set.

2.4. Theorem. *Let X_i, $i \in I$, be compact subsets of M, and let $\{X_i \mid i \in I\}$ be compact in $(P_{comp}(M), \hat{d})$ then $X := \cup \{ X_i \mid i \in I\}$ is compact in (M,d).*

Proof: First we need the following definition: for any finite collection of open sets $U_1, \cdots, U_n$ in M,
$[U_1, \cdots, U_n] := \{X \mid X \subseteq \bigcup_{i=1}^{n} U_i$ and for $i = 1, \cdots, n$ $X \cap U_i \neq \varnothing \}$.
We have that $[U_1, \cdots, U_n]$ is open in $(P_{comp}(M), \hat{d})$. Let G be an open cover of X. Then for all $i \in I$, G is an open cover of X_i, so there is a finite subcollection of G, which covers X_i say $\underline{U_i} = \{U_{i_1}, \cdots, U_{i_n}\}$. Assume for $j = 1, \cdots, n$ $U_{i_j} \cap X_i \neq \varnothing$ because otherwise we could remove it. Let $[\underline{U_i}] := [U_{i_1}, \cdots, U_{i_n}]$ then it is easy to see that $[\underline{U_i}]$ is an open neighborhood of X_i so $\{[\underline{U_i}] \mid i \in I\}$ is an open cover of $\{X_i \mid i \in I\}$. So it has a finite subcover, say $\{[\underline{U_{i_1}}], \cdots, [\underline{U_{i_m}}]\}$. So X is covered by the finite collection $\{U_{i_1 1}, \cdots, U_{i_1 n_{i_1}}, U_{i_2 1}, \cdots, U_{i_2 n_{i_2}}, \cdots U_{i_m 1}, \cdots, U_{i_m n_{i_m}}\}$ $\square$.

We list two properties of compact sets which can be found in any standard work on topology, for example [11]: (i) the continuous image of a compact set is compact, (ii) let $X \subseteq M$ and $Y \subseteq N$, X and Y compact then $X \times Y$ is compact in the product topology for $M \times N$.

2.5. Lemma. *Let (M_1, d_1) be a metric space and (M_2, d_2) a metric space where d_2 is an ultrametric. Let $([M_1 \to M_2], e)$ be the metric space of non distance increasing functions from $M_1 \to M_2$ with the bounded function metric. Then we have the following inequality: $d_2(\phi_1(X_1), \phi_2(X_2)) \leq \max(e(\phi_1, \phi_2), d_1(X_1, X_2))$.*

Proof: $d_2(\phi_1(X_1), \phi_2(X_2)) \leq \max(\, d_2(\phi_1(X_1), \phi_2(X_1)), d_2(\phi_2(X_1), \phi_2(X_2)) \leq \max(e(\phi_1, \phi_2), d_1(X_1, X_2))$ $\square$.

2.6. Lemma. *Let $\phi : M \to P_{comp}(M)$. Define $\hat{\phi} : P_{comp}(M) \to P(M)$ by $\hat{\phi}(X) = \cup\{\phi(x) \mid x \in X\}$. Then we have $\hat{\phi} : P_{comp}(M) \to P_{comp}(M)$, if ϕ is continuous then $\hat{\phi}$ is continuous, if ϕ is contractive then $\hat{\phi}$ is contractive, if ϕ is non distance increasing then $\hat{\phi}$ is non distance increasing.*

3. Definitions

First we define the the set of streams, and a metric on it so we have a metric space on which we can apply the results of the preceding paragraph on topological spaces. Then we give the syntax and the semantics of our little language.

3.1. Streams

Let $V = \{0,1,2, \cdots \}$ be the set of integers. Let V^{str} be the set of finite and infinite sequences of members of V : $V^{str} = V^{*} \cup V^{\omega}$. V^{str} is called the set of streams. Let x and y members of V^{str}.

A metric on the set of streams is defined as follows: $d(x,y) := 2^{-\max\{n \mid x[n] = y[n]\}}$ where x[n] denotes the first n numbers of x, with the conventions that if the length of the stream is smaller than n than x[n] = x and $2^{-\infty} = 0$.

X and Y are typical members of $P_{comp}(V^{str})$. Let $\hat{d}$ be the Hausdorff distance on $P_{comp}(V^{str})$.

3.2. Syntax

Let $v \in Var$, where Var is the set of variables. A set of recursive equations (declarations) in our language will look like $\{v_i \leftarrow S_i\}_i$, where the $v_i \in Var$ are the declared variables that can appear recursively in the expressions $S_i \in Exp$. A member of Exp consists of zero or more formal variables $z \in Fovar$ followed by an expression $s \in Exp_1$. If this s is not preceded by formal variables, the expression S is called a stream expression.

In expressions $s \in Exp_1$ we can use several predefined variables. Let $Pvar$ the class of predefined variables. It is composed of the following subclasses with their typical elements: $g \in Cfvar$: set of contracting function variables, $f \in Nfvar$: set of non distance increasing function variables, $\alpha \in Ifvar$: set of integer function variables, if the arity of α is zero then α is called a constant, $\beta \in Sifvar$: set of stream to integer function variables, so $Pvar = Cfvar \cup Nfvar \cup Ifvar \cup Sifvar$.

Now we come to the main definition of this paragraph:

$S \in Exp$, $s \in Exp_1$, $t \in Exp_2$, $a \in Sexp_1$, $b \in Sexp_2$:

$S ::= \text{var } z_1, \cdots, z_n : s$

$s ::= a \mid z \mid S(s_1) \cdots (s_n) \mid f(s_1) \cdots (s_n) \mid g(t_1) \cdots (t_n) \mid s \cdot t$
$t ::= b \mid tail(s) \mid S(t_1) \cdots (t_n) \mid v(t_1) \cdots (t_n) \mid f(t_1) \cdots (t_n)$

$a ::= \alpha(a_1) \cdots (a_n) \mid \beta(s_1) \cdots (s_n)$
$b ::= \alpha(b_1) \cdots (b_n) \mid \beta(t_1) \cdots (t_n)$

Remarks

Usually we omit the brackets around the arguments of functions or variables.

If an expression s contains a variable v (for example in $s \equiv s'.t$ where $t \equiv v(t_1) \cdots (t_n)$) then that variable is protected by some other expression s', it is called guarded, or it appears unguarded within the arguments of a contracting function variable, but then we also call it guarded. If a variable is guarded then it is not necessary to guard variables that appear within the arguments of that variable. Exp_2 is a class which contains expressions that have appearances of unguarded variables.

It may seem that if one uses a formal variable as a guard we can have unguarded variables. For example in $v \leftarrow \text{var } z : z \cdot v(tail(z))$ we can get an unguarded v if the formal variable z obtains ϵ (the empty stream) as meaning of its corresponding actual parameter. We will define our semantics of a set of declarations in such a way that in these cases a default value is taken.

The classes $Sexp_1$ and $Sexp_2$ are meant as a classes of integers, the basic building blocks of our streams.

The general idea is that the so constructed expressions s are in a certain sense contractive in variables v and non distance increasing in formal variables z.

Examples of functions f would be "$\cup$" (non deterministic choice) and "||" (merge), as defined in [4]. *Fair* merge, however, does not preserve closedness and does not fit naturally into our framework.

3.3. Types and domains

We will use the domains DOM_ω for sets of streams and $DOM_{\omega^*\to\omega}$ for functions on streams.

Let $DOM_\omega = (P_{comp}(V^{str}), \hat{d})$ be the non empty compact subsets of V^{str} with the Hausdorff metric. Let $DOM_{\omega^*\to\omega} = ([P_{comp}(V^{str}) \times \cdots \times P_{comp}(V^{str}) \to P_{comp}(V^{str})], e)$ be the set of non distance increasing functions from $(P_{comp}(V^{str}) \times \cdots \times P_{comp}(V^{str}), d_{\max})$ to $(P_{comp}(V^{str}), \hat{d})$ equipped with the bounded function metric e. Let $DOM = DOM_\omega \cup DOM_{\omega^*\to\omega}$.

Let Env be the class of environments. $\gamma \in Env$ is a total function from $Var \cup Pvar \cup Fovar \to DOM$, which satisfies the following points:

- $f \in Nfvar$ implies $\gamma(f) \in DOM_{\omega^*\to\omega}$ and $\gamma(f)$ is monotone w.r.t. set inclusion,
- $g \in Cfvar$ implies $\gamma(g) \in DOM_{\omega^*\to\omega}$, and moreover, $\gamma(g)$ is contractive. We also require that $\gamma(g)$ is monotone (w.r.t. set inclusion),
- $\alpha \in Ifvar$ implies $\gamma(\alpha) \in P_{finite}(V) \times \cdots P_{finite}(V) \to P_{finite}(V)$,
- $\beta \in Sifvar$ implies $\gamma(\beta) \in P_{comp}(V^{str}) \times \cdots P_{comp}(V^{str}) \to P_{finite}(V)$ and $\gamma(\beta)$ is non distance increasing,
- $z \in Fovar$ implies $\gamma(z) \in DOM_\omega$,
- $v \in Var$ implies $\gamma(v) \in DOM_\omega$ or $\gamma(v) \in DOM_{\omega^*\to\omega}$.

Remarks

(i)$\gamma(\beta) \in DOM_{\omega^*\to\omega}$ because $P_{finite}(V) \subset P_{comp}(V^{str})$, and for $\gamma(\alpha)$ the requirement of being non distance increasing is trivially satisfied.

(ii)The condition that $\gamma(\beta)$ is non distance increasing implies that this function is determined by the first elements of its arguments. At first sight this is very restrictive. However, the arguments can sometimes depend on more elements, and, furthermore, the syntax can be extended by allowing (at some places), functions that are determined by more elements.

(iii)In case a functionvariable f or g is used in an expression s we also require for all $X \in P_{comp}(V^{str})$ $\epsilon \notin \gamma(f)(X)$ and $\epsilon \notin \gamma(g)(X)$.

Type is the set of types. A type τ is either ground or functional. Ground types are ω_0 and ω and functional types are

$$\omega\to\omega, \omega\times\omega\to\omega, \cdots, \omega^n\to\omega, \cdots, \omega_0\to\omega_0, \omega_0\times\omega_0\to\omega_0, \cdots, \omega_0^n\to\omega_0, \cdots, \omega\to\omega_0, \cdots, \omega^n\to\omega_0, \cdots.$$

We consider only expressions that can be typed with typing rules. For example: $\alpha \in Ifvar : type(\alpha) = \omega_0^n \to \omega_0$, $v \in Var : type(v) = \omega$ or $type(v) = \omega^n \to \omega$.

Now we give maps that define the semantics, in the sequel we will prove that the domain of these maps is DOM. The semantics are defined by the following maps:

Let $[\![\cdots]\!] : Exp \to Env \to DOM$ be defined by

$$[\![\text{var } z_1, \cdots, z_n : s]\!]\gamma = \lambda\phi_1.\cdots.\lambda\phi_n.[\![s]\!]_1 \gamma\{\phi_i / z_i\}_{i=1}^n$$

where $\bar{s} \equiv$ if $z_1=\epsilon$ or $\cdots$ or $z_n=\epsilon$ then ϵ else s fi. Remark: the replacement of the s by the if..fi construct is done for two reasons. First we do not want variables to become unguarded. Consider the following set of declarations, where we define a function "v" and a stream "$\bar{v}$": { $v \leftarrow$var z : $z \cdot v(tail(z))$, $\bar{v} \leftarrow 1 \cdot v(1)$ }. Now if "v" obtains ϵ as actual parameter, then it is not clear what this definition means, because the variable v in the body of $v \leftarrow$var z : $z \cdot v(tail(z))$ becomes unguarded.

Second we want $[\![S]\!]\gamma$ for all $\gamma \in Env$ to be a non distance increasing function. Without the if $\cdots$ fi construct this is not always the case. For example, let $S \equiv$ var $z_1,z_2 : z_1 \cdot tail(z_2)$, $\gamma \in Env$, so $[\![\text{var } z_1,z_2 : z_1 \cdot tail(z_2)]\!]\gamma = \lambda\phi_1.\lambda\phi_2.(\phi_1 \cdot tail(\phi_2))$. Now if $[\![S]\!]\gamma$ would be a non distance increasing function, we would have $d([\![S]\!]\gamma(\epsilon)(123),[\![S]\!]\gamma(\epsilon)(1234)) \leqslant d(<\epsilon,123>,<\epsilon,1234>)$ but we have instead $d([\![S]\!]\gamma(\epsilon)(123),[\![S]\!]\gamma(\epsilon)(1234)) = 2.d(<\epsilon,123>,<\epsilon,1234>)$ so $[\![S]\!]\gamma$ is not non distance increasing.

Let $[\![\cdots]\!]_1 : Exp_1 \to Env \to DOM$ be defined by
$$[\![a]\!]_1\,\gamma = [\![a]\!]_a\,\gamma,$$
$$[\![s \cdot t]\!]_1\,\gamma = [\![s]\!]_1\,\gamma \cdot [\![t]\!]_2\,\gamma,$$
$$[\![S(s_1)\cdots(s_n)]\!]_1\,\gamma = [\![S]\!]\,\gamma\ \ [\![s_1]\!]_1\,\gamma \cdots [\![s_n]\!]_1\,\gamma,$$
$$[\![f(s_1)\cdots(s_n)]\!]_1\,\gamma = \gamma(f)\,[\![s_1]\!]_1\,\gamma \cdots [\![s_n]\!]_1\,\gamma,$$
$$[\![g(t_1)\cdots(t_n)]\!]_1\,\gamma = \gamma(g)\,[\![t_1]\!]_2\,\gamma \cdots [\![t_n]\!]_2\,\gamma.$$

Let $[\![\cdots]\!]_2 : Exp_2 \to Env \to DOM$ be defined by
$$[\![b]\!]_2\,\gamma = [\![b]\!]_b\,\gamma,$$
$$[\![v(t_1)\cdots(t_n)]\!]_2\,\gamma = \gamma(v)\ \ [\![t_1]\!]_2\,\gamma \cdots [\![t_n]\!]_2\,\gamma,$$
$$[\![S(t_1)\cdots(t_n)]\!]_1\,\gamma = [\![S]\!]\,\gamma\ \ [\![t_1]\!]_2\,\gamma \cdots [\![t_n]\!]_2\,\gamma,$$
$$[\![f(t_1)\cdots(t_n)]\!]_1\,\gamma = \gamma(f)\,[\![t_1]\!]_2\,\gamma \cdots [\![t_n]\!]_2\,\gamma.$$

Let $[\![\cdots]\!]_a : Sexp_1 \to Env \to DOM$ be defined by
$$[\![\alpha(a_1)\cdots(a_n)]\!]_a\,\gamma = \gamma(\alpha)\,[\![a_1]\!]_a\,\gamma \cdots [\![a_n]\!]_a\,\gamma,$$
$$[\![\beta(s_1)\cdots(s_n)]\!]_a\,\gamma = \gamma(\beta)\,[\![s_1]\!]_1\,\gamma \cdots [\![s_n]\!]_1\,\gamma.$$

Let $[\![\cdots]\!]_b : Sexp_2 \to Env \to DOM$ be defined by
$$[\![\alpha(b_1)\cdots(b_n)]\!]_b\,\gamma = \gamma(\alpha)\,[\![b_1]\!]_b\,\gamma \cdots [\![b_n]\!]_b\,\gamma,$$
$$[\![\beta(t_1)\cdots(t_n)]\!]_b\,\gamma = \gamma(\beta)\,[\![t_1]\!]_2\,\gamma \cdots [\![t_n]\!]_2\,\gamma.$$

We have $type(S) \in \{\omega, \omega \to \omega, \cdots, \omega^n \to \omega, \cdots\}$. Recall that we only consider expressions that can be typed, we usually omit the subscripts of the $[\![\cdots]\!]$ functions.

3.3.1. Theorem. *If an expression S has type τ then we have* $[\![S]\!]\gamma \in DOM_\tau$.

Proof: We prove that for $S \equiv$ var $z_1, \cdots, z_n : s$ we have $[\![S]\!]\gamma \in P_{comp}(V^{str}) \times \cdots \times P_{comp}(V^{str}) \to P_{comp}(V^{str})$.

We have for all $s \in Exp_1$, $n \in \{0,1,\cdots\}$, $z_1, \cdots, z_n \in Fovar$, $\gamma \in Env$
$$[\![\text{var } z_1, \cdots, z_n : s]\!]\gamma \in P_{comp}(V^{str}) \times \cdots \times (V^{str}) \to P_{comp}(V^{str}) \text{ iff } [\![s]\!]\gamma \in P_{comp}(V^{str}) \qquad (*)$$

So we have to prove for all $s \in Exp_1$, $\gamma \in Env$: $[\![s]\!]\gamma \in P_{comp}(V^{str})$. This is proved simultaneously with $[\![t]\!]\gamma \in P_{comp}(V^{str})$, $[\![a]\!]\gamma \in P_{finite}(V)$, $[\![b]\!]\gamma \in P_{finite}(V)$. Induction on the complexity of s,t,a,b. We do not treat all cases.

$s \equiv a$: Either $a \equiv \alpha(a_1)\cdots(a_n)$ or $a \equiv \beta(s_1)\cdots(s_n)$. We treat $a \equiv \alpha(a_1)\cdots(a_n)$. By induction $[\![a_i]\!]\gamma \in P_{finite}(V)$, $i=1,\cdots,n$. So $<[\![a_1]\!]\gamma, \cdots, [\![a_n]\!]\gamma> \in P_{finite}(V) \times \cdots \times P_{finite}(V)$.
We have $\gamma(\alpha) \in P_{finite}(V) \times \cdots \times P_{finite}(V) \to P_{finite}(V)$. Observe $P_{finite}(V) \subset P_{comp}(V^{str})$.

$s \equiv f(s_1)\cdots(s_n)$: By induction $[\![s_i]\!]\gamma \in P_{comp}(V^{str})$, so $<[\![s_1]\!]\gamma, \cdots, [\![s_n]\!]\gamma> \in P_{comp}(V^{str}) \times \cdots \times P_{comp}(V^{str})$.
We have $\gamma(f) \in P_{comp}(V^{str}) \times \cdots \times P_{comp}(V^{str}) \to P_{comp}(V^{str})$.

$s \equiv s \cdot t$: $[\![s]\!]\gamma, [\![t]\!]\gamma \in P_{comp}(V^{str})$ by induction, so $[\![s]\!]\gamma \times [\![t]\!]\gamma = \{<x,y> \mid x \in [\![s]\!]\gamma, y \in [\![t]\!]\gamma\}$ is compact in $V^{str} \times V^{str}$. We have that "." is continuous from $V^{str} \times V^{str}$ so the result follows.

$t \equiv S(t_1)\cdots(t_n)$: $S \equiv$ var $z_1, \cdots, z_n : s$ and by induction we know $[\![s]\!]\gamma \in P_{comp}(V^{str})$, so by (*) we have $[\![S]\!]\gamma = [\![\text{var } z_1 \cdots z_n : s]\!]\gamma \in P_{comp}(V^{str}) \times \cdots \times P_{comp}(V^{str}) \to P_{comp}(V^{str})$.

$a \equiv \alpha(a_1)\cdots(a_n)$: By induction $<[\![a_1]\!]\gamma, \cdots, [\![a_n]\!]\gamma> \in P_{finite}(V) \times \cdots \times P_{finite}(V)$
so $\gamma(\alpha)<[\![a_1]\!]\gamma, \cdots, [\![a_n]\!]\gamma> \in P_{finite}(V)$.

The fact that $[\![S]\!]\gamma$ is non distance increasing will be proved in the main theorem of next section and so we are done □.

4. Declarations

The syntax and the semantics of a set of declarations will be given in this section.

4.1. Syntax

Let d $\in$ Decl be a set of declarations: $d ::= \{v_1 \leftarrow S_1, \cdots, v_n \leftarrow S_n\}$ where $v_i \in Var, S_i \in Exp, i = 1, \cdots, n$. We consider only sets of declarations d such that

- d can be typed,
- for each variable v occurring in some S_j we have that $v \in \{v_1, \cdots, v_n\}$ (this is called closedness of d),
- all z occurring in S_j are in the scope of some var z, and hence, we have no z's occurring in a global way.

4.2. Semantics

To define the semantics we associate with a set of declarations $d \equiv \{v_i \leftarrow S_i\}_i$ a function F:

$$F : DOM_{\tau_1} \times \cdots \times DOM_{\tau_n} \to DOM_{\tau_1} \times \cdots \times DOM_{\tau_n},$$

$$F = \lambda\phi_1^{\tau_1}. \cdots .\lambda\phi_n^{\tau_n}. < [\![S_1]\!] \gamma\{\phi_i / v_i\}_{i=1}^n, \cdots, [\![S_n]\!] \gamma\{\phi_i / v_i\}_{i=1}^n >$$

where $\gamma \in Env$, type$(v_i) = \tau_i$ for i=1,...,n. We will prove that F is contractive on $DOM_{\tau_1} \times \cdots \times DOM_{\tau_n}$ so there exists a unique fixed point of F. This fixed point will be taken as the meaning of a set of declarations.

4.2.1. Lemma. *If for all $S \in Exp$, $v \in Var$, $\gamma \in Env$ $\lambda\phi.[\![S]\!]\gamma\{\phi / v\}$ is contractive, then for all $d \in Decl$ its associated function F is contractive for all $\gamma \in Env$.*

Let $Env^* = \{\gamma \in Env \mid \text{for all } z \in Fovar : \epsilon \notin \gamma(z)\}$.

4.2.2. Lemma. *Let $s \in Exp_1$, and let $z_1, \cdots, z_n \in Fovar$ the free formal variables of s. Then we have $\lambda\phi.[\![\text{if } z_1 = \epsilon \text{ or} \cdots \text{or } z_n = \epsilon \text{ then } \epsilon \text{ else } s \text{ fi}]\!]\gamma\{\phi / v\}$ is contractive for all $\gamma \in Env$ iff $\lambda\phi.[\![s]\!]\gamma\{\phi / v\}$ is contractive for all $\gamma \in Env^*$ and $\lambda\phi.[\![\text{if } z_1 = \epsilon \text{ or} \cdots \text{or } z_n = \epsilon \text{ then } \epsilon \text{ else } s \text{ fi}]\!]\gamma\{\phi / z\}$ is non distance increasing for all $\gamma \in Env$ iff $\lambda\phi.[\![s]\!]\gamma\{\phi / z\}$ is contractive for all $\gamma \in Env^*$ and for all ϕ such that $\epsilon \notin \phi$.*

4.2.3. Lemma. *If $\epsilon \notin \phi_i, i = 1, \cdots, n$ then $\epsilon \notin [\![\text{var } z_1, \cdots, z_n : s]\!]\gamma(\phi_1) \cdots (\phi_n)$ for all $\gamma \in Env$.*

4.2.4. Lemma. *Let $\gamma \in Env^*$. Let length(x) denote the length of a stream x and length(X) = inf$\{$length$(x) \mid x \in X\}$. Then for all $s \in Exp_1$ length$([\![s]\!]\gamma) \geq 1$.*

4.2.5. Theorem. *Let $d \in Decl$. Then F (associated with d) is contractive on $DOM_{\tau_1} \times \cdots \times DOM_{\tau_n}$.*

Proof. By (4.2.1) and (4.2.2) it suffices to prove for all $\gamma \in Env^*$, $v \in Var$, $s \in Exp_1$

$$d([\![s]\!]\gamma\{\phi / v\}, [\![s]\!]\gamma\{\phi' / v\}) \leq c.d(\phi, \phi'), 0 \leq c < 1.$$

This is proved simultaneously with the following facts. For all $v \in Var$, $z \in Fovar$, $s \in Exp_1$, $t \in Exp_2$, $a \in Sexp_1$, $b \in Sexp_2$, $\gamma \in Env^*$

$$d([\![s]\!]\gamma\{\phi / z\}, [\![s]\!]\gamma\{\phi' / z\}) \leq d(\phi, \phi') \text{ for all } \phi, \phi' \text{ such that } \epsilon \notin \phi, \phi',$$

$$d([\![t]\!]\gamma\{\phi / v\}, [\![t]\!]\gamma\{\phi' / v\}) \leq d(\phi, \phi') \text{ for all } \phi, \phi',$$

$$d([\![t]\!]\gamma\{\phi / z\}, [\![t]\!]\gamma\{\phi' / z\}) \leq 2.d(\phi, \phi') \text{ for all } \phi, \phi' \text{ such that } \epsilon \notin \phi, \phi',$$

$$d([\![a]\!]\gamma\{\phi / v\}, [\![a]\!]\gamma\{\phi' / v\}) \leq c.d(\phi, \phi') \text{ for all } \phi, \phi',$$

$$d([\![a]\!]\gamma\{\phi / z\}, [\![a]\!]\gamma\{\phi' / z\}) \leq d(\phi, \phi') \text{ for all } \phi, \phi' \text{ such that } \epsilon \notin \phi, \phi',$$

$$d([\![b]\!]\gamma\{\phi / v\}, [\![b]\!]\gamma\{\phi' / v\}) \leq d(\phi, \phi') \text{ for all } \phi, \phi',$$

$$d([\![b]\!]\gamma\{\phi / z\}, [\![b]\!]\gamma\{\phi' / z\}) \leq 2.d(\phi, \phi') \text{ for all } \phi, \phi' \text{ such that } \epsilon \notin \phi, \phi'.$$

The proof goes by induction on the (structural) complexity of s,t,a,b.

$s \equiv a$: Either $a \equiv \alpha(a_1) \cdots (a_n)$ or $\beta(s_1) \cdots (s_n)$. We treat $\beta(s_1) \cdots (s_n)$.

By induction for $i = 1, \cdots, n$ $d([\![s_i]\!]\gamma\{\phi / v\}, [\![s_i]\!]\gamma\{\phi' / v\}) \leq c.d(\phi, \phi')$

so $d(<[\![s_1]\!]\gamma\{\phi / v\}, \cdots, [\![s_n]\!]\gamma\{\phi / v\}>, <[\![s_1]\!]\gamma\{\phi' / v\}, \cdots, [\![s_n]\!]\gamma\{\phi' / v\}>) \leq c.d(\phi, \phi')$.

$\gamma(\beta)$ is non distance increasing, so we are done. The result for $z \in Fovar$ follows by analogy.

$s \equiv z$: $d([\![z]\!]\gamma\{\phi / v\}, [\![z]\!]\gamma\{\phi' / v\}) = 0 \leq c.d(\phi, \phi')$, $d([\![z]\!]\gamma\{\phi / z\}, [\![z]\!]\gamma\{\phi' / z\}) \leq d(\phi, \phi')$.

$s \equiv f(s_1) \cdots (s_n)$: By induction for $i = 1, \cdots, n$ $d([\![s_i]\!]\gamma\{\phi / v\}, [\![s_i]\!]\gamma\{\phi' / v\}) \leq c.d(\phi, \phi')$, so $d(<[\![s_1]\!]\gamma\{\phi / v\}, \cdots, [\![s_n]\!]\gamma\{\phi / v\}>, <[\![s_1]\!]\gamma\{\phi' / v\}, \cdots, [\![s_n]\!]\gamma\{\phi' / v\}>) \leq c.d(\phi, \phi')$.

$\gamma(f)$ is non distance increasing, so we are done. The result for $z \in Fovar$ follows by analogy.

$s \equiv s \cdot t$: By induction $d([\![s]\!]\gamma\{\phi/v\},[\![s]\!]\gamma\{\phi'/v\}) \leqslant c.d(\phi,\phi')$ and $d([\![t]\!]\gamma\{\phi/v\},[\![t]\!]\gamma\{\phi'/v\}) = d(\phi,\phi')$

By properties of concatenation we are done if $d([\![s]\!]\gamma\{\phi/v\},[\![s]\!]\gamma\{\phi'/v\}) > 0$.

So suppose $[\![s]\!]\gamma\{\phi/v\} = [\![s]\!]\gamma\{\phi'/v\}$. $\gamma\{\phi/v\} \in Env^*$, so by lemma (4.2.4) $length([\![s]\!]\gamma\{\phi/v\}) \geqslant 1$ so

$$d([\![s \cdot t]\!]\gamma\{\phi/v\},[\![s \cdot t]\!]\gamma\{\phi'/v\}) \leqslant \tfrac{1}{2}\ d([\![t]\!]\gamma\{\phi/v\},[\![t]\!]\gamma\{\phi'/v\})$$

For $z \in Fovar$ we have again (because $\epsilon \notin \phi$) $\gamma\{\phi/v\} \in Env^*$.

$t \equiv v'(t_1) \cdots (t_n)$: We have:

$$d(<[\![t_1]\!]\gamma\{\phi/v\}, \cdots ,[\![t_n]\!]\gamma\{\phi/v\}>,<[\![t_1]\!]\gamma\{\phi'/v\}, \cdots ,[\![t_n]\!]\gamma\{\phi'/v\}>) \leqslant d(\phi,\phi').$$

Now if $v \not\equiv v'$ then we have $\gamma(v')$ is non distance increasing and we are done and if $v \equiv v'$ we apply lemma (2.5) and remark that ϕ and ϕ' are non distance increasing.

$t \equiv S(t_1) \cdots (t_n)$: Let $S \equiv$ var $z_1, \cdots ,z_n :s$. By induction we have

$d([\![s]\!]\gamma\{\phi/z\},[\![s]\!]\gamma\{\phi'/z\}) \leqslant d(\phi,\phi')$ for all $\gamma \in Env^*$ and ϕ,ϕ' such that $\epsilon \notin \phi,\phi'$. So by lemma (4.2.2) $[\![S]\!]\gamma$ is non distance increasing for all γ. Now if $[\![S]\!]\gamma\{\phi/v\} \neq [\![S]\!]\gamma\{\phi'/v\}$ we apply lemma (2.5).

Other cases are omitted □.

$$[\![\cdots]\!]_{Decl} : Decl \to DOM_{\tau_1} \times \cdots \times DOM_{\tau_n} \text{ is defined by } [\![\{v_i^{\tau_i} \leftarrow S_i\}_{i=1}^{n}]\!]_{Decl} = Fix(F),$$

the fixed point of F which exists by the Banach theorem. This fixed point can be obtained by iterating from an arbitrary starting point in the space.

5. Programs

5.1. Syntax

A program is a a set of declarations combined with an expression u. This expression u is a member of $Eexp$, a class of expressions. $Eexp$ leaves in a certain sense more freedom than Exp_1 and Exp_2. We do not have to restrict our class of functions. Let δ be a new member of $Fvar$. We do not put any new restrictions on $\gamma \in Env$, so we only know that $\gamma(\delta)$ is a function.

$$u \in Eexp \quad u ::= a \mid v(u_1) \cdots (u_n) \mid \delta(u_1) \cdots (u_n)$$

Let $p \in Prog$ be a program. $Prog$ is defined by $p ::= <d \mid u>$ where $d \in Decl$ and $u \in Eexp$. Assume furthermore that every $p \in Prog$ is syntactically closed, i.e. every $v \in Var$ that appears in u is declared in d. Recall that d itself is closed.

5.2. Semantics

$[\![\cdots]\!]_E : Eexp \to Env \to P(V^{str})$ is defined by

$$[\![a]\!]_E\gamma = [\![a]\!]\gamma,$$
$$[\![v(u_1) \cdots (u_n)]\!]_E\gamma = \gamma(v)[\![u_1]\!]_E\gamma \cdots [\![u_n]\!]_E\gamma,$$
$$[\![\delta(u_1) \cdots (u_n)]\!]_E\gamma = \gamma(\delta)[\![u_1]\!]_E\gamma \cdots [\![u_n]\!]_E\gamma.$$

$[\![\cdots]\!]_{Prog} : Prog \to Env \to P(V^{str})$ is defined by

$$[\![<d \mid u>]\!]_{Prog}\gamma = [\![u]\!]_E\gamma\{\epsilon_i([\![d]\!]_{Decl})/v_i\}_i$$

where $\epsilon_i(\cdots)$ denotes the ith component of $\cdots$.

6. Some extensions and remarks

6.1. Extensions

In this section we want to discuss some extensions and we will see some limitations of our framework. The treatment of these ideas will be brief and not fully worked out. First we look at three possible extensions:

• Use a fully typed lambda calculus. We think there are no new problems when we allow functions of higher order than we have used up to now.

• Allow more declarations: There are sets of declarations that are intuitively correct and are not allowed in our framework. For example $\{v_1 \leftarrow v_2, v_2 \leftarrow 1.(v_2+1)\}$ does not satisfy our syntax. We like to allow such a set of declarations. One way to do this is the derivation of an equivalent correct set of declarations. We can syntactically transform such a set with certain rules. An example of such a rule would be:

Let $v \in Var$ be a variable that is declared in a set of declarations d, i.e. $d \equiv \{ \cdots ,v \leftarrow S, \cdots \}$. Let this variable v also appear in the body of a declaration: there is a $\bar{v} \in Var$ such that $d \equiv \{ \cdots ,\bar{v} \leftarrow \cdots v \cdots , \cdots \}$. Now replace this occurrence of v by its body S.

Note that clashes of formals do not occur due to the absence of global variables. Our example $\{v_1 \leftarrow v_2, v_2 \leftarrow 1.(v_2+1)\}$ could be transformed to $\{v_1 \leftarrow 1.(v_2+1), v_2 \leftarrow 1.(v_2+1)\}$. The latter set of declarations is permitted in our framework.

• In a set of declarations we can define functions. Up to now these functions were all non distance increasing. We can extend our sets of declarations in such a way that it is possible to declare other kinds of functions.

(i) functions from $P_{comp}(V^{str}) \to P_{comp}(V^{str})$ that satisfy for a fixed n $d(\phi(x),\phi(y)) \leq 2^n . d(x,y)$.

We have to make expressions u such that for all $v \in Var$, $z \in Fovar$ $d([\![u]\!]\gamma\{\phi/v\},[\![u]\!]\gamma\{\bar{\phi}/v\}) \leq c.d(\phi,\bar{\phi})$, $d([\![u]\!]\gamma\{\phi/z\},[\![u]\!]\gamma\{\bar{\phi}/z\}) \leq 2^n.d(\phi,\bar{\phi})$.

If we want to use these functions in declarations of non distance increasing functions then we must be careful. For example, suppose we have constructed a function that can make the distance between two streams twice as big. We want to use this function in the definition of a non distance increasing function. This can only be done in places where we were allowed to use the tail function. For $n \geq 2$ relatively minor refinements in the syntactic and semantic framework developed above are necessary. Related questions are discussed by Wadge [22].

(ii) Monotone functions (with respect to set inclusion). We now discuss what happens when we lift the restriction on f and g imposed before. Specifically, we replace f,g by functionsymbols $\delta \in Mofvar$ (Monotone function variables) the meaning of which is required only to be a monotone function from $P_{comp}(V^{str}) \to P_{comp}(V^{str})$. Functions $[\![S]\!]\gamma$ are now no longer non distance increasing, and an additional requirement on the set of declarations is necessary to ensure that $\lambda\phi.[\![S]\!]\gamma\{\phi/v\}$ is contracting.

We define the classes $Mexp, Mexp_1, Mexp_2$. Let $S \in Mexp, s \in Mexp_1, t \in Mexp_2$. We use S,s,t in analogy with our earlier syntax, but they are not the same.

$S ::= \text{var } z_1, \cdots, z_n : s$

$s ::= a \mid z \mid \delta(t_1) \cdots (t_n) \mid S\,(t_1) \cdots (t_n) \mid s.t$

$t ::= a \mid z \mid \delta(t_1) \cdots (t_n) \mid v\,(t_1) \cdots (t_n) \mid S\,(t_1) \cdots (t_n)$

In the definition of the semantics we take the usual precautions to ensure that the guards of a $v \in Var$ can not become ϵ. The formal definition of the semantics is omitted.

Let $d \in Decl$ be a set of declarations, $d = \{v_i \leftarrow S_i\}_i$. We now formulate the restriction on d. First we introduce some terminology. Let $FV(d)$ be the set of formal variables in $\bigcup_{i=1}^{n} S_n$. Let $OF(d) \subset FV(d)$ denote the outer formal variables in d : $OF(d) = \bigcup_{i=1}^{n} \{z_{i_1}, \cdots, z_{i_{n(i)}}\}$ if $S_i \equiv \text{var } z_{i_1}, \cdots, z_{i_{n(i)}} : s_i$. Let $IF(d) = FV(d) - OF(d)$ be the inner formals of d.

Because the set of declarations is well typed, every $z \in IF(d)$ is instantiated with an expression $s \in Exp_1$ or $t \in Exp_2$. Now we want to define what an instantiation means for a $z \in OF(d)$. If $z \in OF(d)$ there is a variable $v \in Var$ such that $(v \leftarrow \text{var} \cdots z \cdots : s) \in d$. Assume that this v is used in the body of a variable $\bar{v} \in Var$, i.e. $(v \leftarrow \text{var} \cdots : \cdots v(t_1) \cdots (t_n) \cdots) \in d$. $\bar{v}$ is not necessarily different from v. Let t_i the expression that appears in the body of $\bar{v}$ as 'actual' expression for z. This t_i is called an instantiation of z.

An expression is *allowed* as argument of a $\delta \in Mofvar$ in a set of declarations $d \in Decl$ if no $v \in Var$ occurs in this expression, and if $z \in Fovar$ occurs in this expression, then all instantiations of z must be allowed.

Now we can formulate the restriction. All arguments of a $\delta \in Mofvar$ that appear in a $d \in Decl$ must be allowed. We omit the proof that this restriction implies the desired contractivity property.

Second, we want to discuss how we can mix monotone functions with sets of declarations of other functions. For simplicity, consider only two kinds of functions: monotone and non distance increasing. Let d be a set of declarations in which we define (simultaneously) these two kinds of functions. There are two kinds of variables: those that will be assigned as meaning a non distance increasing function and those that will be assigned a monotone function. The difference between these two kinds of variables will be denoted by putting a bar on the latter.

Let $S \in Exp$ be expressions that belong to v's and $\bar{S} \in Mexp$ expressions that belong to $\bar{v}$'s, i.e. $d = \{v_i \leftarrow S_i, \bar{v}_i \leftarrow \bar{S}_i\}_i$. We extend Exp and $Mexp$ such that $\bar{v}$ can be used in S and v in $\bar{S}$. In an expression $S \in Exp$ we can use $\bar{v}$ in places where v is allowed, but the arguments of a $\bar{v}$ must be constant expressions. An expression is called constant if it contains no $v \in Var$ or $z \in Fovar$. In an expression $\bar{S} \in Mexp$ v can be used on each place where a $\bar{v}$ is allowed. The conditions together ensure that the v_i are non distance increasing.

In general, monotone functions are not continuous with respect to the Hausdorff distance. Still, we would like to have that finite approximations converge to the result. We illustrate this problem by the permutation function. This function is described by Turner in [20]. It maps a stream to the set of all its permutations. Let x be a stream and $\{x_i\}_i$ a sequence such that $\lim_{n \to \infty} x_i$. The x_i can be considered as approximations of x. We have that a sequence of permutations of successive approximations is not necessarily a converging sequence. Take for example $x = 12345 \cdots$. Let $x[n]$ denote the first n elements of x, i.e. $x[n] = 1 \cdots n$. We have $\lim_{n \to \infty} x[n] = x$, but $\lim_{n \to \infty} perm(x[n])$ does not exist.

A way out could be an extension of the notion of limit we use. Arnold, Nivat [1] consider operators that are only continuous with respect to Painlevé limits. Let *Lim* denote a limit in the Painlevé sense. Then we have

$\underset{n\to\infty}{Lim}\ perm(x[n]) = perm(x)$. See also some of the remarks of Smyth [18] where he compares the Hausdorff metric with the Vietoris topology. They agree on $P_{comp}(V^{str})$ but differ on $P_{closed}(V^{str})$. These are topics for further research.

6.2. Remarks

Up to now, our functions have as domain the collection of compact sets of streams. Sometimes it is more convenient to take as domain the set of streams, and consider functions from $V^{str} \to P_{comp}(V^{str})$. When we want to apply the function to a set of streams we do this in the usual way, i.e. $f[X] = \cup\{f(x) \mid x \in X\}$. An appeal to lemma 2.6. yields that functions extended in this way fit into our framework.

Lemma 2.6. can also simplify proofs. For example, to prove that a (monotonic) function is non distance increasing from $P_{comp}(V^{str}) \to P_{comp}(V^{str})$ it suffices to show that this function is non distance increasing from $V^{str} \to P_{comp}(V^{str})$.

7. References

[1] ARNOLD, A., NIVAT, M., The metric space of infinite trees, algebraic and topological properties, Fund. Inform. III, 4, pp 445-476, 1980.

[2] DE BAKKER, J.W., Mathematical theory of program correctness, Prentice Hall International,1980.

[3] DE BAKKER, J.W., KLOP, J.W., MEYER, J.-J.CH., Correctness of programs with function procedures in Logic of Programs, LNCS 131, proceedings 1981, Kozen, D., Springer, 1982.

[4] DE BAKKER, J.W., ZUCKER, J.I., Compactness in semantics for merge and fair merge in Logic of Programs, LNCS 164, proceedings 1983, Kozen, D., Clarke, E., Springer, 1983.

[5] DE BAKKER, J.W., ZUCKER, J.I., Processes and the denotational semantics of concurrency, Information and Control, 54, pp 70-120, 1982.

[6] BROY, M., Fixed point theory for communication and concurrency, in Bjorner, Ed., IFIP TC 2 Working conference on Formal description of Programming Concepts II, Garmisch, June 1982, pp 125-147, North Holland, Amsterdam, 1983.

[7] BROY, M., BAUER, L., A systematic approach to language constructs for concurrent programs, in Science of Computer Programming 4, pp 103-139, North Holland, 1984.

[8] BURGE, W.H., Stream processing functions, in IBM journal of research and development, 19, pp 12-25, 1975.

[9] DARLINGTON, J., HENDERSON, P., TURNER, D.A. (eds), Functional programming and its applications, Cambridge University Press, Cambridge, 1982.

[10] DENNIS, J.B., WENG, K.K.-S., An abstract implementation for concurrent computation with streams, in Proc. 1979 int. conf. on parallel processing, pp 35-45, 1979.

[11] DUGUNDJI, J., Topology, Allyn and Bacon, Inc., Boston, 1966.

[12] IDA, T., TANAKA, J., Functional programming with streams, in Information Processing, pp 265-270, North-Holland, 1983.

[13] MEERTENS, L.G.L.T., Procedurele datastructuren (in Dutch), in Colloquium Capita Datastructuren (J.C. VAN VLIET (Red)), pp 171-186, MC syllabus 37, Amsterdam, 1978.

[14] MICHAEL, E., Topologies on spaces of subsets, in Trans. AMS 71, pp 152-182, 1951.

[15] NAKATA, I, Programming with streams, in IBM-research report , RJ 3751 (43317) , 1983.

[16] NIVAT, M., Infinite words, infinite trees, infinite computations, in Foundations of computer science III.2 (de Bakker, J.W., van Leeuwen, J. (eds)), 3-52, Mathematical centre tracts 109, 1979.

[17] ROUNDS, W.C., GOLSON, W.G., Connections between two theories of concurrency: Metric spaces and synchronization trees, Information and control 57, pp 102-124, 1983.

[18] SMYTH, M.B., Powerdomains and predicate transformers: a topological view, Proc. 10th ICALP, Barcelona, Spain, Diaz, J. (ed), LNCS 154, pp 662-676, 1983.

[19] TISON, S., DAUCHET, M., COMYN, G., Metrical and ordered properties of powerdomains, Proc. FCT conference, Borgholm, Sweden, Karpinski, M. (ed), LNCS 158, pp 465-474, 1983.

[20] TURNER, D.A., Recursion equations as a programming language, in Darlington, J., Henderson, P., Turner, D.A. (eds), Functional programming and its applications, Cambridge University Press, Cambridge, pp 1-28, 1982.

[21] TURNER, D.A, A new implementation technique for applicative languages, in Software- Practice and experience, 9 ,pp 31-49, 1979.

[22] WADGE, W.W., An extensional treatment of dataflow deadlock, in Theoretical Computer Science 13 (1981), pp 3-15, 1981.

[23] WADLER, P., Applicative style programming, program transformation and list operators, in Proc. functional programming languages and computer architecture, pp 25-32, 1981.

Infinite Streams and Finite Observations in the Semantics of Uniform Concurrency

J.W. de Bakker

Centre for Mathematics and Computer Science &
Free University, Amsterdam

J.-J. Ch. Meyer

Free University, Amsterdam

E.-R. Olderog

Christian-Albrechts-Universität Kiel

ABSTRACT

Two ways of assigning meaning to a language with uniform concurrency are presented and compared. The language has uninterpreted elementary actions from which statements are composed using sequential composition, nondeterministic choice, parallel composition with communication, and recursion. The first semantics uses infinite streams in the sense which is a refinement of the linear time semantics of De Bakker et al. The second semantics uses the finite observations of Hoare et al., situated "in between" the divergence and readiness semantics of Olderog & Hoare. It is shown that the two models are isomorphic and that this isomorphism induces an equivalence result between the two semantics.

1. INTRODUCTION

Infinite streams of actions or states provide a natural and clear concept for describing the behaviour of non-terminating concurrent processes [Br, Ni]. The supporting mathematics, however, tends to get complicated even if some simplifying assumptions on the admissible sets of streams are possible [Br, BBKM]. On the other hand, finite traces of actions or more generally finite observations like ready or failure pairs typically require a rather simple mathematics to justify the semantic constructions [BHR, FLP, OH2]. However, these constructions often seem more "ad hoc" and less clear conceptually. Also, finite observations are in general less expressive than infinite streams, for example in the presence of fairness [He2, OH2].

Our paper now presents an interesting case where infinite streams and finite observations are equally expressive in the sense of an isomorphism. We establish our results for a core language $\mathcal{L}$ of uniform or schematic concurrency [BMOZ] involving uninterpreted atomic actions, sequential composition, nondeterministic choice (local nondeterminism), parallel composition (merge) with communication and recursion. For $\mathcal{L}$ we introduce two versions of (denotational)linear time semantics [BBKM].

The first semantics $\mathcal{D}_{str}$ is based on finite and infinite streams of actions. $\mathcal{D}_{str}$ refines the linear time semantics LT developed in [BBKM] in that it deals more satisfactorily with recursion. This is achieved by using a Smyth-like ordering on sets of streams. When developing the semantics $\mathcal{D}_{str}$ we shall carefully motivate the conditions of flatness and topological closedness for our powerdomain of streams. In particular, topological closedness will be crucial for proving the continuity of the semantic operators. Unfortunately, these proofs are rather complicated [Me, BBKM].

The second semantics $\mathcal{D}_{obs}$ fits into the specification-oriented approach to the semantics of concurrent processes [OH1/2]- a generalization of the specific failure semantics in [BHR]. The starting point for the approach is a simple correctness criterion for processes: a process P satisfies a specification S, denoted by $P\,\mathbf{sat}\,S$, if every observation we can make about P is allowed by S. An observation is a finitely representable information about the computational behaviour of processes. Examples of observations are (finite) traces, traces with divergence information, ready pairs and failure pairs leading to the (increasingly sophisticated) trace, divergence, readiness and failure semantics for concurrent processes [OH2]. Our specific observation semantics $\mathcal{D}_{obs}$ for $\mathcal{L}$ can be seen as "in between" the divergence and the readiness semantics of [OH2].

Our main result is that both approaches to the semantics of $\mathcal{L}$ are isomorphic. This isomorphism has various benefits in the mutual understanding of both approaches:

- the concepts in $\mathcal{D}_{str}$ have a natural translation into $\mathcal{D}_{obs}$: for example, topological closedness in $\mathcal{D}_{str}$ gets translated into prefix closedness in $\mathcal{D}_{obs}$,

- through this translation the constructions for $\mathcal{D}_{obs}$ become clear conceptually,
- most important perhaps, proofs of continuity of the semantic operators in $\mathcal{D}_{str}$ now become very simple via the isomorphism to $\mathcal{D}_{obs}$, involving only the notion of domain finite relations on the side of observations [OH1/2]. Thus through the idea of observation we can circumvent the technically difficult continuity proofs of [BBKM, Me].

Our paper is backed up by the reports [Me] and [OH2]; the linking isomorphism result will be proved fully in its final version.

2. THE LANGUAGE $\mathfrak{L}$

Let A be a finite set of *actions,* with $a,b \in A$, $*: A \times A \xrightarrow{part} A$ be a partial binary operation on A called *communication function,* and *Pvar* be a set of *process variables,* with $x,y \in Pvar$. Then the set of *(concurrent) processes* $\mathfrak{L}$, with $P,Q \in \mathfrak{L}$, is given by the following BNF-syntax:

2.1. Definition

$$P ::= a \mid P;Q \mid P \text{ or } Q \mid P \| Q \mid x \mid \mu x[P]$$

2.2. Remarks. Every action $a \in A$ denotes a process, the one which finishes (terminates successfully) after performing a. $P;Q$ denotes *sequential composition* such that Q starts once P has finished. P **or** Q denotes *nondeterministic choice,* also known as *local nondeterminism* [FHLR]. $P \| Q$ denotes *communication merge* (cf. [BK]) where parallel composition is modelled by arbitrary interleaving plus communication between those actions a of P and b of Q for which $a*b$ is defined. For example, if only $b*c$ is defined, we will obtain the following equation in our semantics:

$$(a;b)\|c = a;b;c \text{ or } a;c;b; \text{ or } c;a;b \text{ or } a;(b*c).$$

Communication merge is inspired by [Mi2, BK, Wi], though we do not assume any algebraic property of $*$.

By varying the communication function $*$, we can express more familiar notions of parallel composition like shuffle (arbitrary merge) or merge with binary communication as in CCS[Mi].

Starting from actions $a \in A$, the operators ;, **or**, and $\|$ can only define concurrent processes P with finite semantic behaviour; infinite behaviours require processes P involving recursion, expressed here by the μ-construct [dB].

3. THE STREAM SEMANTICS $\mathcal{D}_{str}$

Let $\perp \notin A$. Then we define the set of *streams* $Str(A)$, with $u,v,w \in Str(A)$, as follows [Br]:

3.1. Definition. $Str(A) = A^* \cup A^\omega \cup A^*.\{\perp\}$.

3.2. Remarks. $Str(A)$ includes the set $A^\infty = A^* \cup A^\omega$ of finite and infinite words over A [Ni], called here *finished* and *infinite streams,* respectively, and additionally the set $A^*.\{\perp\}$ of *unfinished streams.* The linear time semantics LT of [BBKM] was entirely based on A^∞. The reason for including unfinished streams $u.\perp$ as well is that they allow a more satisfactory treatment of recursion (see Proposition 3.28).

Let ϵ denote the *empty* (finished) stream, $\leqslant$ the *prefix relation* and $<$ *the proper prefix relation* over streams, and $|u|$ the *length* of a stream u, with $|u| = \infty$ for infinite u's. Additionally we use the following approximation relation

3.3. Definition. $u \sqsubseteq v$ iff the following holds
- if u is finished or infinite then $u = v$,
- if u is unfinished, i.e., of the form $u = u'\perp$, then $u' \leqslant v$.

3.4. Examples. $a \leqslant a\perp$, $a\perp \nleqslant a$, $a\perp \nleqslant ab$ but $a \not\sqsubseteq a\perp$, $a\perp \sqsubseteq a$, $a\perp \sqsubseteq ab$.

Consider for a moment an arbitrary cpo $(C, \sqsubseteq_c, \perp_c)$ and a subset $S \subseteq C$.

3.5. Definition. S is called *flat* if $x \sqsubseteq_c y$ implies $x = y$ for all $x,y \in S$. If $C \setminus \{\perp_c\}$ is flat, the cpo $(C, \sqsubseteq_c, \perp_c)$ itself is called flat.

3.6. Proposition. $(Str(A), \sqsubseteq, \perp)$ *is a non-flat cpo.*

To provide meaning to concurrent processes $P \in \mathfrak{L}$ we need (certain) *sets* of streams. Let $\mathcal{P}(Str(A))$ denote the powerset of streams, with typical elements $X,Y \in \mathcal{P}(Str(A))$. Then we will use the following *Smyth relation* [Sm]:

3.7. Definition. $X \sqsubseteq_S Y$ if $\forall v \in Y\ \exists u \in X: u \sqsubseteq v$.

3.8. Remark. $X \supseteq Y$ implies $X \sqsubseteq_S Y$.

It is well-known that the Smyth relation $\sqsubseteq_S$ is not antisymmetric and thus not a partial order on non-flat domains like $\mathcal{P}(Str(A))$ [Ba, Br]. But the Smyth relation is a pre-order which generates an equivalence relation $\equiv_S$ on $\mathcal{P}(Str(A))$:

$$X \equiv_S Y \quad \text{iff} \quad X \sqsubseteq_S Y \quad \text{and} \quad Y \sqsubseteq_S X.$$

What are the sets identified by $\equiv_S$?

3.9. Definition. $\min_S(X)=\{v \in X \mid \neg\exists u \in X: u \sqsubseteq v \wedge u \neq v\}$ is the set of minimal streams in X.

Then $X \equiv_S Y$ if and only if $\min_S(X)=\min_S(Y)$. Thus the sets $\min_S(X)$ form a system of representatives of the equivalence classes under $\equiv_S$. Note that $\min_S(X)$ is flat.

3.10. Definition. $\mathcal{P}_f(Str(A))$ is the set of all flat subsets of $Str(A)$.

3.11. Proposition. *$\mathcal{P}(Str(A))/\equiv_S$ is isomorphic to $\mathcal{P}_f(Str(A))$.*

3.12. Proposition. *$(\mathcal{P}_f(Str(A)), \sqsubseteq_S, \{\perp\})$ is a cpo.*

The proof can be found in [Ba] (see [Me]). Next, we need some auxiliary operators on streams.

Concatenation $u \cdot v$: For $u,v \in A^{\infty}=A^{*} \cup A^{\omega}$ the concatenation $u \cdot v$ is well-known from the theory of infinitary languages [Ni]. We extend this definition to arbitrary streams by imposing the equation $\perp \cdot v = \perp$.

Communication merge $u \| v$: Here we consider only finite streams $u,v \in A^{*} \cup A^{*} \cdot \{\perp\}$. Then $u \| v$ is a *set* of (finite) streams defined by

$$u \| v \; = \; u \,⫫\, v \cup v \,⫫\, u \cup u | v$$

where recursively $\epsilon ⫫ v=\{v\}$, $\perp ⫫ v=\{\perp\}$, $a \cdot u ⫫ v = a \cdot (u \| v)$ and $au|bv=(a{*}b)\cdot(u\|v)$ provided $a{*}b$ is defined; in all other cases $u|v=\emptyset$. This finite recursive definition of $\|$ using $⫫$ and $|$ is due to [BK].

To lift these definitions to flat sets of streams, we use the operator $\min_S$ of Definition 3.9 and the following notion of *n-th approximation* $u^{[n]}$, $n \geq 0$, for streams u: $u^{[n]}=u$ if $|u|<n$ and $u^{[n]}=u'\perp$ if $|u|\geq n$ and $u' \leq u$ with $|u'|=n$. We extend this definition pointwise to subsets $X \subseteq Str(A)$ by putting $X^{[n]}=\{u^{[n]} \mid u \in X\}$. Now let $X,Y \in \mathcal{P}_f(Str(A))$.

Sequential composition

$$X ;^{str} Y \; = \; \min_S(\{u \cdot v \mid u \in X \text{ and } v \in Y\})$$

Local nondeterminism

$$X \textbf{ or } Y \; = \; \min_S(X \cup Y)$$

Parallel composition

For $X,Y \subseteq A^{*} \cup A^{*}.\{\perp\}$ (involving only finite streams) we set

$$X \|^{str} Y \; = \; \min_S(\{w \in Str(A) \mid \exists u \in X,\ v \in Y: w \in u \| v\})$$

and for arbitrary flat $X,Y \subseteq Str(A)$ we work with semantic approximations:

$$X \|^{str} Y \; = \; \bigsqcup_{n=0}^{\infty}{}_S (X^{[n]} \|^{str} Y^{[n]}).$$

3.13. Theorem. *The semantic operators*

$$op^{str}: \mathcal{P}_f(Str(A)) \times \mathcal{P}_f(Str(A)) \rightarrow \mathcal{P}_f(Str(A))$$

with $op \in \{;,\ \textbf{or},\ \|\}$ are both well-defined and $\sqsubseteq_S$-monotonic.

The proof is given in [Me]. Showing monotonicity is not trivial for ; and $\|$. To provide meaning to recursive processes too, we will have to show that the semantic operators op^{str} are also continuous.

3.14. Theorem. $\textbf{or}^{str}$ is continuous under $\sqsubseteq_S$.

Unfortunately, the operators $;^{str}$ and $\|^{str}$ are not continuous on arbitrary flat sets of streams. To rescue the continuity of ; and $\|$, we will restrict ourselves to closed sets of streams.

3.15. Definition [Ba]. $X \subseteq Str(A)$ is *closed* if for every infinitely often increasing chain $<u_n>_{n\geq 0}$ of unfinished streams in $Str(A)$ the property

$$\forall n \geq 0 \exists v_n \in X: u_n \sqsubseteq v_n$$

implies that the stream limit $\bigsqcup_{n=0}^{\infty} u_n \in X$.

At first sight this closedness property looks a bit technical, but it is not. We can show that it coincides with the clear concept of *topological closedness* w.r.t. the following metric topology on $Str(A)$.

3.16. Definition. The *distance* d: $Str(A) \times Str(A) \rightarrow [0,1]$ is given by

$$d(u,v) = 2^{-\min\{n \mid u^{[n]} \neq v^{[n]}\}}$$

with the convention that $2^{-\infty}=0$.

3.17. Examples. $d(abc,aba)=2^{-3}, d(a^n,a^\omega)=2^{-n-1}$.

3.18. Proposition. *$(Str(A),d)$ is a complete metric space.*

Thus, we can talk of *Cauchy sequences* $<u_n>_{n\geq 0}$ of streams, their *topological limits* and of *topologically closed* sets $X \subseteq Str(A)$, i.e. where every Cauchy sequence $<u_n>_{n\geq 0}$ with $u_n \in X$ has its topological limit (which exists in $Str(A)$) inside X.

3.19. Proposition. *A subset $X \subseteq Str(A)$ is closed iff X is topologically closed.*

3.20. Examples. $X=\{a^n ba^\omega \mid n \geq 0\} \cup \{a^\omega\}$ is (topologically) closed, but $Y=\{a^n ba^\omega \mid n \geq 0\}$ is not.

Note that Y typically arises through a *fair merge* of $Y_1=\{a^\omega\}$ and $Y_2=\{b\}$. Hence notions like fairness or eventuality are not expressible using only (topologically) closed sets of streams [He2, Me].

3.21. Definition. $\mathcal{P}_{ncf}(Str(A))$ is the set of all non-empty, closed and flat subsets of $Str(A)$.

The following lemma is crucial for the further development:

3.22. Lemma. *If $<X_n>_{n\geq 0}$ is a $\sqsubseteq_S$-chain of sets $X_n \in \mathcal{P}_{ncf}(Str(A))$, then $\bigsqcup_{n=0}^{\infty}{}_S X_n \neq \emptyset$.*

The proof is rather involved [Me]. We can now establish the following results:

3.23. Proposition. *$(\mathcal{P}_{ncf}(Str(A)), \sqsubseteq_S, \{\perp\})$ is a cpo.*

3.24. Theorem. *The operators $;^{str}$ and $\|^{str}$, when restricted to $\mathcal{P}_{ncf}(Str(A))$, are continuous under $\sqsubseteq_S$.*

The proof uses Lemma 3.2.2 and otherwise follows [BBKM]; the case of $\|$ is difficult.

3.25. Remark. Lemma 3.22 and Theorem 3.24 do not hold, in general, for *infinite* sets A of actions.

We can now define the denotational stream semantics $\mathcal{D}_{Str}$ for $\mathcal{L}$. The set of environments is given by $\Gamma = Pvar \rightarrow \mathcal{P}_{ncf}(Str(A))$, with $\gamma \in \Gamma$. Let, as before, X,Y range over $\mathcal{P}_{ncf}(Str(A))$, and let $\gamma' = \gamma\{X/x\}$ be as γ but with $\gamma'(x)=X$. For a $\sqsubseteq_S$ -continuous function Φ from $\mathcal{P}_{ncf}(Str(A))$ to $\mathcal{P}_{ncf}(Str(A))$ let $\mu\Phi$ denote its least fixed point.

3.26. Definition. The semantic mapping

$$\mathcal{D}_{Str}[\![\cdot]\!]: \mathcal{L} \rightarrow (\Gamma \rightarrow \mathcal{P}_{ncf}(Str(A)))$$

is given by:

(i) $\mathcal{D}_{Str}[\![a]\!](\gamma) = \{a\}$

(ii) $\mathcal{D}_{Str}[\![P;Q]\!](\gamma) = \mathcal{D}_{Str}[\![P]\!](\gamma);^{str}\mathcal{D}_{Str}[\![Q]\!](\gamma)$

(iii) $\mathcal{D}_{Str}[\![P \,\mathbf{or}\, Q]\!](\gamma) = \mathcal{D}_{Str}[\![P]\!](\gamma)\mathbf{or}^{str}\mathcal{D}_{Str}[\![Q]\!](\gamma)$

(iv) $\mathcal{D}_{Str}[\![P \| Q]\!](\gamma) = \mathcal{D}_{Str}[\![P]\!](\gamma)\|^{str}\mathcal{D}_{Str}[\![Q]\!](\gamma)$

(v) $\mathfrak{D}_{Str}[\![x]\!](\gamma) = \gamma(x)$

(vi) $\mathfrak{D}_{Str}[\![\mu x[P]]\!](\gamma) = \mu\Phi_{P,\gamma}$ where $\Phi_{P,\gamma} = \lambda X \cdot \mathfrak{D}_{Str}[\![P]\!](\gamma\{X/x\})$.

A process $P \in \mathfrak{L}$ is called *guarded in* x whenever all occurrences of x in P are within subprocesses of P of the form $Q;(...x...)$. A process P is called *guarded* (cf. [Mil] or [Ni], where *Greibach* replaces guarded) whenever, for each recursive subprocess $\mu y[Q]$ of P we have that Q is guarded in y.

3.27. Examples. $\mu x[a;x \,\mathbf{or}\, b]$ and $\mu x[a;(x \| b)]$ are guarded; $\mu x[x]$, $\mu x[x;a \,\mathbf{or}\, b]$ and $\mu x[x \| b]$ are not.

3.28. Proposition. *In the semantics* $\mathfrak{D}_{Str}$ *all unguarded processes* P *(without free process variables) are identified:* $\mathfrak{D}_{Str}[\![P]\!](\gamma) = \{\perp\}$.

This solution seems more attractive than the results in the linear time semantics LT of [BBKM]. For example, $LT[\![\mu x[x]]\!](\gamma) = A^{\infty}$ but (surprisingly) $LT[\![\mu x[x;b]]\!](\gamma) = A^{\omega}$.

4. THE OBSERVATION SEMANTICS $\mathfrak{D}_{obs}$

4.1. Background.

Motivated by the failure semantics of [BHR], a new approach to the semantics of concurrent processes has been developed in [OH1/2]. It is called "specification-oriented" because it starts from the following simple concept of process correctness: a process P satisfies a specification S, abbreviated P **sat** S, if every observation we can make about P is allowed by S. The idea is that by varying the structure of observations we can express various types of process semantics and process correctness in a uniform way.

The principles of specification-oriented semantics are:

- an observation is a finitely representable information about the operational behaviour of processes,
- therefore the set of possible observations about a process enjoys some natural closure properties with respect to certain predecessor and successor observations,
- sets of observations are ordered by the nondeterminism ordering (reverse set-inclusion) [BHR],
- this ordering leads to a simple mathematics, in particular a very simple continuity argument for the language operators.

Let us now start with an example of a semantics- not treated in[OH2]- which fits into this framework. We use two distinct symbols $\surd, \uparrow \notin A$ to define the following set $Obs(A)$ of *observations*, with $h \in Obs(A)$:

4.2. Definition. $Obs(A) = A^* \cup A^* \cdot \{\surd, \uparrow\}$.

4.3. Remarks. Here observations are finite *traces* or *histories* over A and the extra symbols $\surd$ and $\uparrow$, representing *successful termination* [BHR] and *divergence* [OH2], respectively. Divergence $\uparrow$ stands for an infinite internal loop of a process generated by an unguarded recursion like $\mu x[x]$. Thus in spite of their finite representation, not all observations can be made effectively; a similar concession is also present in the concept of testing due to [dNH].

As for streams we let ϵ denote the *empty* history and $\leqslant$ the *prefix relation* between histories. Apart from $\leqslant$ we do not introduce any further relation on $Obs(A)$ which would correspond to $\sqsubseteq$ on $Str(A)$. Let $\mathfrak{P}(Obs(A))$ denote the powerset of $Obs(A)$, with $H \in \mathfrak{P}(Obs(A))$).

4.4. Definition. $H \subseteq Obs(A)$ is called *saturated* iff the following holds:

(i) H includes the *minimal observation, i.e.* $\epsilon \in H$,

(ii) H is *prefix closed,* i.e.

$$h \in H \quad \text{and} \quad h' \leqslant h \quad \text{imply} \quad h' \in H$$

(iii) H is *extensible,* i.e.

$$h \in H \setminus A^* \cdot \{\surd\} \quad \text{implies} \quad \exists \alpha \in A \cup \{\surd, \uparrow\}: h\alpha \in H$$

(iv) H treats divergence as *chaos,* i.e.

$$h\uparrow \in H \quad \text{and} \quad h' \in Obs(A) \quad \text{imply} \quad hh' \in H.$$

4.5. Remarks. These closure properties are (partly) motivated by looking at saturated H's as the sets of possible observations about a concurrent process:

(i) As long as the process has not yet started, we only observe the empty history ϵ.

(ii) Whenever we have observed a history h, also all its prefixes h' are observable.

(iii) Only histories $h\surd$ indicate the successful termination of the observed process; for all other histories h some *extension* $\alpha \in A \cup \{\surd, \uparrow\}$ is certain to happen, but we do not know which one, by looking at h.

(iv) Identifying divergence $h\uparrow$ after a history h with the *chaotic closure* $h \cdot Obs(A)$ cannot be explained operationally, rather it originates from the desire to ban diverging processes from satisfying any reasonable specification. This idea is familiar from Dijkstra's weakest precondition semantics where a diverging program will not achieve any postcondition [Pl].

Properties (i), (ii) are typical conditions on traces to be found in [BHR, FLP, OH1/2]. Property (iii) is a new "linear version" of the extensibility condition in the readiness [OH2] or failure semantics [BHR]. Property (iv) is typical for a simple, but proper treatment of divergence [OH2]; without $\uparrow$ unsatisfactory results occur [BHR] akin to those in the LT semantics [BBKM] (cf. end of Section 3).

4.6. Definition. $\mathcal{P}_{sat}(Obs(A))$ is the set of all saturated subsets of $Obs(A)$.

On $\mathcal{P}_{sat}(Obs(A))$ we introduce the following *nondeterminism order* $\sqsubseteq_N$ [BHR]:

4.7. Definition. $H_1 \sqsubseteq_N H_2$ iff $H_1 \supseteq H_2$.

4.8. Proposition. *$(\mathcal{P}_{sat}(Obs(A)), \supseteq, Obs(A))$ is a cpo.*

Proving the cpo property for $\mathcal{P}_{sat}(Obs(A))$ is much simpler than for $\mathcal{P}_{ncf}(Str(A))$: cf. Lemma 3.22. But what is the relationship between $\mathcal{P}_{ncf}(Str(A))$ and $\mathcal{P}_{sat}(Obs(A))$ anyway? This is the topic of the next section.

5. THE ISOMORPHISM BETWEEN STREAMS AND OBSERVATIONS

We wish to relate the cpo's $(\mathcal{P}_{ncf}(Str(A)), \sqsubseteq_S, \{\bot\})$ and $(\mathcal{P}_{sat}(Obs(A)), \supseteq, Obs(A))$. To this end we define a mapping Ψ, first as

$$\Psi: Str(A) \rightarrow \mathcal{P}(Obs(A)).$$

For $u \in A^*$ and $v \in A^\omega$ let

$$\Psi(u) = \{h \in A^* \mid h \leqslant u\} \cup \{u\surd\}$$

$$\Psi(v) = \{h \in A^* \mid h \leqslant v\}$$

$$\Psi(u\bot) = \{h \in A^* \mid h \leqslant u\} \cup \{uh \mid h \in Obs(A)\}.$$

5.1. Remarks. A finished streams u is translated into the set of all its prefixes plus $u\surd$ with $\surd$ signalling successful termination of u, an infinite stream is translated into the set of all its *finite* prefixes, and an unfinished stream $u\bot$ is translated into the set of all prefixes of u plus the chaotic closure $u \cdot Obs(A)$ of divergence $u\uparrow$.

We extend Ψ pointwise to a mapping

$$\Psi: \mathcal{P}(Str(A)) \rightarrow \mathcal{P}(Obs(A))$$

by

$$\Psi(X) = \bigcup_{w \in X} \Psi(w)$$

5.2. Examples. $\Psi(\{ab\}) = \{\epsilon, a, ab, ab\surd\}$, $\Psi(\{a^\omega\}) = \{a^n \mid n \geqslant 0\}$, $\Psi(\{\bot\}) = Obs(A)$.

5.3. Theorem. *Ψ is an isomorphism from the cpo $(\mathcal{P}_{ncf}(Str(A)), \sqsubseteq_S, \{\bot\})$ onto the cpo $(\mathcal{P}_{sat}(Obs(A)), \supseteq, Obs(A))$, i.e. Ψ is bijective, yields $\Psi(\{\bot\}) = Obs(A)$ and strongly preserves the partial orders:*

$$X \sqsubseteq_S Y \quad \textit{iff} \quad \Psi(X) \supseteq \Psi(Y)$$

for all $X, Y \in \mathcal{P}_{ncf}(Str(A))$.

5.4. Remarks. $\mathcal{P}_{ncf}(Str(A))$ has been constructed through a chain of clear domain-theoretical notions: streams, sets of streams, Smyth relation, flatness, continuity, topological closure, non-emptiness. The introduction of $\mathcal{P}_{sat}(Obs(A))$ with its saturation property may seem more ad hoc. But the theorem now tells us that $\mathcal{P}_{sat}(Obs(A))$ can in fact be viewed as a *special representation of the general construction* $\mathcal{P}_{ncf}(Str(A))$. This provides us with a new mutual understanding of the closedness properties in both domains: *topological closedness* on streams corresponds to taking *all finite prefixes* as observations, *flatness* of set of streams corresponds to the *chaotic closedness* on observations, *non-emptiness* of sets of streams does *not* simply correspond to the fact that saturated sets of observations include ϵ, but that in addition they are *extensible.*

Whereas the non-emptiness of (lubs of) sets of streams is a global property, the extensibility of observations is a local property where every observation $h \notin A^*\{\uparrow\}$ can be locally extended by another $\alpha \in A \cup \{\surd, \uparrow\}$. This issue of "global" vs. "local" hints at why it is more difficult to prove the cpo property for $\mathcal{P}_{ncf}(Str(A))$ than for $\mathcal{P}_{sat}(Obs(A))$.

6. THE OBSERVATION SEMANTICS $\mathcal{D}_{obs}$: CONTINUED

Let us now continue with the observation semantics $\mathcal{D}_{obs}$. For the operators of $\mathcal{D}_{obs}$ we could well provide indirect definitions using the previous isomorphism. But it will be more illuminating to discuss direct definitions because the ordering $\supseteq$ on sets of observations allows a very simple, uniform proof of (monotonicity and) continuity.

In fact, this uniform argument can be explained independently of the specific structure of observations. Consider two sets $\mathbf{X}, \mathbf{Y}$ and a relation $R \subseteq \mathbf{X} \times Y$. Then R induces an operator

$$op_R : \mathcal{P}(\mathbf{X}) \rightarrow \mathcal{P}(\mathbf{Y})$$

on the subsets of $\mathbf{X}$ by taking for every $X \subseteq \mathbf{X}$ the *pointwise image* of X under R, i.e.

$$op_R(X) = \{y \in \mathbf{Y} \mid \exists x \in \mathbf{X}: xRy\}.$$

6.1. Lemma [OH2]. *The operator op_R is $\supseteq$-monotonic. Moreover, if R is domain finite, i.e. if for every $y \in \mathbf{Y}$ there exist only finitely many $x \in \mathbf{X}$ with xRy, op_R is also $\supseteq$-continuous.*

Let us demonstrate the use of the lemma in the case of *sequential composition*. First we define the corresponding semantic operator

$$;^{obs} : \mathcal{P}_{sat}(Obs(A)) \times \mathcal{P}_{sat}(Obs(A)) \rightarrow \mathcal{P}_{sat}(Obs(A))$$

as follows:

$$\begin{aligned} H_1 ;^{obs} H_2 = \; & \{h_1 \mid h_1 \in H_1 \text{ and } h_1 \text{ does not contain } \surd\} \\ & \cup \{h_1 h_2 \mid h_1 \surd \in H_1 \text{ and } h_2 \in H_2\} \\ & \cup \{h_1 h \mid h_1 \uparrow \in H_1 \text{ and } h \in Obs(A)\} \end{aligned}$$

Well-definedness of $;^{obs}$ has to be checked separately. But monotonicity and continuity of $;^{obs}$ follow from the general Lemma 6.1. Taking $\mathbf{X} = Obs(A) \times Obs(A)$ and $\mathbf{Y} = Obs(A)$ we look for a domain finite relation $R \subseteq \mathbf{X} \times \mathbf{Y}$ such that

$$(*) \quad ;^{obs} = op_R \upharpoonright \mathcal{P}_{sat}(Obs(A)) \times \mathcal{P}_{sat}(Obs(A)).$$

R can be read off from $;^{obs}$ as follows:
$(h_1, h_2) R h$ iff

(i) h_1 does not contain $\surd$, $h_2 = \epsilon$ and $h = h_1$, or

(ii) h_1 ends in $\surd$ and $h = (h_1 \setminus \surd) \cdot h_2$, or

(iii) h_1 ends in $\uparrow$, $h_2 = \epsilon$ and $h \in (h_1 \setminus \uparrow) \cdot Obs(h)$

Here $h_1 \setminus \surd$ and $h_1 \setminus \uparrow$ result from h_1 by removing from h_1 the symbols $\surd$ or $\uparrow$, respectively. Clearly, this R is domain finite. Thus Lemma 6.1 implies:

6.2. Proposition. *The operator $;^{obs}$ is monotonic and continuous under $\supseteq$.*

The discussion of the remaining operators will be brief. *Local nondeterminism* is just set-theoretic union

$$H_1 \mathbf{or}^{obs} H_2 = H_1 \cup H_2.$$

$\mathbf{or}^{obs}$ is well-defined and (by Lemma 6.1) monotonic and continuous under $\supseteq$. *Parallel composition* is defined by

$$H_1 \|^{obs} H_2 = \{h \mid \exists h_1 \in H_1, h_2 \in H_2 : h \in h_1 \| h_2\}$$

where $h_1 \| h_2$ is a set of observations given, similarly to the stream definition in Section 3, by

$$h_1 \| h_2 = h_1 \mathbin{\|\!\!\_} h_2 \cup h_2 \mathbin{\|\!\!\_} h_1 \cup h_1 | h_2$$

with $\epsilon \mathbin{\|\!\!\_} \epsilon = \{\epsilon\}$, $ah_1 \mathbin{\|\!\!\_} h_2 = a \cdot (h_1 \| h_2)$, $\surd \mathbin{\|\!\!\_} h_2 = \{h_2\}$, $\uparrow \mathbin{\|\!\!\_} \epsilon = Obs(A)$ and with $ah_1 | bh_2 = (a{*}b) \cdot (h_1 \| h_2)$ provided $a{*}b$ is defined; in all other cases $h_1 \mathbin{\|\!\!\_} h_2 = \emptyset$ and $h_1 | h_2 = \emptyset$. Lemma 6.1 yields:

6.3. Proposition. *The operator $\|^{obs}$ is well-defined, monotonic and continuous under $\supseteq$.*

6.4. Remarks. In the observation semantics the continuity proof for the operators $;^{obs}$, $\mathbf{or}^{obs}$, $\|^{obs}$ could be reduced to a simple test on domain finiteness. In the stream semantics the operators $;^{str}$ and $\|^{str}$ will *fail* such a test. For example, the infinite stream a^ω can originate from infinitely many pairs of streams u,v in the sense of both $u \cdot v = a^\omega$ and $u \| v = a^\omega$. Thus finite observations are crucial here.

Another advantage of finite observations is that we can define the operators, in particular $\|^{obs}$, without reference to any semantic approximation of its arguments - unlike the stream operator $\|^{str}$ where we put

$$X \|^{str} Y = \bigsqcup_{n=0}^{\infty}{}_S (X^{[n]} \|^{str} Y^{[n]})$$

in the general case.

We can now define the denotational observation semantics $\mathcal{D}_{obs}$ for $\mathcal{L}$. Again we use environments $\gamma \in \Gamma$, but now w.r.t. $\Gamma = Pvar \to \mathcal{P}_{sat}(Obs(A))$.

6.5. Definition. The semantic mapping

$$\mathcal{D}_{obs}[\![\cdot]\!]: \mathcal{L} \to (\Gamma \to \mathcal{P}_{sat}(Obs(A)))$$

is given by

(i) $\mathcal{D}_{obs}[\![a]\!](\gamma) = \{\epsilon, a, a\surd\}$

(ii) $\mathcal{D}_{obs}[\![P;Q]\!](\gamma) = \mathcal{D}_{obs}[\![P]\!](\gamma) ;^{obs} \mathcal{D}_{obs}[\![Q]\!](\gamma)$

(iii) $\mathcal{D}_{obs}[\![P \,\mathbf{or}\, Q]\!](\gamma) = \mathcal{D}_{obs}[\![P]\!](\gamma) \mathbf{or}^{obs} \mathcal{D}_{obs}[\![Q]\!](\gamma)$

(iv) $\mathcal{D}_{obs}[\![P \| Q]\!](\gamma) = \mathcal{D}_{obs}[\![P]\!](\gamma) \|^{obs} \mathcal{D}_{obs}[\![Q]\!](\gamma)$

(v) $\mathcal{D}_{obs}[\![x]\!](\gamma) = \gamma(x)$

(vi) $\mathcal{D}_{obs}[\![\mu x[P]]\!](\gamma) = \mu\Phi_{P,\gamma}$ where $\Phi_{P,\gamma} = \lambda H.\, \mathcal{D}_{obs}[\![P]\!](\gamma\{H/x\})$.

7. THE ISOMORPHISM BETWEEN STREAMS AND OBSERVATIONS: CONTINUED

Here we wish to link the stream semantics $\mathcal{D}_{Str}$ with the observation semantics $\mathcal{D}_{obs}$. Recall that Ψ is the cpo isomorphism from $\mathcal{P}_{ncf}(Str(A))$ onto $\mathcal{P}_{sat}(Obs(A))$.

7.1. Theorem. *For every language operator $op \in \{;\, , \mathbf{or}\, , \|\}$ of $\mathcal{L}$ and all $X, Y \in \mathcal{P}_{ncf}(Str(A))$*

$$\Psi(X\ op^{str}\ Y) = \Psi(X) op^{obs} \Psi(Y)$$

holds.

7.2. Corollary. *For every concurrent process $P \in \mathcal{L}$ and environment $\gamma \in \mathcal{P}var \to \mathcal{P}_{ncf}(Str(A))$*

$$\Psi(\mathcal{D}_{Str}[\![P]\!](\gamma)) = \mathcal{D}_{obs}[\![P]\!](\Psi \circ \gamma)$$

holds.

Together with theorem 5.3 the corollary says that the denotational *semantics* $\mathcal{D}_{Str}$ and $\mathcal{D}_{obs}$ are *isomorphic.*

8. CONCLUDING REMARKS

We have not included any notion of *global* nondeterminism like + [Mi1] or □ [BHR] nor any notion of *deadlock* like *stop* [BHR] or δ [BK] in $\mathcal{L}$. This restriction allows us to work with a linear time approach in the form of streams or linear histories. It is a topic for further research to investigate whether our results can be extended to non-linear approaches like failure [BHR] or branching time semantics [BZ].

REFERENCES

[Ba] R.J.R. Back, *A Continuous Semantics for Unbounded Nondeterminism,* Theoret. Comp. Sci. 23 (1983) 187-210.

[dB] J.W. de Bakker, *Mathematical Theory of Program Correctness* (Prentice Hall International, London, 1980).

[BBKM] J.W. de Bakker, J.A. Bergstra, J.W. Klop, J.-J. Ch. Meyer, *Linear Time and Branching Time Semantics for Recursion with Merge,* TCS 34 (1984) 135-156.

[BZ] J.W. de Bakker, J.I. Zucker, *Processes and the Denotational Semantics of Concurrency,* Inform. and Control 54 (1982) 70-120.

[BMOZ] J.W. de Bakker, J.-J. Ch. Meyer, E.-R. Olderog, J.I. Zucker, *Transition Systems, Infinitary Languages and the Semantics of Uniform Concurrency,* to appear in: Proc. 17th ACM STOC, Providence, R.I., 1985.

[BK] J.A. Bergstra, J.W. Klop, *Process Algebra for Synchronous Communication,* Information and Control, 60 (1984), pp. 109-137.

[BHR] S.D. Brookes, C.A.R. Hoare, A.W. Roscoe, *A Theory of Communicating Sequential Processes,* J. ACM 31 (1984) 560-599.

[Br] M. Broy, *Fixed Point Theory for Communication and Concurrency,* in: D. Bjørner (Ed.), Formal Description of Programming Concepts II (North-Holland, Amsterdam, 1983) 125-146.

[FHLR] N. Francez, C.A.R. Hoare, D.J. Lehmann, W.P. de Roever, *Semantics of Nondeterminism, Concurrency and Communicating,* JCSS 19 (1979) 290-308.

[FL] N. Francez, D.J. Lehmann, A. Pnueli, *A Linear History Semantics for Languages for Distributed Programming,* Theoret. Comp. Sci. 32 (1984) 25-46.

[He1] M.C.B. Hennessy, *Synchronous and Asynchronous Experiments on Processes,* Report CSR-125-82, Dept. of Comp. Sci., Univ. of Edinburgh, 1982.

[He2] M.C.B. Hennessy, *An Algebraic Theory of Fair Asynchronous Communicating Processes,* Manuscript, Dept. of Comp. Sci., Univ. of Edinburgh, 1984.

[Me] J.-J. Ch. Meyer, *Fixed Points and the Arbitrary and Fair Merge of a Fairly Simple Class of Processes,* Tech. Report IR-89/IR-92, Free University, Amsterdam, 1984.

[Mi1 R. Milner, *A Calculus of Communicating Systems,* LNCS 92 (Springer, Berlin, 1980).

[Mi2] R. Milner, *Calculi for Synchrony and Asynchrony,* Theoret. Comp. Sci. 25 (1983) 267-310.

[dNH] R. de Nicola, M.C.B. Hennessy, *Testing Equivalences for Processes,* TCS 34 (1984) 83-134.

[Ni] M. Nivat, *Infinite Words, Infinite Trees, Infinite Computations,* Foundations of Computer Science III. 2, Mathematical Centre Tracts 109 (1979) 3-52.

[OH1] E.-R. Olderog, C.A.R. Hoare, *Specification-oriented Semantics for Communicating Processes,* in: J. Diaz (Ed.), Proc. 10th ICALP, LNCS 154 (Springer, Berlin, 1983) 561-572.

[OH2] E.-R. Olderog, C.A.R. Hoare, *Specification-oriented Semantics for Communicating Processes,* Tech. Monograph PRG-37, Prog. Research Group, Oxford Univ., 1984 (to appear in Acta Informatica).

[Pl] G.D. Plotkin, *Dijkstra's Predicate Transformers and Smyth's Power Domains,* in: D. Bjørner (Ed.), Abstract Software Specification, LNCS 86 (Springer, Berlin, 1980) 527-553.

[Sm] M.B. Smyth, *Power Domains,* JCSS 16 (1978) 23-26.

[Wi] G. Winskel, *Synchronisation Trees,* TCS 34 (1984) 33-82.

IMPOSED-FUNCTIONAL DEPENDENCIES INDUCING HORIZONTAL DECOMPOSITIONS

P. De Bra*
Department of Mathematics
University of Antwerp, U.I.A.
Universiteitsplein 1
B-2610 Antwerp, Belgium

*Research assistent of the N.F.W.O.

ABSTRACT

A new decomposition theory for functional dependencies in the Relational Database Model is given. It uses a horizontal decomposition of a relation into two disjoint subrelations, of which the union is the given relation. This horizontal decomposition is based on a new constraint, the ***imposed-functional dependency (ifd)***, of which the ***conditional-functional dependency (cfd)***, introduced in a previous work, is a special case.

Functional dependencies can be expressed as special cfd's, (which themselves are special cases of ifd's). The horizontal decomposition induces another constraint: the ***afunctional dependency***. The membership problem for mixed ifd's and ad's is solved, and a complete set of inference rules is given. The inheritance problem, i.e. the problem of determining which dependencies hold in the subrelations that result from a horizontal decomposition step, is shown to be solvable in polynomial time.

1. INTRODUCTION

The vertical decomposition of relations into projections of these relations was introduced with the Relational Database Model by Codd [Co]. The horizontal decomposition of relations into restrictions of these relations, suggested in [Sm], has been used in [De1,De2,Pa] for treating exceptions to ***functional dependencies (fd's)***. In those papers no real constraints have been used for inducing horizontal decompositions. In [De3] the horizontal decomposition was formalized using a constraint: the ***conditional-functional dependency*** (cfd).

The main idea behind the decomposition of [De3] is that in the part of a relation without exceptions to some constraint, some other constraints may obviously hold too. The final goal of the decomposition theory that started with [De3] is to allow very general kinds of "partial implications" between constraints.

In this paper we introduce the ***imposed-functional dependency (ifd)***, a generalization of fd's and of cfd's. Also the concept of "goals", used in [De1,De2,Pa] to formalize "fd's with exceptions", can be expressed by means of ifd's. The horizontal decomposition, based on ifd's, induces another constraint: the ***afunctional dependency*** (ad), which also occurs in the decompositions of [De1,De2,De3,Pa].

In Section 2 we define the horizontal decomposition, based on ifd's. We also propose two theoretical tools: the ***Armstrong relation*** and the ***conflict concept***. In Section 3 the membership problem is solved for mixed ifd's and ad's and a complete set of inference rules is given. In Section 4 the inheritance of dependencies is proved to be solvable in polynomial time.

We suppose the reader is aware of the basic definitions and notations of the Relational Database theory [Ul].

2. HORIZONTAL DECOMPOSITIONS

The success of the traditional vertical decomposition, based on functional dependencies (fd's), depends on the presence of fd's in the real world. In many "real world" situations there is a need to allow exceptions to some fd's. In [De1,De2,Pa] it is shown how to treat such situations by means of horizontal decompositions. The exceptions are put in a separate subrelation, inducing the fd in the remaining (and main) part of the relation. Because the fd holds in this main part, it can be used to decompose this subrelation vertically.

When removing the exceptions (by means of a horizontal decomposition) some additional constraints may become obvious in the main part of the relation, i.e. there may be a kind of "ad hoc implication" between some fd's. For instance, if (in a company) a department treats only one job, it may be obvious that every employee can have only one manager for this department. We now show how to express this constraint formally, and then we treat the above example in detail.

Definition 2.1.

Let X be a set of attributes. A set of tuples S in a relation instance is called X-*complete* iff the tuples not belonging to S all have other X-projections than those belonging to S. Formally, if $t_1 \in S$, $t_2 \notin S$ then $t_1[X] \neq t_2[X]$.

A set of tuples S is called X-*unique* iff all the tuples of S have the same X-projection. Formally, if $t_1, t_2 \in S$ then $t_1[X] = t_2[X]$. ∎

The sets of tuples that are both X-complete and X-unique play an important role in the horizontal decomposition theory. They are the sets of all tuples having one and the same X-projection. For convenience we often use the term "X-*value*" to indicate such a set of tuples as well as the X-projection of the tuples in the set.

Definition 2.2.

The *imposed-functional dependency (ifd)* $X \rightarrow Y \supset\!\!- X' \rightarrow Z$, with $X \subseteq X'$, means that in every X-complete set of tuples (in every instance) in which the fd $X \rightarrow Y$ holds, the fd $X' \rightarrow Z$ must hold too. ∎

The constraint of the company-example is

$$department \rightarrow job \supset\!\!- department, employee \rightarrow manager.$$

It means that in every department that treats only one job every employee has only one manager (for this department).

The ifd's contain the *conditional-functional dependencies* (cfd's) of [De3] as a subclass, since cfd's are ifd's $X \rightarrow Y \supset\!\!- X' \rightarrow Z$ with $X = X'$. They also contain the fd's as a subclass. An fd $T \rightarrow U$ is equivalent to the ifd $\emptyset \rightarrow \emptyset \supset\!\!- T \rightarrow U$ as well as a large number of other ifd's, e.g. $T \rightarrow T \supset\!\!- T \rightarrow U$ (which also is a cfd). We usually denote an fd as fd, and not as a special ifd.

The horizontal decomposition separates (in our example) the departments treating only one job from the others. Assuming that in this company most departments are dedicated to only one job, the part of the relation, containing these departments, is almost the entire relation. Hence not much efficiency is lost by allowing some departments to possibly (temporarily) treat several jobs, since the fd's *department→job* and *department, employee→manager* still hold in the main part of the relation.

When separating the exceptions to an fd $X \rightarrow Y$ from the main part of the relation (instance) the X-values must not be split. This "separation" is formalized by defining the following restriction operator:

Definition 2.3.

Let $\mathcal{R}$ be a relation scheme, X, Y be sets of attributes.

For every instance R of $\mathcal{R}$, the *restriction for $X \rightarrow Y$ of R, $\sigma_{X \rightarrow Y}(R)$*, is the largest X-complete subset (of tuples) of R in which $X \rightarrow Y$ holds.

The *restriction for $X \rightarrow Y$ of $\mathcal{R}$, $\sigma_{X \rightarrow Y}(\mathcal{R})$*, is a scheme $\mathcal{R}_1$, (with the same attributes as $\mathcal{R}$,) of which the instances are exactly the restrictions for $X \rightarrow Y$ of the instances of $\mathcal{R}$. ∎

Definition 2.4.

The *horizontal decomposition of a scheme $\mathcal{R}$, according to the ifd $X \rightarrow Y \supset\!\!- X' \rightarrow Z$*, is the pair $\{\mathcal{R}_1, \mathcal{R}_2\}$, where $\mathcal{R}_1 = \sigma_{X \rightarrow Y}(\mathcal{R})$ and $\mathcal{R}_2 = \mathcal{R} - \mathcal{R}_1$. ∎

The horizontal decomposition of a scheme according to a "trivial" ifd like $X \rightarrow Y \supset\!\!- X \rightarrow Y$ is equivalent to the decomposition according to the "goal" (X, Y) (or $X \not\rightarrow Y$ in a more recent notation) as defined in [De1,De2,Pa].

Note that the horizontal decomposition of a scheme, according to $X \rightarrow Y \supset\!\!- X' \rightarrow Z$ does not depend on X' or Z, but it induces the fd $X' \rightarrow Z$ in $\mathcal{R}_1$. In $\mathcal{R}_2$, which contains the "exceptions", the fd $X \rightarrow Y$ is violated for every X-value. This is formalized by means of a constraint:

Definition 2.5.

The *afunctional dependency (ad) $X \not\rightarrow Y$* means that in every nonempty X-complete set of tuples, in every instance, the functional dependency $X \rightarrow Y$ does not hold. [De1].

For every instance R (or scheme $\mathcal{R}$) the instance $R - \sigma_{X \rightarrow Y}(R)$ (resp. $\mathcal{R} - \sigma_{X \rightarrow Y}(\mathcal{R})$) is denoted by $\sigma_{X \not\rightarrow Y}(R)$ (resp. $\sigma_{X \not\rightarrow Y}(\mathcal{R})$) and is called the *restriction for $X \not\rightarrow Y$ of R (resp. $\mathcal{R}$)*. ∎

It is easy to see that $\sigma_{X \not\rightarrow Y}(R)$ is the largest X-complete subset of tuples of R in which $X \not\rightarrow Y$ holds.

From now on we let a relation scheme $\mathcal{R}$ have a set $\mathcal{A}$ of ad's (that hold in $\mathcal{R}$) as well as a set $\mathcal{I}$ of ifd's.

The calculation of the constraints that hold in the restrictions of $\mathcal{R}$ is described in Section 4. The main problem with this calculation is that ifd's and ad's (which hold in $\mathcal{R}$) may not hold in some restrictions of $\mathcal{R}$.

To illustrate the new horizontal decomposition, based on ifd's, consider the following example:

Example 2.6.

Let *COMPANY* be a relation scheme, with attributes D, J, E, M, S, representing *E*mployees working, for a *D*epartment, on a *J*ob, for which they have a *M*anager and earn a *S*alary. In every department which treats only one job, every employee has only one manager and one salary (for this department). This is the ifd $D \rightarrow J \supset\!\!- ED \rightarrow MS$. (Note that this is a much weaker constraint than $EJ \rightarrow MS$, which would mean that every employee would have only one manager and salary for each job.)

Using $D \rightarrow J \supset\!\!- ED \rightarrow MS$ the scheme $COMPANY(\{D \rightarrow J \supset\!\!- ED \rightarrow MS\})$ is decomposed in $COMPANY_1(\{D \rightarrow J, ED \rightarrow MS\}$ and $COMPANY_2(\{D \not\rightarrow J\})$.

Note that the number of managers and salaries that an employee has in a department of $COMPANY_2$ is completely unknown.

Consider the following instance of *COMPANY*:
$COMPANY(\{D \rightarrow J \supset\!\!- ED \rightarrow MS\}) =$

D	J	E	M	S
IN	IN	Jones	Johnson	10000
IN	IN	Smith	Johnson	12000
OUT	OUT	Jones	Harvey	5000
OUT	OUT	Smith	Harvey	6000
INOUT	IN	Jones	Harvey	4000
INOUT	OUT	Jones	Harvey	5000
INOUT	IN	Smith	Harvey	3000

After the decomposition we have the instances:
$COMPANY_1(\{D \rightarrow J, ED \rightarrow MS\}) = \sigma_{D \rightarrow J}(COMPANY) =$

D	J	E	M	S
IN	IN	Jones	Johnson	10000
IN	IN	Smith	Johnson	12000
OUT	OUT	Jones	Harvey	5000
OUT	OUT	Smith	Harvey	6000

$COMPANY_2(\{D \not\rightarrow J\}) = \sigma_{D \not\rightarrow J}(COMPANY) =$

D	J	E	M	S
INOUT	IN	Jones	Johnson	4000
INOUT	OUT	Jones	Harvey	5000
INOUT	IN	Smith	Harvey	3000

■

The presence of both ifd's and ad's in a database scheme may involve a situation of "conflict" between the ifd's and the ad's. For instance the fd $X \rightarrow Y$ (which is a special ifd) and the ad $X \not\rightarrow Y$ cannot both hold in a nonempty instance. The "bad" combination of ifd's and ad's, which must be avoided when designing a database, are defined below.

Definition 2.7.
A set $\mathcal{I} \cup \mathcal{A}$ of ifd's ($\mathcal{I}$) and ad's ($\mathcal{A}$) is said to be ***in conflict*** iff the empty set of tuples is the only instance in which all dependencies of $\mathcal{I} \cup \mathcal{A}$ hold. ■

In Section 3 it is indicated how the detection of conflict can be reduced to the membership problem for fd's, (which is well known).

In Sections 3 and 4 the existence of ***Armstrong relations for fd's*** (described in [Ar,Fa]) plays an important role. In [Del] it is proved that the Armstrong relations of [Ar], (and also the "direct product construction" of [Fa]) satisfy the following property:

Theorem 2.8.
Let $Arm(\mathcal{F})$ denote the ***Armstrong relation*** for a set $\mathcal{F}$ of fd's. In $Arm(\mathcal{F})$ every fd, that is a consequence of $\mathcal{F}$, holds, and for every other fd $X \rightarrow Y$, the "corresponding" ad $X \not\rightarrow Y$ holds. ■

3. THE MEMBERSHIP PROBLEM FOR IFD'S AND AD'S

For cfd's and ad's it is proved in [De3] that the membership problem can be reduced to that of fd's, which is well known [Be,Ber]. In the sequel we shall prove that the membership problem for ifd's and ad's also is closely related to that of fd's.

We use the symbol $\models$ to denote the (logical) implication of a dependency by a set of dependencies. We use the symbol $\vdash$ to denote the derivation of a dependency from a set of dependencies by means of the following inference rules:

$(I1)$: if $Z - X' \subseteq Y - X$ and $X \subseteq X'$ then $X \to Y \supset\!\!- X' \to Z$.
$(I2)$: if $X \to Y \supset\!\!- X' \to Z$ and $W \subseteq V$ then $X \to Y \supset\!\!- X'V \to ZW$.
$(I3)$: if $X \to Y \supset\!\!- X' \to X''$ and $X \to Y \supset\!\!- X'' \to Z$ then $X \to Y \supset\!\!- X' \to Z$
$(I4)$: if $X \to Y \supset\!\!- X' \to Z$ and $X' \to Z \supset\!\!- X'' \to T$ then $X \to Y \supset\!\!- X'' \to T$.
$(I5)$: if $X \to Y \supset\!\!- X' \to Z$ and $X \to X''$ then $X'' \to Y \supset\!\!- X'X'' \to Z$.
$(IA1)$: if $X \to Y \supset\!\!- X' \to Z$ and $X' \not\twoheadrightarrow Z$ then $X \not\twoheadrightarrow Y$.
$(IA2)$: if $X \not\twoheadrightarrow Y$ and $X \subseteq X'$ then $X \to Y \supset\!\!- X' \to Z$ for all Z.
$(FA1)$: if $X \to Y$ and $X \not\twoheadrightarrow Z$ then $Y \not\twoheadrightarrow Z$. ∎

As fd's are special ifd's the use of fd's in these rules is allowed. The reader is invited to deduce the "classical" inference rules for fd's (i.e. reflexivity, augmentation and transitivity [Ul]) from the above rules, as well as the inference rules for cfd's, mentioned in [De3] and the inference rules for mixed fd's and ad's, given in [De1]. It is also possible to deduce a (complete) set of inference rules for mixed cfd's and ad's. (Such a set of rules is not given in [De3].)

Theorem 3.1.
The rules $I1 \ldots I5$, $IA1$, $IA2$ and $FA1$ are sound.

Proof
For $I1 \ldots I5$, and $IA2$ this is very easy and left to the reader. $FA1$ is proved in [De1] (since it uses fd's and ad's only). We only prove $IA1$.

Suppose $X \to Y \supset\!\!- X' \to Z$ holds and $X \not\twoheadrightarrow Y$ does not hold. Consider an X-complete set S of tuples in which $X \to Y$ holds (and hence also $X' \to Z$, because of $X \to Y \supset\!\!- X' \to Z$). Since $X \subseteq X'$ the X-complete set of tuples S is also X'-complete. Hence there is an X'-complete set of tuples (S) in which $X' \not\twoheadrightarrow Z$ does not hold. ∎

In the sequel we first prove that $I1 \ldots I5$ are complete for ifd's, i.e. $I1 \ldots I5$ generate all the consequences of a given set I of ifd's. (We discuss the mixed membership problem later.) In this proof we use a special set of fd's, which also provides the link between the membership problem for ifd's and that of fd's. The reader may notice some resemblance between the construction of the proof and that of the completeness of the rules for cfd's, in [De3]. However, because the new proof is more complicated, it is included in this paper.

Definition 3.2.
$FSAT_I(X,Y)$ is the smallest possible set of fd's, such that:
1) $X \to Y \in FSAT_I(X,Y)$.
2) If $T \to U \in FSAT_I(X,Y)$ and $T \to U \supset\!\!- T' \to V \in I$ then $T' \to V \in FSAT_I(X,Y)$.
3) If $FSAT_I(X,Y) \models T \to V$ then $T \to V \in FSAT_I(X,Y)$. ∎

$FSAT_I(X,Y)$ can be constructed starting from $\{X \to Y\}$ and by repeatedly trying to satisfy 2) and 3) of the definition.

Lemma 3.3.
$FSAT_I(X,Y) = \{P \to Q : I \cup \{X \to Y\} \models P \to Q\}$.

Proof

Consider $Arm(FSAT_I(X,Y))$. By Definition 3.2 and Theorem 2.8 it is clear that I holds in $Arm(FSAT_I(X,Y))$, since for every ifd $T \to U \supset\!\!- T' \to V$ of I either $T \not\to U$ holds (and hence $T \to U \supset\!\!- T' \to V$ by rule $IA2$) or $T \to U$ and $T' \to V$ hold. It is also obvious that $X \to Y$ holds in $Arm(FSAT_I(X,Y))$.

Since I holds, all fd's that are consequences of I also hold in $Arm(FSAT_I(X,Y))$, hence are consequences of $FSAT_I(X,Y)$ (and hence they are in $FSAT_I(X,Y)$ because of step 3) of Definition 3.2). This proves that $\{P \to Q : I \cup \{X \to Y\} \models P \to Q\} \subseteq FSAT_I(X,Y)$. The opposite inclusion is obvious from Definition 3.2. ∎

From the above lemma immediately follows that if $Y \subseteq X$ then $FSAT_I(X,Y)$ is the set of all fd's that are consequences of I. We usually denote this set by $FSAT_I(\emptyset,\emptyset)$.

Note also that for all X, Y the sets $FSAT_{I \cup \{X \to Y\}}(\emptyset,\emptyset)$ and $FSAT_I(X,Y)$ are equal.

Lemma 3.4.
If $P \to Q \in FSAT_I(X,Y)$ then $I \vdash P \to Q$ or $I \vdash P \to X$.

Proof

Let $I = \{X_i \to Y_i \supset\!\!- X'_i \to Z_i : i = 1 \ldots n\}$.

For $P \to Q = X \to Y$ this property is trivial. We prove that it remains valid during the construction of $FSAT_I(X,Y)$ by repeatedly trying to satisfy 2) and 3) of Definition 3.2.

- Let step 2) be the reason for $P \to Q$ to be in $FSAT_I(X,Y)$. Then for some i $P = X'_i$ and $Q = Z_i$ and by induction $I \vdash X_i \to Y_i$ or $I \vdash X_i \to X$.

If $I \vdash X_i \to Y_i = X_i \to X_i \supset\!\!- X_i \to Y_i$ then $X_i \to X_i \supset\!\!- X_i \to Y_i$ and $X_i \to Y_i \supset\!\!- X'_i \to Z_i$ induce $X_i \to X_i \supset\!\!- X'_i \to Z_i$ by $I4$. Hence $I \vdash X'_i \to Z_i = P \to Q$.

If $I \vdash X_i \to X$ then $X'_i \to X$ holds by augmentation, (which is a consequence of $I1 \ldots I5$) , since $X \subseteq X'$.

- Let step 3) be the reason for $P \to Q$ to be in $FSAT_I(X,Y)$. Then there are three possibilities (corresponding to the three well known inference rules for fd's):

a. If $Q \subseteq P$, then $I \vdash P \to P \supset\!\!- P \to Q = P \to Q$ by $I1$.

b. If $P = P_1P_2$, $Q = Q_1Q_2$, $Q_2 \subseteq P_2$ and $P_1 \to Q_1 \in FSAT_I(X,Y)$ then $I \vdash P_1 \to Q_1$ or $I \vdash P_1 \to X$ by induction, hence $I \vdash P_1P_2 \to Q_1Q_2 = P \to Q$ or $I \vdash P_1P_2 \to X = P \to X$ by augmentation.

c. If $P \to O$ and $O \to Q \in FSAT_I(X,Y)$ then $I \vdash P \to O$ or $P \to X$ and $I \vdash O \to Q$ or $O \to X$ by induction. Using the transitivity rule for fd's (a consequence of $I1 \ldots I5$) we obtain $I \vdash P \to Q$ or $I \vdash P \to X$.

The proof is completed by remarking that reflexivity (case a), augmentation (case b) and transitivity (case c) are complete for fd's [Ul]. ∎

Lemma 3.5.
If $I \models X' \to X$ then $I \vdash X \to Y \supset\!\!- XX' \to Z$ iff $X' \to Z \in FSAT_I(X,Y)$. (We write XX' to make sure that $X \subseteq XX'$).

Proof

If $I \vdash X \to Y \supset\!\!- XX' \to Z$ then $I \models X \to Y \supset\!\!- XX' \to Z$ because $I1 \ldots I5$ are sound. Hence $I \cup \{X \to Y\} \models XX' \to Z$ which implies that $XX' \to Z \in FSAT_I(X,Y)$ by Lemma 3.3. $XX' \to Z$ and $X' \to X$ induce $X' \to Z$ hence $X' \to Z \in FSAT_I(X,Y)$.

For the converse we give the same kind of proof as in the previous lemma.

Let $I = \{X_i \to Y_i \supset\!\!- X'_i \to Z_i : i = 1 \ldots n\}$.

If $X' \to Z = X \to Y$ then $I \vdash X \to Y \supset\!\!- XX' \to Z$ by $I1$.

We prove that the property of the lemma remains valid during the construction of $FSAT_I(X,Y)$ by repeatedly trying to satisfy 2) and 3) of Definition 3.2.

- Let step 2) be the reason for $X' \to Z$ to be in $FSAT_I(X,Y)$. Then for some i $X' = X'_i$ and $Z = Z_i$ and $X_i \to Y_i \in FSAT_I(X,Y)$. By Lemma 3.4. $I \vdash X_i \to Y_i$ (and $X'_i \to Z_i$) or $I \vdash X_i \to X$.

If $I \vdash X_i \to Y_i$ (and hence $I \vdash X'_i \to Z_i = X' \to Z$ and hence $XX' \to Z$ by augmentation) then $I \vdash X \to Y \supset\!\!- XX' \to Z$ by $I4$ (on $X \to Y \supset\!\!- X \to X$ and $X \to X \supset\!\!- XX' \to Z$).

If $I \vdash X_i \to X$ then $X \to Y \supset\!\!- XX_i \to Y_i$ (holding by induction), and $XX_i \to Y_i \supset\!\!- XX'_i \to Z_i$ induce $X \to Y \supset\!\!- XX'_i \to Z_i = X \to Y \supset\!\!- XX' \to Z$ by $I4$. ($XX_i \to Y_i \supset\!\!- XX'_i \to Z_i$ is derived by $I5$ from $X_i \to Y_i \supset\!\!- X'_i \to Z_i$ and $X_i \to X$ by $I5$.)

- Let step 3) be the reason for $X' \to Z$ to be in $FSAT_I(X,Y)$

There are three possibilities:

a. If $Z \subseteq X'$ then $I \vdash X \to Y \supset\!\!- XX' \to Z$ by $I1$.

b. If $X' = X''X'''$, $Z = Z'Z''$, $Z'' \subseteq X'''$ and $X'' \to Z' \in FSAT_I(X,Y)$ then by induction $I \vdash X \to Y \supset\!\!- XX'' \to Z'$. Since $Z'' \subseteq X'''$ rule $I2$ generates $X \to Y \supset\!\!- XX''X''' \to Z'Z''$.

c. If $X' \to U$ and $U \to Z \in FSAT_I(X,Y)$ then $I \vdash X' \to U$ or $X' \to X$ and $I \vdash U \to Z$ or $U \to X$, by Lemma 3.4.

If $I \vdash X' \to U$ and $I \vdash U \to Z$ then $I \vdash X' \to Z$ by transitivity, and hence $I \vdash X \to Y \supset\!\!- XX' \to Z$ by $I2$ and $I4$.

If $I \vdash X' \to X$ then $I \vdash X \to Y \supset\!\!- XX' \to U$ by induction.

If also $I \vdash U \to Z$ then $I \vdash X \to Y \supset\!\!- XX' \to Z$ by $I3$.

If on the other hand $I \vdash U \to X$ then $I \vdash X \to Y \supset\!\!- XU \to Z$ by induction, and then $I \vdash X \to Y \supset\!\!- XX' \to Z$ by $I2$ and $I4$ on $X \to Y \supset\!\!- XX' \to U$ and $X \to Y \supset\!\!- XU \to Z$ ∎

Theorem 3.6.

$I1 \ldots I5$ are complete for ifd's.

Proof

Let $I = \{X_i \to Y_i \supset\!\!- X'_i \to Z_i : i = 1 \ldots n\}$.

If $I \models X \to Y \supset\!\!- X' \to Z$ then (by the proof of Lemma 3.3) $X' \to Z \in FSAT_I(X,Y)$ (and $I \models X' \to X$ since $X \subseteq X'$ by the definition of ifd's). Hence by Lemma 3.5. $I \vdash X \to Y \supset\!\!- X' \to Z$.

If $I \vdash X \to Y \supset\!\!- X' \to Z$ then $I \models X \to Y \supset\!\!- X' \to Z$ since $I1 \ldots I5$ are sound. ∎

Because of the completeness of rules $I1 \ldots I5$ we shall abandon the symbol $\vdash$ for ifd's in the sequel, and only use the symbol $\models$.

Corollary 3.7.

$I \models X \to Y \supset\!\!- X' \to Z$ iff $X' \to Z \in FSAT_I(X,Y)$ (and $X \subseteq X'$).

Proof

This immediately follows from Lemmas 3.3. and 3.5. ∎

Corollary 3.7. shows that the membership problem for ifd's is very closely related to that of fd's. In fact one can regard an ifd as an ad-hoc implication between two fd's. The construction of $FSAT_I(X,Y)$ indeed consists of generating the "closure" of a set of fd's, using the normal inference rules (in step 3) and some "additional" rules (the ifd's in step 2). It is not obvious that ifd's should behave this way, since the ifd $X \rightarrow Y \supset\!\!- X' \rightarrow Z$ is a stronger constraint than the expression that "if the fd $X \rightarrow Y$ holds (in the entire relation) then also $X' \rightarrow Z$ holds". However, this "nice" property seems not to hold any longer if the condition $X \subseteq X'$ in the definition of $X \rightarrow Y \supset\!\!- X' \rightarrow Z$ is dropped.

From Corollary 3.7. one can deduce a membership algorithm which verifies whether $X' \rightarrow Z$ is in $FSAT_I(X,Y)$, in $O(n^3 r^2)$ time, where n is the number of ifd's of I and r is the number of attributes of $\mathcal{R}$, denoted $\# \Omega$. The algorithm is omitted because it is similar to that for cfd's, given in the original version of [De3].

In the sequel we consider the presence of ad's as well as ifd's. First we show how conflict can be detected algorithmically.

Lemma 3.8.

$I \cup A$ is in conflict iff for some $T \not\twoheadrightarrow U \in A$ holds $I \models T \rightarrow U$.

Proof

The if-part is trivial.

For the only-if part consider the instance $Arm(FSAT_I(\emptyset,\emptyset))$. In $Arm(FSAT_I(\emptyset,\emptyset))$ I holds, hence if $I \cup A$ is in conflict, then some ad $T \not\twoheadrightarrow U \in A$ does not hold. By Theorem 2.8. this means that $T \rightarrow U$ holds, and is a consequence of $FSAT_I(\emptyset,\emptyset)$. Hence $T \rightarrow U \in FSAT_I(\emptyset,\emptyset)$. By Lemma 3.3. then $I \models T \rightarrow U$. ∎

If n is the number of ifd's of I ($\# I$), m is the number of ad's of A ($\# A$) and r is the number of attributes ($\# \Omega$), then the time-complexity of a conflict detection algorithm (based on Lemma 3.8) and a membership algorithm for ifd's, similar to that of [De3] is $O(n^3 r^2 m)$.

The membership problem for mixed ifd's and ad's is solved in the next two theorems.

Theorem 3.9.

Let $I \cup A$ be not in conflict, $X \not\twoheadrightarrow Y$ an ad. Then $I \cup A \models X \not\twoheadrightarrow Y$ iff $I \cup A \cup \{X \rightarrow Y\}$ is in conflict.

Proof

The only-if part is trivial.

For the if-part, suppose that $I \cup A \cup \{X \rightarrow Y\}$ is in conflict. Then by Lemma 3.8 $I \cup \{X \rightarrow Y\} \models \{T \rightarrow U\}$ for some $T \not\twoheadrightarrow U \in A$. We prove that $I \cup \{T \not\twoheadrightarrow U\} \vdash X \not\twoheadrightarrow Y$. ($\vdash$ because we use our inference rules.)

$T \rightarrow U \in FSAT_I(X,Y)$ by Lemma 3.3. By Lemma 3.4 $I \models T \rightarrow X$, (since $I \not\models T \rightarrow U$ unless $I \cup A$ was in conflict), hence also $I \models T \rightarrow XT$ by augmentation. $TX \rightarrow U \in FSAT_I(X,Y)$ also by augmentation. Hence by Corollary 3.7 $I \models X \rightarrow Y \supset\!\!- XT \rightarrow U$.

- $T \not\twoheadrightarrow U$ and $T \rightarrow XT$ induce $XT \not\twoheadrightarrow U$ by $FA1$.
- $XT \not\twoheadrightarrow U$ and $X \rightarrow Y \supset\!\!- XT \rightarrow U$ induce $X \not\twoheadrightarrow Y$ by $IA1$.

This shows that $I \cup \{T \not\twoheadrightarrow U\} \vdash X \not\twoheadrightarrow Y$. ∎

Using Lemma 3.8 a membership algorithm for ad's (considering the presence of ifd's) can be easily deduced from Theorem 3.9. The time needed to perform a membership test for ad's is the same as for the conflict detection: $O(n^3 r^2 m)$ where $n = \# I$, $m = \# A$ and $r = \# \Omega$.

Theorem 3.10.
Let $I \cup A$ be not in conflict. Then $I \cup A \models X \to Y \supset\!\!- X' \to Z$ (with $X \subseteq X'$) iff $I \models X \to Y \supset\!\!- X' \to Z$ or $I \cup A \models X \not\to Y$.

Proof
The if-part is trivial.
For the only-if-part, assume that $I \not\models X \to Y \supset\!\!- X' \to Z$ and $I \cup A \not\models X \not\to Y$. By Theorem 3.9 $I \cup A \cup \{X \to Y\}$ is not in conflict. Consider $Arm(FSAT_I(X,Y))$, in which $I \cup \{X \to Y\}$ holds. If some ad $T \not\to U$ of A does not hold then $I \cup \{X \to Y\} \models T \to U$ (Theorem 2.8 and Lemma 3.4), a contradiction with $I \cup A \cup \{X \to Y\}$ not being in conflict (by Theorem 3.9). In $Arm(FSAT_I(X,Y))$ $X' \to Z$ does not hold (by Theorem 3.7). Hence $Arm(FSAT_I(X,Y))$ is an instance in which $I \cup A$ holds and in which $X \to Y \supset\!\!- X' \to Z$ does not hold.
Hence $I \cup A \not\models X \to Y \supset\!\!- X' \to Z$. ∎

Because of this theorem a membership algorithm for ifd's takes as much time as a membership algorithm for ad's: $0(n^3 r^2 m)$ with $m = \# I$, $m = \# A$ and $r = \# \Omega$.

The following corollary immediately follows from Theorems 3.6, 3.9 and 3.10:

Corollary 3.11
The rules $I1 \ldots I5$, $IA1$, $IA2$ and $FA1$ are complete for mixed fd's and ad's. ∎

4. THE INHERITANCE OF DEPENDENCIES.

The membership problem must be solved in order to be able to decide whether a decomposition according to an ifd is trivial or not (i.e. whether for $X \to Y \supset\!\!- X' \to Z$ $X \to Y$ or $X \not\to Y$ holds). When decomposing the subschemes further on (using other ifd's) one must know which dependencies already hold in these subschemes. This is called the ***inheritance problem***. The inherited dependencies determine whether a further decomposition step is possible.

Notation 4.1.
In the sequel we treat the horizontal decomposition of a scheme $\mathcal{R}$, with ifd's I and ad's A, according to $X \to Y \supset\!\!- X' \to Z \in I$, into the schemes $\mathcal{R}_1 = \sigma_{X \to Y}(\mathcal{R})$, with ifd's I_1 and ad's A_1, and $\mathcal{R}_2 = \sigma_{X \not\to Y}(\mathcal{R})$, with ifd's I_2 and ad's A_2. We assume that $I \cup A$ is not in conflict, $I \cup A \not\models X \to Y$ and $I \cup A \not\models X \not\to Y$. When we say that a set of dependencies is "the" set of dependencies that hold in a scheme, we mean that this set generates all dependencies that hold in that scheme. In other words, we do not consider complete sets of dependencies. ∎

Remark 4.2.
Since fd's cannot be violated by taking a restriction, all fd's that hold in $\mathcal{R}$ also hold in $\mathcal{R}_1$ and $\mathcal{R}_2$. ∎

Before giving a complete description of the inheritance; we first give some inclusions, which are easy to prove:

Lemma 4.3.
Using the notations of 4.1 we have:
$I_1 \subseteq \{T{\rightarrow}U{\supset\!\!-}T'{\rightarrow}V : I \cup A \cup \{X{\rightarrow}Y\} \models T{\rightarrow}U{\supset\!\!-}T'{\rightarrow}V\}$.
$I_2 \subseteq \{T{\rightarrow}U{\supset\!\!-}T'{\rightarrow}V : I \cup A \cup \{X{\not\twoheadrightarrow}Y\} \models T{\rightarrow}U{\supset\!\!-}T'{\rightarrow}V\}$.
$A_1 \subseteq \{T{\not\twoheadrightarrow}U : I \cup A \cup \{X{\rightarrow}Y\} \models T{\not\twoheadrightarrow}U\}$.
$A_2 \subseteq \{T{\not\twoheadrightarrow}U : I \cup A \cup \{X{\not\twoheadrightarrow}Y\} \models T{\not\twoheadrightarrow}U\}$. ∎

The proof of the inheritance of ifd's and ad's relies on the construction of a special instance with the following property:

Lemma 4.4.
Consider a set $I \cup A$, not being in conflict. Let S be an instance in which $I \cup A$ holds. If $I \cup A \cup \{P{\not\twoheadrightarrow}Q\}$ is not in conflict, then there exists an instance T, containing S as a subset, in which the ad $P{\not\twoheadrightarrow}Q$ holds (and hence also every ifd $P{\rightarrow}Q{\supset\!\!-}P'{\rightarrow}Q$ (where $P \subseteq P'$). ∎

We omit the proof, because it is very similar to that of Lemma 4.4 of [De3]. But since the formal proof is rather complex we indicate the main idea of this construction: if for a P-value there is only one Q-value, then add a tuple with this P-value and with another Q-value, to obtain $P{\not\twoheadrightarrow}Q$. Then add a number of other tuples (in fact a whole Armstrong relation), to keep $I \cup A$ is satisfied. This idea is illustrated by the following example.

Example 4.5.
Consider a scheme R with attributes $\{A, B, C, D\}$, ifd's $I = \{A{\rightarrow}B, B{\rightarrow}A, C{\rightarrow}D, D{\rightarrow}A\}$ and ad's $A = \{A{\not\twoheadrightarrow}C\}$.
Consider the following instance S:

A	B	C	D
a	a	a	a
a	a	b	a
b	b	c	b
b	b	d	b
c	c	e	c
c	c	f	d

In S $I \cup A$ holds, but the ad $A{\not\twoheadrightarrow}D$ does not hold. There are two violations of $A{\not\twoheadrightarrow}D$: {tuples 1 and 2} and {tuples 3 and 4}.
The following instance is an Armstrong relation for $FSAT_I(\emptyset, \emptyset)$:

A	B	C	D
0	0	0	0
1	1	1	1
0	0	2	2
0	0	3	0
1	1	4	4
1	1	5	1
0	0	6	2
1	1	7	4

Let $\overline{P} = \{attribute A : I \models P \rightarrow A\}$, then in our example $\overline{P} = AB$. Let $t = (a,a,a,a)$ and $r = (0,0,0,0)$. After the renaming in $Arm(FSAT_I(\emptyset,\emptyset))$, the union of S and this Armstrong relation is the following instance T:

A	B	C	D
a	a	a	a
a	a	b	a
b	b	c	b
b	b	d	b
c	c	e	c
c	c	f	d
a	a	0	0
1	1	1	1
a	a	2	2
a	a	3	0
1	1	4	4
1	1	5	1
a	a	6	2
1	1	7	4

In T $I \cup \mathcal{A}$ still holds, and the number of violations of $A \not\twoheadrightarrow D$ in T is less than in S: only {tuples 3 and 4} is still a violation of $A \not\twoheadrightarrow D$. By repeating the above construction once more $A \not\twoheadrightarrow D$ becomes satisfied in the final T. ∎

The dependencies that are inherited by both $\mathcal{R}_1$ and $\mathcal{R}_2$ are described by the following "inheritance rules":

($H1$): If $T \not\twoheadrightarrow U$ and $T \rightarrow X$ then $T \not\twoheadrightarrow U$ is inherited by both $\mathcal{R}_1$ and $\mathcal{R}_2$ (when decomposing $\mathcal{R}$ according to $X \rightarrow Y \supset\!\!- X' \rightarrow Z$).

($H2$): If $T \rightarrow U \supset\!\!- T' \rightarrow V$ and $T \rightarrow U$ or $T \rightarrow X$ then $T \rightarrow U \supset\!\!- T' \rightarrow V$ is inherited by both $\mathcal{R}_1$ and $\mathcal{R}_2$. ∎

The soundness of these rules can be easily proved, using the remark that an fd $T \rightarrow X$ means that every X-complete set of tuples is T-complete.

In the sequel we denote the set of the ad's of $\mathcal{A}$ that are inherited by rule $H1$ by $\hat{\mathcal{A}}$. The set of the ifd's of I (or their fd-part) that are inherited by rule $H2$, or that are trivial, is denoted by $\hat{I}$. We include the trivial ifd's because they represent the "goals" of [De1,De2,Pa]. We do not consider them in the lemma and the theorem below, because they are of no importance for the inheritance problem.

Lemma 4.6.
Let $I \cup \mathcal{A}$ be not in conflict. Let S be an instance in which $\hat{I} \cup \hat{\mathcal{A}}$ holds. Then there exists an instance T, containing S as a subset, and in which $I \cup \mathcal{A}$ holds.

Proof
T can be obtained by repeating the construction of Lemma 4.4. for every ad of $\mathcal{A} - \hat{\mathcal{A}}$ and every ifd of $I - \hat{I}$. The final instance T satisfies $I \cup \mathcal{A}$. ∎

Theorem 4.7.
An ifd or ad must hold in $\mathcal{R}_1$ (resp. $\mathcal{R}_2$) iff it is a consequence of $\hat{I} \cup \hat{\mathcal{A}} \cup \{X \rightarrow Y\}$ (resp. $\hat{I} \cup \hat{\mathcal{A}} \cup \{X \not\twoheadrightarrow Y\}$).

Proof

From Lemma 4.3 and the soundness of the inheritance rules it follows that $(\hat{I} \cup \hat{A} \cup \{X \to Y\})^* \subseteq (I_1 \cup A_1)^* \subseteq (I \cup A \cup \{X \to Y\})^*$ and $(\hat{I} \cup \hat{A} \cup \{X \not\to Y\})^* \subseteq (I_2 \cup A_2)^* \subseteq (I \cup A \cup \{X \not\to Y\})^*$, where * means the "closure" operator, i.e. taking all the consequences of a set of dependencies.

We only prove the theorem for the inheritance of an ad in $\mathcal{R}_1$. The three other cases are similar.

Let $T \not\to U \in (I \cup A \cup \{X \to Y\})^* - (\hat{I} \cup \hat{A} \cup \{X \to Y\})^*$. We prove that $T \not\to U \notin (I_1 \cup A_1)^*$.

Since $T \not\to U \notin (\hat{I} \cup \hat{A} \cup \{X \to Y\})^*$, $\hat{I} \cup \hat{A} \cup \{X \to Y\} \cup \{T \to U\}$ is not in conflict, by Theorem 3.9. Hence there exists an instance S in which $\hat{I} \cup \hat{A} \cup \{X \to Y\} \cup \{T \to U\}$ holds. By the construction of Lemma 4.6. an instance R can be build which contains S and in which $I \cup A$ holds. In this construction (explained in example 4.5) a number of modified copies of $Arm(FSAT_I(\emptyset, empty))$ are added to S. Since $X \not\to Y$ holds in $Arm(FSAT_I(\emptyset, \emptyset))$, and since $I \not\models T \to X$ (by the definition of $\hat{A}$), $R_1 = \sigma_{X \to Y}(R) = S$. Hence in $\mathcal{R}_1$ $T \not\to U$ does not hold, which means that $T \not\to U \notin (I_1 \cup A_1)^*$. ∎

From Theorem 4.7. one can easily deduce an algorithm that calculates the inherited dependencies in $O(n^4 r^2 + n^3 m^2 r^2)$ time, where $n = \# I$, $m = \# A$ and $r = \# \Omega$. (This is n times the complexity of an ifd-membership test plus m times the complexity of an ad-membership test.

A decomposition algorithm can be easily constructed for the following normal form:

Definition 4.8.

A scheme $\mathcal{R}$ is said to be in *Imposed Normal Form (INF)* iff for all ifd's $X \to Y \supset\!\!- X' \to Z$ of I either $X \to Y$ or $X \not\to Y$ holds in $\mathcal{R}$.

A decomposition $\{\mathcal{R}_1, \ldots, \mathcal{R}_n\}$ is in *INF* iff all the $\mathcal{R}_i$, $i = 1 \ldots n$, are in INF. ∎

Note that in the "final" subschemes there are no real ifd's anymore, only fd's and ad's. (Otherwise we could decompose the subscheme further on.)

5. TOWARDS MORE GENERAL DEPENDENCIES.

In [De3] the conditional-functional dependencies have been introduced as the first member of a large class of dependencies which express partial implications between constraints. The cfd's look like the formula: $X \to Y \supset\!\!- X \to Z$.

In this paper we have developed the imposed-functional dependencies, which are more general: $X \to Y \supset\!\!- X' \to Z$, where $X \subseteq X'$.

The reader is invited to compare the inference rules for cfd's [De3] with the rules for ifd's. The more general constraint has more natural inference rules. In the future the concept of ifd's should be generalized still further, to obtain a less strict relationship between X and X'.

A first step in that direction would be to change $X \subseteq X'$ into $X' \to X$. However, this "general" imposed-functional dependency is not yet really more general than the ifd: one can easily see that such a general ifd is equivalent to the ifd $X \to Y \supset\!\!- XX' \to Z$ together with the fd $X' \to X$. Hence the advantage of using general ifd's instead of ifd's is that an ifd and an fd can be expressed in only one constraint. As a consequence some inference rules (like $I5$) can be expressed in a more readable way than for (normal) ifd's.

In future work still more general dependencies will be examined. The horizontal decomposition should also be based on other classes of constraints, such as the multivalued dependencies.

References

[Ar] Armstrong W., Dependency structures of database relationships, *Proc. IFIP 74*, North Holland, pp. 580–583, 1974.

[Be] Beeri C., Bernstein P.A., Computational Problems related to the Design of Normal Form Relation Schemes, *ACM TODS*, vol. **4.1**, pp. 30–59, 1979.

[Ber] Bernstein P.A., Normalization and Functional Dependencies in the Relational Database Model, *CSRG-60*, 1975.

[Co] Codd E., Further normalizations of the database relational model, In *Data Base Systems* (R. Rustin, ed.) Prentice Hall, N.J., pp. 33–64, 1972.

[De1] De Bra P., Paredaens J., The membership and the inheritance of functional and afunctional dependencies, Proc. of the Colloquium on Algebra, Combinatorics and Logic in Computer Science, Gyor, Hungary.

[De2] De Bra P., Paredaens J., Horizontal Decompositions for Handling Exceptions to Functional Dependencies, in "Advances in Database Theory", Vol. II, pp. 123–144, 1983.

[De3] De Bra P., Paredaens J., Conditional Dependencies for Horizontal Decompositions, in "Lecture Notes in Computer Science", Vol. 154, pp. 67-82, (10-th *ICALP*), Springer-Verlag, 1983.

[Fa] Fagin R., Armstrong Databases, *IBM RJ 3440*, 1982.

[Pa] Paredaens J., De Bra P., On Horizontal Decompositions, *XP2-Congress*, State Univ. of Pennsylvania, 1981.

[Sm] Smith J., Smith D., Data base abstractions: Aggregation and generalization, *ACM TODS*, vol. **2.2**, pp. 105–133, 1977.

[Ul] Ullman J., Principles of Database Systems, Pitman, 1980.

CHARACTERIZATION OF HIGH LEVEL TREE TRANSDUCERS

Joost Engelfriet and Heiko Vogler*
University of Leiden, P.O.Box 9512
2300 RA Leiden, The Netherlands

1. INTRODUCTION. We introduce (OI) n-level tree transducers as a natural extension of top-down tree transducers [Ro,Th,E1] (n=0) and macro tree transducers [E2,CF, EV1] (n=1). An n-level tree transducer can be considered as an n-level tree grammar [Da] of which the derivations are syntax-directed by an input tree. Thus n-level tree transducers generalize the syntax-directed translation schemes of [AU1,2] (which are regular tree grammars with syntax-directed derivations, i.e., top-down tree transducers [MV,Vo]) in the sense that the handling of context is allowed. Actually, we show in this paper that "high" level tree transducers can perform the composition closure of the class of translations of tree-valued attribute grammars [Kn] (cf. [EF, CM,CF]).

The subject of this paper is the characterization of the class of translations induced by n-level tree transducers for both the nondeterministic and the deterministic case. The class of translations is characterized by tree transducers, which have a regular tree grammar as control and a generalized pushdown device as storage. (For the concept of "grammars with storage" we refer the reader to [E4,E5,EV2,EV3]). The storage type involves the n-iterated pushdown of which a configuration is a pushdown of pushdowns of ... of pushdowns (n-times) [Gr,Ms,E5,DGo]. Hence, we call a tree transducer with the above mentioned control and storage an n-iterated pushdown tree transducer. Actually, we characterize the n-level S transducers for an arbitrary storage type S and then take S to be the "tree storage type". This method allows us to prove our results level by level. This paper should be considered as an introductory presentation; for a detailed version with full proofs we refer to [EV4].

2. PRELIMINARIES. We recall the basic notions concerning objects of high functional types (see [Da]). Let Q be a set of types. For a string $w \in Q^*$ of length k and $i \in [k]$ (where $[k] = \{1,\ldots,k\}$) $w(i)$ is the i-th letter of w. The empty string is λ. A Q-set is a pair $\langle A,\text{type}\rangle$, where A is a set and $\text{type}: A \to Q$ is a mapping; for $q \in Q$, $A^q = \{a \in A \mid \text{type}(a)=q\}$; type(a)=q is abbreviated by a:q. If "type" is understood the Q-set is also denoted by A. For $w \in Q^*$ of length $k \geq 1$, $A^w = \{(a_1,\ldots,a_k) \mid a_i \in A^{w(i)}\}$; $A^\lambda = \{()\}$. For Q-sets $\langle A,\text{type}_A\rangle$ and $\langle B,\text{type}_B\rangle$, $A \subseteq B$ iff $A^q \subseteq B^q$ for every $q \in Q$; if $A \cap B = \emptyset$, then $A \cup B$ is the Q-set $\langle A\cup B,\text{type}\rangle$ with type = $\text{type}_A \cup \text{type}_B$. The set of derived types over Q, denoted by $D^*(Q)$, is defined by $D^0(Q) = Q$, $D^{n+1}(Q) = (D^n(Q))^* \times D^n(Q)$, and $D^*(Q) = \cup\{D^n(Q) \mid n \geq 0\}$. $D^+(Q) = \cup\{D^n(Q) \mid n \geq 1\}$ and $D(Q) = D^1(Q)$. The level of a derived

* The work of the second author has been supported by the Netherlands Organization for the Advancement of Pure Research (Z.W.O).

type $\tau \in D^n(Q)$, denoted by level(τ), is n. Every derived type $\tau \in D^n(Q)$ with $n \geq 0$ can be uniquely written as $\tau = (\alpha n, \ldots(\alpha 2,(\alpha 1,q))\ldots)$ with $\alpha i \in (D^{i-1}(Q))^*$ and $q \in Q$. For any $D^*(Q)$-set <X,type>, the <u>level</u> of $B \in X$, denoted by level(B), is level(type(B)). The $D^*(Q)$-set Y of <u>parameters</u> is the tuple <Y,type>, where $Y = \{y_{i,\tau} \mid i \geq 1, \tau \in D^*(Q)\}$ and type:$Y \to D^*(Q)$ defined by type$(y_{i,\tau}) = \tau$. For $\alpha \in D^n(Q)^*$ of length k, $y\langle\alpha\rangle = (y_{1,\alpha(1)}, \ldots, y_{k,\alpha(k)})$. For a $D^*(Q)$-set X, the $D^*(Q)$-set of <u>applicative terms over</u> X, denoted by AT(X), is the smallest $D^*(Q)$-set AT which satisfies (i) $X \subseteq AT$, and (ii) let $\alpha \in D^n(Q)^*$ of length k for some $n,k \geq 0$, and for every $j \in [k]$ let $\xi_j \in AT^{\alpha(j)}$; let $\nu \in D^n(Q)$ and let $\xi_0 \in AT^{(\alpha,\nu)}$; then $\xi_0(\xi_1,\ldots,\xi_k) \in AT^{\nu}$. Note that every applicative term $\xi \in AT(X)^{\nu}$ for some $\nu \in D^n(Q)$ with $n \geq 0$, has a <u>unique decomposition</u> $B\tilde{\xi}_r \ldots \tilde{\xi}_1$, where $r \geq 0$, $B \in X^{\tau}$, $\tau = (\alpha r, \ldots(\alpha 1,\nu)\ldots)$ for some $\alpha i \in D^{n+i-1}(Q)^*$, and for every $i \in [r]$, $\xi_i \in AT(X)^{\alpha i}$.

From now on let $Q = \{q\}$.

<u>Example 1</u>. Let $\gamma:((q,q)(\lambda,q),(qq,q))$, $\sigma:((q,q),(\lambda,q))$, $\delta:(q,q)$, and $\alpha:q$ be elements of a $D^*(Q)$-set X. Clearly, γ and σ have level 2, δ has level 1, and α has level 0. By part (i) of the definition of applicative terms, $\delta \in AT(X)^{(q,q)}$. Since $\alpha \in AT(X)^q$, it follows from part (ii) of that definition that $\delta(\alpha) \in AT(X)^q$, in the same way it can be checked that $\xi = \gamma(\delta,\sigma(\delta))(\alpha,\sigma(\delta)()) \in AT(X)^q$, where () is the empty list of parameters. □

<u>Remark 1</u>. There is an intuitive way of looking at an applicative term $\xi \in AT(X)^{\tau}$ with $\tau \in D^n(Q)$, $n \geq 0$. Either $\xi \in X^{\tau}$ or $\xi = \xi_0(\xi_1,\ldots,\xi_k)$, where $k \geq 0$, $\xi_0 \in AT(X)^{\nu}$ with $\nu = (\alpha,\tau) \in D^{n+1}(Q)$ for some $\alpha \in D^n(Q)^*$ of length k, and for every $i \in [k]$, $\xi_i \in AT(X)^{\alpha(i)}$. But then, ξ can be viewed as a tree which either consists only of one node labeled by ξ or is a tree with the root labeled by ξ_0 and with ξ_i as the i-th subtree. By iterating this decomposition, we finally obtain a tree of trees ... of trees as a representation of ξ. Figure 1 shows how the term ξ of Example 1 looks like from this point of view. The number of circles by which a symbol is surrounded, coincides with the level of the symbol. □

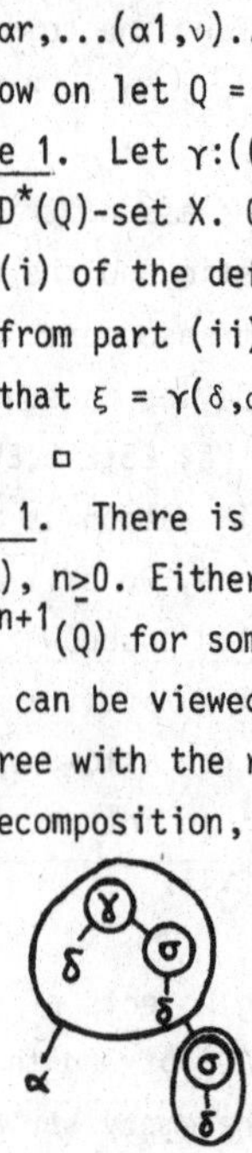

Fig.1: Applicative term viewed as a tree of...of trees.

<u>Remark 2</u>. Every finite D(Q)-set X can be considered as a usual ranked alphabet: for $A \in X$, if type(A) $= (q^k,q)$ with $k \geq 0$, then A has rank k (i.e., rank(A) = k). Hence, $AT(X)^q$ is the usual set of (labeled) trees over X, also denoted by T_X. □

Let ξ be an applicative term, U a set and $\Theta(u)$ an object depending on u; then $\xi[u \leftarrow \Theta(u); u \in U]$ denotes the applicative term obtained by replacing every occurrence of $u \in U$ in ξ by $\Theta(u)$. In particular, for $\alpha \in D^n(Q)^*$ of length k and applicative terms ξ_j, $\xi[y\langle\alpha\rangle \leftarrow (\xi_1,\ldots,\xi_k)]$ abbreviates $\xi[y_{j,\alpha(j)} \leftarrow \xi_j; j \in [k]]$. For sets Ψ and Φ, $\Psi(\Phi) = \{\psi\langle\varphi\rangle \mid \psi \in \Psi, \varphi \in \Phi\}$. If <Ψ,type> is a Q-set, then <Ψ(Φ), type> is also a Q-set, with type$(\psi\langle\varphi\rangle)$ = type(ψ).

3. HIGH LEVEL S TRANSDUCERS. In this section we introduce high level S transducers (where S is any storage type). A storage type S is a tuple (C,P,F,I,E), where C is the set of configurations, P is the set of predicates which are mappings $C \to \{true, false\}$, F is the set of instructions which are partial functions $C \to C$, I is the set of input elements, and E is the set of encodings which are partial functions $I \to C$. For the rest of this paper S denotes the storage type (C,P,F,I,E) if not otherwise specified.

Example 2. - The tree storage type TR = (C,P,F,I,E) contains all trees over an infinite ranked alphabet Ω as configurations, a predicate looks like root=σ ($\sigma \in \Omega$) and is true on a tree t iff the root of t is labeled by σ, and sel_i ($i \geq 1$) is an instruction which selects the i-th (direct) subtree. I = C and E = $\{e | e$ is the identity on T_Σ for some finite subset Σ of $\Omega\}$.

- The trivial storage type S_0 is the storage type ($\{c\},\emptyset,\{id\},\{c\},\{id\}$), where id is the identity on $\{c\}$. □

Let $n \geq 0$. An n-level S transducer M is a tuple (N,e,Δ,η,R), where N is the finite $D^*(Q)$-set of nonterminals such that for every $A \in N$, level(A) $\leq$ n, $e \in E$ is the encoding, Δ is the finite D(Q)-set (i.e., ranked alphabet) of terminals, $\eta \in AT(N)^q$ is the initial term, and R is the finite set of rules of the form $Ay\langle\alpha m\rangle \ldots y\langle\alpha 2\rangle y\langle\alpha 1\rangle \to$ if b then ζ, where b is a boolean combination of predicates in P, $A \in N^\tau$ with τ = $(\alpha m,\ldots(\alpha 2,(\alpha 1,q))\ldots)$, and $\zeta \in AT(N(F) \cup \Delta \cup Y)^q$. Since $y\langle\alpha m\rangle \ldots y\langle\alpha 2\rangle y\langle\alpha 1\rangle$ follows uniquely from type(A), we can abbreviate $Ay\langle\alpha m\rangle \ldots y\langle\alpha 2\rangle y\langle\alpha 1\rangle$ by $A^\wedge$. Note that $A^\wedge$ and ζ are of level 0. An n-level S transducer M is deterministic if for every $c \in C$: if $A^\wedge \to$ if b_1 then ζ_1 and $A^\wedge \to$ if b_2 then ζ_2 are rules in R_1, then $b_1(c)$ = false or $b_2(c)$ = false.

The (OI-) derivation relation of M, denoted by $\Rightarrow_M$ is a binary relation on $AT(N(C) \cup \Delta)^q$. For $\xi_1, \xi_2 \in AT(N(C) \cup \Delta)^q$, $\xi_1 \Rightarrow_M \xi_2$ iff there is a rule $A^\wedge \to$ if b then ζ in R with type(A) = $(\alpha m,\ldots(\alpha 2,(\alpha 1,q))\ldots) \in D^m(Q)$, there are $\xi_i' \in AT(N(C) \cup \Delta)^{\alpha i}$, and there is a $c \in C$ with b(c)=true, such that ξ_2 is the result of replacing the subterm $A\langle c\rangle \xi_m' \ldots \xi_2' \xi_1'$ of ξ_1 by $\zeta[y\langle\alpha i\rangle \leftarrow \xi_i'; i \in [m]][f \leftarrow f(c); f \in F]$ (provided the subterm does not occur in a subterm of the same form: the usual OI-restriction [Fi,Ma,ES,Da,EV1]). The translation induced by M, denoted by $\tau(M)$, is the set $\{(u,t) \in I \times AT(\Delta)^q \mid \eta_{e(u)} \Rightarrow_M^* t\}$, where $\eta_{e(u)} = \eta[A \leftarrow A\langle e(u)\rangle; A \in N]$. Thus, M translates elements of I into trees over Δ. M is total, if dom(τ(M)) = dom(e). The class of translations induced by (total deterministic) n-level S transducers is denoted by (n-$D_tT(S)$) n-$T(S)$.

Example 3. Define the deterministic 2-level TR transducer $M=(N,e,\Delta,A_{in},R)$ as follows. $N=\{A_{in},A,B\}$ with A_{in}:q and A,B:((q,q),(q,q)); e is the identity on T_Σ, where $\Sigma=\{\sigma,\alpha\}$, rank(σ)=1, rank(α)=0. Δ=\{f,a\}, where f:(q,q) and a:(λ,q). R contains the rules

$$A_{in} \to \text{if root}=\sigma \text{ then } A\langle sel_1\rangle(f)(a())$$
$$A(y_{1,(q,q)})(y_{1,q}) \to \text{if root}=\sigma \text{ then } A\langle sel_1\rangle(B\langle sel_1\rangle(y_{1,(q,q)}))(y_{1,q})$$
$$A(y_{1,(q,q)})(y_{1,q}) \to \text{if root}=\alpha \text{ then } y_{1,(q,q)}(y_{1,q})$$

$B(y_{1,(q,q)})(y_{1,q}) \to$ *if* true *then* $y_{1,(q,q)}(y_{1,(q,q)}(y_{1,q}))$.

Note that "true" is a boolean combination of predicates.

Then M can compute on the tree $\sigma(\sigma(\alpha()))$ as follows.

$A_{in}<\sigma(\sigma(\alpha()))> \Rightarrow A<\sigma(\alpha())>(f)(a()) \Rightarrow A<\alpha()>(B<\alpha()>(f))(a()) \Rightarrow B<\alpha()>(f)(a()) \Rightarrow f(f(a()))$.

In fact, $\tau(M) = \{(\sigma^{n+1}\alpha, f^m a) \mid n\geq 0,\ m=2^n\}$, where we denote monadic trees as strings. □

Facts (1). 0-level S transducers are equivalent to the regular tree S transducers defined in[EV3]. Such a transducer has a regular tree grammar as control, that operates on the storage type S. (2). 0-level TR transducers and 1-level TR transducers coincide with top-down tree transducers [Th,Ro,E1] and with (OI-) macro tree transducers [E2,CF EV1], respectively. (3). The ranges of n-level S_0 transducers are generated by the n-level tree grammars. These grammars, introduced in [Da], generate the class of tree languages at the n-th level of the well-known OI-hierarchy [Wa,ES,Da]. □

The aim of this paper is the characterization of n-T(S) by 0-T(S'), where S' is the storage type of n-iterated pushdowns of S-configurations (Theorem 2), for S=TR. However, we prove this characterization for arbitrary S. The result shows the usual trade-off between the complexity of control and the complexity of storage type.

4. APPLICATIVE TERMS, TREE PUSHDOWNS, AND PUSHDOWNS. We first characterize n-T(S) as 0-T(n-AT(S)), where n-AT(S) is the storage type of n-level applicative terms of S. Then we show the (storage type) equivalence of n-AT(S) and the n-iterated tree-pushdown of S, for short $TP^n(S)$ (cf. [Gu,DG2,EV3]), where TP is an operator on storage types which can be iterated: $TP^0(S) = S$, $TP^{n+1}(S) = TP(TP^n(S))$. Since TP(S) is equivalent to the "bounded excursion pushdown of S", for short $P_{bex}(S)$ [EV3], we obtain the equivalence of n-AT(S), $TP^n(S)$, and $P^n_{bex}(S)$, for every $n\geq 1$. This provides the desired characterization of n-T(S).

The storage type n-AT(S) has applicative terms as configurations and imitates with its instructions the rewriting mechnanism of n-level S transducers. As a reservoir of symbols, we fix, for every $n\geq 1$, the $D^n(Q)$-set $<\Xi_n, type_n>$ such that $type_n^{-1}(\tau)$ is an infinitive set for every $\tau\in D^n(Q)$. Let $n\geq 1$. The n-level applicative term of S, denoted by n-AT(S), is the storage type (C',P',F',I',E'), where $C' = AT(\Xi_n(C))^q$, $P' = \{top{=}\gamma \mid \gamma\in\Xi_n\} \cup \{test(p) \mid p\in P\}$, $F' = \{push(\zeta) \mid \zeta\in AT(\Xi_n(F)\cup Y)^q\}$, and for $c' = \delta<c>\xi_n\ldots\xi_1\in C'$ such that $type(\delta) = (\alpha n,\ldots(\alpha 1,q)\ldots)$, and $\xi_i\in AT(\Xi_n(C))^{\alpha i}$ for every $i\in[n]$, $(top{=}\gamma)(c')$ = true iff $\delta = \gamma$, $test(p)(c') = p(c)$, and $push(\zeta)(c') = \zeta[y<\alpha i>\leftarrow\xi_i; i\in[n]][f\leftarrow f(c); f\in F]$. I' = I and E' contains all $\lambda u\in I.\eta_{e(u)}$ and $\eta_{e(u)}\in AT(\Xi_n(\{e(u)\}))^q$ for some $e\in E$. We abbreviate $n\text{-}AT(S_0)$ by n-AT. By Remark 2 a configuration ξ of 1-AT(S) can be viewed as a tree, in which every node is labeled by $\gamma<c>$ for some $\gamma\in\Xi_1$ and $c\in C$; the instruction $push(\zeta)$ of 1-AT(S) applied to ξ replaces the root of ξ by ζ and substitutes for every $y_{i,q}$ the i-the subtree of ξ. This coincides with the definition of the tree-pushdown of S given in [EV3] and denoted TP(S); thus we define here TP(S) to be 1-AT(S). Note that, e.g., $TP^2(S)$ is 1-AT(1-AT(S)).

Lemma 1. For every $n\geq 1$, n-T(S) = 0-T(n-AT(S)). Determinism and totality are preserved. □

0-level n-AT transducers are closely related to the level-n stack automata of [DG1] (denoted by n-STA): range(0-T(n-AT)) = n-STA. Hence, taking $S=S_0$ (see Fact (3)), Lemma 1 reproves the equivalence of n-level tree grammars and level-n stack automata, proved in [DG1].

The next lemma shows how the functional level inherent in n-AT(S), and thus also in n-level S transducers, corresponds to the (iterated) application of the operator TP. The correspondence is expressed using the notion of storage type simulation (see [E5,EV3]), that goes back to [Ho]. Very roughly, the storage type S_1 <u>is simulated</u> by the storage type S_2, for short $S_1 \leq S_2$, if there is a representation function from C_1 to C_2 and for every predicate and instruction φ of S_1 there is an S_2-flowchart which imitates the application of φ to an S_1-configuration c on the S_2-configuration that represents c. An S-flowchart ω is a deterministic flowchart, which uses the predicates and instructions of S, S_1 and S_2 are <u>equivalent</u>, for short $S_1 \equiv S_2$, if $S_1 \leq S_2$ and $S_2 \leq S_1$.

<u>Facts</u> (4). $\leq$ is reflexive and transitive, and $\equiv$ is an equivalence relation. (5). TP is monotonic with respect to $\leq$ and thus preserves $\equiv$ (see [EV4]). (6). If $S_1 \leq S_2$, then $0\text{-T}(S_1) \subseteq 0\text{-T}(S_2)$; determinism and totality are preserved (cf. "justification theorem" 4.18 of [EV3]). □

<u>Lemma 2</u>. For every $n \geq 1$, (n+1)-AT(S) ≡ TP(n-AT(S)). □

<u>Example 4</u>. We illustrate the simulation of $2\text{-AT}(S_0) \leq \text{TP}(1\text{-AT}(S_0))$. Let $\gamma:((q,q)(\lambda,q),(qq,q))$, $\sigma:((q,q),(\lambda,q))$, $\delta:(\lambda,(q,q))$, and $\alpha:(\lambda,(\lambda,q))$ be symbols of Ξ_2. Consider the configuration $t_1 = \gamma(\delta(),\sigma(\delta()))(\alpha()(),\sigma(\delta())())$ of $2\text{-AT}(S_0)$, where we have left out for convenience the configuration c of S_0. The representation of t_1 as a tree-pushdown t_2, i.e., as a configuration of $\text{TP}(1\text{-AT}(S_0))$, is based on the decomposition as explained in Remark 1: $t_1 = \xi_0(\xi_1,\xi_2)$, where $\xi_0 = \gamma(\delta(),\sigma(\delta())) \in AT(\Xi_2)^{(qq,q)}$, $\xi_1 = \alpha()()$ and $\xi_2 = \sigma(\delta())()$, both in $AT(\Xi_1)^q$. This gives already the outer shape of the tree-pushdown t_2. We choose an arbitrary symbol of Ω of rank 2, say v_2, to denote the root of t_2 and associate ξ_0 as configuration to v_2. Actually, since the configuration associated to v_2 must be an applicative term of type q, we slightly modify ξ_0 by replacing every symbol ρ by $\tilde{\rho}$ such that the type of $\tilde{\rho}$ is $\text{dec}(\text{type}_{n+1}(\rho))$. The mapping $\text{dec}:D^+(Q) \to D^*(Q)$ decrements the level of each type in the following way: for $k \geq 0$ $\text{dec}((q^k,q))=q$ and $\text{dec}((\alpha,\nu)) = (\text{dec}(\alpha(1))\ldots\text{dec}(\alpha(k)),\text{dec}(\nu))$ if α has length k. Thus, $\tilde{\gamma}:(qq,q)$, $\tilde{\sigma}:(q,q)$, $\tilde{\delta}:(\lambda,q)$, and $\tilde{\alpha}:(\lambda,q)$. By applying the above mentioned decomposition and type-decrementation to ξ_1 and ξ_2 (and this, in general iteratedly), we obtain the representation t_2 of t_1, viz. $t_2 = v_2<\tilde{\gamma}(\tilde{\delta}(),\tilde{\sigma}(\tilde{\delta}()))>(\tilde{\xi}_1,\tilde{\xi}_2)$ where $\tilde{\xi}_1 = v_0<\tilde{\alpha}()>()$ and $\tilde{\xi}_2 = v_0<\tilde{\sigma}(\tilde{\delta}())>()$, and v_0 is an arbitrary symbol of Ω with rank 0. Now it is easy to see how an instruction of $2\text{-AT}(S_0)$ is simulated. The instruction $f_1 =$ $\text{push}(\delta()(y_{1,(q,q)}(y_{2,q})))$ is simulated by $f_2 =$ $\text{push}(v_1<\text{push}(\tilde{\delta}())>(v_1<\text{push}(y_{1,q})>(y_{2,q})))$. Note that it is easy to construct a flowchart that only executes instruction f_2.
Applying f_1 and f_2 to t_1 and t_2, respectively, yields $t_1' =$ $\delta()(\delta()(\sigma(\delta())()))$ and $t_2' = v_1<\tilde{\delta}()>(v_1<\tilde{\delta}()>(v_0<\tilde{\sigma}(\tilde{\delta}())>()))$. □

<u>Lemma 3</u>. For every $n \geq 1$, n-AT(S) ≡ TP^n(S).

Proof. Immediate from Lemma 2 and Fact 5. □

In [EV3] it is shown that TP(S) is equivalent to the bounded excursion pushdown of S (cf. also [vL]). Before describing this storage type, we recall the definition of the pushdown operator [Gr,E4,EV2,EV3]). The pushdown of S, denoted by P(S), is the storage type (C',P',F',I',E'), where $C' = (\Gamma\times C)^+$ and Γ is a fixed infinite set, $P' = \{top{=}\gamma \mid \gamma\in\Gamma\} \cup \{test(p) \mid p\in P\}$, $F' = \{push(\gamma,f), stay(\gamma), stay \mid \gamma\in\Gamma,\ f\in F\} \cup \{pop\}$, and for $c' = (\delta,c)\beta$ and $\beta\in C'\cup\{\lambda\}$, $(top{=}\gamma)(c') = true$ iff $\gamma = \delta$, $test(p)(c') = p(c)$, $push(\gamma,f)(c') = (\gamma,f(c))(\delta,c)\beta$, $stay(\gamma)(c') = (\gamma,c)\beta$, $stay(c') = c'$, and $pop(c') = \beta$, if $\beta\neq\lambda$. $I' = I$ and $E' = \{\lambda u\in I.(\gamma,e(u)) \mid \gamma\in\Gamma,\ e\in E\}$. The operator P can be iterated in the same way as TP. $P^n(S_0)$ is denoted by P^n. The bounded excursion pushdown of S, denoted by $P_{bex}(S)$, is a modification of P(S) such that for some number $k\geq 0$, to every configuration at most k instructions of the form $push(\gamma,f)$, $stay(\gamma)$, and stay can be applied. For a formal definition see [EV3].

Lemma 4. For every $n\geq 1$, $TP^n(S) \equiv P^n_{bex}(S)$. If S contains the identity on C, then "bex" can be dropped.

Proof. Follows from $P_{bex}(S) \equiv TP(S)$ (Theorem 5.13 of [EV3]) and Fact 5. The second statement is Corollary 5.21 of [EV3]. □

Lemma's 1, 3, 4 and Fact 6, provide the characterization of n-level S transducers by (0-level) n-iterated pushdown of S transducers.

Theorem 1. For every $n\geq 1$, $n\text{-}T(S) = 0\text{-}T(P^n_{bex}(S))$. Determinism and totality are preserved. If S contains the identity on C, then "bex" can be dropped. □

Facts (7). For $S=S_0$, Theorem 1 implies that the n-level tree grammars (equivalent to $range(n\text{-}T(S_0))$, see Fact 3) are equivalent to the 0-level P^n transducers, which can be viewed as top-down tree automata with storage P^n. For n=1, this reproves the result of [Gu] that the OI context-free tree languages are recognized by "restricted pushdown tree automata". (8). Since all constructions preserve monadicness of the terminal alphabet, we obtain in particular $range(n\text{-}T_{mon}(S_0)) = range(0\text{-}T_{mon}(P^n))$, and hence $range(n\text{-}T_{mon}(S_0))$ = 1-way P^n automata. The language class $range(n\text{-}T_{mon}(S_0))$ is generated by the level-n (string) grammars defined in [Da] (the n-th class in the OI-language hierarchy [Da,Wa,ES,E5]). Hence, we reobtain the characterization of n-level languages by 1-way P^n automata, proved in [DGo]. □

5.CHARACTERIZATION OF HIGH LEVEL TREE TRANSDUCERS. Applying the general result of Theorem 1 to the storage type TR, we obtain the characterization of n-level tree transducers by n-iterated pushdown tree transducers. In the total deterministic case we can prove an even nicer characterization: bex can be dropped.

Theorem 2. For every $n\geq 1$, $n\text{-}T(TR) = 0\text{-}T(P^n_{bex}(TR))$ and $n\text{-}D_tT(TR) = 0\text{-}D_tT(P^n(TR))$. □

Another easy description of $n\text{-}D_tT(TR)$ is provided by its decomposition into simple classes of translations, namely the classes $1\text{-}D_tT(TR)$ (induced by macro tree transducers, see Fact 2) and YIELD. YIELD is a class of substitution functions defined algebraically in [Ma,ES,Da] and syntactically in [E3]. If T is a class of relations, then T^n denotes $\{R_1\circ\ldots\circ R_n \mid R_i\in T\}$, and $T^* = \cup\{T^n \mid n\geq 0\}$.

Theorem 3. For every $n\geq 1$,

(a) $n\text{-}D_tT(TR) = 1\text{-}D_tT(TR)^n$

(b) $n\text{-}D_tT(TR) = 0\text{-}D_tT(TR) \circ YIELD^n$.

Proof. (a) follows immediately from Theorem 2, and Theorem 8.11 of [EV3]. (b) is obtained from (a) and Corollary 4.13 of [EV1]. □

We mention two final results.

- Since $\{1\text{-}D_tT(TR)^n | n\geq 1\}$ is a strict hierarchy (Theorem 4.16 of [EV1]), it follows from Theorem 3(a) that the n-level tree transducers form a strict hierarchy with increasing n.

- Consider the translation class AG of attribute grammars viewed as tree translators [EF,CM,CF]. Since $AG^* = 1\text{-}D_tT(TR)^*$ [E3], Theorem 3(a) implies that $*\text{-}D_tT(TR) = AG^*$, where $*\text{-}D_tT(TR) = \cup\{n\text{-}D_tT(TR) \mid n\geq 0\}$. Thus the (total deterministic) high-level tree transductions can be realized by compositions of tree-valued AG's, and vice versa.

REFERENCES

[AU1] A.V. Aho, J.D. Ullman; Translations on a context-free grammar; Inf. and Contr. 19 (1971), 439-475.

[AU2] A.V. Aho, J.D. Ullman; "The Theory of Parsing, Translation, and Compiling" Vol. 1,2, Prentice Hall, Englewood Cliffs, N.J. 1973.

[CM] L.M. Chirica, D.E. Martin; An order algebraic definition of Knuthian semantics; Math. Syst. Theory 13 (1979), 1-27.

[CF] B. Courcelle, P. Franchi-Zannettacci; Attribute grammars and recursive program schemes I, II; TCS 17 (1982), 163-191 and TCS 17 (1982), 235-257.

[Da] W. Damm; The IO- and OI-hierarchies; TCS 20 (1982), 95-206.

[DGo] W. Damm, A. Goerdt; An automata-theoretic characterization of the OI-hierarchy; Proc. 9th ICALP; 1982, Aarhus, pp. 141-153; to appear in Inf. and Control.

[DG1] W. Damm, I. Guessarian; Combining T and level n; Proc. of the 9th Mathematical Foundations of Computer Sciences 1981, LNCS 118, p.262-270, Springer-Verlag.

[DG2] W. Damm, I. Guessarian; Implementation techniques for recursive tree transducers on higher-order data types; Report 83-16, Laboratoire Informatique Theorique et Programmation, Université Paris 7, 1983.

[E1] J. Engelfriet; Bottom-up and top-down tree transformations - a comparison; Math. Syst. Theory 9 (1975), 198-231.

[E2] J. Engelfriet; Some open questions and recent results on tree transducers and tree languages; in: "Formal language theory; perspectives and open problems", (R.V. Book, Ed.), New York, Academic Press, 1980.

[E3] J. Engelfriet; Tree transducers and syntax-directed semantics; TW-Memorandum Nr. 363 (1981), Twente University of Technology; also: Proc. 7th CAAP, March 1982, Lille, pp. 82-107.

[E4] J. Engelfriet; Recursive automata; (1982) unpublished notes.

[E5] J. Engelfriet; Iterated pushdown automata and complexity classes; Proc. 15th STOC, April 1983, Boston, pp. 365-373.

[EF] J. Engelfriet, G. File; The formal power of one-visit attribute grammars; Acta Informatica 16 (1981), 275-302.

[ES] J. Engelfriet, E.M. Schmidt; IO and OI; JCSS 15 (1977), 328-353 and JCSS 16 (1978), 67-99.

[EV1] J. Engelfriet, H. Vogler; Macro tree transducers; Inf-Memorandum Nr. 7 (1982), Twente University of Technology; to appear in JCSS.

[EV2] J. Engelfriet, H. Vogler; Regular characterizations of macro tree transducers; 9th Colloquium on Trees in Algebra and Programming, March 1984, Bordeaux, France (Ed. B. Courcelle), Cambridge University Press, p. 103-117.

[EV3] J. Engelfriet, H. Vogler; Pushdown machines for the macro tree transducer; Technical Report 84-13, Applied Mathematics and Computer Science Dept., University of Leiden, The Netherlands; also to appear as Inf-Memorandum at Twente University of Technology, Netherlands.

[EV4] J. Engelfriet, H. Vogler; Pushdown machines for high level tree transducers; to appear as technical report at University of Leiden.

[Fi] M.J. Fischer; Grammars with macro-like productions; Ph.D. Thesis, Harvard University, USA, 1968.

[Gr] S.A. Greibach; Full AFLs and nested iterated substitution; Inf. and Contr. 16 (1970), 7-35.

[Gu] I. Guessarian; Pushdown tree automata; Math. Syst. Theory 16 (1983), 237-263.

[Ho] C.A.R. Hoare; Proof of correctness of data representations; Acta Informatica I (1972), 271-281.

[Kn] D.E. Knuth; Semantics of context-free languages; Math. Syst. Theory 2 (1968), 127-145; correction:Math. Syst. Theory 5 (1971), 95-96.

[Ma] T.S.E. Maibaum; A generalized approach to formal languages; JCSS 8 (1974),409-439

[Ms] A.N. Maslov; Multi-level stack automata; Probl. of Inf. Transm. 12 (1976), 38-43.

[MV] D.F. Martin, S.A. Vere; On syntax-directed transductions and tree transducers; 2nd Annual ACM Symp. on Theory of Computation, May 1970.

[Ro] W.C. Rounds; Mappings and grammars on trees; Math. Syst. Theory 4 (1970), 257-287.

[Th] J.W. Thatcher; Generalized^2 sequential machine maps; JCSS 4 (1970), 339-367.

[Vo] H. Vogler; Berechnungsmodelle syntaxgeteuerter Uebersetzungen; Diplomarbeit, RWTH Aachen, April, 1981.

[vL] J. van Leeuwen; Notes on pre-set pushdown automata; in "L Systems" (eds. G. Rozenberg, A. Salomaa), Lecture Notes in Computer Science 15, Springer-Verlag, 1974, pp. 177-188.

[Wa] M. Wand; An algebraic formulation of the Chomsky-hierarchy, Category Theory Applied to Computation and Control, LNCS 25, Springer, Berlin, 1975, 209-213.

AMBIGUITY AND TRANSCENDENCE

Philippe FLAJOLET
INRIA
Rocquencourt
78150 Le Chesnay (France)

ABSTRACT

We establish that several classical context free languages are inherently ambiguous by proving that their counting generating functions, when considered as analytic functions, exhibit some characteristic form of transcendental behaviour.

1. INTRODUCTION

We propose here an analytic method for approaching the problem of determining whether a *context-free* language is *inherently ambiguous*. This method (which cannot be universal since the problem is highly undecidable) is applied to several context-free languages that had resisted previous attacks by purely combinatorial arguments. In particular, we solve here a conjecture of Autebert, Beauquier, Boasson, Nivat [1] by establishing that the "Goldstine language" is inherently ambiguous. Our technique is also applied to a number of context-free languages of rather diverse structural types.

There are relatively few types of languages that have been proved to be inherently ambiguous. This situation owes mostly to the fact that classical proofs of inherent ambiguity have to be based on a combinatorial argument of some sort considering *all possible grammars* for the language. Such proofs are therefore scarce and relatively lengthy.

At an abstract level, our methodology is related to a more general principle, namely the construction of *analytical models for combinatorial problems*. Informally, the idea is as follows:

To determine if a problem P belongs to a class **C**, *associate to elements ω of* **C** *adequately chosen analytic objects $\vartheta(\omega)$ so that a (possibly partial) characterization of $\vartheta(\mathbf{C})$ can be obtained. If $\vartheta(P)\notin\vartheta(\mathbf{C})$, then P does not belong to* **C**.

At such a level of generality, this principle is of course of little use. However it has been successfully applied in the past in the derivation of non trivial lower bounds in complexity theory:

1. Shamos and Yuval [18] have obtained interesting lower bounds for the complexity of computing the mean distance of points in a Euclidian space by considering *the Riemann surface associated to the complex multivalued function* (especially its *branch points*) that continues the function defined by the original problem. They obtain in this way an $\Omega(n^2)$ lower bound on the complexity of the problem. The fact that the proof of this particular result was subsequently "algebracized" by Pippenger [13] does not limit the interest of their approach.

2. More recently Ben-Or [3] has obtained a number of lower bounds for membership problems, including for instance the distinctness problem, set equality and inclusion .... His method consists in considering ***the topological structure of the real algebraic variety*** (the number of connected components) associated to a particular problem and relate it to the inherent complexity of that problem.

Our approach here is to examine properties of ***generating functions of context-free languages*** especially when these functions are considered as ***analytic functions*** instead of plain formal power series. The situation in this case is greatly helped by the fact that, from an old theorem of Chomsky and Schutzenberger, the ordinary generating function of an ***unambiguous*** context-free language is ***algebraic*** as a ***series***, and thus also as an analytic ***function***. Therefore, we can simply prove that a context-free language is inherently ambiguous provided we establish that its generating function is a ***transcendental function***.

Proofs of transcendence for analytic functions appear to be fortunately appreciably simpler than for real numbers. A method of choice consists in establishing the transcendence of a function by investigating its ***singularities***, in particular showing that it has a ***non-algebraic singularity*** (the way algebraic functions may become singular is well characterized), or infinitely many singularities or even a ***natural boundary***.

In the sequel, we shall state some useful transcendence criteria for establishing inherent ambiguity of context-free languages, and present a number of applications to specific languages.

A note about our presentation: it should be clear in what follows that we have made no attempt at deriving the simplest or most elementary proofs of inherent ambiguities of languages. We have instead tried to demonstrate the variety of techniques that may be employed here as they should also prove useful in future applications. It should also be clear that a very large number of languages are amenable to these techniques and some random sampling has been exercised to keep this paper within reasonable size limits.

2. SOME INHERENTLY AMBIGUOUS LANGUAGES

A context free grammar G is ***ambiguous*** iff there exists a least one word in the language generated by G that can be parsed according to G in two different ways. A context-free language L is ***inherently ambiguous*** iff ***any*** grammar that generates L is ambiguous.

A prototype of an inherently ambiguous language is

$$L = \{ a^m b^n c^p \mid n=m \text{ or } n=p \} \tag{1}$$

and the proof of its inherent ambiguity proceeds by showing, by means of some iteration theorem, that ***any*** grammar for L needs to generate words of the form $a^n b^n c^n$ at least twice for large enough n. (See *e.g.* Harrison's book [10] for similar classical proofs).

In this paper, we propose to prove the inherent ambiguity of a number of languages of various types that are structurally more complex than the above example:

Theorem 1: [Languages with constraints on the number of occurrences of letters] ***The languages O_3, O_4 are inherently ambiguous, where:***

$$O_3 = \{ w \in \{a,b,c\}^* \mid |w|_a = |w|_b \text{ or } |w|_a = |w|_c \}$$

$$O_4 = \{\, w \in \{x,\bar{x},y,\bar{y}\}^* \mid |w|_x = |w|_{\bar{x}} \text{ or } |w|_y = |w|_{\bar{y}} \}.$$

Theorem 2: [Crestin's language formed with products of palindromes] *The language C is inherently ambiguous, where:*

$$C = \{\, w_1 w_2 \mid w_1, w_2 \in \{a,b\}^* ; w_1 = w_1^t , w_2 = w_2^t \}$$

with w^t *denoting the mirror image of* w.

Theorem 3: [A simple linear language] *The language S is inherently ambiguous, where:*

$$S = \{\, a^n b v_1 a^n v_2 \mid v_1, v_2 \in \{a,b\}^* \}$$

Theorem 4: [Languages with a comb-like structure] *The languages* P_1, P_2 *are inherently ambiguous, where:*

$$P_1 = \{\, \underline{n}_1 \underline{n}_2 n \cdots \underline{n}_{2k} \mid [\text{for all } j \; n_{2j} = n_{2j-1}] \text{ or } [\text{for all } j \; n_{2j} = n_{2j+1}, n_{2k} = n_1] \}$$

$$P_2 = \{\, \underline{n}_1 \underline{n}_2 \cdots \underline{n}k \mid [n_1 = 1, \text{for all } j \; n_{2j} = 2n_{2j-1}] \text{ or } [\text{for all } j \; n_{2j} = 2n_{2j+1}] \}$$

where for integer n, $\underline{n}$ *denotes the unary representation of* n *in the form of* $a^n b$.

Theorem 5: [Languages deriving from the Goldstine language] *The languages* $G_{\neq}$, $G_{<}$, $G_{>}$, $H_{\neq}$ *are inherently ambiguous, where:*

$$G_{\neq} = \{\, \underline{n}_1 \underline{n}_2 \cdots \underline{n}_p \mid \text{for some } j \; n_j \neq j \}$$

$$G_{<} = \{\, \underline{n}_1 \underline{n}_2 \cdots \underline{n}_p \mid \text{for some } j \; n_j < j \}$$

$$G_{>} = \{\, \underline{n}_1 \underline{n}_2 \cdots \underline{n}_p \mid \text{for some } j \; n_j > j \}$$

$$H_{\neq} = \{\, \underline{n}_1 \underline{n}_2 \cdots \underline{n}_p \mid \text{for some } j \; n_j \neq p \}$$

Theorem 6: [Languages obeying local constraints] *The languages* K_1, K_2 *are inherently ambiguous, where:*

$$K_1 = \{\, \underline{n}_1 \underline{n}_2 \cdots \underline{n}_k \mid \text{for some } j \; n_{j+1} \neq n_j \}$$

$$K_2 = \{\, \underline{n}_1 \underline{n}_2 \cdots \underline{n}_k \mid \text{for some } j \; n_{j+1} \neq 2n_j \}$$

Theorem 7: [A language based on binary representations of integers] *The language B is inherently ambiguous, where:*

$$B = \{\, \underset{\sim}{n}_1 \underset{\sim}{n}_2 \cdots \underset{\sim}{n}_k \mid n_1 \neq 1 \text{ or for some } j \; n_{j+1} \neq n_j + 1 \}$$

in which $\underset{\sim}{n}$ *denotes the binary representation of integer* n *followed by a marker.*

Many of these results are actually known but have been included here for the sake of illustrating the power of the methods we employ: the case of languages like O_2, O_3 is easily reduced to the ambiguity of languages like L defined in (1). The language C has been studied combinatorially by Crestin [7] who proved that it is of *inherent unbounded ambiguity*. We establish here the transcendence of its generating function, which proves a conjecture of Kemp. The result concerning language S is a weaker form of a result due to Shamir [17] by which

$$\{\, ucv_1 u^t v_2 \mid u, v_1, v_2 \in \{a,b\}^* \}$$

is infinitely ambiguous. The language P_2 has been studied by Kemp [12] who proved that the asymptotic density of a closely related language is transcendental, thereby establishing its ambiguity.

The other cases seem to be new. In particular, the case of the language $G_{\neq}$, which is exactly the Goldstine language, solves the conjecture of Autebert *et al.*. Although it seems quite plausible at first sight that such languages must be inherently ambiguous, the difficulty owes to the fact that when attempting to apply iteration theorems, (like Ogden's lemma), some of them (most notably the Goldstine language) behave almost like regular languages.

3. AN OVERVIEW OF TRANSCENDENCE CRITERIA USED FOR ESTABLISHING INHERENT AMBIGUITY

To any language $L \subset A^*$ (A a finite alphabet) we associate its *enumeration sequence* defined by:

$$l_n = card\{ w \in L \mid |w| = n \} .$$

This sequence is characterized by its generating function, called the *generating function* of language L:

$$l(z) = \sum_{n \geq 0} l_n z^n .$$

This function is an analytic function in a neighbourhood of the origin, and its radius of convergence ρ satisfies:

$$\frac{1}{card\, A} \leq \rho \leq 1 .$$

Consideration of analytical properties of function $l(z)$ or, in an often equivalent manner, of asymptotic properties of the sequence $\{l_n\}$ permits in a number of cases to establish inherent ambiguity of the context-free language L by means of the following classical theorem of Chomsky and Schutzenberger [5]:

Theorem: *Let $l(z)$ be the generating function of a context-free language L. If L is unambiguous, then $l(z)$ is an algebraic series (function) in one variable.*

This classical theorem is established in a constructive manner by transforming an unambiguous definition of the language into a set of polynomial equations. It will be used in the sequel under the trivially equivalent form:

Corollary: *If the generating function $l(z)$ of a context-free language L is transcendental, then L is inherently ambiguous.*

The above corollary (see [14] for general information on languages and formal power series) therefore permits to conclude as to the inherent ambiguity of a language provided the following two conditions are met:

(i) [The counting condition]: One has at one's disposal a combinatorial decomposition of the language, in a way that gives access to the sequence l_n and permits to "express" $l(z)$.

(ii) [Transcendence condition]: A transcendence criterion is available to establish the non-algebraic character of $l(z)$.

We now proceed with the statement of a few simple transcendence criteria of which applications will be given in the following sections. The first one is obvious:

Theorem A: *Let $l(z)$ be an algebraic series of $Q[[z]]$, ω an algebraic number. Then $l(\omega)$ is algebraic.*

Criterion A: [Transcendence of values at an algebraic point] *If $l(z)$ is a series of $Q[[z]]$, and if $l(\omega)$ is transcendental for some algebraic ω, then $l(z)$ is transcendental*

Theorem B: *An algebraic function $l(z)$ defined by an equation*

$$P(z,l(z))=0$$

has a finite number of singularities that are algebraic numbers satisfying the equation:

$$\text{Resultant}_y[P(z,y),\frac{\partial P(z,y)}{\partial y}]=0\,.$$

This last result is of course a very classical one (see for instance Seidenberg's book [16]) and comes from the implicit function theorem for analytic functions.

Criterion B: *A function having infinitely many singularities (for instance a natural boundary) is transcendental.*

In the sequel, this result is used to establish the ambiguity of Crestin's language C taking advantage of Kemp's determination of its generating function which appears to have infinitely many singularities. Other applications stem from the existence of natural boundaries for *lacunary series* (as an application of theorems of Hadamard, Borel and Fabry).

A more refined way of establishing the transcendence of a series consists in observing the appearance of transcendental elements in local expansions around a singularity. Indeed, for an algebraic function, one has:

Theorem C: *If $l(z)$ is algebraic it admits in the vicinity of a singularity a fractional power series expansion of the type*

$$l(z)=\sum_{k\geq -m} a_k(1-\frac{z}{\alpha})^{kr},\quad m\in\mathbf{N}, r\in\mathbf{Q}^+,$$

where the a_k are algebraic.

The above expansion is nothing but the familiar Puiseux expansion of an algebraic function.

Criterion C: *If $l(z)$ has in the vicinity of a singularity an asymptotic equivalent that is not of the form:*

$$\omega(1-\frac{z}{\alpha})^r$$

with ω and α algebraic and r rational, then $l(z)$ is transcendental.

It is also well known that the local behaviour of a function in the vicinity of its singularities is closely reflected by the asymptotic behaviour of its Taylor coefficients. Corresponding "transfer" lemmas rely on contour integration techniques, like the Darboux method.

Theorem D: *If $l(z)$ is an algebraic function that is analytic at the origin, then its n Taylor coefficient l_n has an asymptotic equivalent of the form:*

$$l_n = \frac{\alpha^n n^s}{\Gamma(s+1)} \sum_{i\geq 0}^{m} C_i \omega_i^n + O(\alpha^n n^t) , \qquad (\Delta)$$

where $s \in \mathbf{Q} / \{-1,-2,-3, \cdots\}$, $t < s$, *α is an algebraic number and the* C_i, ω_i *are algebraic with* $|\omega_i| = 1$.

Criterion D: *Let* $l(z)$ *be a function analytic at the origin; if its Taylor coefficients* l_n *do not satisfy an asymptotic expansion of type* (Δ), *then* $l(z)$ *is transcendental.*

In passing, Criterion D generalizes a result of Berstel [4] who observed that if there exists an integer α such that the limit

$$\lambda = \lim \frac{l_n}{\alpha^n}$$

exists and is a transcendental number, then $l(z)$ is a transcendental function, so that L cannot be an unmabiguous context-free language. Theorem D does provide a *generalized density* characterization for unambiguous context-free languages that extends Berstel's results.

A particularly useful set of applications of Theorem D is for coefficients with asymptotic equivalents of the form:

$$l_n \sim \gamma \alpha^n n^r .$$

If either r is irrational, α transcendental or $\gamma\Gamma(r+1)$ is transcendental, then $l(z)$ is a transcendental function. Therefore the following asymptotic behaviours are characteristic of transcendental functions:

$$O(e^n n^r) \; ; \; O(\alpha^n n^{\sqrt{2}}) \; ; \; O(\frac{\alpha^n}{n}) \; ; \; O(\frac{\alpha^n}{n^2}) \; ; \; \pi^{\frac{1}{2}} 4^n n^{-\frac{3}{2}} \; \ldots$$

(Notice however for the last example that $\pi^{-\frac{1}{2}} 4^n n^{-\frac{3}{2}}$ *does* occur in the expansion of algebraic functions.)

The last batch of methods is based on a theorem by Comtet [6] that any algebraic function satisfies a linear differential equation with polynomial coefficients, a fact which is reflected on its Taylor coefficients by:

Theorem E: *If* $l(z)$ *is algebraic, then there exist a set of polynomials* $p_0(z), \cdots, p_m(z)$ *such that:*

$$\sum_{j=0}^{m} p_j(z) \frac{d^j l(z)}{dz^j} = 0 .$$

Thus, there exist a set of polynomials $q_0(u), \cdots, q_m(u)$ *such that for all* $n \geq n_0$:

$$\sum_{j=0}^{m} q_j(n) l_{n-j} = 0 .$$

Criterion E: *Let* $l(z)$ *be an analytic function. If there does not exist a finite sequence of polynomials* $q_0, q_1, \cdots, q_m$ *such that for n large enough:*

$$\sum_{j=0}^{m} q_j(n) l_{n-j} = 0 ,$$

then $l(z)$ *is transcendental.*

This criterion comes as a useful complement (or as an alternative) to transcendence proofs based on lacunary series mentioned in relation to Criterion B since it applies obviously to any series

$$\sum_{n\geq 0} a_n x^{c_n}$$

such that $\sup(c_{n+1}-c_n) = +\infty$.

4. TRANSCENDENCE OF VALUES OF GENERATING FUNCTIONS

This method is in principle the most direct. However, in practice, it turns out to be rather hard to apply because of the relative scarcity of transcendence results for real numbers. It is applied here to the following languages:

1. The language O_4 is by definition the union of two context-free languages whose intersection has a generating function that is an ***elliptic integral***. Using a classical result in transcendence theory concerning values of such integrals at algebraic points [15,II,Sect. 4], we establish the transcendence of the generating function of O_4.
2. Language P_2: it has a generating function whose expression involves the ***Fredholm series***:

$$F(x) = \sum_{n\geq 0} x^{2^n}$$

and the approximation theorem of Thue-Siegel-Roth [15,I,Sect. 6, Th. 8] shows the value of the series to be transcendental at any point $x=\frac{1}{q}$ for integral q.

This last example is inspired by the construction due to Kemp [12] of a context-free language with a transcendental density.

5. FUNCTIONS WITH INFINITELY MANY SINGULARITIES

Criterion B expresses that any function with infinitely many singularities is transcendental. Such a property may either be apparent on the very expression of the function or it may result from theorems on ***lacunary series***.

1. The language S: a decomposition reveals that its generating function involves rationally the quantity:

$$s(z) = z\sum_{k\geq 0} \frac{z^{2k}}{1-2z+z^{k+1}},$$

a series which not too surprisingly is related to statistics on "***runs***" (repetitive sequences) [8], and accordingly occurs in an analysis by Knuth of carry propagation. It is easy to check that $s(z)$ has infinitely many poles around $\frac{1}{2}$ satisfying:

$$z_k = \frac{1}{2}+2^{-k-1}+o(2^{-k})$$

and it is therefore transcendent.

2. The language C has been introduced by Crestin [7] and Kemp [11] has shown that its generating function is:

$$l(z) = 1+2\sum_{m\geq 1}\psi(m)\frac{z^m(1+z^m)(1+2z^m)}{(1-2z^{2m})^2}$$

where $\psi(m)=\prod(1-p)$, the product being extended to all prime divisors of m. From that expressions easily follows that $l(z)$ has for $|z|\leq 1$ isolated singularities at points:

$$z_{m,j} = 2^{\frac{1}{2m}} e^{\frac{ij\pi}{m}} .$$

3. The Goldstine language $G_{\neq}$ has a generating function related to the *theta functions*:

$$l(z) = \frac{1-z}{1-2z} - \sum_{j\geq 0} z^{j(j+1)}$$

which is clearly non algebraic as can be checked since, for instance, from the theory of lacunary series the sum has the circle $|z|=1$ as a natural boundary. The same treatment applies to $H_{\neq}$.

This last case is the one that initially motivated our study. The reader may consult [2] for some related enumeration issues.

6. LOCAL BEHAVIOUR AROUND SINGULARITIES

This is certainly the most comfortable method to apply. The mere appearance of logarithmic terms in the local expansion of a function around a singularity is sufficient to establish its transcendence. Such local analyses may often be treated by Mellin transform techniques, a fact not too surprising considering the arithmetical character of many of the languages we study.

1. The language K_1 has a generating function whose expression involves the *Lambert series* associated to the arithmetical *divisor function*:

$$D(z) = \sum \frac{z^n}{1-z^n} .$$

The Mellin transform of $D(e^{-t})$ is

$$\int_0^\infty D(e^{-t})t^{s-1}dt = \zeta^2(s)\Gamma(s) ,$$

from which we obtain through a residue calculation:

$$D(z) \sim (z-1)\log(1-z) ,$$

as z tends to 1, a typically transcendent behaviour.

2. The proofs for K_2, P_1 follow by similar arguments.

7. GENERALIZED ASYMPTOTIC DENSITIES

These are based on the existence of generalized densities corresponding to expansion (Δ) of Theorem D.

1. The language $G_>$ has a ***bivariate*** generating function (recording the number of a's and b's in words) that involves the function:

$$b(x,y) = \sum_{j\ge 1} [y^j \prod_{k=1}^{j} \frac{1-x^j}{1-x}] .$$

The function $c(x,y)=b(x,y(1-x))$ has the same transcendence status as $b(x,y)$. The transcendence of c is in turn easily related to that of the function:

$$E(x) = \prod_{j\ge 1} (1-x^j)^{-1}$$

which occurs in the theory of ***integer partitions***. Finally, the transcendence of $E(x)$ we may itself establish if we wish by considering the asymptotic form of its Taylor coefficients that is given by a celebrated theorem of Hardy and Ramanujan [9]:

$$E_n \sim \frac{e^{\pi\sqrt{\frac{2n}{3}}}}{4n\sqrt{3}} .$$

8. POLYNOMIAL RECURRENCES

This last part corresponds to Comtet's theorem:

1. The language B has a generating function where there intervenes the series

$$\Lambda(z) = \sum_{n\ge 1} z^{\lambda(n)} \quad \lambda(n) = 2n + \sum_{p\le n} [\log_2 p]$$

a series which because of large gaps cannot have coefficients that satisfy any fixed order polynomial recurrence.

2. Other cases involving theta series, like the Goldstine language, can be also treated in this way.

9. OPEN PROBLEMS

The following problems naturally suggest themselves: (1) Are there sufficient conditions on generating functions to ensure that a language is ***infinitely*** inherently ambiguous? (2) In which class of transcendental functions do generating functions of (ambiguous) context-free languages lie? For instance, in our work we came nowhere close to expressions involving the exponential function. (3) Accordingly are there results on generalized densities of (ambiguous) context-free languages? For instance, can the number of words of size n in a context-free language grow like $\exp(\sqrt{n})$?

Acknowledgment: This work was started after stimulating discussions with Lois Thimonier and J. Beauquier.

References

1. J-M. Autebert, J. Beauquier, L. Boasson, and M. Nivat, "Quelques Proble'mes Ouverts en Theorie des Langages Alge'briques," *R.A.I.R.O. Theoret. Comp. Sc.* **13** pp. 363-379 (1979).
2. J. Beauquier and L. Thimonier, *Formal Languages and Bernoulli Processes*, (to appear) 1983.
3. M. Ben-Or, "Lower Bounds for Algebraic Computation Trees," *Proc. 15th ACM Symp. on Theory of Computing*, pp. 80-86 (1983).
4. J. Berstel, "Sur la densite' asymptotique des langages formels," *Proc. 1st ICALP Colloquium*, pp. 345-368 North Holland, (1972).
5. N. Chomsky and M-P. Schutzenberger, "The Algebraic Theory of Context-Free Languages," *Computer Programming and Formal Systems*, pp. 118-161 North Holland, (1963).
6. L. Comtet, "Calcul pratique des coefficients de Taylor d'une fonction alge'brique," *Enseignement Math.* **10** pp. 267-270 (1964).
7. J.P. Crestin, "Un langage non ambigu dont le carre' est d'ambiguite' inherente borne'e," *Proc. 1st ICALP Colloquium*, pp. 377-390 North Holland, (1972).
8. W. Feller, *An Introduction to Probability Theory and its Applications*, J. Wiley, New-York (1950).
9. G. H. Hardy, *Ramanujan, Twelve Lectures Suggested by his Life and Work*, Cambridge, The University Press (1940).
10. M. Harrison, *Introduction to Formal Language Theory*, Addison-Wesley, Reading, Mass. (1978).
11. R. Kemp, "On the Number of Words in the Language $\{w \in \Sigma^*\}^2$," *Discrete Math.* **40** pp. 225-234 (1980).
12. R. Kemp, "A Note on the density of Inherently Ambiguous Context-Free Languages," *Acta Informatica* **14** pp. 295-298 (1980).
13. N. Pippenger, "Computational Complexity in Algebraic Function Fields," *Proc. 20th IEEE Symp. F.O.C.S.*, pp. 61-65 (1979).
14. A. Salomaa and M. Soittola, *Automata Theoretic Aspects of Formal Power Series*, Springer-Verlag, New-York (1978).
15. Th. Schneider, *Einfuhrung in die Transzendenten Zahlen*, Springer Verlag, Berlin (1957).
16. A. Seidenberg, *Elements of the Theory of Algebraic Curves*, Addison-Wesley, Reading, Mass. (1965).
17. E. Shamir, "Some Inherently Ambiguous Context-Free Languages," *Inf. and Control* **18** pp. 355-363 (1971).
18. M. I. Shamos and G. Yuval, "Lower Bounds from Complex Function Theory," *Proc. 17th IEEE Symp. F.O.C.S.*, pp. 268-273 (1976).

A FAST ALGORITHM FOR POLYGON CONTAINMENT BY TRANSLATION
(Extended Abstract)

S. J. Fortune
AT&T Bell Laboratories
Murray Hill NJ 07974

ABSTRACT

The polygon containment problem is the problem of deciding whether one polygon, C, can be translated to fit within another polygon N. We present an algorithm that runs in time $O(cn \log cn)$ to solve this problem, in the case that the polygon C is convex. Here c is the number of bounding edges of C, and n is the number of bounding edges of N. The algorithm actually computes the feasible region, that is, a description of the set of all placements of C inside N. The algorithm is close to optimal in that the feasible region may have $O(cn)$ vertices.

1. Introduction

Given polygons C and N, can C be translated so that it is entirely contained in N? This is the polygon containment problem. We present an algorithm that solves this problem, with running time $O(cn\log cn)$, assuming that the polygon C is convex. Here c is the number of bounding segments of C, and n is the number of bounding segments of N. Actually, the algorithm computes the feasible region, that is, the set of all placements of C so that C is completely contained in N. The algorithm is close to optimal in that the feasible region may have $O(cn)$ vertices.

The polygon containment problem has been studied previously by Chazelle[C] and by Baker, Fortune, and Mahaney[BFM]. Chazelle considered the case of containment when both translation and rotation are allowed operations. He derived an $O(n^3)$ algorithm for containment, in the case that both polygons are convex, and an $O(n^7)$ algorithm, if both polygons can be nonconvex. Here n is the sum of the number of bounding edges of the two polygons. Chazelle's algorithms only decide containment, and do not report the feasible region. Baker, Fortune, and Mahaney only consider translation. They derive an algorithm that runs in time $O((n^2+cn)\log cn)$ to decide containment of a convex polygon C with c edges inside a nonconvex polygon N with n edges. Their algorithm actually computes the feasible region.

One application where the elimination of the n^2 term is interesting is the "mover's problem", arising in robotics[LPW],[B]. Consider the problem of finding a collision-free path of a polygonal object C amidst polygonal obstacles, where the orientation of the object is fixed. The polygon containment containment algorithm can be modified to solve this problem. We take N to be the plane with the polygonal obstacles removed from it. The algorithm outputs the feasible region of C inside N. The feasible region can be searched, using any graph search algorithm, to find the desired path. In actual problems arising from robotics, it is quite plausible that the object to be moved has a simple description, i.e., c is small, while there may be many obstacles in the space, i.e. n is large.

The algorithm is based on the construction of the "C-diagram" of N. The C-diagram is similiar to the Voronoi diagram of N [K,Y,S]. The Voronoi diagram of N can be viewed as the set of centers of circles contained in N that touch the boundary of N in at least two places. The C-diagram of N is the set of "centers" of polygons similiar to C, scaled arbitrarily in size, contained in N, and that contact the boundary of N in at least two places. Since there is no obvious definition of the center of a polygon, an arbitrary point of C is chosen, hence the diagram depends upon the choice of point. The Voronoi diagram has been used by C. Ó'Dúnlaing, Sharir, and Yap to solve other cases of the mover's problem[OSY1, OSY2, OSY3].

Section 2 below contains the definition of the diagram of N, and some of its basic properties. As a first application of the Voronoi diagram, section 2 also contains a precise upper bound on the number of vertices of the feasible region of C inside N. Section 3 sketches an $O(cn \log cn)$ algorithm to compute the diagram of N, and from it the feasible region of C inside N.

2. The Diagram of N

Since there will never be any ambiguity, we drop the modifier "C" and always refer simply to the diagram of N. C is a fixed convex polygon with c bounding segments. For simplicity we assume that N is a polygon, a polygon with polygonal holes, or the entire plane less a set of polygons. A definition of the diagram for more general planar figures would be possible. In any event, N is closed, and has n bounding segments.

We use the convention that a polygon or a half plane always contains its boundary, and hence is closed. A *polygonal region* is the finite union of a finite intersections of half planes. For R a subset of the plane, $bd(R)$ denotes the boundary of R, $int(R)$ denotes the interior of R, $\overline{R}$ the complement of R, and coR the closure of $\overline{R}$. Thus if H is a halfplane, coH is the other half plane with bounding line $bd(H)$. If R is a polygonal region, and $v \in R$, then v is a *vertex* if for all neighborhoods N containing v, $N \cap R$ is not N, N intersect a line, nor N intersect a half plane. Vertex $v \in R$ is *isolated* if there is a neighborhood N containing v so that $N \cap R = \{v\}$.

Suppose s is a half plane or is a segment of the boundary of a polygon, and n a unit vector perpendicular to s pointing into the interior of the half plane or polygon. Then the *slope* of s is the tail of n, when the head of n is translated so that it lies at the origin. Note that slopes always lie on the unit circle centered at the origin. Slopes p and q are *parallel* if $p=q$, and *antiparallel* if p is diametrically opposite q. If slopes p and q are not antiparallel, then slope r is *between p and q* if r is contained in the section of the unit circle with endpoints p and q that is smaller than π. Slope r is strictly between p and q if it is between p and q and is not p nor q. Slope p is *counterclockwise* of q if the angle (counterclockwise) from q to p is greater than zero and less than π; p is *clockwise* of q if q is counterclockwise of p.

2.1. Placements and Contacts

How can we specify the placement of C in the plane? One possibility would be to choose a point of C, the reference point, and specify placements of C by placements of the reference point. However, we are also interested in scaling the size of C, so we use the following more general notation.

Suppose q is a fixed interior point of C. Consider the linear transformation $T[p,r]:R^2 \rightarrow R^2$ that scales by r and translates q to p, explicitly $T[p,r](x)=r(x-q)+p$, for $r \geq 0$, $x,p,q \in R^2$. Let $C[p,r]=T[p,r](C)$. Notice that $T[p,r]$ with $r>0$ preserves slope, so $C[p,r]$ is a polygon similiar to C with sides multiplied by r if $r>0$, or is the point p if $r=0$. A *placement of C* is just a choice of p and r. We say $C[p,r]$ is *feasible* if $C[p,r] \subseteq N$.

For $x \in N$, let $s(x)=\text{lub}\{r : C[x,r] \text{ feasible}\}$. The *feasible region of C inside N*, $I(C,N)$, is $\{x:s(x) \geq 1\}$. Notice that $s(x)$ is continuous; this depends upon the reference point being chosen an interior point of C.

We wish to analyze the function $s(x)$. To do this we need to analyze the possible ways that $bd(C[p,r])$ could intersect N, when $C[p,r]$ is feasible. It turns out to be convenient to categorize intersections into edge contacts, which arise when C is slid along an edge of N, and vertex contacts, which arise when an edge of C is slid along a vertex of N. $C[p,r]$ has *edge contact* e if e is an edge of $bd(N)$ and either there is an edge e' of C parallel to e with $T[p,r](e')$ intersecting e, or there is a vertex v of C with the slope of e between the slopes of the edges of $bd(C[p,r])$ incident to v and $T[p,r](v)$ intersects e. $C[p,r]$ has *vertex contact* (v,f) if v is a concave vertex of N, f is a bounding segment of C, the slope of f is strictly between the slopes of the edges incident to v, and $T[p,r](f)$ intersects v. See Figure 2.1. Finally, c is a *contact* if $C[p,r]$ has contact c, for some p,r. Note that the definition of edge or vertex contact does not require feasibility.

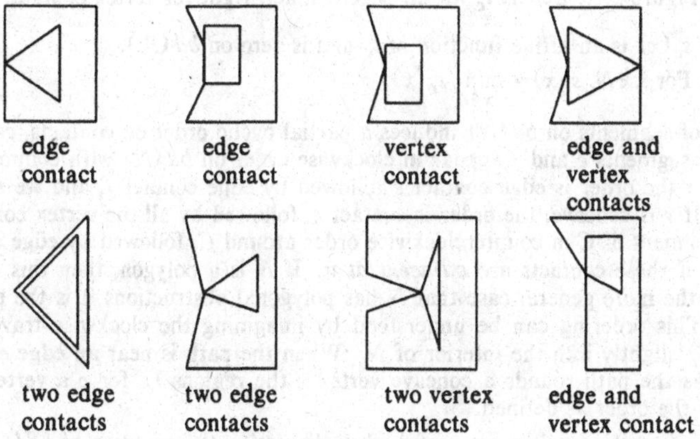

Figure 2.1.

Suppose a vertex of $C[p,r]$ intersects a concave vertex of N. If there is a neighborhood containing the vertices so that, within the neighborhood, $C[p,r] \subseteq N$, then we say the placement has a *vertex-vertex intersection.* This intersection always implies two contacts, which may be two edge contacts, two vertex contacts, or an edge contact and a vertex contact. See Figure 2.1.

The notion of separating halfplane captures the local constraints on motion of C implied by a contact. If c is a vertex contact (v,f), then the *separating halfplane*, P_c, is the halfplane parallel to f through v; if c is an edge contact e, then P_c is the half plane parallel to e through e. Note that P_c is independent of the placement of C, and if $C[p,r]$ has contact c, then $C[p,r] \subseteq P_c$ and $bd(C[p,r]) \cap bd(P_c) \neq \emptyset$.

What does a single contact c imply about the function $s(x)$? Define $t_c = \{p: r\ C[p,r] \text{ has contact } c\}$. If c is a vertex contact (v,f), then t_c is an infinite cone-shaped region with vertex v, and if c is an edge contact e, then t_c is an infinite truncated cone bounded by two half-lines and e. See Figure 2.2. Now for $x \in t_c$, let $s_c(x) = r$, where $C[x,r]$ has contact c.

Proposition 2.1: $s_c(x)$ is an affine function of t_c and is zero on $bd(P_c)$.

Proposition 2.2: For $x \in N$, $s(x) = \min_{c:\, x \in t_c} s_c(x)$.

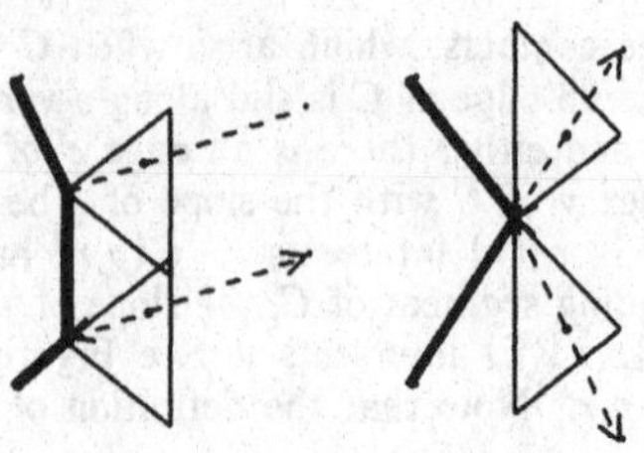

Figure 2.2. Left is t_c for an edge contact, right for vertex contact.

Proposition 2.1: $s_c(x)$ is an affine function of t_c and is zero on $bd(P_c)$.
Proposition 2.2: For $x \in N$, $s(x) = \min_{c:\, x \in t_c} s_c(x)$.

The order of segments on $bd(N)$ induces a partial cyclic order on contacts, called the *global order*. Suppose segments e and f appear in clockwise order on $bd(N)$ with common vertex v. If v is convex, then the order is edge contact e followed by edge contact f, and we say e and f are *adjacent at* v. If v is concave, the order is contact e, followed by all the vertex contacts (v,g) for g a bounding segment of C in counterclockwise order around C, followed by edge contact f. Any successive pair of these contacts are *adjacent at* v. If N is a polygon, then this order is a total cyclic order; in the more general case that N has polygonal obstructions it is the product of total cyclic orders. This ordering can be understood by imagining the clockwise traversal of a path following $bd(N)$ slightly into the interior of N. When the path is near an edge e, the path is in region t_e, and as the path rounds a concave vertex v the regions t_c, for c a vertex contact at v, are traversed in the order as defined.

Canonical intersection points are useful when discussing the partition of $bd(C)$ or $bd(N)$ by contacts. If $C[p,r]$ has contact c, then the *canonical intersection point* ι_c is v if c is a vertex contact (v,f), and is the midpoint of $bd(C) \cap e$ if c is an edge contact e. Canonical intersection points define a second ordering on contacts, called *contact order around* $bd(C[p,r])$. This is the ordering of intersection points clockwise around $bd(C[p,r])$; it is possible that $\iota_c = \iota_{c'}$ for $c \neq c'$, this happens if a vertex of C intersects a vertex of N, either concave or convex. In this case ι_c and $\iota_{c'}$ must be consecutive in global order, and we use global order for the contact order.

2.2. The Diagram and Edges

The *diagram* of N, $D(N)$, is $\{x\colon c,c' \text{ with } P_c \neq P_{c'} \text{ and } s(x) = s_c(x) = s_{c'}(x)\}$. For c, c' contacts with $P_c \neq P_{c'}$, the *cc'-psuedo-edge*, $e_{cc'}$, is $\{x \in t_c \cap t_{c'}\colon s_c(x) = s_{c'}(x)\}$ and the *cc'-edge*, $E_{cc'}$, is $\{x \in t_c \cap t_{c'}\colon s(x) = s_c(x) = s_{c'}(x)\}$. Clearly, $\bigcup_{c,c'} E_{cc'} = D(N)$. Also $E_{cc'} \subseteq e_{cc'}$, and $e_{cc'}$ is empty, a point, a segment, or a halfline, since s_c and $s_{c'}$ are affine and t_c and $t_{c'}$ are convex.

Lemma 2.3: $E_{cc'}$ is the finite union of segments and possibly a halfline.

Proof: There are only finitely many other contacts, hence $\{x\colon x \text{ is an endpoint of } e_{cc'} \cap t_d$, for $d \neq c$, $d \neq c'\}$ is finite. Within any interval of $e_{cc'}$ with endpoints two consecutive points of this set, at most one subinterval is in $E_{cc'}$. □

Suppose c and c' are contacts with $P_c \neq P_{c'}$. If P_c and $P_{c'}$ are not antiparallel, then the slopes of P_c and $P_{c'}$ partition the unit circle into $sl(P_c)$, $sl(P_{c'})$ and two open circular segments $vx(c,c')$ and $cv(c,c')$, where $vx(c,c')$ subtends the smaller (convex) angle and $cv(c,c')$ subtends the larger (concave) angle. $E_{cc'}$ and $e_{cc'}$ if nontrivial are linearly ordered by the value of s_c;

clearly $x<y$ iff the slope of the half line with endpoint x through y is in $cv(c,c')$. If in fact P_c and $P_{c'}$ are antiparallel, then the slopes of P_c and $P_{c'}$ partition the unit circle into $sl(P_c)$, $sl(P_{c'})$, and two equal-angled open segments arbitrarily labelled $vx(c,c')$ and $cv(c,c')$, where $E_{cc'}$ and $e_{cc'}$ are linearly ordered so that $x<y$ iff the slope of the half line with endpoint x through y is in $cv(c,c')$. v is a *left endpoint* (*right endpoint*) of segment s if there is no $w<v$ ($w>v$) in some neighborhood of s containing v. Segments t and u *overlap at* v their intersection properly contains v. Segments t and u *overlap* if they overlap at v for some v.

Lemma 2.4: Suppose $v\in E_{cc'}$.
1) v is the left endpoint of $E_{cc'}$ iff either v is the left endpoint of $e_{cc'}$ or there is a contact d at $C[v,s(v)]$ with $sl(P_d)\in vx(cc')$ and v is not the left endpoint of $t_d\cap e_{cc'}$.
2) v is the right endpoint of $E_{cc'}$ iff either v is the right endpoint of $e_{cc'}$ or there is a contact d at $C[v,s(v)]$ with $sl(P_d)\in cv(cc')$ and v is not the right endpoint of $t_d\cap e_{cc'}$.

Proof:
1) First notice that if $w\in e_{cc'}$ and $w<v$ then for any contact d at $C[v,s(v)]$ with $w\in t_d$, $s_d(w)<s_c(w)$ iff $sl(P_c)\in vx(cc')$.
If: Clearly, if v is the left endpoint of $e_{cc'}$, v is the left endpoint of $E_{cc'}$. Otherwise suppose there is a contact d at $C[v,s(v)]$ with $sl(P_d)\in vx(cc')$ and v is not the left endpoint of $t_d\cap e_{cc'}$. Then there is $w'<v$ on $e_{cc'}$ so that for $w'<w<v$, $w\in t_d$ and $s_d(w)<s_c(w)$.
Only if: We show there is $u<v$ on $e_{cc'}$ so that for all w with $u<w<v$, $s(w)=s_c(w)$. For each d so that d is not a contact at v, $s_d(v)>s_c(v)$, and there is $u_d<v$ on $e_{cc'}$ so that for all w with $u_d<w<v$, $s_d(w)>s_c(w)$. If d is a contact at v, then either $sl(P_d)\notin vx(cc')$, so $s_d(w)\geqslant s_c(w)$ for $w<v$ on $e_{cc'}$, or v is the left endpoint of $t_d\cap e_{cc'}$, so $w\notin t_d$ for $w<n$ on $e_{cc'}$. Hence for all w with $\max\{u_d\}<w<v$, $s(w)=s_c(w)$.
2) Similiar. □

Corollary 2.5:
1) Suppose $v\in E_{cc'}$, c and c' are consecutive in contact order around $C[v,s(v)]$, and $P_c\neq P_{c'}$. Then $E_{cc'}$ is nontrivial.
2) Suppose $E_{dd'}$ is nontrivial and $v\in E_{dd'}$. Then there are c and c' consecutive in contact order so that $E_{cc'}$ overlaps $E_{dd'}$ at v.

What do we now know about the structure of $D(N)$? $D(N)$ contains no isolated points, for if $v\in D(N)$, then $v\in E_{cc'}$ for two contacts c and c' in consecutive contact order, and $E_{cc'}$ is nontrivial by Corollary 2.5. Hence $D(N)$ consists of the union of segments and halflines. $D(N)$ can be naturally decomposed into intrinsic segments and halflines. A segment or halfline is *intrinsic* (to $D(N)$) if it is contained in $D(N)$, its endpoints are vertices of $D(N)$, and no interior point is a vertex. (A vertex of $D(N)$ clearly must be the intersection of two nonparallel segments or halflines.) Then $D(N)$ is the union of its intrinsic segments, which intersect only at vertices of $D(N)$.

The "overlaps" relation is the set of pairs of edges $E_{cc'}$ and intrinsic segments or halflines that overlap. This relation, unfortunately, is badly behaved. It is possible that one intrinsic segment is the union of two different edges $E_{cc'}$ and $E_{dd'}$ (which themselves overlap) and it is possible that $E_{cc'}$ consists of multiple intrinsic segments. The following Lemma describes a situation in which the correspondence is well behaved, and which will be useful in the next section.

Lemma 2.6: The overlap relation is a one-one correspondence between the intrinsic segments or halflines incident to a vertex v of N and the edges $E_{cc'}$, with c and c' adjacent at v.

Proof: Clearly if c and c' are adjacent at v, then $E_{cc'}$ is incident to v. Now every intrinsic segment or halfline must overlap some edge $E_{cc'}$. We show that every intrinsic segment or halfline incident to a vertex of N must overlap some edge $E_{cc'}$, where c and c' are adjacent at some vertex of N. We do this by showing that if c and c' are not adjacent at v, then $E_{cc'}$ is not incident to any vertex v of N. So choose ϵ so small that any two nonintersecting bounding segments of N

are separated by at least ϵ. Then if c and c' are not adjacent at any vertex of N, then $C[v,s(v)]$ fits in a ball of diameter ϵ, and as v is an interior point of $C[v,s(v)]$, there is ϵ' so that v is at least distance ϵ' from any point of N.

To complete the proof of the Lemma, we show that if $E_{cc'}$ overlaps intrinsic segment or halfline s incident to v, then no other $E_{dd'}$ overlaps s. First suppose d and d' are adjacent at v. Since $\{c,c'\} \neq \{d,d'\}$, $E_{cc'}$ and $E_{dd'}$ do not overlap, so $E_{dd'}$ cannot overlap s. Otherwise d and d' are adjacent at $w \neq v$ and $E_{dd'}$ overlaps some intrinsic segment or halfline t incident at w.

We need to show $s \neq t$. Clearly $s \neq t$ if segment $uv \not\subseteq D(N)$, so assume $uv \subseteq D(N)$, we will show there is a vertex $w \in uv$, and $s \neq t$. Clearly $\{P_c, P_{c'}\} \neq \{P_d, P_{d'}\}$. As c,c' are contacts at u, and d,d' are contacts at v, there must be a point $w \in uv$ with at least three contacts with nonparallel separating halfplanes. By Corollary 2.5 there must be three nontrivial edges incident at w, and w is a vertex. □

A plausible hypothesis is that the connected components of $D(N)$ are in one-one correspondence with the connected components of N. Unfortunately, $D(N)$ can be disconnected, even if N is a polygon. See Figure 2.3.

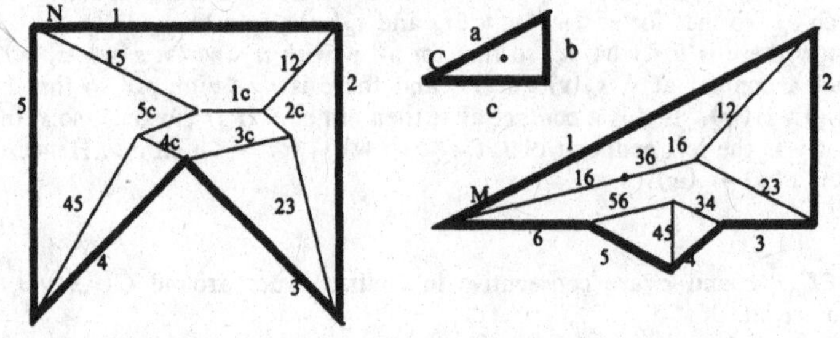

Figure 2.3. Edges of $D(N)$ and $D(M)$ are labelled by contacts. In N there are edge contacts 1, 2, 3, 4, and 5, and a single vertex contact between edge c and the vertex incident to edges 3 and 4. In M there are only edge contacts 1 - 6. Note that E_{36} is a subset of E_{16}.

2.3. A Bound on the Size of $I(C,N)$

We now use the diagram $D(N)$ to give a bound on the number of vertices of $I(C,N)$. Let v be a vertex of $D(N)$. Intrinsic segment or halfline t of $D(N)$ *leaves* v if $s(w) > s(v)$ for $w \neq v$ on t. (Note that s must be affine on t, so if v,w,x are in order on t, then $s(x) > s(w) > s(v)$). Similiarly, t enters v if $s(w) < s(v)$ for $w \neq v$ on t. The *outdegree* of v, $o(v)$, is the number of segments or halflines leaving v. The *intersection count of* v, $i(v)$, is the number of intrinsic segments of $D(N)$ incident to v with opposite endpoints at a concave vertex of N.

Lemma 2.7: $o(v) \leq \min(i(v)+1, 3)$.

Proof Sketch: Suppose intrinsic segment or halfline t leaves v. If c and c' are contacts at v, then (c,c') is a *canonical cone for t at v* if $E_{cc'}$ overlaps t in a neighborhood of v, $sl(P_c)$ is clockwise of $sl(P_{c'})$, and there are no other contact points on $bd(C[v,s(v)])$ from ι_c clockwise to $\iota_{c'}$. Intrinsic segment t always has a canonical cone. If (c,c') and (d,d') are distinct canonical cones, then (d,d') *follows* (c,c') if $\iota_d = \iota_{c'}$ and $P_d \neq P_c$. It can be shown that either (c,c') follows (d,d') or (d,d') follows (c,c'). (c,c') follows (d,d'). It is then immediate that there can be at most three canonical cones, since for every pair of cones, one must follow the other. Furthermore, if (d,d')

follows (c,c'), then there are two distinct contacts at $\iota_{c'}=\iota_d$; this is only possible of $\iota_{c'}=\iota_d$ is a vertex of N, furthermore it must be a concave vertex of N. The last step to establish the Lemma is to show that segment from v to $\iota_{c'}=\iota_d$ is intrinsic. □

For v a concave vertex of N, let $d(v)$ be the number of edges $E_{cc'}$ with c,c' adjacent at v. Clearly $d(v)$ is at most $c-1$. Let VX be the convex vertices of N, and CV the concave vertices of N.

Theorem 2.8: The number of vertices of $I(C,N)$ is at most $|VX|+\sum_{v\in CV} 2d(v)$.

Proof: First notice that if v is a vertex of $I(C[r],N)$, then $v\in D(N)$. For if $v\notin D(N)$, then $s(v)$ is affine in a neighborhood of v. Either $s(v)>r$, and $C[r]$ is feasible in a neighborhood of v, or $s(v)=r$, and $C[r]$ is feasible locally in the halfplane with $s(v)\geqslant r$. Either case contradicts v being a vertex of $I(C[r],N)$.

Now notice, by Lemma 2.6, that the number of intrinsic segments and halflines incident to convex vertices of N is $|VX|$, and to concave vertices is $\sum_{v\in CV} d(v)$.

Choose ϵ so small that $C[\epsilon]$ fits in a ball of diameter less than the length of any intrinsic segment of $D(N)$. Clearly the number of vertices of $I(C[\epsilon],N)$ is bounded by the number of edges incident to vertices of N, that is $|VX|+\sum_{v\in CV} d(v)$. What happens as ϵ increases towards 1? A vertex w of $I(C[\epsilon],N)$ moves along an intrinsic segment of $D(N)$; the number of vertices of $I(C[\epsilon],N)$ does not change until a vertex v of $D(N)$ is encountered. At this point the number of vertices of $I(C[\epsilon],N)$ may increase by the excess of the number of segments or halflines leaving v over the segments entering v. By Lemma 2.7 this is at most $i(v)$. Summing over all vertices of $D(N)$, the number of vertices of $I(C,N)$ is at most $|VX|+\sum_{v\in CV} 2d(v)$. □

Corollary 2.9: There are at most $O(cn)$ segments of $D(N)$.

The bound given by Theorem 2.8 is tight, in that there are examples of polygons C and N with arbitrarily many vertices so that the feasible region $I(C,N)$ has $|VX|+\sum_{v\in CV} 2d(v)$ vertices. See Figure 2.4.

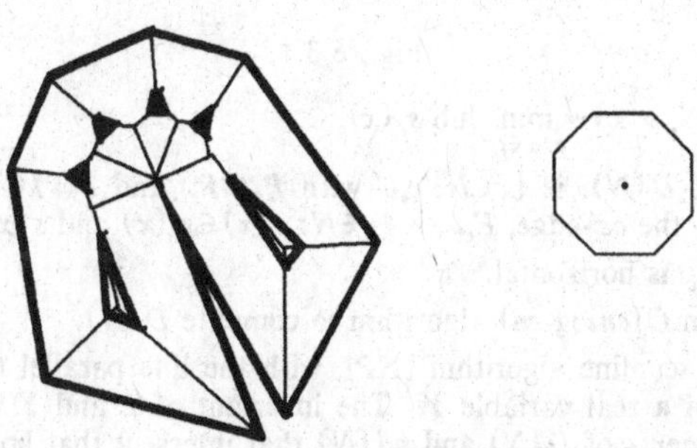

Figure 2.4. $D(N)$ is drawn with light segments, $I(C,N)$ with heavy segments. Notice that N has 8 convex vertices, the single concave vertex v has $d(v)=5$, and $I(C,N)$ has 18 vertices.

3. An Algorithm to Compute $I(C,N)$

We sketch an algorithm to compute a version of $D(N)$, and from it $I(C,N)$. Only the outline of the algorithm appears here; the details will appear in the full paper. We assume that no bounding segment of C or N is horizontal; this condition can be ensured by rotating C and N slightly. We also assume for simplicity that N is a polygon, possibly with polygonal obstacles.

It is not clear how to easily compute $I(C,N)$ when the reference point is chosen to be an interior point of C. We choose the reference point to be the point of $bd(C)$ with maximal y coordinate (necessarily a vertex, since C has no horizontal edges). The motivation for this choice is that any intersection between $bd(C)$ and $bd(N)$ must be at or below the y coordinate of the reference point. Hence if we examine the vertices of $bd(N)$ in y-sorted order, starting with the smallest, at any particular y coordinate we will have already examined the vertices or segments that could have contributed to a contact at a placement of C with that y coordinate.

Unfortunately the diagram $D(N)$ is more complicated when the reference point is a boundary point. As before, we define $s(x) = \text{lub}\,\{r: C[x,r] \text{ feasible}\}$. The first observation is that $s(x)$ is no longer continuous. See Figure 3.1a. The second observation is that the regions t_c, for c a contact, can be degnerate if the reference point lies on $bd(P_c)$. Then t_c can be a segment or a halfline. See Figure 3.1b,c. Furthermore, the value of s_c is no longer determined at a particular placment in t_c but merely is bounded from below. To handle this case we make s_c a set-valued function, specifically $s_c(x) = \{r: C[x,r] \text{ has contact } c\}$.

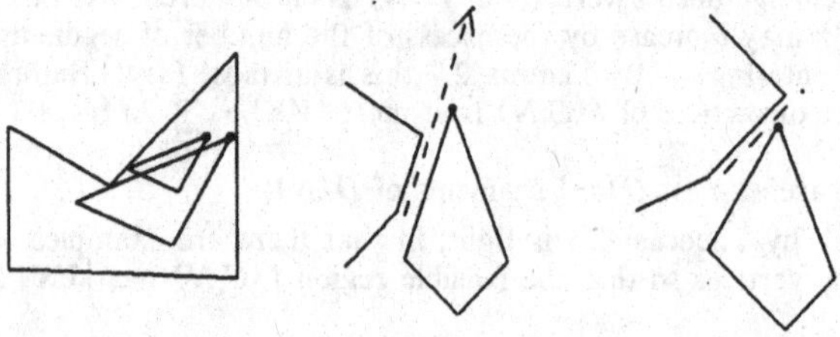

(a) (b) (c)

Figure 3.1.

Proposition 3.1: For $x \in N$, $s(x) = \min_{c:\, x \in t_c} \text{lub}\, s_c(x)$.

The *diagram of* N, $D(N)$, is $\{x \in N: c,c' \text{ with } P_c \neq P_{c'} \text{ and } s(x) \in s_c(x) \text{ and } s(x) \in s_{c'}(x)\}$, and for c,c' with $P_c \neq P_{c'}$ the cc'-edge, $E_{cc'}$, is $\{x \in N: s(x) \in s_c(x) \text{ and } s(x) \in s_{c'}(x)\}$.

Lemma 3.2: No edge $E_{cc'}$ is horizontal.

Theorem 3.3: There is an $O(cn\log cn)$ algorithm to compute $D(N)$.

Proof sketch: We use a scanline algorithm [NP], with the line parallel to the x-axis. The algorithm needs a list L and a real variable Y. The invariant of L and Y is that if Y has value y, then L contains the segments of $D(N)$ and $bd(N)$ that intersect that horizontal line at height y, in order of intersection. Initially L is empty and Y is smaller than the smallest y coordinate of any vertex of $D(N)$.

The variable Y is updated in discrete steps. We keep a queue of events, where each event is actually a point in the plane, and always choose the event with smallest y value. There are two possible events: encountering vertices of $bd(N)$, and encountering intersections of two segments of $D(N)$. The queue can be initialized with all vertices of $bd(N)$, so we need not worry about inserting events of the first kind. To handle intersections of segments of $D(N)$, we use a technique of Bentley and Ottman[BO]. The event queue will always contain the coordinates of the point at which every pair of segments of $D(N)$ adjacent in L will intersect. Since we always choose the minimal event in the queue, if the event is a segment intersection, the segments actually do intersect. The processing of an event includes intersections and deletions of segments on L; these insertions and deletions must as a side effect maintain the intersections scheduled on the event queue.

The event queue must report together events that have identical x and y coordinates, thus there are three kinds of events: a vertex of $D(N)$, an intersection of segments of $D(N)$, and an intersection of segments of $D(N)$ that is also a vertex of $D(N)$. If there are multiple events with the same y coordinate, the order in which the event queue reports the events can be arbitrary.

What is the action at an event that is a vertex v of $bd(N)$? In general, the action is to add to L segments of $D(N)$ arising from contacts adjacent at v. If v is convex there is only one such segment; if v is concave there may be many such. Note that because the reference point is the topmost point of C, all such segments slope upward from v. In the case that v is a convex ceiling vertex (i.e. the slope of the horizontal halfplane open downwards is between the slopes of the segments incident to v), then the segment arising from the contacts at v is already in L, and the action at v is to delete the segment from L.

What is the action at an event x that is the intersection of segments in $D(N)$? Then x is the upper endpoint of those segments, and they should be deleted from L. Exactly one segment of $D(N)$ has lower endpoint x; it must arise from the contacts at x and hence can easily be computed and inserted into L.

The final case is that the event x is both an intersection of segments of $D(N)$ and a vertex of $bd(N)$. Then the action is similiar to the two individual cases. However, all of the segments of $D(N)$ with lower endpoint x actually arise because of contacts adjacent at vertex x.

What is the running time of the algorithm? By the analogue of Corollary 2.9, there are at most $O(cn)$ segments of $D(N)$. We can implement both L and the event queue as balanced tree structures [AHU], hence insertions and deletions take time $O(\log cn)$, since there are never more than $O(cn)$ elements in either structure. Each segment of $D(N)$ is inserted and deleted into L exactly once; each insertion and deletion of a segment causes at most a constant number of operations on the event queue. Hence the total number of operations on either structure is $O(cn)$, and the running time is $O(cn\log cn)$. □

Corollary 3.4: There is an $O(cn\log cn)$ algorithm to compute $I(C,N)$.

Proof sketch: $D(N)$ divides N into polygonal regions, so that within each region the function s is affine. Since $I(C,N) = \{x: s(x) \geq 1\}$, $I(C,N)$ can be computed by examining each region in turn. □

4. References

[AHU] A.V. Aho, J.E. Hopcroft, J.D. Ullman, *The Design and Analysis of Computer Algorithms*, Addison-Wesley, 1975.

[B] R. Brooks, "Solving the Find-Path Problem by Good Representation of Free Space," *IEEE Transactions on Systems, Man, and Cybernetics* 13(3) pp. 190-197 (1983).

[BFM] B. Baker, S. Fortune, S. Mahaney, "Inspection by Polygon Containment," *Twenty-Second Annual Allerton Conference on Communication, Control, and Computing*, October, 1984, submitted to *J. Algorithms*.

[BO] J.L. Bentley, T.A. Ottmann, "Algorithms for Reporting and Counting Geometric Intersections", *IEEE Transactions on Computers*, C-28, pp. 643-647, (1979).

[C] B. Chazelle, "The Polygon Containment Problem," *Advances of Computing Research*, Volume 1, pp. 1-33. JAI Press, Inc.

[K] D. Kirkpatrick, "Efficient Computation of Continuous Skeletons," *20th Annual Symposium on Foundations of Computer Science*, 1979, pp. 18-27.

[LPW] T. Lozano-Perez, M. Wesley, "An Algorithm for Planning Collision-Free Paths among Polyhedral Obstacles," *CACM* 22, pp. 560-570 (1979).

[NP] J. Nievergelt, F.P. Preparata, "Plane-Sweep Algorithms for Intersecting Geometric Figures," *CACM* 25(10), pp. 739-747 (1982).

[OSY1] C. O'Dúnlaing, M.Sharir, C.K. Yap, "Retraction: a New Approach to Motion Planning," 15th Symposium on Theory of Computing, 1983, pp. 207-220.

[OSY2] C. O'Dúnlaing, M.Sharir, C.K. Yap, "Generalized Voronoi Diagrams for a Ladder: I. Topological Analysis," Technical Report 139, Courant Institute of Mathematical Sciences, Nov 1984.

[OSY3] C. O'Dúnlaing, M.Sharir, C.K. Yap, "Generalized Voronoi Diagrams for a Ladder: II. Efficient Construction of the Diagram," Technical Report 140, Courant Institute of Mathematical Sciences, Nov 1984.

[S] M.I. Shamos, "Geometric Complexity," *Proceedings of the Seventh Annual ACM Symposium on Theory of Computing, 1975, pp. 224-233.*

[Y] C.K. Yap, "An $O(n\log n)$ Algorithm for the Voronoi Diagram of Simple Curve Segments," manuscript, Courant Institue of Mathematical Sciences, 1984.

Deterministic and Las Vegas Primality Testing Algorithms

Martin Fürer
Institut für Angewandte Mathematik
der Universität Zürich
CH-8001 Zürich

Abstract

Some deterministic and Las Vegas primality tests are presented. Under certain conditions, they run in polynomial time. In particular, there is a polynomial time Las Vegas algorithm deciding primality of n, when n hat at most 2 prime factors and $n \not\equiv 1 \bmod 24$.

1. Introduction and preliminary results

In order to understand the algorithms presented here, as well as the well-known Monte Carlo primality tests [16 18], it is very helpful to consider the directed graph $G(p^k)$ with certices $V = \mathbb{Z}^{\times}_{p^k}$ and edges $\{(v,v^2) | v \in V\}$. Here $\mathbb{Z}^{\times}_{p^k}$ is the multiplicative group of units in $\mathbb{Z}_{p^k}$, i.e. of those integers modulo p^k which are not multiples of p. Naturally, the squaring operation is unterstood modulo p^k as well. Throughout this paper p, q denote odd primes. Then $\mathbb{Z}^{\times}_{p^k}$ is a cyclic group of order $\varphi(p^k) = (p-1)p^{k-1}$. For this reason, the graph $G(p^k)$ consists of a collection of complete binary trees of height ≥ 0 together with one additional edge from each (old) root and some cycles connecting the new roots, as shown in Figure 1. The vertex 1 is always a (new) root connected to itself by a loop.

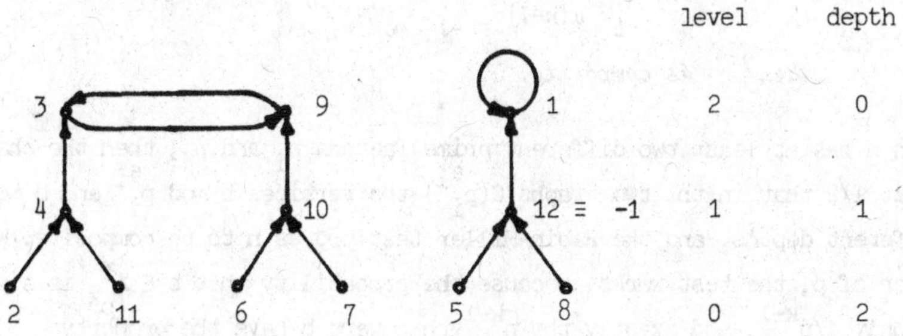

Figure 1: $G(p^k)$ for p = 13 and k = 1 .

Notation

u and v_2 are functions defined by $m = u(m)\, 2^{v_2(m)}$ with u(m) odd.

The depth of $G(p^k)$ is $v_2(p-1)$, and the vertices of level i ($0 \leq i \leq v_2(p-1)$ are 2^i-th powers but not 2^{i+1}-th powers for $i < v_2(p-1)$. In particular, the leaves are exactly the non-squares (modulo p^k).

Let $n = p_1^{e_1} \dots p_k^{e_k}$ be the odd positive integer to be tested for primality. By the Chinese remainder theorem

$$\mathbb{Z}_n^\times \cong \mathbb{Z}_{p_1^{e_1}}^\times \times \dots \times \mathbb{Z}_{p_k^{e_k}}^\times ,$$

and therefore choosing an arbitrary element of $\mathbb{Z}_n^\times$ corresponds to the selection of an arbitrary vertex in each of the graphs $G(p_i^{e_i})$ ($1 \leq i \leq k$).

This leads to the well-known Monte Carlo primality tests, which are extensions of the following test based on Fermat's Little Theorem.

__The Fermat test__ with $b \in \{1,\dots,n-1\}$.
If $b^{n-1} \not\equiv 1 \bmod n$ *then* n *is composite.*

There are composite numbers (the Carmichael numbers, e.g. 561) which are not recognized by this test for all b's prime to n.

__The Rabin-Miller__ test [11,16] with $b \in \{1,\dots,n-1\}$.
If neither $b^{u(n-1)} \equiv 1 \bmod n$,
nor is there an $i \in \{0,1,\dots,v_2(n-1)-1\}$ *with*
$$b^{2^i u(n-1)} \equiv -1 \bmod n,$$
then n *is composite.*

When n has at least two different prime factors p_i and p_j, then the chance is at least 1/2 that in the two graphs $G(p_i^{e_i})$ the vertices b mod $p_i^{e_i}$ and b mod $p_j^{e_j}$ have different depths, and the Rabin-Miller test proves n to be composite. When n is a power of p, the test works, because the probability that $b \in \mathbb{Z}_{p^k}^\times$ is a p^{k-1}-th power is only $1/p^{k-1}$, and exactly the p^{k-1}-th powers b have the property

$$b^{p^k-1} \equiv 1 \bmod p^k.$$

The Monte Carlo primality tests have the disadvantage that a composite number might be declared prime with small probability. Therefore, it would be preferrable to have *Las Vegas algorithms*, which never lie, but have only a fast expected running time for every input.

2. The results

When the factorization of n-1 is known, than n can be tested for primality in Las Vegas polynomial time [14]. In this case, we have also a deterministic polynomial time algorithm. Polynomial time means that the number of steps (e.g. of a Turing machine) is bounded by a polynomial in log n.

Theorem 1. *For every* $c > \frac{1}{2}$, *there is a deterministic polynomial time algorithm deciding primality of* n *after receiving the inputs* $n, r, q_1, s_1, \ldots, q_k, s_k$ *with the properties* $r | n-1$, $r \geq n^c$, $r = q_1^{s_1} \ldots q_k^{s_k}$, $q_1, \ldots, q_k$ *prime. (Here* q_1 *is even, contrary to our usual convention.)*

Assume, we know that n has at most two prime factors, then we can decide fast whether n is prime or composite.

Theorem 2. *For numbers* $n \not\equiv 1 \bmod 24$, *there is a polynomial time Las Vegas algorithm separating the primes from those composites with an even number of prime factors.*

Separation means that for the intersection of the complements, i.e. for composites with an odd number of prime factors, the algorithm is allowed to give either answer.

Theorem 3. *There is a (correct) deterministic algorithm for separating the primes from the numbers with an even number of prime factors. If the Extended Rieman Hypothesis (ERH) holds, then the running time of this algorithm is polynomial.*

Contrary to Miller's primality test [11], it is not the correctness of the algorithm, but only the running time depending on ERH. Furthermore every long run would immediately prove the negation of the ERH.

3. Known factors of n-1

We use the fact that many positive integers have only small prime factors.

Definition

$\psi(x,y) = |\{n \in \mathbb{N} : n \leq x \text{ and } (p|n \Rightarrow p \leq y)\}|$.

Theorem (de Bruijn [4,12]).

$\log \psi(x, \log^\delta x) \sim \log (x^{1-1/\delta})$ for $\delta > 1$.

All logarithms are to the base e, $\log^\delta x$ means $(\log x)^\delta$ and $f(x) \sim g(x)$ stands for $\lim_{x \to \infty} f(x)/g(x) = 1$.

We are only interested in lower bounds for ψ (the easy part of this Theorem). But it is not sufficient to know the asymptotic growth rate. For given x,δ, we actually need to find a fairly small y such that

$$\psi(x,y) \geq x^{1-1/\delta}.$$

We could either prove an effective version of de Bruijn's Theorem (which seems to be tedious), or we use the following Lemma (which includes all we need of de Bruijn's Theorem) and check at run time that our y makes $\psi(x,y)$ sufficiently big.

<u>Lemma</u>

Let $x \geq y \geq 2$, $g(x,y) = \lfloor \log x/\log y \rfloor$ and $f(x,y) = (\pi(y)/g(x,y))^{g(x,y)}$, where $\pi(y) = |\{p : 2 \leq p \leq y \text{ and } p \text{ prime}\}|$.

Then

1. $\psi(x,y) > f(x,y)$.
2. $f(x,\log^{\delta} x) \sim x^{1-1/\delta}$ for $\delta > 1$.
3. $\min(\{x\} \cup \{y : f(x,y) \geq x^{1-1/\delta}\}) = O(\log^{\delta'} x)$ for every $\delta' > \delta > 1$.

<u>Proof</u>

1. For $x \geq y \geq 2$

$$\psi(x,y) \geq \binom{\pi(y)+g(x,y)}{g(x,y)} \geq \left(\frac{\pi(y)+g(x,y)}{g(x,y)}\right)^{g(x,y)} > f(x,y).$$

The binomial coefficient is equal to the number of products $p_1^{e_1} \ldots p_{\pi(y)}^{e_{\pi(y)}}$ with $e_1 + \ldots + e_{\pi(y)} = g(x,y)$.

2. For $x \to \infty$ and $g(x,y) \to \infty$ (hence $y \to \infty$), there is a function h with $h(x,y) \to 1$ and

$$\begin{aligned}\log f(x,y) &= g(x,y) \log \frac{\pi(y)}{g(x,y)} \\ &= g(x,y) \log \left(\frac{y}{\log y} \frac{\log y}{\log x} h(x,y)\right) \\ &\sim \frac{\log x}{\log y} (\log y - \log\log x + \log h(x,y))\end{aligned}$$

and for $y = \log^{\delta} x$ with $\delta > 1$

$$\begin{aligned}\log f(x,y) &\sim \left(1 - \frac{1}{\delta} + \frac{\log h(x,y)}{\log y}\right) \log x \\ &\sim (1 - 1/\delta) \log x .\end{aligned}$$

3. This implies

$$\log f(x,\log^{\delta'} x) > (1-1/\delta) \log x$$

for $\delta' > \delta > 1$ and all sufficiently big x.

Hence

$$\min (\{x\} \cup \{y : f(x,y) > x^{1-1/\delta}\}) = 0 (\log^{\delta'} x)$$

for all $\delta' > \delta > 1$. □

Remarks

1. The prime number theorem $\pi(y) \sim y \log y$ could easily be avoided. Tchebychef's theorem ($\pi(y) = O(y/\log y)$ and $y/\log y = O(\pi(y))$) is sufficient.
2. Minor modifications make this Lemma applicable to products of small primes in algebraic number fields.
3. Given $x \geq 2$ and $\delta > 1$, we can now easily find a small y with $\psi(x,y) > x^{1-1/\delta}$. We try $y = 2,3,\ldots$ at most until $y = x$ or until we find a y with $f(x,y) \geq x^{1-1/\delta}$. As $\pi(y)$ is known exactly, $f(x,y)$ is easy to compute.

Proof of Theorem 1.

Let $\delta = 1/(c-1/2)$ and $y = \min (\{n\} \cup \{z : f(n,z) \geq n^{1-1/\delta}\})$ with the function f of the Lemma. When all primes $p \leq y$ pass the Fermat test, i.e. $p^{n-1} \equiv 1 \bmod n$, then we check which prime powers in the exponent are actually used. For $1 \leq i \leq k$ let t_i be the smallest exponent, such that for $m_i = ((n-1)/q_i^{s_i})q_i^{t_i}$ and all $p \leq y$

$$p^{m_i} \equiv 1 \bmod n .$$

If $t_i \geq 1$, we choose a $p \leq y$ with

$$p^{m_i/q_i} \not\equiv 1 \bmod n .$$

If the divisor $\gcd(p^{m_i/q_i},n)$ of n is not equal 1, then n is composite. Otherwise $m = q_1^{t_1}\ldots q_k^{t_k}$ divides the order $p_j^{e_j-1}(p_j-1)$ of $\mathbb{Z}^{\times}_{p_j^{e_j}}$ for every prime power factor $p_j^{e_j}$ of n. And because no q_i divides n, m even divides p_j-1 . Hence, if $m \geq \sqrt{n}$, then all prime factors p_j of n are greater than $\sqrt{n}$, and n is a prime. On the other hand, if $m < \sqrt{n}$, then the multiplicativity of the Fermat test implies that not only the primes $p \leq y$ but all their products b have the property

$$b^{((n-1)/r)m} \equiv 1 \bmod n .$$

There are $\psi(n,y)$ such b's, and

$$\psi(n,y) > n^{1-1/\delta} = n^{1-c+1/2}$$

by the definition of y and δ. But because of $r \geq n^c$ and $m < n^{1/2}$, the exponent $((n-1)/r)m$ is smaller than $n^{1-c+1/2}$. This means that the equation $z^{((n-1)/r)m} = 1$ of degree $((n-1)/r)m$ has more than $((n-1)/r)m$ solutions in $\mathbb{Z}_n$. Thus $\mathbb{Z}_n$ is not a field and n is not a prime.
The Lemma implies $y = O(\log^{\delta'} n)$ for every $\delta' > \delta$, and it is a routine exercise to verify that this implies a polynomial time algorithm. □

Remark

Under certain conditions prime factors of n^k-1 for $k > 1$ can also be used in deterministic primality tests. E.g. when a non-square mod n of small absolute value is known (which is the case for $n \not\equiv 1 \mod 24$ and under ERH), then prime factors of $n+1$ are as good as those of $n-1$. Furthermore a factor of $n-1$ which does not contain a prime factor smaller than p is as good as a prime factor p of $n-1$.

4. The Las Vegas algorithm A

Let $n = p_1^{e_1} \ldots p_k^{e_k}$ $(e_i\ 1)$. The algorithm of Theorem 2 consists of two parts A and B as shown in Figure 2.

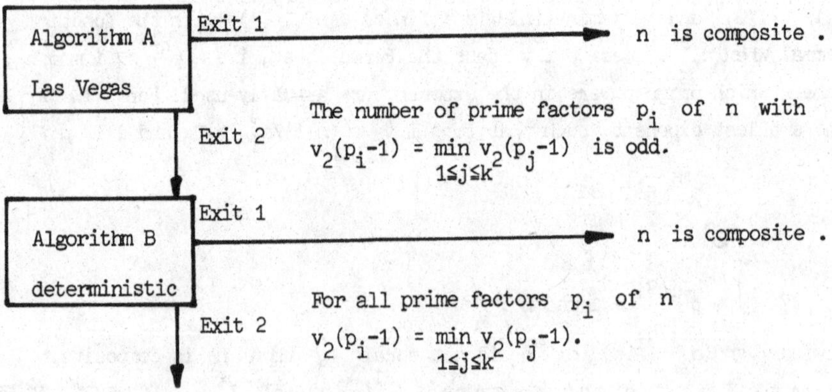
Algorithm A
Las Vegas
Exit 1
n is composite .
Exit 2
The number of prime factors p_i of n with
$v_2(p_i-1) = \min_{1\leq j\leq k} v_2(p_j-1)$ is odd.
Algorithm B
deterministic
Exit 1
n is composite .
Exit 2
For all prime factors p_i of n
$v_2(p_i-1) = \min_{1\leq j\leq k} v_2(p_j-1)$.

Figure 2 : The Algorithm of Theorem 2.

To avoid a misunderstanding, note that we don't claim the algorithm to give any information about the number of factors of composite numbers. With high probability the algorithm then just takes an exit "composite". But there might be numbers n with say three prime factors which (with bad luck) look like primes to the algorithm. It takes then the second exit in both parts and declares carefully, "the number of

Part A is quite simple. It is based on the fact that $v_2(n-1)>m$ if for all i

$$v_2(\varphi(p_i^{e_i})) = v_2((p_i-1)p_i^{e_i-1})=v_2(p_i-1) \geq m$$

and the number of prime factors p of n with $v_2(p-1) = m$ is even. This is easily seen by grouping these primes in pairs and observing that for odd integers u_1, u_2

$$(u_1\cdot 2^m+1)\ (u_2\cdot 2^m+1) = u_1u_2\ 2^{2m}+(u_1+u_2)2^m+1 = u\ 2^{m+1}+1$$

for some integer u.

Algorithm A

repeat

choose $b \in \{1,\dots,n-1\}$ *at random;*

Rabin-Miller test with b

until

the test says "composite" $\longrightarrow$ *exit 1*

or b *is at depth* $v_2(n-1) \longrightarrow$ *exit 2* .

Note that a number b is known to be at depth $v_2(n-1)$ when $b^{(n-1)/2} \equiv -1 \bmod n$. This means that $b \bmod p_i^{e_i}$ is at depth $v_2(n-1)$ in $G(p_i^{e_i})$. And we have just seen, that this is impossible when the number of prime factors p_i with $v_2(p_i-1)$ minimal is even. Hence the algorithm is correct. The expected running time is polynomial, because in each loop the probability of taking an exit is at least $1/2$.

5. The Lucas test

We obtain $\mathbb{Z}_p[\sqrt{d}]$ from $\mathbb{Z}_p$ by formal adjunction of $\sqrt{d}$, i.e.

$$\mathbb{Z}_p[\sqrt{d}] \cong \mathbb{Z}_p[x]\ /\ (x^2-d)\ .$$

When $(\frac{d}{p}) = -1$ for a prime p, then x^2-d is irreducible in $\mathbb{Z}_p = F_p$. Therefore $\mathbb{Z}_p[\sqrt{d}] = \mathbb{Z}_p(\sqrt{d})$ is isomorphic to F_{p^2}, the Galois field with p^2 elements. Furthermore, $\mathbb{Z}_p(\sqrt{d})^\times$ is cyclic of order p^2-1, and

$$\alpha^{p^2-1} = 1 \quad \text{for every } \alpha \in \mathbb{Z}(\sqrt{d})^\times\ .$$

$\mathbb{Z}_p^\times$ is a subgroup of order $p-1$ and α^{p+1} is rational.

Lucas test for $\alpha \in \mathbb{Z}_n[\sqrt{d}]$ *with the Jacobi symbol* $(\frac{d}{n}) = -1$.
If α^{n+1} *is not rational, then* n *is composite.*

A similar deterministic test [6,7] for the primality of Mersenne numbers 2^p-1 has been developed by Lucas [10]. It has been modified and proved correct by Lehmer [9]. When p is prime and $(\frac{d}{p}) = 1$, then by a general version of the Chinese Remainder Theorem [8]

$$\mathbb{Z}_p[\sqrt{d}] \cong \mathbb{Z}_p \times \mathbb{Z}_p ,$$

and an isomorphism is given by

$$a+b\sqrt{d} \mapsto (a+bs,\ a-bs) ,$$

where s is one of the two square roots of d mod p. Then

$$\alpha^{p-1} = 1 \text{ for every } \alpha \in \mathbb{Z}_p[\sqrt{d}]^\times .$$

6. Algorithm B (Theorem 2)

Now we sketch the idea behind Algorithm B. Aussume $p|n$, $q|n$, p and q prime, $v_2(p-1) < v_2(q-1)$, $(\frac{d}{n}) = -1$, $(\frac{d}{p}) = -1$ and $d^{(n-1)/2} \equiv -1 \bmod n$.
Then $v_2(n-1) = v_2(p-1)$ and $(\frac{d}{q}) = 1$.

If many $b \in \mathbb{Z}_n$ pass the Fermat test, then $\gcd(p-1,n-1)$ and $\gcd(q-1,n-1)$ are big. More precisely, if the number of b's less than q passing the Fermat test is greater than $2q^{2/3}$, then $\gcd(q-1,n-1) > 2\,q^{2/3}$.

If many $\alpha \in \mathbb{Z}_n[\sqrt{d}]^\times$ pass the Lucas test, then $\gcd(p+1,n+1)$ and $\gcd(q-1,n+1)$ are big. In particular, if the number of α's in $\mathbb{Z}_q[\sqrt{d}]^\times$ passing the Lucas test (with respect to n) is greater than $q^{1+1/3}$, then $\gcd(q-1,n+1) > q^{1/3}$. Now $\gcd(n-1,\ n+1) = 2$ implies a contradiction, i.e. in this situation n is always recognised as being composite.

In short time, we cannot do many Fermat and Lucas tests. But the argument of the Lemma shows, that it is sufficient to do the tests for all small b's and α's. The multiplicativity of the tests tells us, that their products would pass the tests as well. It is sufficient to do the tests for primes with norm $O(\log^{3+\epsilon} n)$. This is clear for the Fermat tests.

For the Lucas tests the argument is more subtle. We can gerealize the Lemma to the domain of algebraic integers in the number field $Q(\sqrt{d})$. Thereby we use the fact that this domain is a principal ideal domain for the d's considered. And we need to know that there are sufficiently many primes with small coefficients a,b

(what is in equivalent to a small norm for $d<0$ and $|d|$ small) in this number field. This is guaranteed when sufficiently many small rational primes split in the number field $Q(\sqrt{d})$, which follows from the Theorem of Siegel-Walfisz [15], saying that the distribution of primes in arithmetic progressions is sufficiently uniform.

Algorithm B

Choose $d \in \{-1,-2,-3\}$ such that $(\frac{d}{n}) = -1$, and do the Rabin-Miller test with d. Do Fermat tests for all small rational primes and Lucas tests for all primes $a+b\sqrt{d}$ with small norm $a^2 - mb^2$ until sufficiently many primes have been tested.

It is possible to choose such a d, because $n \not\equiv 1 \bmod 24$. The Rabin-Miller test with d ensures that $d \bmod p_i^{e_i}$ lies at the same depth in every $G(p_i^{e_i})$ with $p_i^{e_i}|n$. And $(\frac{d}{n}) = -1$ says that d is in maximal depth $v_2(p_j-1)$ for at least one prime divisor p_j of n.

7. Using the Extended Riemann Hypothesis

The value of the ERH in primality testing is based on the implication proved by Ankeny [2], that for every $n>2$, there exists a $d<c \log^2 n$ with $(\frac{d}{n}) = -1$. (In [13] $c=70$ is claimed and in [3] $c=60$ is proved to be sufficient.) Hence assuming ERH, one can replace all Rabin-Miller tests with random numbers by tests with small primes.

In Theorem 3, we don't need the restriction $n \not\equiv 1 \bmod 24$ of Theorem 2. ERH guarantees a negative d with $(\frac{d}{n}) = -1$ and $|d| = O(\log^2 n)$. For d negative, $|a|$ and $|b|$ are small when $a+b\sqrt{d}$ divides a small rational prime.

For $d<-3$, the situation is more complicated, because the class number $h(d)$ (the index of the subgroup of principal fractional ideals [19] in the multiplicative group of fractional ideals) is usually greater than 1. Fortunately, Siegel's Theorem [15, 17] implies a good upper bound $h(d) = o(d^{1/2+\varepsilon})$. And a Theorem of Minkowski ensures that every ideal class (modulo principal ideals) contains an ideal with norm smaller than $\sqrt{|d|}$ [5,19]. Because $|d|$ is very small, this still enables the implication from the algebraic integers with small norm to a big set of algebraic integers to pass the Lucas test.

8. Conclusion

Naturally, we hope that the approach of this paper might contribute one step towards a deterministic or Las Vegas polynomial time primality test. To some extent, we can now handle the case where the number of prime factors is divisible by two. But a direct generalization to the cases where this number is divisible by 3 or bigger primes does not work. And no algorithm in this spirit seems to be able to beat the almost polynomial $O((\log n)^{c \text{ logloglog } n})$ bound of Adleman, Pomerance and Rumely [1].

References

[1] L.M. Adleman, C. Pomerance and R.S. Rumely, On distinguishing Prime Numbers from Composite Numbers. *Annals of Math.* *117* (1983), 173-206.

[2] N.C. Ankeny, The Least Quadratic Non-Residue. *Annals of Math.* 55 (1952), 65-72.

[3] E. Bach, Fast Algorithms under the Extended Riemann Hypothesis: A Concrete Estimate. 14th STOC (1982), 290-295.

[4] N.G. de Bruijn, On the Number of Positive Integers ≤ x and Free of Prime Factors > y, II. Proc. Koninklijke Nederlandse Akademie van Wettenschappen. Ser. A 69 (=Indag.Math.28) (1966), 239-247.

[5] H. Cohn, Advanced Number Theory. Dover, New York, 1980.

[6] G.H. Hardy and E.M. Wright, An Introduction to the Theory of Numbers. Oxford University Press, Oxford, 1979.

[7] D.E. Knuth, The Art of Computer Programming, Vol. 2: Seminumerical Algorithms. Addison-Wesley, Reading, 1981.

[8] S. Lang, Algebra. Addison-Wesley, Reading, 1984.

[9] D.H. Lehmer, An Extended Theory of Lucas'Functions. *Annals of Math.* *31* (1930), 419-448.

[10] E. Lucas, Théorie des fonctions numériques simplement périodiques. *Amer. J. Math* *1* (1878), 184-239, 289-321.

[11] G.L. Miller, Riemann's Hypothesis and Tests for Primality. *J.of Computer and System Sciences* *13* (1976), 300-317.

[12] K.K. Norton, Numbers with Small Prime Factors, and the Least k-th Power Non-Residue. Memoirs of the AMS No. 106, 1971.

[13] J. Oesterlé, Versions effectives du théorème de Chebotarew sous l'hypothèse de Riemann généralisée, Journées Arithmétiques de Luminy, Astérisque 61 (1979), 165-167.

[14] D.A. Plaisted, Fast Verification, Testing and Generation of Large Primes. *Theoretical Computer Science* *9* (1979), 1-16.

[15] K. Prachar, Primzahlverteilung. Springer, Berlin, 1957.

[16] M.O. Rabin, Probabilistic Algorithm for Testing Primality. *J. of Number Theory* *12* (1980), 128-138.

[17] C.L. Siegel, Ueber die Classenzahl quadratischer Zahlkörper. *Acta Arithm. 1* (1935), 83-86.

[18] R. Solovay and V. Strassen, A Fast Monte-Carlo Test for Primality. *SIAM J. on Computing 6* (1977), 84-85.

[19] I.N. Stewart and D.O. Tall, Algebraic Number Theory. Chapman and Hall, London, 1979.

Efficient Algorithms for Graphic Matroid Intersection and Parity
(Extended Abstract)
by

Harold N.Gabow *
Department of Computer Science
University of Colorado
Boulder, CO 80309
USA

Matthias Stallmann
Department of Computer Science
North Carolina State University
Raleigh, NC 27695–8206
USA

Abstract

An algorithm for matroid intersection, based on the phase approach of Dinic for network flow and Hopcroft and Karp for matching, is presented. An implementation for graphic matroids uses time $O(n^{1/2}\ m)$ if m is $\Omega(n^{3/2}\ lg\ n)$, and similar expressions otherwise. An implementation to find k edge–disjoint spanning trees on a graph uses time $O(k^{3/2}\ n^{1/2}\ m)$ if m is $\Omega(n\ lg\ n)$ and a similar expression otherwise; when m is $O(k^{1/2}\ n^{3/2})$ this improves the previous bound, $O(k^2\ n^2)$. Improved algorithms for other problems are obtained, including maintaining a minimum spanning tree on a planar graph subject to changing edge costs, and finding shortest pairs of disjoint paths in a network. An algorithm for graphic matroid parity is presented that runs in time $O(n\ m\ lg^6\ n)$. This improves the previous bound of $O(n^2\ m)$.

1. Introduction.

Matroid parity generalizes a broad class of combinatorial optimization problems that includes network flow and matching [La]. Yet it can still be solved efficiently [Lo,SG]. This paper presents more efficient algorithms for several cases of the parity problem.

Section 2 develops a phase algorithm for matroid intersection, the "bipartite" parity problem. This generalizes the phase algorithms of Dinic for network flow, Hopcroft and Karp for matching, and Even and Tarjan for 0–1 network flow [D,HK,ET]. It is shown that a phase algorithm for matroid intersection reduces to four matroid problems, the static–base/dynamic–base cycle/cocycle problems. Some of the results in Section 2 overlap recent work of Tovey and Trick [TT], and even more recently Cunningham [C]. The overlap (indicated precisely in Section 2) is not adequate to achieve the time bounds of this paper.

An efficient implementation of the intersection algorithm for graphic matroids is presented in Sections 3–5. Section 3 gives an overview and timing analysis. The time is $O(n^{1/2}\ m)$ if m is $\Omega(n^{3/2}\ lg\ n)$. This is identical to the Hopcroft–Karp bound for matching, a special case of graphic matroid intersection. The four matroid problems mentioned above make other cases more difficult. The time is $O(n\ m^{2/3}\ lg^{1/3}\ n)$ if m is $\Omega(n\ lg\ n)$ and a similar expression otherwise.

Planar graphs can be handled more efficiently because of duality. Section 3 gives a bound of $O(n^{3/2}\ lg\ n)$. The approach also gives an algorithm for maintaining a minimum spanning tree on a planar graph subject to changing edge costs. The time is $O(lg\ n)$ per update, improving the $O(lg^2\ n)$ bound of Frederickson [F].

Section 3 also gives an implementation of the intersection algorithm to find k edge–disjoint spanning trees on a graph. It uses time $O(k^{3/2}\ n^{1/2}\ m)$ if m is $\Omega(n\ lg\ n)$ and a similar expression otherwise. When m is $O(k^{1/2}\ n^{3/2})$ this improves the bound of $O(k^2\ n^2)$ due to Roskind and Tarjan [RT].

---

* This work was supported in part by NSF Grant #MCS–8302648.

Section 4 solves the static–tree cocycle problem used in the graphic intersection algorithm. The solution also speeds an algorithm of Suurballe and Tarjan for finding shortest pairs of disjoint paths in a network [Su T]. The time bound is $O(m + n \lg n)$, improved from $O(m \lg_{m/n+2} n)$. Section 5 solves the dynamic–tree cocycle problem.

Section 6 presents an efficient graphic matroid parity algorithm. The time bound is $O(n\ m \lg^6 n)$, improving the bound of $O(n^2\ m)$ of [SG]. In the parity problem the cycle and cocycle problems involve *pairs* of edges. This seems to make traditional techniques for solving cycle and cocycle problems inapplicable. We reduce the problem to a well–studied problem of computational geometry, range searching.

Many of the ideas of this paper apply to other matroids, such as job scheduling matroids [GT84] and linear matroids. We will discuss these extensions in a future paper.

We close this section with some terminology. The reader is assumed familiar with the basic notions of matroids (see, e.g., [A, La, W]). If e is an element and B a base (or independent set), $C(e,B)$ denotes the *fundamental cycle* of e in B. The *span* of a set of elements A is denoted $sp(A)$. If $T \subset S$ are sets of elements then $S\ /\ T$ denotes the matroid *restricted* to S, with T *contracted*. A *graphic matroid* is derived from an undirected graph; its independent sets are the forests.

Consider a matroid $\mathbf{M}$ over a set of elements E that is partitioned into blocks of size two, called *parity pairs*. Thus each element e has a *mate*, denoted $\bar{e}$, such that $\{e, \bar{e}\}$ is a parity pair. A *matching* M is an independent set consisting of parity pairs, i.e., $e \in M$ if and only if $\bar{e} \in M$. A *maximum matching* has the greatest number of pairs possible. The (*cardinality*) *parity problem* is to find a maximum matching. The *matroid intersection problem* is the "bipartite" version: $\mathbf{M}$ is the direct sum of matroids $\mathbf{M}^i$ on elements $\mathbf{E}^i$, $i = 0,1$, and every parity pair contains one element from each matroid.

Sections 4–5 use these terms for a tree T: $|T|$ denotes the number of vertices in T. For edge vw of T, *v's subtree* is the tree of $T - vw$ containing v.

2. The phase algorithm for matroid intersection.

This section derives results that are needed for a phase algorithm for matroid intersection. It concludes by sketching the algorithm. Some of the results have been recently obtained using different methods. Tovey and Trick [TT] derive a phase algorithm for polymatroidal network flow. This problem, which generalizes network flow and matroid intersection, was introduced by Lawler and Martel [LM], who prove much of the theory for the phase algorithm. Our Corollary 2.1 is similar to [TT]. Cunningham [C] derives equivalents of our Corollaries 2.1–2.2.

We begin with some facts that apply to the matroid parity problem. The basic concept is the augmenting path:

Definition 2.1. An *augmenting path* for a matching M consists of distinct elements $a_i, \bar{a}_i \notin M$, $0 \le i \le k$, $b_i, \bar{b}_i \in M$, $0 < i \le k$, such that the sets

$$M_i^+ = (M + \bar{a}_k) + a_0 + \bar{a}_0 - b_1 - \bar{b}_1 \ldots - \bar{b}_i + a_i \ (0 \le i \le k), \text{ and}$$
$$M_i^- = (M + \bar{a}_k) + a_0 + \bar{a}_0 - b_1 - \bar{b}_1 \ldots + \bar{a}_{i-1} - b_i \ (0 < i \le k)$$

all have the same span, $sp(M + a_0 + \bar{a}_k)$. An *alternating path* for M is defined similarly, except that the last element may be $\bar{a}_k$ (as in an augmenting path), or a_i or b_i.

Note that in an augmenting path, M_k^+ is a matching of rank $|M| + 2$. In [SG] it is shown that a nonmaximum matching has an augmenting path. This can be strengthened as follows.

Theorem 2.1. In a matroid parity problem, let M and N be matchings, with $|N| = |M| + 2k$. Then there is a sequence of paths $P_1, \ldots, P_k$ such that P_i is an augmenting path for

$M_{i-1} = M \oplus P_1 \oplus \ldots \oplus P_{i-1}$, $P_i - M \subset N - M$, $P_i \cap M \subset M - N$, and all paths P_i are disjoint.

Proof. For k=1, modify N to a matching contained in $M \cup N$ whose span includes $sp(M)$. Then use a swapping argument, as in [SG]. For k>1 use induction. ∎

The rest of this section is restricted to the matroid intersection problem. Recall that in matroid intersection the ground set E is the disjoint union of *ground sets* E^i, i = 0,1. It is convenient to extend this notation so that for any set of elements S, $S^i \equiv S \cap E^i$, i = 0,1. Also, without loss of generality restrict the definition of an alternating path (and also augmenting path) so that the first element $a_0 \in E^0$. Thus any $a_i \in E^0 - M$, $\bar{a}_i \in E^1 - M$, $b_i \in M^1$, $\bar{b}_i \in M^0$.

Definition 2.2. If I is an independent set, e,f is a *swap* for I if $sp(I \oplus \{e,f\}) = sp(I)$ and either $e \in M^0$, $f \in E^0 - M$, or $e \in E^1 - M$, $f \in M^1$.

Thus in an alternating path the pairs $\bar{a}_i$, b_{i+1} and $\bar{b}_i$, a_i are swaps.

The cardinality intersection problem is solved by repeatedly finding an augmenting path of shortest length [La], which we call a *sap*. The structure of *saps* is analyzed by introducing a "level" function: For any element e, the *level* $l(e)$ is the length of a shortest alternating path ending with e. In the following discussion, fix a matching M. The level function l is always defined with respect to M, even though other matchings will be constructed. The basic fact about levels is that in a sequence of *saps* of the same length, each *sap* has its elements on consecutive levels. This is proved as follows.

Lemma 2.1. If e,f is a swap for M then $l(f) \le l(e) + 1$.

Proof. If $l(f) > l(e) + 1$, the sequence of swaps defining $l(e)$ preserve the validity of swap e,f, so $l(f) = l(e) + 1$. ∎

For a set of elements S define $S_{jk} \equiv \{e | \ e \in S,\ j \le l(e) \le k\}$. Also define $S_j \equiv S_{jj}$.

Lemma 2.2. Let $N = M \oplus P_1 \oplus \ldots \oplus P_k$ where $k \ge 0$, each P_i is an augmenting path for $M \oplus P_1 \oplus \ldots \oplus P_{i-1}$, and each swap e,f of P_i has $l(f) = l(e) + 1$. Then

$$E^1_{1,i} = sp(N^1_{1,i}), \qquad \text{for } i \equiv 2 \ mod\ 4$$
$$E^0_{i,4s} \subset sp(N^0_{i,\infty} - N_{4s+1}), \text{ for } i \equiv 3 \ mod\ 4.$$

Proof. First suppose $N = M$. Let e be an unmatched element. If $e \in E^1$ then $l(e) \equiv 1$ *mod* 4, and Lemma 2.1 shows the elements of $C(e,M)$ are on level $l(e) + 1$ or lower. If $e \in E^0$ then $l(e) \equiv 0$ *mod* 4, and Lemma 2.1 shows the elements of $C(e,M)$ are on level $l(e) - 1$ or higher.

It is easy to see that the swaps of P_i do not change the spans of the Lemma. ∎

A *sap sequence* is a sequence P_1 ,..., P_k of disjoint paths P_i of the same length, such that P_i is a *sap* for $M \oplus P_1 \oplus \ldots \oplus P_{i-1}$.

Corollary 2.1. Let P_1 ,..., P_k be a sap sequence, and let $P = e_1$,..., e_k be an augmenting path for the matching $M \oplus P_1 \oplus \ldots \oplus P_k$.

(*i*) $l(e_i) \le i$, for all i.

(*ii*) If $|P| = |P_1|$ then $l(e_i) = i$, for all i.

(*iii*) If some edge e_i is in some P_j then $|P| > |P_1|$.

Proof. Prove the Corollary by induction on k. By the inductive assertion (*ii*) holds for all paths P_j, so Lemma 2.2 applies. We first show that (*i*) holds by induction on i. Assume that $l(e_i) \le i$ for some odd level i.

Suppose $i \equiv 1 \mod 4$, so $e_i \in E^1$. The swaps preceding e_i do not change $sp(N^1_{i,i+1})$, by induction and Lemma 2.2. Since $e_i \in sp(N^1_{i,i+1})$, $l(e_{i+1}) \le i + 1$. Since $e_{i+2} = \bar{e}_{i+1}$, $l(e_{i+2}) \le i + 2$, as desired.

Next suppose $i \equiv 3 \mod 4$, so $e_i \in E^0$. The swaps preceding e_i do not change $sp(N^0_{i+4,\infty})$, by induction. Since any element $f \in E^0$ on a level greater than $i + 1$ is in $sp(N^0_{i+4,\infty})$, $l(e_{i+1}) \le i + 1$. Since $e_{i+2} = \bar{e}_{i+1}$, $l(e_{i+2}) \le i + 2$.

We conclude that (i) is true. The same argument shows that if $l(e_j) < i$ for some i then the same holds for all subsequent i, so $|P| > |P_1|$. This implies (ii). For (iii) note that if e_i is in P_j then $l(e_{i+1}) = l(e_i) - 1$. ∎

The matroid intersection algorithm consists of *phases*, where each phase augments a maximal *sap* sequence. The length of a *sap* increases from phase to phase, by Corollary 2.1(iii). The next result allows the number of phases to be bounded precisely.

Corollary 2.2. For a matching M, let s denote the number of matched elements in a *sap*, and let $n = |M| + \Delta$ denote the cardinality of a maximum matching. Then $s\,\Delta \le n$.

Proof. It suffices to show that the Δ disjoint paths P_i of Theorem 2.1 can be chosen so that $|P_{i+1}| \ge |P_i|$. For then each path has $\ge s$ matched elements, so $s\,\Delta \le n$.

The construction of Theorem 2.1 allows P_{i+1} to be chosen as a *sap* for M_i in the matroid $(M_i \cup N) \,/\, (M_i \cap N)$. This implies that $M_{i+1} \cup N \subset M_i \cup N$, and $M_i \cap N \subset M_{i+1} \cap N$. Thus $|P_{i+2}|$ is the length of a *sap* for M_{i+1} in the matroid $(M_{i+1} \cup N) \,/\, (M_{i+1} \cap N)$, which is at least the length of a *sap* for M_{i+1} in the matroid $(M_i \cup N) \,/\, (M_i \cap N)$. By Corollary 2.1($i$) the latter is at least than the length of a *sap* for M_i in the same matroid, which is $|P_{i+1}|$. ∎

For network flow a phase is implemented by repeatedly searching a "level graph" to find a *sap*. For matroid intersection this approach is complicated by the fact that each augment changes the valid swaps, thus changing the level graph. The next result shows how to handle the changes efficiently. Divide the given matroid $\mathbf{M}$ into matroids $\mathbf{M}_i$ corresponding to levels that are paired in swaps. That is, i ranges over all odd levels $\le 4s-1$ and $\mathbf{M}_i = (M \cup E_{i,i+1}) \,/\, (M - M_{i,i+1})$. Note that $M_{i,i+1}$ is a base of $\mathbf{M}_i$.

Lemma 2.3. Let $P_1, \ldots, P_k$ be a *sap* sequence. Let e be an element that is on an odd level $l(e) = i$ and is not in any P_j. Let f be an element with $l(f) = i + 1$. Let g_j, h_j be the swap in P_j with $l(g_j) = i$, $j = 1, \ldots, k$. Then e,f is a swap for $M \oplus P_1 \oplus \ldots \oplus P_k$ if and only if it is a swap for $M_{i,i+1} \oplus \{g_1, h_1, \ldots, g_k, h_k\}$ in the matroid $\mathbf{M}_i$.

Proof. We prove the case $e \notin M$; $e \in M$ is similar. $e \notin M$ implies that e is in the ground set E^1. Let $N = E^1 \cap (M \oplus P_1 \oplus \ldots \oplus P_k)$ and $C = C(e,N)$. It suffices to show that $C_{i,i+1}$ is a cycle in $\mathbf{M}_i$.

First observe that $C_{i,i+1}$ is dependent in $\mathbf{M}_i$: The greatest level in C is $i + 1$, by Lemma 2.2, and no element of $N + e$ is on level 0, so $C = C_{1,i+1}$. Since $C_{1,i-1} \subset N_{1,i-1}$ and $sp(N_{1,i-1}) = sp(M_{1,i-1})$ by Lemma 2.2, $C_{1,i-1} \subset sp(M_{1,i-1})$. Thus $e \in sp(C_{i,i+1} \cup M_{1,i-1})$, as desired.

Next observe that for any $f \in C_{i,i+1}$, $C_{i,i+1} - f$ is independent in $\mathbf{M}_i$: In $\mathbf{M}$, $sp(N_{1,i+1} + e - f) = sp(N_{1,i+1}) = sp(M_{1,i+1})$. Thus $M_{1,i-1} \cup C_{i,i+1} - f \cup M_{i+2,4s}$ is independent. ∎

The algorithm for a phase is as follows:

Step 1: Determine the level $l(e)$ of every element e.

Step 2: Construct the matroid M_i and its base $M_{i,i+1}$, for every odd level $i \leq 4s-1$.
Step 3: Find a path $e_0, ..., e_s$, where $l(e_j) = i$, $\bar{e}_{2i} = e_{2i+1}$, and e_{2i+1}, e_{2i+2} is a swap for the current base of M_{2i+1}. Augment the matching along the path. Repeat this step until the desired path does not exist.

Step 1 is done by breadth–first search. This search is easily programmed using algorithms for two matroid problems: In each problem, a base B is given and does not change. Every matroid element is to be output at most once. The *static–base cycle problem* is to execute a sequence of operations,

cycle(e): For element $e \notin B$, output all elements in e's fundamental cycle (that have not been output already).

The *static–base cocycle problem* is to execute a similar sequence of operations,

cocycle(e): For element $e \in B$, output all elements in e's fundamental cocycle (that have not been output already).

(If f gets output in an operation for e then e,f is a swap.)

Step 3 is done by depth–first search. This search is programmed using algorithms for these dynamic versions of the two problems: A base B is given, but it changes. Every matroid element of the matroid is to be output at most once. The *dynamic–base cycle problem* is to execute a sequence of operations *cycle*(e), defined as above, and also

update(e,f): Execute the swap e,f, thus changing the base B.

The *dynamic–base cocycle problem* is defined similarly.

The depth–first search calls the routine for *cycle*(e) or *cocycle*(e) to find the next element of the path. When the first element is output, the routine is suspended and the search is continued. If the search is unsuccessful, eventually the *cycle* or *cocycle* routine is resumed; the next output element is handled similarly. If the search is successful the routine is aborted. The augment step does *updates* for all swaps that lead to success.

In many matroids the dynamic–base problem is harder than the static. In this case it is more efficient to find the last few *saps* one by one. This leads to following outline for the matroid intersection algorithm. Here p is a parameter, determined by the efficiency of the static– and dynamic–base algorithms.
Step 1. Run p consecutive phases, each phase finding a maximal *sap* sequence and augmenting it. Use the static– and dynamic–base algorithms.
Step 2. Find the remaining *saps* one at a time, augmenting by each one. Use the static–base algorithms.

3. Graphic matroid intersection.

This section presents the graphic matroid intersection algorithm and its analysis. It first outlines algorithms for the two cycle problems. Intersection problems that can be solved using only cycle algorithms– planar graphic matroid intersection and k disjoint spanning trees, are discussed. Then the analysis of the intersection algorithm for general graphic matroids is given. (Details of the cocycle algorithms are in Sections 4–5.)

The static–tree cycle problem is solved by set merging. The algorithm maintains the partition of the vertices of the tree into subtrees formed by the edges that have been output. Since the tree is initially given, the static tree algorithm of [GT83] can be used. The time is $O(m)$.

The dynamic–tree cycle problem is solved by the dynamic tree data structure of [Sl T] and set merging. The given tree is represented as a dynamic tree. In addition, set merging is used to maintain the partition of the vertices into subtrees formed by the edges that have been output but not swapped out (in *update* operations), plus the edges that have been swapped in. The partition allows dynamic tree operations to be done only when at least one edge is output The set merging time is $O(m\ \alpha(m,n))$ [T]. The dynamic tree time is $O(n\ lg\ n)$. This gives a total time of $O(m + n\ lg\ n)$ [T].

In addition to the cycle and cocycle algorithms, the phase algorithm constructs the matroids M_i and bases $M_{i,i+1}$ (see Step 2). For graphic matroids this is done in a depth–first traversal of the spanning forest M. The time is $O(m+n)$.

These algorithms solve two intersection problems of interest. The first is to find k edge–disjoint spanning trees of an (undirected) graph G. This matroid partition problem can be reduced to the matroid intersection of a graphic matroid (k copies of G) and a partition matroid. If the algorithm starts all searches in the partition matroid, only cycle problems are solved in the graphic matroid. The time for a phase is $O(k(m + n\ lg\ n))$, for k static–cycle problems and k dynamic ones. Note that the size of the maximum matching is at most kn. Choosing the parameter p of the algorithm to balance Steps 1 and 2 (see Section 2) gives the following.

Theorem 3.1. k edge–disjoint spanning trees can be found in the following time:
(i) $O(k^{3/2}\ n^{1/2}\ m)$ if m is $\Omega(n\ lg\ n)$;
(ii) $O(k^{3/2}\ n\ m^{1/2}\ lg^{1/2} n)$ if m is $O(n\ lg\ n)$. ■

Variants of this problem can be solved by the same techniques, and have applications to the Shannon switching game [BW] and structural rigidity [I].

The intersection problem on planar graphs can also be solved using only algorithms for cycle problems: The given graph G has a planar dual G^*. A fundamental cocycle in G corresponds to a fundamental cycle in G^*. So the algorithm need only solve cycle problems on the graph G and its dual G^*.

Theorem 3.2. The graphic matroid intersection problem on planar graphs can be solved in time $O(n^{3/2}\ lg\ n)$. ■

This observation improves the results of [F] for maintaining a minimum spanning tree subject to changing edge costs.

Corollary 3.1. The edge–update problem for minimum spanning trees on planar graphs can be solved in $O(lg\ n)$ time per update. ■

Now we give the analysis of the intersection algorithm for general graphic matroids. Let the time for a phase, exclusive of augments (i.e., *updates*), be

$$O(n\ m^r\ lg^s\ n),$$

for some real values $r<1$ and s. Let the time to find one *sap* by itself and augment the matching be $O(m)$. Choose $p = (m^{1-r}\ /\ lg^s\ n)^{1/2}$. So the time for the first p phases (Step 1) is

$$O(n\ (m^{1+r}\ lg^s\ n)^{1/2}). \tag{1}$$

At most n/p more augmenting paths are found (in Step 2, by Corollary 2.2). These searches also use time (1).

To estimate the total augment time, let one *update* on a graph of n vertices and m edges be

$$O(m^t\ lg^u\ n),$$

for some real values $0<t<1$ and u. In an augment for a *sap* with s matched edges, the edges of the given graph are distributed among the s graphs M_i (defined in Section 2). Let M_i have m_i edges. Since

$$\sum_{1}^{s} m_i^t \le s^{1-t}\ m^t\ ,$$

the time for the augment is $O(s^{1-t}\ m^t\ lg^u\ n)$. Since $s \le n/\Delta$ the total of s^{1-t} over all *saps* is at most

$$n^{1-t} \sum_{1}^{n} \Delta^{t-1} = O(n).$$

Thus the total update time for all augments is

(2) $O(n\ m^{t}\ lg^{u}\ n)$.

Section 4 presents a data structure that finds one augmenting path in time $O(m + n\ lg\ n)$. Section 5 presents a data structure that, for any value z, executes a phase (excluding augments) in time $O(m + n(m/z)\ lg\ n)$, and an update in time $O(z + (m/z)^2)$.

Theorem 3.3. The graphic matroid intersection problem can be solved in the following time:

(i) $O(n^{1/2}\ m)$ if m is $\Omega(n^{3/2}\ lg\ n)$;

(ii) $O(n\ m^{2/3}\ lg^{1/3}\ n)$ if m is $\Omega(n\ lg\ n)$ and $O(n^{3/2}\ lg\ n)$;

(iii) $O(n^{4/3}\ m^{1/3}\ lg^{2/3} n)$ if m is $O(n\ lg\ n)$.

Proof. For (ii), choose $z = m^{2/3}\ lg^{1/3}\ n$. In the above calculations this gives $r = 1/3$, $s = 2/3$, $t = 2/3$, $u = 1/3$. Similar calculations give the other cases. ■

4. Static–tree cocycles.

This section presents an $O(m + n\ lg\ n)$ time algorithm for the static–tree cocycle problem. An application to a path problem on graphs is given.

Recall that the static–tree cocycle problem is defined on a graph G with spanning tree T. Edges of T are deleted in an arbitrary order. When an edge is deleted, all edges of its cocycle that remain in G are output and deleted from G. At any point in this process the original tree T has been divided into a number of subtrees, and any edge remaining in G joins two vertices in the same subtree.

The data structure is as follows: Both G and T are represented by adjacency lists. The vertices are numbered by preorder in T. Each adjacency list of G is doubly–linked and sorted by preorder (i.e., in v's list, edge vx precedes vy if x precedes y in preorder). Finally each vertex v has a set,

$$a(v) = \{u \mid \text{edge } uv \text{ is the first or last edge remaining in } u\text{'s adjacency list}\}.$$

To delete edge e and output (the rest of) its cocycle, let $e = pc$ where vertex p is the parent of child c in T. Let T_p (T_c) be p's (c's) subtree. First determine which of T_p and T_c is smaller. Do this by traversing the two subtrees in parallel, stopping when all vertices in the smaller tree have been visited. Then consider two cases:

Case 1: $|T_c| \le |T_p|$. Visit each vertex x of T_c as follows. First remove the two a–set entries for x. Then scan x's adjacency list, first from one end and then from the other. For each edge xy encountered with y a nondescendant of c, output xy and delete it. (Use preorder numbers to check if y descends from c.) Stop each scan when the first descendant z of c is encountered; add x to $a(z)$.

Case 2: $|T_c| > |T_p|$. Visit each vertex y of T_p as follows. For every vertex x in $a(y)$ that is a descendant of c, scan x's adjacency list as in Case 1.

This algorithm is correct, since an edge in e's cocycle joins a descendant of c to a nondescendant. For the timing, account for the time by charging an edge $O(1)$ when it is output, and charging a vertex $O(1)$ each time it is visited. A vertex is visited at most $lg\ n$ times, since each visit halves the size of its subtree.

Theorem 4.1. The static–tree cocycle problem can be solved in $O(m + n\ lg\ n)$ time and $O(m + n)$ space. ■

This algorithm applies to a graph problem of Suurballe and Tarjan [Su T].

Corollary 4.1. In a directed graph with source vertex s and nonnegative edge lengths, a shortest length pair of edge–disjoint paths to every other vertex can be found in $O(m + n \lg n)$ time and $O(m + n)$ space. ∎

5. Dynamic–tree cocycles.

This section proves the following result.

Theorem 5.1. Fix a value $z \leq m/3$. The dynamic–tree cocycle problem can be solved in $O(m + n)$ time for initialization, $O((m/z)\lg n + c)$ time for a cocycle operation that outputs c edges, and $O(z + (m/z)^2)$ time for an update.

The data structure has two levels and is involved. Space allows just an overview.

We begin with some ideas due to Frederickson [F]. Without loss of generality assume that the graph G has maximum degree $\Delta \leq 3$. Let T be a spanning tree. A *cluster* is a subtree S with $z \leq |S| \leq 3z$. A *topological partition* is a partition of the vertices into clusters. The *contracted graph* G^* is derived by shrinking each cluster of a topological partition to a vertex. G^* has $O(m/z)$ vertices and $O((m/z)^2)$ edges. The tree T corresponds to a spanning tree T^* of G^*.

The first level of the data structure is the static–tree data structure of Section 4, on the graph G^*. G^* uses its *inherited preorder*, defined as follows. The cluster containing the root of T is the root of T^*. If a cluster C is joined to children clusters C_i by edges $v_i w_i$, $v_i \in C$, the order of C_i in inherited preorder is given by the preorder of v_i in T. In inherited preorder, the descendants of a vertex v that are not in v's cluster form a set of consecutive clusters. This allows the algorithm of Section 4 to be used. An update is executed using the techniques of [F]. In addition, the adjacency lists of G^* must be sorted on the new inherited preorder, using time $O((m/z)^2)$.

The second level of the data structure is based on topology trees [F]. Let T be a tree with $\Delta \leq 3$. A *topology tree* Σ for T is a binary tree of height $O(\lg |T|)$. The root of Σ corresponds to an edge e that separates T into subtrees T_i, $i=1,2$; the subtrees of the root are topology trees for T_i. The leaves of Σ are the vertices of T. Order the vertices by their left–to–right order as leaves in Σ. The vertices in a node σ of Σ correspond to a subtree of T, and form an interval in this order.

If T is a spanning tree of a graph G, we add the edges of G to the data structure for Σ as follows. Let σ,τ be nodes of Σ with τ a sibling of a node in σ's path to the root. The (directed) *t–edge* $\sigma\tau$ consists of all edges of G with one end in σ and the other in τ. If σ and τ are siblings we store the t–edge $\sigma\tau$ as a search tree S. In S (directed) edges vw in $\sigma\tau$ are ordered on v (using leaf order in Σ). A t–edge $\rho\tau$ (ρ a descendant of σ) is an interval in S. The space for all search trees is $O(m)$, since an edge of G is in at most two search trees.

The second level of the data structure uses topology trees as follows. Every cluster C has a topology tree. Every edge of G joining two vertices of C is represented in the topology tree's data structure. The edges in C that are part of a cocycle are found as $\lg^2 n$ intervals in search trees.

Similarly, each edge CD of G^* has two search trees, each containing all edges of G joining clusters C and D. In C's search tree edges are ordered by preorder of their C–vertex; similarly for D. If edge e is in C, the CD edges in e's cocycle are found as $O(m/z)$ intervals in C's search trees.

6. Graphic matroid parity.

This section outlines an efficient implementation of the matroid parity algorithm on graphic matroids.

First we review the linear matroid parity algorithm of [SG]. The algorithm searches for one augmenting path at a time. The search is breadth–first, i.e., elements are scanned in the order they are labelled. The ith element e to be labelled (scanned) has *serial number* $s(e) = i$. An element is scanned by propogating its label to other elements. This is done in a "grow" or "blossom" step. A *grow step* labels one previously unlabelled element, as is in the algorithms for network flow and matroid intersection. A *blossom step* labels several elements, as in general graph matching. It also combines the blossoms previously containing these elements into a new blossom. (Initially every element is in a blossom by itself.) Further, the blossom step can create a *transform element*. This is an element that is not in the given ground set of the matroid, but gets added to it. In graphic parity a transform consists of two edges that are both matched or both unmatched. (The edges are not necessarily mates). A transform is considered *matched* or *unmatched* depending on the status of its edges. Note that in the following discussion the terms edge, transform, and element are used. To reiterate, an edge is in the given graph; a transform consists of two edges; a (matroid) element is either an edge or a transform.

The main criterion for doing a grow or blossom step for two elements x,y is that they are *adjacent*, i.e., if M is the current matching then $x \in M$, $y \notin M$ and $sp(M - x + y) = sp(M)$. It is convenient to define a set of edges $C(e)$ for an element e as follows: If e is an unmatched edge, $C(e)$ is e's fundamental cycle; if e is a matched edge, $C(e)$ is e's fundamental cocycle. If e is a transform consisting of edges e_1,e_2, then $C(e) = C(e_1) \oplus C(e_2)$. Elements e and f are adjacent if either e is an edge and

$$e \in C(f)$$

or e is a transform consisting of edges e_1,e_2 and

$$\text{exactly one of } e_1,e_2 \in C(f).$$

(Here either of e,f can be the matched element, and f can be an edge or a transform).

When the algorithm scans a labelled element e, a grow step is done for any unlabelled edge f adjacent to e. A blossom step is done for a labelled element f that is adjacent to e and in a different blossom. Blossom steps must be done in the correct order: the next blossom step is for the element f that satisfies the above criterion and has smallest possible serial number $s(f) < s(e)$.

Now we describe how to implement the algorithm by using range searching. The spanning tree of matched edges is numbered in preorder. Hereinafter identify each vertex with its preorder number. Matroid elements are represented as tuples, as follows. An unmatched edge ij is represented as the ordered pair (i,j), where $i<j$. A matched edge joining a vertex l to its parent is represented as the ordered pair (l,h), where h is the greatest (preorder) descendant of l. An transform is represented as an ordered four–tuple (i_1,i_2,i_3,i_4), where (i_1,i_2) and (i_3,i_4) are the pairs representing the two edges of the transform, $i_1 \leq i_3$, and (for an unmatched transform) if $i_1 = i_3$ then $i_2 < i_4$.

Blossoms are numbered in order of their formation. For a labelled element e, $b(e)$ denotes the number of the blossom containing e.

The following constructs are useful for range searching. $[a..b]$ denotes the interval of integers $\{i \mid a \leq x \leq b\}$. Let the universe containing all elements be $[1..n]$, and let S and T be sets. $\overline{S}$ denotes the complement of S. $P(S)$ is the symmetric Cartesian product of S and its complement, i.e., $P(S) = S \times \overline{S} \cup \overline{S} \times S$. If S is the union of $O(1)$ intervals $[a..b]$, then $P(S)$ is the union of $O(1)$ rectangles $[a_1..b_1] \times [a_2..b_2]$. Thus $P(S)$ can be found by making $O(1)$ range queries. For $i \in [1..n]$, $I(i)$ is the set of all intervals that include i, $I(i) = [1..i] \times [i..n]$. For $O(1)$ points i_k, $\oplus I(i_k)$ is the union of $O(1)$ rectangles. Hence it can be found by making $O(1)$ range queries.

The algorithm uses several multi–dimensional universes U to store the elements f that can cause grow or blossom steps. An expression $R(e)$ using the above set constructs gives the elements f that are adjacent to e. So to scan e the algorithm makes range queries to retrieve the sets $R(e) \cap U$, and does grow or blossom steps as appropriate.

Grow steps are done by maintaining two universes that contain all edges f, where f and its mate $\bar{f}$ are both unlabelled. One universe contains matched edges $f, \bar{f}$ and the other contains unmatched edges. The universes are two–dimensional. When an element e is scanned, the grow steps for e are done as follows: All edges f that remain in the appropriate universe and are adjacent to e are found and labelled, and both f and $\bar{f}$ are deleted from the universe.

Now we give the expression $R(e)$ for the edges adjacent to e. *If* e is a matched edge represented as (l,h), an unmatched edge in $C(e)$ joins a descendant of l to a nondescendant. Hence

$$R(e) = P([l..h]).$$

If e is a matched transform e_1,e_2 with e_i represented as (l_i,h_i), an unmatched edge in $C(e_1) \oplus C(e_2)$ joins a vertex descending from exactly one vertex l_i to a vertex descending from zero or two vertices l_i. Hence

$$R(e) = P([l_1..h_1] \oplus [l_2..h_2]).$$

If e is an unmatched edge represented as (i,j), a matched edge (l,h) in $C(e)$ has l an ancestor of exactly one of i,j. Hence

$$R(e) = I(i) \oplus I(j).$$

If e is an unmatched transform of edges e_1,e_2 represented as $(i_1,...,i_4)$, a matched edge (l,h) in $C(e_1) \oplus C(e_2)$ has l an ancestor of one or three of the vertices i_k. (This holds even when two vertices i_k are identical.) Hence

$$R(e) = I(i_1) \oplus ... \oplus I(i_4).$$

Blossom steps are done by maintaining four universes of labelled, scanned elements. Each universe contains either matched elements or unmatched elements, and either edges or transforms. A tuple in a universe consists of the representation of an element e, plus its blossom and serial numbers $b(e)$, $s(e)$. Hence a universe has four or six dimensions.

After an element is scanned it is inserted in the appropriate universe. The procedure for scanning an element e for blossom steps is as follows:

Step 1. Let $L = \{f \mid f$ is an element that is adjacent to e and has smallest possible serial number in its blossom$\}$.

Step 2. Let $b(g)$ be the blossom in $\{b(f) \mid f \in L\} + b(e)$ that has the most elements. For every element h in a blossom of $\{b(f) \mid f \in L\} + b(e) - b(g)$, set $b(h)$ to $b(g)$.

Step 3. Do a blossom step for each element $f \in L$, in order of increasing serial number $s(f)$.

Step 1 constructs L by making range queries on the universes for blossom steps. The edges f adjacent to e are found using the above formulas for $R(e)$. The transforms f adjacent to e are retrieved by a query $R'(e) \cap U$. f is adjacent to e if exactly one of its component edges is in $C(e)$. Hence

$$R'(e) = P(R(e)).$$

Each query finds the element f of smallest serial number in $R(e) \cap U$ or $R'(e) \cap U$, subject to the restriction that $b(f) > b(f)$, where f is the last element found in L.

The coordinates $b(e)$ and $s(e)$ in the blossom universes can be combined into one coordinate, $v(e) = 2mb(e) + s(e)$. (Note that any serial number is less than $2m$.) The query of Step 1 can still be done with a range search. Step 2 changes $b(h)$ by deleting the old tuple for h and inserting a new one. The data structure of [Lu] uses time $O(lg^5 n)$ for each query or update in the higher (five) dimensional universe.

The total time for the parity algorithm is dominated by the time for blossom steps.

This is dominated by the updates in Step 2. An element is modified $O(lg\ m)$ times, since each modification doubles the size of its blossom and a blossom has at most $2m$ elements. So the total time for one element is $O(lg^6\ n)$.

Theorem 6.1. The graphic matroid parity problem can be solved in time $O(nm\ lg^6\ n)$ and space $O(m\ lg^4\ n)$. ■

References

[A] M.Aigner, *Combinatorial Theory*, Springer–Verlag, New York, 1979.

[BW] J.Bruno and L.Weinberg, "A constructive graph–theoretic solution of the Shannon switching game", *IEEE Trans. on Circuit Theory CT–17*, 1, 1970, pp.74–81.

[C] W.H.Cunningham, "Matroid partition and intersection algorithms", Carleton University, preprint.

[D] E.A.Dinic, "Algorithm for solution of a problem of maximum flow in a network with power estimation", *Sov. Math. Dokl. 11*, 5, 1970, pp.1277–1280.

[ET] S.Even and R.E.Tarjan, "Network flow and testing graph connectivity", *SIAM J. Comput.4*, 1975, pp.507–518.

[F] G.N.Frederickson, "Data structures for on–line updating of minimum spanning trees", *Proc. 15th Annual Symp. on Theory of Computing*, 1983, pp.252–257.

[GT83] H.N.Gabow and R.E.Tarjan, "A linear–time algorithm for a special case of disjoint set union", *Proc. 15th Annual ACM Symp. on Theory of Computing*, 1983, pp.246–251.

[GT84] H.N.Gabow and R.E.Tarjan, "Efficient algorithms for a family of matroid intersection problems", *J.Algorithms 5*, 1984, pp. 80–131.

[HK] J.Hopcroft and R.Karp, "An $n^{5/2}$ algorithm for maximum matchings in bipartite graphs", *SIAM J. Comput.2*, 1973, pp.225–231.

[I] H.Imai, "Network–flow algorithms for lower–truncated transversal polymatroids", *J. Operations Res. Soc. Japan 26*, 3,1983, pp.186–210.

[La] E.L.Lawler, *Combinatorial Optimization: Networks and Matroids*, Holt,Rinehart,and Winston, New York,1976.

[Lo] L.Lovasz, "The matroid matching problem", in *Algebraic Methods in Graph Theory*, Colloquia Mathematica Societatis Janos Bolyai, Szeged,Hungary, 1978, pp.495–517.

[Lu] G.S.Lueker, "A data structure for orthogonal range queries", *Proc. 19th Annual Symp. on Foundations of Comp. Sci.*, 1978, pp.28–34.

[LM] E.L.Lawler and C.U.Martel, "Computing maximal 'polymatroidal' network flows",*Math. of Operations Research 7*, 1982, pp.334–347.

[RT] J.Roskind and R.E.Tarjan, "A note on finding minimum–cost edge–disjoint spanning trees", *Math. of Operations Research*, to appear.

[SG] M.Stallmann and H.N.Gabow, "An augmenting path algorithm for the parity problem on linear matroids", *Proc. 25th Annual Symp. on Foundations of Comp. Sci.*, 1984, pp.217–228.

[Sl T] D.D.Sleator and R.E.Tarjan, "A data structure for dynamic trees", *J. Comp. and System Sci. 26*, 1983, pp.362–391.

[Su T] J.W.Suurballe and R.E.Tarjan, "A quick method for finding shortest pairs of paths", *Networks 14*, 1984, pp.325–336.

[T] R.E.Tarjan, *Data Structures and Network Algorithms*, SIAM Monograph, Philadelphia, Pa., 1983.

[TT] C.A.Tovey and M.A.Trick, "An $O(m^4\ d)$ algorithm for the maximum polymatroidal flow problem", Georgia Institute of Technology, preprint.

[W] D.J.A. Welsh, *Matroid Theory*, Academic Press, New York,1976.

OPERATIONAL SEMANTICS FOR ORDER-SORTED ALGEBRA[1]

Joseph A. Goguen, Jean-Pierre Jouannaud[2], and José Meseguer
SRI International, Menlo Park CA 94025
Center for the Study of Language and Information, Stanford University 94305

1. Introduction

Order-sorted algebra (hereafter, OSA) generalizes standard many-sorted algebra by adding a partial ordering $\leq$ on the set S of sorts; this **subsort** relation imposes an additional restriction on an algebra A, namely, if $s \leq s'$ then $A_s \subseteq A_{s'}$ where A_s contains the elements of sort s. [6] generalized many basic results of standard many-sorted algebra to OSA, and [9] simplified and generalized [6]; [5] gives a slightly more complex and less general simplification. [9] also gives sound and complete rules of deduction for OSA, introduces the important concept of "sort constraint", and reduces OSA to standard conditional many-sorted algebra, thus automatically lifting conditional many-sorted algebra results to OSA. After reviewing this, we present here a rewrite rule-based operational semantics for OSA such that:

- A term t in an order-sorted term algebra corresponds to a congruence class modulo a set J of equations in an algebra of "disambiguated" parse trees. J admits a set $\mathcal{J}$ of Church-Rosser rewrite rules, such that each term in the order-sorted term algebra has a unique disambiguated parse, the $\mathcal{J}$-normal form of all disambiguated parses.
- Church-Rosser and terminating rewrites in the order-sorted term algebra correspond to similar rewrites on lowest parses in the disambiguated algebra. This provides an efficient operational semantics that avoids rewriting in J-congruence classes; but it requires carefully constructing disambiguated rules from order-sorted rules; in particular, an order-sorted rule may generate several disambiguated rules for the Church-Rosser property to hold.
- These results apply to both conditional rewriting and to rewriting modulo equations, by using pattern matching in the theory of the equations. We show that pattern matching in an order-sorted theory $\mathcal{E}$ corresponds to pattern matching in a disambiguated theory $\mathcal{E}^{\#}$, but the matchings may be different. Associative matching in the disambiguated theory reduces to standard associative matching, but the reduction is quite subtle.
- There is a very useful form of error-recovery: A term that is not itself well-formed, but becomes well-formed after some rewriting, such as s(4/2) with s the successor function, will recover. We formalize this with retracts, which are left inverses to subsort coercions. An ill-formed term t is parsed with retracts; if it reduces to a well-formed term, then it is called admissible. We prove that rewriting of admissible terms is Church-Rosser and terminating iff standard rewrites are Church-Rosser and terminating for well-formed terms, under the simple hypothesis that the sort of the righthand side of each order-sorted equation is less than or equal to that of its lefthand side.
- These results imply we can check whether an order-sorted specification is Church-Rosser by checking its disambiguated specification with standard Knuth-Bendix, e.g. using REVE [12]. Moreover, once the specification is Church-Rosser, error-recovery comes for free.
- Last but not least, we give operational semantics for sort constraints, generalizing the "declarations" of [6]; these permit defining what would otherwise be partial functions as total functions on an equationally defined subsort, thus giving the power of [1] and [4].

A major motivation is to handle erroneous and meaningless expressions, such as top of an empty stack or division by zero. This has been important from the earliest days of "initial algebra semantics" and was approached awkwardly in [10]. Our results support OBJ2 [3], a programming language with operational semantics based on rewrite rules and mathematical semantics based on

---

[1]Supported in part by Office of Naval Research Contract No. N00014-82-C-0333, National Science Foundation Grant No. MCS8201380 and a gift from the System Development Foundation.

[2]CRIN, Campus Scientifique, BP 239, 54506 Vandoeuvre-les-Nancy Cedex, France; work performed while on leave at SRI and CSLI.

initial OSA semantics, thus giving OBJ2 overloading, polymorphism, multiple inheritance, partial functions as total functions on subsorts, sort constraints, error values, and recovery operations; we have found subsorts enormously helpful in practical examples. [2] shows there need not be a most general unifier when the sorts form a lattice, and [15] shows there are most general unifiers when the sorts form a tree and there is no overloading; both give unification algorithms, and [15] argues for subsorts in resolution and paramodulation. Wadge describes "classified algebra" and Guiho "multi-target" operations. We thank C. Kirchner for help reducing associative OSA rewriting to standard associative rewriting, and K. Futatsugi for many OBJ2 ideas.

2. Order-Sorted Algebra

Given an "index set" S, an S-**sorted set** A is just a family A_s of sets, one for each $s \in S$, written $\{A_s | s \in S\}$. Assume a fixed ordered **sort set** S with partial order $\leq$ and a "top" **universe** sort u such that $s \leq u$ for all $s \in S$.

Definition 1: An **order-sorted signature** Σ is an $S^* \times S$-indexed set $\{\Sigma_{w,s} | w \in S^*, s \in S\}$. □

We may write $\sigma: w \to s$ for $\sigma \in \Sigma_{w,s}$ to emphasize that σ denotes a function with arity w and co-arity ("value") s. When $w = \lambda$ (the empty string) $\sigma \in \Sigma_{\lambda,s}$ denotes a constant of sort s.

Definition 2: Given an order-sorted signature Σ, an **order-sorted Σ-algebra** A consists of a **universe**, also denoted A, a family $\{A_s | s \in S\}$ of subsets of A called the **carriers** of A, and a function $A_\sigma: A_w \to A_s$ for each $\sigma \in \Sigma_{w,s}$ where $A_w = A_{s1} \times ... \times A_{sn}$ when $w = s1...sn$ and A_w is a one point set when $w = \lambda$, such that:

(1) $A_u = A$

(2) $s \leq s'$ in S implies $A_s \subseteq A_{s'}$ and

(3) $\sigma \in \Sigma_{w,s} \cap \Sigma_{w',s'}$ with $s' \leq s$ and $w' \leq w$ implies $A_\sigma: A_w \to A_s$ equals $A_\sigma: A_{w'} \to A_{s'}$ on $A_{w'}$.

We may write $A_\sigma^{w,s}$ for $A_\sigma: A_w \to A_s$ and by (3) we can generally omit the superscript w,s. □

The ordering $\leq$ on S extends to equal length strings by $s_1...s_n \leq s'_1...s'_n$ iff $s_i \leq s'_i$ for $1 \leq i \leq n$, and to pairs $\langle w,s \rangle \leq S^* \times S$ by $\langle w,s \rangle \leq \langle w',s' \rangle$ iff $w \leq w'$ and $s \leq s'$.

Definition 3: Let Σ be an order-sorted signature and let A and B be Σ-algebras. Then a **Σ-homomorphism** h: $A \to B$ is a function from the universe of A to that of B such that:

1. $h(A_s) \subseteq B_s$ for each $s \in S$, and
2. $h(A_\sigma(\underline{a})) = B_\sigma(h(\underline{a}))$ for each $\sigma \in \Sigma_{w,s}$ and $\underline{a} \in A_w$,

where $h(\underline{a}) = \langle h(a1),...,h(an) \rangle$ when $w = s1...sn$ and $\underline{a} = \langle a1,...,an \rangle$ with $ai \in A_{si}$ for $i = 1,...,n$ when $w \neq \lambda$. The Σ-algebras and Σ-homomorphisms form a category denoted $\mathbf{OSAlg}_\Sigma$. □

For regular signatures, the usual term algebra construction yields an initial order-sorted algebra. Regularity says that overloaded operators with argument sorts greater than a given sort string are consistent under restriction to subsorts, thus capturing (for first-order) Strachey's "parametric" polymorphism "locally", while still permitting "ad hoc" polymorphism globally. For example, + can denote addition over the complex numbers and its many subtypes (some of which are disjoint) with parametric polymorphism, as well as Boolean exclusive-or with "ad hoc" polymorphism.

Definition 4: An order-sorted signature Σ is **regular** iff given $w^* \in S^*$ such that there is a $\sigma \in \Sigma_{w,s}$ with $w^* \leq w$ then there is a least $\langle w',s' \rangle \in S^* \times S$ such that $\sigma \in \Sigma_{w',s'}$ and $w^* \leq w'$. □

We let T_Σ denote the standard many-sorted term algebra. The order-sorted Σ-term algebra $\mathcal{T}_\Sigma$ is the least family $\{\mathcal{T}_{\Sigma,s} | s \in S\}$ of sets satisfying:

- $\Sigma_{\lambda,s} \subseteq \mathcal{T}_{\Sigma,s}$ for $s \in S$;
- $\mathcal{T}_{\Sigma,s'} \subseteq \mathcal{T}_{\Sigma,s}$ if $s' \leq s$; in particular, the universe of $\mathcal{T}_\Sigma$ is $\mathcal{T}_\Sigma = \mathcal{T}_{\Sigma,u} = \cup_{s \in S} \mathcal{T}_{\Sigma,s}$;
- if $\sigma \in \Sigma_{w,s}$ and if $ti \in \mathcal{T}_{\Sigma,si}$ where $w = s1...sn \neq \lambda$, then (the string) $\sigma(t1...tn) \in \mathcal{T}_{\Sigma,s}$.

For $\sigma \in \Sigma_{w,s}$ we let $\mathcal{T}_\sigma$: $\mathcal{T}_w \to \mathcal{T}_s$ send t1,...,tn to $\sigma(t1...tn)$; then $\mathcal{T}_\Sigma$ is an order-sorted Σ-algebra.

Lemma 5: Each $t \in \mathcal{T}_\Sigma$ has a **least sort** $s \in S$ such that $t \in \mathcal{T}_{\Sigma,s}$; we denote it LS(t). □

Definition 6: An order-sorted Σ-algebra A is **initial** in the class of all Σ-algebras iff there is a unique Σ-homomorphism from A to any other Σ-algebra. □

Theorem 7: $\mathcal{T}_\Sigma$ is an initial order-sorted Σ-algebra. □

We now discuss equations, beginning with an example:

```
obj BITS is
  sorts Bit NeList List .
  subsorts Bit < NeList < List
  op 0 1 : -> Bit .
  op nil : -> List .
  op __ : NeList NeList -> NeList [assoc]
  op __ : List List -> List [assoc id: nil]
  op head : NeList -> Bit .
  op tail : NeList -> List .
  var L : NeList
  var B : Bit
  eq : head(B L)= B .
  eq : head(B)= B .
  eq : tail(B L)= L .
  eq : tail(B)= nil .
jbo
```

Note that **head** and **tail** are defined only on **NeList**, the non-empty lists, and that **Bit** is a subsort of **NeList**. We now formally develop equations. An S-sorted **variable set** is an S-indexed family $X=\{X_s | s \in S\}$ of *disjoint* sets. Given an S-sorted signature Σ and a variable set X disjoint from Σ, define Σ(X) by $\Sigma(X)_{\lambda,s} = \Sigma_{\lambda,s} \cup X_s$ and $\Sigma(X)_{w,s} = \Sigma_{w,s}$ for $w \neq \lambda$; if Σ is regular, so is Σ(X). Now form $\mathcal{T}_{\Sigma(X)}$ and, viewing it as a Σ-algebra by forgetting the constants in X, denote this Σ-algebra by $\mathcal{T}_\Sigma(X)$. Everything parallels standard many-sorted algebra [13]; in particular $\mathcal{T}_\Sigma(X)$ is the **free** Σ-algebra generated by X, in the following sense:

Theorem 8: Let $\underline{a}$: $X \rightarrow A$ be an **assignment** from X to A. Then there is a unique Σ-homomorphism $\underline{a}^*$: $\mathcal{T}_\Sigma(X) \rightarrow A$ extending f. □

Definition 9: A **Σ-equation** $(\forall X)\ t=t'$ is a triple ⟨X, t, t'⟩, where X is a variable set and $t,t' \in \mathcal{T}_{\Sigma(X)}$. A Σ-algebra A **satisfies** $(\forall X)\ t=t'$ iff $\underline{a}^*(t)=\underline{a}^*(t')$ in A for every assignment $\underline{a}$: $X \rightarrow A$, and A **satisfies** a set Γ of Σ-equations iff A satisfies each member of Γ. □

We now reduce OSA to standard (many-sorted) conditional algebra. The difference, though very useful in applications, is essentially one of viewpoint; mathematically, it is an "equivalence of categories", providing systematic OSA analogues of standard algebraic results. It also implies that standard rewrite-rule techniques can directly implement an OSA programming language like OBJ2. The idea is to provide for each order-sorted signature Σ a corresponding many-sorted signature $\Sigma^\#$ and a set J of conditional equations such that being an order-sorted Σ-algebra is the same (up to isomorphism) as being a many-sorted $\Sigma^\#$-algebra satisfying J. Given Σ, the corresponding $\Sigma^\#$ has the same sort set S, an operator symbol $\sigma_{w,s} \in \Sigma^\#_{w,s}$ for each $\sigma \in \Sigma_{w,s}$ (including constants where $w=\lambda$), and additional **coercion** operators $c_{s,s'} \in \Sigma^\#_{s,s'}$ whenever $s \leq s'$. J contains the following (omitting quantifiers):

1. (identity) $c_{s,s}(x)=x$ for $s \in S$;
2. (injectivity) $x=y$ if $c_{s,s'}(x)=c_{s,s'}(y)$ for $s \leq s'$ in S;
3. (transitivity) $c_{s',s''}(c_{s,s'}(x))=c_{s,s''}(x)$ for $s \leq s' \leq s''$ in S;

4. (homomorphism) whenever σ: $s_1...s_n \to s$ and σ: $s'_1...s'_n \to s'$ are in Σ with $s_i \leq s'_i$ and $s \leq s'$ (including n=0) then $c_{s,s'}(\sigma_{s1...sn,s}(x_1,...,x_n)) = \sigma_{s'1...s'n,s'}(c_{s1,s'1}(x_1),...,c_{sn,s'n}(x_n))$.

We can view an order-sorted Σ-algebra A as a standard $\Sigma^{\#}$-algebra $A^{\#}$ by making $A^{\#}_s = A_s$ for $s \in S$, $A^{\#}_{c_{s,s'}}$ the inclusion $A^{\#}_s \subseteq A^{\#}_{s'}$ (for $s \leq s'$), and $A^{\#}_{\sigma_{w,s}} = A_\sigma : A_w \to A_s$ for $\sigma \in \Sigma_{w,s}$. Then $A^{\#}$ satisfies J by construction. # extends to Σ-homomorphisms f: A→B by letting $f^{\#}_s$: $A^{\#}_s \to B^{\#}_s$ be the restiction of f to $A_s \to B_s$. This gives a functor $(\_)^{\#}$: $\mathbf{OSAlg}_\Sigma \to \mathbf{Alg}_{\Sigma^{\#},J}$ where $\mathbf{Alg}_{\Sigma^{\#},J}$ is the category of standard $\Sigma^{\#}$-algebras satisfying J.

Theorem 10: (Reduction) $(\_)^{\#}$: $\mathbf{OSAlg}_\Sigma \to \mathbf{Alg}_{\Sigma^{\#},J}$ is an equivalence of categories, i.e., there is another functor $(\_)^{\bullet}$: $\mathbf{Alg}_{\Sigma^{\#},J} \to \mathbf{OSAlg}_\Sigma$ such that for each A in $\mathbf{OSAlg}_\Sigma$ and B in $\mathbf{Alg}_{\Sigma^{\#},J}$ there are isomorphisms $A \simeq A^{\#\bullet}$ and $B \simeq B^{\bullet\#}$ natural in A and B respectively. □

Corollary 11: $T^{\bullet}_{\Sigma^{\#},J}$ is an initial order-sorted Σ-algebra and $T^{\bullet}_{\Sigma^{\#}(X),J}$ is a free order-sorted Σ-algebra on X; if Σ is regular, then $\mathcal{T}_\Sigma{}^{\#}$ is an initial $(\Sigma^{\#},J)$-algebra and $\mathcal{T}_\Sigma(X)^{\#}$ is a free $(\Sigma^{\#},J)$-algebra on X. □

3. Order-Sorted Equational Deduction

We review many-sorted equational deduction, define order-sorted equational deduction, and then apply the Reduction Theorem to obtain OSA initiality and completeness. For Σ a many-sorted signature, a term $t \in T_\Sigma(X)$ can be viewed as a **labelled tree**, i.e., a partial function from $\mathcal{N}^*_+$ (sequences of positive naturals) to $\Sigma(X)$ such that its domain $\mathcal{D}(t)$ contains the empty sequence λ, and satisfies $\upsilon i \in \mathcal{D}(t)$ iff $\upsilon \in \mathcal{D}(t)$ and $1 \leq i \leq \mathrm{arity}(t(\upsilon))$. Here $\mathcal{D}(t)$ is the set of **occurrences** of t. Also, t/υ denotes the **subterm** of t at occurrence υ, $t[\upsilon \leftarrow t']$ denotes the result of replacing t/υ by t' in t, and $\mathcal{V}(t)$ denotes the S-sorted set of variables occurring in t, i.e., the smallest X such that $t \in T_\Sigma(X)$. S-sorted assignments $X \to T_\Sigma(Y)$ are denoted by greek letters θ, ρ, etc. and called **substitutions**. The unique homomorphism extending a substitution θ is also denoted θ. The **composition** $\rho \circ \theta$ of two substitutions is just their composition as homomorphisms. If $t' = \theta t$, then t' is an **instance** of t and θ is a **match from** t **to** t'. Many-sorted equations $(\forall X)$ t=t' and conditional equations $(\forall X)$ t=t' *if* C (where C is a finite set of unquantified equations with variables in X) are defined as usual; X can be dropped if all its variables ocurr in t or t'. An equation t=t' (resp. conditional equation t=t' *if* C) is a **rewrite rule** iff $\mathcal{V}(t') \subseteq \mathcal{V}(t)$ (resp. $\mathcal{V}(t') \cup \mathcal{V}(c) \subseteq \mathcal{V}(t)$).

Definition 12: A **one-step rewriting** using an equation $(\forall X)$ t=t' is a triple $\langle Y, t_0, t_1 \rangle$ with a match θ: $X \to T_\Sigma(Y)$ from t to a subterm $\theta(t)$ of t_0 at an occurrence υ such that $t_1 = t_0[\upsilon \leftarrow \theta(t')]$. One-step rewriting using a set Γ of Σ-equations defines a binary relation $\to^{\Gamma}_{(Y)}$ on $T_\Sigma(Y)$, often abbreviated $\to_{(Y)}$. Let the **rewriting** relation associated to Γ, $\overset{*}{\to}_{(Y)}$,be the reflexive, transitive closure of $\to_{(Y)}$ and let $\vdash\!\dashv_{(X)}$ be the symmetric closure of $\to_{(X)}$, called **one-step replacement** on $T_\Sigma(X)$ using Γ. Similarly, $\sim$ is the reflexive, transitive closure of $\vdash\!\dashv$. □

Theorem 13: (Completeness [7, 13]) An equation $(\forall X)$ t=t' is satisfied by all Σ-algebras that satisfy Γ iff $t \sim^{\Gamma}_{(X)} t'$. □

$\sim^{\Gamma}_{(X)}$ is a congruence on $T_\Sigma(X)$, and we let $T_{\Sigma,\Gamma}(X)$ denote $T_\Sigma(X)/\sim^{\Gamma}_{(X)}$, the free (Σ,Γ)-algebra on X [7]. Equational deduction extends naturally to conditional equations: there is a Completeness Theorem, and the free algebra on X satisfying a set Γ of conditional equations, $T_{\Sigma,\Gamma}(X)$, is again a quotient of $T_\Sigma(X)$ by a relation $\sim_{(X)}$ generalizing the above (Proposition

2, [8]). Also [13], given a set of rewrite rules, the rewriting relation $\overset{*}{\rightarrow}_{(X)}$ is independent of X, so $t\overset{*}{\rightarrow}t'$ is unambiguous. We now define $\mathcal{E}$-rewriting when the set of (conditional) equations Γ splits into rules $\mathcal{R}$ and equations $\mathcal{E}$ that cannot be used as rules (e.g., commutativity). We borrow notation from [11], as well as the following fundamental assumption about $\mathcal{E}$: every conditional equation $l=r$ *if* c has $\mathcal{V}(l) = \mathcal{V}(r)$. Note that all our definitions about matching extend to an equational theory $\sim^{\mathcal{E}}$; e.g., an **$\mathcal{E}$-match** from t to t' is a substitution θ such that $t' \sim^{\mathcal{E}} \theta(t)$.

Definition 14: Given a set $\mathcal{R}$ of conditional rewrite rules, the **rewriting relation** $\rightarrow^{\mathcal{R},\mathcal{E}}$ (or more simply $\rightarrow^{\mathcal{R}}$ if $\mathcal{E}$ is empty) is defined by $t\rightarrow^{\mathcal{R},\mathcal{E}}t'$ iff there exist an occurrence υ of $\mathcal{D}(t)$, a rule $l\rightarrow r$ *if* c in $\mathcal{R}$, and a substitution θ such that $t/\upsilon\sim^{\mathcal{E}}\theta l$, $t'=t[\upsilon\leftarrow\theta r]$ and each equality in θC is valid in the free algebra $T_{\Sigma,\Gamma}(X)$. t/υ is called the **redex**, and $\overset{*}{\rightarrow}^{\mathcal{R},\mathcal{E}}$, the reflexive transitive closure of $\rightarrow^{\mathcal{R},\mathcal{E}}$, is called the **derivation relation**. □

Given $\mathcal{R}'$ that may further specialize to $\mathcal{R}$ or even $\mathcal{R},\mathcal{E}$, and a congruence $\mathcal{E}'$ that may further specialize to the congrunce generated by J, we now define rewritings in congruence classes.

Definition 15: Given a rewriting relation $\rightarrow^{\mathcal{R}'}$ and a congruence $\sim^{\mathcal{E}'}$, then **$\mathcal{R}'$ modulo $\mathcal{E}'$** is the **rewriting** relation denoted $\rightarrow^{\mathcal{R}'/\mathcal{E}'}$ defined by $t\rightarrow^{\mathcal{R}'/\mathcal{E}'}t'$ iff there are t_1,t_1' such that $t\sim^{\mathcal{E}'}t_1$ and $t'\sim^{\mathcal{E}'}t_1'$ and $t_1\rightarrow^{\mathcal{R}'}t_1'$. Let $\sim^{\mathcal{R}'}$ denote the smallest congruence generated by the reflexive symmetric transitive closure of $\rightarrow^{\mathcal{R}'}$ and let $\sim^{\mathcal{R}'\cup\mathcal{E}}$ denote the reflexive transitive closure of $\sim^{\mathcal{E}}\cup\sim^{\mathcal{R}}$; both are smallest congruences generated by the corresponding one-step relations. □

The rewrite relation $\mathcal{R}'$ modulo $\mathcal{E}'$ operates on terms, but simulates the rewriting relation induced by $\mathcal{R}'$ on $\mathcal{E}'$-congruence classes. In particular, termination of $\mathcal{R}'$ modulo $\mathcal{E}'$ is equivalent to termination of $\mathcal{R}'$ on $\mathcal{E}'$-congruence classes.

Definition 16: $\mathcal{R}$ is $\mathcal{R}'$-Church-Rosser modulo $\mathcal{E}$ iff for all t_1,t_2 such that $t_1\sim^{\mathcal{R}'\cup\mathcal{E}}t_2$ there are t_1',t_2' such that $t_1\overset{*}{\rightarrow}^{\mathcal{R}'}t_1'$, $t_2\overset{*}{\rightarrow}^{\mathcal{R}'}t_2'$ and $t_1'\sim^{\mathcal{E}}t_2'$. □

This says if t_1 and t_2 can be proved equal using $\mathcal{E}$-equalities and $\mathcal{R}'$-rewritings (both ways), then they can be proved equal by rewriting them to terms t_1' and t_2' that can be proved equal using only $\mathcal{E}$-equalities. Applying this technique requires that $\sim^{\mathcal{E}}$ is decidable and $\rightarrow^{\mathcal{R}'}$ is **terminating** (or **well-founded**); we then take t_1',t_2' to be the normal forms of (respectively) t_1,t_2. The $\mathcal{R}'$-Church-Rosser property implies **$\mathcal{E}$-confluence** of $\mathcal{R}'$: if t reduces to terms t_1 and t_2 using $\mathcal{R}'$-reductions, then t_1 and t_2 reduce to terms t_1 and t_2 that are $\mathcal{E}$-equivalent; but the converse is false when $\mathcal{E}$ is non-empty [11]. Definition 16 specializes to: the standard Church-Rosser property by taking $\mathcal{R}'$ and $\mathcal{E}$ to be respectively $\mathcal{R}$ and the empty congruence; to a Church-Rosser property studied by Huet by taking $\mathcal{R}'$ and $\mathcal{E}$ to be respectively $\mathcal{R}$ and $\mathcal{E}$; and to one studied by Peterson and Stickel and by Jouannaud, taking $\mathcal{R}'$ and $\mathcal{E}$ to be respectively $\mathcal{R},\mathcal{E}$ and $\mathcal{E}$; see [11]. Termination and Church-Rosser together provide a unique normal form for any term.

We now develop OSA deduction. The notions of **substitution** and **match** just replacing $T_{\Sigma}(X)$ by $\mathcal{T}_{\Sigma}(X)$, but **one-step rewriting** is more delicate. Given an equation $(\forall X)$ $t=t'$ in Γ, whenever there is a match θ: $X\rightarrow\mathcal{T}_{\Sigma}(Y)$ from t to a subterm $\theta(t)$ of a term $t_0\in\mathcal{T}_{\Sigma}(Y)$ at some occurrence υ in t_0 then $t_0\rightarrow_{(Y)}t_0[\upsilon\leftarrow\theta(t')]$ *provided* that there is a sort s such that, for x a variable of sort s, $t[\upsilon\leftarrow x]$ is a well-formed term and $\theta(t),\theta(t')\in\mathcal{T}_{\Sigma}(Y)_s$. The proviso avoids replacements that produce ill-formed terms. Let $\vdash\!\dashv_{(Y)}$ (resp. $\overset{*}{\to}_{(Y)}$) be the symmetric (resp. reflexive symmetric) closure of $\to_{(Y)}$ and let $\sim_{(Y)}$ be the reflexive transitive closure of $\vdash\!\dashv_{(X)}$. Generalizing many-sorted conditional equations to OSA is straightforward with the proviso; we obtain a relation $\sim_{(Y)}$ and the one-step replacement $t_0 \to_{(Y)} t_0[\upsilon \leftarrow \theta(t')]$ for a conditional equation $(\forall X)\ t = t'$ **if** C now also requires that $\theta(t_i) \sim_{(Y)} \theta(t_i')$ for each $t_i = t_i'$ in C.

The unique $\Sigma^{\#}$-homomorphism h_X: $T_{\Sigma^{\#}}(X) \to \mathcal{T}_{\Sigma}(X)^{\#}$ provided by Corollary 11 is useful in studying $P(t) = \{t' \in T_{\Sigma^{\#}}(X) \mid h_X(t') = t\}$ for t in $\mathcal{T}_{\Sigma}(X)$, the set of all disambiguated parses of t as a $\Sigma^{\#}$-term; let $P(t)_s$ denote $P(t) \cap T_{\Sigma^{\#}}(X)_s$. There is a least sort s with $P(t)_s$ nonempty. If we need a disambiguated parse but don't care which one, we let p(t) denote one; similarly, for e an order-sorted equation, we let p(e) denote some disambiguated parses for the lefthand and righthand sides of e (they must be the same sort). For Γ a set of order-sorted equations, $P(\Gamma)$ denotes the set of all parses p(e) for each e in Γ. The homomorphic property of h_X and Corollary 11 give a systematic way to relate terms to their parses and to J-deduction between parses. We now reduce satisfaction of OSA equations to satisfaction of standard many-sorted equations.

Theorem 17: (Satisfaction) For Σ a regular order-sorted signature:

(1) A Σ-algebra A satisfies $(\forall X)\ t = t'$ iff the $\Sigma^{\#}$-algebra $A^{\#}$ satisfies any equation (say of sort s) $(\forall X)\ t_1 = t_1'$ such that $h_{X,s}(t_1) = t$ and $h_{X,s}(t_1') = t'$.

(2) Conversely, a $(\Sigma^{\#}, J)$-algebra B satisfies $(\forall X)\ t_1 = t_1'$ (of sort s) iff the order-sorted algebra $B^{\bullet}$ satisfies the equation $(\forall X)\ h_X(t_1) = h_X(t_1')$. □

Corollary 18: For Σ a regular signature and Γ a set of Σ-equations, there is an equivalence of categories $(\_)^{\#}$: $\mathbf{OSAlg}_{\Sigma,\Gamma} \to \mathbf{Alg}_{\Sigma^{\#}, J \cup P(\Gamma)}$. □

Let $X = \{X_s \mid s \in S\}$ be an S-sorted disjoint variable set. A **specialization** of X is an S-sorted partition $\rho(X) = \{\rho(X)_s \mid s \in S\}$ of $\cup_s X_s$ such that if $x \in X_s$ then $x \in \rho(X)_{s'}$ for some $s' \leq s$. The specializations of X are partially ordered pointwise: $\rho'(X) \leq \rho(X)$ iff $\rho'(X)$ is a specialization of $\rho(X)$. If $\rho(X)$ is a specialization of X, then ρ: $X \to \mathcal{T}_{\Sigma}(\rho(X))$ denotes the substitution $x \mapsto x$. The following relates order-sorted and many-sorted deduction:

Lemma 19: For Σ regular, for $t, t' \in \mathcal{T}_{\Sigma}(X)$ and for $e = ((\forall Y)\ t_0 = t_0')$ a many-sorted Σ-equation, $t \to_{(X)} t'$ using e iff there are parses p(t), p(t') and an equation (say of sort s) of the form $e_1 = ((\forall \rho(Y))\ p(t_0) = p(t_0'))$ with $\rho(Y)$ a specialization of Y such that $p(t) \to_{(X)} p(t')$ using e_1; the set of all such e_1 is denoted $\{e\}^{\#}$. □

Theorem 20: (Order-Sorted Completeness) For Σ regular, for $t_1, t_2 \in \mathcal{T}_{\Sigma}(X)_s$ and for Γ a set of Σ-equations, the following are equivalent:

1. $t_1 \sim^{\Gamma}_{(X)} t_2$.
2. The equation $(\forall X)\ t_1 = t_2$ is satisfied by all order-sorted Σ-algebras that satisfy Γ. □

Thus, dividing the universe of $\mathcal{T}_{\Sigma}(X)$ by $\sim^{\Gamma}_{(X)}$ to get $\mathcal{T}_{\Sigma,\Gamma}(X)$ and letting $\mathcal{T}_{\Sigma,\Gamma}(X)_s$ contain the elements with representatives in $\mathcal{T}_{\Sigma}(X)_s$ gives the unique OSA structure on $\mathcal{T}_{\Sigma,\Gamma}(X)$ making the passage to equivalence classes $\mathcal{T}_{\Sigma}(X) \to \mathcal{T}_{\Sigma,\Gamma}(X)$ a Σ-homomorphism.

Corollary 21: (Initiality) For Σ regular and Γ a set of Σ-equations, $\mathcal{T}_{\Sigma,\Gamma}$ is an initial (Σ,Γ)-algebra and $\mathcal{T}_{\Sigma,\Gamma}(X)$ is a free (Σ,Γ)-algebra on X. □

All our results extend naturally to conditional equations. Define a rewrite rule (conditional or not) to be an unquantified order-sorted equation satisfying the same restrictions on variables as in the many-sorted case. $\mathcal{R}$ is **Church-Rosser**, or $\mathcal{R}'$-Church-Rosser modulo $\mathcal{E}$, just as in the many-sorted case. Lemma 19 permits viewing Σ-rewritings with $\mathcal{R}$ as $\Sigma^{\#}$-rewritings modulo J with $\mathcal{R}^{\#}$, so $\mathcal{R}$ is Church-Rosser iff $\mathcal{R}^{\#}$ is Church-Rosser modulo J (Lemma 24 shows the injectivity equation, which doesn't have the same variables on left- and right-hand sides, can be dropped for the initial algebra). Thus reference to X can be dropped from $\sim_{(X)}$ for Church-Rosser OSA rewritings, and similarly for $\mathcal{R}'$-Church-Rosser rewritings modulo $\mathcal{E}$ [14].

4. An Efficient Operational Semantics

We have considered $\mathcal{E}^{\#}$-rewriting in J-congruence classes, and simple rewriting in J-congruence classes when $\mathcal{E}$ is empty. But this is inefficient, since J-congruence classes must be searched for reducible terms. Our more efficient operational semantics requires defining the lowest parse LP(t) of a term t, and a completion process on both the rules of LP($\mathcal{R}$) and the equations of LP($\mathcal{E}$), to recover the Church-Rosser property. Actually, we can define the result of this process without performing it. $T_{\Sigma^{\#},J}(X)$ is simplified by eliminating unecessary coercions $c_{s,s'}$, eliminating the related identity equations, and simplifying homomorphism equations having such coercions. This yields another realization of the free ($\Sigma^{\#}$,J)-algebra over X with simplified signature and equations, still denoted $T_{\Sigma^{\#}}(X)$ and J, with quotient still denoted $T_{\Sigma^{\#},J}(X)$, and with the $\Sigma^{\#}$(X)-homomorphism from $T_{\Sigma^{\#}}(X)$ to $\mathcal{T}_{\Sigma}(X)^{\#}$ still denoted h_X. Now the **construction of** $\mathcal{J}$, the Church-Rosser rules obtained from J (deleting injectivity equations by Lemma 24 below):

1. For each triple (s,s',s") such that $s''<s'<s$, $c_{s',s}(c_{s'',s'}(x)) = c_{s'',s}(x)$ is in $\mathcal{J}$ (transitivity).
2. For each $\sigma\in\Sigma_{s_1...s_n,s}\cap\Sigma_{s'_1...s'_n,s'}$ with $s'_i\leq s_i$ for $1\leq i\leq n$ and $s'\leq s$, the **morphism rule** $\sigma_{s_1...s_n,s}(...,c_{s'_k,s_k}(x_k),...,c_{s''_l,s_l}(x_l),...) = c_{s',s}(\sigma_{s'_1...s'_n,s'}(...,x_k,...,c_{s''_l,s'_l}(x_l),...))$ is in $\mathcal{J}$ for each partition K∪L of [1..n] and each set $\{s''_l \mid l\in L \text{ and } s''_l<s'_l\}$, where all variables are different, x_l is of sort s''_l and x_k is of sort s'_k.

Lemma 22: $\mathcal{J}$ is terminating and Church-Rosser. □

Lemma 23: Each well-formed order-sorted term t has **lowest parse** LP(t) with sort ls, such that a term p(t) of sort s' is a parse of t iff $ls\leq s'$ and $p(t)\sim^{J}c_{ls,s'}(LP(t))$. Moreover, $c_{ls,s'}(LP(t))$ is the unique $\mathcal{J}$-normal form of p(t). □

Lemma 24: Two terms of $T_{\Sigma^{\#}}$ are equal modulo J iff they are equal modulo $\mathcal{J}$. □

Deduction with lowest parses uses a new set $\mathcal{E}^{\#}$ of $\Sigma^{\#}$-equations constructed from $\mathcal{E}$ as follows:

- $\mathcal{E}^{\#}$ is obtained by completing $\mathcal{E}$, assuming that equations l=r *if* c in $\mathcal{E}$ don't change sorts (as defined below) and satisfy $\mathcal{V}(c)\subseteq\mathcal{V}(l)=\mathcal{V}(r)$.
- For each l=r *if* c in $\mathcal{E}$ and for each specialization ρ of the variables $\mathcal{V}$(l), LP(ρl) = LP(ρr) *if* LP(ρc) is an equation of $\mathcal{E}^{\#}$. We assume in the following that LP(ρl) and LP(ρr) are of the same sort, which yields equations in $\mathcal{E}^{\#}$ without top coercions.

These equations are somewhat redundant; a good approximation of the minimal subset is obtained from $\mathcal{E}^{\#}$ by eliminating equations that are instances of others.

Lemma 25: Given order-sorted terms t and t', $t\sim^{\mathcal{E}}t'$ iff $LP(t)\sim^{\mathcal{E}^{\#}}LP(t')$. □

We now treat rewriting with lowest parses, dropping the assumption that the left- and right-hand sides of rules have the same sort after renaming; this may result in rules having coercions on top of their left- and right-hand sides. The **construction of** $\mathcal{R}^{\#}$ is as follows, for all equations l=r *if* c in $\mathcal{R}$ and all specializations ρ of the variables $\mathcal{V}$(l):

- If sr=sl, then LP(ρl) = LP(ρr) *if* LP(ρc) is a rule in $\mathcal{R}^{\#}$;
- If sr<sl, then LP(ρl) = $c_{sr,sl}$(LP(ρr)) *if* LP(ρc) is a rule in $\mathcal{R}^{\#}$;

• Otherwise, for all s∈S, s≥sl and s≥sr, $c_{sl,s}(LP(\rho l)) = c_{sr,s}(LP(\rho r))$ *if* $LP(\rho c)$ is a rule in $\mathcal{R}^{\#}$.

The third kind of rule has important consequences for implementing OSA rewriting: since replacing a lefthand side by a righthand side may yield an ill-formed term, an extra check on the starting term is needed before applying the rule; but this check remains implicit at the level of $T_{\Sigma\#}(X)$, since the matching requires the appropriate coercion to be present.

Lemma 26: (Lifting) For any order-sorted terms t and t′ of sorts s and s′ respectively, $t \xrightarrow{*}_{\mathcal{R},\mathcal{E}} t'$ iff $c_{s,u}(LP(t))\ [\rightarrow_{\mathcal{R}^{\#},\mathcal{E}^{\#}} \circ \xrightarrow{!}{}^{J}_{nf}]^{*}\ c_{s',u}(LP(t'))$. □

Theorem 27: An order-sorted specification is $\mathcal{R},\mathcal{E}$-Church-Rosser and terminating iff its transformed specification is $\mathcal{R}'$-Church-Rosser and terminating on the subset of $T_{\Sigma\#}(X)_u$ of $\mathcal{J}$-normal forms (lowest parses) with $\mathcal{R}' = \rightarrow_{\mathcal{R}^{\#},\mathcal{E}^{\#}} \circ \xrightarrow{!}{}^{J}_{nf}$. □

Our definition of conditional rewriting implied that each time a rule was applied, the condition had to be checked in the algebra $T_{\Sigma\#,\mathcal{E}\#\cup J}(X)$. Validity in this algebra can be checked by equational reasoning, using the completeness theorem for (positive) conditional equations, by rewriting the condition to its normal form, if rewriting is Church-Rosser. This normal form must be a conjunction of equalities deducible from only axioms in $\mathcal{E}^{\#}$ since normal forms are unique up to $\sim^{\mathcal{E}^{\#}}$. Therefore $\mathcal{R}^{\#},\mathcal{E}^{\#}$-reducibility is decidable if $\sim^{\mathcal{E}^{\#}}$ is decidable, $\mathcal{E}^{\#}$-matching is decidable, and the Church-Rosser property is satisfied. Our approach also improves others (e.g., [2] where $\mathcal{E}$ is empty) by using standard matching. Therefore, we can use standard Knuth-Bendix completion for OSA, by processing transformed specifications. For $\mathcal{E}$ non-empty, we used matching in $\mathcal{E}^{\#}$ rather than in $\mathcal{E}$, and doubt that a direct approach would have been so easy. Moreover, matchings under $\mathcal{E}$ and $\mathcal{E}^{\#}$ are equivalent for the usual cases (e.g., associativity), but the equivalence can be delicate. Commutativity is simple, since all equations in $\mathcal{E}^{\#}$ are equational consequences of ordinary commutativity equations. For example, (c x) + y = y + (c x) where c is a coercion and + a binary infix commutative operator, follows from x + y = y + x. Identity and idempotency are similar. Associativity is harder, but the full version of this paper reduces it to standard associative matching.

5. Built-in Error Recovery

Strong typing, even when polymorphic, has some disadvantages. For example, **`head(tail(0 1 0 0))`** is not well-formed according to the **BITS** syntax, since **head**'s arguments should have sort **NeList** but the sort of **`tail(0 1 0 0)`** is **List**, even though **`tail(0 1 0 0)`** evaluates to the nonempty list **1 0 0**. We associate to any order-sorted signature Σ a one-sorted signature Unf(Σ) with the same operators, but with all sorts replaced by the universe sort; call Unf(Σ)-terms **unformed**. Error recovery transforms unformed terms to well-formed terms of an extended order-sorted signature $\Sigma^{\otimes}$ with the same sorts as Σ plus new operator symbols $r_{u,s}$: u→s for each s≠u, called **retracts**, satisfing for each s′≤s the equations $r_{u,s}(x)=x$, for x a variable of sort s′.

Definition 28: A regular order-sorted signature Σ is **coregular** iff for each sort s and operator σ: w′→s′ with s≥s′, there is a greatest (w″,s″) with an operator σ: w″→s″ where s≥s″. □

For Σ corregular, define a lowest parse LP(t) of an unformed term t to be a $(\Sigma^{\otimes})^{\#}$-term. OBJ2 uses retracts to handle unformed order-sorted terms that might become well-formed after reduction, giving them benefit of doubt at parse time by filling gaps between actual and required sorts with retracts. For example, **`head(tail(0 1 0 0))`** reduces to **1** after parsing with retracts and applying rules in **BITS** and a retract rule. On the other hand, the expression **`head(tail(tail(1)))`** also is temporarily accepted, reduced, and unparsed as **`head(`**$r_{U,NeList}$**`(tail(`**$r_{U,NeList}$**`(nil))))`**, a very informative error message. This kind of runtime typechecking, together with the polymorphism provided by subsorts (plus parameterized modules) gives OBJ2 most of the syntactic flexibility of untyped languages with all the advantages of strong typing. Adding retracts is "safe": beginning with an order-sorted signature Σ and a set Γ of

Σ-equations, let us extend Σ to a signature $\Sigma^\bullet$ by adding the retract operators, and similarly extend Γ to $\Gamma^\bullet$ by adding the above retract equations. For retracts to be well-behaved, the extension $(\Sigma,\Gamma)\subseteq(\Sigma^\bullet,\Gamma^\bullet)$ should be **conservative**, i.e., $t \sim^{\Gamma}_{(X)} t'$ iff $t \sim^{\Gamma^\bullet}_{(X)} t'$ for $t,t' \in \mathcal{T}_\Sigma(X)$.

Theorem 29: The extension $(\Sigma,\Gamma)\subseteq(\Sigma^\bullet,\Gamma^\bullet)$ is conservative. □

We also want term evaluation by rewriting to be safe in the presence of retracts, i.e., Church-Rosser and termination should still hold when retracts are added. Call a $\Sigma^\bullet$-term t **admissible** for $\mathcal{R}$ iff there is a Σ-term t' such that $t \sim^{\mathcal{R}^\bullet}_{(X)} t'$.

Theorem 30: If every rule l=r in $\mathcal{R}$ satisfies sort(r)≤sort(l), then $(\mathcal{R}^\bullet)^\#$-rewriting on lowest parses of admissible terms is Church-Rosser and terminating iff $\mathcal{R}$-rewriting on Σ-terms is Church-Rosser and terminating. □

6. Sort Constraints

Conditional sort constraints require the result of an operator be given a sort smaller than expected when the operands satisfy the condition. For example, pushing a bounded stack generally yields an error, but yields a nonempty stack if length(stack)<bound.

Definition 31: For Σ regular, a **sort constraint** is $\delta = \langle X, s, \sigma(x1,...,xn), C\rangle$ with:

1. X a set of variables x1,...,xn of sorts s1,...,sn such that there is an operator σ: s1',...sn'→s' with si'≥si for i=1...n, and s'≥s (s is called the **sort** of the constraint).
2. No operator σ in Σ has arity smaller than w=s1...sn, and all operators σ of arity w have coarity strictly bigger than s (w is called the **arity** of the constraint).
3. C (called the **condition** of δ) is a finite set of Σ equations involving only variables in X.

An order-sorted algebra A **satisfies** the constraint δ iff $A_\sigma(a1,...,an) \in A_s$ whenever $ai \in A_{si}$ for i=1,...,n and C(a1,...,an) holds. A **family** Δ of constraints must have all *different* operators. □

Requirement 2. above ensures that the signature $\Sigma(\Delta)$ obtained from Σ by adding an operator δ: w→s for each constraint ⟨X, s, σ(x1,...,xn), C⟩ of arity w is also regular. Now an example using sort constraints; assuming the variables in X already declared, OBJ2 syntax for a sort constraint is: **as S σ(X1,...,XN) if C .**

```
obj BOUNDED-NAT-STACK is
  extending NAT .
  sorts NeStack Stack ErrStack .
  subsorts NeStack < Stack < ErrStack .
  op empty : -> Stack .
  op overflow : -> ErrStack .
  op bound : -> Nat .
  op push : Nat Stack -> ErrStack .
  op top : NeStack -> Nat .
  op pop : NeStack -> Stack .
  op length : Stack -> Nat .
  var N : Nat .
  var S : Stack .
  as NeStack : push(N,S) if length(S) < bound .
  eq : push(N,S) = overflow if length(S) == bound .
  eq : bound = 50 .
  eq : length(empty) = 0 .
  eq : length(push(N,S)) = inc(length(S)) .
  eq : top(push(N,S)) = N .
  eq : pop(push(N,S)) = S .
jbo
```

Although terms like **length(push(N,S))** and **pop(push(N,S))** are not well-formed, they have a clear meaning for all assignments mapping S to a stack with length<**bound**. Of course, we can regard these as well-formed in the signature obtained by adding **push : Nat Stack -> NeStack** as in $\Sigma(\Delta)$ above; however, we should assume operators lie in the unenlarged signature unless it is impossible to parse without using the enlarged signature. Thus, given sort constraints Δ, the **intended parse** IP(t) should have $h_X(\mathrm{IP}(t))=t$, where h_X: $T_{\Sigma(\Delta)^\#}(X) \to \mathcal{T}_{\Sigma(\Delta)}(X)^\#$. Now an algorithm for IP(t), given a $\Sigma(\Delta)$-term t, and assuming Σ is coregular; IP(t) is actually IP(t,u), for u the universal sort. Let

- $\mathrm{IP}(x,s)=c_{LS(x),s}(x)$ if $s \geq LS(x)$; otherwise undefined.
- $\mathrm{IP}(\sigma(t1,...,tn),s)=$ if there is a σ: $w' \to s'$ in Σ with (w',s') maximum such that $s \geq s'$ (say $w'=s1'...sn'$) then $c_{s',s}(\sigma_{w',s'}(\mathrm{IP}(t1,s1'),...,\mathrm{IP}(tn,sn')))$ else, if there is a constraint $\delta=\langle X, s', \sigma(x1,...,xn), C\rangle$ in Δ of arity w=s1...sn with $s \geq s'$ then $c_{s',s}(\sigma_{w,s'}(\mathrm{IP}(t1,s1),...,\mathrm{IP}(tn,sn)))$ else undefined (this takes care of constants, with n=0).

Conditions for operators in the presence of sort constraints can be extended to terms:

Definition 32: Given a term $t \in T_{\Sigma(\Delta)^\#}(X)$, for each occurence υ in $\mathcal{D}(t)$, define cond[υ] by:

- If $t/\upsilon=\sigma_{w,s}(t1,...,tn)$ with $\sigma_{w,s} \in \Sigma^\#$ or t/u=x with x in X, then cond[υ]=$\emptyset$.
- If $t/\upsilon=\sigma_{w,s}(t1,...,tn)$ with $\sigma_{w,s}$ introduced by a constraint δ with condition C(x1,...,xn) then cond[υ]=C($t/\upsilon 1,...,t/\upsilon n$).

Also, define cond(t)=$\bigcup_{\upsilon \in \mathcal{D}(t)}$cond[$\upsilon$]. □

Given a $\Sigma(\Delta)$-equation in a Σ-algebra A satisfying constraints Δ, and an assignment $\underline{a}$: $X \to A$, we can recursively define an S-sorted partial function $\underline{a}^+$: $T_{\Sigma(\Delta)^\#}(X) \to \{A_s | s \in S\}$ extending $\underline{a}$ homomorphically; we then want to say that if $\underline{a}$ satisfies cond(IP(t)) and cond(IP(t')), then $\underline{a}^+$(IP(t)) and $\underline{a}^+$(IP(t')) are both defined and the equation is satisfied by A if for all such $\underline{a}$ satisfying cond(IP(t)) and cond(IP(t')) we have $\underline{a}^+(\mathrm{IP}(t))=\underline{a}^+(\mathrm{IP}(t'))$. We must show this definition does not beg the question of cond(IP(t)) and cond(IP(t')) being defined at all. The definition of satisfaction for a conditional $\Sigma(\Delta)$-equation is similar. Denote the category of order-sorted Σ-algebras defined by a family Δ of sort constraints and a set Γ of $\Sigma(\Delta)$-equations (conditional or not) by $\mathbf{OSAlg}_{\Sigma,\Delta,\Gamma}$. The following extends the Reduction and Initiality Theorems to sort constraints.

Theorem 33: (<u>Reducing Constraints to Standard Algebra</u>) $\mathbf{OSAlg}_{\Sigma,\Delta,\Gamma}$ has an initial algebra, $\mathcal{T}_{\Sigma,\Delta,\Gamma}$. Also, there is an extension $\Sigma^\$$ of $\Sigma(\Delta)^\#$ and a set of conditional equations $\Gamma^\$$ such that $\mathcal{T}_{\Sigma,\Delta,\Gamma}$ is the image under the equivalence of categories $(\_)^\bullet$ of the minimal $\Sigma^\#$-subalgebra contained in the initial $(\Sigma^\$,\Gamma^\$)$-algebra. □

Given a set $\mathcal{R}$ of $\Sigma(\Delta)$-rewrite rules, to evaluate a term $t \in \mathcal{T}_{\Sigma(\Delta)}$ in the initial algebra $\mathcal{T}_{\Sigma,\Delta,\mathcal{R}}$ we can first form LP(t), lowest $(\Sigma^\bullet)^\#$-parse (with retracts) and then reduce LP(t) using a set $(\mathcal{R}^\bullet)^\#$ of rules containing

- an extension of $\mathcal{J}$ by *conditional* morphism rules for the new operators introduced by Δ and by coercion-retract rules, plus
- conditional $\Sigma(\Delta)^\#$-rules completing by specialization those in $\mathcal{R}$, each having the condition associated to the corresponding righthand side.

Assuming that no rules with coercions on top of lefthand sides are thus generated, we then have

Theorem 34: If $\mathcal{R}^\$$ is Church-Rosser, then for any $t \in \mathcal{T}_{\Sigma(\Delta)}$ such that IP(t) denotes an element of $\mathcal{T}_{\Sigma,\Delta,\mathcal{R}}$ the $\mathcal{R}^\$$-normal form of IP(t) coincides with the $(\mathcal{R}^\bullet)^\#$-normal form of LP(t). □

7. References

1. Benecke, K. and Reichel, H. Equational Partiality. In *Algebra Universalis*, 1984.

2. Cunningham, R. J. and Dick, A. J. J. Rewrite Systems on a Lattice of Types. Imperial College, Department of Computing,1983.

3. Futatsugi, K., Goguen, J., Jouannaud, J.-P., and Meseguer, J. Principles of OBJ2. In *Proceedings, 1985 Symposium on Principles of Programming Languages*, ACM, 1985, pp. 52-66.

4. Gabriel, P. and Ulmer, F. *Lokal Präsentierbare Kategorien*. Springer-Verlag, 1971. Springer Lecture Notes in Mathematics, vol. 221.

5. Gogolla, M. Algebraic Specifications with Partially Ordered Sorts and Declarations. 169, Universitat Dortmund, Abteilung Informatik,1983.

6. Goguen, J. A. Order Sorted Algebra. UCLA Computer Science Department,1978.Semantics and Theory of Computation Report No. 14.

7. Goguen, J. A. and Meseguer, J. "Completeness of Many-sorted Equational Logic." *SIGPLAN Notices 16*, 7 (July 1981), 24-32.Also appeared in *SIGPLAN Notices*, January 1982, vol. 17, no. 1, pages 9-17; extended version as SRI Technical Report CSL-135, May 1982; final version as Technical Report CSLI-84-15, Center for the Study of Language and Information, Stanford University, September 1984, and to be published in *Houston Journal of Mathematics*.

8. Goguen, J. A. and Meseguer, J. Universal Realization, Persistent Interconnection and Implementation of Abstract Modules. In *Proceedings, 9th ICALP*, Springer-Verlag, 1982.

9. Goguen, J. and Meseguer, J. Order-Sorted Algebra I: Partial and Overloaded Operations, Errors and Inheritance. To appear, SRI International, Computer Science Lab,1985.Given as lecture at Seminar on Types, Carnegie-Mellon University, June 1983.

10. Goguen, J. A., Thatcher, J. W. and Wagner, E. An Initial Algebra Approach to the Specification, Correctness and Implementation of Abstract Data Types. RC 6487, IBM T. J. Watson Research Center,October, 1976.Reprinted in *Current Trends in Programming Methodology, IV*, ed. R. Yeh, Prentice-Hall, 1978, pp. 80-149.

11. Jouannaud, J.P. and Kirchner, H. Completion of a Set of Rules Modulo a Set of Equations. In *Proceedings, 11th Symposium on Principles of Programming Languages*, ACM, 1984, pp. 83-92.

12. Lescanne, P. Computer Experiments with the REVE Term Rewriting Systems Generator. In *Proceedings, Symposium on Principles of Programming Languages*, ACM, 1983.

13. Meseguer, J. and Goguen, J. A. Initiality, Induction and Computability. In *Algebraic Methods in Semantics*, M. Nivat and J. Reynolds, Eds., Cambridge University Press, 1985, pp. 459-540.

14. Meseguer, J. and Goguen, J. Deduction with Many-Sorted Rewrite Rules. Technical Report, SRI International, Computer Science Lab.

15. Walther, C. A Many-sorted Calculus Based on Resolution and Paramodulation. In *Eighth International Joint Conference on Artificial Intelligence*, W. Kaufman (Los Altos CA), 1983, pp. 882-891.

A UNIVERSAL DOMAIN TECHNIQUE FOR PROFINITE POSETS

Carl A. Gunter
Department of Computer Science
Carnegie-Mellon University
Pittsburgh, Pennsylvania 15213

Abstract. We introduce a category of what we call *profinite domains*. This category of domains differs from most of the familiar ones in having a categorical coproduct as well as being cartesian closed. Study of these domains is carried out through the use of an equivalent category of pre-orders in a manner similar to the information systems approach advocated by Dana Scott and others. A class of universal profinite domains is defined and used to derive sufficient conditions for the profinite solution of domain equations involving continuous functors. Necessary conditions for the existence of such solutions are also given and used to derive results about solutions of some important equations. A new universal bounded complete domain is also demonstrated using a functor which has bounded complete domains as its fixed points.

1. INTRODUCTION.

For our purposes a domain equation has the form $X \cong F(X)$ where F is an operator on a class of semantic domains (typically, F is an endofunctor on a category $\mathbf{C}$). The solution of such equations is a major component of the Scott-Strachey approach to programming language semantics. The reader is refered to [Stoy 1977] or any other reference on denotational semantics for an explanation of how such equations arise. Techniques for solving them have been worked out for specific categories and in rather general category-theoretic settings as well. Computability considerations have been successfully incorporated into many of these treatments. All of these approaches use one of three techniques. The most general is the inverse limit construction used by Scott [1972] to solve the domain equation $D \cong [D \to D]$ (where $[D \to D]$ is the function space of D). The second uses the Tarski Fixed Point Theorem, which says: if D is a poset with least upper bounds for ω-chains and a least element then any function $f : D \to D$ which preserves such lub's has a least fixed point. The third—which is introduced in [MacQueen *et. al.* 1984]—uses the Banach Fixed Point Theorem, which says: a uniformly contractive function $f : X \to X$ on a non-empty complete metric space X has a unique fixed point. These last two approaches employ what is frequently called a "universal" domain to associate with the operator F a lub preserving or contractive map.

In this paper we examine the problems involved in obtaining solutions to equations over the category of profinite domains which will be defined below. This is a rather natural, and in a sense inevitable, category which contains **SFP** (see [Plotkin 1976]) as a full sub-category. It has the unusual property of being bicartesian closed, *i.e.* it is cartesian closed and has a coproduct. Such categories have a rich type structure and form models of the typed λ-calculus [Lambek and Scott 1984]. Obtaining profinite solutions for domain equations involving the coproduct can be problematic, however. For example, the equation $D \cong 1 + [D \to D]$ where 1 is the one point domain has no profinite solution. We provide a necessary condition which, in effect, reduces the problem of solving such an equation over the profinite domains to one of getting a finite poset which solves a related equation. This condition can be proved sufficient by a variant of the second method described above. Since no single (projection) universal domain for the profinites exists we derive an infinite class of domains which are "sufficiently universal" to apply the method. As a secondary theme we show how to extend the neighborhood or information system approach to one which applies to categories (such as **SFP**) which are larger than the one considered in [Scott 1981a, 1982].

Section two gives some of the basic definitions and explains the equivalence defined by the ideal completion functor. In section three the category of Plotkin orders is introduced and some of its closure properties discussed. Section four discusses normal substructures and defines the category of profinite domains. We also state a result which shows that this category is "maximal" with respect to the conditions of ω-algebraicity and cartesian closure. Section five derives universal domains and in section six these domains are used to show existence of solutions for a significant class of equations. Section six also contains discussion of several specific domain equations and their solutions. Many details and all proofs (including some non-trivial ones) have been excluded due to space considerations. The reader is refered to [Gunter 1985] for details.

2. PRE-ORDERS AND ALGEBRAIC DCPO'S.

A *pre-order* is a pair $\langle A, \vdash_A \rangle$ where $\vdash_A$ is a binary relation which is reflexive and transitive. It is intended that the "larger" element is the one on the left side of the turnstile. Note that $A = \emptyset$ is allowed. To conserve notation we write $A = \langle A, \vdash_A \rangle$ and when A is clear from context the subscript is dropped. A set $S \subseteq A$ is *bounded* if there is an $X \in A$ such that $X \vdash Y$ for every $Y \in S$. Such an X is called a *bound* for S and we write $X \vdash S$. Trivially, any $X \in A$ is a bound for the empty set. A subset $M \subseteq A$ of a pre-order A is *directed* if every finite subset of M has a bound in M. Note, in particular, that every directed set is non-empty.

Definition: An *approximable relation* $f : A \to B$ is a subset of $A \times B$ which satisfies the following axioms for any $X, X' \in A$ and $Y, Y' \in B$:

1. for every $X \in A$ there is a $Y \in A$ such that $X\, f\, Y$;
2. if $X\, f\, Y$ and $X\, f\, Y'$ then there is a $Z \in B$ such that $X\, f\, Z$ and $Z \vdash_B Y, Y'$;
3. if $X \vdash_A X'\, f\, Y' \vdash_B Y$ then $X\, f\, Y$. □

Let $g : A \to B$ and $f : B \to C$ be approximable relations. We define a binary relation $f \circ g$

on $A \times C$ as follows. For each $X \in A$ and $Z \in C$, $X\ (f \circ g)\ Z$ if and only if there is a $Y \in B$ such that $X\ g\ Y$ and $Y\ f\ Z$. Also, for each pre-order A define $\mathrm{id}_A = \vdash_A$. It is easy to verify that $f \circ g$ and id_A are approximable relations. With this composition and identity relation the class of pre-orders and approximable relations form a category which we call **PO**. We let $\mathbf{PO}(A, B)$ be the set of approximable relations on $A \times B$. The approximable relations are partially ordered by set theoretic inclusion.

For pre-orders A and B define the *product pre-order* $A \times B$ to have the coordinatewise ordering. It is easy to show that $\times$ is a categorical product for **PO**. If we take 1 to be the single element pre-order, then for each pre-order A there is a unique approximable relation $1_A : A \to 1$. Thus the pre-orders and approximable relations form a cartesian category with terminal object 1. Moreover, the empty poset 0, is initial in this category, *i.e.* for any object A there is a unique arrow $0_A : 0 \to A$. This 0_A is the "empty relation" and it is trivially approximable. For pre-orders A and B, the *coproduct pre-order* $\langle A + B, \vdash_{A+B} \rangle$ is defined by taking the disjoint union of A and B together with the disjoint union of their respective orders. This, unlike the $+$ operators discussed in many references on domain theory such as [Stoy 1977] or [Scott 1982] is the *categorical* coproduct in **PO**. This shows that **PO** is bicartesian, *i.e.* it has coproduct and initial object as well as product and terminal object.

A *poset* $\langle D, \sqsubseteq \rangle$ (or *partially ordered set*) is a pre-order that is anti-symmetric, *i.e.* if $x \sqsubseteq y$ and $y \sqsubseteq x$ then $x = y$. Using the established convention we write the "larger" element on the right side of the $\sqsubseteq$ symbol. If $x \sqsubseteq y$ then it is sometimes convenient to write $y \sqsupseteq x$. It is frequently desirable to transfer a property of pre-orders to a property of posets and conversely. This is usually possible because pre-orders and posets are closely connected. First of all, every pre-order is isomorphic (in the category with approximable relations as arrows) to a poset. To see this, let $\langle A, \vdash \rangle$ be a pre-order. Define an equivalence relation $\sim$ on A by letting $X \sim Y$ if and only if $X \vdash Y$ and $Y \vdash X$. For each X, let $\tilde{X} = \{Y \in A \,|\, X \sim Y\}$ and set $\tilde{A} = \{\tilde{X} \,|\, X \in A\}$. If we define a binary relation $\sqsupseteq$ on A by letting $\tilde{X} \sqsupseteq \tilde{Y}$ if and only if $X \vdash Y$, then it is easy to check that $\langle \tilde{A}, \sqsubseteq \rangle$ is a poset and the approximable relation $f : \tilde{A} \to A$ given by $\tilde{X}\ f\ Y$ if and only if $X \vdash Y$ is an isomorphism. In addition, posets are isomorphic in the category with approximable relations as arrows if and only if they are isomorphic in the more familiar category with monotone maps as arrows. We can therefore write $A \cong B$ for pre-orders A and B without fear of ambiguity.

A poset $\langle D, \sqsubseteq \rangle$ is said to be a *directed complete* if every directed subset $M \subseteq D$ has a least upper bound $\bigsqcup M \in D$. A monotone function $f : D \to E$ between dcpo's D and E is *continuous* if for every directed set $M \subseteq D$, $\bigsqcup f(M) = f(\bigsqcup M)$. The dcpo's and continuous functions form a category; with a slight over-loading of notation we let $\mathrm{id}_D : D \to D$ denote the identity function. Let $[D \to E]$ be the set of continuous functions from D to E. We order $[D \to E]$ by setting $f \sqsubseteq g$ if for every $x \in D$, $f(x) \sqsubseteq g(x)$. It is easy to check that $[D \to E]$ is itself a dcpo. This definition of dcpo's differs from most other definitions in the literature. We do not require that a dcpo have a least element; indeed, we do not require a dcpo to be non-empty. Much of the usual theory of dcpo's goes through for these "bottomless" cases but there are some non-trivial differences. For example, a continuous function $f : D \to D$ on a dcpo need not have a fixed point. (However, if for some $x \in D$, $x \sqsubseteq f(x)$ then there is a least $y \sqsupseteq x$ such that $f(y) = y$.)

Let D be a dcpo. An element $x \in D$ is *finite* (or compact) if whenever $x \sqsubseteq \bigsqcup M$ for a directed set M, there is a $y \in M$ such that $x \sqsubseteq y$. Let $\mathbf{B}[D]$ denote the set of finite elements of a dcpo D. We say that D is *algebraic* if for every $x \in D$, the set $M = \{x_0 \in \mathbf{B}[D] \mid x_0 \sqsubseteq x\}$ is directed and $\bigsqcup M = x$. In other words, in an algebraic dcpo every element is the limit of its finite approximations. Let **ALG** be the category of algebraic dcpo's and continuous arrows. Suppose $\langle A, \vdash \rangle$ is a pre-order. An *ideal* over A is a directed subset $x \subseteq A$ such that if $X \vdash Y$ and $X \in x$ then $Y \in x$. The *ideal completion* of A is the partial ordering, $\langle |A|, \subseteq \rangle$, of the ideals of A by set-theoretic inclusion. If $X \in A$ then the *principal ideal generated by* X is the set $\downarrow X = \{Y \in A \mid X \vdash Y\}$.

Theorem 1: *If A is a pre-order, then $|A|$ is an algebraic dcpo with $\mathbf{B}[|A|] = \{\downarrow X \mid X \in A\} \cong A$. Moreover, every algebraic dcpo D is representable in this way because $D \cong |\mathbf{B}[D]|$.* □

Definition: If A and B are pre-orders and $f : A \to B$ is an approximable relation then define a function $|f| : |A| \to |B|$ by $|f|(x) = \{Y \mid X \; f \; Y \text{ for some } X \in x\}$. □

It is possible to show that the passage $A \mapsto |A|$, $f \mapsto |f|$ is a functor which defines an equivalence between **PO** and **ALG**. This equivalence extends to several interesting subcategories as well. If $\mathcal{K}$ is a class of pre-orders then let $\mathbf{Id}_{\mathcal{K}}$ be the category which has as objects algebraic dcpo's D such that $\mathbf{B}[D]$ is isomorphic to a pre-order in $\mathcal{K}$ and has as arrows continuous functions. If $\mathcal{K}$ is the class of upper semi-lattices then $\mathbf{Id}_{\mathcal{K}}$ is the category of algebraic lattices. Let us say that a pre-order A is *coherent* if whenever a finite $u \subseteq A$ is pair-wise bounded then it has a least upper bound. If $\mathcal{K}$ is the class of coherent pre-orders then it is possible to show that $\mathbf{Id}_{\mathcal{K}}$ is the category of coherent algebraic dcpo's. A (non-empty) pre-order is *bounded complete* if each of its finite bounded subsets has a least upper bound. Again, if $\mathcal{K}$ is the class of bounded complete pre-orders then it is possible to show that $\mathbf{Id}_{\mathcal{K}}$ is the category of bounded complete dcpo's. Each of these three categories is cartesian closed but none of them has a categorical coproduct. Note also that there is an equivalence between the category of countable pre-orders and the category of countably based algebraic dcpo's.

3. PLOTKIN ORDERS.

In this section we introduce the category of *Plotkin orders* which will be our primary technical tool for studying the profinite domains. Plotkin orders are less abstract than profinite domains and in many ways they are easier to work with. For example, Smyth [1983] proves many facts about strongly algebraic domains by taking a detailed look at the particular class of Plotkin orders which correspond to such domains via ideal completion. Their use makes some arguments more algebraic and simplifies the definitions of some of the functors such as the powerdomains (which we cannot discuss here because of space considerations).

Definition: Suppose A is a pre-order and $S \subseteq A$. We say that S is *normal* in A and write $S \lhd A$ if for every $X \in A$ the set $S \cap \downarrow X$ is directed. □

Note, incidently, that if $S \lhd A$ and $X \in A$ then $X \vdash \emptyset$ and $\emptyset \subseteq S$, so there is an $X' \in S$ such that $X \vdash X'$. Let u be a subset of A. A set u' of upper bounds of u is said to be *complete* if whenever $X \vdash u$, there is an $X' \in u'$ such that $X \vdash X'$. We summarize some more of the properties of the $\lhd$ relation in the following:

Lemma 2: *Let A, B, C be pre-orders.*

1. *Suppose $A \subseteq B$. Then $A \lhd B$ if and only if for every $u \subseteq A$ there is a set $u' \subseteq A$ of upper bounds for u which is complete for u in B.*
2. *If $A \lhd B \lhd C$ then $A \lhd C$.*
3. *If $A \subseteq B \subseteq C$ and $A \lhd C$ then $A \lhd B$.* □

Definition: A pre-order A is a *Plotkin order* if for every finite $u \subseteq A$, there is a finite $B \supseteq u$ such that $B \lhd A$. The category of Plotkin orders with approximable relations will be denoted by **PLT**. □

Intuitively, if $S \lhd A$ then S offers a directed approximation to every element of A. Thus one might think of S as itself an approximation to A. A pre-order A is a Plotkin order just in case it can be built up as a union of finite approximations. Obviously any finite pre-order is a Plotkin order. There are a couple of similar conditions on pre-orders which are frequently useful. An upper bound $X \vdash u$ of u is *minimal* if for each Y, $X \vdash Y \vdash u$ implies $X \sim Y$. If every finite subset of A has a complete set of minimal upper bounds then we say that A has the *(weak) minimal upper bounds property* (or "property m"). If every finite subset of A has a finite complete set of minimal upper bounds then we say that A has the *strong* minimal upper bounds property (or "property M"). Any pre-order which has property M and no ascending chains is a Plotkin order. A proof of this uses König's lemma and can be found in [Smyth 1983]. Let A be a poset and suppose $u \subseteq A$ is finite. If a complete set u' of upper bounds of u is finite then it contains a complete set of minimal upper bounds. If A is a Plotkin order then there is a finite $B \lhd A$ with $u \subseteq B$. Hence, by Lemma 2, u has a finite set of minimal upper bounds in A. It follows, therefore, that a Plotkin order has property M. It is not true, however, that every pre-order having property M is a Plotkin order. A counter-example is illustrated in Figure 1a. Figures 1b and 1c illustrate two other ways in which a poset can fail to be a Plotkin order (by failing to have property M).

It is often easier to work with Plotkin orders which are *posets*. Little is lost by this restriction, since every pre-order is isomorphic (in the category with approximable relations as arrows) to a poset $\tilde{A}$ and it is possible to show that A is a Plotkin order if and only if $\tilde{A}$ is a Plotkin poset. We might have taken the Plotkin posets as our fundamental notion but this would complicate

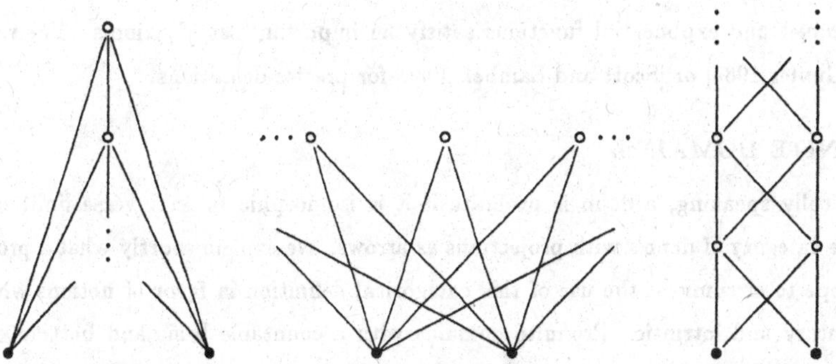

Figure 1: Posets that are not Plotkin orders.

the definitions of some of the functors, and in any event would narrow the scope of discussion unnecessarily. We will, however, sometimes restrict attention to posets in order to simplify the discussion.

Definition: Let A and B be pre-orders. We define the *exponential pre-order* $\langle B^A, \vdash_{B^A}\rangle$ as follows:

1. $p \in B^A$ if and only if p is a finite non-empty subset of $A \times B$ such that for every $Z \in A$, the set $\{(X,Y) \in p \mid Z \vdash_A X\}$ has a maximum with respect to the ordering on $A \times B$.
2. $p \vdash_{B^A} q$ if and only if for every $(X,Y) \in q$ there is a pair $(X',Y') \in p$ such that $X \vdash_A X'$ and $Y' \vdash_B Y$. □

Perhaps it is more intuitive to understand B^A in terms of the familiar concept of a *step function*. If $p \in B^A$, define $\text{step}_p : \tilde{A} \to \tilde{B}$ by $\text{step}_p(\tilde{Z}) = \max\{\tilde{Y} \mid Z \vdash X \text{ and } (X,Y) \in p\}$. Then step_p is a monotone function and for each $p, q \in B^A$, $\text{step}_p \sqsupseteq \text{step}_q$ if and only if $p \vdash_{B^A} q$.

Definition: Let us say that a functor $F : \mathbf{PO} \to \mathbf{PO}$ is *monotone* if for every pair of pre-orders $A \lhd B$, we have $F(A) \lhd F(B)$. A monotone functor is *continuous* if for every pre-order A and directed set $\mathfrak{I}$ of normal substructures of A, we have $F(A) = \bigcup\{F(B) \mid B \in \mathfrak{I}\}$. □

(Warning: this is not quite the same as the standard categorical definition of functor continuity. To be strictly correct more needs to be said about the action of the functor F on the arrows of the category.)

Theorem 3: *If $F : \mathbf{PO} \to \mathbf{PO}$ is a continuous functor and $F(A)$ is finite whenever A is finite then F is an endofunctor on* **PLT**, *i.e. $F(A)$ is a Plotkin order whenever A is a Plotkin order.* □

The definition and theorem can be extended in a straight-forward way to include multi-functors $F : \mathbf{PO}^n \to \mathbf{PO}$. We have the following application.

Corollary 4: *The product, coproduct and exponential functors are continuous and send finite pre-orders to finite pre-orders. Hence they are endofunctors on* **PLT**. □

From this it is possible to show that **PLT** is bicartesian closed. Roughly speaking this means that the product and exponential functions satisfy an important set of axioms. The reader is refered to [Gunter 1985] or [Scott and Lambek 1985] for precise definitions.

4. PROFINITE DOMAINS.

Categorically speaking, a dcpo is profinite if it is isomorphic to an inverse limit of finite posets in the category of dcpo's with projections as arrows. We explain shortly what a projection is but we hope to circumvent the use of this categorical definition in favor of notions which are more elementary and intrinsic. Profinite domains with a countable basis and bottom element are called *strongly algebraic* domains. With continuous functions as arrows they form a cartesian closed category called **SFP** which was introduced by Gordon Plotkin [1976]. Plotkin needed a class of semantic domains closed under the powerdomain operation which he used to provide a denotational semantics for a particular multiprocessing language. To the reader familiar with strongly algebraic domains, a countably based profinite domain is a poset which is isomorphic to a Scott compact open subset of a strongly algebraic domain. In other words, a poset D is ω-profinite if and only if there is a strongly algebraic poset E and a finite set $u \subseteq \mathbf{B}[E]$ such that $E \cong \{x \in D \mid x \sqsupseteq y \text{ for some } y \in u\}$. Thus, if D is ω-profinite then the poset $D_\perp$ (called the *lift* of D) obtained by attaching a least element $\perp$ to D is strongly algebraic. However, it is *not* true, in general, that if $D_\perp$ is strongly algebraic then D is ω-profinite.

Before we give a proper definition of what a profinite domain is, we mention the notion of a projection. Let D and E be dcpo's. A *projection-embedding pair* is a pair $\langle p, q\rangle$ of continuous maps $p : E \to D$ and $q : D \to E$ such that $p \circ q = \mathrm{id}_D$ and $q \circ p \sqsubseteq \mathrm{id}_E$. The function p is the projection and q is the embedding. We abbreviate by writing $\langle p, q\rangle : E \xrightarrow{\mathrm{pe}} D$. The following theorem describes the relationship between projection-embedding pairs and normal substructures (and generalizes the theory exposited in [Scott 1981b]). Let A and B be pre-orders. Write $A \trianglelefteq B$ if there is an $A' \triangleleft B$ such that $A \cong A'$.

Theorem 5: *Suppose $A \triangleleft B$ and $\vdash$ is the order relation on $B \times B$. If $\mathrm{p} = (B \times A) \cap \vdash$ and $\mathrm{q} = (A \times B) \cap \vdash$ then p, q are approximable relations, $\mathrm{p} \circ \mathrm{q} = \mathrm{id}_A$ and $\mathrm{q} \circ \mathrm{p} \subseteq \mathrm{id}_B$. In other words $\langle |\mathrm{p}|, |\mathrm{q}|\rangle : |B| \xrightarrow{\mathrm{pe}} |A|$. Conversely, if $\langle |\mathrm{p}|, |\mathrm{q}|\rangle : |B| \xrightarrow{\mathrm{pe}} |A|$ for approximable relations p and q then $A \trianglelefteq B$. In particular, $A \cong \{Y \in B \mid Y\ (\mathrm{q} \circ \mathrm{p})\ Y\} \triangleleft B$.* □

We will use the theorem in the next section when we discuss universal domains.

Definition: If A is a poset then we denote by $N(A)$ the set of normal substructures of A, ordered by set inclusion. □

Proposition 6: *Let A be a poset. Then $N(A)$ is a dcpo. If A has property* m *then $N(A)$ has a least element called the root of A. It is given by the equation $\mathrm{rt}(A) = \bigcap\{B \mid B \triangleleft A\}$.* □

Actually, if A has property m then $N(A)$ is an algebraic lattice. And if A is a Plotkin poset then $N(A)$ is a locally finite algebraic lattice; that is, $\{x_0 \in \mathbf{B}[N(A)] \mid x_0 \sqsubseteq x\}$ is finite for each

$x \in \mathbf{B}[N(A)]$.

Lemma 7: *If $i : A \trianglelefteq B$ then $N(i) : N(A) \to N(B)$ given by $N(i)(A') = \{i(X) \mid X \in A'\}$ is continuous.* □

Definition: Let D be a dcpo and let M be the set of continuous functions $p : D \to D$ such that $p = p \circ p \sqsubseteq \mathrm{id}_D$ and $im(p)$ is finite. Then D is *profinite* if M is directed and $\bigsqcup M = \mathrm{id}_D$. □

Theorem 8: *A dcpo D is profinite if and only if D is algebraic and* $\mathbf{B}[D]$ *is a Plotkin order. So the cateogry of profinite domains and continuous functions is equivalent to* **PLT**. *Similarly, the category of countably based profinite domains is equivalent to the category* ω**PLT** *of countable Plotkin orders.* □

The proof uses Theorem 5. Smyth [1983] shows that an ω-algebraic dcpo D with a least element is strongly algebraic if and only if $[D \to D]$ is ω-algebraic. This shows that **SFP** is the largest cartesian closed (full) sub-category of the ω-algebraic dcpo's with bottoms. A proof similar to Smyth's can be used to show the following:

Theorem 9: *If D and $[D \to D]$ are ω-algebraic then D and $[D \to D]$ are ω-profinite.* □

A rather obvious consequence of the theorem is that the largest cartesian closed category of (bottomless) ω-algebraic dcpo's has coproducts—a property which **SFP** does not have. In fact there are a great many interesting bicartesian closed proper sub-categories of the profinite domains. Scott has observed that a cartesian closed category **C** of dcpo's with bottom elements induces a bicartesian closed category **C′** as follows. The arrows of **C′** are continuous functions and a dcpo D is an object of **C′** if $D \cong D_1 + \cdots + D_n$ for some n and objects $D_1, \ldots, D_n$ of **C**. That **C′** is bicartesian closed is proved by using the natural isomorphisms invloving $+, \times, \to$ which hold for dcpo's and noting that the equation $(E+F)^D \cong E^D + F^D$ holds when D is a dcpo with a least element. The profinite domains do not arise in this way though; it is not hard to see that sums of strongly algebraic domains are just ω-profinite domains with discrete roots.

5. UNIVERSAL DOMAINS.

We now investigate the mathematical problem of the existence of a profinite universal domain. In the literature there are three primary examples of universal domains. The simplest is the so-called *graph model* $\mathcal{P}\omega$ which is the algebraic lattice of subsets of ω ordered by set inclusion. It receives a detailed study in [Scott 1976] where it is proved that any countably based algebraic lattice is a retract of $\mathcal{P}\omega$. Some domain theorists felt, however, that for applications in denotational semantics of programming languages it would be easier to use a class which did not require the existence of a largest (top) element. Plotkin [1978] showed that the poset T^ω of functions from ω into the lift T of the two point set is universal in the sense that every coherent ω-algebraic dcpo is a retract of T^ω. Since T^ω is itself algebraic and coherent this provided a universal domain for a class of algebraic dcpo's that included the algebraic lattices but contained also certain desired dcpo's without tops. In [Scott 1981a, 1981b, and 1982] yet a third universal domain $\mathcal{U}$ is discussed. Although $\mathcal{U}$ is harder to understand than $\mathcal{P}\omega$ or $\mathcal{T}^\omega$ it has the advantage of having every consistently complete ω-algebraic dcpo as a *projection* (not just as a retract).

Below, we outline a technique for getting universal domains for certain classes of ω-profinite domains. If A is a poset with property m then we remarked in Lemma 6 that $\mathrm{rt}(A)$ is the least element in $N(A)$. Now, if A and B are Plotkin posets and $A \trianglelefteq B$ then $\mathrm{rt}(A) \cong \mathrm{rt}(B)$ so by Theorem 5 no profinite domain can be a continuous projection of a profinite domain that has a different root. Hence there cannot be a projection universal ω-profinite domain. We prove the next best thing: for each finite poset $A \cong \mathrm{rt}(A)$ there is a countable Plotkin poset V_A such that if B is a countable Plotkin poset with $\mathrm{rt}(B) \cong A$ then $B \trianglelefteq V_A$. We offer an outline of the construction below. Kamimura and Tang [1984] use a different approach to get a retraction universal model for the ω-profinite domains having bottoms. Their model, like $\mathcal{P}\omega$ and $\mathcal{T}^\omega$, is locally finite but is somewhat less natural than either of those models. In the opinion of the author, however, the construction described below does the most to reveal the fundamental *idea* that gives the existence result and yields the most detailed description of the model being built. (We are even able to draw a partial picture of it!) We begin by stating an interesting structure theorem for Plotkin posets.

Theorem 10: *(Enumeration) If A is a countable Plotkin poset then there is an enumeration $X_0, X_1, \ldots$ of A such that for each n,* $\mathrm{rt}(A) \cup \{X_i \mid i < n\} \lhd A$. □

Definition: Let $\langle A, \sqsubseteq\rangle$ be a poset. For each $X \in A$, let $\mathbf{X}$ be a constant symbol naming X. Let $\preceq$ be a binary relation symbol which is interpreted by $\sqsubseteq$. A *diagram type* over A is a set Γ of inequalities and negations of inequalities between constant symbols and a variable v, *i.e.* formulas of the form $\mathrm{v} \preceq \mathbf{X}$, $\mathrm{v} \not\preceq \mathbf{X}$, $\mathbf{X} \preceq \mathrm{v}$, or $\mathbf{X} \not\preceq \mathrm{v}$, where $X \in A$. If $A \subseteq B$ and $Z \in B$ then the *diagram type of Z over A* is the set of all such equations (using constant symbols for elements of A) that hold when v is given the value Z and $\preceq$ is interpreted as the order relation on B. A diagram type Γ over A is said to be *realized* in B by Z if Γ is a subset of the diagram type of Z over A. A diagram type Γ over a poset A is said to be *normal* if there is a poset B with $A \lhd B$ such that Γ is realized in B. □

Lemma 11: *If Γ is a normal type over a finite poset B and $B \lhd A$ then there is a finite poset A_1 such that $A \lhd A_1$ and Γ is realized by some $Z \in A_1$ such that* $B \cup \{Z\} \lhd A_1$. □

Lemma 12: *Let A be a finite poset. Then there is a finite poset A^+ such that $A \lhd A^+$ and for every subspace $B \lhd A$ and normal type Γ over B, there is a $Z \in A^+$ such that Z realizes Γ and* $B \cup \{Z\} \lhd A^+$. □

Theorem 13: *Let V be a countable Plotkin poset. Suppose that for every finite $A \lhd V$ and normal type Γ over A, there is a realization Z for Γ such that $A \cup \{Z\} \lhd V$. If B is a countable Plotkin order such that* $\mathrm{rt}(B) \cong \mathrm{rt}(V)$ *then* $B \trianglelefteq V$. □

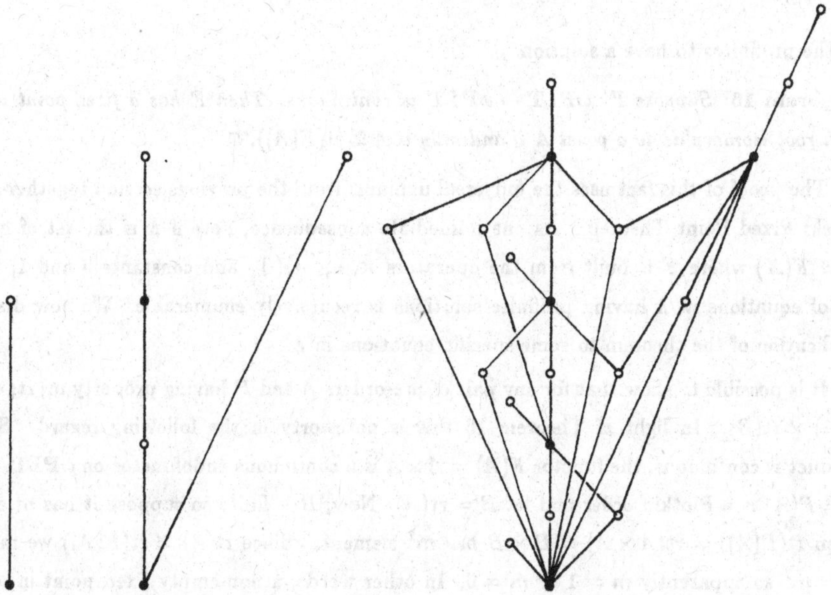

1^+ 1^{++} 1^{+++}

Figure 2: Construction of 1^*.

Corollary 14: ***Let A be a finite poset such that $A \cong \mathrm{rt}(A)$. There is a Plotkin poset A^* such that whenever B is a countable Plotkin order with $\mathrm{rt}(B) \cong A$, then $B \unlhd A^*$.*** □

It is possible to get the A^+ in Lemma 12 by explicit construction. This helps in picturing the universal domain as the limit of the posets $A \unlhd A^+ \unlhd A^{++} \unlhd \cdots$. Figure 2 illustrates the first three stages in the construction of the universal domain with a trivial root.

Before ending the section we mention the *join completion* functor $\mathcal{J}$. For a pre-order A, $\mathcal{J}(A) = \{u \subseteq A \mid u$ is finite and bounded$\}$ and if $u, v \in \mathcal{J}(A)$ then: $u \vdash_{\mathcal{J}(A)} v$ iff $\forall X.\ X \vdash_A u \Rightarrow X \vdash_A v$. The following proposition lists some of the properties of $\mathcal{J}$.

Proposition 15: ***$\mathcal{J}$ is continuous and $\mathcal{J}(A)$ is bounded complete for every non-empty A. Moreover, if A is bounded complete then $A \cong \mathcal{J}(A)$.*** □

The reason for defining $\mathcal{J}$ here in the section on universal domains is this. Suppose A is countable and bounded complete. Then $A \unlhd 1^*$ by Theorem 14. Hence by Proposition 15, $A \cong \mathcal{J}(A) \unlhd \mathcal{J}(1^*)$. This shows that $|\mathcal{J}(1^*)|$ is projection universal for the bounded complete ω-algebraic dcpo's. Although $\mathcal{J}(1^*)$ does not have atoms, adjoining a top element does not produce a boolean algebra, so $|\mathcal{J}(1^*)|$ is not isomorphic to $\mathcal{U}$.

6. FIXED POINTS OF FUNCTORS.

The following theorem states necessary and sufficient conditions for a continuous endofunctor

on the profinites to have a solution.

Theorem 16: *Suppose $F : \omega\mathbf{PLT} \to \omega\mathbf{PLT}$ is continuous. Then F has a fixed point in $\omega\mathbf{PLT}$ with root isomorphic to a poset A if and only if $A \cong \mathrm{rt}(F(A))$.* □

The proof of this fact uses the universal domains from the previous section together with the Tarski Fixed Point Theorem. As one immediate consequence, note if $\mathbf{A}$ is the set of equations $X \cong F(X)$ where F is built from the operators $\times, +, \to, (\cdot)_\perp$ and constants 0 and 1, then the set of equations in $\mathbf{A}$ having profinite solutions is recursively enumerable. We now discuss the application of the theorem to some specific equations in $\mathbf{A}$.

It is possible to show that for any pair of pre-orders A and B having property m, $\mathrm{rt}(A \times B) = \mathrm{rt}(A) \times \mathrm{rt}(B)$. In light of Theorem 16 this is noteworty in the following regard. Since the product is continuous, the functor $F(A) = A \times A$ is a continuous endofunctor on $\omega\mathbf{PLT}$. Suppose $A \cong F(A)$ is a Plotkin order and let $B = \mathrm{rt}(A)$. Now, B is finite so suppose it has m elements. Then $\mathrm{rt}(F(A)) = \mathrm{rt}(A \times A) = B \times B$ has m^2 elements. Since $\mathrm{rt}(A) \cong \mathrm{rt}(F(A))$ we must have $m = m^2$ so apparently $m = 1$ or $m = 0$. In other words, a non-empty fixed point in $\omega\mathbf{PLT}$ of the equation $A \cong F(A)$ must have a least element. This result carries over to the ω-profinite domains, because an ω-profinite solution of the equation $D \cong D \times D$ gives rise to the solution $\mathbf{B}[D] \cong \mathbf{B}[D] \times \mathbf{B}[D]$ in $\omega\mathbf{PLT}$. A similar situation occurs with the diagonal of the coproduct. One can show that if A and B have property m then $\mathrm{rt}(A + B) = \mathrm{rt}(A) + \mathrm{rt}(B)$. Hence the only ω-profinite solution to the equation $D \cong D + D$ is the initial object 0. The diagonal of the function space functor, $F(A) = A^A$ is more problematic, however, because it is *not* true in general that $\mathrm{rt}(B^A) \cong \mathrm{rt}(B)^{\mathrm{rt}(A)}$. Nevertheless, it is possible to show that a finite poset A satisfies $A \cong \mathrm{rt}([A \to A])$ if and only if $A \cong 1$. This shows that a fixed point of the functor F in $\omega\mathbf{PLT}$ must have a least element. Again, this can be used to show that if $D \cong [D \to D]$ is ω-profinite and non-empty then D has a least element. Using Theorem 9 we get the following:

Proposition 17: *If $D \cong [D \to D]$ is ω-algebraic (where the possibility that D has no bottom element is allowed) then it is strongly algebraic.* □

ACKNOWLEDGEMENTS.

This research was carried out under the direction of Dana Scott with funding provided by Carnegie-Mellon University. The author thanks Jon Barwise for introducing him to Scott's work on domain theory. Thanks are also owed to Rick Statman and Gordon Plotkin for helpful conversations and correspondence.

REFERENCES.

GUNTER, C.

1985 **Profinite Solutions for Recursive Domain Equations.** Doctoral Dissertation, University of Wisconsin, Madison, 1985, 181 pp.

KAMIMURA, T. and TANG, A.

1984 *Finitely Continuous Posets.* Technical Report, no. TR-84-1, University of Kansas, 1984, 26 pp.

LAMBEK, J. and SCOTT, P.J.

1984 **Introduction to Higher-Order Categorical Logic** Pre-print, 1984, 200+ pp.

MACQUEEN, D., PLOTKIN, G. D. and SETHI, R.

1984 *An ideal model for recursive polymorhpic types.* In: **Eleventh Symposium on Principles of Programming Languages,** edited by K. Kennedy. Association for Computing Machinery, 1984, pp. 165–174.

PLOTKIN, G. D.

1976 *A powerdomain construction.* **SIAM Journal of Computing,** vol. 5 (1976), pp. 452–487.

1978 *T^{ω} as a universal domain.* **Journal of Computer System Sciences,** vol. 17 (1978b), pp. 209–236.

SCOTT, D. S.

1972 *Continuous Lattices.* In: **Toposes, Algebraic Geometry and Logic,** edited by F. W. Lawvere. **Lecture Notes in Mathematics,** vol. 274, Springer-Verlag, 1972, pp. 97-136.

1976 *Data types as lattices.* **SIAM Journal of Computing,** vol. 5 (1976), pp. 522–587.

1981a *Lectures on a mathematical theory of computation.* Technical Report, no. PRG-19, Oxford University Computing Laboratory, 1981a, 148 pp.

1981b *Some ordered sets in computer science.* In: **Ordered Sets,** edited by I. Rival. D. Reidel Publishing Company, 1981b, pp. 677–718.

1982 *Domains for denotational semantics.* In: **ICALP 82,** edited by M. Nielsen, E. M. Schmidt. **Lecture Notes in Computer Science,** vol. 140, Springer-Verlag, 1982, pp. 577–613.

SMYTH, M. B.

1983 *The largest cartesian closed category of domains.* **Theoretical Computer Science,** vol. 27 (1983), pp. 109–119.

STOY, J. E.

1977 **Denotational Semantics: The Scott-Strachey Approach to Programming Language Theory.** M.I.T. Press, 1977, 414 pp.

A SIMPLE PROOF OF THE SKOLEM-MAHLER-LECH THEOREM

G. HANSEL
Universite de Haute-Normandie
Laboratoire d'Informatique
BP 67, 76130 MONT-Saint-AIGNAN

INTRODUCTION

In [5], T. Skolem proved the following theorem : if $S(z)=\sum_{n \in N} s_n z^n$ is a rational series whose coefficients belong to the field Q of the rational numbers, then $\{n \in N / s_n = 0\}$ is an ultimately periodic subset of N. Skolem's proof uses the properties of analytic functions in p-adic fields.

Then K. Mahler [3] extended Skolem's theorem to the fields of algebraic numbers over Q. His proof generalizes the p-adic method of Skolem and is based on the factorization of the ideals in Dedekind rings.

At last, K. Mahler [4] and C. Lech [2] extended Skolem's theorem to every commutative field with characteristic 0, either by reducing the general case to that of a field of algebraic numbers over Q (Mahler) or by a further generalization of the p-adic method (Lech).

The proofs of these different results are difficult and need thorough previous knowledge. This work aims at giving a simple proof of the general theorem. This is done in three steps : first the case of Q (section II) ; then the case of purely transcendental extensions of Q can be fairby easily reduced to the case of Q (section III) ; after that, the general case is quite immediate (section IV). As an important tool, we use the equivalence between rational and recognizable series established by M.P Schützenberger [6]. For an account of this result and more generally for the properties of rational series, see [1].

We present in this lecture only the case of Q (sections I and II).

I PRELIMINARIES.

I. 1 Recognizable series

Let K be a commutative field and $S(z)=\sum_{n\in N} s_n z^n$ a series with coefficients in K. We note $Ann(S)=\{n\in N / s_n=0\}$.

S is recognizable (over K) iff there exist a square matrix $M=(m_{ij})_{\substack{1\le i\le k\\ 1\le j\le k}}$ a line-vector $\alpha=(\alpha_i)_{1\le j\le k}$ and a column-vector $\beta=(\beta)_{1\le j\le k}$ with coefficients in K such that $s_n=\alpha M^n\beta$, n N. The triple (α,M,β) is a representation of S ; the $\alpha_i, \beta_j, m_{ij}$, $1\le i\le k$, $1\le j\le k$ are the coefficients of this representation, k is its dimension. S is a regular recognizable series iff there exists a representation (α,M,β) of S with M invertible.

M.P. Schützenberger showed [6] that a series S(z) is rational iff it is recognizable.

Following proposition is an immediate consequence of these definitions.

PROPOSITION 1 : Let K a commutative field, $S(z)=\sum_{n\in N} s_n z^n$ a series with coefficients in K. Then the following conditions are equivalent

a) S is a recognizable series (resp. a regular recognizable series) and has a representation (α,M,β) of dimension k.

b) There exist a vector space E of dimension k over the field K, a linear form α' on E, a vector $\beta'\in E$ and an endomorphism (resp. an isomorphism) $f:E\to E$ such that $s_n=\alpha'[f^n(\beta')]$, $n\in N$.

COROLLARY. Let $S(z)=\sum_{n\in N} s_n z^n$ be a recognizable series. Then there exists $m\in N$ such that the series $S_1(z)=\sum_{n\in N} s_{n+M} z^n$ is regular recognizable.

Proof. Let E,α',β', f as in Proposition 1. Since $E\supset f(E)\supset f^2(E)$... there exists $m\in N$ such that f induces an isomorphism g of $f^m(E)$ on itself. Let α'' be the restriction of α' to the subspace $f^m(E)$ and $\beta''=f^m(\beta')$.

Then for all $n\in N$, $s_{n+m}=\alpha'[f^{n+m}(\beta')]=\alpha''[g^n(\beta'')]$. g being invertible, the series $S_1(z)=\sum_{n\in N} s_{n+m}z^n$ is regular recognizable.

1. 2 Periodicity

A subset A of N is ultimately periodic (u.p) (respect. strongly ultimately periodic (s.u.p)) iff there exist two rational integers q_0 and r such that for all $q\ge q_0$, $q\in A$ if and only if $q+r\in A$ (respect. $q\in A$ if and only if $\{q+rn / n\in Z,\ q+rn\ge 0\}\subset A$).

The number r is called a period of A.

Remark 1) A is u.p. iff A is the union of a finite set and of a finite number of arithmetical progressions having the same period.

2) A subset A of N is s.u.p. with period r if and only if for all $j \in \{0,1,\dots,r-1\}$, $\{n\in N / j+rn \in A\}$ is either finite or equal to N.

The aim of the sequel is to prove the

THEOREM (Skolem-Mahler-Lech).
Let K be a commutative field with characteristic 0, $S(z)=\sum_{n\in N} s_n z^n$ a recognizable series over K.

1° If S is a regular recognizable series, then Ann(S) is a strongly ultimately periodic subset of N.

2° In all cases, Ann(S) is an ultimately periodic subset of N.

Remark : The 2) is an immediate consequence of 1° and of the corollary of Proposition 1 : if $\{n\in N/s_{n+m}=0\}$ is a u.p. set, the same is true of $\{n\in N/s_n=0\} = \mathrm{Ann}(S)$.

II RECOGNIZABLE SERIES WITH COEFFICIENTS IN Q

In this section we suppose K=Q the field of the rational numbers.

Let p be a fixed prime number. For every rational number $q\neq 0$ there exists a unique rational integer $u\in Z$ such that $q=p^u \frac{a}{b}$ $a,b\in Z$, a and b not divisible by p. We note $v(q)=u$; moreover we put $v(0)=+\infty$.

The following properties of the mapping v are easy to establish.

A1 For all $q,q' \in Q$, $v(qq')=v(q)+v(q')$

A2 For all q,q' Q, $v(q+q')\geq \inf\{v(q),v(q')\}$

A3 For all $n\in N$, $v(n!)\leq\frac{n}{p-1}$

Let now $P(x)=a_0+a_1+\dots+a_n x^n$ be a polynomial with rational coefficients.
For all $i\in N$, let $v_i(P)=\inf\{v(a_j)/j\geq i\}$ (if $i>n$, $v_i(P)=+\infty$).
From A1 and A2 follows

A4 For all $n\in N$, $v[P(n)]\geq v_0(P)$.

Lemma 1 Let P(x) be a polynomial with rational coefficients and $m\in N$. Let $R(x)=(x-m)P(x)$. Then for all $i\in N$, $v_i(P)\geq v_{i+1}(R)$.

Proof. Suppose $P(x)=a_0+a_1x+\dots+a_nx^n$ and $R(x)=b_0+b_1x+\dots+b_nx^n+b_{n+1}x^{n+1}$, a_n and $b_n\neq 0$. It readily follows that

$a_i = b_{i+1} + mb_{i+2} + m^2 b_{i+3} + \ldots + m^{m-i} b_{n+1}$, $i=0,1,\ldots,$
Using A2 we get $v(a_i) \geq v_{i+1}(R)$, $i \in N$, and then $v_i(P) \geq v_{i+1}(R)$, $i \in N$.

PROPOSITION 2 Let $(d_n)_{n \in N}$ a sequence in Z. For all $n \in N$, let us put $b_n = \sum_{i=0}^{n} \binom{n}{i} p^i d_i$. Then either $\{n \in N / b_n = 0\}$ is a finite set or $(b_n)_{n \in N}$ is the null sequence.

Proof. Let us suppose that $\{n \in N / b_n = 0\}$ is infinite and let us show that $(b_n)_{n \in N}$ is the null sequence. It is sufficient to show that for all $(q,u) \in N^2$, $v(b_q) \geq u$.

1° Let $(R_n(x))_{n \in N}$ be the sequence of polynomials defined by

$$R_n(x) = \sum_{i=0}^{n} \frac{d_i p^i}{i!} x(x-1)\ldots(x-i+1)$$

The sequence $(R_n(x))_{n \in N}$ has the following properties.

i) For all rational integers $m \leq n$, $R_n(m) = R_m(m) = b_m$.

ii) For all $i \in N$, $v_i(R_n) \geq i - \frac{i}{p-1}$: indeed if $R_n(x) = \sum_{i=0}^{n} a_i^{(n)} x^i$, then the coefficient $a_i^{(n)}$ is a linear combination with integer coefficients of the numbers $d_j \frac{p^j}{j!}$, $j \geq i$; but, using A1, A2, A3, we get $v(d_j \frac{p^j}{j!}) \geq j - v(j!) \geq j - \frac{j}{p-1} \geq i - \frac{i}{p-1}$; so, for all $i \in N$, $v(a_i^{(n)}) \geq i - \frac{i}{p-1}$ and then $v_i(R_n) \geq i - \frac{i}{p-1}$.

2° Let us fix $(q,u) \in N^2$.
Let $i \in N$ such that $i - \frac{i}{p-1} \geq u$ and let $m_1 < m_2 \ldots < m_i$ be the i first element of $\{n \in N / b_n = 0\}$. Let $n_0 = \sup\{q, m_i\}$.
By i), the polynomial $R_{n_0}(w)$ can be factorized as $R_{n_0}(x) = (x-m_1)(x-m_2)\ldots(x-m_i)P(x)$.
Then, using Lemma 1, i), ii), A1, A2, and A4 we get

$$v(b_q) = v[R_{n_0}(q)] \geq v[P(q)] \geq v_0(P) \geq v_i(R_{n_0}) \geq i - \frac{i}{p-1} \geq u.$$

So we have $v(b_q) \geq u$.

PROPOSITION 3 Let $S(z) = \sum_{n \in N} s_n z^n$ be a regular recognizable series having a representation (α, M, β) of dimension k and with integer coefficients. If p is a prime number which does not divide det M, then Ann(S) is a strongly ultimately periodic subset of N with a period $r < p^{k^2}$.

Proof. For all $n\in N$, let us denote $\bar{n}$ the class of n in the field Z/p and let $\bar{M}=(\bar{m}_{ij})$ be the matrix with elements in Z/p associated to M.
Since det $\bar{M}=\overline{\det M}\neq 0$, $\bar{M}$ is an invertible matrix over the field Z/p and then there exists a rational integer $r<p^{k^2}$ such that $\bar{M}^r=I$. Consequently, $M^r=I+pM'$, where M' is a matrix with integer elements.
Let then $j\in\{0,1,\dots,r-1\}$; for all $n\in N$, let $d_n=(\alpha M^j)(M'^n)\beta$. We get $s_{j+rn}=\alpha M^{j+rn}\beta=\alpha M^j(I+pM')^n\beta=\sum_{i=0}^{n}\binom{n}{i}p^i d_i$.

By Proposition 2, $\{n\in N/s_{j+rn}=0\}$ is either a finite set or is equal to N.
This assertion being true for all $j\in\{0,\dots,r-1\}$, $\{n\in N/s_n=0\}$ is a s.u.p. subset of N with period r (cf. I-2 Remark 2).

Corollary (Skolem [5]) Let $S(z)=\sum_{n\in N}s_n z^n$ be a recognizable series over Q.

1° If is regular, then Ann(S) is a strongly ultimately periodic subset of N.
2° In all cases, Ann(S) is a ultimately periodic subset of N.

Proof. As it was previously remarked, it suffices to establish 1°.
Let (α,M,β) be a representation of S ; the coefficients of (α,M,β) being rational numbers, for an appropriate $m\in N$, $(m\alpha,mM,m\beta)$ is a representation with integer coefficients of the series $T(z)=m^3S(z)$. T is still a regular recognizable series and Ann(S)=Ann(T). So by Proposition 3, Ann(S) is a s.u.p. subset of N.

References

[1] J. BERSTEL et C. REUTENAUER, Les séries rationnelles et leurs langages, Masson, Paris 1984.

[2] C. LECH, A note on recurring series, Arkiv for Matematik, Band 2 nr22, (1953), p. 417-421.

[3] K. MAHLER, Eine arithmetische Eigenschaft der Taylor coefficienten rationaler Funktionen Proc. Acad.Sci.Amst. 38(1935) p.51-60.

[4] K. MAHLER, On the Taylor coefficients of rational functions, Proc. Cambridge Philos. Soc. 52 (1956) p 39-48.

[5] T. SKOLEM, Skr. norske Videns Akad (1933) n°6.

[6] M.P. SCHUTZENBERGER, On the definition of a family of automata, Information and Control 4, (1961) p 245-270.

On Complete Problems for $NP \cap CoNP$

Juris Hartmanis*
Department of Computer Science
Cornell University
Ithaca, NY 14853

Neil Immerman+
Department of Computer Science
Yale University
New Haven, CT 06520

Abstract

It is not known whether complete languages exist for $NP \cap CoNP$ and Sipser has shown that there are relativizations so that $NP \cap CoNP$ has no $\leq_m^P$-complete languages. In this paper we show that $NP \cap CoNP$ has $\leq_m^P$-complete languages if and only if it has $\leq_T^P$-complete languages. Furthermore, we show that if a complete language L_0 exists for $NP \cap CoNP$ and $NP \cap CoNP \neq NP$ then the reduction of $L(N_i) \in NP \cap CoNP$ cannot be effectively computed from N_i. We extend the relativization results by exhibiting an oracle E such that $P^E \neq NP^E \cap CoNP^E \neq NP^E$ and for which there exist complete languages in the intersection. For this oracle the reduction to a complete language can be effectively computed from complementary pairs of machines (N_i, N_j) such that $L(N_i) = \overline{L(N_j)}$. On the other hand, there also exist oracles F such that $P^F \neq NP^F \cap CoNP^F \neq NP^F$ for which the intersection has complete languages, but the reductions to the complete language cannot be effectively computable from the complementary pairs of machines. In this case, the reductions can be computed from

$$(N_i,\ N_j,\ \text{Proof that } L(N_i) = \overline{L(N_j)}) \quad .$$

Introduction

It is not known whether $P \neq NP$ or $P \neq NP \cap CoNP \neq NP$. Furthermore, it is not known whether complete languages exist in $NP \cap CoNP$. In this paper we investigate the possible existence of complete languages in $NP \cap CoNP$ and study their properties, should they exist.

Sipser [Si] has shown that there exists an oracle C such that $P^C \neq NP^C \cap CoNP^C \neq NP^C$ and that $NP^C \cap CoNP^C$ has no complete languages under many-one polynomial time reductions ($\leq_m^P$-complete). The existence of complete languages in the intersection was shown by collapsing P and NP by the well known BGS method [BGS].

---

*Supported in part by National Science Foundation Grant DCR8301766.
+ Research supported by an NSF Postdoctoral Fellowship.

In this paper we show that there exist $\leq_m^P$-complete languages for $NP \cap CoNP$ if and only if there exist polynomial-time Turing complete languages ($\leq_T^P$-complete). This extends Sipser's result to show that for his oracle C there are neither $\leq_m^P$-complete nor $\leq_T^P$-complete languages in the intersection. Furthermore, we show that there exists an oracle E such that $P^E \neq NP^E \cap CoNP^E \neq NP^E$ for which $NP^E \cap CoNP^E$ has complete languages. At the same time, we show that if $NP \cap CoNP \neq NP$ and $NP \cap CoNP$ has complete languages, then these languages have radically different behaviour than complete languages in NP.

More precisely, let $N_1, N_2, \ldots$ be a standard enumeration for polynomial time clocked nondeterministic Turing machines, let $P_1, P_2, \ldots$ be the corresponding enumeration of deterministic polynomial time clocked machines and let $M_1, M_2, \ldots$ be a standard enumeration of Turing machines. We first show that if $NP \cap CoNP \neq NP$ then there does not exist a recursive function which can bound for all $L(N_i)$ in $NP \cap CoNP$, in the size of N_i, $|N_i|$, the size of a complementary machine N_j such that $L(N_i) = \overline{L(N_j)}$. From this result it follows that if $NP \cap CoNP \neq NP$ and there is a complete language L_0 in the intersection then the reductions of $L(N_i) \in NP \cap CoNP$ to L_0 cannot be effectively computed from N_i. As a matter of fact, the size of the reducing machines is not recursively bounded in $|N_i|$.

We observe that for the above oracle E, the reductions to the complete language L_0 can be effectively computed from complementary pairs of machines (N_i, N_j) such that $L(N_i^E) = \overline{L(N_j^E)}$.

On the other hand, this is not always the case, and we exhibit another oracle F such that $P^F \neq NP^F \cap CoNP^F \neq NP$ and L_0 is a complete for the intersection, but the reductions cannot be effectively computed from the complementary pairs (N_i, N_j) such that $L(N_i^F) = \overline{L(N_j^F)}$. The reductions can be computed from the pair of machines N_i, N_j and the proof that $L(N_i) = \overline{L(N_j)}$.

These results show that there is great logical latitude which permits different relativizations for $NP \cap CoNP$ and if $P \neq NP \cap CoNP \neq NP$ then $NP \cap CoNP$ behaves, in a strict technical sense, differently from NP with respect to complete languages: either they do not exist or the reductions are not effectively computable.

Complete Languages for $NP \cap CoNP$

We will now show that $NP \cap CoNP$ has a $\leq_T^P$-complete language if and only if it has a $\leq_m^P$-complete language.

It has been observed by Kowalczyk [Ko] that $NP \cap CoNP$ has a $\leq_m^P$-complete language if and only if there exists a recursively enumerable set of pairs of complementary machines $\{(N_{i_k}, N_{j_k}) \mid k \geq 1\}$ such that

$L(N_{i_k}) = L(\overline{N_{j_k}})$ and $\{L(N_{i_k}) \mid k \geq 1\} = NP \cap CoNP$.

Theorem 1: There exists a $\leq_T^P$-complete language in $NP \cap CoNP$ if and only if there exists a $\leq_m^P$-complete language.

Proof: If there exists a $\leq_m^P$-complete language L_0 in $NP \cap CoNP$, then $NP \cap CoNP \subseteq P^{L_0}$ and we see that L_0 is also $\leq_T^P$-complete.

Conversely, if for some L_1 in $NP \cap CoNP, L(N_s) = L_1 = \overline{L(N_t)}$, we have $NP \cap CoNP \subseteq P^{L_1}$, then $NP \cap CoNP = P^{L_1}$. To see this, note that for each $L(P_i^{L_1})$ in P^{L_1} we can effectively construct an equivalent machine $N_{\sigma(i)}$. The machine $N_{\sigma(i)}$ simulates $P_i^{L_1}$ and for each oracle querry $N_{\sigma(i)}$ starts N_s and N_t on the querried string. Since $L(N_s) = \overline{L(N_t)} = L_1$, for each querry there is a computation path such that N_s or N_t accepts the querried string. Thus $L(N_{\sigma(i)}) = L(P_i^{L_1})$. As a matter of fact, for each $P_i^{L_1}$ we can effectively construct a pair of complementary machines $N_{\sigma(i)}$ and $N_{\varsigma(i)}$ such that $L(P_i^{L_1}) = L(N_{\sigma(i)}) = \overline{L(N_{\varsigma(i)})}$ and clearly, $\{L(N_{\sigma(i)}) \mid i \geq 1\} = NP \cap CoNP$. But then, by Kowalczyk's Theorem, or an explicit construction of a universal language of the type

$$\{N_{\sigma(i)} \# N_{\varsigma(i)} \# x \# \text{ padding } \mid x \text{ is in } L(N_{\sigma(i)})\},$$

we obtain $\leq_m^P$-complete language for $NP \cap CoNP$. □

Next we show that if $NP \cap CoNP \neq NP$ then there is no recursive succinctness bound in the size of N_i, for $L(N_i)$ in $NP \cap CoNP$, which bounds the size of a complementary machine N_j such that $L(N_i) = \overline{L(N_j)}$.

Succinctness Lemma: If $NP \cap CoNP \neq NP$ then there is no recursive function G such that for all N_i with $L(N_i)$ in $NP \cap CoNP$ there exists an N_j satisfying

$$L(N_i) = \overline{L(N_j)} \text{ and } G(|N_i|) \geq |N_j|.$$

Proof: First we show that

$$\Delta = \{N_i \mid L(N_i) \in NP - NP \cap CoNP\}$$

is a Π_2-complete set in the Kleene Hierarchy [Ro]. To see this, note that Δ can be expressed in a $\forall\exists$ form:

$$\Delta = \{N_i \mid (\forall N_s, N_t)(\exists x)[N_i(x) \neq N_s(x) \text{ or } N_s(x) = N_t(x)]\}.$$

Thus Δ is in Π_2. Its completeness in Π_2 is seen by reducing the Π_2-complete set $\{M_i \mid L(M_i) = 1^*\}$ to Δ as follows. Map M_i onto $N_{\sigma(i)}$, where $N_{\sigma(i)}$ has an n^3-clock and computes in stages. If the clock shuts $N_{\sigma(i)}$ off then the input is rejected. Let $\{(N_{i_k}, N_{s_k}) \mid k \geq 1\}$ be a recursive enumeration of all possible pairs of nondeterministic polynomial time machines.

For input x $N_{\sigma(i)}$ recomputes its previous computations to determine what stage it is in (if this computation is not completed in n^3 steps the input is rejected). In stage k, $k \geq 1$, $N_{\sigma(i)}$, simulates M_i on input 1^k, if it is found that M_i accepts 1^k, then $N_{\sigma(i)}$ checks deterministically on shorter inputs whether $L(N_{\sigma(i)}) \neq L(N_{i_k})$ or $L(N_{i_k}) \neq \overline{L(N_{s_k})}$ (if for all k one of these conditions is satisfied then $L(N_{\sigma(i)})$ is in $NP - NP \cap CoNP$). If neither condition is satisfied in n^2 steps of computation the input x is accepted if and only if x is a satisfiable Boolean formula in CNF, i.e. x is in SAT. Since we have assumed that $NP \cap CoNP \neq NP$, SAT is not in $NP \cap CoNP$ and eventually, for sufficiently long x, one of the above conditions will be found to be satisfied, when this is detected $N_{\sigma(i)}$ enters stage $k+1$.

From the above construction we see that if $L(M_i) = 1^*$ then for all k $L(N_{\sigma(i)}) \neq L(N_{i_k})$ or $L(N_{i_k}) \neq \overline{L(N_{s_k})}$ and $L(N_{\sigma(i)}) \in NP - NP \cap CoNP$, otherwise $L(N_{\sigma(i)})$ is finite and therefore in $NP \cap CoNP$. Thus Δ is Π_2-complete.

If a recursive succinctness bound G would exist, bounding the size of a complementary machine N_j to the size of N_i for each $L(N_i)$ in $NP \cap CoNP$, then

$$\Delta = \{N_i \mid L(N_i) \neq \overline{L(N_j)} \text{ for all } N_j \text{ with } |N_j| \leq G(|N_i|)\}.$$

But then Δ would be recursively enumerable which is a contradiction to Π_2-completeness. Thus no recursive succinctness bound exists. □

Theorem 2: If $NP \cap CoNP \neq NP$ and L_0 is a $\leq_m^P$-complete language for $NP \cap CoNP$, then there is no recursive function G which bounds in the size of N_i, for $L(N_i)$ in $NP \cap CoNP$, the size of the minimal size P_j reducing $L(N_i)$ to L_0. Therefore the reduction of $L(N_i)$ in $NP \cap CoNP$ to L_0 cannot be effectively computable from N_i.

Proof: Let $L(N_{i_0}) = \overline{L(N_{j_0})} = L_0$. Then any P_t reducing $L(N_i)$ in $NP \cap CoNP$ to L_0 defines to machines $P_t \cdot N_{i_0}$ and $P_t \cdot N_{j_0}$ which accept $L(N_i)$ and $\overline{L(N_i)}$, respectively. Since the size of the smallest machine, N_j, accepting $\overline{L(N_i)}$ cannot be recursively bounded in the size of N_i and N_{j_0} is fixed, we see that the size of $P_t \cdot N_{j_0}$ cannot be recursively bounded in the size of N_i and therefore the size of the reducing machine, P_t, cannot be recursively bounded in $|N_i|$. But then P_t cannot be effectively computed from N_i. □

By similar reasoning we get the next result.

Theorem 3: Let L_1 be in $NP \cap CoNP$ and $P^{L_1} = NP \cap CoNP \neq NP$. Then there is no recursive function which bounds in the size of N_i, for $L(N_i)$ in $NP \cap CoNP$, the size of the smallest P_j such that $L(P_j^{L_1}) = L(N_i)$.

Proof: A careful inspection of the proof of Theorem 1 shows that a recursive succinctness bound in this result would imply a recursive succinctness bound for the previous result, contradicting Theorem 2. □

Relativized Computations

Let $h(n) = \log_2 n$. We will use h in several places in our constructions; but, any sufficiently slowly growing unbounded function would do. We will assume for convenience in the next two theorems that deterministic polynomial time turing machine P_i and nondeterministic polynomial time turing machine N_i both have clocks constraining them to run in at most $n^{h(i)}$ steps on inputs of size n.

Theorem 4: There is an oracle E such that

$$P^E \neq NP^E \cap CoNP^E \neq NP^E$$

and such that there exists a many-one complete set for $NP^E \cap CoNP^E$.

Proof: We will construct E as the disjoint union of two sets:

$$E = 00S \cup 1T$$

The prefix for S is 00 in order to leave room for one more set in the next theorem. The set T will code a universal complete set for $NP^E \cap CoNP^E$; and the set S will hide strings in order to insure that $NP^E \neq CoNP^E$. For each string u, T will contain exactly one string uv where $|u| = |v|$. Thus the function f which takes each u to its corresponding v will be computable in $NP^E \cap CoNP^E$;

$$f(u) = v \text{ suchthat } |u| = |v| \text{ and } uv \in T \quad .$$

We will say that the two turing machines N_i^E, N_j^E form a *complementary pair* if they accept complementary languages. We will construct T so that the following two conditions hold concerning f:

(A) The function f is not computable in P^E.

(B) Suppose that N_a^E, N_b^E is a complementary pair; and let $u = (a, b, w, \#^m)$ where $m = |w|^{h(\max(a,b))}$ bounds the number of steps taken by N_a or N_b on input w. Then for all but finitely many $w \in \Sigma^*$ first$(f(u))$ - the first bit of $f(u)$ - will be 1 if and only if N_a^E accepts w.

Condition (B) will insure that the set

$$C(E) = \{(u, x) \mid (\exists v) 1uv \in E; \ \text{first}(v) = x\}$$

is many-one complete for $NP^E \cap CoNP^E$. Condition (A) will insure that $NP^E \cap CoNP^E \neq P^E$ because f is computable in $NP^E \cap CoNP^E$ but not in P^E. We break this condition into infinitely many pieces:

(A_i) The function f is not computed by P_i.

Condition (A_i) will be easy to meet because each P_i can only look at a few of the exponentially many candidates for each $f(u)$.

Finally in the set S we will hide strings to guarantee that $NP^E \neq CoNP^E$. Let

$$L(E) = \{0^m \mid m \in N, (\exists z)(|z| = m, 00z \in E)\} \quad .$$

The following conditions will insure that $L(E) \notin CoNP^E$ and thus that $NP^E \neq CoNP^E$.

(C_i) The language accepted by N_i is not $\overline{L(E)}$.

The Construction

We construct an oracle meeting the above conditions (A), (B), and (C). Assume inductively that E_s, an initial segment of E has been constructed, and that E_s only includes strings of length less than s.

Part (A): Let $i \leq s$ be minimal so that the condition (A_i) has not yet been satisfied. Simulate P_i on input 0^s. Let $w_1, ..., w_k$ be the strings of length at least s queried by P_i. Freeze these strings permanently out of E.

Part (B): Let $k \leq s$ be minimal so that the condition (C_k) has not yet been satisfied. For j going from s to $s^{h(k)}-1$ do the following: For each u with $|u| = j/2$ pick a unique v such that $|v| = |u|$ and add $1uv$ to E. The string v must meet the following two criteria:

- The string $1uv$ has not been previously frozen.
- If $u = (a, b, w, \#^m)$ where $m = |w|^{h(\max(a,b))}$ and N_a accepts w, (necessarily within m steps), then first(v) should be 1. Otherwise first(v) should be 0.

Note that the number of v's excluded by freezing in part (A) is less than $s^{h(s)-1}$ and therefore less than the number of possible v's, i.e. $2^{j/2}$. Thus the above two steps can always be carried out.

Part (C): Recall that k was chosen to be minimal so that the condition (C_k) has not yet been satisfied. Let $r = s^{h(k)}$ and assume that E_r has been constructed correctly so far. Run $N_k^{E_r}$ on input 0^s. If it rejects then freeze E_r. There are no strings of the form $00z \in E_r$ with $|z| = s$. Thus $N_k^{E_r}$ does not accept the complementary language to $L(E)$. If $N_k^{E_r}$ accepts 0^s then pick one of its accepting computations and freeze the strings $y_1, ..., y_t$ queried in this computation. Note that

$$\sum_{j=1}^{t} |y_j| < s^{h(k)} = r$$

because N_k runs in at most $s^{h(k)}$ steps on inputs of size s. Note that some of the y_j's in E may be of the form

$1u_jv_j$ where $u_j = (a, b, w, \#^m)$ with $N_a^{E_r}, N_b^{E_r}$ a valid $NP^{E_r} \cap CoNP^{E_r}$ pair on inputs of length less that s; and such that $m = |w|^{h(\max(a,b))}$. In this case if $N_a^{E_r}$ accepts w then pick one of its accepting computations and freeze it. Otherwise, if $N_b^{E_r}$ accepts w then pick one of its accepting computations and freeze it. In either case we may be forced to freeze some additional strings, $y_1^j, \ldots, y_{t_j}^j$, in E_r. Note that N_a runs in at most m steps, and $m < |y_j|/2$. If follows that

$$\sum_{i=1}^{t_j} |y_i^j| < |y_j|/2 \quad .$$

It easily follows that within $\log r$ interactions all strings to be frozen will have been identified; and that there are fewer than r of them. (In particular their total length is less than $2r$.) Finally, we now pick a string z of length of s such that $00z$ has not been frozen, and add $00z$ to E. Such a z exists because fewer than $2r$ of the 2^s possible z's have been excluded. It follows that we have met the condition that $L(N_k^E)$ is not the complementary language to $L(E)$.

Note that by adding $00z$ to E we may change many of the computations which have been recorded in T. Thus *we must repeat the loop of part* (B) to recompute E_r; but, of course we do not change those strings which have been frozen.

A problem may occur in that some frozen $y = uv$, with $u = (a, b, w, \#^m)$, may now be incorrect. To be incorrect means that $N_a^{E_r}$ and $N_b^{E_r}$ form a valid complementary pair so far; but that first(v) does not reflect the pair's answer on w. How could this have happened? Recall that if either N_a or N_b had accepted w then one of these accepting computations would have been frozen as well. It follows that for an error to have occurred, originally $N_a^{E_r}$ and $N_b^{E_r}$ must both have rejected w. To meet condition (B) we only have to insure that for each valid complementary pair, N_a, N_b, this sort of error happens only finitely often. We insure this by modifying part (C) of the construction as follows:

(Proviso to Part C): **IF** E_r contains a string $y = 1uv$ with $u = (a, b, w, \#^m)$, such that $s \leq |y| < r$; $a + b < h(s)$; $N_a^{E_r}, N_b^{E_r}$ is a complementary pair up to s; and $N_a^{E_r}$ and $N_b^{E_r}$ both reject w **THEN** skip (C) this time.

The effect of the above proviso is that if a very small pair has the potential to mess up the construction then both parts of the pair must now reject some w. If we defer the (C) step and freeze the present initial piece of the oracle then the pair is no longer a complementary pair. It follows that the pair N_a, N_b will never be involved in an error after stage $h^{-1}(a+b)$.

Lemma 5: If the above construction is carried out using Proviso 1, then conditions (A), (B), and (C) are met.

Proof: We must only show that any complementary pair N_a, N_b can be put in error only finitely often; and that the conditions (C_k) are all eventually satisfied.

The first is clear because the pair N_a, N_b cannot be put in error on any input of length s, where $a+b < h(s)$.

It is clear that the second is true as long as the function $h(s)$ grows slowly enough; and a straight forward calculation shows that $h(s) = \log_* s$ does grow sufficiently slowly. This proves the lemma and thus the theorem. □

Corollary 6: There is an oracle E such that $P^E \neq NP^E \cap CoNP^E \neq NP^E$, and such that there is an $NP^E \cap CoNP^E$ complete set, L. Furthermore, the map taking a complementary pair N_a, N_b to its reduction to L is computable.

Proof: By the above construction we know that for N_a, N_b a complementary pair no errors are made after stage $s = h^{-1}(a+b)$. Let $u \in C(E)$, $v \notin C(E)$. Suppose that N_a^E, N_b^E is a complementary pair. Let $e = \max(a, b)$. Put

$$r(w) = \begin{cases} (a,\ b,\ w,\ |w|^e,\ 1) & \text{if } h(w) > a+b \\ u & \text{if } h(w) \leq a+b \text{ and } N_a(w)\downarrow \\ v & \text{otherwise} \end{cases}$$

Then r is a valid reduction of $L(N_a)^E$ to $C(E)$. □

The next theorem shows that there is also an oracle for which there is still a complete set for $NP \cap CoNP$; but, such that the reductions cannot be computed from pairs of complementary machines.

Theorem 7: There is an oracle F such that

$$P^F \neq NP^F \cap CoNP^F \neq NP^F \quad ;$$

such that there exists a many-one complete set, C, for $NP^F \cap CoNP^F$; but, such that reductions are not computable. That is there is no F-computable map, φ^F, such that for each complementary pair, $N_a^F, N_b^F, \varphi^F(a,b)$ converges to an index of a polynomial time reduction of $L(N_a)$ to C.

Proof: We modify the above construction to include parts A, B, and C, as well as a new part D in order to satisfy the following new conditions:

(D_i): The ith partial recursive function, φ_i^F, does not compute reductions to $C(F)$.

In order to foil φ_i's chances of computing reductions, and thus satisfy (D_i) we use an idea from [Si]. For each i, and some $c \in N$ we will consider the following language:

$$L(i, c) = \{(i,\ c,\ w) \mid (\exists v.\ |v| = |w|)((01, i, c, v) \in F \text{ and first } (v) = 1)\} \ .$$

We will modify the construction so that for sufficiently many c we will put exactly one string z of the correct form into F. In these cases the language $L(i, c)$ is in $NP^F \cap CoNP^F$ and will be computed by an appropriate linear time complementary pair $N_{a(i,c)}, N_{b(i,c)}$. We will satisfy (P_i) by making sure that if $\varphi_i^F(a(i, c), b(i, c))$ converges to some polynomial time reduction P_j then P_j does not reduce $L(i, c)$ to $C(F)$.

We will say that D_i *is ready at stage* s if there exists an integer $c \leq s$ as well as integers a, b, j, m, z such that the following two conditions are met:

1. $\varphi_i^{F_s}(a(i, c), b(i, c))$ converges in at most s steps to some polynomial time transducer P_j.

2. $P_j^{F_s}((01, i, c, 0^s))$ converges in at most $s^{h(s)}$ steps to some string $(a, b, w, \#^m, z)$.

We now describe part (D) of the construction. As above we assume that F_s, an initial segment of F, has been computed correctly. F_s includes only strings of length less than s. Let i be minimal so that D_i is ready at stage s; and let a, b, c, j, m, z be the associated values in the definition of being ready. Freeze those strings queried by $P_j^{F_s}((01, i, c, 0^s))$ permanently out of F. Now extend F_s to F_r where $r = s^{h(s)}$; but do this without putting any strings of the form $(01, i, c, v)$ into F where $|u| = s$. We will have foiled P_j as a reduction if the following equivalence does not hold:

$$(a, b, w, \#^m, z) \in C(F) \Leftrightarrow (01, i, c, 0^s) \in L(i, c) \qquad (1)$$

What we do is to freeze the string of the form $(1, a, b, w, \#^m, v) \in F_r$ where $|v| = |(1, a, b, w, \#^m)|$. Then we try to insure that this frozen answer is wrong. There are three cases of interest:

case 1: At least on of $N_a^{F_r}, N_b^{F_r}$ accepts w. In this case we freeze one of the accepting computations as in part (C).[1] Next we put a string of the form $(01, i, c, v)$ into F where $|v| = s$ and first(v) is chosen to make equation (1) false. Finally we recompute F_r.

case 2: Neither of $N_a^{F_r}, N_b^{F_r}$ accepts w; and $a + b \geq i$ or N_1, N_2 is not a correct pair up to s. In this case as above we put a string of the form $(01, i, c, v)$ into F where $|v| = s$ and first(v) is chosen to make equation (1) false. Again we recompute F_r. Note that in this case we may be putting the pair N_a, N_b in error, but we do this at most finitely many times for each pair.

case 3: Otherwise: neither element of the pair accepts w; and the pair is a complementary pair up to s with $a + b$ less than i. In this case we freeze F_r as it is. Thus N_a, N_b will not be a valid pair. Note that we are also causing $N_{a(i,c)}, N_{b(i,c)}$ to be an invalid pair. This is the cost of eliminating N_a, N_b but it can happen to

1 We are assuming that none of the strings in this frozen computation which are in F_r and of the form $(1, a', b', \ldots)$ are potentially in error, where furthermore $a' + b' < i$. Otherwise we freeze the error as in case 3.

φ_i at most i^2 times.

Claim: The construction described above successfully meets condition (D) as well as still satisfying conditions (A), (B) and (C).

Proof: To the reader who has made it through to this point it should be clear that part (D) can only put any given pair in error finitely often. Furthermore for any potentially correct φ_i there will be some stage s at which (D_i) is the minimal ready condition, and all potentially complementary pairs N_a, N_b with $a+b<i$ which will ever be eliminated will already be gone. At this stage case 1 or case 2 will apply, and in either case we will have that P_j, the machine computed by φ_i, is not a valid reduction.

This proves the claim and thus the theorem. □

Acknowledgement

We would like to thank Jim Kadin for valuable discussions and in particular for the formulation of Theorem 1.

References

[BGS]Baker, T., J. Gill and R. Solovay. "Relativization of the $P = ?NP$ Question". *SIAM Journal of Computing* (1975), 431-442.

[GJ]Garey, M.R. and D.S. Johnson. "Computers and Intractability: A guide to the Theory of *NP*-Completeness". W.H. Freeman and Co., San Francisco, 1979.

[Ko]Kowalczyk, W. "Some Connections Between Representability of Complexity Classes and the Power of Formal Systems of Reasoning". Mathematical Foundations of Computer Science, *Lecture Notes in Computer Science 176*. Springer-Verlag 1984, 364-369.

[Ro]Rogers, H., Jr. "Theory of Recursive Functions and Effective Computability". McGraw-Hill, New York, 1967.

[Si]Sipser, M. "On Relativization and the Existence of Complete Sets". Automata Languages and Programming *Lecture Notes in Computer Science 140*. Springer-Verlag 1982, 523-531.

AN ALGEBRAIC THEORY OF FAIR ASYNCHRONOUS COMMUNICATING PROCESSES

Matthew Hennessy
Department of Computer Science
University of Edinburgh

Abstract

A language for defining fair asynchronous communicating processes is presented. The main operator is a binary composition operator $\|$: $p \| q$ represents processes p and q linked together asynchronously but "fairly". In addition the language has a mechanism for abstracting away from internal components of a process. A denotational semantics is given for the language. The domain used consists of certain kinds of finite-branching trees which may have limit points associated with their infinite paths. The semantics is algebraic in the sense that every operator in the language is interpreted as a function over the domain. Each of these functions are continuous, except that associated with $\|$, which is monotonic. The model satisfies a large collection of equations which supports a transformational proof system for processes. The model is also fully-abstract with respect to a natural notion of testing equivalence. Moreover we show that no fully-abstract model can be continuous.

Introduction

In recent papers, [De Nicola 1984], [Hennessy 1983a,b], we have presented models for synchronous and asynchronous processes. These models are very simple kinds of trees which are endowed with an algebraic structure. Moreover, they are completely characterised by sets of inequations, which gives a very powerful method for reasoning about processes. Finally these models are justified using a natural theory of testing: the models distinguish, and will only distinguish, processes which can be differentiated using an appropriate notion of testing. In the present paper we show that a relatively simple extension of this work gives a satisfactory theory of fair asynchronous processes, at least for a restricted idea of fairness.

Consider the two simple processes: $A \Leftarrow aA$, $B \Leftarrow bB$. They can perform the infinite sequence of actions a^ω, b^ω, respectively. If they are placed in parallel, denoted $A|B$ as in [Milner 1980], the resulting process can perform any infinite shuffle of a^ω, b^ω, including either of the sequences a^ω, b^ω. Intuitively, if they are placed in parallel fairly, which we denote by $A\|B$, the resulting process should <u>not</u> be able to perform a^ω nor b^ω. Therefore $A|B$ and $A\|B$ are processes which have different intuitive behaviour. In terms of testing we should be able to produce a test (or experiment) which differentiates between them. Now we cannot test for the presence of an infinite sequence of actions, such as a^ω. But under certain assumptions we can test for the <u>absence</u> of such a sequence. In fact we produce a test e such that $A\|B$ will always pass e whereas $A|B$ may sometimes not pass it. This possibility of failure stems from the ability of A|B to perform the infinite sequence a^ω and is detected in our theory because we connect together the testers and the processes being tested fairly, i.e. using the combinator ‖.

In §1 we define the language we consider, which is based on CCS. The main operator of interest is ‖ but in addition we have hiding operators which allow abstraction from internal details and an internal action, denoted by 1. The operational interpretation we give to ‖ is that called strict fairness in [Hennessy 1984a]. In any infinite (admissible) computation from p‖q both p and q must eventually perform an action (regardless of whether or not it is possible). This interpretation leads to certain oddities. For example if ∅ represents a process which can no nothing then A‖∅ has no infinite admissible computation. In §1.4 we apply the theory of testing developed in [De Nicola 1984], [Hennessy 1983a] to this language, obtaining an operational preorder $\sqsubseteq$. For example A|B $\sqsubseteq$ A‖B but not vice-versa.

In section two we present the model. It consists of certain kinds of finite-branching trees, called ASNT (asynchronous strong nondeterministic trees) together with limit points along paths. For this reason the model is called EASNT (extended asynchronous nondeterministic trees). It is endowed with a complete partial order <. Moreover each operator in the language is interpreted as a monotonic function, all of which are continuous except for ‖. This enables us to interpret the language in the usual algebraic manner in EASNT and we prove that two processes are related in the model, EASNT⟦p⟧ < EASNT⟦q⟧, if and only if for every language context C[ ], C[p] $\underset{\approx}{\sqsubset}$ C[q]; that is the model is fully-abstract with respect to the operational relation $\underset{\approx}{\sqsubset}$.

This result underscores the significance of the model. EASNT is also of interest because it inherits many of the algebraic properties of the simpler model ASNT. In particular it satisfies most of the usual equations associated with CCS-like languages, [Milner 1980], [Hennessy 1983a]. For example it satisfies the so-called τ-laws which enables one to reason about abstract specifications of processes. Although Scott Induction is not consistent for our model (since it presupposes continuity) it can be used to justify other forms of induction such as Recursion Induction. Finally, the model is also of interest because it does not explain fairness using unbounded nondeterminism: the trees are finite-branching.

Full details of the definitions and theorems may be found in [Hennessy 1984b].

§1. The Language

§1.1 The Syntax

The language we use is a variant of CCS, taken essentially from [Hennessy 1983a]. Let X be a set of variables, ranged over by x and M a set of moves or actions, ranged over by μ,γ. We assume M has the structure A ∪ {1}. The elements of A are visible actions and 1 denotes an internal or invisible action. As in [Milner 1980] we assume A has the form $\Lambda \cup \bar{\Lambda}$, where Λ is a primitive set and $\bar{\Lambda} = \{\bar{a}, a \in \Lambda\}$: the action $\bar{a}$ is the complement of the action a and their simultaneous occurrence is denoted by a

1-action. We also say a is the complement of $\bar{a}$, writing $\bar{\bar{a}} = a$. So we use a, b, c, etc. to range over the set of visible actions A.

The set of operators we consider, Σ, are:

Σ^0: $\emptyset$ representing the empty process and Ω representing the totally undefined process.

Σ^1: $\mu.-$ representing prefixing by the action μ and $\restriction E$, where $E \subseteq M$, representing the restriction of actions to those allowed by E.

Σ^2: + representing external nondeterminism, $\oplus$ representing internal nondeterminism and $\|$ representing fair asynchronous parallelism.

We omit the non-fair parallel operator $|$ from our language for convenience only. It merely adds one more case to consider.

The set of recursive terms over Σ, REC_Σ, is then defined in the usual way, by the following BNF-like schema:

$$t ::= x \mid op(t_1,\ldots,t_k),\ op \in \Sigma^k \mid rec_i\tilde{x}.\tilde{t}$$

where $\tilde{x}$, $\tilde{t}$ denote possible infinite sequences of distinct variables, terms respectively. Intuitively $rec_i\tilde{x}.\tilde{t}$ stands for the ith component of the (possibly infinite) mutually recursive definition $\tilde{x} \Leftarrow \tilde{t}$. When the index set is a singleton we abbreviate $rec_1\tilde{x}.\tilde{t}$ by recx.t. Open and closed terms are defined as usual with rec_i binding variables. We use FAP to denote the collection of closed terms, called fair asynchronous processes. We use p, q, r, etc. to range over FAP.

§1.2 Denotational Semantics

A denotational semantics can be given in the usual fashion by interpreting the terms over a Σ-cpo. An interpretation consists of a cpo D, together with a monotonic function of the appropriate arity, op_D, for every operator op in Σ. An interpretation is continuous if each of these functions is continuous. Let ENV_D be the set of D-environments, i.e. mappings from X to D. We then use the usual notation of $D[\![\ ]\!]$ to denote the semantic function from REC_Σ to $(ENV_D \rightarrow D)$; if e is a D-environment $D[\![t]\!]e$ denotes the interpretation of t in D in the environment e. If p is a process then $D[\![p]\!]$ is independent of ENV_D and informally we can view it as an element of D. The actual definition of D is straightforward. See [Stoy 1977].

Most of these interpretations of course are uninteresting. The problem is to discover particular interpretations which are on the one hand aesthetically pleasing and on the other operationally significant; they must be determined by the operational behaviour of processes. In the next section we develop operational criteria for evaluating interpretations. To do so we must define formally the fair computations of a process.

§1.3 Fair Computations

An operational semantics for the language is given in the usual way by defining a labelled transition system $\langle FAP, \overset{\mu}{\to}, M \rangle$. Intuitively $p \overset{\mu}{\to} q$ means that the process p can perform the move μ and thereby be transformed into the process q. The relations $\overset{\mu}{\to}$ are defined in a syntax directed manner, formalising the intuitive meaning of the operators in Σ. The details are now fairly standard and are given for example in [Milner 1980], [Hennessy 1983a]. We use a minor modification of the definitions from the latter where if p has an immediate unguarded recursion then $p \overset{1}{\to} p$. (The operator $\|$ is treated as the asynchronous parallel operator $|$ of [Milner 1980].) Consider the (finite or infinite) derivation

$$p_0 \| q_0 \xrightarrow{\mu_1} p_1 \| q_1 \xrightarrow{\mu_2} p_2 \| q_2 \xrightarrow{\mu_3} \cdots \qquad \text{(D)}$$

By analysing how each individual action is performed (encoded in its proof) we can define two derivations called the projections of D, $proj_1(D)$, $proj_2(D)$, which record the history of p_0, q_0, respectively, and the contributions (if any) they make to each action in (D):

$$p_0 \xrightarrow{\gamma_1} p_1 \xrightarrow{\gamma_2} p_2 \xrightarrow{\gamma_3} \cdots, \quad q_0 \xrightarrow{\gamma_1'} q_1 \xrightarrow{\gamma_2'} q_2 \xrightarrow{\gamma_3'} \cdots$$

Note that in general there is no correlation between the length of D and that of individual projections. For the derivation of D to be fair we require approximately that whenever it is infinite both its projections are infinite. However a formal definition requires further analysis. We first define the set of subderivations, sub(D), of an arbitrary derivation

$$p_0 \xrightarrow{\mu_1} p_1 \xrightarrow{\mu_2} p_2 \xrightarrow{\mu_3} \cdots \qquad \text{(D)}$$

The definition is by structural induction on p_0:

i) p_0 is $q\|r$: Then sub(D) is $sub(proj_1(D)) \cup sub(proj_2(D))$

ii) p_0 is $q \restriction E$: Then we can construct from D the obvious computation D_1 from the process q and sub(D) is $sub(D_1)$

iii) otherwise sub(D) = {D}.

Definition a) The derivation D above is inadmissible if

i) it is infinite, and

ii) it is visible, i.e. for every $n > 0$ there is some $k > n$ such that $\mu_k \neq 1$, and

iii) some subderivation is finite.

b) The derivation D is unfair if some postfix is inadmissible. Otherwise it is fair. □

We need to consider postfixes in part b) because in our language processes can be created dynamically. The definition also requires inadmissible derivation to be visible. Derivations which are not so (i.e. which are invisible) eventually become internal derivations. They do not involve or impinge upon the environment in any way. Consequently an external observer can form no opinion whatsoever on the suitability of invisible derivations. In particular they cannot be deemed to be inadmissible. Of course such derivations represent imperfections and our theory of operational behaviour, given in the next section, reflects this.

Examples

1. Every fair derivation from $A \| B$ must infinitely often perform both an a action and a b action.

2. The process recx.ax+bx, denoted by AB, has the fair derivation

$$AB \xrightarrow{a} AB \xrightarrow{a} AB \xrightarrow{a} \ldots$$

3. Let $\{a_n, n \in \omega\}$ be an infinite set of actions and let A_n denote the cyclic process recx.a_nx. Now consider the process Z_0, defined informally by the infinite set of definitions $Z_n \Leftarrow a_n(A_n \| Z_{n+1})$, $n \geq 0$. Then a fair derivation from Z_0 must perform the action a_k infinitely often, for every $k \geq 0$.

4. The process $A \| \emptyset$ has no infinite fair derivations because the second projection is empty. Similarly $(A \| B) \upharpoonright \{a\}$ also has no infinite fair definitions. □

The last two examples show that the operator $\|$ embodies a strict view of fairness. In $p \| q$ both p and q are obliged to contribute periodically to an overall derivation, even if they are unable to do so! Our language is best viewed as a primitive specification language with $\|$ an operator on specifications rather than a physically realisable construction applicable to processes.

§1.4 An Operational Pre-order

We apply the theory expounded in [Hennessy 1983a] to obtain a natural operational pre-order between processes; approximately $p \lesssim q$ signifies that q passes any test or experiment which p passes. We use a distinguished action w, not in M, to denote the reporting of the successful completion of a test. An experimenter is then a process which may contain occurrences of the distinguished action w. For example, $\bar{a}(\bar{b}w\emptyset + \bar{c}w\emptyset)$ is an experimenter which tests for the ability to perform either of the sequences of actions ab,ac. An application of an experimenter w to the process p is a maximal derivation of the form

$$e \| p = e_0 \| p_0 \xrightarrow{1} e_1 \| p_1 \xrightarrow{1} \ldots \qquad (D)$$

such that $proj_1(D)$ and $proj_2(D)$ are both fair derivations. Such an application is successful if there exists an $n \geq 0$ such that $e_n \xrightarrow{w}$, i.e. if the experimenter reaches a state in which it can report success.

Definition a) p must e if every application of e to p is successful,
b) $p \sqsubseteq q$ if for every e, p must e implies q must e. □

We refer the reader to [De Nicola 1982], [Hennessy 1984], for more motivation of these definitions. As usual we use $\simeq$ for the natural equivalence generated by $\sqsubseteq$ and let $p \sqsubseteq_c q$ if for every context C[ ], $C[p] \sqsubseteq C[q]$.

Examples

1. $AB \sqsubseteq A\|B$ but $A\|B \not\sqsubseteq AB$. The latter follows since $A\|B$ must e, AB m̸ust e, where e is the experimenter $recx.\bar{a}x+\bar{a}w\emptyset$. The fair computation $e\|AB \xrightarrow{1} e\|AB \xrightarrow{1} e\|AB \xrightarrow{1} \ldots$ is an unsuccessful applicationn of e to AB. On the other hand $e\|(A\|B) \xrightarrow{1} e\|(A\|B) \xrightarrow{1} \ldots$ is not fair and so it does not represent an application of e to $A\|B$. All such applications are finite and consequently successful since their terminal element is $w\emptyset\|(A\|B)$.
2. $A \sqsubseteq A\|\emptyset$ but $A\|\emptyset \not\sqsubseteq A$. To see the latter use the same experimenter as in example 1.
3. $A\|A \simeq A$.
4. Let p denote $\bar{b}\emptyset\|(recx.ax+b\emptyset)$ and q be defined by the infinite recursive definition $q \Leftarrow q_1$, $q_1 \Leftarrow q_2 + a\emptyset$, $q_2 \Leftarrow q_3 + aa\emptyset$, etc. These correspond to the two statements b:=false ‖ (while b do x:=x+1) and x:=? from [Apt 1983]. Then $q \sqsubseteq p$ but $p \not\sqsubseteq q$; p must e, where e denotes $1w\emptyset$, but q m̸ust e because q has an immediate unguarded recursion and so $e\|q \xrightarrow{1} e\|q \xrightarrow{1} \ldots$ is an unsuccessful application. Treating these two programs as equivalent amounts to saying to 'fairness' and 'unbounded nondeterminism' are essentially the same phenomenon. In our model this will not be the case; p and q are given different denotations.
5. Let $\mathbb{1}$ denote recx.1x. Then $\mathbb{1}\|a\emptyset \sqsubseteq a\emptyset$ but $a\emptyset \not\sqsubseteq \mathbb{1}\|a\emptyset$; $a\emptyset$ must $aw\emptyset$ whereas $aw\|(\mathbb{1}\|a\emptyset) \xrightarrow{1} aw\|(\mathbb{1}\|a\emptyset) \xrightarrow{1} \ldots$ is an unsuccessful application because the second component is not visible. □

The last example gives an indication of the nature of $\sqsubseteq$. One might expect that $\mathbb{1}\|a\emptyset \simeq a\emptyset$ but we take a different view. Since $\sqsubseteq$ is based on the Smyth ordering possibly divergent processes are considered catastrophic and they are equated with the completely undefined process. Here we interpret 'divergent' as having a divergent subprocess. So that $\mathbb{1}\|a\emptyset$ is equated (via $\simeq$) with the completely undefined process, which happens to be $\mathbb{1}$. This interpretation of 'divergence' may not be entirely satisfactory but it is more or less forced on us, if we wish $\mathbb{1}$ to denote the least element in our model (i.e. be the completely undefined process). We are reluctant to have $\mathbb{1}$ interpreted otherwise since any resulting models would be unnecessarily complex.

§2 The Model

The model consists of a certain brand of nondeterministic trees [Hennessy 1983b] together with limit points of their infinite paths. We call the set of trees ASNT, the asynchronous variety of the Strong Nondeterministic Trees of [Hennessy 1983b]. They are different from the latter only in that i) 1 does not appear as a label on branches and ii) associated with the root of every tree there is a saturated set which represents the "preemptive power" of the tree. The motivation for i) is that the model seek to represent the asynchronous behaviour of processes, which abstracts away from internal moves. The second is required to distinguish 1p from p.

Examples of trees in ASNT are given in Figure 1. Formally a tree t in ASNT is defined by:

i) L(t), a non-empty prefix-closed subset of A*, representing the (finite) paths in the tree.

ii) CL(t), a prefix-closed subset of L(t), representing the paths which lead to closed nodes. These are denoted •, and the other nodes, called open, are denoted by ∘.

iii) A mapping $\mathcal{A}$: CL(t) $\to 2^A$, associating with each closed node a non-empty finite set of finite sets of actions, called the Acceptance set of the node.

iv) P(t) $\subseteq 2^A$, a finite set of finite sets, associated with the root, provided it is closed, called the Preemption set of t.

We use t(s) to denote the node of t determined by s $\in$ A*, and S(t(s)) to denote the set of actions labelling the successor branches of the node t(s). Then the sets above must satisfy:

a) S(t(s)) is finite, i.e. the trees are finite-branching

b) s $\notin$ CL(t) implies sa $\notin$ L(t), i.e. open nodes must be leaves

c) $\mathcal{A}$(t(s)) contains only subsets of S(t(s)) and is saturated, i.e. satisfies: S(t(s)) $\in \mathcal{A}$(t(s)) and X,Y $\in \mathcal{A}$(t(s)), X $\subseteq$ Z $\subseteq$ Y implies Z $\in \mathcal{A}$(t(s)). The element of $\mathcal{A}$(t(s)) represent possible internal states of t after performing s

d) P(t) $\subseteq \mathcal{A}(t(\varepsilon))$ and is also saturated; it represents the preemptive power of t.

The extended model, called EASNT, is trees from ASNT which have limit points associated with certain paths. Examples are given in Figure 2, where the Acceptance sets have been omitted. Formally a limit point can be identified with its path and we present the model in this way. Let EASNT be the set of pairs <t,I> where

i) t $\in$ ASNT

ii) I $\subseteq A^\omega$ with the property that u $\in$ I implies $u_n \in$ CL(t) for every finite prefix u_n of u.

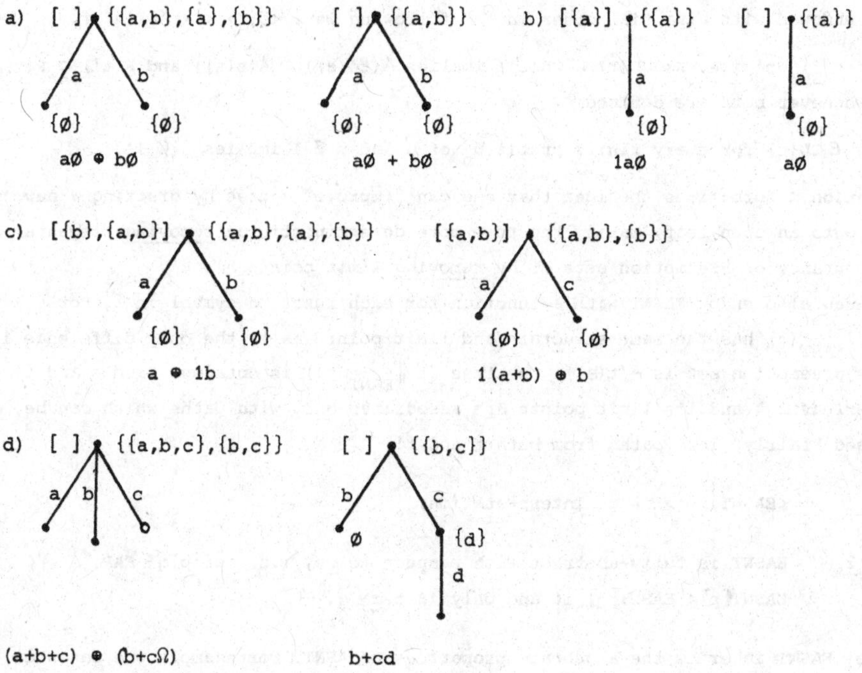

Figure 1

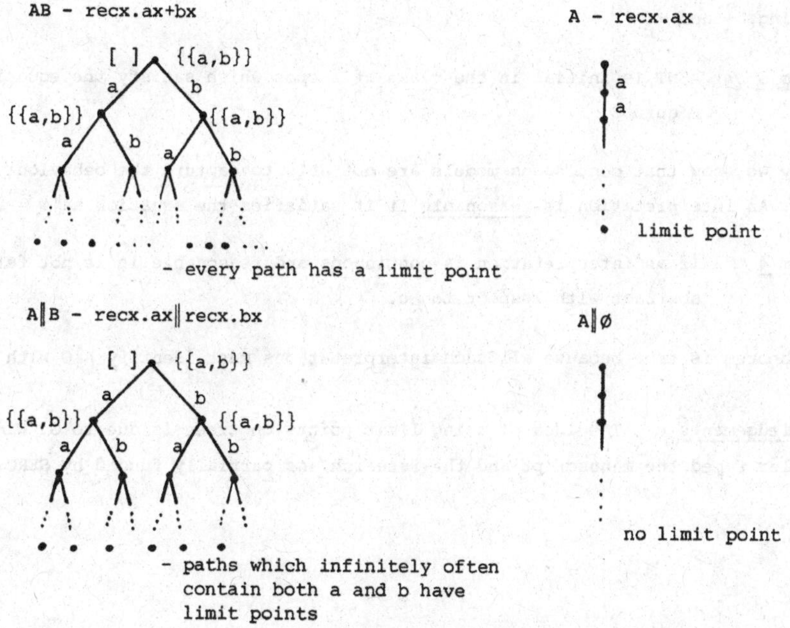

Figure 2

This is endowed with a partial order in the following way: $\langle t,I\rangle < \langle t',I'\rangle$ if

i) $t <_{ASNT} t'$ i.e. $s \in CL(t) \cap CL(t')$ implies $A(t'(s)) \subseteq A(t(s))$ and $P(t') \subseteq P(t)$ whenever both are defined

ii) $u_n \in CL(t)$ for every finite prefix u_n of u and $u \notin I$ implies $u \notin I'$.

The relation $<$ formalises the idea that one can "improve" a tree by grafting a new subtree onto an open leaf, making the tree more deterministic by <u>removing</u> elements from Acceptance or Preemption sets or by <u>removing</u> limit points.

We can also endow EASNT with a function for each function symbol in Σ. For example $1_{EANT}(t)$ has the same structure and limit points as t; the only difference is that its preemption set is $A(t(\varepsilon))$. The tree $(t \parallel_{EANT} t')$ is obtained from t and t' by "interleaving" and its limit points are associated only with paths which can be decomposed "fairly" into paths from both t and t'.

<u>Theorem 1</u> $\langle EASNT, < \rangle$ is an interpretation.

<u>Theorem 2</u> EASNT is fully-abstract with respect to $\underset{\sim}{\sqsubset}c$, i.e. for $p,q \in FAP$, $EASNT[\![p]\!] < EASNT[\![q]\!]$ if and only if $p \underset{\sim}{\sqsubset}c\ q$.

The model EASNT inherits the algebraic properties of ASNT. For example one can show $\parallel$ is associative, commutative and satisfies an interleaving axiom similar to that in [Milner 1980]. In fact ASNT can be characterised by equations over the operators, $\emptyset$ prefixing, + and $\oplus$.

<u>Theorem 3</u> ASNT is initial in the class of Σ-cpos which satisfy the equations in Figure 3.

Finally we show that continuous models are not able to capture the behaviour of terms in FAP. An interpretation is <u>reasonable</u> if it satisfies the equation $ax\parallel\emptyset = a(x\parallel\emptyset)$.

<u>Theorem 4</u> If an interpretation is continuous and reasonable it is not fully-abstract with respect to $\underset{\sim}{\sqsubset}c$.

This theorem is true because all such interpretations must identify $A\parallel\emptyset$ with A.

<u>Acknowledgements</u> The idea of using limit points on trees is due to G. Winskel. K. Møller typed the manuscript and the research was partially funded by SERC.

$$X + Y = X \qquad\qquad X \oplus X = X$$

$$X + Y = Y + X \qquad\qquad X \oplus Y = Y \oplus X$$

$$X + (Y + Z) = (X + Y) + Z \qquad\qquad X \oplus (Y \oplus Z) = (X \oplus Y) \oplus Z$$

$$X + \emptyset = X$$

$$X + (Y \oplus Z) = (X + Y) \oplus (X + Z) \qquad\qquad aX + aY = a(X \oplus Y)$$

$$X \oplus (Y + Z) = (X \oplus Y) + (X \oplus Z) \qquad\qquad aX \oplus aY = a(X \oplus Y)$$

$$X \oplus Y \sqsubseteq X$$

$$1X \sqsubseteq X \qquad\qquad \Omega \sqsubseteq X$$

$$aX \sqsubseteq a1X \qquad\qquad X + \Omega \sqsubseteq X \oplus \Omega$$

$$X + 1Y \sqsubseteq 1(X + Y)$$

Figure 3

References

LNCS denotes Lecture Notes in Computer Science, published by Springer-Verlag.

[Apt, K., 1983] with Olderog, E., Proof Rules and Transformations dealing with Fairness, Science of Computer Programming 3, pp. 65-100.

[Darondeau, P., 1984] Infinitary Languages and Fully Abstract Models for Fair Asynchrony, CNRS-IRISA, Rennes.

[De Nicola, R., 1982], with Hennessy, M., Testing Equivalences for Processes, TCS vol. 34, nos. 1-2, November 1984 (pp. 83-134).

[Hennessy, M., 1983a] Synchronous and Asynchronous Experiments on Processes, Information and Control, vol. 59, nos. 1-3, October 1983 (pp. 36-83).

[Hennessy, M., 1983b] A Simple Model for Nondeterministic Processes, Technical Report CSR-135-83, University of Edinburgh. To appear in JACM.

[Hennessy, M., 1983c] Modelling Finite Delay Operators, Technical Report CSR-153-83, University of Edinburgh.

[Hennessy, M., 1984a] Modelling Fair Processes, Proc. 16th ACM Symposium on Theory of Computing, Washington D.C.

[Hennessy, M., 1984b] An Asynchronous Theory of Fair Asynchronous Processes, Technical Report CSR-171-84, University of Edinburgh.

[Milner, R., 1980] A Calculus for Communicating Systems, LNCS 92.

[Milner, R., 1982] A Finite Delay Operator in Synchronous CCS, Technical Report CSR-116-82, University of Edinburgh.

[Park, D., 1980] On the Semantics of Fair Parallelism, LNCS 86.

[Stoy, J., 1977] Denotational Semantics: The Scott-Strachey approach to programming language theory, MIT Press.

HOARE'S LOGIC FOR NONDETERMINISTIC REGULAR PROGRAMS: A NONSTANDARD COMPLETENESS THEOREM

Mª T. Hortalá-González, M. Rodríguez-Artalejo
Departamento de Ecuaciones Funcionales
Facultad de Matemáticas, Universidad Complutense
28040 Madrid, Spain

Abstract

The paper characterizes formal derivability in a Hoare's calculus for nondeterministic regular programs, by means of a nonstandard semantics which allows certain "infinitely long computations". Our result generalizes a previous one of Csirmaz [10] and uses some properties of a normal form for regular programs which are perhaphs interesting in its own right.

1. Introduction

Hoare's logic [17], inspired by previous work of Floyd [13], is probably the most popular formalism for proving *partial correctness assertions* (p.c.a.'s) about programs. Formal proofs in Hoare's logic require expressing loop invariants in the underlying assertion language, which is usually first order. In some cases this cannot be done, and as a consequence Hoare's logic is not a complete proof system for p.c.a.'s, see [2], [7], [9], [22], [26].

The "natural" invariant for a loop would be the assertion: "The actual computation state can be reached after some finite number of iterations from a state which satisfies the precondition of the loop". To express this one needs non first order notions such as "natural number" and "finite sequence", which explains the eventual undefinability of invariants in a first order language. Several recent works have tried to overcome these difficulties by allowing, more or less explicitly, nonstandard models of number theory to act as "time scale" for computations, while retaining a first order formalism with finitary proof theory. We shall refer to such approaches as *nonstandard semantics* for programs.

The idea may seem unnatural from a practical point of view, but it turns out to be equivalent to usual semantics over "reasonable" data types (see Theorem 3.4. below) and allows semantical characterizations which are not possible in the standard approach. So, Hoare's logic becomes complete w.r.t. an adequately chosen nonstandard semantics, as first shown by Andreka, Németi and Sain [1], [3], see also [10], [12]; and the powers of several known program verification methods correspond to different kinds of induction axioms on time [4], [11], [19], [23],

[24]. These results rely on a nonstandard version of dynamic logic; some related works are [14] and for the propositional case [8], [21]. In [10], Csirmaz obtained a very elegant and general *nonstandard completeness theorem* for Hoare's logic. His result holds for an arbitrary first order theory taken as data type specification and for quite abstract programs which can be written as

(1) **while** $\neg \overset{n}{x} \approx f(\overset{n}{x})$ **do** $\overset{n}{x} := f(\overset{n}{x})$ **od**

where f stands for a first order definable state transformer. Well known normal form results guarantee that this includes, up to equivalence, all deterministic **while**-programs. But two equivalent **while**-programs can behave differently w.r.t. derivability in Hoare's logic, as shown in [6]. To understand in what sense Csirmaz's result applies to arbitrary **while**-programs, a more detailed examination of the proof theoretical properties of normal forms is needed.
In this paper we shall use such an analysis to extend Csirmaz's theorem to a class of nondeterministic regular programs properly including all programs of the form (1). We shall allow *unbounded nondeterminism* through the use of a nondeterministic assignment operator. This construct is known to have practical value for modelling the notion of *fair termination*; see [5] and [16], where other references are given.

2. Nondeterministic regular programs and their partial correctness assertions

We need some basic notions from mathematical logic. Given a finite similarity type τ, we assume *individual variables* $x,y,z,\ldots \in \mathbf{V}$, τ-*terms* $s = s(\overset{n}{x})$, $t = t(\overset{n}{x}),\ldots \in \mathbf{T}^{\tau}(\overset{n}{x})$ using at most the variables $x_1,\ldots,x_n$ and τ-*formulae* (with equality) $\phi = \phi(\overset{n}{x})$, $\psi = \psi(\overset{n}{x}),\ldots \in$ $\in \mathbf{L}^{\tau}(\overset{n}{x})$ with all its free variables among $x_1,\ldots,x_n$. For $\phi \in \mathbf{L}^{\tau}(\overset{n}{x})$ and terms $t_1,\ldots,t_n$, substitution will be denoted by $\phi[\overset{n}{t}/\overset{n}{x}]$ or simply $\phi(\overset{n}{t})$.

Definition 1.1. The set $\mathbf{RP}^{\tau}(\overset{n}{x})$ of *nondeterministic regular programs of type* τ *in variables* $\overset{n}{x}$ is recursively defined by:

$$\rho \in \mathbf{L}^{\tau}(\overset{n}{x};\overset{n}{y}),\quad \chi \in \mathbf{L}^{\tau}(\overset{n}{x}) \Longrightarrow \overset{n}{x}:=?\,\overset{n}{y}.\rho(\overset{n}{x};\overset{n}{y}),\quad \chi(\overset{n}{x})? \in \mathbf{RP}^{\tau}(\overset{n}{x})$$

(*nondeterministic assignment* and *test*)

$$\alpha,\beta \in \mathbf{RP}^{\tau}(\overset{n}{x}) \Longrightarrow (\alpha \cup \beta),\quad (\alpha;\beta),\quad \alpha^{*} \in \mathbf{RP}^{\tau}(\overset{n}{x})$$

(*union*, *composition* and *iteration*) □

The intended meaning of $\overset{n}{x}:=?\overset{n}{y}.\rho(\overset{n}{x};\overset{n}{y})$ is: "nondeterministically replace state $\overset{n}{x}$ by a new state $\overset{n}{y}$ such that $\rho(\overset{n}{x};\overset{n}{y})$". Note that $x_j:=?$ and

$x_j := t(\overset{n}{x})$ can be achieved as $\overset{n}{x} := ?\overset{n}{y}.\Lambda\{y_k \approx x_k / k \in (1..n)-j\}$ and $\overset{n}{x} := ?\overset{n}{y}.(y_j \approx t(\overset{n}{x}) \wedge \Lambda\{y_k \approx x_k / k \in (1..n)-j\})$, respectively. The meaning of the other constructs is the well known one from dynamic logic; they allow to express **if**, **while**, Dijkstra's guarded commands, etc., see [15]. In the sequel we sometimes write $\alpha(\overset{n}{x})$ for $\alpha \in \mathbf{RP}^{\tau}(\overset{n}{x})$.

3. Standard and nonstandard semantics

Given a τ-*structure*

$$A = (A, (c^A)_{c \in \mathbf{C}(\tau)}, (f^A)_{f \in \mathbf{F}(\tau)}, (p^A)_{p \in \mathbf{R}(\tau)})$$

where $\mathbf{C}(\tau)$, $\mathbf{F}(\tau)$ and $\mathbf{R}(\tau)$ are the sets of constants, function symbols and relation symbols in τ, the set of possible *computation states* for programs $\alpha(\overset{n}{x})$ is $S_n(A) = A^n$. Let $\tau_n = \tau + \{R_\alpha : \alpha \in \mathbf{RP}^{\tau}(\overset{n}{x})\}$ be the infinite similarity type which results by adding to τ a new 2n-ary relation symbol for each program. R_α is intended to reflect the *relational semantics* of α as in dynamic logic [15].

Definition 3.1. The *standard interpretation* of $\mathbf{RP}^{\tau}(\overset{n}{x})$ over A is the τ_n-structure $A^{st} = (A; (R_\alpha^{A^{st}} : \alpha \in \mathbf{RP}^{\tau}(\overset{n}{x})))$ univocally determined by the universal closures of the axioms:

$$(:=?)\ R_{\overset{n}{x}:=?\overset{n}{y}.\rho}(\overset{n}{x};\overset{n}{y}) \leftrightarrow \rho(\overset{n}{x};\overset{n}{y}) \qquad (?)\ R_{\chi(\overset{n}{x})?}(\overset{n}{x};\overset{n}{y}) \leftrightarrow \chi(\overset{n}{x}) \wedge \overset{n}{x} \approx \overset{n}{y}$$

$$(\cup)\ R_{\alpha\cup\beta}(\overset{n}{x};\overset{n}{y}) \leftrightarrow R_\alpha(\overset{n}{x};\overset{n}{y}) \vee R_\beta(\overset{n}{x};\overset{n}{y}) \qquad (;)\ R_{\alpha;\beta}(\overset{n}{x};\overset{n}{y}) \leftrightarrow \exists\overset{n}{z}(R_\alpha(\overset{n}{x};\overset{n}{z}) \wedge R_\beta(\overset{n}{z};\overset{n}{y}))$$

$$(*)\quad R_{\alpha*} = R_\alpha^* \quad \text{(Kleene's closure)}$$

Notice that all this axioms except (*) are τ_n-formulae and that $R_\alpha^{A^{st}} \subseteq S_n(A) \times S_n(A)$.

A *continuous interpretation* over A is each τ_n-structure $A^{ct} = (A; (R_\alpha^{A^{ct}} : \alpha \in \mathbf{RP}^{\tau}(\overset{n}{x})))$ which satisfies the axiom set $\mathbf{CT}_n \subseteq \mathbf{L}^{\tau}(\ )$ formed by the universal closures of (:=?) - (;) and

$$(*)_{ct}\begin{cases}\mathbf{refl}_{\alpha*}: R_{\alpha*}(\overset{n}{x};\overset{n}{x}) \quad \mathbf{ext}_{\alpha*}: R_\alpha(\overset{n}{x};\overset{n}{y}) \to R_{\alpha*}(\overset{n}{x};\overset{n}{y})\\ \mathbf{trn}_{\alpha*}: R_{\alpha*}(\overset{n}{x};\overset{n}{z}) \wedge R_{\alpha*}(\overset{n}{z};\overset{n}{y}) \to R_{\alpha*}(\overset{n}{x};\overset{n}{y})\\ \mathbf{ind}_{\alpha*}(\xi): \xi(\overset{n}{x}) \wedge \forall\overset{n}{u}\,\forall\overset{n}{v}\,[R_{\alpha*}(\overset{n}{x};\overset{n}{u}) \wedge \xi(\overset{n}{u}) \wedge R_\alpha(\overset{n}{u};\overset{n}{v})\\ \qquad \to \xi(\overset{n}{v})] \wedge R_{\alpha*}(\overset{n}{x};\overset{n}{y}) \to \xi(\overset{n}{y})\\ \text{for each } \alpha \in \mathbf{RP}^{\tau}(\overset{n}{x}),\ \xi \in \mathbf{L}^{\tau}(\overset{n}{x})\end{cases} \square$$

Standard interpretations are trivially continuous. There are nonstandard continuous interpretations where $R_{\alpha*}^{A^{ct}}$ strictly includes $(R_\alpha^{A^{ct}})^*$. But $R_{\alpha*}^{A^{ct}}$ must obey the induction axioms $\mathbf{ind}_{\alpha*}(\xi)$, which correspond to the *runs* in [10] and to the *continuous traces* of other authors [2], [3]. Intuitively, first order assertions true at the beginning of a trace of

α^* and invariant on it must hold all along the trace; see [18] for examples.

The two following results relate standard and continuous interpretations:

Lemma 3.2. For every *star free* $\alpha(\overset{n}{x})$ there is a formula $\rho_\alpha \in L^\tau(\overset{n}{x};\overset{n}{y})$ which defines $R_\alpha^{A^{ct}} = R_\alpha^{A^{st}}$ in every continuous interpretation.

Proof. Easy induction on α. □

Definition 3.3. A is *expressive* iff $R_\alpha^{A^{st}}$ is definable by a formula $\rho_\alpha \in L^\tau(\overset{n}{x};\overset{n}{y})$ for every program $\alpha(\overset{n}{x})$ (see [20] for other equivalent characterizations). A is *discrete* iff each element $a \in A$ is definable by a formula $\delta_a \in L^\tau(z)$. □

Theorem 3.4. Let A be expressive and discrete. Then A^{st} is the only continuous interpretation over A.

Sketch of proof. For an arbitrary continuous interpretation A^{ct}, we prove $R_\alpha^{A^{ct}} = R_\alpha^{A^{st}}$ by induction on α. For the case $\alpha = \beta^*$, we fix $\overset{n}{a} \in S_n(A)$, take $\delta_{\overset{n}{a}}(\overset{n}{z}) = \Lambda\{\delta_{a_i}(z_i)/i\in 1..n\}$ and apply $\mathbf{ind}_{\beta^*}(\xi)$ with $\xi(\overset{n}{x}) = \exists \overset{n}{z}(\delta_{\overset{n}{a}}(\overset{n}{z}) \wedge \rho_{\beta^*}(\overset{n}{z};\overset{n}{x}))$, where ρ_{β^*} exists by expressiveness. It follows that $A^{ct} \models R_{\beta^*}(\overset{n}{a};\overset{n}{y}) \rightarrow \rho_{\beta^*}(\overset{n}{a};\overset{n}{y})$ for every $\overset{n}{a}$, i.e. $R_{\beta^*}^{A^{ct}} = R_{\beta^*}^{A^{st}}$. □

We define now the semantics of p.c.a.'s.

Definition 3.5. Let $Ax \subseteq L^\tau(\ )$ be a *specification* and $\pi=\{\phi\}\alpha\{\psi\} \in PCA^\tau(\overset{n}{x})$.

(a) π is *true* in A^{ct} (in symbols, $A^{ct} \models \pi$) iff
$A^{ct} \models \forall\overset{n}{x}\,\forall\overset{n}{y}\,(\phi(\overset{n}{x}) \wedge R_\alpha(\overset{n}{x};\overset{n}{y}) \rightarrow \psi(\overset{n}{x}))$ in the sense of first order logic.

(b) π is a *logical consequence* of Ax w.r.t. *standard semantics* ($Ax \overset{st}{\models} \pi$) iff $A^{st} \models \pi$ for every model $A \models Ax$.

(c) π is a *logical consequence* of Ax w.r.t. *continuous semantics* ($Ax \overset{ct}{\models} \pi$) iff $A^{ct} \models \pi$ for every continuous interpretation A^{ct} over each model $A \models Ax$. □

It is the arbitrariness of A in this definition which makes continuous interpretations necessary, in spite of Theorem 3.4. After all, nonstandard data will need nonstandard time to be processed.

4. A Hoare's calculus for nondeterministic regular programs

The following calculus is intended to derive p.c.a.'s $\pi \in PCA^\tau(\overset{n}{x})$ from specifications $Ax \subseteq L^\tau(\ )$.

Axioms

Asignment	*Test*
$\{\phi(\overset{n}{x})\}\overset{n}{x}:=?\overset{n}{y}.\rho(\overset{n}{x};\overset{n}{y})\{\exists\overset{n}{z}\ (\phi(\overset{n}{z})\wedge\rho(\overset{n}{z};\overset{n}{x}))\}$	$\{\phi(\overset{n}{x})\}\chi(\overset{n}{x})?\{\phi(\overset{n}{x})\wedge\chi(\overset{n}{x})\}$

Rules

Choice

$$\frac{\{\phi\}\alpha\{\psi\}\quad \{\phi\}\beta\{\psi\}}{\{\phi\}\alpha\cup\beta\{\psi\}}$$

Composition

$$\frac{\{\phi\}\alpha\{\eta\}\qquad \{\eta\}\beta\{\psi\}}{\{\phi\}\alpha\,;\beta\{\psi\}}$$

Iteration

$$\frac{\{\eta\}\ \alpha\ \{\eta\}}{\{\eta\}\ \alpha^*\{\eta\}}$$

Consequence

$$\frac{\phi\to\phi'\quad \{\phi'\}\alpha\{\psi'\}\quad \psi'\to\psi}{\{\phi\}\alpha\{\psi\}}$$

To apply the consequence rule, the universal closures of $\phi\to\phi'$ and $\psi'\to\psi$ must have been previously derived from Ax. This explains the meaning of "π is Hoare-derivable from Ax", written as $Ax\vdash\pi$.

Soundness Lemma 4.1. Hoare's calculus is sound w.r.t. both standard and nonstandard semantics:

$$Ax\vdash\{\phi\}\alpha\{\psi\}\Longrightarrow Ax\models^{ct}\{\phi\}\alpha\{\psi\}\Longrightarrow\ Ax\models^{st}\{\phi\}\alpha\{\psi\}$$

Sketch of proof. The second implication is trivial. The first one is proved by induction on α, using the induction axioms for the "$\alpha=\beta^*$" case. □

Completeness Theorem for star free programs 4.2. For $\phi,\psi\in \mathbf{L}^{\tau}(\overset{n}{x})$, $Ax\subseteq\mathbf{L}^{\tau}(\ )$ and each star free $\alpha\in\mathbf{RP}^{\tau}(\overset{n}{x})$:

$$Ax\vdash\{\phi\}\alpha\{\phi\}\Longleftrightarrow Ax\models^{ct}\{\phi\}\alpha\{\psi\}\Longleftrightarrow Ax\models^{st}\{\phi\}\alpha\{\psi\}$$
$$\Longleftrightarrow Ax\vdash\ \phi(\overset{n}{x})\wedge\rho_\alpha(\overset{n}{x};\overset{n}{y})\ \to\psi(\overset{n}{y})$$

where ρ_α is the formula from Lemma 3.2.

Sketch of proof. Straightforward induction on α. The same technique would work to prove a *Cook's Completeness Theorem* w.r.t. expressive structures, as in [9]. □

5. A normal form theorem

In this section we show that each nondeterministic regular program is semantically and proof theoretically equivalent to a normalized one which uses the iteration operator only once.

Definition 5.1. Assume $\alpha\in\mathbf{RP}^{\tau}(\overset{n}{x})$, $\hat{\alpha}\in\mathbf{RP}^{\tau}(\overset{n}{x};\overset{n}{u})$, $Ax\subseteq\mathbf{L}^{\tau}(\ )$.

(a) α and $\hat{\alpha}$ are *semantically equivalent* over $\overset{n}{x}$ w.r.t. Ax (in symbols, $Ax\models^{st}\alpha\ \equiv_{\overset{n}{x}}\hat{\alpha}$) iff the universal closures of

$$R_\alpha(\overset{n}{x};\overset{n}{y})\to\forall\overset{m}{u}\ \exists\overset{m}{v}\ R_{\hat{\alpha}}(\overset{n}{x};\overset{m}{u};\overset{n}{y},\overset{m}{v})\quad\text{and}\quad R_{\hat{\alpha}}(\overset{n}{x},\overset{m}{u},\overset{n}{y},\overset{m}{v})\to R_\alpha(\overset{n}{x};\overset{n}{y})$$

hold in A^{st} for every $A\models Ax$.

(b) α and $\hat{\alpha}$ are *proof theoretically equivalent* over $\overset{n}{x}$ w.r.t. Ax (in symbols, $Ax\vdash\alpha\equiv_{\overset{n}{x}}\hat{\alpha}$) iff for every $\phi,\psi\in\mathbf{L}^{\tau}(\overset{n}{x})$:

$$Ax\vdash\{\phi\}\alpha\{\psi\}\Longleftrightarrow Ax\vdash\{\phi\}\hat{\alpha}\{\psi\}\ □$$

Bergstra and Klop [6], examples 7.2 and 7.3, have shown that both notions are independent, even for quite simple **while**-programs.

<u>Normal Form Theorem 5.3</u>. Assume that $\mathbf{T}^{\tau}(\ )$ includes two diferent closed terms **0**, **1**. For every $\alpha \in \mathbf{RP}^{\tau}(\overset{n}{x})$ one can construct $m \in \mathbb{N}$ and $\hat{\alpha} \in \mathbf{RP}^{\tau}(\overset{n}{x},\overset{m}{u})$ such that $\hat{\alpha} = \alpha_1;\ \alpha_2^*;\ \alpha_3$ where $\alpha_1, \alpha_2, \alpha_3$ are star free, and also

$$Ax \overset{st}{\models} \alpha \equiv_{\underset{x}{n}} \hat{\alpha}, \qquad Ax \vdash \alpha \equiv_{\underset{x}{n}} \hat{\alpha}$$

provided that $Ax \vdash \neg \mathbf{0} \approx \mathbf{1}$.

<u>Sketch of proof</u>. The semantical part is a well known fact, at least for deterministic **while**-programs; but in view of Bergstra and Klop's result, the proof theoretical part must be checked with care. Let ε be the trivial program $x_1 := x_1$ without effect. Define $\hat{\alpha} = \alpha_1;\ \alpha_2^*;\ \alpha_3$ recursively on α.

If α is a nondeterministic assignment or a test, put $\hat{\alpha} = \alpha;\ \varepsilon^*;\ \varepsilon$.

If $\hat{\alpha}$ and $\hat{\beta}$ have been already constructed, take new variables u, v not appearing in $\hat{\alpha}$ or $\hat{\beta}$ and put:

$$\begin{aligned}(\alpha \cup \beta)^\wedge = {} & ((u:=\mathbf{0};\ \alpha_1) \cup (u:=\mathbf{1};\ \beta_1));\\ & ((u \approx \mathbf{0}?;\ \alpha_2) \cup (u \approx \mathbf{1}?;\ \beta_2))^*\\ & ((u \approx \mathbf{0};\ \alpha_3) \cup (u \approx \mathbf{1};\ \beta_3))\end{aligned}$$

$$\begin{aligned}(\alpha;\beta)^\wedge = {} & u:=0;\ v:=\mathbf{0};\ \alpha_1;\\ & (((u \approx \mathbf{0} \wedge v \approx \mathbf{0})?;(\alpha_2 \cup (\alpha_3;\ v:=\mathbf{1}))) \cup\\ & ((u \approx \mathbf{0} \wedge v \approx \mathbf{1})?;(\beta_1;\ u:=\mathbf{1})) \cup\\ & ((u \approx \mathbf{1} \wedge v \approx \mathbf{1})?;\ \beta_2))^*;\\ & (u \approx \mathbf{1} \wedge v \approx \mathbf{1})?;\beta_3\end{aligned}$$

$$\begin{aligned}(\alpha^*)^\wedge = {} & u:=\mathbf{0};\\ & ((u \approx \mathbf{0};\ (\alpha_1;\ u:=\mathbf{1})) \cup\\ & (u \approx \mathbf{1};\ (\alpha_2 \cup (\alpha_3;\ u:=\mathbf{0}))))^*;\\ & u \approx \mathbf{0}?\end{aligned}$$

The idea is to combine guards and boolean variables to control the flow of the computation. It is obvious that $\hat{\alpha}$ has the required form. $Ax \overset{st}{\models} \alpha \equiv_{\underset{x}{n}} \hat{\alpha}$ follows easily by induction on α. $Ax \overset{st}{\vdash} \alpha \equiv_{\underset{x}{n}} \hat{\alpha}$ is proved by using various lemmata about Hoare-derivability to translate invariants and intermediate properties from α to $\hat{\alpha}$ and viceversa. Details will be given in a full version of the paper. □

6. <u>A Nonstandard Completeness Theorem</u>

Let us say that $\alpha(\overset{n}{x})$ *has no nested loops* iff for every subprogram β^* of α, β is star free. Notice that programs in the normal form of Theorem 5.3 have no nested loops. The main result of this section is

<u>Theorem 6.1</u>. Given $Ax \subseteq \mathbf{L}^{\tau}(\ )$, $\phi, \psi \in \mathbf{L}^{\tau}(\overset{n}{x})$ and a program $\alpha \in \mathbf{RP}^{\tau}(\overset{n}{x})$ without nested loops:

$$Ax \vdash \{\phi\}\alpha\{\psi\} \iff Ax \overset{ct}{\models} \{\phi\}\alpha\{\psi\}$$

This and Theorem 5.3 yield inmediately:

Nonstandard Completeness Theorem 6.2. Let $Ax \subseteq \mathbf{L}^{\tau}(\ )$ be such that $Ax \vdash \neg 0 \approx 1$. For every $\phi,\psi \in \mathbf{L}^{\tau}(\overset{n}{x})$ and $\alpha \in \mathbf{RP}(\overset{n}{x})$:

$$Ax \vdash \{\phi\}\alpha\{\psi\} \iff Ax \overset{ct}{\models} \{\phi\}\hat{\alpha}\{\psi\}$$

where $\hat{\alpha}$ is the Normal Form from Theorem 5.3. □

Proof of Theorem 6.1. The implication from left to right holds by the Soundness Lemma 4.1. The opposite direction is proved by induction on α.

Induction base. Let α be star free. Then the result holds by Theorem 4.2.

Induction step. We treat here only the two most interesting cases.

(a) *Composition:* α is $(\beta_1^*;\beta_2^*)$ with $\beta_1 \neq \beta_2$. Let IND(β_1^*) be the result of substituting ρ_{β_1} (cfr. Lemma 3.2) for R_{β_1} in the axioms of type (*)ct for β_1^*, and analogously IND(β_2^*). The hypothesis $Ax \overset{ct}{\models} \{\phi\}\alpha\{\psi\}$ implies

$$Ax \cup \text{IND}(\beta_1^*) \cup \text{IND}(\beta_2^*) \models \phi(\overset{n}{a}) \wedge R_{\beta_1^*}(\overset{n}{a};\overset{n}{c}) \wedge R_{\beta_2^*}(\overset{n}{c};\overset{n}{b}) \to \psi(\overset{n}{b})$$

(where $\overset{n}{a}, \overset{n}{b}, \overset{n}{c}$ are new constants) because each model of $Ax \cup \text{IND}(\beta_1^*) \cup \text{IND}(\beta_2^*)$ can be expanded to a model of $Ax \cup \mathbf{CT}_n$. By the compactness of first order logic, we get

$$\models \sigma_1 \wedge \phi(\overset{n}{a}) \wedge R_{\beta_1^*}(\overset{n}{a};\overset{n}{c}) \to (\sigma_2 \wedge R_{\beta_2^*}(\overset{n}{c};\overset{n}{b}) \to \psi(\overset{n}{b}))$$

where σ_1, σ_2 are finite conjunctions of sentences from $Ax \cup \text{IND}(\beta_1^*) \cup \text{IND}(\beta_2^*)$ which can be chosen in such a way that each nonlogical symbol occurring in both of them belongs to τ. By *Craig's interpolation theorem* (see Shoenfield [25]) there is some $\eta \in \mathbf{L}^{\tau}(\overset{n}{x})$ such that

$$\models \sigma_1 \wedge \phi(\overset{n}{a}) \wedge R_{\beta_1^*}(\overset{n}{a};\overset{n}{c}) \to \eta(\overset{n}{c}), \quad \models \eta(\overset{n}{c}) \wedge \sigma_2 \wedge R_{\beta_2^*}(\overset{n}{c};\overset{n}{b}) \to \psi(\overset{n}{b})$$

It follows that $Ax \overset{ct}{\models} \{\phi\}\beta_1^*\{\eta\}$ and $Ax \overset{ct}{\models} \{\eta\}\beta_2^*\{\psi\}$, and hence $Ax \vdash \{\phi\}\alpha\{\psi\}$, by the induction hypothesis and the composition rule.

(b) *Iteration:* Let α be β^* and assume $Ax \nvdash \{\phi\}\alpha\{\psi\}$. Translating Csirmaz's ideas in [10] to a different (and, as we believe, simpler) technical setting, we are going to construct a continuous interpretation over a model of Ax which makes false the p.c.a. $\{\phi\}\alpha\{\psi\}$, thereby contradicting the hypothesis. We shall need some definitions and auxiliary results.

Definition 6.3. For $\Sigma \subseteq \mathbf{L}^{\tau}(\ )$ and $\Phi \subseteq \mathbf{L}^{\tau}(\overset{n}{x})$ the set $\text{Inv}_{\Phi}^{\Sigma}$ of (Σ,Φ)-*invariants* consists of all $\eta \in \mathbf{L}^{\tau}(\overset{n}{x})$ such that (a) $\Sigma \vdash \phi \to \eta$ for some finite conjunction ϕ of formulae from Φ, and (b) $\Sigma \vdash \eta(\overset{n}{x}) \wedge \rho_{\beta}(\overset{n}{x};\overset{n}{y}) \to \eta(\overset{n}{y})$ or equivalently, $\Sigma \vdash \{\eta\}\beta\{\eta\}$ (by Theorem 4.2).

Lemma 6.4. Assume that $Ax \nvdash \{\phi\}\beta^*\{\psi\}$ and let $\overset{n}{a}, \overset{n}{b}$ be new constants. Then

$$\text{Con}(Ax \cup \{\phi(\overset{n}{a}), \neg\psi(\overset{n}{b})\} \cup \text{Inv}_{\{\phi\}}^{Ax}(\overset{n}{b}))$$

where "Con" denotes consistency.

Proof. Accepting that $Ax \not\vdash \{\phi\}\beta^*\{\psi\}$, it must be the case that $Ax \not\vdash \eta \to \psi$, or equivalently $Con(Ax \cup \{\neg\psi(\overset{n}{b}),\eta(\overset{n}{b})\})$, for every $\eta \in Inv^{Ax}_{\{\phi\}}$. As $Inv^{Ax}_{\{\phi\}}$ is closed under finite conjunctions, we get by compactness that $Ax \cup \{\neg\psi(\overset{n}{b})\} \cup Inv^{Ax}_{\{\phi\}}(\overset{n}{b})$ is consistent.

To finish, observe that the sentence $\exists \overset{n}{x}\ \phi(\overset{n}{x})$ belongs to $Inv^{Ax}_{\{\phi\}}$ □

Lemma 6.5. Assuming the conclusion of the previous lemma, there are complete sets $Ax \subseteq \Sigma \subseteq L^{\tau}(\ )$ and $\phi \in \Phi \subseteq L^{\tau}(\overset{n}{x})$ such that

$$Con\ (\Sigma \cup \Phi(\overset{n}{a}) \cup \{\neg\psi(\overset{n}{b})\} \cup Inv^{\Sigma}_{\Phi}(\overset{n}{b}))$$

Proof. See lemmata 3.4 and 3.5 in [10], whose proofs can be straightforwardly translated to our setting. □

In what follows, we assume a fixed choice of Σ, Φ satisfying the previous lemma.

Definition 6.6. A formula $\xi \in L^{\tau}(\overset{n}{x})$ is *evasive* iff for every invariant $\eta \in Inv^{\Sigma}_{\Phi}$ it holds

$$Con(\Sigma \cup \{\exists \overset{n}{u} \exists \overset{n}{v}\ (\eta(\overset{n}{u}) \wedge \xi(\overset{n}{u}) \wedge \rho_{\beta}(\overset{n}{u};\overset{n}{v}) \wedge \neg\xi(\overset{n}{v}))\}) \quad \square$$

Let E denote the set of all evasive formulae, and take new constants $\overset{n}{c}_{\xi}$, $\overset{n}{d}_{\xi}$ for each $\xi \in E$.

Lemma 6.7.

$$Con(\Sigma \cup \Phi(\overset{n}{a}) \cup \{\neg\psi(\overset{n}{b})\} \cup Inv^{\Sigma}_{\Phi}(\overset{n}{b}) \cup \bigcup_{\xi \in E} (Inv^{\Sigma}_{\Phi}(\overset{n}{c}_{\xi}) \cup \{\xi(\overset{n}{c}_{\xi}) \wedge \rho_{\beta}(\overset{n}{c}_{\xi};\overset{n}{d}_{\xi}) \wedge \neg\xi(\overset{n}{d}_{\xi})\}))$$

Proof. As Inv^{Σ}_{Φ} is closed under finite conjunctions, it enoughs by compactness to prove the consistency of

$$\Sigma \cup \Phi(\overset{n}{a}) \cup \{\neg\psi(\overset{n}{b})\} \cup Inv^{\Sigma}_{\Phi}(\overset{n}{b}) \cup$$
$$\{\eta(\overset{n}{c}_{\xi}) \wedge \xi(\overset{n}{c}_{\xi}) \wedge \rho_{\beta}(\overset{n}{c}_{\xi};\overset{n}{d}_{\xi}) \wedge \neg\xi(\overset{n}{d}_{\xi}) : \xi \in E\}$$

for each $\eta \in Inv^{\Sigma}_{\Phi}$ separately. But for fixed $\xi \in E$, $\eta \in Inv^{\Sigma}_{\Phi}$, the definition of evasiveness and the completeness of Σ guarantee that

$$\Sigma \vdash \exists \overset{n}{u} \exists \overset{n}{v}\ (\eta(\overset{n}{u}) \wedge \xi(\overset{n}{u}) \wedge \rho_{\beta}(\overset{n}{u};\overset{n}{v}) \wedge \neg\xi(\overset{n}{v}))$$

which, in view of lemma 6.5, implies the desired result. □

Lemma 6.8.

$$Con\ (\mathbf{CT}_n \cup \Sigma \cup \Phi(\overset{n}{a}) \cup \{R_{\beta^*}(\overset{n}{a};\overset{n}{b}), \neg\psi(\overset{n}{b})\}).$$

Proof. Let A be a model of the set from the previous lemma. Define an interpretation A^{ct} over A by taking

$$R^{A^{ct}}_{\beta^*} = (R^{A^{st}}_{\beta} \cup \{(\overset{n}{a}^{A};\ \overset{n}{c}^{A}_{\xi}) : \xi \in E\} \cup \{(\overset{n}{a}^{A};\ \overset{n}{b}^{A})\})^*$$

and building $R^{A^{ct}}_{\gamma}$ in the standard way from the interpretations of γ's contituents, for any $\gamma \neq \beta^*$.

To prove that A^{ct} is in fact continuous, only the induction axioms $\mathbf{ind}_{\beta^*}(\xi)$ may cause trouble. Reasoning informally, to prove that an arbitrary one of them is true in A^{ct} we assume that

$$(1)\ \ \xi(\overset{n}{x}) \wedge \forall \overset{n}{u} \forall \overset{n}{v}\ (R_{\beta^*}(\overset{n}{x};\overset{n}{u}) \wedge \xi(\overset{n}{u}) \wedge \rho_{\beta}(\overset{n}{u};\overset{n}{v}) \to \xi(\overset{n}{v}))$$

and

(2) $R_{\beta*}(\overset{n}{x};\overset{n}{y})$

are true in A^{ct}. Because of (2) and the definition of $R_{\beta*}^{A^{ct}}$, there is a sequence

$$\overset{n}{x} = \overset{n}{x}_o, \overset{n}{x}_1, \ldots, \overset{n}{x}_i, \ldots, \overset{n}{x}_k = \overset{n}{y}$$

where, for $0 \leq i \leq k$, either (3) or (4) or (5) is true in A^{ct}

(3) $\rho_\beta(\overset{n}{x}_i;\overset{n}{x}_{i+1})$

(4) $\overset{n}{x}_i = \overset{n}{a}$ and $\overset{n}{x}_{i+1} = \overset{n}{c}_\chi$ for some $\chi \in E$

(5) $\overset{n}{x}_i = \overset{n}{a}$ and $\overset{n}{x}_{i+1} = \overset{n}{b}$

Let us reason by induction on i that $\xi(\overset{n}{x}_i)$ is true in A^{ct} for $i = 0,\ldots,k$, implying $\xi(\overset{n}{y})$. The base i=0 is obvious by (1). Assume $\xi(\overset{n}{x}_i)$. If (3) holds, $\xi(\overset{n}{x}_{i+1})$ follows by (1). If (4) holds, ξ cannot be evasive, because if it were we would have $R_{\beta*}(\overset{n}{x};\overset{n}{c}_\xi)$ by virtue of the sequence $\overset{n}{x} = \overset{n}{x}_o,\ldots,\overset{n}{x}_i = \overset{n}{a}, \overset{n}{c}_\xi$ and also $\xi(\overset{n}{c}_\xi) \wedge \rho_\beta(\overset{n}{c}_\xi;\overset{n}{d}_\xi) \wedge \neg\xi(\overset{n}{d}_\xi)$ by evasiveness, contradicting (1). But if ξ is not evasive, then

$$\forall\overset{n}{u}\,\forall\overset{n}{v}\,(\eta(\overset{n}{u}) \wedge \xi(\overset{n}{u}) \wedge \rho_\beta(\overset{n}{u};\overset{n}{v}) \to \eta(\overset{n}{v}) \wedge \xi(\overset{n}{v}))$$

for some $\eta \in Inv_\Phi^\Sigma$, because Σ is complete and η is invariant. As Φ is complete, we have also $\eta \in \Phi$ (because $\eta \in Inv_\Phi^\Sigma$) and $\xi \in \Phi$ (because $\xi(\overset{n}{a})$ is true). We can conclude that $\eta \wedge \xi \in Inv_\Phi^\Sigma$ and as $Inv_\Phi^\Sigma(\overset{n}{c}_\chi)$ is true in A^{ct}, $\xi(\overset{n}{c}_\chi)$ i.e. $\xi(\overset{n}{x}_{i+1})$ is also true. If the pass from $\overset{n}{x}_i$ to $\overset{n}{x}_{i+1}$ is given by (5), we get analogously a formula $\eta \wedge \xi \in Inv_\Phi^\Sigma$ and use the fact that $Inv_\Phi^\Sigma(\overset{n}{b})$ is true in A^{ct}.

To finish the proof of Theorem 6.1, we notice that $\{\phi\}\beta^*\{\psi\}$ fails in A^{ct} due to the states $\overset{n}{a}^A$, $\overset{n}{b}^A$. □

Conlusion

We have characterized Hoare-derivability of a p.c.a. $\{\phi\}\alpha\{\psi\}$ in terms of the behaviour of α's normal form $\hat{\alpha}$ in continuous interpretations. Although this seems to clarify previously known results, it would be nice to get an analogous theorem which refers to α's behaviour directly. This and other aspects of nonstandard semantics, for instance *recursive programs*, will be the subject of further research.

Acknowledgements. We wish to thank Francisca Lucio Carrasco for many fruitful discussions on the subject of this paper.

References

[1] H. Andréka and I. Németi, Completeness of Floyd's program verification method w.r.t. nonstandard time models, Seminar Notes Math. Inst. Hungar. Acad. Sci., SZKI (1977) (in Hungarian).

[2] H. Andréka, I. Németi and I. Sain, Completeness problems in verification of programs and programs schemes, in: J. Bécvar (ed.), Math. Found. of Comp. Sci. 79, Lect. Notes in Comp. Sci. 74 (1979), 208-218.

[3] H. Andréka, I. Németi and I. Sain, A characterization of Floyd's provable programs, in: J. Gruska and M. Chytil (eds.), Math. Found. of Comp. Sci. 81, Lect. Notes in Comp. Sci. 118 (1981), 162-171.

[4] H. Andréka, I. Németi and I. Sain, A complete logic for reasoning about programs via nonstandard model theory, Parts I-II, TCS 17 (1982), 193-212 and 259-278.

[5] K. Apt, Ten years of Hoare's logic: A survey Part II: Nondeterminism, TCS 28 (1984), 83-109.

[6] J.A. Bergstra and J.W. Klop, Proving program inclusion in Hoare's logic, TCS 30 (1984), 1-48.

[7] J.A. Bergstra and J.V. Tucker, Some natural structures which fail to possess a sound and decidable Hoare-like logic for their **while**-programs, TCS 17 (1982), 303-315.

[8] F. Berman, Semantics of looping programs in propositional dynamic logic, Math. Systems Theory 15 (1982), 285-294.

[9] S.A. Cook, Soundness and completeness of an axiom system for program verification, SIAM J. Comp. 7 (1978), 70-90.

[10] L. Csirmaz, Programs and program verification in a general setting, TCS 16 (1981), 199-210.

[11] L. Csirmaz, On the strength of "Sometimes" and "Always" in program verification, Inf. Cntr. 57 (1983), 165-179.

[12] L. Csirmaz and J.B. Paris, A property of 2-sorted Peano models and program verification, Z. f. Math. Logik u. Grund. d. Math. 30 (1984), 325-334.

[13] R.W. Floyd, Assigning meaning to programs, in: J.T. Schwartz (ed.), Math. Aspects of Comp. Sci., AMS 19 (1967), 19-32.

[14] P. Hajek, Making dynamic logic first order, in: J. Gruska and M. Chytil (eds.), Math. Found. of Comp. Sci. 81, Lect. Notes in Comp. Sci. 118 (1981), 287-295.

[15] D. Harel, First-order dynamic logic, Lect. Notes in Comp. Sci. 68 (1979).

[16] D. Harel, Effective transformations on infinite trees, with applications to high undecidability, dominoes and fairness, to appear in J. ACM.

[17] C.A.R. Hoare, An axiomatic basis for computer programming, Comm. ACM 12 (1969), 567-580.

[18] I. Németi, Nonstandard runs of Floyd-provable programs, in: A. Salwicki (ed.), Logics of programs and their applications '80, Lect. Notes in Comp. Sci. 148 (1983), 186-204.

[19] I. Németi, Nonstandard dynamic logic, in: D. Kozen (ed.), Logics of programs '81, Lect. Notes in Comp. Sci. 131 (1981), 311-348.

[20] E.R. Olderog, On the notion of expressiveness and the rule of adaptation, TCS 24 (1983), 337-347.

[21] R. Parikh, The completeness of propositional dynamic logic, in: J. Winkowski (ed.), Math. Found. of Comp. Sci. '78, Lect. Notes in Comp. Sci. 64 (1978), 403-415.

[22] M. Rodríguez-Artalejo, Some questions about expressiveness and relative completeness in Hoare's logic, to appear in TCS.

[23] I. Sain, Structured nonstandard dynamic logic, Z.f. Math. Logik u. Grund. d. Math. 30 (1984), 481-497.

[24] I. Sain, The implicit information content of Burstall's (modal) programverification method, Preprint No. 57/1984, Math. Inst. Hungar. Acad. Sci. Budapest (1984).

[25] J.R. Shoenfield, Mathematical Logic, Addison Wesley Pbl. Co. (1967).

[26] M. Wand, A new incompleteness result for Hoare's system, J. ACM 25 (1968), 168-175.

POWERDOMAINS AS ALGEBRAIC LATTICES

PRELIMINARY REPORT

Karel HRBACEK

City College of the City University of New York

1. Introduction

Mathematical (denotational) semantics of programming languages has been given firm theoretical foundations by the work of Dana Scott extending over the last fifteen years. He has shown that data types can be viewed as objects with a lattice-like structure (called domains), and computations on such data give rise to continuous functions on domains. Scott's theory has been developed in a series of papers (eg. SCOTT [5], [6], [7], [8]), and is quite satisfactory for description of sequential, deterministic computations. However, the denotational approach has met considerable theoretical difficulties in approaching nondeterminism, parallelism and concurrency. In the first place, these features often give rise to noncontinuous, or even nonmonotone, functions. Secondly, even the important case of "continuous", bounded nondeterminism presents problems. PLOTKIN [4] and SMYTH [9] invented powerdomains to represent this kind of nondeterminism in denotational semantics. Smyth powerdomains, based on Smyth ordering, fit well into Scott's theoretical framework, but provide only a rather coarse description. Plotkin uses much finer and more natural Egli-Milner ordering, but Plotkin powerdomains are far from being lattices; i.e., they are not domains in the sense of Scott. Plotkin is thus forced to extend the category of domains. The resulting SFP-objects are rather complicated to define and hard to work with; that is probably the reason why they have not been much used.

Plotkin seems to have considered the possibility of completing SFP-objects into algebraic lattices, but dismissed it as impractical. On p. 463 in [4] he writes: "So converting $\mathbb{P}[D]$ into a lattice would require one to add many points - not just a top element. It is not clear to the author how to keep these separate from the bona-fide elements." And again on p. 482: "...we can embed any SFP-object in $\mathcal{P}(\omega)$... and this gives rise to a lattice with intermediate points. But these intermediate points seem to clutter up the domain...what is wanted is a simple development of $\mathbb{P}[.]$ in the context of $\mathcal{P}(\omega)$ or a similar simple structure. In Scott's words, we want an analytic, not a synthetic, development." The purpose of this work is to do just that. It appears that one can make powerdomains based on Egli-Milner ordering into algebraic lattices. The construction appears to behave quite nicely both in its mathematical properties, and from the point of view of applications to description of nondeterminism. Plotkin powerdomain is embedded as a cofinal subset into this construct, elements of Plotkin powerdomain can be easily distinguished from the "new" elements, and the "new" elements can be given a meaningful intuitive interpretation.

The rest of the paper outlines our approach to powerdomain construction. Many details and all proofs have been left out; they will appear in the full version.

I first learned about Scott's theory in the course of the International Summer School on Theoretical Foundations of Programming Methodology in Marktoberdorf in Summer 1981. I am grateful to the organizers and the NATO Science Committee for supporting my participation.

2. Domains and powerdomains

A poset (D,$\leq$) has the bounded join property (bj) if every finite subset X of D that has an upper bound in D, has a least upper bound lub(X). In particular, $\perp$ = lub($\emptyset$) is the least element of D. A poset (D,$\leq$) is complete if lub(X) exists for every directed subset X of D.

Let (D,$\leq$) be a complete poset with the bj-property. $d \in D$ is a compact element if for every directed $X \subseteq D$, if $d \leq$ lub(X) then $d \leq x$ for some $x \in X$. The poset (D,$\leq$) is algebraic if d = lub($\{x \in D \mid x \leq d$, x compact$\}$) holds for all $d \in D$.

A domain is a complete algebraic poset with the bounded join property.

This definition is equivalent to that of SCOTT [8]. It means that domains are just a slight generalization of algebraic lattices: domains are algebraic lattices without the top element. Since for the purposes of denotational semantics it is more convenient to dispense with the top element, we work with domains, although all our results remain true in the category of algebraic lattices as well.

Let (D,$\leq$) be a poset with the bj-property. $I \subseteq D$ is an ideal if every finite $F \subseteq I$ has an upper bound in D and $x \leq$ lub(F) implies $x \in I$. For any $d \in D$, $(d] = \{x \in D \mid x \leq d\}$ is the principal ideal generated by d. We denote the set of all ideals on D by $|D|$.

<u>Theorem 1.</u> (A proof for algebraic lattices can be found in GRÄTZER [3], Chapter 0.)

(i) Let $(D, \leqslant)$ be a poset with the bj-property. The $(|D|, \subseteq)$ is a domain and the mapping $d \to (d]$ preserves order and finite lubs. Moreover, the principal ideals are precisely the compact elements of $(|D|, \subseteq)$.

(ii) Let $(E, \leqslant)$ be a domain. If E^o is the set of all compact elements of E, then $(E^o, \leqslant)$ is a poset with the bj-property and there is a unique isomorphism i between $(|E^o|, \subseteq)$ and $(E, \leqslant)$ such that $i((e]) = e$ for all $e \in E^o$.

In view of this, every domain can be represented as a domain of ideals on some $(D, \leqslant)$ with the bj-property, ordered by inclusion, and elements of D can be identified with the principal ideals on D. This will be our viewpoint from now on. Intuitively, elements of $|D|$ represent results of some (perhaps infinite) computations, and elements of D are the partial results, obtainable in finite time, of such computations.

If we now consider nondeterministic computations producing results from $|D|$, we see that, at least in case of bounded non-determinism, what is obtainable in finite time is one of a finite number of elements of D. So we let $\mathbb{P}[D]$ be the set of all nonempty finite subsets of D. The natural ordering on $\mathbb{P}[D]$ is the <u>Egli-Milner preordering</u> (see PLOTKIN [4], SMYTH [9]): for $X, Y \in \mathbb{P}[D]$ let

$$X \trianglelefteq Y \Leftrightarrow (\forall x \in X)(\exists y \in Y)\ x \leqslant y \ \ \&\ (\forall y \in Y)(\exists x \in X)\ x \leqslant y.$$

It is well-known that $\trianglelefteq$ is in general not an ordering; if one defines an equivalence relation $\equiv$ on $\mathbb{P}[D]$ by

$$X \equiv Y \Leftrightarrow X \trianglelefteq Y \ \&\ Y \trianglelefteq X,$$

$\trianglelefteq$ induces an ordering on the set $\overline{\mathbb{P}[D]}$ of all equivalence classes of $\mathbb{P}[D]$. To keep our notation simple, we shall work with elements of $\mathbb{P}[D]$ rather than the corresponding equivalence classes, talk about "ordering $\trianglelefteq$ on $\mathbb{P}[D]$" etc., whenever it is unlikely to lead to confusion.

It is also well known that $(\mathbb{P}[D], \trianglelefteq)$ may fail to have the bj-property; thus the set of all ideals (as defined above) on $\mathbb{P}[D]$ is not a domain, only a complete algebraic partial order. In fact, it is exactly the powerdomain in PLOTKIN [4] (see remark on p.471 in [4]).

To obtain a domain, we have to take a different completion, one based on a properly generalized notion of ideal. The right concept is due to FRINK [2].

Let $(P, \leqslant)$ be any poset with the least element $\perp$. $I \subseteq P$ is a (Frink) ideal if every finite $F \subseteq I$ has an upper bound in P and $x \leqslant y$ for all upper bounds y of F implies $x \in I$. If $(P, \leqslant)$ has the bj-property then this definition coincides with the one given earlier; without it, it is more general. Not all (Frink) ideals are directed, but directed ideals will be especially important. We let $|P|$ be the set of all ideals on P. The next theorem is straightforward and known (for algebraic lattices):

Theorem 2. If $(P, \leqslant)$ is a poset with the least element, then $(|P|, \subseteq)$ is a domain. The compact elements of $(|P|, \subseteq)$ are exactly all lubs of finite subsets of P.

Let $(|D|, \subseteq)$ be a domain. $(\mathbb{P}[D], \trianglelefteq)$ is then a poset with the least element $\{\perp\}$; we define the powerdomain of $|D|$ as $(|\mathbb{P}[D]|, \subseteq)$. So the powerdomain is again a domain.

The elements of $|\mathbb{P}[D]|$ are ideals on $\mathbb{P}[D]$; this includes directed ideals, which correspond exactly to elements of Plotkin powerdomain, and can as usual be viewed as representing (partial) results of computations, and also possibly undirected ideals. The first question is, what meaning can we give to the undirected ideals. The next theorem shows that they can be interpreted as "implicit", "hidden" partial results, that eventually resolve themselves into explicit ones.

Theorem 3. Let $\mathfrak{I}$ be an ideal on $(\mathbb{P}[D], \trianglelefteq)$. There exists a unique set $\mathcal{U}_{\mathfrak{I}}$ of mutually $\subseteq$-incomparable directed ideals on $\mathbb{P}[D]$ such that, for every directed ideal $\mathcal{K}$, $\mathfrak{I} \subseteq \mathcal{K} \Leftrightarrow \mathcal{J} \subseteq \mathcal{K}$ for some $\mathcal{J} \in \mathcal{U}_{\mathfrak{I}}$. Moreover, $\mathfrak{I} = \bigcap \mathcal{U}_{\mathfrak{I}}$. If $\mathfrak{I}$ is compact, $\mathcal{U}_{\mathfrak{I}}$ is a finite set of principal ideals (i.e., of elements of $\mathbb{P}[D]$).

For example, let $X, Y \in \mathbb{P}[D]$ be compatible, but have no lub in $\mathbb{P}[D]$. Then the ideal $\mathfrak{I} = \text{lub}\{(X], (Y]\}$ in $|\mathbb{P}[D]|$ is undirected; however, there is a finite set $Z_1,..,Z_n$ of mutually $\trianglelefteq$-incomparable elements of $\mathbb{P}[D]$ such that $(X \trianglelefteq Z \ \& \ Y \trianglelefteq Z) \Leftrightarrow (Z_i \trianglelefteq Z$ for some $i = 1,..,n)$. So $\mathcal{U}_{\mathfrak{I}} = \{ (Z_i] \mid i = 1,...,n \}$. (In terminology of PLOTKIN [4], $Z_1,...,Z_n$ is a complete set of upper bounds of $\{X, Y\}$). We can think of $\mathfrak{I}$ as a "hidden" computational stage, that occurs after completion of both X and Y, but before deciding upon one of the "continuations" $Z_1,\ldots,Z_n$ (which may well be $\trianglelefteq$-incompatible). Theorem 3 shows that the same interpretation can be given to any $\mathfrak{I} \in |\mathbb{P}[D]|$.

So far, the elements of $|\mathbb{P}[D]|$ have been defined as ideals on $\mathbb{P}[D]$; to justify the name powerdomain and make them meaningful as representing nondeterministic computations, we need to be able to view them as subsets of $|D|$. We next show how to do that for directed ideals.

Let $\mathfrak{I}$ be a directed ideal on $\mathbb{P}[D]$. We define a corresponding subset of $|D|$, $[\![\mathfrak{I}]\!]$, as follows:

$$I \in [\![\mathfrak{I}]\!] \Leftrightarrow I \subseteq \bigcup \mathfrak{I} \ \& \ (\forall X \in \mathfrak{I})\ (X \cap I \neq \emptyset).$$

We note that for $\mathfrak{I} = (X]$, the principal ideal generated by $X \in \mathbb{P}[D]$, $[\![\mathfrak{I}]\!] = \mathrm{Con}(X)$ where Con is the convex closure defined for $\mathfrak{X} \subseteq |D|$ by $\mathrm{Con}(\mathfrak{X}) = \{I \in |D| \mid (\exists x_1, x_2 \in \mathfrak{X})\ x_1 \subseteq I \subseteq x_2\}$.
We say that $\mathfrak{X} \subseteq |D|$ is convex if $\mathfrak{X} = \mathrm{Con}(\mathfrak{X})$. $\mathfrak{X}$ is full if $I \in \mathfrak{X}$, $I \subseteq J \subseteq \bigcup \mathfrak{X}$ implies $J \in \mathfrak{X}$. Fullness implies convexity, but not vice versa. A set $C \subseteq \bigcup \mathfrak{X}$ is a cover of $\mathfrak{X}$ if for every $I \in \mathfrak{X}$, $I \cap C \neq \emptyset$. This is equivalent to $C \trianglelefteq \mathfrak{X}$ (the definition of $X \trianglelefteq Y$ given above for $X, Y \in \mathbb{P}[D]$ makes sense for all $X, Y \subseteq |D|$, if one replaces $\leq$ on D by $\subseteq$ on $|D|$). A cover C' is a subcover of C if $C' \subseteq C$. $\mathfrak{X}$ is compact if every cover of $\mathfrak{X}$ has a finite subcover.

Theorem 4.

(a) Let $\mathfrak{I}$ be a directed ideal on $\mathbb{P}[D]$. The set $\mathfrak{X} = [\![\mathfrak{I}]\!]$ is nonempty, full and compact and $\mathfrak{I}$ is the set of all finite covers of $\mathfrak{X}$.
(b) Let $\mathfrak{X} \subseteq |D|$ be nonempty, full and compact. Then the set $\mathfrak{I}$ of all finite covers of $\mathfrak{X}$ is a directed ideal on $\mathbb{P}[D]$ and $\mathfrak{X} = [\![\mathfrak{I}]\!]$.
(c) Let $\mathfrak{I}, \mathfrak{J}$ be directed ideals on $\mathbb{P}[D]$. Then $\mathfrak{I} \subseteq \mathfrak{J} \Leftrightarrow [\![\mathfrak{I}]\!] \trianglelefteq [\![\mathfrak{J}]\!]$ (where $\trianglelefteq$ is the Egli-Milner ordering).

This theorem establishes a 1-1 order-preserving correspondence between directed ideals on $\mathbb{P}[D]$ and certain compact subsets of $|D|$ (in Egli-Milner ordering). The notion of compactness calls for a topology; we next relate it to some of the standard topologies on $|D|$.

Let $(|D|, \subseteq)$ be a domain. The Scott topology (or: the topology of positive information) has for its basis all sets of the form $d^+ = \{I \in |D| \mid d \in I\}$, $d \in D$. Scott topology is T_0, but usually not Hausdorff.

The Lawson topology (or: the topology of positive and negative information) has for its subbasis all sets of the form d^+ and $d^- = \{I \in |D| \mid d \notin I\}$, $d \in D$. Lawson topology is finer than Scott topology, and is Hausdorff.

A set in a topological space is quasicompact if every open cover has a finite subcover; quasicompact sets in Hausdorff spaces are called compact.
For $\mathfrak{X} \subseteq |D|$ we let $\mathfrak{X}\!\uparrow = \{J \in |D| \mid I \subseteq J \text{ for some } I \in \mathfrak{X}\}$.

Theorem 5. The following statements are equivalent:
(1) $\mathfrak{X} = [\![\mathfrak{I}]\!]$ for some directed ideal $\mathfrak{I}$ on $\mathbb{P}[D]$.
(2) $\mathfrak{X}$ is closed in $\mathfrak{X}\!\uparrow$ and quasicompact in Scott topology on $|D|$.
(3) $\mathfrak{X}$ is convex and compact in Lawson topology on $|D|$.

Easy examples show that undirected ideals on $\mathbb{P}[D]$ cannot be identified with subsets of $|D|$ in any meaningful way. However, in view of Theorem 3 we can associate with each ideal $\mathfrak{I}$ on $\mathbb{P}[D]$ a set $\langle\mathfrak{I}\rangle = \{[\![\mathfrak{J}]\!] \mid \mathfrak{J} \in \mathcal{U}_{\mathfrak{I}}\}$ of certain compact subsets of $|D|$ so that

$$\mathfrak{I}_1 \subseteq \mathfrak{I}_2 \Leftrightarrow (\forall \mathfrak{X}_2 \in \langle\mathfrak{I}_2\rangle)(\exists \mathfrak{X}_1 \in \langle\mathfrak{I}_1\rangle)(\mathfrak{X}_1 \trianglelefteq \mathfrak{X}_2).$$

This can be interpreted as: $\mathfrak{I}_2$ provides more information than $\mathfrak{I}_1$ if and only if $\mathfrak{I}_2$ has fewer "continuations" to choose from than $\mathfrak{I}_1$ and each "continuation" available to $\mathfrak{I}_2$ is stronger (in Egli-Milner ordering) than some "continuation" available to $\mathfrak{I}_1$.

In denotational semantics, total computations are represented by maximal ideals. We investigate the relationship between maximal ideals on $\mathbb{P}[D]$ and on D. We note that every maximal ideal on $\mathbb{P}[D]$ is directed.

Theorem 6. Let $\mathfrak{I}$ be a directed ideal on $\mathbb{P}[D]$.
(a) If every $I \in [\![\mathfrak{I}]\!]$ is maximal then $\mathfrak{I}$ is maximal.
(b) If $\mathfrak{I}$ is maximal then for each $I \in [\![\mathfrak{I}]\!]$ there is $J \in [\![\mathfrak{I}]\!]$ such that $I \subseteq J$ and J is maximal.
(c) The converses to both (a) and (b) are false in general.

This shows that a nondeterministic computation that can produce only total results is total, but there are total nondeterministic computations that can produce results that are only partial. However, each such partial result can be extended to a total one.

The above results indicate that the powerdomain construction provides a meaningful representation of bounded nondeterminism, and is helpful in gaining insight into the nature of nondeterministic computations. We mention next some results dealing with mathematical properties of the powerdomain construct. The most important goal is to show that one can solve domain equations in which it occurs.

Scott's theory lives in the category of domains and continuous functions. A function $f\colon |D| \to |E|$ is <u>continuous</u> if $f(\mathrm{lub}^{|D|}(X)) = \mathrm{lub}^{|E|}(f[X])$ holds for every directed $X \subseteq D$. ($f[X] = \{f(x) \mid x \in X\}$.) The first question is whether the powerdomain construct is a functor in this category. Unfortunately, there are difficulties. For each continuous $f\colon |D| \to |E|$ we would like to define a continuous $\mathbb{P}f\colon |\mathbb{P}[D]| \to |\mathbb{P}[E]|$ so that $\mathbb{P}\mathrm{Id}_{|D|} = \mathrm{Id}_{|\mathbb{P}[D]|}$ and $\mathbb{P}(g \circ f) = \mathbb{P}g \circ \mathbb{P}f$. For directed $\mathfrak{J} \in |\mathbb{P}[D]|$ we naturally let

$\mathbb{P}f(\mathfrak{J}) = \{Y \in \mathbb{P}[E] \mid Y \trianglelefteq f[X]$ for some $X \in \mathfrak{J}\}$; this is again a directed ideal (on $\mathbb{P}[E]$). But there are at least two ways how to extend $\mathbb{P}f$ "naturally" to all of $|\mathbb{P}[D]|$:

the "minimal" extension

$$\underline{\mathbb{P}}f(\mathfrak{J}) = \{Y \in \mathbb{P}[E] \mid Y \trianglelefteq Z \text{ for all } Z \trianglerighteq f[X_1], \dots, Z \trianglerighteq f[X_n], \text{ where } X_1, \dots, X_n \in \mathfrak{J}\}$$

and the "maximal" extension

$$\overline{\mathbb{P}}f(\mathfrak{J}) = \{Y \in \mathbb{P}[E] \mid Y \trianglelefteq f[Z] \text{ for all } Z \trianglerighteq X_1, \dots, Z \trianglerighteq X_n, \text{ where } X_1, \dots, X_n \in \mathfrak{J}\}.$$

Both $\underline{\mathbb{P}}f$ and $\overline{\mathbb{P}}f$ are continuous, and one has

(i) $\underline{\mathbb{P}}f(\mathfrak{J}) \subseteq \overline{\mathbb{P}}f(\mathfrak{J})$; $\underline{\mathbb{P}}f(\mathfrak{J}) = \overline{\mathbb{P}}f(\mathfrak{J}) = \mathbb{P}f(\mathfrak{J})$ if $\mathfrak{J}$ is directed;

(ii) $\underline{\mathbb{P}}(g \circ f) \subseteq \underline{\mathbb{P}}g \circ \underline{\mathbb{P}}f$; $\overline{\mathbb{P}}(g \circ f) \supseteq \overline{\mathbb{P}}g \circ \overline{\mathbb{P}}f$;
= holds on directed ideals.

In general, = need not hold, and neither $\underline{\mathbb{P}}$ not $\overline{\mathbb{P}}$ is a functor in the category of domains and continuous functions; it is at present open whether there is a way to define $\mathbb{P}f$ so that one obtains a functor in this category. However, if $f\colon |D| \to |E|$ is continuous and <u>preserves greatest lower bounds</u> (i.e. $f(\mathrm{glb}^{|D|}(X)) = \mathrm{glb}^{|E|}(f[X])$ holds for all $X \subseteq |D|$, $X \neq \emptyset$) then we get $\underline{\mathbb{P}}f = \overline{\mathbb{P}}f =_{\mathrm{def}} \mathbb{P}f$.

Theorem 7. $\mathbb{P}$ is a functor in the category of domains and continuous glb- preserving functions.

Moreover, we also have

Theorem 8. $\mathbb{P}$ preserves projective limits and surjectivity of morphisms (in the category of domains and continuous glb- preserving functions).

This is sufficient to solve domain equations involving $\mathbb{P}$ and the usual functors $\rightarrow$, x, + etc., as shown (for algebraic lattices) in [1], Chapter IV, Section 4 (see especially Scholium 4.9).

One can also define various special functions, such as embedding $i: |D| \rightarrow |\mathbb{P}[D]|$, cartesian product, union and big union (see PLOTKIN [4]) and prove their expected properties.

Some of the complexity of behavior of nondeterministic computations is due to the fact that the set of possible results $X \in \mathbb{P}[D]$ may contain distinct, but compatible elements. We have some results about modelling the situations where it is possible to enforce that the alternatives are mutually exclusive.

Let $\mathbb{P}^W[D]$ be the set of all nonempty finite sets of mutually incompatible elements of D ordered by the Egli-Milner ordering $\trianglelefteq$.

Theorem 9. ($|\mathbb{P}^W[D]|, \subseteq$) is isomorphic to a subdomain of ($|\mathbb{P}[D]|, \subseteq$). Theorem 3 holds for $|\mathbb{P}^W[D]|$ as well, and the ideals in $\mathcal{U}_y$ are mutually $\subseteq$-incompatible.

Theorem 10.

(a) Let $\mathfrak{I}$ be a directed ideal on $\mathbb{P}^W[D]$. The set $\mathfrak{X} = [\![\mathfrak{I}]\!]$ is non-empty and (i) its elements are mutually incompatible;

(ii) every cover of $\mathfrak{X}$ has a finite disjoint subcover.

$\mathfrak{I}$ is just the set of all finite disjoint covers of $\mathfrak{X}$.

(b) Let $\mathfrak{X} \subseteq |D|$ be nonempty and have properties (i) and (ii). Then the set $\mathfrak{I}$ of all finite disjoint covers of $\mathfrak{X}$ is a directed ideal on $\mathbb{P}^W[D]$ and $\mathfrak{X} = [\![\mathfrak{I}]\!]$.

(Since $|\mathbb{P}^W[D]|$ is a subdomain of $|\mathbb{P}[D]|$, the set $[\![\mathfrak{I}]\!]$ is defined for each directed ideal $\mathfrak{I} \in |\mathbb{P}^W[D]|$. A cover C of $\mathfrak{X} \subseteq |D|$ is disjoint if the elements of C are mutually incompatible.)

3. Conclusion

The results outlined in Section 2 indicate that this approach to the powerdomain construction is quite manageable. It is further supported by the fact that it can be generalized to continuous lattices (SCOTT [6]). The powerdomain of a continuous lattice $(D, \leqslant)$ can be defined as a set of all round ideals on $(\mathbb{P}[D], \trianglelefteq)$, ordered by inclusion. The notion of round ideal is defined in GIERZ & KEIMEL [10] for directed ideals; we use an appropriate generalization to Frink ideals. Theorems 3 - 10 of Section 2 can then be proved for continuous lattices (or "continuous lattices without the top element").

After completion of this Preliminary Report I received a letter from Professor Gordon Plotkin with a number of thought-provoking comments on the first draft, as well as some unpublished 1981/82 lecture notes of his. The lecture notes develop Plotkin powerdomain in the category of ω-algebraic posets in a way which seems much closer in spirit to this paper than the original PLOTKIN [4]. In particular, they provide a characterization of the elements of the powerdomain analogous to Theorems 4 and 5. The final version of this paper will discuss the relationship between the two approaches in greater detail; here I can only express my deep thanks to Dr. Plotkin for his interest in my work.

References

[1] A Compendium of Continuous Lattices, ed. by G. Gierz et al., Springer - Verlag 1980.

[2] FRINK, O.: Ideals in partially ordered sets, Amer. Math. Monthly 61 (1954), 223 - 234

[3] GRÄTZER, G.: Universal algebra, 2nd ed., Springer-Verlag 1979

[4] PLOTKIN, G.: A powerdomain construction, SIAM J. Comp. 5 (1976), 452 - 486

[5] SCOTT, D.S.: Outline of a mathematical theory of computation, 4th Annual Princeton Conference on Information Science and Systems 1970, 169 - 176

[6] SCOTT, D.S.: Continuous lattices, Lecture Notes in Math. vol.274, Springer-Verlag 1972, 97 - 136

[7] SCOTT, D.S.: Data types as lattices, SIAM J. Comp. 5 (1976), 522 - 587

[8] SCOTT, D.S.: Lectures on a mathematical theory of computation, Oxford Univ. Computing Laboratory Prog. Research Group - 19, 1981

[9] SMYTH, M.B.: Power domains, JCSS 16 (1978), 23 - 36

[10] GIERZ, G. & K. KEIMEL: Continuous Ideal Completions and Compactifications, in: Continuous Lattices, Lecture Notes in Math. 871 Springer-Verlag 1981, 97 - 124

RANDOM GENERATION OF COMBINATORIAL STRUCTURES FROM A UNIFORM DISTRIBUTION (EXTENDED ABSTRACT)

Mark Jerrum
Department of Computer Science
University of Edinburgh

1 Introduction

A large class of computational problems can be viewed as the seeking of partial information about a relation which associates *problem instances* with a set of *feasible solutions*. Suppose Σ is a finite alphabet in which we agree to encode both problem instances and solutions. A relation $R \subseteq \Sigma^* \times \Sigma^*$ can be interpreted as assigning, to each problem instance $x \in \Sigma^*$, a set of solutions $\{y \in \Sigma^* : xRy\}$. (For technical reasons, we shall assume that this solution set is always finite.) As a paradigm, we might take the relation which associates, with each undirected graph G, the set of 1-factors (perfect matchings) of G:

$$R = \Big\{ \langle x,y \rangle : x \in \Sigma^* \text{ is an encoding of a graph } G, \; y \in \Sigma^* \text{ is an encoding of a 1-factor of } G \Big\}$$

(A *1-factor* of a graph G is a spanning subgraph of G in which every vertex has degree 1.) To each relation of the above form, there correspond a number of naturally defined problems. At least four of these have been identified and considered in previous literature [3]; a fifth is introduced and studied in the present paper. A description of these five categories of problems is given below. Each description is followed, in parentheses, by the interpretation of the problem in the paradigmatic case of the 1-factor relation. Throughout, $x \in \Sigma^*$ represents a problem instance.

1. Existence Does there exist a word $y \in \Sigma^*$ such that xRy? (Does the graph G contain a 1-factor?)

2. Construction Exhibit a word $y \in \Sigma^*$ satisfying xRy, if such exists. (Construct a 1-factor of G.)

3. Optimisation Assume that each solution $y \in \Sigma^*$ has an associated cost, $c(y)$. The optimisation problem associated with R and c involves determining the minimum of the set $\{c(y) : y \in \Sigma^* \text{ and } xRy\}$. (For a weighted graph G, what is the minimum weight of a 1-factor of G?)

4. Counting How many words $y \in \Sigma^*$ satisfy xRy? (How many 1-factors does G possess?)

5. (Uniform) Generation Generate uniformly, at random, a word $y \in \Sigma^*$ satisfying

xRy. (Generate, at random, a 1-factor of the graph *G*. Each 1-factor is to appear with equal probability.)

For a given relation *R*, we may thus speak of the existence, construction, etc. problem associated with *R*. The unifying view of combinatorial problems presented above, has appeared previously in the literature in the form of the *string relations* of Garey and Johnson [3], and the *search functions* of Valiant [12]. It is used here to relate generation problems, which are the main subject of the paper, to more familiar combinatorial problems such as existence and counting.

Previous papers have concentrated on particular instances of the uniform generation problem [1, 2, 14]. In the present paper, however, an attempt is made to analyse the complexity of generation problems *as a class*. Because these problems inherently involve randomisation, we employ, as our model of computation, the *probabilistic Turing machine* (PTM) which is able to make random transitions according to the fall of a fair coin. A generation problem is considered to be tractable if it can be solved (in a sense which is made precise in the next section) by a PTM running in polynomial time.

A relation $R\subseteq\Sigma^*\times\Sigma^*$ is a *p-relation* if it can be "checked fast". Formally we require

1. There exists a polynomial $p(n)$ such that $<x,y>\in R \Rightarrow |y|\le p(|x|)$

2. The predicate $<x,y>\in R$ can be tested in deterministic polynomial time.

Let $R\subseteq\Sigma^*\times\Sigma^*$ be an p-relation. It is not difficult to show that the generation problem associated with *R* can be solved by a polynomial time bounded PTM equipped with a #P oracle. (Essentially, #P is the class of counting problems associated with p-relations [13].) We might summarise this fact informally by saying that uniform generation is no more difficult than counting. Two pieces of evidence are provided in the paper to support the claim that generation is easier, in some sense, than counting. Firstly, it is shown that the generation problem associated with a p-relation *R* can be solved by a polynomial time bounded PTM equipped with a Σ_2^p oracle. (See Stockmeyer [10] for a description of the polynomial hierarchy.) The class #P, on the other hand, is not known to be contained within *any* level of the polynomial hierarchy. This containment result is akin to, and indeed rests upon, a result of Stockmeyer regarding approximate counting [11]. Secondly, a relation is presented for which the associated generation problem is solvable in polynomial time, whereas the associated counting problem is #P-complete. The relation in question is the one which associates each DNF Boolean formula with its set of satisfying assignments. Thus, while *counting* the satisfying assignments to a DNF formula is apparently computationally intractable, the task of *generating* random satisfying assignments is feasible. This result parallels one of Karp and Luby [7], who exhibit a "fully-polynomial randomised approximation scheme" for estimating the number of satisfying assignments to a DNF formula.

Evidence is also presented of a complexity gap between existence (or indeed construction) and uniform generation. (Clearly, generation is at least as difficult as construction.) We show that the existence of a polynomial time bounded PTM for uniformly generating cycles in a directed graph would imply that NP=VPP. (VPP is the class of decision problems which can be solved in polynomial time by a probabilistic algorithm with one-sided error probability [4].) Thus it is rather unlikely that uniform generating of cycles in a directed graph can be accomplished in polynomial time, whereas the *detection* of cycles is an easy matter. Thus we may say, informally, that generation is strictly harder than existence. (The cycle generation example is due to Valiant and Vazirani.)

Further results suggest a strong connection between generation and approximate counting. (The approximate counting problem associated with the relation R, asks for the size of the solution set $\{y : xRy\}$ within a specified relative error.) For many naturally occurring relations R, namely those which are self-reducible in the sense of Schnorr [8], the complexities of the associated approximate counting and generation problems are shown to be within a polynomial factor of one another. Thus, known efficient algorithms for counting can be used to obtain fast algorithms for uniform generation. (Slightly different formulations of these results were obtained independently by Valiant and Vazirani.)

2 Probabilistic Turing Machines

The model of computation we employ is the probabilistic Turing machine, which was first introduced by Gill [4]. A *probabilistic Turing machine* (PTM) is a Turing machine ([6], p.147) equipped with an output tape, and having distinguished coin-tossing states. For each coin-tossing state, and each tape symbol scanned by the tape head, *two* possible transitions of the machine are specified. The computation of a PTM is deterministic, except when the PTM is in a coin-tossing state, in which case the next transition is decided by the toss of a fair coin. If the PTM reaches an accepting state, the *output* of the machine is just the contents of the output tape.

Gill viewed PTM's as language recognisers; in this paper, however, PTM's will be used to generate random outputs, with probability distribution depending on the input x, and on some underlying relation R. We say that the PTM M is a *(uniform) generator* for the relation $R \subseteq \Sigma^* \times \Sigma^*$ iff

1. There exists a function $\varphi \in \Sigma^* \to (0,1]$ such that, for all $x, y \in \Sigma^*$,

$$\Pr(\text{Given input } x,\ M \text{ outputs } y) = \begin{cases} 0 & \text{if } \langle x,y\rangle \notin R \\ \varphi(x) & \text{if } \langle x,y\rangle \in R. \end{cases}$$

2. For all inputs $x \in \Sigma^*$ such that $\{y \in \Sigma^* : xRy\}$ is non-empty,

$$\Pr(M \text{ accepts } x) \geq 1/2$$

Informally, M generates only words in the solution set of x, and each word in the solution set has an equal probability of being selected. Moreover, the probability that M will produce *some* output is bounded away from zero. Note that a machine M, run on input x, signals the fact that the solution set $\{y \in \Sigma^* : xRy\}$ is empty by *never* accepting.

It is easy to see that using j tosses of an unbiased coin it is possible to simulate any biased coin for which the probability of landing "heads" is of the form $i2^{-j}$ $(0 \leq i \leq 2^j)$, and that no other types of coins can be simulated. This restriction on realisable branching probabilites can sometimes be inconvenient. Indeed, the construction of PTM's to compute specified relations would be made easier, and some proofs involving PTM's made simpler, if the definition of PTM were extended to allow more general coin-tossing states. One possibilty is to use a biased coin to determine the next transition of the machine - the bias of the coin being a ratio of two integers computed previously by the machine. The only objection to this extension is that it violates the idea of each computational step of a Turing machine being bounded, that is implementable by some fixed hardware in constant time. Once the decision has been made to use an unbiased coin, the possiblity of M sometimes not accepting its input has to be allowed. For if M were to accept x for all possible sequences of coin tosses, then each word $y \in \Sigma^*$ would be output by M with a probability of the form $i2^{-j}$ for some natural numbers i and j. Thus, for example, M could not compute a relation R for which $|\{y \in \Sigma^* : xRy\}| = 3$ for some input x. Clearly, the model of computation would then be too restrictive.

We say that a PTM M is $f(n)$ time-bounded iff, for all natural numbers n, and all inputs $x \in \Sigma^n$, every accepting computation of M halts within $f(n)$ steps. A PTM M is *polynomially time-bounded* if there exists a polynomial $p(n)$ such that M is $p(n)$ time-bounded. At first sight, this definition may appear unnecessarily severe - we might be tempted to relax it to "the *average* number of steps in an accepting computation is bounded by $f(n)$". The objection to this relaxation is that, although the average length of an accepting computation is short, there may be some words that can only be output by M after a very long computation. That is, solutions might exist which cannot be generated without a prohibitively long delay. Again, technical complications are introduced into proofs by the severity of the definition. In return, the results obtained are seen to relate to an unimpeachable model of resource-bounded computation.

3 Uniform Generation and the Polynomial Hierarchy

For the main result of the section, we make use of a theorem of Stockmeyer. If α, β, r are positive real numbers, with $r \geq 1$, we say that β approximates α within ratio r if $\beta r^{-1} \leq \alpha \leq \beta r$.

Theorem 1: Let $f \in \Sigma^* \to \mathbb{N}$ be a member of #P. Then there exists a function $g \in (\Sigma^* \times \mathbb{N}^+ \to \mathbb{N})$ such that

1. For all $m \in \mathbb{N}^+$, $x \in \Sigma^*$, $g(x,m)$ approximates $f(x)$ within ratio $(1 + m^{-1})$.

2. If the second (integer) argument of g is presented in unary notation, then $g \in \Delta_3^p$.

Proof: See Stockmeyer [11].

(A definition of Δ_3^p can be found in Garey and Johnson [3], page 162.)

Theorem 2: Let $R \subseteq \Sigma^* \times \Sigma^*$ be a p-relation. Then there exist generators for R of the following types

1. A polynomial time bounded PTM equipped with a #P oracle.

2. A polynomial time bounded PTM equipped with a Σ_2^p oracle.

Proof: (Sketch) The proof is conceptually simple and can be informally described in a few lines. Since R is a p-relation, there is a polynomial $p(n)$ such that $\langle x,y \rangle \in R \Rightarrow |y| \leq p(|x|)$. Consider the PTM M which operates in the following manner. On input x, the machine M generates a word y uniformly at random from the set $\{y \in \Sigma^* : |y| \leq p(|x|)\}$. The machine M then tests, in polynomial time, whether xRy; if the test succeeds, M outputs y and accepts. Clearly, M generates each word in the set $\{y \in \Sigma^* : xRy\}$ with equal probability. Unfortunately, since accepting computations of M may form only a small proportion of the total, the probability that M produces *no* output may be very close to 1.

Suppose, however, that each time M enters a coin-tossing state we have available some information concerning the number of accepting configurations which can be reached *given* the fall of the coin. Then we can improve the chances of arriving at an accepting configuration by throwing an *unfair* coin which favours the outcome which leads to the larger number of accepting configurations. In fact, given *exact* information about the number of accepting configurations of M which can be reached from a given configuration, we can so choose the biasing of the coin that

- Only accepting configurations can be reached.

- Each accepting configuration is reached with equal probability.

Part (1) of the theorem is proved by observing that the required information can be obtained using a #P oracle.

If the information about the number of reachable accepting configurations of M is approximate, but sufficiently accurate, we can use a biased coin to arrive at accepting configurations of M with roughly uniform probability. Since the bias of the coin is prescribed, the probability that M will reach a certain accepting configuration is known *a posteriori*. By retaining the output of M with probability inversely proportional to the *a posteriori* probability, and discarding it otherwise, we can force a uniform distribution on the accepting configurations. (A similar technique is used by Bach [1] to generate integers with known factorisation.) Part (2) of the theorem is completed by appealing to theorem 1.

The full proof of the above theorem involves a number of technicalities which arise from the inability of a PTM to branch with other that even probabilities.

4 An Instance where Uniform Generation is Easier than Counting

The previous section provided circumstantial evidence that uniform generation problems *as a class* may be "easier" than counting problems. In this section, we consider a *particular* relation for which the associated counting problem is apparently intractable, whereas the associated generation problem is efficiently soluble. The relation in question associates each Boolean formula F in disjunctive normal form (DNF) with the set of satisfying assignments to F. It is easy to demonstrate that the problem of counting the satisfying assignments to a DNF formula is #P-complete, and hence unlikely to be soluble in deterministic polynomial time. (A description of #P and its completeness class can be found in Valiant [13], or Garey and Johnson [3].) In contrast, a simple and efficient algorithm for generating random assignments to a DNF formula exists, and is presented in this section.

The #P-completeness result is obtained by exhibiting a reduction from #SAT, the problem of counting the number of satisfying assignments to a Boolean formula in conjunctive normal form (CNF). Simon [9] showed #SAT to be #P-complete by a slight modification to the generic transformation used to establish Cook's theorem. Suppose now that F is an instance of #SAT. The formula F can be transformed, using de Morgan's laws, into an equivalent length DNF formula for $\neg F$, the complement of F. This having been done, it merely needs to be noted that the number of satisfying assignments to F *plus* the number of satisfying assignments to $\neg F$ is equal to 2^k, where k is the number of variables occurring in F.

The proposed method for *randomly generating* satisfying assignments to a DNF formula follows closely the Monte Carlo algorithm, presented by Karp and Luby [7], for *estimating their number*. Suppose that $F = F_1 \vee F_2 \vee \cdots \vee F_m$ is a DNF formula in the set of variables X. with each F_i being a conjunction of a number of literals. Let $S_j \subseteq \{0,1\}^X$, $1 \leq j \leq m$, be the set of satisfying assignments to the disjunct F_j, and $S = \cup_k S_k$ the set of satisfying assignments to F itself. The task is to select, uniformly at random, a member of the set S. The algorithm for accomplishing the task is sketched in figure 1.

(1) **for** i:=1 **to** m **do begin**

(2) Select an integer $j \in [1,m]$ randomly, but non-uniformly, such that $\Pr(j=c) = |S_c|(\Sigma_k|S_k|)^{-1}$;

(3) Select $a \in S_j$, uniformly at random;

(4) $N := |\{k \in [1,m] : a \in S_k\}|$;

(5) With probability N^{-1} output a, and **halt**

end

Figure 1: Algorithm for generating a satisfying assignment to a DNF formula.

Consider one iteration of the for loop. Let j_0 be any integer in the range $[1,m]$, and

a_0 any element of S_{j_0}. After line (3) of the for loop is executed, the probability that the variables j and a have the values j_0 and a_0 respectively, is $(\Sigma_k|S_k|)^{-1}$, independent of the choice of j_0 and a_0. Thus the probability that the variable a takes the value a_0, is $N(\Sigma_k|S_k|)^{-1}$, where $N = |\{k\in[1,m] : a_0\in S_k\}|$, and the probability of a_0 being output in line (5) is $(\Sigma_k|S_k|)^{-1}$, independent of the choice of a_0. The algorithm therefore generates each satisfying assignment to F with equal probability. It remains to check that the probability that the algorithm generates no output is bounded away from one. The probability that, on a particular iteration, *some* assignment is output, is greater than m^{-1}. The probability that m iterations occur with *no* output taking place is therefore less than $(1 - m^{-1})^m$, which is bounded above by e^{-1}.

The algorithm given in figure 1, is not, as it stands, directly implementable on a PTM. (The branching probabilities are not of the required form.) This objection can be dealt with, at the expense of introducing some technical complication.

5 Evidence that Uniform Generation is Harder than Construction

Generation problems differ from construction problems in requiring uniformity of the probability distribution on the space of possible outputs. It is natural to ask whether this additional requirement makes uniform generation *strictly* harder than construction. The following theorem suggests that there are naturally occurring relations for which the associated construction and generation problems are of widely differing complexities. Let GENCYCLE be the following problem:

Input Directed graph G.

Output A cycle selected uniformly, at random, from the set of all directed cycles of G.

Clearly, the problem of constructing an arbitrary cycle in a directed graph is easily solved in polynomial time.

Theorem 3: Suppose there exists a polynomial time bounded PTM which solves the problem GENCYCLE. Then NP=VPP.

Proof: It is sufficient to deduce, assuming the condition of the theorem, that VPP contains some NP-complete problem. We choose to work with the problem DHC, of determining whether a directed graph G contains a Hamiltonian cycle [3]. Let G' be the directed graph derived from G by replacing each edge of G by the "chain of diamonds" illustrated in figure 2. The length of the chain is chosen to be $k = \lceil n \lg n \rceil$, where n is the number of vertices in G. Clearly, the transformed graph G' contains a cycle of length $2kn$, if and only if the original graph G contains a Hamiltonian cycle. Now, if G' contains a cycle of length $2kn$ then it contains at least 2^{kn} cycles of this length. Moreover, it is easy to check that the total number of cycles in G' which have length shorter than $2kn$ is bounded by $n^n 2^{k(n-1)}$, which in turn, by choice of k, is bounded by

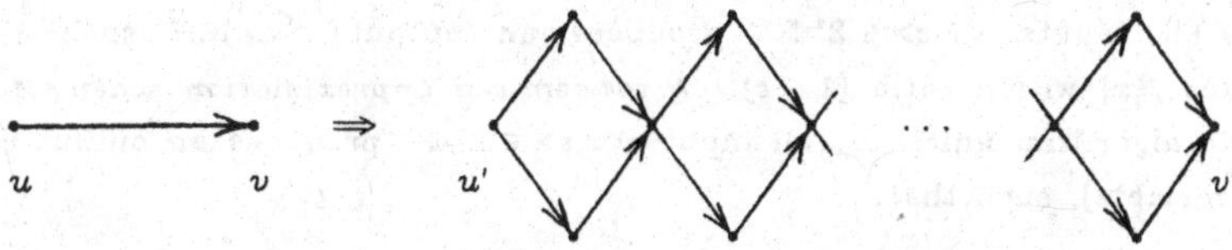

Figure 2: The transformation applied to each edge of G.

2^{kn}. Thus, if G is Hamiltonian, the probability that a randomly generated cycle of G' has length $2kn$ is at least 1/2, whereas, if G is not Hamiltonian, the probability is 0. Membership of DHC in VPP is immediate from this observation.

It would be interesting to find other examples of natural problems which exhibit a complexity gap between their construction and generation variants. One possible candidate is the problem of uniformly generating a 1-factor in an undirected graph. This problem is not known to belong to be polynomial time solvable, but neither is there any convincing evidence of intractability.

6 The Relationship Between Uniform Generation and Approximate Counting

Sections 3 and 4 suggest that uniform generation of combinatorial structures is in some way related to approximate counting of structures, as studied by Stockmeyer [11], and Karp and Luby [7]. It is possible to formalise this connection to a certain extent. Following Schnorr [8] we say that a p-relation $R \subseteq \Sigma^* \times \Sigma^*$ is *self-reducible* iff

1. There exists a polynomial time computable function $g \in \Sigma^* \to \mathbb{N}$ such that $xRy \Rightarrow |y| = g(x)$

2. There exist polynomial time computable functions $\psi \in \Sigma^* \times \Sigma^* \to \Sigma^*$ and $\delta \in \Sigma^* \to \mathbb{N}$ satisfying

   $\delta(x) = O(\lg |x|)$

   $g(x) > 0 \Rightarrow \delta(x) > 0 \qquad \forall x \in \Sigma^*$

   $|\psi(x,w)| \le |x| \qquad \forall x,w \in \Sigma^*$

   and such that for all $x \in \Sigma^*$, $y = y_1 \ldots y_n \in \Sigma^*$,

   $<x, y_1, \ldots, y_n> \in R \iff <\psi(x, y_1, \ldots, y_{\delta(x)}), y_{\delta(x)+1}, \ldots, y_n> \in R$

Intuitively, self-reducibility captures the idea that the solution set associated with a given instance of a problem can be expressed in terms of the solution sets of a number of smaller instances of the same problem. Very many naturally occurring relations are self-reducible; examples include 1-factors in an undirected graph, and satisfying assignments to a CNF or DNF formula.

Suppose $f \in \Sigma^* \to \mathbb{N}$. A (*deterministic*) *approximation scheme* for f is an algorithm which for all inputs $<x,\varepsilon> \in \Sigma^* \times \mathbb{R}^+$ produces an output $g(x,\varepsilon) \in \mathbb{N}$ such that $g(x,\varepsilon)$ approximates $f(x)$ within ratio $(1 + \varepsilon)$. A ***randomised approximation scheme*** for f is an probabilistic algorithm which for all inputs $<x,\varepsilon> \in \Sigma^* \times \mathbb{R}^+$ produces an output $\tilde{g}(x,\varepsilon)$ (now a random variable), such that

$$\Pr\left(\tilde{g}(x,\varepsilon) \text{ approximates } f(x) \text{ within ratio } (1+\varepsilon)\right) \geq 3/4.$$

An approximation scheme (deterministic or randomised) is *fully-polynomial* if its execution time is bounded by a polynomial in ε^{-1} and the length of x.

For self-reducible relations, there is a strong connection between the complexities of the associated uniform generation and approximate counting problems.

Theorem 4: Suppose $R \subseteq \Sigma^* \times \Sigma^*$ is self-reducible. Let $N_R \in \Sigma^* \to \mathbb{N}$ be the counting function associated with R, defined by $N_R(x) = |\{y \in \Sigma^* : xRy\}|$, for all $x \in \Sigma^*$. Then

1. If there exists a polynomial time bounded generator for R, then there exists a fully-polynomial randomised approximation scheme for N_R.

2. If there exists a fully-polynomial deterministic approximation scheme for N_R, then there exists a polynomial time bounded generator for R.

As an example, suppose there were an efficient algorithm for estimating the number of 1-factors of a graph. Then, since the 1-factor relation is self-reducible, the problem of uniformly generating 1-factors of a graph would also be feasible. A second example is provided by spanning trees of a graph. The existence of an efficient algorithm (due to Kirchoff [5]) for counting spanning trees of a graph, immediately implies that the problem of uniformly generating spanning trees of a graph is solvable in polynomial time.

Theorem 4 is not entirely satisfying because of the lack of symmetry between its two parts. The theorem *can* be symmetrised at the expense of replacing uniform generation by a somewhat weaker notion of "approximately uniform" generation. This idea has been pursued by Valiant and Vazirani, who independently obtained results similar in flavour to theorem 4. This work will be detailed in the full version of the paper.

Acknowledgements

I would like to thank Clemens Lauteman and Alistair Sinclair for discussions which helped to clarify the ideas presented in this paper.

REFERENCES

1. Bach, E. How to Generate Random Integers with Known Factorisation. *Proceedings of the 15th ACM Symposium on Theory of Computing*, 1983, pp. 184-188.

2. Dixon, J.D. and Wilf, H.S. The Random Selection of Unlabelled Graphs. *J. Algorithms* 4 (1983), pp. 205-213.

3. Garey, M.R. and Johnson, D.S. *Computers and Intractability*. Freeman, 1979.

4. Gill, J. Computational Complexity of Probabilistic Turing Machines. *SIAM J. on Computing* 6 (1977), pp. 675-695.

5. Harary, F. and Palmer, E.M. *Graphical Enumeration*. Academic Press, 1973.

6. Hopcroft, J.E. and Ullman, J.D. *Introduction to Automata Theory, Languages and Computation*. Addison-Wesley, 1979.

7. Karp, R.M. and Luby, M. Monte-Carlo Algorithms for Enumeration and Reliability Problems. *Proceedings of the 24th IEEE Symposium on Foundations of Computer Science*, 1983, pp. 56-64.

8. Schnorr, C.P. Optimal Algorithms for Self-Reducible Problems. *Proceedings of the 3rd International Colloquium on Automata, Languages and Programming*, EATCS, 1976, pp. 322-337.

9. Simon, J. On the Difference between One and Many. *Proceedings of the 4th International Colloquium on Automata, Languages and Programming*, EATCS, 1977, pp. 480-491.

10. Stockmeyer, L. The Polynomial-time Hierarchy. *Theoretical Computer Science* 3 (1977), pp. 1-22.

11. Stockmeyer, L. The Complexity of Approximate Counting. *Proceedings of the 15th ACM Symposium on Theory of Computing*, 1983, pp. 118-126.

12. Valiant, L.G. The Complexity of Combinatorial Computations: an Introduction. Internal Report CSR-30-78, Department of Computer Science, University of Edinburgh, October, 1978.

13. Valiant, L.G. The Complexity of Computing the Permanent. *Theoretical Computer Science* 8 (1979), pp. 189-201.

14. Wilf, H.S. The Uniform Selection of Free Trees. *J. Algorithms* 2 (1981), pp. 204-207.

Do Rational Equivalence Relations have Regular Cross-Sections? †

J. H. Johnson

Department of Computer Science
University of Waterloo
Waterloo, Ontario, Canada N2L 3G1

ABSTRACT

The following classes of rational equivalence relations are shown to have regular cross-sections: deterministic rational equivalence relations, rational equivalence relations over a one letter alphabet, and rational equivalence relations with bounded separability. Although the general case remains open, it is shown to be reducible to that of locally-finite rational equivalence relations over a two letter alphabet. Two particular cross-sections are shown not to be regular: the set of minimum length words and the set of lexicographically minimal words.

1. Introduction

The familiar Soundex code maps surnames into four-character codes so that similar sounding names are mapped to the same code and different sounding names are mapped to different codes. Thus "Johnson" and "Jansen" are both transformed into the code "J525" indicating an initial letter "J", a letter in the class $\{m,n\}$, a letter in the class $\{c,g,j,k,q,s,x,z\}$, and a letter in the class $\{m,n\}$. It is well known that Soundex is not perfectly accurate in its coding. For example, the common variant spelling "Johnston" is assigned a code "J523". The class "L000" contains all names with a initial "L" and any sequence of vowels and the letters "h" and "w". Many easily distinguishable Chinese surnames fall in this class. For a detailed description of Soundex and a discussion of its use and problems see [10, 12].

In order to improve on Soundex, a number of attempts have been made to construct coding functions that more closely reflect the structure of surnames in the population of interest. For example, the NYSIIS code was designed to achieve greater accuracy on a population with a significant fraction of Spanish surnames. A number of coding functions, including NYSIIS, are discussed by Moore *et al* [11].

One interesting observation [9] is that both the Soundex and NYSIIS functions can be usefully modelled as deterministic GSM's (subsequential functions). This means that they can be computed deterministically from left to right in one pass. It follows immediately that both Soundex and NYSIIS are rational functions and that the relation "has the same code" is a rational equivalence relation on surnames for either Soundex or NYSIIS. Rational relations are discussed by Berstel [1] and Eilenberg [4].

† This work was supported by the Natural Sciences and Engineering Research Council of Canada, Grant No. A0237

The advantage of these coding functions comes primarily from their low cost. Even very large files can be partitioned cheaply according to a code value using any of a number of sorting or hashing algorithms. The coding function needs to be computed only once and so a moderate amount of effort can be directed into computing better codes if the accuracy can be improved. The use of these types of coding functions has been advocated by various authors [3,6,10,11,12,17]. Thus more general equivalence relation models for which reasonable canonical functions are available are worthy of consideration.

It can be shown [9] that any rational equivalence relation has a canonical function computable in $O(n^2)$ time and space or in $O(n^3)$ time and $O(n)$ space where n is the length of the input. If the rational equivalence relation has a rational canonical function, however, it can be computed in $O(n)$ time and space resulting in a significant saving [13,15]. An interesting question is then to identify when a rational equivalence relation has a rational canonical function. It appears that all of them do but seems to be very difficult to prove. In fact, the question is still open. This paper will discuss the current state of this conjecture which is equivalent to that stated in the title.

2. Terminology

Definition: A (binary) **relation** over sets S and T is a subset of $S \times T$.

We will be interested in the usual Boolean operations on relations interpreted as sets as well as the operations composition, inversion (interchange of components), domain, range, identity, cross-product, and application:

$$R_1 \circ R_2 = \{(u,w) \mid \exists v[(u,v) \in R_1 \text{ and } (v,w) \in R_2]\} \qquad R^{(-1)} = \{(v,u) \mid (u,v) \in R\}$$

$$dom R = \{u \mid (u,v) \in R\} \qquad ran R = \{v \mid (u,v) \in R\} \qquad \iota_L = \{(u,u) \mid u \in L\}$$

$$L_1 \times L_2 = \{(u,v) \mid u \in L_1, v \in L_2\} \qquad R(L) = \{v \mid \exists u[u \in L \text{ and } (u,v) \in R]\}.$$

Definition: An **equivalence relation** R over a set S is a relation satisfying the reflexive, symmetric, and transitive laws: $\iota_S \subseteq R$, $R^{(-1)} \subseteq R$, and $R \circ R \subseteq R$.

Definition: The **kernel** of a function $f:S \rightarrow T$ is the equivalence relation over S:

$$ker f = \{(u,v) \in S \times S \mid f(u) = f(v)\} = f \circ f^{(-1)}.$$

Definition: A **canonical function** for an equivalence relation R over S is any function $f:S \rightarrow T$ satisfying $R = ker f$.

Definition: A **cross-section** of an equivalence relation R over S is a set D containing one element from each class of R. Then $f = R \cap (S \times D)$ is a canonical function.

Definition: The **restriction** $R \mid D$ of an equivalence relation R to a set D is the relation formed from R by restricting the domain and range to D. Thus $R \mid D = R \cap (D \times D)$.

Definition: A **thinning** of an equivalence relation R is a restriction whose domain contains at least one member of each equivalence class of R.

Definition: A relation R is **locally-finite** if for any $x \in dom R$, the set $\{y \mid (x,y) \in R\}$ is finite. If R is an equivalence relation then local-finiteness requires that every class be finite in size.

Definition: A **monoid** $<M,\cdot,\Box>$ is a set M with an associative binary operation $\cdot$ and an identity element $\Box$ satisfying: $a \cdot (b \cdot c) = (a \cdot b) \cdot c$, $\Box \cdot a = a = a \cdot \Box \quad \forall a,b,c \in M$.

We can extend concatenation to subsets of M and define the concatenation closure of a subset of M:

$$S \cdot T = \{a \cdot b \mid a \in S, b \in T\} \qquad S^1 = S \quad S^k = S^{k-1} \cdot S \quad S^+ = \bigcup_{i=1}^{\infty} S^i \qquad \forall S,T \subseteq M$$

Definition: The class of **rational subsets** of a monoid $<M,\cdot,\square>$, denoted **Rat**(M), is defined inductively as the following sets (and no others):

(1) All finite subsets of M are rational.

(2) If S and T are rational subsets of M, then $S \cup T$, $S \cdot T$, and S^+ are also rational.

Note that $S^* = \{\square\} \cup S^+$ will be rational if S is.

The first type of monoid that we will consider is the finitely generated free monoid $<\Sigma^*,\cdot,\Lambda>$. The class **Rat**(Σ^*) corresponds to the family of regular languages over Σ^*. It is well known that this class is a Boolean algebra and can be characterized by deterministic finite automata (finite state machines).

Definition: A **lexicographic order** $<$ on Σ^* is the well-order induced by an order on Σ using the rules: $u < uav$, $a < b \Longrightarrow uav < ubw \quad \forall u,v,w \in \Sigma^* \ \forall a,b \in \Sigma$.

The second type of monoid is the direct product of two finitely generated free monoids $<\Sigma^* \times \Delta^*,\cdot,(\Lambda,\Lambda)>$ where the operation $\cdot$ is defined component-wise:

$$(u_1,v_1) \cdot (u_2,v_2) = (u_1 \cdot u_2, v_1 \cdot v_2) \qquad \forall u_1,u_2 \in \Sigma^* \ \forall v_1,v_2 \in \Delta^*.$$

The subsets in the class **Rat**($\Sigma^* \times \Delta^*$) are called (binary) rational relations. They are closed under union, concatenation, and concatenation closure by definition. They are also closed under composition, inversion, domain, range, identity, cross-product, and application:

$$R_1 \in \mathbf{Rat}(\Sigma^* \times \Delta^*) \text{ and } R_2 \in \mathbf{Rat}(\Delta^* \times \Gamma^*) \Longrightarrow R_1 \circ R_2 \in \mathbf{Rat}(\Sigma^* \times \Gamma^*)$$

$$R \in \mathbf{Rat}(\Sigma^* \times \Delta^*) \Longrightarrow R^{(-1)} \in \mathbf{Rat}(\Delta^* \times \Sigma^*),\ dom R \in \mathbf{Rat}(\Sigma^*), \text{ and } ran R \in \mathbf{Rat}(\Delta^*)$$

$$L \in \mathbf{Rat}(\Sigma^*) \Longrightarrow \iota_L \in \mathbf{Rat}(\Sigma^* \times \Sigma^*)$$

$$L_1 \in \mathbf{Rat}(\Sigma^*) \text{ and } L_2 \in \mathbf{Rat}(\Delta^*) \Longrightarrow L_1 \times L_2 \in \mathbf{Rat}(\Sigma^* \times \Delta^*)$$

$$L \in \mathbf{Rat}(\Sigma^*) \text{ and } R \in \mathbf{Rat}(\Sigma^* \times \Delta^*) \Longrightarrow R(L) \in \mathbf{Rat}(\Delta^*).$$

They are not closed under the Boolean operations intersection or set difference although they are closed under domain and range restriction by regular languages:

$$R \in \mathbf{Rat}(\Sigma^* \times \Delta^*),\ L_1 \in \mathbf{Rat}(\Sigma^*), \text{ and } L_2 \in \mathbf{Rat}(\Delta^*) \Longrightarrow R \cap (L_1 \times L_2) \in \mathbf{Rat}(\Sigma^* \times \Delta^*).$$

Definition: A **rational transducer** $\mathbf{T} = <\Sigma,\Delta,Q,q_-,Q_+,E>$ is a 6-tuple where Σ is the tape-one alphabet, Δ is the tape-two alphabet, Q is a set of states, $q_- \in Q$ is a distinguished start state, $Q_+ \subseteq Q$ is a distinguished set of final states, and $E \subseteq (Q \times \Sigma^* \times \Delta^* \times Q)$ is a set of transitions. A path through **T** is a sequence of transitions from E of the form $(q_0,u_1,v_1,q_1)(q_1,u_2,v_2,q_2)(q_2,u_3,v_3,q_3) \cdots (q_{k-1},u_k,v_k,q_k)$. A successful path is one where $q_0 = q_-$ and $q_k \in Q_+$. The label of a path is the concatenation of the labels: $(u_1u_2u_3 \cdots u_k, v_1v_2v_3 \cdots v_k)$. The behaviour $|\mathbf{T}|$ of a transducer **T** is the set of labels of successful paths. Every rational relation has a rational transducer.

Definition: A **deterministic two-tape finite automaton** $\mathbf{A} = <\Sigma,\Delta,Q_1,Q_2,q_-,Q_+,\delta_1,\delta_2>$ is an 8-tuple where Σ and Δ are the tape-one and tape-two alphabets, Q_1 and Q_2 are disjoint sets of states ($Q_1 \cap Q_2 = \varnothing$), $q_- \in Q_1 \cup Q_2$ is a distinguished start state, $Q_+ \subseteq Q_1 \cup Q_2$ is a distinguished set of final states, and $\delta_1 \subseteq (Q_1 \times (\Sigma \cup \{\dashv\})) \times (Q_1 \cup Q_2)$, $\delta_2 \subseteq (Q_2 \times (\Delta \cup \{\dashv\})) \times (Q_1 \cup Q_2)$ are partial functions. A path through **A** is the sequence of transitions of the form $(q_i,t,a_i,\delta_t(q_i,a_i))$ where $t \in \{1,2\}$, $q_i \in Q_t$, $a_i \in \Sigma$ if $t = 1$, and $a_i \in \Delta$ if $t = 2$. A successful path is one from q_- to a state in Q_+. The label of a path is the ordered pair formed by concatenating the Σ labels together as the first component and the Δ labels together as the second component. The behaviour of the automaton is the set of labels of successful paths. It is well known that deterministic two-tape finite automata recognize a sub-class of rational relations [7].

An interesting special case of rational relations occurs when Σ and Δ each contain exactly one letter. This class is also closed under intersection and set difference and is thus a Boolean algebra [8].

The class of all rational relations that are equivalence relations over some regular subset of Σ^* will be denoted **RatEq**(Σ^*). The class of all rational relations that have a rational canonical function whose domain is a regular subset of Σ^* will be denoted **KerRatF**(Σ^*). The set of words that are lexicographically minimal within their classes for a rational equivalence relation R will be denoted by $lexmin(R)$.

3. The Conjecture

The conjecture introduced in this paper can be presented in two equivalent forms:

Conjecture: **KerRatF**(Σ^*) $=$ **RatEq**(Σ^*).

Conjecture: Every rational equivalence relation has a regular cross-section.

Theorem 3.1: $R \in$ **KerRatF**(Σ^*) if and only if $R \in$ **RatEq**(Σ^*) and R has a regular cross-section.

Proof: ($\Leftarrow$) Suppose $R \in$ **RatEq**(Σ^*) and D is a regular cross-section for R. Then ι_D is a rational relation and thus so is $f = R \circ \iota_D$. But f is a canonical function for R since it maps an arbitrary word in $dom R$ into the unique element in the same equivalence class and in D. Thus $R \in$ **KerRatF**(Σ^*).

($\Rightarrow$) By Eilenberg's proposition IX.8.2 [4], for any rational relation X, there is a rational function g such that $g \subseteq X$ and $dom g = dom X$. Suppose $R \in$ **KerRatF**(Σ^*). Then there is an alphabet Δ and a rational function $f:\Sigma^* \to \Delta^*$ such that $R = ker f = f \circ f^{(-1)}$. Since $f^{(-1)}$ is rational, we can find a function $g \subseteq f^{(-1)}$ such that $dom g = dom(f^{(-1)})$. From this we compute $f' = f \circ g$, and we find that $R = ker f'$ and $f' \subseteq R$. Note that $D = ran f'$ is a regular cross-section. ■

Corollary 3.2: **KerRatF**(Σ^*) $\subseteq$ **RatEq**(Σ^*). ■

Corollary 3.3: $R \in$ **KerRatF**(Σ^*) if and only if there is a rational function $f:\Sigma^* \to \Sigma^*$, where $f \subseteq R$ and $R = ker f$. ■

Lemma 3.4: If $R \in$ **KerRatF**(Σ^*), then an f such that $R = ker f$ can be found effectively.

Proof: Consider an enumeration of regular sets over Σ^*: $L_1, L_2, L_3, \cdots$. For each L_i we can compute $f_i = R \circ \iota_{L_i}$. We can test whether f_i is a function [2,16] and whether $dom f_i = dom R$. If these are both true, then $R = ker f_i$. This procedure is guaranteed to terminate. If R has a regular cross-section D then $D = L_i$ for some i so that f_i is the required function. ■

The following sections will outline what is currently known about the conjecture. Section 4 shows that any R with infinite classes can be effectively thinned to one with finite classes. Thus we can assume, without loss of generality, that each class is finite in size. Section 5 shows that the conjecture is true if R has a deterministic two-tape recognizer. Thus we can assume R is inherently non-deterministic. Section 6 shows that the conjecture is true if R is over the one letter alphabet and that R can be coded to two letters if the alphabet has more than two letters. Thus we can assume a two letter alphabet. Section 7 shows that the conjecture is true if we can bound the separability of equivalent words. Section 8 shows that two possible approaches do not work: (1) The set of minimal length words need not be regular. (2) The set of lexicographic minimal words need not be regular. Section 9 presents concluding comments.

4. WLOG R is Locally-Finite

The condition of local-finiteness requires that the size of every equivalence class is finite although not necessarily bounded. For example, the classes of the equivalence relation $EQUAL\_LENGTH \equiv (\Sigma \times \Sigma)^*$ contain all words over Σ of a particular length. Each class is finite although the class size cannot be bounded. The classes of the equivalence relation $STUTTER \equiv \{\bigcup_{x \in \Sigma} \{x\}^+ \times \{x\}^+\}^*$ contain all words that reduce to the same word when sequences of adjacent equal letters are replaced by a single occurrence of the letter. For example, the class containing abc will also contain the words $a^i b^j c^k$ for all $i,j,k \geq 1$. All classes except $\{\Lambda\}$ are infinite so that $STUTTER$ is not locally-finite.

Theorem 4.1: Every rational equivalence relation has a rational locally-finite thinning.

Proof: Assume that we are given a transducer for some rational equivalence relation. The idea of the proof is to consider successful paths that involve a loop reading Λ from tape one and some non-zero length word from tape two. Each such path identifies three words in the same equivalence class: (1) the word on tape one, (2) the word on tape two, and (3) the word on tape two after the loop is removed from the path. The second word is strictly longer than the third word and can be safely removed from the class without fear of deleting the whole class. The substance of the proof involves constructing this set of "long" words and showing that it is regular. Restricting the relation to "short" words will then be a thinning. Proving that the ratio of lengths of related "short" words is bounded then establishes local-finiteness.

Formally, let R be a rational equivalence relation over Σ^*. Then there is a transducer $\mathbf{T} = \langle \Sigma, \Sigma, Q, q_-, Q_+, E \rangle$ recognizing R and satisfying $E \subseteq Q \times (\Sigma \cup \Lambda) \times (\Sigma \cup \Lambda) \times Q$ [1]. We will construct a new transducer $\mathbf{T}'$ which simulates $\mathbf{T}$ but accepts its inputs only if $\mathbf{T}$ accepts using a path with a loop reading Λ from tape one and some non-zero length word from tape two. The simulation will operate in three phases. In phase one, it will simulate $\mathbf{T}$. In phase two, it will simulate $\mathbf{T}$ and trace out a loop that reads Λ from tape one and a non-zero length word from tape two. Phase three will continue the simulation of $\mathbf{T}$.

$$\mathbf{T}' = \langle \Sigma, \Sigma, P_1 \cup P_2 \cup P_3, (q_-,1), Q_+ \times \{3\}, E_{11} \cup E_{12} \cup E_{22} \cup E_{23} \cup E_{33} \rangle$$

$$P_1 = Q \times \{1\} \qquad P_2 = Q \times \{2\} \times Q \qquad P_3 = Q \times \{3\}$$

$$E_{11} = \{ ((q_1,1),x,y,(q_2,1)) \mid (q_1,x,y,q_2) \in E \}$$

$$E_{12} = \{ ((q_1,1),\Lambda,y,(q_2,2,q_1)) \mid (q_1,\Lambda,y,q_2) \in E,\ y \neq \Lambda \}$$

$$E_{22} = \{ ((q_1,2,q_3),\Lambda,y,(q_2,2,q_3)) \mid (q_1,\Lambda,y,q_2) \in E,\ q_3 \in Q \}$$

$$E_{23} = \{ ((q_1,2,q_1),\Lambda,\Lambda,(q_1,3)) \mid q_1 \in Q \}$$

$$E_{33} = \{ ((q_1,3),x,y,(q_2,3)) \mid (q_1,x,y,q_2) \in E \}$$

Note that the transitions in E_{ij} connect states in P_i with states in P_j. Since the start state is in P_1 and the final states are all in P_3 any successful path will be in the set $E_{11}^* \cdot E_{12} \cdot E_{22}^* \cdot E_{23} \cdot E_{33}^*$.

The first component of the state indicates the corresponding state of $\mathbf{T}$ in the simulation. The second component indicates the phase. The third component of states in P_2 remembers the first state of the loop. It is loaded on entry to P_2 by transitions in the class E_{12} and verified on exit from P_2 by transitions in the class E_{23}.

Since the first components of each state in a successful path through $\mathbf{T}'$ identify a successful path through $\mathbf{T}$ with the same label, $|\mathbf{T}'| \subseteq R$.

The set $ran(|\mathbf{T}'|)$ is the desired set of "long" words and is clearly regular. The set of short words is then $K = dom R - ran(|\mathbf{T}'|)$. We must now show that the restriction $R \mid K$ of R to K is (1) a thinning and (2) locally-finite.

(1) To show that it is a thinning, we must show that every equivalence class of R has a representative in K. Otherwise, there must be a class in R with no representatives in K. We can choose a word w of this class that is of minimal length. Since $w \in dom R$ but $w \notin K$, we must have that $w \in ran(|\mathbf{T}'|)$. Thus w is the second component of a label of a successful path in $\mathbf{T}'$. This path can be used to identify a shorter word in the same class as w contradicting the minimality of w.

(2) To show that $R \mid K$ is locally-finite, we will show that any pair of related words u, v in $R \mid K$ must satisfy: $|u| < n(|v|+1)$ and $|v| < n(|u|+1)$ where n is the number of states in Q. The idea of the proof is to show that some loop which reads Λ and writes a non-zero length string must exist and so that $v \in ran(|\mathbf{T}'|)$. The details are omitted. ■

5. WLOG R is Inherently Non-Deterministic

The conjecture will be proven for rational equivalence relations that can be recognized by a deterministic two-tape automaton. If fact, if R is locally-finite then $lexmin(R)$ is defined and regular. Note that we require the condition of local-finiteness. For example, consider the class containing the word ab for the relation $STUTTER$ defined above with $a < b$. For any word that we pick $a^i b^j$, we can pick another that is lexicographically smaller and equivalent: $a^{i+1}b$. We will denote by $lexf(R)$ the function that maps every word w in $dom R$ into the lexicographic minimal element in $R(\{w\})$. For equivalence relations: $lexf(R) = R \cap (dom R \times lexmin(R))$.

Theorem 5.1: If R is a deterministic rational locally-finite relation, then $lexf(R)$ is a deterministic rational function.

Proof: Again the proof is by construction. We will take a deterministic two-tape automaton that recognizes R and construct one that recognizes deterministically a pair of words (u,v) if and only if u and v are in the same class and v is the lexicographic minimal element in the class. We will assume an arbitrary but fixed order on the letters of $\Delta \cup \{\dashv\}$ which will be denoted $<$.

Formally, let $\mathbf{M} = <\Sigma, \Delta, Q_1, Q_2, q_-, Q_+, \delta_1, \delta_2>$ be a deterministic two-tape finite automaton such that $R = |\mathbf{M}|$. We can assume without loss of generality that $Q_+ \subseteq Q_1$. For any set of states $r \subseteq Q_1 \cup Q_2$ we can define $\omega(r)$ as the set of states in Q_1 that are reachable from r only reading from tape 2:

$$\omega(r) = Q_1 \cap \bigcup_{\substack{p \in r \\ w \in \Delta^*}} \delta_2(p,w)$$

where δ_2 has been extended to strings in Δ^* in the usual way.

We can then construct a deterministic two-tape automaton for $lexf(R)$. This automaton will trace out a path through $\mathbf{M}$ and at the same time verify that all paths corresponding to lexicographically smaller words on tape two will fail. The succeeding path is traced out in the first component of the state and the other paths are traced in the second component.

$$\mathbf{M}' = <\Sigma, \Delta, Q_1 \times 2^{Q_1}, Q_2 \times 2^{Q_1}, (q_-, \varnothing), Q_+ \times 2^{(Q - Q_+)}, \delta'_1, \delta'_2>$$

$$\delta'_1((q,r),a) = (\delta_1(q,a), \omega(\delta_1(r,a))) \qquad \forall q \in Q_1 \ \forall r \subseteq Q_1 \ \forall a \in \Sigma \cup \{\dashv\}$$

$$\delta'_2((q,r),a) = (\delta_2(q,a), r \cup \bigcup_{x<a} \omega(\delta_2(q,x))) \qquad \forall q \in Q_2 \;\; \forall r \subseteq Q_1 \;\; \forall a \in \Delta \cup \{\dashv\}$$

To show that $lexf(R) = |\mathbf{M}'|$ we must verify:

(1) $|\mathbf{M}'| \subseteq R$

(2) $(u,v) \in |\mathbf{M}'|$ and $(u,w) \in R \implies v \leq w$

(3) $dom(|\mathbf{M}'|) = dom R$

(1) Suppose $(u,v) \in |\mathbf{M}'|$. Then there is a successful path through $\mathbf{M}'$ with label (u,v). By selecting the first component of each state in this path, we can identify a path through $\mathbf{M}$ with the same label. Thus $(u,v) \in |\mathbf{M}| = R$.

The details of (2) and (3) are omitted. ∎

Theorem 4.1 can be generalized to provide deterministic locally-finite thinnings for deterministic rational equivalence relations.

Lemma 5.2: Every deterministic rational equivalence relation has a deterministic rational locally-finite thinning.

Proof: Deterministic rational relations are closed under domain and range restriction by regular languages. By theorem 4.1, R has a rational locally-finite thinning $R \mid K = R \cap (K \times K)$ where K is a regular set. Thus $R \mid K$ is deterministic if R is. ∎

Combining these two results allows us to find regular cross-sections for any deterministic rational equivalence relation.

Theorem 5.3: If R is a deterministic rational equivalence relation, then R has a regular cross-section.

Proof: A regular cross-section can be found by constructing a locally-finite thinning of R and applying theorem 5.1. ∎

Definition: A **length-bounded** rational transduction R is a rational transduction such that $(u,v) \in R$ implies that $|v| - k \leq |u| \leq |v| + k$ for some k. The length of related words can differ by at most some constant amount.

Corollary 5.4: If R is a length-bounded rational equivalence relation, then R has a regular cross-section.

Proof: In the terminology of Elgot and Mezei [5], any length-bounded rational relation is finite automaton definable (FAD). This means that it can be recognized by an automaton that reads exactly one character from each tape at each step. Each tape is assumed to be padded to the right with an infinite string of end-markers and the machine continues processing until the read head sees end-markers on all tapes. This type of machine can be easily simulated by an deterministic automaton that reads in turn one character from each tape. Thus any length-bounded rational relation is deterministic. The result follows. ∎

6. WLOG Σ has two letters

Theorem 6.1: A rational equivalence relation R over Σ has a regular cross-section if $|\Sigma| = 1$.

Proof: Let $\Sigma = \{a\}$. The relation $R_{>} = \{(a^m, a^n) \mid m > n\}$ is easily shown to be rational. But then $dom R - dom(R \cap R_{>})$ is regular. This is exactly the set of words that are of minimal length within their equivalence classes. Thus R has a regular cross-section.

Theorem 6.2: The conjecture is true for $|\Sigma| = k, k \geq 2$ if and only if it is true for $|\Sigma| = 2$.

Proof: Suppose that the conjecture is true for $|\Sigma| = 2$ and consider a rational equivalence relation R over a k-letter alphabet. Suppose $\Sigma = \{a_0,a_1,\ldots,a_{k-1}\}$ and let h be the morphism satisfying $h(a_i) = a^i b$. Thus h maps the i-th letter in Σ into a sequence of i a's followed by a single b. The equivalence relation $R' = h^{(-1)} \circ R \circ h$ is a rational equivalence relation over $\{a,b\}^* - \{a,b\}^* a$. If R has a regular cross-section L then $h(L)$ will be a regular cross-section for R'. If R' has a regular cross-section L' then $h^{(-1)}(L')$ will be a regular cross-section for R. This follows from the isomorphism between Σ^* and the words in $\{a,b\}^*$ not ending in a. ■

7. WLOG R has Unbounded Separability

Definition: Two words are said to be k-**separable** if there exists a k-state automaton that recognizes one but not the other.

Definition: An equivalence relation is said to have **bounded separability** if there is some value k such that all pairs of equivalent words are k-separable. Otherwise, it is said to have unbounded separability.

Definition: A thinning of an equivalence relation R with respect to a set L is the relation $R\theta L = R \mid (dom R - (R(L) - L))$.

Intuitively, thinning with respect to a set L splits classes that intersect L keeping the part in the intersection. Classes that are disjoint from L are kept in their entirety. If R is a rational equivalence relation and L is a regular language, then $R\theta L$ is a rational equivalence relation.

Theorem 7.1: If R has bounded separability then R has a regular cross-section.

Proof: Suppose that all pairs of equivalent words can be distinguished by automata with k or fewer states. There are only a finite number of these automata, say $\alpha(k)$. Furthermore, they can be enumerated: $L_1, L_2, \ldots, L_{\alpha(k)}$. Suppose that we thin R with respect to each of the L_i in turn: $R' = (\cdots((R\theta L_1)\theta L_2)\theta \cdots)\theta L_{\alpha(k)}$. If $dom R'$ is not a regular cross-section of R then there are two words u and v belonging to the same class of R'. But since they are k-separable, they must be separated by L_j for some $j \leq \alpha(k)$. But then one or the other must have been removed when the thinning with respect to L_j was performed. Thus $dom R'$ must be a regular cross-section of R. ■

8. Two Non-Regular Cross-Sections

It has been established above that rational equivalence relations over a one letter alphabet have a regular cross-section composed of the minimum length words from each class. However, the set of minimal length words is not necessarily regular when we have more then one letter. Similarly deterministic locally-finite rational equivalence relations have a regular cross-section composed of the lexicographic minimal words of each class. This set is not regular for non-deterministic relations.

Theorem 8.1: There is a rational equivalence relation for which the set of minimal length elements is a cross-section but not regular.

Proof: Let $T = \{(a^{2i}b^{4j}, b^{4i}a^{2j+1}) \mid i,j \geq 0\}$, $R = \iota \cup T \cup T^{(-1)}$. Then R is clearly a rational equivalence relation. Furthermore, the set of minimal length elements forms a cross-section:

$$K = \Sigma^* - \left\{ \{a^{2i}b^{4j} \mid i<j\} \cup \{b^{4i}a^{2j+1} \mid i \geq j\} \right\}.$$

This is not a regular set since otherwise $K \cap a^* b^* = \{a^{2i}b^{4j} \mid i \geq j\}$ would also have to be regular. ■

Theorem 8.2: There is a locally-finite rational equivalence relation R for which $lexmin(R)$ is not regular.

Proof: Consider $T = (a,ab)\{(a,ab)\cup(b,ba)\}^*(a,b)$, $R = \iota\cup T\cup T^{(-1)}$. Then R is a locally-finite rational equivalence relation. However, $lexmin(R)$ is not regular if $a<b$ or $b<a$. Consider first the case $a<b$. If $lexmin(R)$ is regular, then $U = \{lexmin(R)\cap a\Sigma^*a\}$ must be regular. Let h be the morphism on $\{a,b\}$ satisfying $h(a) = ab$ and $h(b) = ba$. Then

$$U = \{awa \mid w\in\{a,b\}^* \text{ and } awa<h(a)h(w)b\}$$

There are two cases:

(1) awa is a prefix of $h(a)h(w)b$. In this case awa must be a prefix of the Morse ω-word: *abbabaabbaababbabaababbaabbabaab* · · ·

(2) There is a prefix of awa of the form sa where sb is a prefix of $h(a)h(w)b$ and $s\in\{a,b\}^*$. Note that sb is also a prefix of the Morse ω-word.

Consider a (trim) deterministic automaton that recognizes U and make the following modifications: For every state from which there is both an outgoing a transition and an outgoing b transition, delete the a transition. This will clearly remove all words that not prefixes of the Morse ω-word. The proof (details omitted) demonstrates that arbitrarily long words remain. This is a contradiction since this infinite word is known to be cube-free [14] and so any infinite subset of its prefixes cannot be regular.

The case for $b<a$ can be handled in a similar manner. ■

Note that neither of these results contradicts the conjecture since in each case $K' = \Sigma^* - dom\,T$ is a regular cross-section.

9. Conclusions

Although the truth or falsity of the main conjecture has not been established, considerable progress has been made. In fact, one could argue that, for all practical purposes, the conjecture is true since any counter-example would not correspond to a practical string similarity relation. On the other hand, there is always the prospect of some new class of relations that capture an interesting aspect of string similarity.

If the conjecture is true, it removes another problem with rational equivalence relations. They currently have no good characterization: It is undecidable whether a given rational relation is an equivalence relation [9] and they have no machine model. If the conjecture is true, then rational functions provide such a characterization since it is decidable whether a given rational relation is a function.

Some interesting cases remain unresolved. For example, none of the results say anything about bounds on the cardinality of the equivalence classes. Can we assume, without loss of generality, that at least one class has more than k elements or that all classes have no more than k elements. This question is open even for $k = 2$.

One of the referees suggested another interesting case. We can define a rational transducer T to be unambiguous if for any $(u,v)\in|\mathbf{T}|$ there is exactly one successful path with (u,v) as a label. Does the existence of an unambiguous transducer for R imply that R has a regular cross-section?

10. References

1. J. Berstel, *Transductions and context-free languages*, Teubner, Stuttgart, Germany (1979).
2. M. Blattner and T. Head, Single valued *a*-transducers., *J.C.S.S.* **15** p. 310-327 (1977).
3. L. Davidson, Retrieval of misspelled names in an airline passenger record system, *Commun. ACM* **5**(3) p. 169-171 (1962).
4. S. Eilenberg, *Automata, languages, and machines, vol. A*, Acad. Press, New York (1974).
5. C. C. Elgot and J. E. Mezei, On relations defined by generalized finite automata, *IBM J. of Res.* **9** p. 47-65 (1965).
6. I. P. Fellegi and A. B. Sunter, A theory for record linkage, *J.A.S.A.* **64** p. 1183-1210 (1969).
7. P. C. Fischer and A. L. Rosenberg, Multitape one-way nonwriting automata, *J.C.S.S.* **2** p. 88-101 (1968).
8. S. Ginsburg, *The mathematical theory of context-free languages.*, McGraw-Hill, New York (1966).
9. J. H. Johnson, Formal models for string similarity., PhD. thesis., University of Waterloo (1983). Available as University of Waterloo Research Report CS-83-32.
10. D. E. Knuth, *Sorting and searching*, Addison-Wesley, Reading, Mass (1973).
11. G. B. Moore, J. L. Kuhns, J. L. Trefftzs, and C. A. Montgomery, Accessing individual records from personal data files using non-unique identifiers, NBS Special Publication 500-2, U.S. Department of Commerce–National Bureau of Standards (1977).
12. H. B. Newcombe and J. M. Kennedy, Record linkage: Making maximum use of the discriminating power of identifying information, *Commun. ACM* **5**(11) p. 563-566 (1962).
13. M. Nivat, Transductions des langages de Chomsky, *Ann. de l'Inst. Fourier* **18** p. 339-456. (1968).
14. A. Salomaa, *Jewels of formal language theory.*, Computer Science Press, Rockville, Maryland (1981).
15. M. P. Schützenberger, A remark on finite transducers., *Info. Contr.* **4** p. 185-196 (1961).
16. M. P. Schützenberger, Sur les relations rationelles., *Automata theory and formal languages: 2nd GI Conference* **33** p. 209-213 (1975).
17. G. Wiederhold, *Database design.*, McGraw-Hill, New York (1977).

ON PROBABILISTIC TIME AND SPACE

Hermann Jung
Sektion Mathematik
Humboldt-Universität zu Berlin
DDR-1086 Berlin · PO Box 1297
German Democratic Republic

Abstract. We prove that inequalities of arithmetic expressions over the ring of nxn matrices can be decided by probabilistic Turing machines working simultaneously within O(logn) space and polynomial time. As a corollary we obtain:

$$\text{PrSPACE}(\log n) = \text{PrTISP}(n^{O(1)}, \log n) ,$$

which solves a problem that has been open for a long time.

1. Introduction.

A long standing open question in the theory of computational complexity is the relationship between time and space bounded computations. For any function T(n), it is not known whether all problems solvable in time T(n) are also solvable in space $O(\log^{O(1)} T(n))$. On the other hand, it is obvious that every S(n) tape bounded deterministic (as well as nondeterministic) Turing machine runs in $2^{O(S(n))}$ time (for any constructible $S(n) \geq \log n$). The situation differs for probabilistic tape bounded machines. Gill (1977) proved that the computation time of probabilistic S(n) tape bounded Turing machines can be bounded only by $2^{2^{O(S(n))}}$. Nevertheless, it was an open question whether the double exponential time is essential for solving problems in probabilistic logn tape. Our main theorem, proved in this paper, says that every logn tape bounded probabilistic Turing machine M can be replaced by a probabilistic machine M' which recognizes the same language as M and works simultaneously within logn space and polynomial time. Thus, an exponential speed-up in computation time is obtained. But, for the decrease in computation time, one has to pay with an increase in error probability. In particular, while M may work with bounded error probability, M' will not. The probabilistic Turing machine M' will be defined using a 'fast' probabilistic approximation algorithm for deciding inequalities of arithmetic formulas described in the next section.

2. A probabilistic algorithm for deciding inequalities.

In this section we present a probabilistic algorithm deciding inequalities of the form $F(x_1,\ldots,x_r) \leq F'(y_1,\ldots,y_s)$, where F, F' are multivariate polynomials over the ring of n n matrices. The polynomials are given as arithmetic formulas. Since we need some further structural properties of F (F', resp.) let us recall the definition of arithmetic formulas (or expressions).

Given any ring A with ring operations +,· , the set of formulas over A is defined to be the smallest set $\mathcal{F}$ of finite expressions that satisfies the following conditions:

(i) $x_i \in \mathcal{F}$, for any indeterminate x_i (i=1,2,...)

(ii) $a \in \mathcal{F}$, for every constant $a \in A$

(iii) If $F,F' \in \mathcal{F}$, then $F+F' \in \mathcal{F}$ as well as $(F+F') \in \mathcal{F}$ and $F\cdot F' \in \mathcal{F}$.

Let d(F) denote the depth (i.e., the depth of parentheses) and s(F) the size of F. Furthermore we introduce some additional notions.

A formula F is said to be atomic if F is either an indeterminate or a constant. F is said to be closed if F is either atomic or has the form (F'). It is easy to see that any nonatomic closed formula has the form $(\sum_i \prod_j F_{ij})$, where F_{ij} are closed formulas.

Finally, md(F) denotes the multiplication depth of a closed formula F, defined by:

- if F is atomic, then md(F)=1
- if F is nonatomic and of the form $(\sum_i \prod_j F_{ij})$ (for closed subformulas F_{ij}), then $md(F)=\max_i(\sum_j md(F_{ij})+1)$.

The formula inequality problem (FIN) under consideration is now formulated as follows:

FIN

input: binary encoded formulas $F(x_1,\ldots,x_r),F'(y_1,\ldots,y_s)$ over the ring of n×n matrices over the integers, where the indeterminates are replaced by n×n matrices $A_1,\ldots,A_r,B_1,\ldots,B_s$ with n-bit elements

problem: '$a_{1n} \leq b_{1n}$?' , where $[a_{ij}]=F(A_1,\ldots,A_r)$ and $[b_{ij}]=F'(B_1,\ldots,B_s)$

We characterize the computational complexity of FIN in terms of simultaneously tape and time bounded probabilistic Turing machines (for the definition of probabilistic complexity classes, see Gill, 1977).

<u>LEMMA 1</u>. FIN can be recognized by an O(logN) tape bounded probabilistic Turing machine working simultaneously within polynomial

time, where N is the length of the binary input.
(i.e., $FIN \in PrTISP(N^{O(1)}, \log N)$)

Proof.(Sketch)

We are given formulas F, F' and have to decide whether a_{1n} is not greater than b_{1n}. For simplicity we assume that F and F' are closed formulas with:

- the constants as well as the inputs of F and F' are $n \times n$ matrices with n-bit elements from the interval between -1 and +1
- n is a power of 2 and greater than the maximal size of F and F' .

This can be achieved by multiplying both sides of the inequality with an appropriate constant and by padding the formulas.

In order to decide the inequality we describe a probabilistic algorithm which approximates a certain element of the matrix $\underline{F}(A_1,..,A_r)$ ($\underline{F}'(B_1,...,B_s)$,resp.). The formula $\underline{F}$ ($\underline{F}'$, resp.) is obtained from

$$F = (\sum_{i=1}^{k} \prod_{j=1}^{j_i} F_{ij}) \quad (F', \text{resp.})$$

by substitution according to the following rules:

$$\underline{F} = (\sum_{i=1}^{n} 1/n \cdot I \cdot \prod_{j=1}^{n} \underline{F}_{ij} \cdot n^{-(md(F)-d_i-1)} \cdot I) \quad \text{if } F \text{ nonatomic,}$$

$$\underline{F}_{ij} = 1/n \cdot F_{ij} \quad \text{if } F_{ij} \text{ atomic,}$$

where

- n is fixed during the recursive application of this rule,
- $d_i = \sum_{j=1}^{j_i} md(F_{ij})$,
- $\underline{F}_{ij} = 0$ if $i > k$, and
- $\underline{F}_{ij} = I$ if $i \leq k$ and $j > j_i$.

Thus $\underline{F}$ is a closed formula with size $s(\underline{F})$ bounded by $n^{O(1)}$.

By definition: $\underline{F}(x_1,...,x_r) = n^{-md(F)} \cdot F(x_1,...,x_r)$. The matrix $1/n \cdot I$ is called sum distribution matrix and $n^{-(md(F)-d_i-1)} \cdot I$ is called correction matrix.

The multiplication of F by $n^{-(md(F))}$ will support a probabilistic approximation, i.e.,

- $1/n \cdot I$ provides an easy possibility to branch the stochastic process in order to approximate a matrix sum
- the factor n^{-1} supports the branching in case we have to approximate a matrix multiplication .

Before defining the probabilistic approximation we have to estimate the complexity of computing the formula $\underline{F}$.

Since md(F) ≤ s(F), we can compute md(F) straight foreward by going from the left to the right of F and storing the obtained maximal multiplication depth and the multiplication depth of the actually observed closed subformula (similar to a depth first search in a tree). Thus, the multiplication depth of a formula F as well as $\underline{F}$ can be computed by a deterministic logn tape bounded Turing machine.
Let $[\underline{F}]$ denote the set of all closed subformulas in $\underline{F}$, where each subformula is characterized by both its structure and its position in $\underline{F}$.
We define inductively a mapping of the set $[\underline{F}]$ in the set of finite directed trees:
If $\underline{F}$ is atomic, then the corresponding tree $T(\underline{F})$ is empty.
If $\underline{F}$ has degree one and $\underline{F}=(\sum_{i=1}^{n} 1/n\cdot I\cdot \prod_{j=1}^{n+1} \underline{F}_{ij})$, then the associated tree $T(\underline{F})=(V(\underline{F}),E(\underline{F}))$ is defined by:
$V(\underline{F})=[\underline{F}]$, $E(\underline{F})=E_+(\underline{F})\cup E_.(\underline{F})$, with
$E_+(\underline{F})=\{(\underline{F},\underline{F}_{i1}) : 1\le i\le n\}$, $E_.(\underline{F})=\{(\underline{F}_{ij},\underline{F}_{ij+1}) : 1\le i,j\le n\}$.

Given any $\underline{F}=(\sum_{i=1}^{n} 1/n\cdot I\cdot \prod_{j=1}^{n+1} \underline{F}_{ij})$ with $d(\underline{F})>1$ we define $T(\underline{F})$ by:
$V(\underline{F})=[\underline{F}]$, $E(\underline{F})=E_+(\underline{F})\cup E_.(\underline{F})$, with
$E_+(\underline{F})=\{(\underline{F},\underline{F}_{i1}) : 1\le i\le n\}\cup \bigcup_{i,j} E_+(\underline{F}_{ij})$,
$E_.(\underline{F})=\{(\underline{F}',\underline{F}_{ij+1}) : 1\le i,j\le n \text{ and } \underline{F}' \text{ is a leaf in } T(\underline{F}_{ij})\}$
$\cup \bigcup_{i,j} E_.(\underline{F}_{ij})$.

Note that the matrices $\underline{F}_{in+1}$ are the correction matrices, and that the sum distribution matrices are isolated nodes in $T(\underline{F})$. If we label each node $\underline{F}'$ of $T(\underline{F})$ either with $\underline{F}'$ (if $\underline{F}'$ atomic) or with I (if $\underline{F}'$ nonatomic), we can define the value of a path by the label product of its nodes and the value of $T(\underline{F})$ to be the sum of the values of all paths from $\underline{F}$ to a leaf in $T(\underline{F})$. It is not hard to see that the value of $T(\underline{F})$ is equal to the value of $\underline{F}(A_1,\dots,A_r)$ if we delete the sum distribution matrices in $\underline{F}$.
Now we define a Markov process with the set of states
$S=\{s_1,s_{11},\dots,s_{1n},s'_{11},\dots,s'_{1n},\dots,s_{t1},\dots,s_{tn},s'_{t1},\dots,s'_{tn},s_n,s'_n,\underline{s}\}$
where
- t is the number of closed subformulas in $\underline{F}$, i.e., the number of nodes in $T(\underline{F})$
- s_1 is the initial state of the Markov process
- s_{ij} are the 'positive' and s'_{ij} the 'negative' states

- s_n is the 'positive' and s_n' the 'negative' final state
- $\underline{s}$ is a certain sink of the Markov process .

We split the set of states into groups $S_1,\ldots,S_t$. Each group $S_i=\{s_{i1},\ldots,s_{in},s_{i1}',\ldots,s_{in}'\}$ corresponds to a subformula $\underline{F}_i$ (with respect to a fixed enumeration of $[\underline{F}]$ with $\underline{F}_1=\underline{F}$).

According to the tree structure, the positive transition probabilities of the Markov process can be defined by:

$Pr(s_1 \rightarrow s_{11})=1$

$Pr(s_{ij}\rightarrow s_{kj})=Pr(s_{ij}'\rightarrow s_{kj}')=1/n$ if $(\underline{F}_i,\underline{F}_k)\in E_+(\underline{F})$

$Pr(s_{ij}\rightarrow s_{km})=Pr(s_{ij}'\rightarrow s_{km}')=1/n\cdot p_{jm}$ if $(\underline{F}_i,\underline{F}_k)\in E_.(\underline{F})$, $\underline{F}_i$ is not a correction matrix, and the (jm)-th element p_{jm} of $\underline{F}_i$ is greater than zero

$Pr(s_{ij}\rightarrow s_{km}')=Pr(s_{ij}'\rightarrow s_{km})=1/n(-p_{jm})$ if $(\underline{F}_i,\underline{F}_k)\in E_.(\underline{F})$, $\underline{F}_i$ is not a correction matrix, and the (jm)-th element p_{jm} of $\underline{F}_i$ is negative

$Pr(s_{ij}\rightarrow s_{kj})=Pr(s_{ij}'\rightarrow s_{kj}')=p_{jj}$ if $(\underline{F}_i,\underline{F}_k)\in E_.(\underline{F})$ and $\underline{F}_i$ is a correction matrix with the (jj)-th element p_{jj}

$Pr(s_{in}\rightarrow s_n)=Pr(s_{in}'\rightarrow s_n')=p_{nn}$ if $\underline{F}_i$ is a leaf with the (nn)-th element p_{nn}

(Note that $\underline{F}_i$ is a correction matrix, except in the case that $\underline{F}$ is atomic)

$Pr(s_n\rightarrow s_n)=Pr(s_n'\rightarrow s_n')=Pr(\underline{s}\rightarrow \underline{s})=1$.

With the remaining probabilities the states of the Markov process are falling into the sink $\underline{s}$.

The defined Markov process has the following properties:

(i) After t+1 steps the Markov process, starting in s_1, is, with probability 1, in one of the states $\{\underline{s},s_n,s_n'\}$.

(ii) $Pr(s_1\xrightarrow{*}s_n) - Pr(s_1\xrightarrow{*}s_n') = n^{-md(F)}\cdot a_{1n}$,
where a_{1n} is the (1n)-th element of $F(A_1,\ldots,A_r)$ and $Pr(s_1\xrightarrow{*}s_n)$ ($Pr(s_1\xrightarrow{*}s_n')$, resp.) denotes the probability that the Markov process, starting in s_1, falls into s_n (s_n' ,resp.) after a finite number of steps.

If F is atomic, then (ii) is obvious. It is not hard to prove by induction over k that (ii) is true for any product of k atomic formulas. This can be extended to closed formulas with depth 1. Hence, (ii) can be verified by induction over the formula depth.

The 'computational complexity' of the described Markov process, for a given $\underline{F}$, can be characterized by:

(1) The number of states is polynomially bounded (with respect to n)

(2) The single step transitions for any state of the Markov process can be simulated on a probabilistic Turing machine simultaneously within logn space and polynomial time.

(1) is obvious and (2) is due to the possibility of 'uniform' branching, which can be realized on a complete binary tree of depth logn. Let $\underline{M}$, $\underline{M}'$ are logn tape bounded probabilistic Turing machines which are able to simulate the Markov processes corresponding to $\underline{F}$ and $\underline{F}'$, respectively.

We define a new probabilistic Turing machine M which decides the relation '$a_{1n} > b_{1n}$'. Using $\underline{M}$ and $\underline{M}'$ in parallel, M simulates both Markov processes simultaneously.

If $\underline{M}$ reaches one of the states $\{s_n, s'_n\}$, then $\underline{M}$ stops with probability $n^{-md(F')}$ in this state or goes, with probability $1-n^{md(F')}$, into $\underline{s}$. If $\underline{M}$ has reached $\underline{s}$ (during the past simulation or after the last step described above), then it stops with equal probability either in s_n or in s'_n.

$\underline{M}'$ proceeds in the same way except that $n^{-md(F')}$ is replaced by $n^{-md(F)}$.

There are 3 cases in the outcome of the pair ($\underline{M}$,$\underline{M}'$):

- If $\underline{M}$ stops in s_n and $\underline{M}'$ in s'_n, then M answers $a_{1n} > b_{1n}$.
- If $\underline{M}$ stops in s'_n and $\underline{M}'$ in s_n, then M answers $a_{1n} \leq b_{1n}$.
- If both $\underline{M}$ and $\underline{M}'$ stop in the same state (either s_n or s'_n), then M decides with equal probability either $a_{1n} > b_{1n}$ or $a_{1n} \leq b_{1n}$.

Property (ii) of the described Markov processes implies that M accepts any element of FIN with probability $\geq 1/2$ and rejects any pair not belonging to FIN with probability $> 1/2$. Furthermore, M works simultaneously within O(logn) tape and polynomial time.

Hence, we can find an appropriate constant c and a probabilistic logn tape bounded Turing machine M' which accepts FIN with error probability $\leq 1/2 - 2^{-n^c}$ and works in polynomial time. (For the corresponding method, see Ruzzo/Simon/Tompa,1982, Jung,1984)

3. Concluding remarks.

It is known that any language in PrSPACE(logn) can be reduced by uniform logn depth reductions to a matrix inversion problem (see

Borodin/Cook/Pippenger,1983 and Jung,1984).
Applying Csanky's algorithm (Csanky,1976) the inverse of a nonsingular $n \times n$ matrix can be expressed by a formula with size $n^{O(1)}$ and depth 1, but division occurs. If we consider only the problem of deciding inequalities, we can avoid divisions. Hence, we can reduce any language in PrSPACE(logn) to FIN, restricted to depth one formulas. Thus we obtain:

<u>THEOREM 1</u>.

(i) FIN is complete for PrSPACE(logn) with respect to logn depth reductions.

(ii) PrSPACE(logn) = PrTISP($n^{O(1)}$,logn)

Furthermore, Theorem 1 implies that FIN can be reduced by uniform logn depth reductions to FIN_1, where FIN_1 denotes the inequality problem for formulas with depth one.
The probabilistic approximation method proposed in this paper can be applied to the approximation of the permanent, i.e., it is easy to prove that

$$PER=\left\{ (A,B) : A,B \text{ quadratic matrices over the integers with } per(A) \leq per(B) \right\}$$

is in PrTIME($n^{O(1)}$).
On the other hand, Valiant (1979) observed that computing the permanent is #P-complete. His method can be used for proving that PER is hard for PrTIME($n^{O(1)}$). If we compare the computational complexity of PER with the complexity of

$$DET=\left\{ (A,B) : A,B \text{ quadratic matrices over the integers with } det(A) \leq det(B) \right\}$$

we obtain:

<u>THEOREM 2</u>.

(i) DET is complete for PrSPACE(logn)

(ii) PER is complete for PrTIME($n^{O(1)}$)

For more details about connections between DET and other problems in FIN, we refer to the survey of Cook (1983).

<u>References</u>.

Borodin A., Cook S.A., Pippenger N. (1983), Parallel computation for well-endowed rings and space bounded probabilistic machines. Inf. and Control 58, 113-136

Cook S.A.,(1983), The classification of problems which have fast parallel algorithms. Proc. FCT'83, LNCS 158, 78-93

Csanky L. (1976), Fast parallel matrix inversion algorithms. SIAM J. Comput. 5, 618-623

Gill J. (1977), Computational complexity of probabilistic Turing machines. SIAM J. Comput. 6, 675-695

Jung H. (1984), On probabilistic tape complexity and fast circuits for matrix inversion problems. Proc. ICALP'84, LNCS 172, 281-291

Ruzzo W.L., Simon J., Tompa M. (1982), Space-bounded hierarchies and probabilistic computations. Proc. 14th Annual ACM Symp. on Theory of Computing

Valiant L.G. (1979), The complexity of computing the permanent. Theor. Comp. Science 8, 181-201

THE NEAREST NEIGHBOR PROBLEM ON BOUNDED DOMAINS

Rolf G. Karlsson
J. Ian Munro
Data Structuring Group
Department of Computer Science
University of Waterloo
Waterloo, Ont., Canada N2L 3G1

Edward L. Robertson
Department of Computer Science
Indiana University
Bloomington, Indiana, USA 47405

1. Introduction

This paper deals with maintaining a data structure, containing n elements from $M=\{0,1,...,m-1\}$, that will return its key value nearest to a query point. Our primary interest is in the class of problems in which m is much larger than n, but very small in comparison to 2^n. The problem is the one dimensional, bounded domain restriction of what is sometimes called the "post office problem". Our interest, however, came as a natural generalization of priority queues. Yet another view arises, in this volume, in the work of Chazelle and Guibas on fractional cascading. They are interested in a structure on contiguous segments of the integers $0,..m-1$, that supports the operatons find the segment containing a query point, split a segment at a point, and merge two adjacent segments. This is equivalent to the dynamic formulation of our problem.

The main result is a $\log\log m$ lower bound for the dynamic problem (support insert, delete and find closest) under a reasonable model (all logarithms in this paper are given to base 2). We also present an $O(\log\log m)$ algorithm using $O(n+m^{\epsilon})$ space, for all $\epsilon>0$. Finally, we show that $\log\log m$ is also a lower bound on the static problem (only queries) when allowing only $O(n)$ space. Our point of view is that a bounded domain is interesting and potentially practical. For instance, the common assumption that key values are arbitrary reals contrasts with the fact that computers have a finite precision; in many applications this generality is unrealistic and perhaps even undesirable.

Denote by $M^{(n)}$ the subsets of M of cardinality n and $S \in M^{(n)}$ as the current set of keys. The (dynamic) nearest neighbor problem is to efficiently support the three set operations:

NN(q,S) : retrieve the element in S with a key value closest to q (i.e., find the nearest neighbor to q).

INSERT(q,S) : replace S by $S\cup\{q\}$, where $q\in M$.

DELETE(q,S) : replace S by $S-\{q\}$, where $q\in M$.

It is useful to break up the query in two operations:

PREDECESSOR(q,S) : find the greatest key in S that is less than or equal to q.

SUCCESSOR(q,S) : find the least key in S that is greater than or equal to q.

The nearest neighbor is determined by comparing the predecessor with the successor. The *space* complexity is the amount of storage, in $\log m$ bit words, required by the data structure that provides the solution. The *time* complexity is the number of basic steps on such words necessary to process any of the operations in the worst case.

2. Related Work

A balanced tree, e.g. an AVL tree [1], supports an $O(\log n)$ algorithm for NN, INSERT, and DELETE, using $O(n)$ space. This is within a constant factor of optimal for infinite domains when counting comparisons since the nearest neighbor problem is reducible to sorting, which has an information theoretic lower bound of $n\log n - O(n)$. It was therefore a significant contribution when van Emde Boas [5],[6] presented the stratified tree, an $O(\log\log m)$ algorithm. The main drawback of the stratified tree is its $O(m)$ storage requirement. Johnson [3] developed a more flexible structure than van Emde Boas' with essentially the same run time. His data structure allocates memory blocks as they are needed, but even then the space demand may be unacceptable when the domain size m is high. A slower $O(\sqrt{\log m})$ time algorithm which operates on $O(n)$ words was given by Willard [7]. The time complexities given so far are measured on a uniform RAM. In a less realistic 'cell probe model' Ajtai, Fredman and Komlos [2] gave an $O(1)$ priority queue using $O(n)$ space. They assume a model in which a binary trie can be searched in constant time, hence their result, although very interesting, is in a model of questionable practicality.

3. A Fast Search

Willard [7] proved that van Emde Boas' stratified tree algorithm has an inherent space requirement of $\Omega(n^{3/4}m^{1/4})$. In this section we briefly sketch an $O(\log\log m)$ dynamic algorithm which circumvents that space lower bound, requiring only $O(n+m^{\epsilon})$ storage. Two known data structures are used:

1) The stratified tree [5],[6], a ($\log\log m$ time, m space) implementation of dynamic nearest neighbor search.

2) The q-fast trie [7], a ($\sqrt{\log m}$ time, n space) implementation.

In combining these to form our structure, the stratified tree is simply plugged in, and only a few details of the q-fast trie need be explained. The q-fast trie is basically a (pruned) trie of degree b in which the leaves contain between c and $2c$ elements. The leaves are represented as conventional balanced trees (indeed 2-3 trees). Most of the internal trie nodes will have rather few non-empty branches. Willard uses an Inner tree at each node to store (and quickly update) pointers to non-empty nodes at the next level. His implementation calls for an AVL tree for this purpose. The structure also retains at each node a reference to the leftmost and rightmost leaf in its subtree. Our structure is formed by employing stratified trees as Inner trees in the q-fast trie and optimizing the choice of parameters. Willard [7] observed that this does not improve the run time of q-fast trees if we insist on $O(n)$ space. Our point is that we can improve run time if we sacrifice some space.

Theorem 1: We can process any of the operations NN, INSERT, and DELETE in $O(\log\log m)$ time using $o(n\frac{m^{1/\log\log m}}{\log m})$ storage.

Proof: In the data structure proposed above, there are three time components to consider.

i) The proximity search at internal nodes with branch factor b.

ii) The length of the search path expressed by the trie height h.

iii) The binary search in the key sets appended as trie leaves each containing about c elements.

Emulating the q-fast trie with stratified trees as Inner trees (part i), the total time is

$$T = \log\log b + h + \log c$$

since exact matches in trie nodes are found in constant time, hence at most one proximity search on an Inner tree need be performed. The stratified trees occupy $O(b)$ words each, so the total space demand is $O(nhb/c+n)$. To retain $O(\log\log m)$ run time we choose $c = (\log m)^{\alpha}$ and $h = \beta \log\log m$. The obvious choice of $m = b^h$ makes $b = m^{1/\log\log m}$. These give a family of $O(\log\log m)$ time methods with space decreasing as the parameters increase. We spare the reader the details. The bound quoted in the theorem follows from choosing $\alpha = 2$ and $\beta = 1$. The search and update algorithms are straightforward adaptations of [7] and [5]. □

Hence, if we allow space very slightly superlinear in n, but still $o(m)$, we may obtain a worst case run time of $O(\log\log m)$. In fact, our structure may go below the space lower bound of $n^{3/4}m^{1/4}$ for stratified trees, since $\frac{n}{\log m} m^{1/\log\log m} < nm^{1/\log\log m} < n^{3/4} m^{1/4}$, if $m^{1/\log\log m} < (m/n)^{1/4}$, and thus the space use is $o(n^{3/4} m^{1/4})$ if $n = o(m^{1-4/\log\log m})$.

Johnson [3] also presents a hybrid structure with $O(\log\log m)$ search on $o(m)$ space. He there achieves a minimal space of $O(n \times \log\log m \times m^{1/\log\log m})$. Johnson's scheme with time complexity $O(\sqrt{\log m})$ gives Willard's p-fast trie. In the next section, we show that $\log\log m$ time is the best we can hope for in a reasonable model.

4. A Dynamic Lower Bound

4.1. The Model

We shall demonstrate a $\log\log m$ lower bound on the time to process each of NN, INSERT, and DELETE for sets $S \in M^{(n)}$. The bound applies under a *segment graph model*, defined as follows:

i) A single-source directed graph G represents S, with the input node denoted as the *root*.

ii) Each node represents directly a contiguous subset, a *segment*, of M, and represents indirectly the set of keys contained in the segment; the root, in particular, represents M and S.

iii) A node gives the rightmost (min) and the leftmost (max) key value in its segment, if it is nonempty.

iv) A descendant of a node represents a subsegment of the segment represented by the node.

v) Each answer to a query is given by a path in G.

vi) A constant amount of information may be stored at each node in the graph G, but there is no bound on the total space used in the structure.

In order to derive the lower bound, we mark a node if its segment contains a key. The marks enable us to measure the number of nodes that are necessary to process a query, an insert, or a delete. We judiciously select nodes to probe in order to efficiently find the smallest marked segment including a search element.

We distinguish between three types of nodes in G.

i) the root (the source node).

ii) the m 'leaves', each representing an integer from 1 to m. The marked leaves are linked together.

iii) the internal nodes, which may contain pointers and markers, and deal with subsegments of M.

In this general model, we can describe the stratified tree algorithm [5] in enough detail so that its crucial operations are accounted for.

4.2. The Stratified Tree

Van Emde Boas defines the stratified tree as a hierarchical decomposition of an ordered binary tree into canonical subtrees (CS), hence it is a particular graph fitting our model. To represent the stratified tree work, we shall expand on the marking and introduce *primary* and *secondary* marks. Their use is motivated by the following brief description of the stratified tree.

A stratified tree is formed by recursively applying the following decomposition to a full binary tree T with m leaves. T is sliced at half its height to produce one upper canonical subtree (UCS) with $\sqrt{m}$ leaves (center level nodes in T) and $\sqrt{m}$ lower canonical subtrees (LCS) with $\sqrt{m}$ leaves each. We call the center level nodes, which are the leaves of the UCS and the roots of the LCS (for example, v in Figure 1), the *medial* nodes of T. The decomposition is then applied to the UCS and all LCS.

Van Emde Boas' technique works because S can be represented by recording information very sparsely in the CS. Basically, as long as there is at most one key present in a CS A and all CS containing A have more than one key, the key is stored at the root of A, and the rest of A is empty. If more entries have to be represented, then the corresponding medial nodes of A contain information as well;

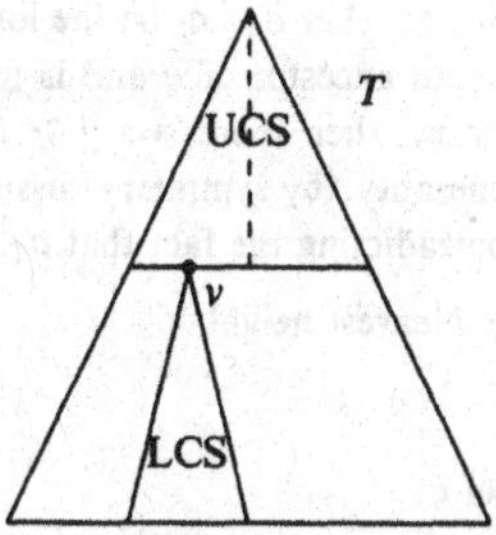

Figure 1: The stratified tree

and so on, recursively. The leaves corresponding to the keys in S and all their ancestors are said to be *present*. A node is a ***branch point*** if it has two present children. The LCS of a node v together with the half of the UCS containing v is called the *reach* of v. A node v is *active* if and only if there exists a branch point in the interior of the reach of v (i.e. not counting a branch point at the UCS root or at the LCS leaves). Branch points are always active. We mark the internal nodes as follows:

1) v receives a *primary* mark if it is a branch point.

2) v gets a *secondary* mark if it is active: if v has a branch point in its LCS, not counting branch points at the leaves, mark it '−', else mark it '+'. Let each secondary mark have a pointer back to the nearest primary marked ancestor.

Van Emde Boas' algorithm looks for the lowest active node, the lowest secondary mark. In a stratified tree an active node most often has no leaves marked present in its subtree. Note that a given node is only in the reach of loglog m other nodes.

The secondary marks reflect the CS framework and correspond to van Emde Boas' upper branch point (ub) field. For our purposes, it is equivalent and conceptually clearer to unwind the stratified tree as a full binary tree. For example, the min and max pointers for a node in the stratified tree give the extremal leaves within its local CS. To find the minimum and maximum keys in the node's segment, van Emde Boas' algorithm performs an O(loglog m) time search down through min and max pointers for local CS. We translate that by passing pointers to min and max keys up through the hierarchical tree levels. The updating of min and max information at intermediate nodes is taken care of as secondary marks are modified.

The edges in a binary tree are labeled 0 (left branch) or 1 (right branch). The tree reflects a binary representation of the keys, with the addresses of nodes at level i expressed by bit representations $q_1 \dots q_i$.

Let each marked internal node point to four extreme values:

the Min and the Max in its left subtree, and
the Min and the Max in its right subtree.

We establish the following equivalence.

Theorem 2: Finding the nearest marked ancestor in a *primary* marked binary tree of height $h = \log m$ is equivalent, within a constant factor, to finding the closest neighbor present in a subset of $\{0,\dots,m-1\}$.

Proof: We first show that by knowing the successor and predecessor, the nearest neighbor can be found in constant time.

Nearest neighbor (NN) => Nearest marked ancestor (NMA).

To mark an arbitrary node with bit representation $a_1 \cdots a_i$, $i \leqslant h$, insert $a_1 \dots a_i 0 \dots 0$ and $a_1 \dots a_i 1 \dots 1$ into the set, where $h-i$ 0's or 1's are appended.

Consider an NMA query on $q = q_1...q_h$. Let $a_1...a_i$ be the longest common prefix of the successor and the predecessor of q. Then $a_1...a_i$ is an ancestor of q and is marked. Indeed, $a_1...a_i$ is the nearest marked ancestor of q. Assume the contrary, then there is a $j > i$ and $a_{i+1}...a_j$ such that $a_1...a_j$ is a marked ancestor of q. Without loss of generality (by symmetry) assume $a_{i+1} = 0$. Then $a_1...a_j1...1$ is less than $a_1...a_i1c_{i+2}...c_h$ and is *in* the set, contradicting the fact that $a_1...a_i1c_{i+2}...c_h$ is the successor of q.

Nearest marked ancestor $\Rightarrow$ Nearest neighbor

To find one neighbor:
find the nearest marked ancestor of q;
select the left or right subtree depending on the next bit of q;
if q is less than or equal to the minimum key α of that subtree **then** α is the successor of q
else the maximum key of the tree is the predecessor of q;

We show that the key $q = q_1...q_h$, with nearest marked ancestor $q_1...q_i$, $i < h$, cannot lie between the min value $q_1...q_ib_{i+1}...b_h$ and the max value $q_1...q_ic_{i+1}...c_h$ in its own subtree.

For some $j \geq i+1$ it must be that $b_{i+1}...b_j = c_{i+1}...c_j$ since at least $b_{i+1} = c_{i+1}$ because they belong to the same subtree of $q_1...q_i$ ($b_{i+1} = c_{i+1} = q_{i+1}$). Consider the largest j satisfying this condition. Either $j = h$, in which case the subtree contains the one key q, or $j < h$ and $b_{j+1} \neq c_{j+1}$. In this latter case the node $q_1...q_ib_{i+1}...b_j$ must be marked. But then either $q \leq q_1...q_ib_{i+1}...b_h$ or $q \geq q_1...q_ic_{i+1}...c_h$ since otherwise $q_{i+1}...q_j = b_{i+1}...b_j$, i.e. $q_1...q_ib_{i+1}...b_j$ is a lower marked ancestor of q than $q_1...q_i$. Assume $q \leq q_1...q_ib_{i+1}...b_h$. Since $q_1...q_i0...0 \leq q$ but the interval from $q_1...q_i0...0$ to $q_1...q_ib_{i+1}...b_h$ is empty, $q_1...q_ib_{i+1}...b_h$ is indeed the successor of q. The case when $q \geq q_1...q_ic_{i+1}...c_h$ follows similarly. Hence, q is either less than the minimum or greater than the maximum key in the subtree rooted at $q_1...q_i$.

An insertion into $\{0,...,m-1\}$ marks the corresponding leaf in the tree. Except for the first entry, this will cause one internal node to be primary marked. The fact that all changes are limited to the leaf and the vicinity of an internal node permit updating the structure efficiently.

Updating after Insert(q):
find the nearest marked ancestor of q, call it nq;
select the subtree A of nq to which q belongs;
let min be the minimum key of A;
if $q <$ min **then**
  form $q_1...q_i$, the longest common prefix of q and min;
  mark the node $q_1...q_i$;
  the minimum and maximum in $q_1...q_i$'s left subtree is set to q;
  the min and max in $q_1...q_i$'s right subtree is set to the min and max in A (Figure 2);
  the min in A is set to q;
else { symmetric case }

The max in nq's right subtree is the max in $q_1...q_i$'s right subtree (case $q <$min), since otherwise $q_1...q_i$ would be marked and closer to q than nq is.

Deletion reverses insertion, observing that the node unmarked when q is deleted may not be the same node that was marked when q was inserted, due to intervening changes in the structure. Still, it is always q's nearest marked ancestor that is unmarked.

The above argument supports a structure which allows constant time nearest neighbor determination, once a marked ancestor is found. □

Theorem 2 enables us to express a bound on NN computations in terms of the equivalent problem of finding a nearest marked ancestor. We then only have to support a consistent marking and may discard the extremal (min and max) information. Our next result shows that we can find the nearest primary marked ancestor in loglog m probes using both primary and secondary marks. Furthermore, the secondary marks may be updated in loglog m changes. To introduce the secondary marks, we conduct a

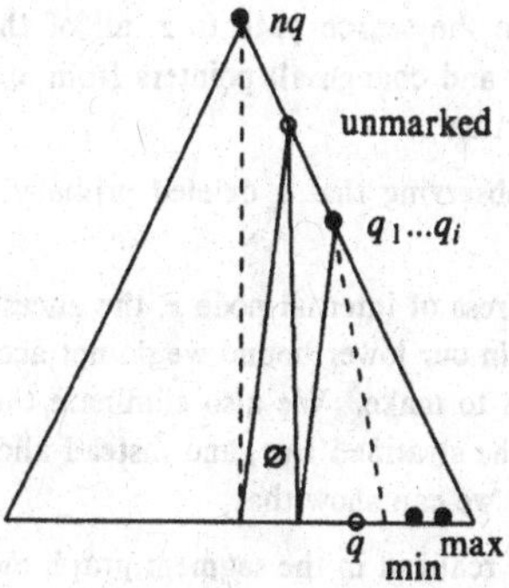

Figure 2

binary search from the root to a lowest primary marked ancestor *nq* of *q*. Every node visited during the search receives a secondary mark.

Theorem 3: The nearest primary marked ancestor of a leaf in a marked binary tree of height *h* may be found in log *h* time by a procedure which uses at most one step which follows an arbitrary pointer.

Proof: Given a leaf *q* which is a descendant of some marked node *x*, we find its nearest marked ancestor as follows. Perform a binary search of the path from root to *q*. If a probed node *v* is marked then bisect the remaining path below *v* to locate the next probe, otherwise probe a node halfway between *v* and the current subtree root. If there are no marks (except at leaves) below *x*, this will lead directly to *x* or to a child of *x*. The search does not terminate at the first primary mark. Unless the search only arrives at *x* on the final probe, it will go beyond *x* and back up to a child of *x*, verifying that there are no marks on that path below *x*. If there is a primary marked internal node below *x*, then the secondary mark pointers will give us the correct marked ancestor to *q*.

To resolve the search ambiguity that a node *y* (Figure 3) in *nq*'s subtree may be primary marked while not being an ancestor to *q*, secondary marks are associated with pointers, leading back to the nearest primary marked ancestor.

We show that this structure can be maintained in log *h* time. All secondary nodes are between two primary nodes. (For simplicity we treat the root as if it was always marked.) Any secondary node between two primary nodes is on the search path to the lower primary node. Hence the primary marking of a node *z* splits the path between exactly two primary nodes *x* and *y*. The portion of the path above *z* is

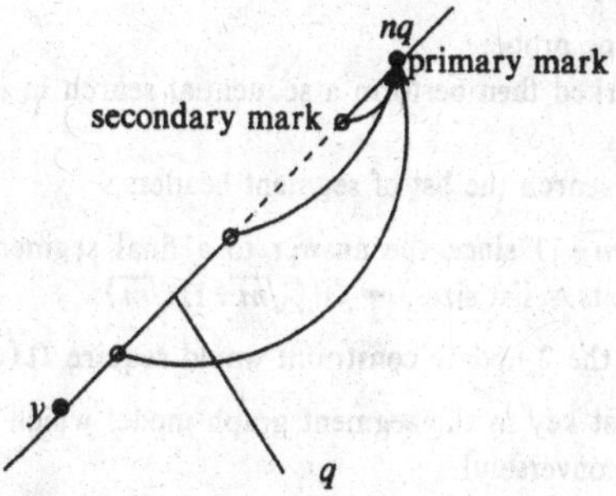

Figure 3: Secondary mark pointers

only changed by secondary marks on the search path to z, all of these nodes will have pointers to x. Below z, follow the search path to y and change all pointers from x to z. This completes the necessary updating for the structure on an insertion.

Deletion is done similarly by observing that a deleted primary mark is only on one path between primary nodes. □

In the preceding proof, the address of internal node z, the ancestor of an inserted (or deleted) key, is not immediately found. However, in our lower bound we do not account for how to find internal nodes to mark, but only how many changes to make. We also eliminate the *father pointers,* which van Emde Boas uses to locate medial nodes in the stratified tree, and instead allow simple address arithmetic in our lower bound model. Omitting details we can show that

Theorem 4: The stratified tree can be realized in the segment graph model.

4.3. A Trade-off Argument

For our lower bound argument the space requirement is of no concern, $O(m)$ or more words are allowed to store the data structure. For simplicity, we limit ourselves to look for the predecessor of a query point; we denote it *the* closest key. In accordance, we only store the maximum key in a marked segment.

For a lower bound, we consider the number of nodes to probe for the retrieval of the closest key, denote this measure $f_1(n,m)$, and the number of changes we have to make for an update, denote this $f_2(n,m)$. At an update, we do not consider *how* to find a key, or *which* key to change. A solid basis for a lower bound is to establish a trade-off between f_1 and f_2, and then to find the point where the two costs are balanced. For the class of algorithms with a trade-off of the form we establish between f_1 and f_2, $\log\log m$ is a lower bound.

Observe that if marks are sparse in the structure, with less information stored, a query is costly to process. Conversely, a dense marking makes updating expensive.

Lemma 5: Finding the closest key in the segment graph model where at most 2 changes are made at an update requires $\sqrt{m}$ probes (Conversely, finding the closest key in a segment graph model in at most $\sqrt{m}$ probes needs at least 2 changes for an update).

Proof: In a segment graph where only one update is made, the worst-case search time clearly is $\Theta(m)$. Now consider a 2-update graph. We have to update a leaf node, and are left with one update for the rest of the structure. An optimal set reduction is to split M in $\sqrt{m}$ segments of size $\sqrt{m}$. The two updates are then performed on segment headers and segment leaves. Define head(q) := q div $\sqrt{m}$, and tail(q) := q mod $\sqrt{m}$.

Update(q): insert or delete a *present* mark at head(q) and tail(q);

Search(q): find head(q) in one probe;
if head(q) is marked **then** perform a sequential search in its segment to find the marked key closest to tail(q)
else sequentially search the list of segment headers;

Total search time is $1+(\sqrt{m}-1)$ since the answer to a final segment probe is given by default. The storage complexity is O(# lists × list sizes) = $O((\sqrt{m}+1)\sqrt{m})$.

Other scenarios under the 2-update constraint would require $\Omega(\sqrt{m})$ probes in the worst case. □

Lemma 6: Finding the closest key in the segment graph model which allows at most $\sqrt{m}$ changes at an update takes 2 probes (and conversely).

Proof: For each node, we store a neighbor pointer to its predecessor. This corresponds to the secondary marking in the stratified tree. Define head(q) and tail(q) as in the proof of Lemma 5.

Search(q): **if** head(q) is marked present **then** return neighbor(tail(q))
else return neighbor(head(q))

Insert(q): **if** head(q) is present **then**
mark tail(q);
if max(head(q)) $< q$ **then** max(head(q)) := q;
update the neighbor pointers for nodes in the head(q) segment
else
mark head(q);
max(head(q)) := q;
update the neighbor pointers for nodes in the list of headers;

Delete(q) is similar to Insert.

Again, the optimal set reduction is to split M in $\sqrt{m}$ segments of size $\sqrt{m}$. □

Lemma 7: Finding the closest key in the segment graph model which allows at most $k+1$ changes at an update requires $m^{1/2^k}$ probes.

Proof: We extend the argument in the proof of Lemma 5. The homogeneous set reduction is essentially given by a recurrence relation:

$$f(k) = \begin{cases} m & \text{, if } k=1 \\ (f(k-1))^{1/2} & \text{, if } k>1 \end{cases}$$

where k is the number of updates allowed. It follows that $f(k) = m^{1/2^{k-1}}$

More precisely, in a k-update structure we start probing at a node p_1, representing a segment s_1 of length $\sqrt{m}$. If p_1 is unmarked (because s_1 contains no keys), then probe a node p_2 closer to the source, representing a larger segment s_2, which includes s_1. If p_1 was marked then probe a node p_3, representing a smaller segment s_3, a subsegment of s_1. Let s_3 be of length $m^{1/4}$, while s_2 represents $m^{1/4}$ (header) nodes at the same distance from p_2 as p_1. The relative length of s_2 is thus $m^{1/4}$. The recursive probing will eventually reach a segment of length $m^{1/2^k}$ which cannot be resolved further on the k update basis; we have to do a sequential search there for the closest key. Compared with Lemma 5 the brute force universe is reduced from $\sqrt{m}$ to $m^{1/2^k}$.

This gives a trade-off

$$\text{update} = k+1 \text{ vs. search} = k+(m^{1/2^k})-1$$

An insert attempts to fill in (mark) a node representing the largest empty segment, while a delete has to unmark a smallest marked segment. Even how to find the first node to change takes O(k) time, and each update then has to assign marks to O(k) subsegments.

In our model, there is no faster way to uniformly decrease a universe of size m than by probing at nodes representing universe sizes $\sqrt{m}$. This in order to select, at each probe, between two equal sized subproblems (depending on a valid marking), for a sequential refinement of the relative universe. The update constraint prevents any other guidance for more judicious probing (i.e., faster search) in the graph. □

The converse also holds.

Lemma 8: Finding the closest key in the segment graph model which allows at most $m^{1/2^k}$ changes at an update requires $k+1$ probes.

Proof: Similar to the proof of Lemma 7. For each node on a segment level that contains a marked node, we include a pointer to its predecessor. This corresponds to the concept of active nodes in the stratified tree. □

Theorem 9: The trade-off between update and search in solving the dynamic nearest neighbor problem for $M^{(n)}$ is balanced at loglog$m$ cost in the segment graph model.

Proof: Given Lemmas 7 and 8, we compute the cut off

$$k+1 = k+m^{1/2^k}-1$$

which gives

$$m^{1/2^k} = 2$$

or approximately

$$k = \log\log m$$

In fact,

$$m^{1/2^k} = \log\log m \text{ , gives } k = \log\log m - \log\log\log\log m$$

□

Corollary 10: The dynamic nearest neighbor problem for sets $S \in M^{(n)}$ has a loglog m time lower bound under the segment graph model.

MIN is given by NN(0), so loglog m is also a lower bound for the priority queue problem. By Theorem 4 and Corollary 10, we conclude

Corollary 11: The stratified tree algorithm is optimal under the segment graph model.

The lower bound depends on the data structures being dynamic. However, for data structures that use O(n) space, we cannot do any better even if just queries are considered.

5. A Static Lower Bound

In [8] and [4] it is shown that loglog m is an upper bound for finding the closest point in $S \in M^{(n)}$ when using O(n) space. In this section, we show that we cannot expect to do better in a reasonable model. We assume loglog $m = o(\log n)$. The bound will apply in the segment graph model given in the previous section, with two additional constraints:

1) An internal node in the graph G represents contiguous segments that contains at least $C(m,n)$ keys. Each leaf contains at most $C(m,n)$ keys.

2) The graph G preserves proximity between segments: descendants are ordered by their domain offsets.

The O(n) space complexity necessitates a compressed selection of segments to be represented as graph nodes. The cluster size $C(m,n)$ is related to the space complexity $S(m,n)$, which in turn affects the time complexity $T(m,n)$.

Given $S(m,n) = n$, we have a trade-off between $C(m,n)$ and $P(m,n)$, the maximal path length in G. If $C(m,n) = 1$, then $P(m,n) = \Omega(\log n)$, and if $C(m,n) = n$, then $P(m,n) = 1$. In between, if $C(m,n) = 2^{\sqrt{\log m}}$ then $P(m,n) = \sqrt{\log m}$. The greater $C(m,n)$ is, the faster we can find the smallest node segment in G including q. But that also implies a higher processing time to resolve the set of $C(m,n)$ keys. Given only the information that a set is ordered, the best way to search it is by repeated bisection. Since the total time then is at least $\log(C(m,n))$, we optimize $C(m,n)$ so that $P(m,n) \leqslant \log(C(m,n))$. Hence the best $C(m,n)$ is determined by the O(n) storage constraint, and by the path length in G necessary to break down the log m bits of q. We formally express this as a lower bound on any search strategy on $P(m,n)$.

Theorem 12: Finding the nearest neighbor in $S \in M^{(n)}$ for any q in M requires $\Omega(\log\log m)$ time in the worst case under a segment graph model, if only O(n) storage is provided.

Proof: Assume q is not present. To find the leaf L including q, we probe judiciously in the graph. The address of the probed node is given by some function of the log m bits representing q. Since a node v in G stores no information on how the sub-graph rooted at v is pruned, the segment address for L in G, giving the proximity of q, has to be retrieved by recursive search. Denote the log m bits of q by $B(q)$. The optimal strategy is to split $B(q)$ in two equal parts, and attempt to map into the address space of G using the address given by the first half of $B(q)$. If the probe locates a node v in G, then we know there is a sub-graph of G descending from v. We continue the search by splitting the second half of $B(q)$, and repeat the probing using the first of these split halves. If the mapping does not correspond to a node address in G, then the path has been pruned, and we have to backtrack the search. We split the first half of $B(q)$, and probe into the address space of G using the resulting first split half. Observe that if we try to map using more than half of the remaining bits of q, then the adversary will force the search to backtrack. This would give us a larger sub-problem than above, for the next step. □

References

[1] Adel'son-Vel'skii, G.M. and Landis, E.M., "An Algorithm for the Organization of Information," *Doklady Akademia Nauk* USSR 146, 2 (1962), 263-266.

[2] Ajtai, M., Fredman, M.L. and Komlos, J., "Hash Functions for Priority Queues," *Proc. 24th Annual IEEE Symposium on Foundations of Computer Science* (1983), 299-303.

[3] Johnson, D.B., "A Priority Queue in which Initialization and Queue Operations Take O(log log D) Time," *Math. Systems Theory 15*, 4 (Dec. 1982), 295-310.

[4] Karlsson, R.G., Algorithms in a Restricted Universe, Ph.D Thesis, University of Waterloo (Nov. 1984), and Computer Science Dept Research Report CS-84-50.

[5] van Emde Boas, P., Kaas, R. and Ziljstra, E., "Design and Analysis of an Efficient Priority Queue," *Math. Systems Theory 10* (1977), 99-127.

[6] van Emde Boas, P., "Preserving Order in a Forest in Less Than Logarithmic Time and Linear Space," *Information Processing Lett. 6*, 3 (June 1977), 80-82.

[7] Willard, D.E., "Two Very Fast Trie Data Structures," *19th Allerton Conference* (1981), 355-363.

[8] Willard, D.E., "Log-logarithmic Worst-case Range Queries Are Possible in Space $\Theta(n)$," *Information Processing Lett.* 17 (Aug. 1983), 81-84.

Routing through a Generalized Switchbox

by

Michael Kaufmann and Kurt Mehlhorn
Fachbereich 10, Angewandte Mathematik und Informatik
Universität des Saarlandes, 6600 Saarbrücken
West Germany

Abstract: We present an algorithm for the routing problem for two-terminal nets in generalized switchboxes. A generalized switchbox is any subset R of the planar rectangular grid with no non-trivial holes, i.e. every finite face has exactly four incident vertices. A net is a pair of nodes of non-maximal degree on the boundary of R. A solution is a set of edge-disjoint paths, one for each net.

Our algorithm solves generalized switchbox routing problems in time $O(n(\log n)^2)$ where n is the number of vertices of R, i.e. it either finds a solution or indicates that there is none.

1. Introduction

Automatic design systems e.g. CALCOS (Lauther) and PI (Rivest) for integrated circuits divide the routing problem into several stages (cf Fig.1).

1) Determine a global routing for every net. A net is a set of points which have to be connected and a global routing fixes the global shape of the realization of the net, i.e. how the net runs with respect to the subcircuits.

2) Cut the routing region into regions of simple shape, e.g. channels, switchboxes.

3) Determine for every net the exact positions where it crosses the boundaries of the regions.

4) Route each region obtained in step 2.

In general, the regions obtained in step 2 are *not* channels (cf. Fig 1). However, if each subcircuit is connected to the chip boundary by a (sequence of) *cut*(s) then the subregions have no non-trivial holes and have all their terminals on the boundary of the infinite face. We call such regions generalized switchboxes.

A subgraph R of the planar rectangular grid is a generalized switchbox if every finite face has exactly four vertices on its boundary (cf Figure 2).

Let $B(R) = \{v|\ v$ node of R and v has degree $\leq 3\}$ be the nodes of non-maximal degree. All nodes of $B(R)$ lie on the boundary of the infinite face of R (henceforth simply called *boundary*). A two-terminal net is an unordered pair of points in $B(R)$.

A *generalized switchbox routing problem* (GSRP) is given by a generalized switchbox R and a set $N = \{(s_i, t_i);\ 1 \leq i \leq m\}$ of nets. A solution of the problem is a set $P = \{p_i; 1 \leq i \leq m\}$ of paths such that

(1) p_i connects s_i and t_i for $1 \leq i \leq m$

(2) p_i and p_j are edge-disjoint for $i \neq j$.

Figure 3 shows a GSRP and a solution of it. Note that a solution consists of edge-disjoint paths: this is frequently called a solution in the knock-knee mode. Also note that a vertex v of R is used by either one or two wires which either go straight through v or bend in v. (cf. Figure 4)

In this paper we present an algorithm which solves standard generalized switchbox routing problems in $0(n \log n)^2)$ where n is the number of vertices of the routing region R. A routing problem is *standard* if $deg(v) + ter(v)$ is even for all nodes v where $deg(v)$ is the degree of node v and $ter(v)$ is the number of nets which have v as a terminal. We call $deg(v) + ter(v)$ the extended degree of node v. For non-standard GSRPs we do slightly worse. We show how to find a solution in time $0(nlog^2 n + |U|^2)$, where U is the set of vertices with odd extended degree.

Previous work on routing problems in knock-knee mode can be found in Preparata/Lipski, Frank, Mehlhorn/Preparata, Becker/Mehlhorn, Kramer/v. Leeuwen, and Brady/Brown. Preparata/ Lipski solve the channel routing problem, Frank and Mehlhorn/ Preparata solve the switchbox routing problem. Becker/Mehlhorn consider a more general problem than the one considered here. They consider arbitrary subsets of the planar grid (holes are allowed!!) and solve the routing problem in time $0(n^{3/2})$. Finally Brady/Brown show that any layout in knock-knee mode can be wired using four conducting layers.

This paper is organized as follows.

In section 2 we review the basic theorem of Okamura/Seymour on multi-commodity flow in planar graph and refine it to the special case of standard generalized switchboxes. Section 3 gives the algorithm for standard GSRPs and analyse the runtime. Finally we deal with non-standard GSRPs. In section 5 we mention some extensions of the work presented here.

2. The theorem of Okamura/Seymour and its application to generalized switchboxes

Let $G = (V, E)$ be a graph and let N be a set of unordered pairs of vertices of G; $N = \{(s_i, t_i); 1 \leq i \leq m\}$. A *cut* is a subset $X \subseteq V$ of the vertices of G. The *capacity* of a cut X is the number of edges in E with exactly one end in X and the *density* of a cut X is the number of nets $(s, t) \in N$ with exactly one terminal in X, i.e.

$cap(X) = |\{e \in E; e = (a, b)$ and $a \in X, b \notin X\}$ and

$dens(X_1, X_2) = \{(s, t) \in N\};\ s \in X_1,\ t \in X_2$ for $X_1, X_2 \subseteq V,\ X_1 \cap X_2 = \emptyset$

We will also use

$CAP(x) = \{e \in E; e = (a, b)$ and $a \in X, b \notin X\}$ and

$dens(X_1, X_2) = \{(s, t) \in N; s \in X_1, t \in X_2\}$ for

$X_1, X_2 \subseteq V, X_1 \cap| X_2 = \emptyset$

Theorem (Okamura/Seymour): If G is planar and can be drawn in the plane such that $s_1, ..., s_m, t_1, ..., t_m$ are all on the boundary of the infinite region and $cap(X) - dens(X)$ is non-negative and even for all cuts $X \subseteq V$ then there are pairwise edge-disjoint paths $p_1, ..., p_m$ such that p_i connects s_i and t_i, $1 \leq i \leq m$.

Okamura/Seymour give a constructive proof of their theorem; their proof leads to the following algorithm which can be made to run in time $O(n^2)$ as shown by Becker/Mehlhorn.

Let $\hat{G}$ be an embedding of G with $s_1, ..., s_m, t_1, ..., t_m$ on the boundary of the infinite face. We may assume w.l.o.g. that $\hat{G}$ is 2-connected. Then the boundary of the infinite face consists of a circuit C which we regard as a subgraph of G. We say that a cut X is *critical* if X is connected, *saturated*, i.e. $cap(X) = dens(X)$, and $CAP(X)$ contains exactly two edges of C. Thus if X is critical then $C|(V(C) \cap X)$ and $C|(V(C) - X)$ are both paths.

We can now describe the algorithm:

let $e = (v, w$ be an arbitrary edge on the boundary C of the infinite face of C;
if there is a critical cut X with $v \in X$, $w \notin X$
then let X be such a critical cut with
let X be such a critical cut with $|(C) \cap X|$ minimal:
let $(s, t) \in N$ be a net with $s \in X$, $t \notin X$ such that the subpath of C from w to t not using v has minimal length; (cf. Figure 5)
remove edge e from G;
replace net (s, t) by the pair (s, v) and (w, t) of nets;
construct a solution for the reduced graph using the algorithm recursively and obtain the path for net (s, t) by connecting the paths for nets (s, v) and (w, t) by edge e.
else remove edge e from G and add net (v, w) to the set of nets;
construct a solution for the reduced graph and throw away the path for net (v, w)
fi

The correctness of this algorithm can be reduced from the paper of Okamura/Seymour; a proof can be found in Becker/Mehlhorn.

We close this section with a collection of observations. For a vertex $v \in V$ let $deg(v)$ be the degree of v and let $ter(v)$ be the number of nets in N which have v as a terminal. We call a routing problem (given as a planar graph and a set of nets) *standard* if the extended degree $deg(v) + ter(v)$ is even for all $v \in V$. We call it *solvable* if it has a solution.

Lemma 1. Let $G = (V, E)$ be a planar graph and let N be a set of nets having their terminals on the boundary of the infinite face

a) The routing problem $G, N)$ is standard iff $cap(X) - dens(X)$ is even for every cut X.

b) A standard routing problem (G, N) is solvable iff no cut X is oversaturated, i.e. there is no cut with $cap(X) < dens(X)$

Proof: a) $cap(X) - dens(X)$ is even for every cut X iff it is even for every singleton set $X = \{x\}$. For a singleton x we have $cap(x) = deg(x)$ and $dens(x) = ter(x)$. Part b) is just a reformulation of the theorem of Okamura/Seymour using part a). ∎

Lemma 1 suggests the importance of standard routing problems.

We will next take a closer look at critical cuts. In our algorithm we process the routing region row by row from top to bottom. Within every row we proceed from left to right, i.e. as edge $e = (v, w)$ we always choose a vertical edge connecting the left upper corner v with its "downward" neighbor w. In other words, e is the leftmost vertical edge in the top row of region R.

Assume now that there is a critical cut X through e, say $v \in X$, $w \notin X$. Let X_0 be a minimal critical cut through e, i.e. X_0 minimizes $|V(C) \cap X_0|$ and among the cuts with the same value of $|V(C) \cap X_0|$ is also minimizes $|X_0|$. Then

1) $R|X_0$ is connected

2) $R|X_0$ is a generalized switchbox

3) every node $x \in X_0$ has degree ≥ 2 except maybe the two endpoints of the path $V(C) \cap X_0$.

We view the "cut" X_0 as a polygonal line S intersecting exactly the edges in $CAP(X_0)$, where S consists of straight line segments $S_1, \ldots, S_k$ where S_1 intersects the edge (v, w) (cf. Figure 6).

By a lengthy but tricky proof we can show the following lemma:

Lemma 2. If X_0 is a minimal critical cut then the line S consists of at most two segments.

This lemma is very crucial for the efficiency of our algorithm. It completely characterizes the form of the minimal critical cuts X_0 through edge (v, w). In figure 7 we indicated all possible forms of a minimal critical cut through edge e. There is one further observation to make. If there is a saturated cut where the second segment bends upwards then cut X_{L+2} in figure 7 is also saturated (move the vertical segment to the left and observe that the cut remains saturated).

3. Implementation and runtime

In this section we describe an implementation of Okamura/Seymour's algorithm for generalized switchboxes. There are two main tasks which we have to solve (efficiently):

(1) find the minimal critical cut X_0 through edge (v, w), if there is any

(2) choose the appropriate net to route across cut X_0.

We use two data structures to solve these tasks efficiently. The first data structure is a range tree for the set of nets and is global to the algorithm. The second data structure is a priority queue for the free capacities of the cuts through edge (v, w) and is local to each row of the routing region. We assume that the vertices on the boundary $C(R)$ of the routing region are numbered in clock-wise order by the integers in range $[1..M]$. As the algorithm proceeds vertices in $C(R)$ are deleted (always a left upper corner) and new nodes become boundary nodes. The new boundary vertices inherit the number from deleted vertices as shown in Figure 8. In this way the numbering of the boundary vertices remains in increasing clockwise order. However, adjacent boundary vertices are not necessarily numbered by consecutive integers. From now on we identify nodes in $C(R)$ with their number.

A net is represented as a pair of integers, namely by the pair of numbers associated with its terminals. The set $N = (s_i, t_i); s_i \leq t_i, 1 \leq i \leq m$ of nets is stored in a range tree. Range trees were introduced by Lueker and Willard; see also Mehlhorn, section VII.2.2..

In our case the range tree requires space $0(nlogn)$ and supports the following operations in time $0(log^2 n)$:

1) Insert a net into N or delete a net from N

2) Given a,b,c,d find nets $(s, t) \in N$ and $(s', t') \in N$ with $a \leq s$, $s' \leq b$, $c \leq t$, $t' \leq d$ and t maximal or s' maximal respectively.

3) Given $a < b$ find the number of nets $(s, t) \in N$ with either $a \leq s \leq b < t$ or $s < a \leq t \leq b$.

Note that in every step in the algorithm we have to update the data structures.

We will next describe the local data structure for each row. Let L be the length of the top-row. We consider cuts consisting of one horizontal segment and one vertical segment or of only a horizontal segment. Let X_i be the cut where the horizontal segment intersects exactly i edges of the routing region. (cf.Figure 7). Let X_{L+2} be the cut which parts the left upper corner from the rest. For every i let

$$fcap(X_i) = cap(X_i) - dens(X_i)$$

be the free capacity of cut X_i. We have to execute the following operations on $fcap(X), 1 \leq i \leq L$:

(4) compute $fcap(X_i), 1 \leq i \leq L$ in order to initialize the local data structure.

(5) find the maximal i with $fcap(X_i) = 0$ in order to find the minimal critical cut X_0 through edge (v,w).

(6) decrease $fcap(X_i)$ by two for $a \leq i \leq b$ in order to update the local data structure.

We show first how to do the fourth task in time $0(L(logn)^2)$. Consider cut X_i. We know that $X_i \cap V(C)$ is a path and hence the numbers of vertices in $X_i \cap V(C)$ form an interval $[h, j]$ with $h \leq j$ or two intervals $[h, M]$, $[i, j]$ with $h > j$. Note that h is the number of vertex v. The integer j is easily found by computing in a preprocessing step for every vertex u of R the highest vertex below u which lies on $C(R)$. The capacity of cut X_i is now readily computed in time $0(1)$ by adding the lengths of its constituting segments. The density of cut X_i is computed in time $0((logn)^2)$ using the third property of range trees derived above.

It remains to show how to solve the other two tasks. We use priority queues with updates as described in Galil/Naamad; see also Mehlhorn, section IV.9.1.. They allow us to perform these tasks in time $0(logn)$ each.

We are now ready to describe how operations 1 to 6 are used to implement the routing algorithm. Suppose that we start to process a new row. Using (4) we will set up the local data structure for the row in time $0(L(logn)^2)$ where L is the length of the row. Next we process the row from left to right. Let $e = (v, w)$ the leftmost vertical edge. We use (5) to find the minimal critical cut in time $0((logn)^2)$. Assume that there is a minimal critical cut, say X_i. We know that $X_i \cap V(C)$ is a path and hence the numbers of the vertices in $V_i \cap V(C)$ form one or two intervals. Next we have to find the net (s, t) to be routed across edge e. We want $|\{s, t\} \cap X_i| = 1$ and the terminal outside X_i to be as close to w as possible. The task of finding such a net is easily formulated as a few operations of type (2). Thus in time $0((logn)^2)$ we can find the net to be routed across edge e. Next we have to delete one net and add to new nets to the global data structures. This is task (1). Finally, the local data structure needs updating (Figure 9 shows a typical situation). This is easily formulated as a few operations of type (6).

In summary we conclude that removal of a single edge takes time $0((logn)^2)$ and that building the local data structure for a row of length L takes time $0(L(logn)^2)$. Thus total running time is $0(n(logn)^2)$.

We want to make one final remark concerning the case that the routing region R splits into two disjoint parts. We then apply the algorithm separately to both parts. It is important to observe that we can use the *same global* data structure for both parts and that we can continue to process the current row, using the current local data structure. We summarize in

Theorem 1. Let (R, N) be a standard generalized switchbox routing problem with a routing region of n vertices. Then a solution (if there is one) can be constructed in time $0(n(logn)^2)$

4. Non-Standard Routing Problems

In this section we briefly discuss non-standard GSRPs. Figure 10 shows that lemma I,b is not true for non-standard problems. Nevertheless, there is a close convertion between standard and non-standard GSRPs as shown in Becker/Mehlhorn. Let (R, N) be a GSRP and let $U = \{v; v \text{ has odd extended degree }\}$. Then, if (R, N) is solvable then there is a solvable standard GSRP $(R, N \cup P)$ where P is a pairing of U. Becker/Mehlhorn show how to find P in time $0(bn)$ where b is the circumference of the routing region. We refine their techniques and show how to find the pairing in time $0(n(\log n)^2 + |U|^2)$.

Theorem 2. Non-standard routing problems with n vertices and U vertices of odd extended degree can be solved in time $0(nlog^2 n + |U|^2)$

4. Conclusions and Extensions

In this paper we have shown that a fairly general routing problem can be solved efficiently. The solution is based on the theory of multi-commodity flows in planar networks and two advanced data structures, namely range trees and priority queues with updates.
We have recently extended the results of this paper.

Theorem 3. (Kaufmann/Mehlhorn): Let R be an arbitrary subgraph of the planar grid with n vertices and let $N = (s_i, t_i), 1 \leq i \leq k$ be a set of nets. Each terminal is required to lie on the boundary of a non-trivial face (finite or infinite). We also assume that a global routing $[p_i]$ is given for each net. Then a routing consistent with this global routing can be found in time $0(n(logn)^2)$

Theorem 3 considerably strengthens the result of this paper; Figure 11 shows an example. In view of the introduction we may say that theorem 3 solves steps 2) to 4) efficiently, at least in the case of two-terminal nets.

5 References

[1] M. Becker/K. Mehlhorn: "Routing and Edge-disjoint paths in planar graphs" *Technical report*, FB 10, Universität des Saarlandes, Aug. 1984

[2] M. Brady/D. Brown: "VLSI Routing: Four Layers Suffice" *MIT VLSI conference*, 1984

[3] A. Frank: "Disjoint Paths in Rectilinear Grids" *Combinatorica* 2, 4 (1982), 361–371

[4] M. Kaufmann/K. Mehlhorn: "Local Routing of two-terminal Nets is easy" *Technical report*, FB 10, Universität des Saarlandes, Okt. 1984

[5] M.R. Kramer/J. van Leeuwen": "Wire Routing is NP-complete" *Technical Report* RUU-CS-82-4, 1982, Utrecht

[6] K. Mehlhorn/F. Preparata: "Routing Through a Rectangle" *Technical Report*, 1983

[7] H. Okamura/ P.D. Seymour: "Multicommodity flows in planar graphs" *Journal of Combinatorial Theory*, Series B, 1981, 75–81

[8] F. Preparata/W. Lipski: "Three Layers are Enough" *23rd FOCS* 1982, 350–357

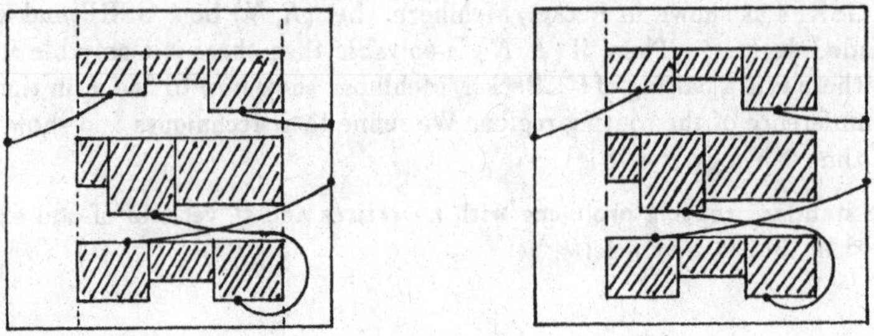

(a) (b)

Figure 1: A typical routing problem in standard cell design. The subcircuits are shown hatched, the global wiring of the nets is indicated by lines, and the subdivision of the routing regions into "simple" regions is indicated by dashed lines. Note that the subregions in (a) are channels with "rugged" borders and the single subregion in part (b) is a generalized switchbox

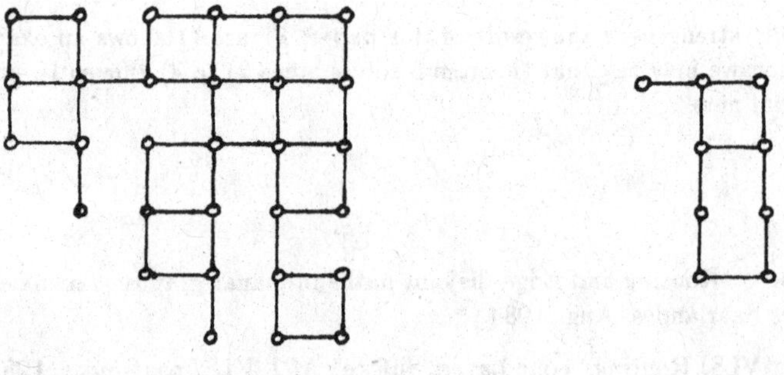

A generalized switchbox Not a generalized switchbox

Figure 2

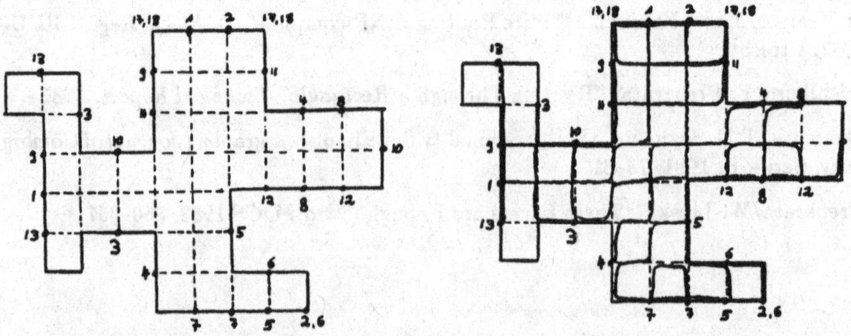

Figure 3: A GSRP and its solution

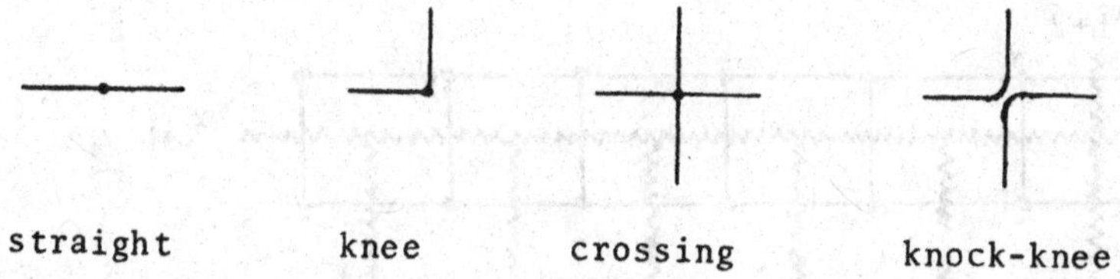

Figure 4

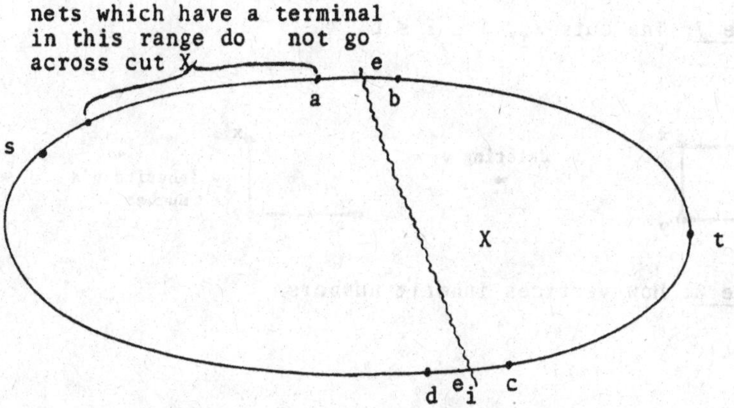

Figure 5: Choice of (s,t)

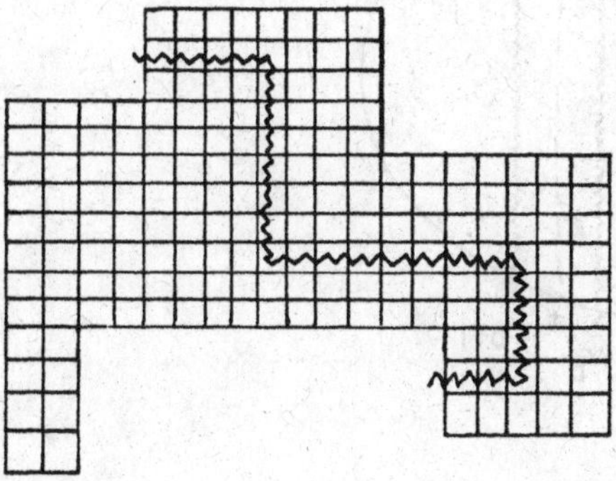

Figure 6: A cut consisting of segments $S_1, \ldots, S_k$.

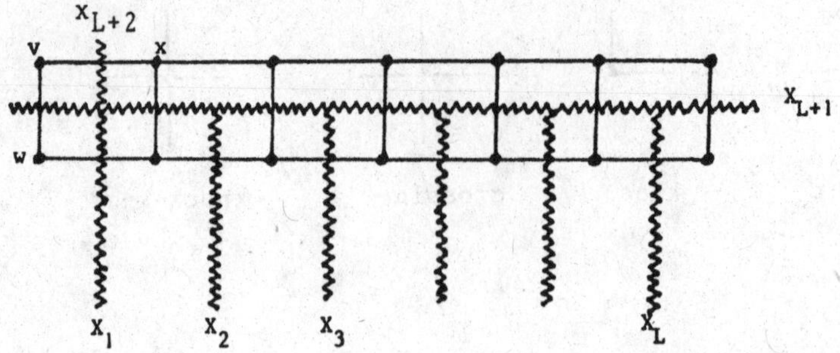

Figure 7: The cuts X_i, $1 \le i \le L$

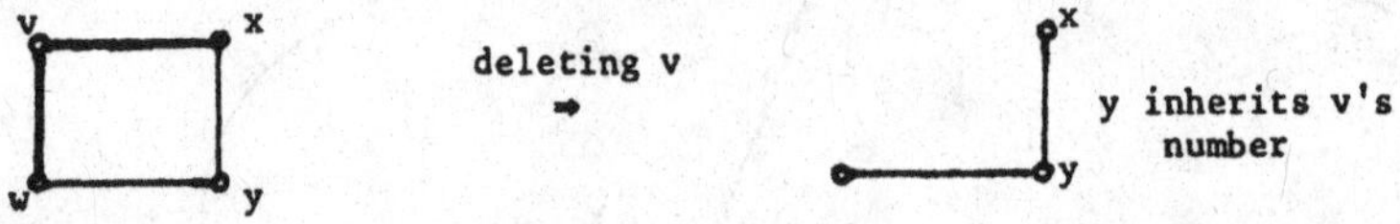

Figure 8: How vertices inherit numbers

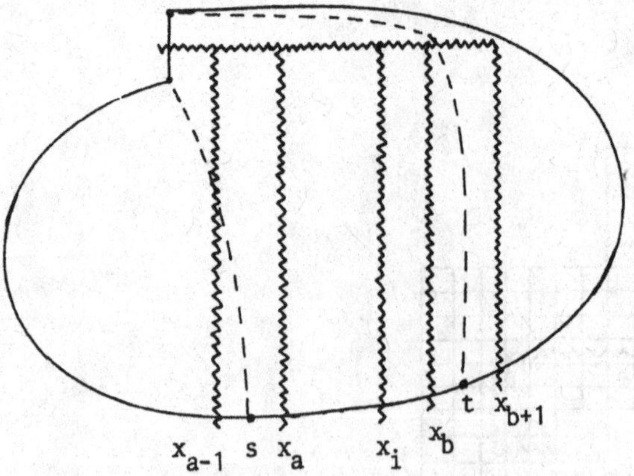

Figure 9: Updating the local data structure. In this example the free capacity $fcap(X_i)$ changes by -2 for $i \le a-1$, by 0 for $a \le i \le b$, and by -2 for $i \ge b+1$

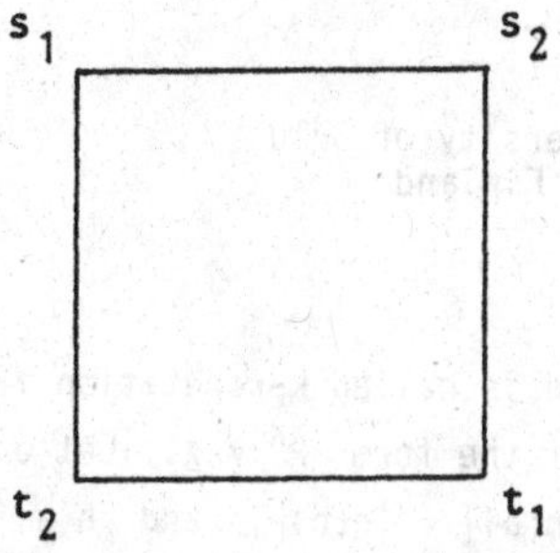

Figure 10: A non-standard problem which has no solution. However fcap(X) ≥ 0 for a cut X.

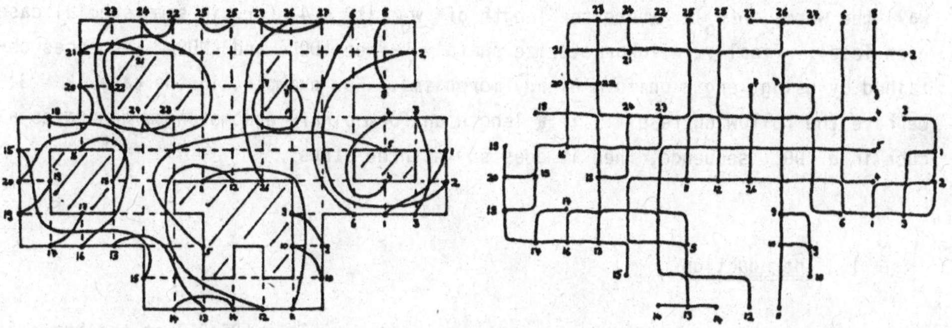

Figure 11: Illustration for theorem 3

ON k-REPETITION FREE WORDS GENERATED BY LENGTH UNIFORM MORPHISMS OVER A BINARY ALPHABET

Veikko Keränen

Department of Mathematics, University of Oulu
Linnanmaa, SF-90570 Oulu, Finland

Abstract. Let an integer $k \geq 3$ be fixed. A word is called k-repetition free, or shortly k-free, if it does not contain a subword of the form $P^k \neq \lambda$. Let a morphism $h: \{a,b\}^* \to Y^*$ be length uniform (meaning that $|h(a)| = |h(b)|$) and $h(a) \neq h(b)$. Assume that P^n, $k \leq n \in \mathbb{N}$, is a subword of $h(w)$, where w in $\{a,b\}^*$ is k-free In this case we give an optimal upper bound for the length of P^n. Moreover, we give outlines for the proof of the following result: when deciding whether a given morphism h, of the form mentioned above, is k-free, one has only to examine (in an easy way) the words $h(w_o)$, where the length of w_o is ≤ 4 (or, in some special cases, even less). Finally, we characterize sharply k-free DOL and NDOL sequences obtained by using length uniform binary morphisms. For example, in the case $k = 3$ we have the following result: if a length uniform binary endomorphism generates a cube in a DOL sequence, then it does so in three steps.

1. Introduction

The investigation of k-free words was started by Thue [35,36] at the beginning of this century. One of his results in [35] was that there exist infinitely long cube-free (i.e. 3-free) words over a binary alphabet. Moreover, he showed that in th case of three letters one can construct infinitely long square-free words, i.e. words containing no repetitions at all. Later on many of Thue's results have been rediscovered, e.g. Morse in [26].

Recently there have been many studies of this subject, e.g. [1-25,27-29,31-34] from which [1,5,9,10,20,22] contain the most interesting results in connection with our work. Basic results are found in [24,31], and for a review we refer to [4].

Most examples of infinitely long k-free words constructed in the literature are obtained by iterating a morphism. This means that the theory of repetitions is close related to the theory of L systems, see e.g. [30]. Very often one desires the resulting word to be an ω-word, i.e. an infinite sequence of letters from left to right Such ω-words are mostly obtained by so-called prefix-preserving morphisms, i.e. by morphisms satisfying $h(a) = aw$ for some letter a and non-empty word w. Nevertheless, our results concerning DOL and NDOL systems hold true even if the morphisms in them were not prefix-preserving.

In [5,9] (cf. also [1,25,36]) it is proved that a length uniform morphism h over any alphabet X, with $card(X) \geq 3$, is square-free if and only if $h(w_0)$ is square-free for every square-free w_0 in X^* of length ≤ 3. In our case, Theorem 6 below characterizes all k-free (for a fixed $k \geq 3$) length uniform morphisms $h: \{a,b\}^* \to Y^*$ very sharply: h is k-free if and only if $h(a)$, $h(b)$, $h(ab)$ are primitive and $h(w_0)$ is k-free whenever w_0 in $\{a,b\}^*$ of length ≤ 4 is so. (A word is called primitive, if it is only a trivial power of another word.) Moreover, if h is k-free, then it is n-free for every integer $n \geq k \geq 3$. It is interesting to compare this property to that in Leconte [22], where it is proved that any morphism h is power-free if and only if h is a square-free morphism and $h(aa)$ is cube-free for each letter a. (A morphism is called power-free, if it is n-free for every $n \geq 2$. Note that in the case of k-freeness, k is fixed.)

The length uniformity condition seems to be quite restrictive, at least when one compares the above-mentioned results to the general results of the same kind in [1,2, 9,13,36]. However, Crochemore proves in [9] that any morphism h over a three letter alphabet X is square-free if and only if $h(w_0)$ is square-free whenever w_0 in X^* of length ≤ 5 is so. Concerning the k-freeness of morphisms in the general case Bean et al. [1] have shown that it suffices to check whether $h(w_0)$ is k-free for all k-free words w_0 of length $\leq k+1$ and whether a certain subword property holds. However, their result only gives sufficient conditions for a morphism to be k-free, whereas in our case Theorem 6 provides also necessary conditions. Furthermore, it is worth mentioning that even if h were not length uniform, the words $h(a)$, $h(b)$ and $h(ab)$ (among other words) have to be primitive, if one desires h to be k-free for some k. Consequently, in the light of Lemma 1 and Corollary 2 (to mention the most important auxiliary results) we conjecture that it is possible to characterize quite as sharply as in Theorem 6 all k-free morphisms over a binary alphabet. However, for the present we do not have an affirmative proof for this conjecture.

2. Preliminaries

For the very basic notations and definitions (concerning e.g. L systems) the reader is referred to [30]. However, for convenience we specify the following concepts.

The set with no elements in it, called the empty set, is denoted by $\emptyset$. For a finite set A, $card(A)$ denotes the number of elements in A. Let $\mathbb{N}$ be the set of non-negative integers and $\mathbb{N}_+ = \mathbb{N} - \{0\}$. For a real number r we denote by $\lfloor r \rfloor$ the largest integer no greater than r, and by $\lceil r \rceil$ the smallest integer no less than r. Thus, for an integer $r = \lfloor r \rfloor = \lceil r \rceil$. By Y we mean an alphabet with $card(Y) \geq 2$. The length of a word w is denoted by $|w|$.

A word u is called a subword [an inner subword] of w, if $w = u_1 u u_2$ for some words [non-empty words] u_1 and u_2. The notation $SW(w)$ $[ISW(w)]$ denotes the set of all subwords [inner subwords] of w. Moreover, we write $XSW(w_1,\ldots,w_n)$

$= XSW(w_1) \cup \cdots \cup XSW(w_n)$ for words w_i and $X = \lambda$ or I. A word w is primitive, if $w = w_o^n$, $n \in \mathbb{N}$, implies $n = 1$ (w is only a trivial power of another word w_o).

Let k be in $\mathbb{N}_+$. We say that a word is k-free, if it does not contain a subword of the form $P^k \neq \lambda$. A word sequence or a language is k-free, if all words in it are k-free, otherwise we say that there is a k-repetition in it. A morphism $h: X^* \to Y^*$ is k-free, if $h(w)$ is k-free for every k-free w in X^*.

A morphism $h: X^* \to Y^*$ is called length uniform, if $|h(a)| = |h(b)|$ for every a and b in X. If, in addition, $|h(a)| = t \geq 2$ for every a in X and a fixed integer t, then, according to Brandenburg [5], h is termed uniformly growing.

3. Auxiliary results

The complete proofs of our results, found in [21], are quite long containing many auxiliary results. From these auxiliary results we present the most interesting two.

Lemma 1. Let u, v and w be non-empty words of equal length such that $u \neq v$ Then

$$w^2 \notin SW(uvu) \quad \text{and} \quad uv \notin ISW(u^2v, vu^2, v^2u, uv^2, w^3).$$

Furthermore, if $uv \in ISW(uvu, vuv)$, then $uv = w_o^r$ for some non-empty word w_o and odd integer $r \geq 3$.

By Lemma 1 it is easy to prove

Corollary 2. Let u and v be different non-empty words of equal length and $A = \{u^2v, vu^2, v^2u, uv^2\}$. Then $A \cap ISW(\alpha\beta\gamma\delta) = \emptyset$ whenever α, β, γ and δ are in $\{u,v\}$.

4. Morphisms

Let $h: \{a,b\}^* \to Y^*$ be a length uniform morphism such that $h(a) = u$ and $h(b) = v$, where $u \neq v$. For the repetitions occurring in the image words of h Corollary 2 means the following: if a word w in $\{a,b\}^*$ is k-free for some fixed k, then $h(w)$ can contain only relatively short subwords of the form P^n, $k \leq n \in \mathbb{N}$, such that $|P| \not\equiv 0 (\text{mod} |u|)$. (Note that $P^n = P^{n-1}P = PP^{n-1}$ and every long P^{n-1} would contain, as a subword, a word in A.) On the other hand, we easily see that $h(w)$ has no subwords of the form P^n, $k \leq n \in \mathbb{N}$, such that $0 < |P| \equiv 0(\text{mod}|u|)$. Consequently, only "short" repetitions of the form P^n, $n \geq k$, can occur in $h(w)$. The optimal upper bound for the length of P^n is provided by the following

Theorem 3. Let an integer $k \geq 3$ be fixed. Let $h: \{a,b\}^* \to Y^*$ be a length uniform morphism such that $h(a) \neq h(b)$, and let a word w in $\{a,b\}^*$ be k-free. If $h(w)$ has a subword of the form P^n, where $k \leq n \in \mathbb{N}$, then $|P^n| < (2k-1)|h(a)|$. If, in addition, neither $a(ba)^{k-1}$ nor $b(ab)^{k-1}$ is a subword of w, then $|P^n| \leq 2(k-1)|h(a)|$.

As an example of the optimality of the upper bound for $|P^n|$, consider the case $n = k = 3$, $h(a) = cdc$ and $h(b) = dcd$. Choosing $P^3 = h(abab) = (cdcd)^3$, we get $|P^3| = 4|h(a)| = 2(k-1)|h(a)|$.

Theorem 3 is interesting in the connection with NDOL sequences. Consider an NDOL system

$$G = (X, Y, g, h, \alpha),$$

where $X = \{a,b\}$, the morphisms $g: X^* \to X^*$, $h: X^* \to Y^*$ are length uniform and $h(a) \neq h(b)$. Assume that the underlying DOL system $G_o = (X,g,\alpha)$ generates a k-free DOL sequence $S(G_o)$ for some $k \geq 3$. Then, Theorem 3 together with Theorem 11 below imply that all subwords of the form P^n, $n \geq k$, occurring in the NDOL sequence $S(G)$, can be found at the beginning of this sequence.

The following Theorem 4 gives us a test set for checking whether a given length uniform morphism h over a binary alphabet is k-free for some given $k \geq 3$. However, this theorem is most interesting in considerations concerning the k-freeness of DOL and NDOL sequences. This is the case, because in Theorem 6 we obtain an even better algorithm (optimal in a certain sense) for testing the k-freeness of h.

Theorem 4. Let $h: \{a,b\}^* \to Y^*$ be a length uniform morphism such that $h(a) \neq h(b)$ [$h(a)$, $h(b)$ and $h(ab)$ are primitive], and let a word w in $\{a,b\}^*$ be k-free for some fixed k. Then $h(w)$ is k-free if and only if $h(w_o)$ is k-free for every subword w_o of w such that

$$|w_o| \leq 4 \qquad \text{for} \quad 3 \leq k \leq 6 \quad [k \geq 3];$$

and

$$|w_o| \leq \tfrac{2}{3}(k+1) \qquad \text{for} \quad k \geq 7.$$

Furthermore, in the general case these upper bounds for $|w_o|$ are as sharp as possible.

The next lemma still improves the result of Theorem 4.

Lemma 5. Let $h: \{a,b\}^* \to Y^*$ be a length uniform morphism such that $h(a) \neq h(b)$, and let x, y, z be letters in $\{a,b\}$ and the word $xyyz$ k-free. Moreover, assume that $h(y)$ is primitive and, in addition, if $k = 3$, cube-free. Then $\alpha P^k \beta \neq h(xyyz)$ whenever $|\alpha|$, $|\beta| < |h(a)|$.

Using Theorem 4 and Lemma 5 it is now straightforward to prove

Theorem 6. Let an integer $k \geq 3$ be fixed. A length uniform λ-free morphism $h: \{a,b\}^* \to Y^*$ is k-free if and only if

(i) $h(a)$, $h(b)$ and $h(ab)$ are primitive;
(ii) $h(w_0)$ is k-free for every w_0 in $\{a,b\}^*$ of length ≤ 3 (differing from a^3 and b^3 if $k = 3$); and
(iii) $h(w_0)$ is k-free for every w_0 in $\{xxyx, xxyy, xyxx, xyxy \mid x,y \in \{a,b\}, x \neq y\}$.

Consequently, if h is k-free, then it is n-free for every integer $n \geq k$.

By Theorem 6 it is easy to decide, for any $k \geq 3$, whether a given morphism h of the considered form, is k-free. Since the words w_0, to be tested, are always of length ≤ 4, the amount of work, needed to solve the problem, does not grow as k gets greater. In fact we get

Corollary 7. Let $h: \{a,b\}^* \to Y^*$ be a length uniform morphism such that $|h(a)| = |h(b)| \geq 2$ and $h(a)$, $h(b)$, $h(ab)$ are primitive. Then h is $(2|h(a)| - 1)$ - free.

As an example, let $h(a) = aab$ and $h(b) = baa$. Then, by Corollary 7, h is 5-free.

5. Endomorphisms

Concerning short words $h(a)$ and $h(b)$ one can still improve the upper bounds for the length of w_0 in Theorem 6. In the case of an endomorphism $(Y = \{a,b\})$ we have obtained the following results using UNIVAC 1100/22 computer and, in spite of and efficient program, hours of CPU time. In the case $k = 3$ we found out that in alphabetical order (taking short words before longer ones) with respect to $g(ab)$

$$g(a) = abbaababaababba, \qquad g(b) = baababbaababaab \tag{1}$$

is the first binary length uniform endomorphism g such that $g(w_0)$ is cube-free for every cube-free w_0 of length ≤ 3, but $g(w_0)$ contains a cube for a cube-free w_0 of length 4. Here $g(abaa)$ contains the cube $(babaababbaa)^3$ (but $g(w_0)$ is cube-free for other cube-free $w_0 \neq abaa$ of length 4). In fact this morphism g is an example showing that in the general case the upper bound 4 for $|w_0|$ in Theorems 4 and 6 is optimal. Since $g(a)$ in (1) is of length 15 we have

Theorem 8. In the case $1 \leq |g(a)| = |g(b)| \leq 14$ a length uniform endomorphis g over the alphabet $\{a,b\}$ is cube-free if and only if (i) $g(a) \neq g(b)$; (ii) g(a and $g(b)$ are primitive; and (iii) $g(w_0)$ is cube-free for every cube-free w_0

in $\{a,b\}^*$ of length ≤ 3.

Also, for $k = 3, 4$ and 5, the following endomorphisms

$k = 3$: $g(a) = abaabba$, $g(b) = baabaab$;
$k = 4$: $g(a) = aabba$, $g(b) = babab$;
$k = 5$: $g(a) = aaabbba$, $g(b) = bababab$

are the first such that g fulfils the primitiveness condition (i) in Theorem 6 and $g(w_o)$ is k-free for every w_o over $\{a,b\}$ of length 1 and 2, but $g(w_o)$ contains a k-repetition for a w_o of length 3 or 4 (consider the word $g(aba)$). These results mean that

Theorem 9. In the case $k = 3$ $[k = 4, k = 5]$ and $1 \leq |g(a)| = |g(b)| \leq 6$ $[\leq 4, \leq 6]$ a length uniform endomorphism g over the alphabet $\{a,b\}$ is k-free if and only if (i) $g(a)$, $g(b)$ and $g(ab)$ are primitive; and (ii) $g(aa)$, $g(bb)$, $g(ab)$ and $g(ba)$ are k-free.

Using our results one can now enumerate k-free endomorphisms for any $k \geq 3$. As an example we consider the lengths $|g(a)| = |g(b)| = 1,\ldots,6$, the repetitions $k = 3, 4, 5$ and give for each $|g(a)|$ and k the first endomorphism g (in alphabetical order with respect to $g(ab)$) such that g is n-free for all integers $n \geq k$ but not $(k-1)$-free. By Theorems 9 and 6 this is easy to do also without any computer program.

		g_1	g_2	g_3	g_4	g_5	g_6
$k = 3$:	a	a	ab	aab	abba	abaab	aababb
	b	b	ba	abb	baab	babba	aabbab
$k = 4$:	a			aab	aaab	aaabb	aaabab
	b			aba	aabb	aabab	aaabbb
$k = 5$:	a			aab	aaab	aaaab	aaaabb
	b			baa	aaba	aaabb	aaabab

6. DOL and NDOL sequences

We consider the decidability of k-freeness of DOL and NDOL sequences generated by length uniform morphisms over the alphabet $\{a,b\}$. It is possible to generate a k-free DOL sequence even if the iterated endomorphism g itself is not k-free. For example, if

$$g(a) = ab, \quad g(b) = aa, \tag{2}$$

then $G = (\{a,b\}, g, a)$ generates a 4-free DOL sequence, as is straightforward to see using Theorem 4. However, here $g(b^{k-1}) = a^{2(k-1)} = a^k a^{k-2}$ showing that g is not k-free for any $k \geq 3$. So, in deciding whether a given DOL or NDOL sequence is k-free for a given k we may have to search (cf. Theorem 4) whether certain words producing k-repetitions are subwords of that sequence. For this purpose we present two results. However, before that consider the DOL system $G = (\{a,b\}, g, a)$, where

$$g(a) = babab, \qquad g(b) = aabaa. \tag{3}$$

Now the sequence S(G) begins as follows:

$$a,\ babab,\ aabaa\,g(abab),\ bababbabab\,g(baa)\,g^2(abab),\ \ldots\ .$$

Hence bb occurs for the first time in $g^3(a)$. Furthermore, a^3 and a^4 occur (as the subwords of g(bb)) for the first time in $g^4(a)$. This means that the following lemma is optimal.

Lemma 10. Let g be a length uniform endomorphism and assume that a word w of length 2 [≤ 4] is a subword of a DOL sequence S(G) generated by $G = (\{a,b\}, g, \alpha)$. Then w is a subword of some $g^i(\alpha)$ with $i \leq 3$ [≤ 4].

The following theorem tells us that for a given DOL sequence S(G) (of the considered form) and a word w one is able to decide whether w occurs as a subword in S(G).

Theorem 11. Let $G = (\{a,b\}, g, \alpha)$ be a DOL system such that $|g(a)| = |g(b)| = q \geq 2$. If w is any non-empty subword of S(G), then it is a subword of some $g^i(\alpha)$ with $i \leq \lceil \log_q |w| \rceil + 3$.

Using Theorem 4, Lemma 10 and Theorem 11 we now obtain

Theorem 12. Let g be a uniformly growing endomorphism over $X = \{a,b\}$, k a fixed integer such that $3 \leq k \leq 6$ [$k \geq 7$] and $B(k,q) = \lceil \log_q(2(k+1)/3) \rceil + 4$ ($q = |g(a)|$). Then

(i) the DOL sequence S(G) generated by $G = (X, g, \alpha)$ is k-free if and only if $g^i(\alpha)$ is so for every $i \leq 5$ [$i \leq B(k,q)$].

(ii) If S(G) is k-free and $h: X^* \to Y^*$, with $card(Y) \geq 2$, is a length uniform morphism for which $h(a) \neq h(b)$, then the NDOL sequence $S(G_1)$ generated by $G_1 = (X, Y, g, h, \alpha)$ is k-free if and only if $h(g^i(\alpha))$ is so for every $i \leq 4$ [$i \leq B(k,q)-1$].

Considering the NDOL sequence $S(G_1)$ and the case $3 \leq k \leq 6$ in Theorem 12 we see that the upper bound 4 is optimal for the steps to be checked at the beginning of $S(G_1)$. This follows by choosing $\alpha = b$, $g(a) = ab$, $g(b) = ba$ and h as the morphism g in (1). Now g is cube-free (see e.g. Corollary 7) and the word abaa occurs for the first time in $g^4(b)$ in the DOL sequence S(G). Hence a cube occurs for the first time in $h(g^4(b))$ in the NDOL sequence $S(G_1)$.

Next we turn to deal with those length uniform morphisms for which the image words of a, b and ab are primitive. In this case we can improve the results of Theorem 12 to the optimum. Furthermore, this case turns out to be very interesting as regards the cube-freeness of DOL and NDOL sequences.

In (3) we considered the endomorphism $g(a) = babab$, $g(b) = aabaa$, for which $g^4(a)$ contains the 4-repetition a^4, but the set $\{g^i(a) \mid i \leq 3\}$ is 4-free (as is easy to see using Theorem 4 and Lemma 5). This indicates that the following theorem is optimal.

Theorem 13. Let g be a length uniform endomorphism over {a,b} such that g(a), g(b) and g(ab) are primitive. Then the DOL sequence S(G) generated by $G = (\{a,b\}, g, \alpha)$ is k-free for some $k \geq 3$ if and only if the set $\{g^i(\alpha) \mid i \leq 4\}$ is k-free.

Although Theorem 13 is optimal in the general case, we shall see below that for the case $k = 3$ its result can be made still one step better.

In [20] Karhumäki shows that any cube-free word over {a,b} of length at least 24 contains as subwords all cube-free words over {a,b} of length 3, i.e. the words aab, baa, abb, bba, aba and bab. Hence a uniformly growing endomorphism g never generates a cube-free DOL sequence unless all the words g(a), g(b), g(ab) and g(ba) are primitive. In the case $k \geq 4$ the situation is very different as indicated by g in (2). This special property makes the cube-freeness problem for DOL sequences (generated by binary length uniform endomorphisms) very easy to solve, at least for short words g(a) and g(b). In fact, using the above-mentioned result in [20] and Theorem 8 we get

Theorem 14. A DOL sequence S(G) generated by $G = (\{a,b\}, g, \alpha)$, where $2 \leq |g(a)| = |g(b)| \leq 14$ and the axiom α is cube-free, is cube-free if and only if the endomorphism g is cube-free.

It should be noted that in the case $|g(a)| = |g(b)| \leq 14$ it is very easy to decide whether the endomorphism g is cube-free. By Theorem 8 one needs only to check the cube-freeness of those $h(w_o)$, for which w_o is cube-free and of length ≤ 3.

Moreover, it is possible that instead of the upper bound 14 for $|g(a)|$ in Theorem 14 we may have even 32, but not more, since the endomorphism g, defined by

$g(a) = aabaabbaabbabbaabaababbabbaabaabb$, $g(b) = aabbabbaabaababbabbaabaabbaabbabb$

is such that $g(w_o)$ is cube-free for every cube-free $w_o \neq baba$ over {a,b} of length ≤ 4, but g(baba) contains the cube $(abbabbaabaabbaabbabbaabaab)^3$. Furthermore, baba is not in $SW\{ g(w_o) \mid w_o \in \{aa,ab,ba,bb\} \}$, and so S(G) is cube-free for every DOL system $G = (\{a,b\}, g, \alpha)$, where α is cube-free and baba $\notin SW(\alpha)$ (see Theorem 4). What the optimal upper bound is for $|g(a)|$ in Theorem 14 remains open for the present.

In [20] it is shown that any binary endomorphism (not necessarily length uniform) generates a cube in a DOL sequence if and only if it does so in less than 11 steps. In our case we obtain as an optimal result the following

Theorem 15. A DOL sequence $S(G)$ generated by $G = (\{a,b\}, g, \alpha)$, where the endomorphism g is length uniform, is cube-free if and only if the set $\{g^i(\alpha) \mid i \leq 3\}$ is cube-free.

Finally, concerning NDOL sequences we can prove for example

Theorem 16. Let g and h be length uniform morphisms over $\{a,b\}$ such that the image words of a, b and ab are primitive for both g and h [for g and $h(a) \neq h(b)$]. Then the NDOL sequence $S(G)$ generated by $G = (\{a,b\}, Y, g, h, \alpha)$, with $card(Y) \geq 2$, is k-free for some fixed $k \geq 3$ if and only if the set $\{h(g^i(\alpha)) \mid i \leq 4 \ [i \leq 5]\}$ is k-free.

Acknowledgements

I want to thank Professor Paavo Turakainen for encouragement and much valuable advice. Also, thanks are due to Jussi Mattila, who made the first computer programs for enumerating and testing morphisms.

References

[1] D.R. Bean, A. Ehrenfeucht and G.F. McNulty, Avoidable patterns in strings of symbols, Pacific J. Math. 85 (1979) 261-294.

[2] J. Berstel, Sur les mots sans carré définis par une morphisme, Springer Lecture Notes in Computer Science 71 (1979) 16-25.

[3] J. Berstel, Mots sans carré et morphismes iteres, Discrete Math. 29 (1979) 235-24

[4] J. Berstel, Some recent results on squarefree words, Proc. STACS 84, Springer Lecture Notes in Computer Science (1984) 14-25.

[5] F.J. Brandenburg, Uniformly growing k-th power-free homomorphisms, Theoret. Comput. Sci. 23 (1983) 69-82.

[6] A. Carpi, On the size of a square-free morphism on a three letter alphabet, Inf Proc. Letters 16 (1983) 231-236.

[7] A. Carpi, On the centers of the set of weakly square-free words on a two letter alphabet, Inf. Proc. Letters 19 (1984) 187-190.

[8] A. Cerny, On generalized words of Thue-Morse, Techn. Report, Univ. Paris VII, L.I.T.P. 83-44 (1983).

[9] M. Crochemore, Sharp characterizations of squarefree morphisms, Theoret. Comput Sci. 18 (1982) 221-226.

[10] M. Crochemore, Regularites evitables (Ph.D. Thesis, Univ. Rouen), Univ. Paris V L.I.T.P. 83-43 (1983).

[11] F. Dejean, Sur un théorème de Thue, J. Combin. Theory, Ser. A, 13 (1972) 90-99.

[12] F. Dekking, On repetitions of blocks in binary sequences, J. Combin. Theory, Ser. A, 20 (1976) 292-299.

[13] A. Ehrenfeucht and G. Rozenberg, Repetitions in homomorphisms and languages, Springer Lecture Notes in Computer Science 140 (1982) 192-196.

[14] A. Ehrenfeucht and G. Rozenberg, Repetitions of subwords in DOL languages, Info and Control 59 (1983) 13-35.

[15] A. Ehrenfeucht and G. Rozenberg, On regularity of languages generated by copying systems, Discrete Appl. Math. 8 (1984) 313-317.
[16] E.D. Fife, Binary sequences which contain no BBb, Trans. Amer. Math. Soc. 261 (1980) 115-136.
[17] T. Harju, Morphisms that avoid overlapping, Univ. Turku (1983).
[18] T. Harju and M. Linna, The equations $h(w) = w^n$ in binary alphabets, Theoret. Comput. Sci. 33 (1984) 327-329.
[19] J. Karhumäki, On strongly cube-free ω-words generated by binary morphisms, Springer Lecture Notes in Computer Science 117 (1981) 182-189.
[20] J. Karhumäki, On cube-free ω-words generated by binary morphisms, Discrete Appl. Math. 5 (1983) 279-297.
[21] V. Keränen, On k-repetition free words generated by length uniform morphisms over a binary alphabet, Preprint, Dep. Math., Univ. Oulu (1984).
[22] M. Leconte, A fine characterization of power-free morphisms, To appear in Theoret. Comput. Sci. (1985).
[23] M. Linna, On periodic ω-sequences obtained by iterating morphisms, Ann. Univ. Turkuensis, Ser. A I 186 (1984) 64-71.
[24] M. Lothaire, Combinatorics on Words (Addison-Wesley, Reading, Massachusetts, 1983).
[25] A. de Luca, On the product of square-free words, Discrete Math. 52 (1984) 143-157.
[26] M. Morse, Recurrent geodesics on a surface of negative curvature, Trans. Amer. Math. Soc. 22 (1921) 84-100.
[27] J.-J. Pansiot, The Morse sequence and iterated morphisms, Inf. Proc. Letters 12 (1981) 68-70.
[28] J.-J. Pansiot, A propos d'une conjecture de F. Dejean sur les répétitions dans les mots, Discrete Appl. Math. 7 (1984) 297-311.
[29] P.A. Pleasants, Non-repetitive sequences, Proc. Cambridge Phil. Soc. 68 (1970) 267-274.
[30] G. Rozenberg and A. Salomaa, The Mathematical Theory of L Systems (Academic Press, London, 1980).
[31] A. Salomaa, Jewels of Formal Language Theory (Computer Science Press, Rockville, Maryland, 1981).
[32] P. Séébold, Sequences generated by infinitely iterated morphisms, To appear in Discrete Appl. Math. (1985).
[33] R. Shelton, Aperiodic words on three symbols I, II, J. reine angew. Math. 321 (1981) 195-209, 327 (1981) 1-11.
[34] R. Shelton and R. Soni, Aperiodic words on three symbols III, J. reine angew. Math. 330 (1981) 44-52.
[35] A. Thue, Über unendliche Zeichenreihen, Norske Vid. Selsk. Skr., I. Mat. Nat. Kl., Christiania, 7 (1906) 1-22.
[36] A. Thue, Über die gegenseitige Lage gleicher Teile gewisser Zeichenreihen, Norske Vid. Selsk. Skr., I. Mat. Nat. Kl., Christiania, 1 (1912) 1-67.

EVERY COMMUTATIVE QUASIRATIONAL LANGUAGE IS REGULAR

Juha Kortelainen
Department of Mathematics
University of Oulu
SF-90570 Oulu 57, Finland

1. Introduction

A nonregular language L is minimal with respect to a language family $\mathcal{L}$ if, for each nonregular language L_1 in $\mathcal{L}$, L is in the rational cone generated by L_1. Minimality is studied in several articles, for instance in [1],[3],[9] and [10]. Let $\mathcal{C}(\mathcal{L})$ be the rational cone generated by the language family $\mathcal{L}$. Denote $\overline{D}_1^* = \{x \in \{a_1,a_2\}^* \mid |x|_{a_1} \neq |x|_{a_2}\}$. In [1],[9] and [10] we can find the following conjecture.

Conjecture 1. If L is a nonregular language in $c(\mathcal{R})$, then $\overline{D}_1^*$ is in $\mathcal{C}(L)$.

Actually this conjecture states that the language $\overline{D}_1^*$ is minimal with respect to $c(\mathcal{R})$, the language family consisting of the commutative closures of all regular languages. We prove the conjecture. A result of Latteux and Leguy [11] then implies

Conjecture 2. Every commutative quasirational language is regular.

Conjecture 2 was stated in [8] and [10]. It was partially proved in [5] and [12]; in [5] it is shown that every commutative linear language is regular and in [12] that every commutative quasirational language over a two-letter alphabet is regular. Moreover, in [13] it is established that all commutative one-counter languages are regular.

2. Preliminaries

A set S is linear if $S = \{u_0+k_1u_1+\ldots+k_ru_r \mid k_j \in \mathbb{N}, j=1,\ldots,r\}$ for some $u_i \in \mathbb{N}^n$, $i=0,1,\ldots,r$. We say that s is the rank of S if there are exactly s linearly independent elements (over Q, the rationals) in $u_1, \ldots, u_r$. The rank of S is denoted by rank(S). Naturally rank(S) $\leq n$. If rank(S)=r, then S is a proper linear set. A subset T of $\mathbb{N}^n$ is semilinear if it is a finite union of linear sets. The rank of T, denot by rank(T), is s if $T = S_1 \cup \cdots \cup S_m$ where each S_i is a linear set and we have $\max_i \text{rank}(S_i) = s$. The convex closure conv(S) of the linear set S is defined by

$$\text{conv}(S) = \{u_0 + \alpha_1 u_1 + \ldots + \alpha_r u_r \mid \alpha_j \in Q,\ \alpha_j \geq 0,\ j=1,\ldots,r\} \cap \mathbb{N}^n .$$

Denote $A(S) = \{\alpha_1 u_1 + \ldots + \alpha_r u_r \mid \alpha_j \in Q,\ j=1,\ldots,r\}$. Note that $A(S)$ is a linear subspace of Q^n. By Lemma 1, conv(S) is a semilinear set.

A linear set $S \subset \mathbb{N}^n$ is fundamental if

$$S = \{(r_1,\ldots,r_n) + k_1(s_1,0,\ldots,0) + \ldots + k_n(0,\ldots,0,s_n) \mid \text{each } k_j \in \mathbb{N}\}$$

for some $r_j, s_j \in \mathbb{N}$, $r_j < s_j$, $j=1,\ldots,n$. If S is fundamental, then obviously rank(S)=n. A semilinear set is called fundamental if it is a finite union of fundamental linear sets.

Let $U \subset \mathbb{N}^n$. The complement of U is the set $\overline{U} = \{v \in \mathbb{N}^n \mid v \notin U\}$. In [6] Ginsburg proves that (i) the intersection of two semilinear sets is a semilinear set; (ii) the complement of a semilinear set is a semilinear set; and (iii) each semilinear set is a finite union of proper linear sets. These facts are extensively used in our proofs.

Let $V, W \subset \mathbb{N}^n$. We define $V + W = \{v+w \mid v \in V, w \in W\}$. Let $e_i \in \mathbb{N}^n$ be the element in which the ith coordinate is one and all the others are equal to zero, $i=1,\ldots,n$. Let $\psi_{<a_1,\ldots,a_n>}$ be the usual Parikh-mapping from $\{a_1,\ldots,a_n\}^*$ onto $\mathbb{N}^n$. When $\psi_{<a_1,\ldots,a_n>}$ is understood, it is denoted by ψ.

Let Σ_1 be an alphabet and $x \in \Sigma_1^*$. Then for each $a \in \Sigma_1$, $|x|_a$ denotes the number of occurrences of the symbol a in x. Let $L \subset \Sigma_1^*$ be a language. Then $x^{-1}L = \{y \in \Sigma_1^* \mid xy \in L\}$. Define

$$c(x) = \{y \in \Sigma_1^* \mid |x|_a = |y|_a \text{ for each } a \in \Sigma_1^*\} \text{ and } c(L) = \bigcup_{x \in L} c(x) .$$

Call c(L) the commutative closure of the language L. If $L = c(L)$, then L is commutative.

For a language L, let Σ_L be the smallest alphabet Σ_1 such that $L \subset \Sigma_1^*$. If $L \subset \{a_1,\ldots,a_n\}^*$, the complement of L with respect to $\{a_1,\ldots,a_n\}$ is the language $\overline{L}(a_1,\ldots,a_n) = \{x \in \{a_1,\ldots,a_n\}^* \mid x \notin L\}$. When $\overline{L}(a_1,\ldots,a_n)$ is understood, it is denoted by $\overline{L}$.

A language $L \subset \{a_1,\ldots,a_n\}^*$ is a SLIP-language if $\psi(L)$ is a semilinear set. If L is commutative and $\psi(L)$ is a linear set, then the convex closure of L is the language $\text{conv}(L) = \psi^{-1}(\text{conv}(\psi(L)))$. A commutative language $R \subset \{a_1,\ldots,a_n\}^*$ is fundamental if $\psi(R)$ is a fundamental semilinear set. Note that if R is fundamental, it is a regular commutative SLIP-language.

It should be clear that $c(\mathcal{R})$ is exactly the family of all commutative SLIP-languages and that $c(\mathcal{R})$ is closed under union, intersection and complementation. Let $D_1^* = c((a_1a_2)^*)$.

3. Main results

We first prove some auxiliary results.

Lemma 1. For each linear set $S \subset \mathbb{N}^n$, conv(S) is a semilinear set.

Proof. Assume $S = \{u_0 + k_1u_1 + \ldots + k_mu_m \mid k_j \in \mathbb{N},\ j=1,\ldots,m\}$ where $u_i \in \mathbb{N}^n$, $i=0,1,\ldots,m$. Let

$$U_0 = \{u_0 + \alpha_1u_1 + \ldots + \alpha_mu_m \mid \alpha_j \in Q,\ 0 \leq \alpha_j < 1,\ j=1,\ldots,m\} \cap \mathbb{N}^n$$

and $U_1 = \{k_1u_1 + \ldots + k_mu_m \mid k_j \in \mathbb{N},\ j=1,\ldots,m\}$. Obviously U_0 is finite and thus $U = U_0 + U_1$ is a semilinear set. It is easy to see that $U = \text{conv}(S)$. □

The following lemma states that a proper linear set is completely characterized by its convex closure and a certain fundamental linear set.

Lemma 2. For each proper linear set $S \subset \mathbb{N}^n$, there exists a fundamental semilinear set $U \subset \mathbb{N}^n$ such that $S = \text{conv}(S) \cap U$.

Proof. Assume $S = \{u_0 + k_1u_1 + \ldots + k_mu_m \mid k_j \in \mathbb{N},\ j=1,\ldots,m\}$ where $u_i \in \mathbb{N}^n$, $i=0,1,\ldots,m$, and the elements $u_1,\ldots,u_m$ are linearly independent. Obviously $m \leq n$. If $m < n$, there are distinct numbers $i_1,\ldots,i_{n-m} \in \{1,\ldots,n\}$ such that the elements $u_1,\ldots,u_m e_{i_1},\ldots,e_{i_{n-m}}$ are linearly independent. In this case denote $u_{m+j} = e_{i_j}$, $j=1,\ldots,n-m$. For each $i \in \{1,\ldots,n\}$, let $m_i \in \mathbb{N}_+$ be the smallest number such that $m_ie_i = r_{i_1}u_1 + \ldots + r_{i_n}u_n$ for some integers $r_{i_1},\ldots,r_{i_n}$. Denote

$$U_0 = \{(t_1,\ldots,t_n) \in \mathbb{N}^n \mid t_i < m_i,\ i=1,\ldots,n\} \cap \{u_0 + \alpha_1u_1 + \ldots + \alpha_nu_n \mid \alpha_i \text{ an integer},\ i=1,\ldots,n\}$$

and $U_1 = \{k_1m_1e_1 + \ldots + k_nm_ne_n \mid k_i \in \mathbb{N},\ i=1,\ldots,n\}$. Then $U = U_0 + U_1$ is a fundamental semilinear set and $S = \text{conv}(S) \cap U$. □

It should be noted that (i) the intersection of two fundamental semilinear sets is either empty or a fundamental semilinear set; and (ii) the complement of a fundamental semilinear set is either empty or a fundamental semilinear set.

Let $S \subset \mathbb{N}^n$ be a semilinear set. Then S is <u>homogenous</u> if there exist proper linear sets $S_1,\ldots,S_m \subset \mathbb{N}^n$ and a fundamental semilinear set $U \subset \mathbb{N}^n$ such that

(i) $S = S_1 \cup \ldots \cup S_m$; and (ii) $S = (\text{conv}(S_1) \cup \ldots \cup \text{conv}(S_m)) \cap U$

By the definition, a homogenous semilinear set is fully determined by the convex closures of the sets $S_1,\dots,S_m$ and by U: the boundaries of S are given by the sets $S_1,\dots,S_m$ and U characterizes the inner structure of S. Lemma 2 implies that each proper linear set is homogenous.

Call a language $L \subset \{a_1,\dots,a_n\}^*$ homogenous if $L \in c(R)$ and $\Psi(L)$ is a homogenous semilinear set. The following lemma is of crucial importance for the later results.

Lemma 3. Let the language $L \in c(R)$ be nonregular. Then there exists a nonregular homogenous language $L' \in C(L)$.

Proof. Without loss of generality we may assume that $\Sigma_L = \{a_1,\dots,a_n\}$. Let $L_1,\dots,L_m \in c(R)$ be languages such that $\Psi(L_i)$ is a proper linear set and $L = L_1 \cup \dots \cup L_m$. By Lemma 2 there exists a fundamental language $R_i \subset \{a_1,\dots,a_n\}^*$ such that $L_i = \text{conv}(L_i) \cap R_i$, $i=1,\dots,m$. Remember that each R_i is regular. Let $s \in \mathbb{N}$ be the greatest number for which there exist $i_1,\dots,i_s \in \{1,\dots,m\}$ such that the language $L \cap \overline{R}_{i_1} \cap \dots \cap \overline{R}_{i_s}$ is nonregular. Since $L \cap \overline{R}_1 \cap \dots \cap \overline{R}_m = \emptyset$, we have $s < m$. Let $I = \{i_1, \dots, i_s\}$ and $J = \{j \mid j \notin I, j \in \{1,\dots,n\}\}$. Let

$$R_0 = \bigcap_{j\in J} R_j \cap \bigcap_{i\in I} \overline{R}_i .$$

By a straightforward argument it can be shown that $L' = L \cap R_0$ is a nonregular homogenous language. Since R_0 is regular, $L' \in C(L)$. □

We next state a technical lemma. Geometrically the result is obvious. We omit the proof since it is somewhat lengthy and tedious.

Lemma 4. Let $S_1,\dots,S_m \subset \mathbb{N}^n$ be proper linear sets such that the rank of $\overline{\text{conv}(S_1)} \cap \dots \cap \overline{\text{conv}(S_m)}$ is n. Then there exists a proper linear set $T \subset \mathbb{N}^n$ such that $\text{conv}(T) \subset \overline{\text{conv}(S_1)} \cap \dots \cap \overline{\text{conv}(S_m)}$ and $\text{rank}(T) = n$.

We can now establish the first part for the proof of Conjecture 1.

Lemma 5. Let L be a homogenous language such that $\Sigma_L = \{a_1,\dots,a_n\}$. Assume $S_1,\dots,S_m \subset \mathbb{N}^n$ are proper linear sets and $U \subset \mathbb{N}^n$ is a fundamental semilinear set for which $\Psi(L) = S_1 \cup \dots \cup S_m$ and $\Psi(L) = (\text{conv}(S_1) \cup \dots \cup \text{conv}(S_m)) \cap U$. If $\text{rank}(\Psi(L)) = \text{rank}(\overline{\Psi(L)} \cap U) = n$, then $\overline{D}_1^* \in C(L)$.

Proof. Since $\text{rank}(\overline{\Psi(L)} \cap U) = n$, we have $\text{rank}(\overline{\text{conv}(S_1)} \cap \dots \cap \overline{\text{conv}(S_m)}) = n$. By the previous lemma, there exists a proper linear set $T_1 \subset \mathbb{N}^n$ such that $\text{conv}(T_1) \subset \overline{\text{conv}(S_1)} \cap \dots \cap \overline{\text{conv}(S_m)}$ and $\text{rank}(T_1) = n$. Since $\text{rank}(\Psi(L)) = n$, there must be S_j, say S_1, such that $\text{rank}(S_1) = n$. Obviously $\text{conv}(T_1) \cap \text{conv}(S_1) = \emptyset$. Using these facts we can find $w_0, w_1,$

$w_2 \in \mathbb{N}^n$ and $\alpha_1, \alpha_2, \beta_1, \beta_2 \in \mathbb{Q}$ with α_1, β_1 positive such that

(i) $W = \{w_0 + k_1 w_1 + k_2 w_2 \mid k_1, k_2 \in \mathbb{N}\} \subset U$;

(ii) $w_0 + k_1 w_1 + k_2 w_2 \in \mathrm{conv}(S_1)$ for each $k_1 > \alpha_1 k_2 + \alpha_2$;

(iii) $w_0 + k_1 w_1 + k_2 w_2 \in \mathrm{conv}(T_1)$ for each $k_1 < \beta_1 k_2 + \beta_2$.

Now $W \subset U$ implies that $w_0 + k_1 w_1 + k_2 w_2 \in \Psi(L)$ if $k_1 > \alpha_1 k_2 + \alpha_2$.

Let $x_i \in \{a_1, \ldots, a_n\}^*$ be words such that $\Psi(x_i) = w_i$, $i=0,1,2$. Then $x_0^{-1}L \in C(L)$ is commutative. Let $h: \{a_1, a_2\}^* \to \{a_1, \ldots, a_n\}^*$ be a morphism defined by $h(a_i) = x_i$, $i=1,2$. The language $L_1 = h^{-1}(x_0^{-1}L) \subset \{a_1, a_2\}$ is commutative by a result in [7]. It is easy to see that L_1 is non-regular. Of course $L_1 \in C(L)$. Then $\bar{D}_1^* \in C(L)$ by the results of [4] and [9]. □

Let $S \subset \mathbb{N}^n$ be a semilinear set. We say that S is <u>unlimited</u> if for each $m \in \mathbb{N}$ there exists $(m_1, \ldots, m_n) \in S$ such that $m_i > m$, $i=1,\ldots,n$.

<u>Lemma 6</u>. Assume $L \in c(R)$ is a language such that $\Sigma_L = \{a_1, \ldots, a_n\}$ and $\mathrm{rank}(\Psi(L)) < n$. If $\Psi(L)$ is unlimited, then $D_1^* \in C(L)$.

<u>Proof</u>. Let $S_1, \ldots, S_m \subset \mathbb{N}^n$ be proper linear sets such that $\Psi(L) = S_1 \cup \ldots \cup S_m$. Let $q \in \{1, \ldots, m\}$ be such that

$$S_q = \{u_0 + k_1 u_1 + \ldots + k_r u_r \mid k_i \in \mathbb{N}, j=1,\ldots,r\}$$

where $u_j \in \mathbb{N}^n$, $j=0,1,\ldots,r$, the elements $u_1, \ldots, u_r$ are linearly independent and $u_1 + \ldots + u_r \in \mathbb{N}_+^n$. Since $\Psi(L)$ is unlimited, such a number q always can be found. Choose q in such a way that $A(S_q)$ is not a proper subset of $A(S_j)$ for any $j \in \{1, \ldots, m\}$. Since $\mathrm{rank}(\Psi(L)) < n$ and S_q is proper, we have $r < n$. Let K be the set of all $k \in \{1, \ldots, m\}$ such that either

(i) $A(S_k)$ is not a subset of $A(S_q)$; or

(ii) $A(S_k) \subset A(S_q)$, but S_k is not a subset of $u_0 + A(S_q)$.

Now it can be shown that there is $w_0 \in S_q$ and $t_0 \in \mathbb{N}_+$ such that for any $k \in K$,

(1) $w_0 + \alpha_1 t_0 e_1 + \ldots + \alpha_n t_0 e_n \notin S_k$

for all $\alpha_j \in \mathbb{N}$, $j=1,\ldots,n$.

Since $r < n$, there must be $d \in \{1, \ldots, n\}$ such that $e_d \notin A(S_q)$. Let $x_i \in \{a_1, \ldots, a_n\}^*$, $i=0,1,2$, be words such that $\Psi(x_0) = w_0$, $\Psi(x_1) = t_0(u_1 + \ldots + u_r - e_d)$ and $\Psi(x_2) = t_0 e_d$. Let $h: \{a_1, a_2\}^* \to \{a_1, \ldots, a_n\}^*$ be a morphism defined by $h(a_1) = x_1$ and $h(a_2) = x_2$. Obviously $x_0^{-1}L$ is a commutative language in $C(L)$. Using (1) it can be shown that $D_1^* = h^{-1}(x_0^{-1}L)$. □

One final lemma is still needed. It is the converse of Lemma 6.

Lemma 7. Assume $L \in c(R)$ is a language such that $\Sigma_L = \{a_1,\dots,a_n\}$. Let $T_1,\dots,T_p$ be proper linear sets and U is a fundamental semilinear set such that $\Psi(L) = T_1 \cup \dots \cup T_p$ and $\Psi(L) = (\mathrm{conv}(T_1) \cup \dots \cup \mathrm{conv}(T_p) \cap U))$. If $\mathrm{rank}(\overline{\Psi(L)} \cap U) < n$ and $\overline{\Psi(L)} \cap U$ is unlimited, then $\overline{D}_1^* \in C(L)$.

Proof. The proof resembles that of Lemma 6. Let $S_1,\dots,S_m$ be proper linear sets such that $\overline{\Psi(L)} \cap U = S_1 \cup \dots \cup S_m$. Let

$$S_q = \{u_0 + k_1u_1 + \dots + k_ru_r \mid k_j \in \mathbb{N},\ j=1,\dots,r\}$$

and K be as in the proof of Lemma 6. We can find $w_0 \in S_q$ and $t_0 \in \mathbb{N}_+$ such that for any $k \in K$

$$(1)\quad w_0 + \alpha_1t_0e_1 + \dots + \alpha_nt_0e_n \notin S_k$$

holds for all $\alpha_j \in \mathbb{N}$, $j=1,\dots,n$. Since U is fundamental there exists $U_1 \subset U$ such that $w_0 \in U_1$ and

$$U_1 = \{v_0 + k_1(m_1,0,\dots,0) + \dots + k_n(0,\dots,0,m_n) \mid k_j \in \mathbb{N},\ j=1,\dots,n\}$$

for some $v_0 \in \mathbb{N}^n$, $m_j \in \mathbb{N}_+$, $j=1,\dots,n$. Let $t' = t_0m_1\cdots m_n$. Now $r<n$ and $u_1 + \dots + u_r \in \mathbb{N}_+$. Since $r<n$, there must be $d \in \{1,\dots,n\}$ such that $e_d \notin A(S_q)$. Let $x_i \in \{a_1,\dots,a_n\}^*$, $i=0,1,2$, be words such that $\Psi(x_0) = w_0$, $\Psi(x_1) = t'(u_1 + \dots + u_r - e_d)$ and $\Psi(x_2) = t'e_d$. Let $h\colon \{a_1, a_2\}^* \to \{a_1,\dots,a_n\}^*$ be the morphism defined by $h(a_1) = x_1$, $h(a_2) = x_2$. Clearly $x_0^{-1}L$ is a commutative language in $C(L)$. It thus suffices to show that $\overline{D}_1^* = h^{-1}(x_0^{-1}L)$.

Assume $a_1^ia_2^i \in h^{-1}(x_0^{-1}L)$ for some $i \in \mathbb{N}$. Then $h(a_1^ia_2^i) \in x_0^{-1}L$ which implies that $x_0h(a_1^ia_2^i) \in L$. This means that

$$\begin{aligned}\Psi(x_0x_1^ix_2^i) &= w_0 + it'(u_1 + \dots + u_r - e_d) + it'e_d\\ &= w_0 + it'(u_1 + \dots + u_r)\end{aligned}$$

is in $\Psi(L)$, a contradiction, since the above element is in $S_q \subset \overline{\Psi(L)}$. Since $h^{-1}(x_0^{-1}L)$ is commutative, we may deduce that $h^{-1}(x_0^{-1}L) \subset \overline{D}_1^*$.

Let $x \in \overline{D}_1^*$. Then $x \in c(a_1^ia_2^j)$ for some $i,j \in \mathbb{N}$, $i \neq j$. To prove that $x \in h^{-1}(x_0^{-1}L)$, it suffices to show that $a_1^ia_2^j \in h^{-1}(x_0^{-1}L)$. Consider the element

$$w_1 = w_0 + it'(u_1 + \dots + u_r - e_d) + jt'e_d\ .$$

Let $w_2 = w_0 + it'(u_1 + \dots + u_r)$. Now $w_1 \notin w_0 + A(S_q)$, since otherwise $w_1 - w_2 = (i-j)e_d \in A(S_q)$ and (since $i \neq j$) $e_d \in A(S_q)$, a contradiction. By the choice of t', $w_1 \notin S_k$ for any $k \in K$. This means that $w_1 \in S = \overline{\Psi(L)} \cap U$. Since $w_1 \in U_1 \subset U$, w_1 must be in $\Psi(L)$. Now $\Psi(x_0x_1^ix_2^j) = w_1$. Since L is commutative, the word $x_0x_1^ix_2^j \in L$, so $x_1^ix_2^j \in x_0^{-1}L$. Obviously $a_1^ia_2^j \in h^{-1}(x_0^{-1}L)$. We deduce that $\overline{D}_1^*$ is a subset of $h^{-1}(x_0^{-1}L)$. □

Theorem 1. If L is a nonregular language in $c(\mathcal{R})$, then $\overline{D}_1^* \in \mathcal{C}(L)$.

Proof. We can assume that $\Sigma_L = \{a_1, \ldots, a_k\}$, $k \in \mathbb{N}$. Note that $k \geq 2$ since each language in $c(\mathcal{R})$ over one symbol is regular. The proof is by induction on k.

Using the results of Berstel and Boasson ([2],[4]), Latteux proves in [9] that the theorem is true when k=2. Assume it holds for each $k = 2, 3, \ldots, n-1$, $n > 2$.

Consider the case $k = n$. By Lemma 3 we may assume that L is homogenous. Let $S_1, \ldots, S_m$ be proper linear sets and U a fundamental semilinear set such that $\Psi(L) = S_1 \cup \ldots \cup S_m$ and $\Psi(L) = (\mathrm{conv}(S_1) \cup \ldots \cup \mathrm{conv}(S_m)) \cap U$.

If $\mathrm{rank}(\Psi(L)) = \mathrm{rank}(\overline{\Psi(L)} \cap U) = n$, then $\overline{D}_1^* \in \mathcal{C}(L)$ by Lemma 5.

Assume that $\mathrm{rank}(\Psi(L)) < n$. If $\Psi(L)$ is unlimited, then $D_1^* \in \mathcal{C}(L)$ by Lemma 6. This naturally implies that $\overline{D}_1^* \in \mathcal{C}(L)$. If $\Psi(L)$ is not unlimited, it is obvious that there exists a language $L' \subset \{a_1, \ldots, a_{n-1}\}^*$ in $c(\mathcal{R})$ such that $\mathcal{C}(L) = \mathcal{C}(L')$. Then we are through by induction.

Assume now that $\mathrm{rank}(\overline{\Psi(L)} \cap U) < n$. If $\overline{\Psi(L)} \cap U$ is unlimited, $\overline{D}_1^* \in \mathcal{C}(L)$ by Lemma 7. If $\overline{\Psi(L)} \cap U$ is not unlimited, it is easy to see tha there exists a nonregular language $L'' \subset \{a_1, \ldots, a_{n-1}\}^*$ in $c(\mathcal{R})$ such that $L'' \in \mathcal{C}(L)$. Again, the theorem is true by induction. □

The family QR of quasirational languages is the substitution closure of linear languages. The family QR is also called "derivation bounded languages" and "standard matching choice languages". Let L QR be commutative. Since L is a context-free language, $L \in c(\mathcal{R})$. In [11] Latteux and Leguy prove that $\overline{D}_1^*$ is not in QR. By the previous theorem L must be regular. We can thus state

Theorem 2. Every commutative quasirational language is regular.

References

[1] J.-M. Autebert, J. Beauquier, L. Boasson and M. Latteux, Very smal families of algebraic nonrational languages, in *Formal Language Theory, Perspectives and Open Problems* (R.V. Book, ed.), Academic Press, New York, 1980, 89 - 107.

[2] J. Berstel, Une hiérarchie des parties rationnelles de $\mathbb{N}^2$, Math. Systems Theory 7 (1973), 114 - 137.

[3] J. Berstel, *Transductions and Context-Free Languages*, B.G. Teubner Stuttgart, 1979.

[4] J. Berstel and L. Boasson, Une suite décroissante de cones rationnels, Lecture Notes Comput. Sci. 14 (1974), 383 - 397.

[5] A. Ehrenfeucht, D. Haussler and G. Rozenberg, Conditions enforcing regularity of context-free languages, Lecture Notes Comput. Sci. 140 (1982), 187 - 191.

[6] S. Ginsburg, *The Mathematical Theory of Context-Free Languages*, Mc-Graw Hill, New York, 1966.

[7] M. Latteux, Cônes rationnels commutativement clos, Rairo Inform. Théor. 11 (1977), 29 - 51.

[8] M. Latteux, Langages commutatifs, Thèse Sc. Math., Lille I, 1978.

[9] M. Latteux, Cônes rationnels commutatifs, J. Comput. System Sci. 18 (1979), 307 - 333.

[10] M. Latteux, Langages commutatifs, transductions rationnelles et intersection, Publication de l'Equipe Lilloise d'Informatique Théorique IT 34.81, 1981.

[11] M. Latteux and J. Leguy, Langages algébriques rationellement satures, Publication de l'Equipe Lilloise d'Informatique Théorique IT 31.81, 1981.

[12] M. Latteux and J. Leguy, On the usefulness of bifaithful rational cones, Publication de l'Equipe Lilloise d'Informatique Théorique IT 40.82, 1982.

[13] M. Latteux and G. Rozenberg, Commutative one-counter languages are regular, J. Comput. System Sci. 1 (1984), 54 - 57.

A PROBABILISTIC DISTRIBUTED ALGORITHM FOR SET INTERSECTION AND ITS ANALYSIS*
(Preliminary Version)

Thomas G. Kurtz
Department of Mathematics
University of Wisconsin
Madison, Wisconsin 53706, U.S.A.

Udi Manber
Department of Computer Science
University of Wisconsin
Madison, Wisconsin 53706, U.S.A.

ABSTRACT

A Probabilistic algorithm for checking set disjointness and performing set intersection of two sets stored at different machines is presented. The algorithm is intended to minimize the amount of communication between the machines. If n is the total number of elements and k is the number of bits required to represent each of the elements, then it is shown that the expected running time of the set disjointness algorithm is $O(\log\log n)$ rounds, each round consisting of exchanging one message with $O(n+k)$ bits and performing $O(n)$ steps of local computation (all the constants are small). The analysis of the algorithm involves approximating Markov chains by deterministic models.

1. INTRODUCTION

This paper considers the problem of computing set intersection of two sets stored at two different machines. We assume that the sets contain elements whose size is quite large. For example, an element may be a line of text, an entry in a database, a picture, or a file. The goal is to avoid sending all of the data to one machine and performing the intersection there. This is essential in cases where communication dominates the computation cost or in cases where there is not enough space in one machine for both sets. We present in this paper a probabilistic distributed algorithm for set intersection that is based on hashing, and in particular, random hash functions [CW79, WC79]. The algorithm efficiently eliminates elements that do not belong to the intersection without sending them over to the other machine. The rate of elimination of elements depends on the relative size of the intersection. We analyze the expected performance of the algorithm and show that if the intersection is small then the improvement in communication cost over any deterministic algorithm is substantial. If the intersection is not small then elements are eliminated at a slower rate. The algorithm can detect this with high probability early and then a deterministic algorithm can be used on the elements that were not eliminated. The additional cost of local computation is not excessive in any case.

The sequential computational complexity of the set intersection problem under a comparison based model is known. It is straightforward to perform set intersection of two sets of size n, using sorting, with $O(n \log n)$ comparisons. Reingold [Re72] proved that $\Omega(n \log n)$ comparisons are necessary to determine if the two sets are disjoint. Manber and Tompa [MT82] extended Reingold's results to probabilistic and nondeterministic decision trees and proved that the same lower bound holds (see also [MSM84]). Manber [Ma84] considered the case of sets of different sizes and showed that $\Theta(m \log n)$ comparisons are necessary and sufficient in order to determine set disjointness of two sets of sizes n and m, $m > n$. The same lower bound holds for probabilistic decision trees as well. These results imply that one has to use more than comparisons to improve on the solution using sorting.

In this paper we show that the set disjointness problem can be solved in $O(n \log\log n)$ expected number of operations. The operations include hashing and comparisons. Moreover, the algorithm we present is very suitable to a distributed environment in which the sets are stored at two different machines. It can be divided into $O(\log\log n)$ rounds, each round consists of

---

* This research was supported in part by the National Science Foundation under Grants DMS-8401360 and MCS-8303134.

exchanging one message with $O(n+k)$ bits (where k is the size of each element) and performing $O(n)$ steps of local computation. (It is possible to modify the algorithm so that only $O(n)$ expected number of bits of communication are required. This is done by reducing the size of the messages as the algorithm progresses. However, more rounds will be required, and in practice (since messages are small anyway) it is an inferior distributed algorithm. We will not discuss this modification in this paper.)

Analysis of probabilistic algorithms is usually quite complicated. This problem is no exception. We analyze the running time for large n by splitting the evolution of the algorithm into two stages, an essentially deterministic initial stage and a random termination stage. We approximate the behavior of the algorithm in the initial stage by a deterministic model and show that this deterministic approximation is good until most of the elements outside the intersection have been eliminated. We then show that the order of magnitude of the running time of the random termination stage is independent of n. The techniques employed here are applicable to models in a variety of fields (cf. [Ku76], [Ku78], and [DK]) and further applications to probabilistic algorithms are anticipated.

Several other similar problems have been studied recently under a distributed model. Rodeh [Ro82] showed that exchanging $\Theta(\log n)$ numbers is necessary and sufficient to compute the median of the union of two sets stored at different machines. Mehlhorn and Schmidt[MS82] considered the following very simplified version of set intersection. Given two sequences $X = (x_1, x_2, \ldots, x_n)$ and $Y = (y_1, y_2, \ldots, y_n)$, such that $X, Y \subseteq \{0, 1, \ldots, 2^n - 1\}$, determine whether there exists i such that $x_i = y_i$. They proved that any deterministic algorithm requires sending n^2 bits, and then showed a probabilistic algorithm whose expected communication cost is only $O(n \log^2 n)$ bits. This serves as another example where probabilistic algorithms are more powerful than deterministic algorithms. In this paper we extend these results to the more general set intersection problem.

Another similar example of the power of probabilistic algorithms is probabilistic counting. Flajolet and Martin [FM83] (see also [St83]) introduced a class of such algorithms to estimate the number of distinct elements in a multiset. They were able to achieve an estimate with typical accuracy of 5-10% by a probabilistic algorithm that runs in linear time and makes only one pass through the data. This is significantly faster than the regular deterministic algorithm which requires sorting.

2. THE ALGORITHM

Let $X = \{x_1, x_2, \ldots, x_n\}$ and $Y = \{y_1, y_2, \ldots, y_m\}$, such that $X, Y \subseteq \{0, 1, \ldots, 2^k - 1\}$. We assume that X is stored in machine M_1 and Y is stored in machine M_2. We want to compute $X \cap Y$. Both machines can exchange messages and perform local computation on the data they hold. We are interested in minimizing both the amount of communication and the amount of local computation.

The algorithm consists of several identical rounds. In each round the sets are reduced by eliminating elements that are certain not to appear in the intersection. The algorithm terminates when either no more elements are left, in which case the sets are guaranteed to be disjoint, or when we are left with a subset of candidates that belong to the intersection with very high probability. In this case we can either conclude that, with high probability, the sets are not disjoint, or exchange the candidates to ensure that they indeed form the intersection. In section 4 we show that if the sets are disjoint the expected number of rounds to eliminate all elements is $O(\log \log n)$.

Each machine ℓ ($\ell = 1,2$) uses a binary table, called B_ℓ, of size $N > \max(m, n)$, $N = O(m+n)$. N determines the size of each message; the larger N is the less messages we expect to have. It is convenient to consider $N = m + n$. The main part of the algorithm is the use of random hash functions introduced by Carter and Wegman [CW79]. These functions are taken at random from a predetermined class of hash functions. For example, the following class of functions is a good candidate: $H_i \equiv [ax + b \pmod p)] \pmod N)$, where $a, b < p$ ($a \neq 0$), are chosen at random, $p > 2^k$ is a prime, and N is the size of the table ($p \gg N$) (see [CW79, WC79] for a description of several other good classes and their properties). We denote the elements that are not eliminated after round i by X^i and Y^i respectively ($X^0 = X$ and $Y^0 = Y$); these elements are called *candidates*. In each round $i \geq 0$ one of the machines, say M_1, selects a random hash function H_i from a class of hash functions H. (Since the number of such functions required by the algorithm is small, it is sufficient in practice to select those functions in advance; however, for the analysis we need the fact that the functions are completely random.)

M_1 sends a description of H_i to M_2 (in the case of the function given above the description includes the parameters a and b). M_1 uses H_i to hash the elements of X^i into B_1 in the following way. $B_1[j]$ is set to *true* iff there exists at least one element $x_s \in X^i$ such that $H_i(x_s) = j$ (i.e. x_s is hashed onto the j'th position). M_2 does the same (using the same hash function) for Y^i. The corresponding tables are then exchanged. This requires sending only N bits. M_1 can now eliminate all elements of X^i that were hashed into position j such that $B_2[j] =$ *false*; M_2 does the same for Y^i. (To find those elements one can either leave pointers with the B tables, or rehash.)

There are several ways to terminate the algorithm. If we are only interested in a disjointness test and we are satisfied with a probabilistic algorithm that may make errors then we can run the algorithm for $c(\log_2 \log_2 n)$ steps, where $c > 1$ is a constant. If not all the elements are eliminated then the sets are not disjoint with very high probability (depending on c). If we want to determine the actual intersection with some probability of error we can terminate at round i when either $X^i = \emptyset$ (notice that $X^i = \emptyset$ implies $Y^i = \emptyset$), or $X^{i-q} = X^{i-q+1} = \cdots = X^i$ (and the same for Y) for some predetermined constant q. We have not yet analyzed this case.

Another approach is to run this algorithm for as long as a significant number of elements are expected to be eliminated and then send the remaining elements (most of which belong to the intersection with high probability) to the other machine. The decision when to stop the algorithm depends on the relative costs of the different steps. More precisely, the cost of the computation is

$$C_m = \sum_{i=0}^{m-1} \left[\alpha\,(X^i + Y^i) + \beta\right] + \gamma\,(X^m + Y^m)$$

if the algorithm is terminated after m rounds. The parameters α, β and γ correspond respectively to the costs of hashing and performing the elimination, sending the bitmaps, and sending the remaining elements at the end (we include both X^m and Y^m for symmetry). Let B be the cardinality of the intersection. We would like to select the first m such that the cost of performing the next round is more than the cost of the extra communication in sending the elements that could have been eliminated in this round, that is

$$\begin{aligned}
&E\left[\gamma\,(X^{m-1} + Y^{m-1}) - \gamma\,(X^m + Y^m)\,|\,X^{m-1}, Y^{m-1}\right] \\
&= \gamma\left[(X^{m-1} - B)\,(1 - N^{-1})^{Y^{m-1}} + (Y^{m-1} - B)\,(1 - N^{-1})^{X^{m-1}}\right] \\
&\leq \alpha\,(X^{m-1} + Y^{m-1}) + \beta.
\end{aligned}$$

Of course this requires an estimate of B. One such estimate (based on least squares after m rounds) is given by

$$\frac{\sum_{i=0}^{m-1} W_{im}\left[\left(X^{i+1} - X^i\left(1 - \Upsilon(Y^i)\right)\right)\Upsilon(Y^i) + \left(Y^{i+1} - Y^i\left(1 - \Upsilon(X^i)\right)\right)\Upsilon(X^i)\right]}{\sum_{i=0}^{m-1} W_{im}\left[\Upsilon(2Y^i) + \Upsilon(2X^i)\right]}$$

where $\{W_{im}\}$ are positive weights, and $\Upsilon(x) = (1 - N^{-1})^x$. The optimal selection of the weights as well as other estimation methods remained to be studied. Termination rules based on a more careful analysis of the stochastic model also need to be explored.

3. EMPIRICAL RESULTS

We simulated the algorithm for checking set disjointness that was described in section 2. We considered two random disjoint sets and measured the mean and standard deviation (over 200 random inputs) of the number of rounds it took to eliminate all elements. We assume that the hash functions map the elements uniformly onto the bitmap tables. The results are given in table 1. Notice that the standard deviation is very small.

set size	mean	standard deviation
16	2.845	0.568
32	3.120	0.476
64	3.205	0.452
128	3.270	0.445
256	3.420	0.495
512	3.760	0.428
1024	3.940	0.238
2048	3.990	0.173
4096	4.015	0.122
8192	4.040	0.196
16384	4.065	0.247
32768	4.100	0.301
65536	4.165	0.372

Table 1: Running times for the set disjointness algorithm

4. ANALYSIS

If we assume that the values of H_i for distinct elements are independent and uniformly distributed, then the algorithm in the previous section is probabilistically equivalent to the following "balls in boxes" model. There are N boxes and red, green, and blue balls. At the i'th round let R_i denote the number of red balls, G_i the number of green balls, and B (which does not depend on i) the number of blue balls. The balls are placed at random in the boxes. If a box contains only red or only green balls then those balls are discarded. The remaining R_{i+1} red, G_{i+1} green, and B blue balls are then collected and the process is repeated. Of course, the red balls correspond to elements in X but not in Y, the green balls to elements in Y but not in X, and the blue balls to elements common to X and Y. We are interested in the behavior of the model if N is large and R_0 and G_0 are $O(N)$.

We omit some of the proofs for lack of space; for more details see [KM84].

As a first step in the analysis, we show that the probabilistic model is well approximated by the following deterministic model. Given r_0, g_0 and b,

$$r_{i+1} = r_i\left(1 - e^{-(b+g_i)}\right) \qquad (4.1)$$
$$g_{i+1} = g_i\left(1 - e^{-(b+r_i)}\right)$$

<u>**Theorem 4.1**</u> For $N = 2, 3, \ldots$, let $\{(R_i^N, G_i^N, B^N)\}$ be the random process described above with N boxes and starting with R_0^N red balls, G_0^N green balls, and B^N blue balls. Define $r_i^N = N^{-1}R_i^N$, $g_i^N = N^{-1}G_i^N$, and $b^N = N^{-1}B^N$. Let $0 < \alpha < 1/2$, and $\{(r_i, g_i)\}$ satisfy 4.1. If for each $\epsilon > 0$,

$$\lim_{N\to\infty} \Pr\left\{N^\alpha\left(|r_0^N - r_0| + |g_0^N - g_0| + |b^N - b|\right) > \epsilon\right\} = 0,$$

then for $\epsilon > 0$

$$\lim_{N\to\infty} \Pr\left\{\sup_i N^\alpha\left(\left|r_i^N - r_i\right| + \left|g_i^N - g_i\right|\right) > \epsilon\right\} = 0. \qquad (4.2)$$

Proof: The theorem is essentially a law of large numbers. Note, letting $e_N = \left(1 - N^{-1}\right)^{-N}$, that the conditional expectations are given by

$$
\begin{aligned}
E\left[r_{i+1}^N \mid r_i^N, g_i^N\right] &= r_i^N \left(1 - e_N{}^{-\left(b^N + g_i^N\right)}\right) \\
&\equiv F_1^N\left(r_i^N, g_i^N\right) \\
E\left[g_{i+1}^N \mid r_i^N, g_i^N\right] &= g_i^N \left(1 - e_N{}^{-\left(b^N + r_i^N\right)}\right) \\
&\equiv F_2^N\left(r_i^N, g_i^N\right)
\end{aligned}
\tag{4.3}
$$

and the conditional variances are

$$
\begin{aligned}
&E\left[\left(r_{i+1}^N - F_1^N\left(r_i^N, g_i^N\right)\right)^2 \mid r_i^N, g_i^N\right] = \\
&N^{-1}\left[r_i^N\left(1 + r_i^N - N^{-1}\right)\left(e_N^{-\left(b^N + g_i^N\right)} - e_{N/2}^{-2\left(b^N + g_i^N\right)}\right)\right. \\
&\left. + \left(r_i^N\right)^2\left(e_{N/2}^{-2\left(b^N + g_i^N\right)} - e_N^{-2\left(b^N + g_i^N\right)}\right)\right]
\end{aligned}
\tag{4.4}
$$

with a similar identity for g_{i+1}^N. The details are omitted. ∎

Remark 4.2 By (4.2), for large N, $|r_i^N - r_i| \leq \epsilon N^{-\alpha}$ and $|g_i^N - g_i| \leq \epsilon N^{-\alpha}$ with high probability.
Our main interest is in

$$
\tau_N = \min\left\{i : R_i^N = G_i^N = 0\right\}. \tag{4.5}
$$

We begin by treating the case in which $G_0^N = 0$.

Proposition 4.3 Suppose $G_0^N = 0$, $B^N > 0$, $N = 2, 3, \ldots$, $\sup_N \left(r_0^N + b^N\right) < \infty$, $\lim_{N\to\infty} \log N \left|b^N - b\right| = 0$, and $R_0^N \to \infty$. Then

$$
\lim_{N\to\infty} \sup_{z\in Z^+} \left|\Pr\{\tau_N \leq z\} - \exp\left\{-R_0^N\left(1 - e^{-b}\right)^z\right\}\right| = 0, \tag{4.6}
$$

and for every $\epsilon > 0$ there is a κ_ϵ such that

$$
\limsup_{N\to\infty} \Pr\left\{\left|\tau_N - \frac{\log R_0^N}{\left|\log\left(1 - e^{-b}\right)\right|}\right| \geq \kappa_\epsilon\right\} \leq \epsilon. \tag{4.7}
$$

Remark 4.3 Let $\xi_1, \xi_2, \cdots$, be independent geometrically distributed random variables with $\Pr\{\xi_i \leq z\} = 1 - (1-p)^z$. Then for large R

$$
\Pr\left\{\max_{1\leq i\leq R} \xi_i \leq z\right\} = \left(1 - (1-p)^z\right)^R \approx e^{-R(1-p)^z}.
$$

Consequently, τ_N behaves as the maximum of R_0^N independent geometrically distributed random variables with parameter $p = e_N^{-b^N}$.

Theorem 4.4 Suppose the conditions of Theorem 4.1 are satisfied with $r_0, g_0, b > 0$. Let $0 < \gamma < \alpha$ and define

$$\sigma_N = \frac{\gamma \log N}{|\log(1 - e^{-b})|}.$$

(Note that $(1 - e^{-b})^{-\sigma_N} = N^{\gamma}$.) Then

$$\lim_{N\to\infty} \sup_{z\in Z^+} \left| \Pr\{\tau_N \le z\} - \exp\left\{-(r_{\sigma_N} + g_{\sigma_N}) N (1 - e^{-b})^{z-\sigma_N}\right\}\right| = 0, \tag{4.8}$$

and for each $\epsilon > 0$ there exists $\kappa_\epsilon > 0$ such that

$$\limsup_{N\to\infty} \Pr\left\{\left|\tau_N - \frac{\log N}{|\log(1 - e^{-b})|}\right| \ge \kappa_\epsilon\right\} \le \epsilon. \tag{4.9}$$

Remark 4.5 Note that

$$r_0 + g_0 \le \frac{r_k + g_k}{(1 - e^{-b})^k} \le r_0 \exp\left\{\frac{e^{-b}}{1 - e^{-b}} \sum_{i=1}^{k} g_i\right\} + g_0 \exp\left\{\frac{e^{-b}}{1 - e^{-b}} \sum_{i=1}^{k} r_i\right\} \le C(r_0, g_0, b) \tag{4.10}$$

for all k, where $C(r_0, g_0, b)$ is a constant.

Consequently there exist constants c_1 and c_2 depending on r_0, g_0 and b such that

$$c_1 N^{-\gamma} \le r_{\sigma_N} + g_{\sigma_N} \le c_2 N^{-\gamma} \text{ and } c_1 \le (r_{\sigma_N} + g_{\sigma_N})(1 - e^{-b})^{-\sigma_N} \le c_2 \tag{4.11}$$

for all N.

Proof: It follows from Theorem 4.1 that for every $\epsilon > 0$

$$\lim_{N\to\infty} \Pr\left\{\left|\frac{r^N_{\sigma_N}}{r_{\sigma_N}} - 1\right| + \left|\frac{g^N_{\sigma_N}}{g_{\sigma_N}} - 1\right| > \epsilon\right\} = 0. \tag{4.12}$$

Let $\tau^R_N = \min\{i : R^N_i = 0\}$, $\gamma^R_N = \min\{i : \tilde{R}^N_i = 0\}$ where for $i > \sigma_N$ $\tilde{R}^N_i$ is the number of red balls that have been in a box with a blue ball at each round j, $\sigma_N < j \le i$. Finally, let $\hat{R}^N_i$, $i > \sigma_N$, be the number of red balls that would remain if at time σ_N all green balls were painted blue, and define $\eta^R_N = \min\{i : \hat{R}^N_i = 0\}$. Note that $\gamma^R_N \le \tau^R_N$ and that

$$\Pr\{\eta^R_N \le z\} \le \Pr\{\tau^R_N \le z\} \le \Pr\{\gamma^R_N \le z\}. \tag{4.13}$$

After round σ_N, $\{\tilde{R}^N_i\}$ and $\{\hat{R}^N_i\}$ behave like the model without green balls analyzed in Proposition 4.3. Consequently, by Proposition 4.3, and the Markov property

$$\begin{aligned} &\lim_{N\to\infty} \sup_{z\in Z^+} \left|\Pr\{\eta^R_N - \sigma_N \le z\} - E\left[\exp\left\{-R^N_{\sigma_N}\left(1 - e_N^{-(b^N + g^N_{\sigma_N})}\right)^z\right\}\right]\right| \\ &= \lim_{N\to\infty} \sup_{z\in Z^+} \left|\Pr\{\eta^R_N - \sigma_N \le z\} - \exp\left\{-r_{\sigma_N} N (1 - e^{-b})^z\right\}\right| = 0 \end{aligned} \tag{4.14}$$

and

$$\begin{aligned} &\lim_{N\to\infty} \sup_{z\in Z^+} \left|\Pr\{\gamma^R_N - \sigma_N \le z\} - E\left[\exp\left\{-R^N_{\sigma_N}\left(1 - e_N^{-b^N}\right)^z\right\}\right]\right| \\ &= \lim_{N\to\infty} \sup_{z\in Z^+} \left|\Pr\{\gamma^R_N - \sigma_N \le z\} - \exp\left\{-r_{\sigma_N} N (1 - e^{-b})^z\right\}\right| = 0. \end{aligned} \tag{4.15}$$

It follows that $\lim_{N\to\infty} \Pr\left\{\gamma_N^R = \tau_N^R\right\} = 1$.

Let τ_N^G and γ_N^G be defined as τ_N^R and γ_N^R.

Note that $\tau_N = \tau_N^R \vee \tau_N^G$ so $\lim_{N\to\infty} \Pr\left\{\tau_N = \gamma_N^R \vee \gamma_N^G\right\} = 1$.
Again applying Proposition 4.3

$$\begin{aligned}
&\lim_{N\to\infty} \sup_{z\in Z^+} \left|\Pr\left\{\gamma_N^R \vee \gamma_N^G - \sigma_N \le z\right\} - E\left[\exp\left\{\left(R_{\sigma_N}^N + G_{\sigma_N}^N\right)\left(1 - e_N^{-b^N}\right)^z\right\}\right]\right| \\
(4.16)\quad &= \lim_{N\to\infty} \sup_{z\in Z^+} \left|\Pr\left\{\tau_N - \sigma_N \le z\right\} - \exp\left\{-\left(r_{\sigma_N} + g_{\sigma_N}\right) N \left(1 - e^{-b}\right)^z\right\}\right| = 0.
\end{aligned}$$

Replacing z by $z - \sigma_N$ gives (4.8).
By (4.8), for N sufficiently large

$$\exp\left\{-c_2 N \left(1 - e^{-b}\right)^z\right\} - \frac{\epsilon}{4} \le \Pr\left\{\tau_N \le z\right\} \le \exp\left\{-c_1 N \left(1 - e^{-b}\right)^z\right\} + \frac{\epsilon}{4}.$$

Select z_1 so that $\exp\left\{-c_1 N \left(1 - e^{-b}\right)^{z_1}\right\} = \frac{\epsilon}{4}$ and z_2 so that $\exp\left\{-c_2 N \left(1 - e^{-b}\right)^{z_2}\right\} = 1 - \frac{\epsilon}{4}$,

and note that

$$z_i = \frac{\log N}{\left|\log\left(1 - e^{-b}\right)\right|} + K_\epsilon^i \quad (i = 1, 2).$$

The theorem follows. ■

In the final case considered, we assume $B^N = 0$ for all N.

Theorem 4.6 Suppose the conditions of Theorem 4.1 are satisfied with $r_0, g_0 > 0$, and that $B^N = 0$ for all N. Let $\sigma_N = \min\left\{i : r_i g_i \le N^{-1}\right\}$. Then

$$\lim_{N\to\infty} \Pr\left\{\tau_N \in \left\{\sigma_N, \sigma_N + 1, \sigma_N + 2\right\}\right\} = 1. \tag{4.17}$$

Specifically, setting $u_N = r_{\sigma_N - 1} g_{\sigma_N - 1}$

$$\begin{aligned}
&\lim_{N\to\infty} \left(\Pr\left\{\tau_N = \sigma_N\right\} - e^{-Nu_N}\right) = 0 \\
(4.18)\quad &\lim_{N\to\infty} \left(\Pr\left\{\tau_N = \sigma_N + 1\right\} - e^{-Nu_N^2}\left(1 - e^{-Nu_N}\right)\right) = 0 \\
&\lim_{N\to\infty} \left(\Pr\left\{\tau_N = \sigma_N + 2\right\} - \left(1 - e^{-Nu_N^2}\right)\right) = 0.
\end{aligned}$$

Remark 4.7 Note that

$$\lim_{i\to\infty} \frac{r_{i+1}}{r_i g_i} = \lim_{i\to\infty} \frac{1 - e^{-g_i}}{g_i} = 1 \tag{4.19}$$

and

$$\lim_{i\to\infty} \frac{r_i}{g_i} = \frac{r_{i-1}\left(1 - e^{-g_{i-1}}\right)}{g_{i-1}\left(1 - e^{-r_{i-1}}\right)} = 1. \tag{4.20}$$

In particular $\lim_{N\to\infty} r_{\sigma_N} g_{\sigma_N} / u_N^2 = 1$. Note also that $\lim_{N\to\infty} e^{Nu_N}\left(1 - e^{-Nu_N^2}\right) = 0$,

Distributed Algorithms

in Synchronous Broadcasting Networks

Extended Abstract

Gad M. Landau [1] Mordechai M. Yung [2,3] and Zvi Galil [1,2,3]

[1] Department of Computer Science, Tel-Aviv University, Tel-Aviv, 69978.
[2] Department of Computer Science, Columbia University, New York, N.Y. 10027.
[3] Supported in part by NSF grant MCS-8303139

Summary of Results

In this paper we consider a synchronous broadcasting network, a distributed computation model which represents communication networks that are used extensively in practice. This is the first work we know of that deals with this model in a theoretical context.

The problem we consider is a basic problem of information sharing, the computation of the multiple identification function. That is, given a network of p processors, each of which contains an n-bit string of information, the question is how every processor can compute the subset of processors which have the same information as itself. The problem was suggested by Yao in his classical paper in communication complexity [17], as a generalization of the two-processor case studied in that paper.

The immediate algorithm which solves this problem takes O(np) time (time= communication time in bits, which is our complexity measure). We present the following algorithms:

- **a. An algorithm which takes advantage of properties of strings, uses a very simple scheduling policy, and does not use arithmetic operations. (In fact, the processor can be a Turing machine). The algorithm's complexity is $O(n\log^2 p+p)$.**

- **b. An algorithm which uses a simulation of sorting networks by the distributed system. If t(p) is the depth of the sorting network of p processors, then our algorithm takes O(n t(p) + p) time. Using recent results on sorting networks we get an O(nlogp+p) (impractical) algorithm. The algorithm also uses addition and subtraction operations.**

- **c. By letting the processor use modular arithmetic operations as well, we can use Yao's probabilistic version, modify our algorithms and get probabilistic algorithms (with small error) where logn replaces n in the complexity expressions.**

To prove lower bounds for the problem we use Yao's result to get an $\Omega(n)$ bound, and we also show an $\Omega(p)$ bound. We suggest open problems concerning new techniques for proving lower bounds in the presence of broadcasting, as well as other problems about efficient use of the model and comparisons between different models of distributed computation.

1. Introduction

The synchronous broadcasting distributed computation model presented here represents existing communication systems (for example, the multiple frequency hopping radio networks or point-to-multipoint networks). Works in theoretical computing have dealt either with routing network models (see [9] [6] [13]) or with one channel broadcasting networks where either transmission order is prearranged [5], or a resource sharing (Ethernet-like) mechanism is used (see [7] [16]). Previous work unjustifiably neglected the network model, defined as follows: The processors in the network are $\{P_1,.......,P_p\}$; without loss of generality $p=2^k$. The network is fully connected (this is the topology we deal with), the communication is via the links, and there is no central common memory. The operation mode is synchronous and the communication operations are *transmission*, in which the processor broadcasts its message, and *reception*, in which the processor chooses a processor to listen to and gets one bit during a single unit of time. The complexity measure is the communication time.

One of the central problems in a distributed environment is information recognition and identification in a global context [3]. In a network each processor has its own local information, and the basic problem is how to let the processors recognize, share and process information which originally belongs to other processors. We find interesting versions of the problem in practice (in distributed sensor networks (DSN) [18] and in distributed systems [15] [11]) as well as in theory [1] [3] [17] [10] [6] [13]. To demonstrate problem solving in a synchronous broadcasting network, we deal with the following problem: Given a network of p processors where each processor has an n-bit string, each processor wants to know the subset (*class*) of processors which have the same information as itself. This problem appears in various situations. For example, the string can be information observed in a DSN where the system tries to compare signals received by different remote sensors and decide their credibility.

The problem is a generalization of the the *identification function* computation: Two processors, one with a string x and the other one with a string y, want to compute the function $f(x,y)= \delta_{x,y}$. ($\delta_{x,y}=1$ iff $x=y$, and 0 otherwise.) Yao [17] proved a lower bound on the communication complexity of this problem and showed that at least n bits have to be transmitted when we allow deterministic two-way communication. He also gave a probabilistic protocol (with small error) in which only O(log n) bits are exchanged. He suggested a generalization to three processors in a very special case where two of them are sending information to the third one, and posed an open question: what is the complexity of the problem where more than two processors are involved ?

The immediate solution to the network of p processors gives an n(p-1) time protocol. We design an $O(n \log^2 p + p)$ time algorithm (by 'algorithm' we mean a distributed one, that is, a protocol). We use string properties, propose a structured organization of the communication, and get an algorithm which uses only communication operations and comparisons of bits. A second algorithm is given where the distributed system simulates a sorting network. In this algorithm a processor must be able to do arithmetic operations and the scheduling is more complicated than in the first one. Using the reduction from sorting we are able to show that using recent results [2] [12], the algorithm takes $O(n \log p + p)$ time (with a very large constant multiplying the n logp term). Both algorithms can be transformed into probabilistic ones if a small error can be tolerated. In the probabilistic versions the n term becomes log n in both complexity expressions.

We show lower bounds of $\Omega(n)$ and $\Omega(p)$ to the problem. Our protocol allows the processors to send messages which include information (i.e. addresses) about other processors. We show that restricting messages to be functions only of the processor's input weakens the model, since any such restricted protocol requires $\Omega(np)$. We suggest some open problems. The most challenging is developing lower bound techniques for broadcasting networks. The synchronous broadcasting model seems to defy all known lower-bound techniques. Those are usually based on weaknesses of the model in information transfer. Our model seems to have no such weaknesses.

2. The Multiple Identification Algorithm

2.1. Relations on Strings

Let $\Sigma = \{0,1\}$ and $x,y \in \Sigma^n$ ($x = x(1)....x(n)$).

We use the following notation and properties of strings and their prefixes.

Definition 1: $\forall i, 0 \leq i \leq n : x\, E_i\, y \Leftrightarrow \forall j, 0 < j \leq i: x(j)=y(j)$. (Remark: $\forall x,y \in \Sigma^n$: $x\, E_0\, y$).

Definition 2: $\forall i, 1 \leq i \leq n$: $x\, F_i\, y \Leftrightarrow$ $(x\, E_{i-1}\, y)$ and $(\neg (x\, E_i\, y))$. (Remark: $x\, F_{n+1}\, y \Leftrightarrow x=y$).

E_i means that the prefix of length i is equal, while F_i means that the prefix of length i-1 is equal and the i-th bit is different.

Fact 1: E_i is an equivalence relation and E_{i+1} is a subset of E_i.

Fact 2: $\forall i, 1 \leq i \leq n : ((x_1\, F_i\, y_1)$ and $(x_2\, F_i\, y_2)$ and $(x_1\, E_i\, x_2)) \Rightarrow$ $(y_1\, E_i\, y_2)$.

2.2. The Information Structures in the Processor

In each processor P_v we have:

1. The string (input) array $x_v = x_v(1),.....,x_v(n)$.
2. Address array $R_v = R_v(1),........,R_v(n)$ to store processor addresses. The algorithm will have the property that if $R_v(i)=w$ then $x_v\, F_i\, x_w$.
3. Processor (output) Array $N_v = N_v(1),.....,N_v(p)$ where $N_v(i) \in \{0,1\}$. N is the result of the computation. It will be shown that at termination $N_v(u)=1$ iff $x_v = x_u$.

2.3. Organization of Communication

Our algorithm is divided into steps. In each step we partition the $p=2^k$ processors into clusters. Processors communicate only with processors of their cluster. The fact that a processor cannot transmit and receive information concurrently can be handled easily.

Definition 3: a 2^m-cluster: In step m the clusters have size 2^m and are called 2^m-clusters. They are defined in the obvious way. For $0 \leq m \leq k$ there are 2^{k-m} 2^m-clusters. The j-th 2^m-cluster is $\{P_{(j-1)2^m+1}, ..., P_{j2^m}\}$.

Obviously, there is one p-cluster, and each processor is a 2^0-cluster. Clusters can be represented by a *cluster tree.* A 2^m-cluster is the father of the two 2^{m-1}-clusters contained in it.

The cluster conference: In step i let S be a cluster. Its left and right sons which are now sub-clusters are denoted by S_l and S_r. Each processor P_v in the cluster is aware of its cluster number, its own number within the cluster and its sub-cluster. The goal of the conference is to let $P_v \in S$ collect the information about strings of processors in S. If $P_v \in S_l$ then it knows the information about strings in this sub-cluster from previous steps and it has to get information from S_r. We will see later what is the information provided by the protocol and we will prove its sufficiency. The arrays R_v and N_v represent the information known to P_v about its cluster. We will show that at the end of step m if P_v and P_w are in the same cluster then $N_v(w)=1$ iff $x_v = x_w$.

2.4. The Multiple Identification Algorithm

The algorithm has logp steps. Before the algorithm starts, each processor P_v assigns the following values: $\forall j$: $R_v(j) := \Phi$ where Φ denotes the null processor, and $N_v(v) := 1$ while for all j: $j \neq v$: $N_v(j) := 0$. We describe the algorithm for a general processor P_v in cluster $S = (S_l \cup S_r)$ where $P_v \in S_l$.

In each step the processor chooses a processor belonging to the other sub-cluster from which it gets the information about this sub-cluster. We call this processor the partner of P_v, denoted by P_w. During the step the processor may change its partners. Sometimes during the step the processor stops working for the rest of the step. The local boolean variable Work tells whether the processor is working or not.

Each step m (m=1,..,logp) has three parts:

Part 1. INITIALIZATION:

P_v chooses a partner P_w (without loss of generality w is $2^{m-1}+v$) and Work:=true.

Part 2. SCANNING:

During the step, P_v scans the string x_v from left to right in n time units. Let P_w be its partner in time unit i. An invariant property of partners' strings is $x_v(1),...,x_v(i-1) = x_w(1),....,x_w(i-1)$ i.e. $x_v E_{i-1} x_w$. P_v receives $x_w(i)$ and $R_w(i)=u$ from its partner P_w. If $u \neq \Phi$ then since $\{(R_w(i)=u) \Rightarrow (x_w\ F_i\ x_u)\}$, P_v concludes that $x_u(1),....,x_u(i-1) = x_w(1),....,x_w(i-1)$ i.e. $x_u E_{i-1} x_v$.
If $x_v(i) \neq x_w(i)$ then $x_w F_i x_v$ and since $R_w(i)=u$ it knows (by fact 2) that $x_u(1),...,x_u(i) = x_v(1),...,x_v(i)$ i.e. $x_u E_i x_v$. Therefore P_v sets $R_v(i) := w$ and in the next time unit u becomes the partner of v (w:=u). By changing partners P_v can always scan the string forward in the next time unit.
If on the other hand $x_v(i) = x_w(i)$, P_v does not change partner and copies $R_w(i)=u$ to $R_v(i)$. (This copying is actually needed only if $R_v(i)=\Phi$). If there is a mismatch (i.e. $x_v(i) \neq x_w(i)$) and $u=\Phi$ then P_v can stop working in the current step since there are no members of its class in the other sub-cluster (Work:=false).

<u>The Scanning Procedure:</u>

```
1.       for j:= 1 to n do
       begin { time unit j }
2.       if Work then begin
2.a                      Send ( x_v(j) , R_v(j) ) ;
2.b                      Get  from P_w ( x_w(j) , R_w(j) ) ;
3.                       'Check'; {whether there is a match; see below}
                         end
4.              else { Work=false } wait a time unit;
      end; { time unit j }
```

The procedure 'Check' summarizes the local operations in a time unit:

<u>The procedure 'Check':</u>

```
   begin { time unit j ( P_v got x_w(j) and R_w(j) ) }
1.     if x_v(j) = x_w(j) { match }
2.       then  if (R_w(j) ≠ Φ) then R_v(j):= R_w(j)
         else
           { mismatch x_v ≠ x_w }
3.             if R_w ≠ Φ
4.               then          { change partner, update partner index }
                   begin   R_v(j) := w ;  w := R_w(j) ; end
5.               else Work := false ;
   end
```

Part 3. UNION CLASS:
After scanning the string, the processor has to identify processors in the other sub-cluster which belong to its class: A processor which is still working knows that its current partner belongs to its class. It gets a sequence of zeros and ones from its partner. The i-th element of this sequence indicates whether the i-th element of the partner's sub-cluster belongs to the class or not.

2.5. Correctness and Complexity of the Algorithm

We need the following relations on processors and strings for describing the algorithm dynamically and for proving its properties.

Definition 4: For a step m we say that $Assemble_m(P_v,P_w) \Leftrightarrow$ P_v and P_w are in the same cluster at the end of step m.

We extend our relation on strings to relations on strings belonging to processors, which are the input of our algorithm. For each step m of the algorithm we define a relation.

Definition 5: $x_v E_i^m x_w \Leftrightarrow (x_v E_i x_w$ and $Assemble_m(P_v,P_w))$

Definition 6: $x_v F_i^m x_w \Leftrightarrow (x_v F_i x_w$ and $Assemble_m(P_v,P_w))$

Definition 7: A partnership sequence for processor $P_v \in S_l$ in step m, which we denote PS(v,m), is: $[l_1 P_{w_1} r_1], [l_2 P_{w_2} r_2], \ldots\ldots, [l_s P_{w_s} r_s]$, where for i:=1,..,s P_{w_i} are processors, and l_i, r_i are time units (or equivalently indices in the arrays R and x) satisfying the following: $l_1=1$, $l_i \leq r_i$, $r_{i-1}=l_i - 1$ and $r_s \leq n$. The sequence describes the behavior of processor P_v in step m: P_{w_i} is P_v's partner during time interval $[l_i, r_i]$ and P_v works in this step till time unit r_s.

We briefly outline the correctness proof. First we prove some properties of the partnership sequence and the information transmitted in a step. (We use R^m and N^m to denote R and N after step m, respectively.)

Claim 1: Let P_v be a processor, and $1 \leq m \leq \log p$.

- (1) If $[l_1 P_{w_1} r_1], [l_2 P_{w_2} r_2], \ldots\ldots, [l_s P_{w_s} r_s]$ is PS(v,m) then $\forall i : P_{w_i} \in S_r$.
- (2) If $R_v^m(j) = u \neq \Phi$ then $Assemble_m(P_v, P_u)$.

The claim holds by induction on the step number m and on the number of the partner in PS(v,m). Notice that the claim holds for the first step. For a general step m, the first partner $P_{w_1} \in S_r$ by the algorithm. Assume $P_{w_i} \in S_r$ and let u be an address transmitted by P_{w_i} in time unit j; then $u = R_{w_i}^{m-1}(j)$. By induction on m, $Assemble_{m-1}(P_{w_i},P_u)$ which implies that $u \in S_r$ and $Assemble_m(P_v,P_u)$. The claim holds since u becomes either $R_v(j)$ or the new partner $P_{w_{i+1}}$ (and P_{w_i} is copied to $R_v(j)$).

This claim describes the properties of the partners and the information collected from each partner separately. The following lemma considers properties of the whole partnership sequence.

Lemma 1: Let P_{w_t} be P_v's partner at time unit j of step m; then:

- (1) $x_{w_t} E_{j-1}^m x_v$.

- (2) $\forall i \leq j$: $\{(R_v(i)=u \neq \Phi) \Rightarrow (x_u F_i^m x_v)\}$

To prove the lemma we have to prove the two assertions together because they are related to each other. We use once more double induction on step number and on the number of the current partner in the partnership sequence. We show that the concatenation of the sub-strings of the x_i's which matched x_v along the sequence is always the current partner string's prefix, which implies (1). To complete the proof, we show that all the updates of R during the step preserve (2).

The following lemma shows that the information collected by each processor represents the full relevant knowledge of all the strings in its cluster, even though it has communicated only with a subset of the cluster.

Lemma 2: $x_v F_j^m x_w \Leftrightarrow \{(R_v^m(j) \neq \Phi)$ and $(R_w^m(j) \neq \Phi)\}$.

The lemma is proven by induction on the step number m. We have to show that two processors which belong to the same cluster, have the same prefix of length j-1, and disagree on x(j), mark in R the fact that there is a processor in their cluster with this property, even though these processors do not necessarily listen to each other during the step in which their sub-clusters were united. Therefore, we prove that it does not matter which processor is chosen to be the first partner, the information collected in a step (that is, the places updated in R) being independent of a specific partnership sequence. We consider two partnership sequences of processor P_v and we check all the cases of possible first (leftmost) difference in updating R along both sequences. We conclude that none of these cases is possible and in the two sequences the same $R_v(i)$'s are updated (perhaps with different values). Furthermore, both sequences have the same length.

The claims of the following lemma imply the correctness of a general step in the algorithm:

Lemma 3: If $P_v \in S_l$ in step m, then:

- (1)If there exists $P_w \in S_r$ with $x_v E_j^m x_w$, then P_v works at least up to time unit j+1 in the step.

- (2) If $P_w \in S_r$ in step m, and $x_v = x_w$, then P_v works in 'Union-Class' of step m. If P_v stops working, then none of the processors in S_r needs its transmissions.

- (3) $\forall P_w$ $\text{Assemble}_m(P_w, P_v) \Rightarrow (x_v = x_w \Leftrightarrow N_v^m(w)=1)$.

Part (1) of the lemma is immediate since the partnership sequence is independent of the choice of the first partner, as explained above, and the fact that P_w can be chosen by P_v to be the first partner.

Part (2) is proven by defining time unit n+1 to be the 'Union-Class' sub-step and by using part 1. By symmetry we show that a processor is working iff its transmission is required by the other sub-cluster.

Part (3) is implied by part 2 and the correctness of 'Union Class', which is shown by induction on the step number.

Theorem 1: The algorithm is correct and its complexity is $O(n \log^2 p + p)$.

Proof: Since at the end of the algorithm $\text{Assemble}_k(P_w, P_v)$ holds for all P_v, P_w we conclude:

$\forall v,w$: $((x_v = x_w) \Leftrightarrow (N_v(w)=1))$.

We have k=log p steps. In each 'Scan' sub-step we have n time units each of communications cost (log p + 1). Therefore the total time of 'Scan's is $O(n \log^2 p)$. The length of 'Union-Class' in a step is the length of the sub-cluster, hence the total time of the unions is $\Sigma_{i=0}^{k-1}$ (2^i) = O(p). *QED*

3. An Algorithm Using Reduction from Sorting Networks

3.1. Simulation of Sorting Network

Constructing sorting networks is one of the most widely studied problems in parallel computation. For a long time the best network to sort N numbers was Batcher's $O(\log^2 N)$-level construction [4]. A recent breakthrough by Ajtai, Komlos and Szemeredi [2] achieved an O(logN)-depth parallel network that sorts N numbers. Their work also provided O(N)-node O(logN)-degree network which sorts N inputs in O(logN) time (depth). Leighton [12] further reduced the degree of such a network to a constant. (These new networks are not practical since either the depth or the number of processors has a huge constant factor.) A sorting network is composed of comparison boxes, each with two inputs and two outputs. In our model a box can be simulated by four processors, two of which contain the input strings of the box; the other two processor receive these strings (as output of the comparison). The broadcasting network can simulate a sorting network and sort p k-bit words in O(klogp) time. One has only to show that each processor can compute quickly the addresses of the other processors involved in each comparison.

3.2. The Multiple Identification Algorithm Using Simulation of Sorting

Part 1. SORTING:

Each processor concatenates its address v to its input x_v. The processors sort the strings $x_v v$, v=1,..p. After the sorting processor P_v receives the string x'v'. Call processors with the same x' a ***group***. As a result of the sorting, the first group of processors starting with P_1, contains (in increasing order) the addresses (v'-s) of the first class (the one with the smallest x), and so on.

Part 2. GROUP BOUNDARIES:

Each processor performs a search to find the boundaries of its group, that is, the smallest and largest processors which got the same string x'. This can be done using one of the following methods:

- 1. The doubling technique: Each processor P_v broadcasts its string 4 logp times. Simultaneously, P_v compares its string to the one of the processor P_{v+1}, P_{v+2}, P_{v+4},.. and so on until its x' is different from the string x' of P_{v+2^j}, and then by binary search it finds the largest processor with the same string. The smallest processor is found symmetrically.

- 2. The method of searching for boundary indicators, suggested by Manfred Warmuth: The processor P_v has two Boolean variables called Left and Right. Each processor compares its string x' with those of its left and right immediate neighbors (p_{v-1} and p_{v+1}) and updates Left and Right according to the result of the comparison. Then the processor broadcasts its Left and Right variables p times and simultaneously listens to its neighbors which are in its group- first to its left neighbor P_{v-1}, then to P_{v-2},.... until it gets an indication that some P_{v-j} is not in the group; then it does the same with its right neighbors.

Part 3. OUTPUT CALCULATION:

The goal of this part is to enable each processor P_v to calculate the output N' of processor $P_{v'}$, whose input string and address (x'v') were received by P_v in part 1. Therefore, P_v needs to know the addresses received by all processors in its group. First, P_v (except if it is the smallest in its group) gets from P_{v-1} the address (v-1)' received by it in part 1. Then P_v computes the difference of the addresses v'-(v-1)'. Now the i-th processor in the group knows the difference between the addresses of the i-th and the (i-1)-th processors of the class which forms the group. Then one by one and in order the members of the group (except the smallest one) broadcast the differences (using a special symbol to denote end-of-message). Each processor, knowing all the differences, can calculate the addresses of the processors in the class. P_v computes a vector N' by assigning 1 to indices corresponding to address of members of the class. (N' is the output vector of processor number v').

Part 4. OUTPUT DISTRIBUTION:
The goal of this part is for $P_{v'}$ to receive its output from P_v (which calculated it). Processor P_v concatenates v' and its own address v. The system sorts v'v. As a result, processor $P_{v'}$ gets v'v, where v is the name of the processor that computed $P_{v'}$'s output. Next $P_{v'}$ receives the output N' from P_v and the algorithm ends.

The time analysis of the algorithm is as follows:
Part 1 takes O((n+log p)log p) sorting time and part 2 takes O(n log p) using the first method or O(n+p) using the second one. Part 4 takes O(p) time for broadcasting of N', dominating the sorting, which takes only $O(\log^2 p)$. The address difference transmissions in part 3 cost O(p), which dominates the time of this part. The total time of the algorithm is therefore O(nlog p +p).

The time analysis of part 3 is based on the observation that the sum of the differences transmitted by a group in this part is bounded by p and on the following claim:

Lemma 4: If $a_1, a_2, \ldots, a_k$ are non-negative integers that satisfy $\Sigma_{i=1}^{k}(a_i) \leq p$, then $\Sigma_{i=1}^{k}(|\log a_i| + 1) = O(p)$.

A practical implementation, which uses Batcher's network, yields an $O(n\log^2 p + p)$ algorithm, which is the same complexity as our first algorithm. However the algorithm that uses simulation of sorting networks requires that processors perform additions and subtractions, while the first algorithm does not.

4. The Probabilistic Algorithms

Karp and Rabin [8] introduced the idea of ***fingerprint function***, which is to choose a random hash function ϕ such that $\phi(x) << x$, and for every collection of strings of a given size there is only a small probability that $x \neq y$ when $\phi(x) = \phi(y)$. Given our set of strings (regarded as a set of binary numbers) we can choose the family of functions to be { x mod q : q prime, q = O(log n + log p) }, namely, the fingerprints are the residues. The analysis given in [8] shows that the probability of an error is very small. After a few repetitions, each time with a random chosen prime, we get a negligible error.

The Probabilistic algorithm is as follows:

- 1. P_1 chooses (probabilistically) a random prime q, q = O(log n + log p), and broadcasts it.
- 2. Each P_i computes $\phi(x_i) = x_i$ mod q.
- 3. The processors execute the algorithm (one of the two algorithms presented), using $\phi(x_i)$ as the information string.

The complexity of the probabilistic version of the first algorithm is $O((\log n \log^2 p) + p)$ while the complexity of the probabilistic algorithm which is based on sorting is O((log n logp)+ p).

5. Lower Bounds

Lemma 5: The multiple identification problem is $\Omega(n)$.
This is proven for the case p=2. The proof is Yao's theorem in [17]. (Our model is not stronger than the model in [17] when p=2.)

Lemma 6: The multiple identification problem is $\Omega(p)$.
Proof: Consider the case where n=1, that is one bit x_i is stored in each processor p_i. Let x be $x_1x_2...x_p$. The address information of a bit is actually its location in x. For a processor P_i, if $x_i=1$ then the output $N_i=x$. Otherwise N_i is the complement string of x. In any algorithm the processor receives a certain number of bits and computes N_i. The transmissions must define the initially unknown part of x, that is a string of length p-1. Call the length of the transmissions LT, and call the Kolomogorov Complexity of x (or its complement string, since they are the same) KC. We claim that LT$\geq$KC, since otherwise LT is a shorter description of the string. Most of the strings of length p-1 have KC= $\Omega(p)$ so LT= $\Omega(p)$. The length of the transmissions received by the processor is $\Omega(p)$ and in each time unit the processor gets one bit; therefore the time of the algorithm is $\Omega(p)$. *QED*

We comment that known techniques used for proving lower bounds, namely information transfer, crossing sequences, fooling sets and arguments involving a network's diameter or a transmission's history (see for example: [14], [17], [10], [13], [9], [5]) do not help us in the broadcasting model. This is because after n units of time all the information was transmitted (while each processor can get only part of it).

Different models restrict the message space differently. In our algorithms processors send data information and address information. We trade address transmissions for the necessity of exchanging information with all the processors. This address-data transmission trade-off is the idea that made the protocol superior to any protocol which allows only transmission of input data. Using [17] it is easy to show that any such restricted protocol requires $\Omega(np)$ time. This demonstrates the differences between the two-processor case, which is the case dealt with by communication complexity (modeling VLSI), and multi-processor communication (modeling communication networks).

6. Conclusions and Open problems

The main open problem is improving the lower bound for the multiple identification and developing techniques for proving lower bounds for multi-processor problems when we allow broadcasting and transmission of information which is not restricted only to the input strings. This interesting topic requires further extending the approaches used here and in the field of communication complexity. Tools for comparing different communication models need to be developed as well.

We showed the power of the synchronous broadcasting model. The cluster tree and simulating sorting networks are efficient schemes for communication organization. Developing methods of communication organization for different communication schemes and network topologies is a crucial step in distributed-algorithm design. Developing efficient algorithms for the model presented in the paper is a challenge as well.

7. Acknowledgement

We thank Manfred Warmuth for helpful discussions and Bruce Abramson and Stuart Haber for their comments on earlier versions of the paper.

References

1. Abelson, H. Lower Bounds on Information Transfer in Distributed Computation. Symposium on Foundation of Computer Science, IEEE, October, 1978, pp. 151-158.

2. Ajtai M., J. Komlos and E. Szemeredi. An O(n logn) Sorting Network. Symposium on Theory of Computing, ACM, April, 1983, pp. 1-9.

3. Angluin D. Local and Global Properties in Network of Processors. Symposium on Theory of Computing, ACM, May, 1980, pp. 82-93.

4. Batcher K. Sorting Networks and their Applications. AFIPS Spring Joint Computer Conference, 32, 1968, pp. 307-314.

5. Chandra A. K., M. L. Furst and R. J. Lipton. Multi-Party Protocols. Symposium on Theory of Computing, ACM, April, 1983, pp. 94-99.

6. Gafni E., M.C. Loui, P. Tiwori, D.B. West and S. Zaks. Lower Bounds on Common Knowledge in Distributed Algorithms, with Applications. University of Illinoi at Urbana-Champaign, March, 1984.

7. Greenberg A.G. On the Time Complexity of Broadcast Communication Schemes. Symposium on Theory of Computing, ACM, May, 1982, pp. 354-364.

8. Karp R.M. and M.O. Rabin. Efficient Randomized Pattern-Matching Algorithms. University of California, Berkley, 1981.

9. Pachl J., E. Korach, and D. Rotem. A Technique for Proving Lower Bounds for Distributed Maximum-Finding Algorithms. Symposium on Theory of Computing, ACM, May, 1982, pp. 378-382.

10. Papadimitriou C. H., and M. Sipser. Communication Complexity. Symposium on Theory of Computing, ACM, May, 1982, pp. 196-200.

11. Saltzer, J.H. Naming and Binding of Objects. In *Operating Systems: an advanced course*, Bayer, R., R. M. Graham, and G. Seegmuller, Ed.,Springer-Verlag, 1978, pp. 99-208.

12. T. Leighton. Tight Bounds on the Complexity of Parallel Sorting. Symposium on Theory of Computing, ACM, May, 1984, pp. 71-80.

13. Tiwari P. Lower Bounds on Communication Complexity in Distributed Computer Networks. Symposium on Foundation of Computer Science, IEEE, October, 1984, pp. 109-117.

14. Ullman J. D.. *Computational Aspects of VLSI.* Computr Science Press, Rockville, Maryland, 1984.

15. Watson, R.W. Identifiers (Naming) in Distributed Systems. In *Distributed Systems- Architecture and Implementation: an advanced course*, Lampson B.W., M. Paul, and H.J. Siegert, Ed.,Springer-Verlag, 1983, pp. 191-210.

16. Willard D. Log-logarithmic Protocol for Resolving Ethernet and Semaphore Conflicts. Symposium on Theory of Computing, ACM, May, 1984, pp. 512-521.

17. Yao A.C. Some Complexity Questions Related to Distributive Computing. Symposium on Theory of Computing, ACM, May, 1979, pp. 209-213.

18. Yemini Y. and A. Lazar. Towards Distributed Sensor Networks. Conference on Information Science and Systems, Princton University, March, 1982.

A CONTEXT DEPENDENT EQUIVALENCE BETWEEN PROCESSES

Kim Guldstrand Larsen
Department of Computer Science
University of Edinburgh

ABSTRACT In recent years several equivalences between nondeterministic and concurrent processes have been proposed in order to capture different notions of the extensional behaviour of a process. Usually the equivalences are congruences wrt. the process constructing operations in order to support hierarchic development of systems. With the purpose of achieving more flexible hierarchic development methods we suggest parameterizing the equivalences with information about contexts. We carry out the suggestion in full for the bisimulation equivalence, which we parameterize with a special type of context information called environments. As a Main Theorem we offer a useful characterization of the information ordering on environments. Also a Modal Characterization of the parameterized bisimulation equivalence is presented.

1. MOTIVATION

In recent years several equivalences between nodeterministic and concurrent processes have been proposed in order to capture different aspects of the extensional behaviour of a process [1, 4, 6, 5, 8, 11, 14, 15]. Often sound and complete axiomatizations [7, 13, 15] as well as modal characterizations characterizations [1, 3, 7, 12, 18, 19, 20] of the various equivalences have been given. One motivation for equivalences is to relate specifications and implementations. Normally therefore much care is taken to ensure that the equivalences are congruences wrt. the process constructing operations in order to support hierarchic development and modular decomposition. That is, given only the specifications of components (not their implementations) one can deduce whether the components in a particular context will implement (or satisfy) some overall specification.

Now consider the following hierarchic development method, the so called *stepwise refinement method*: A specification, **SPEC**, of some desired nondeterministic or concurrent process has been given . The task is to find an implementable version of SPEC, **IMP**, s.t. IMP≡SPEC (≡ being the equivalence under consideration). Using the stepwise refinement method IMP is constructed in the following way. First decide on which process construction, C, to use and write down a subspecification, **SUBSPEC**, s.t. C[SUBSPEC]≡SPEC. Now find - using the stepwise refinement method recursively if SUBSPEC is not computationally feasible already - an implementation **SUBIMP** of SUBSPEC, i.e. SUBIMP≡SUBSPEC. Then taking IMP to be C[SUBIMP] will clearly give an implementation of SPEC under the assumption that ≡ is a congruence.

Looking carefully at the stepwise refinement method as stated above we notice that it requires SUBIMP and SUBSPEC to be proved congruent. I.e. interchangeable in *any* context and not just interchangeable in the context C in which they are actually going to be placed. We are therefore brought to prove more than what seems necessary. In order to reduce this work, we will *parameterize* the equivalence ≡ with *information* about contexts. The required proof of SUBIMP≡SUBSPEC can then be replaced by a proof of the more specific SUBIMP$\equiv_e$SUBSPEC, where e is information about the context C. Now assume that all the possible information relevant to parameterizing our equivalence ≡, is collected in a *domain of information I*. Then for any context C we may associate a subset, *Inf*(C), of *I* defined by:

$$e \in Inf(C) \overset{\Delta}{\Longleftrightarrow} \forall p,q \in P.\ p \equiv_e q \Rightarrow C[p] \equiv C[q]$$

where P is the set of processes. Thus any $e \in Inf(C)$ can be seen as *valid* information about C and can as such be used in the proof of $SUBIMP \equiv_e SUBSPEC$. However, not all $e \in Inf(C)$ contains the same amount of information about C. In particular if $e,f \in Inf(C)$ st. $\equiv_f \subseteq \equiv_e$, we would consider e as being more (or more accurate, not less) informative than f since e agrees more closely to the equivalence induced by C: namely that of "interchangeability in the context C". Thus we define the preorder $\propto$ on information as follows:

$$f \propto e \iff^{\Delta} \equiv_f \subseteq \equiv_e$$

We shall denote the opposite ordering of $\propto$ by $\sqsubseteq$, and read $e \sqsubseteq f$ as "f is at least as discriminating as e". Now define for any information $e \in I$ the set of contexts, $Con(e)$, of which e is valid information, ie.:

$$Con(e) = \{ C \mid e \in Inf(C) \}$$

Let us assume that the domain of information I does not exceed the expressive power of contexts, in the sense that incompatible information (under $\propto$) can be distinguished by some context C. Then the following is easily shown to hold:

$$e \sqsubseteq f \iff Con(e) \subseteq Con(f)$$

ie. e is at least as informative as f if and only if any context for which e is valid information f is also valid information. As such, if there exists an element Δ in I st. $\equiv_\Delta = \equiv$ then Δ will be a member of $Inf(C)$ for any context C, since $\equiv$ is a congruence. Thus Δ will be the maximal element under $\sqsubseteq$ or equivalently for all $e \in I$ $\equiv_\Delta \subseteq \equiv_e$.

Let us now return to the stepwise refinement method. As already mentioned SUBIMP may itself have been obtained by a stepwise refinement. Ie., for some context D, SUBIMP is D[SUBSUBIMP] where SUBSUBIMP is an implementation of SUBSUBSPEC with $D[SUBSUBSPEC] \equiv SUBSPEC$. However, by using the parameterized equivalence we only have to prove $SUBIMP \equiv_e SUBSPEC$ so the above can be replaced by taking SUBIMP as D[SUBSUBIMP], where $D[SUBSUBIMP] \equiv_e D[SUBSUBSPEC]$ and $D[SUBSUBSPEC] \equiv_e SUBSPEC$. When C is a context and e is information then we define $Inf^+(C,e) \subseteq I$ as:

$$d \in Inf^+(C,e) \iff^{\Delta} \forall p,q \in P.\ p \equiv_d q \Rightarrow C[p] \equiv_e C[q]$$

(Note, that Inf^+ generalize Inf since $Inf(C) = Inf^+(C,\Delta)$). Then, in order to obtain a proof of $D[SUBSUBIMP] \equiv_e D[SUBSUBSPEC]$ it should be enough to prove $SUBSUBIMP \equiv_d SUBSUBSPEC$ for some $d \in Inf^+(D,e)$.

So far we have tried to motivate the idea of parameterizing process equivalences with information about contexts, by indicating its use in the stepwise refinement method. However, much is still left vague by the above description. First of all, what is "information about contexts" and secondly, how is this information used in parameterizing existing equivalences? Once these two questions have been answered we must provide ways of deducing when some information e is *valid* about a context C or more general, when:

$$e \in Inf^+(C,d)$$

for a context C and information d. In case there exists a minimal discriminating (ie. minimal wrt $\sqsubseteq$ or equivalently maximal wrt $\propto$) element, $min(C,d)$, in $Inf^+(C,d)$, we can reduce the above problem to:

$$min(C,d) \sqsubseteq e$$

since $Inf^+(C,d)$ is upward closed under $\sqsubseteq$. Note, that with this reduction, the ordering $\sqsubseteq$ has become even more important. As an analogy to Dijkstra's *weakest precondition* , [2], we could term the element *min*(C,d) the *weakest inner information* of d under C, and view contexts as *weakest inner information transformers*. However we shall not pursue this analogy any further in this paper.

Instead we shall concentrate on parameterizing the bisimulation equivalence [11, 14] with a special type of information called *environments*. In section 2 we give a short description of how to view *processes* and their behaviour as *labelled transition systems.* We define and investigate the notions of *simulation* and *bisimulation* . In section 3 we introduce the concept of *environments* as elements of a labelled transition system and we define a parameterized version of the bisimulation equivalence. Section 4 contains our *Main Theorem*, giving an important and simple (ie. to state but not prove) characterization of the discrimination ordering, $\sqsubseteq$. Section 5 outlines a *Modal Characterization* of the parameterized bisimulation equivalence.

2. PROCESSES AND BISIMULATION EQUIVALENCE

In this section we give a short description of how to model processes and their operational behaviour by labelled transition systems. We define the notions of simulation and bisimulation and state those of their properties relevant for this paper. For a full treatment resp. a related notion we refer to [11, 14] resp. [10].

Let P be a set of objects which we may think of as *processes* or *agents*. Let A be a set of *atomic actions* and let $\rightarrow$ be a subset of P×A×P called the *derivation relation*. For $(p,a,q)\in\rightarrow$ we will usually write $p \xrightarrow{a} q$ which is to be interpreted "p may perform the action a and become q in doing so". Thus processes and their operational behaviour are described by the labelled transition system $\mathcal{P}=(P,A,\rightarrow)$ (For more information about labelled transition systems and how they can be used in giving operational semantics to programming languages see [9, 17]). Often we shall write $p \xrightarrow{a}$ as an abbreviation for $\exists q\in P.\ p \xrightarrow{a} q$. Thus $p \xrightarrow{a}$ reads "p may perform the action a".

Definition 2.1: A *simulation* R is a binary relation on P st. whenever pRq and $a\in A$ then

$$\text{(i)} \quad p \xrightarrow{a} p' \Rightarrow \exists q'.q \xrightarrow{a} q'.\ p'Rq'$$

A process q is said to simulate a process p if and only if there exists a simulation R with pRq. We write $p\leq q$. □

For $R\subseteq P^2$ let $\mathcal{S}(R)$ be the set of pairs (p,q) satisfying the clause (i) above. Then R is a simulation iff $R\subseteq\mathcal{S}(R)$, ie. iff R is a postfixpoint for $\mathcal{S}$. $\mathcal{S}$ is actually a monotonic endofunction on the complete lattice of binary relations under inclusion, and has as such a maximum fixpoint (which moreover is the maximum post fixpoint), which is simply $\leq$. This implies that $\leq$ itself is a simulation (the maximum). Now if $\mathcal{S}$ is *anticontinuous*, ie. for any decreasing sequence R_n of relations $\mathcal{S}(\cap_n R_n) = \cap_n \mathcal{S}(R_n)$, then we know from standard fixpoint theory that the maximum fixpoint, $\leq$, is given as $\cap_n \mathcal{S}^n(P^2)$. A (sufficient) condition for $\mathcal{S}$ to be anticontinuous is that the transition system $\mathcal{P}=(P,A,\rightarrow)$ is *imagefinite*, meaning that for all $p\in P$, $a\in A$ the set of a-derivatives of p, $\{p' \mid p \xrightarrow{a} p'\}$, is finite (see [7]).

Two processes, p and q, are considered equivalent if they have the same set of potential first actions and can remain having equal potentiality during the course of execution. This idea of equivalence is formalized by the following notion of *bisimulation* between processes (see [14, 16]).

Definition 2.2: A binary relation R on P is a *bisimulation* if and only if both R and $R^T = \{(q,p) \mid (p,q)\in R\}$ are simulations. Two processes, p and q, are said to be bisimulation equivalent if and only if there exists a bisimulation R with pRq. We write p~q. □

Let for $R\subseteq P^2$, $\mathcal{F}(R) = \mathcal{S}(R)\cap(\mathcal{S}(R^T))^T$. Then R is a bisimulation iff $R\subseteq\mathcal{F}(R)$. Since $\mathcal{S}$, $\cap$ and $\_^T$ are monotonic functions so is $\mathcal{F}$. As such $\mathcal{F}$ has a maximum postfixpoint, which is simply ~, implying that ~ itself is a bisimulation. ~ is moreover an equivalence relation and a congruence wrt. the CCS process constructing operations [11]. Since $\cap$ and $\_^T$ are anticontinuous $\mathcal{F}$ is anticontinuous if $\mathcal{P}$ is imagefinite.

Example 2.3: Let $\mathcal{P}$ be given by the diagrams below:

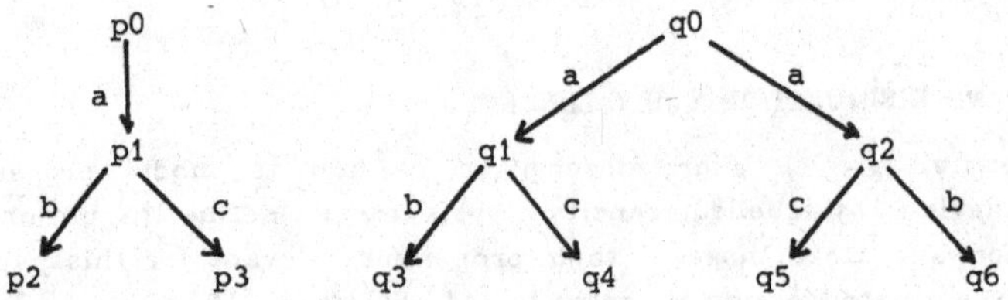

Then R={(p0,q0),(p1,q1),(p1,q2),(p2,q3),(p2,q6),(p3,q4),(p3,q5)} is a bisimulation with p0Rq0. Thus p0~q0. □

3. PARAMETERIZING THE BISIMULATION EQUIVALENCE

In this section we shall introduce the concept of environment and show how it can be used in parameterizing bisimulation equivalence.

The view we are taking is that an environment e is an object which *consumes* the actions produced by a process in it. However the environment's ability of consuming actions might be limited, so if $p \xrightarrow{a} p'$ but e cannot consume the action a then the derivation $p \xrightarrow{a} p'$ will never be considered when p is executed in the environment e. Similar to the assumption that a process may change after having performed/produced an action we will assume that an environment may change after having consumed an action. Thus environments and their behaviour can be described by a labelled transition system $\mathcal{E}=(E,A,\Rightarrow)$, where E is the set of environments, A is the set of actions (identical to the set of actions used in the transition system of processes) and $\Rightarrow$ is a subset of E×A×E called the *consumption relation*. $e \overset{a}{\Rightarrow} e'$ is to be read "e may consume the action a and in doing so become the environment e' ".

Now let us face the question of how to parameterize bisimulation equivalence with environments. Informally two processes, p and q, are considered equivalent in an environment e if they have the same set of potential first actions *that can be consumed by e* and they remain having equal potentiality during the course of execution *under all environment changes of e*. More formally we define the parameterized bisimulation equivalence as follows:

Definition 3.1: Let $\mathcal{E}=(E,A,\Longrightarrow)$ be a transition system of environments. Then an *$\mathcal{E}$-parameterized bisimulation*, R, is an E-indexed family of binary relations, $R_e \subseteq P^2$ for $e \in E$, st. whenever pR_eq and $e \overset{a}{\Longrightarrow} f$ then

(i) $p \overset{a}{\rightarrow} p' \Rightarrow \exists q'.q \overset{a}{\rightarrow} q' \wedge p'R_fq'$

(ii) $q \overset{a}{\rightarrow} q' \Rightarrow \exists p'.p \overset{a}{\rightarrow} p' \wedge p'R_fq'$

Two processes p and q are said to be bisimulation equivalent in an environment $e \in E$ if and only if there exists an $\mathcal{E}$-parameterized bisimulation, R, such that pR_eq. This we write $p \sim_e q$. □

To put this another way: whenever R is an E-indexed family of binary relations over P, let $\mathcal{F}(R)$ be the E-indexed family of binary relations over P, such that $\mathcal{F}(R)_e$ is the set of pairs (p,q) satisfying the clauses (i) and (ii) above whenever $e \overset{a}{\Longrightarrow} f$. Then R is an $\mathcal{E}$-parameterized bisimulation iff $R \subseteq \mathcal{F}(R)$ (ie. for all $e \in E$. $R_e \subseteq \mathcal{F}(R)_e$). $\mathcal{F}$ is actually a monotonic endofunction on the complete lattice of E-indexed families of binary relations ordered by (componentwise) inclusion. As such $\mathcal{F}$ has a maximum fixpoint. It is easily shown that the E-indexed family $\{\sim_e | e \in E\}$ equals this maximum fixpoint implying that $\{\sim_e | e \in E\}$ itself is an $\mathcal{E}$-parameterized bisimulation.

Theorem 3.2: For all $e \in E$, $\sim_e$ is an equivalence relation.
Proof: Show that the E-indexed family of relation ID, with ID_e being the identity relation on P, is an $\mathcal{E}$-parameterized bisimulation. Show that composition and converse of $\mathcal{E}$-parameterized bisimulations (composition and converse taken componentwise) are $\mathcal{E}$-parameterized bisimulations. The theorem will then follow from the definition of parameterized bisimulation equivalence. □

As indicated in the introduction $\sim_e$ is for all environments e a weaker (and thus perhaps easier to prove) equivalence than the original (unparameterized) bisimulation equivalence $\sim$.

Theorem 3.3: For all $e \in E$ and for all $p,q \in P$ $p \sim q$ implies $p \sim_e q$.
Proof: Take for all $e \in E$ $R_e = \sim$ and show that R is an $\mathcal{E}$-parameterized bisimulation. □

Example 3.4: Let $\mathcal{E}$ and $\mathcal{P}$ be given by the diagrams below:

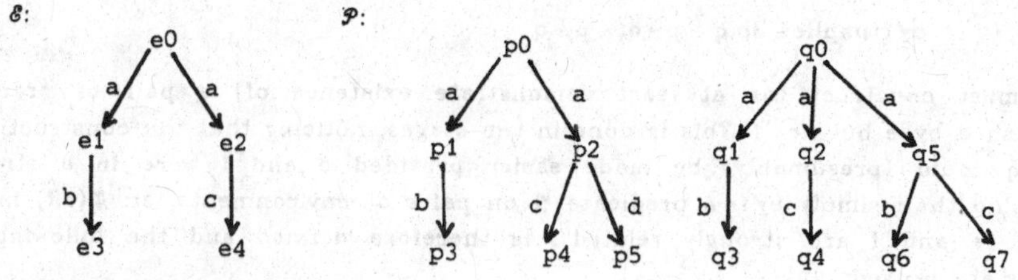

Then the E-indexed family R with:

$R_{e0} = \{(p0,q0)\}$
$R_{e1} = \{(p1,q1),(p2,q2),(p1,q5)\}$
$R_{e2} = \{((p2,q2),(p1,q1),(p2,q5)\}$
$R_{e3} = \{(p3,q0),p3,q3)\}$
$R_{e4} = \{(p4,q7),(p4,q4)\}$

is a parameterized bisimulation. Thus $p0 \sim_{e0} q0$. Note that $p0 \not\sim q0$. □

4. MAIN THEOREM

In this section we state our Main Theorem, which gives a very useful characterization of the discrimination ordering, $\sqsubseteq$. The theorem simply says that the discrimination ordering is nothing more than the *simulation ordering* form definition 2.1. Though easy to state the theorem was by no means easy to prove: only after several months search a proof was found. The fact that the discrimination ordering has this intuitively appealing characterization strengthen our belief in the naturalness of our definition of parameterized bisimulation equivalence. Let us restate the definition of the discrimination ordering.

Definition 4.1: Let $\mathcal{E}=(E,A,\Rightarrow)$ be an environment system and let $e,f\in E$. Then $e\sqsubseteq f$ if and only if $\sim_f\subseteq\sim_e$. □

In some environment systems there are minimal and maximal environments wrt. $\sqsubseteq$:

Lemma 4.2:
(i) If $e\in E$ such that for all $a\in A$ not $e\overset{a}{\Rightarrow}$ then e is a minimal environment wrt. $\sqsubseteq$. Actually $\sim_e=P^2$.
(ii) If $e\in E$ such that for all $a\in A$ $e\overset{a}{\Rightarrow}e$ then e is a maximal environment wrt. $\sqsubseteq$. Moreover $\sim_e=\sim$. □

However we can say much more about $\sqsubseteq$ as stated in the following *Main Theorem*:

Theorem 4.3: If $\mathcal{E}$ and $\mathcal{P}$ are imagefinite transition systems and $\mathcal{P}$ contains $\mathcal{E}$ and is closed under action prefixing and finite sums then for all environments e and f:

$$e \sqsubseteq f \quad \text{iff} \quad e \leq f \qquad \square$$

Since the full proof is rather long we shall just outline the proof strategy. The full proof will appear in an extended version of this paper.

Proof Strategy:
"$\Leftarrow$": Prove that the E-indexed relation, R, with $R_e = \{(p,q) \mid \exists f.\ e\leq f \wedge p\sim_f q\}$ is a bisimulation. Then if $e\leq f$ and $p\sim_f q$ we have $pR_e q$ and therefore $p\sim_e q$.
"$\Rightarrow$": This is the hard direction. We must prove $e\not\leq f$ implies $e\not\sqsubseteq f$ or equivalently:

$$(1) \qquad e\not\leq f \text{ implies } \exists p,q.\ \ p\sim_f q \wedge p\not\sim_e q$$

ie. we must construct (or at least demonstrate existence of) a pair of processes distinguished by e but not f. This is done in two stages, noticing that the construction of p and q could (presumably) be made easier provided e and f were in a stronger relationship than simply $e\not\leq f$. A predicate $\mathfrak{P}$ on pairs of environments, st. $\mathfrak{P}(e,f)$ implies $e\not\leq f$ and "e and f are strongly related", is therefore defined and the following two theorems are proved:

$$(2) \qquad e\not\leq f \text{ implies } \exists e',f'.\ \ e'\leq e \wedge f\leq f' \wedge \mathfrak{P}(e',f')$$

$$(3) \qquad \mathfrak{P}(e,f) \text{ implies } \exists p,q.\ \ p\sim_f q \wedge p\not\sim_e q$$

Since $\leq\subseteq\sqsubseteq$ is already known (2) and (3) trivially implies (1). In this strategy the choice of $\mathfrak{P}$ is the crucial factor. On the one hand, we want $\mathfrak{P}$ as strong as possible, in order to make the construction in (3) as easy as possible (from past experience this rules out the simple choice of $\mathfrak{P}(e,f)=e\not\leq f$). On the other hand $\mathfrak{P}$ cannot be too strong since (2) is required to hold. □

The statement of the theorem - at least as far as the present proof is concerned - requires both $\mathcal{P}$ and $\mathcal{E}$ to be imagefinite. Also the set of processes must be "sufficiently rich". Clearly if the set of processes is empty the theorem is not valid in general (especially not the "⟹"-direction). (For an operational semantics of action prefixing and finite sums see [11]). A natural next step would be to generalize the theorem to include the imageinfinite cases as well. However, we have proved that a simple generalization of the predicate $\mathfrak{D}$ to include imageinfinite environments fails to generalize the present proof. Thus a new predicate $\mathfrak{D}$ with the properties (2) and (3) or a totally new technique will be needed.

Example 4.5: Let e and f be environments with the following behaviour:

e:

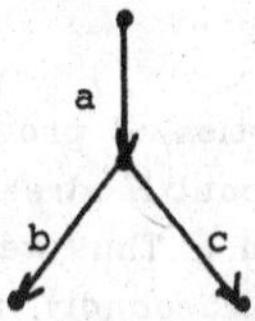

f:

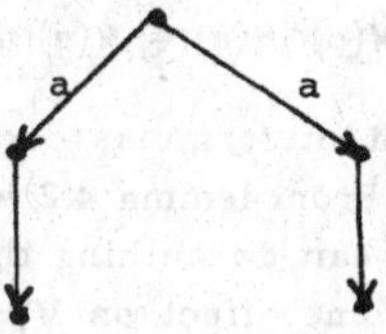

then $e \not\leq f$. Also $\mathfrak{D}(e,f)$. Let p and q be processes with the following behaviour:

p:

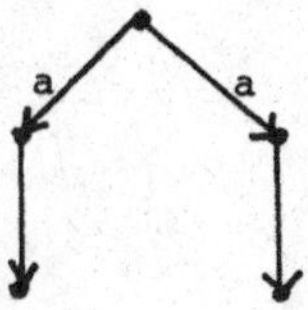

q:

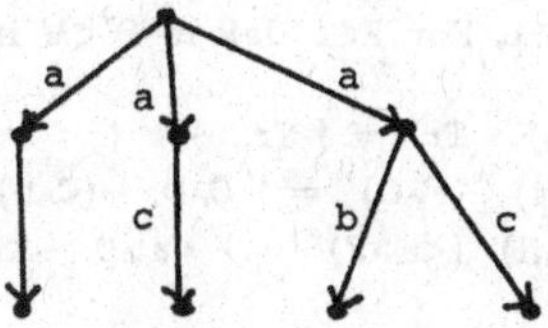

then $p \sim_f q$ but $p \not\sim_e q$. p and q are actually the two processes that will be constructed by the proof of theorem 4.4. □

5. MODAL CHARACTERIZATION

In this section we present a modal characterization of the environment parameterized bisimulation equivalence pointed out to us by Colin Stirling. First we recall some standard characterization results from [7]:

Let the modal language M be the least set of formulas such that:

(i) $Tr \in M$
(ii) $F,G \in M \Rightarrow F \wedge G \in M$
(iii) $F \in M \Rightarrow \neg F \in M$
(iv) $a \in A,\ F \in M \Rightarrow \langle a \rangle F \in M$

Let L be the sublanguage of M consisting of the formulas not containing $\neg$. The *satisfaction relation* $\models \subseteq P \times M$ is the least relation such that:

(i) $p \models Tr$ for all $p \in P$
(ii) $p \models F \wedge G$ iff $p \models F$ and $p \models G$
(iii) $p \models \neg F$ iff not $p \models F$

(iv) $p \models \langle a \rangle F$ iff $\exists p'.\ p \xrightarrow{a} p' \wedge p' \models F$

Now define for $p \in P$ the sets of formulas:

$$\mathcal{M}(p) = \{ F \in \mathcal{M} \mid p \models F \}$$
$$\mathcal{L}(p) = \{ F \in \mathcal{L} \mid p \models F \}$$

Then, provided $\mathcal{P}$ is imagefinite, we have the following characterization results [7]:

(A) $p \sim q$ iff $\mathcal{M}(p) = \mathcal{M}(q)$
(B) $p \leq q$ iff $\mathcal{L}(p) \subseteq \mathcal{L}(q)$

Now, $p \sim_e q$ means that the behaviours of p and q are equivalent "relative" to e. Hence, bearing the characterization result A in mind, we would expect a characterization of $\sim_e$ to be of the form:

$$p \sim_e q \text{ iff } \mathcal{M}(p) \cap \mathcal{H}(e) = \mathcal{M}(q) \cap \mathcal{H}(e)$$

where $\mathcal{H}(e)$ is a set of formulas corresponding to properties of processes which can be examined under e. From lemma 4.2 we know two things about $\mathcal{H}$ already. First, if e is the environment which can do nothing then $p \sim_e q$ for all p and q. Thus we expect $\mathcal{H}(e)$ in this case to have the same effect on $\mathcal{M}(p)$ for all processes p. Secondly, if e is the universal environment (ie. capable of reproducing itself under all actions), then $p \sim_e q$ iff $p \sim q$. Thus, we expect $\mathcal{H}(e) = \mathcal{M}$ in this case. We now offer $\mathcal{H}$.

Definition 5.1: For $F \in \mathcal{L}$ define $F^+ \subseteq \mathcal{M}$ inductively as:

(i) $Tr^+ = \{ Tr, \neg Tr \}$
(ii) $(F \wedge G)^+ = \{ C \wedge D, \neg(C \wedge D) \mid C \in F^+ \text{ and } D \in G^+ \}$
(iii) $(\langle a \rangle F)^+ = \{ \langle a \rangle C, \neg \langle a \rangle C \mid c \in F^+ \}$ □

Thus, F^+ is simply the set of formulas derived form F by inserting arbitrary negations. We extend $(\_)^+$ to sets of $\mathcal{L}$-formulaes by defining for $X \subseteq \mathcal{L}$ $X^+ = \{G \mid \exists F \in X.\ G \in F^+\}$. We can now state the Modal Characterization Theorem:

Theorem 5.2: Provided $\mathcal{E}$ and $\mathcal{P}$ are imagefinite transition systems then for all $p,q \in P$ and $e \in E$:

$$p \sim_e q \text{ iff } \mathcal{M}(p) \cap \mathcal{L}(e)^+ = \mathcal{M}(q) \cap \mathcal{L}(e)^+ \ \square$$

Hence, the set $\mathcal{H}(e)$ is simply $\mathcal{L}(e)^+$. Intuitively this seems correct since $\mathcal{L}(e)^+$ only contains formulas based on what e can perform and thus detect. It also matchs the two things we know already. If e is the empty environment then $\mathcal{L}(e)^+ = \{Tr, \neg Tr, Tr \wedge Tr, Tr \wedge \neg Tr, \ldots\}$ and if e is the universal environment then $\mathcal{L}(e) = \mathcal{L}$ and therefore clearly $\mathcal{L}(e)^+ = \mathcal{M}$. We now outline the proof of theorem 5.2:

Proof:
"$\Rightarrow$": Suppose $p \sim_e q$. We prove by induction on $F \in \mathcal{M}$ that $F \in \mathcal{M}(p) \cap \mathcal{L}(e)^+$ iff $F \in \mathcal{M}(q) \cap \mathcal{L}(e)^+$. We consider only the cases $F = \neg G$ and $F = \langle a \rangle G$ leaving the two simpler cases to the reader:

<u>$F = \neg G$:</u> If $\neg G \in \mathcal{M}(p) \cap \mathcal{L}(e)^+$ an easy argument shows that $G \in \mathcal{L}(e)^+$ and $G \notin \mathcal{M}(p)$. Thus $G \notin \mathcal{M}(p) \cap \mathcal{L}(e)^+$ and therefore by the induction hypothesis $G \notin \mathcal{M}(q) \cap \mathcal{L}(e)^+$. Since $G \in \mathcal{L}(e)^+$ $G \notin \mathcal{M}(q)$ and thus $\neg G \in \mathcal{M}(q)$. Hence, $\neg G \in \mathcal{M}(q) \cap \mathcal{L}(e)^+$.

$F=\langle a\rangle G$: If $\langle a\rangle G\in M(p)\cap L(e)^+$ an easy argument shows that there exists a $C\in L$ such that $\langle a\rangle C\in L(e)$ and $G\in C^+$. Hence $e\overset{a}{\Rightarrow}e'$ with $e'\models C$ for some e'. Also $p\overset{a}{\rightarrow}p'$ with $p'\models G$ for some p'. However, $p\sim_e q$. Hence $q\overset{a}{\rightarrow}q'$ with $p'\sim_{e'}q'$ for some q'. We know $G\in C^+\subseteq L(e')^+$ and $G\in M(p')$. So by induction hypothesis $G\in M(q')$. Hence $\langle a\rangle G\in M(q)$ and finally $\langle a\rangle G\in M(q)\cap L(e)^+$.

"$\Leftarrow$": We show that the E-indexed family R with:

$$R_e = \{ (p,q) \mid M(p)\cap L(e)^+ = M(q)\cap L(e)^+ \}$$

is a parameterized bisimulation. Assume not. Then for some e, p and q pR_eq but:

$$e\overset{a}{\Rightarrow}e' \text{ and } p\overset{a}{\rightarrow}p' \text{ and } \forall q'.\ q\overset{a}{\rightarrow}q' \Rightarrow \neg(p'R_{e'}q')$$

Using the image finiteness assumption for $\mathcal{P}$ let $\{q_1,\dots,q_n\} = \{q' \mid q\overset{a}{\rightarrow}q'\}$. If this set is empty $\langle a\rangle Tr\in M(p)\cap L(e)^+$ but $\langle a\rangle Tr\notin M(q)\cap L(e)^+$, contradicting pR_eq. Otherwise $\exists A_1,\dots,A_n\in M$ and $\exists B_1,\dots B_n\in L$ such that:

(i) $\forall i.\ A_i\in B_i^+$
(ii) $\forall i.\ B_i\in L(e')$
(iii) $\forall i.\ p'\models A_i$ and $q_i\not\models A_i$

Clearly $B_1\wedge..\wedge B_n\in L(e')$ and by definition $A_1\wedge\dots\wedge A_n\in(B_1\wedge..\wedge B_n)^+$. We know $p\models\langle a\rangle(A_1\wedge..\wedge A_n)$ whereas $q\not\models\langle a\rangle(A_1\wedge..\wedge A_n)$. Moreover $\langle a\rangle(B_1\wedge..\wedge B_n)\in L(e)$ and $\langle a\rangle(A_1\wedge..\wedge A_n)\in(\langle a\rangle(B_1\wedge..\wedge B_n))^+$. However this contradicts pR_eq. □

Example 5.3: Let e, p and q be given as in example 4.5. Then $\langle a\rangle(\langle b\rangle Tr \wedge \langle c\rangle Tr) \in M(q)\cap L(e)^+$ but not $\langle a\rangle(\langle b\rangle Tr \wedge \langle c\rangle Tr) \in M(p)$. Thus $p\not\sim_e q$. □

6. CONCLUSION

In this paper we have presented an environment parameterized version of the bisimulation equivalence [11, 14]. As a Main Theorem we have proved that the discrimination ordering between environments is nothing more than the wellknown simulation ordering. This theorem will be of great significance for the future work in this area as pointed out in the introduction. To give a further indication of the Main Theorem's importance, consider a future complete proof system for $\sim_e$. We would naturally expect such a system to have an inference rule of the form:

$$\frac{e\sqsubseteq f \qquad p\sim_f q}{p\sim_e q}$$

However, from our Main Theorem we know that $e\sqsubseteq f$ iff $e\leq f$ and $\leq$ should be relatively straigthforeward to axiomatize. Thus, we can hope for a genuine complete proof system and not "just" a relative one. As pointed out in section 4 one problem still remains open: the extension of the Main Theorem to include image infinite process and environment systems. However the Main Theorem seems to generalize directly to a parameterized version of the *weak bisimulation equivalence* [11, 14]. Finally we presented a Modal Characterization of the parameterized bisimulation equivalence. Due to the intuitively appealing characterization of $\sqsubseteq$ and the simple Modal Characterization of $\sim_e$ we fell confident about the naturalness of our definition of parameterized bisimulation equivalence.

ACKNOWLEDGEMENTS: The author would like to thank Robin Milner and Colin Stirling for many interesting discussions and for their constant support during the long period of search for a proof of the Main Theorem. Also thanks to Colin Stirling for pointing out the Modal Characterization in secton 5.

REFERENCES

1. Brookes, S. D. and Rounds, W. C. "Behavioural Equivalence relations induced by programming logics." *LNCS* 154 (1983).

2. Dijkstra. *Series in Automatic Computation*. Volume : *A discipline of programming*. Prentice-Hall, 1976.

3. Graf, S. and Sifakis, J. A Modal Characterization of observational congruence on finite terms of CCS. Tech. Rept. Technical Report no. 402, IMAG, 1983. To appear in ICALP'84

4. Hennessy, M. and Plotkin, G. D. "A term Model for CCS." *LNCS* 88 (1980). Proceedings of 9th MFCS Conference

5. Hennessy, M. A Term model for Synchronous Processes. Tech. Rept. CSR-77-81, University of Edinburgh, Department of Computer Science, 1981.

6. Hennessy, M. and Milner, R. "On Observing Nondeterminism and Concurrency." *LNCS* 85 (1980). Proceedings of 7th ICALP

7. Hennessy, M. and Milner, R. Algebraic Laws for Nondeterminism and Concurrency. Tech. Rept. CSR-133-83, University of Edinburgh, Department of Computer Science, 1983. To appear in JACM

8. Hoare, C.A.R., Brookes, S.D. and Roscoe, A.W. A Theory of Communicating Sequential Processes. Tech. Rept. PRG-16, Oxford University Computing Laboratory, Programming Research group, 1981.

9. Keller, R. "A fundamental theorem of asynchronous parallel computation." *Parallel Processing* , (1975). Ed. T: Feng, Springer Verlag

10. Milner, R. "An Algebraic Definition of Simulation between Programs." *in: Proc. 2nd International Conference on Artificial Intelligence* (1971).

11. Milner, R. "A Calculus of Communicating Systems." *LNCS* 92 (1980).

12. Milner, R. "A modal characterisation of observable machine-behaviour." *LNCS* 112 (1981).

13. Milner, R. "A Complete Inference System for a Class of Regular Behaviours." *CSR*-111-82 (1982). University of Edinburgh, Department of Computer Science

14. Milner, R. "Calculi for Synchrony and Asynchrony." *Theoretical Computer Science* 25 (1983), 267-310.

15. Nicola, R. de and Hennessy, M. Testing Equivalences for Processes. Tech. Rept. SCR-123-82, University of Edinburgh, Department of Computer Science, 1982.

16. Park, D.J. "Concurrency and Automata on Infinite Sequences." *LNCS* 104 (1981).

17. Plotkin, Gordon D. A Structural Approach to Operational Semantics. Tech. Rept. DAIMI FN-19, Computer Science Department, Aarhus University, Denmark, September, 1981.

18. Stirling, C. A Proof Theoretic Characterization of Observational Equivalence. Tech. Rept. CSR-132-83, University of Edinburgh, Department of Computer Science, 1983. In Proceedings FCT-TCS Bangalore (1983), To appear in TCS

19. Stirling, C. A Complete Modal Proof System for a Subset of SCCS. To appear in CAAP'85

20. Stirling, C. A Complete Modal Proof System for a Subset of CCS. To appear

LOWER BOUNDS BY KOLMOGOROV-COMPLEXITY (Extended Abstract)

Ming Li*
Department of Computer Science
Cornell University
Ithaca, New York 14853

Abstract
Using Kolmogorov-complexity, we obtain the following new lower bounds.

For on-line nondeterministic Turing machines,

(1) simulating 2 pushdown stores by 1 tape requires $\Omega(n^{1.5}/logn)$ time; together with a newly proved $O(n^{1.5}\sqrt{logn})$ upper bound [L3], this basically settled the open problem 1 in [DGPR] for 1 tape vs. 2 push-down case (the case of 1 tape vs 2 tapes was basically settled by [M]);

(2) simulating 1 queue by 1 tape requires $\Omega(n^{4/3}/logn)$ time; this brings us closer to a newly proved $O(n^{1.5}\sqrt{logn})$ upper bound [L3];

(3) simulating 2 tapes by 1 tape requires $\Omega(n^2/lognloglogn)$ time; this is a minor improvement of [M]'s $\Omega(n^2/log^2nloglogn)$ lower bound; it is also claimed (full proof contained in [L3]) that the actual languages used in [M] (also here) and [F] do not yield $\Omega(n^2)$ lower bound.

To cope with an open question of [GS] of whether a k-head 1-way DFA (k-DFA) can do string matching, we develop a set of techniques and show that 3-DFA cannot do string matching, settling the case $k=3$. Some other related lower bounds are also presented.

1. Introduction

Obtaining good lower bounds has been one of the most important issues in theoretical computer science. This paper represents a continuous effort in searching for good lower bounds by means of Kolmogorov-complexity (K-complexity). Some important open questions are answered (or partially answered) and new techniques are developed along with the solution of each problem.

In the traditional lower bound proofs, complicated counting arguments are usually involved. The messy counting arguments blur the essence of the problem, increase the level of difficulty, and therefore limit our ability to understand and obtain better lower bounds. However, the beauty of simplicity and intuition is brought back in the lower bound proofs by a recently discovered tool, the K-complexity. The concept of K-complexity was independently introduced by Kolmogorov [K] and Chaitin [Cha]. The use of K-complexity as a tool in lower bound proofs was first introduced by Barzdin and Paul [P]. Since then, many interesting results have been obtained (e.g. [P1], [P2], [PSS], [RS1]).

Definition 1.1: The *K-complexity* of a finite string X, written as $K(X)$, is the size of the smallest TM (may be nondeterministic) which, starting from empty input tape, prints X.

Definition 1.2: The *K-complexity* of X, relative to string Y, written as $K(X|Y)$, is the length of smallest TM (deterministic or nondeterministic), with Y as its extra information, that *accepts* (or *prints*) only X.

Definition 1.3: String X is *random* if $K(X) \geq |X|-1$. String X is *random relative* to string Y if $K(X|Y) \geq |X|-log|Y|$.

Fact 1: More than half of the finite binary strings are random.

Fact 2: If $X=uvw$, and X is random, then $K(v|uw) \geq |v|-log|X|$. That is, random strings are locally almost random.

Fact 3: If F is any formal system, X is random and $|X| >> |F|$, then it is not provable in F that '*X is random*'.

The paper is organized as follows: in Section 2 we prove new lower bounds (and present new upper bounds) for on-line computations; in Section 3 we obtain lower bounds on string matching. Many proofs we omitted (due to space limitation) may be found in [L2]. This paper will concentrate on lower bound proofs, the proofs for all the upper bounds claimed will appear in a companion paper [L3].

---

* This work was supported in part by an NSF grant DCR-8301766.

2. Lower bounds for on-line computation

In this Section we consider on-line computations which are generally used for investigating the dependency of the computational power on the number of tapes. We call a TM M a k-tape *on-line* machine if M has a 1-way read only input tape and k work tapes. Without explicit indication, all the machines in this section will be on-line machines. An on-line machine M works in *real time* if each time M reads an input symbol it makes only a constant number of moves. A k-pushdown machine is like a usual pushdown automaton, but has k pushdown stores. Similarly, a k-queue machine has k (first in first out) queues instead of k-pushdowns.

One classical question about TM's is how much power an additional work tape gives a machine. For real time deterministic computations, early in 1963, Rabin [R] proved 2 tapes are better than 1. Eleven years later Aanderaa [A] generalized Rabin's result to $k+1$ versus k. In 1982, Duris and Galil [DG] proved, by the crossing sequence technique, that two tapes are better than one in the nondeterministic case. In 1982 Paul [P] proved, using Kolmogorov-complexity, that on-line simulation of $k+1$ tapes by k tapes requires $\Omega(n(logn)^{1/k+1})$ time. Duris, Galil, Paul, and Reischuk [DGPR] later proved that for nondeterministic machines simulating 2 tapes by 1 tape requires $\Omega(nlogn)$ time and simulating k tapes by k pushdown stores requires $\Omega(nlog^{1/(k+1)}n)$ time (for deterministic machines). The following open questions (open problems 1 and 6) were listed in [DGPR]: Can the gaps between the Hartmanis-Stearns [HS] $O(n^2)$ upper bound and the $\Omega(nlogn)$ lower bound in both deterministic case and nondeterministic case for 1 tape simulating k tapes (pushdowns) can be narrowed? Notice that according to [HS1], 2 tapes can deterministically simulate k tapes in time $tlogt$; and according to [BGW] 2 tapes can nondeterministically simulate k tapes without losing any time. For deterministic on-line machines Maass [M], the author [L], and Vitanyi [V] independently proved: it requires $\Omega(n^2)$ time to deterministically simulate 2 tapes (pushdown stores) with 1 tape. (Note, a preliminary $\Omega(n^{2-\epsilon})$ lower bound of Maass antidates both of [L] and [V].) This settled the deterministic case (open question 6 in [DGPR]). In addition, Vitanyi [V] also obtained an $\Omega(n^2)$ lower bound for 1 tape simulating 1 queue. In the nondeterministic case, the situation is quite different: Maass obtained an $\Omega(n^2/log^2nloglogn)$ lower bound for 1 tape vs 2 tapes via a ingenious language and a nice combinatorial lemma, but it does not apply to 1 tape vs 2 pushdown case.

In this section we try to complete our knowledge on nondeterministic case of above open question. An $\Omega(n^{1.5}/logn)$ optimal lower bound, which is obtained in parallel to above deterministic results, is presented for the 1 tape vs 2 pushdown store question. This greatly improves the $\Omega(nlogn)$ bound of [DGPR]. It is optimal because of a recently discovered new simulation by the author that shows unexpectedly: 1 nondeterministic tape can simulate 2 pushdown stores, or 1 queue in time $O(n^{1.5}\sqrt{logn})$ [L3]. (Here is an upper bound that is stimulated by the lower bound research.) We will also obtain an $\Omega(n^{4/3}/logn)$ lower bound for 1 tape nondeterministically simulating 1 queue, which is the first lower bound in this case. For the case of 1 tape versus 2 tapes, we improve the Maass' lower bound to $n^2/lognloglogn$. Unlike above results, this result is based on on Maass' proof. Surprisingly, we claim that that the actual language used by [M] (and a similar language, in a different context but for the same purpose, used by Freivalds [F] seven years ago) can be accepted by a one tape machine in $O(\frac{n^2loglogn}{\sqrt{logn}})$ time. Therefore the $\Omega(n^2)$ lower bound, whose existence we doubt, needs a new language.

Throughout this paper, variables X, Y, x_i, y_i ... denote strings in Σ^* for $\Sigma=\{0,1\}$. Consider a 1-tape on-line machine M. We call M's input tape head h_1, and its work tape head h_2.

Definition 2.1: Let x_i be a block of input, and R be a region on the work tape. We say that M *maps* x_i *into* R if while h_1 is reading x_i h_2 never goes out of region R; We say M maps x_i *onto* R if in addition h_2 travels the *entire* region R while h_1 reads x_i.

A crossing sequence (c.s.) for a point on the work tape of M is a sequence of ID's, where each ID is of form (state of M, h_1's position). We write $|c.s.|$ to mean the space needed to represent the c.s.

Remark 2.1: Since h_1 only moves to the right, we can represent the *ith ID* (ID_i) in a c.s. as follows:

ID_i=(state of M, current h_1's position − h_1's position of ID_{i-1}),

where ID_0=(−,0). Thus if a c.s. has d ID's and the input length is n, then $|c.s.| \le d|M| + logk_1 + ... + logk_d$, with $\sum_{i=1}^{d} k_i = n$. This is less than $d|M| + dlog(n/d)$ by a standard calculation (i.e. maximize the function).

Remark 2.2: Let $x_1, \ldots, x_k$ be blocks of equal length C on the input tape. Suppose d of these blocks are deleted, and that we want to represent the remaining blocks in the smallest space possible but still remember their relative distances. We can use following representation,

$$m\bar{x}_1\bar{x}_2 \cdots \bar{x}_k(p_1,d_1)(p_2,d_2)....$$

where m is the number of (non-empty) $\bar{x}_i$'s; $\bar{x}_i$ is x_i if it is not deleted, and is empty string otherwise; (p_i,d_i) indicates that the next p_i consecutive x_k's (of length C) are one group (adjacent to each other), and followed by a gap of d_iC long. m, the p_i's, and the d_i's are self-delimited. (A string x is self-delimited if each bit of x is doubled and with '01' at both ends. For instance, 01001100111101 is the self-delimited version of 01011.) By a standard calculation (similar to Remark 2.1), the space needed is $\sum_{i=1}^{k} |\bar{x}_i| + dlog(n/d)$.

We now prove an intuitively straightforward lemma which coincides with our intuition that a small region with short c.s.'s around it cannot hold a lot of information. Stated formally:

Jamming Lemma: Suppose on input beginning $x_1x_2 \cdots x_k\#$ ..., where the x_i's have equal length, M maps each of $x_{i_1}, \cdots, x_{i_l}$ into region R by the time h_1 reaches # sign. Then the contents of the work tape of M at that time can be reconstructed by using only $\{x_1, \cdots, x_k\}-\{x_{i_1},...,x_{i_l}\}$, the contents of R, and the two c.s.'s on the left and right boundaries of R.

Remark 2.3: Roughly speaking, if $\sum_{j=1}^{l} |x_{i_j}| > 2(|R|+2|c.s.|+|M|)$, then the Jamming Lemma implies the either $X=x_1...x_k$ is not random or some information about X has been lost.

Proof of Jamming Lemma: Name the two positions at the left boundary and the right boundary of R to be l and r, respectively. We now simulate M. Put input $\{x_1,...,x_k\}-\{x_{i_1},...,x_{i_l}\}$ at their correct positions on the input tape (as indicated by the c.s.'s). Run M with h_2 staying to the left of R: whenever h_2 reaches point l, the left boundary of R, we interrupt M (in the nondeterministic case we also match the current state and h_1 position) and consider the next ID in the c.s. at point l, using this we relocate h_1, adjust state of M and then go on running M. After we finish at the left of R, we do the same thing at the right of R. Finally we put the contents of R into region R. Notice that although there are many empty regions on the input tape corresponding to those unknown x_i's, h_1 never reads those regions because h_2 never goes into R. □ (Jamming Lemma)

Remark 2.4: If M is nondeterministic, then we need to rephrase 'contents of work tape' as 'legal contents of work tape' which simply means some computation path on the same input would create this work tape contents.

Define $L=\{x_1\$x_0\$x_2\$x_0 \cdots \$x_t\$x_0\#x_1x_2 \cdots x_t \mid x_i \in \{0,1\}^* \text{ for } i=0,...,t\}$.

Theorem 2.1: It requires $\Omega(n^{1.5}/logn)$ time to nondeterministically simulate 2 pushdown stores by 1 tape.

The theorem will follow from Lemma 2.1. We shall concentrate on explaining the ideas of the proof.

Lemma 2.1: It requires $\Omega(n^{1.5}/logn)$ time to accept L by any 1-tape nondeterministic on-line machine.

Proof of Lemma 2.1: Suppose a nondeterministic 1-tape M accepts L in time $o(n^{1.5}/logn)$. We fix a large n and a large constant C such that all the subsequent formulas are meaningful.

Fix a random string X of length n. Equally partition X into $x_0x_1 \cdots x_k$, where $k=n^{1/2}/Clogn$. Consider input $Y=x_1\$x_0\$x_2\$x_0 \cdots \$x_k\$x_0\#x_1x_2 \cdots x_k$ to M. Observe that $|Y|<3n$. M should accept this input Y. Let us fix a *shortest* accepting computation P of M on input Y. We shall show that P is long.

Consider the k pairs $x_i\$x_0\$$ in Y. If half of them are mapped *onto* some regions of sizes larger than n/C^3, then M uses time $O(n^{1.5}/logn)$, a contradiction. Thus in the following we will assume that for more than half of the above such pairs, M maps each into some region of size $\leq n/C^3$. Let S be the set of such pairs. When h_1 gets to # sign, we consider two cases:

Case 1: (Jammed) Assume there do not exist two pairs in S that are mapped into 2 regions n/C^2 apart. In this case, it is clear that all the pairs in S are mapped into a region R of size $3n/C^2$, since every pair in S is mapped into a region of size $\leq n/C^3$. Consider the two regions R_l and R_r of length $|R|$, left and right neighboring to R respectively. Find a point l in R_l and a point r in R_r with shortest c.s. in R_l and R_r, respectively. If either of the two c.s.'s is of length more than $n^{0.5}/C^4logn$ then M uses $O(n^{1.5}/logn)$ time. If they are both shorter than $n^{0.5}/C^4logn$, then the Jamming Lemma can be applied. We can reconstruct the contents of the work tape at the time when h_1 gets to # sign by a short program. By Jamming Lemma, the construction only requires the following information:

(1) $\{x_0, x_1, \cdots, x_k\}-\{x_i \mid x_i x_0 \in S\}$, which, by Remark 2.2, requiring less than $2|X|/3$ space;

(2) two c.s.'s that require lees than $|X|^{1/2}$ space; and

(3) the tape contents of regions R, R_l, and R_r which requires no more than $9|X|/C^2$ (note $C>>9$) space.

We then find X as follows: for each Y such that $|Y|=|X|$, equally divide $Y=y_0y_1 \cdots y_k$ as dividing X. Check if $y_0=x_0$. Attach $y_1 \cdots y_k$ after # sign and continue to simulate M with the work tape constructed as above; M accepts iff $Y=X$. This program is short, showing $K(X)<|X|$. One might worry about the nondeterminism here, but notice that the nondeterminism is also defined in the K-complexity, and we can simply simulate M nondeterministically in the above, making sure that the c.s.'s are matched.

Case 2: (not Jammed) Assume there are two pairs, say $x_i\$x_0$ and $x_j\$x_0$, that are mapped n/C^2 apart, that is, the distance between the two regions *onto* which these two pairs mapped is $\geq n/C^2$. Let R_0 be the region between above two regions. Hence $|R_0| \geq n/C^2$. As before we search for a shortest c.s in R_0. If the shortest c.s. is longer than $n^{1/2}/C^3logn$, then M runs for $O(n^{1.5}/logn)$ time. Otherwise we record this short c.s. and try to reconstruct x_0 in below. But notice that a simple minded approach such as finding a shortest c.s. in the middle is not enough here, because some other x_0's can be mapped on both side of the c.s.

To overcome above difficulty, observe that since the size of shortest c.s. is $n^{1/2}/C^3 \log n$ there can only be this many bits in x_0 that are mapped to both sides of the c.s. From this observation, we reconstruct x_0 as below.

(1) In each *ID* of the shortest c.s., we add a bit which specifies the current bit read by h_1. Fortunately, this does not cause the increase of c.s. size: for the c.s. of length $n^{1/2}/C^3 \log n$, less than $2n^{1/2}/C^3$ space is needed by Remark 2.1.

(2) For each Y such that $Y=X$, we equally divide $Y=y_0 y_1 \cdots y_k$. Check if $y_i=x_i$ for all $i>0$. If not, then $Y \neq X$; otherwise, arrange y_i's in their corresponding positions on the input tape.

(3) Simulate M only at the left of the shortest c.s. Every time h_2 meets the c.s., M check if the current *ID* matches the current state of M (including the bit added in (1)), and then take the next *ID* continuing the simulation. $Y=X$ iff the simulation ends with everything coincides.

The above program uses the information of $x_1, \cdots, x_k$ and the c.s. which needs less than $|x_0|/2$ space to represent. This contradicts the relative randomness of x_0. □ (Lemma 2.1)

Proof of Theorem 2.1: The language L can be easily accepted by a two tape machine. For two pushdown stores, we modify L: reverse $x_1 x_2 ... x_k$ following # sign. The modified L can be accepted by $\overline{M}$ with two pushdown stores in linear time as follows: put x_1 in stack1, put next x_0 in stack1 and in stack2, put x_2 in stack2, put next x_0 in stack1 and stack2, and x_3 in stack1, ..., and so on. When the input head reads to #, $\overline{M}$ starts to match in an obvious way. To make this process real time we further modify L by simply putting a $1^{2|x_0|}$ padding after every other reversed x_i. Since all these changes do not hurt our lower bound proof in Lemma 2.1, the proof is complete. □ (Theorem 2.1)

Combined with Theorem A below recently proved in [L3], we essentially close the gap for 1 tape vs 2 pushdown stores, answering the open question 1 of [DGPR].

Theorem A: 2 pushdown stores or 1 queue can be simulated by 1 nondeterministic tape in $O(n^{1.5}\sqrt{\log n})$ time (for both on-line and off-line machines). (The proof is contained in [L3].)

Theorem 2.2: It requires $\Omega(n^{4/3}/\log n)$ time to nondeterministically simulate 1 queue by 1 tape.

Idea of the Proof: At first glance, one might think the language L in above can be used (and therefore an $\Omega(n^{1.5}/\log n)$ optimal lower bound). Unfortunately, with a second thought, a 1 queue machine probably has no way to accept L in linear time. But if you persist, the following observation can be made. If $|x_0|=n^{1/3}$, and $|x_{i\geq 1}|=n^{2/3}$, then 1 queue machine can accept in linear time on the condition that it could *count fast*. How does a queue count fast? Probably no way. But this leads us to the following language

$$L_{pad}=\{x_1 x_0 x_2 x_0 \cdots x_k x_0 \# x_1 \cdots x_k \# 1^{k|x_0|^2}\}.$$

We claim that a 1 queue machine can accept L_{pad} in linear time, but a 1 tape machine would need $\Omega(n^{4/3}/\log n)$ in the worst case. We leave the detail to the final paper. □ (Theorem 2.2)

Theorem 2.2 brings us closer to the $O(n^{1.5}\sqrt{\log n})$ upper bound of Theorem A, although a gap is still to be closed. This is also the first lower bound for 1 tape vs 1 queue in the nondeterministic case. For deterministic case a $\Omega(n^2)$ lower bound was proved in [V].

For the nondeterministic case of 1 tape vs 2 tapes, Maass [M] obtained an $\Omega(\frac{n^2}{(\log n)^2 \log\log n})$. Recently, the author was surprised by a theorem 7 years ago by Freivalds [F] (Theorem 2 in [F], without proof) which, if true, would immediately imply the tight $\Omega(n^2)$ lower bound. Both [F] and [M] independently constructed two similar ingenious languages (although the language by [F] was less complete).

In [M], although a very general language L_f was introduced, only a simple subset, $\hat{L}$, of it was used. The language $\hat{L}$ can be defined as follows (w.l.g. let k be odd).

$$\hat{L}=\{b_0{}^1 b_1{}^1 \cdots b_k{}^1$$
$$b_0{}^2 b_0{}^3 b_1{}^2 b_2{}^2 b_1{}^3 b_3{}^2 \cdots b_{2i}{}^2 b_i{}^3 b_{2i+1}{}^2 \cdots b_{k-1}{}^2 b_{(k-1)/2}{}^3 b_k{}^2$$
$$b_0{}^4 b_{(k+1)/2}{}^3 b_1{}^4 b_2{}^4 b_{(k+3)/2}{}^3 b_3{}^4 \cdots b_{2j(\mathrm{mod}\,k+1)}{}^4 b_j{}^3 b_{2i+1(\mathrm{mod}\,k+1)}{}^4 \cdots b_{k-1}{}^4 b_k{}^3 b_k{}^4$$
$$|\ b_i{}^1=b_i{}^2=b_i{}^3=b_i{}^4 \text{ for } i=0,\cdots,k\}$$

The length of each $b_i{}^j$ (a binary string) may be different. We can also define a delimited version L' of $\hat{L}$ where every $b_i{}^j$ in $\hat{L}$ is replaced by $*b_i{}^j*$ of an uniform length.

The language, B, constructed in [F] is similar (but less complete) if we let $c(i)=a(i)b(i)$ and replace each single $a(i)$ or $b(i)$ by $c(i)$ in the following. Here is the construction of [F]. Let B' consist of all strings

$$a(1)b(1)a(2)b(2) \cdots a(2n)b(2n)2a(2n)b(2n)b(2n-1)a(2n-1)b(2n-2)b(2n-3) \cdots$$
$$\cdots a(n+1)b(2)b(1)$$

where all $a(i)$ and $b(i)$ are from {0,1}. B is defined to be the set of all strings $0x$ or $1y$, where $x \in B'$ and $y \in \overline{B'}$. [F] claimed that it requires $\Omega(n^2)$ time for a 1 tape nondeterministic on-line TM to accept B.

Theorem B [L3]: $\hat{L}$ (L' and B) can be accepted in $O(\frac{n^2 loglogn}{\sqrt{logn}})$ time by a 1-tape *nondeterministic* on-line machine. (Proof contained in [L3])

Lemma B [L3]: Let $S=\{0,1,\cdots,k-1\}$ where $k=2^l$ for for some integer l. Let R be a binary (neighboring) relation defined on S such that, for s_1 and s_2 in S, s_1Rs_2 if

(1) $s_1=2*s_2(modk)$ or $s_1=2*s_2+1(modk)$, or

(2) $s_1=s_2+1$, or

(3) s_2Rs_1.

Then there exists a partition of S into two sets S_1 and S_2 such that,

(a) $|S_1|=|S_2|$.

(b) $S_1\cap S_2=\phi$,

(c) $|N|=O(k/\sqrt{logk})$, where $N=\{s_1\in S_1 \mid s_1Rs_2$ for some $s_2\in S_2\}$. (N is the set of elements in S_1 that are 'neighbors' of some elements in S_2.) (Proof contained in [L3].)

Remark: This gives an upper bound on Theorem 3.1 of [M] and Lemma 2.3 below.

Remark: Assertion (c) in Lemma B is true for any partition as long as for all $s_1\in S_1$ and $s_2\in S_2$, $\#bin(s_1)\leq\#bin(s_2)$ where $\#bin(x)=\#$ of 1's in binary x. It is this property which is used in the proof of Theorem B.

Corollary B [L3]: Language L' and B can be accepted by a 1 tape deterministic on-line machine in $O(n^2 loglogn/\sqrt{logn})$ time. B can be accepted by a 1 tape nondeterministic on-line machine in time $O(n^{1.5}\sqrt{logn})$ □ (Proof contained in [L3])

Remark: Other upper bounds have also been obtained. For example, 1 nondeterministic tape can probabilistically simulate 2 tapes in less than square time with any fixed small error ϵ (*i.e.* reject with $Pr(exist\ accepting\ path)\leq\epsilon$ accept if there is a path P, $Pr(P\ accepts)>1-\epsilon$. Also W. Ruzzo showed that a multitape Σ_k ATM running in time T can be simulated by a 1 tape $\Sigma_{k'}$ ATM in time $O(TlogT)$ where $k'=k+1$ if k is odd, $k'=k$ otherwise [R2], the $k=1$ case has been proved by N. Pippenger [R2].

In the rest of this section, trying to meet above lower bound, we improve the [M]'s lower bound to $\Omega(\frac{n^2}{lognloglogn})$. Unlike Theorem 2.1 (which was obtained in parallel to those of [M] and [V]), the next theorem is based on [M]'s approach. We assume the reader is familiar with [M].

Theorem 2.3: It requires $\Omega(n^2/lognloglogn)$ time to nondeterministically simulate 2 tapes by 1 tape.

We will show that the language L' (and $\hat{L}$) requires $\Omega(n^2/lognloglogn)$ time for 1 tape machines. We will only give ideas to show where and how the improvement is made. We refer the readers to [M] for details. In [M], Maass proved an important combinatorial lemma (Theorem 3.1 in [M]) which is generalized below,

Lemma 2.3: Let S be a sequence of numbers from $\{0,..,k-1\}$, where $k=2^l$ for some l. Assume that every number $b\in\{0,..,k-1\}$ is somewhere in S adjacent to the number $2b(mod\ k)$ and $2b(mod\ k)+1$. Then for every partition of $\{0,..,k-1\}$ into two sets G and R such that $|G|$, $|R|>k/4$ there are at least $k/clogk$ (for some fixed c) elements of G that occur somewhere in S adjacent to a number from R.

The proof of this lemma is a simple reworking of [M]'s proof. An $n/\sqrt{logn}$ upper bound of this lemma is contained in Lemma B.

Notice that any sequence S in L' satisfies the requirements in Lemma 2.3. Let n be the length of a random string that is divided into $k=n/loglogn$ blocks. A sequence S in L' is constructed from these k blocks. A new idea is to find *many* (instead of 1 as in [M]) 'deserts' on the work tape.

Lemma 2.4: ('Many Desert Lemma') For some constant C, and for large n, there are $I=logn/C$ regions $D_1, D_2, \cdots, D_I$ on the work tape such that,

(1) for all $i\neq j$, $D_i\cap D_j=0$;

(2) for each i, $|D_i|=n/c^{12}logn$, where $c\geq2$ is the constant in Lemma 2.2;

(3) for each i, at least $k/4=(n/4loglogn)$ blocks are mapped to each side of D_i.

Proof of Lemma 2.4: Again we only give the ideas behind the proof. Divide the whole work tape into regions of length $n/c^{13}logn$. By the Jamming Lemma, no region can hold more than $n/c^{11}logn$ blocks. By a standard counting argument, we can find regions $D_1, D_2,..., D_{logn/C}$ for some constant C in the 'middle' of work tape such that (1), (2), and (3) above are satisfied. □ (Lemma 2.4)

To prove Theorem 2.3, we apply the proof of [M] for each desert D_i in Lemma 2.4 Instead of using Theorem 3.1 of [M] we use Lemma 2.3 above. Notice that since each D_i is 'short', the total number of blocks mapped outside D_i is more than $k-(k/c^9logk)$. Therefore Lemma 2.2 can be applied. Now for each region D_i, M has to spend $O(n^2/(logn)^2loglogn)$ time. We sum up the time M spent at all $O(logn)$ regions, getting the

$\Omega(n^2/lognloglogn)$ lower bound. □ (Theorem 2.3)

3. Lower bounds on string-matching

The string-matching problem is defined [GS] as follows: given a character string x, called the *pattern* and a character string y, called the *text*, find all occurrences of x as a subword of y. The string-matching problem is very important in practice.

Since the publication of linear algorithms by [BM], [C2], and [KMP], there has been a constant effort to search for better algorithms which run in real time and save space. Finally, Galil and Seiferas [GS] showed that string-matching can be performed by a six-head *two-way* deterministic finite automaton in linear time. They ask whether a k-head one-way deterministic finite automaton (from now on k-DFA) can perform string-matching. In [LY], we answered this question for case $k=2$ by showing that 2-DFA cannot do string-matching. Efforts have been made for the cases where $k>2$, but even the case $k=3$ has not been solved. It is believed that a solution to the case of $k=3$ would give some important insights into the general case.

Towards answering the Galil-Seiferas conjecture, we develop a set of techniques which enable us to settle the case of $k=3$ negatively. We hope that the methods used here combined with that of [LY] would help in providing useful techniques for the general problem.

In addition, we obtain lower bound on string-matching by 2-way k-head DFA with k-1 heads blind, and on probabilistic matching and moving strings on one Turing machine tape.

Because of the space limitation, we assume the familiarity of automata theory [HU] and we have to omit many proofs. The details can be found in [L1, L2]. We assume that the standard input to M is $\#pattern\$text¢$, where $pattern, text \in \Sigma^*$ for the alphabet $\Sigma=\{0,1\}$. M starts with all heads at # sign.

An *ID* of M *on* input I is the $k+2$ tuple: $(I, q, i_1, i_2, \cdots, i_k)$ where q is a state and i_j for $1 \le j \le k$ is the position of the j-th head. An $\overline{ID}_t$ of M on input I is the *ID* of M without I at time t.

Let I_1 and I_2 be *ID*'s. We write $I_1 \vdash I_2$ if M, started in *ID* I_1, reaches *ID* I_2 in one step. We write $I_1 \vdash_* I_2$ either if $I_1=I_2$ or if M, started in *ID* I_1, reaches *ID* I_2 in a finite number of steps.

Superscripts are used to denote different occurrences of the same string. Subscripts are used to denote different binary strings. Everything in the following concerns a fixed 3-DFA M, and a long random string $Y=kXk'$. M and Y will be chosen in Theorem 3.1

We name the three heads of M as h_a, h_b, h_c. We will also use h_1, h_2 and h_3 to mean the leading head, the second head, and the last head respectively at a specific time. So, h_a, h_b, and h_c are fixed names, whereas h_1, h_2, and h_3 are only transient names.

We use $p(h)$ to denote the phrase 'the position of the head h'. Let x be a string (a segment of M's input) of length greater than 0. At a particular step in the simulation of M, we make the following definitions: $p(h_i)=x$ denotes that the position of h_i is at the last bit of x; $p(h_i)>x$ means that h_i has passed the last bit of x; $p(h_i)<x$ means that h_i has not reached the first bit of x.

a_0 always stands for the *pattern* which is going to be of form $1^kX1^{k'}$ where $Y=kXk'$. In the following, we always consider input of form $\#1^kX1^{k'}\$text¢$. X is always equally partitioned into six parts $X=x_1x_2...x_6$. In general, given strings s or $x_{uv\ w}$, without explicit definition, we always implicitly assume that they are equally partitioned into six parts, and written as $s_1s_2 \cdots s_6$ or $x_{uv\ v1}x_{uv\ v2}...x_{uv\ v6}$, respectively. When the ranges of the indices are not explicitly stated, they are always assumed to be from 1 to 6.

If $X=xyz$, then $X-y=xz$. If y is not a substring of X, then $X-y=X$.

Definition 3.1 The *text* in the input $\#1^kX1^{k'}\$text¢$ is *regular* if it is concatenated, no more than 1000 times, from the following blocks:

(1) $1^l01^l0 \cdots 1^l0$, where 1^l is repeated less than $log|X|$ times and $K(l) \le log|X|+2|M|$;

(2) X;

(3) X', where X' is obtained from X by replacing a substring x (only one) by x' that has an equal length and satisfies $K(x'|X) \le 100log|X|$;

(4) Prefixes of X;

(5) $\overline{X}$, where $\overline{X}$ is obtained from X by replacing a substring x (only one) by $\overline{x}$ that has an equal length and satisfies $K(\overline{x}|X-x) \le |k|+|k'|+100log|X|$;

(6) 1^k and $1^{k'}$.

The *text* is *easy* if only blocks from (1)-(4) are allowed in above. □ (Definition 3.1)

Proposition 3.1: If the *text* is *easy* then: (1) the *text* can be constructed from $|X|$ and $O(log|X|)$ information; (2) there is a constant C_0 ($<<k,k'$) not depending on k or k' such that each head position in the *text* at a specific time can be described by $|k|+C_0$ information, and further, if a head h is in an occurrence of X, X', or some prefix of one of them, then $p(h)$ can be specified by $C_0log|X|$ information. □

Definition 3.2: Let x be a string segment of an *easy text*. x is *independent* (with respect to *text*) if for every string X', or its prefix in Definition 3.1 that appears in the *text*, $K(X'-x\,|X-x) \leq 50\log|X|$. □ (Definition 3.2)

Definition 3.3: Let x be *independent*. We say x *is compared with* y if (1) $|x|=|y|$, and (2) there is a time when one head, say h_i, is at x and simultaneously another head, say h_j, is at y (excluding the first bit and last bit of x and y). If y is just another occurrence of x, then we say this occurrence of x *is matched*, or matched by (h_i,h_j). We also say (h_i,h_j) did the matching. Let x^1 and x^2 be different occurrences of string x in text of above input. We say x^1 is *matched* to x^2 if there is a sequence of occurrences of x's starting from x^1 and ending with x^2, each being compared with the next. An occurrence of x is *well-matched* if this occurrence of x is matched to the x of a_0. □ (Definition 3.3)

The idea behind the proof of next theorem comes from the following observation: Let kXk' be a random string. Suppose that there is a time that all three heads have left the *pattern* $1^kX1^{k'}$ and no head is reading the ¢ sign, the *text* is *easy* with no occurrences of *pattern*, and two heads are reading some occurrences of X. Then we would lose the information of either k or k'. At this time we attach $1^lX1^{l'}$ to the end of *text*, if the machine does string-matching correctly, we would be able to recover k and k' by finding the minimum l and l' such that the machine finds a matching. Therefore, we show that kXk' is not random. So our goals are to (1) make *text easy* and (2) drive the heads out of *pattern* (or 1^k of *pattern*). To make *text easy* we construct *text* to be (essentially) a sequence of a_i's and block of 1's, where $a_i=1^mX1^m$ for some non-random m greater than k and k'. To drive the heads out of the *pattern*, we have to do an exhaustive adversary proof. The goal is to 'construct an *text easier* than the *pattern*'

Theorem 3.1: No 3-DFA accepts L$=\{\#a_0\$text¢\,|\,a_0$ is a substring of $text\}$.

Proof of Theorem 3.1 (*idea*): Suppose a 3-DFA M accepts L. Fix a long enough random string Y, as mentioned before. We will show that Y is not random for a contradiction. Divide $Y=kXk'$, where $|k|=|k'|$, $|X|^{1/4}>>|k|$, $|X|>>\sqrt{|X|}$, and $|k|>>\log|X|$. Let $m=\min\{2^j\,|2^j>k,k'\}$. X is divided into $x_1x_2x_3x_4x_5x_6$ of equal length. Consider only inputs of form $\#1^kX1^{k'}\$text¢$ to M. That is, $a_0=1^kX1^{k'}$. We will always assume that we are in the process of simulating M.

The following strategy **P** is needed to play our adversary proof. The purpose of **P** is to obtain an invariant value such that after h_1 has passed a block of 1's, many more 1's can be added without changing the status of M. Further this block of 1's can be used to recover k if it is followed by $X1^m$. To understand it better, one may want to read **P** later when **P** is called.

Strategy P(x): Given $\#a_0\$text¢$ on tape, $p(h_1)=text$ with corresponding state of M and h_2,h_3 positions. The parameter x is a substring of X.

$i:=1$;

repeat

append $b_i=1^{m|Q|}0$ to the input (before ¢);

continue to simulate M until $p(h_1)=b_i0$;

$i:=i+1$

until $S_1 \vee S_2 \vee S_3=true$;

The three predicates S_1, S_2, and S_3 are defined as below:

S_1: A matching of one occurrence of x (parameter of **P**) to another occurrence of x by (h_2,h_3) happened in the last loop;

S_2: Neither h_2 nor h_3 moved more than $|Q||X|$ steps in the last loop;

S_3: h_1 and h_2 are separated by only 1-blocks.

If S_2 is true, then there exist constants $C_1,C_2<|Q||X|+1$ such that for all l, should we let $b_{i-1}=1^{C_1+l*C_2}$ in the input, M would be in a fixed state with same h_2,h_3 positions when $p(h_1)=b_{i-1}$. Replace the last appended $b_{i-1}=1^{m|Q|}0$ by $a_l=1^{C_1+l*C_2}X1^m$ where $l=1$ at this moment.

If S_1 or S_3 is true, do nothing.

end_P.

Claim P: (1) Only one of the S_i's can be true; (2) The number of times that the *repeat* loop is executed is less than twice the number of X-blocks and 1-blocks in the input. □ (Claim P)

Nine technical lemmas are needed in the process of simulating M. Note that the $a_{i>0}$'s used in each of the following lemmas are all 'local', that is, they have no relation with any $a_{i>0}$'s used in the proofs of other lemmas or main theorem.

Lemma 1 (The Matching Lemma): Let the *text* be *regular* (Def. 3.1) and with exactly one occurrence, a_g, of a_0 in it. Let x be a segment of X such that (1) x is *independent* (Def. 3.2), and (2) $|x|>\sqrt{|X|}$. Then the occurrence of x in a_g, must be well-matched.

Proof of Lemma 1: Suppose Lemma 1 is not true. Let x^l, for $l=1,2, \cdots l_0 \leq 1000$, be all the occurrences of x, including the one in a_g, that are not well-matched in the *text*. Now for each x^l, we record 3 pairs of information for the 3 heads,

h_a pair: (positions of h_b and h_c and state of M when h_a enters this occurrence of x^l, positions of h_b and h_c and state of M when h_a leaves this x^l.);

h_b pair: exchange h_a and h_b in above;

h_c pair: exchange h_a and h_c in h_a's pair.

We now show that Y is not random by giving a short program which accepts only Y. For input Y',

(1) Compare Y' with Y except the x part which we do not need.

(2) Construct the *pattern* and the *text* with x' of Y' (the corresponding part of x) replacing all x's. Then for each of the above three pairs, starting from the first component, we simulate M until some *ID* of M coincides with the second component of the pair. If there is no such coincidence, we reject this Y'.

If Y' passes tests (1) and (2), then $Y'=Y$ (otherwise M does not accept L). Notice that we used only the following information: (i) X-x and $5(|k|+|k'|)$ amount of information for constructing the regular text (excluding the x part), and (ii) h_a,h_b,h_c pairs for each x^l. The total amount of information that we used in the above program is less than $|Y|$ because of the assumption $|X|^{1/4}>>|k|$ and the fact $|x|>\sqrt{|X|}$. □ (Lemma 1)

Corollary: (1) Lemma 1 is true for a k-NFA, for any k; (2) 2-DFA cannot do string matching (see [LY]).

Remark: Combined with the ideas from [YR], the proof of a theorem by Yao and Rivest [YR], which states that a k-DFA is better than a $(k-1)$-DFA, can be simplified.

Lemma 2 (The 2-head Lemma): Let s, $|s|>\sqrt{|X|}$, be an independent (Def. 3.2) segment of X. For input $I=\#1^kX1^{k'}\$Z0a_10a_2...a_{l+2}0\not c$, where $a_i=1^mX1^m$, let Z be regular (Def. 3.1) with no occurrence of a_0 and no more than l occurrences of s in it. If there is a time when $p(h_1)=(s \text{ of } a_{l+2})$, $p(h_2)<(s \text{ of } a_1)$, and s in $a_{1\leq i\leq l+2}$'s are not matched, then X is not random.

Remark on Lemma 2: We have presented a simplified form of Lemma 2. When it is actually applied, the a_i's and contents of Z can be intermingled. Since the proofs are the same, we preferred to present a simplified version.

The next lemma suggests the basic idea of the proof of our main result.

Lemma 3 (The Easiness Lemma): Let the *text* be *easy* and contain no occurrence of a_0. If at some step t, two heads of M are out of a_0 and their positions can be described by $10log|X|$ long information, and if no head is in 1^k of a_0 or at the $\not c$ sign, then Y is not random.

Lemma 4 (The Replacement Lemma): Assume the *text* is *easy*. At time t in the simulation of M, if a segment s of X is not matched, then there exists s' such that, (1) $|s|=|s'|$, (2) $s\neq s'$, (3) s' can be constructed from X and $O(log|X|)$ information, and (4) if h_i passed s at time t, then replacing s by s' will not change the status of M when $p(h_i)=s'$ (or s).

Lemmas 4-1, 4-2, 4-3 are variants of the Replacement Lemma that are needed in the application.

Lemma 4-1: In Lemma 4, if the condition that s is not matched is removed, then we can conclude that all not well-matched occurrences of s can be replaced by some s' so that (1)-(4) in Lemma 4 are still true. □ (Lemma 4-1)

Lemma 4-2: Let *text* be *easy* and contain C full occurrences of a_0, say $b_1, \cdots, b_C$. Assume that at some time t in the simulation of M, for each b_i there is a substring s_i of X not well-matched. For $i=1,..,C$, let $|s_i|\geq|X|/1000$ (s_i's may be all different). Let s_1 be independent and s_1 appears in text less than D times. Here C and D are small constants less than, say, 20. Then *text* can be changed by substituting s_i's so that:

(1) *text* is easy and does not contain any occurrence of a_0;

(2) There is a time t' such that, $\overline{ID}_{t'}$ on the changed input is same to $\overline{ID}_t$ on the old input.

(3) There is a substring e of s_1 which remains unchanged in s_1 after replacement. $|e|\geq|s_1|/2C$ and e is independent.

Lemma 4-3: Lemma 4-2 can be modified so that b_1 is not changed. That is, the resulting *text* contains exactly one occurrence b_1 of a_0.

Lemma 5: Let *text* in input $\#a_0\$text\not c$ be easy and contain no occurrence of a_0. Let s be a substring of X where s is independent with respect to *text* and $|s|>\sqrt{|X|}$. If there is a time t of M such that $p(h_3)>(1^k$ of $a_0)$, and $p(h_1)<\not c$, then Y is not random.

Lemma 6: Let the *text* in input $\#a_0\$text¢$ be *easy*. Let there be exactly one occurrence of a_0 in $a_{j>0}$ in a_j is not well-matched (to a_0), (4) s is not matched to other occurrences of s that h_2 can still see, and (5) $|s|>|X|/1000$. Then Y is not random.

Now we continue to prove Theorem 3.1. We construct an *easy text*. Let the partial input be

(A) $\#a_0\$a_10\cdots$,

where $a_1=1^mX1^m$. Consider the time t when $p(h_1)=(X$ of $a_1)$. Note, at t, $p(h_3)<(X$ of $a_0)$, since otherwise we can remove second 1^m from a_1 and apply Lemma 3.

(1) All x_i's of a_1 are matched (by h_1,h_2), then there is a time of M such that $p(h_1)=(x_2$ of $a_1)$, and $p(h_2)>(x_1$ of $a_0)$. Change a_1 to $a_1'=1^mx_1x_2$. Add $a_2=1^mX1^m0$ to get the partial input

(B) $\#a_0\$a_1'0a_20\cdots$

Simulate M on the new input and consider time $p(h_1)=(X$ of $a_2)$ for the new input (B). There must exist an x_p in a_2 not yet matched (assuming $p(h_3)<(1^k$ of $a_0)$). We go on constructing the input by the following process.

(C) *For* $t=3$ to 8 *repeat* the following. Add $a_t=1^mX1^m$ to the input and and run M on the new changed input. Consider time $p(h_1)=(X$ of $a_t)$. If all x_i ''s of a_t are matched, then let $a_t=1^mx_1x_2x_3$.

Now at time $p(h_1)=(X$ of $a_8)$. We consider following cases.

(1.1) If, for $j=1,..,6$, all x_{pj} of a_2 are matched to some $a_{i>2}$'s, we find the smallest i such that x_{p4} of a_2 is matched to x_{p4} of a_i. Change *text* to

(D) $...a_20a_30...a_{i-1}01^mx_{p1}...x_{p4}0¢$.

Simulate M on the new input (D) until $p(h_1)=text$. We then apply $\mathbf{P}(x_p)$ which results exactly one of S_1, S_2, or S_3 true. If S_1 is true, then $p(h_3)>(1^k$ of $a_0)$, we apply Lemma 4-2, then Lemma 5. If S_3 is true, then x_{p5} of a_2 cannot be well-matched, to satisfy the conditions of Lemma 1 we apply Lemma 4-3; If S_2 is true, then $\mathbf{P}$ adds $a_f=1^{C_1+l*C_2}X1^m$ to the input, and we simulate M on the new input and stop M as soon as one of the following cases happens.

(1.1.1) $p(h_3)=(1^k$ of $a_0)$. Then x_{p6} of a_2 is not well-matched. Other un-matched x_j's in $a_{i>2}$ remain un-matched. We delete second 1^m from a_f and we are done by Lemma 4-2 and Lemma 5.

(1.1.2) $p(h_2)>(x_{p5}$ of $a_2)$. If (h_1,h_2) did not match x_{p5} of a_f to that of a_2, then x_{p5} of a_2 has not been matched yet. Delete second 1^m of a_f, then apply Lemma 4-3 followed by Lemma 6. If (x_{p5} of a_2) is matched to (x_{p5} of a_f), then case (1.1.3) applies.

(1.1.3) $p(h_1)>(x_4$ of $a_f)$. Then $x_{p1}x_{p2}x_{p3}$ of a_f is not matched, because when $p(h_1)=(x_4$ of $a_i)$ we have $p(h_2)>(x_3$ of $a_2)$. And x_{p2} of a_2 is not well-matched. Also for every a_i in between a_2 and a_f there is a long not well-matched part. Now continue to run M and stop M as soon as one of the following cases happens.

(1.1.3.1) h_2 reaches a_f. Apply Lemma 4-3 so that only a_2 still contains a_0 and s, which is a long sub-string of x_{p2}, is *independent*. If s is not a substring of the changed a_f then the Matching Lemma can be applied; suppose it is, since s in a_f is not matched, there must be a substring s' of s in a_2, satisfying $|s'|\geq|s|/i$ where i is defined in (D), that cannot be well-matched, again we can apply the Matching Lemma.

(1.1.3.2) (h_2,h_3) do some matching of X. If h_1 is not at ¢, we are done by Lemma 4-2 and Lemma 5. And if $p(h_1)=¢$ we apply Lemma 4-3 so that only a_f contains a_0 and *text* is *easy*, then we can vary l to find k by the method of Lemma 3. This shows Y is not random.

(1.2) There exists j such that x_{pj} is not matched to any $a_{i>2}$.

(1.2.1) $p(h_2)>a_2$. Apply Lemma 4-3 so that only a_2 contains a_0, then use Lemma 6;

(1.2.2) $p(h_2)\leq a_2$. Since many a_t's are left in form of 1^mX1^m, with some common part un-matched, in (C), the 2-head Lemma can be applied.

(2) Some x_p in a_1 is not matched. We construct new input by process (C), and exactly the same argument as in (1.1)&(1.2) applies. (Change a_2 to a_1.) □ (Theorem 3.1)

Remark: (1) We hope the idea of easier text and harder pattern suggests some possible approaches to the general $k>3$ case. (2) Though almost all the lemmas we proved can be generalized, to keep them readable we chosed not to. However, we do hope the techniques and the lemmas developed here find themselves applications elsewhere, like the Matching Lemma in the proof of Yao and Rivest Theorem.

A 2-way k-DFA is just like a k-DFA but each head can go both directions. A head is *blind* if it can see only end-markers. In [DG] it is proved that 2-way 2-DFA with one head blind cannot do string-matching. Obviously 2-way 3-DFA with 2 heads blind can do string-matching. Here in contrast to the impossibility result of Theorem 3.1, we prove a lower bound on the time to do string-matching required by a 2-way k-DFA with k-1 blind heads. We hope this can shed some light on the other important open problem concerning the lower bound of doing string-matching by a 2-way 2-DFA.

Theorem 3.2: String-matching requires $\Omega(n^2/\log n)$ time for a k-head two way DFA with $k-1$ heads blind, where n is the length of the input.

Theorem 3.3: $\bar{L}=\{\#x\$yx\not{c}\}$ (used in above proof) can be accepted by a 2-way 3-DFA with 2 heads blind in time $O(n^2/\log n)$.

Remark: It is proved in [LY] that $\bar{L}$ defined above cannot be accepted by a 1-way 2-DFA. By a similar proof the language $L'=\{\#a_0\$a_1*a_2*\ldots*a_l\not{c} \mid a_0=a_i \text{ for some } i\}$, defined and shown to be not acceptable by a 2-way 2-DFA with one head blind in [DG], is acceptable in time $n^2/\log n$ by a 2-way 4-DFA with three blind heads.

It has been an interesting philosophical question [W]: is (probabilistic) checking easier than (probabilistic) generating? For example, given matrix A, B, and C, Freivalds showed (see [W]) that we can probabilistically check AB=C in n^2 time, but no one knows how to calculate AB in $O(n^2)$ time even probabilistically (open problem 2.6 in [W]). Also similarly it is known [W] that given polynomials $p_1(x),p_2(x),p_3(x)$, the probabilistic checking of $p_1(x)p_2(x)=p_3(x)$ can also be done faster than the known generating ($p_3(x)$) algorithms. Here we shall provide an example which does show that checking is easier than generating.

A PTM [G] is a TM equipped with a random number generator. It decides the next move by a random choice from two possible branches. A PTM P performs a task with error probability ϵ if it outputs the correct answer with probability $1-\epsilon$. Language L is accepted by a PTM P in time $t(n)$ if there exist an $\epsilon<1/2$ such that if $x\in L$ then P accepts x in with probability greater than $1-\epsilon$ in time $t(n)$, otherwise P accepts x with probability less than ϵ in time $t(n)$. In this section, we solely consider the 1-tape probabilistic machines (1-tape PTM's) without an extra input tape, i.e., the input is presented on this single work tape at the beginning of the computation.

Freivalds [F] proved a very interesting result that a 1-tape PTM can match two strings on 1-tape in time $O(n\log n)$ with any fixed error probability $\epsilon>0$. In contrast we show the following.

Theorem 3.4: Consider a 1-tape PTM M, with input $x\#^{|x|}0^{|x|}$ presented on its only work tape. To move x to the 0's positions with a fixed error probability $\epsilon<1/2$, (i.e., to output $x\#^{|x|}x$ where $x\#^{|x|}$ stays at original position) M requires $\Omega(n^2)$ time.

Remark: Comparing to the $n\log n$ probabilistic algorithm for accepting $x\#^{|x|}x$ (with any fixed small error ϵ) by a 1-tape PTM [F], this lower bound leads us to an interesting conclusion: checking is indeed easier than generating. Notice that this is not true for 1-tape deterministic or nondeterministic machines since a n^2 lower bound for accepting the palindromes were proved long time ago by Hennie [H2].

4. Open problems

There are several open questions: (1) Close the gap for 1 tape vs. 1 queue; (2) Prove that k-DFA cannot do string matching, and give a simple proof of Theorem 3.1; (3) Can 1 tape nondeterministically simulate 2 tapes in less than square time? (This question will be discussed in [L3].) Most open problems listed in [DGPR] are still open except 1 (not completely solved) and 6 (completely solved). Similar questions for off-line machines also need to be answered.

5. Acknowledgements

I am greatly indebted to Juris Hartmanis, my thesis advisor, for his guidance, criticism and encouragement. I also wish to thank Chanderjit Bajaj, Zvi Galil, John Gilbert, Luc Longpre, Joel Seiferas, Yaacov Yesha, and Zhen Zhang for very helpful discussions on various topics contained in this paper.

6. References

[A] S.O. Aanderaa, On k-tape versus (k-1)-tape real time computation, in Complexity of Computation. R. Karp Ed. (1974) pp. 75-96.

[BGW] R.V. Book, S.A. Greibach, and B. Wegbreit, Time- and tape-bound Turing acceptors and AFL's, JCSS 4,6 (Dec. 1970) pp. 606-621.

[BM] R.S. Boyer and J.S. Moore, A fast string searching algorithm, CACM 20, 10 (Oct. 1977) pp. 762-772.

[Cha] G. Chaitan, Algorithmic Information Theory, IBM J. Res. Dev. 21 (1977) pp. 350-359.

[C2] S.A. Cook, Linear time simulation of deterministic two-way pushdown automata, Proc. IFIP Congress 71, TA-2. North-Holland, Amsterdam (1971) pp. 172-179.

[DGPR] P. Duris, Z. Galil, W.J. Paul, and R. Reischuk, Two nonlinear lower bounds, Proc. 15th ACM STOC (1983) pp. 127-132. (Revised June 1983)

[DG] P. Duris and Z. Galil, Two tapes are better than one for nondeterministic machines, Proc. 14th ACM STOC (1982) pp. 1-7.

[DG1] P. Duris and Z. Galil, Fooling a two-way automaton or one pushdown store is better than one counter for two way machines, Proc. 13th ACM STOC (1981) pp. 177-188.

[F] R. Freivalds, Probabilistic machines can use less running time, Info. Processing, 77 (1977) pp. 839-842.

[F1] M. Furer, The tight deterministic time hierarchy, Proc. 14th ACM STOC (1982) pp. 8-16.

[GS] Z. Galil and J.I. Seiferas, Time-space optimal string-matching, Proc. 13th ACM STOC (1981) pp. 106-113.

[G] J. Gill, Computational complexity of probabilistic Turing machines, SIAM J. Comp. 6 (1977) pp. 675-695.

[HS] J. Hartmanis and R.E. Stearns, On the computational complexity of algorithms, Trans. Amer. math. Soc. 117 (1965) pp. 285-306.

[H2] F.C. Hennie, One-tape off-line Turing machine computations, Inf. and Control 8 (1965) pp. 533-578.

[HS1] F.C. Hennie and R.E. Stearns, Two tape simulation of multitape Turing machines, J.ACM, 4 (1966) pp. 533-546.

[HU] J.E. Hopcroft and J.D. Ullman, Introduction to automata theory, languages, and computation, Addison-Wesley (1979).

[K] A. Kolmogorov, Three approaches to the quantitative definition of information, Problems of Information Transmission, 1-1, 1-7, Jan-Mar (1965).

[KMP] D.E. Knuth, J.H. Morris, Jr., and V.R. Pratt, Fast pattern matching in strings, SIAM J. Comp. 6, 2 (Jun. 1977) pp. 323-350.

[L] M. Li, On 1 tape versus 2 stacks, TR-84-591, Dept. of Comp. Sci., Cornell University (Jan. 1984).

[L1] M. Li, Lower bounds on string-matching, TR-84-636, Dept of Comp. Sci., Cornell University (July 1984).

[L2] M. Li, Lower bounds in computational complexity, Ph.D. Thesis, Cornell University (Jan. 1985).

[L3] M. Li, Simulating two pushdowns by one nondeterministic tape in $O(n^{1.5}\sqrt{logn})$ time, abstract (Jan. 1985).

[LY] M. Li and Y. Yesha, String-matching cannot be done by a two-head one-way deterministic finite automaton, TR 83-579, Department of Computer Science, Cornell University (Oct. 1983).

[M] W. Maass, Quadratic lower bounds for deterministic and nondeterministic one-tape Turing machines, Proc. 16th ACM STOC (May 1984) pp. 401-408. (Revised summer 1984).

[P] W.J. Paul, Kolmogorov complexity and lower bounds, 2nd International Conference on Fundamentals of Computation Theory (1978).

[P1] W.J. Paul, On heads versus tapes, Proc. 22nd IEEE FOCS (1981) pp. 68-73.

[P2] W.J. Paul, On-line simulation of $k+1$ tapes by k tapes requires nonlinear time, Proc. 23rd IEEE FOCS (1982) pp. 53-56.

[P3] W.J. Paul, On time hierarchies, Proc. 9th ACM STOC (1977) pp. 218-222.

[PSS] W.J. Paul, J.I. Seiferas, and J. Simon, An information-theoretic approach to time bounds for on-line computations, Proc. 12th ACM STOC (1980) pp. 357-367.

[R] M.O. Rabin, Real time computation, Israel J. of Math, 1,4 (1963) pp. 203-211.

[R1] A. Rosenberg, On multihead finite automata, IBM J., (1966).

[R2] W. Ruzzo, *Private communication*. (1984)

[RS1] S. Reisch and G. Schnitger, Three applications of Kolmogorov-complexity, Proc. 23rd IEEE FOCS (1982) pp. 45-52.

[V] P.M.B. Vitanyi, One queue or two pushdown stores take square time on a one-head tape unit, Report CS-R8406, Center for Mathematics Computer Science, Amsterdam (Mar. 1984).

[W] D.J.A. Welsh, Randomized Algorithms, Discrete Applied Math. 5 (1983) pp. 133-145.

[YR] A.C. Yao and R. Rivest, $k+1$ heads are better than k, J. ACM, 25 (1978) pp. 337-340.

A Bidirectional Shortest-Path Algorithm With Good Average-Case Behavior (Preliminary Version)

Michael Luby
University of Toronto

Prabhakar Ragde
University of California at Berkeley

1. Introduction

The two-terminal shortest-path problem is a well-studied problem in graph theory. It is an essential subroutine in algorithms dealing with such diverse problems as network flow [EK], approximations to the travelling salesman problem [BT], and problem-solving systems in artificial intelligence [Po]. Previous probabilistic analyses include Spira's result [S] for the all-pairs shortest path problem, and Perl's analysis [Pe] of the single-source all-destinations problem. The fastest algorithm known is due to Dijkstra [D]; it performs a unidirectional search outward from the source node s towards the destination node d. A natural alternative, termed bidirectional search, is to simultaneously search forward from s and backwards from d. In the worst case this is roughly twice as slow as unidirectional search, but empirical results suggest that it is faster in practice ([Po],[Ma]).

In this paper we present an algorithm that is a multiplicative factor of $\sqrt{n}$ faster than the unidirectional algorithm in the average case. Our results hold for a large class of probability distributions on random graphs, including both directed and undirected graphs, sparse as well as dense graphs, and graphs where the length of each edge is drawn from a different probability distribution. In the last case, we require only that the distributions be "similar and well-behaved" for a very small initial portion of the distributions. In section 8 of the paper, we state the explicit properties that the edge probability distributions must satisfy for our analysis to hold.

2. Definition of a Random Graph

We assume that the number of nodes in the graph is fixed at n, and that the graph is a complete directed graph. A random instance of a graph is drawn by choosing the length of each edge independently from a common exponential distribution. More formally, let l_e be the length of edge e. Then $Pr[l_e \leq x] = 1 - \lambda e^{-\lambda x}$, for some fixed $\lambda > 0$.

We use this probabilistic model throughout our presentation for expository purposes. In section 8 we shall relax our requirements on the probability distribution. Our results require a more technical analysis under these weaker assumptions, but the main ideas behind the analysis and the results obtained are essentially the same as for the common exponential distribution.

The following properties of the exponential distribution are essential to our analysis. Let $1, 2 \ldots k$ be edges whose lengths are chosen as above. For each $1 \leq i \leq k$,

1) $Pr[l_i \leq x_i + y | l_i \geq x_i] = Pr[l_i \leq y]$.
2) Given that for all j, $l_e \geq x_j$, $Pr[l_i - x_i \leq \min_{1\leq j\leq k}\{l_j - x_j\}] = \frac{1}{k}$.

3. A Quick Review of Dijkstra's Algorithm

The input to the algorithm is a directed graph $G = (V, E)$, a length for each edge in E, and two specified nodes s and d. The output of the algorithm is a shortest directed path from s to d.

The algorithm maintains a set S of nodes for which the shortest path from s is known, and a tree of shortest paths from s to each node in S. Initially the tree is empty and S consists of the single node s. The general step of the algorithm is to add an edge (u, v) to this tree, where $u \in S$ and $v \notin S$. This edge is chosen such that the distance from s to u plus the length of (u, v) is minimum over all such edges; v then enters S. Such an edge is called *external*, as opposed to edges with both ends in S, which are called *internal*. When d enters S, the algorithm halts.

The algorithm can be implemented using priority queues [AHU] if the adjacency list for each node is sorted by edge length. The priority queue will contain only the shortest unused edge leaving each node in S. We draw from the queue until an external edge is drawn. Our analysis will assume this implementation. Running times for this algorithm can be expressed in terms of queue operations. Later, we will discuss how our results apply when the adjacency lists are not sorted.

4. Average-Case Analysis of Unidirectional Search

We will describe a procedure which will be used to simulate the behavior of the unidirectional search algorithm on a random graph, and use the properties of the exponential distribution to analyze it. The procedure will have associated with it a real-valued variable L, which starts at zero and increases in a continuous manner. The edge-lengths are chosen from the exponential distribution, but are unknown to the procedure. All edges are initially *inactive*. At some point, the procedure may make an edge e *active*, when $L = t_e$. When $L = t_e + l_e$, the edge is *discovered* by the procedure. An edge that has been discovered is no longer considered active.

To start the procedure, we make all edges leaving s active, and $L = 0$. L is increased until an edge (s, v) is discovered, when $L = t_v$. We add v to S, activate all the edges leaving v, and continue to increase L. If the next edge to be discovered is (v, w) (when $L = t_w$), then the length of (v, w) is $t_w - t_v$, and the shortest path to w uses edges (s, v) and (v, w), and is of length t_w. Similarly, if (s, w) had been discovered first, at time t'_w, then the shortest path to w would consist of the edge (s, w), of length t'_w. In either case, we add w to S, activate all edges leaving w, and continue.

In a general snapshot of the algorithm, all edges directed out of nodes in S are active, except possibly for some internal edges which have been discovered. The first external edge (u, v) to be discovered will bring some node v into S when L has some value t_v, and the shortest path from s to v will be of length t_v. All edges leaving v are activated when this occurs. When an edge entering d is discovered, a shortest path between s and d will have been found, and the algorithm halts.

The edges discovered by the procedure correspond exactly to the edges drawn from the priority queue, which will be our measure of the running time of the algorithm. Thus, we need to study the number of edges discovered. The analysis hinges on the following fact: by property 2 of the exponential distribution, any active edge is equally likely to be the next one discovered.

We say the algorithm is in *stage k* when $|S| = k$. In stage k, there are $k(n-k)$ external edges leaving S, the discovery of any of which would end the stage. Of these, only k go to d. Thus the probability that d is added to S in stage k, given that stage k is reached, is $\frac{1}{n-k}$. The following theorem is then a simple consequence.

Theorem 1. *Let X be the number of nodes in S at the end of the algorithm. Then* $Pr(X = k) = \frac{1}{n-1}$, *and* $E(X) = \Theta(n)$. ∎

Since the discovered external edges form a spanning tree of S, the expected number of discovered edges is $\Omega(n)$. Internal edges may also be discovered during the course of the algorithm. These discoveries do not terminate a stage; but they do correspond to queue operations. Let Y be the number of internal edge discoveries. The expectation of Y is bounded above with the aid of the following lemma, which is also the basis for much subsequent reasoning. Let T_1 be an interval of values of L such that at the beginning of the interval, there is a set of p active edges labelled *good*, and T_1 ends when a good edge is discovered for the first time. Let T_2 be an interval of values of the same length as T_1, such that at the beginning of the interval, there is a set of q active edges labelled *bad*.

Lemma 2. *Let k be the number of bad edges that are discovered in* T_2. *Then:*

1) $Pr[Y \geq k] \leq \left[\frac{q}{q+p}\right]^k$

2) $E[Y] \leq \frac{q}{p}$

The lemma is easily proved using property 2 of the exponential distribution. Applying the lemma, we see that in stage k, there are $k(n-k)$ external (good) edges active, and at most k^2 internal (bad) edges active; thus the expected number of internal edges discovered in stage k is at most $\frac{k}{n-k}$. Summing over all stages, one can show:

Theorem 3. *The expected number of internal edge discoveries in unidirectional search is* $O(n)$. ∎

Theorems 1 and 3 demonstrate that the expected number of queue operations in unidirectional search is $\Theta(n)$.

5. Bidirectional Search

The bidirectional search algorithm proceeds in two phases. In the first phase, we alternate between two unidirectional searches: one forward from s, growing a tree spanning a set of nodes S for which the minimum distance from s is known, and the other backwards from d spanning a set D of nodes for which the minimum distance to d is known. Phase 1 alternately adds one node to S and one node to D, continuing until $S \cap D$ becomes nonempty. At this point, the shortest path is known to lie within the search trees associated with S and D except for at most one edge from S to D. We defer discussion of Phase 2, in which this minimum path is found.

We say phase 1 is in stage k when both S and D contain k nodes. During a stage, there are several types of active edges. *S-internal* (resp. *D*-internal) edges have both ends in S (resp. D). *S-external* (resp. *D*-external) edges have their tails (resp. heads) in S (resp. D), and their other ends in $V-(S \cup D)$. *Cross-edges* have their tails in S and their heads in D.

The description of the procedure for unidirectional search is now modified to simulate bidirectional search. We define L_S to be the distance searched forward from s, and L_D to be the distance searched backward from d. The procedure initializes both L_S and L_D to zero, with all edges leaving s S-active, and all edges entering d D-active. L_S increases until an edge (v, w) is discovered with $w \notin S$. w is added to S, and all edges directed out of w are made S-active. The procedure then searches back from d in a similar manner.

The notions of activation and discovery of an edge are more complicated for bidirectional search than for unidirectional search, because of cross-edges. S-internal and S-external edges are S-active but not D-active; D-internal and D-external edges are D-active but not S-active. Cross edges are both S-active and D-active. Consider a cross edge (v, w) which became S-active when L_S was t_1, and D-active when L_D was t_2. Edge (v, w) cannot possibly be discovered in the S-search unless $L_S - t_1 \geq L_D - t_2$. Thus, we say cross-edge (v, w) is *S-enabled* if $L_S - t_1 \geq L_D - t_2$, and *D-enabled* if $L_s - t_1 \leq L_D - t_2$. For ease of notation, S-internal and S-external edges are considered to be S-enabled (similarly for D). During the S-search, all S-enabled edges are equally likely to be next discovered, and a similar statement can be made for the D-search.

Since there are two priority queues in the implementation of bidirectional search, an edge may be accessed twice (once in each queue). Discovery of an edge in the procedure corresponds to the first access.

6. Analysis of Phase 1

Stage k is the last stage of phase 1 if a cross-edge is discovered during either of the two searches. Let E be this event.

Lemma 4. *Given that stage k is reached, $\frac{k}{2n} \leq Pr[E] \leq \frac{2(k+1)}{n-k}$.*

Proof: First, we prove the upper bound. In stage k the S-search proceeds until an external edge or cross-edge is discovered. There are $k(n-2k)$ S-external edges, and k^2 cross-edges. If all cross-edges are S-enabled, the probability that a cross-edge is the first external edge discovered in the S-search is $\frac{k}{n-k}$. Similarly, there are $k(n-2k-1)$ D-external edges and $k(k+1)$ cross-edges during the D-search. Thus the probability that a cross edge is discovered in either search is at most $\frac{2(k+1)}{n-k}$.

To prove the lower bound, we note that the same end result is obtained if we run the procedure in the following fashion: increase both L_S and L_D simultaneously, at the same rate, until some edge is discovered. If it is a cross-edge, Phase 1 is over. If it is an S-external edge, then L_D is increased until a D-enabled edge is discovered, and stage k will be over; if it is a D-external edge, then L_S is increased.

When L_S and L_D are increased simultaneously, every cross-edge is either S-enabled or D-enabled. Thus every external edge is equally likely to be the next one discovered. There are $2k(n-2k)$ external edges and k^2 cross-edges. Thus the probability that a cross-edge is the first discovered is at least $\frac{k}{2n}$. ∎

Using Lemma 4, we can give the following characterization of the distribution of the running time of phase 1.

Theorem 5. *Let X be the number of nodes in $S \cup D$ at the end of phase 1, and let P_ℓ be the probability that $X \geq \ell\sqrt{n}$. Then*

$$e^{\frac{-(\ell-1)(\ell-2)}{4}} \geq P_\ell \geq e^{\frac{-3(\ell+1)(3\ell+4)}{2}}$$

where the upper bound holds for $0 \leq \ell \leq \sqrt{n}$, and the lower bound holds for $0 \leq \ell \leq \sqrt[4]{n}/5$.

Proof: We use the following inequality from [Mi], valid when $x < a$, $a \geq 1$.

$$x^2 e^{-x}/a \leq (1 - x/a)^a \leq e^{-x}$$

We will prove the upper bound. Let $t = \lfloor\sqrt{n}\rfloor$. Then

$$\prod_{i=k(t+1)+1}^{(k+1)(t+1)} \left[1 - \frac{i}{2n}\right] \leq \left(1 - \frac{k(t+1)+1}{2n}\right)^{t+1}$$

$$\leq \left(1 - \frac{k}{2\sqrt{n}}\right)^{\sqrt{n}}$$
$$\leq e^{-k/2}$$

From the lower bound in Lemma 4, we conclude

$$P_\ell \leq \prod_{i=1}^{\ell\sqrt{n}} \left(1 - \frac{i}{2n}\right)$$
$$\leq \prod_{k=0}^{\ell-2} \prod_{i=k(t+1)+1}^{(k+1)t} \left(1 - \frac{i}{2n}\right)$$
$$\leq \prod_{k=0}^{\ell-2} e^{-k/2}$$
$$\leq e^{-(\ell-1)(\ell-2)/4}$$

The lower bound is proved in a similar fashion. ∎

Corollary: $E[X] = \Theta(\sqrt{n})$

The total number of edges discovered in phase 1 is X plus the number of internal edges that are discovered. The following theorem completes the analysis of phase 1, by showing that the expected number of queue operations is $O(\sqrt{n})$.

Theorem 6. *The expected number of internal edges discovered in phase 1 is $O(\log n)$.*

Proof: Let Y_i be the number of S-internal edges discovered during stage i of phase 1, and $Y = \sum_{i=1}^{n} Y_i$. Then, since there are at most i^2 S-internal edges and $i(n-2i)$ S-external edges, by Lemma 2 we have an upper bound of $q_i = \frac{i}{n-i}$ on the probability that the first edge discovered in stage i is internal. In fact, $Pr[Y_i = \ell] \leq (q_i)^\ell(1-q_i)$.

Now let Y_i^* be such that $Pr[Y_i^* = \ell] = q^\ell(1-q)$, where $q = \dfrac{k\sqrt{n}}{n - k\sqrt{n}}$, and $k \leq \sqrt{n}/4$. Since $q_i \leq q$ for $i \leq k\sqrt{n}$,

$$Pr\left[\sum_{i=1}^{k\sqrt{n}} Y_i^* \geq \ell\right] \geq Pr\left[\sum_{i=1}^{k\sqrt{n}} Y_i \geq \ell\right]$$

Using Chebyshev's inequality and properties of the geometric distribution, we obtain

$$Pr\left[\left|\sum_{i=1}^{r} Y_i^* - \frac{rq}{1-q}\right| \geq \frac{\epsilon rq}{1-q}\right] \leq \frac{1}{\epsilon^2 qr}$$

Substituting for q and r and simplifying, we get

$$Pr\left[\sum_{i=1}^{k\sqrt{n}} Y_i^* \geq \frac{(\epsilon+1)k^2 n}{n - 2k\sqrt{n}}\right] \leq \frac{n - k\sqrt{n}}{\epsilon^2 k^2 n}$$

For $\epsilon \geq 1$, $k < \sqrt{n}/4$, we have

$$Pr\left[\sum_{i=1}^{k\sqrt{n}} Y_i^* \geq 4\epsilon k^2\right] \leq \frac{1}{(\epsilon k)^2}$$

Now, let $k = 4\sqrt{\log n}$. Then

$$Pr\left[\sum_{i=1}^{4\sqrt{n \log n}} Y_i \geq 64\epsilon \log n\right] \leq \frac{1}{16\epsilon^2 \log n}$$

Since

$$Pr[Y \geq \ell] \leq Pr\left[\sum_{i=1}^{k\sqrt{n}} Y_i \geq \ell\right] + Pr[X > k\sqrt{n}]$$

and the second term is $O(n^{-4})$ by Theorem 5,

$$E[Y] = \sum_{\ell=1}^{n^2} Pr[Y \geq \ell]$$
$$\leq 64 \log n + \sum_{\ell=64\log n}^{n^2} Pr[Y \geq \ell]$$
$$\leq 64 \log n \left(1 + \sum_{\epsilon=1}^{\infty} \frac{1}{16\epsilon^2 \log n}\right) + O(n^{-2})$$
$$= O(\log n)$$

A similar analysis will take care of D-internal edge discoveries. ■

7. Description And Analysis of Phase 2

In general, the s-d path found at the end of phase 1 is not necessarily the shortest s-d path. However, it is easy to prove that the shortest s-d path lies entirely within the search trees associated with S and D except for at most one cross-edge. The aim of phase 2 is to find the shortest path among this restricted set of paths.

Let U be the sum of L_S and L_D at the end of phase 1. U is at least as large as the length of the s-d path discovered at the end of phase 1, and so can be used in our procedure as an upper bound on the length of a shortest s-d path.

The shortest path may go through any node in S or D. Phase 2 is a process of node elimination. A node is *eliminated* when we are sure that any further undiscovered paths through that node are at least as long as the shortest path found so far. We first increase L_S until we can eliminate the last node added to D in phase 1.

The reasoning behind the elimination is as follows. Let v be the last node added to D at phase 1. Let t_v be the value of L_D when v was added to D (the shortest distance from v to d is t_v). We increase L_S until $L_S + t_v \geq U$. At this point, the length of any undiscovered path from s to d via v is at least $L_S + t_v$; hence we can eliminate v from D. Any cross-edges that are discovered while we are increasing L_S define s-d paths, which are candidates for the shortest s-d path.

We then increase L_D until we can eliminate the last node added to S in phase 1, in a similar manner. These two steps are repeated, eliminating nodes from S and D in the reverse order which they were added in phase 1, until both S and D are empty. At this point the shortest path has been found.

In practice, drawing a single S-external edge from the queue may eliminate several nodes from D, and any shorter paths found by drawing cross-edges can be used to update the value of U. In the analysis, however, we assume pessimistically that the latter never occurs, since decreasing U can only help eliminate nodes faster.

The following theorem shows that the expected number of queue operations in bidirectional search is $\Theta(\sqrt{n})$.

Theorem 7. *The expected number of edges discovered during phase 2 is $O(\sqrt{n})$.*

Proof: Consider the following two time intervals. Let T_1 be the interval in phase 1 when L_S is being increased between the value when the ith node s_i was added to S, and the value when the $(i+1)^{st}$ node s_{i+1} is added to S. Let T_2 be the interval in phase 2 when L_D is being increased, between the value at which s_{i+1} is eliminated from S and the value at which s_i is eliminated from S. By the definition of elimination, the lengths of T_1 and T_2 are equal. Let Z_i be the number of edges that are discovered in T_2, and let $Z = \sum_{i=1}^{n} Z_i$. Z is the total number of edges discovered while eliminating nodes from S.

We can apply Lemma 2 in this situation. The good edges are the S-external edges in T_1; there are $i(n-2i)$ of these. The bad edges are the D-enabled edges during T_2; there are at most in of these. If we define $q_i = \frac{n}{2n-2i}$, and Z_i^* to be a random variable such that $Pr[Z_i^* = \ell] = q_i^\ell(1-q_i)$, then $Pr[Z_i \geq x] \leq Pr[Z_i^* \geq x]$. We note

$$E[Z] = \sum_{i=1}^{n} E[Z|X=i]Pr[X=i]$$

$$= \sum_{i=1}^{n} E\left[\sum_{j=1}^{i} Z_i | X = i\right] Pr[X = i]$$

$$\leq \sum_{i=1}^{n} E\left[\sum_{j=1}^{i} Z_i^* | X = i\right] Pr[X = i]$$

$$\leq \sum_{i=1}^{n} E[Z_i] Pr[X \geq i]$$

But $E[Z_i^*] \leq \frac{n}{n-2i} \leq 2$ for $i \leq n/4$, and $Pr[X \geq n/4] \leq e^{-n^2/64}$ by Theorem 5. Thus

$$E[Z] \leq 2E[X] + O(n^2 e^{-n^2/64})$$

and $E[Z]$ is therefore $O(\sqrt{n})$. A similar analysis holds for edges discovered while eliminating nodes from D. ■

Following the same line of reasoning as in the proof of Theorem 6, we can give a characterization of the distribution of Z. We get

$$Pr\left[\sum_{i=1}^{k\sqrt{n}} Z_i^* \leq 4\epsilon k\sqrt{n}\right] \leq \frac{2}{\epsilon^2 k\sqrt{n}}$$

for $\epsilon \geq 1, k \leq \sqrt{n}/4$. Letting $k = 4\sqrt{\log n}$, we can show that for $\epsilon \geq 1$,

$$Pr\left[\sum_{i=1}^{4\sqrt{n \log n}} Z_i \leq 16\epsilon\sqrt{n \log n}\right] \leq \frac{1}{8\epsilon^2\sqrt{n \log n}}$$

8. Relaxation of Assumptions

All of the statements and theorems in this section hold for both unidirectional and bidirectional search. The key to the analysis of the running time for the exponential distribution is that all active edges are equally likely to be the next discovered. We first relax this condition to require only that there is a constant $c_b \geq 1$ such that for any two active edges e_1 and e_2, e_1 is at most c_b times more likely than e_2 to be next discovered.

More formally, let f be the p.d.f. and F the c.d.f. for the edge length distribution. We define $\phi(x) = \frac{f(x)}{1 - F(x)}$. Informally, $\phi(x)$ is the probability that the length of the edge is x, given that it is at least x. Let t lie between 0 and 1. We say that the edge length distribution is c_b-bounded over $[0, t]$ if $\frac{\phi(x)}{\phi(y)} \leq c_b$ for all x, y such that $F(x), F(y) \leq t$.

Theorem 7. *The bounds on the probabilities and expectations in the previous sections hold to within a constant multiplicative factor, depending only on c_b, when the exponential distribution is relaxed to a distribution that is c_b-bounded over $[0, 1]$, i.e., everywhere.* ■

The next relaxation in the assumptions is based on the observation that the algorithm examines only the shortest edges leaving a node. More precisely,

Theorem 8. *If the edge length distribution is c_b-bounded everywhere, then for sufficiently large c_a (depending only on c_b), the probability that the algorithm examines more than $c_a \log n$ edges leaving any node is $o(n^{-2})$.*

Proof Sketch: We shall sketch the proof of this fact for phase 1 and for the exponential distribution. First, we note that $Pr[X \geq n/4] \leq e^{-n^2/64}$, and thus with high probability no more than $n/4$ stages occur. Let $c_a = c_1 c_2$; since s is the node that participates in the most stages, let P be the probability that more than $c_a \log n$ edges leaving s are discovered. If we can show P is $o(n^{-3})$ for c_1, c_2 sufficiently large constants, then the statement of the theorem will hold.

Let P_1 be the probability that a discovery is made in more than $c_1 \log n$ stages, P_2 be the probability that a discovery is made in less than $c_1 \log n$ stages but more than $c_1 c_2 \log n$ edges are discovered. Clearly $P \leq P_1 + P_2$.

To bound P_1, let $X_i = 1$ if a discovery from s occurs at the ith stage, 0 otherwise. There are n edges leaving s, $(i-1)(n-2i)$ external edges leaving other nodes; thus $Pr[X_i] \leq \frac{n}{i(n-2i+2)}$. Let $X = \sum_{i=1}^{n} X_i$. Let X_i^* be a 0-1 random variable that is 1 with probability $\frac{n}{i(n-2i+2)}$, and $X^* = \sum_{i=1}^{n} X_i^*$. Then $Pr[X \geq x] \leq Pr[X^* \geq x]$. We use a result of Bernstein's [R, p. 386]:

$$Pr\left[X^* - M \geq \lambda D(1 + \tfrac{\lambda}{6D} e^{\frac{\lambda}{D}})\right] \leq e^{\frac{-\lambda^2}{2}}$$

where $M = E[X^*]$, $D^2 = \sum \sigma^2(X_i^*)$. We can bound M above by $2\log n$, and bound D^2 between $\log n$ and $2\log n$. Let $\lambda = c\sqrt{\log n}$. Then

$$Pr\left[X^* \geq 2\log n\left(1 + c + \frac{ce^{c/2}}{6}\right)\right] \leq n^{\frac{-c^2}{2}}$$

For c sufficiently large this is $o(n^{-3})$. The bound for P_1 follows by letting $c_1 = 2(1 + c + \frac{ce^{c/2}}{6})$.

To bound P_2, we note that as long as the number of stages is less than $n/4$, the probability of the next edge to be discovered from s being an external edge (which ends a stage) is at least 1/2. We wish to determine Y, the number of edges discovered from this node by the kth stage in which there is a discovery from this node ($k = c_1 \log n$). This is dominated by a negative binomial distribution:

$$Pr[Y = ik] \leq \binom{ik-1}{k-1}\left(\frac{1}{2}\right)^{ik}$$
$$\leq \frac{1}{\sqrt{2\pi k}}\left(\frac{ie}{2^i}\right)^{k}$$

and

$$Pr[Y = (i+1)k] \leq \left(\frac{3}{4}\right)^{k} Pr[Y = ik]$$

Then

$$P_2 \leq \sum_{j=c_2 k}^{\infty} Pr[Y = j]$$
$$\leq k \sum_{i=c_2}^{\infty} Pr[Y = ik]$$
$$\leq k Pr[Y = c_2 k] \sum_{j=0}^{\infty} \left(\frac{3}{4}\right)^{kj}$$
$$\leq \sqrt{\frac{c_1 \log n}{2\pi}} \left(\frac{c_2 e}{2^{c_2}}\right)^{c_1 \log n} \frac{1}{1 - (3/4)^{c_1 \log n}}$$

and for c_2 sufficiently large this is $o(n^{-3})$. ∎

The following theorem can be shown using elementary probability theory.

Theorem 9. *Let $G_{p,n}$ be a random directed graph with n nodes such that each edge in the graph exists with probability p. With probability $1 - o(n^{-2})$, there are at least $c_a \log n$ edges leaving and entering every node in $G_{p,n}$ if $p \geq \frac{c_r \log n}{n}$, where c_r is a constant depending on c_a.* ∎

Let c_r be a constant. A c_r*-short edge* is an edge of length l, where $F(l) \leq \frac{c_r \log n}{n}$. From theorems 8 and 9, we can conclude:

Theorem 10. *For fixed c_b, there is a sufficiently large constant c_r such that if the edge length distribution is c_b-bounded everywhere, then with probability $1 - o(n^{-2})$ the algorithm examines only c_r-short edges.* ∎

This says that the algorithm is oblivious to the distribution of edges that are not c_r-short. Hence the distribution need only be c_b-bounded for such edges. In other words,

Theorem 11. *The bounds on the probabilities and expectations in the previous section*

hold to within a constant multiplicative factor (depending only on c_b), when the exponential distribution is relaxed to a distribution c_b-bounded over $\left[0, \frac{c_r \log n}{n}\right]$, where c_r is sufficiently large depending on the value of c_b. ■

This theorem is quite general. If, for a given distribution, there exist positive constants a, b and ϵ such that $0 < a \leq f(x) \leq b$ for $x \in [0, \epsilon]$, then for sufficiently large n, constants c_b and c_r can be found so that the distribution satisfies the conditions of Theorem 11. The uniform distribution over $[0, x]$, $x \leq 1$, is an example of a distribution for which our results hold. Random sparse graphs can be dealt with by considering them as complete graphs in which the lengths of nonexistent edges are infinite.

Finally, the analysis for directed graphs can be adapted to hold for undirected graphs.

9. Implementation Details

In an implementation of unidirectional or bidirectional search using priority queues, there are at most n edges in a queue at any one time, one for each node in the S or D sets. Hence each queue operation takes $O(\log n)$ time, and the expected running time of bidirectional search (given an input distribution satisfying the conditions of the previous theorem) is $O(\sqrt{n} \log n)$. Unidirectional search will require $O(n \log n)$ time on the average, by the same reasoning.

If the edge-lists are not sorted, Dijkstra's algorithm is typically implemented by the method of temporary and permanent labels [L]. Instead, we suggest the following implementation. We still use priority queues. The only change is that each time a node is first reached by the algorithm, its edge list is made into a priority queue, and this queue is used to ensure that the shortest unused edge leaving the node is always in the main search priority queue. If a is the average length of an adjacency list, this operation takes expected $O(a)$ time [AHU]. Since a must be at least $\Omega(\log n)$ for our results to hold, the cost of these operations dominate all others. Expected running times are $O(an)$ for unidirectional search and $O(a\sqrt{n})$ for bidirectional search.

10. Acknowledgements

We wish to thank Richard Karp for suggesting this as a research problem and for his guidance and inspiration. The empirical results in [Ma], which suggested our direction of attack, were obtained under his supervision. We are also indebted to Alberto Marchetti for his helpful suggestions for simplifying and clarifying our paper.

References

[AHU] Aho, A.A., Hopcroft, J.E., and Ullman, J.D. The Design and Analysis of Computer Algorithms. Addison-Wesley, 1974.

[BT] Balas, E., Toth, P., "Branch and Bound Methods for the Traveling Salesman Problem", *MSRR 488*, Carnegie-Mellon University, March 1983

[D] Dijkstra, E.W. "A Note on Two Problems in Connection With Graphs", *Numerische Mathematik*, 1(1959), pp. 260-271.

[EK] Edmonds, J., Karp, R.M. "Theoretical Improvements in Algorithmic Efficiency for Network Flow Problems", *Journal of the ACM*, Vol. 19, No. 2, April 1972, pp. 248-264

[L] Lawler, E.L. Combinatorial Optimization: Networks and Matroids. Holt, Rinehart and Winston, 1976.

[Ma] Ma, Y. "A Shortest Path Algorithm with Expected Running Time $O(\sqrt{V} \log V)$", Master's Project Report, UC Berkeley.

[Mi] Mitrinovic, D.S. Analytic Inequalities. Springer-Verlag, 1970.

[Pe] Perl, Y. "Average Analysis of Simple Path Algorithms", *Tech. Report UIUCDCS-R-77-905*, University of Illinois at Urbana-Champaign, 1977.

[Po] Pohl, I. "Bidirectional Search." *Machine Intelligence*, 6(1971), pp. 127-140.

[R] Renyi, A. Probability Theory. North-Holland, 1970.

APPLICATIONS OF AN INFINITE SQUAREFREE CO-CFL*

Michael G. Main[1], Walter Bucher[2] and David Haussler[3]

KEYWORDS: Context-free languages, repetitions, pumping lemmas, syntactic monoids, locally linear languages.

1. INTRODUCTION

A *square* is an immediately repeated nonempty string, *e.g.*, *aa, abab, newyork-newyork.* A string x is called *square-containing* if it contains a substring which is a square. For example, the string *mississippi* contains the segment *iss* twice in a row; in fact, *mississippi* contains a total of five squares. On the other hand, *colorado* contains no squares (the character *o* appears several times, but not consecutively). A string without squares is called *squarefree.*

In a study of context-free languages, Autebert *et al* [2,3] collected several conjectures about square-containing strings. One of the weakest conjectures was that no context-free language (CFL) could include all of the square-containing strings and still have an infinite complement. Contrary to this conjecture, such a language has recently been constructed [13]. This construction is summarized here, together with applications to some other combinatorial problems about CFLs.

The path to the language is via the "parity sequence", given in section 2. From this sequence we construct a CFL with an infinite complement that contains only *cubefree* strings (no nonempty substring of the form xxx). Using this result, together with closure properties, we can construct a CFL with an infinite squarefree complement (section 3). The final section uses the square-containing CFL to solve several other problems, and to ask some new questions. Perrot's conjecture [14,2] that the

*The authors gratefully acknowledge the support of NSF grants IST-8317918 and the Austrian Bundes Ministerium fur Wissenschaft und Forschung.

[1] Department of Computer Science, University of Colorado, Boulder, CO 80309, USA.
[2] Intitutes for Information Processing, Technical University of Graz, A-8010 Graz, AUSTRIA.
[3] Department of Mathematics and Computer Science, University of Denver, Denver, CO 80208, USA.

syntactic monoid of a non-regular CFL must have an element of infinite order is shown to be false, as is a related conjecture about iterative pairs. We also use the language to generate a 1-locally linear full AFL of CFLs, strictly greater than the regular languages. This answers a question of van der Walt [18,2].

Notation: Notation is standard from Hopcroft and Ullman's text [11]. The length of a string x is denoted by $|x|$.

2. A CFL with an Infinite Strongly-Cubefree Complement

A *cube* consists of three consecutive occurrences of a nonempty string, such as *aaa*, *ababab*, or *abaabaaba*. A string is called *cubefree* if no substring is a cube. A string is called *strongly cubefree* if it has no substring of the form xxa, where x is a nonempty string and a is the first character of x. For example, *mississippi* is cubefree, but not strongly cubefree (because of *ississi*). A language is called *strongly cubefree* if every string in the language is strongly cubefree. This section gives a CFL with an infinite strongly-cubefree complement.

The construction begins with a sequence $p = p_1p_2p_3\cdots$, called the parity sequence. The ith character of the sequence, denoted p_i, is defined to be 0 if the binary representation of i contains an even number of 1s; otherwise p_i is 1. So, the first few characters of the sequence are 110100110010. Thue showed that the parity sequence is strongly cubefree, and since then the sequence has had a number of rediscoveries with a variety of applications [7,10,16,17]. (See Braunholtz [5] for an elegant proof of the fact that the sequence is strongly cubefree.)

For our purposes, we need an inductive definition of the parity sequence:

(1) $p_1 = 1$.

(2) $p_{2i+1} \neq p_{2i}$ $(i \geq 1)$.

(3) $p_{2i} = p_i$ $(i \geq 1)$.

Define L to be the set of strings over $\{0,1\}$ which are *not* prefixes of the parity sequence. Clearly L has an infinite, strongly-cubefree complement (the prefixes of p). It remains to show that L is context-free. But, it is easy to build a nondeterministic pushdown automaton, with input alphabet {0,1}, which accepts exactly L. The PDA accepts a string x (with length $|x|$) iff at least one of these conditions holds:

(1) $x_1 = 0$, or

(2) for some i ($\frac{|x|}{2} > i \geq 1$): $x_{2i+1} = x_{2i}$, or

(3) for some i ($\frac{|x|}{2} \geq i \geq 1$): $x_{2i} \neq x_i$.

The first two conditions can be checked by a finite automaton. The third condition can be checked by nondeterministically guessing an i where it holds, and using the stack to confirm or deny this.

3. A CFL with an Infinite Squarefree Complement

Let p be the parity sequence defined in section 2. From p, we can define a new sequence $s = s_1 s_2 s_3 \cdots$, over the alphabet {0,1,2}, as follows:

(1) $s_1 = 2$.

(2) for $i > 1$: s_i = the number of 1s between the ith 0 and the $(i+1)^{th}$ 0 in p.

Braunholtz [5] gives a nice proof that s contains only the characters {0,1,2}, and is squarefree.

Define M to be the set of strings over {0,1,2} which are *not* prefixes of s. Clearly M has an infinite squarefree complement (*i.e.*, every string in the complement is squarefree). M is also context-free, because it can be obtained as an inverse homomorphic image of the CFL L, given in section 2. Specifically, let $h(0) = 0$, $h(1) = 10$, and $h(2) = 110$. Then

$$M = h^{-1}(L) = \{x \mid h(x) \text{ is not a prefix of } p\}.$$

Since CFLs are closed under inverse homomorphisms (for example, see [9, page 208]), this implies that M is context-free.

4. Applications and Open Problems

The CFL from section 3 has an infinite squarefree complement. The conjecture that no such language exists was actually a weak version of several older conjectures dating back to 1973. Here are these conjectures, which are solved by the language M of section 3. We also list some problems that remain open.

Problem 1 (solved): The syntactic monoid of a language L consists of the equivalence classes induced by the relation $x \equiv y$ iff for all strings u and v, $uxv \in L \iff uyv \in L$. With the operation of concatenation, this forms a monoid. Perrot [14,2] conjectured that any non-regular CFL must have an element of infinite order (i.e., a string x such that the equivalence classes for x, xx, xxx,... are all distinct). The language M of section 3 violates this conjecture, since $xx \equiv xxx$ for any string x.

Problem 2 (solved): For a language L, an iterative pair is a tuple (u,v,w,x,y) such that for all $i>0$, $uv^iwx^iy \in L$. The iterative pair is called very degenerate if $uv^*wx^*y \subseteq L$ and it is positive degenerate if $uv^+wx^+y \subseteq L$. Boasson [4] proved that when every iterative pair of a CFL is very degenerate, then the language is regular. It was conjectured that the result still holds if every iterative pair is positive degenerate [2], but again, M from section 3 provides a counterexample.

Problem 3 (solved): A language L is called 1-*ll* (locally linear) provided that there exists some integer n such that whenever $w \in L$ and there are n "marked" positions in w, then w may be factorized as $w = xyz$, where each of x, y and z contain a marked position, and $xy^*z \subseteq L$. These are the languages that can be "pumped" almost anywhere, and were introduced by van der Walt [18]. It was conjectured that any cylinder of 1-*ll* context-free languages contained only regular languages [1,2,3]. (Recall a cylinder is a family of languages which is closed under inverse homomorphism and intersection with a regular set.) We disprove this conjecture with the following lemma, which is based in part on [1]:

Lemma: *Let ρ be an infinite squarefree sequence over an alphabet Δ and define*

$$L = \{x \in \Delta^* \mid x \text{ is } not \text{ a prefix of } \rho\}.$$

Let $R \subseteq \Sigma^*$ be a regular language, and let $h:\Sigma^* \to \Delta^*$ be a homomorphism. Then $h^{-1}(L) \cap R$ is a 1-ll language.

Proof: Let R be recognized by a deterministic finite automaton with q states, and let $p>1$ be $\max\{|h(a)| : a \in \Sigma\}$. Given $(q+1)^2(q+1+p)$ marked positions in a string $w \in h^{-1}(L) \cap R$ we will find a factorization $w=xyz$ such that each of x, y and z contain a marked position and $xy^*z \subseteq h^{-1}(L) \cap R$. Actually, it will be sufficient to show $xy^*z \subseteq R$ and $h(xz) \in L$, since $h(xy^iz) \in L$ whenever $i \geq 2$ (recall that $\overline{L}$ is squarefree). We proceed with two cases:

Case 1: Suppose that there is a substring u of w such that u contains $q+1$ marked positions and $h(u)=\epsilon$ (the empty string). Then there are two marked positions in u such that the finite automaton for R is in the same state immediately after these two different positions. This gives us a factorization $w=xyz$ such that $xy^*z \subseteq R$ and $h(y)=\epsilon$. Therefore, $h(xz) = h(xyz) \in L$, as required.

Case 2: Suppose that whenever there is a substring u of w with $h(u) = \epsilon$, then u contains at most q marked positions. We then pick out certain substrings of w, as follows: the first substring, u_1, begins at the leftmost marked position of w and continues until we have included exactly $q+1$ positions which are not erased by h (call these the non-erased positions of u_1). The next substring, u_2, begins at the next marked position of w (after u_1) and continues until it has exactly $q+1$ positions which are not erased by h. We continue in this way to find substrings u_3, $u_4 \cdots$, until w is exhausted. Note that by the condition of case 2, each u_i has at most $(q+1)^2$

marked positions. Since w has a total of $(q+1)^2(q+1+p)$ marked positions, we have identified at least $(q+1+p)$ substrings.

For each substring u_i, we define a vector of states $\overline{v_i} = (s_1, \cdots, s_{q+1})$, where s_k is the state of the finite automaton for R immediately after reading the kth non-erased character of u_i. Every such vector has at least one repeated state, since there are a total of q states. Moreover, among the first $q+1$ vectors, there are two vectors, $\overline{v_i}$ and $\overline{v_j}$ (with $1 \leq i < j \leq q+1$), which contain the same state twice each. Call this state s. We can now factorize w as $w = w_0 w_1 w_2 w_3$, where:

- w_0 is the prefix of w up to the point in u_i where the finite automaton reaches state s for the first time. This includes a marked position (the first character of u_i).
- w_1 is a portion of u_i which takes the finite automaton back to state s, including at least one non-erased position. Note that $1 \leq |h(w_1)| \leq (q+1)p$, since u_i contains only $q+1$ non-erased positions.
- w_2 contains the portion of w after w_1 and up to some point in u_j where the finite automaton is back in state s. This includes a marked position (the first character of u_j).
- w_3 is the rest of w. Since $j \leq q+1$, this suffix must contain at least p of the u_m substrings. Hence, it contains some marked positions and also $|h(w_3)| \geq (q+1)p \geq |h(w_1)|$. This inequality will be used below.

Now, each of w_0, w_2 and w_3 contains a marked position and both $w_0(w_1 w_2)^* w_3 \subseteq R$ and $w_0 w_1 w_2^* w_3 \subseteq R$. To complete the proof we must show either $h(w_0 w_3) \in L$ or $h(w_0 w_1 w_3) \in L$. In order to reach a contradiction, assume $h(w_0 w_3) \notin L$ and $h(w_0 w_1 w_3) \notin L$. Then both $h(w_0 w_3)$ and $h(w_0 w_1 w_3)$ are prefixes of ρ, which implies that $h(w_3)$ is a prefix of $h(w_1 w_3) = h(w_1)h(w_3)$. But $1 \leq |h(w_1)| \leq |h(w_3)|$, which implies that $h(w_1)$ is a non-empty prefix of $h(w_3)$. This implies that $h(w_0 w_1 w_3)$ contains two adjacent copies of the non-empty string $h(w_1)$ -- which cannot be since $h(w_0w_1w_3)$ is a prefix of the squarefree sequence ρ. By this contradiction we conclude that either $h(w_0w_3) \in L$ or $h(w_0w_1w_3) \in L$, as required. □

Corollary 1: *The cylinder of languages generated by the CFL M of section 3 contains only 1-ll langugages.* □

Corollary 2: *The full-AFL of languages generated by the CFL M of section 3 contains only 1-ll langugages.*

Proof: The full AFL generated by *M* is the closure of the cylinder under the operations homomorphism, union, concatenation and Kleene star. It is easy to show that 1-*ll* languages are closed under these four operations (see [18]). □

Problem 4 (open): A permuted square (or *permutation*) is a nonempty string of the form xy, where x has the same characters as y, but maybe in a different order. For example: *abcabaca*. A string is called *permutation-free* if no substring is a permutation, and a language is permutation-free if every string in it is permutation-free. For a three letter alphabet, the longest permutation-free string has length seven. For a five letter alphabet, Pleasants has shown that there are infinite permutation-free sequences [15]. (The question of four letters remains open.) The question asked here is whether there is any CFL with an infinite, permutation-free complement.

Problem 5 (open): This is a more specific version of problem 4. A string is called *permutation-containing* if it has a permutation as a substring. Is the set of permutation-containing strings context-free? For an alphabet of three or fewer characters, the answer is yes -- in fact it is regular, since its complement (the permutation-free strings) is finite. For sixteen or more characters, the answer is no, as shown by the "Interchange Lemma" [12]. What about four to fifteen characters?

Problem 6 (open): Let L be a language over an alphabet Σ. It is not hard to show that $\Sigma^*L\Sigma^*$ is regular iff CORE(L) is regular, where

$$\mathrm{CORE}(L) = \{x \in L \mid x \text{ has no proper substring in } L\}.$$

It would be useful to have a similar characterization of when $\Sigma^*L\Sigma^*$ is context-free. Also along these lines: is there any context-free language L such that L has an infinite squarefree complement and $L = \Sigma^*L\Sigma^*$? Such a language would disprove conjecture A from [6].

Problem 7 (open): Ehrenfeucht, Parikh and Rozenberg have provided a necessary and sufficient pumping lemma for regular languages which involves the complement of the language being examined [8]. Is there such a lemma for context-free languages? One consequence of the languages constructed in sections 2 and 3 is this: there is no possibility of any sort of pumping lemma for co-CFLs (languages whose complement is context-free). This fact should be taken into account in any search for a necessary and sufficient pumping lemma for CFLs.

References

(1) J.M. Autebert, L. Boasson and G. Cousineau, A note on 1-locally linear languages, *Information and Control* 37(1978), 1-4.

(2) J.M. Autebert, J. Beauquier, L. Boasson and M. Nivat, Quelques problems ouverts en theorie des languages algebriques, *RAIRO Informatique theorique / Theoretical Informatics* 13 (1979) 4, 363-378.

(3) J.M. Autebert, J. Beauquier, L. Boasson and M. Latteux, Very small families of algebraic nonrational languages, in *Formal Language Theory: Perspectives and Open Problems* (R. Book, Ed.), Academic Press (1980), New York, 89-108.

(4) L. Boasson, Un critere de rationalite des lanages algebriques, in: *International Conference on Automata and Programming Languages*, (M. Nivat, ed.), (North-

Holland, 1972), 359-365.

(5) C.H. Braunholtz, Solution to problem 5030, *Am. Math. Mo.* 70 (1963), 675-676.

(6) W. Bucher, A. Ehrenfeucht and D. Haussler. On Total Regulators Generated by Derivation Relations, pre-publication manuscript.

(7) A. Cobham Uniform tag sequences, *Math. Sys. Theory* 6 (1972), 164-191.

(8) A. Ehrenfeucht, R. Parikh and G. Rozenberg, Pumping lemmas for regular sets, *SIAM J. of Computing* 10, 1981.

(9) M. Harrison, *Introduction to Formal Language Theory*, Addison-Wesley, Reading, MA., (1978), 36-40.

(10) G.A. Hedlund, Remarks on the work of Axel Thue on sequences, *Nord. Mat. Tidskr.* 16 (1967), 148-150. MR 37 (1959), #4454.

(11) J.E. Hopcroft and J.D. Ullman, *Introduction to Automata Theory, Languages and Computation*, Addison-Wesley, Reading, MA., 1979.

(12) M.G. Main, Permutations are not context-free: an application of the interchange lemma, *IPL* (1982), 68-71.

(13) M.G. Main, An infinite squarefree co-CFL, *IPL*, to appear.

(14) J.F. Perrot, Introduction aux monoides syntactiques des langages algebriques, in: *Languages Algebriques* (J.P. Crestin and M. Nivat, eds), (1973), p. 167-222.

(15) P.A.B. Pleasants, Nonrepetitive sequences, *Proc. Cambridge Phil. Soc.* 68 (1970), 267-274.

(16) A. Thue, Uber unendliche Zeichenreihen, *Norske Videnskabers Selskabs Skrifter Mat.-Nat. Kl. (Kristiania)* (1906), Nr. 7, 1-22.

(17) A. Thue, Uber die gegenseitige Lage gleicher Teile gewisser Zeichenreihen, *Norske Videnskabers Selskabs Skrifter Mat.-Nat. Kl. (Kristiania)* (1912), Nr. 1, 1-67.

(18) A.P.J. van der Walt, Locally linear families of languages, *Information and Control* 32(1976), 27-32.

SPECIAL RELATIONS IN AUTOMATED DEDUCTION

Zohar Manna
Computer Science Department
Stanford University

Richard Waldinger
Artificial Intelligence Center
SRI International

ABSTRACT

Two deduction rules are introduced to give streamlined treatment to relations of special importance in an automated theorem-proving system. These rules, the *relation replacement* and *relation matching* rules, generalize to an arbitrary binary relation the paramodulation and E-resolution rules, respectively, for equality, and may operate within a nonclausal or clausal system. The new rules depend on an extension of the notion of *polarity* to apply to subterms as well as to subsentences, with respect to a given binary relation. The rules allow us to eliminate troublesome axioms, such as transitivity and monotonicity, from the system; proofs are shorter and more comprehensible, and the search space is correspondingly deflated.

1. INTRODUCTION

In any theorem-proving system, the task of representing properties of objects is shared between axioms and rules of inference. The axioms of the system are easier to introduce and modify, because they are expressed in a logical language. However, because axioms are declarative rather than imperative, they are given no individual heuristic controls. The rules of inference, on the other hand, cannot be altered without reprogramming the system, and they are usually expressed in the system's programming language. However, the rules can be given individual heuristic controls and strategies.

It is customary to use rules of inference to express properties of the logical connectives, which are the same from one theory to the next, and to use axioms to express properties of constants, functions, and relations, which may vary. It is hazardous, however, to express certain properties of functions and relations by axioms. Some properties of the equality relation, for example, are rarely represented axiomatically. For one thing, in a first-order system indefinitely many axioms are necessary to represent the substitutivity property of this relation, depending on how many function and relation symbols are in the vocabulary of the theory. More importantly, axioms for equality are difficult to control strategically, because they have many irrelevant consequences.

In response to this problem, some theorem-proving researchers have paraphrased their theories to avoid explicit mention of the equality axiom (e.g., Kowalski [79]). Others have adopted special inference rules for dealing with equality. In resolution systems, two equality rules, paramodulation (Wos and Robinson [69]) and E-resolution (Morris [69]) have been found to be effective. Variations of these rules are used in many theorem provers today (e.g., Boyer and Moore [79], Digricoli [83]). By a single application of either of these rules, we can derive conclusions that would require several steps if the properties of equality were represented axiomatically. The proofs are markedly shorter, and the search spaces are even more dramatically compressed because the axioms and intermediate steps are not required. Within their limited domain of application, theorem-proving systems using these rules surpass most human beings in their capabilities.

Special Relations

The authors became involved in theorem proving because of its application to program synthesis, the derivation of a program to meet a given specification. We have been pursuing a deductive approach to this problem, under which computer programming is regarded as a theorem-proving task. In the proofs required for program synthesis, certain relations assume special importance. Again and again, proofs require us to reason not only about the equality relation, but also about the less-than relation $<$ (over the integers or reals), the subset relation $\subseteq$, the sublist relation $\preceq_{list}$, or the subtree relation $\preceq_{tree}$. To represent the transitivity and other properties of these relations axiomatically leads to many of the same problems that were faced in dealing with equality: the axioms apply almost everywhere, spawning innumerable

This research was supported in part by the National Science Foundation under grants MCS-82-14523 and MCS-81-05565, by the Defense Advanced Research Projects Agency under contract N00039-84-C-0211, by the United States Air Force Office of Scientific Research under contract AFOSR-81-0014, by the Office of Naval Research under contract N00014-84-C-0706, and by a contract from the International Business Machines Corporation.

consequences that swamp the system. Yet we would not want to implement a new inference rule for each of the relations we find important.

Both the paramodulation and the E-resolution rules are based on the *substitutivity* property of equality, that if two elements are equal they may be used interchangeably; i.e., for any sentence $\mathcal{P}\langle x, y\rangle$, the sentence

if $x = y$
then if $\mathcal{P}\langle x, y\rangle$ *then* $\mathcal{P}\langle y, x\rangle$

is valid. Here $\mathcal{P}\langle y, x\rangle$ is the result of replacing in $\mathcal{P}\langle x, y\rangle$ certain (perhaps none) of the occurrences of x with y, and certain (perhaps none) of the occurrences of y with x. (The notations we use here informally will be defined systematically later on. We assume throughout that sentences are quantifier-free.)

We observe that many of the relations we regard as important exhibit substitutivity properties similar to the above property of equality, but under restricted circumstances. For example, over the nonnegative integers, we can show that

if $x < y$
then if $a \leq x \cdot b$ *then* $a \leq y \cdot b$

and, over the lists, we can show that

if $x \preceq_{list} y$
then if $u \in x$ *then* $u \in y$.

Knowing that $x < y$ or that $x \preceq_{list} y$ does not allow us to use x and y interchangeably, but it does allow us to replace certain occurrences of x with y, and vice versa.

Based on such substitutivity properties, we can introduce two deduction rules that generalize the paramodulation and E-resolution rules for equality to an arbitrary relation, under appropriate circumstances. Just as the equality rules enable us to drop the transitivity and substitutivity axioms for equality, the new relation rules enable us to drop the corresponding troublesome axioms for the relations of our theory.

Polarity

For the equality relation, knowing that $x = y$ allows us to replace in a given sentence any occurrence of x with y and any occurrence of y with x, obtaining a sentence that follows from the given one. For an arbitrary binary relation $\prec$, knowing that $x \prec y$ still may allow us to replace certain occurrences of x with y and certain occurrences of y with x. We describe a syntactic procedure that, for a given relation $\prec$, identifies which occurrences of x and y in a given sentence can be replaced, provided we know that $x \prec y$.

More precisely, we identify particular occurrences of subexpressions of a given sentence as being positive (+), negative (−), or both, or neither, with respect to $\prec$. If $x \prec y$, positive occurrences of x can be replaced with y, and negative occurrences of y can be replaced with x. In other words, we can establish the substitutivity property that, for any sentence $\mathcal{P}\langle x^+, y^-\rangle$, the sentence

if $x \prec y$
then if $\mathcal{P}\langle x^+, y^-\rangle$ *then* $\mathcal{P}\langle y^+, x^-\rangle$

is valid (over the theory in question). Here $\mathcal{P}\langle y^+, x^-\rangle$ is the sentence obtained from $\mathcal{P}\langle x^+, y^-\rangle$ by replacing certain positive occurrences of x with y and certain negative occurrences of y with x. With respect to the equality relation, every subexpression is both positive and negative; therefore, if we take $\prec$ to be $=$, this property reduces to the substitutivity of equality.

The new rules, like the equality rules, allow us to perform in a single application inferences that would require many steps in a conventional system. Proofs are shorter and closer to an intuitive argument; the search space is condensed accordingly.

Nonclausal Deduction

The paramodulation and E-resolution rules are formulated for sentences in clausal form (a disjunction of atomic sentences and their negations); on the other hand, the two corresponding rules we introduce apply to free-form sentences, with a full set of logical connectives (cf. Manna and Waldinger [80], Murray [82], Stickel [82]). By adapting such a nonclausal system, we avoid the proliferation of sentences and the disintegration of intuition that accompany the translation to clausal form. Also, it is awkward to express the mathematical induction principle in a clausal system, because we must do induction on sentences that may require more than one clause to express. On the other hand, our rules are also immediately and directly applicable to clausal theorem-proving systems.

This is an abbreviated version of a full paper (Manna and Waldinger [85a]), from which we have omitted some results, all proofs, and many examples.

2. PRELIMINARIES

Before we can define our central notion, that of polarity of a subexpression with respect to a relation, we must introduce some concepts and notations. We will be brief and informal, because we believe that this material will be familiar to most readers.

Expressions

We consider *terms* composed (in the usual way) of constants, variables, and function symbols. (We reserve the symbols u, v, w, x, y, z, with optional subscripts, as variables.) The constants are identified with the 0-ary function symbols. We also consider *propositions* composed from terms, relation symbols, and the truth symbols (logical constants) *true* and *false*, and *sentences* composed from propositions and logical connectives. (We regard logical connectives as relations over the truth values $\{T, F\}$.) Note that we do not include the quantifiers $\forall$ and $\exists$ in our language.

The *operators* consist of the function and the relation symbols. The *expressions* consist of the terms and the sentences; the *ground* expressions are those that contain no variables. The expressions that occur in a given expression are its *subexpressions*. They are said to be *proper* if they are distinct from the entire expression.

Replacement

We introduce the operation of replacing subexpressions of a given expression with other expressions. We actually have two distinct notions of replacement, depending on whether or not every occurrence of the subexpression is to be replaced.

Suppose s, t, and e are expressions, where s and t are either both sentences or both terms. If we write e as $e[s]$, then $e[t]$ denotes the expression obtained by replacing every occurrence of s in $e[s]$ with t; we call this a *total replacement*. If we write e as $e\langle s\rangle$, then $e\langle t\rangle$ denotes the expression obtained by replacing certain (perhaps none) of the occurrences of s in $e\langle s\rangle$ with t; we call this a *partial replacement*. We do not require that $e[s]$ or $e\langle s\rangle$ actually contain any occurrences of s; if not, $e[t]$ and $e\langle t\rangle$ are the same as $e[s]$ and $e\langle s\rangle$, respectively. Also, while the result of a total replacement is unique, a partial replacement can produce any of several expressions. For example, if $e[s]$ is $p(s,s,b)$, then $e[t]$ is $p(t,t,b)$. On the other hand, if $e\langle s\rangle$ is $p(s,s,b)$, then $e\langle t\rangle$ could be any of $p(s,s,b)$, $p(t,s,b)$, $p(s,t,b)$, or $p(t,t,b)$. If we want to be more specific about which occurrences are replaced, we must do so in words.

We can extend the definition to allow the replacement of several subexpressions at once. Suppose $s_1, \ldots, s_n, t_1, \ldots, t_n$, and e are expressions, where the s_i are distinct and, for each i, s_i and t_i are either both sentences or both terms. If we write e as $e[s_1, \ldots, s_n]$, then $e[t_1, \ldots, t_n]$ denotes the expression obtained by replacing simultaneously every occurrence of each expression s_i in e with the corresponding expression t_i; we call this a *multiple total replacement*. If we write e as $e\langle s_1, \ldots, s_n\rangle$, then $e\langle t_1, \ldots, t_n\rangle$ denotes any of the expressions obtained by replacing simultaneously certain (perhaps none) of the occurrences of some of the expressions s_i in e with the corresponding expression t_i; we call this a *multiple partial replacement*.

Substitutions

We have a special notation for a substitution, indicating the total replacement of variables with terms. A theory of substitutions was developed by Robinson [65], in the paper in which the resolution principle was introduced. A fuller exposition of this theory appears in Manna and Waldinger [81].

For any distinct variables $x_1, x_2, \ldots, x_n$ and any terms $t_1, t_2, \ldots, t_n$, a *substitution*

$$\theta: \ \{x_1 \leftarrow t_1,\ x_2 \leftarrow t_2,\ \ldots,\ x_n \leftarrow t_n\}$$

is a set of replacement pairs $x_i \leftarrow t_i$. The *empty substitution* $\{\,\}$ is the set of no replacement pairs. For any substitution θ and expression e, we denote by $e\theta$ the expression obtained by *applying* θ *to* e, i.e., by simultaneously replacing every occurrence of the variable x_i in e with the expression t_i, for each replacement pair $x_i \leftarrow t_i$ in θ. We also say that $e\theta$ is an *instance* of e.

3. RELATIONAL POLARITY

We are now ready to define our key notion, the polarity of (an occurrence of) a subexpression with respect to a given binary relation. We actually define the polarity of a subexpression with respect to two binary relations, $\prec_1$ and $\prec_2$. This notion is to be defined so that, if the subexpression is positive, replacing that subexpression with a larger expression (with respect to $\prec_1$) will make the entire expression larger (with respect to $\prec_2$). Similarly, if the subexpression is negative, replacing that subexpression with a smaller expression (with respect to $\prec_1$) will make the entire expression larger (with respect to $\prec_2$).

Definition (polarity for the arguments of an operator):
Let f be an n-ary operator (i.e., function or relation) f and $\prec_1$ and $\prec_2$ binary relations. Then

- f is *positive* over its ith argument with respect to $\prec_1$ and $\prec_2$ if the sentence

$$\begin{array}{l} \textit{if } x \prec_1 y \\ \textit{then } f(z_1, ..., z_{i-1}, x, z_{i+1}, ..., z_n) \prec_2 f(z_1, ..., z_{i-1}, y, z_{i+1}, ..., z_n) \end{array}$$

is valid. In other words, replacing x with a larger element y makes $f(z_1, ..., z_{i-1}, x, z_{i+1}, ..., z_n)$ larger.

- f is to be *negative* over its ith argument with respect to $\prec_1$ and $\prec_2$ if the sentence

$$\begin{array}{l} \textit{if } x \prec_1 y \\ \textit{then } f(z_1, ..., z_{i-1}, y, z_{i+1}, ..., z_n) \prec_2 f(z_1, ..., z_{i-1}, x, z_{i+1}, ..., z_n) \end{array}$$

is valid. In other words, replacing y with a smaller element x makes $f(z_1, ..., z_{i-1}, y, z_{i+1}, ..., z_n)$ larger. ▟

When we say that a relation $p(z_1, \ldots, z_n)$ is positive or negative over its ith argument with respect to a single relation $\prec_1$, without mentioning a second relation $\prec_2$, we shall by convention take $\prec_2$ to be the *if-then* connective. Every relation is both positive and negative over each of its arguments with respect to the equality relation $=$. Also, every connective is both positive and negative over all its arguments with respect to $\equiv$. Note that a binary relation $\prec$ is transitive if and only if it is negative with respect to $\prec$ itself over its first argument, and $\prec$ is transitive if and only if it is positive with respect to $\prec$ over its second argument.

When we say that a connective is positive or negative over its ith argument, without mentioning any relations $\prec_1$ and $\prec_2$ at all, we shall by convention take both $\prec_1$ and $\prec_2$ to be the *if-then* connective. Polarity in this sense is close to its ordinary use in logic; for example, the negation connective *not* is negative in its first (and only) argument.

We are now ready to define polarity for the subexpressions of a given expression. The definition is inductive.

Definition (polarity of a subexpression):
Let $\prec_1$ and $\prec_2$ be binary relations. Then an expression s *is positive* [or *negative*] *in* s itself with respect to $\prec_1$ and $\prec_2$ if the sentence

$$\textit{if } x \prec_1 y \textit{ then } x \prec_2 y \quad [\text{or} \quad \textit{if } x \prec_1 y \textit{ then } x \succ_2 y\,]$$

is valid.

Let f be an n-ary operator and $e_1, e_2, \ldots, e_n$ be expressions. Consider an occurrence of s in one of the expressions e_i. Then the occurrence of s is *positive* [or *negative*] in $f(e_1, e_2, \ldots, e_n)$ with respect to $\prec_1$ and $\prec_2$ if there exists a binary relation $\prec$ such that the polarity of the occurrence of s in e_i with respect to $\prec_1$ and $\prec$ is the same as [is opposite to] the polarity of f over its ith argument with respect to $\prec$ and $\prec_2$. ▟

Note that if s has both polarities in e_i, or if f has both polarities over its ith argument, then s automatically has both polarities in $f(e_1, e_2, \ldots, e_n)$. We may indicate the polarity of a subexpression s by annotating it s^+, s^-, or $s^\pm$. For example, suppose our theory includes the theories of sets and nonnegative integers. The occurrence of s in the sentence $card(s^-) < m$ is negative with respect to the subset relation $\subseteq$ and the *if-then* connective. For note that *card* is positive over its argument with respect to $\subseteq$ and $\leq$ and that $<$ is negative over its first argument with respect to $\leq$ and *if-then*. Therefore, we know that s is positive in $card(s)$ with respect to $\subseteq$ and $\leq$ and that $card(s)$ is negative in $card(s) < m$ with respect to $\leq$ and *if-then*. By the definition, taking $\prec_1$ to be $\subseteq$, $\prec$ to be $\leq$, and $\prec_2$ to be *if-then*, we conclude that s is negative in $card(s) < m$ with respect to $\subseteq$ and *if-then*.

When we say that an occurrence of a subexpression is positive or negative in a sentence with respect to a single relation $\prec_1$, without mentioning a second relation $\prec_2$, we shall again take $\prec_2$ to be the *if-then* connective. When we say that an occurrence of a subsentence is positive or negative in a sentence, without mentioning any relation at all, we shall again take both $\prec_1$ and $\prec_2$ to be *if-then*.

We can now establish the fundamental property of polarity.

Proposition (*polarity replacement*): For any binary relation $\prec$ and sentence $\mathcal{P}\langle x^+, y^-\rangle$, the sentence

$$\begin{array}{l} \textit{if } x \prec y \\ \textit{then if } \mathcal{P}\langle x^+, y^-\rangle \textit{ then } \mathcal{P}\langle y^+, x^-\rangle \end{array}$$

is valid. Here $\mathcal{P}\langle y^+, x^-\rangle$ is the result of replacing in $\mathcal{P}\langle x^+, y^-\rangle$ certain positive occurrences of x with y and certain negative occurrences of y with x, where polarity is taken in $\mathcal{P}\langle x^+, y^-\rangle$ with respect to $\prec$. ┘

The proposition allows us to replace occurrences of both x and y in the same sentence and (trivially) admits the possibility that no replacements are made.

Example: Suppose our theory includes the theories of finite sets and integers. Take $\mathcal{P}\langle x^+, y^-\rangle$ to be the sentence

$$\mathcal{P}\langle x^+, y^-\rangle: \quad a < card(x^+ \sim y^-) \textit{ and } card(y^- \sim x^+) \leq b.$$

Take $\prec$ to be the subset relation $\subseteq$. Note that, with respect to $\subseteq$, both occurrences of x are positive and both occurrences of y are negative in $\mathcal{P}\langle x^+, y^-\rangle$, as indicated by the annotations. Therefore, according to the proposition, the following sentence (among others) is valid:

$$\begin{array}{l} \textit{if } x \subseteq y \\ \textit{then if } a < card(x \sim y) \textit{ and } card(y \sim x) \leq b \\ \qquad \textit{then } a < card(x \sim x) \textit{ and } card(y \sim y) \leq b, \end{array}$$

for which one occurrence of x and one occurrence of y in $\mathcal{P}\langle x^+, y^-\rangle$ has been replaced. ┘

4. NONCLAUSAL DEDUCTION

In this section we present a basic nonclausal deduction system, without any special-relation rules. This system bears some resemblance to those of Murray [82] and Stickel [82]; it is based on the system of Manna and Waldinger [80], but is simplified in several respects.

The Deduced Set

The deduction system we describe operates on a set, called the *deduced* set, of sentences in quantifier-free first-order logic. We attempt to show that a given deduced set is unsatisfiable, i.e., that there is no interpretation under which all the sentences are true. We do not require that the sentences be in clausal form; indeed, they can use the full set of connectives of propositional logic, including equivalence ($\equiv$) and the conditional (*if-then-else*). If the truth symbol *false* belongs to the deduced set, the set is automatically unsatisfiable, because the sentence *false* is not true under any interpretation.

Because the variables of the sentences in the deduced set are tacitly quantified universally, we can systematically rename them without changing the unsatisfiability of the set; that is, the set is unsatisfiable before the renaming if and only if it is unsatisfiable afterwards. The variables of the sentences in the deduced set may therefore be *standardized apart*; in other words, we may rename the variables of the sentences so that no two of them have variables in common.

For any sentence $\mathcal{F}$ in the deduced set and any substitution θ, we may add to the set the *instance* $\mathcal{F}\theta$ of $\mathcal{F}$, without changing the unsatisfiability of the set. In particular, if the deduced set is unsatisfiable after the addition of the new sentence, it was also unsatisfiable before. Note that in adding the new sentence $\mathcal{F}\theta$, we do not remove the original sentence $\mathcal{F}$.

The Deductive Process

In the deductive system we apply *deduction rules*, which add new sentences to the deduced set without changing its unsatisfiability. Deduction rules are expressed as follows:

$$\mathcal{F}_1, \mathcal{F}_2, \ldots, \mathcal{F}_m \Rightarrow \mathcal{F}.$$

This means that, if the *given* sentences $\mathcal{F}_1, \mathcal{F}_2, \ldots, \mathcal{F}_m$ belong to the deduced set, the *conclusion* $\mathcal{F}$ may be added. Such a rule is said to be *sound* if the given sentences $\mathcal{F}_1, \mathcal{F}_2, \ldots, \mathcal{F}_m$ imply the sentence $\mathcal{F}$. If a deductive rule is sound, its application will preserve the unsatisfiability of the deduced set.

The deductive process terminates successfully if we introduce the truth symbol *false* into the deduced set. Because deduction rules preserve unsatisfiability, and because a set of sentences containing *false* is automatically unsatisfiable, this will imply that the original deduced set was also unsatisfiable.

In the basic systems, the only deduction rule is:
• The **resolution** rule, which performs a case analysis on the truth of matching subsentences.
This rule is described in this section. In later sections, we augment the basic system with two new classes of rules:
• The **replacement** rule, which replaces subexpressions with other expressions (not necessarily equivalent or equal).
• The **matching** rule, which introduces new conditions to be proved that enable subexpressions to be matched.

Resolution Rule

The resolution rule applies to two sentences of our set, and performs a case analysis on the truth of a common subsentence. Instances of the sentences can be formed, if necessary, to create a common subsentence; however, we present here only the *ground version* of the rule, which does not form instances of these sentences.

Rule (resolution, ground version): For any ground sentences $\mathcal{P}$, $\mathcal{F}[\mathcal{P}]$, and $\mathcal{G}[\mathcal{P}]$, we have

$$\mathcal{F}[\mathcal{P}],\ \mathcal{G}[\mathcal{P}] \ \Rightarrow\ (\mathcal{F}[\mathit{false}]\ \mathit{or}\ \mathcal{G}[\mathit{true}]). \quad \lrcorner$$

In other words, if $\mathcal{F}[\mathcal{P}]$ and $\mathcal{G}[\mathcal{P}]$ are sentences in our deduced set with a common subsentence $\mathcal{P}$, we can add to the set the sentence ($\mathcal{F}[\mathit{false}]$ *or* $\mathcal{G}[\mathit{true}]$) obtained by replacing every occurrence of $\mathcal{P}$ in $\mathcal{F}[\mathcal{P}]$ with *false*, replacing every occurrence of $\mathcal{P}$ in $\mathcal{G}[\mathcal{P}]$ with *true*, and taking the disjunction of the results. We shall assume that $\mathcal{F}[\mathcal{P}]$ and $\mathcal{G}[\mathcal{P}]$ have at least one occurrence each of the subsentence $\mathcal{P}$. We do not require that $\mathcal{F}[\mathcal{P}]$ and $\mathcal{G}[\mathcal{P}]$ be distinct sentences. Because the resolution rule introduces new occurrences of the truth symbols *true* and *false*, it is always possible to simplify the resulting sentence immediately afterwards. These subsequent simplifications will be regarded as part of the resolution rule itself.

Murray's [82] *polarity strategy* allows us to consider only those applications of the resolution rule under which at least one occurrence of $\mathcal{P}$ is positive (or of no polarity) in $\mathcal{F}[\mathcal{P}]$ and at least one occurrence of $\mathcal{P}$ is negative (or of no polarity) in $\mathcal{G}[\mathcal{P}]$. In other words, not all the subsentences that are replaced with *false* are negative and not all the subsentences that are replaced with *true* are positive. This strategy blocks many useless applications of the rule and rarely interferes with a reasonable step. The intuitive rationale for the polarity strategy is that it is our goal to deduce the sentence *false*, which is falser than any other sentence. By replacing positive sentences with *false* and negative sentences with *true*, we are moving in the right direction, making the entire sentence falser.

The general version of the rule, which we omit, allows us to instantiate the variables of the given sentences as necessary to create common subsentences.

The resolution rule presented here is an extension of the rule of Robinson [65] to the nonclausal case. Nonclausal resolution was developed independently by Manna and Waldinger [80] and Murray [82]. The resolution rule (with simplification) has been shown by Murray to provide a complete system for first-order logic. An implementation of a nonclausal resolution theorem prover by Stickel [82] employs a connection graph strategy.

5. THE RELATION REPLACEMENT RULE

We now begin to extend our nonclausal deduction system to give special treatment to a binary relation $\prec$. The two new rules of the extension allow us to build into the system instances of the *polarity replacement* proposition, just as the paramodulation and E-resolution rules allow us to build in instances of the substitutivity of equality.

With respect to a given relation $\prec$, the rule allows us to replace subexpression occurrences with larger or smaller expressions, depending on their polarity. The ground version of the rule which applies to sentences with no variables, is as follows:

Rule (relation replacement, ground version): For any binary relation $\prec$, ground expressions s and t, and ground sentences $\mathcal{F}[s \prec t]$ and $\mathcal{G}\langle s^+, t^-\rangle$, we have

$$\mathcal{F}[s \prec t],\ \mathcal{G}\langle s^+, t^-\rangle \ \Rightarrow\ (\mathcal{F}[\mathit{false}]\ \mathit{or}\ \mathcal{G}\langle t^+, s^-\rangle).$$

Here $\mathcal{G}\langle t^+, s^-\rangle$ is obtained from $\mathcal{G}\langle s^+, t^-\rangle$ by replacing certain positive occurrences of s with t and replacing certain negative occurrences of t with s, where polarity is taken in $\mathcal{G}\langle s^+, t^-\rangle$ with respect to $\prec$. $\lrcorner$

In other words, if $\mathcal{F}[s \prec t]$ and $\mathcal{G}\langle s^+, t^-\rangle$ are sentences in our deduced set, we can add to the set the sentence $(\mathcal{F}[\mathit{false}]\ \mathit{or}\ \mathcal{G}\langle t^+, s^-\rangle)$.

For a particular relation $\prec$, we shall refer to this rule as the $\prec$-replacement rule: thus, we have a $<$-replacement rule, a $\leq$-replacement rule, and so forth. Although the rule allows us to replace occurrences in $\mathcal{G}\langle s^+, t^-\rangle$ of both expressions s and t at the same time, it is typically applied to replace occurrences of one or the other expression, but not both. Subsequent simplification, to remove occurrences of the truth symbols *true* and *false*, may be regarded as part of the relation replacement rule itself.

There is a polarity strategy for the relation replacement rule, which allows us to apply the rule only if some occurrence of $s \prec t$ is positive (or of no polarity) in $\mathcal{F}[s \prec t]$.

In illustrating the rule we draw boxes around the matching occurrences of s and t.

Example: In the theory of the nonnegative integers, suppose our deduced set contains the sentences

$$\mathcal{F}: \quad \mathit{if}\ p(s)\ \mathit{then}\ (\boxed{s} < t)^+ \qquad \text{and} \qquad \mathcal{G}: \quad s < (\boxed{s}^+)^2.$$

Note that the boxed occurrence of s in $\mathcal{G}$ is positive with respect to the less-than relation $<$. Therefore we can apply the $<$-replacement rule to replace the occurrence of s in $\mathcal{G}$ with t, to deduce

$$[\mathit{if}\ p(s)\ \mathit{then}\ \mathit{false}]\ \ \mathit{or}\ \ s < t^2,$$

which simplifies to

$$[\mathit{not}\, p(s)]\ \ \mathit{or}\ \ s < t^2.$$

The above application of the rule is in accordance with the polarity strategy, because the occurrence of $s < t$ is positive in $\mathcal{F}$. Note that not every occurrence of s in $\mathcal{G}$ was replaced in applying the rule. ┛

The general version of the rule, which we omit, applies to sentences with variables and allows us to instantiate the variables as necessary to create common subexpressions. We illustrate it.

Example: In the theory of sets, suppose our deduced set contains the sentences

$$\mathcal{F}: \quad \begin{array}{l} \mathit{if}\ p(x) \\ \mathit{then}\ (\boxed{h(x,a)} \subset \boxed{b})^+\ \ \mathit{or}\ \ (\boxed{h(b,y)} \subset \boxed{x})^+ \end{array}$$

and

$$\mathcal{G}: \quad (c \in \boxed{h(u,a)}^+ \sim v)\ \ \mathit{or}\ \ q(u,v),$$

where $\sim$ is the set difference function.

Note that: (1) $\mathcal{F}$ contains the [positive] subsentences $h(x,a) \subset b$ and $h(b,y) \subset x$. (2) The boxed subterms $h(x,a), h(b,y)$, and $h(u,a)$ and the boxed subterms b and x are simultaneously unifiable, with most-general unifier $\theta : \{x \leftarrow b,\ u \leftarrow b,\ y \leftarrow a\}$. (3) The boxed occurrence of $h(u,a)$ is positive in $\mathcal{G}$ with respect to $\subset$. Therefore we can apply the $\subset$-replacement rule, replacing all occurrences of $h(b,a) \subset b$ in $\mathcal{F}\theta$ with *false*, replacing the occurrence of $h(b,a)$ in $\mathcal{G}\theta$ with b, and taking the disjunction of the results, to obtain

$$\left[\begin{array}{l} \mathit{if}\ p(b) \\ \mathit{then}\ \mathit{false}\ \mathit{or}\ \mathit{false} \end{array}\right] \ \ \mathit{or}\ \ (c \in b \sim v)\ \ \mathit{or}\ \ q(b,v).$$

This sentence simplifies to

$$(\mathit{not}\, p(b))\ \ \mathit{or}\ \ (c \in b \sim v)\ \ \mathit{or}\ \ q(b,v).$$

The above application of the rule is in accordance with the polarity strategy. ┛

Use of the relation replacement rule allows a dramatic abbreviation of many proofs. For this reason and because the rule enables us to eliminate troublesome axioms from the deduced set, the search space is constricted. We have not established completeness results for the rule; judging from the corresponding theorem for paramodulation (Brand [75]), we expect such results to be difficult.

The most important instance of the relation replacement rule is obtained by taking the relation $\prec$ to be the equality relation $=$. This special case of the rule, which allows us to replace equals with equals, is a nonclausal version of the paramodulation rule. Another important instance of the relation replacement rule is obtained by taking the relation $\prec$ to be the equivalence connective $\equiv$. This is possible only because we regard connectives as relations over truth values.

6. FURTHER RESULTS

We briefly outline some of the techniques that are presented in the full version of this paper (Manna and Waldinger [85a]).

Strengthening

The relation replacement rule does not always allow us to draw the strongest possible conclusion. In the full paper, we establish a stronger form of the relation replacement rule.

We motivate the strengthening of the rule with an example. In the theory of the integers, suppose our deduced set contains the sentences

$$\mathcal{F}: \ \boxed{s} < t \qquad \text{and} \qquad \mathcal{G}: \ a \le \boxed{s}^{+} + 2.$$

Because the occurrence of s in $\mathcal{G}$ is positive with respect to the less-than relation $<$, the $<$-replacement rule allows us to replace s with t and deduce that (after simplification)

$$a \le t^{+} + 2.$$

From these two sentences, however, we should be able to deduce the stronger result

$$a < t + 2.$$

Similarly, from the sentence $s < t$ and *not* $(a - s > b)$, we should be able to deduce *not* $(a - t \ge b)$ rather than merely *not* $(a - t > b)$.

Unfortunately, the rule as we have presented it does not yield these more useful conclusions; the strengthened relation-replacement rule does.

The Relation-Matching Rule

The so-called "relation-matching rule" is not a rule in itself but an augmentation of the other rules. The resolution and relation replacement rules draw a conclusion when one subexpression in our proof unifies with another. The relation-matching augmentation allows these rules to apply even if the two expressions fail to unify, provided that certain conditions can be introduced into the conclusion. We omit a precise statement of the rule, but illustrate the augmentation of the resolution rule in the ground case with an example.

Example: In the theory of lists, suppose that our deduced set includes the sentences

$$\mathcal{F}: \ p(\ell) \ \textit{or} \ \boxed{c \in (tail(\ell))^{+}}^{+} \qquad \text{and} \qquad \mathcal{G}: \ \textit{if} \ \boxed{c \in \ell^{+}}^{-} \ \textit{then} \ q(\ell).$$

The two boxed subsentences are not identical. The subterm $tail(\ell)$ is positive in $c \in tail(\ell)$ with respect to the proper-sublist relation $\prec_{list}$. The other boxed subsentence $c \in \ell$ can be obtained by replacing this subterm with ℓ. We can apply the resolution rule with $\prec_{list}$-matching to obtain

$$\begin{array}{l} \textit{if } tail(\ell) \preceq_{list} \ell \\ \textit{then } p(\ell) \ \textit{or} \ \textit{false} \\ \qquad \textit{or} \\ \qquad \textit{if true then } q(\ell), \end{array}$$

which simplifies to

$$\begin{array}{l} \textit{if } tail(\ell) \preceq_{list} \ell \\ \textit{then } p(\ell) \ \textit{or} \ q(\ell). \end{array}$$ ▟

In the case in which the relation $\prec$ is taken to be the equality relation $=$, the resolution rule with relation matching reduces to a nonclausal variant of the E-resolution rule.

The relation matching and relation replacement rules play complementary roles, and one might expect that a single deductive system would employ one or the other rule but not both. After all, in clausal equality systems, paramodulation and a variant of E-resolution have each been shown to be complete (Anderson [70], Digricoli [83], and Brand [75]) without including the other. Moreover, by incorporating both rules, we admit a troublesome redundancy: The same conclusion can be derived in several ways. On the other hand, it often turns out that a proof that seems unmotivated or tricky using only one of the rules seems more straightforward using a combination of both. We expect that by including both rules together in a system we shall be able to apply more restrictive strategies to each of them. Consequently, we shall obtain a smaller search space than if we had included either of the rules separately.

7. EXTENSIONS

The concepts in this paper are being extended in several directions. We briefly indicate several of these here.

Explicit Quantifiers

The system we have described deals with sentences that have had their quantifiers removed by skolemization. It is impossible, however, to remove quantifiers that occur within the scope of an equivalence ($\equiv$) connective or in the *if*-clause of a conditional (*if-then-else*) connective without first paraphrasing the connective in terms of others. If several of these connectives are nested, the paraphrased sentence becomes alarmingly complex.

In an earlier work (Manna and Waldinger [82]), we extend the deductive system to sentences that may have some of their quantifiers intact. In many cases, we can complete the proof without removing all the quantifiers. If these quantifiers are in equivalences or *if*-clauses, we need not paraphrase the offending connectives. Thus, we not only retain the form of the original sentence, but also can use the equivalences we retain in applying the equivalence replacement rule.

Planning and the Frame Problem

Theorem-proving techniques have often been applied to problems in automatic planning. One approach to this application has been the formulation of a *situational logic*, a theory in which states of the world are regarded as domain elements, denoted by terms. Typically, an action in a plan is represented as a function mapping states into other states. The effects of an action can be described by axioms.

In a situational logic, a problem may be expressed as a theorem to be proved. For example, the problem of achieving the condition that block a is on block b and block b is on block c might be phrased as the theorem

$$(\exists z)\left[on(a,b,z)\ \ and\ \ on(b,c,z)\right].$$

The *frame problem*, which occurs when planning problems are approached in this way, is connected with the requirement that we need to express not only what conditions are altered by a given action, but also what conditions are unchanged. For example, in addition to the primary effect of putting one block on top of another, we must state explicitly that this action has no effect on other relations, such as color; otherwise, we shall have no way of deducing that the color of a block after the action is the same as its color before. Therefore, we must include in our deduced set the *frame* axiom

$$\begin{array}{l} \textit{if } clear(x,w) \textit{ and } clear(y,w) \\ \textit{then if } color(z,u,w) \\ \qquad \textit{then } color(z,u,puton(x,y,w)). \end{array}$$

In other words, if the action of putting block x on top of block y is legal and if block z is of color u in state w, then z will also be of color u in the resulting state $puton(x,y,w)$.

We need a separate frame axiom not only for the color of blocks, but also their size, shape, surface texture, and any other attributes we wish to discuss in our theory. Adding all the frame axioms to our deduced set aggravates the search problem, because the axioms have many consequences irrelevant to the problem at hand. By use of an appropriate "conditional polarity with respect to a function," we can drop all the frame axioms from our deduced set. Of course, the information that certain actions and relations are independent must still be expressed, but this can be done by polarity declarations rather than by axioms.

DISCUSSION

The theorem-proving system we have presented has been motivated by our work in program synthesis, and the best examples we have of its use are in this domain. We have used the system to write detailed derivations for programs over the integers and real numbers, the lists, the sets, and other structures. These derivations are concise and easy to follow: they reflect intuitive derivations of the same programs. A paper by Traugott [85] describes the application of this system to the derivation of several sorting programs. A paper by Manna and Waldinger [85b] describes the derivation of several binary-search programs. Our earlier informal derivation of the unification algorithm (Manna and Waldinger [81]) can be expressed formally in this system.

An interactive implementation of the basic nonclausal theorem-proving system was completed by Malachi and has been extended by Bronstein to include some of the relation rules. An entirely automatic implementation is being contemplated. The relation rules will also be valuable for proving purely mathematical theorems. For this purpose they may be incorporated into clausal as well as nonclausal theorem-proving systems.

Theorem provers have exhibited superhuman abilities in limited subject domains, but seem least competent in areas in which human intuition is best developed. One reason for this is that an axiomatic formalization obscures the simplicity of the subject area; facts that a person would consider too obvious to require saying in an intuitive argument must be stated explicitly and dealt with in the corresponding formal proof. A person who is easily able to conduct the argument informally may well be unable to understand the formal proof, let alone to produce it.

Our work in special relations is part of a continuing effort to make formal theorem proving resemble intuitive reasoning. In the kind of system we envision, proofs are shorter, the search space is compressed, and heuristics based on human intuition become applicable.

ACKNOWLEDGEMENTS

The authors would like to thank Alex Bronstein, Neil Murray, David Plaisted, Mark Stickel, and Jon Traugott for their suggestions and careful reading. Jon Traugott suggested extending the notion of polarity from one relation to two, making the rules more powerful and the exposition simpler. The manuscript was prepared by Evelyn Eldridge-Diaz with the TEX typesetting system.

REFERENCES

Anderson [70]
R. Anderson, Completeness results for E-resolution, *AFIPS Spring Joint Computer Conference*, 1970, pp. 652–656.

Boyer and Moore [79]
R. S. Boyer and J S. Moore, *A Computational Logic*, Academic Press, New York, N.Y., 1979.

Brand [75]
D. Brand, Proving theorems with the modification method, *SIAM Journal of Computing*, Vol. 4, No. 2, 1975, pp. 412–430.

Digricoli [83]
V. Digricoli, *Resolution By Unification and Equality*, Ph.D. thesis, New York University, New York, N.Y., 1983.

Kowalski [79]
R. Kowalski, *Logic for Problem Solving*, North Holland, New York, N.Y., 1979.

Manna and Waldinger [80]
Z. Manna and R. Waldinger, A deductive approach to program synthesis, *ACM Transactions on Programming Languages and Systems*, Vol. 2, No. 1, January 1980, pp. 90–121.

Manna and Waldinger [81]
Z. Manna and R. Waldinger, Deductive synthesis of the unification algorithm, *Science of Computer Programming*, Vol. 1, 1981, pp. 5–48.

Manna and Waldinger [82]
Z. Manna and R. Waldinger, Special relations in program-synthetic deduction, Technical Report, Computer Science Department, Stanford University, Stanford, Calif., March 1982.

Manna and Waldinger [85a]
Z. Manna and R. Waldinger, Special relations in automated deduction, Journal of the ACM (to appear).

Manna and Waldinger [85b]
Z. Manna and R. Waldinger, Origin of the binary search paradigm, in the Proceedings of IJCAI-85, Los Angeles, August 1985.

Morris [69]
J. B. Morris, E-resolution: extension of resolution to include the equality relation, *International Joint Conference on Artificial Intelligence*, Washington, D.C., May 1969, pp. 287–294.

Murray [82]
N. V. Murray, Completely nonclausal theorem proving, *Artificial Intelligence*, Vol. 18, No. 1, 1982, pp. 67–85.

Robinson [65]
J. A. Robinson, A machine-oriented logic based on the resolution principle, *Journal of the ACM*, Vol. 12, No. 1, January 1965, pp. 23–41.

Robinson [79]
J. A. Robinson, *Logic: Form and Function*, North-Holland, New York, N.Y., 1979.

Stickel [82]
M. E. Stickel, A nonclausal connection-graph resolution theorem-proving program. *National Conference on AI*, Pittsburgh, Pa., 1982, pp. 229–233.

Traugott [85]
J. Traugott, Deductive synthesis of sorting algorithms, Technical Report, Computer Science Department, Stanford University, Stanford, Calif. (forthcoming).

Wos and Robinson [69]
L. Wos and G. Robinson, Paramodulation and theorem proving in first order theories with equality, in *Machine Intelligence 4* (B. Meltzer and D. Michie, editors) American Elsevier, New York, N.Y., 1969, pp. 135–150.

Dynamic Interpolation Search

by

Kurt Mehlhorn and Athanasios Tsakalidis

Fachbereich 10, Angewandte Mathematik und Informatik
Universität des Saarlandes, D-6600 Saarbrücken
West Germany

Abstract: We present a new data structure called Interpolation Search tree (IST) which supports interpolation search and insertions and deletions. Amortized insertion and deletion cost is $O(\log n)$. The expected search time in a random file is $O(\log \log n)$. This is not only true for the uniform distribution but for a wide class of probability distributions.

1. Introduction

Interpolation search was first suggested by Peterson [9] as a method for searching in sorted sequences stored in contiguous storage locations. The expected running time of interpolation search on random files (generated according to the *uniform* distribution) of size n is $\Theta(\log \log n)$. This was shown by Yao/Yao [11], Pearl/Itai/Avni [7], and Gonnet/Rogers/George [2]. A very intuitive explanation of the behavior of interpolation search can be found in Pearl/Reingold [8] (see also Mehlhorn [5]).

Dynamic interpolation search, i.e. data structures which support insertions and deletions as well as interpolation search, was discussed by Frederickson [1] and Itai/Konheim/Rodeh [3]. Frederickson presents an implicit data structure which supports insertions and deletions in time $O(n^\epsilon)$, $\epsilon > 0$, and interpolation search with expected time $O(\log \log n)$. The structure of Itai/Konheim/Rodeh has expected insertion time $O(\log n)$ and worst case insertion time $O((\log n)^2)$. It is claimed to support interpolation search, although no formal analysis of its expected behavior is given. Both papers assume that files are generated according to the uniform distribution.

Willard [10] extended interpolation search into another direction: *non-uniform* distributions. He introduces a variant of interpolation search and shows that its expected running time is $O(\log\log n)$ on *static* μ-random files where μ is any *regular* probability density. A density μ is regular if there are constants b_1, b_2, b_3, b_4 such that $\mu(x) = 0$ for $x < b_1$ or $x > b_2$, $\mu(x) \geq b_3 \geq 0$ and $|\mu'(x)| \leq b_4$ for $b_1 \leq x \leq b_2$. A file is *μ-random* if its elements are drawn independently according to density μ. It is important to observe that Willard's algorithm does *not* have to know the density μ. Rather, its running time is $O(\log\log n)$ on μ-random files provided that μ is *regular*. Thus his algorithm is fairly robust.

In this paper we combine and extend the research mentioned above. We present two new data structures called *simple* and *augmented interpolation search tree* respectively (SIST, AIST) which have the following properties.

1) They require space $O(n)$ for a file of cardinality n, the constant being smaller for SISTs than for AISTs.

2) The amortized insertion and deletion cost is $O(\log n)$; the expected amortized insertion and deletion cost is $O(\log\log n)$.

3) In augmented interpolation search trees the expected search time on files generated by μ-random insertions and random deletions is $O(\log\log n)$ provided that μ is a *smooth* density. An insertion is μ-random if the key to be inserted is drawn from density μ. A deletion is random if every key present in the current file is likely to be deleted. These notions of randomness are called I_r and D_r respectively in Knuth[4]. A density μ is *smooth* if there are constants d and $\alpha < 1$ such that for all $a < b < c$, a, c, b, and all integers m and n , $m = \lceil n^\alpha \rceil$,

$$\int_{c-(b-a)/m}^{c} \hat{\mu}(x)dx \leq dn^{-1/2}$$

where $\hat{\mu}(x) = O$ for $x < a$ or $x > b$ and $\hat{\mu}(x) = \mu(x)/p$ for $a \leq x \leq b$ where $p = \int_a^b \mu(x)dx$.

We want to point out that every regular (in Willard's sense) density is smooth and that there are smooth densities which are not regular.

4) In simple interpolation search trees the expected search time on files generated by uniform-random insertions and random deletions is $O(\log\log n)$, and the expected search time on files generated by μ-random insertions and random deletions is $O((\log\log n)^2)$ provided that μ is regular.

5) The worst search time is $O((\log n)^2)$.

6) The data structures support sequential access in linear time and operations Predecessor, Successor and Min in time $O(1)$. In particular, they can be used as priority queues.

This paper is structured as follows. In section 2 SISTs and AISTs are defined and insertion and deletion algorithms are analysed. In section 3 we turn to the expected behavior of interpolation search trees. First some lemmas relevant to both simple and augmented ISTs are derived. Then AISTs are discussed in section 3.1 and SISTs are discussed in sections 3.2.1 (uniform distribution) and 3.2.2 (regular distribution).

We omit all proofs because of lack of space. For the details we refer the reader to the full paper [6].

2. The Interpolation Search Tree

In this section we introduce simple (SIST) and augmented (AIST) interpolation search trees and discuss the insertion and deletion algorithms. We use IST to denote either SIST or AIST. An IST is a multiway tree where the degree of a node depends on the cardinality of the set stored below it. More precisely, the degree of the root is $\Theta(\sqrt{n})$. The root splits a file into $\Theta(\sqrt{n})$ subfiles. We will not postulate that the subfiles have about equal size and in fact our insertion and deletion algorithms will not enforce any such condition. In *ideal* ISTs the subfiles have about equal size. In this case the subfiles have size $\Theta(\sqrt{n})$ and hence the sons of the roots of an ideal IST have degree $\Theta(\sqrt{\sqrt{n}})$. In particular, ideal ISTs have depth $O(\log\log n)$. The search algorithm (we will describe several) for ISTs use interpolation search in every node of the IST in order to locate the subfile where the search should be continued. Since we want to use interpolation search in the nodes of an IST it is necessary to use arrays for the nodes of an IST. In augmented ISTs (AIST) we will in addition associate with each node an approximation to the inverse distribution function which allows us to interpolate perfectly for a sample of values of size n^α where $\alpha, 1/2 \le \alpha < 1$, is a parameter.

Definition : 1:

Let a and b be reals, $a < b$. A simple interpolation search trees (SIST) with boundaries a and b for a set $S = \{x_1 < x_2 \ldots < x_n\} \subseteq [a, b]$ of n elements consists of

1) A set REP of representatives $x_{i_1}, x_{i_2}, \ldots, x_{i_k}$, $i_1 < i_2 < \ldots < i_k$ stored in an array REP[1...k], i.e.

REP$[j] = x_{i_j}$. Futhermore, k satisfies $\sqrt{n/2} \le k \le 2\sqrt{n}$.

2) Interpolation search trees $T_1, \ldots, T_{k+1}$ for the subfiles $S_1, \ldots, S_{k+1}$ where $S_j = \{x_{i_{j-1}+1}, \ldots, x_{i_j-1}\}$ for $2 \le j \le k$, $S_1 = \{x_1, \ldots, x_{i_1-1}\}$, and $S_{k+1} = \{x_{i_k+1}, \ldots, x_n\}$. Furthermore, tree $T_j, 2 \le j \le k$, has boundaries $x_{i_{j-1}}$ and x_{i_j}, T_1 has boundaries a and x_1, and T_{k+1} has boundaries x_k and b.

3) In augmented ISTs (AITS) there is in addition an array $ID[1 \ldots m]$, where m is some integer, with $ID[i] = [j]$ iff

$$REP[j] < a + i(a-b)/m \le REP[j+1]$$

Moreover, the subtrees of AISTs are again AISTs. ∎

An array REP contains a sample of the file S. In ideal ISTs we require this sample to be equally spaced. Ideal ISTs will be built by the insertion and deletion algorithms at *appropriate* time intervals. In AISTs these algorithms also have to construct the array $ID[1 \ldots m]$. For reasons to become clear below we require $m = n^\alpha$ for some α, $1/2 \le \alpha < 1$.

Definition : 2:

An IST for set S, $|S| = n$, is *ideal* if $i_j = j\lfloor\sqrt{n}\rfloor$ for all $j \ge 1$, and if the interpolation search trees $T_1, \ldots, T_{k+1}$ are again ideal. In an ideal AISTs with parameter α we require in addition that $m = \lceil n^\alpha \rceil$. ∎

The following Lemma is almost immediate.

Lemma 1.

Let $1/2 \le \alpha < 1$. Then an ideal AIST for set S, $|S| = n$, can be built in time $O(n)$ and requires space $O(n)$. It has depth $O(\log\log n)$ ∎

We are now ready for insertion and deletion algorithms. We follow a very simple principle. Suppose that we have an ideal IST for a file of size n. We will then leave the root node unchanged for the next $n/4$ insertions and deletions into the file and then build a new ideal IST for the new file. The same principle is applied to the subfiles. Note that this strategy will *not* enforce any balancing criterion between subfiles. In particular, if all insertions go into the same subfile then the size of this subfile grows from $\sqrt{n}$ to $\sqrt{n} + n/4$. This is in marked contrast to ordinary balanced trees. Deletions are performed by marking (tagging) the element to be deleted. The element is not physically removed. It is removed when a subtree containing it is removed.

Definition : 3:

a) If V is a node of an IST then T_v is the subtree with root v.

b) The *weight* $w(v)$ of a node is the number of (marked or unmarked) keys which are stored in T_v. The size $size(v)$ of a node v is the number of *unmarked* keys which are stored in T_v.

c)*Rebuilding* T_v is to replace the subtree T_v by an ideal IST for the set of unmarked keys stored in T_v.

In our implementation of nterpolation search trees we associate with each node v of the subtree a counter $C(v)$. It counts the number of insertions and deletions into the subfile stored in tree T_v. Whenever we rebuild a subtree T_w for some node w we initialize the counters of all nodes of the (new) subtree T_w to zero. Moreover, the counter $C(v)$ *overflows* whenever its value exceeds $W/4$ where W *is the size* of node v when the tree was built, i.e. when the counter $C(v)$ was reset to 0 for the last time. ▮

We execute the insertions and deletions as follows. We first give a short informal description and then give more detailed algorithms below.

Insertion of a key x

1) Find the position where x should be inserted and insert x. Increase the counters of all nodes v on the path of search by one.

2) Find the highest node, say z, on the path of search such that $C(z)$ overflows. Rebuild the subtree with root z.

Deletion

1) Mark the element to be deleted and increase the counters of all nodes of the search path.

2) as 2) above.

The *intuition* behind these algorithms is as follows.

1) Good worst behavior for searches can be achieved if the weights along any path from the root to a leaf are geometrically decreasing, because this will guarantee logarithmic depth of the tree. The counters do exactly that; cf. lemma 2 below. Good worst case behavior for insertions/deletions (at least in an amortized sense) can be achieved if nodes of size W remain unchanged for a time which is proportional to W. This is also achieved by the counters. Note that a tree T_v of (initial) size W is only rebuilt after $W/4$ insertions/deletions into that subtree.

2) Good average case behavior for searches can be achieved if interpolation search (or a variant of it) can be used to search the arrays of representatives. In order for that to work we need to know that the array of representatives stored in a node v is a "fair" sample of the file stored in subtree T_v. We achieve this goal by *not* enforcing any criterion which relates the size of the files stored in the direct sons of a node v. Note that in ordinary balanced trees an "overflow" at a node v changes not only node v but also v's father. In particular, in ordinary balanced trees an "overflow" at node v changes the set of representatives stored in v's father. We found it impossible to do a satisfactory expected case analysis of any such scheme and therefore have chosen update algorithms which do not enforce any balancing condition between brother nodes. This will imply in particular, that the files which are stored in brother can be treated as independent files.

We give the detailed insertion and deletion algorithm next. In these algorithms we use isize(V) (for *initial size*) to denote the size of node v when $C(v)$ was reset to zero for the last time. Moreover, we assume that the position where key x has to be inserted, deleted is known. This position can be found using the search algorithm described in the next section.

```
(1)   proc  Insert (x);
(2)         colet T be the current tree, let v₀,v₁,...,vₖ
(3)         be a path from a new node v₀ at the appropriate
(4)             position to the root vₖ;oc
(5)         store x into node v₀ and set
(6)         C(v₀) := ∅; isize(v₀) := 1
(7)         for i from 1 to k do C(u) := C(vᵢ) +1 od;
(8)         let i be maximal such that C(vᵢ) ≥ isize (vᵢ)/4;
```

```
(9)          if i exists
(10)         then Rebuild (T_{v_i}) fi
(11) end
```

and

```
(1) proc  Delete (x)
(2)       let T be the current tree, let v_1, ..., v_k be
(3)       a path from the node v_1 containing key x to
(4)       the root v_k;
(5)       mark key x;
(4)-(7)   as (7)-(10) above;
(8) end
```

Finally procedure Rebuild is given by

```
(1) proc  Rebuild (T)
(2)       build an ideal IST for the set of unmarked keys
          stored in tree T, set C(v) := 0 for all nodes
          of the new tree and set isize(v) to the
          appropriate value of all nodes of the new tree
(3) end
```

From now on we reserve the name **interpolation search tree** for those ISTs which can be generated from the empty initial tree by a sequence of insertions and deletions. We have

Lemma 2.

The depth of an IST for a file of n keys is $O(\log n)$. It requires $O(n)$ space. ∎

Lemma 2 can explain why we restrict the parameter α to be strictly less than 1 in AISTs. If $\alpha < 1$ then storage requirement is linear, if $\alpha \geq 1$ then storage requirement is non linear.

Lemma 3.

The amortized cost of an insertion or deletion (not counting the time for the preceding search) is $O(\log n)$, i.e. the total cost of the first n insertions and deletions is $O(n \log n)$. ∎

3. Searching in Interpolation Search Trees

In this section we will introduce several algorithms for searching in interpolation search trees. We will also analyse the worst case and expected case running time of these algorithms. More precisely, we discuss three algorithms: one for searching AISTs and two for searching SISTs. The two following algorithms for searching SISTs differ in their expected running time and in the class of distribution to which they apply. Whilst the first algorithms has expected running time $O(\log \log n)$ but works only for the uniform distribution, the second algorithm has expected cost $O((\log \log n)^2)$ but works for all regular densities.

The expected case running time is defined with respect to random files and trees which we define next. We will also derive some properties of random trees which will be useful for the analysis of all three searching strategies.

Let μ be a probability density function on the real line. We will later put various restrictions on μ. A random file of size n is generated by drawing independently n reals according to density μ. A *random IST* of size n is generated as follows.

3.1. Searching Augmented Interpolation Search Trees

Searching AISTs is quite simple. Supposed that we have to search for $y \in \mathbf{N}$. We can use the approximation ID to the inverse distribution function to obtain a very good estimate for the position of y in the array of representatives. From this initial guess we can then determine the actual position of y by a simple linear search. The details are as follows.

Let T be an AIST with boundaries a and b. Let REP[1 ... k] and ID[1 ... m] be the array of representatives and approximation to the inverse distribution respectively associated with the root.

(1) $j := \mathrm{ID}[\lfloor((y-a)/(b-a))m\rfloor]$
(2) **while** $y \geq \mathrm{REP}[j+1]$ **and** $j < k$
(3) **do** $j := j+1$ **od**
(4) search the j-th subtree using the same algorithm recursively

The correctness of this algorithm is fairly obvious.
Let $i := \lfloor(y-a)m/(b-a)\rfloor = (y-a)m/(b-a) - \epsilon$ for some $0 \leq \epsilon < 1$. Then

$$\mathrm{REP}[j] \leq a + i(b-a)/m \leq \mathrm{REP}[j+1]$$

This proves $y \geq \mathrm{REP}[j]$ and hence establishes correctness. The worst case search time $WT(n)$ in an AIST of size n is also easily derived. Clearly at most $O(\sqrt{n})$ time units are spent in the root array. Also the subfile to be searched has size at most $n/2$ and hence

$$WT(n) \leq O(\sqrt{n}) + WT(n/2)$$

which solves for $WT(n) = O(\sqrt{n})$. The worst case search time is easily improved to $O((\log n)^2)$ by using exponential and binary search instead of linear search. More precisely, compare y with REP[j], REP[$j+2^0$], REP[$j+2^2$], until an l is found with $\mathrm{REP}[j+2^{l-1}] < y \leq \mathrm{REP}[j+2^l]$. Then use binary search to finish the search. With this modification worst case search time in the array is $O(\log n)$ and hence total worst case search time is $O((\log n)^2)$.

Finally observe that the number of search steps used by exponential + binary search is O(number of steps taken by linear search) and hence the expected case analysis done below also applies to exponential + binary search. Let us turn to expected search time next.

Definition : 5:

A density μ is *smooth* for a parameter $\alpha < 1$ if μ has finite support $[a, b]$ for some a, b and if there is a constant d such that for all c_1, c_2, c_3, $a \leq c_1 < c_2 < c_3 \leq b$, and all integers m and n; $m = \lceil n^\alpha \rceil$

$$\int_{c_2-(c_3-c_1)/m}^{c_2} \mu[c_1, c_3](x)dx \leq dn^{-1/2}$$

Note that there is no smooth density for $\alpha < 1/2$. This can be seen as follows. Let $c_1 = a$, $c_3 = b$. Then there is c_2 such that

$$\int_{c_2-(b-a)/m}^{c_2} \mu[a, b](x)dx \geq 1/m$$

and hence $m = n^\alpha$, $\alpha \leq 1/2$ is impossible. This explains that we restrict α to be at least $1/2$. ∎

1) Take a random file F of size n' for some n' and build an ideal IST for it.

2) Perform a sequence $Op_1, \ldots, Op_m$ of μ-random insertions and random deletions in the sequence then $m = i + d$ and $n = n' + i - d$. An insertion is μ-random if it inserts a random real drawn according to density μ into the tree. A deletion is random if it deletes a random element from the file, i.e. all elements in the file are equally likely to be chosen for the deletion. These notions of randoms are called I_r and D_r respectively in Knuth [4]

The following two properties of random ISTs are very helpful: subtrees of random trees are again random and the size of subtree stays **rootic** with high probability.

Definition : 4:

a) Let v be a density function on the real line and let a, b be reals with $a < b$. The density $v[a,b]$ is defined by

$$v[a,b](x) = \begin{cases} v(x)/p & \text{if } a \le x \le b \\ 0 & \text{otherwise} \end{cases}$$

where $p \int_a^b v(x)dx$.

b) A density function v has finite support $[a,b]$ if $v = v[a,b]$ ∎

Lemma 4.

Let μ be a density function with finite support $[a,b]$, let T be a μ-random IST with boundaries a and b and let T' be a subtree of T. Then there are reals c, d such that T' is a $\mu[c,d]$-random IST. ∎

Lemma 5.

Let μ be a density function with finite support $[a,b]$, let T be a μ-random IST of size n, and let T' be a direct subtree of T. Then the size of T' is $O(n^{3/4})$ with probability at least $1 - O(n^{-1/2})$ ∎

Lemma 5 illustrates the self=organizing feature of ISTs. The Array of representatives in the root node is a sample reflecting the underlying file and hence is fairly dense in regions of high density of the distribution. This leads to the effect that the size of the subtrees stays reasonably balanced no matter what the distribution is.

In the next section we describe search algorithms for ISTs. The analysis of these algorithms is according to the following pattern.

1) We show that the worst case search time in an IST of size n is $O(\sqrt{n})$. (One can with slightly more work achieve time $O((\log n)^2)$.

2) We show that the expected search time in the root array (the array of representatives associated with the root) is $O(g(n))$ where $g(n) = 1$ in sections 3.1 and 3.2.1 and $g(n) = \log\log n$ in section 3.2.2.

Lemma 6.

Let μ be a density with finite support $[a,b]$ and let $T(n)$ be the expected search time in a μ-random IST of size n. Then

$$T(n) \le O(g(n)) + T(O(n^{3/4})) + O(n^{-1/2})O(n^{1/2})$$

and hence $T(n) = O(\log\log n)$ if $g(n) = 1$ and $T(n) = O((\log\log n)^2)$ if $g(n) = \log\log n$.

Lemma 8.

Let μ be a smooth density for parameter $\alpha < 1$ and let T be a μ-random AIST with parameter α. Then the expected search time in the root array is $O(1)$.

Theorem 1.

Let μ be a smooth density for parameter $\alpha < 1$. Then the expected search time in a μ-random AIST size is $O(\log\log n)$

3.2. Searching simple Interpolation Search Trees

In this section we show how to search in simple interpolation search trees; in section 3.2.1 we deal with uniformly generated files and in 3.2.2 we deal with more general distributions.

3.2.1 Uniform Distribution.

In AISTs we used the array ID, an approximation to the inverse distribution function, to obtain a good initial guess for the location of the search key y. In simple ISTs we have to do without the array. However, if the file is generated according to the uniform distribution then the identity function is a good (indeed perfect) approximation. This leads to the following algorithm.

(1) $j := \lfloor (y-a)k/(b-a) \rfloor$;
(2) **if** $y \geq \text{REP}[j]$
(3) **then** lines (2)-(4) of the algorithm of section 3.1
(4) **else** lines (2)-(4) of the algorithm of section 3.1
with +1 replaced by −1
(5)**fi**

The correctness of this algorithm is obvious. Also worst case search time is $O(\sqrt{n})$ by the same argument as in section 3.1. For the analysis of expected search time we follow Perl and Reingold [8].

Lemma 9.

The expected search time in the root of a random SIST T for the uniform distribution is $O(1)$.

Theorem 2.

The expected search time in a uniform-random SIST of size n is $O(\log\log n)$.

3.2.2. Regular Distribution

We will now describe how to search in SISTs for regular distributions.

Regular distributions were introduced by Willard in his analysis of interpolation search. Our discussion is inspired by Willard's results; however our treatment is slightly simpler than his since we perform interpolation search on the set of representatives and not on the file itself.

Definition : 6:

Let $c \geq 0$ and $a < b$. A density function μ with finite support $[a, b]$ is c-regular if

$\max\{|\mu'(x)|; a \leq x \leq b\}/min\{|\mu(x)|; a \leq x \leq b\} \leq c$ ∎

Before we describe the search algorithm we draw some simple consequence from this definition.

Lemma 10.

Let $c \geq 0$, $a < b$ and let μ with finite support$[a, b]$ be c-regular. Let $\ell = b - a$, let a', b' be such that $a \leq a' < b' \leq b$ and let $\ell' = b' - a'$.

a) $\mu[a', b']$ is also c-regular
b) $\max\{\mu(x); a \leq x \leq b\} / \min\{\mu(x); a \leq x \leq b\} \leq 1 + c\ell$
c) Let $G(x) = \int_a^x \mu(y)dy$. Then

$$|G(x) - (x - a)/\ell| \leq c\ell/2$$

d) Let $p = \int_{a'}^{b'} \mu(x)dx$. Then

$$\ell p/(1 + c\ell(1 - p)) \leq \ell \leq \ell p(1 + c\ell)/(1 + c\ell) \blacksquare$$

Lemma 10 lists some important properties of regular distributions. Part b) states that the deviation from uniformity goes to *zero* as ℓ goes to *zero*. In particular it suggests that interpolation search (or a variant of it) can be used to search c-regular files provided that ℓ is small. Part c) gives another look at the deviation from the uniform distribution; note that $G(x) = (x - a)/\ell$ if μ is uniform. Part d) relates the length $\ell' = b' - a'$ of a subinterval $[a', b']$ and its probability p.

We also need the following property of μ-random files.

Lemma 11.

Let $a \leq a' < b' \leq b, c \geq 0$ and let $\mu = \mu[a, b]$ be a $c-$*regular* density. For a μ-random file F of N reals in the range $[a, b]$ let $R(F)$ be the number of reals in subinterval $[a', b']$. $R(F)$ is a random variable.

Let $p = \int_{a'}^{b'} \mu(x)dx$. Then

$$\text{prob}(|R(F) - pN| \geq t) \leq p(1 - p)N/t^2 \leq N/4t^2 \qquad \blacksquare$$

We are now ready for search time algorithm. Let T be a SIST with boundaries A and B and a root array REP$[1 \ldots k]$. Let F_0 be the μ-random initial file for T, i.e. the file which existed when T was rebuilt for the last time. Then $|F_0| = n$ where $k = \lceil\sqrt{n}\rceil$. Let $y \in [A, B]$. We show how to locate y in array REP in expected time $O(\log\log n)$.

The search proceeds in two phases. In the first phase we use binary search. Binary search halves the cardinality of the file in every step; we will show that it also reduces the length of ℓ of the file by a multiplication factor < 1 in every step with high probability. We use binary search until the length of the file to be searched is small enough so as to make interpolation search work. The first case has excepted cost $O(1)$.

In the second phase we use interpolation search. In contrast to ordinary interpolation search we use two interpolation indices ($j-$ delta) and ($j+$ delta). Here j is the ordinary interpolation index and delta is a relaxation factor. The factor delta is chosen such that REP$[j - delta] \leq y \leq$ REP$[j + delta]$ and $\ell' :=$ REP$[j + delta]$ - REP $[j - delta] = O(\ell^{3/2})$ has probability at least 1/2. The details follow.

$a := A; b := B; L := B := A;$
$d_1 := min(1/(4c(1 + cL))^2, 1/2)$
$low := O; high := k + 1;$
$\ell := b - a;$

while $\ell \geq d_1$
do middle := $(low + high)/2$
if $y \leq$REP$[middle]$

```
        then high := middle; b :=REP[middle]
        else low := middle; a :=REP[middle]
        fi
        ℓ:= b − a; m := high − low + 1;
    od;

    while high − low + 1 ≥ 9
    do  ℓ:= b − a; m := high − low + 1;
        j:= ⌈(y − a)m/ℓ⌉
        delta:= max(4, cmℓ)
        cases
        y < REP[j − delta] :    high := j − delta; b := REP [j − delta]
        y ≥ REP[j + delta] :    low := j + delta; a := REP [j + delta]
        REP [j − delta] ≤ y ≤ REP [j + delta]:  low := j − delta;
                                    high := j + delta; a :=REP [j − delta];
                                    b := REP [j + delta];
        esac
    od
    complete the search in time O(1) using linear search.
```
∎

For the analysis of the algorithm we use the following notation: ℓ' and m' denotes the values of ℓ and m in the next iteration. Also F denotes the elements of file F_0 between REP[*low*] and REP[*high*]. Note that $|F| = m\sqrt{n}$.

Lemma 12.

The expected number of iteration of phase 1 is $O(1)$. ∎

We turn to phase 2 next. We call an iteration of phase 2 a type 1 iteration if delta=$c\ell m$ and a type 2 iteration if delta=4.

Lemma 13.

a) the expected number of type 1 iterations is $O(\log\log n)$
b) the expected number of type 2 iterations is $O(1)$.

∎

Theorem 3.

The expected search time in a μ-random SIST of size n is $O((\log\log n)^2)$ for any regular density μ. ∎

4. Conclusions

We see two achievements in this paper.

a) We made interpolation search dynamic, i.e. we found a data structure with $O(\log\log n)$ expected search time, $O((\log n)^2)$ worst serach time, $O(\log\log n)$ expected amortized insertion and deletion cost and $O(\log n)$ worst case amortized insertion and deletion cost.

b) We extended interpolation search to a wide class of density functions.

References

[1] G. Frederickson: "Imlpicit Data Structures for the Dictionary problem" *Journal of ACM* Vol. 30 No. 1, 80–94 (1983)

[2] G. Gonnet, L. Rogers, J. George: "An Algorithmic and Complexity Analysis of Interpolation Search" *Acta Informatica* 13(1), 39–52 (1980)

[3] A. Itai, A.G. Konheim, M. Rodeh: " A Sparse Table Implementation of Priority Queues" *Proc. ICALP 81, LNCS 115*, 417–431 (1981)

[4] D. E. Knuth: "Deletions that preserve Randomness" *IEEE Trans. Software Engrg. SE 3*, 351–359

[5] K. Mehlhorn: "Data Structures and Algorithms" *Vol. 1, Sorting and Searching, Springer Verlag, EATCS Monographs in Theoretical Computer Science* 1980

[6] K. Mehlhorn and A. Tsakalidis: "Dynamic Interpolation Search" *Technischer Bericht A84/05* FB 10 Universität des Saarlandes, 1984, submitted to Journal of ACM.

[7] Y. Pearl, A. Itai, H. Avni: "Interpolation Search- A Log Log N Search" *Communications of ACM*, 21(7), 550–554 (1978)

[8] Y Pearl and E. M. Reingold: "Understanding the Complexity of Interpolation Search" *Inform Proc. Letters* 6(6), 219–222 (1977)

[9] W.W. Peterson: "Addressing for Random Storage" *IBM J. Res. and Develop.* 1, 131–132 (1957)

[10] D.E. Willard: "Searching Nonuniformly Generated Files in a Log Log N Runtime" *SIAM Journal of Computing*, in press

[11] A.C. Yao and F.F. Yao: "The Complexity of Searching an Ordered Random Table" *Proc. 17th Annual Symp. Foundations of Computer Science* 173–177 (1976)

POLYNOMIAL LEVELABILITY AND MAXIMAL COMPLEXITY CORES

Pekka Orponen[1], David A. Russo[2] and Uwe Schöning[3]

[1]Department of Computer Science, University of Helsinki, SF-00250 Helsinki 25, Finland.

[2]Department of Mathematics, University of California, Santa Barbara, Ca. 93106, U.S.A.

[3]Institut für Informatik, Universität Stuttgart, D-7000 Stuttgart 1, West Germany.

ABSTRACT

It is known that any set A not in P contains an infinite complexity core, that is, a set $C \subseteq A$ such that any algorithm for A takes superpolynomial time almost everywhere on C. We investigate the conditions under which an intractable set A can possess a core that is maximal with respect to inclusion; such a core could be understood as containing exactly the "inherently hard" instances of A. We show that although intractable sets with maximal cores do exist, this property seems to be highly unnatural. In particular, no known complete sets for NP and PSPACE are of this type. We observe that a recursive set contains a maximal core if and only if it contains a maximal P-subset, and so our results apply equally to show the nonexistence of maximal "approximations" to natural intractable sets by P-sets.

This work was supported in part by the Emil Aaltonen Foundation, the Academy of Finland, the Deutsche Forschungsgemeinschaft, and the National Science Foundation under Grant No. MCS83-12472. The work was carried out while the first author was visiting the Department of Mathematics, University of California at Santa Barbara.

1. INTRODUCTION

Assume that a recursive set A is not in P. Then Lynch [9] has shown that A contains an infinite **complexity core**, that is, a set $C \subseteq A$ such that given any algorithm M for A and polynomial p, the running time of M exceeds $p(|x|)$ on almost all x in C. A very attractive interpretation of this result would be provided by thinking of the core as consisting of "inherently hard" instances of the decision problem for A. Then the theorem would translate to: a problem is intractable if and only if it has infinitely many hard (yes-)instances. This interpretation is, however, complicated by the fact that cores are seldom unique. Obviously any subset and finite variation of a core is again a core, and the same is easily seen to hold for finite unions of cores. Still, the issue here is not really uniqueness in this strict sense, but whether a set not in P contains a complexity core that is **maximal** modulo finite variations. Such a core could be interpreted as describing exactly the inherently hard (yes-)instances of the corresponding decision problem.

The existence, or rather nonexistence of maximal complexity cores is the main topic of this paper. For reasons to be explained later, a set that does **not** possess a maximal core is called **polynomially levelable**, or **P-levelable** for short. It seems - unfortunately for the purpose of explaining intractability in terms of complexity cores - that most natural intractable sets are P-levelable. We argue this by showing that levelability is a consequence of several well-known "naturalness" properties, such as paddability [3], self-reducibility [11,15], and completeness for a deterministic time class. Thus, our results apply to sets such as SAT, QBF etc. - assuming, of course, that $P \neq NP$, P $\neq$ PSPACE etc. We note in passing the surprising fact that all P-levelable sets have the same structure of complexity cores, as ordered by inclusion modulo finite sets [12].

It is often more convenient to think of P-levelable sets from a complementary point of view. In [13] it was proved that a recursive set has a maximal complexity core if and only if the set is the disjoint union of a set in P and a P-immune set (i.e. a set that has no infinite P-subsets [5]). From this result it easily follows that P-levelability of recursive sets can also be characterized as the property of not possessing a **maximal P-subset** (modulo finite variations). We take this as our definition. This is also the reason for our choice of the term "levelable"; the term was suggested by K. Ko [8] in analogy with a related notion in axiomatic complexity theory [4,17]. Also the P-subset structures of all P-levelable sets turn out to be isomorphic [14].

This abstract is organized as follows: In the next section we prove that recursive "honestly paddable" sets [3,18] not in P are P-levelable, and a stronger version of this result for the common "invertibly paddable" sets. These results apply to all the natural NP- and PSPACE-complete sets: SAT, QBF etc. Then we observe that also Young's "honestly k-creative" sets [18] are P-levelable, thus covering all the known NP-complete sets. In the third section we extend our analysis to sets that are "positive self-reducible" [11,15,16], or complete for a deterministic time class. In the fourth and last section we consider the problem of proving the levelability of all NP- and PSPACE-complete sets, and introduce a levelability preserving subclass of the polynomial time many-one reductions.

2. P-LEVELABILITY AND PADDABILITY

In this section we prove that all known NP-complete sets are P-levelable. This argument consists of two parts: our basic theorem asserts that "honestly paddable" sets not in P are P-levelable. (A stronger version of this result holds for "invertibly paddable" sets.) Young's "honestly k-creative" NP-complete sets, which are not known to be paddable, are covered by another theorem. The paddability results naturally apply also to many non-NP-complete sets. Let $\Sigma = \{0,1\}$ be the basic alphabet.

2.1 **Definition.** A set $A \subseteq \Sigma^*$ is **P-levelable** if for any $E \subseteq A$, $E \in P$, there exists another $E' \subseteq A$, $E' \in P$, such that the difference $E' - E$ is infinite.

From the results in [13] it follows that a recursive set is P-levelable if and only if it does not contain a maximal complexity core, and that a recursive set is **not** P-levelable if and only if it is the disjoint union of a set in P and a P-immune set.

A set $A \subseteq \Sigma^*$ is **paddable** [3,18] if there exists a polynomial time computable function pad: $\Sigma^* \times \Sigma^* \to \Sigma^*$ that is one-one in its second argument and satisfies: $x \in A$ if and only if $pad(x,y) \in A$, for all $x,y \in \Sigma^*$. If there exists a polynomial p such that $p(|pad(x,y)|) \geq |x| + |y|$, for all $x,y \in \Sigma^*$, then A is **honestly paddable.** If there exists a polynomial time computable function decode: $\Sigma^* \to \Sigma^*$, such that $decode(pad(x,y)) = y$ for all $x,y \in \Sigma^*$, then A is **invertibly paddable.** It was observed in [10] that if a set is invertibly paddable, then it has a padding function that can be inverted in both arguments. From this it easily follows that invertibly paddable sets are also honestly paddable.

Examples of honestly, even invertibly paddable sets include all the "natural" complete sets for NP, co-NP, and PSPACE (canonical examples would be SAT, TAUT, and QBF, respectively), and also some sets not known to be complete (e.g. ISO, the set representing the Graph Isomorphism problem).

2.2 **Theorem.** Let A be a recursive set not in P. If A is honestly paddable, then A is P-levelable.

Proof. Let pad(x,y) be an honest padding function for A, with a nondecreasing polynomial bound p on compression. Define

$$f(x) = pad(x, 0^{p(|x|)+1}).$$

Then $|f(x)| > |x|$ and $f(x) \in A$ iff $x \in A$, for all $x \in \Sigma^*$.

Assume that A is not P-levelable, so that it contains a maximal P-subset E. Consider the following "boundary" set of E:

$$B = \{x \mid x \notin E, f(x) \in E\}.$$

Clearly B is a P-subset of A, and $B \cap E = \emptyset$. We prove that B is infinite, contradicting the maximality of E.

For any $x \in A$, the set $\{x, f(x), f(f(x)), \ldots\}$ is an infinite P-subset of A. Hence, by the maximality of E, it is a.e. contained in E. In particular, for each $x \in A - E$ there is a smallest $n > 1$ such that $f^{(n)}(x) \in E$. For this n, $f^{(n-1)}(x) \in B$. Hence, from each $x \in A - E$ begins a length-increasing sequence x, f(x), f(f(x)),... of strings in A - E, ending in a string $y \in B$. Because $A \notin P$, A - E is infinite. But because of the increase in length, only finitely many sequences can end in each $y \in B$. Thus B is infinite. □

If we assume the padding to be invertible, we can improve on this greatly. Say that a set A is **nonsparse P-levelable** if for any $E \subseteq A$, $E \in P$, there exists another $E' \subseteq A$, $E' \in P$, such that the difference $E' - E$ is nonsparse [3]. The following result extends one by Meyer and Paterson [11], who observed that for a paddable set A not in P, the difference A - E must be nonsparse for any P-subset E of A.

2.3 Theorem. Let A be a recursive set not in P. If A is invertibly paddable, then A is nonsparse P-levelable.

Proof(sketch). Assume to the contrary that A has a P-subset E that is maximal up to sparse variations. Consider the following boundary set of E:

$$B = \{z \mid z \notin E, \text{ but } z = pad(x,y) \text{ and } pad(x,yb_1b_2) \in E \text{ for some } b_1,b_2 \in \{0,1\}\}.$$

Clearly $B \in P$ and $B \subseteq A - E$, so B must be sparse.

Let M be any algorithm for A. We may assume, without loss of generality, that E contains the P-set

$$E_\emptyset = \{pad(x,y) \mid M \text{ accepts } x \text{ in } |y| \text{ steps}\}.$$

Given any finite set $F \subseteq A$, the set

$$F^* = \{pad(x,y) \mid x \in F,\ y \in \Sigma^*\}$$

is a.e. contained in $E_\emptyset$. The proof is now based on the fact that if $F \subseteq A - E$, the number of strings in F^* increases at an exponential rate with the length of the padding y, whereas the boundary B admits only a polynomial "flow" of strings from A - E to E. By choosing the basis set F so that it has a certain "critical mass", we can make the difference $F^* - E$ infinite, leading to a contradiction. □

Berman and Hartmanis conjectured in [3] that all NP-complete sets are polynomially isomorphic. This conjecture, which of course would imply the P-levelability of all NP-complete sets, was motivated by the observation that all NP-complete sets known at the time were easily seen to be invertibly paddable, and invertibly paddable NP-complete sets can be shown to be isomorphic [3,18]. Recently, however, Young [18] introduced a new class of apparently nonpaddable NP-complete sets, which he calls "k-creative". The proof technique above can be used t establish also the P-levelability of all the k-creative sets exhibite in [18].

Let $\{M_i\}$ be a standard enumeration of nondeterministic Turin machines (see, e.g., [6]). Machine M_i **witnesses** $L(M_i) \in NP^{(k)}$ if it running time is bounded by a k:th degree polynomial. A set $A \in NP$ i **k-creative** if there exists a polynomial time computable function f called a **productive** function, such that for each M_i witnessin $L(M_i) \in NP^{(k)}$, $f(i) \in L(M_i)$ if and only if $f(i) \in A$.

It was shown in [18] that every honest, one-one, polynomial tim computable function f is a productive function for some k-creative set and that all k-creative sets with honest productive functions ar NP-complete. We have the following theorem (whose proof we omit).

2.4 **Theorem.** All k-creative sets with honest productive functions ar P-levelable, unless P = NP. □

3. SELF-REDUCIBILITY AND COMPLETENESS

In this section we extend our P-levelability analysis to sets tha are "positive self-reducible" or complete for a deterministic tim class. We begin with self-reducibility.

A set $A \subseteq \Sigma^*$ is (polynomial time) **self-reducible** [11,15] if ther exist a well-founded partial order $\leqslant$ on Σ^* and a polynomial tim deterministic oracle Turing machine M, such that $L(M,A) = A$, and M o any input x queries only strings that strictly precede x in the order $\leqslant$ If the self-reducing machine is such that for all $X, Y \subseteq \Sigma^*$, $X \subseteq$ implies $L(M,X) \subseteq L(M,Y)$, A is said to be **positive** self-reducible [16] Positive self-reducibility is a relatively strong generalization of th common "disjunctive" and "conjunctive" reducibilities.

Let M be a positive self-reducing machine, and let the sequence $A_\emptyset \subseteq A_1 \subseteq A_2 \subseteq \ldots$ be defined by:

$$A_\emptyset = \emptyset;$$

$$A_{i+1} = L(M, A_i), \text{ for } i \geq \emptyset.$$

It can be shown that $A = \bigcup_i A_i$. Consider the following condition on M:

(D) For each $x \in \Sigma^*$ there is some $i \geq \emptyset$ such that if $y \in A$ depends on x, then $y \in A_i$,

where "y depends on x" means that there is a sequence of strings $y = y_\emptyset$, $y_1, \ldots, y_n = x$, such that M on input y_k and oracle A queries y_{k+1}. Condition (D) is not entailed by the general definition of self-reducibility, but all the usual self-reductions can be constructed so as to satisfy it. (To witness, Karp and Lipton in [7] define "self-reducibility" in a much more restrictive way.)

3.1 Theorem. Let A be a recursive set not in P. If A is positive self-reducible via a machine satisfying (D), then A is P-levelable.

Proof (idea). Given any P-subset E of A, the assumptions on M can be shown to force $L(M,E) - E$ to be infinite. Since $L(M,E) \in P$ and $L(M,E) \subseteq A$, E cannot be maximal. □

Interesting examples of apparently nonpaddable sets that can be shown P-levelable by Theorem 3.1 are, e.g.,

FACTOR = {<m,a,b> | m,a,b natural numbers, $1 < a < b < m$, m has a factor between a and b} [7,11]; and

for any nondeterministic Turing machine M:

L_M = {<x,c> | c codes an initial segment of an accepting computation of M on input x}.

Our final P-levelability result concerns deterministic time complete sets, its most interesting application being probably to the class EXPTIME.

3.2 Theorem. Let A be a recursive set not in P. If A is complete for some deterministic time class, then A is P-levelable.

Proof. Assume that A is not P-levelable. Then A is the disjoint union of an infinite P-immune set C and a set in P [13]. It is easy to see that if A is complete for some class of sets, then so is C. However, L.Berman proved in [2] that infinite P-immune sets cannot be complete for deterministic time classes.□

4. REDUCTIONS AND P-LEVELABILITY

In this section we pinpoint the reason why our levelability results do not extend to all NP- and PSPACE-complete sets via $\leq_m^P$-reductions. This is briefly because $\leq_m^P$-reductions can behave very badly on polynomial time recognizable subsets - a reduction can map a set in P onto any r.e. set. We show that if a reduction behaves well "locally" on P-sets, then it preserves the "global" property of P-levelability. A subclass of the well-behaved reductions also gives us a natural reducibility characterization of sets that are not P-levelable, similar to the characterization of bi-immune sets in [1].

4.1 Definition. A polynomial time many-one reduction f: A -> B is **P-to-P** if for each $E \subseteq A$, $E \in P$, the image set f[E] is in P. The reduction is **P-to-finite** if f[E] is finite for each $E \subseteq A$, $E \in P$.

A well known class of P-to-P reductions is formed by the polynomial time isomorphisms of Berman and Hartmanis [3]. Their conjecture that all NP-complete sets are isomorphic implies, of course very strongly that these sets are related by P-to-P reductions.

We have the following characterization:

4.2 Theorem. A recursive set A is not P-levelable if and only if there is a P-to-finite reduction from A to some recursive set B.□

This characterization can be used to establish the preservation result:

4.3 Theorem. Let A and B be recursive sets, and let A be P-to- reducible to B. Then A is P-levelable implies that B is P-levelable.□

We omit the proofs.

We conjecture that all NP-complete sets are related by P-to-P reductions, and so are P-levelable if P ≠ NP. This is a very weak consequence of the Berman-Hartmanis conjecture: it is even vacuously true if P = NP, in which case the latter conjecture fails badly [10].

REFERENCES

[1] J.L.Balcázar and U.Schöning, Bi-immune sets for complexity classes. To appear in **Math. Syst. Theory.**

[2] L.Berman, On the structure of complete sets: almost everywhere complexity and infinitely often speedup. **Proc. 17th IEEE Symp. Foundations of Computer Science** (1976), 76-80.

[3] L.Berman and J.Hartmanis, On isomorphism and density of NP and other complete sets. **SIAM J. Comput.** 6 (1977), 305-322.

[4] M.Blum and I.Marques, On complexity properties of recursively enumerable sets. **J. Symb. Logic** 38 (1973), 579-593.

[5] P.Flajolet and J.M.Steyaert, On sets having only hard subsets. **Proc. 2nd Int. Colloq. Automata, Languages, and Programming** (1974), Springer-Verlag, 446-457.

[6] J.E.Hopcroft and J.D.Ullman, **Introduction to Automata Theory, Languages, and Computation.** Addison-Wesley, Reading, Ma., 1979.

[7] R.Karp and R.Lipton, Some connections between nonuniform and uniform complexity classes. **Proc. 12th ACM Symp. on Theory of Computing** (1980), 302-309.

[8] K.Ko, Non-levelable sets and immune sets in the accepting density hierarchy in NP. Manuscript (1984), submitted for publication.

[9] N.Lynch, On reducibility to complex or sparse sets. **J. Assoc. Comput. Mach.** 22 (1975), 341-345.

[10] S.R.Mahaney and P.Young, Orderings of polynomial isomorphism types. Manuscript (1983), submitted for publication.

[11] A.R.Meyer and M.S.Paterson, With what frequency are apparently intractable problems difficult? Tech. Rep. TM-126, Laboratory of Computer Science, Massachusetts Institute of technology, Cambridge, Ma., 1979.

[12] P.Orponen, A classification of complexity core lattices. Manuscript (1984), submitted for publication.

[13] P.Orponen and U.Schöning, The structure of polynomial complexity cores. **Proc. 11th Symp. Math. Foundations of Computer Science** (1984), Lecture Notes in Computer Science 176, Springer-Verlag, 452-458.

[14] D.A.Russo and P.Orponen, A duality between recursive complexity cores and polynomial time computable subsets. Manuscript (1984), submitted for publication.

[15] C.P.Schnorr, Optimal algorithms for self-reducible problems. **Proc. 3rd Int. Colloq. Automata, Languages, and Programming** (1976), Edinburgh Univ. Press, 322-337.

[16] A.L.Selman, Reductions on NP and P-selective sets. **Theoret. Computer Sci.** 19 (1982), 287-304.

[17] R.Soare, Computational complexity, speedable and levelable sets. **J. Symb. Logic** 42 (1977), 545-563.

[18] P.Young, Some structural properties of polynomial reducibilities. **Proc. 15th ACM Symp. Theory of Computing** (1983), 392-401.

FINITE GROUP TOPOLOGY AND p-ADIC TOPOLOGY FOR FREE MONOIDS.

J.E. PIN, Université Paris VI et CNRS, LITP
Tour 55-65, 4 place Jussieu
75230 Paris Cedex 05, FRANCE

The finite group topology for free groups was first introduced by M. Hall Jr [2] and extended by Reutenauer [5] to the case of free monoids. This is the initial topology $\mathcal{T}$ defined by all morphisms from the free monoid into a discrete finite group. The p-adic topology $\mathcal{T}_p$ is defined in the same way by replacing "group" by "p-group" in the definition. (Similarly the "profinite topology" recently introduced by D. Scott [8] is obtained by replacing "group" by "monoid" in the definition, but we are not concerned with this topology in this paper). The aim of this paper is to study the topologies $\mathcal{T}$ and $\mathcal{T}_p$ and their connexions with formal languages.

Standard methods show that $\mathcal{T}$ and $\mathcal{T}_p$ can be defined by linear (ultra) metrics. Moreover if a free monoid is topologized by $\mathcal{T}$ or $\mathcal{T}_p$, then it becomes a topological monoid and every morphism between two free monoids is continuous.

Our first result shows that open sets of these topologies are closed under some classical operations of language theory : union, concatenation, plus operation, left and right quotients by an arbitrary set. We also show that if $L_0, \ldots, L_k$ are open and $a_1, \ldots, a_k$ are letters, then $L_0 a_1 L_1 \ldots a_k L_k$ is also open. As a consequence we show that every surjective length-preserving morphism between two free monoids is <u>open</u> (that is, the image of an open set is also open). All these results hold for both $\mathcal{T}$ and $\mathcal{T}_p$.

Our second result shows that in the case of recognizable languages, topological properties have a nice algebraic counterpart. Indeed, we prove that if a recognizable language is open or closed in $\mathcal{T}$ (resp. $\mathcal{T}_p$), then the regular $\mathcal{D}$-classes of its syntactic monoid M are Brandt semigroups (resp. Brandt semigroups whose groups are p-groups). Furthermore, if P denotes the image of L in M, P satisfies a simple condition.

(*) For all $s,t \in M$ and for all idempotent $e \in M$, $st \in P$ implies $set \in P$.
A similar result holds for closed subsets of A . If L is closed then P satisfies

(**) For all, $s,t \in M$ and for all idempotent $e \in M$, $set \in M$ implies $st \in P$.
Now, two natural questions arise :

1) Does there exist an algorithm to decide whether a given recognizable language is closed, open or both ?

2) Does there exist an algorithm to compute the topological adherence (resp. interior) of a given recognizable set ? In particular is this adherence (interior) also recognizable ?
Notice that (1) is a special case of (2). We conjecture that condition (**) (resp. (*)) characterizes closed (resp. open) recognizable sets. This conjecture, if true, would give a nive solution to the first question. Two partial results give some evidence that the conjecture might be true. First a recognizable submonoid of A^* is closed iff it satisfies (**).-see theorem 6.4 for more details.- Second, a recognizable language L is clopen (that is, open and closed) iff it satisfies (*) and (**). In fact it is easy to see that this last condition is equivalent to say that L is a group-language (resp. a p-group language in the case of $\mathcal{C}_p$).

Our last result relates the second question to an important problem of semigroup theory. Indeed we show that computing the kernel of a finite semigroup -an old problem due to Rhodes [7]- reduces to solve positively question 2. In particular, this would solve the membership problem for Inv, the variety of finite monoids generated by finite inverse monoids. The conjecture, presented at the previous ICALP [3], states that $M \in$ Inv iff idempotents of M commute. In terms of language theory this would solve positively the membership problem for $A^* \mathcal{I}nv$, the boolean algebra generated by languages of the form LaK where $a \in A$ and L and K are group (resp. p-group) languages.

Except for the last section, the proofs are language theoretic. In particular, we need to study an operation an languages that counts, in some sense, the ambiguity of the concatenation product.

After a preliminary section, definitions and basic properties are presented in section 2. Section 3 is self contained and devoted to the counting operation mentionned above. The results of section 3 are then used in section 4 to list operations that preserve open sets and in section 5 to study length preserving morphisms. In section 6 we present the algebraic properties of recognizable open languages and we discuss questions (1) and (2). Finally applications of question (2) are presented in the last section. Detailed proofs will be published elsewhere.

1. Preliminaries

$|S|$ will denote the cardinality of a set S. Let A be a finite alphabet and let A^* be the free monoid over A. A language L is recognizable (= rational, regular) iff it is recognized by a finite automaton or, equivalently, if its syntactic monoid is finite.

Given a prime number p, a p-group is a finite group whose order is a power of p. A language L is a group language (resp a p-group language) iff its syntactic monoid is a finite group (resp. p-group) or equivalently iff L is recognized by a finite group automaton (resp. p-group automaton).

Let $u,v \in A^*$. Following Eilenberg [1] we denote by $\binom{u}{v}$ the number of distincts factorizations of u of the form $u = u_0 a_1 u_1 a_2 \ldots a_n u_n$ where $a_1,\ldots,a_n \in A$ $a_1 \ldots a_n = v$ and $u_0,\ldots,u_n \in A^*$. For instance $\binom{abab}{ab} = 3$. For $0 \leq i < p$, and $u \in A^*$, set $L(u,i,p) = \{v \in A^* \; \binom{v}{u} \equiv i \bmod p\}$

The next result gives a complete description of p-group languages.

Theorem 1.1 [1] A language L is a p-group language iff it is a boolean combination of languages of the form $L(u,i,p)$ for $u \in A^*$ and $0 \leq i < p$.

No such description is known for group languages.

2. The finite group-topology and the p-adic topology.

Let $F(A)$ be the free group over A. The Hall topology for the free group [2] is the coarsest topology such that every group morphism from $F(A)$ into a finite discrete group is continuous. Reutenauer [5] extended this definition for the free monoid.

Definition 2.1 The finite group topology on A^* is the coarsest topology such that every (monoid) morphism from A^* into a discrete finite group is continuous.

Similarly, we have

Definition 2.2 The p-adic topology on A^* is the coarsest topology such that every (monoid) morphism from A^* into a discrete finite p-group is continuous.

We shall denote by $\mathcal{T}_H$ the Hall topology for the free group, by $\mathcal{T}$ the finite group topology for the free monoid and by $\mathcal{T}_p$ the p-adic topology. Observe that if $A = \{a\}$ then A^* (resp. $F(A)$) is isomorphic to $\mathbb{N}$ (resp. $\mathbb{Z}$) and that our "p-adic topology" is, in this case, the usual p-adic topology on integers. The next propositions will give some more explicit definitions of these topologies.

Proposition 2.1 [5] $\mathcal{T}$ is the restriction of $\mathcal{T}_H$ to A^*. That is, a set L of A^* is open (closed) iff there exists an open (closed) set S of $F(A)$ such that $L = S \cap A^*$.

Proposition 2.2 [5] A set L of A is open in $\mathcal{T}$ (resp $\mathcal{T}_p$) iff it is (infinite) union of group (resp. p-group) languages.

For each $u,v \in A^*$, set

$$e(u,v) = \min\{n \in \mathbb{N} \mid \text{there is a morphism } \varphi : A^* \to G \text{ into a finite group of order } n \text{ such that } u\varphi \neq v\varphi\}.$$

We make the usual convention that $\min \emptyset = \infty$, so that $e(u,u) = \infty$. Now we set

$$d(u,v) = 2^{-e(u,v)}$$

and we have the following properties, for all $u,v,w \in A^*$

(1) $d(u,v) = 0 \Leftrightarrow u = v$
(2) $d(u,w) \leqslant \max(d(u,v), d(v,w))$
(3) $d(u,v) = d(v,u)$
(4) $d(wu,wv) = d(uw,vw) = d(u,v)$

The first three properties say that d is an ultrametric distance and condition (4) says that d is linear. Then we have

Proposition 2.3 The distance d defines the finite group topology on A^*. In particular A^* is a topological Hansdorff space.

Furthermore

Proposition 2.4 (A^*,d) is a topological monoid (i.e. the multiplication is continuous) and every morphism between free monoids is continuous.

Similar results hold for $\mathcal{C}_p$ by replacing "group" by "p-group" in the definition of $e(u,v)$. Here is a useful result on limits.

Proposition 2.5 [2] For every $u \in A^*$, $\lim_{n\to\infty} u^{n!} = 1$ in $\mathcal{C}$ and $\lim_{n\to\infty} u^{p^n} = 1$ in $\mathcal{C}_p$.

It is time to give a first series of examples.

Example 1 Given $0 \leqslant r < n$, the set of all words of length congruent to r modulo n is clopen. In particular, the set $(A^n)^*$ is clopen.

Example 2 Let $A = \{a\}$. Then the sets

$S = \{a^n | n$ is square-free$\}$ and $P = \{a^n | n$ is prime$\}$ are closed

Indeed $S = a^* \setminus \bigcup_{k \geqslant 2} (a^{k^2})^*$ and $P = a^* \setminus \bigcup_{p,q \geqslant 2} (a^{pq})^*$

Example 3 Let $\bar{A}$ be a copy of A and let $\pi : (A \cup \bar{A})^* \to F(A)$ be the natural morphism onto the free group defined by $a\pi = a$ and $\bar{a}\pi = a^{-1}$. Then π is a continuous mapping from $(A \cup \bar{A}), \mathcal{C})$ onto $(F(A), \mathcal{C}_H)$. Now since $\{1\}$ is closed in $F(A)$, the Dyck language $D^* = 1\pi^{-1}$ is closed.

Other examples will be given further on in the paper.

3. A counting operation

In this section we introduce a new operation on languages that will be used intensively in the next sections. This operation is a slight generalization of Straubing's counting [9] and also appeared in a different form in the work of Thérien [10]. But let us give the formal definition.

Definition 3.1 Let $L_0,\dots,L_k$ be languages of A^*, $a_1,\dots,a_k$ be letters of A and $0 \leq r < n$ be two integers. Then $(L_0a_1L_1\dots a_kL_k)_{r,n}$ is the set of all words $u \in A^*$ such that the number of factorizations of u of the form $u = u_0a_1u_1\dots a_ku_k$ with $u_0 \in L_0,\dots, u_k \in L_k$ is congruent to r modulo n.

Given monoids $M_0,\dots,M_k$ recognizing $L_0,\dots,L_k$ respectively, we shall now describe a monoid recognizing $(L_0a_1L_1\dots a_kL_k)_{r,n}$. Let $M = M_0 \times M_1 \times\dots\times M_k$ and let $K = \mathbb{Z}/n\mathbb{Z}\langle M\rangle$ be the ring of all polynomials over M with coefficients in $\mathbb{Z}/n\mathbb{Z}$. Thus every element of K can be written in the form $\sum_{m\in M} \lambda_m m$ where $\lambda_m \in \mathbb{Z}/n\mathbb{Z}$ and $\lambda_m \neq 0$ for a finite number of m only. Addition is defined by

$$(\sum_{m\in M} \lambda_m m) + (\sum_{m\in M} \mu_m m) = \sum_{m\in M}(\lambda_m + \mu_m)m$$

and product by the formula

$$(\sum_{m\in M} \lambda_m m)(\sum_{m\in M} \mu_m m) = \sum_{m\in M} (\sum_{st=m} \lambda_s \mu_t)m$$

Finally let $M_{k+1}(K)$ be the ring of matrices of size $(k+1)\times(k+1)$ over K and let R be the multiplicative submonoid of $M_{k+1}(K)$ consisting of all matrices p satisfying the following conditions.

(1) For $i > j$, $p_{ij} = 0$ (that is, p is upper-triangular)

(2) For $i=j$, $p_{ii} = (1,\dots,1\ m_i,1,\dots,1)$ for some $m_i \in M_i$. (That is, if we write p_{ii} as $\Sigma\, \lambda_m m$, then $\lambda_m = 0$ for all m except for exactly one $m = (1,\dots, 1,m_i,1,\dots,1)$)

(3) For $i < j$, $p_{ij} \in \mathbb{Z}/n\mathbb{Z}\langle 1 \times\dots\times 1 \times M_i \times\dots\times M_j \times 1 \times\dots\times 1\rangle$ (that is, if $p_{ij} = \Sigma\, \lambda_m m$ then $\lambda_m = 0$ unless m has the form $(1,\dots, 1, m_i,\dots,m_j,1,\dots,1)$ for some $m_i \in M_i$, $m_{i+1} \in M_{i+1},\dots,m_j \in M_j$)

We shall denote by $\mathbb{Z}/n\mathbb{Z}\Diamond(M_0,\dots,M_k)$ this monoid R, which belongs to the same family as the Schützenberger product (in fact the Schützenberger product is obtained by replacing the ring $\mathbb{Z}/n\mathbb{Z}$ by the boolean semiring in the previous construction). We can now state

Theorem 3.1 Let $L_0,\dots,L_k$ be languages of A^* recognized by monoids $M_0,\dots,M_k$ respectively, let $a_1,\dots,a_k$ be letters of A^* and let $0 \leq r < n$ be two integers. Then $(L_0a_1L_1\dots a_kL_k)_{r,n}$ is recognized by the monoid $\mathbb{Z}/n\mathbb{Z}\Diamond(M_0,\dots,M_k)$.

Corollary 3.2 If $L_0,\dots, L_k$ are recognizable languages of A^*, so is $(L_0a_1\dots a_kL_k)_{r,n}$ for all $0 \leq r < n$ and $a_1,\dots, a_k \in A$.

This last result can be specialized for group languages and for p-group languages.

Corollary 3.3 If $L_o,\dots, L_k$ are group languages, then $(L_o a_1 L_1 \dots a_k L_k)_{r,n}$ is a group language for all $0 \leq r < n$ and $a_1,\dots, a_k \in A$.

Corollary 3.4 If $L_o,\dots, L_k$ are p-groups languages, then $(L_o a_1 L_1 \dots a_k L_k)_{r,p^n}$ is a p-group language for all r,n such that $0 \leq r < p^n$ and $a_1,\dots, a_k \in A$.

This last result can be specialized for group lanquages and for p-group lanquages.

Example 4 $(A^* a_1 A^* \dots a_k A^*)_{r,n} = \{u \in A^* \mid \binom{u}{a_1 \dots a_k} = r \bmod n\}$ is clopen in $\mathcal{C}$.

Similarly

$$(A^* a_1 A^* \dots a_k A^*)_{r,p^n} = \{u \in A^* \mid \binom{u}{a_1 \dots a_k} = r \bmod p^n\} \text{ is clopen in } \mathcal{C}_p.$$

4. Operations that preserve open sets

In this section we show that open sets are preserved under various operations. Let us start with the right and left quotients. Recall that if X and L are languages, then $X^{-1}L = \{u \in A^* \mid \exists x \in X\ xu \in L\}$ and $LX^{-1} = \{u \in A^* \mid \exists x \in X\ ux \in L\}$.

Proposition 4.1 Let X,L be languages of A^*. If L is open in $\mathcal{C}$ (resp. $\mathcal{C}_p$), so are $X^{-1}L$ and LX^{-1}.

Proof We have $X^{-1}L = \{u \in A^* \mid \exists x \in X\ xu \in L\} = \bigcup_{x \in X} x^{-1}L$. Since open sets are closed under union, it suffices to prove the result for $x^{-1}L$ where x is a word. Now the map $\varphi : A^* \to A^*$ defined by $u\varphi = xu$ is continuous since the multiplication is continuous (proposition 2.4). Therefore if L is open, $L\varphi^{-1} = x^{-1}L$ is also open. The proof for LX^{-1} is dual.

Theorem 4.2 Let $L_o,\dots, L_k$ be group (resp. p-group) languages and let $a_1,\dots,a_k$ be letters. Then $L_o a_1 L_1 \dots a_k L_k$ is open in $\mathcal{C}$ (resp. $\mathcal{C}_p$).

Proof We give the proof for $\mathcal{C}_p$ only, but the proof for $\mathcal{C}$ is similar. Let r and n be integers such that $0 \leq r < p^n$. Then by corollary 3.4. $(L_o a_1 L_1 \dots a_k L_k)_{r,p^n}$ is a p-group language and thus is open. Now we have

$$L_o a_1 L_1 \dots a_k L_k = \bigcup_{\substack{o < r < p^n \\ n > o}} (L_o a_1 L_1 \dots a_k L_k)_{r,p^n}$$

Thus $L_o a_1 L_1 \dots a_k L_k$ is union of open sets and hence open.

This theorem has many interesting consequences.

Corollary 4.3 Let $L_o,\dots, L_k$ be open sets of $\mathcal{C}$ (resp. $\mathcal{C}_p$) and let $a_1,\dots, a_k$ be letters of A. Then $L_o a_1 L_1 \dots a_k L_k$ is open in $\mathcal{C}$ (resp. $\mathcal{C}_p$).

Proof By proposition 2.2, every L_i is union of group (p-group) languages. Now concatenation distributes over union and thus $L = L_0 a_1 L_1 \dots a_k L_k$ is union of languages of the form $L = K_0 a_1 K_1 \dots a_k K_k$ where $K_0, \dots, K_k$ are group (p-group) languages. Since each K is open by theorem 4.2, L is also open.

Corollary 4.4 Open sets of $\mathcal{T}$ (resp. $\mathcal{T}_p$) are preserved under union, concatenation and plus operation.

Proof Let $K, L \subset A^*$ be two open sets of $\mathcal{T}$ (resp. $\mathcal{T}_p$). Then $K \cup L$ is open by definition of a topology. Moreover we have

$$KL = \bigcup_{a \in A} Ka(a^{-1}L) \text{ if } 1 \notin L, \text{ and}$$

$$KL = K \cup \bigcup_{a \in A} Ka(a^{-1}L) \text{ if } 1 \in L.$$

Now for each $a \in A$, $a^{-1}L$ is open by proposition 4.1 and $Ka(a^{-1}L)$ is open by corollary 4.3. Thus KL is union of open sets and hence is open. Finally $L^+ = \bigcup_{n>0} L^n$. But L^n is open for all $n > 0$ and thus so is L^+.

Given two languages L and K, the shuffle of L and K is the language $L \sqcup\!\sqcup K = \{w \in A^* \mid w \text{ factorizes as } w = u_0 v_1 u_1 v_2 \dots v_n u_n \text{ where } u_0, u_1, \dots, u_n, v_1, \dots, v_n$ are words such that $u_0 u_1 \dots u_n \in L$ and $v_1 \dots v_n \in K\}$

Corollary 4.5 For every language $L \subset A^*$, $L \sqcup\!\sqcup A^*$ is open.

Proof We have $L \sqcup\!\sqcup A^* = \bigcup_{u \in L} u \sqcup\!\sqcup A^*$. Now if $u = a_1 \dots a_k$, $u \sqcup\!\sqcup A^* = A^* a_1 A^* \dots a_k A^*$. But A^* is open and thus $A^* a_1 A^* \dots a_k A^*$ is open by corollary 4.3. Therefore $L \sqcup\!\sqcup A^*$ is union of open sets and hence is also open.

5. Length preserving morphisms between free monoids.

The goal of this section is to prove the following result.

Theorem 5.1 Let $\varphi : A^* \to B^*$ be a surjective length-preserving morphism. Then φ is an open map. This result holds for both $\mathcal{T}$ and $\mathcal{T}_p$.

Proof Since every open set of $\mathcal{T}$ (resp. $\mathcal{T}_p$) is union of (p)-group languages, it suffices to show that if L is a (p)-group language, then $L\varphi$ is open. Let $\eta : A^* \to G$ be a morphism onto a (p)-group G that recognizes L. Consider for each letter $a \in A$, an injective morphism $\varphi_a : B^* \to A^*$ such that $\varphi_a \varphi = Id_{B^*}$ and $a\varphi\varphi_a = a$ (such a morphism always exists since φ is surjective and length-preserving). Finally define a substitution $\sigma : A^* \to 2^{B^*}$ by setting $a\sigma = a\eta\eta^{-1}\varphi_a^{-1}$.

Then we have for every $a \in A$

$$a\varphi \in a\varphi_a^{-1} \subset (a\eta\eta^{-1})\varphi_a^{-1} = a\sigma \subset (a\eta\eta^{-1})\varphi$$

It follows, for every $u \in A^*$, $u\varphi \in u\sigma \subset (u\eta\eta^{-1})\varphi$ and thus

$$L\varphi \subset L\sigma \subset (L\eta\eta^{-1})\varphi = L\varphi, \text{ that is, } L\varphi = L\sigma.$$

Now, for every $a \in A$, $a\eta\eta^{-1}$ is open by definition and $(a\eta\eta^{-1})\varphi_a^{-1} = a\sigma$ is also open since φ_a is continuous (proposition 2.4).

Furthermore open sets are preserved under concatenation (corollary 4.4) and thus $u\sigma$ is open for every $u \in A^+$. It follows that if $L \subset A^+$,

$L\varphi = \bigcup_{u \in L} u\sigma$ is open. Finally if $1 \in L$, then we have

$L\varphi = (L\backslash 1)\varphi \cup (1\eta\eta^{-1})\gamma^{-1}$ where $\gamma : B^* \to A^*$ is any morphism such that $\gamma\varphi = Id_{B^*}$. It follows that $(1\eta\eta^{-1})\gamma^{-1}$ is open and $(L\backslash 1)\varphi = \bigcup_{u \in L\backslash 1} u\sigma$ is open. Thus $L\varphi$ is open in every case and this conclude the proof. □

Let us conclude this section by giving some examples of context-free open sets.

<u>Corollary 5.6</u> The complement of the Dyck language D^* is a deterministic, context-free and open language. Furthermore, open context-free languages are preserved under inverse morphisms, surjective length-preserving morphisms and intersection with rational open languages.

6. <u>Algebraic properties of recognizable open sets</u>

In this section we give some syntactic properties of recognizable languages that are open or closed in $\mathcal{T}$ or $\mathcal{T}_p$. Throughout this section, L denotes a recognizable language of A^*, $\eta : A^* \to M$ denotes its syntactic morphism and we set $P = L\eta$ (and thus $P\eta^{-1} = L$). We can state

<u>Theorem 6.1</u> 1) If L is open in $\mathcal{T}$ (resp. $\mathcal{T}_p$), then for each $s,t \in M$ and each idempotent $e \in M$, $st \in M$ implies $set \in P$. (*)

2) If L is closed in $\mathcal{T}$ (resp. $\mathcal{T}_p$), then for each $s,t \in M$ and each idempotent $e \in M$, $set \in M$ implies $st \in P$. (**)

<u>Proof</u> We just prove 2) for the finite group topology. Others proofs are similar. Assume that L is closed and let $s,t \in M$ and let $e \in M$ be an idempotent such that $set \in P$. Let $u \in s\eta^{-1}$, $x \in e\eta^{-1}$ and $v \in t\eta^{-1}$. Then since e is idempotent, we have $(x^{n!})\eta = e$ for all $n > 0$ and thus $ux^{n!}v \in P\eta^{-1} = L$ for all $n > 0$. Now $\lim_{n\to\infty} x^{n!} = 1$ by proposition 2.5 and since the multiplication is continuous, we have $\lim_{n\to\infty} ux^{n!}v = uv$. Since L is closed, it follows that $uv \in L$ and consequently $(uv)\eta = st \in P$. □

Let us recall the definition of Green relations. Let $x,y \in M$. Then

$x \mathcal{R} y$ iff there exist $a,b \in M$ such that $xa = y$ and $yb = x$.
$x \mathcal{L} y$ iff there exist $c,d \in M$ such that $cx = y$ and $dy = x$.
$x \mathcal{D} y$ iff there exist $a,b,c,d \in M$ such that $axb = y$ and $cyd = x$.
$x \mathcal{H} y$ iff $x \mathcal{R} y$ and $x \mathcal{L} y$.

A $\mathcal{D}$-class is called regular if it contains an idempotent. A well known result of semigroup theory states that every regular $\mathcal{D}$-class can be represented by an "egg-box picture" like this one.

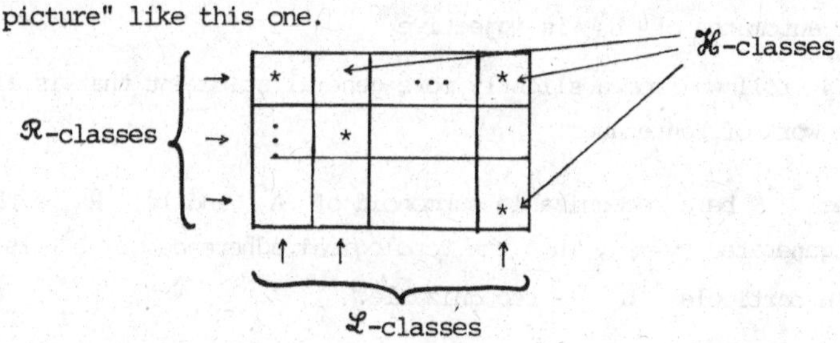

In this picture rows represent $\mathcal{R}$-classes, columns represent $\mathcal{L}$-classes and boxes represent $\mathcal{H}$-classes. A star in a box means that the corresponding $\mathcal{H}$-class H contains an idempotent e. In this case H is a group with unit e. A further condition says that there is at least one star in each row and in each column. We can now state

Theorem 6.2 1) If L is open or closed in $\mathcal{C}$ (or $\mathcal{C}_p$) then the regular $\mathcal{D}$-classes of M are Brandt semigroups, that is, the egg-box pictures have the following form

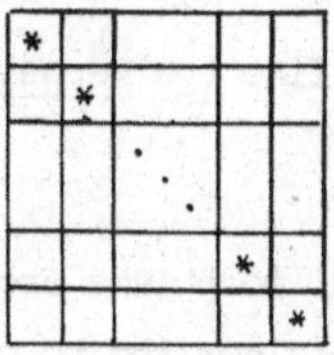

(square, with stars only on the diagonal).

2) If L is open or closed in $\mathcal{C}_p$, then furthermore the groups appearing in the $\mathcal{D}$-classes are p-groups.

We conjecture that condition (*) (resp. (**)) of theorem 6.1 characterizes open (closed) recognizable languages. This conjecture is true in two particular cases.

Corollary 6.3 Let L be a recognizable language. Then the following conditions are equivalent :

(1) L is clopen in $\mathcal{C}$.
(2) L satisfies conditions (*) and (**)
(3) L is a group language.

A similar result holds for $\mathcal{T}_p$: L is clopen in $\mathcal{T}_p$ iff it is a p-group language. The second particular case is a consequence of Reutenauer results [5,6]

Theorem 6.4 Let L^* be a recognizable submonoid of A^* and let H be the subgroup of F(A) generated by L^*. Then the following conditions are equivalent :

(1) L^* is closed in $\mathcal{T}$.

(2) $L^* = H \cap A^*$

(3) L^* satisfies (**)

(4) The minimal automaton of L^* is injective

Theorem 6.4 follows from a slightly more general statement that is also a consequence of the work of Reutenauer.

Theorem 6.5 Let L^* be a recognizable submonoid of A^* and let H be the subgroup of F(A) generated by L^*. Then the topological adherence of L^* is $\bar{L}^* = H \cap A^*$. In particular $\bar{L}^*$ is recognizable.

In this case one can effectively compute the adherence of a recognizable language. It is not known whether this is always the case. As we show in the next section, this problem has some surprising applications.

7. Some applications.

Let M and N be two monoids. Recall that a relational morphism $\tau : M \to N$ is a map from M into the subsets of N such that

(1) for each $m \in M$, $m\tau \neq \emptyset$

(2) for each $m_1, m_2 \in M$ $(m_1\tau)(m_2\tau) \subset (m_1m_2)\tau$

(3) $1 \in 1\tau$

For each $n \in N$, we set $n\tau^{-1} = \{m \in M | n \in m\tau\}$. Define the kernel of a monoid M as the set

$$K(M) = \bigcap_{\tau : M \to G} 1\tau^{-1}$$

where the intersection is taken over all relational morphisms from M into a finite group G. Rhodes [7] asked whether there is an algorithm to compute the kernel of a finite monoid. This question first arose in the study of the complexity problem but has other interesting applications. Here we show that the question reduces to compute the adherence of a recognizable language.

Let M be a finite monoid and let $A = M \setminus 1$. Then there is a natural morphism $\eta : A^* \to M$. For each $m \in M$ set $L_m = m\eta^{-1}$ and let F be the (finite!) union of all adherences $\bar{L}_m$ such that $1 \in \bar{L}_m$. Then F is a closed subset of A^* not containing 1. Therefore $A^* \setminus F$ is open and contains a group language recognized by a certain finite group G. Let $\pi : A^* \to G$ be the corresponding morphism and let $\gamma : M \to G$ the relation defined by $m\gamma = \bar{L}_m \pi$. Then we can state

Theorem 7.1 $\gamma : M \to G$ is a relational morphism and $1\gamma^{-1} = K(M)$

Corollary 7.2 If there is an algorithm to compute the adherence of a recognizable set, then the membership problem for the variety of finite monoids Inv is decidable.

Proof It was shown in [3] that $M \in$ Inv iff $K(M)$ is idempotent and commutative.

Acknowledgement Part of these results were obtained in Naples (Italy) as I was visiting Prof. A. De Luca. I would like to thank him for his invitation and for many useful discussions. I am also very grateful to one of the anonymous referees for the new and simple proof of theorem 5.2.

REFERENCES

[1] S. Eilenberg, Automata, languages and Machines, Academic Press, Vol B (1976)

[2] M. Hall Jr., A topology for free groups and related groups, Ann. Math. 52 (1950) 127-139.

[3] S.W. Margolis and J.E. Pin, Languages and inverse semigroups, 11th ICALP LNCS 172, (1984), 337-346.

[4] J.E. Pin, Variétés de langages formels, Masson, Paris (1984)

[5] Ch. Reutenauer, Une topologie du monoïde libre, Semigroup Forum 18, (1979) 33-49.

[6] Ch. Reutenauer, Sur mon article "une topologie du monoïde libre", Semigroup Forum 22, (1981), 93-95.

[7] J. Rhodes and B. Tilson, Improved lower bounds for complexity of finite semigroups, Journal of Pure and Applied Algebra 2 (1972), 13-71.

[8] D. Scott, Infinite words, unpublished.

[9] H. Straubing, Families of recognizable sets corresponding to certain varieties of finite monoids, J. Pure and Applied Algebra, 15, (1979), 319-327.

[10] D. Thérien, Sur les monoïdes dont tous les groupes sont résolubles, Semigroup Forum 26, (1983), 89-101.

ON THE USE OF RELATIONAL EXPRESSIONS IN THE DESIGN OF EFFICIENT ALGORITHMS

(Extended Abstract)

Seppo Sippu
Department of Computer Science
University of Jyväskylä
Seminaarinkatu 15
SF-40100 Jyväskylä, Finland

Eljas Soisalon-Soininen
Department of Computer Science
University of Helsinki
Tukholmankatu 2
SF-00250 Helsinki, Finland

Abstract. Relational expressions have finite binary relations as arguments and the operations are composition (·), closure (*), inverse ($^{-1}$), and union (U). The efficient computation of the relation denoted by a relational expression is considered, and a tight bound is established on the complexity of the algorithm suggested by Hunt, Szymanski and Ullman. The result implies a unified method for deriving efficient algorithms for many problems in parsing. For example, optimal algorithms are derived for strong LL(1) and strong LL(2) parser construction and an efficient polynomial-time algorithm is derived for determining the inessential error entries in an LR(1) parsing table.

1. INTRODUCTION

Simple algorithms can often be described by defining a relation R on a finite set A such that the desired result is R*(B), for B ⊂ A, or R*, or is easily obtained from R*. Here R* denotes the reflexive transitive closure of R and R*(B) denotes the image of B under R*. Hunt, Szymanski and Ullman (1974,1977) have extended this idea by defining "relational expressions" that are expressions whose arguments are relations and whose operators are chosen from among · (composition), * (closure), $^{-1}$ (inverse), and U (union). They give an algorithm for evaluating a relational expression, and they use relational expressions in deriving efficient algorithms for many context-free grammar problems. Examples are an $O(n^2)$ algorithm for computing Wirth-Weber precedence relations and an $O(n^2)$ algorithm for testing whether a grammar is SLR(1). Here n denotes the size of the grammar.

The algorithm given by Hunt, Szymanski and Ullman (1974,1977) for evaluating a relational expression is based on a graph representation of the expression. The relation denoted by the expression is obtained in a straightforward way from the reflexive transitive closure of the graph. The time bound obtained for evaluating relational expression E is O(n·size(E)), where n denotes the upper bound on the size of the domain and on the size of the range of any argument in E and size(E) is the sum of the sizes of the arguments in E.

In this paper we show how the strong components algorithm of Tarjan (1972) can be applied to the graph representation of a relational expression in order to get a more efficient algorithm for the evaluation. In this way we obtain a single-traversal, O(t·size(E)) time-bounded algorithm for computing the relation denoted by relational expression E. Here t is the time spent on a single set operation (union, assignment) on sets of size min{d,r}, where d is the size of the domain of E and r is the size of the range of E. This improvement is essential in many context-free grammar problems. For example, a relational expression that defines the lookahead symbols of an LALR(1) parser contains relations defined on large sets having size of the LR(0) parsing machine, but the range of the ultimate relation is only the set of terminal symbols (DeRemer and Pennello, 1982).

The approach yields a unified method for deriving efficient or even optimal algorithms for many problems in parsing. Some of these results have been obtained earlier using special complicated algorithms. In the approach, an algorithm is given to evaluate any relational expression efficiently, and special-purpose algorithms are then obtained by defining suitable relational expressions.

The work of S.Sippu was supported by the Finnish Cultural Foundation. The work of E. Soisalon-Soininen was supported by the Academy of Finland.

We summarize in the following the problems we shall consider and the time bounds obtained. We denote by $|G|$ the size of a context-free grammar G, defined as the sum of the lengths of all rules in G. The terminal alphabet is denoted by T. The time spent on a single set operation on subsets of T is denoted by t.

(1) The time needed to construct the strong LL(1) parser for G is $O(t\cdot|G|)$. This bound is sharp because the parser requires $O(|T|\cdot|G|)$ space. Under the condition that no nonterminal produces only the empty string this result has been obtained by Johnson and Sethi (1975).

(2) The time needed to construct the strong LL(2) parser for G is $O(t\cdot|T|\cdot|G|)$. Also in this case the bound is sharp.

(3) The time needed to test whether or not grammar G is SLR(2) is $O(|T|\cdot|G|^2)$. This extends the method of SLR(1) testing by Hunt, Szymanski and Ullman (1974,1977) to SLR(2) testing. The bound obtained by Hunt, Szymanski and Ullman is $O(|G|^2)$ for SLR(1) testing but only $O(|G|^{k+2})$ for SLR(k) testing, $k \geq 2$ (also see Hunt, Szymanski and Ullman, 1975).

(4) The time needed to compute the lookahead symbols for the reduce actions of the LALR(1) parser for grammar G is $O(t\cdot|G|\cdot|Q|)$, where Q is the set of states in the LR(0) parsing machine for G. This bound can be regarded as optimal because the look-ahead sets for each pair (state, reduce action) require space $O(|T|\cdot|P|\cdot|Q|)$, where P is the set of rules in G. The result is obtained using a relational expression composed (with minor modifications) of the relations given in DeRemer and Pennello (1982).

(5) The time needed to determine the "inessential" (or "don't care") error entries in an LR(0)-based LR(1) parsing table for grammar G is $O(|T|\cdot|G|^2\cdot|Q|^2)$, where Q is the set of states in the LR(0) parsing machine for G. Previously no polynomial-time algorithm was known for computing the entire set of inessential error entries. In Soisalon-Soininen (1982) the problem is analyzed in detail, but the algorithm given may leave some inessential error entries undetected. A relational expression for this simpler algorithm yields a time bound $O(|T|\cdot|G|\cdot|Q|)$.

2. EVALUATING RELATIONAL EXPRESSIONS

To obtain efficient algorithms by means of relational expressions it is essential to allow the relational expressions to contain argument relations with different domains and ranges. Of course, the domains and ranges must be compatible with the operations. In a relational expression of the form $E_1\cdot E_2$ or E_1E_2 (composition) the range of E_1 and the domain of E_2 must be the same. In a relational expression of the form E^* (closure) the domain and range of E must be the same. In a relational expression of the form $E_1 \cup E_2$ (union) the domains of E_1 and E_2 must be the same and so must their ranges.

The <u>size</u> of relation R, denoted by size(R), is defined as the sum $|R|+|A|+|B|$, where A is the domain and B the range of R. (For any finite set A, $|A|$ denotes the number of elements in A.) The <u>size</u> of relational expression E, denoted by size(E), is defined as the sum of the sizes of its arguments.

To evaluate a relational expression E, we construct a directed graph $G_E = (V_E, R_E)$ such that the relation denoted by E will be obtained as a certain subset of R_E^*.

<u>Lemma 1</u>. (Hunt, Szymanski and Ullman, 1974,1977) Let E be a relational expression with domain A and range B. Then there is a directed graph $G_E = (V_E, R_E)$ and injections IN: $A \to V_E$ and OUT: $B \to V_E$ such that the following conditions are satisfied:
(1) IN(A), the set of "input nodes", and OUT(B), the set of "output nodes", are disjoint.
(2) $R_E(V_E) \cap IN(A) = \emptyset$, that is, no input node is entered by an edge.
(3) $R_E^{-1}(V_E) \cap OUT(B) = \emptyset$, that is, no output node is left by an edge.
(4) For all a in A and b in B:

$$a\ E\ b \text{ if and only if } IN(a)\ R_E^*\ OUT(b).$$

Moreover, the graph G_E and the injections IN and OUT can be constructed from E in time O(size(E)). □

Theorem 2. Let E be a relational expression with domain A and range B and let A' be a subset of A.

(a) The image, E(A'), of A' under the relation denoted by E can be computed in time O(size(E)).

(b) The relation denoted by E can be computed in time $O(t\cdot|E|)$, where t is the time spent on a single set operation (union, assignment) on sets of size $\min\{|A|,|B|\}$.

Moreover, these computations can be performed during a single traversal of the directed graph G_E.

Proof. For claim (a), perform the standard depth-first traversal starting from the nodes in IN(A') and marking all visited nodes. E(A') is obtained as the set of those b in B for which OUT(b) is marked.

For claim (b), we assume that $|B| \leq |A|$. (If $|A| < |B|$, consider the relational expression E^{-1}, compute its value, and finally take its inverse.) First note that the standard depth-first traversal of $G_{E^{-1}}$ readily gives an $O(|B|\cdot|E|)$ algorithm: compute for each b in B the set $E^{-1}(b)$. However, this algorithm is inefficient in that portions of the graph are traversed several times. To obtain a single-traversal, and $O(t\cdot|E|)$ time-bounded, algorithm we use an observation by DeRemer and Pennello (1982) They showed that the strong components algorithm of Tarjan (1982) is easily augmented to compute efficiently any function of the form

$$F(x) = \bigcup_{xR^*y} F_0(y),$$

where $G = (V,R)$ is the directed graph in question and $F_0\colon V \to 2^W$, for some set W, is a function whose values are known. The complexity of the original algorithm is only increased by assignments of the forms $F(x):=F_0(x)$, $F(x):=F(x) \cup F(y)$, and $F(y):=F(x)$. The time taken by one such assignment is $O(t)$, where t is the time taken by a single set operation on subsets of W. Thus, the complexity of the augmented algorithm remains as $O(t\cdot|G|)$. The relation denoted by relational expression E is obtained by computing F, when $G = G_E$ and F_0 is defined as follows:

$$F_0(y) = \begin{cases} \{OUT^{-1}(y)\}, & \text{when } y \text{ is an output node;} \\ \emptyset, & \text{otherwise.} \end{cases}$$

Observe that the range of F_0 is 2^B and that for all a in A and b in B, b belongs to F(IN(a)) if and only if IN(a) R_E^* OUT(b), that is, if and only if a E b. □

Observe that the time bound $O(t\cdot|E|)$ can be regarded as linear in $|E|$ when either A or B is a small set and when vector operations are available. In any case the time bound is $O(\min\{|A|,|B|\}\cdot|E|)$.

3. APPLICATIONS

We denote a (context-free) grammar by G = (N,T,P,S'), where N is the nonterminal alphabet, T is the terminal alphabet, P is the set of rules, and S' is the start symbol in N. For convenience, we assume that our grammars are augmented: the only rule in which S' appears is S' → \$S\$\$, where \$ is a terminal not appearing elsewhere. We denote nonterminals by A,B,C,D,E,S', terminals by a,b,c, symbols in NUT by X,Y,Z, terminals strings by x,y,z,w, strings in (NUT)* by $\alpha,\beta,\gamma,\delta,\omega$, and the empty string by ε.

String α is nullable if it derives the empty string, that is, $\alpha \Rightarrow^* \varepsilon$. The size of G, denoted by |G|, is the sum of all $|A\omega|$, where $A \to \omega$ is a rule of G. For any rule $A \to \alpha\beta$ of G, the dotted rule $A \to \alpha\cdot\beta$ is called an LR(0) item (or item, for short Observe that |G| equals the number of distinct items of G.

For other definitions and notations pertaining to context-free grammars and parsing, see Aho and Ullman (1972,1973).

Basic relations

We begin by defining for grammar G some simple relations, which will be used throughout this section. Most of these relations come from Hunt, Szymanski and Ullman (1974,1977). The relations are defined by:

X terminal a, whenever a is a terminal of G and X = a.

A has-rule $A \to \omega$, whenever $A \to \omega$ is a rule of G.

$A \to \omega$ has-first-item $A \to \cdot\omega$, whenever $A \to \omega$ is a rule of G.

$A \to \omega$ has-last-item $A \to \omega\cdot$, whenever $A \to \omega$ is a rule of G.

$A \to \alpha\cdot X\beta$ passes-null $A \to \alpha X\cdot\beta$, whenever $A \to \alpha X\beta$ is a rule of G and X is nullable.

$A \to \alpha\cdot X\beta$ passes-any $A \to \alpha X\cdot\beta$, whenever $A \to \alpha X\beta$ is a rule of G.

$A \to \alpha\cdot X\beta$ points X, whenever $A \to \alpha X\beta$ is a rule of G.

X begins A, whenever G has a rule $A \to \alpha X\beta$, where α is nullable.

X ends A, whenever G has a rule $A \to \alpha X\beta$, where β is nullable.

A derives X, whenever G has a rule $A \to \alpha X\beta$, where α and β are nullable.

For any grammar G, these relations are of size $O(|G|)$ and can be computed from G in time $O(|G|)$. Observe that the set of nullable nonterminals in G can be determined in time $O(|G|)$ (Harrison, 1978). Also observe that the relations begins and ends could have been obtained via the other relations, as the values of the following relational expressions:

begins = points^{-1} (passes-null^{-1})* has-first-item^{-1} has-rule^{-1}.

ends = points^{-1} passes-any passes-null* has-last-item^{-1} has-rule^{-1}.

However, we have included these relations among the set of basic relations for G because they are "small" (i.e., of linear size) and are anyway easily computed from G.

Strong LL(1) parser construction

Consider the relational expressions (cf. Hunt, Szymanski and Ullman, 1974,1977):

adjoins = points^{-1} passes-any passes-null* points.

first-of = terminal begins*.

follows = first-of adjoins^{-1} (ends^{-1})*.

has-lookahead = has-first-item passes-null* (points first-of^{-1} $\cup$
has-last-item^{-1} has-rule^{-1} follows^{-1}).

Here relational expression names appearing as arguments in other expressions mean subexpressions, not their values. For example, follows is actually the expression

(terminal begins*) (points^{-1} passes-any passes-null* points)$^{-1}$ (ends^{-1})*.

Lemma 3. In any reduced grammar G,
(1) X adjoins Y iff G has a rule $A \to \alpha X\gamma Y\beta$, where γ is nullable.
(2) a first-of Y iff $a \in FIRST_1(Y) \setminus \{\varepsilon\}$.
(3) a follows Y iff $a \in FOLLOW_1(Y)$.
(4) $A \to \omega$ has-lookahead a iff $a \in FIRST_1(\omega FOLLOW_1(A))$, for rule $A \to \omega$. □

Theorem 4. (Johnson and Sethi, 1975) Given any reduced grammar $G = (N,T,P,S')$,
(1) the collection of all sets $FIRST_1(X)$, $X \in NUT$, can be computed in time $O(t\cdot|G|)$;
(2) the collection of all sets $FOLLOW_1(X)$, $X \in NUT$, can be computed in time $O(t\cdot|G|)$;
(3) the strong LL(1) parser for G can be constructed in time $O(t\cdot|G|)$.
Here t is the time taken by a single set operation on subsets of T.

Proof. Consider (3). Constructing the strong LL(1) parser means essentially the computation of the relation denoted by the relational expression has-lookahead. Every argument in has-lookahead is only of size $O(|G|)$ and can be computed from G in time $O(|G|)$ (although it is true that there are subexpressions, e.g. adjoins, which denote relations having size nonlinear in $|G|$). Thus the size of has-lookahead is $O(|G|)$ and it can be constructed from G in time $O(|G|)$. As the range of has-lookahead is T, we conclude by Theorem 2 that the relation it denotes can be computed in time $O(t\cdot|G|)$. □

Strong LL(2) parser construction

The key idea is to fix a terminal a in T and to consider strings ab, b in T. For each a in T, define the relations a-begins and passes-a by setting:

Y a-begins A, whenever G has a rule $A \to \alpha X\gamma Y\beta$, where α and γ are nullable and X derives* a.

$A \to \alpha{\cdot}X\beta$ passes-a $A \to \alpha X{\cdot}\beta$, whenever $A \to \alpha X\beta$ is a rule of G and X derives* a.

For each a in T, these relations are of size $O(|G|)$. Moreover, they can be computed from G in time $O(|G|)$ because by Theorem 2 the set $(\text{derives*})^{-1}(\{a\})$ can be computed in time $O(|G|)$.

Then consider, for a in T, the relational expressions:

a-adjoins = points^{-1} passes-any passes-null* passes-a passes-null* points.

a-first-of = terminal begins* a-begins begins*.

a-follows = first-of a-adjoins^{-1} (ends^{-1})* ∪
first-of a-begins begins* adjoins^{-1} (ends^{-1})*.

has-a-lookahead = has-first-item passes-null* (points a-first-of^{-1}
∪ passes-a passes-null* (points first-of^{-1} ∪
has-last-item^{-1} has-rule^{-1} follows^{-1})
∪ has-last-item^{-1} has-rule^{-1} a-follows^{-1}).

Lemma 5. In any reduced grammar G,
(1) X a-adjoins Y iff G has a rule $A \to \alpha X\gamma Y\beta$, where $\gamma \Rightarrow^* a$.
(2) b a-first-of Y iff $ab \in FIRST_2(Y) \cap T^2$.
(3) b a-follows Y iff $ab \in FOLLOW_2(Y)$.
(4) $A \to \omega$ has-a-lookahead b iff $ab \in FIRST_2(\omega FOLLOW_2(A))$, for rule $A \to \omega$. □

Theorem 6. Given any reduced grammar $G = (N,T,P,S')$,
(1) the collection of all sets $FIRST_2(X)$, $X \in N \cup T$, can be computed in time $O(t \cdot |T| \cdot |G|)$;
(2) the collection of all sets $FOLLOW_2(X)$, $X \in N \cup T$, can be computed in time $O(t \cdot |T| \cdot |G|)$;
(3) the strong LL(2) parser for G can be constructed in time $O(t \cdot |T| \cdot |G|)$.
Here t is the time taken by a single set operation on subsets of T.

Proof. Consider (3). By Theorem 2, the relation denoted by has-a-lookahead can be computed in time $O(t \cdot |G|)$, for each fixed a in T. Repeating this procedure for all a in T gives the strong LL(2) parser, taking total time $O(|T| \cdot t \cdot |G|)$. - In proving (1) observe that the strings in $FIRST_2(X) \cap T$ are obtained as (derives* terminal)({X}). □

SLR(2) testing

We need some relations on pairs of items and nonterminals defined by:

$(A \to \alpha{\cdot}X\beta,\ B \to \gamma{\cdot}X\delta)$ goes-to $(A \to \alpha X{\cdot}\beta,\ B \to \gamma X{\cdot}\delta)$.

$(p,\ A \to \alpha{\cdot}B\beta)$ points-right (p,B).

$(p,\ B)$ expands-right $(p,\ B \to {\cdot}\omega)$.

$(A \to \alpha{\cdot}B\beta,\ p)$ points-left $(B,\ p)$.

$(B,\ p)$ expands-left $(B \to {\cdot}\omega,\ p)$.

Here p is any item or nonterminal. The relations are all of size $O(|G|^2)$ and can be computed from G in time $O(|G|^2)$. This means, by Theorem 2, that the relation on items and nonterminals defined by

mutually-accesses = (goes-to ∪ points-right ∪ expands-right ∪ points-left ∪
expands-left)*({(S',S')})

can be computed in time $O(|G|^2)$.

Lemma 7. $A \to \alpha{\cdot}\beta$ and $B \to \gamma{\cdot}\delta$ are items in the same state of the LR(0) parser if and only if

$A \to \alpha{\cdot}\beta$ mutually-accesses $B \to \gamma{\cdot}\delta$.

□

The following relational expression can be used to derive an $O(|G|^2)$ algorithm for SLR(1) testing (Hunt, Szymanski and Ullman, 1974):

$$\underline{\text{has-common-lookahead-with}} = \underline{\text{has-last-item}}^{-1}\ \underline{\text{has-rule}}^{-1}\ \underline{\text{follows}}^{-1}\ (\underline{\text{points}}^{-1} \cup \underline{\text{follows}}\ \underline{\text{has-rule}}\ \underline{\text{has-last-item}}).$$

Observe that a reduced grammar G is SLR(1) if and only if the relation denoted by

$$\underline{\text{has-common-lookahead-with}} \cap \underline{\text{mutually-accesses}}$$

is included in the identity relation.

For SLR(2) testing we need, for a in T, the relation defined by:

$A \to \alpha{\cdot}a\beta$ directly-passes-a $A \to \alpha a{\cdot}\beta$.

Now consider, for a in T, the relational expression

$$\underline{\text{has-common-a-lookahead-with}} = \underline{\text{has-last-item}}^{-1}\ \underline{\text{has-rule}}^{-1}\ \underline{\text{a-follows}}^{-1}$$
$$(\underline{\text{first-of}}\ \underline{\text{points}}^{-1}\ (\underline{\text{passes-null}}^{-1})^*\ \underline{\text{directly-passes-a}}^{-1} \cup$$
$$\underline{\text{follows}}\ \underline{\text{has-rule}}\ \underline{\text{has-last-item}}\ (\underline{\text{passes-null}}^{-1})^*\ \underline{\text{directly-passes-a}}^{-1}$$
$$\cup\ \underline{\text{a-follows}}\ \underline{\text{has-rule}}\ \underline{\text{has-last-item}}).$$

Lemma 8. A reduced grammar G is SLR(2) if and only if the relation denoted by

$$\underline{\text{has-common-a-lookahead-with}} \cap \underline{\text{mutually-accesses}}$$

is included in the identity relation, for all a in T. □

Theorem 9. Given any reduced grammar G = (N,T,P,S'), it is solvable in deterministic time $O(|T|\cdot|G|^2)$ whether or not G is SLR(2).

Proof. For each a in T, the relational expression has-common-a-lookahead-with is of size $O(|G|)$, has domain and range of size $|G|$, and can be constructed from G in time $O(|G|)$. By Theorem 2, the relation it denotes can be computed in time $O(|G|^2)$. Repeat this for all a in T. □

Computation of LALR(1) lookahead

Let M be the LR(0) parsing machine for grammar G. We consider the problem of computing the LALR(1) lookahead symbols for the reduce actions in M. We denote by Q the set of states of M and by GOTO the transition function of M. We define some relations on the set of pairs (q,A) in Q×N and $(q, A \to \omega)$ in Q×P. In pair (q,A) the state q has a transition on the nonterminal A and in pair $(q, A \to \omega)$ the state q contains the item $A \to \omega{\cdot}$. The relations are defined by:

(q,A) goes-to GOTO(q,A), whenever q has a transition on A.

q has-transition-on X, whenever q has a transition on X.

q has-null-transition (q,B), whenever q has a transition on B and B is nullable.

$(\text{GOTO}(q,\alpha),A)$ includes (q,B), whenever q has a transition on B and G has a rule $B \to \alpha A\beta$, where β is nullable.

$(\text{GOTO}(q,\omega), A \to \omega)$ lookback (q,A), whenever q has a transition on A.

The relations includes and lookback come from DeRemer and Pennello (1982), who also consider the relations denoted by the relational expressions

$$\underline{\text{directly-reads}} = \underline{\text{goes-to}}\ \underline{\text{has-transition-on}}\ \underline{\text{terminal}},$$

$$\underline{\text{reads}} = \underline{\text{goes-to}}\ \underline{\text{has-null-transition}}.$$

The relations goes-to, has-transition-on, has-null-transition, includes, and lookback are of size $O(|G|\cdot|Q|)$ and can be computed from G and M in time $O(|G|\cdot|Q|)$. Observe that this is not the case with the relations denoted by directly-reads and reads.

Now consider the relational expression

$$\underline{\text{has-LALR-lookahead}} = \underline{\text{lookback}}\ \underline{\text{includes}}^*\ \underline{\text{reads}}^*\ \underline{\text{directly-reads}}.$$

Lemma 10. (DeRemer and Pennello, 1982) In a reduced grammar, terminal a is an LALR(1) lookahead symbol for the reduce action by rule $A \to \omega$ at state q if and only if

$(q, A \to \omega)$ has-LALR-lookahead a.

□

The relational expression has-LALR-lookahead is of size $O(|G|\cdot|Q|)$, has range T, and can be constructed from G and M in time $O(|G|\cdot|Q|)$. By Theorem 2 we have:

Theorem 11. Given a reduced grammar G and its LR(0) parsing machine M with state set Q, the sets of LALR(1) lookahead symbols for the reduce actions can be computed in time $O(t\cdot|G|\cdot|Q|)$, where t is the time taken by a single set operation on subsets of T. □

Determining the inessential error entries

We consider any LR(0)-based LR(1) parser M for grammar G. The set of states, Q, of M consists of sets of valid LR(0) items. A parsing table entry (q,a) in M is an error entry if ACTION(q,a) = "error", that is, terminal a is not acceptable at state q. Error entry (q,a) is essential if it is actually consulted sometimes. That is, there is an input string w such that M, when started at the initial parsing configuration for w, will enter, after zero or more moves, a configuration in which state q is on top of the stack and terminal a is the current input symbol. Error entry (q,a) is inessential (or don't care) if it is not essential.

Fact 12. Any error entry (GOTO(q,b),a), where b is a terminal, is essential. □

In the following we define several relations on the set of pairs of the forms $(q, A \to \alpha\cdot\beta)$, $(q, \cdot B)$, and $(q, B\cdot)$. In pair $(q, A \to \alpha\cdot\beta)$ the state q always contains the item $A \to \cdot\alpha\beta$ and in pairs $(q, \cdot B)$ and $(q, B\cdot)$ the state q always contains some item of the form $A \to \alpha\cdot B\beta$. First define:

$(GOTO(q,\alpha), B\cdot)$ symbol-in $(q, A \to \alpha B\cdot\beta)$.

$(q, A \to \alpha\cdot B\beta)$ points $(GOTO(q,\alpha), \cdot B)$.

$(q, \cdot B)$ expands $(q, B \to \cdot\omega)$.

$(q, A \to \alpha X\cdot\beta)$ entered-by X.

For terminal a in T define:

$(q, B \to \omega\cdot)$ on-a-reduces-to $(q, B\cdot)$,

whenever ACTION(GOTO(q,ω),a) = "reduce by $B \to \omega$".

$(q, A \to \alpha\cdot B\beta)$ directly-on-a-passes-null $(q, A \to \alpha B\cdot\beta)$,

whenever ACTION(GOTO(q,α),a) = "reduce by $B \to \varepsilon$".

$(q, A \to \alpha\cdot\beta)$ error-entry-on-a $(GOTO(q,\alpha), a)$,

whenever ACTION(GOTO(q,α),a) = "error".

The above relations are all of size $O(|G|\cdot|Q|)$ and can be computed from G and M in time $O(|G|\cdot|Q|)$.

Then consider the relational expression

directly-descends = points expands

and, for a in T, the relational expressions

may-on-a-access = (on-a-reduces-to symbol-in ∪ directly-descends* directly-on-a-passes-null)*,

may-imply-a-essential = terminal entered-by^{-1} may-on-a-access error-entry-on-a.

Lemma 13. For any terminal a in T,

$(q, A \to \alpha\cdot\beta)$ may-on-a-access $(q', B \to \gamma\cdot\delta)$

whenever there is a parsing configuration with state GOTO(q,α) on top of the stack and terminal a as the current input symbol such that M, when started at this configuration, will enter, after zero or more moves, a configuration with state GOTO(q',γ) on top of the stack and the same terminal a as the current input symbol. □

Fact 12 and Lemma 13 imply:

Lemma 14. Whenever (q,a) is an essential error entry, then

b may-imply-a-essential (q,a)

for some b. □

In practice, also the converse of Lemma 14 seems to hold. That is, if for some b b may-imply-a-essential (q,a), then (q,a) is an essential error entry. An example of a grammar for which this is not the case is:

S' $\to$ \$S\$\$, S $\to$ bABb|bba|cAB, A $\to$ b, B $\to$ CD, C $\to$ ε, D $\to$ E, E $\to$ ε.

In a typical LALR(1) parser using default reduce actions we have:

b terminal entered-by^{-1} (GOTO(q_0,c),A $\to$ b$\cdot$) on-a-reduces-to symbol-in (q_0,S $\to$ cA$\cdot$B) directly-descends (GOTO(q_0,cA),B $\to$ $\cdot$CD) directly-on-a-passes-null (GOTO(q_0,cA),B $\to$ C$\cdot$D) directly-descends (GOTO(q_0,cAC),D $\to$ $\cdot$E) directly-on-a-passes-null (GOTO(q_0,cAC),D $\to$ E$\cdot$) = (GOTO(q_0,bAC),D $\to$ E$\cdot$) on-a-reduces-to symbol-in (GOTO(q_0,bA),B $\to$ CD$\cdot$) on-a-reduces-to symbol-in (q_0,S $\to$ bAB$\cdot$b) error-entry-on-a (GOTO(q_0,bAB),a),

although the error entry (GOTO(q_0,bAB),a) is inessential. (q_0 is the initial state.)

The relational expression

may-imply-essential = may-imply-a_1-essential $\cup$ ... $\cup$ may-imply-a_n-essential,

where $\{a_1,\ldots,a_n\}$ = T, can be used to derive an $O(|T|\cdot|G|\cdot|Q|)$ algorithm for determining most of the inessential error entries. Observe that the set of essential error entries is included in may-imply-essential(T) and that the relational expression may-imply-essential is of size $O(|T|\cdot|G|\cdot|Q|)$. To determine exactly the set of inessential error entries we need some additional relations. Define:

(q,B$\cdot$) left-corner-in (q,A $\to$ B$\cdot\beta$),

and, for a in T,

(q,A $\to$ $\alpha\cdot$Bβ) on-a-passes-null (q,A $\to$ αB$\cdot\beta$),

whenever (q,A $\to$ $\alpha\cdot$Bβ) may-on-a-access (q,A $\to$ αB$\cdot\beta$).

The relation left-corner-in is of size $O(|G|\cdot|Q|)$ and can be computed in time $O(|G|\cdot|Q|)$. The relation on-a-passes-null is a subrelation of that denoted by may-on-a-access, has size $O(|G|\cdot|Q|)$, and can be computed in time $O(|G|^2\cdot|Q|^2)$ because by Theorem 2 the relation denoted by may-on-a-access can be computed in time $O(|G|^2\cdot|Q|^2)$.

Now consider, for a in T, the relational expressions

on-a-accesses = (on-a-reduces-to symbol-in $\cup$ on-a-passes-null)*
(on-a-reduces-to left-corner-in $\cup$ directly-descends $\cup$
on-a-passes-null)*,

implies-a-essential = terminal entered-by^{-1} on-a-accesses error-entry-on-a.

Lemma 15. For any terminal a in T,

(q,A $\to$ $\alpha\cdot\beta$) on-a-accesses (q',B $\to$ $\gamma\cdot\delta$)

if and only if there is a parsing configuration with state GOTO(q,α) on top of the stack and terminal a as the current input symbol such that M, when started at this configuration, will enter, after zero or more moves, a configuration with state GOTO(q',γ) on top of the stack and the same terminal a as the current input symbol. □

Fact 12 and Lemma 15 imply:

Lemma 16. (q,a) is an essential error entry if and only if

b implies-a-essential (q,a)

for some b. □

Lemma 16 implies that the set of essential error entries is obtained as the image of T under the relation denoted by the relational expression

implies-essential = implies-a_1-essential ∪ ... ∪ implies-a_n-essential,

where $\{a_1,\ldots,a_n\}$ = T. By Theorem 2 we have:

Theorem 17. The set of inessential error entries in any LR(0)-based LR(1) parser M for grammar G = (N,T,P,S') can be determined in time $O(|T|\cdot|G|^2\cdot|Q|^2)$, where Q is the set of states in M. □

REFERENCES

Aho AV, Ullman JD (1972,1973) The theory of parsing, translation, and compiling, Vols 1 and 2. Prentice-Hall, Englewood Cliffs, N.J.

DeRemer FL, Pennello TJ (1982) Efficient computation of LALR(1) lookahead sets. ACM Trans. Prog. Lang. Syst. 4: 615-649

Harrison MA (1978) Introduction to formal language theory. Addison-Wesley, Reading, Mass.

Hunt HB III, Szymanski TG, Ullman JD (1974) Operations on sparse relations and efficient algorithms for grammar problems. In: 15th Annual IEEE Symp. on Switching and Automata Theory, Oct 1974. IEEE, New York, pp 127-132

Hunt HB III, Szymanski TG, Ullman JD (1975) On the complexity of LR(k) testing. Comm. ACM 18: 707-716

Hunt HB III, Szymanski TG, Ullman JD (1977) Operations on sparse relations. Comm. ACM 20: 171-176

Johnson DB, Sethi R (1975) Efficient construction of LL(1) parsers. Technical Report No. 164, Computer Science Department, The Pennsylvania State University, University Park, Penn.

Soisalon-Soininen E (1982) Inessential error entries and their use in LR parser optimization. ACM Trans. Prog. Lang. Syst. 4: 179-195

Tarjan RE (1972) Depth-first search and linear graph algorithms. SIAM J. Comput. 1: 146-160

The Complementation Problem for Büchi Automata with Applications to Temporal Logic (extended abstract)

A. Prasad Sistla
University of Massachusetts

Moshe Y. Vardi
Stanford University

Pierre Wolper
AT&T Bell Laboratories

ABSTRACT

The problem of complementing Büchi automata arises when developing decision procedures for temporal logics of programs. Unfortunately, previously known constructions for complementing Büchi automata involve a doubly exponential blow-up in the size of the automaton. We present a construction that involves only an exponential blow-up. We use this construction to prove a polynomial space upper bound for the propositional temporal logic of regular events and to prove a complexity hierarchy result for quantified propositional temporal logic.

1. Introduction

For many years, logics of programs were tools for reasoning about the input/output behavior of programs. When dealing with concurrent or non-terminating processes (like operating systems) there is, however, a need to reason about infinite computation paths. These are the sequences of states that the computation goes through. In the propositional case they can be viewed as infinite sequences of propositional truth assignments. In [Pn81], temporal logic was proposed to reason about such sequences. Later it was incorporated into the process logics of [Ni80], [HKP82], and [VW83].

Recent works [Sis83, WVS83] established a close relationship between temporal logic and the theory of ω-regular languages. The ω-regular languages are the analogue of the regular languages, but defined on denumerable words rather than finite words. The notion of ω-regularity is robust and has a well-developed theory [Ch74, Ei74, TB73]. There are several characterization of ω-regular languages, one of which is by Büchi automata [Bu62]. A Büchi automaton is a finite automaton operating on denumerable words. An infinite word is accepted by a Büchi automaton iff there is some run of the automaton on that word in which some state from a designated set of states appears infinitely often.

In [Sis83, WVS83] several temporal logics are shown to have exactly the expressive power of Büchi automata; in other words, the class of sets of sequences described by those logics coincides with the class of ω-regular languages. One method to decide satisfiability for these logics is to build a Büchi automaton that accepts exactly the strings satisfying the formula. Since these logics are closed under negation, building this automaton involves complementing Büchi automata. That is, given a Büchi automaton A, one has to find a Büchi automaton $\bar{A}$ such that $L(\bar{A})=\Sigma^*-L(A)$, where $L(A)$ denotes the language accepted by A.

The complementation problem for Büchi automata was first studied by Büchi [Bu62]. He showed that his automata are indeed closed under complementation. His proof, however, was not explicitly constructive. Later on, several explicit constructions were given [Bu73, Ch74, McN66, Sie70]. All these constructions, however, involve at least a doubly exponential blow-up. That is, there is a constant $c>1$ such that if A has n states, then $\bar{A}$ has c^{c^n} states. This blow-up is very expensive computationally and causes the decision procedures using the complementation of Büchi automata to be highly inefficient. For example, the decision procedure described in [WVS83] for the temporal logic *ETL*, runs in exponential space, while the known lower bound for this logic is PSPACE.

In this paper we reexamine the complementation problem for Büchi automata. We prove, using Büchi's original ideas [Bu62], that Büchi automata can be complemented with only an exponential blow-up. We then use the construction to show that the non-emptiness of complement problem for Büchi automata, i.e., the problem of whether for a given Büchi automaton A we have $L(\overline{A})\neq\emptyset$, is PSPACE-complete. (The analogous result for finite automata on finite words was proven by Meyer and Stockmeyer [MS72]).

These results turns out to be very useful in deciding satisfiability for various temporal logics. We first reconsider ETL_r, an extended temporal logic that directly reasons about ω-regular events [WVS83]. As mentioned earlier, the best known decision procedure for this logic runs in exponential space. Using our results about Büchi automata, we improve the upper bound for ETL_r to polynomial space, which matches the lower bound.

We then turn to $QPTL$, a quantified propositional temporal logic [Sis83]. While this logic has the same expressive power as ETL_r, its complexity is nonelementary, since $S1S$, the second-order theory of one successor, which is known to be nonelementary [Me75], is easily reducible to $QPTL$. Using our result about Büchi automata we prove that the class of $QPTL$ formulas with k alternations of quantifiers, is complete for $SPACE(exp^k(p(n)))$ (i.e., a stack of k exponentials), where $p(n)$ is a polynomial in n. We believe that this result is of general theoretical interest, since $QPTL$ is the first nonelementary logic we know of, where each alternation of quantifiers increases the space complexity by exactly one exponential.

2. Büchi Automata and their Complementation Problem

A *Büchi automaton* is a nondeterministic finite automaton on denumerable words. Formally, it is a tuple $A=(\Sigma,S,\rho,s_0,F)$, where Σ is an alphabet, S is a set of states, $\rho:S\times\Sigma\rightarrow 2^S$ is a nondeterministic transition function, $s_0\in S$ is a starting state, and $F\subset S$ is a set of designated states. A *run* of A over a denumerable word $w=a_1a_2\cdots$, is a sequence $s_0,s_1,\cdots$, where $s_i\in\rho(s_{i-1},a_i)$, for all $i\geq 1$. A run $s_0,s_1,\cdots$ is *accepting* if there is some designated state that repeats infinitely often, i.e., for some $s\in F$ there are infinitely many i's such that $s_i=s$. The denumerable word w is *accepted* by A if there is an accepting run of A over w. The set of denumerable words accepted by A is denoted $L(A)$.

We consider the problem of complementing Büchi automata. That is given a Büchi automaton A that accepts the language $L(A)$, we want to construct an automaton $\overline{A}$ that accepts the language $\overline{L(A)}=\Sigma^\omega-L(A)$. This problem was first studied by Büchi [Bu62]. He showed that his automata are indeed closed under complementation. His proof, however, was not explicitly constructive. Later on, explicit versions of Büchi's original proof were given [Bu73,Sie70]. These explicit constructions, however, involve a doubly exponential blow-up. That is, there is a constant $c>1$ such that if A has n states, then $\overline{A}$ has c^{c^n} states. Other construction for complementing Büchi automata were given by McNaughton [McN66] and by Rabin [Ra69] (see also [Ch74]). McNaughton's construction is also doubly exponential, while Rabin's construction is nonelementary.

Here we describe a construction, based on Büchi's original proof, that given a Büchi automaton A with n states, yields a Büchi automaton with $O(16^{n^2})$ states that accepts the complement of $L(A)$.

2.1. A Generalized Subset Construction

To complement a Büchi automaton $A=(\Sigma,S,\rho,s_0,F)$, we first built a family $\{\hat{A}_i\}$ of deterministic automata on finite words that captures the essential behavior of the automaton. The behavior that we are trying to capture is as follows. Given a finite nonempty word x and two states $u,v\in S$:

1. is there a run of A on x starting with u and ending with v?
2. is there a run of A on x starting with u, ending with v, and containing some state in F?

To construct the automata $\{\hat{A}_i\}$, we use a construction that can be viewed as a generalization of Rabin and Scott's *subset construction* [RS59].

Let $S=\{s_1,\ldots,s_n\}$ be the set of states of A. Define $S'=S\times\{0,1\}$ and $S^*=(2^{S'})^n$. S^* has m states, denoted $p_1,\ldots,p_m$, where $m=4^{n^2}$. Intuitively, a state in S^* is an n-tuple of sets of states of S labeled by 0 or 1. We need an n-tuple of sets rather then a single set, because we are trying to capture information about runs that can start in any state of S. The label on the state (0 or 1) indicates whether the run contains a state in F. The state set of the $\hat{A}_i$'s is $\hat{S}=S^*\cup\{p_0\}$, i.e., we add to S^* a special starting state.

The deterministic transition function $\hat{\rho}:\hat{S}\times\Sigma\rightarrow S^*$ is defined as follows:

- $<S_1,\ldots,S_n>=\hat{\rho}(p_0,a)$ iff $S_i=\{<u,0>:u\in\rho(s_i,a)\}\cup\{<u,1>:u\in\rho(s_i,a)\cap F\}$.

- $<S_1,\ldots,S_n>=\tilde{\rho}(<T_1,\ldots,T_n>,a)$ iff

$$S_i=\{<u,0>:u\in\rho(v,a) \text{ for some } <v,j>\in T_i\}\cup\{<u,1>:u\in\rho(v,a) \text{ for some } <v,1>\in T_i\}\cup$$
$$\{<u,1>:u\in\rho(v,a)\cap F \text{ for some } <v,j>\in T_i\}.$$

We now define $\tilde{A}_i$, $1\le i\le m$, as the deterministic automaton on finite words $(\Sigma,\tilde{S},\tilde{\rho},p_0,\{p_i\})$. Let X_i be the set of finite words accepted by $\tilde{A}_i$, i.e., $X_i=L(\tilde{A}_i)$. The following lemma follows immediately from the fact that the $\tilde{A}_i$'s are deterministic.

Lemma 2.1: $X_1,\ldots,X_m$ is a partition of Σ^+. □

The next lemma describe how the $\tilde{A}_i$'s capture the behavior of A.

Lemma 2.2: Let $p_i=<S_1,\ldots,S_n>$ and $x\in\Sigma^+$. Then $x\in X_i$ iff for all pairs of states s_j,s_l of A:

1. there is a run $u_0,\ldots,u_k$, $1\le k$, of A over x such that $u_0=s_j$ and $u_k=s_l$ iff $<s_l,0>\in S_j$.
2. there is a run $u_0,\ldots,u_k$, $1\le k$, of A over x such that $u_0=s_j$, $u_k=s_l$, and $u_h\in F$ for some $1\le h\le k$ iff $<s_l,1>\in S_j$. □

In the next section we show how the generalized subset construction can be used to complement Büchi automata. We believe that this construction is of general usefulness. Two recent applications are the determinization of Büchi automata [Va85] and emptiness of hybrid automata [VS85].

2.2. The Complementation Construction

Consider now the languages $Y_{ij}=X_iX_j^\omega$ where $1\le i,j\le m$. We can prove the following results about these languages.

Lemma 2.3: $\cup_{ij}Y_{ij}=\Sigma^\omega$

Proof: The proof is based on Ramsey's Theorem and is similar to the proof of Lemma 2.1 in [Bu62]. Ramsey's theorem tells us that given a partition of all pairs of natural numbers into finitely many disjoint sets $C_1,..,C_n$, there exists an infinite sequence of natural numbers $i_1<i_2<\cdots<i_q<\cdots$ and a set C_k such that $(i_p,i_q)\in C_k$ for all pairs i_p,i_q with $i_p<i_q$. Let us consider a denumerable word $w=w_0w_1\cdots$. By Lemma 2.1, the word w, in combination with the languages X_i defined in the previous section, define a partition of all pairs of natural numbers into m sets, $C_1,\ldots,C_m$, such that $(i,j)\in C_k$ iff $w_i\cdots w_{j-1}\in X_k$. By Ramsey's Theorem, there is a sequence $i_1<i_2<\cdots<i_q<\cdots$ and a set C_k such that $(i_p,i_q)\in C_k$ for all pairs i_p,i_q with $i_p<i_q$. This implies that the word x can be partitioned into $w_1=w_0\cdots w_{i_1-1}$, $w_2=w_{i_1}\cdots w_{i_2-1}$, $w_3=w_{i_2}\cdots w_{i_3-1},\cdots$, where for $l>1$, $w_l\in X_j$ and $w_1\in X_i$ for some i. Thus, for some i,j, $x\in Y_{ij}$. □

Lemma 2.4: For $1\le i,j\le m$, either $L(A)\cap Y_{ij}=\emptyset$ or $L(A)\cap Y_{ij}=Y_{ij}$.

Proof: We will prove that if one word $w\in Y_{ij}$ is in $L(A)$, then all words in Y_{ij} are in $L(A)$. Indeed, a word $w\in Y_{ij}$ can be decomposed into $w_iw_j^1w_j^2\cdots$ where $w_i\in X_i$ and for all $k>0$, $w_j^k\in X_j$. Consider a run of A on w and denote by s_i the state reached in that run at the end of w_i, s_j^1 the state reached at the end of $w_iw_j^1$, etc. The run is accepting iff the path taken through the automaton between s_j^k and s_j^{k+1} contains a state in F for infinitely many k. Now, any other word $y\in Y_{ij}$ can be decomposed similarly to w into $y_iy_j^1y_j^2\cdots$ By Lemma 2.2, there will also be a run of A on y such that the state reached at the end of y_i will be s_i, the state reached at the end of $y_iy_j^1$ will be s_j^1, etc. Moreover, there will be a path between s_j^k and s_j^{k+1} containing a state of F and labeled by y_j^k iff there is such a path labeled by x_j^k. Hence, if x is accepted by A, so is y. □

Lemma 2.5: $\overline{L(A)}=\cup\{Y_{ij}\mid Y_{ij}\cap L(A)=\emptyset\}$.

Proof: Immediate from Lemmas 2.3 and 2.4. □

We now construct a Büchi automaton $\bar{A}$ that accepts $\overline{L(A)}$.

Theorem 2.6: Let $A=(\Sigma,S,\rho,s_0,F)$ be a Büchi automaton, with $|S|=n$. Then we can construct a Büchi automaton $\bar{A}$ with $O(16^{n^2})$ states, such that $L(\bar{A})=\overline{L(A)}$.

Proof: From the automata $\tilde{A}_i$ and $\tilde{A}_j$ (each of size $m+1=4^{n^2}+1$), it is easy to build a Büchi automaton for Y_{ij} with $2m+1$ states. Then, by Lemma 2.6, we only need to take the union of the automata for the languages Y_{ij} such that $Y_{ij}\cap L(A)=\emptyset$. Thus $\bar{A}$ will be a union of at most m^2 Büchi automata, each with at most $2m+1$ states. The resulting automaton will thus have as many as $m^2(2m+1)=O(64^{n^2})$ states. However, this construction is rather wasteful. Indeed, it contain as many as m^2 copies of the automata $\tilde{A}_i$'s. A more careful construction can use only $m+1$ copies of these automata. So, we can construct an $\bar{A}$ that has at most $O(16^{n^2})$ states. □

Note that the above proof is not fully constructive, since we did specify how we can check for each Y_{ij} whether $Y_{ij} \cap L(A) = \emptyset$ or not. We will address this issue in the next section.

2.3. Decision Problems

Two problems that we will have to solve for Büchi automata are the non-emptiness and the non-emptiness of complement problems; that is, given a Büchi automaton, determine whether there is some word it accepts (the non-emptiness problem), and whether there is some word it does not accept (the non-emptiness of complement problem). To solve the non-emptiness problem, we prove the following lemma in the full paper.

Lemma 2.7: A Büchi automaton accepts some word iff there is a designated state of the automaton that is reachable from the initial state and is reachable from itself. □

This will enables us to prove the following:

Theorem 2.8: The non-emptiness problem for Büchi automata is logspace complete for NLOGSPACE. □

We now turn to the non-emptiness of complement problem for Büchi automata. Given a Büchi automaton A, the obvious way to solve this problem is to construct the automaton $\bar{A}$ and then use the algorithm for non-emptiness on $\bar{A}$. This gives an algorithm that uses exponential time and space as $\bar{A}$ is of size exponential in the size of A. However, as the fact that the non-emptiness problem is in NLOGSPACE indicates, it is possible to solve the non-emptiness of complement problem using only polynomial space. The argument is that it is not necessary to first build the whole automaton $\bar{A}$ before applying the algorithm for non-emptiness. In the rest of this paper, we will have to deal several times with the same type of construction: given an instance of a problem, construct a Büchi automaton which is exponentially big in the size of the problem, then determine if the Büchi automaton accepts some word. Each time, we will be able to show that the problem can be solved using only polynomial space. To avoid repeating the same argument several times, we prove the following lemma in the full paper.

Lemma 2.9: Given a problem P and a Büchi automaton A which can be constructed from P, if

1) the size of the states of A is polynomial in the size of P,
2) the initial state of A can be constructed in space polynomial in the size of P,
3) it can be checked if a state is designated in space polynomial in the size of P, and
4) each transitions of A can be constructed in space polynomial in the size of P (i.e., given a state of A, one can construct each transition from that state in polynomial space),

then determining if A accepts some word can be done in space polynomial in the size of P. □

So, to show that the non-emptiness of complement problem for Büchi automata is in PSPACE, we only need to establish that the complement of a Büchi automaton satisfies the conditions of Lemma 2.9. To do this, the only non-obvious step is to show that the correct languages Y_{ij} can be selected in polynomial space. We thus show the following:

Lemma 2.10: The problem of determining if $Y_{ij} \cap L(A) \neq \emptyset$ is in PSPACE for any of the languages Y_{ij}.

Proof: This can be done by constructing a Büchi automaton A_{ij} that accepts the language $L(A) \cap Y_{ij}$ and checking whether it is empty or not. The automaton A_{ij} can be constructed with at most $O(n4^{n^2})$ states (cf. [VW84]). Furthermore, A_{ij} satisfies the conditions of Lemma 2.9. So we can check its emptiness in polynomial space. □

From Theorem 2.6 and Lemmas 2.9 and 2.10, we can then prove:

Theorem 2.11: The non-emptiness of complement problem for Büchi automata is logspace complete in PSPACE. □

We note that our technique yields a polynomial space upper bound for the equivalence problem of Büchi automata. The previously known algorithm for this problem runs in exponential time and space [Al84].

3. Extended Temporal Logic

In [Wo83], an extension of temporal logic that incorporates nondeterministic finite automata as connectives was introduced. In [WVS83], three different versions of this extension were defined and studied further. The difference between the three versions is the type of acceptance conditions used for the finite automata defining the connectives. The three types of acceptance are *finite acceptance* (some prefix is accepted by the standard notion of acceptance for finite words), *looping acceptance* (the automaton has some infinite run over the word) and *repeating acceptance* (the automaton has a Büchi acceptance condition). These acceptance conditions give rise to three logics: ETL_f, ETL_l, and ETL_r, correspondingly.

These logics all have the same expressive power. Nevertheless, while there is a linear translation from ETL_f and ETL_l to ETL_r, the best known translation from ETL_r to ETL_f or ETL_l is triply exponential. This suggest that ETL_r is much more succinct than ETL_f and ETL_l. Moreover, while the decision problem for ETL_f and ETL_l is PSPACE-complete, the decision procedure for ETL_r presented in [WVS83] required exponential space. Nevertheless, using our new results on Büchi automata, we will now show that the decision problem for ETL_r is also in PSPACE, hence it is PSPACE-complete. Note, however, that the decision procedure for ETL_f and ETL_l requires space $O(n^2)$, while the decision procedure for ETL_r requires space $O(n^4)$.

3.1. Definition of the Logic

Formulas of ETL_r are built from a set of atomic propositions P by means of

- Boolean connectives, and
- automata connectives: every Büchi automaton $A=(\Sigma,S,\rho,s_0,F)$, where Σ is the input alphabet $\{a_1,\ldots,a_l\}$, S is the set of states, $\rho:\Sigma\times S\to 2^S$ is the transition function, $s_0\in S$ is the initial state, and $F\subseteq S$ is a set of designated states, is considered as an n-ary temporal connective. That is, if $f_1,\ldots,f_l$ are formulas, then so is $A(f_1,\ldots,f_l)$.

A structure for our logic is an infinite sequence of truth assignments, i.e., a function $\pi:N\to 2^P$ that assigns truth values to the atomic propositions in each state. We use π^i to denote the i-th "tail" of π, i.e., $\pi^i(k)=\pi(k+i)$. We now define satisfaction of formulas by induction. Satisfaction of a formula f by a structure π is denoted $\pi\models f$.

- for an atomic proposition p, $\pi\models p$ iff $p\in\pi(0)$.
- $\pi\models f_1\wedge f_2$ iff $\pi\models f_1$ and $\pi\models f_2$.
- $\pi\models\neg f$ iff not $\pi\models f$.
- $\pi\models A(f_1,\ldots,f_l)$, where $A=(\Sigma,S,\rho,s_0,F)$, iff there there exists an infinite word $w=w_0w_1\cdots$ over Σ, accepted by A, such that for all $j\geq 0$, if w_j is a_k, then $\pi^j\models f_k$.

3.2. Decision Procedure for ETL_r

To give the PSPACE decision procedure for ETL_r, we first need to introduce the notion of the closure of an ETL_r formula f, denoted $cl(f)$. Given an automaton $A=(\Sigma,S,\rho,s_0,F)$, for each $s\in S$ we define A_s to be the automaton (Σ,S,ρ,s,F). The closure is then defined as follows:

- $f\in cl(f)$
- $f_1\wedge f_2\in cl(f)\to f_1,f_2\in cl(f)$
- $\neg f_1\in cl(f)\to f_1\in cl(f)$
- $f_1\in cl(f)$ not of the form $\neg f_2\to\neg f_1\in cl(f)$
- $A(f_1,\ldots,f_l)\in cl(f)\to f_1,\ldots,f_l\in cl(f)$
- $A(f_1,\ldots,f_l)\in cl(f)\to A_s(f_1,\ldots,f_l)\in cl(f)$, for all $s\in S$.

If we define the size of an automaton connective to be equal to the number of states of the automaton, then for an ETL_r formula f, the size of $cl(f)$ can easily be seen to be at most $2n$ where n is the length of f.

To establish a decision procedure for ETL_r, we reduce the satisfiability problem to the emptiness problem for Büchi automata over the alphabet $2^{cl(f)}$. To this end we extend the function $\pi:N\to 2^P$ to a function $\psi:N\to 2^{cl(f)}$ in a natural way: for every $i\in N$ and every formula $g\in cl(f)$, we have that $g\in\psi(i)$ iff π^i satisfies g. Sequences that correspond to models satisfy some special properties.

A *Hintikka sequence* for an ETL_r formula f is a function $\psi:N\to 2^{cl(f)}$ that satisfies the following conditions:

1) $f\in\psi(0)$

and, for all elements $i\in N$

2) $g\in\psi(i)$ iff $\neg g\notin\psi(i)$,
3) $g_1\wedge g_2\in\psi(i)$ iff $g_1\in\psi(i)$ and $g_2\in\psi(i)$,
4) If $A(f_1,\ldots,f_l)\in\psi(i)$, where $A=(\Sigma,S,\rho,s_0,F)$, then there exists an infinite word $w=w_0w_1\cdots$ over Σ, accepted by A, such that for all $j\geq 0$, if w_j is a_k, then $f_k\in\psi(i+j)$.

5) If $\neg A(f_1, \ldots, f_l) \in \psi(i)$, then there is no infinite word $w = w_0 w_1 \cdots$ over Σ, accepted by A, such that for all $j \geq 0$, if w_j is a_k, then $f_k \in \psi(i+j)$.

Lemma 3.1: A ETL_r formula f has a model iff it has a Hintikka sequence

Proof: Given in the full paper. □

The next step in obtaining a decision procedure for ETL_r is to construct a Büchi automaton that accepts exactly the Hintikka sequences for a formula. To do this, we will actually build three automata. The *local automaton*, A_L, will check Hintikka conditions 1-3, the *positive automaton*, A_P, will check Hintikka condition 4 and the *negative automaton*, A_N, will check Hintikka condition 5. The local automaton is straightforward to construct and we leave it to the reader.

The Positive Automaton

The positive automaton is actually the result of taking the intersection of a collection of automata, one for each formula of the form $A(f_1, \ldots, f_l)$ in $cl(f)$. We will now describe how to build each of these automata. We need to construct an automaton defined over $2^{cl(f)}$ that will run A for each j such that $A(f_1, \ldots, f_l) \in \psi(j)$. We will build this automaton from A in several steps.

Let $A = (\Sigma, S, \rho, s_0, F)$, where $\Sigma = \{a_1, \ldots, a_l\}$. First, we will transform A into an automaton A^0 over $2^{cl(f)}$. The states of A^0 are the same as those of A and we have that $s' \in \rho^0(\mathbf{a}, s)$ iff for some j, $s' \in \rho(a_j, s)$ and $f_j \in \mathbf{a}$

We now need to transform the automaton A^0 so that it checks the sequence each time $A(f_1, \ldots, f_l)$ appears. To do this, we will use a construction similar to the "flag construction" described in [Ch74, Ra70]. Details will be given in the full paper.

The Negative Automaton

The most straightforward way to deal with this case is to build, for each formula of the form $\neg A(f_1, \ldots, f_m)$, the complement of the automaton A and then apply the flag construction as in the preceding case. This, however, would lead to a doubly exponential blow-up and it is possible to be more efficient. We do that by first building an automaton that tries to find an occurrence of $\neg A_p(f_1, \ldots, f_l)$ that does not satisfy condition 5, and then taking the complement of this automaton.

We start by constructing the automaton A^0 exactly as in the previous case. We then build an automaton A^1. The automaton A^1 has the same states as the automaton A^0 plus a dormant state 0. Its transition function is the one of A^0 extended, for all $\mathbf{a} \in 2^{cl(f)}$, by $0 \in \rho^1(\mathbf{a}, 0)$; and, for all $\mathbf{a}$ such that $\neg A(f_1, \ldots, f_n) \in \mathbf{a}$, it is extended by $s \in \rho^1(\mathbf{a}, 0)$ for each s such that $s \in \rho^0(\mathbf{a}, s_0)$. Acceptance is defined exactly as for A. The automaton we have built stays in the dormant state until it sees an element containing $\neg A(f_1, \ldots, f_l)$ and then either stays in the dormant state or starts running exactly as A^0. The sequences it accepts are thus those in which $\neg A(f_1, \ldots, f_n)$ appears at some point and that satisfy $A(f_1, \ldots, f_l)$ from that point. This is exactly the complement of the set of sequences we are checking for. We now take A^2 to be the union of the automata A^1 for each formula of the form $\neg A(f_1, \ldots, f_l)$ in $cl(f)$. A^2 has at most $n+1$ states, where n is the length of f. Now A_N is taken to be the complement of A^2, using the construction we described in Section 2. A_N has $O(16^{n^2+2n})$ states.

We now have:

Proposition 3.2: Let f be an ETL_r formula. Then, one can construct a Büchi automaton of size exponential in the length of f such that a sequence $\psi: N \to 2^{cl(f)}$ is accepted by that automaton iff it is a Hintikka sequence for f.

Proof: The automaton that corresponds to the intersection of the local, positive, and negative automata for f is the required automaton. This automaton has $O(c^{n^2+n\log n})$ states, for some constant c. □

Proposition 3.3: The satisfiability problem for ETL_r is log space complete in PSPACE.

Proof: The hardness result follows easily from the hardness results in [SC82]. To prove that the problem is in PSPACE, it is sufficient to observe that the automata, A_L, A_P, and A_N satisfy the conditions of Lemma 2.9. Thus the automaton corresponding to their intersection also satisfies the conditions of Lemma 2.9, and the problem of determining if this automaton accepts some word, which is equivalent by Proposition 3.1 to determining if the formula is satisfiable is in PSPACE. □

The above proof shows that the decision procedure for ETL_r requires nondeterministic space $O(n^2)$, and consequently deterministic space $O(n^4)$. In contrast, the decision procedures for ETL_l and ETL_r requires nondeterministic space $O(n)$, and consequently deterministic space $O(n^2)$.

4. Quantified Proposition Temporal Logic

In the previous section, we proved a result about one possible extension of temporal logic. There are other ways to extend temporal logic, one of which is to introduce quantification over propositions. This extension, quantified propositional temporal logic (*QPTL*), was described in [Sis83]. It turns out that it has exactly the same expressive power as the extended temporal logic we studied in section 3 [Wo82, WVS83]. However, as we will see, from a complexity point of view it has very different properties.

Formulas of *QPTL* are built from a set of atomic propositions P using:

- boolean connectives
- the temporal operators X (next) and F (eventually). We will also use G as an abbreviation for $\neg F \neg$.
- Quantification over propositions (i.e., if $f(p)$ is a formula, then so is $\exists p\ f(p)$. We will also use $\forall$ as an abbreviation for $\neg\exists\neg$.

We will say that a *QPTL* formula is in *normal form* if it can be written as:

$$Q_1p_1Q_2p_2 \cdots Q_kp_k\ f$$

where each Q_i is either $\forall$ or $\exists$ and f is a quantifier-free formula. (Every *QPTL* formula is equivalent to a formula in normal form.) If Q_1 is $\exists$ and there are k alternations of quantifiers, we say that the formula is in the set Σ_k^{QPTL}.

QPTL formulas are interpreted over infinite sequence of truth assignments, i.e., functions $\pi: \mathbf{N} \to 2^P$ that assigns truth values to the atomic propositions in each state. We use π^i to denote the i-th "tail" of π, i.e., $\pi^i(k)=\pi(k+i)$. We now define satisfaction of formulas inductively.

- for an atomic proposition p, $\pi \models p$ iff $p \in \pi(0)$.
- $\pi \models f_1 \wedge f_2$ iff $\pi \models f_1$ and $\pi \models f_2$.
- $\pi \models \neg f$ iff not $\pi \models f$.
- $\pi \models Xf$ iff $\pi^1 \models f$
- $\pi \models Ff$ iff there is a $i \geq 0$ such that $\pi^i \models f$
- $\pi \models \exists p\ f$ iff there is some π' that agrees with π except for the proposition p and such that $\pi' \models f$

Before stating our complexity results on *QPTL*, we need one definition. Let us define $g(k,n)$ as follows:

$$g(0,n) = n$$
$$g(k+1,n) = 2^{g(k,n)}.$$

(i.e., $g(k,n)$ has a stack of k exponents.)

We prove the following:

Theorem 4.1: The satisfiability problem for Σ_k^{QPTL} is complete for SPACE($g(k,p(n))$), where $p(n)$ is a polynomial. □

We note that this result also holds for *weak QPTL*, in which all predicate are finite, i.e., they are eventually false forever. A result closely related to ours was proven by Robertson [Ro74]. Robertson studied *WS1S*, the theory of natural numbers of successor with quantification over finite sets, which is equivalent to weak *QPTL*. He showed that Σ_k^{WS1S} is in NTIME($g(k+1,p(n))$), and is logspace hard for NTIME($g(k,p(n))$). Thus we improve his results both by closing the gap between lower and upper bounds, and by being able to deal also with quantification over infinite sets. We believe our result to be of general theoretical interest, since *QPTL* is the first nonelementary logic we know of, where each alternation increases the complexity by exactly one exponential.

4.1. Upper Bounds

The proof of our upper bounds, will be based on the construction of a Büchi automaton that accepts exactly the sequences satisfying a Σ_k^{QPTL} formula. More precisely, we prove the following.

Lemma 4.2: Given a Σ_k^{QPTL} formula f of size n, one can construct a Büchi automaton of size $g(k+1,p(n))$ that accepts exactly the sequences satisfying f.

Proof: The proof proceeds by induction.

Base case ($k=0$): In this case one deals with quantfier free formulas and the construction given in [WVS83] can be used.

Inductive Step: We have to establish the result for formulas in Σ_k^{QPTL} knowing the result for formulas in Σ_{k-1}^{QPTL}. First, notice that a formula in Σ_k^{QPTL} can be written as

$$\exists \neg f_1$$

where f_1 is a formula in Σ_{k-1}^{QPTL}. Now, if we can build an automaton of size $g(k,p(n))$ for f_1, we can construct an automaton for $\exists\neg f_1$ by complementing that automaton and projecting it on a smaller alphabet to eliminate the quantified propositions. If we use the complementation algorithm for Büchi automata described in Section 2, the result will be an automaton of size $g(k+1,p(n))$. □

We can now establish our upper bounds.

Theorem 4.3: Satisfiability for formulas of Σ_k^{QPTL} is in SPACE($g(k,p(n))$).

Proof: Let us first consider the case $k=0$. We have to show that satisfiability for quantifier free temporal logic formulas is in PSPACE. This was done in [SC82]. Also, this is an immediate consequence of the fact that the Büchi automaton we constructed for this case satisfies all the conditions of Lemma 2.9.

In the case $k\geq 1$, we have a formula f of the form $\exists\neg f_1$ where $f_1 \in \Sigma_{k-1}^{QPTL}$. By Lemma 4.2, we know that we can construct an automaton for f_1 using space $g(k,p(n))$. Now, to check if the formula f is satisfiable, it is sufficient to check that there is some word not accepted by the automaton for f_1. By Lemma 2.11, this can be done in space polynomial in the size of the automaton for f_1 and hence in SPACE($g(k,p'(n))$) for some polynomial p'. □

4.2. Lower Bounds

We will now show the lower bound for Σ_k^{QPTL}. To do this, we first need to show how to construct a formula $Q_{k,m}(p,q)$ such that p and q are true exactly once and are separated by a distance greater than $g(k,m)$. More precisely, we prove the following lemma.

Lemma 4.4: Given $k>0$ and $m>0$, one can construct in space log(m) a formula $\phi_{k,m}(p,q) \in \Sigma_{k-1}^{QPTL}$ such that if $\pi \models \phi_{k,m}(p,q)$ then

1) p and q are each true at exactly one point.
2) If $\pi^i \models p$ and $\pi^j \models q$ then $j = i + N_{k,m}$ for some number $N_{k,m}$ such that $N_{k,m} \geq g(k,m)$.

Proof:

The proof will proceed by induction. We show how to construct $\phi_{1,m}$ and then show how to construct $\phi_{k+1,m}$ given $\phi_{k,m}$. Before proceeding further, we need to define the notion of a *proper sequence of numbers*. Let $c_0, c_1, \cdots, c_{l-1}$ be a sequence of binary numbers each of size s. We let $v(c_i)$ denote the integer value of the number c_i, and c_{ij} denote the jth bit in the number c_i (the 0th bit is the least significant bit). We say that the above sequence is a proper sequence of numbers iff $v(c_0)=0$, $v(c_{i+1}) = v(c_i)+1$ for $0\leq i<l-1$, and $v(c_{l-1}) = 2^s-1$. Clearly for a proper sequence $l = 2^s$. It is easy to write the relation between the bits in successive numbers. For $0\leq i<l-1$ and, $0\leq j<s$ we have

$$c_{(i+1)j} = c_{ij} \text{ iff } \exists\, r<j \text{ such that } c_{ir} = 0$$

We can now show how to construct $\phi_{1,m}(p,q)$. For this we use m existentially quantified propositions $q_0, q_1, \ldots, q_{m-1}$. At each point in a sequence, the truth values of these propositions define a binary number. The formula $\phi_{1,m}$ asserts that the sequence of these numbers starting at the point i where p is true form a proper sequence of numbers. The formula will also assert that there is exactly one point just before the point where q is true where all the propositions $q_0, \ldots, q_{m-1}$ are true. It is fairly straightforward to construct these formulas. Thus, $\phi_{1,m}$ can be constructed and it will be of length $O(m^2)$. It satisfies condition 2 of the lemma if we take $N_{1,m} = 2^m$.

We now show how to construct $\phi_{k+1,m}$ given $\phi_{k,m}$ for $k\geq 1$. Intuitively, the formula $\phi_{k+1,m}(p,q)$ will state that there is a proper sequence of numbers each of length $N_{k,m}$ between the points i,j where p and q are true respectively. Each number will occupy $N_{k,m}$ positions in the sequence and its value will be given by the truth values of a proposition b on those positions. The formula will also use a proposition r which will be true at each position corresponding to the beginning of a number. The formula $\phi_{k+1,m}(p,q)$ will be the conjunction of formulas stating the following conditions:

1. The proposition p holds at exactly one point, say i, and q holds at exactly one point say j. The proposition r is true at i and j, and is false at all points before i and after j.

2. The successive points where r is true, are separated by a distance $N_{k,m}$. We can satisfy this by requiring that for all points k,l, if k and l are separated by a distance $N_{k,m}$ then there is exactly one instance between k and l where r is true.

By this condition we can consider the truth values of b, between successive instances where r is true, to be a binary number of size $N_{k,m}$. We consider the right most bit of a number to be its least significant bit.

3. The proposition b is false throughout the subsequence between the first and second positions where r is true. This asserts that the value of the first number is 0.

4. The value of each succeeding number is equal to the value of the preceding number incremented by 1. This can be expressed by giving the relation between the values of the bits in corresponding positions of successive numbers. Such positions are those between i and j, which are separated by a distance $N_{k,m}$.

5. In the last number, that is the one before j, b is true at all points in the number.

6. In all numbers other than the last number there is at least one position where b is false. This condition guarantees that 5 does not hold in any other number.

Let f' be the conjunction of the formulas expressing conditions 1-6 and let f be the result of converting f' into standard form. In the full paper, we will show that $\phi_{k+1,m}(p,q) = \exists b \forall p_{i_k} p_{i_k}(f)$. Also, we will show that since $\phi_{k,m} \in \Sigma_{k-1}^{QPTL}$, $f \in \Pi_{k-1}^{QPTL}$. Thus, $\phi_{k+1,m} \in \Sigma_k^{QPTL}$ and $\phi_{k+1,m}$ satisfies the second condition of the lemma for an $N_{k,m}$ satisfying

$$N_{k,m} = N_{k-1,m} \cdot 2^{(N_{k-1,m})} \text{ for } k \geq 2$$

Given that the construction for $\phi_{1,m}$ gave us $N_{1,m} = 2^m$, we clearly have that $N_{k,m} \geq g(k,m)$. Finally, it is easily seen that the length of $\phi_{k,m}$ is $O(m^2)$, and it can be obtained in $SPACE(\log m)$. □

We are now ready to prove our lower bounds.

Theorem 4.5: Every language in SPACE($g(k,p(n))$) is log space reducible to the satisfiability problem for Σ_k^{QPTL}

Proof: Let $M = (Q,\Sigma,\rho,V_A,V_I)$ be a one tape deterministic turning machine that is $g(k,p(n))$ space bounded. The elements in M are the set of states, the alphabet, the next move function, the accepting state and the initial state respectively. Let ID_0, $ID_1, \cdots$ be a sequence of IDs that describe the computation of M on some input of length n. Let $m = p(n)$. Without los of generality we assume that each ID is of length $N_{k,m}$. If $N_{k,m} \geq g(k,m)$ then M uses only the initial $g(k,m)$ cells in each ID. Using a formula f of $QPTL$ we express the computation of M on input w.

We use the propositions P_σ for each $\sigma \in (Q \times \Sigma) \cup \Sigma$, where the elements in $Q \times \Sigma$ are the composite symbols. We use a proposition B which marks the beginning of IDs. The sequence between successive instances where B holds defines an ID. We briefly describe how we can obtain a formula f that expresses the computation of M. The formula f will be the conjunction of the formulas expressing the following conditions.

1. All the IDs are of length $N_{k,m}$.
2. Each ID is a valid ID.
3. Each successive ID is obtained from the previous one by one move of M, i.e. the contents of a cell in an ID depend on the contents of this cell and its neighbor's contents in the preceding ID.
4. ID_0 is an initial ID, and eventually a final ID appears.

Given that $\phi_{k,m} \in \Sigma_{k-1}^{QPTL}$, we will show in the full paper that each of the conditions 1-4 can be expressed by a formula in Π_{k-1}^{QPTL}. Thus the conjunction f of these formulas will also be in Π_{k-1}^{QPTL} and the formula g obtained by introducing an existential quantification over each free variable in f is in Σ_k^{QPTL}. Moreover, g is a satisfiable formula iff w is accepted by M and it can be obtained using space $O(\log n)$. □

5. References

[Al84] H. Alaiwan, "Equivalence of Infinite Behavior of Finite Automata", *Theoretical Computer Science* 31(1984), pp. 297-306.

[Bu62] J. R. Büchi, "On a Decision Method in Restricted Second Order Arithmetic", *Proc. Internat. Congr. Logic, Method and Philos. Sci. 1960*, Stanford University Press, 1962, pp. 1-12.

[Bu73] J. R. Büchi, "The Monadic Theory of ω_1", In *Decidable Theories II*, Lecture Notes in Mathematics, v. 328, Springer-Verlag, 1973, pp. 1-127.

[Ch74] Y. Choueka, "Theories of Automata on ω-Tapes: A Simplified Approach", *J. Computer and System Sciences*, 8 (1974), pp. 117-141.

[Ei74] S. Eilenberg, *Automata, Languages and Machines*, vol. A, Academic Press, New York, 1974.

[HKP82] D. Harel, D. Kozen, R. Parikh, "Process Logic: Expressiveness, Decidability, Completeness", *Journal of Computer and System Science* 25, 2 (1982), pp. 144-170.

[McN66] R. McNaughton, "Testing and Generating Infinite Sequences by a Finite Automaton", *Information and Control* 9 (1966), pp. 521-530

[Me75] A. R. Meyer, "Weak Monadic Second Order Theory of Successor is not Elementary Recursive", *Proc. Logic Colloquium*, Lecture Notes in Mathematics, v. 453, Springer-Verlag, 1975, pp. 132-154.

[MS72] A. R. Meyer, L. J. Stockmeyer, "The Equivalence Problem for Regular Expressions with Squaring Requires Exponential Time", *Proc. 13th IEEE Symp. on Switching and Automata Theory*, Long Beach, CA, 1972, pp. 125-129.

[Ni80] H. Nishimura, "Descriptively Complete Process Logic", *Acta Informatica*, 14 (1980), pp. 359-369.

[Pn81] A. Pnueli, "The Temporal Logic of Concurrent Programs", *Theoretical Computer Science* 13(1981), pp. 45-60.

[Ra69] M.O. Rabin, "Decidability of Second Order Theories and Automata on Infinite Trees", *Trans. AMS*, 141(1969), pp. 1-35.

[Ra70] M.O. Rabin, "Weakly Definable Relations and Special Automata", *Proc. Symp. Math. Logic and Foundations of Set Theory* (Y. Bar-Hillel, ed.), North-Holland, 1970, pp. 1-23.

[Ro74] E. L. Robertson, "Structure of Complexity in the Weak Monadic Second-Order Theory of the Natural Numbers", *Proc. 6th ACM Symp. on Theory of Computing*, Seattle, 1974, pp. 161-171.

[RS59] M. O. Rabin, D. Scott, "Finite Automata and their Decision Problems", *IBM J. Res. & Dev.*, 3(2), 1959, pp 114-125.

[SC82] A.P. Sistla, E.M. Clarke, "The Complexity of Propositional Linear Time Logics", *Proc. 14th ACM Symp. on Theory of Computing*, San Francisco, 1982, pp. 159-168, to appear in *J. ACM*.

[Sie70] D. Siefkes, *Decidable Theories I - Büchi's Monadic Second-Order Successor Arithmetics*, Lecture Notes in Mathematics, v. 120, Springer-Verlag, 1970.

[Sis83] A. P. Sistla, *Theoretical Issues in The Design and Verification of Distributed Systems*, Ph.D. Thesis, Harvard University, 1983.

[TB73] B. A. Trakhtenbrot, Y. M. Barzdin, *Finite Automata Behavior and Synthesis*, North Holland, Amsterdam, 1973.

[Va85] M.Y. Vardi, "*On deterministic ω-automata*", to appear.

[VS85] M.Y. Vardi, L. Stockmeyer, "Improved Upper and Lower Bounds for Modal Logics of Programs", *Proc. 17 ACM Symp. on Theory of Computing*, Providence, May 1985.

[VW83] M. Y. Vardi, P. Wolper, "Yet Another Process Logic", in *Logics of Programs*, Springer-Verlag Lecture Notes in Computer Science, vol. 164, Berlin, 1983, pp. 501-512.

[VW84] M. Y. Vardi, P. Wolper, "Automata Theoretic Techniques for Modal Logics of Programs", IBM Research Report, October 1984. A preleminary version appeared in *Proc. ACM Symp. on Theory of Computing*, Wahington, April 1984, pp. 446-456.

[WVS83] P. Wolper, M. Y. Vardi, A. P. Sistla, "Reasoning about Infinite Computation Paths", *Proc. 24th IEEE Symp. on Foundations of Computer Science*, Tucson, 1983, pp. 185-194.

[Wo82] P. Wolper, "Synthesis of Communicating Processes from Temporal Logic Specifications", Ph. D. Thesis, Stanford University, 1982.

[Wo83] P. Wolper, "Temporal Logic Can Be More Expressive", *Information and Control*, 56(1983), pp. 72-99.

A COMPLETE COMPOSITIONAL MODAL PROOF SYSTEM FOR A SUBSET OF CCS*

Colin Stirling
Department of Computer Science
Edinburgh University
Edinburgh, U.K.

Abstract

Logical proof systems for concurrent programs are notoriously complex, often involving arbitrary restrictions. One of the main reasons for this is that unlike other major programming concepts parallelism does not appear to have a logical correlate. Using a simple semantic strategy we tentatively propose one and offer an example compositional modal proof theory for a subset of Milner's CCS. The proof rules are reminiscent of Gentzen introduction rules except that there are also introduction rules for the combinators of CCS.

Introduction

Logical proof systems for concurrent programs are notoriously complex often involving arbitrary restrictions: a small representative sample is [AFR,L,LG,OG,ZBR]. When p is a program and $p \models A$ means that p satisfies (the property expressed by) the formula A and $\|$ is a binary commutative and associative parallel operator there is little hope of finding an interesting binary function * on arbitrary formulas which validates an unrestricted implication of the form:

if $p \models A$ and $q \models B$ then $p \| q \models A * B$

Failure of such a principle is testimony to the complexity of concurrency: there does not seem to be a clean way of reasoning from the parts of a concurrent system to the whole. Many theorists have responded by analysing away concurrency, appealing instead to a model of the program. This practice has resulted in 'endogenous' logics, logics which are not syntax directed.

In this paper we tentatively propose a general method for reasoning about concurrent programs and offer an example proof system. The proposal is a rationalization of ideas in [BKP] and arises from a simple semantic strategy. Let $\models_B$ be another semantic relation relativized to a formula B: $p \models_B A$ is stipulated to mean

for any program q, if $q \models B$ then $q \| p \models A$

B, therefore, in $\models_B$ (partially) describes an environment. (See [La] for an account of environment.) By definition information can be derived about $q \| p$ when $q \models B$ and $p \models_B A$. An immediate consequence of associativity of $\|$ is:

if $p \models_A B$ and $q \models_B C$ then $p \| q \models_A C$

* This work was supported by the Science and Engineering Research Council of the U.K.

Let r be any program satisfying A, then $r \| p \models B$ and therefore, also, $(r\|p)\| q \models C$: by associativity $r \| (p\|q) \models C$ and consequently $p\| q \models_A C$. This, therefore, suggests a general method for reasoning about concurrent programs with arbitrary numbers of components. In principle, we also have a compositional semantics for $\|$ in terms of the pair of semantic relations.

This semantic ploy suggests we introduce two proof-theoretic consequence relations $\vdash$ and $\vdash_B$ to coincide with the semantic pair. Resulting proof rules (introduction rules) for $\|$ are then straightforward:

$$\frac{p \vdash B \quad q \vdash_B C}{p\|q \vdash C} \qquad \frac{p \vdash_A B \quad q \vdash_B C}{p\|q \vdash_A C}$$

Unlike most logics for parallel programs, these rules will not presuppose (as a proof proceeds) either a fixed or a bounded number of potential concurrent subcomponents. They allow one to treat $\|$ as a first class program operator on a par with sequential composition ';'. Computationally the formula B in $\models_B$ suggests an environment description. Logically it suggests an assumption: $p \models_B A$ could be written $B,p \models A$. The proposed proof rules for $\|$ are, therefore, analogous to Gentzen's cut rule [G] in the form: $\dfrac{A, \Gamma \vdash B \quad B, \Delta \vdash C}{A, \Gamma, \Delta \vdash C}$. The second rule is also analogous to the Hoare sequential composition rule.

In [St2] we used this strategy to provide a sound and complete modal proof system for a subset of Milner's Synchronous Calculus of Communicating Systems, SCCS [Mi3], where the binary parallel operator is a synchronous parallel, a tight coupling. An asynchronous parallel, with all its attendant complications, is a better test of the strategy. So here we offer a sound and complete modal proof system for a subset of Milner's Calculus of Communicating Systems [Mi1]. The modal language used is Hennessy-Milner logic [HM] which has the virtue, unlike more standard programming logics, of tying its expressiveness to a logic independent criterion, namely bisimulation equivalence. Together with the theoretical simplicity of CCS this aids the development of the modal proof system. The proof rules are introduction rules not only for the logical connectives but also for the combinators of the program language. The parallel introduction rules include the pair above. This work is closely related to [Wi1,Wi2] and extends results in [St1].

The paper consists of four sections. The first two are introductory, describing Hennessy-Milner logic, its logic independent criterion of expressibility, and the subset of CCS we build a proof theory for. Section 3 introduces some of the proof rules while section 4 contains the full proof system. More details together with proofs will be contained in a full version.

1. Transition Systems, Bisimulation Equivalence and Hennessy-Milner Logic

A nondeterministic or concurrent program may communicate repeatedly with its environment. A simple input/output function is, therefore, too austere as a model of such a program: two programs determining the same input/output function may behave very differently in the same environment. Transition systems have long been recognized as a richer model [K,P1,Si1]. More recently they have been used extensively as models of concurrent programs within the framework of tense (temporal) logic [EH, HS,MP,QS]. Here our interest is transition systems whose transitions are labelled.

Definition 1.1 A transition system is a triple $\langle P, Act, \rightarrow\rangle$ where

P is a set (of processes) and Act is a set (of actions)

$\rightarrow$ is a mapping which associates with each $a \in Act$ a relation $\xrightarrow{a} \subseteq P \times P$.

A transition system T is finite branching provided that each relation $\xrightarrow{a}$, $a \in Act$, is image finite: $\xrightarrow{a}$ is image finite if for each $p \in P$ the set $\{q : p \xrightarrow{a} q\}$ is finite.

In [HM] the authors offer, in effect, a very intuitive understanding of a transition system. The set Act is viewed as a set of atomic experiments. An atomic experiment on a process (program) $p \in P$ is understood as an attempt to communicate with p. Communication may change a process depending on its internal structure. The relations $\xrightarrow{a}$, $a \in Act$, are intended to capture the effect of experimentation: $p \xrightarrow{a} q$ means that p can evolve to q in response to an a experiment; or q is the result of a successful a experiment on p. A computation can be viewed as a successful sequence of experiments (communications). Similar ideas are also contained in [Ab,DeH,HBR, Ho,Mo].

Hennessy and Milner propose that two processes (programs) should be equivalent (have the same meaning) when no amount of finite experimentation distinguishes them. A formal criterion, observation equivalence, is proffered which is the same as bisimulation equivalence when T is finite branching.

Definition 1.2 A relation $R \subseteq P \times P$ on T is a bisimulation just in case

if pRq then i. $\forall a \forall p'$ if $p \xrightarrow{a} p'$ then $\exists q'.\ q \xrightarrow{a} q'$ and $p'Rq'$

ii. $\forall a \forall q'$ if $q \xrightarrow{a} q'$ then $\exists p'.\ p \xrightarrow{a} p'$ and $p'Rq'$

A relation is a bisimulation on T if it has the property given in this definition. (The identity relation, for instance, is a bisimulation). Such relations give rise to a natural equivalence, bisimulation equivalence, on processes in T:

$p \sim_T q$ iff there exists a bisimulation R such that pRq

It is straightforward to check that $\sim_T$ is an equivalence and is also the maximal bisimulation under inclusion. Bisimulation equivalence is a very fine equivalence. If two processes have the same computations (respond successfully to the same sequence of experiments) then this does not guarantee their equivalence. Strong interconnections between their intermediate states are also necessary. It is precisely these kinds of connection that are, in general, needed for comparing the behaviours of concurrent programs. Bisimulations were introduced in [Pa] and have been further investigated in [Mi3,Si2].

Hennessy and Milner present a modal logic which characterises bisimulation equivalence on finite branching transition systems [HM]. Here we offer a negation free version of their logic: the avoidance of negation aids the development of the modal proof theory provided in the sequel. Let $T = (P, Act, \longrightarrow)$ be a transition system and L_T the modal language:

$$A ::= \quad Tr \mid Fal \mid A \wedge A \mid A \vee A \mid \langle a \rangle A \mid [a]A \quad \text{for} \quad a \in Act$$

L_T is reminiscent of propositional dynamic logic [Ha]. However, here, only atomic actions appear within the modal operators. Unlike dynamic logic, the satisfaction relation $\models_T$ is defined between processes (programs) and formulas. $\models_T \subseteq P \times L_T$ is the least relation such that:

$p \models_T Tr$ for any $p \in P$ $\qquad$ $p \not\models_T Fal$ for any $p \in P$

$p \models_T A \wedge B$ iff $p \models_T A$ and $p \models_T B$ $\qquad$ $p \models_T A \vee B$ iff $p \models_T A$ or $p \models_T B$

$p \models_T \langle a \rangle A$ iff $\exists q. p \xrightarrow{a} q$ and $q \models_T A$ $\qquad$ $p \models_T [a]A$ iff $\forall q. p \xrightarrow{a} q$ implies $q \models_T A$

Tr and Fal are the only atomic formulas: Tr stands for true which every process satisfies whereas Fal does not hold of any process. $p \models \langle a \rangle A$ means that p can evolve under some successful a experiment to a process satisfying A. Similarly $p \models [a]A$ means that every process which is the result of a successful a experiment on p satisfies A. In particular, $p \models [a]Fal$ means that p is a-deadlocked: no a experiment on p can be successful. This modal language is, therefore, expressively rich; it can say of processes not only what they can do but also what they cannot do. This discriminating power is required for the characterization of bisimulation equivalence. Let $L_T(p) = \{A : p \models_T A\}$. Then Hennessy and Milner (in effect) prove the following characterization theorem:

<u>Theorem 1.3</u> If T is finite branching then $L_T(p) = L_T(q)$ iff $p \sim_T q$

The properties expressible in L_T are tied to the distinguishing powers of bisimulation equivalence: formulas of L_T cannot differentiate processes which are bisimulation equivalent and vice versa. The assumption that T be finite branching can be discarded if infinite disjunctions and conjunctions are allowed [HS,Mi2]. Further modal characterizations of equivalences can be found in [BR,GS,HS,Mi2].

In the following we develop a proof theory on L_T for a particular process language containing a binary commutative and associative parallel operator. The process language chosen is a subset of Milner's CCS.

2. A Subset of CCS

Milner proposed his Calculus of Communicating Systems, CCS, as a tractable model of asynchronous systems which may also synchronize [Mil]. It is a transition system $(P, Act, \rightarrow)$ whose set of processes P is generated from a small set of combinators; each combinator is intended to capture a distinctive intuitive concept. Here we only consider a subset of CCS: CCS without restriction, value passing and the renaming operator. These further features will be examined in the full version of this paper.

Processes in CCS may evolve asynchronously and may also synchronize. To capture synchrony Milner offers a small structure on the set of actions Act. Let Δ be a set of atomic actions and $\bar{\Delta}$ be a set of co-actions disjoint from Δ and in bijection with it. The bijection is $\bar{\ }$: $\bar{a} \in \bar{\Delta}$ stands for the co-action of $a \in \Delta$. Using $\bar{\ }$ for the inverse means that a is also the co-action of $\bar{a}$. Synchronization is only allowed between co-actions and is represented by τ. We let $Act = \Delta \cup \bar{\Delta} \cup \{\tau\}$ with a,b,c, ranging over this set. The set P of CCS processes we consider is given by the closed expressions of the following process language. We let X,Y,Z range over process variables:

$$p ::= Z \mid \mathbb{0} \mid ap \mid p+p \mid \text{fix } Z.p \mid p|p$$

$\mathbb{0}$ (which we use instead of NIL) is the nullary process which cannot respond to any experiment. The process ap responds to a and thereby evolves to p. The combinator + represents non-deterministic choice which may be resolved by an experimenter. Potentially infinite behaviour is allowed via the recursion combinator fix Z which binds free occurrences of Z in p in the process fix Z.p. A syntactic restriction is imposed on fix Z.p, that Z is guarded in p: every free occurrence of Z in p is within a subexpression aq of p. Finally, | represents the asynchronous parallel operator which also allows for synchronization of co-actions.

The remaining undefined feature of the transition system for this subset of CCS is the transition relation $\rightarrow$. This is defined as the least set such that:

i. $ap \xrightarrow{a} p$

ii. $p+q \xrightarrow{a} r$ if $p \xrightarrow{a} r$ or $q \xrightarrow{a} r$

iii. $\text{fix } Z.p \xrightarrow{a} q$ if $p[\text{fix } Z.p/Z] \xrightarrow{a} q$ where $[./.]$ is substitution

iv. $p|q \xrightarrow{a} p'|q'$ if $p \xrightarrow{a} p'$ and $q' = q$ or $q \xrightarrow{a} q'$ and $p' = p$
or $\exists b.\ p \xrightarrow{b} p'$ and $q \xrightarrow{\bar{b}} q'$ and $a = \tau$

When $a \neq b$ (in contrast to when $a = b$) the experimenter may resolve the choice in $ap + bq$ by offering an a or a b experiment. The parallel operator | models asynchrony by interleaving and allows for synchronization of co-actions. An important feature of CCS is that the number of concurrent subcomponents may increase in response to an experiment: for instance, if $p = \text{fix } Z.(aZ|bZ)$ then $p \xrightarrow{a} p|bp$. This possibility of growth must be reflected in any logical proof system for CCS. For a full discussion of CCS with examples see [Mil].

Bisimulation equivalence is a natural equivalence on CCS processes. It is also a congruence: process contexts preserve equivalence [Mi1,Mi3]. The following fact implies that CCS processes as presented here are finite branching.

<u>Fact 2.1</u> $\forall p \in CCS\{q : \exists a.p \xrightarrow{a} q\}$ is finite.

By theorem 1.3 we know that the modal logic L_{CCS} characterizes bisimulation equivalence (on CCS). Two processes are indistinguishable by formulas of L_{CCS} just in case they are bisimulation equivalent. The following fact states that $|$ is both commutative and associative (up to bisimulation equivalence).

<u>Fact 2.2</u> $p|q \sim_{CCS} q|p$ and $p|(q|r) \sim_{CCS} (p|q)|r$

This means that formulas of L_{CCS} cannot distinguish between these equivalent processes

3. Towards a Compositional Modal Proof System

The successful construction of a sound and complete modal proof system on L_{CCS} should result in a proof-theoretic relation $\vdash_{CCS}$ equivalent to $\models_{CCS}$. A stringent constraint, we impose, is that the proof rules be Gentzen style introduction rules [G] However, it is also necessary to take into account the structure of processes. The theoretical simplicity of the process language suggests that introduction rules also be offered for the combinators. These rules are the topic of this section, a prelude to the full proof system. Throughout we omit the CCS index from $\vdash_{CCS}$ and $\models_{CCS}$.

The introduction rules below for action prefixing are at the same time introducti rules for <a> and [a]. Their justification is that ap must evolve to p under any a experiment.

$$\frac{p \vdash A}{ap \vdash \langle a\rangle A} \qquad \frac{p \vdash A}{ap \vdash [a]A}$$

A global + introduction rule of the form $\frac{p \vdash A \quad q \vdash B}{p+q \vdash A * B}$ where * is truth functio al (and not the uninteresting constant true function) is unsound [St1]. Restricted versions which depend on the form of A and B can be found:

$$\frac{p \vdash \langle a\rangle A}{p+q \vdash \langle a\rangle A} \qquad \frac{q \vdash \langle a\rangle A}{p+q \vdash \langle a\rangle A} \qquad \frac{p \vdash [a]A \qquad q \vdash [a]A}{p+q \vdash [a]A}$$

Their justification is that p+q can only evolve to a process p evolves to or a proces q evolves to.

A global $|$ introduction rule suffers the same fate as a global + one. But, unlike the + case, restricted versions which depend on the forms of A and B are inadequa It would be necessary to also examine the modal subformulas of A and B. Even if such rules could be found they would then be in opposition to the type of rules we are prop osing. An alternative approach outlined in the introduction, based on ideas in [BKP], is now offered.

The semantics of L are extended by introducing a further semantic relation $\models_B$ for any formula $B \in L$ $p \models_B A$ is stipulated to mean :

for any q if $q \models B$ then $q|p \models A$

Recall Fact 2.2 that $|$ is both commutative and associative (up to bisimulation equivalence). From associativity follows a significant transitivity property:

<u>Fact 3.1</u> If $p \models_A B$ and $q \models_B C$ then $p|q \models_A C$

For suppose $r \models A$ then $r|p \models B$ and $(r|p)|q \models C$: by associativity $r|(p|q) \models C$ and consequently, $p|q \models_A C$. In principle, this property allows us to treat $|$ as a first class programming operator (on a par with sequential composition). Natural $|$ introduction rules arise when a further proof-theoretic consequence relation $\vdash_B$ coinciding with $\models_B$ is introduced:

$$\frac{q \vdash A \quad p \vdash_A B}{q|p \vdash B} \qquad \frac{q \vdash_A B \quad p \vdash_B C}{q|p \vdash_A C}$$

Commutativity of $|$ justifies replacement of $q|p$ with $p|q$ in the conclusion of these rules. Computationally A in $p \models_A B$ can be understood as an 'environment' description, a partial summary of any process q having the property that $q|p \models B$. Logically A can be viewed as an assumption : $p \vdash_A B$ could be written as $A,p \vdash B$. This suggests a logical analogy to $|$ introduction, Gentzen's cut rule [G] in the form: $\dfrac{A,\Gamma \vdash B \quad B,\Delta \vdash C}{A,\Gamma,\Delta \vdash C}$

There is also a similarity to Hoare's introduction rule for sequential composition. From now on $A,p \models B$ $(A,p \vdash B)$ is written instead of $p \models_A B$ $(p \vdash_A B)$.

Relativizing $\models$ creates problems for introduction rules for combinators other than $|$. For instance, neither 1 nor 2 is valid unlike for the unrelativized $\models$ when A is omitted throughout:

1. $A,p \models \langle a \rangle B$ or $A,q \models \langle a \rangle B$ implies $A,p+q \models \langle a \rangle B$
2. $A,p \models [a]B$ and $A,q \models [a]B$ implies $A,p+q \models [a]B$

1 fails when $p = b\mathbb{O}$, $q = c\mathbb{O}$, $A = \langle a \rangle([b]\mathrm{Fal} \wedge [c]\mathrm{Fal})$ and $B = [b]\mathrm{Fal} \vee [c]\mathrm{Fal}$. Underlying this difficulty is that the environment may respond to an a experiment instead of p,q and p+q. For the parallel is asynchronous. (Both 1 and 2 hold when the parallel is strictly synchronous [St2].) It appears that more information is needed than our current symbolism allows. A solution is to extend the logical language by adding two subsidiary modal operators $\langle \underline{a} \rangle$ and $[\underline{a}]$. More information is to be carried by these operators than their L counterparts in the context of the relativized relation: $A,p \models \langle \underline{a} \rangle B$ $([\underline{a}]B)$ is only to tell us about p's responses to a experiments. (Hence $p \models \langle \underline{a} \rangle B$ would have to be equivalent to $p \models \langle a \rangle B$.) Instead of simply extending L we define two new languages:

$\langle\rangle L = \{\langle \underline{a} \rangle B : B \in L \text{ and } a \in Act\}$ $[\,]L = \{[\underline{a}]B : B \in L \text{ and } a \in Act\}$

Moreover, we always assume that in $p \models A$ and $A,p \models B$ the formula A is in L whereas B may also be in <>L or []L.

The semantics of the new languages for CCS are completed by:

$$A,p \models \langle \underline{a} \rangle B \text{ if } \quad \text{i. if } \exists r.r \models A \text{ then } \exists q.p \xrightarrow{a} q \text{ and } A,p \models B$$
$$\text{or } \quad \text{ii. } a = \tau \text{ and } \exists b \neq \tau \;\; \exists q.p \xrightarrow{\bar{b}} q \text{ and}$$
$$\forall r.r \models A \text{ implies } \exists s.r \xrightarrow{b} s \text{ and } s|q \models B$$

$$A,p \models [\underline{a}]B \text{ if } \quad \text{i. } \forall q.p \xrightarrow{a} q \text{ implies } A,q \models B$$
$$\text{and } \quad \text{ii. If } a = \tau \text{ then } \forall b \neq \tau \; \forall q.p \xrightarrow{b} q \; \forall r.r \models A$$
$$\text{if } r \xrightarrow{\bar{b}} s \text{ then } r|q \models B$$

Their awkwardness is due to the possibility that $a = \tau$: p's responses to τ include p's synchronization with the environment. Clearly, if $A,p \models \langle \underline{a} \rangle B$ then $A,p \models \langle a \rangle B$: but not the converse which leaves open the possibility that the environment alone responds to a. (Moreover if $A,p \models [a]B$ then $A,p \models [\underline{a}]B$.) Successful introduction rules for + are a direct consequence of the following pair:

1'. $A,p \models \langle \underline{a} \rangle B$ or $A,q \models \langle \underline{a} \rangle B$ implies $A,p+q \models \langle \underline{a} \rangle B$

2'. $A,p \models [\underline{a}]B$ and $A,q \models [\underline{a}]B$ implies $A,p+q \models [\underline{a}]B$

Action prefix introduction rules are also $\langle \underline{a} \rangle$ and $[\underline{a}]$ introduction rules which come now in pairs due to the possibility of synchronization with the environment. The $\langle \underline{a} \rangle$ rules are:

$$\frac{A,p \vdash B}{A,ap \vdash \langle \underline{a} \rangle B} \qquad \frac{A,p \vdash B}{\langle \bar{b} \rangle A,bp \vdash \langle \underline{\tau} \rangle B}$$

The $[\underline{a}]$ rules are similar. Remember the language restrictions here: both A and B must be in L.

Introduction rules for <a> and [a] are still needed. But, now, they become global, independent of the main combinator in p:

$$\frac{A,p \vdash \langle \underline{a} \rangle B}{A,p \vdash \langle a \rangle B} \qquad \frac{A,p \vdash B}{\langle a \rangle A,p \vdash \langle a \rangle B} \qquad \frac{[a]A \wedge B,\ p \vdash [\underline{a}]C \qquad A,p \vdash C}{[a]A \wedge B,\ p \vdash [a]C}$$

The first rule exploits the relationship between $\langle \underline{a} \rangle$ and $\langle a \rangle$. The possibility that the environment alone responds to a is covered by the second rule. $[\underline{a}]$ is weaker that [a]: in the third rule then the first premise is strengthened (by the second) to take account of environment responses to a experiments.

The origin of our difficulties was the relativized relation $\models_A$. Untackled is the question whether the | composition rules remain sound for <>L and []L. Clearly the first rule is untouched because both A and B must belong to L. But what about the second: $\dfrac{A,q \vdash B \quad B,p \vdash C}{A,q|p \vdash C}$. Here both A and B $\in$ L but C may not be. However, if $C = \langle \underline{a} \rangle D$ then the rules hold because p is a subcomponent of $q|p$. On the other ha the rule can fail when $C = [\underline{a}]D$. The conclusion tells us about the responses of $q|p$ to any a experiment whereas the second premise only tells us about q's response. We also need to know about p's response. The solution is a more symmetric | introduction rule in the presence of []L formulas:

$$\frac{A,p \vdash B \qquad B,q \vdash [\underline{a}]C \qquad A,q \vdash D \qquad D,p \vdash [\underline{a}]C}{A,p|q \vdash [\underline{a}]C}$$

This rule insists upon information about both p and q's responses to a experiments in the premises. This accounts for the definitions of <>L and []L and for the strictures on $A,p \models B$. Fact 3.1, then, only holds for $C \in L \cup \langle\rangle L$.

Left ignored is the fix combinator. However, the behaviour of fixZ.p is fully determined by repeated 'unfolding': an unfolding of fixZ.p is p[fixZ.p/Z]. Contextual introduction rules for fix which appeal to this unfolding are offered. The rules depend upon the modal degree of a formula A, m(A), which is inductively defined as the maximum depth of modal operators in A [HM]:

$$m(Tr) = m(Fal) = 0\ ;\ m(A \vee B) = m(A \wedge B) = \max(m(A), m(B))$$

$$m(\langle a\rangle A) = m([a]A) = m(\langle \underline{a}\rangle A) = m([\underline{a}]A) = 1 + m(A)$$

If $p \models A$ and $m(A) = n$ then A is a property of p's evolution in response to experimenting whose 'depth' is at most n. When p = fixZ.q the guardedness condition on Z in q guarantees that A is at most a property of the nth 'unfolding' of p. We can, therefore, appeal to standard approximation techniques. When p = fixZ.q then p^n for $n \geq 0$ is inductively defined: $p^0 = \mathbb{O}$; $p^{n+1} = q[p^n/Z]$. For instance if p = fixZ.aZ then $p^0 = \mathbb{O}$ and $p^n = \underbrace{aa\ldots a}_{n\,\text{times}}\mathbb{O}, n > 0$. A process p = fixZ.q, therefore, must respond in the same way as p^n, $n \geq 0$, to any sequence of experimenting of length less than or equal to n: such experimenting is summed up by formulas whose modal degree is at most n. The result is the following pair of rules, suggested by Gerardo Costa, where p = fixZ.q:

$$\frac{p^n \vdash A}{p \vdash A}\ m(A) \leq n \qquad\qquad \frac{A,p^n \vdash B}{A,p \vdash B}\ m(B) \leq n$$

4. A Complete Modal Proof System for the Subset of CCS

The full modal proof system for the fragment of CCS appears below. The combinator and modal introduction rules are as in the previous section. The new features are the axioms and the logical introduction rules which are straightforward. Recall the language conventions covering $p \vdash A$ and $A,p \vdash B$ that A is always in L whereas B may not be. Only one explicit restriction on languages is, therefore, necessary in the rules.

We illustrate some of the rules with a partial proof where $A = [\bar{a}]Tr \wedge [\bar{c}]Fal$; $B = \langle b\rangle Tr$; $p = ab\mathbb{O} + c\mathbb{O}$; and $q = \bar{a}b\bar{a}b\bar{a}b\mathbb{O}$:

Axioms

$$p \vdash Tr \qquad \mathbf{0} \vdash [a]A \qquad A,p \vdash Tr \qquad Fal,p \vdash B \qquad A,\mathbf{0} \vdash [a]B$$

$$ap \vdash [b]A \text{ when } a \neq b \qquad A,bp \vdash [\underline{a}]B \text{ when } a \neq \tau \text{ and } a \neq b$$

∨I

$$\frac{p \vdash A}{p \vdash A \vee B} \qquad \frac{p \vdash B}{p \vdash A \vee B} \qquad \frac{A,p \vdash B}{A,p \vdash B \vee C} \qquad \frac{A,p \vdash C}{A,p \vdash B \vee C} \qquad \frac{A,p \vdash C \quad B,p \vdash C}{A \vee B,p \vdash C}$$

∧I

$$\frac{p \vdash A \quad p \vdash B}{p \vdash A \wedge B} \qquad \frac{A,p \vdash C}{A \wedge B,p \vdash C} \qquad \frac{B,p \vdash C}{A \wedge B,p \vdash C} \qquad \frac{A,p \vdash B \quad A,p \vdash C}{A,p \vdash B \wedge C}$$

<a>I

$$\frac{p \vdash A}{ap \vdash \langle a\rangle A} \qquad \frac{A,p \vdash \langle \underline{a}\rangle B}{A,p \vdash \langle a\rangle B} \qquad \frac{A,p \vdash B}{\langle a\rangle A,p \vdash \langle a\rangle B}$$

<a̲>I

$$\frac{A,p \vdash B}{A,ap \vdash \langle \underline{a}\rangle B} \qquad \frac{A,p \vdash B}{\langle \bar{b}\rangle A,\ bp \vdash \langle \underline{\tau}\rangle B}$$

[a]I

$$\frac{p \vdash A}{ap \vdash [a]A} \qquad \frac{[a]D \wedge E,\ p \vdash [\underline{a}]B \quad D,p \vdash B}{[a]D \wedge E,\ p \vdash [a]B}$$

[a̲]I

$$\frac{A,p \vdash B}{[\bar{b}]A,\ bp \vdash [\underline{\tau}]B} \qquad \frac{A,p \vdash B}{A,bp \vdash [\underline{b}]B}$$

+I<>

$$\frac{p \vdash \langle a\rangle A}{p+q \vdash \langle a\rangle A} \qquad \frac{q \vdash \langle a\rangle A}{p+q \vdash \langle a\rangle A} \qquad \frac{A,p \vdash \langle \underline{a}\rangle B}{A,p+q \vdash \langle \underline{a}\rangle B} \qquad \frac{A,q \vdash \langle \underline{a}\rangle B}{A,p+q \vdash \langle \underline{a}\rangle B}$$

+I[]

$$\frac{p \vdash [a]A \quad q \vdash [a]A}{p+q \vdash [a]A} \qquad \frac{A,p \vdash [\underline{a}]B \quad A,q \vdash [\underline{a}]B}{A,p+q \vdash [\underline{a}]B}$$

fixI

$$\frac{p^n \vdash A}{p \vdash A}\ p = fixZ.q \text{ and } n \geq m(A) \qquad \frac{A,p^n \vdash B}{A,p \vdash B}\ p = fixZ.q \text{ and } n \geq m(B)$$

|I

$$\frac{p \vdash A \quad A,q \vdash B}{p|q \vdash B} \qquad \frac{p \vdash A \quad A,q \vdash B}{q|p \vdash B} \qquad \frac{A,p \vdash B \quad B,q \vdash C}{A,p|q \vdash C}\ C \in []L \qquad \frac{A,q \vdash B \quad B,q \vdash C}{A\ q|p \vdash C}\ C \in []L$$

$$\frac{A,p \vdash B \quad B,q \vdash [\underline{a}]C \qquad A,q \vdash D \quad D,p \vdash [\underline{a}]C}{A,\ p|q \vdash [\underline{a}]C}$$

$$[\tau]I\ \frac{Tr,\ b\mathbf{0} \vdash B}{[\bar{a}]Tr,\ ab\mathbf{0} \vdash [\underline{\tau}]B} \qquad \frac{Fal,\ \mathbf{0} \vdash B}{[\bar{c}]Fal,\ c\mathbf{0} \vdash [\underline{\tau}]B}\ [\tau]I$$

$$\wedge I\ \frac{[\bar{a}]Tr,\ ab\mathbf{0} \vdash [\underline{\tau}]B}{A,\ ab\mathbf{0} \vdash [\underline{\tau}]B} \qquad \frac{[\bar{c}]Fal,\ c\mathbf{0} \vdash [\underline{\tau}]B}{A,\ c\mathbf{0} \vdash [\underline{\tau}]B}\ \wedge I$$

$$+I[]\ \frac{A,\ ab\mathbf{0} \vdash [\underline{\tau}]B \qquad A,\ c\mathbf{0} \vdash [\underline{\tau}]B}{A,\ p \vdash [\underline{\tau}]B}$$

$$\wedge I\ \frac{A,\ p \vdash [\underline{\tau}]B}{[\tau]B \wedge A,\ p \vdash [\underline{\tau}]B} \qquad \frac{Tr,\ p \vdash Tr}{B,\ p \vdash B}\ \langle b\rangle I$$

$$[\tau]I\ \frac{[\tau]B \wedge A,\ p \vdash [\underline{\tau}]B \qquad B,\ p \vdash B}{[\tau]B \wedge A,\ p \vdash [\tau]B} \qquad \frac{q \vdash [\tau]B \wedge A}{fixZ.\bar{a}bZ \vdash [\tau]B \wedge A}\ fixI$$

$$|I\ \frac{[\tau]B \wedge A,\ p \vdash [\tau]B \qquad fixZ.\bar{a}bZ \vdash [\tau]B \wedge A}{(ab\mathbf{0} + c\mathbf{0})\ |\ fixZ.\bar{a}bZ \vdash [\tau]\langle b\rangle Tr}$$

The modal system above is sound. This is the content of the following theorem:

Theorem 4.1 if $p \vdash B$ then $p \models B$ and
if $A,p \vdash B$ then $A,p \models B$

Completeness can be understood in two ways:

weak completeness : if $p \models B$ then $p \vdash B$

strong completeness : weak completeness and if $A,p \models B$ then $A,p \vdash B$

The modal system is weak complete. Constructing a strongly complete system is problematic. One difficulty is that if A is CCS-valid, true of every CCS process, then $B,p \models A$ for any B. In fact, there is not a simple dichotomy between weak and strong completeness: a weak completeness result depends on a corresponding strong result to justify $p|q \models A$ implies $p|q \vdash A$. Full details of the strong result is contained in the full version. Here we simply state the weak completeness theorem:

Theorem 4.2 if $p \models A$ then $p \vdash A$

Acknowledgements

I would like to thank Gerardo Costa, Kim Larsen and Robin Milner for helpful comments on the topic of this paper and Heather Carlin and Dorothy McKie for typing.

References

LNCS abbreviates Lecture Notes in Computer Science, Springer-Verlag

[Ab] S. Abramsky 'Experiments, powerdomains and fully abstract models for applicative multiprogramming' LNCS Vol. 158 pp. 1-13 (1983).

[AFR] K. Apt, N. Francez and W. de Roever 'A proof system for communicating sequential processes' TOPLAS pp. 359-385 (1980).

[BKP] H. Baringer, R. Kuiper and A. Pnueli 'Now you may compose temporal logic specifications' CS84-09, Dept. of Applied Maths, Weizmann Institute of Science (1984).

[BR] S. Brookes and W. Rounds 'Behavioural equivalence relations induced by programming logics' LNCS Vol.154, pp. 97-108 (1983).

[DeH] R. de Nicola and M. Hennessy 'Testing equivalences for processes' in LNCS Vol. 154 pp. 548-560 (1983).

[EH] E. Emerson and J. Halpern 'Sometimes and not never revisited: on branching versus linear time' pp. 127-140 POPL Proceedings (1983).

[G] G. Gentzen 'Investigations into logic deduction' in 'The Collected Works of Gerhard Gentzen' ed. Szabo, North-Holland (1969).

[GS] S. Graf and J. Sifakis 'A modal characterization of observational congruence on finite terms of CCS', LNCS Vol.172 pp. 222-234 (1984).

[Ha] D. Harel 'First-Order Dynamic Logic' LNCS Vol.68 (1979).

[HBR] C. Hoare, S. Brookes and A. Roscoe 'A theory of communicating sequential processes', Technical Monograph Prg-16, Computing Lab, University of Oxford (1981).

[HM] M. Hennessy and R. Milner 'Algebraic laws for nondeterminism and concurrency' Technical Report CSR-133-83 (and to appear in JACM) (1983).

[Ho] C. Hoare 'A model for communicating sequential processes'. Technical Monograph, Prg-22, Computing Lab, University of Oxford (1982).

[HS] M. Hennessy and C. Stirling 'The power of the future perfect in program logics' LNCS Vol.176 pp. 301-311 (1984).

[K] R. Keller 'A fundamental theorem of asynchronous parallel computation' in Parallel Processing ed. T. Feng, Springer-Verlag (1975).

[L] L. Lamport 'The 'Hoare logic' of concurrent programs' Acta Informatica pp.21-37 (1980).

[La] K. Larsen 'A context dependent equivalence between processes' This volume.

[LG] G. Levin and D. Gries 'A proof technique for communicating sequential processes' Acta Informatica pp. 281-302 (1981).

[Mi1] R. Milner 'A Calculus of Communicating Systems' LNCS Vol.92 (1980).

[Mi2] R. Milner 'A modal characterisation of observable machine-behaviour' LNCS Vol. 112, pp. 25-34 (1981).

[Mi3] R. Milner 'Calculi for synchrony and asynchrony' Theoretical Computer Science, pp. 267-310 (1983).

[Mo] E. Moore 'Gedanken-experiments on sequential machines' in 'Automata Studies' ed. C. Shannon and J. McCarthy, Princeton University Press, pp. 129-153 (1956).

[MP] Z. Manna and A. Pnueli 'How to cook a temporal proof system for your pet language' POPL Proceedings pp. 141-154 (1983).

[OG] S. Owicki and D. Gries 'An axiomatic proof technique for parellel programs I' Acta Informatica pp. 319-340 (1976).

[Pa] D. Park 'Concurrency and automata on infinite sequences' LNCS Vol.104 (1981).

[Pl] G. Plotkin 'A structural approach to operational semantics'. Lecture Notes, Aarhus University (1981).

[QS] J. Queille and J. Sifakis 'Fairness and related properties in transition system - a temporal logic to deal with fairness' Acta Informatica 19, pp. 195-220 (198

[Si1] J. Sifakis 'A unified approach for studying the properties of transition system Theoretical Computer Science, pp. 227-258 (1982).

[Si2] J. Sifakis 'Property preserving homomorphisms of transition systems' Technical Report, IMAG (1982).

[ST1] C. Stirling 'A proof theoretic characterization of observational equivalence' in Procs. FCT-TCS Bangalore (1983). (To appear in TCS).

[St2] C. Stirling 'A complete modal proof system for a subset of SCCS' To appear in CAAP '85.

[Wi1] G. Winskel 'On the composition and decomposition of assertions'. Tech. Report 59 Computer Laboratory, University of Cambridge (1985).

[Wi2] G. Winskel 'A complete proof system for SCCS with modal assertions'. To appear

[ZBR] J. Zwiers, A. de Bruin and W. de Roever 'A proof system for partial correctness of dynamic networks of processes' Technical Report RUU-CS-83-15, Dept. of Computer Science, University of Utrecht (1983).

On Matrix Multiplication Using Array Processors +

P.J. Varman
Department of Electrical and Computer Engineering
Rice University
Houston, TX-77001

I.V. Ramakrishnan
Department of Computer Science
University of Maryland
College Park, MD-20742

Abstract

Array processor models in the past have assumed constant storage per processor. Such an assumption leads to a lower bound of $\Omega(n^2)$ time complexity to multiply two $n \times n$ matrices on a one-dimensional array processor.

In this paper it is shown that relaxing the restriction of constant storage per processor leads to a lower bound of $\Omega(n\sqrt{n})$ time complexity to multiply two $n \times n$ matrices on a one-dimensional array processor. Furthermore, an optimal matrix multiplication algorithm is described for such an array that uses $O(n\sqrt{n})$ processors and requires $O(n\sqrt{n})$ time. The algorithm is well suited for fault-tolerant VLSI implementation.

1. Introduction

Parallel algorithms for multiplying two $n \times n$ dense matrices on several models of parallel computation have been investigated [1,3,4,5,9,14]. In [6], Gentleman addressed the question of the complexity of matrix multiplication on a model in which communication costs (that is, the time required to move data between processors) were explicitly included. The model was characterized by a function, $\sigma(k)$, defined to be the maximum number of processors to which data initially available at a single processor could be made available in k or fewer data movement steps. In particular, he showed that under the assumption that no two elements of the same matrix be initially stored in the same processor, matrix multiplication requires at least s data movements where $\sigma(2s) \geq n^2$. Furthermore, the proof of this lower bound suggests that the minimum number, s, of data movements *cannot be overlapped in time*, since at least one data element has to be moved s processors away from its initial position. Thus, if we assume that it takes unit time to move a single data element between adjacent processors, the results imply a lower-bound of s time units on the time required for matrix multiplication. In particular, on a one-dimensional linear arrangement of processors, for which $\sigma(k)=2k+1$, the time required for matrix multiplication in the above model is $\Omega(n^2)$. ++

In this paper we reexamine the model used in the analysis in [6]. We show that the $\Omega(n^2)$ lower-bound on time arises because of the overly restrictive assumption in the model that no two elements of the same matrix be initially stored in the same processor, thereby requiring $\Omega(n^2)$ processors. By relaxing just this assumption, we obtain a lower-bound of $\Omega(n\sqrt{n})$ on the time required by any matrix multiplication algorithm that computes n^3 scalar products on a one-dimensional linear arrangement of processors. Furthermore, we will also describe an algorithm that uses $n\sqrt{n}$ processors and performs matrix multiplication in $O(n\sqrt{n})$ time steps. The array is well-suited for fault-tolerant VLSI implementation.

The rest of the paper is organized as follows. In Section 2 we introduce the computation model and analyze the complexity of matrix multiplication on such a model. We observe that the $\Omega(n^2)$ bound in Gentleman's model [6] arises due to the fact that we have too *many* processors ($\Omega(n^2)$) and that by reducing the number of processors we can do much *better* in time performance. In Section 3 we present an $O(n\sqrt{n})$ time algorithm using $O(n\sqrt{n})$ processors to multiply two $n \times n$ dense matrices. In Section 4 we discuss the relationship of our model to previously proposed schemes for

---

+ This material is based on work supported in part by the National Science Foundation under grant number ECS-84-04399, in part by the Office of Naval Research under Contract N00014-84-K-0530 and an IBM faculty development award.

++ $f(n)=O(g(n))$ iff there exists constants c and n_0 such that $f(n) \leq c\, g(n)$ for $n \geq n_0$ and $f(n)=\Omega(g(n))$ iff $f(n) \geq c\, g(n)$ for $n \geq n_0$.

fault-tolerance of VLSI arrays, and indicate its superior performance in this regard. The proof of correctness of our algorithm appears in the Appendix.

2. Computation Model

The computation model consists of an unlimited number of processors each with its own local memory. Each processor has an index from the set of integers I={...,-1,0,1,...} and the processor with index i (henceforth referred to as cell i) has communication links to cell i-1 and cell i+1 ($\forall i \in I$). The processors may thus be visualized as being arranged along a line as illustrated in Fig. 2.1.

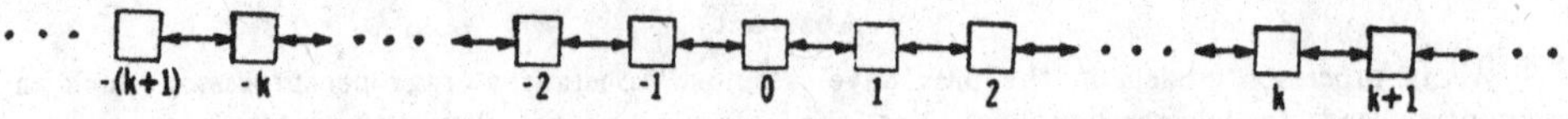

Fig. 2.1

We will assume that it takes one time step to transfer a data element from cell x to cell x+1 or to cell x-1. Thus in k ($k \geq 0$) time steps a data element at cell x can be made available to at most 2k+1 cells, namely, to those with indices in the range [x-k,..,x+k]. Note, however, that there is no limit on the number of data items that may be transferred from cell i to cell i+1 or cell i-1 in one time step. This fact was implicit in Gentleman's model [6] as well.

The elements of the matrices A and B are initially stored without duplication in the local memories associated with the cells. The cell in whose local memory an element of matrix A or B is initially stored will be referred to as the *home cell* of that element. In our model the home cell for any $a_{ij} \in A$ and $b_{ij} \in B$ is unique.

We place no restrictions on the number of data elements that may initially be stored in each cell's memory, that is, several elements of matrix A (B) may have the same home cell. This is in contrast to the restriction in [6], which required that no two elements of the same matrix be initially stored in the local memory of the cell. This restriction, therefore, required that there be at least n^2 processors to hold the elements of the $n \times n$ matrices A and B and consequently (as our proof suggests), spread the elements so far apart that the total time to multiply the two matrices was dominated entirely by the time to *communicate* the data to the requisite cells.

Finally, we assume that a scalar multiplication and/or addition also takes one time step. In this model we will now establish a lower-bound of $\Omega(n\sqrt{n})$ on the time required to multiply two $n \times n$ matrices by any algorithm that computes n^3 scalar products.

Lemma 2.1: Let d denote the maximum number of cells away from its home cell that any data element a_{ij} or b_{ij} participates in the computation of a scalar product. Let t denote the *earliest* time by which any element of matrix C gets its final update (that is, it has accumulated all its product terms). Then all the n^3 scalar products are computed in at most 1+8 max(t,d) cells.

Proof: Without loss of generality, let c_{ij} be the first element of C to get its final update at time t in cell w. Now c_{ij} requires each of a_{ik} and b_{kj} ($\forall k=1,..,n$) in its computation. Hence, if any of them had its home cell more than t cells away from cell w then they could not have contributed to c_{ij} by time t. Thus, the home cells of a_{ik} and b_{kj} must be in the range [w-t,..,w+t].

Now consider an arbitrary a_{is}. All the n scalar products $a_{is}b_{sq}$ must be computed within d cells of the home position of a_{is}, that is, in the range [w-t-d,..,w+t+d]. Since no data element could have participated in the computation of a scalar product more than d cells away from its home position, the home cells for all b_{sq} must be in the range [w-t-2d,..,w+t+2d]. Since s ($1 \leq s \leq n$) was arbitrary, it follows that $\forall s$ and $\forall q$, b_{sq} must have its home cell in the range [w-t-2d,..w+t+2d].

Finally, it follows that all n^3 scalar products must be computed within at most d cells of the home cells of all b_{sq}, that is, in the range [w-t-3d,..,w+t+3d]. Thus, all n^3 scalar products are computed in at most 2t+6d+1 cells, which is less than 1 + 8 max(t,d). □

Theorem 2.1: Any matrix-multiplication algorithm that computes n^3 scalar products on the model described above must take time $T=\Omega(n\sqrt{n})$.

Proof: By definition of d and t in Lemma 1, it follows that $T \geq t$ and $T \geq d$. Hence,

$$T \geq \max(t,d) \quad ..(1)$$

By Lemma 1, at most $1+8\max(t,d)$ cells participate in the computation of the n^3 scalar products. Thus,

$$T \geq \frac{n^3}{1+8\max(t,d)}.$$

Since $t \neq 0$, $T \geq \frac{n^3}{9\max(t,d)}$ ..(2)

From (1) and (2), $T^2 \geq \frac{n^3}{9}$ and hence, $T = \Omega(n\sqrt{n})$. □

Theorem 2.2: If two $n \times n$ matrices are multiplied by forming n^3 scalar-products in time $O(n\sqrt{n})$ on the model described above, then the number of processing cells required is $\Omega(n\sqrt{n})$.

Proof: Since n^3 scalar-products have to be computed within time $cn\sqrt{n}$ (for some constant $c>0$) at least $\frac{n^3}{cn\sqrt{n}}$ of these must be computed in every machine cycle. Thus the number of cells required is at least $\frac{1}{c}n\sqrt{n}$ which is $\Omega(n\sqrt{n})$. □

3. Matrix Multiplication Algorithm

We will begin with a description of the cell and array model. We will assume that n, which is the size of the matrices being multiplied, is k^2 for some integer k.

Let A, B and C denote three $n \times n$ matrices, where $C = A \times B$. The row and column indices of each matrix range from 1 to n. The $n\sqrt{n}$ cells used for matrix multiplication are indexed $1,2,..,n\sqrt{n}$ and arranged along a line as shown in Fig. 3.1 below for the case n=4.

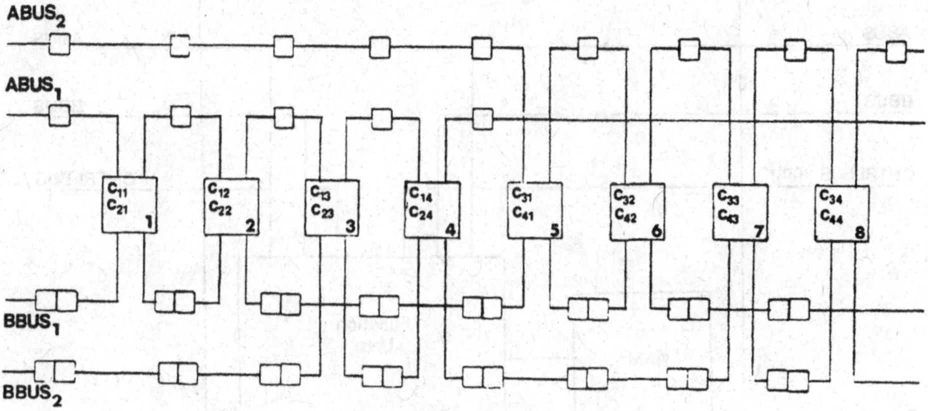

Fig. 3.1: 1-D Arrangement of Processors for n=4

Each cell has $\sqrt{n}$ words of local storage, with addresses ranging from 1 to $\sqrt{n}$. The n^2 elements of matrix C (all initialized to 0) are stored in the local memories of the cells, one per word, and updated in-situ as elements of matrices A and B are made available to the cells. Let α and β be two integers such that $0 \leq \alpha, \beta < \sqrt{n}$ and let $i = \alpha\sqrt{n}+\beta+1$. Then, element c_{ij} is stored in memory location $\beta+1$ in cell $\alpha n+j$. The array is driven by a global clock.

The cells are interconnected by a system of busses that run parallel to the line along which the cells are arranged. There are four distinct types of busses which transport elements of matrix A (henceforth referred to as ABUS), elements of matrix B (BBUS), and control signals (CNTRLBUS) from the I/O port at the left end of the array to the different cells. There are $\sqrt{n}$ busses of each type. The busses of each type are assigned indices 1,2,..., $\sqrt{n}$. Let $(ABUS)_i$, $(BBUS)_i$ and $(CNTRLBUS)_i$ denote the ith ABUS, BBUS and CNTRLBUS respectively. Each cell is connected to exactly one ABUS, BBUS and CNTRLBUS as follows. Let $1 \leq p,q \leq \sqrt{n}$ and $1 \leq r \leq n$. Then $(ABUS)_i$ and $(CNTRLBUS)_i$ are connected to cells $(i-1)n+r$ and $(BBUS)_i$ is connected to cell $(i-1)\sqrt{n} + (p-1)n + q$. For instance, in Fig. 3.1, $(ABUS)_1$ is connected to cells 1, 2, 3 and 4 and $(ABUS)_2$ to cells 5, 6, 7 and 8. $(BBUS)_1$ is connected to cells 1, 2, 5 and 6 whereas $(BBUS)_2$ is connected to cells 3, 4, 7 and 8. The organization of CNTRLBUS is similar to that of ABUS and hence has been omitted in Fig. 3.1.

We will denote two processors i and j as *logically* adjacent with respect to a bus if i and j are connected to the same bus and there is no processor with an index k which lies between i and j, that is also connected to the same bus. Thus, in Fig. 3.1, cells 1 and 2 are logically adjacent with respect to $(BBUS)_1$. Cells 2 and 5 are also logically adjacent with respect to the same bus. Associated with each bus is a delay equal to the number of clock ticks required to move a data element travelling along the bus between consecutively indexed cells i and i+1. The delay associated with the ABUS and CNTRLBUS is 1, as shown by the "unit-delay" buffers on these busses('s in Fig. 3.1). Similarly, the delay in traversing between adjacent cells i and i+1 along the BBUS is 2 clock ticks('s in Fig. 3.1). Note that if cells i and j ($i < j$) are logically adjacent with respect to a BBUS then it would take 2(j-i) clock ticks to transport an element from cell i to cell j along that BBUS. Since cells i and j are separated by a physical distance proportional to j-i, no element has to traverse more than a fixed physical distance in one clock cycle and this distance is *independent* of the *size* of the array.

We will now describe the function of each cell in the array. A model of a cell is shown in Fig. 3.2.

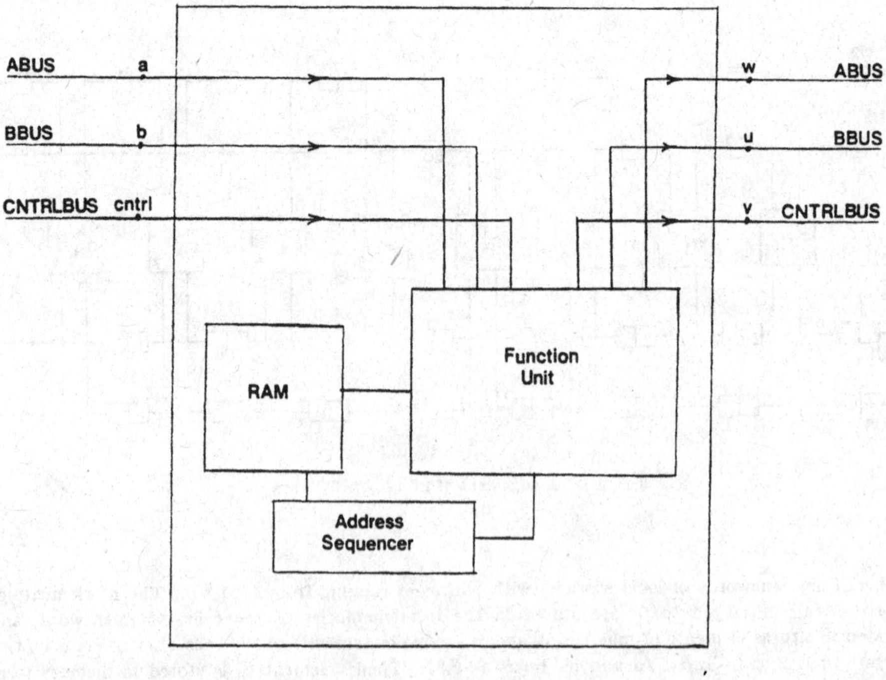

Fig. 3.2: A Cell Model

Φ_L, Φ_U, Φ_T and Φ_C are load,unload,transport and compute control signals respectively that are transported along the CNTRLBUS. These four control signals can be encoded using two bits. (A two-bit wide control port is therefore adequate.) In every cycle, the cell decodes the control signals and either allows the signals to pass through the cell without performing any action (if Φ_T is true) or updates some c_{uv} stored in its local memory. A Φ_L signal causes the cell to latch-in the data available on its BBUS (at point *b*) into an internal buffer BBUF and a Φ_U control signal causes the cell to unlatch the data stored in its BBUF onto the BBUS (at point *u*). On receiving a Φ_T signal, the cell merely transmits all the data at its input ports (*a*,*b* and *cntrl*) onto the corresponding output ports (*w*, *u*, and *v*) without performing any action. Every cell has a memory address register (MAR) that is reset to 1 when it receives a Φ_L control signal and is incremented by 1 every time it receives a Φ_C or Φ_U signal. The program executed by a cell in every cycle is described below. MEM[MAR] denotes a memory location in the RAM (random access memory) pointed to by MAR. Comments in the program appear within "/*..*/".

```
begin
 decode control signals at cntrl;
 If ΦT
  then begin
          transfer data at b to u;
          go to exit;
         end else
         begin
          If ΦL
          then begin
                  MAR ← 1;
                  latch data at b onto BBUF;
                 end else MAR ← MAR +1;
          /* if control signal is ΦL,ΦU or ΦC then */
          /* accumulate the product terms of an element in matrix C */
          MEM[MAR] ← MEM[MAR] + (element at a)*BBUF;
          If ΦU then transfer BBUF to u;
          end;
   exit: transfer data at cntrl to v;
         transfer data at a to w;
end.
```

Observe that the locations in the RAM are accessed in a cyclic sequence and hence it can be replaced by a more compact set of cyclically rotating registers.

The algorithm consists of a host inserting the elements of matrices A,B and control signals at appropriate clock ticks described as follows. Let n be the size of the matrices being multiplied where $n=k^2$. The array consists of nk cells that are indexed 1,2,...,nk. Let α and β be two integers such that $0\leq\alpha,\beta<\sqrt{n}$. The algorithm consists of the following steps.

1. Let $i=\alpha\sqrt{n}+\beta+1$. Then, insert a_{ij} into $(ABUS)_{\alpha+1}$ at tick $t_0+\alpha(n+\sqrt{n}-1)+\beta+(j-1)(2\sqrt{n}-1)$.
2. Let $j=\alpha\sqrt{n}+\beta+1$. Then, insert b_{ij} into $(BBUS)_{\alpha+1}$ at tick $t_0+(i-1)(2\sqrt{n}-1)-\alpha\sqrt{n}-\beta$.
3. Insert a Φ_L signal and a Φ_U signal along with $a_{(\alpha\sqrt{n}+1)j}$ and $a_{(\alpha\sqrt{n}+\sqrt{n})j}$ respectively into $(CNTRLBUS)_{\alpha+1}$.
4. Let x be an integer such that $1<x<\sqrt{n}$. Then, insert a Φ_C control signal along with $a_{(\alpha\sqrt{n}+x)j}$ into $(CNTRLBUS)_{\alpha+1}$.
5. Insert a Φ_T signal into $(CNTRLBUS)_{\alpha+1}$ at other times.

Theorem 3.1: The time-complexity of the algorithm is $O(n\sqrt{n})$.

Proof: The first element to be inserted in the array is b_{1n}. It is inserted at time $t_0-(n-1)$. $a_{nn}b_{nn}$ is the last product term that is evaluated by the array. It is evaluated at time $t_0+4n\sqrt{n}-n-3\sqrt{n}$. Unloading of the c_{ij}'s can be done in $O(n\sqrt{n})$ using $\sqrt{n}$ busses.

Example: We will illustrate the operation of the algorithm for the case n=4, on the array of 8 cells shown in Fig. 3.1. We will assume that the time at which a_{11} is inserted in the array is 0. Therefore

t_0=0.

The elements inserted into $(ABUS)_1$ and $(ABUS)_2$ and the times at which they are inserted are derived from step (1) of the algorithm, and summarized in Tables 3.1(a) and 3.1(b) respectively. Let t_0=0.

i \ j	1	2	3	4
1	0	3	6	9
2	1	4	7	10

Table 3.1(a)-Insert times at $(ABUS)_1$

i \ j	1	2	3	4
3	5	8	11	14
4	6	9	12	15

Table 3.1(b)-Insert times at $(ABUS)_2$

Similarly, the elements inserted into $(BBUS)_1$ and $(BBUS)_2$ and the times at which they are inserted are derived from step (2) of the algorithm and summarized in Tables 3.2(a) and 3.2(b) respectively.

i \ j	1	2
1	0	-1
2	3	2
3	6	5
4	9	8

Table 3.2(a)-Insert times at $(BBUS)_1$

i \ j	3	4
1	-2	-3
2	1	0
3	4	3
4	7	6

Table 3.2(b)-Insert times at $(BBUS)_2$

The insertion time for control signals into $(CNTRLBUS)_1$ and $(CNTRLBUS)_2$ are summarized in Tables 3.3(a) and 3.3(b) respectively. Φ_C and Φ_T are not shown for the following reason. Firstly, Φ_T is always inserted in a tick if none of the other control signals are inserted in that tick. Secondly, in general, Φ_C is inserted in all ticks following the tick in which Φ_L is inserted and preceding the tick in which Φ_U is inserted. However, for the case n=4 Φ_L and Φ_U are inserted in consecutive ticks.

Φ_L	Φ_U
0	1
3	4
6	7
9	10

Table 3.3(a)-Insert times at $(CNTRLBUS)_1$

Φ_L	Φ_U
5	6
8	9
11	12
14	15

Table 3.3(b)-Insert times at $(CNTRLBUS)_2$

We will now trace the computation of the four product terms ($a_{31}b_{11}, a_{32}b_{21}, a_{33}b_{31}, a_{34}b_{41}$) of c_{31}. Now b_{11} is inserted into $(BBUS)_1$ at tick 0 and a Φ_L signal is also inserted into $(CNTRLBUS)_1$ at tick 0. So b_{11} is latched in cell 1 at tick 0. It is unlatched at tick 1 as a Φ_U signal appears at cell 1 at tick 1 on $(CNTRLBUS)_1$. At tick 3 it reaches cell 2 which merely transmits it along $(BBUS)_1$ (the transmit signal Φ_T inserted into $(CNTRLBUS)_1$ at tick 2 appears at cell 2 in tick 3). b_{11} then reaches cell 5 at tick 9 after traversing the three buffers along $(BBUS)_1$ between cells 2 and 5 (see Fig. 3.1) each of which delays it by 2 ticks. Now a_{31} and a Φ_L signal are inserted into $(ABUS)_2$ and $(CNTRLBUS)_2$ respectively at tick 5. They encounter 4 buffers on their respective busses before reaching cell 5. Each buffer delays them by a tick and hence they reach cell 5 at tick 9. Now $(BBUS)_1$, $(ABUS)_2$ and $(CNTRLBUS)_2$ are connected to cell 5. So the first product term $a_{31}b_{11}$ gets computed at tick 9 in cell 5 and stored in location 1 of its local memory (since a Φ_L signal resets the address pointer to 1).

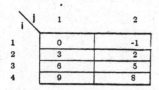

Similarly, it can be verified that a_{32} and b_{21} appear at tick 12, a_{33} and b_{31} appear at tick 15 and a_{34} and b_{41} appear at tick 18 in cell 5.

4. Concluding Remarks

We compare the matrix-multiplication algorithm proposed in this paper with some other matrix-multiplication schemes for VLSI that have appeared in the literature [9]. Many of the matrix-multiplication algorithms proposed in [9] employ either a two-dimensional hexagonal or a mesh-connected array to multiply $n \times n$ matrices in $O(n)$ time using $O(n^2)$ processors. Two-dimensional arrays, however, are not as well suited to fault-tolerant implementations (necessary for wafer-scale integration [8]) as linear arrays which are their one-dimensional counterparts. However, linear arrays, due to their limited connectivity, require $O(n^2)$ time steps to multiply two $n \times n$ matrices [2,7,11,12].

Rosenberg [13] proposed the *Diogenes* approach to designing easily testable fault-tolerant arrays. In this scheme, the processors in the array are placed along a line and interconnected by means of busses that run parallel to the line along which processors are arranged. Faulty processors are by-passed by setting switches on the busses passing through a processor. The reader is referred to [13] for a detailed description.

The array proposed in this paper for matrix multiplication has certain similarities to that obtained by using the Diogenes approach applied to a two-dimensional array. Fig. 4.1 shows the "collapsing" of a 3×3 mesh array onto a line.

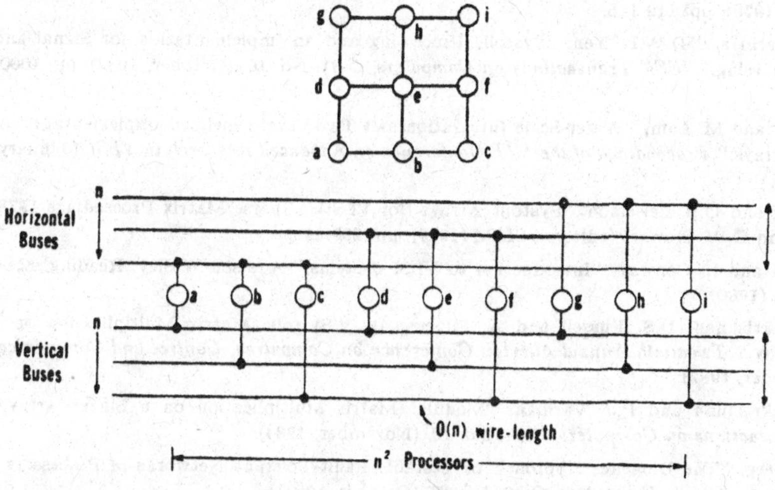

Fig. 4.1

The primary disadvantage of this scheme is that, processors which were physically adjacent in the two-dimensional arrangement are now physically separated by a distance of $O(n)$ (see for instance, cells c and f in Fig. 4.1). Accounting for signal propagation times, which may grow proportionately to the length of the signal path [10], matrix-multiplication algorithms of $O(n)$ time complexity on a mesh, can take up to $O(n^2)$ time in such an implementation. Note that this would be the case *even if the busses had buffers* to pipeline several elements along a bus.

In our scheme, however, the time complexity of matrix multiplication is only $O(n\sqrt{n})$ cycles. Furthermore, we require only $n\sqrt{n}$ cells (rather than the n^2 cells that is required if we collapse an $n \times n$ mesh onto a straight line using the Diogenes approach) and only $\sqrt{n}$ horizontal and $\sqrt{n}$ vertical busses (rather than n of each that is required using the Diogenes approach). The total area ocuupied by the $n\sqrt{n}$ processors is $O(n^2)$ (as each processor requires $\sqrt{n}$ storage). Also, each bus is $n\sqrt{n}$ long and hence the wiring area occupied by all the $\sqrt{n}$ busses is $O(n^2)$. Thus the total area occupied by our array is $O(n^2)$. Note however that the straightforward collapsing of a mesh onto a straight line would require $O(n^3)$ area. Thus our scheme preserves much of the advantages of the Diogenes approach and has better resource utilization and better time performance as well.

Finally, we note that the array proposed in this paper is a unidirectional logical one-dimensional array for which efficient fault-tolerant schemes, based on retiming have been proposed [8,15].

In conclusion, in this paper we have presented an optimal algorithm to multiply two $n \times n$ matrices that uses $O(n\sqrt{n})$ processors and requires $O(n\sqrt{n})$ time steps. The algorithm executes on an array that is well suited for fault-tolerant VLSI implementation.

References

[1] E. Arjomandi, "A Study of Parallelism in Graph Theory,"Ph.D. Thesis, Department of Computer Science, University of Toronto, (December,1975).

[2] J. Bentley and T. Ottmann, "The Power of One-Dimensional Vector of Processors," Universitat Karlsruhe, Bericht 89, (April, 1980).

[3] L.E. Cannon, "A Cellular Computer to Implement the Kalman Filter Algorithm," Ph.D. Thesis, Montana State University, (1969).

[4] A. Chandra, "Maximal Parallelism in Matrix Multiplication," IBM Tech. Report, RC 6193, (September, 1976).

[5] M. Flynn and S.R. Kosaraju, "Processes and their Interactions," Kybernetics, 5(1976),pp. 159-163.

[6] W.M. Gentleman, "Some Complexity Results for Matrix Computations on Parallel Processors," *JACM*, 25(1978), pp. 112-115.

[7] A.V. Kulkarni and D.W.L. Yen, "Systolic Processing and an Implementation for Signal and Image Processing," *IEEE Transactions on Computers,* C-31, No. 10, (October, 1982), pp. 1000-1009.

[8] H.T. Kung and M. Lam, "Wafer-Scale Integration and Two-Level Pipelined Implementation of Systolic Arrays," *Proceedings of the MIT Conference on Advanced Research in VLSI,* (January, 1984).

[9] H.T. Kung and C.E. Leiserson, "Systolic Arrays (for VLSI)," Sparse Matrix Proceedings 1978, I.S. Duff and G.W. Stewart (editors), SIAM (1979), pp. 256-282.

[10] C.A. Mead and L. Conway, "Introduction to VLSI Systems," Addison-Wesley, Reading, Massachusetts, (1980).

[11] I.V. Ramakrishnan, D.S. Fussell and A. Silberschatz, "Systolic Matrix Multiplication on a Linear Array," *Twentieth Annual Allerton Conference on Computing, Control and Communication,* (October, 1982).

[12] I.V. Ramakrishnan and P.J. Varman, "Modular Matrix Multiplication on a Linear Array," *IEEE Transactions on Computers,* C-33, No. 10, (November, 1984).

[13] A. Rosenberg, "The Diogenes Approach to Testable Fault-Tolerant Networks of Processors," *IEEE Transactions on Computers,* C-32, No. 10, (October, 1983).

[14] F. Van Scoy, "Parallel Algorithms in Cellular Spaces," Ph.D. Thesis, University of Virginia, (1976).

[15] P.J. Varman, "Wafer-Scale Integration of Linear Processor Arrays," Ph.D. Thesis, The University of Texas at Austin, (August, 1983).

Appendix

Lemma 1: No two distinct a_{pq} and a_{rs} ever appear simultaneously at the same input port of any cell in the array.

Proof: First we will show that if a_{pq} and a_{rs} are inserted into the same bus at the same time then p=r and q=s. Second, since the a_{ij}'s travel at the same speed through the array, the lemma follows.

Let $p=\alpha\sqrt{n}+\beta+1$ and $r=\gamma\sqrt{n}+\delta+1$ where $0 \le \alpha,\beta,\gamma,\delta < \sqrt{n}$. Since a_{pq} and a_{rs} are inserted into the same bus, $\alpha=\gamma$. As they are inserted at the same time, we equate their insertion times. Hence, from step 1 of the algorithm we obtain the following equality:

$$\beta-\delta = (s-q)(2\sqrt{n}-1) \quad ...(1)$$

Now $0 \leq |\beta-\delta| \leq (\sqrt{n}-1)$ and $\forall n \geq 1$, $(2\sqrt{n}-1) > (\sqrt{n}-1)$ and hence (1) can never be satisfied unless $\beta=\delta$ and q=s. If $\beta=\delta$ and $\alpha=\gamma$ then p=r. □

An element b_{ij} from matrix B is latched in $\sqrt{n}$ of the $n\sqrt{n}$ cells. We will now identify the cells in which they are latched.

Lemma 2: Let $0 \leq \alpha, \beta, u < \sqrt{n}$ and $j=\alpha\sqrt{n}+\beta+1$. Let b_{ij} be an element in matrix B. Then,

1. $\forall u$, b_{ij} is latched in cell un+j at time $t_{ij}+u(2n+\sqrt{n}-1)+2(j-1)$ where t_{ij} is the time at which it is inserted into $(BBUS)_{\alpha+1}$.
2. b_{ij} is not latched into any other cell.

Proof: We establish the result by induction on u. For the basis u=0, we need to show that b_{ij} is latched in cell j. To do so, we first establish that it is not latched in any cell s where $s=\alpha\sqrt{n}+\gamma+1$ and $0 \leq \gamma < \beta$. Assume to the contrary that it is latched in cell s. In order for this to happen a load control signal and b_{ij} must appear simultaneously at the input port of cell s. Let $\Phi_L(x)$ denote this load signal. Now cell s is connected to $(CNTRLBUS)_1$ (since s lies between 1 and n-1) and hence $\Phi_L(x)$ must be inserted along with some a_{1f} at time $t_0+(f-1)(2\sqrt{n}-1)$. Equating the time it takes $\Phi_L(x)$ and b_{ij} to reach cell s, we obtain the following equality:

$$(i-f)(2\sqrt{n}-1) = \beta-\gamma \quad ...(1)$$

Now $0 \leq |\beta-\gamma| < \sqrt{n}$ and hence for (1) to be satisfied, $\beta=\gamma$ and i=f. Therefore this contradicts $\beta<\gamma$. It can be easily verified that $\Phi_L(x)$ inserted along with a_{1i} reaches cell j at time $t_{ij}+2(j-1)$ and this is also the time when b_{ij} reaches cell j and is therefore latched.

For the induction, assume the lemma is true for some fixed u. We will first have to show that b_{ij} is released from cell un+j at time $t_{ij}+u(2n+\sqrt{n}-1)+2(j-1)+\sqrt{n}-1$. (In order for it to be released an unload control signal, say $\Phi_U(x)$, must appear at the input port of cell un+j at this time.) Now $(CNTRLBUS)_{u+1}$ is connected to this cell. We can easily show that if $\Phi_U(x)$ is inserted along with $a_{(u\sqrt{n}+\sqrt{n})i}$ into $(CNTRLBUS)_{u+1}$ then $\Phi_U(x)$ reaches cell un+j at the required time (that is, $t_{ij}+u(2n+\sqrt{n}-1)+2(j-1)+\sqrt{n}-1)$) and hence b_{ij} is released from it.

We will now have to show that it does not get latched in any cell between $un+\alpha\sqrt{n}+\beta+1$ and $(u+1)n+\alpha\sqrt{n}+\beta+1$. First, assume to the contrary that it does get latched in any cell $un+\alpha\sqrt{n}+\delta$ where $\beta+1 \leq \delta < \sqrt{n}$. This means it must have met a load control signal, say $\Phi_L(x)$, travelling along $(CNTRLBUS)_{u+1}$ in this cell. $\Phi_L(x)$ must be inserted along with some $a_{(u\sqrt{n}+1)f}$. Equating the time it takes for b_{ij} to reach cell $un+\alpha\sqrt{n}+\delta$ (after it is released from cell $un+\alpha\sqrt{n}+\beta+1$) and for $\Phi_L(x)$ to reach this cell we obtain the following equality:

$$(f-i)(2\sqrt{n}-1) = \delta-\beta+\sqrt{n}-2 \quad ...(2)$$

Now $\max(|\delta-\beta|) \leq \sqrt{n}$ and hence (2) cannot be satisfied unless f=i. If f=i then $\delta=\beta-\sqrt{n}+2$ which is outside the permissible range for δ.

Now assume to the contrary that b_{ij} is latched in any cell $(u+1)n+\alpha\sqrt{n}+\delta$ where $1 \leq \delta \leq \beta$. This means it must have met met a load control signal $\Phi_L(x)$ travelling along $(CNTRLBUS)_{u+2}$ in this cell. Now $\Phi_L(x)$ must have been inserted along with some $a_{((u+1)\sqrt{n}+1)f}$. Equating the time it takes for b_{ij} to reach cell $(u+1)n+\alpha\sqrt{n}+\delta$ and for $\Phi_L(x)$ to reach this cell we obtain the following equality:

$$(f-i)(2\sqrt{n}-1)=\delta-\beta-1 \quad ...(3)$$

Now $\max(|\delta-\beta|) \leq \sqrt{n}$ and hence (3) cannot be satisfied unless f=i. If f=i then $\delta=\beta+1$ which is the outside the permissible range for δ.

It can again be verified that b_{ij} meets $\Phi_L(x)$ that is inserted along with $a_{((u+1)\sqrt{n}+1)i}$ in cell $(u+1)n+\alpha\sqrt{n}+\beta+1$ at time $t_{ij}+(u+1)(2n+\sqrt{n}-1)+2(j-1)$ and is therefore latched. □

Having identified the cells in which the b_{ij}'s are latched and released, we can now establish the following result.

Lemma 3: No two distinct b_{ip} and b_{js} ever appear simultaneously at the same input port of any cell in the array.

Proof: Let $0 \leq u, \alpha, \beta, \gamma, \delta < \sqrt{n}$ and assume to the contrary that b_{ip} and b_{js} appear simultaneously at the input port of cell $un+\alpha\sqrt{n}+\delta+1$. Now this cell is connected to $(BBUS)_{\alpha+1}$. So b_{ip} and b_{js} must travel in this bus. Therefore, let $p=\alpha\sqrt{n}+\beta+1$ and $s=\alpha\sqrt{n}+\gamma+1$ We need only show that they do not clash at the input port of cells at which either b_{ip} or b_{js} are latched into. Hence either $\delta=\beta$ or $\delta=\gamma$ and without loss of generality let $\beta<\gamma$.

Consider the first case where $\delta=\beta$. Equating the time it takes b_{ip} and b_{js} to reach cell $un+\alpha\sqrt{n}+\delta+1$ (after being released from cells $(u-1)n+\alpha\sqrt{n}+\beta+1$ and $(u-1)n+\alpha\sqrt{n}+\gamma+1$ respectively) we obtain the following equality:

$$(j-i)(2\sqrt{n}-1)=\sqrt{n}-1+\beta-\gamma \quad ...(1)$$

For (1) to hold $i=j$ and $\gamma=\beta$. If $\gamma=\beta$ then $p=s$ and hence b_{ip} and b_{js} are not distinct. We can arrive at a similar contradiction for the second case also. □

We are now ready to establish that every element in matrix C accumulates their correct product terms.

Lemma 4: Let $0\leq\alpha,\beta,\gamma,\delta<\sqrt{n}$. Then $\forall k$, $1\leq k\leq n$, $a_{(\alpha\sqrt{n}+\beta+1)k}$ meets $b_{k(\gamma\sqrt{n}+\delta+1)}$ in cell $\alpha n+\gamma\sqrt{n}+\delta+1$.

Proof: Let t_a and t_b denote the times at which $a_{(\alpha\sqrt{n}+\beta+1)k}$ and $b_{k(\gamma\sqrt{n}+\delta+1)}$ respectively are inserted into the array. The time at which $a_{(\alpha\sqrt{n}+\beta+1)k}$ reaches cell $\alpha n+\gamma\sqrt{n}+\delta+1$ is $t_a+(\alpha n+\gamma\sqrt{n}+\delta)$ which on substituting for t_a becomes $t_0+\alpha(n+\sqrt{n}-1)+(k-1)(2\sqrt{n}-1)+(\alpha n+\gamma\sqrt{n}+\delta)+\delta$.

From Lemma 2, the time at which $b_{k(\gamma\sqrt{n}+\delta+1)}$ is latched in this cell can be simplified to $t_0+\alpha(n+\sqrt{n}-1)+(k-1)(2\sqrt{n}-1)+(\alpha n+\gamma\sqrt{n}+\delta)$.

It is unlatched $(\sqrt{n}-1)$ clock ticks later whereas $a_{(\alpha\sqrt{n}+\beta+1)k}$ meets it β clock ticks later where $\beta\leq\sqrt{n}-1$. The address pointer in the cell points to location $\beta+1$ where $c_{(\alpha\sqrt{n}+\beta+1)(\gamma\sqrt{n}+\delta+1)}$ is stored and hence it is correctly updated. □

OPTIMAL PARALLEL PATTERN MATCHING IN STRINGS

(Extended summary)

Uzi Vishkin*

ABSTRACT

Given a text of length n and a pattern, we present a parallel linear algorithm for finding all occurrences of the pattern in the text. The algorithm runs in O(n/p) time using any number of $p \leq n/\log n$ processors on a concurrent-read concurrent-write parallel random-access-machine.

I. Introduction

The family of models of computation used in this paper is the parallel random-access-machines (PRAMs). All members of this family employ p synchronous processors all having access to a common memory. The present paper refers to two members of the PRAM family. Our presentation focuses on the concurrent-read concurrent-write (CRCW) PRAM. This model allows simultaneous reading from the same memory location as well as simultaneous writing. In the latter case, the smallest serial numbered among the processors that attempt to write succeeds. In the full paper we show that a weaker concurrent-read concurrent-write PRAM model, where several processors may attempt to write at the same memory location only if they seek to write the same thing, actually suffices for the strongest results in this paper. There, we also show how to implement some of the results on a concurrent-read exclusive-write (CREW) PRAM, where simultaneous reading into the same memory location but not simultaneous writing is allowed. See [Vi-83a] for a survey of results concerning the PRAM family.

Let Seq(n) be the fastest known worst-case running time of a sequential algorithm, where n is the length of the input for the problem being considered. Obviously, the best upper bound on the parallel time achievable using p processors without improving the sequential result is of the form O(Seq(n)/p). A parallel algorithm that achieves this running time is said to have optimal speed-up or more simply to be optimal. A goal, in serial computation, is to design linear time algorithms (O(n) time). Analogously, a goal, in parallel computation, is to design Algorithms whose running time is proportional to n/p, where p is the number of processors used. In this case we say that a parallel algorithm achieves parallel linear running time.

---

*Courant Institute, New York University and (present address) Department of Computer Science, Tel Aviv University, Tel Aviv 69 978, Israel. This research was supported by DOE grant DE-AC02-76ER03077 , by NSF grants NSF-MCS79-21258 and NSF-DCR-8318874 and by ONR grant N0014-85-K0046.

The list of optimal speed-up parallel algorithms (or algorithms which are within a factor of log n from this goal) obtained so far is short in spite of the interest in them. Let us mention them: computation of partial (prefix) "sums" of n variables, where the word "sum" stands for any associative binary operation, [SV-81] for finding the maximum among n elements and merging, [Vi-83b] for finding the k smallest out of n elements, [AKS-83], [RV-83] (a randomized algorithm) and [SV-81] for sorting, [PVW-83] for various operations on 2-3 tree. [Vi-84b] for ranking a linked list (a randomized algorithm), [G-84] for string matching (where the symbols are taken from an alphabet whose size is bounded), [CLC-81], [HCS-79], [R-84] (a randomized algorithm), [SV-82a] and [Vi-84] for computing connected components of graphs, [TC-84] and [TV-83] for computing biconnected components of graphs, [SV-82b] for finding maximum flow in a network, [AIS-84] and [AV-84] for finding Euler tours, [TV-83] and [Vi-84c] for computing various functions on trees, [Vi-84c] for strong orientation of undirected graphs, and [BV-84] for generation of a computation tree form of an arithmetic expression and for finding matches in a sequence of parentheses.

The string matching problem is defined as follows. Input. Two arrays PATTERN and TEXT whose lengths are m and n, respectively. Output. A Boolean array MATCH of length n. MATCH(i), $1 \leq i \leq n$, indicates if an occurence of PATTERN starts at TEXT(i).

The main contribution of this paper is in presenting an original parallel linear algorithm for the general case of this problem which runs in O(log n) time on a CRCW PRAM. The text analysis part of the algorithm achieves this efficiency on a CREW PRAM. The algorithm can also be implemented as a parallel linear algorithm which runs in time $O(\log^2 n)$ on a CREW PRAM.

There are two known linear time serial algorithms for this extensively studied problem, due to [BM-77] and [KMP-77]. Recall that every parallel linear algorithm is, in particular, a linear time serial algorithm. The present result is stronger than theirs in the sense that it gives a parallel linear algorithm while their serial algorithms do not seem to imply satisfactory parallel linear algorithms. Moreover, our algorithm is not more complicated than theirs. Some parts of it (particularly, the analysis of the text) are even considerably simpler.

The string matching algorithm of [G-84] also runs in O(log n) time using n/log n processors but requires the size of the alphabet to be fixed. However, it needs n processors in order to obtain O(log n) time for the general case considered here, and simulating it by a single processors takes O(nlog n) time. Unlike his algorithm,ours does not use the "Four Russians Trick" ([AHU-74]). There, O(log n) bits are packed into a single register and then each instruction concerning this register is counted as one operation. We use a few ideas from Galil's paper but are able to improve his result due to the following:

(1) Novel algorithmic ideas for the string matching problem. We sketch briefly

one such notable idea. A formal presentation of this idea is given in Section 3. The pattern is preanalyzed and the following table is constructed. Consider the following proposition: "The suffix starting at position i of the pattern is a prefix of the pattern". For each i, $1 \leq i \leq m$, the table will either indicate that the proposition is true, or point to a single character following i that provides a counter example to the proposition. Let $j_1 > j_2$ be two locations of the text such that $j_1 - j_2 < m$ and the suffix starting at position $j_1 - j_2 + 1$ of the pattern is not a prefix of the pattern. Following the analysis of the pattern, position $j_1 - j_2 + 1$ of the table points to a counter example, say w. That is, $PATTERN[j_1-j_2+w] \neq PATTERN[w]$. The duel idea. (See also Fig. 1). It is impossible that occurrences of the pattern start both at location j_1 and j_2 of the text. Moreover, the $j_1 - 1 + w$ position of the text can be either the w position of the pattern, the $j_1 - j_2 + w$ position of the pattern or neither (but not both). The idea of a duel between j_1 and j_2 is to compare this position of the text with each of these positions of the pattern. Thereby, we can eliminate the possibility that an occurrence of the pattern starts in at least one of j_1 or j_2.

Now, consider the set of locations of the text such that at time t of an algorithm the possibility that an occurrence of the pattern starts at each of them has not (yet) been ruled out. Applying duels between successive pairs of these locations enable us to decrease by a factor of two a bound on the cardinality ("density") of this set.

(2) A careful assignment of processors to their jobs (using Brent's theorem).

The text analysis part of the algorithm is described in Section 3 and the pattern analysis part in Section 4.

II. Preliminaries

Most of this section is devoted to definitions and known facts regarding periodicity in strings.

Let u,w be two strings. u is a period of w if w is a prefix of u^k for some k, or equivalently if w is a prefix of uw. We call the shortest period of a string w the period of w. w has period size P if the length of the period of w is P. If w is at least twice longer than its period we say that w is periodic. Let u be a string. $|u|$ is the number of characters in the string.

We will use some simple facts about periodicities.

Proposition 1. Let v be a periodic string and let w, $|w| \leq |v|/2$, be a period of v. Suppose w itself is periodic and u is a period of w such that $w = u^k$, $k > 1$. Then u is a period of v.

Proof. v is a prefix of w^s for some $s > 1$. Hence, v is a prefix of u^{ks}.

Proposition 2 (The Periodicity Lemma [LS-62]): If w has two periods of of size P and Q and $|w| \geq P + Q$, then w has a period of size gcd(P,Q).

In the rest of this section an <u>occurrence</u> of some pattern <u>at j</u> will mean that the pattern is a substring beginning at position j of a given fixed string z. For proof of propositions 3-6 below, see [G-84].

<u>Proposition 3</u>: If v occurs at j and $j + \hat{P}$, for any $\hat{P} \leq |v|/2$, then (1) v is periodic with a period of length $\hat{P}$, and (2) v occurs at j + P, where P is the period size of v.

In the rest of this section we consider a periodic string $v = u^k u'$, $k > 1$, u the period of v, u' a proper prefix of u, and $|u| = P$.

<u>Proposition 4</u>: If v occurs at j and j + mP, $m \leq k$, then $u^{k+m}u'$ occurs at j.

<u>Proposition 5</u>: If v occurs at j and $j + \Delta, \Delta \leq |v| - P$, then Δ is a multiple of P.

We call an occurrence of v at j <u>important</u> if v <u>does not</u> occur at j + P.

<u>Proposition 6</u>: If there are two important occurrences of v at r and s, $r > s$, then $r - s > |v| - P$.

<u>Theorem (Brent)</u>. Any synchronous parallel algorithm of time t that consists of a total of x elementary operations can be implemented by p processors within a time of $\lceil x/p \rceil + t$.

<u>Proof of Brent's theorem</u>. Let x_i denote the number of operations performed by the algorithm in time i ($\sum_1^t x_i = x$). We now use the p processors to "simulate" the algorithm. Since all the operations in time i can be executed simultaneously, they can be computed by the p processors in $\lceil x_i/p \rceil$ units of time. Thus, the whole algorithm can be implemented by p processors in time of

$$\sum_1^t \lceil x_i/p \rceil \leq \sum_1^t (x_i/p + 1) \leq \lceil x/p \rceil + t. \qquad \square$$

<u>Remark</u>. The proof of Brent's theorem poses two implementation problems. The first is to evaluate x_i at the beginning of time i in the algorithm. The second is to assign the processors to their jobs.

III. <u>Analysis of the text</u>.

The algorithm has three steps. In the first step an analysis of the pattern is performed. This analysis is used in the second step to find a sparse set of "suspicious" indices of the text. By suspicious indices we mean indices of the text in which occurrences of the pattern may start. The last step applies a character by character check to find in which of the suspicious indices an occurrence of the pattern really starts. In this section we describe the last two steps. The first step is described in the next section.

<u>Definition</u>. Suppose that PATTERN[j,j+1,...,m] is not a prefix of PATTERN[1,...,m] for some j, $2 \leq j \leq m$. That is, there exists an integer w, $1 \leq w \leq m-j+1$, such that PATTERN(w) $\neq$ PATTERN((j-1)+w). We say that w is a

witness to this mismatch. Observe that w is a witness against the existence of a period of size $j - 1$ in PATTERN.

Output of Step 1. For each j, $2 \leq j \leq \lfloor m/2 \rfloor + 1$, Step 1 determines whether PATTERN has a period of size $j - 1$ (WITNESS(j) will be 0) and computes a witness if not (it assigns such a witness to WITNESS(j)).

Steps 2 and 3

For $k \geq 0$, the set of k-blocks is $\{TEXT[1,\ldots,2^k],\ldots,TEXT[\ell 2^k+1,\ldots,(\ell+1)2^k],\ldots\}$. Steps 2 and 3 depend considerably on whether the pattern is periodic.

Case 1. The pattern is not periodic.

Step 2.

Initialize. for all i, $1 \leq i \leq n-m+1$ pardo
MATCH(i) := T

Recall that the goal of our algorithm is that MATCH(i) = T if and only if an occurrence of the pattern starts at i, for any i, $1 \leq i \leq n-m+1$.

Let us define the k-sparsity property: For each k-block at most one value of MATCH is T. Namely, each of $MATCH[1,\ldots,2^k],\ldots,MATCH[\ell 2^k+1,\ldots,(\ell+1)2^k],\ldots$ contains at most one T.

The goal of Step 2 is to satisfy $(\lfloor \log m \rfloor-1)$-sparsity. However, at the end of Step 2 it will still be possible that MATCH(i) is T while there is no occurrence of PATTERN that starts at TEXT(i).

LEFT(a,k) contains the entry of the leftmost T in TEXT of k-block number a, $1 \leq a \leq \lceil n-m+1/2^k \rceil$, or an indication that there is no such T.

Let us describe stage k of Step 2. (The input to stage k satisfies (k-1)-sparsity.)

Stage k, $1 \leq k \leq \lfloor \log m \rfloor-1$: Satisfy k-sparsity.

The procedure given below is performed in parallel for all k-blocks. Let a be an integer satisfying $1 \leq a \leq \lceil n-m+1/2^k \rceil$. We describe the procedure for k-block a. k-block a is the union of two (k-1)-blocks: 2a and 2a-1.

```
if LEFT(k-1,2a) = 'null'
then LEFT(k,a) := LEFT (k-1,2a-1)
else if LEFT(k-1,2a-1) = 'null'
     then LEFT(k,a) := LEFT(k-1,2a)
     else see below.
```

(k-1)-sparsity implies that following stage $k - 1$ there is at most one index j_1 in (k-1)-block 2a and at most one index j_2 in (k-1)-block 2a-1 such that $MATCH(j_1) = MATCH(j_2) = T$. The remaining case is where both indices j_1 and j_2 exist. We use the concept of a duel (which was described informally in the introduction) to eliminate one of these T - s using information that exists in WITNESS following Step 1.

Let w be $WITNESS(j_1-j_2+1)$. Let $x = PATTERN(w)$, $y = PATTERN(j_1-j_2+w)$ and $z = TEXT(j_1-1+w)$. Since j_1 and j_2 belong to the same k-block, $j_1-j_2 < 2^k$.

For $k < \lfloor \log m \rfloor - 1$, this implies $w \neq 0$. w is a witness that PATTERN[$j_1 - j_2 + 1$, ..., m] is not a prefix of PATTERN. Namely, $x \neq y$.
If an occurrence of PATTERN starts at j_1 then $x = z$.
If an occurrence of PATTERN starts at j_2 then $y = z$.
$x \neq y$ implies that only one of the later two equalities can be satisfied and therefore at most one of these two occurrences may hold. We use z to eliminate the possibility of (at least) one of these occurrences:

```
if  z ≠ y
then MATCH(j_2) := F
if  z ≠ x
then MATCH(j_1) := F
```

Finally,

```
if MATCH(j_2) = T
then LEFT(k,a) := j_2
else if MATCH(j_1) = T
     then LEFT(k,a) := j_1
     else LEFT(k,a) := 'null'
```

Complexity. Stage k of Step 2 needs $O(n/2^k)$ operations and $O(1)$ time. Therefore, Step 2 needs a total of $O(n)$ operations and $O(\log n)$ time.

Step 3.

For each α, $1 \leq \alpha \leq n-m+1$, such that MATCH(α) = T check, character by character, if an occurrence of the pattern starts at α.

```
for all j, 1 ≤ j ≤ ⌈(n-m+1)/2^(⌊log m⌋-1)⌉, pardo
  for all i, 1 ≤ i ≤ m, pardo
    (Denote t(j) = LEFT(⌊log m⌋-1,j))
    if t(j) ≠ 'null
    then if TEXT(t(j)+i-1) ≠ PATTERN(i)
         then MATCH(t(j)) := F (simultaneous writes are possible)
```

This results in MATCH(i) = T (for any i, $1 \leq i \leq n-m+1$) if and only if an occurrence of the pattern starts at location i of the text as we wanted.
Complexity. $O(mn/2^{\lfloor \log m \rfloor - 1}) = O(n)$ operations and $O(1)$ time.

Case 2. The patters is periodic.

Say that the pattern is $u^s v$ where u is the period of the pattern, $|u|=P$, and $|v|<P$ and let $Q = |v| = m-sP$ ($<P$).

Step 2.1 Rerun Step 1 for PATTERN[1,...,2P] instead of the whole pattern.

Step 2.2 Perform $\lfloor \log P \rfloor$ rounds of duels with respect to the text (similar to Step 2 of Case 1 above). As a result each $\lfloor \log P \rfloor$-block of the text will have at most one index, where an occurrence of the period u may start (to be called a suspicious index, as before). Observe that since the information in WITNESS is based now only on u^2, every index of the text in which an occurrence of u^2 starts is suspicious.

Step 3.1. For every suspicious index check, character by character, if an occurrence of $u^2 v$ starts at it (similar to Step 3 of Case 1 above).

Steps 2.1, 2.2 and 3.1 result in the following: for every i, $1 \leq i \leq n-2P-Q+1$, MATCH(i)=T if and only if there is an occurrence of u^2v at i.
These steps need a total of O(n) operations and O(log n) time.

Step 3.2. Our present goal is to find for each such i the maximum k such that an occurrence of u^kv starts at i. Then, if $k \geq s$ we conclude that an occurrence of the pattern starts at i. The full paper brings the slightly tedious implementation of Step 3.2. It needs O(log n) time using n/log n processors.

IV. Step 1 - Analysis of the pattern.

The pattern is the input for Step 1. Step 1 consists of manipulating the array WITNESS, whose length is m. Recall that in the previous section we already specified what WITNESS must include following Step 1. It is initialized as follows.

for all j, $1 \leq j \leq m$ pardo
  WITNESS(j) := 0 (Interpretation. PATTERN[j,j+1,...,m] is
  "suspected" to be a prefix of the pattern.)

In this section, the set of k-blocks refers to the pattern. It is {PATTERN[1,...,2^k],...,PATTERN[$\ell 2^k$+1,...,$(\ell+1)2^k$],...}.

Step 1 consists of [log m]-2 or [log m]-3 iterations (called stages) and a terminal stage. Only in the full paper, we describe the terminal stage and how to determine the exact number of iterations to be performed and prove correctness. Following stage k, the following three properties are satisfied.

(1) The k-certainty property. For j, $1 \leq j \leq 2^k$, WITNESS(j) = 0 if and only if an occurrence of PATTERN[1,...,2^{k+1}-j+1] starts at PATTERN(j). That is, for $1 \leq j \leq 2^k$, WITNESS(j) = 0 indicates that we are certain that there is such an occurrence at j. The k-centainty property can alternatively be presented as follows. Imagine that PATTERN[1,...,2^{k+1}] was the whole pattern. Then, WITNESS[1,...,2^k] has its final values as required by the output definition of Step 1.
Obviously, WITNESS(1) must be always zero.

(2) The k-sparsity property. (In this section it will apply to the pattern). If WITNESS[2,...,2^k] does not have any zero then WITNESS of each k-block has at most one zero. (That is, each of WITNESS[1,...,2^k],...,WITNESS[$\ell 2^k$+1,...,$(\ell+1)2^{k+1}$],... contains at most one zero).

(3) The k-lookahead property. WITNESS(i) $\leq 2^{k+1}$ for every index i of the pattern.

Satisfying the k-certainty and the k-sparsity properties is a fairly intuitive goal, while satisfying the k-lookahead property may seem counter-intuitive. Particularly, since satisfying it implied in several places not using available information which seemed as if it will speed up the algorithm. Therefore, our presentation focuses on satisfying the first two properties. In the full paper we prove that the k-lookahead property is satisifed as well.

We describe now informally stage k + 1 of Step 1. (A more detailed description can be found in the full paper). We follow closely the illustrative description which is given in Fig. 2.

After stage k we must be at either the arrow leading to Box 2 or at the arrow leading to Box 4. In either case "k-certainty" is satisfied.

"k-sparsity" is satisfied when we enter Box 2. k-sparsity need not be satisfied at a periodic mode (i.e., if we were at Box 4 in stage k and proceeded to stage k + 1 at Box 4).

LEFT(a,k) relates in this section to the pattern. It contains the entry of the leftmost zero in WITNESS of k-block number a, $1 \leq a \leq \lceil m/2^k \rceil$, or an indication that there is no such zero. If PATTERN[$1,\ldots,2^{k+1}$] has a period of size $\leq 2^k-1$ then PERIODICITY(k) contains the period size.

Let us specify the instructions in each of the boxes. The instructions for boxes 2-5 assume that they are activated in stage k + 1.

Box 1. (Start)

```
for all j, 1 ≤ j ≤ m pardo
  WITNESS(j) := 0
if PATTERN(1) ≠ PATTERN(2)
then start stage 1 at Box 2
else start stage 1 at Box 4 (enter a periodic mode)
```

Box 2. (Upon entering Box 2, k-sparsity and k-certainty are satisfied. WITNESS[$2,\ldots,2^k$] has no zeros.)

If suspected periodicity has been found start stage k + 2 at a periodic mode (Box 4). Otherwise, progress to Box 3.

Box 3. (k-sparsity and (k+1)-certainty are satisfied. For every $2 \leq j \leq 2^{k+1}$, WITNESS(j) ≠ 0.)

Satisfy (k+1)-sparsity.

k-sparsity implies that there is at most one index j_1 in k-block 2a and at most one index j_2 in k-block 2a-1 such that WITNESS(j_1) = WITNESS(j_2) = 0. The interesting case is where indices j_1 and j_2 exist. Here enters again the concept of a duel. We perform a duel between these indices in which one of these zeros will be eliminated, similar to the previous section.

(Implementation Remark 1. In the present description, we ignore the case where j_1 - 1+w > m (or when there is reference to an index of the pattern which is >m). The algorithm proceeds as if PATTERN(j_1-1+w) matches any possible character. However, the k-lookahead property prevents this case from affecting the correctness of the algorithm as explained in the presentation of the terminal stage of Step 1 in the full paper.)

Box 4. Periodic mode. (Recall that we are presently describing stage k + 1). (Say that the last transition from Box 2 or 5 occurred at stage k_1+1. k-certainty and k_1-sparsity are satisfied. Say the period size of PATTERN[$1,\ldots,2^{k+1}$] (the suspected periodicity) is P).

We pick indices j of the first (k+1)-block such that WITNESS(j) = 0 and j - 1 is not divisible by P. The fact that k-certainty was satisfied upon entering Box 4, implies that each such j must belong to the second k-block. For each such index j, we select the index i, such that $j - P < i < j$ and $i - 1$ is divisible by P and perform a "one way" duel between i and j in which only an assignment into WITNESS(j) can be performed.

Claim. Suppose P is not a period of PATTERN$[1,\ldots,2^{k+2}]$. Then for at most four indices j that satisfied the first if condition WITNESS(j) remains 0.

Check whether the periodicity continues until index 2^{k+2} of the pattern. If yes, start stage $k + 2$ at Box 4. (Observe that (k+1)-certainty is satisfied). Suppose the periodicity does not continue until index 2^{k+2}. Consider the possibilities that any multiple of P, which is $< 2^{k+1}$, is a period of PATTERN$[1,\ldots,2^{k+2}]$. The character of the pattern which caused the assignment into WITNESS(P+1) is also a counter example to any of these possibilities. Update this into WITNESS. As a result WITNESS$[2,\ldots,2^{k+1}]$ will have at most four zeros whose indices are $> 2^k$ (the claim). Check, character by character, if any of these zeros represents a period of PATTERN$[1,\ldots,2^{k+2}]$ and update WITNESS appropriately. Obviously at most one of this zeros represents a period of PATTERN$[1,\ldots,2^{k+1}]$ (Proposition 2). Proceed to Box 5. (Observe that (k+1)-certainty is satisfied).

Box 5. ((k+1)-certainty is satisfied. WITNESS$[2,\ldots,2^k]$ has no zeros. k_1-sparsity is satisified).

Satisfy k-sparsity. This is done in $k - k_1$ iterations. In iteration t, $1 \leq t \leq k-k_1$, (k_1+t)-sparsity is satisfied. Each iteration is similar to the way in which (k+1)-sparsity is satisfied in Box 3. If WITNESS$[2^k+1,\ldots,2^{k+1}]$ has a zero (PERIODICITY(k+1) $\neq$ 'null') then start stage $k + 2$ at Box 4. Otherwise, proceed to satisfy (k+1)-sparsity at Box 3.

Complexity analysis. Stage k: Each of boxes 2,3 and 4 is visited at most once in each stage. Box 2 needs $O(2^k)$ operations and $O(1)$ time. Box 3 needs $O(1)$ operations and $O(1)$ time per each of the $\leq \lceil m/2^k \rceil$ k-blocks in order to satisfy k-sparsity. Box 4 needs $O(2^k)$ operations and $O(1)$ time. Since k increases from 1 to $\leq \lfloor \log m \rfloor - 2$, we have so far $O(m)$ operations and $O(\log m)$ time. Box 5: For each i, we satisfy i-sparsity at most once during these stages. As in Box 3 satisfying i-sparsity needs $O(m/2^i)$ operations and $O(1)$ time, and the same total bound of $O(m)$ operations and $O(\log m)$ time applies.

Apply Brent's theorem to get $O(\log m)$ parallel running time using $m/\log m$ processors.

The terminal stage. Determine WITNESS(j), $2 \leq j \leq \lfloor m/2 \rfloor + 1$. (Note that the only problem that may arise in arguing that we have already achieved this goal relates to Implementation Remark 1 in Box 3. There, we described a situation where the information in WITNESS implies a comparison with a character of the pattern whose index is $> m$. By implementation Remark 1 the outcome of such a comparison would not affect the values in WITNESS.)

Overall complexity of Step 1. Step 1 requires $O(m/p)$ time using $p \leq m/\log m$

processors.

Conclusion. We presented a new linear time serial algorithm for the string matching problem in which the analysis of the text is particularly simple. The algorithm is parallel linear for a very wide range for the number of processors. The exact range depends on the model of computation being used.

ACKNOWLEDGEMENT. I am grateful to Zvi Galil for encouraging me to continue improving the results in this paper and for quite a few insights through both discussions and his paper. Helpful comments by Dennis Shasha are also gratefully acknowledged.

REFERENCES

[AHU-74] A.V. Aho, J.E. Hopcroft and J.D. Ullman, The Design and Analysis of Computer Algorithms, Addison-Wesley, Reading, MA, 1974.

[AIS-84] B. Awerbuch, A. Israeli and Y. Shiloach,"Finding Euler circuits in logarithmic parallel time", Proc. 16th Annual ACM Symp. on Theory of Computing (1984), 249-257.

[AKS-83] M. Ajtai, J. Komlós, and E. Szemerédi, "An O(n log n) sorting network," Combinatorica 3, 1 (1983), 1-19.

[AV-84] M.J. Atallah and U. Vishkin, "Finding Euler tours in parallel", to appear in JCSS.

[Ba-78] T.P. Baker, "A technique for extending rapid exact-match string matching to arrays of more than one dimention", SIAM J. Comput. 7,4 (1978), 533-541.

[BM-77] R.S. Boyer and J.S. Moore, "A fast string searching algorithm", Comm. ACM 20(1977), 762-772.

[BV-84] I. Bar-On and U. Vishkin, "Optimal parallel generation of a computation tree form", Proc. 1984 International Conf. on Parallel Processing, 490-495. To appear in ACM Trans. on Programming languages and systems.

[CLC-81] F.Y. Chin, J. Lam and I. Chen, "Optimal parallel algorithms for the connected component problems," Proc. 1981 International Conf. on Parallel Processing (1981), 170-175.

[G-84] Z. Galil, "Optimal parallel algorithms for string matching", Proc. 16th ACM Symp. on Theory of Computing, 1984, 240-248.

[FRW-83] F.E. Fich, R.L. Radge and A. Wigderson, "Relation between concurrent-write models of parallel computation", preprint, Div. of Computer Science, Univ. of Calif., Berkeley, 1983.

[HCS-79] D.S. Hirschberg, A.K. Chandra and D.V. Scywate, "Computing connected components on parallel computers', Comm. ACM 22(1979), 461-464.

[KMP-77] D.E. Knuth, J.H. Morris and V.R. Pratt, "Fast pattern matching in strings", SIAM J. Comp. 6 (1977), 322-350.

[LS-62] R.C. Lyndon and M.P. Schutzenberger, "The equation $a^M = b^N c^P$ in a free group", Michigan Math. J. 9 (1962), 289-298.

[PVW-83] W. Paul, U. Vishkin and H. Wagener, "Parallel dictionaries on 2-3 trees", Proc. 10th ICALP, Lecture Notes in Computer Science 154, Springer-Verlag, 1983, 597-609.

[R-84] J.H. Reif,"Optimal parallel algorithm for graph connectivity", TR-08-84, Aiken Computation Lab., Harvard Univ.

[RV-83] J.H. Reif and L.G. Valiant, "A logarithmic time sort for linear size networks", Proc. 15th Annual ACM Symp. on Theory of Computing (1983), 10-16.

[SV-81] Y. Shiloach and U. Vishkin, "Finding the maximum merging, and sorting in a parallel computation model," J. Algorithms 2 (1981), 88-102.

[SV-82a] Y. Shiloach and U. Vishkin, "An O(log n) parallel connectivity algorithm", J. Algorithms 3(1982), 57-67.

[SV-82b] Y. Shiloach and U. Vishkin, "An $O(n^2 \log n)$ parallel max-flow algorithm", J. Algorithms 3 (1982), 128-146.

[TC-84] Y.H. Tsin and F.Y. Chin, "Efficient parallel algorithms for a class of graph theoretic problems", SIAM J. COMPUT. 13 (1984), 580-599.

[TV-83] R.E. Tarjan and U. Vishkin, "An efficient parallel biconnectivity algorithm", TR 69, Dept. of Computer Science, Courant Institute, NYU, 1983. To appear in SIAM J. Comput..

[Vi-83a] U. Vishkin, "Synchronous parallel computation - a survey", TR 71, Dept. of Computer Science, Courant Institute, NYU, 1983.

[Vi-83b] U. Vishkin, "An optimal parallel algorithm for selection", preprint, 1983.

[Vi-84a] U. Vishkin, "An optimal parallel connectivity algorithm", Discrete Applied Mathematics 9 (1984), 197-207.

[Vi-84b] U. Vishkin, "Randomized speed-ups in parallel computation", Proc. 16th Annual ACM Symp. on Theory of Computing (1984), 230-239.

[Vi-84c] U. Vishkin, "On efficient parallel strong orientation", to appear in Information Processing Letters.

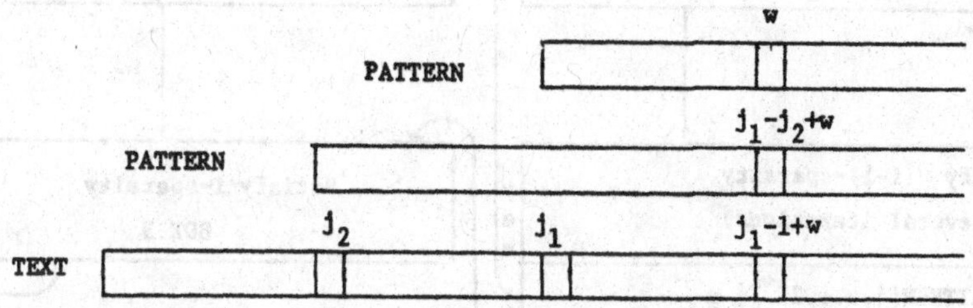

Figure 1. A duel between positions j_1 and j_2 of the text.

- PATTERN(w) $\neq$ PATTERN(j_1-j_2+w)
- If TEXT(j_1-1+w) $\neq$ PATTERN(w) then there is no occurrence of the pattern at j_1.
- If TEXT(j_1-1+w) $\neq$ PATTERN(j_1-j_2+w) then there is no occurrence of the pattern at j_2.

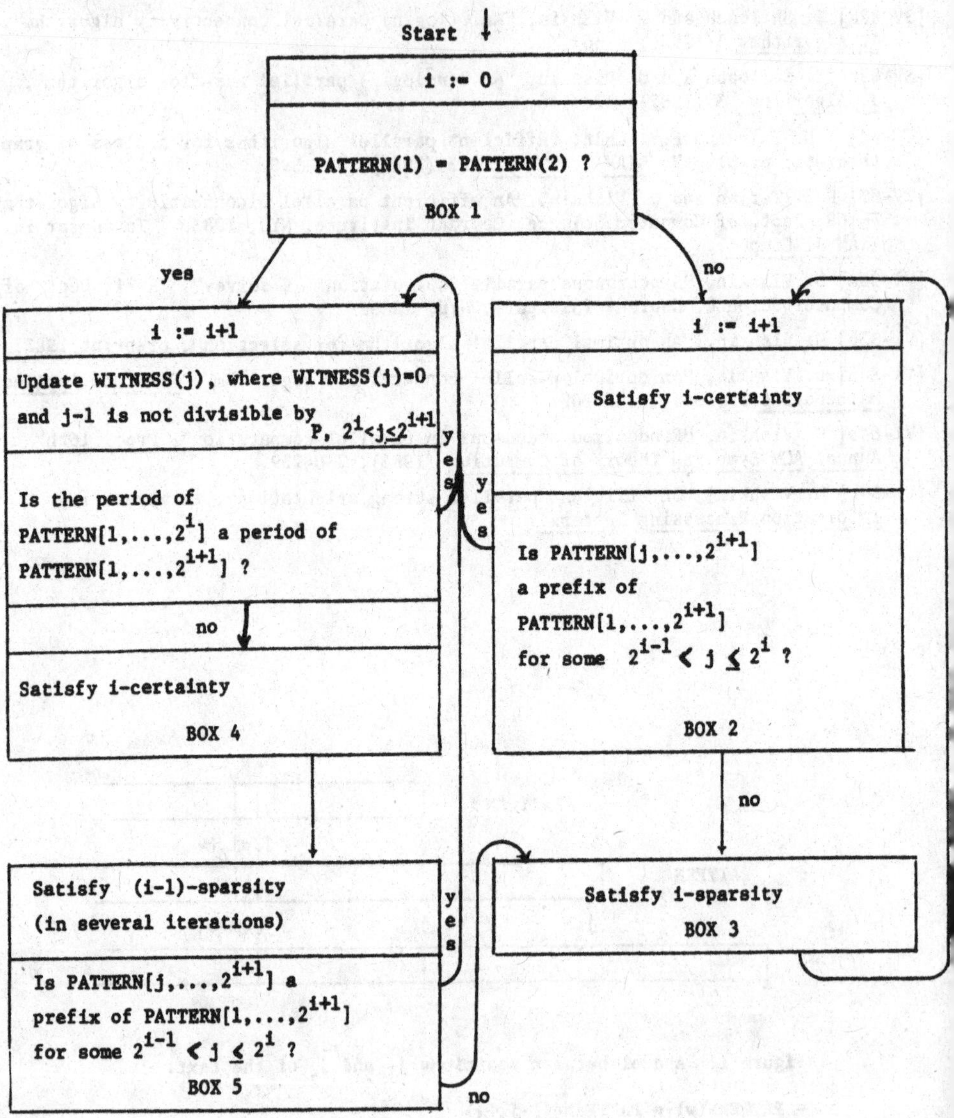

Figure 2. Step 1.

COMPOSITIONALITY AND CONCURRENT NETWORKS:
Soundness and Completeness of a Proofsystem

Job Zwiers – Department of Computer Science, University of Nijmegen, Toernooiveld, 6525 ED Nijmegen, the Netherlands.
Willem Paul de Roever – Dept. of Computer Science, University of Nijmegen and Dept. of Computer Science, University of Utrecht, P.O. Box 80.002, 3508 TA Utrecht, the Netherlands.
Peter van Emde Boas – Departments of Mathematics and Computer Science, University of Amsterdam, Roetersstraat 15, 1018 WB Amsterdam, the Netherlands.

ABSTRACT

Specification,construction and verification of programs should be done in a *compositional* way. This means that for each syntactic programming construct it should be possible to infer a specification for the whole construct from *specifications* of the constituent syntactic components of that construct. A compositional proofsystem is presented for a language that includes parallel executing networks and recursive creation of subnetworks. This system is then shown to be arithmetically complete.

1. Introduction

By now there is general agreement in the state-of-the-art of program correctness, e.g. [Lam], [BK], [MC], [Lam2], [CH], [OH], [MC2], [O2], that the specification, construction, and verification of programs should be done compositionally. By compositionality the following is meant: For each syntactic programming construct it has to be possible to infer a given specification for the whole construct from *specifications* of the constituent components of that construct, without additional knowledge of the internal (syntactic) structure of these components. The rules for parallel composition of statements in the systems of [OG] and [AFR] are not compositional, since the "interference freedom test" in [OG] and the "cooperation test" in [AFR] must be applied to the proofoutlines of the components of a parallel construct, i.e. containing the program texts of those components, which do represent their internal structure.
On the other hand, Lamport's "Concurrent Hoare Logic" in [Lam] *is* compositional. Here the specifications are "generalized Hoare formulae" of the form $\{p\}S\{q\}$, meaning that, if execution is begun anywhere in S while p is true, then p will remain true until S terminates, and q will be true if and when S terminates. Lamport's proofrule for parallel composition has the following form:

$$\frac{\{p\}S_1\{p\} \quad , \quad \{p\}S_2\{p\}}{\{p\}S_1\|S_2\{p\}}$$

The important observation is here that the assertions in the specifications for S_1 and S_2, and as well for $S_1\|S_2$, are *identical*. Although compositional in the strict sense as defined above, this aspect is debatable. Namely, the very reason for requiring compositionality is that the problem of verifying a program can be split up into subproblems which are each simpler to deal with than the original problem. One such subproblem, nl. how the proof of $\{p\}S_1\|S_2\{p\}$ splits into subproofs for S_1 and S_2, is very simple indeed. But there is no reduction in complexity of the assertions associated with S_1 and S_2, since they are the same as for the whole construct. Proofrules for parallel composition that do allow for independent specifications of the component processes of a parallel construct have been given in [Lam2], [BK], [MC]. The rules in [Lam2] and in [BK] rely on a specification language which is sufficiently powerful to express, within a version of temporal logic, the usual mathematical semantics of parallel composition, for instance in [BK] as a set of "conjoinment axioms". Although conceptually straightforward, it is not clear whether such transcriptions of the metalanguage for describing the semantics are easy to manipulate in practice.
In this paper, we study a proofsystem for *partial correctness* specifications for a CSP-like language called DNP. ("Dynamic Networks of Processes") Our objectives are:

- To describe not merely a rule for parallel composition, but rather a proofsystem for a *complete* language including sequential composition, nondeterminism, communication between processes and (recursive) expansion of processes into networks of concurrently executing processes.
- To keep the specification language as simple as possible without loosing the possibility of expressing independent compositional specifications.
- To keep the proofrules simple.
- To establish a sound and relatively complete proofsystem, and to give rigorous proofs thereof.

One of our results is the fact that a relatively complete system *can* be given. A result of Clarke [Cla] implies that for certain programming languages there exists no Hoare-like proofsystem for partial correctness which is relatively complete. This is the case whenever an interpretation for assertions and programming language exists, such that:

(a) The programming language has an undecidable halting problem,
(b) The assertion language is expressive, that is, strongest postconditions are expressible,
(c) The validity problem for formulae in the assertion language is decidable.

Clarke's result can be understood as follows: In a partial correctness system, there exists a formula stating that a program S does *not* terminate, nl., $\{true\} S \{false\}$. From (b), (c) and the relative completeness of the system, it would follow that such formulae can be recursively enumerated, contradicting (a).
A formula expressing nontermination of S exists in our system too. Now, if the assertion language is a usual first order predicate language with (only) program variables acting as the variables in the predicate formulae, then (b) and (c) can be satisfied by chosing a *finite* interpretation as shown in [Cla]. For the language DNP it is possible to program Turing machines *even* when we chose such a finite interpretation for program variables, so (a) is satisfied in this case. However, our assertion language is essentially a first order language with *two* types of variables, nl. variables ranging over the domain for program variables, and so called trace variables, ranging over finite sequences. These sequences are required because the sequence of values communicated along a certain channel between two concurrently executing processes can be explicitly denoted; such a sequence is called a *trace*. The length of these traces, which also can be explicitly denoted, cannot be bounded from above, so we cannot chose a finite domain of interpretation for traces without rendering the language inexpressive. So in fact we establish *arithmetical* completeness, in the sense that a standard model of Peano arithmetic can be defined in our assertion language whenever this language is expressive.

Prior to giving a detailed description of the programming language DNP, we like to point out some underlying ideas and their connection with our specifications. The object of study is a simple language which describes dynamically changing networks of processes. In such a network, primarily sequential programs, called processes, execute in parallel and communicate (exclusively) via interconnecting channels. However, processes can expand temporarily into parallel subnetworks. This happens recursively, since the so formed subnetwork can contain new copies of the original (expanded) process. After termination of all component processes of a subnetwork, the expanded process contracts (shrinks) again, and continues its original mode of execution.
Hence, processes act as transformers of states and traces. This combination of state-based and communication-based programming is characteristic for our specifications, which have the following form:

$$I : \{p\} S \{q\} \qquad (*)$$

Here, I is an invariant describing (exclusively) the communication behaviour of S, i.e. I does not refer to any internal state which S passes through during execution. Hence, I expresses the behaviour of S as far as relevant to other *concurrently* executing processes. On the other hand, the pre- and postconditions p and q, resp., describe the combined state-trace transformations, much in the same way as formulae of the usual Hoare calculi are related to state transformations. Informally, the meaning of (*) is the following:

> If S is started in an initial state and with an initial trace for which p holds, then the invariant I will hold for the trace of S at any moment during execution of S (including the moment of termination, if S terminates). Also, whenever S terminates, q will hold for the final state and trace of S.

2. The language

In the following syntax of DNP, x and u stand for program variables, E and D for channel names, P for procedure names, e for expressions and b for boolean expressions. *Lists* of names like "$E_{in-1},\ldots,E_{in-k}$" are abbreviated as "$\bar{E}_{in}$".

Statements: $S ::= skip \mid x{:=}e \mid b \mid D!e \mid D?x \mid S_1;S_2 \mid S_1 \square S_2 \mid co\ N\ co \mid P(\bar{E}_{in};\bar{E}_{out};\bar{u})$

Networks: $N ::= S_1 \| S_2$

Procedure declarations: $Dec ::= P(\bar{D}_{in};\bar{D}_{out};\bar{x}) : begin\ S\ end$

Programs: $Prog ::= \langle Dec \mid S \rangle$

The intuitive meaning of $skip$, $x{:=}e$ and $S_1;S_2$ should be clear. $S_1 \square S_2$ stands for nondeterministic choice between S_1 and S_2. Boolean expressions are incorporated as statements. They function as "guards": whenever b evaluates to *true*, the guard can be passed, i.e. it is equivalent to "*skip*" in this case. When b evaluates to *false* the guard cannot be passed and the computation is aborted. As far as *partial* correctness is concerned, a construct as if b *then* S_1 *else* S_2 *fi* can be regarded as equivalent to $b;S_1 \square \neg b;S_2$. We will freely use such "derived" constructs in our examples. A network $S_1 \| S_2$ calls for concurrent execution of S_1 and S_2. In such a network, S_1 and S_2 are not allowed to have *shared* program variables. The two component processes of a network can communicate with each other (only) along named, directed channels. Communication along a channel, say "D", occurs when an output command "$D!e$" is executed by one of the component processes simultaneously, i.e. synchronized, with an input command "$D?x$" of the other one. The value of e is then assigned to the program variable x and both processes continue their execution.

In DNP, channels always connect exactly two processes. So a process cannot both read from and write to one and the same channel, nor are two different processes allowed to both read from or both write to some common channel. A channel from which some process reads or to which it writes is called an *external* channel of that process. When two processes are bound together into a network, their *common* channels, along which they communicate, are said to be *internal* channels of that network.
When dealing with *nested* networks, i.e. networks as $S_1 \| S_2$ in which S_1 and S_2 are themselves (or contain) subnetworks, it is possible that some subnetwork has an internal channel with the same name as some channel of the main network. This is even unavoidable when the subnetwork and the main network belong to different incarnations of the same procedure body in case of a recursive procedure call. Such channel name "clashes" are resolved by introducing a kind of block structure with the " *co N co* " construct, which *hides* internal channels, i.e. no *internal* channel of $S_1 \| S_2$ is visible anymore outside of the process co $S_1 \| S_2$ co.
So in $S \equiv co\ S_1 \parallel co\ S_2 \parallel S_3\ co\ co$ with $S_1 \equiv D?x$, $S_2 \equiv D!0$, $S_3 \equiv D?y$, the S_2 process communicates with S_3 along the D channel internal to $S_2 \| S_3$, and not with S_1.
In agreement with the modular character of DNP, we have for recursive procedures a scope concept different from that of Algol like languages. All variables used in some procedure body (which is bracketed by *begin* – *end*) are assumed to be *local* variables, i.e., there are no references to any kind of *global* variables possible. (Correspondingly, there is no explicit variable declaration mechanism needed in DNP.)
The parameter list of a procedure consists of input channels, followed by output channels, followed by value/result-variable parameters. To simplify matters technically, we impose the restriction that all names in a (formal or actual) parameter list be distinct. This avoids any kind of "aliasing" that could introduce unwanted sharing of program or channel variables by two processes.

3. A semantics for DNP

For CSP-like languages, a number of semantic definitions have been given ([FHLR], [FLP], [CH], [Mil], [Bro], [Bru]). In general these definitions differ considerably with respect to the degree in which they abstract from behavioral properties of processes. In this article we are interested in partial correctness properties only. Therefore, a semantics is used in which the nondeterminism is considered to be *angelic,* in the terminology of [Bro]. That is, whenever a process, after performing some communications, has a possibility to deadlock or to diverge, but it has *also* the possibility of terminating or performing another communication, then the former possibility is not represented in our semantics.

The basic domain of denotations for the semantics of processes consists of *sets of trace–state pairs.*

A *trace* τ is a finite sequence of pairs consisting of a channelname and a communicated value. Special cases are the *empty* trace <>, and the trace $<(D,v)>$ with only one communication, nl., of value v along channel D. Concatenation of traces τ_1 and τ_2 is denoted by $\tau_1\tau_2$. A trace τ_1 is an initial prefix of τ_2, written as $\tau_1 \leq \tau_2$, iff there exists a trace τ such that $\tau_1\tau = \tau_2$. For a trace τ and a set of channelnames *cset*, the *projection* $\tau|cset$ is defined as the trace obtained from τ by omitting all communications *not* referring to the channels in *cset*.
Relabeling a channelname D by E for a trace τ, that is, substituting the name E for all occurences of D, is written as $\tau[E/D]$. The set of all traces is denoted by *Trace*.

A *state* s is a function assigning values to program variable names. Program variables can assume *integer* values as well as the special value ω; ω might be viewed as standing for *undefined*, since it is used to initialize local variables of procedures. The set of integers unioned with ω is denoted by *Val*. The *everywhereundefinedstate* is the unique state Ω for which $\Omega(x) = \omega$ for all variable names x.

The variant $s[v/x]$ of a state s is defined as usual:

$$s[v/x](x) = v$$
$$s[v/x](y) = s(y) \quad \text{for } y \neq x.$$

For a state s and a set of program variable names *var*, the *restriction* $s|var$ is given by:

$$(s|var)(x) = s(x) \quad \text{if } x \in var,$$
$$= \omega \quad \textit{otherwise.}$$

If the states s_1 and s_2 agree on the intersection of their domain, that is, if for all x, if both $s_1(x) \neq \omega$ and $s_2(x) \neq \omega$, then $s_1(x) = s_2(x)$, then the union $s_1 \oplus s_2$ is defined as:

$$\begin{aligned} s_1 \oplus s_2(x) &= s_1(x) \quad \text{if } s_1(x) \neq \omega \\ &= s_2(x) \quad \text{if } s_2(x) \neq \omega \\ &= \omega \quad\quad\;\; \text{if } s_1(x) = s_2(x) = \omega. \end{aligned}$$

The set of all states is denoted by *State*.

A *trace-state pair* is a pair (τ,s), where τ is a trace, and where s is a state as defined above or the special symbol $\perp$. A pair (τ,s) with $s \neq \perp$ indicates a possible computation which after performing the communications in τ, *terminates* in state s.
A pair $(\tau,\perp)$ indicates an *unfinished* computation, that is, a computation that has already performed the communications in τ, but has not yet terminated. Unfinished computations are *not* the same as diverging, i.e. nonterminating, computations. They serve to order sets of trace-state pairs, as follows:

$$(\tau_1,s_1) \leq (\tau_2,s_2) \quad \Leftrightarrow \quad \tau_1 = \tau_2 \wedge s_1 = s_2 \quad \vee \quad \tau_1 \leq \tau_2 \wedge s_1 = \perp.$$

The ordering of *sets* of trace-state pairs, the so called *Hoare* order, is defined as follows:

$$U \leq V \quad \Leftrightarrow \quad \forall(\tau_1,s_1) \in U \; \exists(\tau_2,s_2) \in V \; [\, (\tau_1,s_1) \leq (\tau_2,s_2) \,].$$

In fact this defines only a preorder, since for two different sets U and V with the same maximal elements, we still have $U \leq V$ and $V \leq U$. The Hoare order is turned into a partial order by requiring sets to be *prefix closed*. A set of trace-state pairs U is prefix closed iff for all pairs (τ_1,s_1), (τ_2,s_2) we have that:

$$(\tau_2,s_2) \in U \text{ and } (\tau_1,s_1) \leq (\tau_2,s_2) \text{ implies } (\tau_1,s_1) \in U.$$

The Hoare order for prefix closed sets boils down to the usual set inclusion order. Therefore, the least upperbound of a collection of prefix closed sets always exists and equals the union of these sets. We chose as our basic domain of denotations the set **D** of all *nonempty* prefix closed sets of trace-state pairs. From the foregoing it follows that **D** is a complete partial order (cpo), with the singleton $\{(<>,\perp)\}$ as least element. The cpo structure on **D** is needed to describe the semantics of recursive procedures.
The reason for excluding the empty set $\varnothing$ from **D**, is that in some situations inclusion of $\varnothing$ as (necessarily) least element gives rise to undesirable representations of infinite communications. E.g., a call of the procedure P, defined as: $P(D) : begin \; D!0 \; ; P(D) \; end$, should *not* have the empty set as denotation, but rather the following set, where the infinite communication "$<(D,0),(D,0),(D,0),...>$" is represented as an infinite collection of unfinished computations:

$$\{(<>,\perp),(<(D,0)>,\perp),(<(D,0),(D,0)>,\perp),...\}.$$

Both sets are possible solutions to the fixedpoint equation used when defining the semantics of this procedure call, but only the second solution corresponds to the unique least fixedpoint in our domain **D**.

For a trace-state pair set U, *Close*(U) is defined as the least prefix closed set containing U.

Also, we extend the projection operator for traces to sets of trace-state pairs in the following way:

$$U|cset = \{(\tau|cset,s) \mid (\tau,s) \in U \}.$$

Now we are able to define the meaning of statements and networks S. This meaning $[S]$, is essentially a mapping from initial states to sets of trace-state pairs. Because of the possibility of procedure calls in S, the meaning $[S]$ depends on a procedure environment η determining the meaning of these calls. If we denote the set of procedure environments by *Env*, then $[S]$ is a function:

$$[S] : Env \rightarrow (State \rightarrow \mathbf{D}).$$

The intuition is that S, when started in state s can produce any of the trace-state pairs in $[S]\,\eta\, s$, where the meaning of calls of procedure P is given by $\eta(P)$.
With this in mind it will be clear that $\eta(P)$ must be an element from a domain **B** consisting of functions:

$$\beta : Chan^* \times Chan^* \times Var^* \rightarrow (State \rightarrow \mathbf{D}),$$

so that the meaning of a call $P(\overline{E}_{in};\overline{E}_{out};\overline{u})$ can be obtained as $\eta(P)(\overline{E}_{in},\overline{E}_{out},\overline{u})$.
The domains $(State \rightarrow \mathbf{D})$ and **B** are provided with a cpo structure by using pointwise ordering of functions in the usual way. (For a set X and a cpo Y, the functions in $X \rightarrow Y$ are ordered by: $\phi \leq \psi$ iff $\forall x \in X : \phi(x) \leq \psi(x)$. This yields a cpo again.)

The definition of sequential composition requires the following extension of "[ ]" to sets of trace-state pairs U:

$$[S]^+ \,\eta\, U = \{(\tau_u,\perp) | (\tau_u,\perp) \in U\} \;\cup\; \{(\tau_u\tau,s) \mid \exists s_u : (\tau_u,s_u) \in U, \, s_u \neq \perp \wedge (\tau,s) \in [S]\,\eta\, s_u \}.$$

Note that $[S]^+\eta\, U$ is prefixed closed if U is.

Finally, we come to the definition of the semantics for DNP. For expressions e and boolean expressions b, the value of e and b, evaluated in state s, is denoted by $[e]\, s$ and $[b]\, s$, resp..

Definition
For a statement S, network N, environment η, state s, (i.e, $s \neq \bot$):

$[skip]\,\eta\, s = Close\,\{(<>,s)\}$

$[x:=e]\,\eta\, s = Close\,\{(<>,s[[e]s/x])\}$

$[b]\,\eta\, s = Close\,(if\ [b]s\ then\ \{(<>,s)\}\ else\ \{(<>,\bot)\})$

$[D!e]\,\eta\, s = Close\,\{(<D,[e]s)>,s)\}$

$[D?x]\,\eta\, s = Close\,\{<(D,v)>,s[v/x]) \mid v \in Val\}$

$[S_1;S_2]\,\eta\, s = [S_2]^{+}\eta\,([S_1]\eta\, s)$

$[S_1 \square S_2]\,\eta\, s = [S_1]\,\eta\, s\ \cup\ [S_2]\,\eta\, s$

$[P(\bar{E}_{in};\bar{E}_{out};\bar{u})]\,\eta\, s = \eta(P)(\bar{E}_{in},\bar{E}_{out},\bar{u})(s)$

$[co\ N\ co]\,\eta\, s = ([N]\,\eta\, s) \mid chan(co\ N\ co)$

$[S_1 \| S_2]\,\eta\, s = \{(\tau,s') \mid (\tau|chan(S_i),s_i') \in [S_i]\,\eta\, s_i\ \text{ for } i=1,2\ \wedge\ \tau = \tau|chan(S_1,S_2)\}$,

where $s_1 = s|complement(var(S_2))$,
$s_2 = s|complement(var(S_1))$,
$s' = s_1' \oplus s_2'$ if $s_1' \neq \bot$ and $s_2' \neq \bot$,
$= \bot$,otherwise.

$[<Dec\,|\,S>]\,\eta\, s = [S](\eta[\beta/P])\, s$,

where β is derived from the declaration: $Dec \equiv P(\bar{D}_{in};\bar{D}_{out};\bar{x}) : begin\ S_0\ end$,

as the least solution (in the domain **B**) of the equation:

$\beta(\bar{E}_{in};\bar{E}_{out};\bar{u})s = \{(\tau[\bar{E}_{in}/\bar{D}_{in},\bar{E}_{out}/\bar{D}_{out}],s[[\bar{x}]s'/\bar{u}]) \mid (\tau,s') \in [S_0]\,(\eta[\beta/P])\,(\Omega[[\bar{u}]s/\bar{x}])\}$.

End definition

We remark here that the functional defining the semantics of recursive procedures can be shown to be continuous. Also, the righthand sides of the semantic equations above all define *nonempty prefix closed sets* indeed. Furthermore, if for the union $s_1' + s_2'$ in the equation for the parallel construct $S_1 \| S_2$ there is some x with $s_1'(x) \neq \omega$ and also $s_2'(x) \neq \omega$, then it can be seen that $x \in complement(var(S_1,S_2))$, and so that $s_1'(x) = s(x) = s_2'(x)$. So s_1' and s_2' agree for the value assigned to x in this case. We conclude that the semantics is well defined.

The role of the clause "$\tau = \tau|chan(S_1,S_2)$" in the semantics of parallelism is to enforce that τ contains *exclusively* communications along channels from S_1 and S_2.

The semantics of recursive procedures can be understood as follows. When procedure P is called with actual parameterlist "$\bar{E}_{in};\bar{E}_{out};\bar{u}$", the body S_0 of P starts executing in a state for which all variables are *"undefined"*, except that the formal parameters $\bar{x}$ are initialized to the values $[\bar{u}]s$ of the corresponding actuals. Communications performed by this body S_0 along the "formal" channels $\bar{D}$, are redirected via the corresponding actual channels $\bar{E}$. When the execution of the body terminates, the final state s' of the body, is *not* the final state according to the *caller* of the procedure. Instead, the state s in which P was called is preserved during the call and upon termination of P only the values of the parameters $\bar{x}$ in s' are copied back to the corresponding actual parameters $\bar{u}$.

A *closed* program is defined as a program for which all procedures called in this program are *defined* in the procedure declaration. It is easily seen that the semantics of a closed program does not depend on the "environment" argument η. For such closed programs, we introduce the convention that if the "environment" argument for the semantics of the program is omitted, it is assumed to be equal to the *empty* environment Θ.

4. The language for specifications

Our language for assertions in correctness formulae is a first order predicate language with two types of logical variables, nl. *integer variables* v and *trace variables* t. Logical variables that occur free in assertions are also called *ghost variables*. Logical variables cannot occur in a program text, so the value they denote is not affected by program execution. Program variables x on the other hand, and also *trace projections* π_{cset} denote values that *are* affected by program execution. For a given statement and set of channel names *cset*, the trace projection π_{cset} denotes the sequence of communications actually performed up to some moment during the execution of that statement. The channel name and the communicated value of the n-th communication of π_{cset} are represented by terms $chan(\pi_{cset}[n])$ and $val(\pi_{cset}[n])$, resp.. The term $|\pi_{cset}|$ stands for the *length* of π_{cset}. We remark that there is no term in the language representing the whole trace as such, i.e. only *projections* can be denoted. This will be of considerable importance when formulating a proofrule for parallel composition in the next section. The syntax of terms, i.e. expressions, channel names and trace expressions, and of assertions is the following:

Expressions: $e ::= 0 \mid 1 \mid \omega \mid v \mid x \mid val(texp[e]) \mid \ |texp| \ \mid e_1 + e_2$

Channel names: $c ::= D \mid chan(texp[e])$

Trace expressions: $texp ::= t \mid \pi_{cset} \mid (texp|cset)$

Assertions: $p ::= e_1 = e_2 \mid c_1 = c_2 \mid p_1 \wedge p_2 \mid \neg p \mid \exists v.[p] \mid \exists t.[p]$

The program variables and channel names in trace projections of an assertion p are denoted by $var(p)$ and $chan(p)$, resp.. The logical (integer) variables and trace variables of p are refered to as $lvar(p)$ and $tvar(p)$.

Trace projections π_D onto a *single* channel D are abbreviated as D, that is, a channel name itself stands for the trace projection on this channel. Also we will freely use abbreviations such as "texp1 = texp2" which can easily be transformed into assertions within the language above.

An assertion p is *interpreted* in a logical variable environment γ and a trace-state pair (τ,s), where $s \neq \perp$. We write $[p]\,\gamma\,(\tau,s)$ for this interpretation. *Ghost* variables, i.e. free occurrences of *logical* integer variables v or trace variables t, are interpreted as the values $\gamma(v)$ and $\gamma(t)$, resp..
Program variables x are interpreted as $s(x)$, and the value of a *trace projection* π_{cset} is taken to be $(\tau|cset)$.

The interpretation of assertions *not* containing program variables is of course independent of the state component s. A typical example is the invariant I in correctness formulae $I:\{p\}\,S\,\{q\}$. For such assertions I, we use $[I]\,\gamma\,\tau$ as an abbreviation for $[I]\,\gamma\,(\tau,\Omega)$.

An assertion p is called *valid*, denoted by $\models p$, iff $\forall\gamma\ \forall(\tau,s).\ s\neq\perp \Rightarrow [p]\,\gamma\,(\tau,s)$ holds.

Substitution in assertions of expressions for variables is defined as usual, taking care that possible name "clashes" are avoided. Substitution in assertion p of expression e for variable v is denoted by $p[e/v]$.

Substitution of a trace expression *texp* for a trace projection π_{cset} in an assertion p is defined only when *cset* includes all channel names occurring in trace projections in p. If $\pi_{\overline{cset}}$ is an occurrence of a projection with $\overline{cset} \subseteq cset$, then it is replaced by $(texp|\overline{cset})$ under the substitution $p[texp/\pi_{cset}]$. A special case is the substitution $p[\pi_{cset}\langle(D,v)\rangle/\pi_{cset}]$, which we abbreviate as $p[D\langle\underline{v}\rangle/D]$. As can be seen, in this case it suffices to replace projections $\pi_{\overline{cset}}$ for which D is among the channels *cset*, by $\pi_{\overline{cset}}\langle(D,v)\rangle$, i.e. the concatenation of $\pi_{\overline{cset}}$ with $\langle(D,v)\rangle$.

After these preparations, we can give a formal definition of correctness formulae. They are of the form:

$\langle Dec \mid I:\{p\}\ S\ \{q\}\rangle$,where $var(I) = \emptyset$.

(I.e. with the restriction that the invariant I does not contain program variables, but only trace projections and logical variables.)
In this formula the dependence of S on the procedure declaration *Dec* is made explicit. Whenever this declaration is clear from context, we use $I:\{p\}\ S\ \{q\}$ as a shorthand.

We define a correctness formula to be *valid*, written as: $\models \langle Dec \mid I:\{p\}\ S\ \{q\}\rangle$, iff

$$\forall\gamma\ \forall\eta\ \forall(t,s).\ s\neq\perp \Rightarrow [\,[p]\,\gamma\,(t,s) \ \Rightarrow\ \forall(\tau,s)\in[S]\,\bar\eta\,s.[\,[I]\gamma(t\tau)\ \wedge\ (s\neq\perp \Rightarrow [q]\,\gamma\,(t\tau,s))\,]\,] ,$$

with the procedure environment $\bar\eta = \eta[\beta/P]$, β being derived from the declaration *Dec* as in the definition of the semantics for DNP.

This definition can be understood as follows:

Let t,s be some initial trace and state for which p holds, then:

- I is required to hold for all possible extensions $t\tau$ of the initial trace t, produced by executing S. Note that, because of prefix closedness of $[S]\,\bar\eta\,s$, this amounts to the same as requiring that I holds at all moments during execution of S!

- q is required to hold for the final state and trace, if and when S terminates, since such terminated computations are represented by pairs (τ,s) with $s\neq\perp$ in $[S]\,\bar\eta\,s$.

As can be seen, due to the quantifier "$\forall\gamma$" in the definition above, ghost variables v and t are in fact interpreted as if they were universally quantified as: $\forall v\ \forall t.\ [\ \langle Dec|I:\{p\}\ S\ \{q\}\rangle\ ]$

(This last formula however, is not a legal correctness formula as defined above).

5. A proof rule for parallel composition

A compositional proof rule for parallel composition can be based upon restricting specifications of programs to those specifications that cannot be interfered with by parallel execution of other programs. For DNP we achieve this by imposing the restriction that a specification only refers to program variables and channel names in trace projections that actually occur in the program. This restriction can be relaxed somewhat by (also) allowing variables and channel names to occur in specifications if they do not occur in *any* of the programs executing in parallel. The intuition here is that an invariant I for a program S, obeying this restriction, is preserved under execution of some other program S' in parallel, since communication along a channel referred to by I, if any, can occur only in cooperation with S, so the specification for S guarantees that I is preserved. Furthermore, our *specification language* is such that if S' communicates along a channel, *not* occurring in I, then the value of all expressions and trace expressions in I remains the same, and so I is preserved in this case too. This leads to the following proof rule:

$$\frac{I_1:\{p_1\}\ S_1\ \{q_1\}\quad,\quad I_2:\{p_2\}\ S_2\ \{q_2\}}{I_1\wedge I_2:\{p_1\wedge p_2\}\ S_1\|S_2\ \{q_1\wedge q_2\}}$$

,with the restrictions: $var(p_i,q_i)\cap var(S_j)=\emptyset$,
$chan(I_i,p_i,q_i)\cap chan(S_j)\subseteq chan(S_i)$, for (i,j) = (1,2) and (i,j) = (2,1).

6. The sequential composition rule

In a top down development of programs, the invariant I describing the "communication protocol" of some program S executing in parallel with other programs, is designed without knowing the syntactic structure of S. This has certain consequences when, as a next step in the development, S is split up as a *sequential* composition "$S_1;S_2$". For then specifications for S_1 and S_2 have to be invented with the communication protocol I for S already fixed. Now if I is to be an *invariant* for S, both S_1 and S_2 should preserve this invariant. This suggests specifications for S_1 and S_2 containing the *same* invariant I as for S. Reduction in complexity of specifications is achieved here much in the same way as for usual Hoare calculi, nl. by chosing an appropriate intermediate assertion r as postcondition for S_1 and as precondition for S_2. The fact that pre- and postconditions can express properties of the communication trace is crucial here, since it allows for *simpler* specifications of S_1 and S_2, while retaining the *same* communication protocol for both. With the specifications for S_1, S_2 and S as above, the specification for S can be proven from those for the components S_1 and S_2 with the following rule for sequential composition:

$$\frac{I:\{p\}\ S_1\ \{r\}\quad,\quad I:\{r\}\ S_2\ \{q\}}{I:\{p\}\ S_1;S_2\ \{q\}}$$

The following tiny example tries to clarify the usage of this rule. Suppose we have a specification:

$I:\{\pi_{D,E}=\langle\rangle\}\ S\ \{true\}$, with $I\equiv\exists v.[\pi_{D,E}\leq\langle(D,v),(E,v)\rangle]$ (1)

An obvious decomposition of S is: $S\equiv S_1;S_2$, with specifications:

$I:\{\pi_{D,E}=\langle\rangle\}\ S_1\ \{\exists v.[\pi_{D,E}=\langle(D,v)\rangle\wedge x=v]\}$ (2)
$I:\{\exists v.[\pi_{D,E}=\langle(D,v)\rangle\wedge x=v]\}\ S_2\ \{true\}$ (3)

Here we introduced a program variable x to store the value v send along D.
It will be clear that (1) can be proven from (2) and (3) using the sequential composition rule.

7. The proof system

We present a proof system for specifications as introduced in the previous sections. For convenience, we restrict ourselves to programs with only *one* procedure. However, the system can be easily generalized to deal with more than one procedure declaration. Many rules are simple adaptations of rules as can be found in usual Hoare calculi. A short example at the end of this section explains the role of some of the rules presented here. Apart from the recursion rule, we have that for all other axioms and rules, the procedure declarations *"Dec"* in the premisses and conclusions of these rules are all the same. Therefore, except for the recursion rule, we omit the declaration in correctness formulae, assuming that the procedure environment is clear from context.
The rules for skip, assignment, boolean test, communication commands and procedure call have in common that an implication "$p\rightarrow I$" has to be checked to prove $I:\{p\}\ S\ \{q\}$. Therefore in actual proofs it is convenient to adopt the convention that an invariant I in a specification is implicitly attached (as a conjunct) to both pre- and postcondition of that specification. With this convention, implications "$p\rightarrow I$" as mentioned above are trivialized. The rules for atomic statements below reflect this convention.

$I : \{p \wedge I\}\ skip\ \{p \wedge I\}$ (skip)

$I : \{p[e/x] \wedge I\}\ x{:=}e\ \{p \wedge I\}$ (assign)

$I : \{p \wedge I\}\ b\ \{p \wedge b \wedge I\}$ (test)

$$\frac{I \wedge p \rightarrow (I\,[D<e>/D] \wedge q\,[D<e>/D])}{I : \{p \wedge I\}\ D!e\ \{q \wedge I\}} \quad (output)$$

$$\frac{I \wedge p \rightarrow \forall v.[\, I\,[D<v>/D] \wedge q\,[D<v>/D,v/x]\,]}{I : \{p \wedge I\}\ D?x\ \{q \wedge I\}} \quad (input)$$

We proceed with rules for the other constructs in DNP. Since the rules for sequential and parallel composition were already presented in sect. 6 and 5 resp., they are not repeated here.

$$\frac{I{:}\{p_1\}\ S_1\ \{q_1\} \ ,\ I{:}\{p_2\}\ S_2\ \{q_2\}}{I{:}\{p_1 \wedge p_2\}\ S_1 \square S_2\ \{q_1 \vee q_2\}} \quad (choice)$$

A salient point is the following axiom which states that the trace existing on the moment that S starts executing, can only be *extended*, i.e. that the *initial* part remains fixed.

$(\ \pi_{cset} \geqslant t\ ) : \{\pi_{cset} = t\}\ S_1 \| S_2\ \{\pi_{cset} \geqslant t\}$ (extension)

,where $cset = chan(S_1 \| S_2)$, and where t is some (logical) trace variable.

$$\frac{I{:}\{p\}\ N\{q\}}{I{:}\{p\}\ co\ N\ co\ \{q\}} \quad \text{(hiding)}$$

,where N is a *network* $S_1 \| S_2$, and provided that $chan(I,p,q) \subseteq chan(co\ N\ co)$
(Remark: $chan(co\ S_1 \| S_2\ co)$ has been defined as the channels of S_1 and S_2 with the channels *connecting* S_1 and S_2 omitted). So I,p and q cannot contain references to *internal* channels of the network.

The next rule is a *subsidiary deduction* type of rule, that is, if the derivation required by the "premiss" of the rule does exist, then the conclusion of the rule holds. Note that the declaration part of the formulae in this subsidiary deduction does not include the declaration of procedure P anymore.

$$\frac{<\ |\ I{:}\{p \wedge I\}\ P(\overline{D}_{in};\overline{D}_{out};\overline{x})\ \{q\}> \ \ |{-}{-}\ \ <\ |\ I{:}\{p \wedge I \wedge \overline{y}{=}\overline{\omega}\}\ S_0\ \{q\}>}{<P(\overline{D}_{in};\overline{D}_{out};\overline{x}){:}\,begin\ S_0\ end\ |\ I{:}\{p \wedge I\}\ P(\overline{D}_{in};\overline{D}_{out};\overline{x})\ \{q\}>}$$

,provided that $var(p,q) \subseteq \overline{x}$, and where $\overline{y}$ denotes the list of local variables of S_0, excluding the parameters $\overline{x}$.

$$\frac{I{:}\{p\}\ P(\overline{D}_{in};\overline{D}_{out};\overline{x})\ \{q\}}{I[\bullet/\bullet] : \{p[\bullet/\bullet]\}\ P(\overline{E}_{in};\overline{E}_{out};\overline{u})\ \{q[\bullet/\bullet]\}} \quad (parameter\ substitution)$$

,where $[\bullet/\bullet] \equiv [\overline{E}_{in}/\overline{D}_{in}, \overline{E}_{out}/\overline{D}_{out}, \overline{u}/\overline{x}]$,

and provided that: $\overline{u} \cap var(p,q) \subseteq \overline{x}$ and $(\overline{E}_{in} \cup \overline{E}_{out}) \cap chan(I,p,q) \subseteq (\overline{D}_{in} \cup \overline{D}_{out})$.

We continue with a collection of auxiliary rules, all of which are adaptations of rules encountered in proofsystems for recursive procedures as e.g. in [Apt].

$$\frac{\begin{array}{c} I'{:}\{p'\}\ S\ \{q'\} \\ I' \rightarrow I\ ,\ p \rightarrow p'\ ,\ q' \rightarrow q \end{array}}{I{:}\{p\}\ S\ \{q\}} \quad \text{(consequence)}$$

$I : \{p \wedge I\}\ S\ \{p \wedge I\}$ (*invariance*)

,provided that: $var(p) \cap var(S) = \varnothing$ and $chan(I,p) \cap chan(S) = \varnothing$. Remark: the soundness of this axiom depends heavily on the fact that assertions refer to traces by means of projections only.

$$\frac{I_1 : \{p_1\}\ S\ \{q_1\} \ ,\ I_2 : \{p_2\}\ S\ \{q_2\}}{I_1 \wedge I_2 : \{p_1 \wedge p_2\}\ S\ \{q_1 \wedge q_2\}} \quad (conjunction)$$

$$\frac{I{:}\{p\}\ S\ \{q\}}{I[e/v,f/t]{:}\{p[e/v,f/t]\}\ S\ \{q[e/v,f/t]\}} \quad (ghost\ variable\ substitution\ I)$$

,where v and t are a logical integer variable and trace variable, resp., and where e and f are an integer expression and a trace expression, not containing program variables or channelnames occurring free in S.

$$\frac{I:\{p\}\ S\ \{q\}}{I:\{p[e/v,f/t]\}\ S\ \{q\}} \quad \textit{(ghost variable substitution II)}$$

,where v and t are a logical integer variable and trace variable not occurring free in I or q, and where e and f are an *arbitrary* integer expression and trace expression, resp..

7.1 Example of a proof

The following example shows the typical use of some of the proof rules above, in particular of the extension axiom. The abbreviation "$\pi_{D,E} \leqslant <D,E,D,E>$" stands for an assertion which expresses that communication occurs *alternatingly* between channels D and E. (The communicated values are irrelevant to the proof). Now we want to prove correctness of the specification:

$$I : \{\pi_{D,E} = <D,E>\}\ S_1 \| S_2\ \{true\},$$

with $I \equiv \pi_{D,E} \leqslant <D,E,D,E>$, $\quad S_1 \equiv D!0\ ;\ F!0$ and $S_2 \equiv F?x\ ;\ E!0$.

Because of the syntactic restrictions associated with the parallel composition rule, the specification for S_1 cannot contain the channelname E, and likewise, the specification for S_2 cannot contain D. Therefore, if the extension axiom had not been present, one could do no better than:

- prove: $(\pi_{D,F} \leqslant <D,D,F>) : \{\pi_{D,F} = <D>\}\ S_1\ \{true\}$
  and: $(\pi_{E,F} \leqslant <E,F,E>) : \{\pi_{E,F} = <E>\}\ S_2\ \{true\}$
- apply the parallel composition rule and the consequence rule, yielding:

$$(\pi_{D,E} \leqslant <D,D,E,E> \vee \pi_{D,E} \leqslant <E,D,D,E> \vee \pi_{D,E} \leqslant <D,E,D,E>) :$$
$$\{(\pi_{D,E} = <D,E> \vee \pi_{D,E} = <E,D>) \wedge \pi_F = <>\}\ S_1 \| S_2\ \{true\}.$$

The fact that the trace $\pi_{D,E}$ starts as $<D,E...>$ and not as $<D,D...>$ or $<E,D...>$ has been lost in the invariant of this last specification! However, one can improve upon this by using the following instance of the extension axiom:

$$\pi_{D,E,F} \geqslant t : \{\pi_{D,E,F} = t\}\ S_1 \| S_2\ \{\pi_{D,E,F} \geqslant t\}$$

We apply substitution rule (I) to this formula, substituting $<D,E>$ for t. Then, one obtains:

$$\pi_{D,E,F} \geqslant <D,E> : \{\pi_{D,E,F} = <D,E>\}\ S_1 \| S_2\ \{\pi_{D,E,F} \geqslant <D,E>\}$$

We combine this with the formula derived with the parallel composition rule above, using the conjunction rule:

$$\pi_{D,E} \leqslant <D,E,D,E> : \{\pi_{D,E} = <D,E> \wedge \pi_F = <>\}\ S_1 \| S_2\ \{true\}$$

Finally, one removes the conjunct "$\pi_F = <>$" from the precondition by applying substitution rule (II). To do so, substitute $<>$ for π_F, and use again the consequence rule:

$$\pi_{D,E} \leqslant <D,E,D,E> : \{\pi_{D,E} = <D,E>\}\ S_1 \| S_2\ \{true\}$$

This shows that the desired specification is indeed derivable.

8. Completeness of the proofsystem

In this section we show that the proofsystem as described is relatively complete. Note that we have fixed the interpretation of the assertion language in section 4. As already argued in the introduction, the fact that this interpretation includes the standard interpretation for the integers is a necessity, since otherwise the language would have been inexpressive. The expressiveness of our particular interpretation is stated as lemma 1 of this section. So by "relative completeness" we mean that

if $\models <Dec \mid I:\{p\}\ S\ \{q\}>$ then $Tr \vdash\!\!-- <Dec \mid I:\{p\}\ S\ \{q\}>$.

Here, "$Tr \vdash\!\!--$ ..." denotes derivability in the proofsystem of section 7 with all valid assertions of the language of section 4 added as axioms.

We start with the introduction of *strongest invariants* and *strongest postconditions*.

First a semantic characterization:

Definition : The strongest invariant *SI* and strongest postcondition *SP* of a closed program $<Dec \mid S>$, relative to a precondition p, are defined as:

$$SI(<Dec \mid S>)(p)\ \gamma\ \tau \ \equiv\ \exists \tau_0,s_0.[\ [p]\ \gamma\ (\tau_0,s_0) \wedge \exists(\tau_1,s_1) \in [S]\ \bar{\eta}\ s_0.[\ \tau|chan(S,p) = \tau_0\tau_1\ ]\ ]$$

$$SP(<Dec \mid S>)(p)\ \gamma\ (\tau,s) \equiv \exists \tau_0,s_0.[\ [p]\ \gamma\ (\tau_0,s_0) \ \wedge$$
$$\exists(\tau_1,s_1) \in [S]\ \bar{\eta}\ s_0.[\ \tau|chan(S,p) = \tau_0\tau_1 \wedge s \neq \perp \wedge s|var(S,p) = s_1\ ]]$$

,where $\bar{\eta}$ is the procedure environment $\Theta[\beta/P]$, derived from *Dec* as usual. (The "empty" environment Θ is used here, since the programs under consideration are closed.)

Lemma 1   *SI* and *SP* are *representable as assertions*.

So there exist assertions $sinv(<Dec|S>)(p)$ and $sp(<Dec|S>)(p)$ *in the language of section* 4 which are interpreted as $SI(<Dec|S>)(p)$ and $SP(<Dec|S>)(p)$, resp.. The rather longwinded proof is omitted here.

Our first concern is that the "strongest invariant and -postcondition" are a *valid* invariant and postcondition indeed, and that they are as strong as possible. This is the contents of the following two lemmas; (proofs omitted here).

Lemma 2   For a closed program $<Dec|S>$ we have:

$$\models\ <Dec \mid sinv(<Dec|S>)(p) : \{p\}\ S\ \{sp(<Dec|S>)(p)\}>$$

Lemma 3   For a closed program $<Dec|S>$,

if $\models\ <Dec|I:\{p\}\ S\ \{q\}>$ *then* $\models sinv(<Dec|S>)(p) \rightarrow I$
and $\models sp(<Dec|S>)(p) \rightarrow q$

To show completeness of the proofsystem, it suffices to show:

$$Tr \vdash\!\!-\ <Dec|sinv(<Dec|S>)(p) : \{p\}\ S\ \{sp(<Dec|S>)(p)\}> \quad (*),$$

For if $\models\ <Dec|I : \{p\}\ S\ \{q\}>$,

then $Tr \vdash\!\!-\ <Dec \mid I : \{p\}\ S\ \{q\}>$ follows from (*) with the *consequence rule*.

The rest of this section aims at proving (*). First, we state a lemma which allows the expression of the strongest invariant and postcondition of a parallel construct in terms of the strongest invariants and postconditions of the constituent components of that construct. What is remarkable is that a simple conjunction of invariants and postconditions of the components is not sufficient.

Lemma 4   If p_1, p_2 are assertions, S_1, S_2 statements with:

$var(p_i) \cap var(S_j) = \emptyset$, *and* $chan(p_i) \cap chan(S_j) \subseteq chan(S_i)$, for (i,j)=(1,2) or (2,1),
$c_i = chan(S_i, p_i)$ for i=1,2, $c_{12} = c_1 \cup c_2$, and t is some trace variable not occurring in p_1 or p_2,

then: $\models [\ sinv(<Dec|S_1\|S_2>)(p_1 \wedge p_2 \wedge \pi_{c_{12}} = t) \Leftrightarrow$

$(sinv(<Dec|S_1>)(p_1 \wedge \pi_{c_1} = t|c_1) \wedge sinv(<Dec|S_2>)(p_2 \wedge \pi_{c_2} = t|c_2) \wedge \pi_{c_{12}} \geq t)\ ]$

and: $\models [\ sp(<Dec|S_1\|S_2>)(p_1 \wedge p_2 \wedge \pi_{c_{12}} = t) \Leftrightarrow$

$(sp(<Dec|S_1>)(p_1 \wedge \pi_{c_1} = t|c_1) \wedge sp(<Dec|S_2>)(p_2 \wedge \pi_{c_2} = t|c_2) \wedge \pi_{c_{12}} \geq t)\ ]$

The rather intricate proof is omitted here. The properties of *"sinv"* and *"sp"*, needed in the completeness proof for sequential composition, choice and hiding are somewhat simpler than for parallel composition. We collect these properties in the following lemma.

Lemma 5   Let $I_{12} \equiv sinv(<Dec|S_1;S_2>)(p)$,
$J_{12} \equiv sinv(<Dec|S_1 \Box S_2>)(p)$, $q_{12} \equiv sp(<Dec|S_1 \Box S_2>)(p)$,
$I \equiv sinv(<Dec|\ co\ S_1\|S_2\ co>)(p)$, $q \equiv sp(<Dec|\ co\ S_1\|S_2\ co>)(p)$,

then the following holds:

(i) $\models\ <Dec|I_{12}:\{p\}\ S_1\ \{sp(<Dec|S_1>)(p)\}>$, $\models\ <Dec|I_{12}:\{sp(<Dec|S_1>)(p)\}\ S_2\ \{sp(<Dec|S_1;S_2>)(p)\}>$,
(ii) $\models\ <Dec|J_{12}:\{p\}\ S_i\ \{q_{12}\}$, for i=1,2, and
(iii) $\models\ <Dec|I;\{p\}\ S_1\|S_2\ \{q\}$.

Finally we arrive at the completeness proof.

Theorem.   For a closed program $<Dec|S>$,

if $\models\ <Dec|I:\{p\}\ S\ \{q\}$ then $Tr \vdash\!\!-\ <Dec|I:\{p\}\ S\{q\}>$. (**)

The proof proceeds by induction on the structure of S. From the foregoing it follows that it suffices to show:

$$Tr \vdash\!\!-\ <Dec \mid sinv(<Dec|S>)(p) : \{p\}\ S\ \{sp(<Dec|S>)(p)\}>, \quad (*)$$

where we can assume (**) "by induction" for the constituent components of S, if S is not an atomic statement. To show (*), we distinguish a number of cases, according to the structure of S. Here we treat only some interesting cases.

- If $S \equiv S_1;S_2$, then (*) follows immediately from lemma 5 (i), the induction hypothesis (**) and the sequential composition rule.
- If $S \equiv S_1 \Box S_2$, idem, but using lemma 5 (ii) and the choice rule.
- If $S \equiv co\ S_1\|S_2\ co$, idem, now using lemma 5 (iii) and the hiding rule.

Parallel composition is treated as follows:

We abbreviate $sinv(<Dec|S_1\|S_2>)(p)$ *as* I_{12}, and $sp(<Dec|S_1\|S_2>)(p)$ *as* sp_{12}.
Also we use the following notations: $\bar{x}_i = var(S,p) - var(S_j)$ for (i,j) = (1,2) or (2,1),
$c_i = (chan(p) - chan(Sj)) \cup chan(S_i)$ for (i,j) = (1,2) or (2,1), $c_{12} = c_1 \cup c_2 = chan(S_1,S_2,p)$. We assume that $\bar{v}_1$, $\bar{v}_2$ and t are two lists of ghost variables and a trace variable, not occurring free in I_{12}, p or sp_{12}.

Now if $\models <Dec|I_{12}:\{p\}\ S_1\|S_2\ \{sp_{12}\}>$ then also $\models <Dec|I_{12}:\{\bar{p}\}\ S_1\|S_2\ \{sp_{12}\}>$,

where $\bar{p} = p \wedge \bar{x}_1=\bar{v}_1 \wedge \bar{x}_2=\bar{v}_2 \wedge \pi_{c_{12}}=t$. This $\bar{p}$ can be split into p_1, p_2 and p_n, as follows:

$$p_i \equiv \bar{p}[\bar{v}_1/\bar{x}_1, \bar{v}_2/\bar{x}_2, t/\pi_{c_{12}}] \wedge \bar{x}_i=\bar{v}_i \wedge \pi_{c_i}=t|c_i, \text{ for } i=1,2, \qquad p_n \equiv (\pi_{c_{12}} = t).$$

Note that $var(p_i) \cap var(S_j) = \emptyset$ and $chan(p_i) \cap chan(S_j) \subseteq chan(S_i)$ for (i,j)=(1,2) or (2,1),
and that $\bar{p} \Leftrightarrow p_1 \wedge p_2 \wedge p_n$. Therefore, if we abbreviate $sinv(<Dec|S_1>)(p_1)$, $sinv(<Dec|S_2>)(p_2)$, and "$\pi_{c_{12}} \geq t$" as I_1, I_2 and I_n resp., then lemma 4 applies, so, also using the definition of strongest invariant:

$$I_1 \wedge I_2 \wedge I_n \Leftrightarrow sinv(<Dec|S_1>)(p_1) \wedge sinv(<Dec|S_2>)(p_2) \wedge I_n \Leftrightarrow sinv(<Dec|S_1\|S_2>)(p_1 \wedge p_2 \wedge p_n) \Rightarrow I_{12}.$$

Analogously, again applying lemma 4: $sp_1 \wedge sp_2 \wedge I_n \Rightarrow sp_{12}$,

where $sp(<Dec|S_1>)(p_1)$ *and* $sp(<Dec|S_2>)(p_2)$ are abbreviated as: sp_1 and sp_2 resp..

Now, with lemma 2: $\models <Dec|I_1:\{p_1\}\ S_1\ \{sp_1\}>$, and: $\models <Dec|I_2:\{p_2\}\ S_2\ \{sp_2\}>$.

so, by induction: $Tr \mid\!-\!- <Dec|I_1:\{p_1\}\ S_1\ \{sp_1\}>$, and: $Tr \mid\!-\!- <Dec|I_2:\{p_2\}\ S_2\ \{sp_2\}>$. (1)

From (1), by the parallel composition rule: $Tr \mid\!-\!- <Dec|I_1 \wedge I_2:\{p_1 \wedge p_2\}\ S_1\|S_2\ \{sp_1 \wedge sp_2\}>$. (2)

Next, we introduce an instance of the extension axiom: $\mid\!-\!- <Dec|I_n:\{p_n\}\ S_1\|S_2\ \{I_n\}>$. (3)

We combine (2) and (3) with the conjunction rule:

$$Tr \mid\!-\!- <Dec|I_1 \wedge I_2 \wedge I_n:\{p_1 \wedge p_2 \wedge p_n\}\ S_1\|S_2\ \{sp_1 \wedge sp_2 \wedge I_n\}>$$

Finally, applying the consequence rule yields the desired result, also using substitution rule (II).

$$Tr \mid\!-\!- <Dec|I_{12}:\{p\}\ S_1\|S_2\ \{sp_{12}\}>$$

This concludes the case of parallel composition, and therefore of the completeness proof.

REFERENCES

[AFR] Apt, K.R., Francez, N, de Roever, W.P. A proofsystem for Communicating Sequential Processes. TOPLAS 2 (3) '80

[BK] Barringer, H. Kuiper, R. A temporal logic specification method supporting hierarchical development.

[Bro] Broy, M. Fixed point theory for communication and concurrency. Proc. of IFIP conf. on formal description of prog. concepts II, '82

[Bru] Bruin, A. de and Bohm, A.P.W. The denotational semantics of dynamic networks of processes. report RUU-CS-82-13, University of Utrecht.

[CH] Chen, Z., Hoare, C.A.R. Partial correctness of CSP. IEEE Int. Conf. on Dist. Comp. Systems '81.

[Cla] Clarke,E.M. Programming constructs for which it is impossible to obtain good Hoare like axiom systems. JACM 26 (1) jan '79.

[FHLR] Francez, N., Lehman, D. and Pnueli, A. A linear History Semantics for Distributed languages. Proc. IEEE FOCS Symposium '80.

[Lam] Lamport, L. The Hoare Logic of concurrent programs. Acta Informatica 14 '80

[MC] Misra, J. and Chandy, M. Proofs of Networks of Processes. IEEE SE 7 (4) '81.

[MC2] Misra, J. Reasoning about Networks of Communicating Processes. INRIA Advanced Nato Study Institute on Logics and Models for Verification and Specification of Concurrent Systems '84

[Mil] Milner, R. A Calculus of Communicating Systems. Springer LNCS 92 '80.

[OG] Owicki, S. and Gries, D. An axiomatic proof technique for parallel programs. Acta Informatica 6 '76.

[OH] Olderog, E.R. and Hoare, C.A.R. Specification oriented semantics for communicating processes. Proc. of the 10th ICALP conference '83 LNCS 154.

[O2] Olderog, E.R. Specification oriented programming in TCSP. INRIA Advanced Nato Study Institute on Logics and Models for Verification and Specification of Concurrent Systems '84

[Pnu] Pnueli, A. Compositional verification of concurrent programs using temporal logic. INRIA Advanced Nato Study Institute on Logics and Models for Verification and Specification of Concurrent Systems '84

[ZBR] Zwiers, J. de Bruin, A. de Roever, W.P. A proof system for partial correctness of Dynamic Networks of Processes Proc. of Conference on Logics of Programs, '83, LNCS 164 '84.

AUTHOR INDEX

D. Beauquier 33
M. Ben-Or 43
G. Bilardi 53
L. Bougé 63
W. Bucher 71, 404
B. Chazelle 80, 90
M. Chroback 101
R. Cole 111
M. Coppo 120
P.-L. Curien 130
J.W. de Bakker 140, 149
P. de Bra 158
W.P. de Roever 509
H. Edelsbrunner 80
A. Ehrenfeucht 71
J. Engelfriet 171
Ph. Flajolet 179
J.F. Fortune 189
M. Fürer 199
H. Gabow 210
Z. Galil 363
J.A. Goguen 221
O. Goldreich 43
L. Guibas 90
C.A. Gunter 232
G. Hansel 244
J. Hartmanis 250
D. Haussler 71, 404
M. Hennessy 260
T. Hortalá-González 270
K. Hrbacek 281
N. Immerman 250
M. Jerrum 290
J.H. Johnson 300
J.-P. Jouannaud 221
H. Jung 310
R.G. Karlsson 318
M. Kaufmann 328
V. Keränen 338
J.N. Kok 140
J. Kortelainen 348
T.G. Kurtz 356
G.M. Landau 363
K.G. Larsen 373
M. Li 383
L. Lovász 1
M. Luby 394
M.G. Main 404
U. Manber 356
Z. Manna 413
K. Mehlhorn 328, 424
J. Meseguer 221
J.-J.Ch. Meyer 149
S. Micali 43
J.I. Munro 318
M. Nivat 33
E.-R. Olderog 149
P. Orponen 435
J.E. Pin 445
A. Pnueli 15
F.P. Preparata 53
P. Radge 394
I.V. Ramakrishnan 487
R.L. Rivest 43
E.L. Robertson 318
M. Rodríguez-Artalejo 270
D.A. Russo 435
S. Sippu 456
A.P. Sistla 465
E. Soisalon-Soininen 456
U. Schöning 435
M. Stallmann 210
C. Stirling 475
A. Tsakalidis 424
P. van Emde Boas 509
M.Y. Vardi 465
P.J. Varman 487
U. Vishkin 497
H. Vogler 171
R. Waldinger 413
P. Wolper 465
M.M. Yung 363
J. Zwiers 509

Vol. 142: Problems and Methodologies in Mathematical Software Production. Proceedings, 1980. Edited by P.C. Messina and A. Murli. VII, 271 pages. 1982.

Vol. 143: Operating Systems Engineering. Proceedings, 1980. Edited by M. Maekawa and L.A. Belady. VII, 465 pages. 1982.

Vol. 144: Computer Algebra. Proceedings, 1982. Edited by J. Calmet. XIV, 301 pages. 1982.

Vol. 145: Theoretical Computer Science. Proceedings, 1983. Edited by A.B. Cremers and H.P. Kriegel. X, 367 pages. 1982

Vol. 146: Research and Development in Information Retrieval. Proceedings, 1982. Edited by G. Salton and H.-J. Schneider. IX, 311 pages. 1983.

Vol. 147: RIMS Symposia on Software Science and Engineering. Proceedings, 1982. Edited by E. Goto, I. Nakata, K. Furukawa, R. Nakajima, and A. Yonezawa. V. 232 pages. 1983.

Vol. 148: Logics of Programs and Their Applications. Proceedings, 1980. Edited by A. Salwicki. VI, 324 pages. 1983.

Vol. 149: Cryptography. Proceedings, 1982. Edited by T. Beth. VIII, 402 pages. 1983.

Vol. 150: Enduser Systems and Their Human Factors. Proceedings, 1983. Edited by A. Blaser and M. Zoeppritz. III, 138 pages. 1983.

Vol. 151: R. Piloty, M. Barbacci, D. Borrione, D. Dietmeyer, F. Hill, and P. Skelly, CONLAN Report. XII, 174 pages. 1983.

Vol. 152: Specification and Design of Software Systems. Proceedings, 1982. Edited by E. Knuth and E.J. Neuhold. V, 152 pages. 1983.

Vol. 153: Graph-Grammars and Their Application to Computer Science. Proceedings, 1982. Edited by H. Ehrig, M. Nagl, and G. Rozenberg. VII, 452 pages. 1983.

Vol. 154: Automata, Languages and Programming. Proceedings, 1983. Edited by J. Díaz. VIII, 734 pages. 1983.

Vol. 155: The Programming Language Ada. Reference Manual. Approved 17 February 1983. American National Standards Institute, Inc. ANSI/MIL-STD-1815A-1983. IX, 331 pages. 1983.

Vol. 156: M.H. Overmars, The Design of Dynamic Data Structures. VII, 181 pages. 1983.

Vol. 157: O. Østerby, Z. Zlatev, Direct Methods for Sparse Matrices. VIII, 127 pages. 1983.

Vol. 158: Foundations of Computation Theory. Proceedings, 1983. Edited by M. Karpinski, XI, 517 pages. 1983.

Vol. 159: CAAP'83. Proceedings, 1983. Edited by G. Ausiello and M. Protasi. VI, 416 pages. 1983.

Vol. 160: The IOTA Programming System. Edited by R. Nakajima and T. Yuasa. VII, 217 pages. 1983.

Vol. 161: DIANA, An Intermediate Language for Ada. Edited by G. Goos, W.A. Wulf, A. Evans, Jr. and K.J. Butler. VII, 201 pages. 1983.

Vol. 162: Computer Algebra. Proceedings, 1983. Edited by J.A. van Hulzen. XIII, 305 pages. 1983.

Vol. 163: VLSI Engineering. Proceedings. Edited by T.L. Kunii. VIII, 308 pages. 1984.

Vol. 164: Logics of Programs. Proceedings, 1983. Edited by E. Clarke and D. Kozen. VI, 528 pages. 1984.

Vol. 165: T.F. Coleman, Large Sparse Numerical Optimization. V, 105 pages. 1984.

Vol. 166: STACS 84. Symposium of Theoretical Aspects of Computer Science. Proceedings, 1984. Edited by M. Fontet and K. Mehlhorn. VI, 338 pages. 1984.

Vol. 167: International Symposium on Programming. Proceedings, 1984. Edited by C. Girault and M. Paul. VI, 262 pages. 1984.

Vol. 168: Methods and Tools for Computer Integrated Manufacturing. Edited by R. Dillmann and U. Rembold. XVI, 528 pages. 1984.

Vol. 169: Ch. Ronse, Feedback Shift Registers. II, 1–2, 145 pages. 1984.

Vol. 171: Logic and Machines: Decision Problems and Complexity. Proceedings, 1983. Edited by E. Börger, G. Hasenjaeger and D. Rödding. VI, 456 pages. 1984.

Vol. 172: Automata, Languages and Programming. Proceedings, 1984. Edited by J. Paredaens. VIII, 527 pages. 1984.

Vol. 173: Semantics of Data Types. Proceedings, 1984. Edited by G. Kahn, D.B. MacQueen and G. Plotkin. VI, 391 pages. 1984.

Vol. 174: EUROSAM 84. Proceedings, 1984. Edited by J. Fitch. XI, 396 pages. 1984.

Vol. 175: A. Thayse, P-Functions and Boolean Matrix Factorization, VII, 248 pages. 1984.

Vol. 176: Mathematical Foundations of Computer Science 1984. Proceedings, 1984. Edited by M.P. Chytil and V. Koubek. XI, 581 pages. 1984.

Vol. 177: Programming Languages and Their Definition. Edited by C.B. Jones. XXXII, 254 pages. 1984.

Vol. 178: Readings on Cognitive Ergonomics – Mind and Computers. Proceedings, 1984. Edited by G.C. van der Veer, M.J. Tauber, T.R.G. Green and P. Gorny. VI, 269 pages. 1984.

Vol. 179: V. Pan, How to Multiply Matrices Faster. XI, 212 pages. 1984.

Vol. 180: Ada Software Tools Interfaces. Proceedings, 1983. Edited by P.J.L. Wallis. III, 164 pages. 1984.

Vol. 181: Foundations of Software Technology and Theoretical Computer Science. Proceedings, 1984. Edited by M. Joseph and R. Shyamasundar. VIII, 468 pages. 1984.

Vol. 182: STACS 85. 2nd Annual Symposium on Theoretical Aspects of Computer Science. Proceedings, 1985. Edited by K. Mehlhorn. VII, 374 pages. 1985.

Vol. 183: The Munich Project CIP. Volume I: The Wide Spectrum Language CIP-L. By the CIP Language Group. XI, 275 pages. 1985.

Vol. 184: Local Area Networks: An Advanced Course. Proceedings, 1983. Edited by D. Hutchison, J. Mariani and D. Shepherd. VIII, 497 pages. 1985.

Vol. 185: Mathematical Foundations of Software Development. Proceedings, 1985. Volume 1: Colloquium on Trees in Algebra and Programming (CAAP'85). Edited by H. Ehrig, C. Floyd, M. Nivat and J. Thatcher. XIV, 418 pages. 1985.

Vol. 186: Formal Methods and Software Development. Proceedings, 1985. Volume 2: Colloquium on Software Engineering (CSE). Edited by H. Ehrig, C. Floyd, M. Nivat and J. Thatcher. XIV, 455 pages. 1985.

Vol. 187: F.S. Chaghaghi, Time Series Package (TSPACK). III, 305 pages. 1985.

Vol. 188: Advances in Petri Nets 1984. Edited by G. Rozenberg with the cooperation of H. Genrich and G. Roucairol. VII, 467 pages. 1985.

Vol. 189: M.S. Sherman, Paragon. XI, 376 pages. 1985.

Vol. 190: M.W. Alford, J.P. Ansart, G. Hommel, L. Lamport, B. Liskov, G.P. Mullery and F.B. Schneider, Distributed Systems. Edited by M. Paul and H.J. Siegert. VI, 573 pages. 1985.

Vol. 191: H. Barringer, A Survey of Verification Techniques for Parallel Programs. VI, 115 pages. 1985.

Vol. 192: Automata on Infinite Words. Proceedings, 1984. Edited by M. Nivat and D. Perrin. V, 216 pages.1985.

Vol. 193: Logics of Programs. Proceedings, 1985. Edited by R. Parikh. VI, 424 pages. 1985.

Vol. 194: Automata, Languages and Programming. Proceedings, 1985. Edited by W. Brauer. IX, 520 pages. 1985.